Warlord

CARLO D'ESTE

Warlord

*A Life of Churchill
at War, 1874–1945*

ALLEN LANE
an imprint of
PENGUIN BOOKS

ALLEN LANE

Published by the Penguin Group
Penguin Books Ltd, 80 Strand, London WC2R ORL, England
Penguin Group (USA) Inc., 375 Hudson Street, New York, New York 10014, USA
Penguin Group (Canada), 90 Eglinton Avenue East, Suite 700, Toronto, Ontario, Canada M4P 2Y3
(a division of Pearson Penguin Canada Inc.)
Penguin Ireland, 25 St Stephen's Green, Dublin 2, Ireland
(a division of Penguin Books Ltd)
Penguin Group (Australia), 250 Camberwell Road, Camberwell, Victoria 3124, Australia
(a division of Pearson Australia Group Pty Ltd)
Penguin Books India Pvt Ltd, 11 Community Centre, Panchsheel Park, New Delhi – 110 017, India
Penguin Group (NZ), 67 Apollo Drive, Rosedale, North Shore 0632, New Zealand
(a division of Pearson New Zealand Ltd)
Penguin Books (South Africa) (Pty) Ltd, 24 Sturdee Avenue, Rosebank, Johannesburg 2196, South Africa

Penguin Books Ltd, Registered Offices: 80 Strand, London WC2R ORL, England

www.penguin.com

First published in the USA by HarperCollins Publishers 2008
This amended edition first published in Great Britain by Allen Lane 2009

3

Copyright © Carlo D'Este, 2008, 2009
Maps copyright © Jason Petho, Petho Cartography

The moral right of the author has been asserted

Set in 10.5/14 pt PostScript Linotype Sabon
Typeset by Rowland Phototypesetting Ltd, Bury St Edmunds, Suffolk
Printed in England by Clays Ltd, St Ives plc

ISBN: 978-0-713-99753-8

www.greenpenguin.co.uk

For Sue and Harry Brack,
esteemed friends who helped to make this book possible; and
for my wife, Shirley Ann.
In memory of Airman Shirley Barton Eldridge, one of the many
thousands who gave their lives in the cause of the Second World War.

Contents

CONTENTS

List of Illustrations

List of Maps

Introduction:
Born for War

The largest human being of our time.   – Sir Isaiah Berlin

Long before he became a statesman, Winston Churchill was first a soldier. War and soldiering were in his blood, inspiring his earliest fantasies as a child and his greatest adventures as a young man, before in old age he took over their direction as Britain's wartime leader.

His fascination with soldiering began in the nursery, where he waged imaginary battles with armies of toy soldiers. His experiences as a young cavalry officer and war correspondent led him to distant and exotic places and exposed him to war in its many aspects, including its gruesome horrors. Even as prime minister and one of the world's most powerful men during the Second World War, Churchill never lost his love of soldiering, often lamenting that he had missed his calling by not winning fame as a battlefield warrior.

Churchill was one of those rare figures in history, men such as Frederick the Great, Oliver Cromwell and his own famous ancestor, the Duke of Marlborough, who were 'born for war', as Napoleon once described himself. These were war leaders who 'instinctively understood it in all of its aspects: strategic, political, diplomatic, moral and psychological'. Moreover, as one of Churchill's most astute biographers, Sebastian Haffner, has observed: 'No one will ever understand the phenomenon that was Churchill by regarding him simply as a politician and statesman who was ultimately destined like Asquith or Lloyd George, Wilson or Roosevelt, to conduct a war; he was a warrior who realized that politics forms a part of the conduct of war.'

It is not so well known that Churchill was a military visionary with ideas of astonishing, if sometimes impractical, originality. As first lord of the Admiralty in 1915, he conceived and approved the design and construction of an enormous Trojan horse-like armoured vehicle that would transport in safety between eighty and one hundred troops across no man's land to assault the German trenches; and in 1939, again as first lord, he conceived 'Nellie', a gargantuan trench digger that would be used to permit the infantry to overwhelm the powerful defences of the Siegfried Line in safety. Although both projects ultimately failed, they were nevertheless examples of the remarkably innovative ideas that poured forth from Churchill's fertile mind.

In 1912, well before others could see the warning signs, Churchill foretold a potential great conflict. In a prophetic letter to his cousin and close friend Charles 'Sunny' Churchill, the ninth Duke of Marlborough, he warned of the threat of war emanating from the unstable situation in the Balkans, and noted: 'The European situation is far from safe and anything might happen. It only needs a little ill will or bad faith on the part of a great power to precipitate a far greater conflict.'

Despite having personal experience of war at Omdurman in 1898, and as a participant in the last cavalry charge in the history of the British army, Churchill nevertheless held a Victorian's somewhat romanticized view of war, and of Britain's greatness of empire as the most powerful nation on earth. One perceptive observer, the newspaperman Cecil King, described Churchill as 'a man of the 19th, if not the 18th century; he knows little and cares less for the political currents of the day. To him war is a vast pageant with himself in a scarlet uniform on a white horse, baton in hand, leading the British forces forward through the smoke of battle.'

As a twenty-two-year-old junior officer fresh from the Royal Military College at Sandhurst, Churchill was torn between his youthful enthusiasm for putting his life on the line and the horror of the wars he fought in. His military experience as a soldier exposed him to the grit, blood and death of war in its cruellest forms. His exploits left him with an abhorrence of war, and during the first three decades of the twentieth century his was a frequent, often strident, but forlorn voice preaching preparedness and other means of *avoiding* war. However, when war engulfed the world for the second time in twenty-five years, Churchill answered the call. Where others talked of peace with Nazi Germany, his was the strongest voice among those determined to resist tyranny.

Although he became perhaps the most famous politician in British history, Churchill never strayed far from his military roots. While political office and its myriad powers were his ultimate goal, he used soldiering, writing and his experience as a war correspondent to that end. Politics may have dominated his life, but soldiering was a passion he never lost during his political rise. During the Second World War, he was frequently seen in the uniform of the Royal Air Force or in that of an army colonel. As one writer has noted, 'Wellington was a soldier who felt it his duty to be a politician. Churchill was a politician who wanted to be a soldier . . . A nation which since Cromwell has always felt uncomfortable with all but its most eccentric military leaders, was led in its most dangerous battle by a war leader in a zip-suit and carpet slippers.'

Churchill possessed an unfulfilled lifelong ambition to become a warrior-hero in the Napoleonic mould, which even service in the squalor of the front lines as a lieutenant colonel commanding a rifle battalion in France in 1916 failed to cure. Later in life he called war 'the greatest of all stimulants'. As early as 1911, one of his critics remarked with insight, 'He is always unconsciously playing a part – an heroic part. And he is himself his most astonished spectator. He sees himself moving through the smoke of battle – triumphant, terrible, his brow clothed with thunder, his legions looking to him for victory, and not looking in vain. He thinks of Napoleon; he thinks of his great ancestor [the Duke of Marlborough] . . . [in his] fervid and picturesque imagination there are always great deeds afoot, with himself cast by destiny in the Agamemnon role.'

Warts and all, Winston Churchill nevertheless represented the indomitable spirit of a defiant nation under siege. His oratory was stirring and, like FDR's, his words galvanized his fellow countrymen. His predecessor as prime minister, Neville Chamberlain, regarded Hitler as 'the commonest little dog', but was duped and coerced by the German dictator's signature on the meaningless Munich agreement in September 1938, a vaguely worded covenant that 'lacked even the ringing affirmation of nonaggression treaties'. Chamberlain's well-intentioned declaration of 'peace in our time' was actually a death warrant for France and a guarantee that Britain was destined for another war with Germany. When he learned of Munich, Churchill remarked: 'This is only the first step, the first foretaste of a bitter cup which will be proffered to us year by year unless by a supreme recovery of moral health and martial vigour we arise again and take our stand for freedom.' Once war had come, and the foreign secretary, Lord Halifax, suggested that Britain make peace with Hitler, Churchill not only declined but instead vowed to rescue 'mankind from the foulest and most soul-destroying tyranny which has ever darkened the stained pages of history'.

The Second World War was the greatest test of all, and much of the credit for Britain's survival belongs to Churchill, who simply refused to lose. His defiance of 'Corporal Hitler', as he scornfully referred to the Nazi leader, was on full display throughout the war, from his 'we shall fight on the beaches' to his 'we shall fight on for ever and ever and ever.'

In no particular order, Churchill was brilliant, pampered, petulant, romantic, pragmatic, courageous, egotistical, eccentric, possessed of enormous perseverance, opinionated beyond measure and impossibly demanding. He drank too much, suffered from depression (his 'black dog'), 'waddled rather than walked' and by almost any criterion ought to have been too old to carry the enormous burden of a prolonged war that threatened Britain's very existence. As a young man he once said, 'If I had two lives I would be a soldier and a politician: but as there will be no war in my time, I shall have to be a politician.' In the event Winston Churchill was both.

Although Churchill has been the subject of hundreds of biographies, very little has been written about the military Churchill. More than forty years since his death in 1965, his attraction for historians and biographers continues unabated, even more so in the wake of 11 September 2001. He has been praised, condemned for a host of sins real and imagined, and, in recent years, made the subject of a number of revisionist biographies notable mainly for their portrayal of a man with feet of clay. Despite the plethora of books about Churchill the politician and political leader, there has yet to be an objective, total examination of his crucial role as military leader. It is as a soldier of both the nineteenth and the twentieth centuries that this biography will, in contrast to others, appraise Churchill's extraordinary life.

When he became prime minister in May 1940, during Britain's darkest time, Churchill was already beyond the age when most men had retired. For the next five years, which included an illness in 1943 that many thought he would not survive, he bore perhaps the greatest pressures ever placed upon any statesman or war leader. His grasp of the military art ranged from genius one moment to misjudgment the next. He experienced the euphoria of success and tasted the bitter cup of failure (to his death Churchill never fully recovered from the sting of his role in the Dardenelles disaster in 1915). Nothing that concerned the war escaped his attention, often to the despair of his military chieftains. Whether grilling his generals, admirals and airmen around a conference table with penetrating questions, pursuing strategic issues with Roosevelt and Stalin, or planning the invasion of France before the ashes of Dunkirk had even cooled, Churchill was a war leader with a formidable grasp of detail. He might make unorthodox, often maddening diversions his military advisers deemed irrelevant and sometimes downright damaging, but on far too many occasions for it to be mere happenstance he also displayed sheer brilliance.

This then is the story of the military life of Winston Churchill – the descendant of Marlborough who, despite never having risen above the rank of lieutenant colonel, came eventually to direct the military campaigns of his nation and, more than any other man, to save Britain from tyranny during his and his nation's finest hour.

Prologue: 10 May 1940

Perhaps the darkest day in English history.   – Sir Henry 'Chips' Channon

In Berlin on Wednesday, 8 May 1940, CBS news correspondent William L. Shirer recorded in his diary that he 'could not help noticing a feeling of tension' emanating from the German Foreign Ministry: 'Something is up.' In his radio broadcast the following night, Shirer warned his listeners in the United States, 'The war will be fought and decided before the summer is over.'

Some hours earlier a black Mercedes with darkened windows had inconspicuously driven away from the Reich Chancellery and merged with the weekday traffic on the streets of Berlin. To all outward appearances the Mercedes was an ordinary motor car transporting a Nazi official, perhaps even a high-ranking bureaucrat. In the northern suburb of Berlin-Finkenkrug it entered a small, remote railway station that had been cordoned off from prying eyes by the Sicherheitsdienst (the German Security Service, or SD). It halted by a platform, next to a military train that consisted of two locomotives and eight ordinary green Reichsbahn railway carriages. Amid tight security the occupant disembarked and without ceremony boarded one of the carriages. Punctually at 4.38 p.m. the train (which had been assigned the unusual code name *Amerika*), steamed away from the station on northbound tracks, ostensibly headed towards Hamburg and its expected destination, Denmark. After nightfall, however, it turned west, and by midnight on a moonless night it reached Hanover, where it was switched, this time on to westbound tracks.

After an all-night journey the train at last arrived at its destination, a tiny, secluded station situated in the village of Euskirchen, in the rugged and sparsely populated Eifel region near the German border with

Belgium and Luxembourg. The train's occupants stiffly disembarked in the chill of the pre-dawn darkness and climbed into three specially converted three-axle Mercedes limousines suitable for driving in rough terrain. The procession headed west into the hilly country deep inside the Eifel, passing through silent villages whose names had been removed and replaced with yellow signs bearing a variety of military markings. After half an hour the vehicles halted near a series of former anti-aircraft emplacements recently converted into secure bunkers.

The principal occupant of the train had come to witness at first hand the culmination of a massive, top-secret military operation called Case Yellow, worked on for months by the German general staff.

As the sun began to rise into the dawn of a promising spring day, the only sound was of birds chirping in the nearby trees. The small entourage gathered around the man who was plainly dressed in a military greatcoat and an officer's cap topped by an eagle with a swastika clutched in its talons. Within minutes the serenity was shattered as the thunder of guns was heard from the west. He pointed his arm in the general direction of the noise and announced, 'Gentlemen, the offensive against the Western powers has just started.' The man was Adolf Hitler, the supreme leader of Nazi Germany, and he had come to witness the opening salvoes of the Second World War in the west, and the display of a formidable new type of warfare: the blitzkrieg, which had first been tested against the hapless Poles in September 1939.

This day was to be the realization of what Hitler had ardently told his generals in August 1939: 'Our opponents are little worms . . . What matters in beginning and waging war is not righteousness but victory. Close your hearts to pity. Proceed brutally.'

One of Hitler's adjutants pointed silently to his watch as if to record the moment for history. The time was 5.35 a.m., Friday, 10 May 1940.

The Allies, Britain and France, had long ruled out the possibility of an invasion of the west through the vast Ardennes Forest by an armoured force, relying instead on the textbook theory that, with its inadequate, narrow winding roads, the region was impassable for tanks. What the Allies would learn on this critical day was that the German army was capable of employing the same element of surprise that had so confounded the French in 1914, when it had followed the Schlieffen Plan, by which the Germans invaded France by first invading Belgium.

2

Thus, on the morning of 10 May, what was thought to have been impossible became a reality when, across the length of the Ardennes and along more than two hundred miles of Germany's western border with Belgium, Holland and the Grand Duchy of Luxembourg, there came the distinctive clanking sound of armoured vehicles on the move.

At dawn the Germans unleashed massive blitz attacks into all three countries. In all an enormous force of 137 German divisions, including more than two thousand tanks, was massed along and behind the German border. The panzer divisions were positioned, one behind the other, like giant building blocks; the rear ranks of the panzers were nearly fifty miles east of the Rhine, and had they been placed end to end, the tail would have extended into East Prussia. In support of the invasion were as many as 3,800 aircraft of Hermann Göring's Luftwaffe. However, Plan Yellow was so highly secret that the first time the airmen knew of the invasion was the pre-dawn hours of 10 May, when they were abruptly awakened and given fifteen minutes' notice to attend operational briefings. 'There was no time even to shave. Shortly before sunrise every available aircraft left its field.'

Although the Allies were on high alert, the German offensive came as a complete surprise. The French inspector general of artillery was in Metz on the morning of 10 May to assure the artillery commanders of the Third Army that modern guns would be ready 'next spring'. He naively inquired of an aide: 'Where are they holding the manoeuvres?' The aide replied, 'That, *mon Général*, is the start of the German offensive.'

One of the few strategies available to the Dutch was to open their dykes and canal locks and flood key areas around their border with Germany. Before they could react, however, German divisions had swarmed across the borders of Holland and Belgium, their spearheads slicing through scant opposition. A German parachute division was dropped from the sky and landed by glider on key targets throughout Holland. Bridges in Rotterdam and other key cities were seized almost before the Dutch knew what had hit them, and although they fought heroically they were simply outgunned and outmanned. 'Initiative, speed and surprise [were] the new German technique,' notes Len Deighton. '[General Freiherr Wolfram von] Richthofen's Stuka dive-bombers were their artillery.' From the North Sea to the Rhone Valley, massed Luftwaffe aircraft suddenly appeared at daybreak, with the sun rising behind them in the east, and attacked airfields, railway yards and roads in France, Belgium and Holland. The Luftwaffe attacked seventy airfields in all three countries, destroying three or four hundred aircraft, and providing Hitler with uncontested air superiority.

The Luftwaffe bombers that attacked Holland flew out over the North Sea and then turned east, thus gaining even greater surprise. 'They flew low over acres of tulip fields in bloom, where girls working there in the early morning waved to them, not noticing the markings on their wings.'

In another sector of the Eifel, the 7th Panzer Division, like all the invasion forces, had only been alerted the night of 9 May. War was hardly on the minds of its soldiers, many of whom had visions of being given passes to enjoy the Whitsun holiday that weekend. The 7th Panzers were led by one of the Wehrmacht's brightest and most innovative young commanders, forty-eight-year-old Major General Erwin Rommel. In a brief letter to his wife he wrote: 'You'll get all the news for the next few days from the papers. Don't worry yourself, everything will go all right.' At 5.32 a.m. Rommel's panzers were among the first to invade Belgium as one of the spearheads of Colonel General Fedor von Bock's Army Group B.

Hitler had spent a restless night aboard the *Amerika*. 'I did not sleep a wink,' he later admitted. 'Principally, I was kept awake by anxiety over the weather.' When dawn arrived fifteen minutes earlier than his meteorologists had predicted, he flew into a rage. He was soon calmed by a flurry of signals from his commanders in the vanguard of the blitz, chief among them the electrifying news at 7.00 a.m. that, at Liège, German paratroopers had been landed by gliders directly inside and had seized the supposedly impregnable Fort Eben Emael, the principal fortification of the Belgian defensive system along the Meuse river. Its capture opened up the plains of Belgium and the cities of Brussels and Antwerp for the German panzers. At Maastricht, another main entry point into Belgium, the Germans encountered scant resistance. One by one key bridges over the Meuse, the Albert Canal and at Rotterdam and other Dutch cities fell, sometimes with scarcely a shot being fired.

This flurry of attacks, the commando raids, the mining of the harbours of ports in Holland and Belgium by the Luftwaffe, and the relentless onslaught by the four armies of Bock's Army Group B firmly planted the impression the Germans wished to convey: that the main thrust of their invasion was aimed at seizing Holland and Belgium. The ruse would soon draw the bulk of the British Expeditionary Force and three French armies into Belgium, into a carefully laid trap that would lead to the fall of France, crush Holland and Belgium and inflict on the British army the greatest humiliation in its celebrated history. When Hitler was informed of the British and French troop movements, he later recalled, 'I could have wept for joy: they had fallen into the trap.'

The 10th of May 1940 was also the day that Winston S. Churchill became prime minister. In the weeks ahead, as the Dutch, Belgian and French armies collapsed and the British withdrew their remaining forces from the beaches of Dunkirk, Hitler turned his thoughts to the invasion of Britain. Churchill, as he later wrote, 'felt as if I were walking with destiny, and that all my past life had been but a preparation for this hour and for this trial'.

I

Toy Soldiers

The toy soldiers turned the current of my life.   – Churchill

He rather resembles a naughty, little sandy-haired bulldog, and seems backward
except for complicated games with toy soldiers.
                                   – Clara Jerome, Churchill's grandmother

It was only fitting that Winston Leonard Spencer Churchill was born
'amid velvet muffs, fur coats and plumed hats' in the early-morning
hours of St Andrew's Day, 30 November 1874, at Blenheim Palace in
Oxfordshire, the ancestral home of the Marlboroughs. According to his
parents his arrival in a temporary cloakroom adjacent to the grand
ballroom was unexpected. As the newest descendant of one of the icons
of British history, Winston Churchill began life in a hurry, a trait he
would never relinquish.

His cousin and close friend Shane Leslie once noted that his birth
seems to have been hastened by a gala event at Blenheim that night, the
annual St Andrew's Ball, in which his mother Jennie participated with
her customary ardour. 'His previous and perhaps presumptuous arrival
[his mother] alluded to as Winston's effort to make his first speech . . .
and historians will suppose that the band struck up martial music for
his entry.' In fact his birth was probably accelerated because his mother
had not only fallen during a shooting party six days earlier but had
taken a jarring ride in a pony carriage that afternoon and was dancing
enthusiastically when her labour pains began. His parents had intended
his birth to take place in their London home in Curzon Street, Mayfair,
but, as he would throughout his long and tumultuous life, Winston
Churchill could be counted upon to do the unexpected.

An announcement in *The Times* three days later read: 'On the 30th

Nov, at Blenheim Palace, the Lady Randolph Churchill, prematurely, of a son.'

Not only is the declaration by his parents that he was born some two months prematurely highly dubious, but in that day it would have been a medical miracle had he even survived. Hardly anyone in the Churchill family's immediate circle of friends fell for the ruse. Churchill himself seems not to have believed it, once remarking with evident amusement, 'Although present on the occasion, I have no clear recollection of the events leading up to it.'

Churchill's parents have been unflatteringly described as 'remote and tantalizingly glamorous. Randolph's glittering, bulging eyes and oversize whiskers hiding a small, intense face caused him to resemble a tenacious miniature Schnauzer, while darling "Mummy" was another spectacle altogether.' Indeed the descendants of the first and only notable Marlborough 'were a thoroughly disreputable family, in debt, had scandalous relationships with women, and were incredibly rude to people, with only smatterings of respectability'. Randolph and Jennie Churchill were exceptions; they captivated English political and social circles. 'Neither Randolph nor Jennie needed to out-dazzle each other,' observed Shane Leslie. 'They both shone of their own light unlike the usual conjugal pairs who reflected each other like the moon and the sun.'

Few who met her ever forgot Churchill's mother, Jennie Jerome, a vivacious, raven-haired American. She was one of the best-known and most fascinating young women of Victorian England, for her great beauty, joie de vivre and marriage to one of Parliament's rising stars, and as a woman of considerable repute, with a legion of lovers. She was the product of a traditional silver-spoon, upper-class upbringing that included a finishing school in Paris, where she met her future husband. Jennie was one of three daughters of a formerly ultra-wealthy New York financier, co-founder of the famed Jockey Club and former owner of the *New York Times*, Leonard Jerome, who had lately fallen on hard times as a result of the stock market collapse of 1873. The Jerome sisters, Jennie, Leonie and Clara, were once described by a contemporary wit as, respectively, 'the Beautiful, the Witty and the Good'. Jennie Jerome Churchill's admiring nephew Shane Leslie depicted her as 'a magnificent type whose fierce yet faithful character [was] so utterly fearless towards those she loved, so scornful of those she disliked'.

As a parent Jennie left a great deal to be desired. She typified the upper-class women of her age for whom parenting did not rank high on their scale of priorities. Life in Victorian England as the wife of Lord Randolph Churchill was meant to be one of hedonistic pleasure, whether in the bedrooms of her lovers or in the endless round of social events, parties, hunts and attendance at high-profile racing events at Ascot and the annual regatta at Henley.

As Shane Leslie wrote, 'Destiny had not slipped her into the world to play with Princes or to tread the Primrose path of politics. She had been furnished with some virile qualities of steel in her veins ... Men she could consider and treat as they generally treated women. There was the pantheress ... in her temper – otherwise it would have been impossible for her to fulfil her only real destiny and duty which was to breed Winston.' Herbert Henry Asquith's second wife, Margot Tennant, did not know who Jennie was when she first encountered her in 1887 at a race meeting. 'She had a forehead like a panther's and great wild eyes that looked through you ... Had Lady Randolph Churchill been like her face, she could have governed the world.'

Jennie was a woman of great contradictions who possessed far more than mere beauty. She disdained the Victorian dictates determining a woman's place in society. Her single-mindedness (which she passed to her two sons) was reflected in her commanding nature. After her boys had grown up her causes ranged from founding a magazine to work aiding the wounded in South Africa during the Boer War.

In Jennie Churchill's self-centred world, motherhood was simply not permitted to become a distraction. The messy and time-consuming business of changing nappies and looking after the myriad needs of a child was not part of the glamorous milieu she inhabited. This was not a particularly unusual feature of life in Victorian society; parents of sufficient means and social standing generally consigned their children to nannies, and shipped them off to boarding school at an early age. On social occasions in the Churchill household Winston and his brother John, born in Dublin in 1880 and called Jack by the family (and thought by some to have been sired by one of Jennie's many lovers), were fetched and put on display like trophies in front of their guests before being swiftly relegated back to the care of the nannies.

The rich, the well connected and the powerful graced the Churchill salon in Mayfair. Whether it was entertaining Disraeli at dinner or welcoming a hunt amid the splendour of Blenheim, life for the parents of young Winston Churchill was a constant round of socializing of almost dizzying proportions. Nevertheless Jennie had little patience for and was easily bored by what to most observers was a grand life epitomized by the Churchill stronghold of Blenheim Palace, a place that held scant appeal for her adventurous nature.

Although she cared deeply about her sons, Jennie never let either of them interfere with her whirlwind social life. Of his mother Winston wrote in his 1930 memoir, *My Early Life*, that she 'always seemed to me a fairy princess: a radiant being possessed of limitless riches and power' who made 'a brilliant impression upon my childhood's eye. She shone for me like the Evening Star.' More telling, however, was his observation, 'I loved her dearly – but at a distance.'

During the years 1882 to 1895, when Winston was attending various schools, her letters to him were as rare as her visits. When she did write, it was often about herself. An 1893 letter from Paris was typical: 'I am sorry not to have been able to write to you before – but I am so "hunted" here I haven't had *one* moment to myself . . . I am enjoying myself immensely, ride & skate to the races dine and even dance!'

A member of the House of Commons at the age of thirty, Lord Randolph Churchill perceived that his Conservative Party was missing a golden opportunity by failing to woo the ordinary working class of Britain. He proposed the insightful but controversial idea that the Tories not only must cater to the workers and their needs but could actually win them over.

Largely thanks to Lord Randolph the Conservatives regained a majority in Parliament in 1886, a turnaround that catapulted him into the forefront of British politics and gave him the unique distinction of being both one of the nation's most admired and one of its most hated politicians. As chancellor of the exchequer and leader of the House of Commons under Prime Minister Lord Salisbury, not only was he a powerful figure in his own right, but many thought him a future prime minister – until his career self-destructed after he foolishly overestimated his own importance and committed what amounted to political suicide by resigning his office in December 1886 over a minor issue. Salisbury had had his fill of his imperious chancellor and rid himself of Randolph simply by accepting his resignation. Lord Randolph's appalling misjudgment left him a virtual pariah and doomed his career to the same political wilderness that his son would endure in the 1930s. The difference was that the son's career was resurrected to undreamed-of heights whereas Lord Randolph's led to unfulfilled promise, obscurity and an early death.

As a result of his journey into the political wilderness, the Churchills fell upon lean times. Lord Randolph turned down numerous director-ships of banks and insurance companies that might have earned him as much as forty thousand pounds a year, explaining, 'When failure comes, I cannot answer to the Widow and the Orphan whose funds have been invested in my name.' His refusal to sell his name was a selfless moral gesture that left him and his family impoverished, and with no financial legacy for his sons, both of whom had to earn their own living.

Lord Randolph Churchill was an impatient man with little sense of moderation, and possessed of a venomous tongue that lashed out with the sting of a whip whenever anyone crossed him. In fact, as a family, the Churchills were a quarrelsome lot who argued and fought with one another. Lord Randolph's coldness, rudeness, self-promotion and penchant for sarcasm extended to his relationship with his elder son. Although Winston wanted nothing more than to please the father he adored, that affection was never visibly reciprocated during his child-hood. Despite the incessant criticism that was heaped upon him, Churchill doggedly sought Lord Randolph's approval and respect. Not surprisingly, there are no known photographs of the father with his sons.

Winston's recollections of his father verged on fantasy. Describing him as 'The greatest and most powerful influence in my early life', the son, who was time and again rejected and belittled, went to extraordi-nary lengths to glorify the man who had withheld the warmth and love he craved. Although his aunts doted on him, the ruthless drive and towering ambition Churchill brought to adulthood is directly attribu-table to a childhood bereft of both parental warmth and attention. Churchill, 'needing outlets for his own welling adoration ... created images of [his parents] as he wished they were, and the less he saw of them, the easier that transformation became.'

Winston Churchill spent a lifetime in denial of the neglect by his parents that formed what can only charitably be described as an unhappy childhood. Yet there were benefits to being the progeny of influential parents. During his youth Churchill met Queen Victoria, sailed with his mother and the Prince of Wales on the royal yacht, and saw Buffalo Bill perform, and when he could get away with it, would avidly eavesdrop, with an ear to the wall or through a door left ajar, on conversations between his parents and their many visitors.

It was inevitable that young Winston would be relegated to the care of a nanny, Mrs Elizabeth Everest, a widow engaged by Randolph shortly after his birth, who for all practical purposes acted as his surrogate mother and was the dominant force in his early life. 'The infant Winston was consigned to the unflagging, unfailing Mrs Everest,' and later, as a schoolboy, he was in the care of Jennie's sister Leonie, while Jennie 'adventured – politically, gallantly, socially'. Churchill's granddaughter Celia Sandys has written that Mrs Everest 'gave him this undemanding, unconditional love and was the rock upon which his real childhood was built'. Winston and his brother Jack affectionately nicknamed her 'Woom' or 'Woomany'. In his only novel, *Savrola*, published in 1900, Churchill draws a thinly disguised portrait of his beloved surrogate parent: 'She had nursed him from his birth with a devotion and care which knew no break. It is a strange thing, the love of these women. Perhaps it is the only disinterested affection in the world. The mother loves her child; that is maternal nature . . . but the love of a foster-mother for her charge appears absolutely irrational.'

Winston Spencer Churchill was an unruly, manipulative and often difficult child, given to unpredictable behaviour. From the time he first learned to speak, the child with the slightly dishevelled red hair and eyes that bore a resemblance to those of his father (who had earned the dubious nickname of 'Gooseberry Churchill' at Eton), rarely stopped talking. Before he was seven it was already clear that he was headstrong, highly opinionated and virtually impossible to control. The tart tongue and lack of tolerance that Churchill became so famous for as a politician and prime minister were in early evidence. When a family governess earned his ire, the small child demanded, 'Take Miss Hutchinson away; she is very cross.' The young woman was soon employed elsewhere.

He did whatever it took to get what he wanted, whether through tears, scorching rhetoric or a temper tantrum – of which there were many. His frequent raids into the kitchen, run by the family cook Rose Lewis, finally earned him retribution when she deliberately dropped a ladle on his head one day. It was Lewis who anointed Churchill with the nickname 'Copper-top'. On one occasion he ran wild in a Knights-bridge square after a party, 'rapping every knocker while butlers and governesses appealed in vain for the police'. His grandmother Clara Jerome thought he resembled 'a naughty, little sandy-haired bulldog', who seemed 'backward except for complicated games with toy soldiers'.

As much as he adored Mrs Everest, young Winston would resort to any means that would gain him his own way; once, searching 'in his mind for the one thing that would strike his nurse as wickedest, he would "go and worship idols" '.

Churchill's playmates were almost exclusively male, though he was clearly aware of girls. Once when one of Queen Victoria's grand-daughters, Princess Marie of Edinburgh, was 'spooning' with a young man under a table at Clarence House, the Edinburghs' family home, 'a red-haired pugnacious boy crawled in and out and insisted on telling "Missy" how lovely she looked. Master Winston had spotted her.'

At an early age Churchill, a voracious reader, became engrossed by the grand adventure tales of the day. One of his favourite books was *Treasure Island*, but his first literary idol was H. Rider Haggard, whose most famous novel, *King Solomon's Mines*, he read at least a dozen times. Not surprisingly Churchill and his cousins all yearned to visit South Africa, where the story was set. In January 1888 he expressed a desire to meet the author, who agreed to see him. Having been warned that Churchill was no ordinary young man, Haggard wrote, 'I will call next Sunday about 4 to see the youthful prodigy. I hope he will not put me through a cross-examination about my unworthy productions.' To Churchill's delight the two met, and Haggard was subjected to what, in later years, would be a typical Churchillian cross-examination, always probing for answers to seemingly endless questions. He demanded to know what Haggard meant by a particular statement in his book, 'and the author confessed he did not know himself.' Afterwards Haggard sent him a copy of *Allan Quartermain*, no doubt relieved to be free of the clutches of this unusual young man.

Another of Churchill's youthful adventures was a trip to the Tower of London. However, 'he declined both train and bus as too prosaic a means of conveyance. Finally, he sent cheerful word home that he had started "with a drunken cabman and a frisky horse!" '

*

What social graces and life lessons Churchill learned were taught by the wise Mrs Everest, who became confessor, life guide and soother of fears and the usual physical and emotional wounds of an active boy. On a rare occasion when Mrs Everest was granted a brief holiday, the care of the rumbustious child fell to Jennie, who was driven to exhaustion by Winston's incessant demands for playing a variety of games such as 'Hunt the Slipper' well into the night, and by his refusal to sleep like a normal child. 'Winston, you are impossible,' she complained; to which he replied, 'Yes indeed, and a miserable business for us both.'

It was also Mrs Everest who introduced the boy to the delights of toy soldiers and the romantic world of soldiering. Winston found solace in manoeuvring his growing army of German-made lead soldiers (which eventually approached fifteen hundred pieces) on the floor of his nursery room, organized into an infantry division and a cavalry brigade. Shane Leslie recalled, 'Winston was particularly ingenious in demanding and manipulating his toys,' chief of which were the 'lead soldiers who were always standing in action even when their owner slept'. Jack was allowed to participate in Winston's military games, but only in a secondary role that guaranteed he would never be on the winning side. As the commander of the opposition native troops, he was given no artillery and obliged perpetually to lose his battles against his brother's powerful army as a victim of what Winston called his self-created 'Treaty for the Limitation of Armaments'. At no time apparently did it cross Churchill's mind that he would ever serve in any other capacity than that of the commander.

Churchill, recalled another of his cousins, Clare Sheridan, was 'a large schoolboy' who had 'a disconcerting way of looking at me critically and saying nothing. He filled me with awe. His playroom contained from one end to the other a plank table on trestles, on which were thousands of lead soldiers arranged for battle. He organized wars. The lead battalions were manoeuvred into action, peas and pebbles committed great casualties, forts were stormed, cavalry charged, bridges were destroyed – real water tanks engulfed the advancing foes. Altogether it was a most impressive show, and played with an interest that was no ordinary child game.' Shane Leslie once had the temerity to ask the young generalissimo 'for whom were we waiting and was sternly told we were waiting for the enemies of England!'

No one but Churchill and his brother was permitted to touch or play with his soldiers. When one of his toy soldiers broke, it was of no further use to him, and he usually presented its remains to his brother or a relative. Only the able-bodied were eligible to serve in his army.

By 1890 Churchill had graduated from drilling his toy soldiers in imaginary battles in his nursery to outdoor 'wars', in which his real-life soldiers were his brother, several of his cousins and anyone else he could induce to play. There were numerous Churchill cousins: the four sons of Jennie's sister Leonie, and Clara's two sons and a daughter, Clara or Clare, a free spirit who achieved her own unique renown in later life as an acclaimed sculptor, bohemian and world traveller.

Many of Churchill's youthful military adventures took place at Banstead Manor, a small country house near Newmarket in Suffolk, first rented, then purchased, by Lord Randolph. There Winston constructed the 'Den', an intricate sort of Robinson Crusoe thatched cabin with its own drawbridge and homemade catapult, whose ammunition was a plentiful supply of green apples. Everyone who participated in Churchill's military games came under his authoritative 'ruling'. 'There were only two rules – first that Winston always remained General. Secondly there was no promotion.' One of their victims was a cow whose mistake was to stray too close to the young warriors.

That young Churchill took his military duties seriously was to become all too evident during one of these wars which took place in 1893 at the vast estate near Bournemouth of his aunt Cornelia (a sister of Lord Randolph). Winston, finding himself cornered on a bridge and in peril of imminent capture, refused to surrender and leaped off the bridge intending to break his fall on a tree. Instead he fell some thirty feet and was badly injured.

Churchill's prowess with his toy soldiers engendered a desire to become a soldier in his own right. One day his father paid a rare visit to his nursery to inspect his son's army. Afterwards Randolph asked Winston if he would like to enter the army, 'so I said "Yes" at once: and immediately I was taken at my word. For years I thought my father . . . had discerned in me qualities of military genius.' Only later did the young man learn that the true reason for his father's question was that he believed Winston was not clever enough to become a barrister. 'However that may be,' recalled Churchill, 'the toy soldiers turned the current of my life. Henceforward all my education was directed to passing into Sandhurst, and afterwards to the technical details of the profession of arms.'

In 1882, a few weeks before his eighth birthday, he was packed off to his first boarding school, St George's, in Ascot, where boys destined to attend elite establishments such as Eton and Harrow were groomed. The loneliness he felt at being cast into a strange and unfriendly environment was exacerbated by the fact that throughout his education Churchill was rarely visited by either of his parents. 'How I hated this school, and what a life of anxiety I lived there for more than two years,' he wrote in his memoir. 'I counted the days and the hours until the end of every term, when I should return home from this hateful servitude and range my soldiers in line of battle on the nursery floor.'

Young Winston's tenure at St George's began badly. He was routinely and savagely beaten, often until he bled, and verbally abused by the headmaster, the Reverend H. W. Sneyd-Kynnersley, a man of shallow intellect and a brutal sadist who took a particular delight in tormenting and punishing the young man. Several times a month the entire school was assembled in the library, and the two top boys took the selected delinquents away to a nearby room. Roger Fry, the head boy at St George's (later a celebrated art critic), was obliged to assist in the floggings and he later wrote, 'It took only two or three strokes for drops of blood to form everywhere and it continued for 15 or 20 strokes when the wretched boy's bottom was a mass of blood ... sometimes there were scenes of screaming, howling and struggling which made me almost sick with disgust.' One pupil was flogged so hard that he let fly with faeces. 'The irate clergyman instead of stopping at once went on with increased fury until the whole ceiling and walls of his study were spattered with filth.' Churchill never forgot the humiliation of these beatings and years later wrote with vehemence that 'they were flogged until they bled freely, while the rest sat quaking, listening to their screams.'

Never one to accept the inevitable, Churchill rebelled against his tormentor in ways that earned him even more beatings. On one occasion he was flogged for removing the headmaster's straw hat from its perch and stomping it to pieces. It did not help that Churchill was often his own worst enemy. He had learned some bad language in the stables at Blenheim and could not resist imparting his knowledge to his fellow puplils, once leaping on a table in a classroom and singing a ribald song, with predictable results. Churchill later realized more fully the extent of what had been done to him, and while at Sandhurst returned to Ascot 'to settle matters but found his old enemy had suddenly died to the relief of his pupils', at the age of thirty-eight.

Churchill's attendance at St George's has been described as 'one long feud with authority'. But his battles with the headmaster were not his only form of rebellion. He was deliberately defiant in both his Latin and his Greek lessons, which earned him the label of a below-average student. He later wrote of his stubbornness, 'In all the twelve years I was at school no one ever succeeded in making me write a Latin verse or learn any Greek except the alphabet.' As it would throughout his school years, Churchill's unruly behaviour and his readiness to defy authority made him an unsympathetic and unpopular figure with the other students. One, a German named Kessler, described Churchill as quarrelsome and an exhibitionist whose 'attitude got on everyone's nerves'. The conventional correctness of British youth who were taught to buckle down was anathema to Churchill.

For some time his plight remained unknown to his parents. On the contrary, on the basis of negative reports about virtually all aspects of his deportment and academic progress, they believed him a disappointment. His letters were routinely censored by the headmaster and revealed no clues to his unhappiness, which was made worse by the failure of either of his parents to visit him. There is an aura of almost overwhelming sadness in his pleas for them to come and see him, entreaties that were routinely disregarded, and the majority of his letters went unanswered. On one occasion, while a cadet at Sandhurst, Churchill wrote to his mother: 'Thank you very much for writing to me. Longing to see you, I remain, Ever your loving son Winston S. C.'

Only the faithful Mrs Everest made regular visits and noted the scars. When, after two terms, she revealed to Jennie and Randolph the extent of their son's troubles, his father withdrew him from St George's and sent him to a school in Hove.

Churchill's horrific experience of St George's scarred him for life. It haunted him so deeply that when Shane Leslie's daughter, Anita, visited him many years later, he said: 'If my mother hadn't listened to Mrs Everest and taken me away I would have broken down completely. Can you imagine a child being *broken down*? ... I can never forget that school. It was *horrible*.'

2

'A Barren and Unhappy Period of My Life'

These were the bad years.   – London *Sunday Dispatch*, 1939

After his painful experience at St George's School, the next four years of Winston Churchill's life were relatively tranquil. His father enrolled him at a school in Hove, near Brighton, run by two kindly spinsters named Kate and Charlotte Thomson. Although the experience 'makes a pleasant picture in my mind', in no small part because he was able to study subjects more to his liking (history and French), and was permitted to swim and ride horses, Churchill nevertheless seemed unable to avoid conflict with his fellow pupils and remained something of a loner. Once, when asked if he had ever erred, he replied, 'Nein!' and then claimed he was merely cultivating German. 'I used to think him', said his teacher, Eva Moore, 'the naughtiest small boy in the world.' An incident involving a pocketknife and a classroom scuffle with another boy resulted in a trip to the doctor to repair a gash to his chest that might have had tragic results. It also very nearly earned him expulsion.

Churchill made use of his status as the son of a famous man, soliciting autographs from his father (and later his mother) which he sold to other boys to augment his meagre funds. It was the start of a lifetime proclivity for spending wildly and living well beyond his means. In addition to his propensity for finding trouble, if not to seek it out actively, Churchill developed continuing health problems, which became a great concern to his mother. He was diagnosed with an inner-ear disorder that may have affected his balance; he also suffered the various childhood maladies – measles, mumps, influenza, toothaches – and two concussions, both the result of youthful exuberance.

At this early age Churchill became so fixated on his fragile health that for the rest of his life he kept a thermometer handy, which he used daily to check his temperature. In 1886 he contracted pneumonia and very nearly died. His temperature rose to a near-lethal 104.3 degrees during a grave five-day ordeal before the crisis passed. His ailments left him so frustrated that he once wrote to his mother about being 'cursed with so feeble a body'.

He also suffered from a speech defect that was a cross between a lisp and a stutter – no one has ever been quite sure how to categorize it. A throat specialist found nothing definitive, but throughout his life Churchill had trouble pronouncing the letter *s*. Despite working assiduously to overcome the problem through elocution drills and constant practice, he never entirely succeeded in ridding himself of his impairment, which tended to slur his speech and sometimes give the false impression that he was inebriated.

In 1887 Randolph broke the tradition of six generations of Churchills who had attended Eton by enrolling Winston at Harrow, primarily in the belief that the air atop one of the hills of outer London would somehow be more conducive to his health than that of Eton. The four and a half years from April 1888 to December 1892 that Churchill spent at one of Britain's elite schools were chiefly a continuation of his stormy passage into adulthood.

Situated in north-west London with a commanding view of the city and its environs, the town of Harrow dates back to the Romans, who considered the heights of military significance. The school was founded by a local yeoman named John Lyon to educate the poor of the town, and was granted a royal charter by Elizabeth I in 1572. By the time Churchill started there in 1888, Harrow had become one of Britain's most prestigious public schools and a place where the British upper classes sent their sons to be educated. Its old boys are a Who's Who of British history and include poets, historians, men of the arts and literature, a prime minister of India – Jawaharlal Nehru – and six British prime ministers, among them Robert Peel, Stanley Baldwin, Lord Palmerston and of course Churchill himself. Other Old Harrovians of note include Lord Byron, the historian George Macaulay Trevelyan and the Nobel laureate John Galsworthy.

Though the savage beatings he had routinely endured at Ascot were largely absent, mischief and misery seemed to hang over Churchill at Harrow like a pall, much of it of his own making. Although good-hearted by nature, he would deliberately court trouble and continued to be a hugely unpopular, disruptive, impatient and undisciplined pupil. His self-importance and bragging served only to antagonize others. He was, for example, fond of diving into the swimming pool to grab the legs of unsuspecting boys in the shallow end and then drag them underwater. Inevitably there came the day he was caught in the act and trampled underwater by several angry schoolboys who were fed up with his high jinks. An alert master dived in to save him from drowning. Afterwards Churchill's only comment was typically dismissive. He could 'deal with a few but not with the whole lot'.

On another occasion, he crept up behind a sixth-form boy named Leo Amery, who was standing by the edge of the swimming pool, stripped off his towel and shoved him into the pool. 'I emerged sputtering . . . to meet the gleeful grin of a small, freckled, red-haired boy whom I had never seen before,' recalled Amery. Retribution was swift. 'I fled, but in vain,' said Churchill. 'Swift as the wind my pursuer overtook me, seized me in a ferocious grip, and hurled me into the deepest part of the pool.' The following day Churchill explained to Amery that he hadn't realized he was a sixth-former but merely thought that he was 'small enough to be the most suitable victim to hand'. As the editor of the *Harrovian*, Amery recalled that Churchill submitted articles critical of the school administration, one of which he described as 'scurrilous'. 'I can still see the look of misery in his eyes as I blue-pencilled out some of his best jibes.' Somewhat surprisingly, given the rough beginning of their relationship, the two boys bonded, and, notes Celia Sandys, they formed 'an academic alliance in which Amery helped Churchill with his Latin translations while the future Nobel Prize-winner dictated the older boy's English essays'. Little did they know that their schoolboy friendship would turn into a half-century association that was by turns affable and contentious.

The headmaster, the Reverend J. E. C. Welldon, was a fair and kindly man, of whom Churchill once remarked, 'I can always talk around the Headmaster.' Not quite. The 'Punishment Book' maintained by Welldon records Churchill's name several times during his period at Harrow, and two entries (for cutting class and a breaking-and-entering incident, 'doing damage') earned him a flogging of seven strokes. Other misbehaviours registered were bathing twice in one day (punished by detention) and his last offence, in March 1892, disobedience and 'impertinence' (for which he was 'kept back at end of term'). On the whole, however, Churchill's disciplinary record at Harrow differed little from that of other boys who violated the school's strict regulations.

Those of Churchill's articles that Amery did publish did not endear him to Welldon, who 'summoned the young author to his study and addressed him in the following terms: "I have observed certain articles in the *Harrovian* newspaper lately, not calculated to increase the respect of the boys for the constituted authorities of the school. As articles in the *Harrovian* are anonymous, I shall not dream of inquiring who wrote them. But if any more of the same character appear it may be my painful duty to swish *you*." '

The child who evolved into the obdurate, exuberant, opinionated adult was already clearly evident. Even though Headmaster Welldon had taken an interest in Churchill, he too was subjected to his pupil's sharp tongue. On one occasion Churchill was summoned and told, 'I have grave reason to be displeased with you.' Replied the cheeky young man, 'And I, Sir, have very grave reason to be displeased with you.' It was obvious that Churchill had yet to discern the difference between insolence and foolhardiness, or between fearlessness and prudence.

Churchill's indiscretions during his years at Harrow included defiant behaviour, fights and disrepect that sometimes led to his own humiliation. Harassment and punishments failed to dissuade the young man from routinely hurling opinions and challenges. His frequent brushes with authority and with his contemporaries had the effect of hardening him. Whatever he engaged in was done with a full measure of passion and assertiveness. Churchill was good at billiards but played so aggressively that windows that happened to be in the line of fire were sometimes shattered. Contrition was simply never part of his makeup. A chilling incident was indicative of his persistence in the face of adversity. One day, the Reverend Frederick C. Searle, Churchill's under-housemaster, heard a fierce commotion and arrived to find him jammed helplessly into a folding bed with water of varying temperatures being poured on him by a group of bullies as punishment for his impertinence towards the bigger boys in his house. Searle rescued Churchill, whose face was scarlet with rage and dripping with water. Instead of displaying fear he exhibited an unbridled fury at his tormentors. 'The smaller, red-faced boy showed no tendency towards humility but walked up and down cursing and orating to the effect that he would be a great man and that his persecutors would come to nothing and he would crush them to the ground. The effect was tremendous especially over the cursing. The boys were really cowed.' On another occasion Churchill returned home from school with his jacket torn, and when questioned remonstrated: 'How should I not be out at elbows when my father is out of office?'

Already there existed the trait that would define him: what the historian Ronald Lewin has described as his 'glowering ferocity in the face of opposition, almost animal in its instinctive hostility, [that] was a constant throughout Churchill's life'. A badge of his nonconformity was his refusal to do the accepted thing. Any form of public intimacy was scorned at Harrow. Yet on one occasion when Mrs Everest visited him, Churchill flouted this unwritten rule. As a jeering group of boys followed them and the taunts reached a crescendo, he courageously kissed his beloved nanny goodbye.

His schooldays at Harrow left few pleasant memories. He preferred history, poetry and essay writing to the traditional Harrow emphasis on Latin and mathematics. That he had even been admitted was itself something of a minor miracle. During the entrance examination he was unable (and probably unwilling) to answer a single question on the Latin portion, and turned in a blank paper. Years later he grumbled over his dislike of examinations: 'I should have liked to be asked to say what I knew. They always tried to ask me what I did not know. When I would have willingly displayed my knowledge, they sought to expose my ignorance.'

Fortunately the Reverend Dr Welldon had seen enough promising qualities in young Churchill to admit him to Harrow. However, instead of being assigned to learn Latin and Greek, he was sent to the dunce class, where English was taught. After Churchill had become one of the foremost writers of the English language, he later boasted that it was a blessing that served him well. His debt to his English teacher, Robert Somervell, he said, was great. Somervell 'was charged with the duty of teaching the stupidest boys the most disregarded thing – namely to write mere English . . . I learned it thoroughly. Thus I got into my bones the essential structure of the ordinary British sentence – which is a noble thing.' Nevertheless the stigma of being at the tail end of his class rankled, particularly when, in front of an audience of parents and visitors, his name was one of the last to be called during the traditional roll call. His father had resigned that year as chancellor of the exchequer, and the Churchill name attracted more than normal attention. 'I frequently heard the irreverent comment, "Why, he's last of all!"'

His slovenliness, tardiness and dismissive attitude frustrated his tutor and housemaster, H. O. D. Davidson, who wrote to Jennie that her son was 'so regular in his irregularity, that I really don't know what to do ... But if he is unable to conquer this slovenliness ... he will never make a success of public school ... As far as ability goes he ought to be at the top of his form, whereas he is at the bottom.' Yet, like Dr Welldon, Davidson saw genuine promise in Churchill. 'He is a remarkable boy in many ways ... [and] I am very much pleased with some history work he has done for me.'

Another of Churchill's strong traits that emerged at Harrow was his ability to absorb and memorize large volumes of words. He may have been an indifferent student, but his memory was prodigious. Upon discovering that he could earn a prize in a school competition by remembering a thousand lines of poetry and reciting them to the headmaster, Churchill learned not one thousand but twelve hundred lines of Macaulay's poetry and won outright. In addition to memorizing poetry, he also composed a prizewinning poem entitled 'The Influenza' (about the spread of the disease throughout Europe in 1890). Churchill was proud that the *Harrovian* published it, and although the poem dealt with influenza it also included a verse that dealt with a subject that would remain a centrepiece of his political and military thought: the sanctity of the British Empire.

> God shield our Empire from the might
> Of war or famine, plague or blight
> And the power of Hell,
> And keep it ever in the hands
> Of those who fought 'gainst other lands,
> Who fought and conquered well.

He proudly wrote home that Mrs Everest should bring him proper clothes so that he could accept his award in appropriate sartorial splendour. Churchill could also recite from memory entire scenes from three of Shakespeare's plays. Not surprisingly, his interest in Shakespeare focused on the warrior kings: Richard III, Henry IV and Henry V. Thus, when he actually put his mind to it, he became an adept pupil who had the good fortune to have been taught history, English literature and mathematics by three exceptional teachers, L. M. Moriarty, Robert Somervell and C. H. P. Mayo.

Churchill was not a religious man, although he was confirmed in the Church of England while at Harrow. His mother thought the event might 'steady him', although Dr Welldon held the clearer view that he wished to participate 'only because it will get him off other work!' Thereafter religion played no meaningful role in his life.

In November 1891 Welldon suggested that Churchill would benefit from a visit to France and a stay with a French family during the forthcoming Christmas holidays. Randolph was due to return from a trip to South Africa, and Winston preferred to be home to see his father and then travel to France, but strictly on his own terms, and certainly not with 'a vile, nasty, fusty, beastly French "Family"'.

'Please have a little regard for my happiness,' he later complained to his mother. After being rebuffed by Jennie, he responded with the typical tart replies that would later characterize Churchill the impatient and demanding prime minister. Jennie wrote on 8 December 1891: 'The tone of your letter is not calculated to make one over lenient . . . When one wants something in this world, it is not by delivering ultimatums . . . You can be quite certain my darling that I will decide for what is best, but I will tell you frankly that I am going to decide not *you*.' When he persisted, an exasperated Jennie retorted: 'I have only read one page of yr letter and I send it back to you – as its style does not please me . . . you won't gain anything by taking this line.'

Never disposed to take no for an answer, even as a child, Churchill, at his most petulant, replied in a manner designed to lay guilt upon his mother:

My darling Mummy,

Never would I have believed that you would have been so unkind. I am utterly miserable. That you should refuse to read my letter is most painful to me . . . I can't tell you how wretched you have made me feel – instead of doing every thing to make me happy you go and 'cut the ground away from under my feet' like that . . . I am so unhappy but if you don't read this letter it will be the last you'll have the trouble to send back . . . don't be so cruel to

Your loving son,
WINNY

Ultimately Winston won his war of words and rather than having to live with the dreaded 'beastly French "Family"' was permitted to travel to France under the tutelage of his French master.

The most dismal aspect of his clash with his mother was that it was clearly a matter of indifference to Jennie whether her son spent the Christmas holiday at home or not. As during his earlier schooldays, Randolph and Jennie rarely visited their son. Randolph, in fact, did not make his first visit until November 1890, two and a half years after Winston entered Harrow. Their apathy was partly mitigated by a charming family friend, Laura, Countess of Wilton, who took pity on Churchill and wrote to him on a regular basis, occasionally including money, and always signing her letters with the words, 'Yr Deputy Mother, Laura Wilton'. She also sent him food hampers and oranges and often invited him to her home near Windsor during the summer break.

Randolph's resignation as chancellor in 1886 was catastrophic and self-destructive, not only to himself but to his elder son. Randolph became an embittered and 'wishful wanderer upon the earth', as if he were on a relentless quest for his own form of the Holy Grail. While he was travelling abroad, Jennie was involved with her paramour of the moment, a debonair Austrian diplomat, Count Charles Kinsky. In the summer of 1891 Kinsky took Winston to the Crystal Palace exhibition hall to view an exhilarating programme of performances by wild animals and the London fire brigade, which drilled with precision in honour of Queen Victoria's grandson, the visiting kaiser Wilhelm II. Churchill was enormously impressed not only by the kaiser's colourful white uniform, complete with a steel breastplate, high white leather boots and 'a helmet of bright Brass surmounted by a white eagle nearly 6 inches high', but also by a spectacle that 'was perfectly splendid. There were nearly 2000 firemen & 100 Engines. They all marched past the Emperor to the music of a band of infantry.' Afterwards there were fireworks to end what was one of the most exciting days of young Churchill's life, which also included his first taste of champagne. Once home he lost no time in drawing a picture of the kaiser's helmet and his boots. Sixteen years later Winston Churchill and the kaiser would meet in Germany under very different circumstances.

For young Winston, Randolph's descent into melancholy brought only prolonged misery. Although he clearly adored his father, Winston lived a life of denial of his constant rejection by a stern (and, in his final years, seriously ill) parent who invariably seemed to find only the worst qualities in his son. Indeed the litany of criticism that verged on the abusive would have crushed a lesser mortal than Winston Churchill. In his father's eyes Winston rarely earned praise, but rather deserved heaps of scorn for the ordinary mistakes and growing pains of a youth struggling to find his own identity and place in the adult world. Churchill's stubborn single-mindedness was his strength and his weakness both as a schoolboy and as an adult. More important, his indefatigability was a driving force that would serve him well when he had to contend with one crisis after another as Britain's leader fifty years later.

After Winston's first two years at Harrow, Randolph had come to the conclusion that his elder son was little better than a wastrel with a poor future, who was unworthy of being sent to Oxford to further his education and become a lawyer. Randolph was slowly descending into madness and an illness that would claim his life at the age of forty-five. His political disappointment, combined with his growing dismay over what appeared to be his son's uncertain future, led to a mutual decision between father and son that the army should be Winston's career of choice. There is little doubt that the family's declining financial situation encouraged Randolph in his conclusion.

What Churchill could never overcome was his distant relationship with his father. The harder he tried to please him, the less he seemed to succeed. His closest friend at Harrow was Jack Milbanke, a baron's son, who would later win a Victoria Cross in the Boer War before being killed in action in 1915 at Gallipoli. Although Churchill deeply admired Milbanke, in *My Early Life* he painfully recalled how forlorn he felt on the rare occasions when Randolph visited Harrow and took both boys to lunch at a nearby pub. Jack and Randolph talked as if they were equals, while Winston was largely ignored. 'How I should have loved to have that sort of relationship with my father! But alas, I was only a backward schoolboy and my incursions into the conversation were nearly always awkward or foolish.'

To the end of his life Churchill was haunted by his father's rejection. From the time of his entry into Sandhurst, and particularly after Randolph's early death in 1895, he spent the rest of his life proving to himself and to the ghost of his dead parent that indeed he was not a failure. A painful fantasy occurred in November 1947 at Chartwell,

Churchill's home in Kent. A well-wisher had purchased a portrait of his father and given it to Churchill, who placed it on an easel in his studio. On this particular afternoon he suddenly felt a presence in the room and saw his father sitting in his leather armchair. The two men began to talk as Randolph quizzed his son on the events of British history since his death. As Churchill attempted to explain to his father what he had done with his life, Randolph, in death, was as unimpressed with his son as he had been in life. He recalled Winston's 'stupidity' at school and said he would not talk politics 'with a boy like you ever'. However, as their conversation progressed, Randolph seemed impressed by his son's understanding of the historical events of the twentieth century and wondered why he hadn't gone into politics. Before Churchill could explain what he had accomplished, his father lit a cigarette and promptly vanished. Churchill's daughter Mary Soames once inquired if there was anything he would have liked to accomplish during his extraordinary life that he hadn't. 'And it didn't take him very long to think. He said, "Oh, yes. I would like my father to have lived long enough to see that I was going to be some good."'

His veneration of his failed father was tempered by sadness. Once he said to his own son, Randolph, after the two had spent a day together, 'We have had more conversations in this one holiday than I had with my father in his entire lifetime.' Occasions of intimacy between father and son were so rare that they became cause for elation. One such instance was in the autumn of 1891. While on holiday at Banstead, Churchill fired a double-barrelled shotgun at a rabbit he had spied on the lawn. The gun went off beneath Randolph's window, and brought down his wrath upon Winston. For once, however, he took pains to reassure his distressed son and in his own way to apologize for his outburst. He 'proceeded to talk to me in the most wonderful and captivating manner about school and going into the Army and the grown-up life which lay beyond. I listened spellbound to this sudden complete departure from his usual reserve, amazed at his intimate comprehension of all my affairs.'

Lord Randolph was not alone in his distress at his son's performance at Harrow. Shortly before Winston was to take the preliminary examination for admission to Sandhurst in the summer of 1890, Dr Welldon, convinced he would not pass, declined to let him sit it. This brought Winston a blast of displeasure from Jennie. 'You work in such a fitful inharmonious way, that you are bound to come out last ... I daresay you have 1000 excuses ... your work is an insult to your intelligence. If you would only trace out a plan of action for yourself & carry it out & be *determined* to do so – I am sure you could accomplish anything you wished. It is that thoughtlessness of yours which is your greatest enemy.' Refusing to accept any blame, Churchill attempted to dismiss the problem by writing, 'I am afraid some enemy hath sown tares in your mind,' and laying responsibility for the setback on 'being put under a master whom I hated & who returned that hate'. After promising to pass the examination, Churchill lived up to his word in November 1890 and was one of the twelve (of twenty-nine) from Harrow to do so, thus validating his mother's insistence that he could succeed whenever he chose to do so. But he still had to pass the 'further' or principal entrance examination.

At Harrow, Churchill's interest in soldiering had taken a more practical turn. During the last three of his four and a half years there he became a proficient horseman, excelled at swimming and fencing (for which he earned a prize) and won a shooting competition. Passing the preliminary examination for Sandhurst enabled him to enrol in the army class, and he enthusiastically undertook his first military training by joining what was called the Rifle Corps. The military part of the Harrow curriculum was designed to prepare its young candidates for admission to either Sandhurst or Woolwich, for those pursuing commissions in respectively the infantry or cavalry and the Royal Artillery or Royal Engineers. Although Churchill scorned most of his instructors, it was fitting that he deeply respected Moriarty, the master who taught the army class and who frequently lectured on the Crimean War.

In November 1888 an American colonel named Gouraud, who had fought in the Battle of Gettysburg, visited Harrow to demonstrate a new invention, the phonograph, into which he sang and recorded 'John Brown's Body'. The stirring music and the mere presence of a soldier who had fought in one of history's great battles seem to have fired Churchill's imagination, and this experience is thought to have influenced his decision more than fifty years later to direct that 'The Battle Hymn of the Republic' be sung at his funeral.

On another occasion a noted swordsman visited Harrow to give a lecture. When he offered to slice in half an apple off the head of any boy present willing to volunteer, no one spoke up. 'The Monitors swallowed hard, and each was trying to pluck up courage when a small red-haired boy from the fourth form climbed on to the stage and offered his services. It was young Winston.'

One element of his military training was mock battles fought against other schools. Between 1888 and 1892 Churchill participated in five such events. In 1892 he became the fencing champion of Harrow, perhaps the highest honour he won there, and in 1892 he won the Public Schools Fencing Championship, only the second Harrovian ever to have achieved this distinction. The *Harrovian* noted that Churchill fenced in an unorthodox manner, 'chiefly due to his quick and dashing attack which quite took his opponents by surprise'. It was a skill that would serve him well as an officer.

Outside his fantasy world of toy soldiers, however, he possessed little actual military background or knowledge except for what he learned during lectures he attended. Yet for a young man relatively unschooled in the military arts, Churchill's first military paper, written some time in 1889, when he was fourteen, was a remarkable endeavour. Written as an essay for his English teacher, Robert Somervell, 'The Engagement of "La Marais", July 6, 1914', imagined a military campaign in Russia by a British army twenty-five years in the future. Told in diary form through the words of the aide to the commanding general, his sixteen-page paper described how a British force came under Russian attack while moving to relieve a garrison marooned at Kharkov in the Ukraine. Appended to the paper were six detailed, hand-drawn maps of surprising imagination and initiative, complete with military dispositions.

Churchill's lifelong romanticism about war was reflected in this first military paper, which contained such phrases as 'moving lines & columns of red surmounted by the glimmering bayonet', and 'enemy's shells bursting in the masses of our cavalry killing and wounding dozens of them at a time'. His imagination was fired by what he described as a 'magnificent' scene. When the British finally won the terrible battle, his hero, Colonel Seymour, exclaimed that he could 'sleep to-night under the influence of victory which is the best narcotic in the world'.

Despite his rebellious nature and penchant for blaming others, Churchill had been well looked after at Harrow by men like Welldon, Moriarty and Somervell, and had learned far more than he ever cared to admit.

Although still prone to nagging ailments and youthful injuries, physically he had developed into a wiry, hardy young man, a trait very likely inherited from his American grandfather, Leonard Jerome. More important, he had willingly and enthusiastically embraced his first military training.

On the subject of his experiences at the school, Churchill was largely silent in his memoir. It was as if he had wiped away all traces of what was essentially an important but depressing time in his life. Years later, as a member of Parliament, he was given a rude reminder of his restless days there, when he returned to show the school to a friend and was pelted with balls by a group of boys. Of his education in general Churchill wrote with obvious bitterness, 'I was on the whole considerably discouraged by my school days ... I would far rather have been apprenticed as a bricklayer's mate, or run errands as a messenger boy, or helped my father to dress the front windows of a grocer's shop ... It would have taught me more ... Also, I should have got to know my father, which would have been a joy to me.'

Churchill completed his formal schooling relatively uneducated, a victim of his own stubborn nature, and by the standards of the British class system an abject failure who had not played the game by its traditional rules. He was largely ignorant of the world and, as a young man of privilege, unequipped for a successful career. He left Harrow in December 1892 having failed to acquire some of the appropriate skills – with the exception of fencing – required of a proper young English gentleman. He was, remembered Shane Leslie, 'deficient in cricket, Latin Verse and other accepted tests of Victorian success ... His father told Jennie that the boy had not the brains to fit him for Oxford.' His father's harsh pronouncement that his son was a good-for-nothing failure was a crushing burden to bear. However, if Churchill could pass the tough entrance examination for admission to Sandhurst, he might yet redeem Randolph's unforgiving judgment.

3
Sandhurst

No one who was not a congenital idiot could avoid passing thence into the Army.
– My Early Life

The British Empire into which Winston Churchill was born in 1874 was at its zenith, eclipsing any in history. Lord Curzon called it 'the greatest instrument for good the world has ever seen'. The Union Jack flew from flagpoles throughout Britain's vast domain, which extended from the Middle East to the far corners of Asia, North America, the Pacific and South Africa – fully one-fifth of the world's land area and one-quarter of its population. The Royal Navy was the most powerful military force in the world, and 'Rule, Britannia' and the Rock of Gibraltar were far more than merely the mottoes and emblems of Britain's empire. Henry V's army of archers and Wellington's regiments, which ended the reign of Napoleon, were renowned. Yet the era of Pax Britannica from 1815 to the mid-1880s was one of almost constant warfare in the outposts of the empire. During this period there were thirteen major colonial wars, ranging from the Opium Wars with China, the Indian Mutiny, the Sikh wars and the Zulu wars to the costly Crimean War against Russia. Niall Ferguson notes, 'In all, there were seventy-two separate British military campaigns in the course of Queen Victoria's reign – more than one for every year of the so-called *pax Britannica.*'

Years later Churchill would become the principal believer in and protector of Britain's dwindling and increasingly irrelevant empire, an anachronism which was already on its deathbed in the wake of the worldwide nationalism that followed the First World War, and which effectively expired with the creation of the independent states of India and Pakistan in 1947.

In his time membership of the army's officer corps was the exclusive province of the British upper class. 'Because they were the leisured class, they were also the fighting class,' writes David Cannadine. They were 'duty-bound and historically conditioned to protect civil society from invasion and disruption. Honour and glory, courage and chivalry, gallantry and loyalty, leadership and horsemanship were quintessential patrician attributes, inculcated in the country house and learned on the hunting field.' That the officer corps was recruited primarily from the upper classes had little or nothing to do with these officers' qualifications to command men. Queen Victoria's nephew the Duke of Cambridge once observed that the British commander in chief 'should be a gentleman first and an officer second', and Nelson himself once declared that 'you cannot be a good officer without being a gentleman.' The Duke of Wellington proclaimed that 'the best officers in the world' were gentlemen of the upper classes. From the time of Waterloo, in fact, the British army had remained virtually unchanged, its virtues, its tactics and its traditions untouched.

Britain was primarily a naval power, and its relatively small army had never been on a level numerically with those in Europe, where much larger standing armies such as those of France were the norm. Bismarck was once asked what he would do should the British army ever appear in Prussia; he was said to have replied that he would 'send a policeman and have it arrested'.

Until 1870 commissions in the cavalry or infantry were acquired by purchase. A candidate had to produce suitable evidence that he had attained 'the education of a gentleman'. To sustain a military career an officer not only had to possess sufficient wealth but also had to come from the upper class. The sons of the wealthy were not expected to work, and those who did not join the army often served in the Church of England or went into politics. The British army did not provide pensions for retired officers; instead when an officer retired he generally sold his commission. A field-grade officer (major or lieutenant colonel) could finance his retirement by selling his commission for as much as ten thousand pounds – the more prestigious the regiment, the higher the value of a commission.

An officer had to win the consent of the colonel commanding the regiment he wished to join and, perhaps most important of all, 'to produce a substantial sum which was both proof of his standing in society and a bond for good behaviour'. One of the primary weaknesses of the British system was that, once commissioned, an officer remained entitled to serve in his chosen regiment for ever, no matter what his age or physical condition. The result was a fossilized system in which some regiments were commanded by similarly fossilized officers, sometimes in their eighties, who were nevertheless entitled to (and did) remain on active service or in command. Promotions were based strictly on seniority within the regiment.

All of this combined to produce an army in which social standing, the proper connections and wealth undermined merit and discouraged the leadership qualities essential in any successful military force. This concept was the result of generations of tradition relatively unchanged by time or the technology of war. To be successful an officer need not be particularly well educated or possess a strong intellect; however, he was expected to meet the standards of bravery, dedication and leadership where it counted – on the battlefield. Field Marshal Lord Wolseley, for example, distrusted officers who read too many textbooks, once remarking that he 'hoped that the British officer would never "degenerate into a bookworm"'. That despite this the system managed to produce a great many effective and successful military leaders such as Marlborough, Wellington and Nelson was a tribute to the British character. Even as late as the Second World War, officers who attained high command but whose origins were in the lower or poorer elements of society were disparaged. Field Marshal Sir Bernard Montgomery was a perfect example of the absurd class consciousness of the British military. In the elitist British army Montgomery was the ultimate outsider, a black-sheep 'colonial' in an exclusive old-boys' club where one's lineage and social standing counted for more than one's ability.

Churchill's towering ambition and ruthless climb up the ladder of success hardly qualified him as a gentleman but in no way detracted from his determination to succeed as an officer or his fascination with all things military and his romanticized view of war. Later on his stormy relations with high-ranking officers from the time of Omdurman in 1898 through two world wars are indicative of his rejection of the dubious premise that being a 'gentleman' somehow counted for more than competence.

The military commission Winston Churchill sought as a matter of necessity was nothing less than a career path that would separate him from his contemporaries, whose entry into the ranks of the military had mostly to do with social and class obligation. Churchill saw it entirely differently: a commission was a stepping-stone to a political career.

The Royal Military College (now called the Royal Military Academy), located at Sandhurst both in Churchill's time and in our own day, is Britain's training school for future officers. Sandhurst was created to remedy the abuses of the purchase system and in response to the disastrous performance of the army during the early campaigns of the French Revolutionary Wars in the 1790s. It was clear that a better means had to be developed to train officers, and a cavalry officer, Major General John Gaspard Le Marchant, established the Royal Military College in 1800. What was called the Junior Department of the College was formed in 1802 – the same year that West Point was founded – in a converted country house at Great Marlow in Buckinghamshire. However, unlike West Point, where the course of instruction is of four years' duration, Sandhurst in Churchill's day trained future officers during three terms, over a period of sixteen months. In 1812 the college moved to its present site at Sandhurst Park, Berkshire.

The mission of Sandhurst in the 1890s was to train gentlemen cadets to be junior army officers, and admission was based on the results of a competitive written examination. Churchill's appointment to Sandhurst was a struggle that he won only narrowly. He first sat the principal entrance examination in July 1892 and failed badly, ranking only 390th of 693 candidates. The minimum admission standard for the cavalry was 6,457 marks; Churchill's score was only 5,100. Welldon wrote frankly to him that 'it is essential that in coming back to school you should come resolved to work not only by fits & starts but with regular persistent industry . . . all depends on yourself.'

On 10 January 1893, shortly after he sat the examination for the second time, he suffered the spectacular accident at his aunt Cornelia's estate when he deliberately jumped off a bridge and attempted to slide down a fir tree to evade capture while playing war games. The accident might well have been his obituary or, at the very least, ended his chances of attaining an army commission. Churchill later grossly exaggerated the extent of his accident, claiming that he was unconscious for three days and ruptured a kidney (had he actually ruptured one of his kidneys he would have bled internally and died, probably within the hour).

Lord Randolph, who was in Ireland at the time of the accident, hastened back to England and summoned a surgeon to his son's bedside. The injuries laid Churchill low until early March, and the medical bills made a serious dent in the family's already depleted pocketbook. Although his parents' extravagant lifestyle had by 1893 nearly bled them dry, they spared no expense when either of their sons required the best available medical attention. 'I was shocked and also flattered to hear of the enormous fees they had paid,' Churchill wrote some years later.

He endured a painful two-month recuperation, and 'for a year I looked at life round a corner.' Most of his convalescence was spent with one of his favourite relatives, his aunt Lily, the Duchess of Marlborough, who also had American roots and was another of his kindly relatives who both encouraged and pampered Churchill, often helping out financially when his parents were pinching pennies, which by 1893 was most of the time. His father's friend and racing partner, Lord Dunraven, drily summed up Churchill's failed attempt at acrobatics: 'I suppose boys will be boys, but I see no necessity for them believing themselves to be birds or monkeys and acting as such.' Whenever the untoward occurred Churchill's lifelong tendency was to rationalize. In the case of this foolishness he argued that the idea of jumping and 'embracing' the top of a fir tree was correct, 'only the data were absolutely wrong'.

To add insult to real injury, the results of his recent examination bore no fruit; he had failed again. Although he did better, scoring 6,106 marks and coming 203rd out of 664 aspirants, it was still not good enough. Lord Randolph wrote seeking Welldon's advice and was told that if Winston was to have any reasonable chance of passing he needed to be a sent to a crammer. Welldon recommended an elite school in west London run by a former army officer, Captain Walter H. James, who had had great success preparing young men for the Sandhurst examination.

When Churchill reported for remedial instruction Captain James found the same lackadaisical attitude his other teachers had encountered. At one point Churchill insolently suggested to his new mentor that 'his knowledge of history was such that he did not want any more teaching in it.' James wrote to Randolph, 'He is distinctly inclined to be inattentive and to think too much of his abilities . . . The boy has very many good points in him but what he wants is very firm handling.' Captain James was neither the first nor the last person to recognize that trying to 'handle' Winston Churchill was hopeless.

On his third try, at the end of June 1893, Churchill was at last successful – but not comfortably so. Although he finished first in the mandatory history paper, his cumulative marks did not qualify him for a future commission in the infantry, which was the elite arm of the British military. In fact they were barely sufficient to meet the criteria for acceptance at Sandhurst as a cavalry cadet.

Churchill was not troubled by his failure to qualify for the infantry and indeed looked forward to the more romantic and adventurous-sounding cavalry. Telegrams to various family members expressed his elation. However, if Winston thought his father would be pleased with his news, he misjudged badly. Lord Randolph was indignant and pelted his hapless son with words that stung like hail. Winston, he thundered, had not finished high enough and was plainly a failure. 'The first extremely discreditable feature of your performance was missing the infantry, for in that failure is demonstrated beyond refutation your slovenly happy-go-lucky harum scarum style of work for which you have always been distinguished at your different schools . . . With all the advantages you had, with all the abilities which you foolishly think yourself to possess . . . this is the grand result that you come up with among the 2nd and 3rd rate class who are only good for commission in a cavalry regiment.'

Lord Randolph concluded with a diatribe so hurtful that one charitably hopes it had more to do with his deteriorating mental condition than with his true feelings. 'Do not think', he wrote, 'I am going to take the trouble of writing to you long letters . . . again on these matters & you need not trouble to write any answer to this part of my letter, because I no longer attach the slightest weight to anything you may say about your own acquirements & exploits. Make this position indelibly impressed on your mind, that if your conduct and action at Sandhurst is similar to what it has been in the other establishments in which it has sought vainly to impart to you some education, then my responsibility for you is over . . . I am certain that if you cannot prevent yourself from leading the idle useless unprofitable life you have had during your schooldays . . . you will become a mere social wastrel one of the hundreds of the public school failures, and you will degenerate into a shabby unhappy & futile existence.'

Lord Randolph's rage was also manifested by the hit to his pocketbook of an additional two hundred pounds a year for horses and their care. 'As soon as possible I shall arrange your exchange into an infantry regiment of the line.' The issue was soon resolved when Churchill was notified that he was being admitted to Sandhurst under an infantry cadetship after all, some other candidates having withdrawn. Randolph fully expected that Winston would become an infantry officer, and he died without ever learning that his rebellious son would eventually spurn a more prestigious infantry commission and instead become a cavalry officer.

Incapable of demonstrating affection for his elder son, Randolph nevertheless was fearful that his future was bleak. His criticisms of his son were exceptionally harsh and were undoubtedly exacerbated by his illness, but they were not entirely without merit. Although he was unwilling to admit it, what grated was that his son clearly had ability but, for reasons he was unable to understand, refused to use his gifts in a responsible manner. From his first schooldays at Ascot Churchill had demonstrated a complete disdain for education except on his own terms. When the spirit moved him he worked and studied hard; when it did not, which was usually, his marks suffered accordingly. And while Lord Randolph may have questioned his son's brains, those who taught him knew that his abilities far exceeded his underemployed talent. Nor could his father possibly have predicted his rebellious son's achievements and fame.

Churchill's reply was contrite and masked his shock and disappointment at his father's stern disapproval. 'I am very sorry you are displeased with me ... [I] will try to modify your opinion of me by my work & conduct at Sandhurst.' Writing to his mother he also concealed his feelings, noting that at Sandhurst 'my fate is in my own hands & I have a fresh start.'

Lord Randolph used his friendship with the Duke of Cambridge, the commander in chief of the British army, to have Winston commissioned in the 60th Rifles (King's Royal Rifle Corps), one of the elite regiments of the British army, when he completed his training. Churchill duly entered Sandhurst at the beginning of September 1893 as an infantry cadet.

As the son of a famous politician Churchill was typical of the young men admitted to Sandhurst and Woolwich who were public schoolboys from the 'proper' social and economic backgrounds. What made Sand-hurst unique for Winston Churchill was that for the first time in his life he took a genuine interest in his education. Being there had a purpose and a goal – and for Churchill having a good reason to do anything was paramount.

The discipline was strict, the accommodation was spartan and the hours were long and tiring, but none of this seemed to bother him much. Not only did he have a fresh start, but also 'I was deeply interested in my work, especially Tactics and Fortification,' he later recalled. In addition to learning the discipline of marching and drilling on the parade ground, cadets were taught a variety of subjects including security; military law; army administration; rudimentary map reading and draw-ing; how to construct various types of field fortifications, cut railway lines and blow up bridges; and gymnastics. His father helpfully enabled him to acquire a small military library.

Churchill had great enthusiasm for horses and horsemanship and spent a great deal of the funds sent to him by his parents hiring horses at a nearby livery stable. He became proficient at riding, a skill he would of course need to master as a cavalry officer. 'Horses were my greatest pleasure at Sandhurst,' he later wrote. He participated in steeplechases and point-to-point events. Father and son even displayed evidence of a newfound intimacy. Lord Randolph sent Winston to a riding school in order to help improve his skills, though his learning was tempered by 'biting the tan' (being thrown from his horse) on numerous occasions. In his memoir Churchill advised those of his readers who were parents: 'Don't give your son money. As far as you can afford it, give him horses.'

During drill, however, he still had trouble distinguishing his left foot from his right, and for a time was consigned to the 'Awkward Squad', which consisted of remedial training for cadets who required 'smartening up'. In his first year, Churchill's examinations were satisfactory but placed him far from the top of his class. His conduct was 'good but unpunctual'. For the remainder of his course his marks and class standing would improve dramatically, but he remained unashamedly unpunctual.

Although Churchill's endurance markedly improved at Sandhurst, he required assistance after a mandatory three-quarter-mile run with full field pack. 'I am cursed with so feeble a body that I can hardly support the fatigues of the day; but I suppose I shall get stronger during my stay here,' he lamented. Yet the occasional bumps, bruises and other assorted scrapes failed to dampen his newfound enthusiasm: 'One could feel oneself growing up almost every week.'

With no source of funds to support his education, Churchill relied on Lord Randolph to come to his assistance. Only later did he learn of his parents' severe financial straits. His father managed to send him ten pounds a month, which usually met his needs. Still, Churchill would also sometimes approach his mother in his quest to augment his monthly stipend. Although his appeals often worked, they also brought stern warnings from his mother to mend his spendthrift ways or face being cut off.

His father's disapproval weighed heavily upon Churchill, who wrote wistfully to Jennie: 'I am awfully sorry that Papa does not approve of my letters. I take a great deal of pains over them & often re-write entire pages. If I write a descriptive account of my life here, I receive a hint from you that my style is too sententious & stilted. If on the other hand I write a plain and excessively simple letter – it is put down as slovenly. I can never do anything right.' Nevertheless for the first time his father seemed proud of his son's achievements, often praising him to his friends with Winston present. But privately Lord Randolph still insisted on treating him as a child in need of constant reproof rather than as a young adult about to make his own way. Despite the approval of Winston's company officer, he refused permission for his son to take what was called 'unrestricted leave' from Sandhurst during periods of free time, such as weekends, a status routinely granted most cadets. Of his father's refusal to trust him, and his constant faultfinding, Churchill wrote, 'I suppose I shall go on being treated as "that boy" until I am 50 years old.'

There is no better example of Churchill's fragile relationship with his father than an incident in 1894 involving a gold pocket watch engraved with the Churchill coat of arms that had been presented to him by Randolph. After it was damaged one day when another cadet ran into him as he was placing it in a protective leather case, Churchill had the watch secretly repaired without telling his father of the incident. However, not long afterwards, to his utter dismay, it fell out of his pocket while he was walking along the edge of a nearby pond and sank in six feet of water. He stripped off his clothes and waded into the pond in an attempt to retrieve it. Faced with a choice between hypothermia and leaving the watch, Churchill gave up, but he returned the following day after securing permission from the commandant to do whatever it took to find the watch – provided of course that he paid for it.

What he did next was a preview of Winston Churchill at his audacious best. Where others would have simply written off the watch and faced the music, he 'borrowed 23 men from the Infantry Detachment – dug a new course for the stream – obtained the fire engine and pumped the pool dry and so recovered the watch.' Unfortunately for Winston, Lord Randolph also happened to visit the watchmaker a short time later and learned of both incidents. His condemnation was swift. That Winston was 'stupid' was the crux of it, but what must have hurt just as deeply was his father's reference to his brother Jack as one who never did 'stupid things' and 'is vastly your superior'.

Not all of Lord Randolph's letters were censorious. A short time before, he had written to urge his son to buckle down. 'Now is the time to work & work hard,' and 'if you desire to be thought smart & well trained & well informed about all the details of your profession you should still keep up all your Sandhurst acquirements. Why do I write all this. Because when you go into the army I wish you to make your one aim the ambition of rising in that profession by showing to your officers superior military knowledge skill & instinct. This is all written in perfect kindness to you. If I did not care about you I would not trouble to write long letters to you.'

Although Lord Randolph was adamant that his son join the 60th Rifles, it was not long after entering Sandhurst that Winston fell in love with the cavalry and its glamour and wanted no part of becoming a foot soldier. About this time an old friend of the family, the commanding officer of the 4th Hussars, Colonel John P. Brabazon, invited Churchill to Aldershot to dine in the regimental mess. The occasion and the spectacle of twenty to thirty officers brilliantly dressed in blue and gold uniforms so impressed him that his decision to join the cavalry became irrevocable. 'It was like a State banquet . . . an all-pervading air of glitter, affluence, ceremony and veiled discipline.' Brabazon indicated that he would be pleased to have Churchill as a member of his regiment when he was commissioned. Winston's intention to spurn an infantry commission displeased and embarrassed both Lord Randolph and the Duke of Cambridge. In a gesture of goodwill the duke indicated he could still find a place for Winston in the 60th Rifles.

Although he admired Brabazon as 'one of the finest soldiers in the army', Randolph grumbled that he 'had no business to go and turn that boy's head about going into the 4th Hussars'. What Churchill's parents failed to recognize was their son's growing independence; he was beginning to make his own life decisions.

His diligence paid off when he triumphed in his exams and graduated in December 1894 with honours from Sandhurst, eighth in a class of 150 cadets. It had been, he wrote, 'a hard but happy experience ... I passed out of Sandhurst into the world. It opened like Aladdin's Cave.' He was now eligible to receive his commission from Queen Victoria.

In 1894 Lord Randolph Churchill became gravely ill with an unspecified condition that was widely believed to have been complications from syphilis, but in recent years has been considered as more likely to have been a brain tumour or some other neurological disorder. In June, Winston was summoned home from Sandhurst to see his father off on what was to be the longest of his numerous escapist journeys, this one to take him around the world on a fruitless search in exotic places for an elixir that might restore his failing health. In addition to Jennie, Randolph's entourage included a family doctor, his longtime manservant Thomas Walden – and a lead coffin, in the event of his death during the trip. Lord Randolph was by this time a mere shadow of his former self: 'His face looked terribly haggard and worn with mental pain. He patted me on the knee in a gesture which however simple was perfectly informing ... I never saw him again, except as a swiftly fading shadow.'

In late November, Lord Randolph's condition worsened in India, then improved slightly before again degenerating when they reached Egypt. His behaviour ranged from bizarre to outright insane. For Jennie the trip was a horrible ordeal. 'He is quite unfit for society ... you cannot imagine anything more distracting & desperate than to watch it & see him as he is,' she wrote to her sister Clara.

None of Winston's thirty-six letters sent to them during his parents' journey was answered. One, written on 9 December 1894, described how he was one of only fifteen cadets in his class picked for what was called the Riding Examination, a stiff competition that included jumping fences with and without stirrups or reins, jumping with the hands behind the back, and other challenging tests of riding skills. The fifteen riders were reduced to a final four still in contention for a coveted prize, one of whom was Churchill. The event was witnessed and judged by a cavalry general and other senior cavalry officers from Aldershot. 'I was wild with excitement and rode I think better than I have ever done before but failed to win the prize by 1 mark being 2nd with 199 out of 200 marks. I am awfully pleased with the result, which in a place where everyone rides means a great deal . . . I hope you will be pleased.' It is doubtful that Churchill's letter recording his exemplary feat of horsemanship ever reached his ailing father.

To the end Lord Randolph remained the same cantankerous and certainly unhappy man he had become since his ignominious fall from power. From the moment of his return to England on Christmas Eve 1894 until his death aged forty-five on 24 January 1895 at his mother's house in Grosvenor Square, 'the family awaited his death with miserable resignation . . . [until] the numbing fingers of paralysis laid that weary brain to rest.' Winston was asleep in the house of a neighbour when he was summoned with the news of his father's passing. He ran through the snow to join his mother, devastated by the news. Lord Randolph's death seemed to galvanize young Churchill, and as Shane Leslie, who witnessed the event, explained, 'Winston emerged like a strong-willed being that had been hitherto a caterpillar, and had now taken charge. He stood with a silent glare receiving the visits of his father's friends in the hall. Later it was whispered by nurses that he stood with his elbow against his father's coffin. This was as it should be for he had already decided to take his father under biographical protection.'

Churchill would write of his father's death, 'All my dreams of comradeship with him, of entering Parliament at his side or in his support, were ended. There remained for me only to pursue his aims, and vindicate his memory. This I have tried to do.' For the remainder of his long life Winston would relentlessly chase – but never catch – the ghost of his dead father.

Lord Randolph Churchill was buried on a chilly winter day in the churchyard in the village of Bladon, within sight of Blenheim, the estate he had coveted but never owned. His son's description, written some years later, was of a 'landscape brilliant with sunshine', over which 'snow had spread like a glittering pall'.

A memorial service was held in Westminster Abbey, dutifully attended by members of the Conservative government, and by Randolph's nemesis, Lord Salisbury. His son was determined that his father's legacy (dubious though it actually was) would not be forgotten, and that one day he would write the story of his life, a promise he kept in 1906.

An unfulfilled relationship with his son was not the only thing Lord Randolph Churchill left behind in the wake of his death. His unpaid debts ravaged the inheritance left to his family. What the creditors did not take, Jennie managed to consume through her profligate spending. Winston candidly admitted to a cousin, 'We are damned poor!' and some years later observed that relative poverty had probably been fortunate. 'Perhaps it was a very good thing that we lost the Jerome millions. Suppose we had inherited them as Grandpa's male heirs. Where would we be now? . . . It was a good thing that we never had that money to spend on yachts and horses, on gambling and women. Why by now we should have long reached the gutters of Monte Carlo!' Indeed it obliged both Winston and Jack to fend for themselves and become financially independent. Nevertheless in his own way Churchill carried on the family tradition and was himself an incorrigible spender, living beyond his means for most of his life, his writing his primary source of income.

A week after Lord Randolph's burial Churchill forcefully declared his independence by persuading his mother to telegraph Colonel Brabazon with a request that he be given a place in his regiment. The colonel immediately gave his blessing, and correspondence between Jennie and the Duke of Cambridge brought about the desired result: Churchill would be commissioned as a cavalry officer.

What Lord Randolph never lived to see was that his son's future as a cavalry officer not only was auspicious but would offer him opportunities to succeed in a manner that would hardly have been possible had he become an infantry officer. Winston's military training at Sandhurst was rudimentary at best, and, as is true with any school, practical application of his profession would soon become his best teacher.

4

A Young Man on the Make:
The 4th Queen's Own Hussars

Winston Leonard Spencer Churchill, Gentleman Second Lieutenant, Land Forces.   – By Her Majesty's Command

On 14 February 1895, the newly minted second lieutenant Winston S. Churchill reported to the army barracks at Aldershot, Surrey, for duty with his new regiment, the 4th Queen's Own Hussars. His long-coveted commission from the queen arrived six days later and formalized his entry into the army.

Officially a 'gentleman' by virtue of his commission, Churchill was expected to live by a convoluted gentleman's code. Among the unwritten provisions was the obligation to pay one's gambling debts without delay, although other debts might often remain unpaid with impunity. Thus, six years after he was commissioned Churchill had inexcusably failed to pay his tailor for his uniforms. The fact that Churchill was a gentleman by royal decree did not necessarily make it so. In fact, the young man who stumbled into adulthood from a stormy and rebellious childhood was hardly admirable in any respect. Virtually friendless and exceedingly self-absorbed, Churchill fully merits the observation by the biographer Richard Holmes that a close study of his letters to his mother, to whom he frequently made outrageous demands during this period of his life, reveals a very disagreeable personality.

The British army of 1895 had not participated in a major conflict since the Crimean War of 1854–6, notable for the Charge of the Light Brigade at Balaklava, the last great cavalry action. It seemed to Churchill that he had joined the army at the wrong time; he had no way of knowing that within the space of five years he would take part in a sufficient number of wars to satisfy even the most ardent adventurer.

The heart and soul of the British army was its regiments, each with a cherished battle history carved into its identity like engraving in a stone. Regiments consisted of a variable number of battalions and companies. In 1895 the British army comprised 225,000 men, organized into 140 battalions. Fewer than 17,000 were cavalrymen assigned to one of the army's twenty-eight cavalry regiments. At any one time more than half the army was based overseas.

Tradition was the bond that drew men like Churchill to its ranks. Tradition meant past glories won in exotic places, and none were greater than those of a handful of regiments that symbolized the battles of fame, and sometimes infamy, in defence of the British Empire. John Keegan has noted that regiments were (and still are) like tribes, and 'regimental loyalty was the touchstone of their lives. A personal difference might be forgiven the next day. A slur on the regiment would never be forgotten, indeed would never be uttered.' For all practical purposes the British regiment was a separate world.

The 4th Queen's Own Hussars was a light cavalry regiment that possessed one of the army's finest pedigrees, a lineage dating to 1685, and battles fought in the far corners of the empire, from the Peninsula to Balaklava, Sevastopol and Afghanistan. In 1893 it had been relocated from Ireland to the Aldershot garrison. Colonel Brabazon, its dashing commander, was a veteran of the Afghan wars of 1878 and 1879, and the very embodiment of how a professional soldier should look and act. His inability (whether real or affected was never clear) to pronounce the letter *r* made Churchill feel more comfortable with his own speech impediment. The 4th Hussars offered Churchill the excitement of being a cavalry officer and the expectation of one day becoming a warrior in his own right in some far-flung corner of the empire.

Junior lieutenants begin their military careers at the very bottom of the chain of command, and are paid and treated accordingly. Pay was abysmal and dated from rates established in 1806, so that subalterns like Churchill received annual pay of ninety-five pounds. (Clerks in the War Office were paid nearly twice as much.) Outside income was not only essential but expected. By the time Churchill was commissioned, pay was approximately £150 per annum, whereas £650 was deemed the bare minimum to maintain the standard of living expected of a regimental cavalry officer. As a graduation present from Sandhurst, Aunt Lily promised him a charger (a horse trained to go into battle in a cavalry charge with the rider using one hand on the reins and holding a sword or pistol in the other). However, her new husband Lord William Beresford instead purchased a racing pony, which was no help in fulfilling Churchill's immediate needs. Moreover, significantly greater expenses remained if Churchill was to enjoy the lifestyle of an officer and meet a cavalryman's requirement of a minimum of one charger, three polo ponies and two hunter-jumpers. In addition officers were obliged to furnish their own quarters, and meet other expenses consistent with their status.

Of greater importance than his finances were the complex challenges that came with an officer's commission. To be effective he had not only to become militarily proficient but also – and this was the hard part – to earn the respect of those under whom he served as well as of those whom he commanded. Although authority is conferred by virtue of a commission, respect is earned. To be rated 'not good with soldiers' was the ultimate condemnation.

New officers were required to complete a basic training programme of six months' duration, the same instruction given to private soldiers. The regimental riding master was an ill-tempered, tyrannical major nicknamed 'Jocko', an unsparingly tough taskmaster who seemed to relish ridiculing the slightest mistake by his charges, particularly if the offender happened to be an officer. Although officially an officer and a gentleman, Churchill in Jocko's eyes was merely a raw, untrained recruit who had to be taught the ways of cavalry drill. He was among the victims of Jocko's sharp tongue and later ruefully recalled that it was difficult to maintain one's dignity while sprawled in the dirt after falling off a horse during a mounting-and-dismounting drill. 'Many a time did I pick myself up shaken and sore from the riding-school tan and don again my little gold braided pork-pie cap . . . with what appearance of dignity I could command, while twenty recruits grinned furtively but delightedly.' When he tore a muscle in his thigh he could not admit it – the prospect of enduring Jocko's public scorn was sufficient incentive to fight through the pain. Churchill was unaccustomed to mutely accepting criticism or abuse from anyone, but in Jocko he met his match, and for once he wisely kept his own counsel.

New officers also had to acquire certain skills before being pro-nounced qualified for regimental service. The daily routine of garrison duty in peacetime lacked excitement. A typical day at the Aldershot garrison began with breakfast in bed (which years later would become one of Churchill's trademarks), followed by a gruelling two hours of riding school, care and grooming of the horses, and private-practice carbine exercises with a sergeant, which would enable him to catch up with training already under way.

The afternoon was taken up with drill – which Churchill loathed – followed by hot baths to ease the aches and pains from riding. Evenings were spent in the mess socializing and playing various card games, at which he did not excel. (Whatever he did not excel at he dismissed as boring or pointless.) Riding school normally lasted twelve months, but Churchill's skills were better than average, and he was advised that three months would be adequate. He was soon playing polo and steeple-chasing (against his mother's wishes), and escaped serious injury in March 1895 when he was thrown, nearly breaking a leg.

His primary challenge, however, remained finding sufficient funds to meet his obligations as an officer. As if that were not enough, his mother's escalating debts would soon entangle her sons, who felt obliged to come to her aid. His money woes notwithstanding, Churchill was enamoured of his new existence; despite its austerity, it 'was a gay and lordly life that now opened upon me'. He loved the pomp and pageantry. While he was still a cadet at Sandhurst, Queen Victoria had travelled to Aldershot in May 1894 for a gala parade in her honour. The entire twenty-five-thousand-man garrison was assembled, resplendent in their colourful dress uniforms of blues, reds and gold, swords glittering in the sunlight. Churchill was part of a Sandhurst guard of honour, and the occasion made a tremendous impression.

While his life revolved around the army, Churchill was already study-ing politics and politicians with a keen eye and forming ideas. He was a young man of infinite ambition, and it was clear that he never intended to make a career of military service, particularly when it was thought that war was unlikely. His military obligation was for four years, and as he wrote to his mother, 'four years of healthy and pleasant exercise, combined with both responsibility & discipline can do no harm to me – but rather good. The more I see of soldiering the more I like it, but the more I feel convinced it is not my *métier*. Well, we shall see.'

Thirty-five years later he would still sing the praises of the 'thrill and the charm' in the 'glittering jingle' of a squadron of cavalrymen manoeuvring in synchronized formation, while bemoaning the fact that war by then had turned impersonal, greedy and base with the advent of the aeroplane, the machine gun and artillery, all of which could kill indiscriminately. 'The Dragoon, the Lancer and above all, as we believed, the Hussar, still claimed their time-honoured place upon the battlefield. War, which used to be cruel and magnificent, has now become cruel and squalid.' Churchill's idea of war was to assemble the warring parties in a venue similar to that of the Olympic Games and settle the problem in an honourable, civilized manner. War, he believed, should not be left in the hands of incompetent politicians and amateurs who, he pointedly noted, 'reduced it to a mere disgusting matter of Men, Money and Machinery'.

With the British army numbering only 225,000 men in the 1890s, Churchill was not alone in believing that never again would it engage in a European conflict. Looking back in 1930 at his early years in the army, Churchill was disillusioned that the values and expectations he possessed as a young officer had all been overturned. 'Everything I was sure or taught to be sure was impossible, has happened,' he pensively wrote. His education as the future warlord of his nation had begun with the belief that his warrior skills would never be put to the test. What neither Churchill nor anyone else could foresee in the 1890s was that, despite the usual minor clashes in out-of-the-way places, Britain's almost unprecedented period of peace was swiftly coming to an end. The final years of the nineteenth century and the early years of the twentieth would see war on a scale no one would have believed possible.

In early July 1895 Churchill suffered a shattering blow with the death from peritonitis at the age of sixty-two of his beloved nanny, Mrs Everest. He had been to visit her shortly before her death. 'She was delighted to see me . . . and I think my coming made her die happy,' he sorrowfully told his mother. 'I shall never know such a friend again . . . I feel very low – and find that I never realized how much poor old Woom was to me.' She had been let go by Lord Randolph in the autumn of 1891 primarily because Jack, at the age of eleven, had no further need of a nanny. Winston protested in vain, but perhaps because of her long service to the Churchills, his grandmother, Fanny, the dowager Duchess of Marlborough, hired her.

In October 1893, however, Fanny also discharged Mrs Everest, provoking outrage from Winston, who wrote to his mother protesting the shabby manner in which she had been dismissed by a terse letter and without final wages. His protests fell upon deaf ears; his mother had never been close to her son's nanny, a common phenomenon with such relationships in the British upper classes. Although Jennie made no effort to intervene on Mrs Everest's behalf with her mother-in-law, Lord Randolph arranged for a small monthly stipend to be sent to her. In his study of Churchill's character, Richard Holmes suggests, 'It did not occur to him to moderate his own financial demands in return for a small continuing payment to the woman he claimed to love so much.'

She had been the rock of Winston's life, the one steadfast constant he could always count on for love and sympathy, for moral support and for understanding him as his parents never did. Throughout their long relationship Churchill had always been her 'darling precious boy'. Winston and Jack paid for Mrs Everest's headstone and attended her burial, and for a number of years thereafter Churchill paid a florist to maintain the grave. 'Until the end of his life her photograph hung in his room,' and as Shane Leslie has remarked, 'England may be grateful to that dear and dutiful woman.'

In the peacetime British army the year was broken into a seven-month period of training and a winter season of five months, during which officers were granted two and one-half months of unrestricted leave to do as they pleased. Garrison duty had already become boring and, with no extra funds for extracurricular activities such as hunting, de rigueur for any self-respecting officer, Churchill was determined to make good use of his first year's leave in the winter of 1895–6 and cast about for somewhere he could indulge his thirst for adventure. Seeking out a war was a highly acceptable alternative. One of the few places where there was conflict that year was Cuba, where rebels were fighting a lengthy guerrilla war with the Spaniards.

Determined to get to Cuba, Churchill used family connections to write to an old friend of his father, Sir Henry Drummond Wolff, the British ambassador to Spain, who was happy to oblige and not only arranged for the necessary permissions but paved the way for him to be warmly received in Havana by the Spanish authorities. He also embarked on his first journalism assignment by persuading a London newspaper, the *Daily Graphic*, to pay him the sum of five guineas each for letters from Cuba about the war.

It was the first of many occasions when Winston Churchill engaged in the practice of 'doing business with the people at the top'. He was also recruited by the director of military intelligence to collect statistics and information, and given maps and background on the situation in Cuba. However the request may have been phrased, Churchill and his companion, Reginald Barnes, an officer from his regiment and a future divisional commander in France in the First World War, were acting as spies.

The two men travelled to Cuba via New York in November 1895 aboard a Cunard Royal Mail steamship. Americans, Churchill told Jack, were good-hearted, crude, strong, lusty and charming, but American journalism was 'vulgarity divested of truth. Their best papers write for a class of snotty housemaids and footmen . . . mind you, that vulgarity is a sign of strength . . . which may well be the envy of older nations of the earth.' The two officers were given a private tour of the cruiser *New York*. Churchill wrote that its sailors 'impressed me more than the ship itself, for while any nation can build a battleship – it is the monopoly of the Anglo-Saxon race to breed good seamen'. He was also taken on a tour of the US Military Academy at West Point and was shocked by the rigid discipline, calling it 'positively disgraceful'. Given Churchill's own rebellious nature towards authority, this view was not altogether surprising. Those who give up their personal liberty, as the cadets at West Point are obliged to do, 'can never make good citizens or fine soldiers', he complained. His conclusion was enigmatic: 'A child who rebels against that sort of control should be whipped – so should a man who does not rebel.'

Churchill and Barnes arrived in the Spanish colony of Cuba on 20 November. The island had been the scene of unrest off and on for most of the nineteenth century. When insurrection erupted anew in 1895, Spain sent a seven-thousand-man expeditionary force to suppress it. However, all attempts had failed, and by the time Churchill arrived, there was open support in both Britain and the United States for the rebels.

Churchill had never seen action, and his idealism and belief in the sanctity of war were untested. 'From very early youth I had brooded about soldiers and war, and often I had imagined in dreams and day-dreams the sensations attendant upon being for the first time under fire.

It seemed to my youthful mind that it must be a thrilling and immense experience to hear the whistle of bullets all around and to play at hazard from moment to moment with death and wounds.'

His first glimpse of Cuba inflamed his romanticism. 'I felt as if I sailed with Captain Silver and first gazed on Treasure Island,' he wrote. 'Here was a place where real things were going on . . . a scene of vital action . . . Here I might leave my bones.' However, as he later admitted, his musings were detached, given the arrival of breakfast and 'the hurry of disembarkation'.

The two young officers wasted no time in journeying by armoured train to eastern Cuba, where sporadic fighting was taking place. In contrast to the exotic grandeur of Havana, this was 'a forsaken place', largely jungle, unspoiled vistas and incredible heat and humidity, where 'smallpox and yellow fever are rife'. What they found was a messy guerrilla war that had no front, no battle lines and none of the glory or spectacle Churchill had imagined war to be. While there was lots of shooting (though with few casualties), the 'war' consisted largely of a ragtag rebel force conducting ambushes, attacking railway lines and trains, but avoiding all-out conflict with the heavily manned and armed Spaniards in battles they could not win.

Churchill and Barnes were warmly received by the Spanish commander, General Álvaro Suárez Valdés, who entertained them in his mess and proclaimed it an honour to have a pair of English officers accompanying him on a two-week march with a force of nearly four thousand Spanish troops deep into Cuba's interior in search of the rebels. The Englishmen were provided with horses and accorded the same amenities as Spanish officers. Communication with their hosts was by means of 'execrable French'. What little they saw of the Cuban insurgency was only from the perspective of the Spaniards and taught them very little about the nature of war, other than as an example of futility. It seemed as if they were chasing ghosts who would fleetingly appear from time to time but never long enough to pin down.

Churchill's twenty-first birthday was an auspicious occasion, when 'for the first time I heard shots fired in anger and heard bullets strike flesh or whistle through the air.' Dressed in uniforms unsuitable for the humid jungle, Churchill and Barnes were accompanying a search party when rebels began taking potshots. The only casualty was a horse behind him, which was mortally wounded by a bullet Churchill thought passed within a foot of his head and therefore qualified him as having been 'under fire'. He also observed the horse die a painful death from a bullet that might well have ended his own life. He would later recall that, as a result of the experience, 'I began to take a more thoughtful view of our enterprise than I had hitherto done.'

Although both men were non-combatants in a godforsaken place, they were nevertheless in harm's way, devoutly hoping not to be killed or wounded. Churchill was convinced that, for all the irrationality of charging off into the jungles of an island thousands of miles from Britain, 'there were very few subalterns in the British Army who would not have given a month's pay to sit in our saddles.' In this respect he was no different from other young men for whom the thrill of adventure far outweighs consideration for their safety or their lives.

Before they left Cuba the two men were decorated with the Spanish Red Cross (a medal given only to officers) for their service there, but once back in England they were informed by the War Office that under no circumstances were they to wear the medal. While the army was quite prepared for its peacetime officers to seek out risky ventures like Cuba, it was hardly willing to call formal attention to that fact.

Churchill's participation with the Spaniards drew condemnation in both the United States and Britain. In the first of what would be countless such occurrences, he became a controversial figure in British public life. His dispatches made public the fact that he was in Cuba with the Spaniards. One newspaper wondered what business a British officer had mixing himself up in a foreign dispute. 'Spending a holiday in fighting other people's battles is rather an extraordinary proceeding even for a Churchill,' noted the *Newcastle Leader*. Moreover, by some he was seen as merely a mouthpiece for the Spaniards, to whom he was thought to be beholden.

Churchill's five dispatches to the *Daily Graphic*, under the byline 'From Our Own Correspondent', were well written and long on descriptions of the countryside but necessarily short on anything of substance. At best he saw a handful of rebels at a distance melting into the protective shelter of the Cuban landscape. He complained about the absurd amounts of ammunition fired by both sides, but primarily by the Spaniards: 99 per cent of this ammunition never hit anyone. 'It has always been said ... that it takes 200 bullets to kill a soldier, but as applied to the Cuban war 200,000 shots would be closer to the mark.'

Part of him was sympathetic to the rebels' cause, although he was revolted by and disdainful of them and their cruelty. In 1896 Churchill wrote an article about the war for the *Saturday Review*, in which he characterized the rebels as fighting neither bravely nor effectively. 'They cannot win a single battle or hold a single town. Their army, consisting to a large extent of coloured men, is an undisciplined rabble.' The Spaniards may have been bad, but a Cuban government would be even worse, 'equally corrupt, more capricious, and far less stable'.

Churchill's Cuban adventure lasted less than three weeks. What he actually witnessed in Cuba was the death knell of Spanish colonialism and an omen of the future of Britain's own vast empire. The United States recognized the rebels in 1896 and would go to war three years later against the Spaniards in a short but bloody conflict. American sympathy was somewhat at Churchill's expense. His and Barnes's presence in Cuba did not go unnoticed in the US press; Churchill was interviewed by the *New York World* in an article which pointed out that other newspapers had printed 'many flaming editorials' condemning the presence in Cuba of 'emissaries of the British government sent to teach [Marshal Arsenio Martínez] Campos [the commander in chief of Spanish forces in Cuba] how to whip the secessionists' in what was clearly a case of Britain 'throwing more bricks at the Monroe Doctrine'.

That notion that two wholly inexperienced young British officers were in Cuba to teach experienced Spanish officers anything was almost comical, but then as now the press never shied away from a newsworthy story, particularly when it was starved of information and had in Churchill (back in New York City on his way home to England) a talkative and quotable Englishman who thrived in the limelight of public attention. 'The country is well nigh ruined,' he opined to the *New York Herald*, 'and a speedy peace seems to be the only thing that can save its people from a general bankruptcy.' But as a young man taught from birth to believe in the concept of British colonialism, Churchill could hardly have been expected to side with a cause that would end Spanish rule. His loquaciousness got him into considerable trouble with Sir Henry Drummond Wolff, who wrote in February 1896 from Madrid: 'I should be very glad if you could avoid saying things unpalatable to the Spaniards, having obtained the letters on your behalf which secured your good treatment I am reproached for the unfavourable commentaries you make . . . this kind of thing places me in a painful dilemma.'

Although his first real test of bravery was yet to come, Cuba was nevertheless a useful learning experience. One of its lessons was the value of a siesta. Churchill found the Spanish practice of long afternoon naps during the heat of the day very much to his liking and adopted it as his own for the rest of his life.

It was the regular practice of the British army for regiments stationed in Britain periodically to replace units that had been stationed overseas for a number of years. In 1896 the 4th Hussars were alerted for a nine-year deployment to India and were to sail in September. The prospect of dreary peacetime service in India held no appeal, and Churchill sought ways to escape accompanying the regiment. His brief forays into politics at various events in London left him with the idea that perhaps politics was where he belonged. When he learned that General Sir Herbert Kitchener, the commander in chief of the British army in Egypt, was mounting an expedition to the Sudan to avenge the killing of Major General Charles 'Chinese' Gordon at Khartoum ten years earlier, he made representations to be assigned to Kitchener's headquarters. When that ploy failed, Churchill, who by now considered himself an accomplished journalist, sought assignments in exotic places from various newspapers. One newspaper, the *Daily Chronicle*, offered a handsome remuneration to report on the unrest in Crete but required him to pay his own travel expenses. The cash-strapped Churchill had to decline. Towards the end of the summer of 1896 his opportunities to avoid duty in India dwindled. As a very junior officer only just returned from Cuba, he had virtually no chance of dodging such service unless pressure was exerted in high places. The prospect in no way deterred him from shamelessly using his father's name and his mother's influence in a quest to gain permission for temporary leave from his regiment. His efforts not only were unsuccessful but also drew the unfavourable notice of the army.

By August 1896 Churchill had become ill tempered and frustrated by his inability to realize duty either with Kitchener or in South Africa. After learning that the 9th (Queen's Royal) Lancers were being sent to South Africa, and possibly to Rhodesia to quell a native rebellion, he somehow managed to persuade Colonel Brabazon to recommend his temporary posting to that regiment. He also wrote to his mother to demand her immediate help in his quest to avoid having to accompany the 4th Hussars to India. 'The future to me is utterly unattractive,' he complained in what was perhaps the most candid letter he ever wrote to her. 'I look upon going to India with this unfortunate regiment – (which I now feel so attached to that I cannot leave it for another) – as useless and unprofitable exile. When I speculate upon what might be and consider that I am letting the golden opportunity go by I feel that I am guilty of an indolent folly that I shall regret all my life.' Churchill's rationale was shamelessly self-serving. A chestful of medals, he reasoned, was the key to a political career. 'A few months in South Africa would earn me the S.A. [South Africa] medal and in all probability the [British South Africa] company's Star. Thence hot foot to Egypt – to return with two more decorations in a year or two – and beat my sword into an iron despatch box.'

By the age of twenty-two Churchill had already adopted his lifelong maxim of never taking no for an answer. Generally when he wrote to Jennie it was to plead for money. However, on this occasion his letter was a blatant and bullying demand that she come to his aid – at once.

I cannot believe that with all the influential friends you possess and all those who would do something for me for my father's sake – that I could not be allowed to go – were those influences properly exerted.

It is useless to preach the gospel of patience to me. Others as young are making the running now and what chance have I of ever catching up. I put it down here – definitely on paper – that you really ought to leave no stone unturned to help me . . . It is a little thing for you to ask and a smaller thing for those in authority to grant . . . three months leave is what I want & you could get if for me . . . you cant realize how furiously intolerable this life is to me when so much is going on a month away from here.

There is no known reply from Lady Randolph. Churchill's various attempts to escape duty in India eventually came to naught. Fresh out of options he sailed with his regiment from Southampton on 11 September 1896.

5

The Jewel of Empire: India, 1896–1897

*Such was 'the long, long Indian day' as I knew it for three years; and not such a
bad day either.* — My Early Life

When Winston Churchill arrived in Bombay in early October 1896, the
British presence in India was already 287 years old. India's civilization
had existed for more than five thousand years, a span that made it one
of the world's oldest. The first outsiders were Aryan tribes from the new
world which arrived some time around 1500 BC and eventually merged
with indigenous tribes to evolve into what became the Indian people.
Arabs, Portuguese and Dutch preceded the British East India Company,
established in 1609 to trade in the rich textiles and spices that abounded
throughout Asia. The East India Company became the world's most
powerful private enterprise and, after Robert Clive led the British to
victory in the Battle of Plassey in 1757, a *de facto* government.

The British believed that everything noble about their empire was on
display in India. When the hugely successful Empire of India Exhibition
opened in London's Earl's Court in 1895, its premise was that the
supervision and control of India by a mere quarter of a million British
troops and administrators were evidence of British brilliance. Certainly
it was the epitome of condescension when the viceroy of India, Lord
Curzon, proclaimed that 'governing India was the fulfilment of a mandate from God', and that the result was 'the miracle of the world'.
However, the reality was that India had become far more than the crown
jewel of Britain's vast empire: its immense riches were a vital economic
necessity.

The Victorian world of empire was the foundation of Winston
Churchill's beliefs and upbringing. Now, in 1896, he would see for
himself what had inspired Kipling's mesmerizing writing about India,

and he would experience what he and his countrymen regarded as a modern version of the divine right of kings. However, policing the sprawling empire was another matter altogether, and as Britain's influence spread and it acquired territories in faraway places ranging from Egypt to South Africa and India, its security problems multiplied.

The East India Company had an insatiable and irresponsible appetite for profit, and its imperial administration of India was marred by a succession of Anglo-Sikh wars and by the bloody Sepoy Mutiny of 1857–8, after which Britain disbanded the company. In 1873 a governor general was installed and the British colonial system of administration created. Along with the Indian army, the British army became the instrument for enforcing security and internal order.

Famine, starvation, floods, crushing poverty, sickness and sectarian violence beset the India of the British Empire, while the caste system condemned much of the population to lives of deprivation. The gulf between the tiny minority of wealthy Indians and the remainder of the population was enormous. A succession of British prime ministers, possessed of good intentions, faced but could not resolve the twin dilemmas of Ireland (whose nationalists wanted Home Rule) and India.

Churchill's arrival in Bombay after the twenty-three-day voyage from England was inauspicious. Eager to be the first to do something, he and several other officers were given permission to disembark before the main party and hired a small skiff to take them ashore. As they reached the notoriously dangerous quayside, the heavy swells caused the skiff to rise four or five feet, and when Churchill grabbed an iron stanchion while attempting to transfer to the dock, he lost his grip and slipped on the wet steps, painfully wrenching and probably dislocating his right shoulder. The injury was serious enough for it to bother him for the remainder of his life; his shoulder would frequently displace, sometimes from the simplest of motions, such as reaching for a book, swimming or making an expansive gesture during a speech in the House of Commons. He was unable to play tennis and in order to play polo had to strap his arm to his chest. Of greater importance was that he could no longer use a sword and instead relied on a Mauser pistol for close combat. The injury, he recalled, was 'a grave embarrassment in moments of peril, violence and effort'.

The 4th Hussars settled into their permanent duty station at

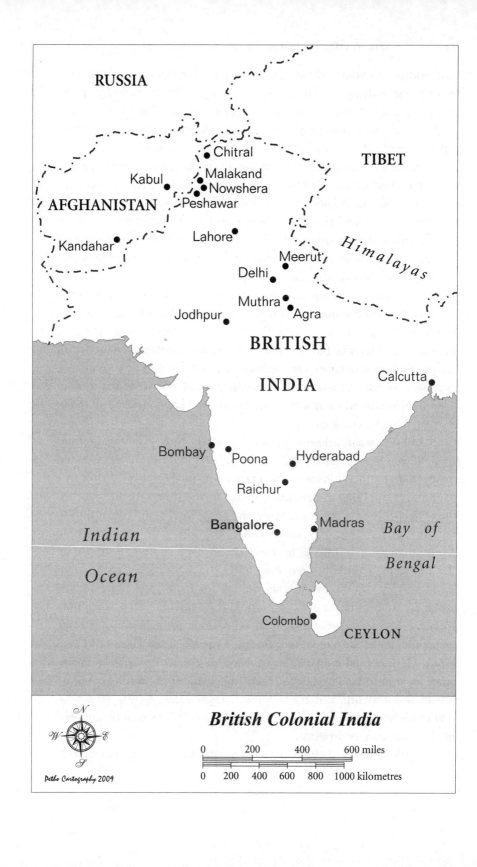

British Colonial India

Bangalore, on the high plains of southern India. At three thousand feet above sea level Bangalore had a moderate climate that spared its residents the insidious heat and humidity common to most of India. A city of lakes, parks and ancient temples, it was as close to ideal as anywhere in the subcontinent.

Bangalore was also an idyllic place to enjoy the benefits army service bestowed on an officer. With Britain at peace, military duties and recreation were equal partners. Indeed it had been so long since the British army had waged war that there were few officers below the rank of major with any war experience at all. At the turn of the century a general observed that duty in India had little to do with war. 'In the summer there was the individual training, polo, a little pigsticking, bathing in the Commissioner's swimming bath, the long, long Indian days, the weary nights and the howling of dogs, the siesta, the burning heat and dust.'

Churchill, Reginald Barnes and another officer lived in a spacious pink-and-white bungalow covered in bougainvillaea. Each was pampered by a butler and a servant who waited on him hand and foot, and at the stables there was a groom for his horse and polo ponies. Churchill's day began at the crack of dawn, when he was awakened by the gentle hands of his servant lathering his face and shaving him with a straight razor. 'If you liked to be waited on and relieved of home worries, India . . . was perfection . . . Princes could live no better than we.'

In India, Churchill indulged what would be a lifelong love of horticulture. The previous occupant of his cottage had left behind a fine collection of roses that he proudly praised in letters to his mother and brother. His fondness for animals and gardening became passions that only those admitted to his inner circle ever saw. When he was in positions of power the rest of the world would know only Churchill's unrelenting and uncompromising side.

He also began collecting butterflies, a hobby he had begun at Banstead and now renewed with great enthusiasm. His collection numbered some sixty-five species before a rat destroyed it. Although Churchill's terrier (somewhat pretentiously named 'Winston') caught and killed the rodent, the incident left him distraught.

With no wars to wage, sports took their place. The lives of the officers revolved principally around their military duties and the grand sport of polo, which was played avidly both for recreation and in a quest for the coveted Inter-Regimental Cup, awarded to the best team in India. Despite his nagging shoulder injury, Churchill was a member of the regimental team and played the demanding sport skilfully. Polo was a near obsession, 'the serious purpose of life', as he described it. He insisted on playing no fewer than eight chukkas per session, and sometimes as many as twelve, an exhausting regimen for the fittest of men, far more so for a one-armed player. Normally it took several years for a newly arrived regiment to be able to compete with any degree of success in the fierce inter-regimental competition against other, veteran units. Rising to the challenge, the determined polo-playing officers of the 4th Hussars decided it was time for an exception to the rule, and within two months of their arrival were competing for another coveted cup in Hyderabad that they were thought to have no chance of winning. Neither the heavily favoured 19th Hussars (the regiment the 4th had just relieved) nor the crowd took the fledgling team from Bangalore seriously, particularly when they appeared on the field with a one-armed player as a member of their team.

Polo matches in colonial India were more than sporting events; they were magnificent spectacles, possessed of pomp worthy of the best of the British Empire. The day began with a formal military parade. Attired in gleaming dress uniforms, the soldiers marched past the official dignitaries and were joined by teams of cannon-pulling elephants, all trained to raise their trunks in unison in salute. The romantic Churchill later lamented the abolition of this ritual. 'We now have clattering tractors drawing far larger and more destructive guns. Thus civilization advances. But I mourn the elephants and their salutations.'

The laughter that greeted the underdog visitors at the start of the afternoon match quickly subsided when they scored a record number of goals and routed the 19th Hussars. Churchill does not tell us how many goals he scored, but he played a noteworthy part in his regiment's stunning victory. His team might not have been taken so lightly had it been realized that the 4th Hussars had taken the unusual step of purchasing the entire polo stud of the Poona Light Infantry Regiment. Thus fortified with a stable of experienced polo ponies, Churchill's team underwent rigorous preparations that paid off triumphantly in Hyderabad.

Patrick Thompson, a contemporary of Churchill, said that 'to get at Churchill's angle in life' one had only to see him play polo. The sheer intensity with which he played left an indelible impression on Thompson. 'He rides in the game like heavy cavalry getting into position for the assault. He trots about, keenly watchful, biding his time, a master of tactics and strategy. Abruptly he sees his chance, and he gathers his pony and charges in, neither deft nor graceful, but full of tearing physical energy . . . He bears down opposition by the weight of his dash and strikes the ball. Did I say "strikes"? He slashes the ball.'

For men like Churchill polo *was* war; it was like a miniature battlefield. Bloodshed and injury to horse and rider were common, and the faint of heart need not apply. Indeed, during Churchill's time polo was perhaps the closest officers got to a battlefield without actually killing one another, though this too sometimes happened to both rider and animal. Colliding, slashing and spills are an integral part of the sport. Polo ponies give their all and sometimes die on the field from heart attacks and broken legs. Polo is the toughest physical training a cavalryman can engage in and keeps him in top physical shape. Courage and audacity on the polo field translate into savvy and audacity on the battlefield. Many famous soldiers, among them General George S. Patton, forged their skills and tested themselves daily on the polo field. They believed that the training and initiative they learned there were vital when it came to fighting. Lasting friendships were also cemented on the polo field and have been known to influence the choice of battlefield generals.

The youthful Churchill was more than a mere player; he was a combatant. Looking ahead, we can see that he played polo with the same aggressive attitude he would demand of his generals during the Second World War, a standard that was to cause considerable frustration when most of them failed to live up to his high expectations.

Yet such an existence came at a price, one that Churchill was more than happy to pay. Frugality had always been a concept he had failed to embrace, and in India, in part seduced by the cheap and plentiful labour and easy living, he consistently lived well beyond his means, often borrowing money from the very local moneylenders he had been specifically warned to avoid at all costs. In early 1897 Jennie strongly censured her son for deliberately overdrawing his bank balance by cashing a cheque for his quarterly allowance from her even though '*you knew* you had nothing in the bank . . . I *must* say I think it is *too* bad of you – indeed it is hardly honourable knowing as you do that you are dependent on me & that I give you the biggest allowance I *possibly can*, more than I can afford.' Although more than justified, Jennie's complaints about her son's reckless spending had as much to do with the stress it placed on her own finances as they did with motherly concern for her headstrong son. She demanded he learn to live within his means. 'You cannot but feel ashamed of yrself . . . I haven't the heart to write more.' Churchill dismissively blamed his 'stupid' banker. In fact, this behaviour was all too typical of his egotism and utter disregard for anyone but himself.

For most young bachelor army officers like Churchill, service in India meant a splendid opportunity not only for polo and other sports but also for romance. The cream of the many eligible young English ladies who journeyed to India arrived every year with the single purpose of finding romance and, if they were fortunate, a husband. This pool of single young women was drolly referred to as 'the fishing fleet'.

Although neither was looking for marriage, at a polo match during Churchill's first months in India he met Pamela Plowden, the attractive, intelligent and vivacious daughter of Sir Trevor Chichele-Plowden, the British resident (a position similar to that of a consul) of Hyderabad. For the first time in his life he was love-struck. Pamela, he confided to Jennie, was 'very beautiful and clever'. Their courtship, interrupted by Churchill's forays to other places to play polo, included a romantic elephant ride through Hyderabad. Although their friendship lasted a lifetime, their relationship could never progress to marriage because her father refused to grant his daughter's hand.

Even after he became famous for his exploits in the Boer War and might have won her father's consent, Churchill does not seem to have pursued Pamela with sufficient ardour, and she eventually became convinced of his inability ever to commit to another, once complaining that he was incapable of affection. He was stung by her honesty (and accuracy) and duly protested. 'I am no fickle gallant capriciously following the fancy of the hour. My love is deep and strong . . . [and] will remain true till death.'

Her later observation of Churchill was astute. 'The first time you meet Winston, you see all his faults, and the rest of your life you spend in discovering his virtues.' The correspondence between Winston and Pamela spanned sixty-three years and was sold at auction by Christie's in 2003 for nearly three hundred thousand pounds. One item was a passionate letter in which he wrote: 'I have lived all my life seeing the most beautiful women London produces . . . never have I seen one for whom I would for an hour forego the business of life. Then I met you . . . were I a dreamer of dreams, I would say "marry me – and I will conquer the world and lay it at your feet."' By 1901 even Jennie was convinced they would marry, and Winston had written that 'she is the only woman I could ever live happily with,' but his inertia ultimately killed their romance, and in 1902 she married another and became the Countess of Lytton.

As he had been during his years at Harrow, Churchill, while not unpopular with his colleagues in India, was viewed as somewhat irrepressible. They found him a bit too glib and something of a loner but nevertheless regarded him as one of their own. Most of the young regimental officers he found shallow and uninteresting. Most of them had scant interest in discussing politics or military science and disliked (and perhaps envied) his conversational skills. Around them Churchill was his usual opinionated self, aggressive in his opinions and always ready to discourse on any given subject. 'His brother officers liked him but thought him bumptious and held it their duty to keep him in his place.' One night a group of disgruntled subalterns organized a raid to rough him up, but he had given his room to another officer, who gave them a rude reception.

In 1898 the 4th Hussars participated in the Inter-Regimental polo matches at Meerut, fourteen hundred miles to the north, near Delhi. Although his team lost in the second round, Churchill distinguished himself. At the conclusion of the matches a great dinner was held in the host regiment's mess. When the interminable toasts and speeches by the winners and losers finally ended, there was a sigh of relief: the assembled officers were ready for the usual (often silly) games that were a part of such festivities. Suddenly Churchill bounded to his feet and announced that the assembled officers would no doubt 'like to hear me address you on the subject of polo'. In his memoir of India, Sir Robert Baden-Powell – the future hero of Mafeking and the founder of the Boy Scout movement – wrote, 'There were cries of: "No, we don't! Sit down!"' Ignoring their protests, he began to pontificate on the laws of polo. 'He proceeded to show how it was not merely the finest game in the world but the most noble and soul-inspiring contest in the whole universe, and having made that his point, he wound up with a peroration which brought us all cheering to our feet.' Finally one of the officers rose and said: 'Well, that is enough of Winston for this evening,' and they decided to teach him a lesson. He was thereupon shoved under a large divan, and the two heaviest subalterns sat down on it, trapping him underneath 'with orders not to allow him out for the rest of the evening'. A somewhat dishevelled Churchill soon managed to break free and defiantly declare: 'You can't keep me down like that.'

With ample time on his hands Churchill underwent an epiphany of sorts. Lord Randolph's death seemed to have spurred him into setting goals for his future life and career. 'I resolved to throw myself into life's battles with the utmost seriousness of energy, to repair the neglects of my school days, to read and study, to think and fit myself, as far as I could, to mingle in the great world of politics in which he had lived; and to seek adventures of all kinds in the hope of winning distinction. These adventures were not slow in coming.' More to the point, in school Churchill had been required to read and study – and he rebelled – but now that he was free to make his own decisions, those activities suddenly held great appeal. In India he determined that the time had come when he absolutely had to make up his educational deficiencies. Just as a future ally and friend named Dwight Eisenhower would undergo a similar epiphany after being commissioned in the US army, Winston Churchill suddenly felt impelled to make up for his lost education.

He admitted to being conscious of the lapses in his learning in 1895 while at Aldershot, complaining to his mother that his schooling had been too utilitarian and, unlike Oxford or Cambridge, had not produced 'a liberal education' or the intellectual polish he now deemed essential. He convinced himself of the need to improve his knowledge one evening in the regimental mess when he attempted to show off, only to be corrected by the better-read Brabazon. (The colonel was one of the few who could take him to task and still retain his friendship and esteem.)

Churchill's godson, the second Earl of Birkenhead, would later write that he became 'a one-man university without dons', in which he confronted 'an ocean of ignorance' by throwing himself into his studies with what amounted to a frenzied 'passion with which he sought enlightenment'. He began to read and study with zeal the great masters of economics, history and philosophy: Plato, all eight volumes of Gibbon's massive *Decline and Fall of the Roman Empire*, Macaulay (whom Churchill would later recall as 'the prince of literary rogues, who always preferred the tale to the truth'), Darwin, Malthus and Schopenhauer were among those whose works he devoured, often reading four or more books at a time.

His mother fed his reading appetite by sending parcels filled with his latest requests. 'Poked away in a garrison town which resembles a 3rd rate watering place, out of season & without the sea, with lots of routine work and a hot and trying sun – without society or good sport – half my friends on leave and the other half ill – my life here would be intolerable were it not for the consolations of literature. The only valuable knowledge I take away from India (soldiering apart) could have been gathered equally well in Cumberland Place. Notwithstanding all this I have not been unhappy, though occasionally very bored' – 'unfulfilled' might have been a better description of Churchill's state of mind. Years later his memory had softened when he wrote: 'Such was "the long, long Indian day" as I knew it for three years; and not such a bad day either.'

Enthusiasm, however, is sometimes fleeting and, with no prospect of wriggling free of his duties in India to seek adventure, it soon flagged. He continued to put pressure on his mother. 'I long for excitement of some sort and the prospect of joining an English expedition attracts me immensely. I do hope you will not relax your efforts,' he wrote to her in early 1897.

For a young man of limited experience, Churchill seemed to have an opinion about virtually every subject. When the secretary of state for war, Lord Lansdowne, proposed to increase the strength of the army, Churchill was quick to criticize both the proposal and Lansdowne's 'stupid speech . . . I hoped no one would be so foolish as to advocate the expenditure of more money on the army.' Later, after he had himself entered Parliament, Churchill again took a stand against a proposal to increase the army's size.

In 1897 it was decided that the Guards regiments would serve overseas, a move scorned by Churchill, who blamed the 'meddling & muddling' of the War Office for the decision. He also insisted that he would 'infinitely prefer any Highland regiment or any Rifle Regiment to the Grenadiers, Coldstreams or Scots Guards, either to serve in or with', an ironic statement given that he would be tutored in a unit of the Grenadier Guards in 1915 and command a Scottish battalion in 1916.

During his tour of duty in India, Churchill continued to be accident prone. In April 1897 he was supervising the marking of targets in the pits of the practice rifle range when a bullet hit the frame of a nearby target, splintering it in all directions. One deeply penetrated his left thumb but 'to the mercy of God' missed his eyes. His hand was badly wounded by the errant splinter and had to be cleansed and rebandaged daily. Although the wound was so severe that he could barely lift his arm to comb his hair or brush his teeth, it did not stop him from playing polo with the reins fastened to his wrist. Such a manoeuvre was daring and highly dangerous, and could easily have resulted in the pony dragging him by his arm in the event of a fall – a fairly common occurrence in the rough-and-tumble sport of polo.

By the time he had been in India for eight months he had fallen into the typical routine of colonialism. For the most part those who served in the British army in the subcontinent lived in their own restricted world of transplanted customs, clubs, messes and other trappings that replicated life in Britain. Churchill's knowledge of the Indian people and their problems was admittedly 'barren', and 'if I stay here twenty years as a soldier I see no prospect of my acquiring any knowledge worth knowing of Indian affairs.' Soldiers traditionally grouse about their existence. 'I have lived the life of a recluse out here,' he complained. 'Outside the regiment I know perhaps three people who are agreeable and I have no ambitions to extend my acquaintance . . . Life out here is stupid, dull & uninteresting . . . and unless I get *good letters of introduction* to the *very best* (not socially best) people out here my stay is likely to be *very* valueless.'

Broke and bored, and with no wars in the offing to attract his attention, Churchill was clearly disenchanted with military service, and chafed at the notion of spending the remainder of his service commitment in garrison duty in India. Yet he was a good soldier and performed his duties well and conscientiously. His troop sergeant, S. Hallaway, recalled the enthusiasm with which Churchill approached his tasks, often arriving at the stables with a notebook and various coloured pencils. He would quiz his more experienced sergeant: how was a certain manoeuvre conducted? Why this, why that, always the inquisitive 'why' and 'how' things were done. The lieutenant's incessant questions sometimes irked Sergeant Hallaway, who was more concerned with tending to the horses.

During reconnaissance training he became so badly blistered by the sun that dressings had to be placed around his throat, but rather than complain he was proud that he had been given the responsibilities of a brigade major – 'a most important duty and one which in England could never have been obtained under 14 or 15 years service . . . I am becoming my dear Mamma a very "correct" soldier. Full of zeal . . . Responsibility is an exhilarating drink.'

Other letters described his pleasure at being given the role of acting regimental adjutant. 'The colonel consults me on all points . . . my soldiering prospects are at present very good . . . I have eleven subalterns below me and should I continue to serve I might easily become a Captain in 3½ more years . . . I have also given satisfaction to my superior officers and polo & other things quite apart, I have every reason to believe that I shall be reported in the Annual Confidential Report as one of the two most efficient officers in my rank.'

Nevertheless Winston's constant complaints brought swift rebuttal from Jennie. 'I am quite disheartened about you. You seem to have no real purpose in life & won't realize at the age of 22 that for a man life means work, & hard work if you mean to succeed . . . It is useless my saying more – we have been over this ground before – it is not a pleasant one.' Her remonstrations that he stay in India and show 'that you can work hard and do something' had no effect. Determined to leave India, he saw an opportunity in April 1897 when two ancient enemies, Greece and Turkey, went to war over Crete.

'By good fortune I am possessed of the necessary leave and I propose, with your approval, to go to the front as a special correspondent,' he told Jennie. 'Which side to go on. This my dearest Mamma must depend on you.' His lengthy letter halfheartedly stated that if she objected he would not go but that it was up to her to find him a sponsor.

This latest scheme to find a conflict to cover was further evidence that Churchill still regarded war as an abstraction and viewed it as merely an occasion to 'see the fun and tell the tale'. It came to nothing the following month when Greece averted hostilities and sued for peace with Turkey. Churchill had already sailed from Bombay, and with no war to report toured Italy and visited his brother Jack, who was on holiday in Paris, and spent a leisurely summer in England.

Churchill's voyage from India in 1897 was to have one lasting benefit: He met Colonel Ian Standish Monteith Hamilton, an up-and-coming officer who was to play a major role in his life and achieve infamy at

Gallipoli in 1915. A veteran of numerous campaigns, including the Second Afghan War of 1879, Hamilton bonded with Churchill during hours of discussion about politics and warfare. As a result of their chance meeting the two men formed a lifelong friendship that lasted until Hamilton's death in 1947.

Churchill's troubles with money and his boredom with garrison duty with not even a scent of war were forgotten in August 1897. While he was relaxing on the stately lawns of the Goodwood racecourse in Sussex, a real opportunity arose when he learned that Pathan tribesmen in the North-West Frontier had revolted. 'I read in the newspapers that a Field Force of three brigades had been formed, and that at the head of it stood Sir Bindon Blood.'

Churchill had first met General Sir Bindon Blood at Aunt Lily's in 1896. An old friend of her husband, Lord William Beresford, and an influential officer, Blood had just returned from India, where he had commanded an expeditionary force. The two had talked at length, and by the time they parted Churchill had persuaded Blood to promise him duty with his unit should he ever return to India. The Blood family name had been emblazoned in British history ever since his ancestor, Colonel Thomas Blood, a famous adventurer and former Irish landowner, stole the crown jewels from the Tower of London in 1671. Although caught and imprisoned in the Tower, Blood managed to escape execution for treason by making a personal appeal to King Charles II, who not only pardoned him but restored his lands, which had been lost after the English civil war, and granted him a handsome pension of five hundred pounds per year.

True warriors, soldiers like Wellington, Napoleon and Bindon Blood, are a breed apart from other men, and although Churchill possessed the warrior spirit, his motives, unlike those of most soldiers whose primary motivation in combat is survival, were purely selfish. For someone of his youth and inexperience, the path to a coveted seat in Parliament seemed to pass through the army, which offered opportunities to attain public attention through heroic deeds. Surely such a possibility now existed in the wilds of the North-West Frontier, where ambition could comfortably combine with valour.

The rebellion was the first opportunity since Cuba for Churchill to participate in a real war, and he was determined, to the point of obsession, to do so. He telegraphed Blood that he should make good his promise and hastened to return at once to India, praying that the war would last long enough for him to see action.

6

A Taste of War:
The North-West Frontier, 1897

*Being in many ways a coward – particularly at school – there is no ambition
I cherish so keenly as to gain a reputation of personal courage.*

– Churchill, December 1897

The North-West Frontier of colonial India encompassed some of the
most rugged and forbidding terrain on earth, which to this day is populated by fiercely independent tribesmen, smugglers, bandits and warlords. Much though they fought among themselves, in a wilderness
where the only law was that of the warlord and the tribe, the men of the
Indian frontier were united in their hatred of British colonialism. They
traditionally resented British intrusion into their land, and the signs of
imperial settlement in the region in the form of roads and forts were
clear evidence of the British intention to remain permanently.

Armed primarily with rifles, these feral tribesmen not only were
unafraid of the British sent to rein them in but actually welcomed the
challenge of fighting – and killing – them. Churchill would later write:
'At a thousand yards the traveller falls wounded by the well-aimed bullet
of a breech-loading rifle. His assailant, approaching, hacks him to death
with the ferocity of a South-Sea Islander. The weapons of the nineteenth
century are in the hands of the savages of the Stone Age.'

The origin of the current unrest in the North-West Frontier was an
1895 rebellion that threatened the British fort at Chitral. A bloody battle
in Malakand Pass between twelve thousand Chitral tribesmen and a
British relief force of fifteen thousand soldiers sent from Peshawar left
some two thousand tribesmen dead or wounded against British losses
of a mere sixty-nine killed or wounded. This latest in a long history of
uprisings occurred in what today is the border region between Pakistan
and Afghanistan that is the home base of the Al Qaeda terrorist network.

In July 1897 the Mullah of Swat ('the Mad Mullah'), a Muslim holy man, incited the native Pathan tribesmen to rebel against British control over territory they believed was rightfully theirs. The insurgents attacked the Gibraltar-like fort at Chakdara and the garrison posted at Malakand Pass, both of which secured access to the Swat Valley, the only road to the British garrison at Chitral, one hundred miles to the north at the furthest reaches of the North-West Frontier.

The uprisings were deemed a threat to the authority and prestige of the British Empire, so they could not be ignored. With the garrisons in peril, a call for reinforcements by the British commander led to the formation of the Malakand Field Force under General Sir Bindon Blood. Unlike the 1895 expedition, Blood's punitive force was relatively small, consisting of about two thousand men, mostly Indian army troops commanded by white officers, matched against some twelve thousand Pathans.

*

71

Churchill was in such a rush to return from London to India that he left behind a pile of new books, his pet dog and, all too predictably, a pile of unpaid bills. After a sweltering and thoroughly miserable voyage that he described as like being in 'a vapour bath', he was bitterly disappointed when he arrived in Bombay to find that there was no telegram from Blood notifying him of his inclusion in the Malakand force. He returned to duty in Bangalore with fading optimism and wrote gloomily to Jennie that apparently 'someone at Headquarters has put a spoke in my wheel. I have still some hopes – but each day they grow less and less. It is an object lesson of how much my chances of success in the army are worth.'

Churchill's suspicion that someone was out to derail his dream was soon proved wrong when he received a letter from Blood saying that, although there was no staff position for him, he could nevertheless come as a press correspondent and would be appointed to fill the first available vacancy. Having only just returned from his long annual leave, Churchill had to exert considerable effort before he was somehow able to persuade his superiors to grant him a month's further leave to join the Malakand Field Force.

The problem was that he would be denied permission to travel to the North-West Frontier as a war correspondent without a special pass – and to obtain that pass he would have to be accredited to a suitable newspaper, a process which could prove difficult. Whatever the obstacles that stood in his way, Churchill simply refused to be denied this opportunity. He planned to take his own horses with him (this idea proved impractical) and if denied entry to the frontier zone, he was prepared to take his chances by riding through the mountains on his own. 'It might not have been worth my while, who am really no soldier, to risk so many fair chances on a war which can only help me directly in a profession I mean to discard. But I have considered everything and I feel that the fact of having seen service with British troops while still a young man must give me more weight politically – must add to my claims to be listened to and may perhaps improve my prospects of gaining popularity with the country. Besides this – I think I am of an adventurous disposition and shall enjoy myself not so much *in spite of* as *because* of the risks I run.'

A year later, after he had survived one of the most gruesome battles in British military history, Churchill would not be so quick to pronounce war enjoyable. Instead he would begin to grasp the meaning of Alexander Hamilton's dictum, prompted by the Founding Father's experience in the American Revolution, 'War, like most other things, is a science to be acquired and perfected by diligence, by perseverance, by time, and by practice.'

He managed to become accredited to an Indian newspaper, the *Allahabad Pioneer*, for which Kipling had once written. He was to submit a daily piece of three hundred words. In London, Jennie persuaded the *Daily Telegraph* to engage her son as its correspondent, although he was required to pay his own expenses in return for a fee of five pounds per column. His editor demanded 'picturesque forceful letters' (he would not be disappointed). Churchill had asked for ten pounds per article, but at least now armed with the necessary accreditation and an approved leave, he set out on the arduous journey from southern India to the North-West Frontier.

Train travel in India was a unique undertaking, just as it is today. Trains were generally crowded to overflowing, often with passengers leaning out of the carriage windows or sitting on the roofs. Besides people, all manner of animals were common, ranging from chickens to goats, pigs and occasionally even deadly snakes carried in baskets that did not invite closer inspection. Churchill travelled first class (how else?) and seems to have been spared the usual teeming conditions. His carriage was kept relatively cool by shutters to block out the sun and by 'a circular wheel of wet straw which one turned from time to time'. He passed the time composing letters and reading by lamplight. Writing to his brother he enthusiastically endorsed the importance of punishing the upstart rebels 'who have dared violate the Pax Britannica'. Repayment in kind 'is now at hand. It is impossible for the British government to be content with repelling an injury – it must be avenged.'

The 2,028-mile trip took six days, including a stop-over at Rawalpindi, during which Churchill spent an evening in the 4th Dragoons' sergeants' mess listening to a sing-song. 'Nothing recalls the past so potently as a smell,' he wrote some years later. 'In default of a smell the next best mnemonic is a tune. I have got tunes in my head for every war I have been to . . . Some day when my ship comes home, I am going to have them all collected in gramophone records, and then I will sit in a chair and smoke my cigar while pictures and faces, moods and sensations long-vanished return; and pale but true there gleams the light of other days.'

At Nowshera, the railway's northernmost terminus, he hired a tonga

– 'a kind of little cart drawn by relays of galloping ponies' – that stirred clouds of choking yellow dust as it sped through the almost lunar landscape on the forty-mile journey to the Malakand Pass, where Bindon Blood had established his headquarters.

In this inhospitable sector of India the British had three enemies to overcome: the rebels, the unforgiving climate, and the bleak, arduous terrain, which strongly favoured the defender. Churchill well remembered years later that, in conditions unlike any he had ever encountered, 'You could lift the heat with your hands, it sat on your shoulders like a knapsack, it rested on your head like a nightmare.'

The conditions in Cuba had been disagreeable, but this new challenge failed to dampen his single-minded desire to be a part of the Malakand campaign and to win recognition and decorations for bravery. Covered from head to toe in dust, Lieutenant Churchill reported for duty at the headquarters of the Malakand Field Force.

Sir Bindon Blood was an imposing figure, a deeply experienced frontier soldier and a warrior who personified the image of a field general. With his white hair, large bushy moustache and piercing eyes, Blood exuded confidence and professionalism. His carriage and persona were those of a man confident of his abilities: a born soldier who was exceptionally proud of the deeds of his intrepid ancestor. On one occasion when his encampment was attacked by snipers and bullets were flying everywhere, with several men wounded, he coolly continued eating his dinner as if nothing untoward was occurring. The foundation of Bindon Blood's success as a colonial commander was a combination of audacity and a deep understanding of the native population. As a veteran of the Indian and British armies, he was better equipped and trained than anyone else to deal with the mountain tribesmen. His memoirs, published in 1933, contain these words:

> The good old Rule
> The simple Plan
> That he shall take who has the Pow'r
> And he shall keep who can!

When Churchill arrived, Blood was away pacifying a native tribe, a mission which he accomplished without bloodshed. As a member of the Malakand officers' mess, Churchill learned for the first time to drink whisky in a place where water was in short supply and accordingly precious. Although he enjoyed wine, champagne and the occasional brandy, he found his first experience of Scotch unpleasant. He was a man who had spent most of his life spurning conformity, but as an outsider at the Malakand HQ he seemed compelled to adopt the custom of his fellow officers even though he all but held his nose while doing so. 'Once one got the knack of it, the very repulsion from the flavour developed an attraction of its own,' he wrote. Although he would later temper his criticism, in 1897, not yet twenty-four, he railed against drunkenness and the bad habits of university students, which he thought should be firmly reined in. 'Subalterns in those days were an intolerant tribe; they used to think that if a man got drunk or would not allow other people to have a drink, he ought to be kicked.'

The debate over Churchill's use of alcohol has consumed writers, historians and revisionists eager either to defend or to discredit him. However, during his Indian army days his drinking was clearly more a means of conforming – alcohol was 'the main basic standing refreshment of the white officer in the East'.

Before he could join a fighting unit he was required to purchase several horses and engage a groom to maintain them. It was customary for the horses and personal effects of dead officers to be auctioned off. Churchill arrived at a propitious moment and took advantage of the misfortune of others to outfit himself at minimal cost, writing rather tactlessly that 'unluckily for them, but very conveniently for me, several officers had been killed in the preceding week.'

He used his idle hours to good advantage to write the first nine of what would eventually number fifteen dispatches to the *Daily Telegraph*. Each was published under the byline 'A Young Officer', a decision made by Jennie on the advice of a family friend. Although it displeased Churchill, Jennie faithfully made it known in the right London circles who the author was. In one commentary he went well beyond merely reporting the situation in the North-West Frontier to offer stern criticism of British policy, specifically the refusal of the politicians to heed the advice of their military men in the field – a familiar theme in any war, and one that many of his generals during the Second World War would apply to Churchill himself.

While not writing, Churchill rode on several patrols with the 11th Bengal Lancers, looking for but failing to find action. The days of relative leisure at the force base camp soon ended, however. As the encounters escalated, it had been decided to burn rebel villages and crops in retribution. 'All who resist will be killed without quarter,' he wrote to Reginald Barnes. 'The Mohmands need a lesson – and there is no doubt we are a very cruel people.'

Blood led the Malakand Field Force west towards the Mamund Valley, a virtual cul-de-sac, in search of Pathan rebels. Although the British had no particular quarrel with the Mamunds, another warlike tribe whose home was in the valley, what ought to have been peaceful suddenly turned bloody when the Mamunds (in the belief that the British were there to wage war on them) attacked the Malakand base camp.

Churchill's wish to see action was now realized. In his memoirs Blood wrote: 'Lieut. Winston Churchill of the 4th Queen's Own Hussars ... joined me as an extra A.D.C. – and a right good one he was!' The general sent for Churchill and suggested he join one of the fighting units. 'He was all for it, so I sent him over at once and he saw more fighting than I expected and very hard fighting too! He was personally engaged in some very serious work.'

Blood sent a brigade on a reprisal mission to locate and destroy the rebels. Instead it was badly mauled, at which point he ordered his troops to lay waste the valley. Churchill wrote impersonally that 'with fire and sword in vengeance ... we proceeded systematically, village by village, and we destroyed the houses, filled up the wells, blew down the towers, cut down the great shady trees, burned the crops and broke the reservoirs in punitive devastation.'

Greatly outnumbered, the punitive expedition was itself punished in humiliating fashion. What had once been a twelve-hundred-man brigade was soon broken in disarray into small bands of soldiers who fought a series of battles in widely scattered parts of the valley. In one of these the commanding general and a battery of artillery fought for their lives on a dark night in chaotic hand-to-hand combat with tribesmen armed with rifles and long knives in a rabbit-warren village of mud huts. Churchill described 'an awful rout in which the wounded were left to be cut up by these wild beasts'.

The war in the mountains of the North-West Frontier was fierce and without quarter. There were deadly ambushes, battles fought with rifles at point-blank range reminiscent (on a far smaller scale) of the American civil war. It was common to hear bugle calls sounding 'Charge!'

Churchill attached himself first to a cavalry unit and then to a Sikh rifle company. He had come to find action, and action is what he got.

This undermanned rifle unit consisted of only five British officers and some eighty-five Sikhs. Their objective was to destroy a village high in the hills at the head of the valley. As they moved upward, Churchill recalled his Sandhurst training about dispersal of forces and realized that his company was not nearly strong enough to defend against a concerted rebel attack. With the place apparently deserted, it was decided to withdraw to a sounder position behind a knoll a short distance below the village, but before they could do so, all hell broke loose. Suddenly the hillside erupted with menacing howls and a hail of rifle fire from a force of Pathans hidden in the rocks above them.

Almost instantly five men were cut down. One of the British officers was shot through the eye. Churchill grabbed the Martini-Henry rifle of a wounded Sikh and began returning fire. 'We had certainly found the adventure for which we had been looking,' was his droll description of a bloody life-and-death small-unit engagement.

At one point a group of Pathan tribesmen approached within yards of Churchill's ragtag force, which was now in full retreat with its wounded. The battalion adjutant, who had come forward to order a 'retirement' (a polite word often used in place of 'retreat') from the village, was among the wounded. It is a solemn point of honour in most armies that the dead and wounded are never left on the battlefield and the Malakand Field Force of 1897 was no exception. Unfortunately, in this particular skirmish panic overtook honour. As the adjutant was being lifted to safety, a group of sword-bearing Pathans appeared. The men carrying the adjutant abruptly dropped him to the ground and fled. The rebel leader slashed at the helpless officer. Almost blind with fury, Churchill drew his sword and prepared to engage the man. 'I forgot everything else at this moment except a desire to kill this man.' As he advanced, the tribesman awaited his arrival, his sword brandished for combat. With other enemy tribesmen near by, Churchill decided that common sense should prevail over the quixotic notion of a duel to the death he would almost certainly have lost. Instead he pulled out his revolver and began firing, hitting no one. It suddenly dawned on him that he was all alone and in serious peril. If he was to live to fight another day, it was imperative to beat a hasty retreat, however inglorious it might be. 'I ran as fast as I could. There were bullets everywhere.' He

77

reached the safety of his own lines unharmed. One officer and a dozen or so Sikhs were not so fortunate. Those who had not been killed in the initial skirmish and could not be evacuated to friendly lines had to be abandoned and were hacked to pieces. Churchill's unit was now surrounded by several hundred tribesmen and might have met the same fate but for the timely arrival of a relief force.

As his outnumbered force withdrew into defensive positions, it was relentlessly attacked. Some rebels without guns threw stones at them. 'I felt no excitement and very little fear,' Churchill reported. 'All the excitement went out when things became really deadly.' With his pistol ineffective, Churchill used the rifle of a wounded soldier and fired off some forty rounds 'with some effect at close quarters. I cannot be certain, but I think I hit 4 men. At any rate they fell.'

Churchill returned from the debacle in Mamund Valley with the blood on his trousers of a wounded sepoy he had dragged to safety. He had passed his first test of combat and, more important, had lived to tell the tale. Unlike his fellow subalterns, who 'were highly delighted at a few bullets that whistled about' and considered it 'a tremendous escape', he found little to boast about. 'They have not yet seen what it means to be well punished,' he noted, always mindful of what these events meant to his career.

To his grandmother Fanny, Churchill confided that war was unforgiving and that the British were as cruel as their enemy. 'I wonder if people in England have any idea of the warfare that is being carried on here . . . no quarter is ever asked or given. The tribesmen torture the wounded & mutilate the dead. The troops never spare a man who falls into their hands – whether he be wounded or not . . . The picture is a terrible one . . . I wish I could come to the conclusion that all this barbarity – all these losses – all this expenditure – had resulted in a permanent settlement being obtained, I do not think however that anything has been done – that will not have to be done again.'

Churchill's first real taste of war also left him more avid than ever for recognition. 'I rode my grey pony all along the skirmish line where everyone else was lying down in cover. Foolish perhaps but I play for high stakes and given an audience there is no act too daring or too noble. Without the gallery things are different . . . I should like to come back and wear my medals at some big dinner or some other function.'

In mid-September, in the aftermath of the valley war, he was attached to a Punjab infantry unit that had been badly mauled. 'A change from British cavalry to Native Infantry! Still it means the medal and also that next time I go into action I shall command a hundred men – and possibly I may bring off some '*coup*'. Besides I shall have some other motive for taking chances than merely love of adventure.' One of only three British officers who were not dead or wounded, he spoke no Punjabi and could convey his instructions only though hand signals and the few words he had learned, including *maro* ('kill'). He led his colonial troops in several minor skirmishes and again emerged unscathed. Many of his brother officers were not so fortunate. Over a two-week period one of Bindon Blood's brigades lost 245 killed and wounded, twenty-five of them officers.

During his service with the Malakand Field Force everything else in Churchill's prior existence became like a distant memory, a typical reaction of soldiers whose lives are on the line, when only survival counts. 'I do not look ahead more than a day – or further than the hills that surround the valley . . . Europe is infinitely remote. – England infinitely small – Bangalore a speck on the map of India – but here everything is life size and flesh colour.' A short time later he made a point of stating that although 'it is a war without quarter . . . I have not soiled my hands with any dirty work – though I recognize the necessity of some things.'

Although he respected the fighting ability of the hill tribesmen, in one of his dispatches to the *Daily Telegraph* he called them 'little savages whose principal article of commerce is their women – wives and daughters – who are exchanged for rifles . . . It is impossible to imagine a lower type of beings or a more dreadful state of barbarism.'

Despite his close calls, the danger, the heat, the extreme physical discomfort and the sobering sight of the dead and wounded, Churchill persisted in treating his experience as mostly a lively diversion, having little regard for the possibility that he might become one of the unlucky men to be wounded or killed. 'I have faith in my luck,' he reassured his mother. 'Meanwhile the game amuses me – dangerous though it is – and I shall stay as long as I can. It is a strange life. Here I am lying in a hole – dug two feet deep in the ground – to protect me against the night firing – on a mackintosh with an awful headache – and the tent & my temperature getting hotter every moment as the sun climbs higher and higher. But after all, food and a philosophic temperament are man's only necessities.'

His flawed vision that heroism was the key to political success persisted, his desire to be noticed and rewarded reaching the point of recklessness when he proudly announced his gratification that 'my follies have not been altogether unnoticed . . . Bullets – to a philosopher my dear Mamma – are not worth considering. Besides I am so conceited I do not believe the Gods would create so potent a being as myself for so prosaic an ending.'

Churchill's romanticism was dangerously unabated despite the harsh examples of war he had personally experienced. More troubling, however, was his misguided confidence that he, unlike his comrades in arms, would be somehow exempt from death before achieving a great destiny.

War invariably exacts a painful cost, and in the aftermath of battle there are the inevitable funerals of those who have paid the ultimate price. Churchill's description of one such event, while moving, was a curious mixture of romanticism and realism that somehow made clear his failure fully to grasp that war is not a stage for ambition:

The funerals of the British officers and men, killed the day before, took place at noon . . . but all the pomp of military obsequies was omitted, and there were no Union Jacks to cover the bodies, nor were volleys fired over the graves . . . To some the game of war brings prizes, honour, advancement, or experience; to some the consciousness of duty well discharged; and to others – spectators, perhaps – the pleasure of the play and the knowledge of men and things. But here were those who had drawn the evil numbers – who had lost their all, to gain only a soldier's grave. Looking at these shapeless forms, coffined in a regulation blanket, the pride of race, the pomp of empire, the glory of war appeared but the faint and unsubstantial fabric of a dream; and I could not help realising with Burke: 'What shadows we are and what shadows we pursue.'

When the uprising was finally quelled and the Malakand campaign ended, Churchill had to settle for a mention in dispatches from General Blood, who noted that his commander in the field 'has praised the courage and resolution of Lieutenant W. L. S. Churchill, 4th Hussars, the correspondent of the *Pioneer* newspaper with the force who made himself useful at a critical moment.' Blood also wrote to Colonel Brabazon to praise Churchill's service. 'He is now pro tem an officer of native infantry . . . I have put him in when he was the only spare officer within reach, and he is working away equal to two ordinary subalterns.' Blood also believed that even greater accolades awaited Churchill, and that 'if he gets a chance he will win the VC or a DSO [Distinguished Service Order].' Churchill was pleased that 'Sir Bindon has made me his orderly officer, so that I shall get a medal and perhaps a couple of clasps.' He called his service with the Malakand Field Force 'the best I have ever had in my life' and 'one which I aim to repeat'. However, instead of a VC or DSO, Churchill had to settle for a 'Punjab Frontier, 1897–98' clasp to his India Medal, which was basically nothing more than a decoration for having served in India. When Blood's dispatches were published, Churchill was thrilled and grateful. 'I had no military command and only rode about trying to attract attention – when things looked a little dangerous.'

In the meantime his leave had expired, and although Blood sought to keep Churchill as his aide, the army high command in India blocked his transfer, and it was only through Blood's intervention that he was given a two-week extension until a replacement could be sent to relieve him. Churchill was furious, calling the decision 'as dirty a tale of childish malice as was ever told'. Unless he got his own way, even such magnanimous gestures as the six weeks' leave accorded him by his regiment were not enough, nor was there even a remote sense of appreciation for the opportunity given to him. Instead he indulged in a juvenile temper tantrum reminiscent of his childhood, petulantly blaming 'the pettiness which induces high military officers to devote so much time and attention to annoying a poor wretch of a subaltern . . . It has been a severe object lesson to me, one which I shall not ever forget – of the petty & evil intrigue on which appointments in India depend.'

In an effort to avoid returning to his regiment, Churchill attempted to join another expeditionary force being formed to deal with yet another rebellion, this one in the Tirah Mountains, beyond the Khyber Pass. One of its brigades was commanded by his new friend, Colonel Ian Hamilton, who Churchill expected would aid his scheme to extend his leave and participate in this new adventure. However, his dream of further glory ended when Hamilton was thrown from his horse, breaking a leg – an injury that cost him his command. Churchill's request to extend his leave was summarily denied, and he was ordered back to duty in Bangalore. This order ended his stirring adventures on the North-West Frontier. He would later grumble that the leaders of the 1898 Tirah expedition 'had been very selfish in not letting me come with them', failing to recall that it was his own regimental commander who had curbed his venturesome ways.

If Churchill thought he would return to a hero's welcome in the regimental mess at Bangalore, he was mistaken. Although his fellow officers treated him with civility, for the most part they regarded him as a medal and glory seeker – a fairly accurate perception. There was a strong whiff of unseemliness about an indulgent, self-important young man presuming to tell his superiors how to fight wars and politicians how to conduct their business that violated the Victorian standards of gentlemanly conduct.

Churchill found the monotonous routine of peacetime regimental duty more boring and irrelevant than ever. Having tasted war, he thirsted for yet more adventure, and his heart and dreams were with the Tirah Expeditionary Force. He found himself engaged in mock manoeuvres, firing blanks instead of real bullets in make-believe battles. Soldiers who have been in battle often find it difficult to adapt to garrison duty under peacetime conditions, and Churchill was no exception. Henceforth anything less than the real thing seemed superfluous to him, and the news of the forming of the Tirah expedition left him chafing over his inability to join it. 'I am more ambitious for a reputation for personal courage than anything else in the world,' he confided to his mother. 'A young man should worship a young man's ideals . . . As for deserving such an honour – I feel that I took every chance and displayed myself with ostentation wherever there was danger – but I had no military command and could not expect to receive credit for what should after all be merely the behaviour of a philosopher – who is also a gentleman.'

The Tirah Field Force soon met its match in the Afridi tribesmen who harassed and inflicted heavy casualties on the British from the high mountain ridges, eventually forcing them into a humiliating withdrawal before winter set in, with little to show for their incursion.

Believing that there would be a second Tirah expedition in the spring of 1898, Churchill redoubled his efforts to be released from the 4th Hussars and once again employed the good offices of his mother. Jennie appealed on her son's behalf to Field Marshal Lord Roberts (the former commander in chief, India, who now held a similar position in Ireland), asking that he intervene on Winston's behalf. This time, however, her efforts achieved nothing when both Roberts and Field Marshal Lord

Wolseley (since 1895 the commander in chief of the British army) elected not to intercede. Churchill was angry that a man with whom his father had had a close friendship should deny him and lamented that Roberts's refusal was 'a good instance of ingratitude in a fortunate and very much overrated man'.

The best he could manage was ten days' leave at Christmas 1897, and although he toyed with the idea of journeying to the North-West Frontier, he soon realized that there was insufficient time and, more important, that it was a foolish notion. 'The military pussycat is a delightful animal, as long as you know how to keep clear of her claws,' he later wrote of his decision not to test the system any further.

His return to garrison duty provided time to write his first book, *The Story of the Malakand Field Force*. When he learned that someone else was also writing an account he redoubled his efforts and wrote furiously, determined not to be outdone. Within six weeks he had produced a manuscript, having already alerted his mother that she should not only immediately find a publisher but also negotiate suitable terms of not less than three hundred pounds, plus a royalty on each copy – an enormous sum. In addition Churchill was adamant that he would not permit any revisions to be made other than 'bad sentences polished & any repetitions of phrase or fact weeded out'.

If this was a form of penance for neglecting her son during his childhood, Jennie was rapidly discharging the debt. She soon found a literary agent who secured a contract with Longmans, a respected London publisher. The illusion of a three-hundred-pound payment *and* royalties, however, became instead an advance of fifty pounds *against* royalties, which meant it had to be earned back through sales before he received any additional payment. All the same Churchill was satisfied and regarded the book's publication as 'certainly the most noteworthy act of my life', although he qualified this description by adding, 'Up to date (of course)'.

He wrote to Jennie: 'I am pleased with it chiefly because I have discovered a great power of application which I did not think I possessed.' The book remains to this day the best account of that forgotten war in spite of his admission that he wrote it primarily 'for the impression my words produce & the reputation they give me . . . I vy often yield to the temptation of adapting my facts to my phrases.' Nevertheless, although it expressed an enigmatic realization (quite at odds with his own behaviour) that war is evil, it also inevitably reflected the long-standing romanticism that his first real experience of war had failed to dampen. His account of the British relief of Chakdara is one example of such sentiments: 'In that moment the general, who watched the triumphant issue of the plans, must have experienced as fine an emotion as is given to man on earth.'

Churchill's rather idealistic vision of generalship became one of the foundations of the expectations he later had for men whom he appointed to lead when he became Britain's war leader. 'The general who avoids all "dash", who never starts in the morning looking for a fight and without any definite intention, who does not attempt heroic achievements, and who keeps his eyes on his watch, will have few casualties and little glory.'

To his credit Churchill's experience on the North-West Frontier left him with firm ideas about war that were, to say the least, unusually perceptive for a young man of his limited military education. Unlike most other Victorians he believed that compassion for a defeated enemy was necessary. ' "Never despise your enemy" is an old lesson, but it has to be learnt afresh, year after year, by every nation that is warlike and brave,' he wrote.

Now free of his writing duties, he was more restless than ever and was determined to see further action. His son, Randolph, would later write: 'He did not think that the risks he had run with the Malakand Field Force had gained him the reputation he believed he had deserved.' His high expectations for himself notwithstanding, Churchill had a great deal to show for the experience, including his life. He had proved his bravery, his dispatches were widely read, and he would soon publish a highly acclaimed first book at the age of twenty-four (eight thousand copies were in print by early 1899). Moreover, unlike his regimental contemporaries, he was now a battle-tested officer. Of course he never saw it that way – as long as there were battles to be fought, Churchill believed it was his duty to search out and participate in them, and to continue earning the capital he believed necessary for entry into politics. If his destiny did not lie in India, he would make sure he found it elsewhere.

7

Soldier of Fortune

I must now go to Egypt . . . my life here is not big enough to hold me.
                                              – Churchill, October 1897

As he would throughout his life, Churchill refused to take no for an answer when denied the chance to join the Tirah Expeditionary Force. Although recovered from his accident, Ian Hamilton had no immediate vacancy for him in his brigade. Instead Churchill pinned his hopes on securing a position on the staff of the commander in chief of the Tirah Expeditionary Force, General Sir William Lockhart, whose headquarters were in Peshawar. It was a huge risk on Churchill's part, and one that if not successful would have had serious consequences. His willingness to act recklessly was a measure of his obsession with escaping from what he disdainfully called 'a third rate watering place'. Rather than return to Bangalore (a three-day trip) after participating in a regimental polo match in Meerut, Churchill elected to gamble that he could somehow talk his way on to Lockhart's staff. He could not possibly travel to Peshawar (six hundred miles north-west of Meerut) and return to his regiment in three days, at which point he would be deemed absent without leave and subject to disciplinary action, a prospect to which Churchill gave scarcely a passing thought. Instead of returning to Bangalore with the polo team, he boarded a train for the three-day trip to Peshawar.

On arrival he contacted Lockhart's adjutant, Captain Aylmer Haldane, a Scottish officer who had served in the Gordon Highlanders with Ian Hamilton. The general had told Churchill that Haldane was a man of 'immense influence . . . if he were disposed towards you, everything could be arranged . . . If you came up here you might with your push and persuasiveness pull it off.'

85

With no advance warning Churchill presented himself at Lockhart's office and 'with a beating heart' asked to see Captain Haldane. And 'pull it off' was exactly what he did; in barely half an hour the glib young lieutenant stated his case, extolled his own virtues and won over a 'none too cordial but evidently interested' Haldane, who said: 'Well, I'll go and see the Commander-in-Chief and see what he says.' Before long Haldane returned to declare: 'Sir William has decided to appoint you an extra orderly officer on his personal staff. You will take up your duties at once. We are communicating with the Government of India and your regiment.'

Once again an audacious act paid handsome dividends, as Churchill became the newest member of the Tirah Expeditionary Force. In the months that followed, although he and Haldane, who was twelve years his senior, became friends, Churchill nevertheless privately criticized him as 'indiscreet – over-bearing – irritating [in] manner – possessed by a great desire to confer favours – but in some ways a remarkable man', and 'an able fellow' – all traits that might well have characterized Churchill himself.

Haldane would later say of Churchill's brief time with the Tirah Field Force that it enabled him 'to form an opinion of the young cavalry officer who was widely regarded in the Army as super-precocious, indeed by some as insufferably bumptious, and realize that neither of these epithets was applicable to him'. Instead the Churchill whom Haldane knew in India was neither arrogant nor controversial. 'He struck me at almost first sight as cut out on a vastly different pattern from any officer of his years I had so far met . . . I had a feeling that such a prodigy would go far.'

Churchill saw no action, and in the spring of 1898 the Tirah Expeditionary Force was disbanded. He returned to his regiment to begin plotting his escape from India at the earliest opportunity.

In 1898 Britain was entering a period that would see wars in the Sudan and, the following year, in South Africa against the rebel Boers. For decades both Britain and France had made major investments in Egypt, which had become an important commercial centre. In 1882, when unrest threatened Egypt's stability, the Liberal government of William Gladstone had intervened to restore order, ensure control of the vital Suez Canal and forestall a similar annexation by the French. Although

Egypt remained hypothetically an independent nation, it was in practice under British rule.

The Egyptian empire included the Sudan, where unrest prevailed and control was tenuous at best. In 1881 the Mahdist movement erupted when a former boatbuilder and carpenter named Muhammad Ahmad declared himself the 'Mahdi' (the Guided One) and recruited a large Islamic fundamentalist army in order to expel the Egyptians and attain Islamic self-rule. What his Dervish army lacked in military training and modern weapons they more than made up for in religious fanaticism and a readiness to die for their cause in a jihad (holy war). The Mahdist uprising swept the Sudan, and in November 1883 the rebels not only defeated a force of forty thousand Egyptians that was lured into a deadly ambush in the desert south of Khartoum, but captured its weapons, including machine guns and artillery. By 1884 the Mahdist army was threatening the capital of Khartoum.

Major General Charles George Gordon (who had earned the nickname 'Chinese Gordon' for his success in defending Shanghai and helping to defeat the Taiping rebellion in the 1860s) and a small force of one thousand British troops arrived in Khartoum to carry out an evacuation of British and Egyptian subjects. Gordon, however, believed himself an agent of Providence, answerable only to God, and disobeyed his orders by electing to defend Khartoum in the name of Christianity. The Mahdists laid siege to the city and in January 1885 killed Gordon and every single member of his relief expedition.

In London successive Liberal and Conservative governments promised that the martyred Gordon's death would be avenged, and the reconquest of the Sudan became a top priority. Churchill would later write in one of his newspaper dispatches that a stonemason ought to be commissioned to carve the word 'Avenged' into the pedestal of Gordon's statue in Trafalgar Square.

In 1895 the British formed an expeditionary force under Major General Sir Horatio Herbert Kitchener, the Sirdar (commander in chief) of the Egyptian army, to retake the Sudan and reinstate Anglo-Egyptian rule. Kitchener's force consisted primarily of Egyptian units, augmented over time by British regiments. For three years the Sirdar, with the support of a flotilla of gunboats in the Nile, ponderously advanced towards the Sudan, moving at a snail's pace as a railway line was extended for the sole purpose of resupplying his army. The Sudan

Military Railway was an incredible feat of engineering constructed under the worst possible conditions by Kitchener's brilliant chief engineer, Édouard Girouard, and the sweating men (Egyptians, former Mahdist prisoners of war and a variety of native tribesmen) of his Railway Battalion. The railway eventually penetrated as far south as Atbara, where in April 1898 Kitchener's army fought a major battle and routed a force of sixteen thousand Mahdists who formed the last major obstacle to his advance on Khartoum, some two hundred miles distant.

By the summer of 1898 Kitchener was positioned for the final campaign to retake Khartoum and at last avenge Gordon. Reports of his expedition to reclaim the Sudan reached Churchill as early as October 1897. He had long relished an assignment to Egypt as his eventual ticket out of India, and wrote to Jennie, 'I must now go to Egypt and you should endeavour to stimulate the Prince [of Wales, one of Jennie's friends] into writing to Kitchener on the subject . . . my life here is not big enough to hold me. I want to be up and doing and cannot bear inaction or routine . . . I become more in need of serious occupation every day.'

In early 1898 he learned that his mother was on holiday in Cairo and wrote that, aided by her considerable influence, he intended to proceed there by the end of June. 'You should make certain of my being employed then,' he insisted. 'It is a pushing age and we must shove with the best.' A short time later he tried flattery. 'Your wit & tact & beauty should overcome all obstacles,' he said. Jennie tried hard and bombarded Kitchener with letters – all to no avail. Not only did Kitchener spurn her representations, but her current lover, Major Caryl Ramsden, nicknamed 'Beauty' for his exceptional good looks, jilted her: Jennie found him *in flagrante* with the wife of an army general.

Churchill had entrusted the editing and proofreading of his Malakand book to his aunt Clara's husband, Moreton Frewen, known in the family as 'Mortal Ruin'. Frewen, a noted horseman and a well-meaning entrepreneur, was singularly unsuccessful and unlucky in virtually every business venture he ever undertook. The results of his editing appalled Churchill, who complained to his mother that Frewen had ruined his book with his emendations, leaving 'only shame that such an impertinence should be presented to the public . . . I writhed all day yesterday afternoon – but today I feel nothing but shame and disappointment.' Nevertheless he tactfully refrained from expressing his true feelings to his uncle, and praised his work on his behalf.

Churchill need not have worried. The book was an instant success, widely read by men in high places and earning praise from reviewers and a warm letter from the Prince of Wales in which he strongly advised Churchill to remain in the army before seeking entry into Parliament. 'You have plenty of time before you, and should certainly stick to the Army before adding M.P. to your name,' he advised. The success of *The Story of the Malakand Field Force* was a remarkable departure for a young man who was accustomed to nothing but criticism from his elders. 'I had never been praised before. The only comments which had been made upon my work at school had been "Indifferent", "Untidy", "Slovenly", "Bad".'

In 1898 Churchill declared his financial independence from his mother. Jennie's extravagances had multiplied in the years since Randolph's death, and she had accumulated such extraordinarily high debts that she was obliged to seek a loan of seventeen thousand pounds. The bank refused to guarantee such a sizeable sum unless Churchill would guarantee to pay a premium of seven hundred pounds to cover the interest owed. Although he reluctantly agreed, he refused to take on any of her future debts. That declaration included legal action against his mother to protect himself and to prevent her from sharing his inheritance (such as it was) should she ever remarry: a perceptive decision because Jennie did remarry in 1900, an army officer twenty years her junior. Although the dispute damaged Winston's relationship with his mother for a time and left 'a dirty taste in my mouth', Jennie continued to use her influence in high places on his behalf.

With his prospects growing dimmer by the day, Churchill recognized that his best hope lay in returning 'to the centre of the Empire'. He was granted three months' leave from his regiment and left India in mid-June 1898 for the three-week journey to London to plead his case in person to anyone willing to hear him. If the army would not send him to Egypt, he was determined to leave the military to find more 'adventure' and to write a book about it, 'without the blunders which disfigure my first attempt'.

His zeal was boundless: he petitioned friends and acquaintances of his family, used the good offices of anyone even remotely capable of helping him fulfil his ambition, and unreservedly exploited his mother to that end. Ever since Randolph's death Jennie had become the spearhead of his every quest. Whether he was insisting that she arrange to have his book published, facilitate a newspaper assignment or orchestrate a transfer from India to Egypt, by outright demand or through flattery she was repeatedly put on notice that it was her obligation to make his wishes come true; 'relax not a volt of your energy', was typical of his exhortations. Such intense focus and total disregard for the feelings of others would later become the hallmark of Churchill the war leader.

In 1898 Churchill's centre of attention was Herbert Horatio Kitchener, an undisputed warlord who brooked no interference from London (or anywhere else). The Sirdar was twenty-five years older than Churchill, and, whereas Churchill was aggressive and outspoken, Kitchener was stolid, courageous, a superb organizer, ambitious beyond measure, but never a 'thruster' – an aggressive commander such as Nelson, Wellington, Napoleon, Patton or Rommel.

An Ulster-born Protestant, Kitchener had been commissioned in the Royal Engineers and brought to his profession an engineer's methodical mind-set. During his early years in the army he toiled in obscurity as a relatively junior officer. However, his service surveying Palestine in the 1870s led to a mastery of Arabic, a skill that would help propel him to the attention of the War Office when, as a major in the early 1880s, he served in the Intelligence Department in Cairo. He went on to hold a variety of other posts in Egypt, including governor of Suakin, a remote Sudanese town on the Nile, and adjutant general of the Egyptian army. In 1892 he was promoted to his current high post.

Without guile, Kitchener won his battles by sound organization and the application of slow-moving but overwhelming force. The War Office deemed him imperious and unreceptive, and indeed he had established himself as a virtual law in Egypt, disregarding Whitehall whenever it suited him, including rejecting recommendations for the assignment of British officers to his command. With his thick black moustache, Kitchener was a formidable figure despised for his arrogance and for the contemptuous way in which he treated his officers and men. Utterly ruthless, he had no tolerance whatsoever for failure. To question one of his decisions was the professional kiss of death for his subordinates.

It did not help Churchill's chances that Kitchener loathed war correspondents, particularly those who sought to pull strings. And while he tolerated their presence when ordered to do so by the prime minister, he did everything within his power to make their task as difficult as possible. On the rare occasions when he permitted them to enter his presence, Kitchener treated them with complete disdain. Although noted for his exacting attention to detail, he possessed a streak of almost childish pettiness that would manifest itself over rather trivial matters. Thus it was that the proposed assignment of a mere subaltern to one of his units provoked his displeasure.

Like Churchill, Kitchener was deeply wedded to the principle of Victorian imperialism; however, in the Sirdar's case the campaign in the Sudan was something of a holy undertaking to save the empire from infidels. Not for the first time would Western civilization and Islam clash violently, and in Kitchener the British had a commander who intended to carry out his task with extreme ruthlessness.

Churchill now faced a major hurdle. His Malakand adventure and his writings had thoroughly annoyed many of the army's old guard, who believed that subalterns should be seen and not heard. His reputation preceded his return to London, and despite the great publicity he had received after the publication of his book, he was widely seen within the establishment as an egotistical young upstart who shamelessly employed his family's good name to his own ends. His brazen disregard of protocol, his quest for medals and glory, all became well known, and his highly opinionated dispatches had earned him a number of enemies in high places and a warning from the Prince of Wales that his duties as an officer were at odds with those of a war correspondent. None of the criticism or the whispering dampened Churchill's zeal to fight in yet another military campaign, however, whatever the cost to his reputation, which he earnestly believed would one day be acknowledged and admired – and lead to a seat in Parliament. His son would later point out, 'He was penniless; indeed, in debt. He was a soldier of fortune. He had to make his way, he had to make his name.'

With a late-summer campaign in the Sudan now certain, Churchill applied to the War Office for a transfer to the 21st Lancers, a cavalry regiment formerly stationed in India. Despite Churchill's reputation for grandstanding, the War Office did not obstruct his application, which was favourably passed on to Kitchener's command and summarily rejected. The adjutant general, Sir Evelyn Wood, wrote to Kitchener: 'I strongly recommend Churchill as good value for you and the Army.' The Sirdar refused to budge: 'Do not want Churchill as no room.' Jennie and Mary Jeune, an influential London matron and family friend, both lobbied intensively on his behalf. Lady Jeune went so far as to telegraph Kitchener: 'Hope you will take Churchill. Guarantee he won't write.' Kitchener wasn't buying it.

What made Churchill's chances of a post in Egypt even dimmer was the open hostility of Kitchener, who wanted no part of him. The Prince of Wales had written a glowing letter praising his book, but this too carried no weight with Kitchener. Although Churchill called those who opposed him 'ill-informed and ill-disposed', an almost impenetrable barrier had been erected with his name on it.

Despite continued entreaties from Jennie and others of influence in London, Kitchener's reluctance to accept nominations for positions within his command ultimately hurt Churchill, who later admitted, 'The obstacle of my going to Egypt was at once too powerful and too remote to be within [my mother's] reach.'

While he was in England, Churchill conducted a personal reconnaissance of possible parliamentary seats and tested the political waters in a well-received speech at Bradford, but otherwise devoted his efforts to lobbying. He heard from the prime minister, Lord Salisbury, who was among those who had read his book and wanted to speak to him personally. That it was Lord Salisbury is ironic, for this was the same man who, during an earlier term as prime minister in the 1880s, had freely accepted his father's resignation as chancellor of the exchequer. At No. 10 Downing Street, Churchill was warmly greeted and later remembered the kind words and old-fashioned courtesy shown him by the instrument of Lord Randolph's downfall. During their thirty-minute meeting Salisbury praised Churchill's book and observed, 'I myself have been able to form a truer picture of the kind of fighting that has been going on in these frontier valleys from your writings than from any other documents which it has been my duty to read.' Their cordial discussion concluded with the prime minister's saying, 'If there is anything at any time that I can do which would be of assistance to you, pray do not fail to let me know.'

Salisbury's words were music to Churchill's ears. Surely a recommendation from the prime minister himself would sway Kitchener into accepting his assignment. It was now nearly the end of July, and Churchill knew that Kitchener's campaign to recapture Khartoum was due to commence the following month. Time was therefore perilously short when he wrote to Salisbury and brazenly explained his reasons. 'I want to go, first, because the recapture of Khartoum will be a historic event: second, because I can, I anticipate, write a book about it which from a monetary, as well as from other points of view, will be useful to me.' Salisbury obligingly wrote to the civil administrator of Egypt, Lord Cromer (who was nominally Kitchener's boss), to make the case for Churchill to Kitchener, who rebuffed his prime minister by wiring back and not only refusing to accept Churchill but also declaring that other officers on a waiting list would be given priority.

His project seemed to be at a dead end when, from out of the blue, came his acceptance. A lieutenant in the 21st Lancers had, opportunely for Churchill, just died, and he was approved to replace him as a supernumerary, apparently through the intervention of Sir Evelyn Wood, who had asserted the authority of the War Office over assignments to the British contingent of Kitchener's army. However, Churchill would again have to travel at his own expense and was curtly informed that in the event of his death the army would incur no financial liability.

Although he now had permission to join the 21st Lancers, Churchill did not have permission to relinquish his assignment in India. Uncertain whether he would be released from the 4th Hussars, he chose the novel, Churchillian solution of simply disregarding the possibility that his request might be turned down. Instead he immediately fled London for Cairo by a somewhat slow, indirect route through Marseille aboard what he described as 'a filthy French tramp [steamer] manned by these detestable French sailors'. If the Indian authorities decided to recall him, Churchill reasoned, they would first have to locate him – and once he was safely in Cairo there would surely be little they could do about it.

Although Lady Jeune had assured Kitchener that Churchill would not be a correspondent 'in this war', he had in fact already arranged to write dispatches for the London *Morning Post* for a rather more significant sum than had been the case in India – fifteen pounds per dispatch. The *quid pro quo* of Lady Jeune's promise was that officially Churchill was merely another officer being assigned to the 21st Lancers; unofficially he had no intention of permitting such a minor detail to stand in the way of his reporting on the war. The deal he cut was through a close friend, Oliver Borthwick, the son of the proprietor of the *Morning Post*. The paper would publish letters purportedly written by a soldier to a friend at home who just happened to have forwarded them to the newspaper because of their possible interest to the public. In this manner Churchill could claim anonymity and thus escape Kitchener's wrath. He would shortly write to Aylmer Haldane, noting with tongue in cheek, 'If you look in the *Morning Post* it is possible that you will see that one of my friends has committed and continues to commit an unpardonable breach of confidence by publishing letters of mine. Don't give away the pious fraud as I do not want to be recalled.'

When he arrived in Cairo on 29 July 1898, there were no messages from India recalling him. And while he had indeed outfoxed his regiment, it can be fairly assumed that, for their part, the 4th Hussars had tired of his antics and were happy to be rid of him. Whatever the reasons the saga of Churchill's stormy service with the Indian army was over, although he now faced the peril of Kitchener's ire.

8

Omdurman

It was not a battle, but an execution.

— G. W. Steevens, war correspondent, London *Daily Mail*

When Churchill arrived in Cairo to join the 21st Lancers, two of the regiment's four squadrons were already en route to join Kitchener's army, now encamped deep inside the Sudan at Atbara, and the other two were in the process of deploying from their barracks. Had Churchill arrived a day or two later, he would have had to make the fourteen-hundred-mile journey to the Sudan on his own – and at his own expense.

To his dismay he learned that, although he had been slated to command a troop, uncertainty over his assignment and time of arrival had led to the appointment of another officer in his place. Lieutenant Robert Grenfell happily wrote to his family of his good fortune: 'Here I have got the troop that would have been Winston's.'

There was no time for the usual assimilation into a military unit. Churchill was immediately put to work assisting with the loading of the train that was to carry the squadrons on the first leg of their trip deep into the heart of East Africa.

The deployment of the 21st Lancers was a very complex undertaking. More to the point, the repositioning of a military unit is, at best, organized chaos. For a cavalry unit the two-week journey into the Egyptian and Sudanese wilderness was even more difficult. Their horses were Arabian stallions, skittish by nature, which had to be loaded on to confining rail wagons. In addition the animals required considerable quantities of forage that were not available in the desert. Logistics – the provisioning, maintenance and timely resupply of an army – is a dull but essential aspect of warfare that is rarely written about. Yet, as Napoleon learned the hard way during his abortive campaign in Russia in 1812, without competent logisticians battles are usually lost. Many years later, before the D-day landings in Normandy on 6 June 1944, Prime Minister Winston Churchill, who never fully appreciated the subject, would complain: 'The destinies of two great empires seemed to be tied up in some God-damned things called LSTs [landing ships, tank – the workhorse vessels of the invasion fleets of the Second World War].'

In his first dispatch Churchill accurately described the business of deployment as 'a wearying affair'. With cavalry 'the difficulties [were] more than doubled' as horses, soldiers and weapons and equipment were loaded on a long train bound for the southern terminus of the military railway at Berber, a city on the Nile near Atbara. To the strains of a band playing 'Auld Lang Syne', there were final handshakes and goodbyes exchanged with those on the platform who were remaining behind. Then the train slowly steamed away for the lengthy journey into the wilderness of deepest Africa.

It took a while before Churchill lost his fear that Kitchener would somehow rescind his assignment and have him recalled. His imagination ran wild with various scenarios, all of which ended badly. Every time the train stopped or the steamers carrying the regiment up the Nile docked, he expected to see a staff officer bearing the dreaded orders. 'I was pursued and haunted by a profound, unrelenting fear . . . I suppose a criminal flying from justice goes through the same emotions . . . Thank God, there was no wireless in those days or I should never had have a moment's peace.' Kitchener, however, had more important things on his mind than the assignment of Lieutenant Winston Churchill to his army, and the recall never came.

After an exhausting twenty-four-hour journey by rail, the Lancers toiled to transfer men and equipment to barges towed by steamers that transported them up the Nile to the ancient city of Luxor, famous for its temples, where there was a brief stop-over. It gave Churchill enough time to indulge his love of history and his recollection of H. Rider Haggard's *Cleopatra*, and to see the temples he had long fantasized about visiting. He was enthralled by the Nile, 'the great waterway of Africa. It is the life and soul of Egypt.'

Clad in khaki uniforms better suited to more temperate climates, the men of the 21st Lancers were subjected to the relentless rays of the sun during their final advance towards Khartoum; a movement of eight to ten miles a day was routine. Churchill's dispatches and his later memoir are rhapsodic in recounting his love affair with the Nile. His vivid descriptions of the journey were so evocative that his readers could almost feel the incredible heat, experience the utter desolation of the desert and sense the visual impact of the mighty Nile. 'How delicious it was in the evenings,' Churchill wrote, when 'we filed down in gold and purple twilight to drink and drink and drink again from the swift abundant Nile.' The river, he said, 'grows on me day by day. It colours all one's thoughts.'

Churchill was not the only war correspondent accompanying the expeditionary army. A photograph taken aboard one of the Nile steamers shows him as one of sixteen correspondents, each of whom was hoping to write a headline account for a British public eager for news of the expedition. As it turned out, the young freelance soldier of fortune in their midst would have the lion's share of publicity for the bloody battle soon to occur at Omdurman.

Late one afternoon, during the long march south, for reasons that he never specified but that involved military duties of some sort, Churchill was left behind on the east bank of the Nile at Atbara. All he knew was that his regiment was supposed to be encamped some fifteen miles away in the desert. After crossing to the west bank on a small ferry, he asked where he was supposed to go and was told: 'It is perfectly simple. You just go due south until you see the campfires, then turn towards the river.' Churchill had gone scarcely a mile when the sun suddenly sank and he was left to navigate by means of the North Star, which he kept at his back as he rode deeper into the wilderness, until the sky clouded over in total darkness. Rather than roam aimlessly with no exact idea where his unit was encamped, and filled with a sense of utter helplessness, he curled up in a sandy spot behind a rock, his pony's reins grasped tightly in his hand. Expecting to eat dinner with his regiment, he had begun his journey without rations and, what was worse, without water for either himself or his pony.

Towards dawn the sky cleared and, navigating by the constellation Orion, he eventually stumbled upon the river. 'Jumping off my horse I walked into the Nile until it rose above my knees, and began to drink its waters, as many a thirsty man has done before; while the pony, plunging his nose deep into the stream, gulped and gulped in pleasure and relief as if he could never swallow enough.' In daylight, with the

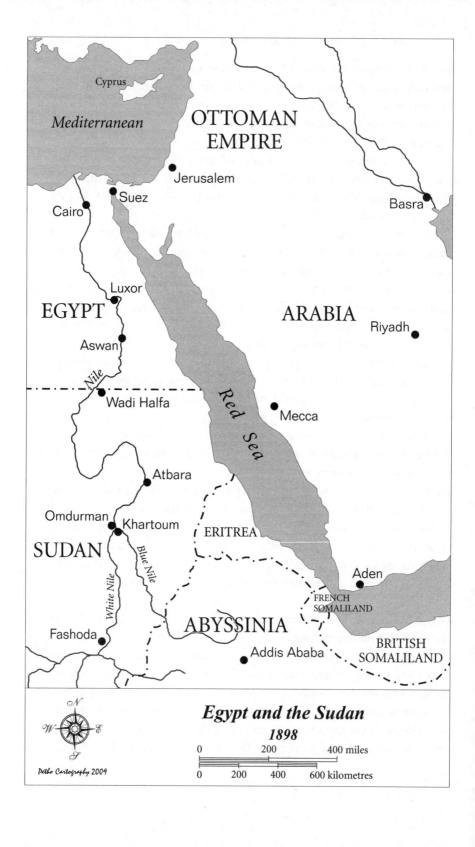

Cyprus

Mediterranean

OTTOMAN
EMPIRE

Jerusalem

Suez

Cairo

Basra

Luxor

EGYPT

ARABIA

Riyadh

Aswan

Nile

Wadi Halfa

Red Sea

Mecca

Atbara

Omdurman

Khartoum

ERITREA

SUDAN

Blue Nile

White Nile

Aden

FRENCH
SOMALILAND

Fashoda

ABYSSINIA

Addis Ababa

BRITISH
SOMALILAND

N
W *E*
S

Petho Cartography 2009

Egypt and the Sudan
1898

0   200   400 miles

0   200   400   600 kilometres

help of a villager with whom he communicated by gestures, Churchill eventually located his unit, thus ending his nerve-racking one-man trek through the wilderness.

Above Aswan the Nile descends into a deep, rocky gorge – the first of many great cataracts during its immense journey from its headwaters deep in Africa to the Mediterranean – making further passage by steamer impossible. An army of coolies and convicts in chains assisted in yet another change of venue to a town some six miles south, where new steamers awaited them for the next leg of their four-day journey to Wadi Halfa, the southernmost Egyptian garrison town, on the border with the Sudan. From Wadi Halfa the journey evolved into a four-hundred-mile train trip on the recently completed Sudan Military Railway.

Kitchener's punitive army consisted of 8,200 British and 17,600 Egyptian and Sudanese troops. His firepower was an awesome array of field artillery (5-inch howitzers that fired a fifty-pound shell), deadly Maxim guns, Royal Navy gunboats providing support from the Nile and a huge number of animals to carry both men and equipment: more than 3,500 camels, nearly 2,500 horses, 896 mules and 229 donkeys – and an enormous cache of food and supplies.

By late August the force was assembled on the plain outside the fortress of Omdurman. Churchill seemed mainly concerned with wearing a medal on his breast rather than with his safety or the forthcoming battle. Considering that he saw no combat with the Tirah Expeditionary Force, he wrote irrationally to Haldane to complain about Kitchener and to request that he expedite the award of 'a medal and two clasps for gallantry for the hardships & dangers I encountered with the T.E.F. I am of a keen desire to mount the ribbon on my breast while I face the Dervishes here. It may induce them to pause.'

After the siege of 1885 Khartoum lay in ruins. Shortly thereafter the Mahdi, who had become the undisputed ruler of the Sudan, established a theocratic Mahdist state with Omdurman as the new capital and began to lead a life of unbridled excess, naively believing that he would go on to conquer both Egypt and the world.

Across the Nile from Khartoum, the river branches into the White Nile and the Blue Nile. On the White Nile, just below the confluence of the two rivers, was a former mud fort erected by the Egyptians.

Extending some six miles in length along the White Nile, Omdurman had by 1898 evolved into a substantial city of about 150,000 inhabitants, most of whom lived in mud huts on narrow, foul-smelling streets. Surrounding the city was a fortress consisting of a great wall and substantial defensive works to fend off assaults, particularly from the Nile. Six months after Khartoum, the Mahdi suddenly died (whether from his excesses or poison is not certain). An enormous, yellowish brown tomb for him, visible from miles away, was erected in the centre of the city. His handpicked successor was Khalifa Abdullah, a man described as 'sly, suspicious, vain, quick-tempered, unbelievably cruel and despotic', yet possessed of 'a certain ruthless charm' – a man whose delusions may have exceeded those of the Mahdi.

In the years between 1885 and 1898 there had been uprisings, plots, incursions by the Abyssinians, an abortive invasion of Egypt and savage internal struggles. However, the Khalifa's army remained intact and in 1898, despite its crushing defeat at Atbara, was thought to number about 52,000. Confrontation between the two opposing armies was now only a question of time and place.

On 1 September 1898, two years of laborious preparation were about to come to fruition. Kitchener's army had established its main battle position with its rear element along the Nile, where it was protected by British gunboats. Initially, several thousand yards to the north-west, the cavalry and the camel corps were positioned astride a rocky ridgeline called the Kerreri Hills. Rather than attack the Mahdist army, however, Kitchener's strategy was to remain in essentially defensive positions and by his mere presence provoke them into attacking.

Kitchener's army consisted of 'great brown masses of infantry with a fringe of cavalry dotting the plain for miles in front, with the Camel Corps – chocolate-coloured men on cream-coloured camels – stretching into the desert . . . and the gunboats stealing silently up the river on the left, scrutinizing the bank with their guns'.

What Churchill witnessed that day deep in the heart of Africa was a sight no man could forget. Between their position and Omdurman were a long, low ridge and a rolling sandy plain, interspersed with small knolls, that Churchill realized would be the battlefield. Eerily, not a soul could be seen. Late that morning he watched in astonishment as, some four miles to the south-west, a great dark mass of men appeared over the crest of a hill, in all at least forty thousand and possibly as many as fifty thousand Mahdist troops, arranged in five separate formations. Although spears honed to a lethal sharpness were their predominant weaponry, an estimated twenty thousand warriors were armed with antiquated single-shot Martini-Henry rifles, which fired a .45-calibre bullet that packed a powerful and usually deadly punch.

The spectacle was both awe-inspiring and chilling, reminding Churchill of the crusaders of the twelfth century he had once studied:

Lines of men appeared over the crest, and while we watched, amazed by the wonder of the sight, the whole face of the slope became black with swarming savages. Four miles from end to end, and in five great divisions, this mighty army advanced . . . The whole side of the hill seemed to move . . . Above them waved hundreds of banners, and the sun, glinting on perhaps forty thousand hostile spear-points, spread a sparkling cloud. It was, perhaps, the impression of a lifetime.

Churchill's regimental commander ordered him to report the situation personally to Kitchener. Churchill felt understandable trepidation over what effect his appearance would have on the Sirdar, and he had good reason for concern. A week earlier he had learned of Kitchener's disapproval of his presence. Frank Rhodes, a retired army colonel, now a correspondent for *The Times*, had spoken to the general about him: 'Kitchener said he had known I was not going to stay in the army – was only making a convenience of it; that he had disapproved of my coming in place of others whose professions were at stake & that E. [Sir Evelyn] Wood had acted wrongly & had annoyed him by sending me. But that I was quite right to try my best.'

Churchill rode towards the colourful Anglo-Egyptian army, drawn up in mass formation, its banners flying in the breeze. At the head of his army rode Kitchener, his staff several paces behind. Churchill drew alongside but to the rear of the Sirdar and crisply saluted: 'Sir, I have come from the Twenty-first Lancers with a report.' Kitchener nodded his assent, signalling that the subaltern should continue. Churchill outlined the enemy's dispositions and after a long pause Kitchener asked: 'How long do you think I've got?' In a flash Churchill replied: 'You have got at least an hour and a half, sir, even if they come on at their present rate.'

Thus ended Churchill's first, uneventful encounter with the man he both feared and, for the time being, admired. Afterwards he was taken in hand by Kitchener's intelligence chief, Sir Reginald Wingate, and enjoyed an elegant and civilized lunch, of bully beef, pickles and wine, complete with knives and forks, served atop a white oilcloth. Churchill was seated next to Major Adolf von Tiedemann, an observer from the German general staff, who said to him: 'This is the 1st of September. *Our* great day and now *your* great day.' (Baron von Tiedemann was referring to the Prussian victory over France in 1870, which paved the way for German unification.) The conversation turned to the forthcoming battle, about which there was great confidence. 'Everyone was in the highest spirits and best of tempers. It was like a race luncheon before the Derby ... It was really a good moment to live, and I, a poor subaltern who had thought of himself under a ban, plied my knife and fork with determination amid the infectious gaiety of all these military magnates.'

Buoyed by his unexpected good fortune, Churchill afterwards strolled along the riverbank with another officer when they were hailed by the commander of a nearby gunboat anchored in the Nile. The officer was a Royal Navy lieutenant dressed in a spotless white uniform. A 'jolly talk' ensued, along with an offer of naval hospitality. A bottle of champagne suddenly flew through the air; Churchill failed to catch it before it fell into the river, whence he happily retrieved it. The officer was future admiral of the fleet and first sea lord Lieutenant David Beatty.

The Khalifa's army marched en masse to within several miles of Kitchener's positions, and on what seemed to be a single command halted like a well-drilled parade formation. Most battles are preceded by considerable preliminary fighting and bombardments, but here the two sides merely gazed warily at each other, neither prepared to make the first move. The riflemen fired off bursts in the air in what Churchill described as 'a great roar – a barbaric *feu de joie*', and, at a second command, this massive army simply lay down on the ground, explicitly conveying that the great confrontation would not occur on this day.

There were minor skirmishes on 1 September, and British artillery destroyed the eighty-foot-high dome of the Mahdi's tomb, raising large clouds of red dust. That the desecration of the Mahdi's tomb would further enrage his enemy seemed of no consequence to Kitchener. If anything it was a sign of his contempt for those he would on the morrow slay pitilessly on a battlefield some seven miles north of Omdurman.

Churchill viewed the coming battle as something of a lark. 'This kind of war was full of fascinating thrills,' he wrote in 1930. 'It was not like the Great War. Nobody expected to be killed . . . but to the great mass of those who took part in the little wars of Britain in those vanished light-hearted days, this was only a sporting element in a splendid game.'

Beneath a glorious sunrise that would soon turn the sands blood red, there commenced on the morning of 2 September 1898 what history has recorded as the Battle of Omdurman, which might better be described as the Massacre of Omdurman. Though it is unlikely that any slept well if at all that night, at 4.30 a.m. bugles sounded throughout the Anglo-Egyptian army, summoning its troops to arise for battle. The Egyptian cavalry was immediately sent forward to make contact with the enemy, and, at first light the great mass of the Khalifa's army became visible in the distance.

Churchill was ordered to take a patrol forward and later claimed to have been the first to see the advancing enemy, and 'certainly the first to hear their bullets. Never shall I see such a sight again. At the very least there were 40,000 men – five miles long in lines with great humps and squares at intervals – and I can assure you that when I heard them all shouting their war songs from my coign of vantage on the ridge of Heliograph Hill I and my patrol felt very lonely. And though I never doubted the issue – I was in great awe.'

The two opposing armies resembled gladiators awaiting a signal to begin what would be not a sporting event but a fight to the death. Ominously circling overhead were a hundred large and ugly vultures that had suddenly appeared, seemingly sensing that a feast would shortly be awaiting them.

At 6.30 the massed forces of the Khalifa's army began methodically advancing on the Anglo-Egyptian positions, flags fluttering brilliantly in the sunlight, the spears of thousands of warriors waving in the air, their voices roaring approval of Allah and their leader, with continuous chanting in Arabic of 'There is one God and Muhammad is the Messenger of God.'

Behind one of the formations rode the Khalifa himself on a donkey, attended only by a small retinue. 'They came very fast, and they came very straight,' wrote the *Daily Mail* correspondent G. W. Steevens, 'and then presently they came no farther. With a crash the bullets leaped out of the British rifles,' and 'they poured out death as fast as they could load and press the trigger.'

The Khalifa's army was divided into five separate forces. Its tactics were simple: advance, outflank and overcome the enemy under the protection of Allah. Two of these forces moved forward to Kitchener's positions astride the Kerreri Hill mass, while the other three wheeled right and advanced towards the main Anglo-Egyptian positions near the river in a suicidal frontal attack. What occurred within the space of perhaps two hours was, as Steevens wrote, 'not a battle but an execution.'

The massed Dervish infantry moved steadily forward as shells began raining down on them, wreaking appalling carnage. The roar of voices, guns and fire was earsplitting. Bullets indiscriminately shattered some, while others were blown to pieces by artillery shells. Churchill described it as 'a terrible sight, for as yet they had not hurt us at all, and it seemed an unfair advantage to strike thus cruelly when they could not reply . . . Eight hundred yards away a ragged line of men were coming on desperately struggling forward in the face of the pitiless fire – white banners tossing and collapsing.' Not many managed to get closer than three hundred yards.

Yet on they came, with absolute fearlessness, undaunted by the fires of hell that engulfed them or by the masses of dead and dying all around them. Churchill later described how the twelve thousand Anglo-Egyptian infantrymen 'were engaged in that mechanical scattering of death which the polite nations of the earth have brought to such monstrous perfection'. At the end of as savage a battle as has ever taken place, the dead were strewn across the battlefield. Omdurman was in reality no contest. Though Kitchener's army was greatly outnumbered, it possessed the means of sheer slaughter with its deadly artillery, rifles and Maxim guns, the great killing machines that cut down the tribesmen like blades of grass by a lawnmower. The writer Hilaire Belloc would later write of the Battle of Omdurman:

> Whatever happens we have got
> The Maxim gun and they have not.

The Khalifa's army was destroyed by Kitchener's guns. Dervish warriors died in their thousands; no one ever ascertained the exact number, but no fewer than ten thousand brave men lay dead on the sands outside Omdurman, and between ten thousand and sixteen thousand were wounded, many lying untended and in mortal agony where they fell.

According to Churchill's account, entitled *The River War*, there were also five thousand captured. By 8.00 a.m. it was nearly over. Towards noon Churchill wrote: 'Sir H. Kitchener shut up his [field] glasses . . . remarking that he thought the enemy had been given "a good dusting".'

Churchill's description tells of the steady drum of bullets 'shearing through flesh, smashing and splintering bone' and of 'valiant men . . . struggling on through a hell of whistling metal, exploding shells, and spurting dust – suffering, despairing, dying'.

Despite the one-sided slaughter, the Battle of Omdurman might well have ended in disaster – not for the Dervish army, but for Kitchener, who committed a near-fatal blunder. Believing that the battle was won, he ordered his main forces to advance and secure Omdurman, leaving only a reserve brigade under the command of Lieutenant Colonel Hector Archibald MacDonald, consisting of three thousand Egyptian and Sudanese troops, three batteries of artillery and eight Maxim guns, a mile or so to the north. Because the bulk of his army had turned and was marching in column formation towards the city, his rear element was especially vulnerable to a flank attack. What Kitchener did not know was that a large force of perhaps twenty thousand flying the black flag of the Khalifa was bearing down on MacDonald's brigade. Suddenly in great peril, MacDonald – an experienced and astute soldier who had risen through the ranks from private to command of a brigade and had seen as much service as anyone in the British army – without a second thought disobeyed the orders from Kitchener to rejoin the army and formed a hasty defence as the full fury of the Dervish attack fell upon his brigade. His troops fought off one wave after another of attacks that nearly overran them. In the end it was his foresight and initiative that saved Kitchener from potential disaster. Churchill would later suggest that, had the Khalifa attacked simultaneously with his main force, 'the position of MacDonald's brigade must have been almost hopeless. In the actual event it was one of extreme peril.'

Then Kitchener committed a second blunder. Although the battle had turned in his favour and British casualties were almost nonexistent, he was understandably concerned about having to fight in the narrow alleys of Omdurman and wanted insurance that a major part of the Dervish army should not be permitted to fall back and take up positions within the city. He decided that the battle had been won and, without first ordering a

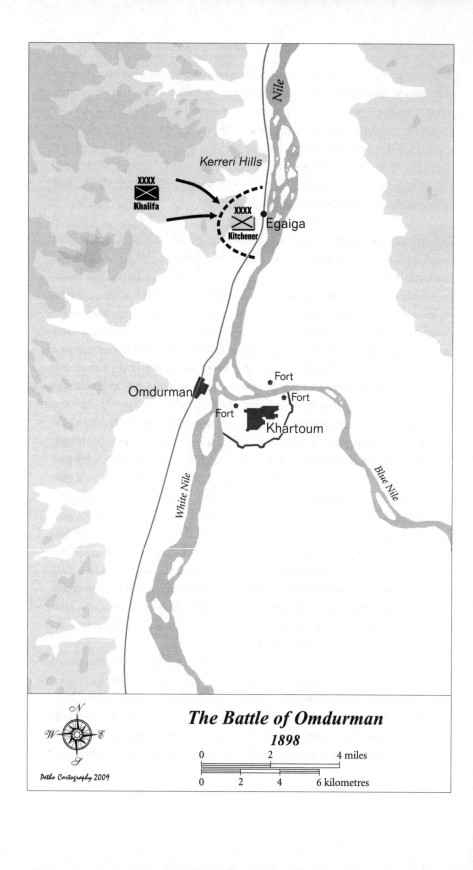

The Battle of Omdurman
1898

reconnaissance to determine the location and strength of the enemy, ordered his cavalry to turn towards Omdurman and enter the city.

At 8.30 a.m. about four hundred cavalrymen of the 21st Lancers began advancing to the left flank of the Anglo-Egyptian front. Suddenly, beyond a ridge where they had halted, 'thousands of Dervishes could be seen.' Then, without warning, matters suddenly turned deadly. Churchill was in command of a patrol on the right flank, and as they advanced the cavalry expected little resistance and intended to 'spear them till we could not sit on our horses'. About 250 yards from the massed Dervish force they encountered what appeared to be a straight line of some 150 men blocking their path. Intending to outflank them, Churchill's Lancers moved to their right only to be fired upon by what were obviously not mere spearmen but sharpshooters, who began pouring heavy fire into the Lancers. 'The distance was too short for it to be harmless on so big a target and I realized there were only two courses open,' wrote Churchill. One was to back off and regroup; the other was to charge the enemy. Under intense fire the cavalry acted instinctively, as they had been trained to do, and 'while the trumpet was still jerking we were all at the gallop towards them.'

History has since immortalized the cavalrymen of Omdurman in portraits and literature in what was the last and perhaps most famous charge of the British cavalry. Churchill's survival that day may well have hinged on the 1896 accident in Bombay that had crippled his right shoulder. At the commencement of the charge his brother officers had all drawn their swords as they galloped full speed ahead towards the riflemen. Churchill quickly realized it would have been useless to attempt to make use of his sword with his right arm and instead drew his Mauser pistol.

As the two sides converged in close combat the scene became chaotic. Suddenly a large, undetected Dervish formation hidden in a nearby wadi exploded from concealment and enveloped the mounted Lancers. They had ridden directly into a carefully laid trap involving an estimated three thousand warriors. 'The blunders of British cavalry are the fertile seed of British glory,' wrote G. W. Steevens in his account of Omdurman.

'It is very rarely', wrote Churchill in one of his dispatches, 'that stubborn and unshaken infantry meet equally stubborn and unshaken cavalry ... In this case the two living walls crashed together with a mighty collision.' Although Churchill said, with hindsight, 'capital – the more the merrier', no one facing such an extreme life-threatening situation would have felt such bravado. The Dervishes stood their ground and stabbed, hacked and shot at the British cavalry. Horses were slashed and fell horribly wounded, their riders falling to the ground, where many were impaled by as many as a dozen men with a ferocity seldom seen on a battlefield; riderless horses galloped free of the killing zone; other Lancers, most of them wounded, who had been thrown from their mounts, clung precariously to reins or stirrups as they were dragged, hanging on literally for their lives. A sergeant who had been slashed had strips of skin cut from his face that hung in shreds.

Through the cauldron rode the regimental commander, Colonel R. M. Martin. Although his charger fell, Martin emerged unscathed and ordered a halt to further charges by his cavalrymen. Many of the Lancers wanted more. 'There were gnashings of teeth and howls of speechless rage,' but common sense ultimately prevailed. The Lancers then opened fire with their carbines at close range.

As for Churchill, 'I remember no sound,' he wrote. 'The whole event seemed to pass in absolute silence. The yells of the enemy, the shouts of the soldiers, the firing of many shots, the clashing of sword and spear were unnoticed by the senses, unregistered by the brain. Others say the same. Perhaps it is possible for the whole of a man's faculties to be concentrated in eye, bridle-hand, and trigger-finger, and withdrawn from other parts of the body.'

Still alive and unwounded on the rim of the cauldron, Churchill quickly determined that he was not yet out of harm's way. The force the charge had broken through was about four deep, 'But they all fell knocked A.O.T. [arse over tip] . . . then we emerged into a region of scattered men and personal combats. The troop broke up and disappeared. I pulled into a trot and rode up to individuals firing my pistol in their faces and killing several – 3 for certain – 2 doubtful – one very doubtful.' A mere twenty yards away, some of the Dervishes began reforming their ranks and two of them aimed their rifles right at Churchill, 'and I looked at them stupidly for what may have been 2 seconds . . . and for the first time the danger & peril came home to me. I turned and galloped. The squadron was reforming nearly 150 yards away. As I turned shots were fired and at that close range I was grievously anxious. But I heard none of their bullets – which went Heaven knows where.'

Hundreds of bloody individual battles played out before the Lancers broke free, dismounted and began surgically cutting down the surviving warriors with carbine fire until the Dervishes at last retreated. 'In one hundred and twenty seconds five officers, sixty-six men, and one hundred and nineteen horses out of less than three hundred had been killed or wounded,' wrote Churchill. To his cousin Sunny Marlborough he pointed out that 'No regiment has sustained such a proportion and such a loss since the Light Brigade – forty years ago.'

That he had narrowly escaped death seems not to have unduly bothered Churchill, who wrote rather glowingly of his experience. 'The Battle was a wonderful spectacle. I had the good luck to ride through the charge unhurt – indeed untouched – which vy few can say.' Although he was certainly fearless, for perhaps the first time in his life he experienced genuine fear. 'I felt myself absolutely alone,' he wrote of his isolation after riding through the ranks of the enemy. 'I thought those riflemen would hit me, and the rest devour me like wolves.' To charge recklessly into such a violent battle as Churchill did, with no thought of the consequences, and to perform bravely under such conditions was the ultimate test of courage. Any soldier who has ever been in a life-and-death combat situation will readily acknowledge that one feels a combination of gut-wrenching fear and the dread of letting down one's comrades in arms. Time stands still, as Churchill pointed out, and whatever the reaction, it is virtually instinctive and, for better or worse, the result of one's training. Field Marshal Viscount Slim would later say of combat that 'the dominant feeling of the battlefield is loneliness,' and Epaminondas (the Theban general who bested Sparta) described a field of battle as 'a dancing floor of Ares [the god of war]'.

Although he later made light of the dangers he faced as merely another exploit in his military repertoire, and 'not in the least exciting', Churchill admitted at the time, 'It was I suppose the most dangerous 2 minutes I shall live to see.'

The Battle of Omdurman lasted some five terrible hours, during which the Dervish army suffered about 95 per cent losses. On 2 September 1898, Omdurman, which is today a thriving suburb of Khartoum with a population of 1.5 million, was a scene of devastation. In *My Early Life* and in *The River War*, Churchill wrote, 'Thus ended the Battle of Omdurman – the most signal triumph ever gained by the arms of science over barbarians.'

Two officers and a private of the 21st Lancers were later awarded the Victoria Cross for gallantry during this action. However, there was nothing glorious about the battlefield, which was strewn with thousands of dead and wounded men, many of whom became a feast for the hungry vultures. The nauseating smell of death would permeate the barren landscape for weeks.

Among the British dead was Lieutenant Robert Grenfell, the officer whose troop Churchill was to have commanded. That troop, on Churchill's left flank, suffered the heaviest casualties of the 21st Lancers, and the lieutenant himself had been hacked to death. Fate sometimes turns on seemingly insignificant events. Little did Churchill know that what he had first deemed bad luck – arriving too late in Cairo to take command of the troop – later spared his life.

If there were lessons for Winston Churchill in the Battle of Omdurman, they may be read from his stunned reaction to Grenfell's death. 'War,' he wrote, 'disguise it as you may, is but a dirty, shoddy business, which only a fool would play at.'

9

David versus Goliath

Victory at Omdurman was disgraced by the inhuman slaughter of the wounded
... Kitchener was responsible for this. – Churchill to Jennie, 26 January 1899

The second Sudan War was more than merely a military victory. 'What happened in the Sudan on 2 September 1898 was the zenith of late Victorian imperialism' and 'the apogee of the generation that regarded world domination as a racial prerogative', notes the historian Niall Ferguson. Britain remained the master of a vast global empire, the principal banker of the world and a supreme power whose likes had never been seen nor would ever be seen again. However, the cost of maintaining its empire was an endless series of small wars and insurrections that the British army was obliged to fight – more than seventy-two of them during the reign of Queen Victoria.

Although the decline and eventual dissolution of the British Empire lay in the future, in 1898 there was near-universal approval in Britain that Gordon had been avenged. Kitchener had carried out his orders to retake the Sudan, and despite the carnage he became a national hero. Almost as important, the British victory at Omdurman and the subsequent reclaiming of the Sudan checked Britain's principal rival, blocking French territorial ambitions in East Africa. Control of Egypt was now firmly in Britain's hands, thus protecting its vital link to India.

There was, however, another, far more ominous consequence of Omdurman. The German military observer Baron von Tiedemann, with whom Churchill had shared a pleasant lunch, 'duly noted the devastating impact of the British Maxim guns, which one observer reckoned accounted for around three-quarters of the Dervish casualties. To Tiedemann the real lesson was obvious: the only way to beat the British was to match their firepower.' That message was made clear to the German general staff. The Maxim gun had already changed the face of war and would in a few more years be a weapon that all modern armies would employ, with devastating results.

British and Egyptian flags now flew in Khartoum in triumph over the ruins of what had once been the residence of the governor general. A memorial service was held for Gordon as British gunboats in the Nile boomed a salute and 'a Catholic chaplain prayed that God might "look down . . . with eyes of pity and compassion on this land so loved by that heroic soul", words that moved Kitchener and other officers to tears.' The hard-boiled Kitchener is reported to have been so 'shaking with sobs' that he was obliged to call off the remainder of the ceremony. Queen Victoria wrote in her diary, 'Surely he [Gordon] is avenged.' There were, however, no tears and no compassion for the warriors of the Khalifa's defeated army – only appalling retribution.

Although the Khalifa escaped along with some ten thousand of his once proud army into the wilderness of the southern Sudan, Kitchener relentlessly tracked him down in October 1899, and in a near repeat of Omdurman, the Khalifa and a thousand of his warriors were killed, mostly by British machine-gun fire, and some nine thousand survivors captured. 'Mahdism is now a thing of the past,' Kitchener wrote, a logical conclusion at the time but a prediction whose obverse has in the twenty-first century become an everyday reality, the spear replaced by the suicide bomber, the hijacker, the improvised explosive device (IED) and the car bomb.

The bloodbath of Omdurman was an awakening for Churchill, who not only experienced war at its malevolent worst but also witnessed the commission by the victorious Anglo-Egyptian army of what today would be called war crimes. In 1898 there was no Geneva Convention to protect warring parties, and Kitchener's soldiers, mostly Sudanese and Egyptians but also some British, carried out barbaric reprisals that would later cast a stain on the honour of an otherwise reputable army.

Those Dervishes who did not escape from Omdurman suffered a horrifying fate. As outrage followed outrage, widespread killings, rape, looting and pillaging were carried out, and the tomb of the Mahdi was desecrated. It was as if the savagery of ordinarily decent soldiers could not be turned off and instead became the excuse for acts of bloodletting no civilized person would dream of committing. Kitchener not only did nothing to stop the brutality but also authorized the defiling of the Mahdi's tomb, which was razed to the ground, ostensibly because it was so badly damaged that it posed safety concerns. He acquired the skull of the Mahdi (the bones were secretly tossed into the Nile), and displayed it on his desk for possible future use as a drinking cup or an inkstand, later deciding that perhaps it should be sent to the Royal College of Surgeons in London.

Kitchener deliberately limited the number of doctors in his force, and the wounded Dervishes were either left untreated on the battlefield or slaughtered with bayonets where they had fallen. One of his officers ordered anyone connected with the Khalifa leadership to be instantly executed. In London some outraged MPs attempted but failed to block a reward of thirty thousand pounds to Kitchener, but the outrage was overshadowed by public acceptance of him as the hero of the Sudan. He was fêted all over Britain, given the freedom of various cities, and not only appointed governor general of the Sudan (as well as retaining his post as Sirdar) but also granted a peerage, thereafter styling himself Lord Kitchener of Khartoum.

Although Kitchener denied all charges of cruelty and maintained that it had been necessary to destroy the tomb and the Mahdi's corpse in order to prevent the site from becoming a shrine and a second Mecca, his clumsy handling of the matter left Queen Victoria privately unconvinced that he had acted with propriety. The government accepted his version and to quieten public opinion issued a White Paper to that effect. Kitchener's manipulation of the truth of what had really occurred at Omdurman may have ended the matter at the time, but truth usually has a way of winning out in the end. There was an impeccable witness to describe it all, a troublesome young officer and war correspondent who would not only publicly criticize the desecration of the Mahdi's tomb but also take on the mighty Kitchener himself.

Three days after the battle, in the company of another officer, Churchill rode on to the battlefield with its dead strewn about like so much litter, and it gave him pause. The Dervish dead were piled three deep in places, while the wounded survivors lay in the torrid sun stoically awaiting death. 'Three days of burning sun had done their work. The bodies were swollen to almost gigantic proportions ... The smell redoubled the horror.' In a graphic dispatch and later in *The River War*, Churchill informed his readers: 'In a space not exceeding a hundred yards square more than four hundred corpses lay festering. Can you imagine the postures in which man, once created in the image of his maker, had been twisted? Do not try, for were you to succeed you would ask yourself with me: "Can I ever forget?"'

The experience left Churchill shaken. 'It has been said that the Gods forbade vengeance to mankind because they reserved for themselves so delicious and intoxicating a drink,' he wrote, 'and it may well be that vengeance is sweet. But one should not drain the cup quite to the bottom. The dregs are sometimes filthy tasting.'

It also dawned on Churchill that war was in fact a dangerous under-taking and that he had been very fortunate to escape death on the sands of Omdurman. The death of Lieutenant Grenfell, an officer Churchill liked and admired and with whom he had travelled and bivouacked, made a deep impression. He wrote to Sunny Marlborough: 'Had I started when I meant to from London I should have had Grenfell's troop and ridden where he rode . . . I have seen more war than most boys my age, probably more than any. I am not squeamish, but I have seen acts of great barbarity perpetrated at Omdurman and have been thoroughly sickened of human blood. I have tried to gild war, and to solace myself for the loss of dear and gallant friends, with the thought that a soldier's death for a cause that he believes in will count for much.'

Before departing Omdurman he visited the newly created British cem-etery, where Grenfell and the other Britons who had died in the battle were buried. 'Such is the melancholy end of brave men who fall in war,' he reflected. The experience so moved Churchill that he wept at the sight of 'a last tribute to those who had paid the bill for all the fun and glory of the game'. In one of his dispatches he compared the service for a dead British soldier, invested with elegiac words and solemn music, all of which deprived the act of death of its squalor, with the awful scenes he had witnessed on the battlefield of Omdurman. 'But there was nothing *dulce et decorum* about the Dervish dead. Nothing of the dignity of unconquerable manhood. All was filthy corruption. Yet these were as brave men as ever walked the earth.'

Churchill also experienced the exhilaration that comes with superior leadership of soldiers. He proudly wrote to Jennie that he firmly believed his men 'would have followed me as far as I would have gone and that I may tell you and you only – was a very long way – for my soul becomes very high at such moments'. Omdurman left him still wedded to his romantic notions of war but also aware of its terrible costs. Nevertheless forty years on he would make such inane statements as 'This kind of war was full of fascinating thrills' and 'Death was a sporting element in a splendid game.' His godson and admirer the Earl of Birkenhead would write of him: 'In spite of what he had seen . . . in spite of the losses and horrors of battle – war continued to hold for Winston a powerful and glittering lure. It required the mechanized butchery of the Great War to dispel this illusion, and even that not completely.'

In the months after Omdurman, Churchill began urgently to chronicle the battle. When the result was published in the autumn of 1899 in two lengthy volumes, *The River War* revealed as much about Churchill himself as it did about the battle. His compassion shone brightly when both in his dispatches and in his book he paid tribute to the bravery of the Dervishes while also railing against the racism of his countrymen and others. In so doing he stood virtually alone. ' "Mad fanaticism" is the deprecating comment of their conquerors. I hold this to be a cruel injustice. Nor can he be a very brave man who will not credit them with a nobler motive, and believe that they died to clear their honour from the stain of defeat.' Churchill then posed a question that would later have great significance: 'Why should we regard as madness in the savage what would be sublime in civilized men? For I hope that if evil days should come upon our own country, and the last army which a collapsing Empire could interpose between London and the invader were dissolving in rout and ruin, that there would be some – even in these modern days – who would not care to accustom themselves to a new order of things and tamely survive the disaster.' His lifelong friend Violet Bonham Carter (*née* Asquith) later commented: 'Can any doubt that if in 1940 the Battle of Britain had ended in defeat he would have been one of these?'

Churchill was indeed fortunate to have been at Omdurman as an officer first and a war correspondent second. His colleagues in the fourth estate did not fare so well. Kitchener kept them at arm's length, and it took Salisbury's intervention before they were even permitted to accompany the main force and witness the battle from a distance. After it was over Kitchener retaliated by ordering them back to Egypt. In *The River War*, Churchill called him 'the bitterest opponent of the Press that modern militarism has yet produced in England'.

Churchill was thus virtually the only correspondent to view Omdurman first hand from the battlefield itself. *The River War* brilliantly, if somewhat over-vividly, captured the extraordinary drama and gave the most comprehensive picture of the Battle of Omdurman that has been written. Moreover, that he was at its epicentre enabled him to describe the event and the last great cavalry battle fought by the British army. Unquestionably the experience was exactly the stuff of his youthful dreams, of defining his manhood and of proving his courage under fire.

Although he would tone down his remarks in *The River War*, Churchill was filled with bitterness towards Kitchener and told Sunny that he was 'a vulgar common man'. Thus the book reverberates with both implied and overt criticism of his erstwhile commander in chief. Although he would extend an olive branch when he became first lord of the Admiralty, as the years passed Kitchener did not lose his simmering resentment, believing that 'that bounder' Churchill had falsely accused him of wrongdoing.

The Victorian era, which evolved into the much briefer Edwardian period at the start of the twentieth century, continued to promote a curious ethic that decreed bravery in the midst of futility, and assumed that to die in vain was the most honourable thing one could do. At Balaklava, during the Crimean War, the cavalry of the Light Brigade had ridden 'in all the pride and splendour of war straight into the arms of death', an act of valour immortalized by Alfred, Lord Tennyson but actually brought about by a combination of incompetence and misunderstanding on the part of the British commanders.

The glorification of bravery was a concept that Winston Churchill never quite relinquished – and one that would occasionally cloud his thinking during the Second World War. And while he embraced courage, he refused to be silenced over acts of dishonour such as had occurred at Omdurman. Ever the Victorian, Churchill, while shocked and repelled by 'the inhumane slaughter of the wounded', nevertheless did not deplore the use of force as a means of upholding British imperialism. 'My faith in our race & blood was much strengthened,' he wrote to Ian Hamilton.

If Churchill's military writings are somewhat inflated paeans to British imperialism, his descriptions of battle remain unexcelled. His mental capacity for retaining detail was as remarkable as the ability of a relatively unschooled young man to produce a major work like *The River War*. Indeed from the rebellious, opinionated and immature young man who had become an officer in 1894 Churchill had progressed to a polished and even more opinionated writer and journalist in 1898, and his dispatches from Britain's latest battlefield left nothing to the imagination.

But even as an imperialist Churchill was enigmatic. One of his dispatches from Omdurman was a scathing and mocking comment on the nature of Britain's empire in all its diverse forms and on the characters who peopled it: 'the odd and bizarre potentates against whom British arms are continually turned', the mad mullahs, the imperial pashas, the Khalifa and other insurgents who led various rebellions or controlled bits of territory under the umbrella of the empire. 'Perhaps the time will come', he wrote, 'when there will be no more royal freaks to conquer. In that gloomy period there will be no more of these nice little expeditions – "the image of European war without its guilt and only twenty-five per cent of its danger"; no more medals for the soldiers, no more peerages for the generals, no more copy for the journalists.'

Despite the mixed signals he sometimes gave out, the distinction between Churchill the Victorian imperialist and Churchill the soldier was clear. Of the British Empire he once said, 'We in this small island have to make a supreme effort to keep our place and status, the place and status to which our undying genius entitles us.' However, Churchill the soldier had ambivalent feelings about war. Its glory was directly tied to his personal quest for medals and the recognition they conferred, but his exposure to its darker side certainly resulted in revulsion against the high cost imposed by glory. Shane Leslie astutely observed of him: 'By this time he believed, like many men, that he had a star. In consequence he took risks whether from horseback at polo or whenever bullets were in or about.'

Churchill's African venture brought him the Queen's Sudan Medal and the Khedive Sudan Medal 'Khartoum' clasp, the same decorations awarded to others. Queen Victoria personally honoured the 21st Lancers for valour at Omdurman, and thereafter it proudly bore the designation 'Empress of India'. It was also the only cavalry regiment accorded the battle honour 'Khartoum'. The recognition was not enough to cure either Churchill's passion for danger or his thirst for financial security. The war in the Sudan would continue for another year before the Khalifa and his army were destroyed; however, it was not exciting enough to induce Churchill to report it. The time had come to move on.

Three days after the Battle of Omdurman, Kitchener decided that the cavalry was of no further use to him and ordered the 21st Lancers and the other regiments to return to their base in Cairo. Churchill left Africa one step ahead of his nemesis. From the time of his arrival in Egypt, he had believed that the Sirdar was angered by his presence – and he was quite right. He had attempted to send a telegram describing the battle and the action of the Lancers through army headquarters. Hubert Howard, the *Times*'s correspondent at Omdurman, and a friend, had been killed in the cavalry battle by friendly fire, and its only other correspondent, Colonel Rhodes, had been wounded. Rhodes would recover from his shoulder wound and become the editor of *The River War*. In an act of generosity the telegram Churchill proposed to send was intended for the *Times*'s correspondent in Cairo, but Kitchener blocked it. The editor of *The Times* telegraphed from London to engage Churchill as the paper's new correspondent, although the offer came too late. Given Kitchener's displeasure with him, remaining in Africa was not really an option he cared to pursue.

The identity of the anonymous author of the Sudan dispatches, for those who had not already worked it out, was revealed in his last report on 20 September (published on 13 October), when Churchill concluded by stating: 'Because no man should write that of which he is either ashamed or afraid, I shall venture in conclusion to subscribe myself – Yours truly, WINSTON SPENCER CHURCHILL.'

Out of what Churchill declared was 'pure spite', Kitchener ordered him 'to take transport back "by long slow marches" to Atbara'. Churchill would have none of it and, ignoring his orders, instead accompanied a battalion of the Grenadier Guards in the comfort of a sailing boat down the Nile, where he began working on his account of the campaign. Because he had been attached only to the 21st Lancers, Churchill deemed himself free to leave and made plans to return to London. Both men benefited: Kitchener rid himself of a thorn in his side, and Churchill received both acclaim and censure for his reporting and, later, for his chronicle of the Sudan campaign.

In London he pondered his exit from the army while continuing at a swift pace to write his account of the war and to use every occasion to make himself known in political circles. During his brief visit Churchill began laying the foundation for standing as a candidate for a parliamentary seat as a member of the Conservative Party. He had made three times as much money from his writings as from what the government had paid him for his military service, which was not even close to a living wage. 'I therefore resolved with many regrets to quit the service betimes,' not, however, before returning to India to play polo for his regiment.

He also was criticized both publicly in the press and privately by the Prince of Wales, who wrote to him, 'I fear in matters of discipline in the Army I may be considered old fashioned – & I must say that I think that an officer serving in a campaign should not write letters for the newspapers or express strong opinions of how the operations are carried out.' The prince suggested that Churchill's future career lay elsewhere: '. . . I cannot help feeling that Parliamentary & literary life is what would suit you best as the monotony of military life in an Indian station can have no attraction for you – though fortunately some officers do put up with it or else we should have no Army at all!'

An anonymous general expressed his displeasure at the upstart young subaltern who had dared to criticize his elders. In a letter to the editor of the *Army and Navy Gazette* he denounced Churchill and his war reporting, remonstrating that 'prompt measures ought to be taken in the interest of Her Majesty's Service to put a stop to it.' The general's letter impelled 'a field officer' to grumble that 'soldiering is about the last thing the young officer [Churchill] thinks about.'

The criticism was swiftly rebutted. Never one to avoid a fight, Churchill (by now back in India) responded immediately with a scathing letter to the editor that derided the general for his anonymity and criticized the army for not insisting that retired senior officers should resolve such criticism with the War Office and not in a public forum with junior officers like himself. It is difficult to imagine any other young officer daring to challenge a senior officer so publicly; Churchill gave it barely a second thought. As with Kitchener, it may have seemed to be an instance of David versus Goliath, but typically when challenged he responded in kind, often impetuously but always with words that cut deeply and were intended to inflict a literary *coup de grâce* on his adversary.

The controversy over Churchill's war reporting eventually resulted in a prohibition by the War Office: soldiers could not be correspondents and correspondents could not be soldiers. Churchill would later refer to himself as 'that hybrid combination of subaltern officer and widely followed war-correspondent which was not unnaturally obnoxious to the military mind'. The notion of a young officer reporting various campaigns and 'discussing the greatest matters of policy and war with complete assurance and considerable acceptance, distributing praise and blame among veteran commanders, apparently immune from regulation or routine, and gathering war experience and medals all the time – was not a pattern to be encouraged or multiplied'.

Such was Churchill's love of the 'emperor of games' that in November 1898 he sailed back to India for duty with the 4th Hussars solely for the purpose of participating in the Inter-Regimental Cup polo tournament at Meerut in February 1899. His many writings tell us nothing about his reception from his brother officers, only that he quickly earned a coveted place on the regimental team. One night before the matches began he fell on some stone stairs, spraining both ankles and reinjuring his chronic right shoulder, which left his arm virtually useless. He attempted to take himself out of contention, arguing that his presence on the field of play would be detrimental to the team, which should therefore use a reserve player. The team met and decided that despite his apparent inability to hit the ball he was too important to leave out.

On the day of the first of the round-robin matches Churchill took the field with his elbow strapped to his side and contributed to the ensuing victory by his teamwork and horsemanship both in defending and in riding off his opposite number when his team scored goals. His team reached the championship match, in which Churchill, despite his handicap, managed to score two goals in a hard-fought contest that was not decided until the final seconds of the last chukka, when the 4th Hussars survived a furious onslaught to emerge as the champions of all India.

When he was not playing polo Churchill was working furiously to complete The River War. He and Haldane met one day in Calcutta, and after Churchill showed his friend some of the proofs of his book, the Scotsman wrote in his diary that Churchill would rise high in political life. In his memoirs Haldane also recounted a conversation with Churchill's former headmaster at Harrow, now the new bishop of the diocese of Calcutta, the Right Reverend J. E. C. Welldon. The two men exchanged amusing anecdotes about Winston Churchill. Welldon remarked how birching Churchill had had no effect and that 'on one occasion Churchill even had the audacity to tell him how to perform his duties.'

By the spring of 1898 Churchill had fulfilled his four-year commitment to the British army. Military service was no longer a worthwhile proposition that could even begin to support his way of life. At a dead end professionally, unable to earn enough on a soldier's pay to get out of debt and with enemies in high places who were prepared to block further use of soldier–war correspondents, Churchill made good his decision to resign his commission shortly after the 1899 tournament. To his grandmother he professed mixed feelings. 'I have thought a great deal about it and although it is possible I may live to regret it, I don't think I shall ever regard it as unreasonable . . . It has nevertheless been a great wrench and I was vy sorry to leave all my friends & put on my uniform & medals for the last time.'

Taking leave of the 4th Hussars was not without considerable nostalgia. He recalled that his fellow officers 'paid me the rare compliment of drinking [to] my health the last time I dined with them. What happy years I had had with them and what staunch friends one made! It was a grand school for anyone. Discipline and comradeship were the lessons it taught; and perhaps after all these were just as valuable as the lore of the universities. Still one would like to have both.'

In retrospect Churchill's four years of military service as an army officer were enormously successful. Although he was on the lowest rung of the officer ranks, his name was now well known throughout the British army – and had been often in the public eye. The publication of *The River War* would attract even more attention and acclaim.

To read Churchill's wide-ranging account is like having a travel guide escort one through the myriad cultural, historical and geographical aspects of Egyptian and Sudanese culture. So that they could understand the battle Churchill wanted his readers to be familiar with the background to the war, why the Mahdists fought and what they fought for, their culture and their warrior ethos. However, with Churchill as a sometimes none too subtle guide, the discerning reader of *The River War* came away with a sense of far more than a series of battles whose outcome was all but preordained. To give a sense of the great sweep of history was his goal. Buried in what some thought was an overwritten account was not only the genesis of a war but thoughts about and criticisms of war and warriors, tactics and strategy, subjects that were mostly lost in the unchanging Victorian concepts of war and British dominance. But, more important, Omdurman was a valuable learning experience that would help form Churchill's developing warrior persona.

He had proved his courage beyond any doubt, both on the polo field and on the terrifying field of battle. Although his insatiable passion for public recognition was scarcely quenched, no young man at the age of twenty-four could have asked for more. Still, he would write to his mother the following month, 'What an awful thing it will be if I don't come off. It will break my heart for I have nothing but ambition to cling to.' The price of that overweening ambition was the loss of Pamela Plowden as his bride.

Although Churchill left the army in the spring of 1899, his military adventures were far from over and his return to civilian life was short lived. His focus may have been politics and Parliament, but far greater tests of a military nature lay ahead.

IO

The Boer War

I naturally desired to find some war to go to in order to gain experience and authority among my brother officers.
                                                  – Churchill, London *Sunday Dispatch*, 1939

In the autumn of 1899 Britain became embroiled in a war in southern Africa that it expected to win handily in three months but that instead became the forerunner of a new century of warfare and changed the way future wars would be fought.

Its roots, like those of most nineteenth-century wars, were directly attributable to British imperialism, in this instance a clash with a race of otherwise peace-loving people who wanted only to be left alone to pursue their singular way of life and practise their stern Calvinist religion. Dutchmen had been in South Africa since 1652, when the Dutch East India Company established a base on the Cape of Good Hope that became an important port of call on the sea route between Europe and the Dutch East Indies. Dutch settlers soon followed and began farming and raising cattle to resupply ships calling at the Cape. Many, however, objected to the control exercised by the Dutch East India Company and began migrating into the immense grasslands of the African veld to establish farms and their own communities and culture.

They called themselves Boers ('farmers'), and eventually their language evolved from pure Dutch into their own unique language, Afrikaans. The descendants of these hardy Dutch colonists began to think of themselves as Afrikaners. Intensely religious, God-fearing and increasingly independent and nationalistic, with their own customs, the Boers deeply resented British intrusion into their tight-knit world, just as their forefathers had railed against the Dutch East India Company.

By the early nineteenth century Britain had expanded its empire by annexing the Cape and colonizing southern Africa. To escape the heavy hand of British rule the Boers undertook the so-called Great Trek, moving their colony to Natal, and in 1840 they established the Boer Republic. Although by the 1850s they had expanded their homeland and established themselves in the Transvaal and the Orange Free State, their rich economy, spawned by the discovery of diamonds at Hopetown and at Kimberley in the late 1860s, led to a diamond rush by settlers and prospectors. Boer resistance to British rule was intensified by Britain's annexation of the Transvaal in 1877 as a crown colony. After gold was discovered in the Transvaal, the heavy British hand was again in evidence in Zululand, and a bloody war on the scale of Omdurman ensued with the slaughter of the Zulus in 1879.

War inevitably followed when the Boers, led by the Transvaal's first president, Paul Kruger, rebelled and the first Boer War was fought in 1880–81, leading to partial independence for the Boers and ushering in a period of growing unease. Britain had already annexed Natal and Bechuanaland, and the annexation of Zululand in 1887 not only severely limited the Boers' access to the Indian Ocean but left the Transvaal all but surrounded by British-controlled territories.

Despite the fervent, unwavering desire of the Boers to remain independent, British intentions were clear: the Transvaal and its independent neighbour and ally, the Orange Free State, were both targets of annexation. With more gold discovered in 1886 at Witwatersrand, the Transvaal became too tempting a target to be ignored for much longer.

Relations with Britain continued to deteriorate after 1889 when Cecil Rhodes, the great empire builder and entrepreneurial genius, and brother of *The Times*'s Colonel Rhodes, established the British South Africa Company and the following year became prime minister of the Cape Colony. Rhodes, the founder of the De Beers diamond cartel and the British colony later named after him (now Zimbabwe), was perhaps the quintessential agent of British imperialism, suiting action to his deeply held conviction that it was incumbent upon the Anglo-Saxon races to enlighten and rule the world, and to extend the empire to ever further corners of the uncivilized world. While a young student at Oxford in 1877, Rhodes had written, 'The more of the world we occupy the better it is for the human race.'

In the 1890s that meant southern Africa. What stood in his way of establishing British domination in the Transvaal were the obstinate

Boers. By 1899 they had grown from restive to rebellious. The removal of Cecil Rhodes as the major player in southern Africa did not end the drift towards war, and when peace talks that concluded in early June that year at Bloemfontein failed to bring about a rapprochement, the two sides were on the brink of conflict. The Salisbury government arrogantly believed that the Boers could be intimidated into ceding their precious independence. Southern Africa was a trouble spot waiting to boil over, and boil over it did that autumn when what the British thought would be a short little skirmish with a horde of ragamuffin Boer farmers turned instead into a prolonged and punishing war that drained a great deal of the mystique from the fabled British Empire.

The end of the nineteenth century was the high point of Britain's smugness over its grand empire, a boastfulness repeatedly emphasized during Queen Victoria's Diamond Jubilee celebrations in 1897. One of the centrepieces of this imposing event was the British army. When the queen attended a service of thanksgiving at St Paul's Cathedral, fifty thousand splendidly arrayed troops lined the streets in a grand formal salute to their sovereign. 'A postage stamp was produced showing a map of the world and bearing the legend: "We hold a vaster Empire than has ever been." Maps showing its territory coloured an eye-catching red hung in schools all over the country. Small wonder the British began to assume they had the God-given right to rule the world.' Lost amid this British self-satisfaction was the fact that the Boers of the Transvaal were not only unmoved but also determined to resist British rule – by force if necessary. With both sides spoiling for a fight, war was certain.

In October 1899 the Boers pre-emptively invaded Natal and the Cape Colony. The British, overconfident of victory against a motley army composed mainly of scruffy-looking farmers, believed that the war would be over by Christmas, revenge for their ignominious and bloody defeat at the hands of the Boers in 1881 at Majuba Hill.

War with the Boers, however, would soon prove very different from that in the Sudan, where the outcome was predestined. Indeed it would soon become appallingly evident that in warring with the Boers the British had invested in a struggle that would last three years, involve 450,000 British and other colonial troops, and exact a ruinous cost of more than two hundred million pounds and a staggering hundred thousand casualties.

Winston Churchill was familiar with the problem of Britain's deteriorating relationship with the Boers and had actually written an unpublished paper on the subject some time around December 1896 entitled 'Our Account with the Boers'. As he had done with all military operations throughout the British Empire during his military service, Churchill had taken full note of the Jameson raid. (Instigated by Cecil Rhodes and led by Leander Jameson, the raid was a failed attempt during the New Year's weekend of 1895–6 by a small mounted force to trigger an uprising in the Transvaal to overthrow President Paul Kruger.) Not surprisingly his thoughts reflected the prevailing attitude in Britain: 'Imperial troops must curb the insolence of the Boers,' he wrote. 'There must be no half measures . . . Sooner or later, in a righteous cause or a picked quarrel . . . for the sake of our honour, for the sake of the race, we must fight the Boers.' It was heady stuff and rather prescient about what occurred three years later.

In July 1899 Churchill made his first venture into politics when he was asked to stand as a Conservative candidate in a parliamentary by-election in the working-class town of Oldham near Manchester. His programme emphasized the status quo: the virtues of the empire, the sanctity of the Church of England and the robust state of the British economy. Although he lost by thirteen hundred votes in a fairly close race, Churchill had at last tested the political waters, had acquitted himself well and was soon encouraged by Arthur Balfour, a future prime minister, then leader of the House of Commons, who told him that 'this small reverse will have no permanent ill effect on your political fortunes.' His loss at Oldham would ultimately prove to have been a blessing in disguise.

When his massive two-volume *The River War* was published in the autumn of 1899, it was widely reviewed and commented on in the British press, on the whole positively. More than a century after its publication it can still be appreciated as an example of Churchill's finest writing. Unremarkably, it infuriated Kitchener, who was unused to public criticism, and especially resented it when it came from that young upstart Winston Churchill.

Although his writing was rewarding to him both critically and financially, Churchill's future was still murky. His ambition was fully fuelled, but the practical reality was that he had no actual strategy for achieving the fame he hungered for, knowing only that unless he did ' "unusual" things it is difficult to see what chance I have of being more than an average person'. The advent of the Boer War would solve the problem.

The outbreak of the second Boer War, the lure of a new battlefield experience in South Africa and the chance once more to don the uniform of an officer in the British army (with its potentially rich rewards for his career) were simply too great for Churchill to ignore. By September 1899 he not only was certain there would be war but had already advanced plans to report it. When the *Daily Mail* attempted to secure his services as its war correspondent, he turned again to the *Morning Post* and suggested to its proprietor that he engage him – for an exceptionally large sum, of course. Thanks to the possibility of his defecting to the *Daily Mail*, Churchill secured for himself an undreamed-of remuneration, one he would earn every pound of in South Africa. His compensation included all expenses, exclusive copyright and one thousand pounds for four months' work – an enormous sum that also set the salary bar much higher for other war correspondents.

Covering a war as a civilian had a downside; access to information would be far more difficult than it had been as an officer–correspondent. Above all there were no medals to be won as a civilian, and without medals there could be no glory. Although he had been a civilian for barely five months, Churchill attempted to reverse course and secure a commission in the Royal Buckinghamshire Yeomanry. As far as he was concerned the War Office ban on soldier–correspondents was merely a minor impediment to be overcome. His choice of regiment was calculated. He reckoned that his chances of another commission were enhanced because a family friend commanded the 9th Yeomanry Brigade and was the adjutant to General Sir Redvers Buller, who had been selected by the War Office to command British forces in South Africa. The plan seemed a repeat of his earlier experiences in India and the Sudan but without the obstacle of Kitchener. To aid his quest Churchill persuaded two senior government ministers to send letters of recommendation to Sir Alfred Milner, the governor general of the Cape Colony.

He obtained passage on a Royal Mail steamship, the *Dunnottar Castle*, for the two-week voyage to Cape Town. Also aboard were Buller and his staff, along with a contingent of correspondents. The ship was given a grand send-off on 14 October by dignitaries and by a band on the Southampton dock playing 'Rule, Britannia' and 'God Save the Queen'.

During his trips to and from India and Egypt, Churchill had learned to loathe sea travel, and the voyage from England to South Africa bore out his dislike. 'What an odious affair is the modern sea journey,' he complained in his very first dispatch for the *Morning Post*. The voyage met his worst expectations; he was 'grievously sick' for a time, but his spirits brightened as the seas calmed. When a tramp steamer heading towards Britain was sighted, the *Dunnottar Castle* signalled for information about the war. As the two ships drew abreast, the tramp displayed a message on a large blackboard declaring that three battles had already been fought and the Boers had lost them all. Churchill and all aboard despaired that the war would probably be over before they had even arrived.

None of it was true; instead of easy victories British forces were already under siege and in danger of annihilation at Mafeking, a small town in the northern tip of the Cape Colony near the border with Bechuanaland and the Transvaal that would remain surrounded for 217 days, and at Kimberley, the diamond-mining centre on the border between the Cape Colony and the Orange Free State.

The travel may have been inconvenient, but Churchill had no intention of permitting the unpleasantness of sea travel to interfere with his personal luxury or with his need to secure favours from influential people through gifts of the wine and spirits that were an essential part of his baggage. Indeed Churchill travelled to Cape Town with provisions more suited to a potentate than to a young war correspondent: Scotch whisky, fine French wine and other luxuries, all charged to his employer. He was also the only correspondent to travel with his own personal valet, Thomas Walden, who had performed similar duties for his father during Lord Randolph's wanderings just before his death.

Churchill used the time well to ingratiate himself with Buller and his staff, and in cultivating friendships. J. B. Atkins, a veteran war correspondent of the *Manchester Guardian*, first encountered Churchill aboard the *Dunnottar Castle*. He was hard to miss: 'the slim, red-haired young man plunging along the deck "with neck thrust out" . . . Shy he was not.' Atkins, who would become both a friend and an admirer, observed that, with his usual brashness, Churchill displayed none of the usual deference reserved for men of superiority, but instead 'talked to them as if they were his own age, or younger'.

The *Dunnottar Castle*'s arrival in Cape Town's Table Bay on 31 October 1899 coincided with the first real news that the war was not going quite as well as Churchill and others had been led to believe. Not only were the British under siege at Mafeking and Kimberley, but the death of Major General Sir Penn Symons and 447 other British soldiers in the first pitched battle of the war on 20 October at Dundee, in northern Natal, should have been a sign that the war would certainly not be over by the end of the year. Even more ominous, in Ladysmith, Natal's second-largest city and a key railway link with the Orange Free State and the Transvaal, the Boers had succeeded in surrounding and trapping the 9,600-man garrison of the Natal Field Force under the command of Lieutenant General Sir George White.

The Boers were a predominantly do-it-yourself army of farmers who wore no uniforms, elected their own officers, fought unconventionally and with deadly accuracy as commandos in small units, lived off the land and were in every possible sense the paradigm of the citizen–soldier. They suited their tactics to the terrain and were skilled horsemen, thus giving their ranks a mobility and freedom of movement in country they knew intimately, advantages not possessed by their foe.

Not for the first time would over-confidence engender a hellish war. The British engaged the Boers with blinkers on, secure in the belief that the enemy posed no serious threat. (Churchill would later point out government parsimony and War Office folly over troop levels and over the resources needed to win the war.) The War Office ignored its own detailed and, as it turned out, all-too-accurate intelligence, which stated that 200,000 men would be required. Instead it took on the Boers with a fraction of that number. British army strength in 1899 was only 106,000 men, and if the estimates were to be acted upon, Britain would have to call upon other members of its empire to augment its somewhat meagre numbers. There were a mere 14,000 troops in the Cape Colony and Natal when the Boers struck. In September 1899 the War Office ordered the dispatch of Buller's corps of 47,000 men. Before the war ended in 1902 the British would commit 450,000 men to the conflict.

From the outset the Boers took maximum advantage of their ability to mount guerrilla-style warfare, often firing from dug-in positions that protected them from direct fire and were used, in turn, to rain accurate rifle fire on their enemy, often with devastating effect. When the circumstances suited them, they would attack from ambush and then disappear as silently as they had come. The British army was trained to fight setpiece battles against a visible enemy, and in South Africa was ill equipped, mentally unprepared and generally untrained for this new kind of warfare.

Churchill, as he had done in India and the Sudan, began yet another lengthy journey to a distant war. His initial destination was Durban, the capital of the Natal. He and Atkins had decided to team up and beat their competition to besieged Ladysmith. By train it was a four-day, seven-hundred-mile journey to East London, much of it across some of the wildest terrain in southern Africa. Like the Nile, however, the place enthralled Churchill with its untamed beauty.

His first letter to Jennie was an uncannily perceptive assessment of the future course of the war. 'We have greatly underestimated the military strength and spirit of the Boers. I vy much doubt whether one Army Corps will be enough to overcome their resistance – at any rate a fierce and bloody struggle is before us in which at least ten to twelve thousand lives will be sacrificed and from which the Boers are absolutely certain that they will emerge victorious.' His mature vision of events did not extend to the Boers. In his first dispatch from South Africa, Churchill, with excessive vitriol, described them as barbarians, 'gross, fierce and horrid – doing the deeds of the devil with the name of the Lord on [their] lips'.

From East London he and Atkins travelled by coastal steamer to Durban. The trip was a nightmare, as the ship was buffeted by what Churchill described as a gale so violent 'that I lay prostrate in all the anguish of sea-sickness and perpetual nausea'. During their few hours in Durban, Churchill visited a hospital ship berthed near by to look for familiar faces and gather information about the war. To his dismay he encountered a seriously wounded Reggie Barnes. While leading a charge against a Boer force entrenched on a hill during the Battle of Elandslaagte (a town north of Ladysmith), his longtime friend had been wounded in the groin, and the injury had paralysed his right leg. Barnes told Churchill that almost 30 per cent of his battalion had been lost in this bloody battle and warned him that the Boers were not to be taken lightly.

Churchill also learned that Ian Hamilton had been one of the last to arrive in Ladysmith before the railway line to Durban was permanently cut, and that Boer forces were now freely roaming the area. The presence of his friend fired his imagination: Hamilton 'would look after me and give me a good show'.

Despite the news that Ladysmith was now cut off and under siege, Churchill and Atkins penetrated into the hill country of the Natal as far as Pietermaritzburg, where they hired a special train. It was able to carry them only to Estcourt, a small, sprawling hill town of tin-roofed buildings forty miles south of Ladysmith that Atkins described as 'a village sunk in a cup of the pleasant and grassy uplands of Natal'. Beyond Estcourt the railway line to Ladysmith had been cut. In the far distance they could hear the boom of guns at the besieged town.

Estcourt, once the heart of agriculture in the surrounding district, was now important for its railway yards, which were the end of the line for train travel further inland. The only remaining forces in Natal that were not trapped in Ladysmith were an assorted collection of perhaps two thousand British and Natal troops based in Estcourt. However, the town was virtually indefensible, and plans were under way to withdraw its garrison. As the situation in Estcourt remained increasingly uncertain, the highlight and principal diversion of each day was the departure and return of the armoured train employed to reconnoitre the countryside north of Estcourt. Atkins was not alone in believing that the train was an iron death trap that would eventually fall victim to a Boer attack.

Shortly after their arrival the garrison commander began the evacuation of Estcourt. Over dinner one evening Churchill and the other correspondents clearly heard the sound of guns being loaded on to trains. Atkins recounts that it was Churchill who spoke up to argue that to abandon Estcourt to the Boers was a grave mistake, and that General Petrus Jacobus 'Piet' Joubert, the Boer commander in Natal, was too conservative to attack beyond the safety of the Tugela river, which passed through Colenso (some twenty miles south-east of Ladysmith). What is more, Churchill said, willingly to cede Estcourt would merely open the way for the Boers to advance towards Durban unhindered. A short time later the sound of the artillery being *un*loaded was heard, leading Churchill to proclaim somewhat smugly: 'I did that.' Thinking better of it, he added: '*We* did that.' Whether the order to abandon Estcourt was reversed solely because of Churchill's urging is unproven; moreover Joubert and a force of two thousand Boers did indeed advance beyond the river but only as far as Chieveley, another town on the railway line, about twenty miles north-west of Estcourt. The actual reason Estcourt was not attacked was the mistaken belief of the Boers that the town was more heavily defended and not worth the risk.

George Clegg, the Estcourt stationmaster, permitted Churchill and Atkins to pitch a tent in the railway yard where, with the aid of Winston's remaining stash of fine wines and liqueurs, they proceeded to make their stay as comfortable as possible. They were joined by the old Harrovian Leo Amery, now the most senior of *The Times*'s war correspondents in South Africa. With no place to stay Amery gladly accepted an invitation to share their tent. Churchill was also re-united with a friend from India, Captain Aylmer Haldane, who had been slightly wounded in the same battle as Reggie Barnes and was unable to rejoin his battalion, now trapped in Ladysmith. Churchill's chance meeting with Haldane would prove fateful.

During leisurely evenings spent around a campfire, Churchill began to unburden himself to Atkins. Despite his many recent successes he still wondered if they were due to his own merits or because he was the son of Lord Randolph Churchill. Was he really his own man or merely the reincarnation of his father? Atkins diplomatically impressed upon Churchill that it was not necessary for him to rely on his father's memory to propel him to success. Churchill admitted to being fearful not only of an early death like that of Lord Randolph but of being a failure. 'The worst of it is', he said, 'that I am not a good life. My father died too young. I must try to accomplish whatever I can by the time I am forty.'

Churchill's future intimate friend Violet Asquith (the eldest daughter of Herbert H. Asquith, Liberal prime minister from 1908 to 1916), would remark of the distress she felt over Churchill's feelings of destiny and his conviction that he must compress great accomplishments into the few years left to him because his father had died young and so would he. She thought Churchill an enigma: wedded to the belief that he would die young but nevertheless confident that he would succeed. 'He had no doubts about his star . . . Even in those early days he felt that he was "walking with destiny", and that he had been preserved from many perils to fulfil its purpose.' However, her insistence that he was not destined to die young like Lord Randolph would be ignored. Therein lay one of the many riddles of Winston Churchill: 'His zest, vitality, activity and industry were inexhaustible. He seemed to have been endowed by Nature with a double charge of life,' yet he was possessed of an obsessive belief in an early death.

Churchill and Atkins also discussed military tactics and strategy. Churchill believed that each was 'just a matter of common sense' that any competent soldier could grasp and successfully carry out. 'Put all the elements of a problem before a civilian of first-rate ability and enough imagination, and he would reach the right solution, and any soldier could afterwards put this solution into military terms.' However simplistic, it was very likely the first expression by Churchill of what a civilian leader should do in a time of war. Despite his relative inexperience at this juncture of his military career, he understood the pitfalls of war, that strategy and tactics were evolving, and that the British army had yet to adapt to warfare in what would be the most violent century in the history of mankind. Nevertheless, as he would learn the hard way, his brilliance at analysing and reporting a war and at applying simple logic to its problems around a campfire would prove a very different proposition from actually directing it and bearing responsibility for its consequences.

Churchill's patience with his enforced inaction was short lived. Before long he joined the armoured reconnaissance train that travelled as far as Colenso without encountering any sign of the Boers. He also purchased a horse from a local trader in order to make his own forays into the lush hill country around Estcourt; at other times he employed a hired carriage. He quickly became a well-known figure, sometimes dressed rather elegantly and incongruously in a dark suit and bow tie, restlessly prowling about town, trolling for any useful scrap of information about Ladysmith and, with his usual inquisitiveness, asking endless questions of military personnel and civilians. Clegg would later write: 'He wanted to know all about everything. He made daily excursions over the hills towards Colenso' on horseback, getting acquainted with the terrain and writing a series of his usual colourful dispatches for the *Morning Post*. Another observer, the eminent British artist Mortimer Menpes, described his impressions of a young man who at times seemed content to listen to others talk – as long as the conversation remained of interest to him. Churchill, he thought, was also 'a man who might be unpopular because of his great cleverness. He is too direct and frank to flatter.'

Years later Clegg's granddaughter would write to Churchill's son

Randolph: 'Many evenings over the camp fires and in the bar your Father would tell of his adventures as a reporter in India and Egypt. These tales were often so fantastic that my Father and his friends did not believe half of them and would laugh and accuse your Father of telling "tall stories" to impress them. Then one day your Father said, "Mark my words, I shall be the Prime Minister of England before I'm finished," only to be greeted by more laughter. The years passed and World War II was upon us, then one morning my Father read in the headlines of the *Natal Mercury* – Winston Churchill – Prime Minister – and suddenly he exclaimed "By jove, he's done it." '

(Churchill himself was not the only one to make such a prediction. Another tale to emerge from South Africa relates to the period after the 118-day siege of Ladysmith had been broken in February 1900 when he was back in the army. A young officer boldly walked up to the commander of British forces in Ladysmith, Sir George White, and 'with a good deal of sang-froid and not much ceremony' began engaging him in conversation in 'a very audible voice'. When later asked by another officer, 'Who on earth is that?' White replied: 'That's Randolph Churchill's son Winston; I don't like the fellow, but he'll be Prime Minister of England one day.')

Churchill also used the time on his hands to write to the adjutant general, Sir Evelyn Wood, to alert him to the dismal state of affairs in Natal. 'The present situation here is bad and critical,' he declared. 'It is astonishing how we have underrated these people.' He also pointed out that the Boers had captured twice as many British soldiers as had been wounded, 'not a very pretty proportion . . . I think we ought to punish people who surrender troops under their command – and let us say at once – No exchange of Prisoners.' Celia Sandys would later point out, 'This last remark reflected Churchill's lifelong philosophy, encapsulated in a Second World War speech by the words "Never give in." ' As it happened, 'within a week, he would have cause to remember, somewhat ruefully, his strictures on those who surrendered.'

Although Churchill thought fleetingly about attempting to make a forty-mile dash by horseback through enemy lines to Ladysmith, common sense prevailed, and he, like the others in the small garrison, settled down to await reinforcements. Soon, however, he began searching for someone willing and able to escort him through the lines to the besieged city. Reputed to have offered as much as two hundred pounds, he eventually found a volunteer willing to accept the assignment for a mere five pounds. He would have slipped away from Estcourt the following morning but for the intervention of what can only be described as one of the two most fateful events of his life.

On 14 November the alarm was raised when Boers were seen in the hills outside the town. The garrison went to full alert, and everyone became jumpy in the belief that an attack was imminent. It was in this atmosphere that on the morning of 15 November Captain Haldane was ordered to take 120 troops aboard an armoured train on a reconnaissance probe towards Colenso. The armoured train was a creature of the Boer War, and although the premise was sound, in practice it was clumsy and vulnerable to attack and disablement without warning. It also ran on a predictable schedule, usually every other day at roughly the same time. Moreover, not only were the railway lines the logistical lifeblood of the British and the sole means by which they could move men, equipment and supplies over the vast expanse of southern Africa, but they were equally the prime target of the Boers – for the very same reason.

The train consisted of an engine, a tender and six trucks, arranged as follows: a flat wagon on which was mounted a 7-inch naval gun (manned by a crew of sailors) that Churchill described as 'an antiquated toy', two armoured trucks, the engine and its tender in the middle, followed by two more armoured trucks, and in the rear a fifth truck containing a breakdown crew complete with tools and equipment. There was also a telegrapher aboard to signal messages back to Estcourt. The trucks were without roofs, and to gain access, troops had to clamber up and over the sides, a climb which was often difficult for smaller men. Like the warships of old, these trucks contained steel gun ports along each side through which riflemen could fire. Soldiers of the Dublin Fusiliers and the Durban Light Infantry (a unit of Natal volunteers) were crammed inside like so many cattle, and owing to the trucks' low walls they had to sit or crouch to avoid becoming exposed targets for a Boer marksman.

Boer activity had increased around Estcourt, thus persuading the garrison commander to order yet another reconnaissance using the armoured train. The folly of employing such a sitting duck was that a handful of cavalry would have had the advantage of speed and flexibility to accomplish the same task with far less risk and a far greater chance of survival.

Churchill learned of the reconnaissance the previous night from Haldane, who expressed misgivings about the mission but nevertheless invited him along. Unable to resist the lure of an adventure, Churchill was not about to pass up another chance to report the war. Amery, too, was aware of the mission, but whether deliberately or from forgetfulness (hardly the trait of a man like Churchill) Winston neglected to inform Atkins until the early hours of 15 November, when he awakened his friend, who declined the invitation and went back to sleep.

Atkins later wrote that Churchill sensed what was to come. He had 'a sort of intuition "that if I go something will come of it. It's illogical, I know."' Thus forewarned, Churchill arrived at the station on a cold, miserable morning armed with the Mauser he had used at Omdurman, several clips of ammunition tucked into his tunic, and his field glasses. He later explained that he elected to accompany Haldane 'out of comradeship, and because I thought it was my duty to gather as much information as I could for the *Morning Post*'. He also admitted that 'because I was eager for trouble, I accepted the invitation without demur.' And trouble was precisely what Churchill got that morning, setting in motion a series of events that would change his life for ever.

11

The Great Escapade

I certainly hated every minute of my captivity more than I have ever hated any other period in my whole life.   – Churchill on being a prisoner of war

The chill in the air and a damp mist aptly fitted the mood of the British garrison as the armoured train bearing Churchill rumbled out of the Estcourt station at 5.30 a.m. on 15 November 1899, towards a fiery reception from the Boers. Steaming cautiously north towards Colenso, the train passed through the village of Frere and arrived in Chieveley (fourteen miles north of Estcourt), without incident or any sign of Boer activity. It stopped briefly while the telegrapher reported their safe arrival, noting also that an estimated one hundred Boers had been observed north of the town but appeared to pose no threat. Haldane was ordered to proceed no further north but instead to return to Frere.

An unflatteringly accurate account written by Leo Amery in the aftermath of that November morning commented: 'It is typical of British military methods that though the train had been running up to Chieveley almost daily, the officer selected to command [Haldane] had never been up the line before. That the train was certain to be caught in a trap, sooner or later, was the outspoken conviction of every officer in Estcourt, but no precautions were taken to accompany it by a few mounted men to scout on both sides of the railway.'

Indeed, before the train could complete the return journey to Frere a Boer force of unknown size was spotted occupying a hillside overlooking a point where the train had to negotiate a long downward slope, then a sharp curve before a half-mile run to Frere station. It was clear that, for the train to reach the town safely, Haldane's small force would have to fight its way through. Although there would certainly be a skirmish, no one expected it to be a serious problem. As Churchill watched through his field glasses, the train came level with the hill; at that moment a thunderous sound of guns erupted as the Boers opened fire with rifles, Maxims and two field guns.

While the naval gun went into action and the infantry crouched inside the trucks began returning fire, the train's driver, Charles Wagner, put on a burst of speed to outrun the ambush – which was precisely what the Boers wanted him to do. As the train steamed at full speed around the curve it came upon a pile of stones that had been wrestled on to the track since its earlier passage. The truck carrying the breakdown crew (now the lead truck) crashed into the stones. The impact violently derailed several trucks, one of which carried the Durban Light Infantry.

The naval gun was quickly hit and disabled as a hail of fire descended on the train and its startled passengers. The first three trucks were either derailed completely or on their sides, blocking the track. Wagner emerged from the engine cab dazed, slightly wounded from a cut to his head, and angry that he, a civilian, was suddenly in the midst of a raging battle. He intended to flee but succumbed to Churchill's power of persuasion: if he stayed 'he would be mentioned for distinguished gallantry in action.' Wagner apparently accepted Churchill's absurd assurance, 'No man is hit twice on the same day.'

The only way out of a well-laid ambush is instantly to return fire and attempt to get clear of the killing zone by any means. Churchill ran to the rear of the train to find Haldane, who by his own later admission had been stunned and confused by the crash, and for a while appeared unsure of what to do. Happy to have Churchill's assistance, he quickly agreed that the only way out of the Boer ambush was somehow to clear the stones from the track, then for the locomotive to use the tender as a battering ram to shove the derailed trucks out of the way and dash to Frere. Their hastily contrived plan was for the infantry inside the armoured trucks to pin down the Boers with rifle fire while the track was being cleared.

Haldane would later suggest not only that he acted as deputy to Churchill but that his friend took complete charge of events. True leaders act in a time of crisis, and never for an instant did it occur to Churchill that he was a mere civilian with no authority whatever. On the contrary it was always in his nature to be in control of his life and the events surrounding it, and he unhesitatingly made this moment of grave danger his own, using persuasion and the power of his personality. He began to organize the perilous task by asking for twenty volunteers from the Durbans. Only nine men stepped forward for what now became Churchill's personal war. Where others would be rightfully terrified, he relished the chance to shine, in his element doing the unthinkable. Acting calm and very much in control, he was described by a captain of the Durbans as 'a very brave man but a damned fool'.

It was an apt description of young Winston Churchill who, riveted by the exhilaration and challenge of a menacing situation, seemed oblivious to the danger. From the dramatic moments of the next hours would come numerous tales of his actions that day – many of them of dubious authenticity – and while the exact details may never be known, what is clear is that during this period of extreme danger he performed heroically.

Churchill and his band of intrepid volunteers spent about seventy minutes (an eternity in war) under relentless, frightening but largely ineffective fire. He would later write, 'My only wonder is that our losses were not greater.' Eventually the track was cleared of stones sufficiently to enable the locomotive to push a derailed truck aside and ease past the crash site. At that point the trucks behind the engine came loose, and only the engine and its tender were left intact. One of the trucks carried the Durban Light Infantry, most of whom, while severely shaken, emerged unhurt. Standing motionless in the killing zone, the locomotive nevertheless somehow managed to remain unscathed by artillery fire, thanks to the abysmal aim of the Boer gunners.

The task of clearing the track completed, Churchill turned next to supervising the loading of some forty wounded aboard the engine, 'the greater part of whom', he later wrote, were packed like sardines inside the tight confines of the cab, many of them seriously hurt, with blood everywhere. As the train began accelerating, its firebox aflame and water spewing from holes made by Boer rounds, Haldane and those still able-bodied enough ran alongside, using the train as cover from the fire above, their objective a group of houses ahead that offered a place of defence. However, when the fire became too heavy, Wagner opened the throttle in order to save the wounded. The train shot forward at a speed too great for Haldane's men to keep pace, leaving them behind to fend for themselves. The infantry became scattered, and soon Boer horsemen rode among them, taking prisoners, while others died or were wounded attempting to escape. The situation was chaotic. Concerned for their safety and determined to help organize a last stand at the houses, Churchill dropped off the locomotive into a shallow cutting alongside the track. What he did not know until it was too late was that the men he was determined to save had already been captured. His last words to Wagner were, 'I can't leave those poor beggars to their fate.'

Instead of encountering friendly troops he found himself all alone. Spotting what he thought were two of the train's civilians a hundred yards ahead, he quickly realized they were Boers. This was not a time for heroics. One man with a pistol against two Boer marksmen with rifles was an uneven match, and Churchill turned and ran in the other direction. A Boer horseman drew near and waved at him to halt. For a brief moment he debated attempting to fire on the man but realized that in his haste he had left his Mauser in the cab of the locomotive and was unarmed – thus avoiding a temptation that more than likely would have cost him his life. Discretion having triumphed over what would have been improvident courage, Churchill quietly surrendered. 'Then I was herded with the other prisoners in a miserable group, and about the same time I noticed that my hand was bleeding, and it began to pour with rain.'

In addition to Churchill, Haldane and fifty-six of his men were captured; at least four were dead and another thirty wounded. The prisoners were taken to an area crawling with what Churchill estimated were three thousand Boers. With his usual bravado he lost no time in letting his captors know his name and that he was a war correspondent and a non-combatant and should not be treated as a prisoner of war. He insisted on being taken to see the commander of Boer forces in Natal, Piet Joubert. His demands were ignored. Instead his captors crowded around him with sudden interest, and one man announced, 'You are the son of Randolph Churchill,' and when Churchill insisted again that he should not be held prisoner, there was laughter. 'Oh, we do not catch lords' sons every day.'

Churchill was eventually taken to Joubert's tent to argue for his release. Among those present was a twenty-nine-year-old lawyer named Jan Christiaan Smuts, the future leader of the Republic of South Africa, who, as a field marshal, would become one of Churchill's closest friends and trusted advisers and a member of his War Cabinet in the Second World War. In 1899 Smuts was the state attorney of the rebel Transvaal republic. He later vividly recalled their first meeting. 'Winston was a scrubby, squat figure of a man, unshaved. He was furious, venomous, just like a viper.' When Churchill complained that it was outrageous to keep him a prisoner, Smuts disagreed, pointing out: 'You have been taken armed [with ammunition] and in command of troops.' His request was denied. Although given no hint of his fate, Churchill was sent to Pretoria along with the other captured British officers. Wet, miserable, still indignant at being captured, in his wildest fantasy he had no conception that his valiant actions that morning and subsequent capture would be merely the opening chapter of the Churchill saga in the Boer War.

Trudging beside Haldane, Churchill seemed buoyed by the experience and more interested in the recognition his feat would bring him than in his plight. Having taken a star turn with his derring-do in clearing the tracks, he felt that the survivors would surely be singing his praises and that it would help him win a seat in Parliament. In this sense Churchill was quite in character: he still treated war as if it were an activity being conducted solely for his personal advancement.

After being herded for six hours through wet fields in drenching rain, the dog-tired group eventually arrived in Colenso and were crowded into an unlighted storage shed near the railway station. Outside the Boers built campfires and began to sing their traditional evening psalm. Churchill later recounted to J. B. Atkins, 'It struck the fear of God into me. What sort of men are these we are fighting? They have a better cause – and cause is everything.' And, as the rain pelted down on the corrugated iron roof during his first night in captivity, Churchill was left wondering if the war might be unjust after all.

About the time Churchill was being captured, the engine and its tender were limping into Estcourt station with men clinging to the cowcatcher and the footplates and hanging on to the sides of the tender. When the alarm was raised both J. B. Atkins and Leo Amery hastened to Frere and began interviewing survivors of the ambush. 'We heard how Churchill had walked round and round the wreckage while the bullets were spitting against the iron walls, and had called for volunteers to free the engine; how he had said, "Keep cool, men!" and "This will be interesting for my paper!" ' Several attested to his bravery, including a private of the Durbans who later wrote that Churchill 'walked about in it all as coolly as if nothing was going on & called for volunteers to give him a hand . . . His presence and way of going on were as much good as fifty men would have been.'

When his colleagues immediately filed dispatches, what was little more than a small event in an expanding war became instead headline news. Churchill's capture became an overnight sensation in Africa and throughout Britain out of all proportion to his status as a mere war correspondent. What enhanced the event was that he was the son of Randolph Churchill, whose name still evoked recognition and respect in southern Africa.

A distraught Thomas Walden wrote to Jennie that he was certain from conversations with the engine-driver Wagner that 'Mr Winston' had not been wounded and that his heroics would earn him recognition. 'Every officer in Estcourt thinks Mr C. and the engine-driver will get the V.C.' Neither ever did – because both were regarded as civilians, decorations for valour were not considered. Moreover, despite Haldane's glowing report of Churchill's gallantry, any award would have had to come from the very establishment he had so harshly criticized in his books and dispatches. Although Churchill would petition the colonial secretary, Joseph Chamberlain, for recognition in 1901, in what his granddaughter describes as an all too obvious case of 'medal-hunting', the War Office was not interested.

From his very first moments as a prisoner Churchill was determined to escape, intending to make his first attempt by hiding under some straw on the floor of the shed in Colenso. He was unable to do so before the next day's march began, and in any case the idea that he could have gone unmissed seems ludicrous: the Boers were certainly not inattentive enough to have lost sight of their celebrity prisoner that easily. They endured another difficult forced march, churning through gooey khaki-coloured mud, across rivers and through bogs. As they passed around the Boer lines near Ladysmith, Churchill could hear the sounds of battle. They spent their second night camped in the open before another five-hour march brought them to the Elandslaagte railway station, where Churchill was locked in the ticket office away from the other prisoners. A Boer soldier later recalled how Churchill stood slightly to the side all the while 'constantly scanning the horizon and all activity around him, unlike the other prisoners, who were downcast and dejected'.

Throughout his ordeal Churchill's fatigue and dismay did not prevent him from being his usual inquisitive self. He never missed an opportunity to question his captors and to probe for a means of escaping. For the final leg of their journey, the prisoners were herded on to a train bound for Pretoria, where officers were separated from the other ranks. Tired but still defiant, Churchill accompanied the officers to what had previously been the Staats (State) Model School for young men and was now a Boer detention facility for enemy officers.

What Churchill had treated as more of a game was now a grim reality that had taken away his freedom. He found captivity intolerable, 'painful and humiliating', and reflected on the irony of men trying to kill each other one moment, then seeking a measure of compassion from their enemy when captured. Suddenly small things became important: food, water and shelter 'the victor must supply or be a savage, but beyond these all else is favour.'

For a prisoner-of-war facility, the State Model School was relatively luxurious, with decent living conditions and minimal regulations. Churchill's quarters were in a communal dormitory shared with Haldane and four other officers. Mail was freely permitted, so he was able to send his dispatches to the *Morning Post*, though not without some censorship.

Churchill repeatedly demanded his release on the same grounds as before: he was a war correspondent and non-combatant and would agree to observe this status if released. Despite his persistent belief that he would not long remain a prisoner, his entreaties met with indifference. He wrote to his mother that she should not worry, he expected to be released shortly, but she should do 'all in your power to procure my release'. He would not have been considered quite so innocuous had the Boers searched him immediately upon his capture. In his tunic pocket were ammunition clips for his Mauser, which would clearly have identified him as a combatant. Moreover, as one writer points out, his ammunition was 'vicious soft-nosed bullets . . . he had no business to be carrying arms or taking part in an operation. If he had been dealing with an enemy more ruthless than the Boers . . . he might have been shot at once.' Although he managed surreptitiously to dispose of one clip, his captor discovered the second, which Churchill claimed to have just picked up. His ploy worked and the unsuspecting Boer tossed the clip away.

Churchill's letters to the Boer secretary of state for war, Louis de Souza, failed to gain his release, even though de Souza personally visited him on several occasions and the two men formed a friendly relationship. At one of their meetings de Souza inquired: 'Mr Churchill, you have no complaints, I hope.' To which Churchill shot back: 'My only complaint is the fact that I am in this place!' The Boer government, however, had no intention of releasing its prize catch, and in fact considered Churchill 'one of the most dangerous prisoners in our hands' who should under no circumstances be released. Thus, instead of enjoying his freedom, Winston Churchill spent a miserable twenty-fifth birthday as a prisoner of war. 'I am 25 today,' he wrote, 'it is terrible to think how little time remains.'

A captured soldier's duty is to try to escape. Although only a civilian, Churchill acted as any good soldier would in such circumstances. He was determined 'to find some way, by force or fraud, by steel or gold, of regaining my freedom'.

While others thought about merely escaping, he had far grander ideas. As Britain's wartime leader during the Second World War, he would advance numerous audacious schemes. In prison in 1899 he conceived a bold plan, not just for a prison break but also to seize the entire city of Pretoria. The city's security forces were minimal, most of them caretakers with little military experience. With a body of only ten men Churchill envisaged seizing rifles and escaping from their guardians, releasing the two thousand British soldiers and NCOs confined at Pretoria's racecourse, then quickly taking control of the forts that protected the city, along with the important railway terminus, so as to disrupt rail traffic throughout the Transvaal. Most notable was Churchill's intention to capture President Kruger and the entire Boer government, which, he believed, might lead to peace. In short he intended almost single-handedly to win the war. 'If we got Pretoria we could hold it for months. And what a feat of arms! . . . It was a great dream,' and would of course have been a splendid feather in his own cap. However, the senior officers held with him vetoed the plan despite his conviction that they ought at least to have tried.

Escape plots flourished, among them one by Captain Haldane and a regimental sergeant major in the Imperial Light Horse named Brockie, an Afrikaner from Johannesburg who had passed himself off as an officer in order to be confined at the State Model School. Well advanced with their own escape plan, they were deeply annoyed when Churchill muscled his way in and insisted on being included. As the highest-profile prisoner he was drawing far too much attention to himself, and the guards would quickly notice his absence. Nor did Haldane believe that with his bad shoulder Churchill could successfully scale the six-and-a-half-foot corrugated-iron fence, on the periphery of the school grounds, that was to be their means of escape. Attempts to dissuade him failed, but because of his heroics in saving the armoured train Haldane would not turn him down. Churchill was relentless and persuasive, reminding Haldane of his sacrifice after the ambush, when he could have remained on the train, and plainly intimating that it was a debt to be repaid. Haldane thus reluctantly included him, later ruefully remarking that 'the wine was drawn and it had to be drunk.'

The three planned to escape on the night of 11 December but had to abort the attempt when a sentry accidentally stood near by and would have noticed anyone trying to scale the iron fence that formed the wall of a latrine at the poorly lit rear of the school grounds. After enduring another day of anxiety, they intended to try again the following night. Haldane thought that Churchill was being far too overt as he paced excitedly back and forth in the compound during the day, and that evening there was once again a vigilant sentry too close to the site of their escape. Brockie told Churchill the escape was off again and departed, as did Haldane, leaving Winston alone inside the latrine.

Thoroughly frustrated and restless at the prospect of yet another delay, Churchill impulsively ignored the risk of exposure and managed to scale the wall and jump down undetected into a garden adjoining the compound, where he hid among the shrubs awaiting the other two. At this point the versions of what actually occurred vary. After approximately one hour Brockie and Haldane returned to the latrine for yet another atttempt but were unable to scale the wall without being detected. Churchill relates that he whispered to Haldane from the garden that he could not climb back over the fence, and that his friend wished him good luck and told him that he must now escape on his own. Publicly all a tight-lipped Haldane would ever state is that matters 'did not go according to plan'.

Churchill's epic escape from Pretoria and his harrowing journey to freedom have been chronicled in great detail by the only witness to the event: Churchill himself. His escape required that – with a slouch hat jammed firmly on his head – he stroll boldly past a sentry stationed only a few yards away from the garden gate, all the while repeating to himself the words (borrowed from Frederick the Great) a twentieth-century warrior named Patton would make his own: 'L'audace! l'audace!' Strolling inconspicuously through Pretoria, 'humming a tune' to himself as if he were just another burgher minding his own business, Churchill eventually reached the outskirts of the city without incident.

He had four bars of chocolate and seventy-five pounds in his pocket, but not the maps and compass the three men had intended to use. Without being able to speak Afrikaans or Dutch, and with only a vague idea that he needed to find a way to Delagoa Bay and the port city of Lourenço Marques in Portuguese East Africa, some three hundred miles to the east, Churchill recalled his plight in 1898 when he was lost in the desert and relied on the constellation Orion to guide him. Realizing he had very little time before his escape was noticed and a search mounted, he decided his only hope of evading capture was to smuggle himself aboard a train heading east. To many the seemingly hopeless situation he now found himself in would have been cause for despair; for Churchill it was yet another life-altering challenge.

Although bitterly disappointed by what they regarded as Churchill's betrayal – his unexpected decision to escape without them – Haldane and his colleagues made every attempt to support his escape by placing a dummy in his bed that remained unnoticed until well into the following morning, when he was finally discovered missing at the 9.30 roll call. The embarrassed Boers were not amused by the bold escape of their best-known prisoner. Handbills were immediately issued offering a reward of twenty-five pounds for his capture: DEAD OR ALIVE, THE ESCAPED PRISONER OF WAR, CHURCHILL. Rumours abounded, including the wild assertion in a Pretoria newspaper that he was thought to be disguised as a woman; a short time later he was said to be posing as a policeman, then as a waiter. This greatly amused his incarcerated friends in the State School, 'who could hardly imagine a man less fitted for the job'.

Indeed, the hunt for young Winston Churchill became absurdly comical: the homes of suspected sympathizers were ruthlessly searched, including that of the bishop of Pretoria, and a nurse was expelled from the Transvaal for allegedly being his lover and aiding his escape. Hoping to claim the reward a constable 'captured' someone who turned out to be a perplexed Swede. For a time it was as if the whole focus of the war was on the capture of what the Boer government called 'a very dangerous individual'. Mostly, however, the Boers were humiliated by having permitted Churchill to escape, and frustrated that they hadn't a clue where he was. Had he remained in Pretoria he would have been delighted by the widespread publicity he was garnering. However, during the days it took him to escape their clutches he felt only anxiety that he would be recaptured and possibly killed.

During the night of 12 December and the early hours of 13 December 1899, he hiked eastward, navigating by the stars, eventually reaching a railway line. After several hours he reached another railway terminus and hid in a ditch until he heard the rumble of an approaching train that he gambled was heading east. It was moving slowly enough to enable him to hop aboard and hide himself under empty bags that had once carried coal from a colliery in the eastern Transvaal. Fortunately he had correctly chosen a train heading east along the Delagoa Bay Railway. Before dawn and possible discovery, he jumped off and began walking through the empty landscape towards some hills where he intended to stay undetected until the following night. Hungry, miserable and all too aware of his precarious state, perhaps for the first time in his life Winston Churchill, never a religious man, actually prayed for divine help. The thought of being recaptured and sent back to prison he 'dreaded and detested more than words can express . . . I prayed long and earnestly for help and guidance.'

It was midsummer in South Africa, and the daytime heat was stifling. Churchill hid in a stand of trees on the side of a ravine in the company of a 'gigantic vulture, who manifested an extravagant interest in my condition, and made hideous and ominous gurglings from time to time'. In the evening Churchill resumed his eastward journey, walking parallel to the railway line with the intention of hopping another train. Although he successfully avoided all signs of habitation and bridges guarded by armed Boers, his usual self-confidence was beginning to crumble. Further along, at another station, he observed three goods trains loading, but their destination was unknown, and in any case there was too much activity for him to slip aboard any of them unnoticed. By now he was utterly exhausted and desperately hungry and thirsty after covering some sixty miles during his first twenty-four hours of freedom. Then, not for the first time in his young life, fortune smiled on Winston Churchill and his prayers were answered.

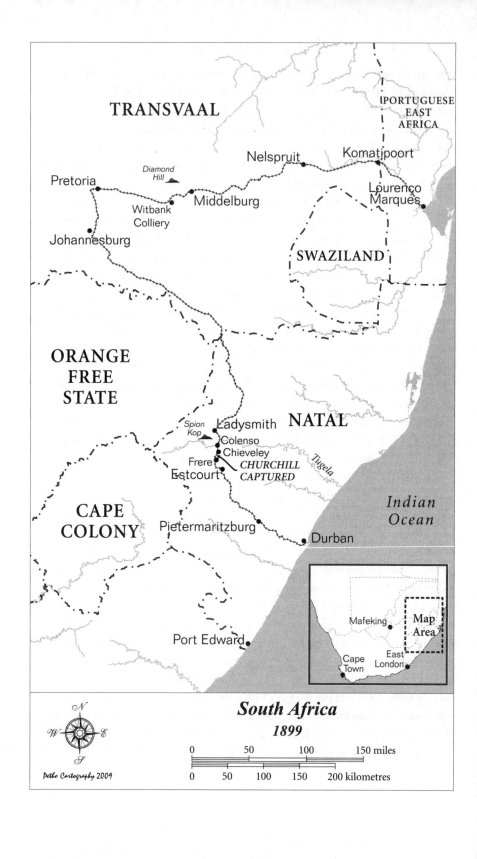

TRANSVAAL

PORTUGUESE
EAST
AFRICA

Nelspruit   Komatjpoort

Diamond
Hill

Pretoria   Lourenço
                    Middelburg   Marques
        Witbank
        Colliery

Johannesburg

                                SWAZILAND

ORANGE
FREE
STATE

                                        NATAL
            Spion Ladysmith
            Kop   Colenso
                  Chieveley
            Frere   CHURCHILL   Tugela
        Estcourt   CAPTURED

                                        Indian
CAPE   Ocean
COLONY   Pietermaritzburg

                            Durban

                            Mafeking   Map
                                              Area

Port Edward
                            Cape   East
                            Town   London

South Africa
1899

0   50   100   150 miles

0   50   100   150   200 kilometres

Petho Cartography 2009

In the distance he thought he saw fires, but when he got closer they turned out to be flames from the engines of a coal mine. Adjacent to the mine was a house and, by now far too exhausted to be unduly troubled, Churchill took the risk of knocking on its door. It was 1.30 a.m., 14 December. He was in the town of Witbank, and the man who was roused from his sleep answered the knock with a revolver in his hand. He was an Englishman named John George Howard, the manager of the Transvaal & Delagoa Bay Collieries.

Before him stood a blue-eyed, red-haired young man who Howard thought must be a Boer spy. He kept the weapon trained on his uninvited nocturnal intruder as Churchill absurdly attempted to pass himself off as 'Dr Bentick', who was in need of help after falling off a train and hurting his shoulder. Howard wasn't buying this obviously tall tale, and his unkempt guest soon admitted that his name was Winston Churchill and that he was an escaped British prisoner of war. 'Will you help me?' Churchill asked. Howard did far more: he put down the revolver and welcomed his unexpected guest, pointing out that he was very lucky to have picked his particular house. 'Thank God you have come here! It is the only place for twenty miles where you would not have been handed over. We are all British here and we will see you through.'

The Boers' search had extended to the towns east of Pretoria, including Witbank, where suspicion was automatically directed at the Britons living there, all of whom had taken an oath of neutrality. Before Churchill's arrival a Boer policeman had already visited Howard. For the next two days, Howard and his sympathetic British colleagues hid Churchill – with only candles, cigars, a bottle of whisky and a chamber pot for company – deep in the mine. The place was infested with white rats that shared the scraps of food Howard was able to provide for him without raising the suspicions of his servants over his sudden uncharacteristically ravenous appetite. According to Churchill he remained hidden in the mine until the evening of 15 December when Howard deemed it safe for him to emerge and breathe fresh air. However, the real reason that Churchill was removed from the mine seems to have been that he had become ill. For the next three days he was hidden behind some packing cases and grain bags in a room next to Howard's office and was treated by Dr James Gillespie, the mine doctor in whom Howard was obliged to confide.

To help smuggle Churchill out of the Transvaal, Charles Burnham, a shipping agent and the part owner of a nearby trading store, became a key player in his escape. 'He purchased large quantities of wool from the neighbouring farmers and arranged for its export to Lourenço Marques.' In the early hours of 19 December Churchill was led to a siding where three railway trucks were being loaded with bales of Burnham's wool. He was secreted in a hollowed-out space in the middle of the bales, covered with a tarpaulin and given some food, cold tea and a revolver. Burnham boarded the train as a passenger, ostensibly to look after his wool shipment but in reality to ensure that his secret passenger made it to safety.

As the train slowly proceeded towards the border, Churchill was able to keep track of its progress through a slit in the wall of his truck. After sitting in a siding for eighteen hours at the border station of Komatipoort, the train at last reached the safety of Portugese East Africa. For the final leg of the trip to Lourenço Marques he no longer had to hide and emerged euphorically to sing, shout and fire his revolver in the air. Late on the afternoon of 21 December 1898, his ordeal ended, and with tongue in cheek Burnham telegraphed Howard: 'Goods arrived safely.'

Filthy and dishevelled, the 'goods' turned up at the British consulate, where at first he was almost turned away. The bravado that had been absent during his weeklong ordeal quickly returned. Mere hours after his arrival the brash young Englishman impudently cabled Louis de Souza, 'Escape not due to any fault of your guards.' He also cabled the *Standard & Diggers News* in Johannesburg: 'Am now writing how I escaped from the Boers but regret cannot for obvious reasons disclose many interesting details. Shall be happy to give you any you may require when next I visit Pretoria. – Churchill.'

He had left behind on his bed in Pretoria a letter for de Souza that was both mischievous and conciliatory. It said, in part: 'I do not consider your Government justified in holding me, a press correspondent and a non-combatant, a prisoner and I have consequently resolved to escape.' The letter went on to offer his thanks for 'the kindness which has been shown to me and the other prisoners by you' and the other Boer authorities. Churchill also expressed his hope that once the war ended 'a state of affairs may be created which shall preserve at once the national pride of the Boers and the security of the British and put a final stop to the rivalry and enmity of both races.' It concluded with Churchill's regrets that 'the circumstances have not permitted me bid you a personal farewell'.

Fortuitously a coastal steamer sailing to Durban was scheduled to depart Lourenço Marques that same evening. Anxious to get Churchill out of Portuguese East Africa without arousing publicity, the British consul arranged for his passage, and, escorted by a band of armed Englishmen, Churchill boarded the SS *Induna* and sailed away to safety.

News of his escape had preceded him to Durban, and upon his arrival Churchill was greeted as a conquering hero. A large crowd on the quay cheered as he bowed from the bridge of the steamer. A high-powered committee composed of the mayor, a general and an admiral welcomed the young hero to Durban. For the first of countless times during the remainder of his long life, he was the apple of the public's eye and his words would carry a hero's weight. After a brief speech Churchill was carried through the streets of Durban to the strains of 'Rule, Britannia'.

In newspapers from Africa to Europe, and in the United States and Asia, headlines and stories abounded of the great escapade; letters and telegrams flowed from friends, acquaintances and complete strangers. The most notable came in the form of a brief telegram to Jennie: 'Thank God – Pamela.' From Churchill came a surprisingly contrite and rare admission: 'There is a God that looks after Winston.'

For a young man who had been so soundly rejected by his father and told he would never amount to anything, it was heady stuff indeed. Moreover, not only had Churchill become a heroic example of British courage, but also his escape had been about the only encouraging news for Britain in what was becoming a lengthy and costly war. Tales about Churchill became embellished from fact into folklore, thus conferring a cult status on Britain's hero of the hour. Thirsting for positive news, the press shamelessly exploited exaggerated tales of his heroics. Music-hall comedian T. E. Dunville, who performed in Lancashire, incorporated this into his routine:

> You've heard of Winston Churchill;
> This is all I need to say –
> He's the latest and the greatest
> Correspondent of the day.

The skipper of the Royal Navy cruiser *Terrible* wrote in March 1900, 'I feel certain that I shall someday shake hands with you as Prime

Minister of England, you possess the two necessary qualifications genius and plod, combined I believe nothing can keep them back.'

What he had accomplished exceeded even his most vivid dreams of success. Before the Boer War, Churchill was known only to those who read his books or knew of him as the author of dispatches from the far corners of the empire. Such was the growing fame of the young man who had been uncertain he would ever succeed in pleasing his dead parent or of living until he could amount to much: his was now a household name throughout Britain and its empire.

I2

'The Red Gleam of War'

We are not interested in the possibilities of defeat. They do not exist.

– Queen Victoria

Churchill's exuberant response to the public adoration heaped upon him was soon overshadowed by the reality that he was in South Africa to report on a war. His original goal had been to witness the relief of Ladysmith, and it was to the scene of the frustrating and fruitless battles being waged by the British army around the besieged city that he now returned to report. Buller warmly welcomed Churchill, who freely passed along the details of his escapades, his observations about Boer tactics, and other information he thought might be useful. The general thought Churchill was wasted as a war correspondent. 'I wish he was leading irregular troops instead of writing for a rotten paper. We are very short of good men, as he appears to be, out here.'

Churchill was also reunited with Leo Amery and J. B. Atkins. They found him haggard from his experience and despite the wonderful publicity still smarting over his capture, 'rounding us up, like cattle! The greatest indignity of my life!' Churchill also continued to muse about the Boers; 'he sits in my tent with a new and lively conviction of the Boer military genius,' wrote Atkins.

One of the many people who met Winston Churchill during the war was the artist Mortimer Menpes, who drew one of the best-known sketches of him as a young man. Menpes has supplied us with a brilliant picture of Churchill in 1900, a young man in a great hurry who 'can be either epigrammatic or sarcastic, and is often both . . . he speaks in an almost flippant manner, giving his views in an apparently careless way, but with the greatest assurance.' Moreover, 'Mr Churchill . . . struck me as a man who, in certain circles, might be termed unpopular, and accused of an arrogance which, to any but a jaundiced vision, would appear for what it undoubtedly is, frankness and perfect manliness.'

In January 1900 Buller conferred upon Churchill a lieutenant's commission in the South African Light Horse Regiment. Once again he had defied convention as the only war correspondent–officer covering the Boer War, in direct contravention of the new War Office decree. Undoubtedly his famous escape contributed to Buller's generosity. Churchill, however, showed his gratitude by proclaiming at his exasperating best that perhaps he had been accorded this privilege 'to qualify me for some reward they might care to give me'.

Churchill also helped his brother acquire a lieutenant's commission in the South African Light Horse. However, in his first and, as it turned out, only action, Jack was wounded in a skirmish near Ladysmith. His war over, Jack Churchill was evacuated from South Africa on the hospital ship *Maine*, the very vessel for which his mother had raised funds and for which she had organized volunteers to care for the wounded. By a stroke of fate one of her first patients was her own son, fortunately with only a minor wound. Atkins wryly commented that it seemed Jack Churchill 'had paid his brother's debts'.

Dispatches began flying from Winston's pen as he again exposed himself to danger while covering the futile battles to relieve Ladysmith. He wrote candidly of Buller and of the inability of the British to learn how to fight the Boers, who continued to exploit their ability to mount guerrilla warfare. Once-obscure place-names on the map of southern Africa now became enshrined in British and South African military history: Kimberley, Ladysmith, Mafeking, Diamond Hill, Magersfontein, Colenso and Spion Kop. The British people craved favourable news of the war; what they got instead was defeat piled on defeat, assuaged only by Robert Baden-Powell's stalwart defence of Mafeking, as 'general after general buried his reputation behind the kopjes [small hills rising up from the African veld].'

Neither side gave quarter, and although the toll on both sides escalated, the British suffered the lion's share of the casualties. One of the bloodiest battles of the war was fought to relieve Kimberley where, not for the first or last time, British tactics played directly into the hands of the outnumbered Boers. The famed Scottish Highlanders suffered devastating losses in an ill-conceived operation to capture Magersfontein Hill, an important piece of terrain that was key to lifting the siege.

Having failed to reconnoitre, the Highland Brigade was ambushed in open ground by massive fire from Boer positions astride the hill. Some nine hundred British soldiers died in this bloodbath. In the Black Watch Regiment alone, losses were more than 80 per cent killed.

After the battle a soldier of the Black Watch who survived the massacre wrote the following famous lines:

> Why weren't we told of the trenches?
> Why weren't we told of the wire?
> Why were we marched up in column?
> May Tommy Atkins enquire.
> Why were scouts not sent forward?
> Who made the mistake? Give his rank?
> Do they know his incompetence yet?
> Tommy has learnt to his sorrow,
> And Tommy can never forget.

British tactical incompetence led to humiliating defeats at Stormberg and at Colenso, ten miles from Ladysmith, when Redvers Buller attempted to lift the siege by foolishly sending his artillery out ahead of his infantry, exposing his guns and men to heavy Boer fire at a cost of one thousand casualties. Colenso and Bullers's bungling of other battles yet to come would earn him relief from command and the derisive nickname, 'Sir *Reverse* Buller'.

Although he liked Buller personally, Churchill was scathingly critical of his military competence, describing him as a commander who 'plodded on from blunder to blunder and from one disaster to another, without losing either the regard of his country or the trust of his troops, to whose feeding as well as his own he paid serious attention'.

In each of these battles British commanders had recklessly believed that superior numbers would win out. The Battles of Magersfontein, Colenso and Stormberg would henceforth be collectively remembered as 'Black Week', demonstrating conclusively that British tactics were outdated and invariably wrong, and that British commanders habitually failed to adapt to the Boers, who refused to play by the rules. But their worst failing was sheer arrogance: the belief that because they were British they were destined to succeed.

'Black Week' sent shock waves throughout Britain, nowhere more so than in Buckingham Palace. 'Queen Victoria, ever a keen observer of the army's exploits, made her feelings abundantly clear: "We are not interested in the possibilities of defeat. They do not exist,"' she declared.

The siege of Ladysmith had yet to be broken when Buller repeated the folly of Colenso on a hill called Spion Kop. Churchill wrote a chilling description of the massive force assembled by Buller, with many soldiers marching to their death in the pouring rain, a 'ceaseless living stream – miles of stern-looking men . . . hurrying forward under the cover of night – and before them a guiding star, the red gleam of war'. The Battle of Spion Kop on 23–24 January 1900, was the largest and one of the bloodiest fought during the Boer War and a classic example of how British commanders were outfoxed by the Boers. As an eyewitness Churchill saw the dead piled high and was sickened. Of the two thousand men who fought this needless and ultimately futile battle, three hundred died, with another thousand men wounded and two hundred captured – all for nothing.

Churchill's graphic dispatches left no doubt in his readers' minds of the horror taking place in southern Africa. In unsparing detail he chronicled not only how the war was being ineptly fought but also the carnage of dead and horribly wounded, young and old men alike, of both sides; of a sixty-year-old Boer whose leg had been shattered by a bullet, who slowly bled to death, a letter from his wife clutched in his hand; or of 'two poor [British] riflemen with their heads smashed like eggshells . . . ah, horrible war, amazing medley of the glorious and the squalid, the pitiful and the sublime.' The day before he had encountered a fresh-faced young cavalry subaltern he had known at Harrow who was looking 'to get a job'. The young officer was killed the next day at Spion Kop, leading Churchill to write that he had 'joined in the evening, [been] shot at dawn . . . Poor gallant young Englishman; he had soon "got his job". The great sacrifice had been required of the Queen's latest recruit.'

As he had in the past, he believed himself impervious to the danger in which he routinely placed himself. A distraught Pamela Plowden had pleaded with him to get out of harm's way and return to England. Instead he wrote that, for better or worse, he was committed to continuing to report the war. Of his conviction that he would come to no harm and must see the war through to its end, Churchill asserted: 'I should forefeit my self respect for ever if I tried to shield myself like that behind an easily obtained reputation for courage . . . I have a good belief that I am to be of some use and therefore to be spared . . . My place is here: here I stay – perhaps forever.'

War has a way of humbling those who disrespect its unpredictability. On the basis of his combat experience he should have appreciated that bullets do not discriminate, and at least once even Churchill had good reason to question his over-confidence while atop a hill observing and writing when the Boers began shelling it. 'I was vy nearly killed two hours ago by a shrapnel,' he thoughtlessly wrote to Pamela, whose reaction can only have been fear for his life. 'But though I was in the full burst of it, God preserved me. Eight men were wounded by it. I wonder whether we shall get through and whether I shall live to see the end . . . The war is vy bitter.'

The siege of Ladysmith continued until the end of February 1900, when Buller's forces at long last reached the beleaguered garrison. For Churchill it had been a rather bizarre journey, but now he became one of the first to enter the liberated city in the company of the commander of the mounted forces, Douglas Mackinnon Baillie Hamilton, the twelfth Earl of Dundonald. 'Never shall I forget that ride,' he informed his readers, the exhilaration clear in his words, as he described how, with guns firing in support, the horses galloped over hill and dale until 'there before us lay the tin houses and dark trees we had come so far to see and save.' They were met by a score of gaunt British soldiers in tattered uniforms, most able only to cheer feebly and weep. Inside Ladysmith, Churchill dined with Sir George White, the garrison commander, and his old friend Ian Hamilton. 'Never before had I sat in such brave company nor stood so close to a great event.'

Hubert de la Poer Gough, the future commander of the British Fifth Army in France in 1918, has hotly disputed Churchill's claim. A cavalry major in the Boer War, Gough served in the North-West Frontier under Bindon Blood, and his force was the first into Ladysmith. He vehemently challenged Churchill's descriptions in *My Early Life* of the fighting and his version of its relief, calling it 'a totally inaccurate account and pure fabrication' – including Churchill's assertion that he had met Sir George White in the street, 'faultlessly attired. Then we all rode together into the long beleaguered, almost starved out Ladysmith. It was a thrilling moment.' According to Gough, Churchill never met White until he burst into his dining room, nor did he accompany Gough into Ladysmith as he told his readers in his dispatch of 9 March 1900.

With the siege of Ladysmith lifted, by the spring of 1900 the war in Natal was largely over, but Churchill's brushes with death had only begun. During the British campaign in the Orange Free State in the spring, he accompanied a brigade of the Imperial Yeomanry commanded by his friend and former regimental commander John Brabazon, now a brigadier. In another spur-of-the-moment decision reminiscent of the armoured-train incident, Churchill elected to accompany a fifty-man mounted force of the Montmorency Scouts (a native unit of volunteers) that attempted to seize a nearby key kopje near Dewetsdorp before a force of some two hundred like-minded Boers could do so. When the scout commander, Major Angus McNeill, a former schoolmate, declared, 'Come with us, we'll give you a show now – first-class,' Churchill promptly accepted for reasons he later cited as 'in the interests of the *Morning Post*', and galloped off in a mad dash to beat the Boers.

When they ascended the kopje McNeill's scouts encountered a dozen Boers who had arrived first and now occupied the protective rocks at the crest, aiming their rifles at the exposed scouts. Suddenly under fire, McNeill ordered a hasty retreat, but as Churchill attempted to spring on to the saddle of his horse it loosened and slipped under its belly, and the animal galloped off in terror. 'Most of the scouts were already two hundred yards off. I was alone, dismounted, within the closest range, and a mile at least from cover of any kind.' And, 'for the second time in this war', Churchill 'ran for my life on foot from the Boer marksmen', all the while thinking, 'here at last I take it.'

Once again luck shone on Winston Churchill, and he was saved from death or capture by the sudden appearance of one of the scouts, 'a tall man, with skull and crossbones badge and on a pale horse. Death in Revelation, but life to me!' Churchill yelled at him to 'give me a stirrup', and the scout stopped while 'I ran up to him, did not bungle the business of mounting, and in a moment found myself behind him on the saddle,' hanging on for dear life. As bullets whizzed wildly around them, the two men rode for their lives. Soon they were out of range of the Boer guns, though not before the gallant horse had been hit by a dumdum bullet. Churchill felt he 'had thrown double sixes again'.

His saviour, Trooper Clement Roberts, was distraught: 'My poor horse, oh, my poor horse; shot with an explosive bullet.' With inappropriate frivolity Churchill rejoined, 'Never mind, you've saved my life.' Though he later described this incident as 'a most exciting adventure', to his mother he was more candid: 'I had another disagreeable adventure near Dewetsdorp: indeed I do not think I have ever been so near destruction.'

Churchill took leave of the South African Light Horse and once again became a civilian war correspondent even though he faced execution as a spy if recaptured by the Boers. However, his critical dispatches deeply angered the British commander in chief, Lord Roberts, once a friend and now one of his sternest critics. Roberts rebuffed his request to cover the campaigns in the Orange Free State but was eventually persuaded to relent and allow Churchill to accompany his army. Churchill received a terse and decidedly unfriendly note from Roberts's private secretary that read: 'Lord Roberts desires me to say that he is willing to permit you to accompany this force as a correspondent – *for your father's sake.*' The note riled Churchill, who in a letter to Jennie queried 'the justice of making me accept as a favour what was already mine as a right'. Grumble he might, but once again his friendships with men of influence had saved the day. However, Roberts would never again acknowledge Churchill, who seems never to have got over the snub.

To his delight he was reunited with his cousin Sunny, who had secured a commission and was assigned to Lord Roberts's staff. It was even more fortunate that Ian Hamilton (now an acting lieutenant general) was commanding part of a one-hundred-thousand-man force during the first major British offensive into the Orange Free State and the Transvaal. Churchill had little trouble persuading Hamilton to include him and Sunny in his entourage.

On 5 June 1900, Hamilton's force liberated Pretoria. Churchill and Sunny were on horseback as part of a group of British officers halted at the closed gates of a railway crossing on the edge of city when a train bearing armed Boers began steaming past. 'Rifles bristled from every window. We gazed at each other dumbfounded at three yards' distance. A single shot would have precipitated a horrible carnage on both sides. Although sorry that the train should escape, it was with unfeigned relief that we saw the last carriage glide away past our noses.'

Upon entering Pretoria the two immediately went in search of the officer POW compound, which Churchill knew had been moved from the States Model School after his and other escapes. They soon found the new prison and, quite unaided, faced armed Boer sentries who could easily have shot them dead. From inside the compound the prisoners saw one of the two unidentified horsemen raise his hat and gave a loud hurrah. One officer recorded that 'suddenly Winston Churchill came galloping over the hill and tore down the Boer flag', as the newly liberated prisoners cheered.

Sunny was in full uniform and demanded that the commandant surrender the place. Someone unlocked the gates, the prisoners rushed out, seized the Boer weapons and raised an improvised Union Jack. It was a supreme moment – not one but two Churchills had liberated them.

Churchill's African adventure ended soon afterwards but not before a couple more narrow escapes. The first occurred at Diamond Hill, one of the anchors of the Boer defences east of Pretoria. The Boers held the high ground, and to capture it Hamilton's troops would have to advance upward under heavy fire. As a furious battle ensued, Hamilton recorded that 'Winston who had been attached to my column . . . somehow managed to give me the slip and climb this mountain . . . and ensconced himself in a niche not much more than a pistol shot directly below the Boer commandos . . . Had even half a dozen of the Burghers run twenty yards over the brow they could have knocked him off his perch with a volley of stones. Thus it was from his lofty perch Winston had the nerve to signal me . . . with his handkerchief on a stick, that if I could only manage to gallop up at the head of my mounted infantry we ought to be able to rush this summit.' Hamilton proceeded to do this, and in the process won the Battle of Diamond Hill, thus preventing the Boers from mounting an offensive to recapture Pretoria.

Hamilton later called it the turning point of the war. Churchill's heroics remained unknown until 1944, when Hamilton published his account. Churchill himself failed even to mention his action in either *My Early Life* or his dispatch of 14 June describing the battle. His heroics notwithstanding, he had instinctively discerned the only weakness in the Boer defences and acted accordingly. Yet his undertaking such a dangerous venture can be explained only by his propensity for doing what others would never dare.

The recognition Churchill desperately wanted from the Boer War but did not attain was the coveted Victoria Cross. Although Ian Hamilton thought he deserved one for his action on Diamond Hill, and recommended he receive it, with both Roberts and Kitchener (now in South Africa) as insurmountable obstacles it was never remotely possible – 'he had only been a Press Correspondent – they declared – so nothing happened.'

As he would during two future world wars, Churchill came and went from battlefields when it suited him. After the Battle of Diamond Hill he decided there was little left for him to accomplish in Africa; the Boer War was entering a new phase and might soon be over, and he was eager to exploit his newfound fame in a bid for a seat in Parliament. It was time to go home to England. Yet the story did not quite end there. He was en route to Cape Town aboard a troop train when it suddenly halted. The line ahead had been methodically destroyed and a bridge over a deep gorge blown up. As Churchill stepped from the train, 'at the same moment there arrived almost at our feet a shell from a small Boer gun. It burst with a startling bang, throwing up clods from the embankment.' Confusion reigned, but Churchill understood from his earlier experience that the train needed to get away from the threat – without delay. 'I therefore ran along the railway line to the engine, climbed into the cab, and ordered the engine-driver to blow his whistle to make the men re-entrain, and steam back instantly' to a nearby station. 'He obeyed,' as most men did when Winston Churchill issued an order. A Boer force had ambushed an earlier train and cut the tracks, and a fierce battle was under way. As the train steamed backwards Churchill took one last opportunity to wage his own personal war by fitting his Mauser with a wooden stock and shooting at a group of Boers near a burning bridge ahead. As far as he was concerned he believed (quite wrongly) that he had just experienced the last shots that would ever be fired at him in anger. Several days later he boarded the *Dunnottar Castle* at Cape Town for the return journey to England, where he arrived on 20 July 1900, his African adventure at an end.

13

Lessons Learned

I have always urged fighting wars and other contentions with might and main till overwhelming victory, and then offering the hand of friendship to the vanquished.
– My Early Life

Queen Victoria's death in 1901 not only marked the end of the great Victorian era but also saw the advent of modern warfare on an unprecedented and deadly scale. Kitchener was sent to South Africa in January 1900 as Roberts's chief of staff and in November succeeded him, after Roberts became too ill to continue as commander in chief of British forces. Under Kitchener's whip hand the British employed brutal, scorched-earth measures that laid waste the two Boer republics. Civilians were rounded up and interned in abysmal conditions in camps where disease ran rampant. Looting was widespread, entire towns were burned to the ground, farmhouses and crops were destroyed, and both sides perpetrated unspeakable cruelties that hardened the animosity between them. Although there is said to have existed at least a semblance of chivalry between the warring parties in that Boer wounded were sometimes treated in British field hospitals – the military historian J. F. C. Fuller proclaimed it 'the last of the gentleman's wars' – there was nothing chivalrous or gentlemanly about the manner in which each side killed the other.

The war dragged on until 1902, and the ensuing peace treaty resulted in the disarming of fourteen thousand defeated but still defiant Boer fighters. Although mere signatures on a piece of paper could hardly assuage the bitterness of the Boers or restore their devastated lands, the treaty that formally ended the war was signed on 31 May 1902, in Pretoria. Incredibly, after the last signature had been affixed 'and the

Boer leaders rose to leave, Kitchener went round giving each a handshake and saying, "We are good friends now." '

The Boer War left Churchill with much to ponder and a great deal to say about it for his newspaper. The dozens of dispatches he wrote reflected not only his observations (and often criticism) but also his growing knowledge of weapons, their capabilities, their employment – and their frequent misuse. They were in fact a primer enabling a discerning reader to gain a profound impression of the war and how it was fought. The war also significantly enhanced the military education of Churchill himself, and the lessons he learned from its few triumphs and myriad blunders were all duly noted and many years later put to effective use in other wars. In particular the alarming effectiveness of the Boer commandos was something he never forgot.

Churchill quickly recognized that the late-Victorian army was dreadfully ill suited to fight a modern war, its senior officers mostly incompetent and its tactics woefully outdated. His impatience with the inept or the timid among his Second World War commanders was directly attributable to his South African experience, as was his disdain for the lazy and the incompetent who needlessly killed their own men. Officers like Robert Baden-Powell, who performed brilliantly in the defence of Mafeking, were rare exceptions.

What is less explicable is how a young man of his limited education and experience, untrained as he was in strategy and high command, could have achieved such a deep understanding of the Boer War. His military education at Sandhurst taught only the basics of soldiering, and his experiences in India and the Sudan, while informative, were also seen from the perspective of an ordinary soldier on the battlefield. Yet it is clear from both his dispatches and his books that Churchill discerned what his own government was blind to – and incapable of correcting. His criticism of the mostly obsolete colonial thinking and leadership of the British army, however disrespectful, was mostly right on the mark.

To his credit Churchill was one of the few who saw beyond the current war to the larger questions of the consequences of waging war. In 1930, reflecting on the Boer War and Britain's mistakes, he wrote a prophetic warning ignored by more than one modern statesman: 'Let us learn our lessons. Never, never, never believe any war will be smooth or easy, or that anyone who embarks on the strange voyage can measure the tides and hurricanes he will encounter. The Statesman who yields to war fever must realize that once the signal is given, he is no longer the master of policy but the slave of unforeseeable and uncontrollable events.' From the time of the Franco-Prussian War of 1870, and certainly during the Boer War, it should have been – but clearly was not – evident that Europe was entering a new age of warfare, one of weapons far more deadly than the Maxim gun and one in which the simple slaughter of poorly armed tribesmen was no longer applicable.

A national enmity towards the Boers that in Britain verged on hysteria did not dissuade Churchill from writing sympathetically about an enemy he knew far better than most. His wartime dispatches were deeply resented by many in a British military establishment that viewed criticism by one of their own as impudent and inappropriate. Among his fiercest critics was General Sir John French, the future commander of the British Expeditionary Force during the first months of the First World War. In 1900 Churchill reported on the war as an observer in a cavalry division commanded by French, a bitter rival of his friend and former commander John Brabazon. Although in later years he would become a close friend, French not only ignored Churchill's presence but also deeply resented his daring criticisms. In a book of essays entitled *Great Contemporaries*, written in 1937, Churchill recalled French's antipathy towards him in the passage already cited about 'that hybrid combination of subaltern officer and widely followed war-correspondent ... distributing praise and blame among veteran commanders'.

Churchill's fabulous escape was not without lingering and sometimes controversial after-effects. Publicly it provoked a combination of anger, resentment and considerable envy of and admiration for his audacity. While most of Britain (and indeed the world) was captivated by his escape, not all of the British or South African press was uncritical. Several newspapers wondered what business a civilian had aboard the armoured train in the first place. When the *Durban Daily Nation* questioned his honour Churchill bristled at the criticism, calling it 'ungenerous'.

In later years there was criticism from various quarters, which Churchill met with ferocious counterattacks defending his actions and his reputation. His combative nature was never more in evidence than over the matter of his role in the great escape from Pretoria. Had he in fact abandoned his colleagues in what was to have been a joint venture, or did Churchill merely take full advantage of the opportunity to escape handed to him on the evening of 12 December 1899? Whenever challenged he instinctively resisted and immediately retaliated. As books and articles appeared extolling his escapades in South Africa, Churchill became protective of *his* version of the event, to the point where anyone who dared to offer so much as a conflicting opinion or criticism was either threatened or sued – or both.

Churchill's escape brought repercussions for the other incarcerated officers, although it greatly enlivened their boring existence in captivity. The Boers tightened security and imposed harsher restrictions. Louis de Souza's wife thought that Churchill must have bribed the guards and noted that the consequences would probably fall upon the others left behind. In his memoir Adrian Hofmeyr, a Dutch clergyman prisoner who had supplied Churchill with the slouch hat that enabled him to remain anonymous as he strolled through the streets of Pretoria, wrote that Churchill's escape had unintended consequences by stopping 'the whole machinery of state. It paralysed the officials . . . even the war was forgotten.'

What is far more certain is that Churchill left behind two very angry partners whose likelihood of escaping had been compromised by a self-centred young civilian. Haldane, while publicly only mildly critical of Churchill, nevertheless recorded his bitter dismay that his former friend had actually pleaded with him for only Brockie to accompany him solely because he spoke the native languages. Rather lamely Churchill insisted that he had acted properly and that there had never been an agreement that they would all act in concert.

It was not until March 1900 that Haldane, Brockie and another officer were able to escape by laboriously digging a tunnel that extended under a wall of their compound. Haldane followed the same route across the vast African veld to Witbank, where John Howard once again risked his life and his own freedom in the dangerous business of aiding an escaped prisoner. Like Churchill before him, Haldane was smuggled into Lourenço Marques hidden among bales of wool. However, unlike Churchill, when he arrived in Durban Haldane avoided the press correspondents who wanted to interview him about his escape.

A lesser-known aspect of Churchill's African adventure was the problems faced by the six brave men of the Witbank colliery who smuggled him into Portugese East Africa. The mother of Charles Burnham, the station agent who arranged for his escape inside the wool bales aboard a freight train, called Churchill ungrateful, arrogant, profane and generally unlikeable. He was, she said, 'very tense, very rude, and very abrupt. And I didn't like his manners.'

Whether or not they liked him personally there was never the slightest hesitation in helping a fellow Briton obtain his freedom. John Howard and his colleagues at the colliery might have paid a serious price for aiding Churchill, and they were among the first to come under suspicion. Howard was visited in early 1900 by a Boer commandant and five burghers from Pretoria who intended to arrest him.

Realizing that he was to be taken to the Boer capital for questioning and was almost certain to be jailed, Howard decided he had only two options: kill all six men or bribe them to keep quiet. With both hands in his coat pockets, in which he gripped two revolvers, he convinced them that the war would end badly and that they would be better served by collectively accepting an immediate bribe of fifty pounds, with another two hundred pounds after the war. Materialism trumped obligation, the offer was accepted and a false report was rendered that Howard had vanished.

In 1902 Churchill acknowledged his debt by sending each man an open-faced watch that had his name engraved on the outside and on the inside an inscription that read: 'From Winston S. Churchill, in recognition of timely help afforded him in his escape from Pretoria, during the South African War. Dec. 13, 1899.'

After the war a myth invented by Churchill took root. It was that the Boer commander, General Louis Botha, had personally captured him on 15 November 1899. A Natal native, Botha was the most successful Boer commander of the war, who had masterminded the stunning victory at Spion Kop that led directly to his appointment as commander in chief of the Boer forces. One of the signatories of the 1902 peace treaty with Britain, Botha became prime minister of the Transvaal in 1907, and in 1910 the first president of the new nation of South Africa.

In 1902 Botha and a group of former Boer generals visited London seeking British assistance for their war-torn land. Botha and Churchill met at a private luncheon where Churchill recounted the tale of his capture. According to Churchill, Botha silently listened, then said: 'Don't you recognize me? I was that man. It was I who took you prisoner, I myself.' There was no other witness present. Whether Churchill invented the episode or simply misunderstood Botha's halting English, or whether Botha simply lied to foster better relations, there is clear evidence that it was mythical. It is ludicrous to believe that on the day of the incident, as the commander of a large Boer force, Botha was performing picket duty with the ambushing force. Whether Churchill was actually convinced of the story's truth or simply found it convenient to enhance his reputation remains unresolved. However, as late as 1939 he was still publicly insisting that Botha had captured him, and complaining that the twenty-five-pound reward for his capture had been miserly. What is not in doubt is that in both the armoured-train ambush and his escape from Pretoria, Churchill exhibited an audacity that would forever cement his reputation as a leader and a risk taker.

Questions about Churchill's escape and motives lingered almost to the end of his life. In 1900, when one of the incarcerated officers, also a war correspondent, Lord Rosslyn, published a book critical of his behaviour, Churchill threatened to sue for libel. He also persuaded the publisher, William Blackwood, to remove the unflattering words in later editions of the book. The matter did not end there; in 1912 Churchill, then a powerful cabinet minister, sued *Blackwood's Magazine* for libel when an article appeared that claimed he had violated his parole while imprisoned. He noted in his statement of claim that the Boers had never accepted his offer of parole. To support his case he demanded that Haldane, then a brigadier on the verge of assuming command of an infantry brigade in Yorkshire, testify on his behalf.

The trial in London in May 1912 was uncontested by *Blackwood's*. Despite Churchill's insistence Haldane had no wish to testify either for or against him, and instead offered only to make 'a qualified statement, to the effect that Winston had not realized his escape was unfair to Brockie and himself'. In his diary Haldane recorded that Churchill attempted to browbeat him into testifying and endeavoured to put words of his own choosing into his mouth. Haldane refused, saying only that he would support Churchill's statement that he had behaved correctly and honourably.

What is troubling about this affair is Churchill's use of any means to get his own way, even if it meant bullying one who not only had befriended him but had helped advance his career from the time of their first meeting in 1897. Haldane was a distinguished, self-effacing man of strong character, and too honourable a soldier to engage in a public brawl, though had Churchill pressed the matter of his testifying for him, such a brawl might well have come to pass.

The two versions of the escape will never be reconciled and are as different as the temperaments of the two men: one impulsive and driven to action, the other just as gallant but more prudent. Churchill insisted: 'My conscience is absolutely clear on the whole episode; I acted with perfect comradeship and honour the whole way through . . . We were all fully resolved that we must at all costs get over on the night of the 12th.' Missing from Churchill's somewhat self-righteous argument is any acknowledgment that his split-second decision to act on his own not only put all three men in peril of compromising and exposing the escape but also undermined his own chance of evading capture. The fact that he was successful was pure good fortune.

Haldane's private belief that they were all to have escaped together was as circumspect as his decision never publicly to embarrass his erstwhile friend. Moreover, had he so chosen, Haldane could have publicly attacked Churchill by publishing his diary. Instead he confined his feelings of considerable resentment to his journal, which reads in part:

Had Churchill only possessed the moral courage to admit that, in the excitement of the moment, he saw a chance of escape and could not resist the temptation to take advantage of it, not realizing it would compromise the escape of his companions, all would have been well. A frank admission of that nature, made early after his escape, would have gone far to disarm much criticism as might have followed. I myself would have been the first publicly to do anything in my power to silence the tongues of any who might rail at him or taunt him with 'not having played the game'.

After Churchill had published My Early Life in 1930, Haldane wrote privately to friends to affirm his intention not to publish anything critical. 'I do not wish to harm him and though I have not much faith in him, I admire his undoubted courage, physical and moral, and we can't afford in these days of sloppy statesmen to ignore that quality.' It is doubtful, however, that Haldane's last words on the matter would have bothered Churchill. Haldane had merely joined the legion of critics who would, while admiring him, question his judgment.

*

The Boer War was a literary windfall for Churchill. Upon his return from South Africa, he turned his war experiences into working capital that provided his first real financial independence. A collection of the thirty-eight dispatches he produced for the *Morning Post* was incorporated into two books published in 1900. The first, *The Relief of Lady-smith*, recounted his adventures and was favourably reviewed by the *Spectator*, which declared that his dispatches were far more than merely battle pictures: 'The writer has a political head and sees with a states-man's eye rather than those of a soldier or a mere word-painter.'

Because of his willingness to take controversial stands, Churchill's dispatches during the final months he was in South Africa infuriated Lord Salisbury's Conservative government. On the subject of war in general and the Boer War in particular, his outlook remained Victorian. Over time his views of the Boer War softened, and during the darkest days of 1940, when London was being pounded day and night by the Luftwaffe, he reflected on both the beauty of the African veld and his remembrance of that long-ago time. It was, he said, 'the last enjoyable war', hardly a description he would have dreamed of using in the early 1900s.

In 1930 Churchill claimed that he had generally taken unpopular positions, among them his insistence that the only way to win wars was to fight them 'with might and main till overwhelming victory, and then offering the hand of friendship to the vanquished . . . Never indeed was it more apt than in South Africa . . . I always get into trouble because so few people take this line.' When, on one occasion, he was asked to write the inscription for a monument to be erected in France, he wrote, 'In war, Resolution. In defeat, Defiance. In victory, Magnanimity. In peace, Goodwill.' Churchill's rationale was simple: 'Those who can win a war well can rarely make a good peace, and those who could make a good peace would never have won the war. It would perhaps be pressing the argument too far to suggest that I could do both.' It would take another world war to substantiate this viewpoint.

Another – and perhaps the most important – reason why Churchill took advantage of what he deemed a golden opportunity to escape was his absolute dread of being imprisoned, of having his life regulated by others. In conversations with J. B. Atkins after his escape, his feelings were palpable. In *My Early Life* he entitled the chapter about his captivity 'In Durance Vile'.

In spite of criticism by those who disliked him and disparaged his escape as a clear violation of the so-called Victorian gentleman's code of honour, the act was vintage Churchill. That he would elect to remain in captivity when he had the slightest chance of freedom would have been out of character for a man so driven by action and danger: rules were for others.

Churchill's adventures between 1894 and 1900 only sharpened his ambition to acquire fame. Yet, as he would later write of the prosperous and triumphant period of Queen Victoria's reign, no one then envisaged that a terrible and ruinous peril lay ahead in the new century.

The Boer War marked the real beginning of the renown that would both reward and trouble Churchill for the rest of his life. Nor was it by any means the end of his military adventures or his education. Ahead lay a shining career in politics in which his rise to power would be as spectacular as his fall; where he would advance from outsider to actually wrestling with the problems of war at the highest level as first lord of the Admiralty, and in the front lines of the Great War as an ordinary infantry officer.

14

Star Bright

The best English politicians are necessarily adventurers.   – Shane Leslie

For the next fifteen years Churchill eschewed soldiering for politics, an arena in which his rise to prominence was as rapid as his sudden celebrity as a correspondent and war hero. Yet it was the military Churchill who made possible the political Churchill. His sojourn in South Africa achieved his aim of being not only noticed but also hailed as a national hero. He lectured in England and gave a public speech in St James's Hall in Piccadilly with Lord Wolseley in the chair. His longed-for political career took flight as he ascended from a mere junior parliamentarian to ever increasing positions of power – and controversy. What never changed was Churchill's obsession with work and with advancing himself.

Life was good, and as he rode a wave of public adoration he was the object of endless speculation and gossip. Other changes in his life included the marriage of his mother in July 1900 to a penniless, handsome twenty-five-year-old Scots Guards officer, Captain George Cornwallis-West, considered the 'best-looking man in England'. 'Sporting George', nicknamed for his passion for all things sporting, particularly game hunting and fishing – and his love affairs – put more effort into his social life than any enthusiasm he exhibited for work. A godson of the Prince of Wales, George was described by another officer as 'a good-looking fellow; bit short on brains'. One of Cornwallis-West's proclivities was for older women. Thus it was hardly surprising when he and Jennie began a torrid affair in the summer of 1898 in what might best be described as lust at first sight. The two lovers fuelled endless gossip in the salons of London, and even Jennie's circle of friends, although accustomed to her romantic liaisons, were aghast at their ill-concealed relationship. The marriage was doomed from the start.

Cornwallis-West may have excelled at upper-class pastimes but he was a failure as a businessman and landed in deep debt that his spendthrift wife, mired in her own unpaid bills, was in no position to ease. Although they seemed to have remained in love, Cornwallis-West proved a better adulterer than an entrepreneur, and engaged in affairs with a number of women. He filed for divorce in 1913, and the marriage was dissolved in 1914. On the subject of his new stepfather, a mere sixteen days older than himself, Churchill remained largely silent.

In the autumn of 1900 Churchill took advantage of his newfound stature as a well-known and heroic figure to stand for Parliament again in the general election as a Conservative candidate for a seat in Oldham, and this time he won by slightly more than two hundred votes. Not yet twenty-six years of age, he became one of the youngest MPs, and one of the best-known public figures in Britain. With the exception of the years 1922–4, he remained an MP for the rest of his political life.

Churchill toured the United States and Canada during the winter of 1900 and claimed to have enlarged his bank account by the astonishing sum of ten thousand pounds through a series of lectures about his war experiences. His reputation preceded him; in New York Mark Twain flatteringly introduced him as the 'hero of five wars, author of six books, and future Prime Minister of England'.

Outspokenness was Churchill's mantra, and his entry into politics did nothing to diminish his willingness to criticize whatever he deemed wrong – or to make political and personal enemies in the process. His long-planned and carefully scripted maiden speech in the House of Commons in February 1901 was such an event and at once marked him out as a maverick. The speech was preceded by the fiery oration of an outspoken Welshman named David Lloyd George, leader of the radical wing of the Opposition Liberal Party, who skewered the British policy in South Africa of torture, starvation and the establishment of concentration camps (the term was first used during the Boer War), all tactics instituted by Churchill's enemy, Field Marshal Kitchener. So vitriolic was Lloyd George's speech that the colonial secretary, Joseph Chamberlain, stormed out of the House. Word quickly circulated that young Winston Churchill was about to make his maiden speech, and soon every seat in the chamber and the galleries was filled. Many came merely to observe 'Randolph's boy'.

Into this atmosphere came Churchill who, for the next thirty minutes, speaking from the very same seat once occupied by his famous father, delivered a confident and well-reasoned address that focused on the Boer War and what he believed was Britain's pressing need to end the war honourably by offering both the carrot and the stick. That carrot included a plea for leniency towards the Boers. By his willingness to take a reasoned but unpopular position over treatment of the Boers he served notice that his colleagues could expect to deal with a very uncommon politician. His colleagues also soon took note of the fact that they were dealing with a master of the quick and rapier-like retort.

Churchill firmly believed that his military experience gave him an authoritative advantage when debating military issues that was atypical in a Parliament consisting primarily of politicians whose notions of war and hardship were rather narrow. Indeed, being able to speak from experience had been one of Churchill's considerations in pursuing his military career, and it was now paying off. He deemed it an irreplaceable asset and thenceforth propounded his belief that military men who performed heroically in war should campaign for seats in Parliament.

Churchill made his parliamentary presence felt during the military debate in May 1901. The state of the British military establishment had been his focus since his arrival in Parliament, and quite late in the evening of 13 May, he rose in the jam-packed House to deliver a lengthy speech he had been preparing for six weeks as a response to a controversial reform proposed by the secretary of state for war, William St John Brodrick, that would have created a large standing army – which his critics argued was scarcely more than an overseas expeditionary force in waiting.

History abounds with examples of politicians who have encouraged war without the faintest idea of its consequences. Typically the vast majority have never heard a shot fired in anger or experienced the hardships, fear and anxiety which soldiers are obliged to endure in combat. For Britain the Boer War was the latest example, and when he joined Parliament in 1901 Churchill was one of its few members who understood that war was more than political debates, agendas and a rush to arms. It was perhaps ironic that it took what many regarded as a young upstart to advance the notion that war was too serious a business to be treated with less than full respect for its consequences. Such an occasion was the debate in the House on 13 May 1901, in which Churchill strenuously challenged the proposed government reforms.

His most important message that evening was less about his opposition to the reforms and more about the nature of war itself. 'I have frequently been astonished since I have been in this House', he said, 'to hear with what composure and how glibly Members, and even Ministers, talk of a European war.' Britain, he said, had a military force too large 'to fight savages' but too inadequate to wage a European war. Its true weapon was not the army but the Royal Navy, and its supreme command of the seas.

The speech also presented a disturbing preview of the First World War. A European war, he declared, 'cannot be anything but a cruel, heart-rending struggle, which, if we are ever to enjoy the bitter fruits of victory, must demand, perhaps for several years, the whole manhood of the nation, the entire suspension of peaceful industries, and the concentration to one end of every vital energy in the community . . . a European war can only end in the ruin of the vanquished and the scarcely less fatal dislocation and exhaustion of the conquerors.'

There was, however, another rationale for Churchill's rather unexpected opposition. Logic dictates that having experienced war personally he would have been more supportive. But his antagonism appears to have been a case of the son emulating the father. Lord Randolph had similarly opposed military spending in 1886, and had argued that the Royal Navy was the sole foundation of Britain's security. Although Churchill ultimately won his argument against the Brodrick plan when the Salisbury government backed off in 1901, the reform initiative dragged on for another two years before expiring of inertia. In 1903 Churchill was still attacking the plan with strong arguments for the supremacy of the navy in war. His persistence reflected a fundamentally flawed assumption that Britain would not fight a land war against Germany.

For a future war leader, Churchill was surprisingly unmilitary during his first years in Parliament and appeared to be doing nothing less than picking up the standard of Lord Randolph. It seems that his desire to continue fighting his father's battles trumped his support for the military establishment. In retrospect it is clear that Churchill would not become his own man until he broke free of his perceived burden of carrying out the legacy of his dead father.

His seemingly anti-military stance was part of the Churchill enigma:

he had strongly supported the war, understood its nature far better than most, yet opposed the government's attempts to increase the size of the military. The debate left the Conservatives wondering what sort of young radical had been foisted upon them. Churchill with his acid tongue and haranguing manner easily eclipsed their real political enemy, the Liberal Party opposite.

In 1908, when the new secretary of state for war, Richard Burdon Haldane (a cousin of Churchill's colleague General Aylmer Haldane), proposed reforms designed to strengthen the army, Churchill proposed the exact opposite, arguing in Parliament only for maintaining the army in India and a home force of one hundred thousand to protect against an invasion, and the necessary organizational structure to mobilize for war. Even if it were doubled or reduced by half, he said, 'the existing army would be equally incompetent to meet the threat.'

Churchill's very unpredictability was both an asset and a source of frustration even to his friends. Outspokenness, opinionatedness and persistence: the qualities he had exhibited as a soldier and war correspondent were in full flower in his first years in Parliament. His oratory was all too often violent and confrontational, earning him enemies on both sides of the floor and in high places, since he never hesitated to criticize cabinet ministers. Perhaps it was the arrogance of youth, but nothing at this stage of his life seemed to dissuade or faze him. His positions on issues of the day were unyielding and relentlessly presented. Whether it was tariff reform or a growing interest in social questions, Churchill was never ambiguous. A strong supporter of free trade, which had made the Victorian era so successful, he vehemently denounced proposed fundamental changes in the British economic system. In his opinion it wasn't broken and therefore didn't need fixing.

There was a certain hypocrisy in his cavalier attitude that anyone who rejected his views on a given matter should be automatically marked as an enemy. During those early years in Parliament hardly anyone who mattered escaped his wrath. Chief among his targets was Arthur Balfour, who replaced his uncle Lord Salisbury as prime minister in 1902. When it suited him Churchill mocked and relentlessly criticized Balfour even when he was out of office. Despite being mere backbenchers, he and Lloyd George, each with his own unique style, became the *enfants terribles* of British politics.

From the time of his entry into the House of Commons, Churchill endlessly sought the limelight, attaining it with singular success but at a price. He was annoying, became increasingly unpopular and was just as determined in politics as he had been in the military to make a difference – by any means and regardless of the personal consequences. Sometimes he baited those with whom he disagreed or feuded; at other times he turned on the charm; and occasionally, in private, he cursed them to their faces. The son of Lord Randolph eventually managed greatly to exceed his father's willingness to take and defend unpopular and controversial positions. Moreover, to his detriment, Churchill's great knowledge and silver tongue were too often overshadowed by his obvious opportunism, which generated distrust among other politicians and among the British people.

His towering ambition and monumental ego left him relatively impervious to the opinions of others and once prompted him to quote a line from Milton: 'Better to reign in Hell than serve in Heaven.' His son Randolph would later write, 'Churchill knew it was good tactics to take on the men at the top,' and as Winston himself bluntly expressed it, 'I have always preferred . . . to cut off the heads of the tall poppies.'

His confrontational positions on issues of the day and his attacks on various ministers and establishment figures resulted in his being blackballed by numerous clubs and rendered him unwelcome in many salons. (When he was captured by the Boers some of the smart London clubs 'expressed hope they would keep him'.) His first speech as a minister of state in 1906 was so severely critical of Lord Milner, now in charge of reconstruction in South Africa, that an enraged Lord Castlereagh and other supporters of Milner were 'determined to unhorse Winston in Rotten Row and if possible to horsewhip him on the ground'. They were disappointed when Churchill evaded them.

Consistent with his maverick image Churchill also became the newest member of a group of boisterous, mischievous, youthful, like-minded backbenchers who refused either to bow to convention or to toe their own party line. Nicknamed the 'Hooligans' or 'Hughligans' (after their unofficial leader, Lord Hugh Cecil), this group became a consistent thorn in the sides of both the Salisbury government and Arthur Balfour during his term as prime minister from 1902 to 1905. Among the most outspoken of this rebellious group was Churchill, who took no notice of the accepted tradition that junior parliamentarians were expected to defer to their party leaders, and continued to argue that the reforms of the army proposed by the government would be wholly ineffective.

Cecil, who would be Churchill's best man at his wedding in 1908, later described his friend during this period: 'From the first Churchill was obviously a clever young man. His ability was unmistakable. But in those days I thought him rather superficial, rather sentimental, addicted to the sort of sentiment that hangs on a phrase and is not very profound ... He liked to speak of the British Flag and the Freedom that went under it ... But he grew older and changed ... Pitt matured at 24. Palmerston at 70. Sir Winston is in the Palmerston class. He did not reach his great period until 1940 to 1945.'

Not for the last time would Churchill be out of step with his own party. By 1902 he was already becoming disillusioned with his fellow Tories, a reaction that was probably exacerbated by the fact that he had begun to write his father's biography and was reliving Lord Randolph's trials and justifying his decisions. Moreover it had become obvious to him that he was not destined ever to hold high office as long as he remained in the Conservative Party. In contrast the Liberals exhibited fresh thinking and a vitality wholly lacking among the old-school Tories.

In 1904, in what for most would have been an act of political suicide reminiscent of his father's in 1886, Churchill famously bolted from the Conservatives and crossed the floor of the Commons to become the newest member of the Liberal Party. Whereas arrogance ruined Lord Randolph's political career, his son's insubordination merely placed him in a far better position to move up in the political world. Whether Churchill truly regarded himself as a Tory or a Liberal is unclear; what was beyond doubt was that he was an opportunist – and that he greatly improved his prospects as a Liberal. Although he received a warm welcome from the Opposition benches, his desertion infuriated the Conservatives. While his defection rid them of an unmanageable trouble-maker, it also inspired genuine loathing from party members and the Tory press. It was a dubious accomplishment that in only three years – as one of his party's most junior members – Churchill had managed to become one of the most detested MPs in Parliament, a young man widely regarded as a buccaneer. When he arose to make his first speech as a Liberal, Prime Minister Arthur Balfour and the other Tories left the House in protest.

The price of what many saw as sheer arrogance was delight at his misfortunes – and there were many of these, including ostracism and being blackballed for admission to an exclusive polo club. Churchill's defection also obliged him to seek a parliamentary seat in different constituencies, where in succeeding years he would both win and lose elections. 'When he lost his Manchester Conservative seat the gentlemanly Stock Exchange telegraphed "What is the use of a W.C. without a seat?" '

Throughout his political career Churchill lost a number of elections in various constituencies, only to find another and win anew. At one point Jennie lamented, 'Must everyone hate my Winston?' (In 1910 former President Theodore Roosevelt visited England, where he lectured and received honorary degrees from both Cambridge and Oxford. Although he was wined and dined by politicians, royalty and such luminaries as Kipling and Arthur Conan Doyle, he made it a point to avoid Winston Churchill, whom he deemed a devious self-promoter.)

In January 1906 the Liberals were swept into power with a huge majority. Churchill's decision to change parties paid off immediately, when the new prime minister, Sir Henry Campbell-Bannerman, appointed him under-secretary of state for the colonies, his first government post and one that he held until 1908, when he became a member of the cabinet as president of the Board of Trade.

Churchill's tenure at the Colonial Office heralded the manner in which he would function throughout the remainder of his political career. Chafing at being merely a junior minister, he adopted as his own, every issue that might enhance his reputation, no matter how insignificant or irrelevant, a practice which only intensified the frenzied atmosphere in which he habitually worked. He was a difficult and often obstinate subordinate who sorely tested his secretary of state, but his talents were obvious, as were his independent mind and his willingness to take on any cause, no matter how unpopular. After another harsh attack in Parliament on Lord Milner in 1906, he even managed to incur the wrath of King Edward VII, the first of several British monarchs whom he would infuriate.

One of Churchill's first actions as colonial under-secretary was to appoint a personal secretary, and his choice, an obscure clerk then toiling in the basement of the Colonial Office, Edward Howard Marsh, proved to be a brilliant one. Eddie Marsh became a lifelong friend and confidant who served Churchill for twenty-three years in eight different ministries. A patron of the arts, author and translator of poetry, he was a friend of many of the great and near great of British arts and letters, among them J. M. Barrie, D. H. Lawrence, the composer Ivor Novello, George Bernard Shaw and – most memorably – the poet Rupert Brooke.

Although the two men could not have been more dissimilar in their interests and temperaments, Marsh was the perfect servant for a volatile master like Churchill, who came to rely on him like a brother. In turn Marsh, a man of uncommon dignity and humanity, was a faithful and devoted assistant to his difficult and demanding boss. He often bore the brunt of Churchill's wrath but came to understand that 'having my head bitten off' was temporary, and that soon 'he would be fitting it back on my neck with care and even with ceremony.' Always at Churchill's side, Marsh accompanied him on his numerous trips abroad, including a memorable 1909 tour of the Blenheim battlefield in Bavaria, site of the Duke of Marlborough's great victory over the forces of Louis XIV in 1704. He never forgot the experience, recalling especially 'Winston's explanations . . . so lucid that for a fleeting instant I saw the campaign with the clear eye of History, or at least of Topography'.

Among Churchill's accomplishments during this busy period of his life was the publication in 1906 of his two-volume biography of his father. Although hailed as a masterpiece of political biography, the book yields only the positive side of Lord Randolph and virtually nothing about his relationship with his elder son.

Early in his political career Churchill had been drawn to David Lloyd George, the aggressive, outspoken Liberal Welshman, whose eloquence and intellect were cut from the same rebellious cloth as his own. The two men made a formidable pair, and each became a titanic political power. Commenting on their fundamentally different perspectives, Asquith once said, 'Lloyd George has no principles and Winston no convictions.' Violet Bonham Carter may have put it best when she described Churchill as an intellectual who reasoned with his mind and Lloyd George as having an undisciplined mind, few convictions or abiding principles, and no historical perspectives: 'His mind had no anchor. He lived by instinct and it served him well.'

In 1908, as only these two glib men could, Lloyd George and Churchill joined forces strongly and eloquently to oppose plans by the Royal Navy for the construction of six of the new dreadnought-class battleships. During this period of his political life Churchill remained an unrepentant isolationist, rather self-righteous in his belief that Britain was capable of buying adequate time to raise an army of sufficient size to fight a land battle under the protective wing of the Royal Navy, which would keep the British Isles safe from foreign invasion.

Of the many battles Churchill fought during his life, his struggle with what he called his 'black dog' was perhaps the most troubling. It may well be traceable to his childhood, but given what we now know about this condition, it is likely to have been genetic in origin. Churchill's 'black dog' appears to have been a mild form of depression that struck at various times during his life and that he constantly sought to overcome. In his later years he spoke candidly about the condition with his personal physician, Sir Charles Wilson (later Lord Moran). In December 1943 Wilson noted: 'Winston has never been at all like other people. No Churchill is. Five out of the last seven Dukes of Marlborough suffered from melancholia. And Winston himself . . . in his early days was afflicted by fits of depression that might last for months . . . He dreaded these bouts and instinctively kept away from anyone or anything that seemed to bring them on.'

His early years in Parliament were the worst in this respect. In August 1944 he reflected on this period of his life: 'For two or three years the light faded out of the picture. I did my work. I sat in the House of Commons, but black depression settled on me. It helped me to talk to [his wife] Clemmie about it. I don't like standing near the edge of a platform when an express train is passing through. I like to stand right back and if possible to get a pillar between me and the train. I don't like to stand by the side of a ship and look down in the water. A few drops of desperation. And yet I don't want to go out of the world at all in such moments.'

There was a form of irrationality about Churchill that both defined and exacerbated his larger-than-life personality. It was this tendency at times to act with both haste and certainty that earned him great success but on other occasions got him into trouble. Violet Asquith, who probably understood Churchill better than anyone else, instinctively perceived that he 'belonged to a different species. It was impossible to measure him against others. He demanded a yardstick all his own. He was compounded of imponderables – heady impulses, blind spots about the obvious – and with them flashes of divination which at our first meeting I had recognized as the light of genius.'

Churchill had been attracted to but never seemed to have genuinely pursued relationships with women other than Pamela Plowden. His interest in (and perhaps love for) some of the great beauties of the time never led to marriage. By the time he entered his thirties he began to have more serious thoughts about the need for a wife. He proposed to two beautiful women, one of whom was an heiress named Muriel Wilson. Both rejected him. He was also smitten with the actress Ethel Barrymore, whose close friend was the author Richard Harding Davis. After learning that Churchill hoped to marry her, Davis implored the actress not to accept; Churchill, he said, 'was a cad'. Although she reciprocated Winston's esteem and would remain a good friend, Ethel Barrymore could not envisage marriage to a politician, particularly such a high-profile, and high-maintenance, individual as Winston Churchill, whom she gently rebuffed.

Others were less gentle. As Shane Leslie wrote, 'Some repulsed him rather rudely like one who told him that she disliked both his politics and his wispy moustache,' to which he shot back that 'she need not worry herself as she was not likely to contact either!' (Easily Churchill's most famous put-down was his riposte at a dinner party to a lifelong critic, the American socialite and member of Parliament Nancy Astor, who is credited with telling him that if she were his wife she would poison his coffee; he supposedly retorted, 'And if I were your husband, madam, I would drink it.')

As with Pamela Plowden, his obsession with succeeding and his colossal ego ensured that women would always play a secondary role in his life. Although he hadn't the slightest inkling of it at the time, Churchill's life changed for ever when he was introduced to the twenty-three-year-old Clementine Hozier in the summer of 1904. Clementine was the eldest surviving daughter of estranged parents: Sir Henry Montagu Hozier, a respected and decorated former colonel of the Dragoon Guards, and Lady Blanche Hozier, the daughter of a Scottish laird. Their first meeting was disastrous and left Clementine decidedly unimpressed. Churchill just stood and stared at her: 'He never uttered one word and was very gauche – he never asked me for a dance, he never asked me to have supper with him. I had of course heard a great deal about him – nothing but ill.' If there was even the tiniest spark between Winston Churchill and Clementine Hozier, it clearly fizzled out during their first meeting. Four years passed before they met again, at another dinner party, in March 1908. Although he doted on Clementine that evening, their conversation was, as usual, mainly about him.

Nor was Clementine alone in her disdain; the first time Churchill met Violet Asquith she found her dinner companion glum and withdrawn. When he learned that she was only nineteen, he went into his familiar lament about an early death. 'And I am thirty-two already ... Curse ruthless time! Curse our mortality! How cruelly short is the allotted span for all we must cram into it!' Then, in words that shocked the young woman, he said, 'We are all worms. But I do believe that I am a glowworm.'

Romance finally blossomed in 1908. On 11 August, the day he decided to propose to Clementine, Winston, as was his custom, arose late and had to be reminded by Sunny that if he intended to propose to her that day he'd better get a move on because she was due to return to London shortly. It was a predictable pattern of behaviour: Clementine was invariably punctual while Winston was habitually late. For one of the few times in his life he hurriedly dressed and that afternoon he proposed marriage in Blenheim's Temple of Diana while rain fell outside. Clementine accepted.

Their marriage on 12 September 1908 tells us a great deal about his priorities. As his youngest daughter Mary Soames has said: 'Winston was a loving husband, and he always wanted Clementine to "be there"; but his self-centredness, combined with his total commitment to politics, did not make him a very companionable one.' Nevertheless in its own curious, almost illogical way the marriage worked. Clementine left Winston to his career, and though his personal and political actions sometimes drove her to near distraction, they never affected their lifelong bond, in which 'she sustained him by her love and her belief in his destiny.' Edward Marsh, who became a close friend of hers, described Clementine as a 'most delightful compound of flagrant worldliness and eternal childhood, in thrall to fashion and luxury (life didn't begin for her on the basis of less than forty pairs of shoes)' and as a woman of 'steadfast and pugnacious courage'.

It was typical of Churchill that on the day of his marriage he slipped away from his own wedding reception for a political discussion with Lloyd George. Nor was their European honeymoon free of work. Both at Blenheim, where the honeymoon commenced, and later in Venice, Churchill left Clementine alone while he worked on a book called *My African Journey*, based on a five-month trip the previous year to Europe, the Mediterranean and Africa.

Given their utterly divergent patterns of life, their marriage was hardly conventional. They slept in separate bedrooms and led their lives by entirely different schedules: Winston, the late riser, preferred break-fasting by himself in bed and invariably retired in the early hours of the morning, while Clementine was the exact opposite. (One of the many unusual habits she had to adapt to was her new husband's peculiar choice of pale-pink silk underwear.)

Although never entirely reconciled to Winston's customary indiffer-ence to her, she understood and accepted that it was a trait that came with the man she had married. Yet Clementine was no wallflower but rather a strong-willed woman with ideas and opinions that were often at odds with those of her mercurial husband. They clashed, particularly when Winston behaved thoughtlessly. One of his most enduring bad habits was his practice of acting without consulting her, as when he bought Chartwell in 1922 when they could ill afford it. Another was bringing home dinner guests with little or no notice and expecting Clementine like a genie instantly to produce suppers for them. Even more vexing, he used these occasions to conduct business or to network with influential men, while excluding her.

Over the years many of his friends annoyed and dismayed her, not only for their political views but also for their personalities. Among those for whom she had little or no use were the three Bs: Brendan Bracken, Lord Beaverbrook (the Canadian businessman, newspaper tycoon and Conservative MP William Maxwell Aitken) and the Earl of Birkenhead the Liberal MP F. E. Smith. Although she was long suffering over Winston's friends, there were limits to her largesse. Sometimes a guest made the mistake, rarely repeated, of crossing her.

Winston, however, had no intention of altering his habits to accom-modate a wife, and it took a great deal of forbearance from the new Mrs Churchill to make their marriage work so well. One of his worst habits was that he tended to talk *at* rather than *to* others, a practice that would madden his Second World War chiefs of staff during endless nights of non-stop monologues.

Although Violet Asquith and Clementine Churchill became friends, during the early years of her marriage Clementine was jealous of Violet's close relationship with her husband and viewed her as a threat. As Violet's memoir of Churchill makes clear, he often confided his innermost thoughts to her, feelings and confidences that he may not have shared with Clementine.

Regardless of whom he married, Winston was determined to have his way, to live his life according to his own timetable of duties, likes and aversions. While she was equally strong willed, Clementine recognized early in their marriage that the key to its success lay in deferring to her husband. There were, of course, limits and exceptions to what she put up with from her often thoughtless and demanding spouse. When provoked or talked down to, she would react with a sudden fury that gave Winston pause. Their differences never interfered with their need and love for each other. Churchill's political and military career separated them for considerable periods that would have destroyed less stable marriages. Over the years they wrote hundreds of letters to each other that form a major part of the story of their marriage.

Clementine found that she could not compete effectively with Winston in oral argument and often resorted to writing him notes about issues or other things that were bothering her, even when they were together in the same house or the same room. Like most couples, they fought, sometimes vehemently. When under fire from Clementine, Winston became obstinate and she became exasperated and 'once she actually shied a dish of spinach at him: it missed, but left a tell-tale mark on the wall ... but rarely did the sun go down on their anger. Throughout their long exchange there are some touching Winston notes – probably slipped under her bedroom door – expressing contrition and love, and signed with penitent pigs or pugs.'

In July 1909 Clementine gave birth to Diana, their first child; over the years four more followed: Randolph (1911), Sarah (1914), Marigold (1918) and Mary (1922). At the end of *My Early Life* Churchill summed up his marriage to Clementine in a single pithy sentence, declaring that in 1908 'I married and lived happily ever after.'

15
The Odd Couple

No two men had ever agreed and disagreed more often and more passionately.
                                                      – Violet Bonham Carter

In less than a decade after his adventures in South Africa, Churchill had moved up in the political world and was gradually attaining his ultimate goal of holding high office. Yet despite being in his political element, he could never entirely divorce himself from military life. It invaded his thoughts and actions, ranging from attendance at German, French and British military manoeuvres in order to soak up advances in the military arts and information on the readiness of their armies, to dreams of high command. During his tenure at the Board of Trade from 1908 to 1910, he shocked various friends and colleagues by daring to compare his career to that of Napoleon. And, as one Labour politician said of him, 'Churchill was, and always has remained, a soldier in mufti. He possesses inborn militaristic qualities, and is intensely proud of his descent from Marlborough.' Although his life's ambition was to become a successful politician, soldiering was still in his blood. He never lost his keen interest in war and the armed services, and could never quite come to terms with the fact that he was no longer a soldier.

Germany's growing militarism attracted his attention in the summer of 1906. In August, he wangled an invitation from Kaiser Wilhelm II (King Edward VII's nephew) to attend the annual German military manoeuvres held at Breslau (now Wroclaw), Silesia, as his personal guest. Already on holiday in the French resort of Deauville to play polo and lounge on the yacht of a friend, Churchill accepted with alacrity. He also received an unambiguous admonition from the prime minister Campbell-Bannerman. The king, he wrote, 'asked me to warn you against being too communicative and frank with his nephew', and stressed that he should, 'as the penny-liners say, "Exercise a wise discretion."' This none-too-subtle warning from his monarch to behave himself was undoubtedly the result of Churchill's penchant for pugnacity and candid utterances both in Parliament and in print, the most recent of which had been his withering attack on Lord Milner.

'There is a massive simplicity & force about the German military arrangements which grows upon the observer,' he wrote from Vienna to the colonial secretary, Lord Elgin, adding, 'Although I do not think they have appreciated the terrible power of the weapons they hold & modern fire conditions, and have in that & in minor respects much to learn from our army, yet numbers, quality, discipline & organisation are four good roads to victory.' Nor did Churchill care for either the German language ('beastly') or the Germans whom he met.

The kaiser appeared attired in his finest military uniform, astride a 'magnificent horse at the head of a squadron of cuirassiers . . . surrounded by Kings and Princes while his legions defiled before him in what seemed to be an endless procession'. Then came the dazzling 'spectacle of German military and Imperial splendour so brilliantly displayed to foreign eyes', but the fifty thousand troops, 'avalanches of field guns' and 'squadrons of motor cars' that passed in review before the kaiser for more than five hours represented, Churchill recorded, 'only a twentieth of the armed strength of the regular German Army before mobilization'.

The manoeuvres were great theatre, carefully choreographed and pretentious in the extreme, involving thousands of participants densely packed into formations that reminded Churchill of the Dervish masses at Omdurman waiting for slaughter. Their pageantry aside – most of it was to indulge the kaiser and his make-believe leadership of his army – Churchill correctly found them of questionable military value. He noted the disgust exhibited by some of the German officers at the pretence that the manoeuvres actually mattered and at the sight of a German princess in full military uniform riding at the head of one regiment in a blatant example of royal privilege. He was also astonished that the Germans were employing the same tactics he had seen eight years earlier at Omdurman, where massed infantry and cavalry had charged headlong into the teeth of an enemy force. 'We had said to ourselves after Omdurman, "This is the end of these sorts of spectacle. Never will there be such fools in the world again."'

Churchill took away from this event an appreciation the size of the massive German army compared with that of 'our tiny British Army, in which the parade of a single division and a brigade of Cavalry at Aldershot was a notable event.' Back in London he wrote to thank the kaiser for his hospitality and to remark on the 'magnificent & formidable army whose operations I was enabled by Your Majesty's kindness to study so pleasantly'. To his aunt Leonie he acknowledged that he was 'very thankful there is a sea between that army and England'. In 1916 Leonie's son Shane Leslie would write: 'Some have since seen reason to give thanks that he [Churchill] had the supervision of that sea.'

While the sheer size of the German army was unsettling, Churchill would have been truly alarmed had he known that Germany had by this time accepted the premise that it would one day fight a two-front war against Russia and France, and that the chief of the German general staff, Count Alfred von Schlieffen, was already well advanced in drawing up a master plan for a lightning invasion of France. The plan that evolved from the fertile mind of this brilliant military strategist would have immense implications for Winston Churchill, not only in the First World War but also in the ensuing world war and in the destiny of Britain in 1940.

Churchill now held a major's commission in the Territorial Army and commanded a squadron of cavalry in the Queen's Own Oxfordshire Hussars. The highlight of each year was the annual week-long summer camp, often held in the parkland of Blenheim, which perhaps explains why he chose a commission in this regiment. Clementine was not entirely persuaded that the opportunity for her husband to indulge in his passion for gambling (of which she thoroughly disapproved but never cured him) and for drinking with the 'boys' were not stronger reasons than participation in the military exercises he attended in May 1909. He described for her the climactic event, the field day in which the eight yeomanry regiments participated. It was, he said, 'amusing', with 'lots of soldiers & pseudo soldiers galloping about'. Churchill's return to summer-soldier status inspired thoughts of a command of his own. Junior-grade officers typically aspire to command of a company, a battalion or possibly a regiment. Not Churchill: 'Do you know I would greatly like to have some practice in the handling of large forces,' he wrote to Clementine. 'I have much confidence in my judgment on things, when I see clearly, but on nothing do I seem to *feel* the truth more than in tactical combinations. It is a vain and foolish thing to say – but *you* will not laugh at it. I am sure I have the root of the matter in me – and never I fear in this state of existence will it have a chance of flowering – in bright red blossom.'

What Churchill did not acknowledge was that the annual exercises of his regiment of cavalry were of the same questionable value as those he had witnessed three years earlier at Breslau. The advent of massed trench warfare five years later would make the role of the cavalry obsolete. Yet old traditions die hard, particularly one as famously romantic as horsemen attired in colourful uniforms charging with lances poised and sabres gleaming. By 1914 the age of the cavalry had passed, but the few officers who actually dared to say so were regarded as heretics. Churchill was not at the point where he would acknowledge that the cavalry he cherished had no future in twentieth-century warfare. Instead he continued to revel in the opportunity to mix soldiering with social pleasures.

Later that summer Churchill returned to Germany again to view the annual manoeuvres, again at the personal invitation of the kaiser. They were held in Franconia (in and around Würzburg), and though he found them somewhat boring in their initial stages, as they progressed they proved far more disturbing than what he had witnessed three years earlier. Pomp and impressive ceremony had characterized the 1906 exercises, but 'the manoeuvres at Wurzburg', he wrote,

showed a great change in German military tactics. A remarkable stride had been made in modernizing their Infantry formations and adapting them to actual war conditions. The absurdities of the Silesian manoeuvres were not repeated. The dense masses were rarely, if ever, seen. The Artillery was not ranged in long lines, but dotted about wherever conveniences of the ground suggested. The whole extent of the battlefield was far greater. The Cavalry were hardly at all in evidence, and then only on distant flanks. The Infantry advanced in successive skirmish lines, and machine-guns everywhere had begun to be a feature. Although these formations were still to British eyes much too dense for modern fire, they nevertheless constituted an enormous advance upon 1906.

In a revealing letter to Clementine, he wrote: 'This army is a terrible engine. It marches sometimes 35 miles a day. It is in number as the sands of the sea – & with all the modern conveniences. There is a complete divorce between the two sides of German life – the imperialists and the Socialists. Nothing unites them. They are two different nations. With us there are so many shades. Here it is all black & white (the Prussian colours). I think another 50 years will see a wiser & gentler world.' Not even Winston Churchill could have predicted that the two most devastating wars in history would take place in those years, or that our world in the twenty-first century would remain dogged by war and international terrorism. 'How easily men could make things much better than they are – if only all tried together!' he mused with uncharacteristic mellowness.

As for war itself, he was both captivated and repulsed by it. 'Much as war attracts and fascinates my mind with its tremendous situations, I feel more deeply every year – & can measure the feeling here in the midst of arms – what vile & wicked folly & barbarism it all is.'

The manoeuvres ended 'with a tremendous cannonade in a fog. I had only two minutes speech with the Emperor – just to say goodbye & thank him for letting me come.' Nevertheless he was in the kaiser's company long enough for a photograph of the two men to be taken; it depicts Churchill in full military uniform, strolling with the kaiser as they engage in conversation.

Churchill also made a point of attending the annual manoeuvres of the British army, and in 1910 he appeared in full military dress with Clementine at the Territorial Army manoeuvres held at Aldershot. However, the event smacked more of a social outing than of serious military business.

Churchill's education in naval warfare began purely by chance in the spring of 1907, when he was introduced while on a holiday in Biarritz to the first sea lord, Admiral Sir John Arbuthnot 'Jackie' Fisher. An innovator and reformer as well as a colourful and controversial character, Fisher is remembered as the father of the modern Royal Navy; and the 'Fisher era', the period from October 1904 to January 1910, when he utterly dominated the navy, was like no other in its history. During his fifty-five years of naval service, Fisher rose from young midshipman in the age of the sailing ship to architect of the dreadnought that ushered in a new era of naval warfare.

When he had been commander in chief of the Mediterranean fleet from 1899 to 1902, Fisher's aim was not only to instil a sense of urgency in his charges but to recognize and accept innovations and new technology in what had become a complacent military power. 'On the British Navy rests the British Empire,' he declared. After an officer had performed badly in a naval exercise, Fisher told him that had his failure occurred at a time of war, 'I would have had you shot.' When he was first sea lord his touchstone was 'We must be ruthless, relentless and remorseless!' He preached the notion that war was not for the faint of heart. 'Moderation in war is imbecility,' he once said. It was music to Churchill's ears.

Fisher understood what the traditionalist mandarins of the navy failed to recognize, namely that with the German naval build-up it was crucial for the Royal Navy not only to be capable of guaranteeing Britain's security and competing on an equal footing with the new class of German warships, but also to manage to do so without crippling the annual budget in the process. As then constituted the Royal Navy was not up to the challenge, hence the introduction of armoured, heavily gunned battle cruisers capable of taking on and defeating any enemy naval force. Fisher's brainchild, the new class of battleship first appeared with the launching of HMS *Dreadnought* – after which it was named – in 1906. With a main armament that hurled 850-pound shells from its ten 12-inch guns, the dreadnought was the first in a series of powerful new warships that would heat up the naval race between Britain and Germany. Under Fisher's auspices, between 1906 and 1909 the Royal Navy built ten of these new battleships and six less heavily armoured but faster battle cruisers.

The naval historian Arthur Marder aptly describes Fisher during his tenure as first sea lord as 'a tornado of energy, enthusiasm and persuasive power . . . He fell on the old regime with a devastating fury . . . There was no rest for anyone connected with the Service. "It was as though a thousand brooms were at work clearing away the cobwebs." ' Fisher tackled reform of not only the ships in which the navy fought but the means by which it did so, consistent with advances in technology. The Fisher reforms helped pave the way for Churchill, who, when he became first lord of the Admiralty, made it his task to carry them out fully, while somehow healing the rifts that had split the naval service. (Until 1964 the Royal Navy was administered by a Board of Admiralty consisting of admirals, called naval lords or sea lords. From 1806 the president of the board was always a civilian political appointee and a member of the cabinet called the first lord of the Admiralty. The first sea lord was the senior naval lord and the professional head of the Royal Navy, Britain's highest naval post. The second sea lord was the chief of naval personnel; the third sea lord was the comptroller of the navy; the fourth sea lord was in charge of logistics; and in the twentieth century the fifth sea lord was chief of the naval air services.)

A terrifying figure who disdained paperwork and would often walk the halls of the Admiralty demanding that someone give him work to do, Fisher saw what others simply ignored, such as the threat posed by the submarine and its deadly torpedo that could sink the largest fighting ship in the fleet in minutes. First developed in the 1880s by an Irish nationalist named John Philip Holland, the new submersible was now capable of changing the entire nature of naval warfare. Some failed to realize this – Sir Arthur Wilson, Fisher's successor as first sea lord, foolishly dismissed it as 'underhanded, unfair, and damned un-English'. Only a few, like Fisher, understood its gravity and pressed to add the submarine as a modern weapon of the Royal Navy and give Britain the lead in the race for domination of the seas.

Fisher's term as first sea lord was explosively controversial, and centred on his bitter rivalry with Admiral Lord Charles Beresford, a Tory MP and a wealthy landed Irishman with English ancestors and prominent royal connections (and an elder brother of Lord William Beresford), who juggled successful careers in Parliament and the Royal Navy. As one of the navy's most famous and admired sailors, Beresford represented in the public mind everything the service stood for. 'To most Britons, he was John Bull the Sailor,' the everyman, and an esteemed, reassuring symbol that 'England was safe as long as Lord Charles and the navy were on guard.'

A hero celebrated for his bravery in command of a gunboat during the bombardment of Alexandria in July 1882, Beresford was a man of towering ambition whose intrigues and self-promotion paid handsome dividends in advancing both his careers. As the leading traditionalist, he was the most visible example of why the navy needed change. Not only did he represent the substantial naval faction that espoused nepotism and the status quo and vigorously opposed all attempts by Fisher to modernize the navy, but by 1903, as the commander in chief of the prestigious Channel fleet, he was also one of the navy's most influential men.

Relations between Fisher and Beresford were rancorous: Fisher referred to Beresford as a 'gasbag' and Beresford returned the ridicule by calling Fisher 'our dangerous lunatic', and by using his considerable influence, both as a senior admiral and as a politician, to undermine him at every opportunity. The essence of their feud lay in Fisher's support for modernization and his battles with the traditionalists who argued that 'wars were not won by material factors, but solely by the blood and guts of the British sailor.' Beresford aspired to become first lord of the Admiralty should the Conservatives return to office; however, his ambition was thwarted when the Liberals easily won the general election of December 1910. Although Churchill could not know it at the time, the Fisher–Beresford schism in the Royal Navy would make his task when he became first lord of the Admiralty all the more difficult.

When Churchill and Fisher first met in 1907 they made an incongruous pair: the young, ambitious politician and the quirky, brilliant and outspoken admiral more than twice his age. Invariably their discussions turned to naval affairs, and Churchill, with his usual interest in all things military, absorbed the knowledge his new friend willingly imparted, listening hour after hour as Fisher spun tales about the Royal Navy. Churchill became more captivated by Fisher than perhaps anyone else he had ever befriended. One of Fisher's biographers describes their remarkable relationship in this way: ' "Fell in love with Winston Churchill," wrote Jack Fisher when they first met at Biarritz in 1907. "You are the only man in the world I really love," Churchill told Fisher, at least by Jack's account. Indeed they sometimes seemed, for all the differences in their ages, like a couple of lovers. Edward VII called them "the chatterers", so fond were they of closeting themselves away in lively talk . . . They were, as Violet Asquith saw, "sparks from the same fire".'

During those two weeks in Biarritz Churchill received a primer on the Royal Navy: 'He told me wonderful stories . . . all about Dreadnoughts, all about submarines, all about the new big guns and splendid Admirals and foolish miserable ones, and Nelson and the Bible . . . I remembered it all. I reflected on it often.'

Churchill and Fisher shared very similar characteristics. Fisher's incredible drive, dominance and zeal to revamp the navy were a mirror image of Churchill's. Both men worked extraordinarily long hours and would stop at nothing to bend others to their will. Arthur Marder's description of Fisher cited above might also have been applied to

Churchill. Fisher worked so hard that the king took the unusual step of ordering him not to work on Sunday – a royal decree that Fisher simply ignored. Both were outspoken to a fault and refused to suffer fools. They differed only in Fisher's contempt for politicians, which Churchill managed – most of the time – to overcome in the admiral's estimation until their bitter feud in 1915. And, as Violet Bonham Carter said, 'No two men had ever agreed and disagreed more often and more passionately.'

Churchill also learned just how ruthless Fisher could be when he spoke freely of his beliefs, his feuds, his numerous animosities and his intention to ruin the careers of those who opposed his policies. He branded some 'traitors' and railed that 'their wives should be widows, their children fatherless, their homes a dunghill.' It was therefore hardly surprising that he was one of the most controversial first sea lords in the history of the Royal Navy. Given that they were two of the most strong-minded men in British public life, the Fisher–Churchill relationship would inevitably prove to be as exhilarating as it was explosive.

Although the pair had long since fallen out when Churchill wrote his six-volume history of the First World War, *The World Crisis*, he nevertheless paid tribute to Fisher's accomplishments. 'He gave the Navy the kind of shock which the British Army received at the time of the South African War. After a long period of serene and unchallenged complacency, the mutter of distant thunder could be heard. It was Fisher who hoisted the storm-signal and beat all hands to quarters ... He shook them and beat them and cajoled them out of slumber into intense activity.' Fisher was deeply alarmed by Germany's naval build-up and on several occasions broached the subject of launching a preventive war, only to be strongly rebuffed by both the king and the prime minister.

In April 1908 Herbert Asquith became prime minister and, in forming his cabinet, is alleged to have invited Churchill to join his government as first lord of the Admiralty. Although it is not certain that Asquith actually offered this important post to such an inexperienced young man, he might have done. Although Randolph Churchill makes no mention of an offer of the Admiralty in the official biography of his father, Asquith's daughter is unequivocal in asserting that 'my father, divining his real vocation, offered him the Admiralty ... and ... he refused it.' What is not in doubt is that in the weeks leading up to his appointment as prime minister, Asquith had mentioned the post to Churchill. The two men met in early March, and Churchill wrote to Asquith on the 14th of that month to acknowledge their conversation, adding, 'You also mentioned the Admiralty to me.' It was, he said, 'a glittering post in the Ministry. If however I were given my choice between the Admiralty & the Colonial Office, I should feel bound to stand by my own work here upon purely public grounds.' In the end Asquith offered Churchill neither post but instead invited him to head the Board of Trade, a position he intended to elevate to cabinet status in his new administration. Churchill immediately accepted.

According to Violet Asquith, when Churchill informed Fisher that he had turned down the Admiralty, Fisher 'exploded and overwhelmed him with reproaches', contending that together they would have done great things: 'What a heaven-sent opportunity he had thrown away!' Fisher's fiery objections notwithstanding, Churchill gave every indication that he was entirely focused on home-front politics. 'He saw himself as a social reformer of the most radical kind, and for this role the Board of Trade offered ample scope.' In any event, even if Churchill had changed his mind, it was too late; the Admiralty had already gone to Reginald McKenna. The truth was that in 1908 Churchill was not yet ready to assume such an important post. A formal collaboration between Fisher and Churchill would have to wait until 1914.

In 1907 three nations united to create a military defence accord called the Triple Entente. Great Britain, Russia and France were more concerned about defending against German expansionism than they were about past political and territorial issues with one another. Because this new alliance in effect surrounded Germany, there was deep concern in Berlin that led to even more distrust. In 1908 the *Daily Telegraph* published an interview with the kaiser in which he was highly critical of Britain and cast doubt on the sincerity of Anglo-German relations. The British press, he said, misunderstood German intentions and his offers of friendship. 'You English are mad, mad as March hares. What on earth has come over you that you should harbour such suspicions against us, suspicions so unworthy of a great nation.' He also criticized the naval race, denying that the German navy was doing anything more than protecting its international trade routes. Thus by 1908 the kaiser's abiding paranoia over Britain, and his untimely meddling in German foreign policy, combined with the Austrian annexation of Bosnia and Herzegovina, part of the Turkish Empire, left the Great Powers even more wary of one another. The result was further turmoil and an ever tightening web of mistrust that now involved the crumbling Ottoman Empire.

Despite this period of uncertainty in Europe, Churchill and Fisher clashed again in 1909 when Churchill and Lloyd George vigorously opposed the naval estimates presented to Parliament by Reginald McKenna which envisaged the construction of new dreadnoughts. Because of the enormous cost of the Boer War, Churchill had come to the conclusion that the cost of maintaining the empire had to be scaled back; that meant cutting the military budgets, particularly that of the navy. In fact his position was ambivalent and contradictory: he had become isolationist, relying on the might of the Royal Navy to guard Britain's shores and its interests, but parsimonious over naval funding, unconvinced of the German naval threat or by Fisher's insistence that the Royal Navy have a 6-to-4 ratio of battleships to less heavily armoured battle cruisers.

Fisher had raised the stakes by increasing the size of the main armament of the battle cruiser from 12 to 13.5 inches, thus creating the capability to fire at even more distant targets with a 1,250-pound shell. Fisher wanted a total of twelve battle cruisers built, of which four were either completed or nearing completion. Churchill circulated a detailed paper to the cabinet, complete with tables comparing German and British naval strengths and expenditures. When Reginald McKenna rebutted Churchill's memo, he produced another, rebutting the rebuttal. It was monumental chutzpah even by Churchill's standards, on a matter that was not even related to his official duties. The controversy became very public and very vocal, with demands of 'We want eight and we won't wait.' After considerable debate within the Asquith government, Fisher won the war of the battle cruisers, over the opposition of Churchill and Lloyd George. As Churchill facetiously noted: 'The Admiralty had demanded six ships; the economists offered four; and we finally compromised on eight.' It would be several more years before Churchill grasped the error of his ways.

He later maintained that the dispute centred on what he believed was an exaggeration by the Admiralty of the threat posed by the German naval building programme – which by 1912 McKenna and Fisher adamantly believed would leave the Royal Navy in a bind. Although the 1912 forecast proved premature, as soon as he was in McKenna's shoes as first lord Churchill freely admitted that he had been wrong and welcomed the additional warships 'with open arms'.

Fisher, however, had other, more serious internal problems within the Admiralty, where there was strenuous opposition to his emphasis on the construction of battle cruisers and his plan to replace the battleship with the battle cruiser as the navy's primary weapon. The dissension within the Admiralty – and Beresford's sponsorship of a public inquiry into his performance as first sea lord – ultimately led to Fisher's downfall. Although he was exonerated, Fisher felt that the government's report was halfhearted, and in January 1910 he resigned as first sea lord and retired from the Royal Navy. His status as Baron Fisher of Kilverstone became that of a naval elder statesman who emerged from his self-imposed exile to fire occasional derogatory broadsides at his friend Churchill.

The rift between the two men was relatively short lived, and in March 1910 Fisher initiated a fresh and friendly dialogue but nevertheless could not help reprimanding Churchill with the observation that he and the Liberal Party had made 'such an awful hash' of the current annual budget. 'I hope I am not kicking your shins! But I do detest cowardice whatever party it is!' Pleased that their falling out was repaired, Churchill admitted that he 'deeply regretted [ever] since that I did not press for the Admiralty in 1908. I think it would have been easily possible for me to obtain it. I believe it would have been better for us all.'

In February 1910 Asquith appointed Churchill home secretary. Churchill maintained a high profile, and his naturally combative nature asserted itself in his new role. He routinely bombarded Asquith with lengthy memos setting out his views on various subjects, and routinely spoke volubly and with characteristic forcefulness in cabinet meetings, leading the prime minister once to observe tartly, 'Winston thinks with his mouth.'

All government business seemed fodder for Churchill, and in his new post he remained a lightning rod for controversy. The women's suffrage movement was in full cry, and Churchill basically dodged the issue by publicly speaking in favour of the principle of a woman's right to vote though declining to pledge his support of specific legislation to effect it.

The suffragettes disrupted the general election campaign of 1910 and made it their business to voice their feelings publicly about Churchill, whenever possible interrupting gatherings where he spoke; one took such umbrage that she attacked him with a dog whip in Bristol.

Whether it was putting down labour unrest by miners or dock or railway workers, Churchill quickly earned a reputation as a hard-nosed politician willing, as always, to do the unpopular thing, with predictable results for his reputation. His lasting memories of his incarceration by the Boers led him to take a compassionate interest in social reform of the British penal system. However, his interest in reform went too far; in December 1910 he proposed the forced sterilization of the feeble-minded on the absurd grounds that their reproduction threatened to taint the British race – a bizarre idea that in the view of a later commentator 'would have been better suited to the Germany of the Third Reich than to the England of George V'. Fortunately Asquith had the good sense to ignore this outlandish scheme, whose most troubling aspect was that Churchill 'could defend a sound or an unsound idea with equal persuasiveness'.

In conjunction with Lloyd George, Churchill continued to push for changes in the Royal Navy. As he put it, 'A resolute effort must be made to curb Naval expenditure ... It is an ugly and thankless job. Still I think I could do it.' There was no challenge that Churchill did not feel capable of taking on and conquering, but the post of first lord of the Admiralty would remain out of his reach until the autumn of 1911, when he would be handed one of the most challenging undertakings of his political career.

16

'Alarm Bells Throughout Europe'

I could not think of anything else but the peril of war.

– Churchill, summer 1911

The death of Queen Victoria in January 1901 after sixty-three years on the throne could hardly fail to mark the end of an era, for the rest of Europe almost as much as for Britain. Yet as the new century got under way there were few indications that it would turn horrific thirteen years later. And while there were small, troubling wars like the one in South Africa, it was a time of relative peace, and by all indications it seemed that the people of Europe were at a zenith of achievement in science, technology, industry and wealth. If anything the new century seemed to promise even greater ones.

The last decade of the nineteenth century and the early years of the twentieth saw the creation of a series of alliances among the Great Powers of Europe that were to ignite the most catastrophic war the world had ever known. In the late nineteenth century the balance of power in Europe had been kept relatively stable, owing largely to the genius and intrigues of the German chancellor Otto von Bismarck, who prevented Germany's arch-enemy France from becoming a threat. France had neither forgotten nor forgiven the loss of its most recent war with Germany in 1870–71, which had cost it Alsace-Lorraine and resulted in the creation of a powerful and militaristic Second German Reich presided over by the Prussian 'Iron Chancellor'. Bismarck used the new German Empire's power shrewdly to create and maintain a delicate balance of power that kept its principal enemies, France and Russia, at bay and Europe at peace through the application of *Realpolitik*. To that end he created the Triple Alliance – Germany, Austria and Italy – in 1882, primarily as a deterrent to Russian ambitions against Austria, whose empire was heading for collapse.

As for Britain, Bismarck never lost his disdain for Britain's military prowess. The man who had once contemptuously remarked that if the British army set foot in Germany he would send a policeman to arrest it, later rephrased that observation, telling Grand Admiral Alfred von Tirpitz in 1897 that 'we would slay them with the butt ends of our rifles.' For all his astuteness as a statesman, Bismarck typified the inability of Europeans to accept that Britain, despite having created the greatest colonial empire in history, and despite possessing a powerful and dominant navy, was any better than the 'nation of shopkeepers' Napoleon had jeered at. But while critics expressed both envy and derision that an island nation the size of Britain, which had to import most of its food, could manage to rule such an empire with a puny army, there were no such doubts about the Royal Navy, which guarded Britain's shores, protected its rule of the seas and maintained its status as a great power. As Napoleon also said, 'Give me six hours' control of the Strait of Dover and I will gain mastery of the world.'

What Bismarck had held together so effectively began to unravel slowly with the death of Kaiser Wilhelm I and that of his son, Friedrich III, both in 1888, and his succession by his grandson, Wilhelm II. The son of Queen Victoria's eldest child, Princess Victoria, Willy, as he was called within his family, was a rebellious youth who grew to manhood with near-hysterical feelings of bitterness and scorn for England and his English kinfolk. His uncle Bertie (who became Edward VII upon the death of Queen Victoria) once said of his nephew, 'Willy is a bully and most bullies, when tackled, are cowards,' and declared him to be 'the most brilliant failure in history'.

Yet Wilhelm admired the Royal Navy and took great pride in being dubbed an 'Admiral of the Fleet' by his English relatives when he visited Britain. However, he would rant endlessly about Britain and protest that he was misunderstood and treated unfairly by the English side of his family, once declaring, 'One cannot have enough hatred for England.'

Although Wilhelm symbolized a new era in German history and was an imposing figure when he appeared in public in military uniform, his quick intellect was negated by visions of military glory and by delusions of grandeur: he felt that he was the modern equivalent of the rulers of the Holy Roman Empire. Wilhelm's most dangerous trait was the fantasy that he and he alone made policy, not his ministers.

Wilhelm's early life revolved around ships and the sea, and his visits to the ships of Queen Victoria's fleet were a never-to-be-forgotten experience that left him with visions of presiding over a German navy even larger and stronger than that of Britain. The kaiser wanted nothing more than to don his uniform and take the salutes of his admirals and sailors.

More important, the Prussian militarism that Bismarck had so carefully controlled and contained within a vibrant and ever productive society became the impetus for the expansion of Germany's empire. In the hands of the new kaiser militarism was a recipe for confrontation and, eventually, war.

Wilhelm hid his shortcomings behind rather grandiose ideas of creating a larger German place in the world: economically, territorially and militarily. He dismissed Bismarck and set Germany upon a more aggressive military course by throwing the Iron Chancellor's caution to the winds of rearmament. Envy of British sea power and an inferiority complex when it came to Britain sparked his aspirations for German greatness. To meet this challenge Wilhelm put his secretary of state for the Imperial Navy, Admiral von Tirpitz, in charge of creating a great battle fleet. There were parallels between Tirpitz and Fisher: both were tough sailors zealously wedded to their profession. Ruthless and aggressive, Tirpitz was a Prussian who, like Fisher, had started his career on the bottom rung of the navy and climbed his way to the top during a career that spanned more than a half century (his favourite drink was reputed to be 'North Sea foam'). He was convinced that the key to protecting the German economy was sea power. Under his aegis there began Germany's ambitious new course, 'a game, but with dangerous toys', and the transition from Bismarck's cautious *Realpolitik* to an expansionist *Weltpolitik*.

In response France and Russia concluded their own Dual Alliance, in which each agreed to come to the aid of the other if attacked by Germany. As the Great Powers began assembling protective alliances with one another, a dangerous tripwire was put in place that could be set off by only a single misstep.

Thus the balance of power in Europe began to tilt towards a newly aggressive Germany with an expanding army and navy. In 1895 a great engineering feat of military significance was completed with the opening of the Kiel Canal. The German High Fleet was based in Kiel, and the new canal made possible its rapid deployment between the Baltic and North Seas.

At first Germany's new militarism and its modern navy seemed to pose no threat to Britain, and it was not until well into the first decade of the twentieth century that it finally became apparent that the German fleet posed a genuine danger in the event of war. Despite what he had seen for himself in Germany, Churchill was among the last to discern that the kaiser, far from being a bumbling amateur, was in fact a menace. So it was that while he and Lloyd George pursued cuts in Royal Navy expenditure, the decade between 1904 and 1914 became an unprecedented, all-out arms race to see which navy could build up its muscle more rapidly.

When Britain upped the stakes in 1906 by producing the first of Fisher's new dreadnought battleships Tirpitz regarded it as a hostile act. Germany responded at once, and a naval rivalry now existed in earnest, with each nation regarding the other's actions as provocative.

Growing unease over Germany's increasingly aggressive posture and its openly worsening relations with France exploded in July 1911 at Agadir, a port city situated far down Morocco's Atlantic coast. Agadir became the focus of a potentially dangerous confrontation when Germany dispatched the gunboat *Panther* to protect what were alleged to be German business interests there. The use of gunboat diplomacy by Germany was a leaf taken directly from the British imperial book, and it was a measure of the bad temper of the times that Agadir became an international incident leading to threats of retribution and even war. Such was the already precarious mood of the European powers that the movement of a puny gunboat caused alarm in its capitals and precipitated what came to be known as the Agadir crisis. As Churchill later wrote, 'All the alarm bells throughout Europe began immediately to quiver.' Under the terms of a 1904 treaty between Britain and France, Morocco was part of France's sphere of influence, and any attempt by Germany to establish a commercial or military presence there was deemed a threat to both nations.

The *Panther* became a pawn in a much larger international chess game that involved threats and counter-threats. Britain not only became an unwilling party to a quarrel between France and Germany but ended up trading invective with Berlin, sparked by an uncharacteristically warlike speech by Lloyd George (then chancellor of the exchequer) delivered at the Mansion House in London. He not only rejected German claims but asserted that Britain was prepared to go to war to protect its (and France's) rights. Should it be necessary, that war would not only be on the sea but also include the dispatch of an expeditionary force to the European continent. An equally belligerent Kaiser Wilhelm interpreted Lloyd George's speech as highly provocative and dangerous to the peace of Europe, and recalled his ambassador, Count Metternich. The speech, wrote Churchill at the time, came as 'a thunder-clap to the German Government'. After the First World War, Churchill said: 'It now seems probable that the Germans did not mean war on this occasion. But they meant to test the ground; and in so doing were prepared to go to the very edge of the precipice.'

The kaiser later told General Sir John French at the annual manoeuvres in 1911 that Britain and Germany were natural allies and should stand shoulder to shoulder against the real threat of the future, which was racial, in particular the 'Yellow Peril'; however, if Britain interfered with German interests it would pay the price.

Churchill later reflected on the not unreasonable belief that war was unthinkable. Surely civilization had progressed beyond that point in a new century, when nations were more and more dependent upon one another for commerce and common sense had rendered such conflict ludicrous.

Even so Home Secretary Winston Churchill was belligerent over Agadir and wrote a note to Clementine, who was holidaying on England's south coast, that Britain was responding with 'pretty plain language to Germany ... to tell her that if she thinks Morocco can be divided up without John Bull, she is jolly well mistaken'.

War was avoided, and although the crisis passed without further talk or threat of war, the incident left Britain more mistrustful than ever of German intentions and determined to build and maintain a fleet of superior size. It certainly left Churchill deeply concerned. Indeed he was alarmed upon learning that the Royal Navy's cordite reserves were stored in magazines for whose safety he was responsible as home secretary. He immediately began lobbying the Admiralty to send Royal Marines to guard them.

What no one had yet fully grasped – but what would become glaringly clear in 1914 – was the fragile nature of Great Power relations: if war could ensue over a relatively trivial incident like Agadir, other circumstances might easily ignite conflict.

Agadir also stirred the military Churchill into thoughts of war and a flurry of activity. Although his duties as home secretary had little to do with war planning, that hardly dissuaded him from developing a war strategy for Britain. The result was a plan of action for how a war with Germany might play out, which he presented to the Committee of Imperial Defence (CID). His central thesis was that the French army was not strong enough to invade Germany; therefore, 'Her only chance is to conquer Germany in France.' With a military force superior in numbers (2.2 million versus 1.7 million), the Germans, he wrote, would attack France and break the defences of the River Meuse by D+20 days. The French would fall back to defend Paris and be augmented by the dispatch of 107,000 British troops upon a declaration of war, with another 100,000 to be sent from India to arrive in France no later than D+40. Eventually France would prevail in 'a decisive trial of strength'.

Churchill went on to outline measures to be taken for the home defence of Britain. This paper, one of the most important documents he ever wrote, included a detailed analysis of how the German advance would be slowed and ultimately stopped short of Paris. When the Germans invaded France three years later his predictions came true virtually to the day: the Germans broke the line of the Meuse on D+21 days, and the French army held at the Marne to the east of Paris on D+33 days.

At the time, however, the CID ignored Churchill's thoughtful memorandum. Among his detractors was the director of military operations, General Sir Henry Wilson, later a field marshal and the chief of the Imperial General Staff from 1918 to 1922. In 1911 Wilson's focus was the coming war with Germany. In a diary entry written before the committee meeting on 23 August, Wilson disparaged both the paper and the amateur strategist who wrote it. 'Winston has put in a ridiculous and fantastic paper on a war on the French and German frontier, which I was able to demolish. I believe he is in close touch with Kitchener and French, neither of whom knows anything at all about the subject.' As it would turn out, Wilson and Churchill were not all that far apart in their ideas; they differed only in their means.

Henry Hughes Wilson was a diligent student of war and an indefatigable practitioner of the concept that to understand war one must inspect the ground upon which it will be fought. In 1912, and again the following year, Lieutenant George S. Patton toured Normandy, convinced he would one day command troops in a battle there. In 1909 Wilson spent ten days, partly on a bicycle, touring the French and Belgian frontiers to gain a perspective on how and where the Germans might invade the West; he returned three or four times a year for the next four years to visit the 1870 battlefields and sites in the Ardennes and Lorraine, where he believed future battles might be fought. Wilson also conferred with France's leading military thinker, General Ferdinand Foch, then the director of the French War College.

When he assumed the post of director of military operations in 1910, Wilson was troubled to discover that there were no plans in existence either for mobilization of the British army or for sending an expeditionary force to assist France. His office wall was covered with an enormous map of Belgium 'with every road by which he thought the Germans could march in heavy black'. In 1911 no one in Britain, not even Churchill, was a greater student of war or a greater proponent of planning how to fight a war on the European continent than Wilson. Churchill would later credit him as 'the man from whom I learned most' about a potential war with Germany.

A secret meeting of the CID was convened on 23 August 1911, for the purpose of briefing Asquith on the war plans of the two services. All the major players of the government were present, including the foreign secretary, Sir Edward Grey; Lloyd George; the secretary of state for war, Lord Haldane; the first lord of the Admiralty, Reginald McKenna; the chief of the Imperial General Staff, General Sir William Nicholson; the first sea lord, Admiral Sir Arthur Wilson; and Churchill, who had no official reason to be there but whose participation was ensured by virtue of his memorandum – and his own resourcefulness.

Sir Henry Wilson conducted the army's lengthy briefing of what he described as a group of 'ignorant men'. Using a huge map placed on the wall of the conference room for reference, Wilson outlined in great detail (with what Churchill later admitted was to prove 'extreme accuracy') just how Germany would attack France if war came, and how Britain would come to the aid of France with six divisions to reinforce the vital left flank of the French defensive line. Wilson's plan varied very little from Churchill's in conception.

After lunch it was the Royal Navy's turn, during a stormy afternoon session that revealed deep and seemingly irreconcilable differences. Churchill would later describe Admiral Sir Arthur Wilson, a gallant sailor who had won the Victoria Cross in the Sudan, as 'without any exception, the most selfless man I have ever met . . . he feared nothing – absolutely nothing.'

Arthur Wilson scoffed at Henry Wilson's premise of British involvement in a ground war, even arguing that it was impossible, owing to the language barrier with the French. Admiral Wilson's briefing was rambling, had been poorly prepared and amounted to a clear indication that the navy did not want even to be present that day. Its war plan could be summed up in a single word: 'blockade'. It would seal off the seas, and the only expeditionary force it projected to land on the Continent was a small one in the Baltic, on the northern shores of Germany, to 'draw off more than its weight of numbers from the German fighting line'. This plan precipitated a strong rebuttal from the army, which pointed out that such decisions were not the province of the navy. When Nicholson asked Wilson if the Admiralty possessed a map of the German railway system, 'Sir Arthur replied it was not their business to have such maps,' and a testy exchange ensued.

The truth was that, if the Admiralty actually possessed a war plan, it was known only to the first sea lord. Arthur Marder has written: 'It was locked up in his own brain, though one story has it that it was scratched out on a single sheet of paper locked up in a safe to which only he had the key!' The Admiralty's rationale was based on the flimsy argument that such plans had to be kept secret lest they be compromised. Wilson ridiculed the whole notion of a war staff, saying that the 'naval War Staff at the Admiralty consisted of himself – assisted by every soul inside the Admiralty, including the charwoman who emptied the waste-paper baskets full of plans of amateur strategists – Cabinet or otherwise'.

Some of the most probing questions asked during the conference came from Churchill, who was pleased by General Wilson's forceful replies and dismayed by Admiral Wilson's evasions and poor responses. The Admiralty, he concluded, was 'cocksure, insouciant and apathetic'. In fact the admiral's position was unchanged from that of his predecessor, Jackie Fisher. In 1908, when war clouds were hanging over France and Germany, Fisher had rebuffed the notion of British assistance to the French, and, when asked by Asquith if the navy could transport one hundred thousand men across the Channel, he had responded with a diatribe that doing so would be 'suicidal folly'. The might of the Royal

Navy, he argued, was the only bulwark that would keep the German army out of Paris.

Herbert Asquith's frustrations over the disunity between the Admiralty and the War Office had been simmering for a long time before Agadir proved the last straw. The 23 August conference left the prime minister and his key ministers deeply disturbed by its clear exposure not only of the lack of a coherent war policy but of the divergent, intransigent views of the navy, whose admirals remained a virtual law unto themselves that no one had yet successfully challenged. Of this significant meeting Churchill recorded, 'Apprehension lay heavy on the minds of all who had participated in it.' Asquith not only sided with the army but, more importantly, realized that there was an urgent need for a shake-up at the Admiralty. Lord Haldane had done a brilliant job of reorganizing and reforming the army and was disconcerted by the navy's attitude. He reiterated to Asquith the vital need for the War Office and the Admiralty to work with a common purpose, an effort doomed to failure unless the navy created its own war staff. With Haldane threatening resignation unless there was sweeping reform at the Admiralty, there was now a motive for action. Reginald McKenna was too deeply committed to the admirals' views to bring about the necessary reform and Asquith now resolved to replace him.

The prospect of war with Germany haunted Churchill. He later wrote that during a holiday in the country in August 1911 'I could not think of anything else but the peril of war.' As always he proclaimed himself convinced of the correctness of his thinking: 'I had no doubts whatsoever what ought to be done in certain matters, and my only difficulty was to persuade or induce others.' He wrote to Lloyd George to express anew his concerns and proposed moving the bulk of the Royal Navy fleet 'to its Scottish station, where it wd be at once the most effective & least provocative support to France, & a real security for this country. It is not for Morocco, nor indeed for Belgium, that I wd take part in this terrible business. One cause alone cd justify our participation – to prevent France from being trampled down & looted by the Prussian junkers – a disaster ruinous to the world, & swiftly fatal to our country.'

The years 1911 to 1914 were exceptionally important in the develop-ment of Churchill's military thought and experience. The first important step was his belated realization that war was possible, even likely. By 1912, two years before the assassination of the Austrian archduke Franz Ferdinand in Sarajevo, that concern had grown to the point where he wrote prophetically to his cousin Sunny of the unstable situation in Europe and the Balkans.

Agadir also exposed the gaping deficiency in Britain's war planning. The pre-First World War British army had created a general staff along the lines of the German one, and despite its relatively small size it was well organized and trained. The problem was that the only accepted doctrine was that of attack, with the anticipation of heavy losses but eventual victory through mobility, 'offensive spirit and moral force', the same tactics employed successfully at Omdurman and disastrously in the Boer War. Nor were the army's senior commanders particularly well trained for the sort of warfare they would encounter on a European battlefield of the twentieth century. 'There was little stress on independence of mind, and the result was a strictly hierarchical army headed by largely unimaginative leaders,' which, as the military visionary J. F. C. Fuller would point out, was sterile, feared initiative and was terrified of originality and afraid of criticism. The English practice of 'muddling through' any situation, while admirable, was to prove detrimental when it came to determining how modern wars were fought.

Despite reforms of the army, the British military was beset with inter-service rivalries both within the Royal Navy and in the ranks of the army among the infantry, cavalry and artillery. No better example exists of the lack of vision and co-operation between the army and navy than the Royal Navy's refusal, at the 23 August meeting, to provide any assurance that it would transport the expeditionary force in a timely manner – something it regarded as a wasteful recipe for disaster.

By his tacit acquiescence in the admirals' view, the first lord, Reginald McKenna, became part of the problem. The plain truth was that the Royal Navy had become complacent and had for too long rested on the laurels of Trafalgar while ignoring both the realities and the dangers that lurked ahead in a new century. Although Jackie Fisher is widely regarded as the architect of the modern sea force that Winston Churchill would preside over, the colourful first sea lord also personified the long tradition of the Royal Navy and its insular mind-set. One of his rare public remarks was made in 1903 during a brief after-dinner speech at the Royal Academy. With the secretary of state for war (St John

Brodrick) in attendance, Fisher uttered the famous dictum that sought to encapsulate the place of the Royal Navy in British history: 'On the British Navy rests the British Empire. Nothing else is of any use without it, not even the army . . . No soldier of ours can go anywhere unless a sailor carries him there on his back.' With the great weight of his authority as the voice of the Royal Navy, Fisher concluded by reminding Britons that 'you may sleep quietly in your beds.' That attitude prevailed throughout British society. A Liberal politician, Sir Charles Dilke, a former Foreign Office under-secretary, once summed it up by declaring, 'The oceans are in fact a British possession.'

That may have been true in 1903, but by 1911 the situation in Europe had changed so completely that, as the 23 August meeting had revealed, the Admiralty needed a thorough reorganization. Both McKenna and Sir Arthur Wilson had persistently refused all attempts to form a war staff, which the prime minister and others in the government deemed vital. In the wake of the August conference, Asquith was no longer willing to ignore the navy's intransigence: hence his intention to replace McKenna. Agadir was the turning point that persuaded Churchill to lobby the prime minister for the post. He bombarded Asquith with letters asking questions about the navy and what was being done to solve various naval problems.

Churchill was not the only candidate for the job – Lord Haldane was the other; and on the basis of the outstanding work he had done reforming the army, including the creation of a general staff along the lines of what the navy required, Haldane fully expected to get the post until he learned that his competition was Churchill. Each man strongly pressed his own case to Asquith. Haldane was hindered by his member-ship of the House of Lords – the first lord should in Asquith's view be a member of the House of Commons – and by the fact that the navy would resist the appointment of an obvious reformer. Churchill's strongest champion was none other than Asquith's daughter Violet, who took every opportunity to promote her friend.

Ultimately Asquith saw Churchill as better suited to inject new blood into the hidebound Royal Navy, and he announced that in October Churchill and McKenna would exchange jobs. Asquith was shrewd enough to grasp that in Churchill he had a man willing to take unpopular actions and positions, one who would not be intimidated by the navy brass, and who would bring about needed reform. As Sebastian Haffner has written, 'Having diagnosed the warrior that lurked within the radical, Asquith rightly concluded that he had only to set the warrior a task to be rid of the radical.' Moreover Asquith seemed to recognize that Churchill's forte was that of a leader more than a politician. He also killed two birds with one stone: to shake up the Admiralty and remove a volatile source of controversy as the head of the Home Office and replace him with a more even-handed custodian.

Churchill was ecstatic on learning of his appointment, but for the prime minister there was a loose end: pacifying King George V, who had succeeded his father the previous year. The king mistrusted Churchill and only after considerable persuasion reluctantly accepted his appointment as first lord. (A striking parallel would occur years later when George V's second son, George VI, was unhappily obliged to accept Churchill as Neville Chamberlain's replacement as prime minister on 10 May 1940.)

Churchill was staying with Asquith at Archerfield House, a country estate in East Lothian lent to the prime minister by a relative. The night of his appointment Churchill went to bed with thoughts of the threat Germany posed:

I thought of the peril of Britain, peace-loving, unthinking, little prepared, of her power and virtue, and of her mission of good sense and fair-play. I thought of mighty Germany towering up in the splendour of her Imperial State and delving down in her profound, cold, patient, ruthless calculations. I thought of the army corps I had watched tramp past, wave after wave of valiant manhood, at the Breslau manoeuvres of 1907 . . . I thought of the sudden successful wars by which her power had been set up.

Churchill would later recall that this historic day ended on a note of epiphany when, as he was preparing to retire in a guest bedroom, he spotted a large Bible on a table and decided to open it at random. It fell open at a page of Deuteronomy. He began to read the following passage: 'Hear, O Israel: Thou art to pass over Jordan this day, to go in to possess nations greater and mightier than thyself, cities great and fenced up to heaven . . . Understand therefore this day, that the Lord thy God is he which goeth over before thee; as a consuming fire he shall destroy them, and he shall bring them down before thy face: so shalt thou drive them out, and destroy them quickly, as the Lord hath said unto thee' (9:1, 3).

Years later he wrote, 'It seemed a message of reassurance.' Thus, only weeks shy of thirty-seven, Winston Churchill found himself the steward of the world's most powerful fleet. 'This is a big thing,' he said. 'The biggest thing that has ever come my way – the chance I should have chosen before all others. I shall pour into it everything I've got.'

17

First Lord of the Admiralty

He had served it [the Admiralty] with the passion of a lover and the dedication of a friar. — Violet Bonham Carter

Into the treacherous waters of Britain's oldest and most venerated military establishment sailed Winston Churchill, with a fierce and fearless determination to bring about badly needed reforms from top to bottom. To be first lord of the Admiralty carried a grave responsibility.

The Royal Navy in 1911 was the real custodian of British power and the most powerful military force on earth, ruling its seas; its famous battles and feats were legendary, and men like Sir Francis Drake and Horatio Nelson were idolized as the very essence of what made Britain a great power. It was also the more old-fashioned of the British military services. Tradition ruled. Although both he and his official biographer disavowed the remark, Churchill is said to have replied sarcastically once to an admiral who had spoken deferentially of the traditions of the Royal Navy: 'What are the traditions of the Navy? Rum, sodomy and the lash!' Apocryphal or not, the comment has nevertheless become rooted in the Churchill legend.

The reform of the Royal Navy was not an undertaking for the faint of heart. Not only was it Britain's first permanent military establishment, dating as far back as 1347, when an assemblage of ships ferried an army of King Edward III across the English Channel to invade France; it had also become very much the king's navy, and it was to the sovereign that it owed its primary allegiance. It would require the approval of the king for a change in naval regulations to create a war staff. Despite its dependence upon the purse strings of Parliament and the decisions of prime ministers regarding its employment, the Royal Navy looked first and foremost to the monarch. Its attitude was one of reluctance even to answer to Parliament.

The Royal Navy of Churchill's time was encrusted with a nepotism and grandeur that had more to do with self-indulgence than with military preparedness. At the time of Queen Victoria's Diamond Jubilee in 1897 the fleet was all glitz and glamour, spit and polish, but very little attention was paid to military proficiency, new tactics or advancing naval technology. Although mandatory, even gunnery practice was deemed a waste of time rather than a necessity, and was carried out halfheartedly (sometimes not at all), often with the admirals ashore to avoid the bothersome noise of the guns. There had been few advances in the art of naval gunnery since the time of Nelson, and the peacetime navy seemed content to rest smugly upon the laurels of Trafalgar. Its admirals had no experience of modern warfare, its rules were unchanged and its naval exercises were rigidly scripted and predictable. When he became the second sea lord in 1902, Fisher 'remarked that the ideas of warfare of his colleagues were of the bow-and-arrow epoch'.

The admirals were wary of the newly appointed first lord, whose reputation as an outspoken, forceful, cost-cutting politician, and as an opponent of the dreadnought programme, was strongly resented. Whatever their resentments, however, Churchill's arrival at the Admiralty left little doubt about who was in charge. Instead of the acquiescent McKenna, the admirals now had to deal with a mover and shaker who was not daunted by their lofty positions, their traditions or their resistance to change.

During what he called 'the four most memorable years of my life', Churchill brought to his task a healthy new awareness of the urgent need for naval preparedness. He was far more than a new broom sweeping clean the debris of past mistakes; his arrival at the Admiralty brought the winds of change – a signal that things would be done very differently on his watch.

One of his first actions was to affix a map of the North Sea to the wall behind his desk. Each evening the duty officer identified the location of the principal ships of the German navy by means of small flags. The first thing Churchill did each morning was study the map, thus enabling himself to keep track of the location of the kaiser's fleet. The map was the most visible indication of Churchill's concern about Germany's growing naval power.

The new first lord found himself in a somewhat awkward position because he had avidly supported Lloyd George, then chancellor of the exchequer, over reduced naval expenditures for new dreadnoughts at the very time when the naval arms race with Germany was at its peak. Though the change in his attitude was nothing less than astonishing, his shift from the narrow political approach he had taken as an opponent of rearmament to a passionate backing of preparedness was a direct reflection of Agadir and of a steady infusion of advice from Admiral Lord Fisher.

He correctly deemed it his primary responsibility 'to prepare for an attack by Germany as if it might come next day'. It took him a mere four days to set in motion one of the main tasks for which he had been sent to the Admiralty: the formation of a naval war staff, which Asquith and others had long sought. It was an enormous and challenging task not only to overcome the opposition of the admirals but also to confront the reality that to create an effective staff would normally take a generation – a luxury he did not enjoy.

As already noted, its creation required the approval not only of the Asquith government but of the king, who duly signed off on his proposal in early 1912, thus clearing the way for an important and far-reaching reform. Churchill wanted the naval war staff directly under his personal control, a proposition that was resisted; control was assigned instead to the first sea lord (where it properly belonged). Although not warmly embraced by the old guard, the war staff created by Churchill slowly evolved and over time began to show the promise and effectiveness he had envisaged.

Although Churchill respected the traditions of the Royal Navy, heads nevertheless quickly rolled. The first to go was Sir Arthur Wilson, who remained deliberately ignorant of land warfare, opposed the employment of a land force in France in the event of war and was tenaciously resistant to the war staff that Churchill had insisted upon. In his stead Churchill appointed Admiral Sir Francis Bridgeman, the commander in chief of the Home Fleet. However, Bridgeman did not measure up to Churchill's demanding standards, and in November 1912, he too was summarily replaced, this time by Admiral Prince Louis of Battenberg, an experienced and able sailor who had joined the navy at the age of twelve and was currently the second sea lord. In all, during his first year in office Churchill forced the resignations of four sea lords, drawing the enmity of, among others, Lord Charles Beresford, who once called him a 'Lilliput Napoleon'.

There were other tempests, the most contentious of which erupted during one of Churchill's visits to the fleet, when a junior officer criticized his commanding officer for a decision he had made. Without hearing the other side of the story, 'Churchill sent for the Captain and told him the young officer's view was to be accepted,' thus precipitating a furious controversy that rippled through the naval chain of command. Not only had Churchill imprudently involved himself in a matter that impugned the authority of a ship's commanding officer, but he then compounded the problem by attempting to silence the second sea lord, Sir John Jellicoe, over correspondence regarding the quarrel. The upshot was a revolt of the sea lords and threats of resignation that came dangerously close to being carried out. Although the matter blew over, it seriously harmed Churchill's standing in the Royal Navy and gave ammunition to his political enemies.

He unrelentingly exhibited his capacity to intimidate and to get his own way by out-talking his admirals and wearing them down through gruelling back-and-forth discussions. The director of naval intelligence, Captain William Hall, told of being pressured by Churchill to the point where he once muttered, 'My name is Hall because if I listen to you much longer I shall be convinced that it's Brown.' On this occasion Churchill saw the humour and did not pursue the matter; other sessions dragged on like marathons.

There was another, more disturbing aspect to Churchill's style of governance. Lord Esher, a founding member of the CID, put his finger on it when he wrote that Churchill 'handles great subjects in rhythmical language, and becomes quickly enslaved by his own phrases. He deceives himself into the belief that he takes broad views, when his mind is fixed upon one comparatively small aspect of the question.' This propensity would frustrate and infuriate those who served under him during the Second World War, when he would fixate on certain military operations, such as his insistence in 1940 on an invasion of Pantelleria (a small island between Sicily and North Africa), an operation that had no strategic importance. On such occasions he became the centre of his own universe and was difficult, if not impossible, to dissuade.

Yet Churchill brought to his new office an infectious enthusiasm for the Royal Navy that even his critics could not help noticing. 'Everything about the Admiralty excited him, from the twin stone dolphins guarding the building's entrance to the furniture within . . . dating from Nelson's time.'

Another of Churchill's first actions as first lord was to turn to his tutor, confidant and foil, Lord Fisher, with whom he had resumed friendly relations. With Fisher in the wings to suggest and urge certain reforms, Churchill moved forward with a speed never before seen in the Admiralty. For the next three years the old admiral became an almost Rasputin-like mentor, advising, cajoling and shamelessly prodding the younger man. Dealing with Fisher was a risk Churchill was willing to take. Fisher's correspondence with Churchill makes lively reading, ranging from fulsome praise to insulting comments whenever his self-proclaimed protégé failed to act as he had suggested. Virtually every compliment in his letters was offset by at least one insult or taunt. Nevertheless Churchill tolerated Fisher's barbs with astonishing equanimity.

For all his brilliance and dedication to the navy, Fisher was an incorrigible intriguer who used others to his own ends. When Churchill appointed Admiral Sir John Jellicoe to the post of second in command of the Home Fleet, Fisher praised his Nelsonian qualities and emphatically exhorted him 'to get Jellicoe Commander-in-Chief of the Home Fleet prior to October 21, 1914', the date he believed war would come. However, in 1912 Churchill made several key appointments of which Fisher disapproved and so was denounced for betraying the navy, once being referred to as 'a Royal pimp'. Nevertheless in letters and face-to-face meetings the Fisher–Churchill relationship blossomed as the old sailor became the inexperienced first lord's personal consigliere.

Although Churchill was tempted to recall Fisher to active duty as first sea lord, he saw the pitfalls of being second-guessed on a daily basis by the crusty admiral, who would hardly have tolerated playing second fiddle to, or taking orders from, him. Moreover, with Fisher back at the Admiralty all the long-standing animosities that endured within the Royal Navy old guard would have been instantly revived. Churchill already had enough problems without incurring more ill will than he himself had already brought about. Thus during the pre-war years the relationship between the two men was conducted at long distance.

Churchill's battles were not limited to Fisher; he also became embroiled in an ill-advised and testy row with King George V over the naming of the Royal Navy's newest ships. Among the names Churchill wanted for one of the new battleships was *Oliver Cromwell*, a name the king rejected and diplomatically had his private secretary suggest was obviously a mistake on the first lord's part, as the name had already been rejected the previous year. Perhaps only Churchill would have failed to accept what amounted to an order from his monarch to cease and desist. Instead he foolishly persisted with arguments for why it was a good idea, only to be soundly reproved, not once but twice before acknowledging defeat. He said, 'I bow to the King's wish,' only to incense the king again the following year by insolently suggesting that perhaps His Majesty might prefer not to be consulted in the future over such matters.

It was no surprise that Churchill reached outside the mainstream of the naval pecking order to select a promising young officer to fill a key appointment, that of private secretary to the first lord. His choice was Rear Admiral David Beatty, then the Royal Navy's youngest admiral and the same officer who had tossed Churchill a bottle of champagne from his gunboat on the Nile the night before the Battle of Omdurman. Beatty was one of the navy's rising stars who seemed to have it all. Debonair and married to an American heiress of the Marshall Field fortune, he was the type of officer who appealed to Churchill's romanticism about leaders who not only performed well but also looked the part. One of their first exchanges was memorable: 'You seem very young to be an admiral,' opined Churchill. Beatty immediately replied, 'And you seem very young to be first lord.' It was the sort of quick-witted, slightly risky, touché type of rejoinder that Churchill liked from an enterprising officer. Against the advice of some that his star had risen much too fast, he at once appointed Beatty, who became a fixture during his time at the Admiralty and one of his key advisers on a wide range of naval matters.

For his part Beatty did not return the affection accorded him by his new boss. Often obliged to accompany Churchill on his numerous and lengthy forays aboard the Admiralty yacht, he once complained to his wife that being in his company 'bores me to tears. Winston talks about nothing but the sea and the Navy and all the wonderful things he is going to do. Mrs Winston is a perfect fool.'

*

Churchill's most significant accomplishments and challenges also occurred very early in his tenure as first lord. The Admiralty was riddled with intrigue, in no small part the result of the long-running Fisher–Beresford feud. With each side distrusting the other, Churchill's first challenge was somehow to make peace with the notoriously fickle admirals and officers while at the same time taking firm control of the Admiralty – all of which was merely a prologue to accomplishing his real mission of preparing the Royal Navy for war.

When it came to Britain's naval future he displayed neither fear nor hesitation in making two critically important decisions, both of which were heavily influenced by Fisher, whose vision was that the Royal Navy should consist of a combination of the newer battle cruisers and submarines. As the father of the dreadnought, Fisher had in the new first lord a willing convert to the 'bigger is better' concept that was clearly in agreement with Churchill's philosophy of fighting 'with might and main till overwhelming victory'.

His stance unleashed resistance and hostility and embroiled him in the unresolved war within the Admiralty over the role of the battleship versus the battle cruiser. The upshot was his acceptance of the case put by both sides and the initiation of a programme to build new Queen Elizabeth-class battleships 'which were to be equipped with the big guns and oil propulsion that Fisher wanted, but also heavy armour and strong secondary armament, which he did not'.

Churchill went one better by adding a 15-inch supergun to these behemoths. The five new super-dreadnoughts took three years to construct, and their 15-inch guns fired a massive projectile weighing just under a ton an astonishing thirty-five thousand yards (nearly twenty miles) at unseen targets over the horizon. The decision to arm the Queen Elizabeth-class vessels was fraught with risk. The addition of the larger armament added some 20 per cent to their cost, and required more armour and larger turrets. Churchill preferred testing a prototype before committing to the expensive construction of a super-dreadnought. 'I went back to Lord Fisher. He was steadfast and even violent. So I hardened my heart and took the plunge . . . From this moment we were irrevocably committed to the whole armament, and every detail in these vessels was redesigned to fit them.'

The other innovation that Churchill introduced was the conversion of the navy's fuel from coal to oil, which not only was more efficient but, more importantly, enabled ships to run at higher and thus more manoeuvrable speeds. The decision was somewhat risky. Coal was a plentiful resource in Britain; oil was not, and it would have to be imported and storage facilities constructed. A royal commission headed by Fisher fully endorsed the idea, and in 1914, to ensure an adequate supply of oil, which had to come from the Middle East, Churchill orchestrated the purchase of a majority share of the Anglo-Persian Oil Company.

Both decisions proved advantageous, and the most lethal weapon on the high seas was born. During the Battle of Jutland in 1916 the real worth of Churchill's bold decisions was proved, and until well into the Second World War this new class of battleship became the backbone of the Royal Navy.

On the other hand Churchill was slow to accept the principle articulated by Fisher that future warfare would allow submarines to torpedo and sink unarmed merchant ships. It tested Churchill's Victorian upbringing and his unflagging belief that wars should be fought at a certain level of honour, such as that exhibited between the combatants during the Boer War. He viewed the notion of submarine warfare as something no civilized nation would dare engage in, perhaps forgetting that the slaughter of poorly armed Zulus and Dervish warriors hardly qualified as 'civilized'. Fisher thought Churchill naive, and within months his prediction would prove chillingly accurate.

Churchill thus became a somewhat reluctant convert to the submarine as another important part of the navy's arsenal of defence of Britain's home waters. Once he accepted its necessity he pursued the unsuccessful development of a fast submarine in the two years prior to the war, draining away funds that would have been better spent on patrol submarines, which Fisher envisaged as a key element in his strategy for the employment of the navy in time of war.

In early 1912 the Germans initiated a naval bill that would increase the size of their fleet that spring, heightening British concerns over the kaiser's intentions. Wilhelm gave a copy of the document to Haldane in February during what has been called the Haldane Mission, an effort to improve the deteriorating relations between the two nations and ease tensions by seeking a formula for curbing the naval race. 'It was the last Anglo-German attempt to find a common ground of understanding, and it failed,' noted the historian Barbara Tuchman. The talks left Haldane convinced that German ambitions to dominate Europe would have to be checked by force.

Haldane turned the German document over to Churchill, who found its contents highly disturbing. It proposed 20 per cent increases in German naval manpower and in the number of destroyers and submarines. Three days before obtaining the document from Haldane, Churchill had already given warning of British plans. In Glasgow he delivered his first policy speech as first lord, making it clear that while 'the purposes of British naval power are essentially defensive,' increases in German naval strength would be matched, and that Britain had no intention of being trumped on the seas. 'There is no chance whatever of our being overtaken in naval strength unless we want to be . . . As naval competition becomes more acute . . . our margin of superiority will become larger, not smaller, as the strain grows greater.'

Churchill's speech sparked outrage in Germany, did nothing to ease tensions and drew criticism from his colleagues in the government, although Lord Haldane pointed out that 'so far from being a hindrance to him in his negotiation, the Glasgow speech had been the greatest possible help.' Churchill's belligerent tone was not surprising given his passion for fighting fire with fire. Wilhelm believed that Churchill, a man he regarded as a friend and to whom he had shown great hospitality, had stabbed him in the back. However, his insistence on an apology from Churchill was silently ignored.

In the House the following month Churchill went one step further, articulating Britain's 'big punch' response to the new German naval bill by proclaiming that for every ship Germany built, Britain would lay two keels 'on all increases above the [previous] German Navy Law'. The new principles were: 'Sixty per cent in Dreadnoughts over Germany as long as she adhered to her present declared programme, and two keels to one for every additional ship laid down by her.'

While Churchill was adamant that Britain must be militarily prepared to fight Germany, he was no warmonger. In April 1912 he reached out to the kaiser in an attempt to ease tensions between the two countries by employing the office of first lord to propose a 'Naval Holiday' that would, at least temporarily, halt the arms race between their two navies. The kaiser stonily responded that such an agreement was possible only between allies. Churchill wrote privately to a friend, who passed the letter along to Wilhelm, once again attempting to smooth the troubled waters by assuring him that Britain was 'innocent of any offensive design'. His olive branch failed to bring Germany to the negotiating table. After the failure of his proposal to halt the naval race with Germany, Churchill believed he had no other choice than to build expensive and untested new warships if he was to fend off his Conservative critics, who would have liked nothing better than to bring down Asquith's Liberal government over the issue of naval security. In May 1912 he gave the final go-ahead to construct the new Queen Elizabeth-class fast battleships.

Churchill used the occasion of a speech at the Royal Academy on 4 May to articulate in plain language the mission of the Royal Navy in war. It was also a statement of the first principle of war: 'the development of the maximum war power at a given moment and at a particular point and object'. That principle would lead, he said, to the manifestation 'of a few minutes of shattering, blasting, overpowering, force'. The use of such absolute force, Churchill insisted, was necessary for Britain to maintain its great position in the world. His message also left no doubt of the perils of possessing great war-making power, but, he warned, 'If any of the great civilized and scientific nations of the world become engaged in war, they will be heartily sick of it long before they have got to the end.' Before a different audience eleven days later, Churchill told the Shipwrights' Company that although war threatened appalling horrors, 'It is much more likely . . . that war will never come in our time and perhaps will have passed from the world.'

Another lamentable shortcoming Churchill found in the Admiralty was that its officers were not required to study naval warfare nor even, he said, to 'pass the most rudimentary examination in naval history'. The Royal Navy had made no contribution to naval literature. 'The standard work on sea power was written by an American admiral [Alfred Thayer Mahan] . . . We had competent administrators, brilliant experts of every description, unequalled navigators, good disciplinarians, fine sea-officers, brave and devoted hearts: but . . . we had more captains of ships than captains of war.' He estimated that it would take at least fifteen years to correct the problem, 'and we were to have only thirty months!'

An example of the reform so desperately needed throughout the navy became obvious in June 1912, during a gunnery exercise conducted in the waters off Malta by the Mediterranean fleet. Accompanied by Asquith and Kitchener (who was visiting from Cairo), Churchill observed the exercise and afterwards asked the admiral in command how many hits the gunners had scored on the target towed by a destroyer. 'None,' replied the admiral. Aghast, he asked for an explanation and was condescendingly informed, 'Well, you see, First Lord, the shells seem to have either fallen *just* short of the target or else *just* a little beyond it.' Violet Asquith recorded in her diary, 'I will not describe what followed.'

Since its publication in 1895, Mahan's landmark book, *The Influence of Sea Power upon History*, had reached far beyond Britain. The book was widely read throughout the German navy, and deeply inspired the kaiser, who even began memorizing some of its passages, convinced that it provided the key to Germany's rightful 'place in the sun'. Its chief argument was that the nation that controlled the sea controlled its own destiny, a rationale that struck a chord with the ambitious Wilhelm. And so Germany accepted Mahan's thesis that it would never be a great power unless it possessed a navy capable of countering that of Britain. By 1911, when Churchill assumed stewardship of the Royal Navy, this fateful decision had put Germany and Great Britain on an inevitable collision course. It became Churchill's monumental task to meet that challenge head-on in what would turn out to be the all too brief thirty months at his disposal.

Churchill's lifelong habit was to begin each day by working and breakfasting in bed, then, with an hour's break for an afternoon nap, to work late into the night at the Admiralty, where he routinely overwhelmed and wore down the admirals, a practice he carried into the Second World War with exhausting effects on his hapless victims.

His primary virtue was his tireless focus on whatever problem he was dealing with. It was as if each one was the only subject requiring his attention. His whirlwind travels took him not only all around Britain to visit virtually every naval installation and ship in the Royal Navy, but also to its overseas establishments in the Mediterranean and the islands of Malta, Corsica and Sicily. He had exclusive use of one of the great perks of his office, a three-thousand-ton Admiralty steam yacht appropriately called the *Enchantress* that became his home away from home for eight months during his first three years as first lord. Clementine did not often join him on board; indeed she rarely saw her husband during this time, and their primary means of communication was by letter.

Churchill's incessant curiosity was combined with a fiery determination to grasp the reins of every single aspect of naval operations. A contemporary photograph depicts a formation of sailors drawn up in ranks at attention, with their rifles on their shoulders, as the first lord, in a top hat and carrying a walking stick, peers intently at a sailor whom he is inspecting. At each stop on his tours 'he would arrive, beaming and alert, his pockets bulging with notes and questions – probing, pertinent and detailed.' Lloyd George grumbled that Churchill had become overly obsessive about the navy and complained, 'You have become a water creature.'

The technical aspects of naval warfare attracted Churchill, and he asked endless questions of anyone and everyone, from ordinary sailors to the admirals, who were obliged to get used to being grilled by their boss. The new first lord seemed to possess a bottomless pit of questions, demands that studies be made and requests for information about tactics, gunnery, the specifications of weapons, equipment and all things nautical. To the annoyance of the naval brass Churchill rarely bothered with the chain of command and instead turned up unannounced on vessels, demanding to be shown everything from the engine room to the punishment cells. By his concern for their welfare, he won the respect of the ordinary bluejackets who manned His Majesty's ships for low pay and under harsh working conditions. Among the unchanged aspects of naval life was a promotion system that was badly in need of modernization that Churchill supported. As home secretary he had been particularly interested in prison reform; thus it was not surprising that he took an interest in the harsh discipline that was part and parcel of life in the Royal Navy.

A proposal to raise the pay and to effect other reforms met the fate of many such worthy endeavours, and was emasculated by the tightfisted Treasury, but he nevertheless became the first head of the Admiralty in nearly sixty years to bring about even a modest increase in the miserable pay and allowances of the Royal Navy men.

Churchill's obsession with control sometimes led him to exceed his authority. During the 1912 naval manoeuvres, for example, he interfered mightily by sending instructions from the Admiralty by wireless to the flag officers conducting the exercise, and then lecturing them 'on how the manoeuvres should have been conducted before the chief umpire had rendered his report'. His habit of meddling in every corner of naval business may have infuriated many, but the results were often positive. When he encouraged sailors and junior officers to criticize their commanding officers, however, there was outrage at the first lord's impertinence, and in the corridors of the Admiralty the resentment was palpable.

Once, after visiting the cells of a cruiser, the lieutenant who escorted him was chided by his fellow officers: 'Why didn't you lock him up?' Admiral Sir William James wrote: 'His curiosity about the service . . . seemed to many of the older officers almost indecent.' No civilian before him had ever acquired such knowledge of the Royal Navy or displayed the fierce determination and speed with which he grasped its reins and mastered the details. Churchill was also aware of what it meant to him as first lord. 'Who could fail to work for such a service? Who could fail when the very darkness seemed loaded with the menace of approaching war?' It was as if a marriage of sorts had taken place between Churchill and the Royal Navy.

Gradually he began to win over most, though certainly not all, of the sceptics by a blend of his enthusiasm, his passion to understand and improve the navy and the sheer force of his personality. When he learned that Admiral Sir Percy Scott, one of the navy's most innovative thinkers, had developed a new system for improving gunnery, he took an immediate interest. The antiquated system then in use called for each gun to lock on to a target by means of individual gun layers who would gradually adjust the angle of each gun by trial and error. No better examples existed of the ineptness of Royal Navy gunnery than the bombardment of Alexandria in 1882, in which Scott claimed that of three thousand shells fired a mere ten were direct hits. Also fresh in Churchill's mind was the dismal exercise he had witnessed off Malta in 1912.

Scott advocated a new concept by which one master gunner would direct the fire of all guns in tandem from a position high within the ship, not obscured by the usual smoke from the guns that blinded the gunners to the movements of their target. The wisdom of Scott's innovation was put to the test in November 1912 during a gunnery trial that Churchill approved over the opposition of the old guard. Two dreadnoughts fired at a moving target, one that boasted the best record in the fleet and employed the system of individual gunners versus one that was controlled by a master gunner employing Percy Scott's new system. It was no contest: the latter scored numerous direct hits, besting by a wide margin the dreadnought using the traditional firing method, which 'could barely find the target at all'. It was a measure of the traditionalists' reluctance to change anything that, despite the overwhelming success of Scott's system, there remained considerable opposition to its acceptance, even though it offered a vital improvement in the Royal Navy's fighting capability.

In the summer of 1912, accompanied for once by Clementine, Asquith, Asquith's daughter Violet and other dignitaries, Churchill made an extended inspection trip aboard *Enchantress* to the Mediterranean. At each of his numerous stops he was greeted with pomp and ceremony to the strains of 'Rule, Britannia' and 'God Save the King'. Local dignitaries resplendently turned out in uniforms and finery were piped aboard and extravagantly indulged with food and wine. During a stop-over at Tunis the French pulled out all the stops for their visitors. On a sandy plain some four thousand French and colonial infantry, cavalry, Zouaves and Chasseurs d'Afrique were assembled to parade in a dazzling display of colourful uniforms in honour of the first lord and his party. The event ended with the cavalry, mounted on magnificent Arabian horses, carrying out a mock charge with sabres flashing. Nearly thirty-one years later, in February 1943, Churchill would again be the most important VIP at a parade in Tripoli, when the victorious British Eighth Army marched past the prime minister to commemorate the defeat of the German and Italian armies in North Africa. Such events were the perks of office that stirred the military spirit in Churchill, who never seemed to tire of martial pageantry.

Asquith was both pleased and amused by his new first lord. During one gunnery exercise Churchill was not content to merely observe but felt obliged actually to participate, and on this occasion he was 'dancing behind the guns, elevating, depressing, and sighting'. The spectacle prompted Asquith to remark: 'My young friend yonder thinks himself Othello, and blacks himself all over to play the part.'

Churchill's obsession with war and its weapons was never more clearly demonstrated than in this diary entry by Violet Asquith: 'As we leaned side by side against the taffrail, gliding past the lovely, smiling coastline of the Adriatic, bathed in sun, and I remarked "How perfect!" he startled me by his reply: "Yes, range perfect – visibility perfect – If we had got some six-inch guns on board how easily we could bombard" . . . and details followed showing how effectively we could lay waste the landscape and blow the nestling towns sky-high.'

Yet there were days when his absence from his family and his 'black dog' intruded. 'Alas I have no vy good opinion of myself,' he wrote to Clementine on 3 November 1913. 'At times, I think I cd conquer everything – & then again I know I am only a weak vain fool. But your love for me is the greatest glory & recognition that has or will ever befall me . . . I only wish I were more worthy of you & more able to meet the inner needs of your soul.'

After a year as first lord, Churchill wrote to Sunny: 'The Admiralty is a most exacting mistress. I have given up all others for her – except Clemmie.' Although being first lord was exhilarating, it was tempered by the fact that Britain was drawing ever closer to the war he feared.

18

Lighting the Bonfire

I think he was the only Minister of the Crown who wept in the House at the declaration of war.
— Shane Leslie

Churchill was an early advocate of the great potential of flight and its military applications. He was particularly fascinated by the new flying machines that had been pioneered by the Americans, Wilbur and Orville Wright, whose first experimental flights on the beaches of Kitty Hawk, North Carolina, in 1903 changed the course of history. Charles Stewart Rolls, co-founder of the Rolls-Royce car company and a pioneer in aviation, ballooning, racing and motor cars, purchased a Wright aeroplane and in 1909 offered his services to the government in exploring its benefits.

Unlike others Churchill was never constrained by technology and was not afraid to use it to any end that enhanced the fighting capability of the Royal Navy. Indeed his vision far exceeded that of more noted military luminaries of that era, men such as Field Marshal Douglas Haig and Foch, who spurned the many advances in technology available in the years preceding the First World War. Haig, for example, thought the machine gun was 'a much over-rated weapon', Kitchener would write off the tank as a 'toy' and Foch treated the telephone as if it were a live hand grenade and in 1910 dismissed the potential of aviation: 'L'avion c'est zéro!'

A report issued by a subcommittee of the CID in 1909 noted that Churchill, then heading the Board of Trade, had suggested that 'the problem of the use of aeroplanes was a most important one, and we should place ourselves in communication with Mr Wright himself, and avail ourselves of his knowledge.'

Fisher, too, was a strong proponent of the establishment of a naval air arm, and Churchill needed no further encouragement. In December 1911 he actively promoted the creation of the Naval Air Service within the Admiralty, minuting the second sea lord that a means should be found 'to make aviation for war purposes the most honourable, as it is the most dangerous profession a young Englishman can adopt'. His enthusiasm was not shared by the parsimonious Treasury, which rebuffed him three times before authorizing funding in 1912.

A steady stream of minutes, memos and letters relating to every facet of aviation poured forth from Churchill's desk. He supported the use of the new zeppelin, which fell into disfavour with the sea lords, who were dubious about airships after an accident to one of the first experimental craft. As a member of the aviation subcommittee of the CID, Churchill found himself at loggerheads with his own former first sea lord, Sir Arthur Wilson, who, though retired, sat as a committee member. Wilson fiercely opposed the employment of airships yet became the advocate of a brilliant idea for what later changed the character of naval aviation: the aircraft carrier.

Churchill fought two battles over aviation: one to gain a share of military aviation from the army and another to create an official naval air service. The army formed the Royal Flying Corps in May 1912. By the end of the year it consisted of some thirty-six biplane fighters and a dozen manned balloons. The War Office claimed full proprietary rights over aviation and the aerial defence of Britain but failed to acquire sufficient funding to carry out the latter function. Not to be outdone by the army, the Royal Navy formed its own unsanctioned aviation service, and a good-natured competition arose between Churchill and his friend and counterpart at the War Office, Colonel Jack Seely, both of whom were 'like schoolboys with a new toy'. Such a rivalry could easily have escalated into ill will, stymying progress. Instead both men recognized that each service had a role in aviation, and in 1913 they brokered a deal that was a rare model of inter-service co-operation. Despite howls of outrage within the army, the navy gained a fleet of airships, and in return the Admiralty provided the cash-strapped War Office with a credit of twenty-five thousand pounds.

Seely and Churchill can claim credit as co-founders of Britain's military aviation. Britain's pre-war air force consisted of an army flying service (the Royal Flying Corps) and a naval aviation arm (the Royal Naval Air Service), both of which were under the nominal control of an

Air Committee, functioning under the aegis of the CID. Although the navy was already actively engaged in flying, a proposal to establish a naval air service dragged on until February 1913, when approval was granted for the navy to assume control of developing aircraft to be used in support of naval operations. Unfortunately 'it was too late, and the navy started the war with no airship capable of operating with the fleet in the reconnaissance role.' One can state nevertheless that the Royal Naval Air Service was unilaterally created by Churchill.

Although there was considerable activity in the years leading up to to the First World War, there might have been far more progress had the naysayers not greatly outnumbered the proponents of aviation. When war came in 1914 and the sceptics abruptly changed their minds about aviation, a future admiral and winner of the Victoria Cross exclaimed, 'They have pissed on Churchill's plant for three years – now they expect blooms in a month.'

In 1912 and 1913 the navy successfully tested the concept of using torpedoes dropped into the sea from an aircraft, and experimented with dropping bombs and firing machine guns mounted on the fuselage. By 1914 approximately 120 pilots had been trained to fly the new Naval Air Service's fifty-two seaplanes, its thirty-nine aircraft and its several airships. Without Churchill's percipient interest and initiative, it is questionable whether the air service would have been this far advanced. Even though Churchill was not the father of British naval aviation, he certainly was its nursemaid at a time when funds were tight and others who lacked his vision regarded the air arm as a wasteful extravagance.

A naval flying school was established at Eastchurch on the Isle of Sheppey, on the northern coast of Kent; from its aerodrome Churchill was later to fly frequently as a student. C. S. Rolls had learned to fly in 1909 at Eastchurch by towing a glider with his new Rolls-Royce motor car to the top of a nearby hill, and became the first airman to fly non-stop across the English Channel and back in June 1910. Hardly a month later he became the first of the many intrepid early flyers who were killed in aircraft accidents.

In 1913 it was deemed unsafe for anyone older than thirty-two to fly an aeroplane; however, given Churchill's deep curiosity and thirst for adventure it was inevitable that he would take up flying. Despite attempts to dissuade him, he refused to be put off and used the power of his office to arrange for lessons. He was fascinated by every aspect of flying, particularly the instruments, which he predicted would one day prove more important than the existing method whereby pilots flew by the seat of their pants. On one occasion he paid so much attention to a new device called an airspeed indicator that he lost his focus and nearly overshot the runway. 'He couldn't bear to make mistakes,' recalled Group Captain Ivon Courtney of the day Churchill bent an under-carriage on landing and insisted on going right back in the air. 'As an instructor, one was *over*-careful with WSC. We were all scared stiff of having a smashed First Lord on our hands.' Churchill was considered a fair pilot once in flight, but his instructors were reluctant to let him take the controls for take-offs and landings. Although he logged some twenty-five hours of flight time, he never flew solo. His instructors were understandably fearful, in part because he had been tossed from one to another like a hot potato, as no one wanted to have responsibility any longer than necessary. Moreover, to have had the first lord of the Admiralty killed or injured under their tutelage would hardly have been a recipe for career advancement. Not content with flying with the Royal Navy, Churchill also took lessons at the Army Central Flying School in Upavon, Wiltshire, where the assistant commandant was Colonel Hugh Trenchard, the future father of the Royal Air Force.

Trenchard and Churchill had met under circumstances that made them both rather bad-tempered, on a polo field in India in 1896 during a match between the 4th Hussars and the Royal Scots Fusiliers. The two young men butted heads after Churchill smacked the neck of his opposite number's pony with his mallet, a flagrant foul usually calling for a penalty shot. The irate fusilier barked: 'Play to the rules and take that stick out of my eye.' Furious at being challenged, Churchill attempted to unseat his opponent. 'Locked together like centaurs in a three-legged race, they careered along until the sheer deadlock brought them straining and swearing to a standstill.' Unaccustomed to being confronted without responding in kind, even when he was the initiator, Churchill scowled angrily at Trenchard and snapped: 'Who the devil were you talking to? If you've a complaint, speak to the umpire.' Trenchard retaliated by knocking Churchill's mallet from his hand before galloping away.

By the time the two men met again at Upavon in 1913 each had advanced his career. Trenchard never thought much of Churchill the polo player and thought even less of him as a pilot. Churchill, he said, wallowed about in the sky and 'seemed altogether too impatient for a good pupil'. However, some years later Trenchard would pay Churchill a handsome compliment. 'He would arrive unexpectedly, usually without pyjamas or even a handkerchief, see what he wanted to see, and stay the night – or what was left of it when he'd finished talking. Everything, including flying, was subordinated in his mind to a single purpose: getting the fleet ready for a war in which Germany would be the enemy. If the Admiralty had grasped his view of what aviation could do to help, the history of air-power might have taken a different turning.'

Courtney recalled that Churchill's demeanour before flying was the antithesis of the typical student flyer's. Where most are nervous and show it in various mannerisms, Churchill was calm, once reviewing papers with Jellicoe over breakfast before announcing, 'Well, Courtney, let us fly.' And fly he did, by his account more than 140 times, sometimes as often as ten times in a single day. Of the many endeavours he undertook during his lifetime, none was more rewarding. The sheer thrill of flying during the formative years of aviation provided a release from his everyday cares.

Churchill routinely flew in the skies over Kent well before the RAF pilots who fought the Battle of Britain had even been born. He seemed happiest when able to combine his inspection trips with flying, and those occasions were no coincidence. During a trip to Sheerness in October 1913 he wrote glowingly to Clementine of flying in a seaplane 'for a beautiful cruise at about 1,000 feet . . . She is a vy satisfactory vessel, and so easy to manage that they let me steer her for a whole hour myself . . . It has been as good as one of those old days in the S. African war, & I have lived entirely in the moment, with no care for all these tiresome party politics & searching newspapers, and awkward by-elections.' He also reflected on how far the naval air service had come under his guidance. 'In another year – if I am spared ministerially, there will be a gt [great] development. When I have pumped in another million the whole thing will be alive & on the wing.'

One of his favorite instructors was a Royal Marine officer, Captain Gilbert Wildman-Lushington, a member of a group of resolute young men with whom he easily bonded and whose company he cherished. Once, in 1913, as they ate wild duck shot especially for him, Churchill interjected a note of seriousness into an otherwise lighthearted occasion by delivering a brief talk on the future military uses of aviation, including the probability that aircraft could be turned from mere reconnaissance vehicles into an offensive role by installing weapons. That possibility was tested in May 1912 off Weymouth, where, with Asquith and the king observing, aircraft were used to detect submerged submarines and to drop explosives on them.

The cost of pioneering aviation was high, and a short time later Wildman-Lushington was killed instantly when he lost control of his biplane and crashed during a landing at the aerodrome at Eastchurch, which became the home base of the Royal Naval Air Service.

Churchill's flying caused great distress to his family and friends, who feared for his life. Clementine, already coping with two young children, was pregnant with their third child, and the absence of her husband and his dangerous pursuit of flying heightened a difficult and tense time in her life. Cousin Sunny wrote a blunt note in March 1913 exhorting Winston to cease his activities, remarking, 'I do not suppose that I shall get the chance of writing you many more letters if you continue your journeys in the Air . . . It is really wrong of you,' a view shared by his wife who implored him on several occasions to 'please be kind & don't fly any more just now.' H. G. Wells castigated Churchill as 'a very intractable, a very mischievous, dangerous little boy . . . Only thinking of him that way can I go on liking him.' Wildman-Lushington's death prompted a terse note from Churchill's friend and fellow Liberal MP F. E. Smith: 'Why do you do such a foolish thing as fly repeatedly? Surely it is unfair to your family, your career & your friends.'

Churchill, however, remained oblivious to these pleas and continued to fly at virtually every opportunity, and his flights included at least one mishap when a seaplane was forced to make an emergency landing in the waters off East Anglia too close to a pier for comfort. His frequent and vivid references to his flying exploits, such as a letter he wrote just before Lushington's fatal crash, did nothing to ease Clementine's anxiety; in fact they had the opposite effect. 'I have been very naughty today about flying,' he said, but he reassured her that 'with twenty machines in the air at once and thousands of flights made without mishap, it is not possible to look upon it as a vy serious risk. Do not be vexed with me.'

All too aware of the hazards posed by flight, and of the vulnerability of pilots flying these dangerous machines, when each and every flight was little better than a game of chance, with death the penalty for failure, he carried on flying. Despite the accidental deaths that had already taken enough lives to convince even the most unperceptive of the perils, he simply took it for granted that exposing himself to danger was part and parcel of his life and his duties and never seems seriously to have weighed the consequences.

His public bravado for the benefit of his instructors notwithstanding, two occasions brought the point home with extreme clarity. The first occurred the day after his maiden flight, when his instructor was killed while flying the same aircraft. The second was after he had flown in a new-model seaplane over the waters off Southampton. A short time later it crashed, killing all aboard.

From his flight experience came a fresh stream of memos about all aspects of the new air service. Churchill may well have been among the first to describe a modern airfield and flight control, writing: 'Landing places should be made visible to airmen from aloft. To this end metal signs, coloured and numbered, should be planted in the same way as motor-car guides are now fixed on our roads. Flags or other conspicuous aviation landmarks should be erected along the main aerial routes, like light-houses at sea, so as to enable navigation to proceed with sureness. It ought to be possible for an airman flying along an aerial route to pick up a succession of points which would enable him to verify his position exactly in relation to each of which well-known landing places exist.'

Although resigned to her husband's stubbornness, Clementine continued her entreaties. 'I cannot help knowing that you are going to fly as you go to Sheerness & it fills me with anxiety,' she wrote in June 1914, still pregnant with Sarah, who would be born in October. This message was followed by a grim letter in which she wrote of having dreamed she had had the baby, but it was 'a gaping idiot . . . I wanted the doctor to kill it . . . Every time I see a telegram now I think it is to announce that you have been killed flying . . . You are probably at it again at this very moment.' The letter was signed, 'Goodbye Dear but Cruel One, Your loving Clemmie'.

As the losses among airmen piled up, Churchill at last acknowledged that his flying days were nearly over. The day after Clementine's mournful letter (but before he received it), he wrote to her: 'I will not fly any more until at any rate you have recovered from your kitten & by then or perhaps later the risks may have been greatly reduced. This is a wrench, because I was on the verge of taking my pilot's certificate . . .

But I must admit that the numerous fatalities this year wd justify you in complaining if I continued to share the risks – as I am proud to do – of these good fellows. So I give it up decidedly for many months & perhaps for ever. This is a gift – so stupidly am I made – wh costs me more than anything wh cd be bought with money. So am vy glad to lay it at your feet, because I know it will rejoice & relieve your heart.'

Churchill's decision to stop flying had less to do with the relief it would bring to his long-suffering wife and more to do with the effect it had upon him personally. In his letter he went on to lament his decision and reflect on his flying experiences. 'I have been up nearly 140 times, with many pilots, & all kinds of machines, so I know the difficulties the dangers & the joys of the air . . . Though I had no need & perhaps no right to do it – it was an important part of my life during the last 7 months & I am sure my nerve, my spirits & my virtue were all improved by it. But at your expense my poor pussy cat! I am so sorry.' As Clementine would discover several years later, Winston's abstention was only temporary.

In May 1914, to redress the lack of schooling received by naval officers, Churchill issued a detailed memorandum on the military education and training of future staff officers. The practice of sitting on one's laurels was over. Thereafter not only would officers be properly educated in all aspects of warfare but a war college would be established at Greenwich, with admission by competitive examination.

This was the thoughtful, rational Churchill in full flower. There was, however, another, idiosyncratic side to him: a boundless thirst for adventure that simply refused to allow for inaction, an obsession with proving himself over and over again, and of not wasting a moment of his life, that dated to his unhappy childhood. This craving for action, combined with his occasional bouts of depression, seems to have spurred his relentless pursuit of anything that struck his fancy.

While visiting the Temple of Zeus at Paestum in southern Italy in 1912, he was less interested in its magnificence than in catching the elusive little green geckos that darted into and out of the cracks in the ancient stones. Refusing to be defeated at this brand-new sport, he focused his entire attention on the task, enlisting the services of Admiral Beatty and a civilian friend as beaters, 'muttering to himself' that 'we must be more scientific about our strategy. There is a science to catching lizards and we must master it.' A short time later, however, he seemed to forget his latest obsession long enough to pick armfuls of wildflowers with Violet Asquith.

In 1913, during a second Mediterranean excursion, he participated in a wild-pig hunt at three o'clock in the morning and also managed to create a bizarre version of 'fishing' as a leisure sport. To cast a line and sit quietly while waiting for a fish to take the bait was simply not for him; instead he turned the venture into a military operation, in one instance employing depth charges dropped from a small boat to stun the fish, which were duly netted as they surfaced. While this tactic worked effectively, it soon proved boring. Churchill decided that a more challenging strategy was called for and employed some fifty hapless sailors to drag the shallows of a bay with an enormous net as he directed them with expansive gestures, entreaties, shouts and precise instructions, as if he were a general attacking an enemy position. He was, as Violet Asquith put it, 'incapable of lotus-eating even for a few hours'.

Churchill's competitive nature was reflected in virtually everything he did. At the game of bridge he played aggressively and dangerously, usually heedless of the consequences. Aboard *Enchantress* in 1912 those who played with him were united in a common bond of misfortune and frustration. Asquith ('an eager and execrable player') used 'to sit in agony while Winston declared, doubled and redoubled with wild recklessness', then watched 'disillusioned and dumbfounded' as his impetuous partner invariably discarded the wrong card, leading to defeat. When questioned, Churchill would dismiss any suggestion of error and insist, 'The cards I throw away are not worthy of observation or I should not discard them. It is the cards I *play* on which you should concentrate your attention.' No one wanted to be Churchill's bridge partner, and those who took up that position were looked upon with pity.

The affectionate side of Winston Churchill was rarely on public display, yet throughout his travels and time away from his home, wife and children, he managed to write frequently. His letters to Clementine, whose health was never robust and often troubling, were surprisingly loving and passionate. They had pet names for each other: she called him her 'Pug' or 'Pug Dog', and he called her his beloved 'Kat', although her letters typically ended with 'Clem', 'Clemmie' or sometimes 'Clem-Pussy-Bird', and were often decorated with drawings of cats in various poses. One typical letter written in 1909 ended with 'Your most loving Clemmie Kat – Miaow', followed by a drawing of a cat reposing with its tail curled. These letters formed what their daughter Mary Soames has appropriately called a 'lifelong dialogue'.

By late 1913 there were war clouds of another sort over the high cost of increasing the Royal Navy to the size Churchill and Fisher believed essential. Asquith's cabinet consisted of a 'peace at any cost' wing of the Liberal Party, led by the chancellor Lloyd George, who still believed that rapprochement with Germany would prevent war. Churchill, the outsider, was not one of them and at times – as it would before the Second World War – his became a lonely voice of warning.

The bone of contention was the forthcoming naval estimates for 1914–15, the first that were solely Churchill's – the earlier ones of his tenure having been inherited from his predecessor. In December 1913, with widespread support within the Liberal Party, Lloyd George not only opposed the estimates but also proposed to negate the 60 per cent standard of supremacy over that of the German navy, established by Churchill and previously endorsed by the government. If enacted, Lloyd George's proposal would have placed in serious jeopardy the construction of four new battleships that Churchill required to keep the Royal Navy at the prescribed ratio.

Few politicians in British history can have been more eloquent – or more devious – than Lloyd George, who took his case to the people on New Year's Day 1914 in an interview published by the *Daily Chronicle*. In this he both attacked Churchill's naval budget and argued that there was no reason for war with Germany. Continued spending, he said, would needlessly escalate the arms race. The answer was disarmament, not armament. To add insult to injury upon Churchill – then conveniently away from London – Lloyd George calculatingly linked his opposition to the fierce resistance of one of his predecessors as chancellor of the exchequer, Lord Randolph Churchill, who had railed in 1886 against what he deemed extravagant Admiralty estimates.

Blindsided by Lloyd George's clever attack, Churchill brooded while some six members of Asquith's cabinet, including Reginald McKenna, who continued to nurse his resentment at being eased out as first lord, openly hoped that he would resign or be forced out – in no small part because of their aspiration themselves to reap the financial benefits of scaled-back naval expenditures. Although by nature stubborn and a fighter when challenged, Churchill realized he might not survive Lloyd George's damaging attack, divulging to a colleague in mid-January that he was not certain how long he could remain in office: 'The position is acute. I cannot make further economies. I cannot go back on my public declarations.' However, he had survived far worse situations and resolved: 'The old Cromwellian spirit still survives. I believe I am watched over.'

The whole affair was more than a dispute over funding; it also reflected an ideological clash within the ivory-tower element of the Liberals, who believed that German intentions were peaceful. The naval budget called for expenditure of more than £50 million, a figure that would soon rise to nearly £53 million, the largest in history, when Churchill presented a supplementary budget that destroyed Lloyd George's plan for reductions of £4 to £5 million. Clearly on a collision course, Churchill fought back – and won. The resolution of a political mess that threatened the very existence of the Asquith government was achieved through a combination of indisputable justification of the navy's needs and the support of the prime minister, who – displeased by Lloyd George's unilateral power play – did not back away from a fight with his fiery chancellor. Although Lloyd George threatened to resign, Asquith called his bluff, upheld Churchill and threatened to dissolve the government and call a general election. He thus ended the crisis that might otherwise have brought about the first lord's resignation at a crucial point in British history.

In March 1914, while presenting his revised naval estimates, Churchill warned the House of Commons in blunt language: 'The causes which might lead to a general war have not been removed ... The world is arming as it was never armed before. Every suggestion for arrest or limitation has so far been ineffectual.'

Germany had isolated itself and was friendless except for the crumbling Habsburg Empire. The blood ties of the great houses of Europe and Britain ultimately meant little in an atmosphere better suited to a hall of mirrors in which nothing is real. To the end the kaiser clung to the futile hope that Britain would not join a Continental war.

By the summer of 1914 the bonfire had been prepared, and it only remained for the right combination of events to set it alight. The assassination in Serbia of Archduke Franz Ferdinand and his wife, Sophie, in Sarajevo on 28 June went relatively overlooked until late July, when there was a frenzied exchange of diplomatic notes, threats, counterthreats and offers of various compromises emanating from Berlin, St Petersburg, Vienna, Paris and London, which ultimately achieved nothing. Europe's Great Powers were hurtling along a collision course and no one could halt them. The Gordian knots of the alliances seemed to trump all else, and just when it was most needed, diplomacy failed utterly and was replaced by bellicose threats.

In Britain even Churchill seemed unfazed as he ordered the fleet to stand down from a test mobilization in the English Channel that was unrelated to the war clouds hanging over Europe. The event in July was of limited military value and ended in the usual naval pageantry on a grand scale, as seventy battleships and other vessels representing each of the Royal Navy's fleets sailed in review past King George V aboard the royal yacht at Spithead on 19 July.

Asquith reported to the king on 24 July that Britain expected to be only a spectator in whatever unfolded in Europe. The real focus was on domestic problems and the lingering issue of Irish Home Rule – a tinderbox that was on the verge of exploding into civil war between the Unionist Protestants of Ulster and the Irish nationalists. By 26 July, however, the crisis in Europe had deepened, in the wake of an Austrian ultimatum that would have virtually ended Serbian sovereignty. After a telephone discussion with the first sea lord Prince Louis, on his own initiative Churchill withdrew the order for the fleet to stand down. He had been enjoying a rare leisurely weekend with his family at a rented seaside cottage near Cromer, along the Norfolk coast, but rushed back to the Admiralty that evening.

On 28 July Austria declared war on Serbia, thus setting in motion a conflict that no one except perhaps Germany wanted. In Churchill's view the Home Fleet was not only in the wrong location as a result of the test mobilization but was also in mortal danger should German U-boats launch sneak torpedo attacks. Fearful of continued indecisiveness by the cabinet, Churchill met privately with Asquith that evening and pointed out that 'the admiral commanding the Home Fleet was the only man in Europe who could "lose the war in the course of an afternoon".' He informed the prime minister that he intended to order the fleet to its wartime battle stations off Scotland that night.

Asquith assented, and in a convoy that stretched for eighteen miles the Home Fleet was safely relocated.

In the critical days before the declaration of war Churchill emerged as the only member of Asquith's cabinet prepared to act decisively rather than wring his hands. 'When he smelled battle afar off, Winston Churchill resembled the war horse in Job,' notes Barbara Tuchman. 'He was the only British minister to have a perfectly clear conviction of what Britain should do and to act upon it without hesitation.'

Churchill was horrified by the prospect of war. In the thirty months he had been first lord of the Admiralty he had made significant progress in preparing the Royal Navy for conflict with Germany. Its actions would now be in the hands of its officers and men. At his order the fleet was mobilized.

On 24 July Winston wrote to Clementine: 'Europe is trembling on the verge of a general war. The Austrian ultimatum to Serbia being the most insolent document of its kind ever devised.' The riddle of this complex man, his fascination with and aversion to war, was never better illustrated than four days later, as Britain stood on the brink. At midnight in the Admiralty, surrounded by his maps and a pervasive sense of crisis, he wrote Clementine an even grimmer note:

Everything trends towards catastrophe & collapse. I am interested, geared-up & happy. Is it not horrible to be built like that? The preparations have a hideous fascination for me. I pray to God to forgive me for such fearful moods of levity – Yet I wd do my best for peace & nothing wd induce me wrongfully to strike the blow – I cannot feel that we on this island are in any serious degree responsible for the wave of madness wh has swept the mind of Christendom. I wondered whether those stupid Kings & Emperors cd not assemble together & revivify Kingship by saving the nations from hell, but we all drift on a kind of dull cataleptic trance.

Britain, he said, was quite prepared to wage war if necessary. 'The sailors are thrilled and confident . . . But war is the Unknown & the Unexpected! God guard us and our long accumulated inheritance. You know how willingly & proudly I wd risk – or give if need be – my period of existence to keep this country great & famous & prosperous & free . . . I feel sure however that if war comes we shall give them a good drubbing.'

Still, as the crisis deepened Churchill held out the slender hope that war might be averted, writing to the Liberal MP Arthur Ponsonby on 31 July, 'So long as no treaty obligations or true British interest is involved I am of your opinion that we shd remain neutral.' When pressed the following day by Lloyd George to say if he would publicly commit himself to war should Belgium be invaded by Germany, Churchill sent a one-word reply, 'No', a position that was short lived. At first the cabinet was deeply divided (twelve of its eighteen members were initially against going to the aid of France if it was attacked by Germany), and three of its members resigned in protest; the remainder, including Churchill, supported British intervention.

In the United States the assassination of the archduke in Sarajevo had raised barely a ripple of public response or interest. American newspapers called the event simply 'another mess in the Balkans' and had no expectation that it would escalate into a devastating war. Theodore Roosevelt had long been suspicious of German intentions and followed events in Europe with deep interest, convinced that Britain must go to war. He admitted that 'I have never liked Winston Churchill,' but in late July, addressing Colonel Arthur Lee, a British military attaché, he grudgingly acknowledged Churchill's 'admirable conduct and nerve in mobilizing the fleet' and asked that Lee extend his congratulations. Although he and Churchill would never be friends, even Roosevelt could not help admiring his enterprising conduct.

By 1 August 1914, the Great Powers had mobilized their armies. Each was on a war footing and, like gunfighters, they waited to see who would draw first. That same day Churchill was finally convinced that war could not be averted. The next day he wrote dolefully to Clementine, 'It is all up. Germany has quenched the last hopes of peace by declaring war on Russia & the declaration against France is momentarily expected . . . the world has gone mad.' When the cabinet met that night, Asquith recorded, 'Winston, who has got on all his war-paint, is longing for a sea-fight in the early hours of tomorrow morning.'

Although war meant the greatest challenge of his political and military life he had yet faced, Churchill seems to have been guided by William Blake's admonition in 'A War Song to Englishmen', which he later quoted in *The World Crisis*:

Prepare, prepare the iron helm of war,
Bring forth the lots, cast in the spacious orb;
The Angel of Fate turns them with mighty hands,
And casts them out upon the darkened earth!
Prepare, prepare!

On 2 August Germany demanded the right of free passage for its armies through Belgium. It was the trigger that brought Britain into the war. The Belgian government refused, and the Germans invaded the next day. As Sir Michael Howard has explained, 'Ever since the sixteenth century it had been an article of faith in British naval policy that the Low Countries should not be allowed to fall into hostile hands, and this belief had become almost visceral, irrespective of party politics.' On 3 August the foreign secretary Sir Edward Grey arose in the Commons to declare: 'It is clear that the peace of Europe cannot be preserved.' Last-ditch diplomacy failed, thus casting the die of war. In London, Big Ben sounded the last hours of peace as a large crowd gathered outside Buckingham Palace to cheer and sing 'God Save the King' throughout the night of 3 August 1914.

On Tuesday, 4 August, 'Downing Street was full of anxious and excited people' as Asquith and his wife were driven from the House of Commons. 'Some stared, some cheered, and some lifted their hats in silence.' That night, as the key figures of the government sat silently, smoking, in the cabinet room of No. 10, there was no response to the British ultimatum, which gave Germany until midnight (11.00 p.m. British time) to provide assurances that Belgian neutrality would not be violated.

When 11.00 p.m. passed with no word from Germany, the declaration of war Churchill had so dreaded was now a reality. 'We were at war,' recorded Margot Asquith, who sat absently beside her husband throughout the long night 'with a feeling of numbness in my limbs'. The ill will that as early as 1912 Churchill had feared would develop into war now drew Britain into its deadly embrace.

The series of complex treaties that bound the various Great Powers to one another now brought about the most terrible war in the history of mankind – one that needn't have been fought. Britain and Germany had misread each other's intentions. What followed was one of history's gravest misjudgments.

Churchill ordered the Admiralty to signal all elements of the Royal Navy: 'Commence hostilities against Germany.' Margot Asquith claims to have seen Churchill 'with a happy face striding toward the double doors of the Cabinet room' of No. 10. Shane Leslie, however, would later write in sorrow, 'I think he was the only Minister of the Crown who wept in the House at the declaration of war.'

19

The Architect of War

I am inclined sometimes almost to shiver when I hear Winston say that the last thing he would pray for is Peace. – Herbert H. Asquith

When war suddenly shattered one of Europe's most glorious summers in memory, during a month traditionally devoted to leisurely holidays, the same wishful thinking that had occurred in the Boer War gripped the British public: there was the widespread belief, even among some in public office who ought to have known better, that the war no one wanted would surely be over by Christmas. What ensued was beyond comprehension. The First World War demonstrated with horrific consequences that modern warfare had evolved well beyond the slaughter seen on a smaller scale at Omdurman, and had far outpaced what the Boer War had foretold. Over the next four years there would occur unprecedented bloodshed. It was as if the civilized world had gone mad. A century that had started with such promise was suddenly and fatally thrust into a conflict that eventually engulfed much of the world and claimed the lives of an estimated twenty million civilians and soldiers, wounding another twenty-one million. Ever since, historians have pondered in vain the need for this war, and wondered what recklessness turned an attainable peace into a conflict that should never have been. John Keegan has asked the lingering question why 'the principle of the international treaty' brought Britain into a war 'that scarcely merited the price eventually paid for its protection'.

With their nations thus committed, it was the thousands of ordinary young men on each side of the conflict who paid the terrible price for the intransigence of their political leaders in what, in retrospect, was the most colossal folly in the history of mankind. As Churchill would later observe so perceptively in 1930, and as others have learned in other times and places, committing a nation to war sets in motion events that run beyond all control. What began in Europe quickly spread like a pandemic, and many nameless places became memorable only for their toll of death. From the mud and trenches of Belgium and France it spread to the Dardanelles, the forbidding rocky landscape of Gallipoli, and to eastern Europe, where, at Tannenberg and on other battlefields, men fought and died for scraps of terrain that were often measured in yards and were of questionable military value. The ugly scar that defined the front lines of the combatants defaced western Europe from the North Sea to Switzerland. Before it ended, once-placid sites like Verdun and the Somme, Passchendaele and Ypres, entered the lexicon of horror and pointless death, their only legacy the cemeteries of white and black crosses and memorials that still shock visitors by their sheer size.

The so-called Great War was 'great' only in the sense of the prodigious numbers of men who were killed. Nearly an entire generation of young men on all sides of the conflict would die. In Britain alone more than six hundred cemeteries would be constructed to bury the dead. In all, the death toll for the gross miscalculations of Europe's leaders was startling: nearly one million British and empire, approximately 1,380,000 French, 1,700,000 German, and 1,700,000 Russians. In addition to the military casualties, as many as ten million civilians are believed to have perished.

None of this seemed even remotely possible in August 1914 when the Great Powers went to war. Yet within days *The Economist* was already presciently calling it 'perhaps the greatest tragedy in human history'.

In the First World War, Winston Churchill learned the hard way that waging war was far more difficult than merely applying logic and common sense, as he had expressed it to J. B. Atkins during the Boer War. Indeed, because he was one of its leading architects in 1914 and 1915, the experience of being powerful as well as accountable for his decisions would have untold consequences for both his career and his state of mind. In less than one fateful year, everything that was so brilliant and so flawed about him would be on full display, from the heights of power to political ruin and the depths of despair, and penance at the front.

Although he had hoped war could be averted, when it did come Churchill embraced it as his own – too much so in the opinion of many.

There were two reasons for this: he had a natural tendency to take charge of any situation in which he found himself and, just as important, Britain in 1914 lacked a true wartime leader. Asquith being, by his own admission, wholly unsuited to that role, the prime minister all but ceded control and decision making in military matters to the two strongest-willed men in his government. Indeed, from Asquith's almost daily letters to the young woman with whom he was infatuated, Venetia Stanley, the war seemed more like a distant abstraction than a grave national crisis.

The British approach to the First World War was self-destructive. With the exception of Churchill, the politicians tended to defer to the generals and the admirals on the grounds that they were the experts and knew best, though as the war progressed they too would prove incompetent. The dangers of ineffective and rudderless political leadership were a lesson Winston Churchill would learn well and vow not to repeat during the Second World War.

With the exception of Field Marshal Lord Kitchener, whom Asquith made secretary of state for war, Churchill was the only important figure in the British government who had seen active service. Thus it was these two powerful men who emerged to dominate the first months of the war in Britain.

It was soon evident to Churchill that there was a void at the top that urgently needed filling. The void was great, and while his motives were clearly patriotic, it did not hurt that successful initiatives would enhance his personal and political standing. Having observed first hand how the Boer War had been botched, he had justifiable misgivings about the wisdom of leaving war strictly to the generals and admirals. Much like the Royal Navy, the British army had retained in its ranks too many dinosaurs left over from the Victorian era who still occupied commands they were barely competent to hold. Churchill's lack of faith would be amply justified over the next four troubled years, as thousands of lives were squandered in futile battles of attrition that mostly provided full employment for the graves registration units.

As the conflict degenerated into a state of paralysis and static warfare, Britain's war leaders deluded themselves into believing that each new year would bring victory though, instead, it brought only more misery and death. The result was a bloody and prolonged stalemate with neither side capable of breaking the deadlock.

Colonel Maurice Hankey, the secretary of the CID, accurately described Churchill as 'a man of a totally different type from all his colleagues. He had a real zest for war. If war there must be, he at least could enjoy it. The sound of guns quickened his pulses.' Churchill's zeal aside, Hankey noted a more important asset: 'When all looked black and spirits were inclined to droop, he could not only see, but could compel others to see, the brighter side of the picture . . . He brought an element of youth, energy, vitality and confidence that was a tower of strength to Asquith's Cabinet in those difficult early days.' Nor was it merely naval operations with which Churchill involved himself in the war's first months. His activities encompassed all three aspects of warfare: land, sea and air. He was bursting with ideas every day on how to end the stalemate and win the war. One of them was his offer of British logistical support for a Russian attack on Germany from the Baltic, whereby troops would land near Danzig (now Gdansk), drive on Berlin and quite probably end the war by capturing the German capital.

Churchill constantly lobbied Asquith with suggestions and proposals of a military nature. The British army, he insisted, was too small and would have to grow dramatically. Arthur Balfour reported a conversation on 8 September 1914 over dinner with Asquith and Churchill in which the first lord spoke 'airily of a British Army of a million men, and tells me he is making siege mortars at Woolwich as big, or bigger, than the German ones, in order to crush the Rhine fortresses'. Such enormous numbers in the first days of the war implied full conscription at a time when no one at the top level of the British government wanted to hear such a daunting prediction from a hawk like Churchill. Ultimately his estimate was but a drop in the manpower bucket. By the time the war ended in November 1918 the British would have mobilized 6.2 million men and suffered 740,000 dead.

When the War Office was unable to take over the aerial defence of the British homeland, Churchill readily accepted the mission for the Royal Navy in September 1914, thus becoming Britain's *de facto* air lord. As such he controlled not only aircraft of the Royal Naval Air Service but also a number of the army's Royal Flying Corps aircraft. Under his direction anti-aircraft barrage balloons and searchlights were emplaced in and around London. In October he learned that the new flying-boat aircraft had been successfully tested in the United States and immediately directed the Admiralty: 'Order a dozen as soon as possible.'

The naysayers grumbled (not too loudly, lest they cross the first lord) that the navy had no business flying aeroplanes or defending British cities. The unadventurous fourth sea lord, who not only 'left no stone unturned to discredit the Air Department', also disparaged the use of searchlights in the anti-aircraft defence of London against zeppelin raids as 'the most foolish contrivance it is possible to imagine'. Another senior naval officer, fearful that the flag flying over the Admiralty would attract unwelcome attention, lobbied to have it hauled down. Churchill scoffed at this idea and summarily rejected it. Tradition dictates that the Admiralty flag is lowered only upon the death of the sovereign.

Nevertheless Churchill's reputation for controversy and self-aggrandizement left many suspicious of his motives and doubtful of his judgment. Asquith himself had mixed feelings: he admired Churchill's dedication and initiative but soon questioned his seemingly unquenchable appetite for battle. The war was less than two months old when the prime minister wrote: 'War is a hellish business at the best – and I am inclined sometimes almost to shiver when I hear Winston say that the last thing he would pray for is Peace.'

Leadership in a time of war is a very sharp, double-edged blade which only the strong-willed should wield. Those with a zeal to lead who act decisively, and succeed, during a time of crisis attain heroic status. In the words of John F. Kennedy, 'leadership and learning are indispensable to each other,' a lesson Churchill was to take from the First World War. What separated him from others was that, having been stung by failure in one world war, he dared to grasp the reins of leadership in a second world conflict.

On the eve of the war Field Marshal Kitchener had arrived in England from Egypt to be invested as an earl, becoming Lord Kitchener. With Asquith present, on 28 July Churchill had Kitchener to lunch at Admiralty House, where they discussed the prospect of a Franco-German war. Both Asquith and Churchill came away impressed by Kitchener's argument that 'if we don't back up France when she is in real danger, we shall never be regarded or exercise real power again.' Despite their former enmity, Churchill thought it important to make use of Kitchener's experience and authority, and it was he who urged Asquith to appoint him secretary for war. Asquith agreed and tendered an offer the field marshal could not refuse. Like so many military men Kitchener mistrusted politicians but accepted the post as his patriotic duty, with the cautionary note: 'May God preserve me from the politicians.'

It was certainly one of the oddities of the time that Churchill and Kitchener – one a former lieutenant and stern critic of the celebrated victor of Omdurman and the other now a field marshal and a peer – became two of the key figures in Asquith's War Cabinet. Although they would have serious disagreements in the course of the war, the hatchet had been largely buried between them.

The Royal Navy's role was primarily defensive and was aimed at blockading the German navy by controlling the North Sea and the approaches to the English Channel. The genesis of this strategy lay in the navy's longtime guardianship of the British Empire and its trade routes. The pre-war plan to strangle the Germans through a close blockade of their ports and sea-lanes was scrapped and replaced by a distant blockade, the antithesis of Churchill's 'seek out and destroy' mentality. His aggressive approach to war extended to his view that the Royal Navy should engage and defeat the German navy at sea. Both he and Fisher seemed to have visions of another Battle of Trafalgar, with the Royal Navy triumphant and Jellicoe (appointed commander of the fleet by Churchill, at Fisher's instigation) as Horatio Nelson redux.

The battle lines were thus drawn between the first lord and his admirals, who vehemently disagreed with him, arguing that it would be a mistake to underestimate the German navy. Other than the ships used in the blockade, the bulk of the British fleet remained immobile in the Scottish harbours of Scapa Flow and Rosyth. The trouble was that this left the Germans in control of events; they would decide when, where and how to fight the Royal Navy. Tirpitz's navy may have been outnumbered and outgunned, but as subsequent events would prove, it was highly competent and not afraid of a showdown. The Germans scored an early success by the effective use of their submarine fleet. On 22 September the U-12 sank three British cruisers off the Dutch coast, killing more than fourteen hundred men, including a number of naval cadets as young as fourteen. Fisher had warned of the dangers posed by the submarine as the new factor in naval warfare, and although Churchill was quite aware of the U-boat menace, the British public was shocked by the sinkings. It was yet another sign that this was not to be another 'gentlemen's war'.

Although the deadly undersea war continued with more U-boat action, the German fleet remained at anchorage, refusing for the present to take the bait, leaving Churchill more and more frustrated with each passing day. He took considerable heat for a speech in Liverpool, the day before the cruisers were sunk, in which he proclaimed that if the German navy 'do not come out and fight they will be dug out like rats from a hole'. His ill-timed threat further estranged him from King George V, whose distrust of the first lord was magnified when he repeated a remark about Asquith that the king had made to him in strict confidence – that the prime minister was 'not quite a gentleman'.

Churchill's fascination with new concepts of war continued to drive him, never more so than in the development of the tank. Warfare was slowly evolving into the age of mechanization. The invention of the internal combustion engine was already in evidence in the new air services in Germany, France and Britain. The possible uses of new machines on land actually dated back to the 1880s and the invention, by a man named James Cowan, of a self-propelled vehicle that has been described 'a locomotive land battery fitted with scythes to mow down infantry'. In 1903 Churchill is likely to have read an article by the ever imaginative H. G. Wells in the *Strand Magazine*, which described his conception of 'a "Land Ironclad" like a large blockhouse 80 to 100 feet in length that could cross trenches'.

By the end of 1914 Churchill's was one of many minds searching for new ways to help break the emerging stalemate in France and the relentless rain of death that was wasting countless lives for no discernible purpose. French and British casualties were already more than a million and mounting daily, most of them the result of artillery fire.

Others were also formulating ideas to overcome the increasingly bleak situation on the western front. Lieutenant Colonel Ernest Swinton, the British official correspondent attached to the British Expeditionary Force (BEF), and the only journalist appointed by the War Office who was permitted to report from the front, received a letter from a friend telling him about 'a Yankee tractor which could climb like the devil'. After observing a gun being towed by a mechanized tractor, first designed in the United States in 1885 by the Holt Company, which was fitted with caterpillar-like tracks, Swinton immediately recognized its potential and sent a memorandum to Hankey proposing the idea of an armoured vehicle that would be protected from rifle and machine-gun fire. Hankey liked Swinton's idea and circulated a memo about the creation of new mechanical devices that soon reached Churchill's desk and that of the prime minister. Asquith was sufficiently impressed by the memorandum to note in late December: 'Hankey suggests the development of a lot of new mechanical devices, such as armed rollers to crush down barbed wire, bullet-proof shields and armour.'

Quite independently Churchill had been thinking along the same lines and was working closely with the Coventry Ordnance Works to produce a new 15-inch artillery weapon that could be towed by the Holt tractor. The involvement of the Royal Navy in the creation of the tank might seem incongruous but it was, in fact, rooted in expediency and Churchill's natural resourcefulness. Not only was he interested in self-propelled artillery, but the navy had also deployed a number of armoured cars early in the war to protect Allied airfields in Belgium, particularly in the defence of Antwerp. For Churchill, who had directed the construction of an armoured car capable of crossing trenches, the development of an armoured tracked vehicle was a simple extension of logic.

After reading Hankey's memo in January 1915, Churchill indicated his support for developing new methods of coping with trench warfare by means of what he was soon calling a 'land ship'. 'A committee of engineer officers and other experts ought to be sitting continually at the War Office to formulate schemes and examine suggestions, and I would repeat that it is not possible in most cases to have lengthy experiments.' The cost would be minimal, and 'the worst that can happen is that a comparatively small sum of money is wasted.' Kitchener voiced his support too and the project was referred to the Ordnance Department. After some preliminary work the ordnance men were unconvinced that an armoured vehicle could be developed. Churchill would later insist that the initiative died of inertia, 'and was decently interred in the archives of the War Office' until the continuing death toll in France resulted in Kitchener's renewed interest and, in early 1916, in the first War Office field trials.

However, with Churchill in the forefront, it was the Admiralty rather than the War Office that took over responsibility for the development of the first tanks used by the British in the First World War. The development of the tank might have remained in limbo had it not been for a fortuitous encounter in February 1915 at a dinner held by the Duke of Westminster, where Churchill met Flight Commander Thomas Hetherington, one of the first volunteers to join the Royal Flying Corps in 1912. Hetherington was involved with producing and field-testing armoured cars and, though aware that the War Office was conducting experiments, had independently noted the need for some type of armoured vehicle on the battlefield. He proposed to his superior, Captain (in 1915, Commodore) Murray F. Sueter, the director of the Air Department, the construction of 'a giant wheeled vehicle for cross-country travelling, which was to have wheels of such large diameter and to be provided with such great propelling power that it could travel indiscriminately over all but the greatest natural and artificial obstacles. It was to be armoured against hostile gun-fire and to be armed with a naval 12-inch gun.' This huge machine, thought Hetherington, would roam behind enemy lines, destroying trenches and artillery batteries and breaking railways by literally ripping out the tracks.

Hetherington told Churchill he was convinced that an armoured vehicle equipped with machine guns and capable of manoeuvring over open terrain under fire was entirely feasible and might turn the tide of the war. The officer, recorded Churchill, 'spoke with force and vision on the whole subject, advocating the creation of land battleships on a scale far larger than has ever been found practicable'.

Already favourably disposed towards any new idea of possible military importance, Churchill directed Hetherington to submit a proposal for his consideration. The next day the young officer submitted his ideas and Churchill immediately summoned one of his top naval architects, Captain Eustace Tennyson d'Eyncourt, presented him with Hetherington's proposal, and sent him off to investigate and, if possible, design a 'land ship'.

Despite being confined to his bedroom with the flu, Churchill immediately convened the first official Admiralty talks about the creation of the tank. This landmark meeting resulted in the formal creation of what was called the Land Ship Committee, chaired by d'Eyncourt. Adamant that the Germans should not learn of the project, Churchill directed that strict secrecy be maintained. The enterprise was identified as 'water-carriers for Russia' until Colonel Swinton pointed out that the War Office was bound to classify it as 'WCs for Russia', thus causing inevitable bafflement and unwanted speculation about why the Admiralty was concerning itself with designing toilets for the tsar. To avoid such confusion the project was renamed 'water tanks for Russia', and, at Swinton's suggestion, the name was eventually shortened to 'tanks'.

Although initially stymied by the belief that the only vehicle that could be produced would be too heavy, d'Eyncourt reacted with unusual speed by producing the first rough designs within a matter of days, earning from Churchill a response of 'Press on.' From there development progressed to field trials the following year that finally convinced the army it was time to take the concept seriously.

In addition to the 'land ship' project under the direction of d'Eyncourt and his team, Murray Sueter was overseeing a separate project to turn an armoured car into an armoured tracked vehicle. Many of the old-school Admiralty brass were already appalled by the folly of Churchill and his damned air service; now the first lord was absorbed in producing a silly land ship, and, as if this were not bad enough, there were also the newfangled armoured cars the air service was using. Opposition simmered, kept in check only by the presence of Churchill. The fourth sea lord complained (not loudly enough for Churchill to hear) that this was not the business of the navy, and a plainly irritated second sea lord sent for Sueter and demanded: 'What do you mean by allowing those awful armoured cars of yours with their objectionable smells to fly the White Ensign?' Sueter pointed out that it was upon Churchill's order and invited the second lord's presence at a demonstration the next day that would be attended by Churchill. 'The Second Lord declined, saying he was not interested in the armoured cars or those stupid Caterpillar landships.'

The first makeshift demonstration took place on 16 February 1915. In one of the most remarkable sights ever encountered in Whitehall, a prototype land ship was pulled around the historic Horse Guards Parade by a large white horse in what was derisively referred to by some as 'Winston's folly'. While the horse towed a small, engineless tracked vehicle, Sueter briefed Churchill on the characteristics and capabilities of the engine-powered version he planned to build. 'I pushed the caterpillar truck, loaded with large stones, about with my hands,' he wrote, 'to show Mr Churchill how easily it could be manipulated.' Churchill himself then pushed the contraption 'about the Horse Guards Parade and was amazed at the ease with which the truck with a full load of large stones could be moved. Although Mr Churchill does not shine at his best in dealing with mechanical matters,' wrote Sueter in his memoirs, 'he has the sharpest brain for grasping a new idea that I have ever met.' Observers from the War Office were unimpressed by the demonstration and doubted the vehicle would ever work in the conditions of trench warfare. Undeterred by the criticism of others and firmly convinced that something had to be done to save lives and help shorten the war, Churchill ordered Sueter to build eighteen of the new land ships.

Self-propelled artillery, the armoured car and a land ship were not the only new inventions Churchill was pursuing early in the war. Always searching for an edge, he began to conceive of another radically new device. In mid-January 1915, he summoned Commodore Sueter and subjected him to a passionate harangue that would typify his leadership in two world wars. Warming to his subject, Churchill strode back and forth as he outlined what he wanted accomplished, stopping only to declare: 'We must crush the trenches in. It is the only way. We must do it. We will crush them. I am certain it can be done.'

What Churchill had specifically in mind was a mechanized steam-roller. 'I wish the experiment made at once,' he commanded. 'Two ordinary steam-rollers are to be fastened together side by side with very strong steel connections ... covering a breadth of at least twelve to fourteen feet ... The ultimate object is to run along a line of trenches, crushing them all flat and burying the people in them ... The matter is extremely urgent ... Really the only difficulty you have got to surmount is to prevent the steam-rollers from breaking apart ... In a fortnight I wish to see these trials.' With that Sueter was dismissed.

The project was a disappointing failure; the machine proved incapable of crushing trenches and usually became mired in the mud and soft earth. Although the problem was never solved, it was not for lack of trying by Churchill, who doggedly pursued the idea whenever he met with Sueter, instructing him to 'put your best brains into this'.

Many resourceful people had a hand in the development of the first tanks. After the war an independent royal commission investigated and attempted to sort out the claims of individuals to monetary rewards, and to having been first. Ernest Swinton sought that honour, but though he may have been the first to articulate the need for a land ship, that was the extent of his involvement. He had no influence over the creation and design of the first tanks. Pioneer thinkers and doers like Hetherington and Sueter deserve the lion's share of the credit. If Swinton can claim to have fathered the tank, Winston Churchill can more appropriately be termed its midwife.

Did Churchill overstate his role? Hardly. His memoir of the First World War actually understates his achievement. 'There never was a person about whom it could be said "this man invented the tank,"' he wrote. Nevertheless the royal commission gave him far more credit, concluding that it 'was primarily due to the receptivity, courage and driving force of the Rt. Hon. Winston Spencer Churchill that the general idea of the use of such a machine as the "Tank" was converted into practical shape'.

Churchill took special pride in recounting how he had daringly spent seventy thousand pounds of public money on such a speculative venture. 'I did not inform the Board of Admiralty to share this responsibility with me. I did not inform the War Office, for I knew they would raise objections to my interference in this sphere.' Nor did he bother to inform the master general of ordnance, whom he knew to be sceptical, and perhaps most important of all, 'Neither did I inform the Treasury,' from whose jealously guarded purse strings all things monetary flowed.

While the Royal Navy struggled through accelerated research and development, the war dragged on during 1915 with no consensus on when (or even if) the land ship would ever be seen on a battlefield. By 1916, however, the value of the tank as a weapon of war had become more evident, and in 1917 its employment would have effects so dramatic they would change the future course of warfare.

By late August 1914 the situation in France had become chaotic, and victory seemed within the Germans' grasp as French and British units fell back almost to Paris. British forces had already retreated 150 miles under the relentless German onslaught, losses were extremely heavy and some units were in a state of disarray resulting in a dramatic headline in *The Times*: BROKEN BRITISH REGIMENTS. The British commander in chief, General Sir John French, was proposing to retire the BEF to the port of Le Havre, in effect throwing in the towel and gravely imperilling the French left flank. With the fragile Anglo-French alliance seemingly on the verge of collapse, the situation so alarmed the British government that Asquith dispatched Kitchener to France to stiffen French's resolve and restore order. Tact was never Kitchener's strong suit, and his mission was a fiasco that served only to embitter French at a time when one of the key battles of the war was being fought on the Marne and France was saved from defeat by the heroic actions of both the British and the French armies.

The Marne fighting signalled an abrupt change in the direction of the war. Although Churchill's brilliant forty-day prediction of 1911 came to pass, it was in no small part a result of the fateful Battle of the Marne. After the valiant stand by both French and British forces, the German high command, instead of continuing its offensive, elected to pull back to positions along the River Aisne, thereby losing the initiative and ultimately turning what might have been victory into a bloody four-year stalemate.

Churchill's prediction did not go unnoticed; he was praised by, among others, Haldane ('extraordinarily accurate . . . & shows great insight'), Balfour ('a triumph of prophecy'), Ian Hamilton ('masterly') and Fisher, who called it both 'astonishing and exhilarating! *It makes one trust your further forecast!*' Asquith told Haldane that Churchill was 'the equivalent of a large force in the field & this is true. You inspire us all by your courage & resolution.'

In the wake of his abortive trip to France, Kitchener requested that Churchill act as his emissary to Sir John French. He wanted him to persuade the British commander in chief to reposition the BEF, then disposed along the Aisne, to a new location on the Channel coast to ensure that the Germans could not outflank the Allied front. Churchill succeeded where Kitchener had failed, and French agreed to the plan. It is a measure of the dysfunction of the British government during the First World War that the first lord of the Admiralty should have been asked to mediate in a purely army matter.

Churchill took full advantage of his presence in France to tour the entire British front, observing artillery duels, visiting troop units, watching with bated breath as a British aircraft dodged German ack-ack, discussing the war atop a haystack with a corps commander, Lieutenant General Sir Henry Rawlinson. 'I saw the big black German shells, "the coal boxes" and "Jack Johnsons" as they were then called, bursting . . . When darkness fell I saw the horizon lighted with the quick flashing of the cannonade. Such scenes were afterwards to become commonplace: but their first aspect was thrilling.'

*

As already noted, during the first days of the war there was no immediate attempt by the German navy to engage the British. In the Mediterranean the Royal Navy botched orders to intercept the German battle cruiser *Goeben* and the light cruiser *Breslau*, both of which eluded pursuit as they emerged from Messina in Sicily and escaped through the Dardanelles to Constantinople (now Istanbul).

By the summer of 1914 Churchill had anticipated that the Germans might attempt to bomb London with their zeppelins based in Cologne, Friedrichshafen, Cuxhaven and Düsseldorf, and took action to deploy his new naval air arm to France. The original idea, however, seems to have come from Sueter, who obtained Churchill's approval to move it to Dunkirk to establish 'a temporary advanced air base for keeping the Channel under close observation for enemy submarines during the passage [to France] of the Expeditionary Force'. Under the command of one of the navy's pioneer airmen, Commander Charles R. Samson, Churchill's fledgling air force consisted of three squadrons, each of which was led by a pilot who had been one of Churchill's pre-war flight instructors.

On 1 September Churchill drafted a memo to Sueter directing that 'the largest possible force of naval aeroplanes should be stationed in Calais or Dunkirk.' He proposed taking the fight directly to the Germans by launching preventive strikes to hunt down and destroy the zeppelins on their home bases in Germany. The naval airmen proved their worth by destroying both in the air and in their sheds six zeppelins during the first year of the war. To protect its precious fleet of aircraft the navy purchased every Rolls-Royce motor car it could lay its hands on, some sixty in all, slapped on makeshift protective armour, mounted each with a Maxim gun and sent them and some two hundred Royal Marines to France to help secure the British airfields at Calais and Dunkirk. Air and ground reconnaissance became a daily fixture during the month of September.

On 4 September what may be considered the first British combined air–ground operation took place when, with one of Commander Samson's aircraft flying overhead and acting as a spotter, two naval armoured cars engaged a motor vehicle containing six German soldiers with Maxim fire. As events in the Great War this and other such engagements were wholly insignificant; however, they were the first tiny steps in the evolution of three-dimensional warfare (air, sea and ground) that has become standard military doctrine. For his part Churchill merits recognition for having unleashed the enormous future potential of airpower.

A short time later, on 10 September, accompanied by Sueter and two admirals, Churchill returned to France to assess what role his little air force could play in defending the French coastal ports from the advancing Germans, and to offer advice and encouragement to the French, who were reinforcing Dunkirk's port against a possible German attack. Afterwards the British consul informed the Foreign Office that Churchill's visit had done a great deal to bolster French morale.

This was merely the first of a series of trips by Churchill to France and Belgium in the early days of the war, one of them carried out by conscripting a light cruiser to carry him across the Channel. His absences from meetings of the cabinet did not go unnoticed, but under Asquith's loose rein he was generally able to do what he pleased. The fact that these journeys were seen by his critics as escapism instead of legitimate military missions failed to deter him. Nevertheless his post-war defence of his role comes across, in retrospect, as somewhat self-serving. While admitting that he could have left such activities to others, he insisted that he was the best-qualified man for the task by virtue of 'the special knowledge which I possessed, and the great and flexible authority which I wielded in this time of improvisation . . . I acted for the best'.

The French commander in chief, General (later Marshal) Joseph Jacques Joffre, appealed to Kitchener to send reinforcements to bolster the defences of Dunkirk and by so doing confuse the Germans by creating the impression that the British were assembling a large, potentially threatening force in the Pas de Calais. Churchill and Kitchener conferred, and it was agreed that the navy would send the Royal Marine Brigade provided the War Office supplied a regiment of yeomanry. Kitchener was happy to comply and selected Churchill's own Oxfordshire regiment, in which his brother Jack was a major. The unit was far from combat ready, prompting Herbert Asquith to observe, 'There are about 450 of them, all told, and if they encounter the Germans in any force I fear we shall see very few of them back again.'

The regimental colonel in chief (an honorary position) just happened to be Churchill's cousin Sunny, the Duke of Marlborough. In a brazen display of nepotism, Churchill arranged for the Royal Navy to provide a small fleet of transports solely for the use of the regiment, a luxury not provided for any other British army unit in France. And, in an emulation of the famously conscripted Parisian taxis that ferried French troops to the Marne, he also commandeered fifty buses from the streets of London to accompany the troops to France and ferry them from place to place, as well as a bevy of naval vehicles for the personal use and comfort of his cousin and his officers. The mission of this force was to divert German forces away from Joffre's beleaguered French army. What Churchill's critics derisively dubbed the 'Dunkirk Circus' began appearing in towns up and down the Pas de Calais region in ultimately harmless grandstanding that the Germans scarcely noticed.

The 'Dunkirk Circus' served as a perfect excuse for Churchill to travel to France to supervise what an amused Herbert Asquith called Winston's 'own little army'. Asquith had reason to be concerned about the possible fate of the Oxfordshire Yeomanry; the fun and frolics in the grounds of Blenheim during annual manoeuvres had done little to prepare the regiment to face a real enemy. Fortunately their mission in France turned out to be bloodless and mostly *opéra bouffe*, manifested by Churchill's appearance on one occasion clad in the full-dress uniform of an Elder Brother of Trinity House, which made him resemble a tug-boat captain dressed in a pea jacket and seaman's cap. A French officer who saw him exclaimed, 'Mon Dieu!'

20

Churchill's Private Army

Winston . . . is like a torpedo. The first you hear of his doings is when you hear the swish of the torpedo dashing through the water.   – Lloyd George

Despite the demanding business of supervising the Royal Navy in wartime, Churchill soon began to chafe over his role in the war. He abhorred being tied to his desk performing ministerial duties, pacing about the Admiralty awaiting reports from the fleet, now guarding the sea-lanes, and eyeing his battle map. His itch to expand his role was undisguised, and he followed events in France and Belgium closely. Determined to escape his deskbound existence, he took advantage of any convenient pretext to visit the front and to become more actively involved. In the process he seems to have lost sight of the enormity of his responsibility as first lord of the Admiralty.

Clementine became alarmed by his obsession with adventure and his growing discontent with his post as first lord. On 19 September 1914 she sent her mercurial husband a letter, pointing out: 'It makes me grieve to see you gloomy & dissatisfied with the unique position you have reached thro' years of ceaseless industry & foresight – The P.M. leans on you & listens to you more & more. You are the only young & vital person in the Cabinet. It is really wicked of you not to be swelling with pride at being 1st Lord of the Admiralty during the greatest War since the beginning of the World.' Clementine's admonitions went unheeded. Her husband remained single-minded about seeing his first military action since the Boer War.

There is an inexplicable but powerful fascination in placing one's life in harm's way – and living to tell the tale. Living dangerously was nothing new to Churchill. Time and again he had been lured by danger's embrace, much as unsuspecting mariners were drawn to their deaths on the rocks of the Rhine by the sirens of German legend. With Churchill, however, the thirst for action ran even deeper. He 'saw himself in the role of a Commander cast in the Napoleon mould', said the biographer Robert Rhodes James. That he needlessly placed himself in peril was, his critics argued, a failure of judgment that defined his character: brilliant but acutely unpredictable. Churchill simply brushed off such criticism.

The trait he brought to the Admiralty and to his role in the First World War was the urge to lead, to take charge of the moment, to be in full command, whatever the cost or the circumstances. During his numerous visits to France during the first two months of war, he had merely been an engrossed observer. In October 1914, however, he realized a long-held dream when an occasion arose that enabled him personally to pull the levers of war as a *de facto* field commander in a desperate venture.

In both world wars Antwerp, with its extensive dock and port facilities, the largest in Europe, was of immense strategic importance and was coveted by both the Germans and the Allies: 'It was felt in England that, as Napoleon is said to have remarked, Antwerp in the hands of a great continental power was a pistol levelled at the English coast.' The Germans were as determined to seize Antwerp as the British were to hold it. The French had likewise long recognized its importance in the defence of their country. Any German attack designed to capture the port was certain to include an offensive through Flanders.

Throughout September 1914 Antwerp was the object of increasing British concern as German forces began massing five divisions consisting of about sixty thousand reserve troops outside the city for an all-out assault. Its defences covered an enormous perimeter that extended well outside the city, guarded by some sixty-five thousand troops of the Belgian army and as many as eighty thousand garrison troops. In late September the forts guarding its approaches came under heavy siege. Although the Belgians were numerically superior to the Germans, they were no match for the heavy guns that relentlessly pounded the city and its forts. The Belgian army was a fragile entity, neither particularly well equipped nor ably led, its morale flagging and its lack of experience about to prove ruinous. Thus, despite the superior numbers, it was now certain that Antwerp would soon fall unless reinforced. The Belgian government sent urgent requests to Paris and London for artillery and aircraft.

Admittedly the situation in Antwerp was hardly clear when viewed from London on the basis of observer reports and telegrams. Yet, for all its professed apprehension, Britain failed to come to the aid of the Belgians in September 1914. The War Office was too burdened to respond to the pleas for assistance, and a harried Kitchener, already hard-pressed sending critically needed supplies and reinforcements to the BEF, rebuffed the request with the observation that Antwerp's danger was exaggerated. By the end of September, he would have good reason to change his mind, when the consequences of Antwerp's capture by the Germans became starkly evident.

Initially it was Churchill who stepped in to fill the void and sent all the naval guns and ammunition he could spare. Although the consensus was that Britain could do little or nothing to prevent the city's fall, he regarded Antwerp as a clarion call to action. There was ample basis for concern. Should it fall before the French anchored the Allied left flank on the North Sea, General Alexander von Kluck's First Army might have been able to capture the Channel ports of Ostend, Calais and Dunkirk. Not only would this imperil the BEF, but also the ports might become a base from which the Germans could even invade Britain. Conversely, in Allied hands Antwerp was a base from which attacks could be mounted upon the German rear. 'WE MUST HOLD ANTWERP,' Churchill wrote to Edward Grey on 7 September.

On the evening of 2 October Grey received a telegram from the Belgians signalling their intention to shift their government from Antwerp to Ostend the next morning. The principals in London met to deal with the crisis. Churchill was absent but his presence was deemed crucial. He had left London a short time earlier by special train to Dover, where he was to embark on yet another cross-Channel trip to Dunkirk. The train was stopped en route and sent back to Victoria Station, from which Churchill was driven to a meeting with Kitchener, Grey and the first sea lord, Prince Louis. Collectively they decided that Antwerp had to be held and that Churchill should travel there at once to assess the situation. This decision reversed an earlier proposal by Churchill, rejected by Kitchener, on 7 September to send British territorial troops to help defend the city. With the promise of immediate aid the Belgian government agreed to defer its decision to leave Antwerp.

Asquith had been in Wales when the decision was made but neverthe-less supported it. 'I don't know how fluent [Churchill] is in French,' he reported to Venetia Stanley, 'but if he was able to do himself justice in a foreign tongue, the Belges will have listened to a discourse the like of which they have never heard before. I cannot but think that he will stiffen them up to the sticking point.'

Antwerp was another prime example of the inept manner in which the British government waged the First World War. At critical times early in the war, even during meetings, Asquith and Venetia's future husband, Edwin Montagu, a Liberal MP and junior government minis-ter, were both composing love letters to her while the business of war took second place.

Shortly after noon on 3 October, Churchill reached the besieged city of Antwerp determined to persuade the Belgians to continue the fight. He did not merely arrive – he blew in like a strong wind off the North Sea. When his vehicle screeched to a halt at the front steps of Antwerp's *hôtel de ville*, the car door was thrown violently open and out bounded Churchill dressed in the same uniform he had worn in France, that of an Elder Brother of Trinity House. His grand entrance was pure melodrama. An eyewitness recorded, 'As he darted into the crowded lobby ... he flung his arms out in a nervous characteristic gesture, as though pushing his way through a crowd. It was a most spectacular gesture' that seemed to announce his arrival as 'the hero dashes up bare-headed on a foam-flecked horse, and saves the heroine ... The Burgomaster stopped him, introduced himself, and expressed anxiety regarding the fate of the city.' Before he could even finish Churchill interrupted him in a loud voice heard by everyone present. "I think everything will be all right now, Mr Burgomaster," he called ... "You needn't worry. We're going to save the city." '

After learning of Churchill's persuasive words to the Belgian prime minister, Count de Broqueville, that all was not lost, the Belgian govern-ment agreed to continue defending Antwerp for a further ten days provided the Allies mounted a major relief operation within seventy-two hours. What Churchill did not tell the Belgians was that neither Britain nor France had much manpower to spare.

By the time of his arrival, plans were already being made to send the two thousand men of the Royal Marine Brigade from Dunkirk, but significantly more reinforcements were urgently required. That night he telegraphed Kitchener and Grey that the Admiralty's two reserve naval brigades should be sent to Antwerp at once. 'When can they arrive?' he demanded. Addressing the grim situation, he noted the vital need for those connected with Antwerp's defence to do their utmost. 'I must impress on you the necessity of making these worn and weary men throw their souls into it, or the whole thing will go with a run.' Kitchener, Grey and Asquith supported Churchill's request, and by the morning of 4 October the War Office had set in motion the immediate dispatch of this force and had arranged with the French government for further reinforcements.

In mid-August 1914 Churchill had created what was called the Royal Naval Division, consisting of some 3,500 naval reservists whom he intended to form into four battalions and eventually integrate into the existing marine brigade. Within the government Churchill's new formation drew praise and requests from politicians such as the future prime minister Andrew Bonar Law for places in the unit for their nephews. Within the Admiralty there was scepticism that this was 'the best possible use of surplus naval reservists', in what many still saw as Churchill's own private army. Captain Herbert Richmond, the assistant director of operations, later an admiral and a distinguished academic, angrily declared that Churchill was 'not sane ... What is this force to do? Heaven only knows. Winston is pleased as Punch! This is the beginning of a great war in which our whole future rests upon the proper use of the Navy!! It is astounding. These men who are thus to be employed in soldiering know nothing about the business. They are all amateurs ... the whole thing is so wicked that Churchill ought to be hanged before he should be allowed to do such a thing ... how the [Admiralty] Board can permit him to indulge in such foolery, without a word of serious protest, I don't know.'

Although *The Times* extolled the new force, the first lord's critics, according to his official biographer, deemed it 'a provocative step, suggesting that Churchill, not content with the naval forces under his command, wanted to control land operations as well'. The men conscripted into this new unit expressed mixed emotions, but all thought of themselves as Churchill men. When they were in action against the Germans and the situation was favourable, they dubbed themselves

'Churchill's Pets'; however, in times of crisis their nickname quickly changed to 'Churchill's Innocent Victims'.

In October 1914 his new creation was put to the test at Antwerp, where, as Ian Hamilton would later describe it, he 'handled the Naval Division as if he were Napoleon and they were the Old Guard, flinging them right before the enemy's opening jaws'.

On Sunday morning, 4 October, Churchill inspected Antwerp's outer defences. The ring of forts guarding the city was being relentlessly pounded by German artillery, and what the first lord encountered was a tired and dispirited Belgian army hanging on by a thread. Part of the Belgian defences was a familiar remembrance of the Boer War, an armoured train mounting naval guns and manned by Royal Navy personnel. Churchill inspected the train while it was under German fire.

Throughout the day he held meetings with various military and civilian officials. 'Mr Churchill was energetic and imperative,' commented Henry Stevens, the young British seaman in charge of his transportation. 'To me it appeared that Mr Churchill dominated the proceedings and the impression formed that he was by no means satisfied with the position generally. He put forward his ideas forcefully, waving his stick and thumping the ground with it.' His impatience with Antwerp's defences was clear in his angry demeanour. 'At one line of trenches he found the line thinly held and asked where "the bloody men were". He certainly was not mollified when he was told that was all that were available at that point.' A telegram he fired off to Kitchener that the Belgian troops defending the city were 'weary and disheartened' was hardly an optimistic sign.

For all of Churchill's exposure to danger from artillery shells or bullets from a good marksman, nothing deterred him from indulging his need for luxury. He settled in at Antwerp's first-class Hotel Saint-Antoine, 'happily giving orders and eating an excellent dinner', and set up his headquarters there.

As he was inspecting the defences on the morning of 4 October, the two naval brigades were marshalling at Dover after hastily assembling what little equipment they possessed and receiving immunizations against typhoid. Not until the early days of the Second World War in 1940 would a less prepared military unit exist. Churchill's reasoning (like Kitchener's) was that, although ill trained, the men would respond to veteran leadership sufficiently to mount a defence of Antwerp.

However, they lacked vital equipment such as ammunition clips and medical supplies; many had just been recruited, had been given as little as two days' military training, and had never so much as fired a weapon. The officers carried empty revolvers. The composition of this motley force ranged from working-class men, such as Welsh miners, to men of the upper classes, including Herbert Asquith's son, the poet Rupert Brooke and a young, British-born New Zealand dentist named Bernard Freyberg, who would later earn a Victoria Cross and two DSOs serving in the army and command his nation's forces during the Second World War. As much as Asquith had faith in Churchill, he had good cause for anxiety about the safety of his son.

What Churchill saw during his inspection of the city's defences on 4 October convinced him that there now existed an opportunity to make his dream of command a reality. The following day, in what Asquith has described as 'a real bit of tragic-comedy', he telegraphed the prime minister to announce that he desired to 'take formal military charge of the British forces in Antwerp and tender my resignation of the office of First Lord of the Admiralty'. His offer of resignation included the proviso that 'I be given the necessary military rank and authority, and full powers of a commander of a detached force in the field'. Churchill later asserted that Kitchener had recommended 'that it should be, and wished to give me the necessary military rank'. While it is true that Kitchener favoured promoting him to the rank of lieutenant general, Asquith instantly denied Churchill's request, thus ending the matter. 'His offer, when read out to the Cabinet, provoked only "roars of incredulous laughter".' With Asquith's rejection of Churchill as the military commander of Antwerp, the War Office ordered General Rawlinson to take command of a forty-thousand-man British relief force.

Although Asquith wanted him back in England post-haste, and telegraphed him to that effect on 5 October, Churchill was unwilling to leave Antwerp at a time when there was no overall military commander to take charge of the city's defence. His determination hardened when Rawlinson reported utter confusion in mustering the relief force at Dunkirk. Some units and heavy naval guns destined for Antwerp had yet to arrive, and he estimated that his force would not reach Belgium for possibly another three or four days. With French marine reinforcements likewise delayed, the adverse news from both Paris and London meant that the burden of defending Antwerp would fall squarely on the three brigades of untested, ill-trained reservists. 'In view of the situation and developing German attack, it is my duty to remain here and combine my direction of affairs unless relieved by some person of consequence,' he telegraphed to Kitchener.

He may have been denied military rank, but Churchill acted every bit the military commander of British forces in Antwerp. Left to his own devices, he issued orders, sent telegrams and cajoled commanders, ordinary troops and politicians to hold firm. A steady stream of orders demanding supplies bore his name and burned the telegraph wires to London. They ranged from guns of various calibres, entrenching tools and steel wire rope to duffel suits for the crews of the armoured trains. He visited the marine brigade dug in south-east of the city and was observed smiling and calmly smoking one of his large cigars under what an Italian reporter described as 'a rain of shrapnel, which I can only call fearful . . . it is not easy to find in the whole of Europe a Minister who would be capable of smoking peacefully under that shellfire.'

As the battle for Antwerp unfolded, Captain Richmond wrote with chilling accuracy of his fear for the fate of the Royal Marine force. 'The 1st Lord is sending *his* army there. I don't mind his tuppenny untrained rabble going, but I do strongly object to 2000 invaluable marines being sent to be locked up in the fortress & become prisoners of war if the place is taken . . . No Board of Admiralty with two pennyworth of knowledge & backbone would have allowed marines to be used in such a way . . . It is a tragedy that the Navy should be in such lunatic hands at this time.'

To enthusiastic cheers from the Belgians, the six thousand men of Churchill's two naval brigades arrived in Antwerp during the night of 5–6 October after an exhausting trip from Dover and Dunkirk, some bivouacking in the gardens of the royal palace but most hustled forward to man defensive positions selected by Churchill. From there things got steadily worse under a deluge of German artillery fire. From a small party of Royal Marines forced to abandon their positions came a disheartening message: 'God help you.' As they dug trenches shivering in the cold, Able Seaman Jack Bentham, later a flying officer in both wars, recorded Churchill's final visit to the front. 'We cursed a car containing Churchill who came out to see what was going on & we were glad when he departed.'

'Winston persists in remaining there, which leaves the Admiralty here without a head,' Asquith complained to Venetia Stanley on the afternoon of 6 October, while admitting that 'he has done good service in the way of starching & ironing the Belges.' Jack Seely, the former secretary of state for war, sent to Antwerp by Sir John French as his emissary, was one of the last to evacuate the besieged city. Seely arrived the same day as Churchill and remained to witness the city's defence by his longtime friend. 'From the moment I arrived it was apparent that the whole business was in Winston's hands. He dominated the whole place – the King, Ministers, soldiers, sailors. So great was his influence that I am convinced that with 20,000 British troops he could have held Antwerp against any onslaught.'

Rawlinson arrived unaccompanied late that same afternoon, his troops still assembling along the Channel ports, and after conferring with Churchill and the Belgian authorities, took formal command of the British forces defending the city. With Rawlinson's presence Churchill no longer had a valid reason to remain in Antwerp, and he reluctantly departed, arriving in London on the morning of 7 October to report to Asquith and the cabinet. 'Winston is in great form & I think has thoroughly enjoyed his adventure,' the prime minister duly reported to his lady friend. 'He is certainly one of the people one would choose to go tiger hunting with, tho' as you very truly say he ought to have [been] born in the centuries before specialism. He was quite ready to take over in Belgium, and did so for a couple of days.'

Lloyd George was less charitable over Antwerp. 'Winston is becoming a great danger . . . [He] is like a torpedo. The first you hear of his doings is when you hear the swish of the torpedo dashing through the water.'

Churchill was not quite finished with Antwerp. When he learned that the commander of his marine brigade, Major General Archibald Paris, proposed to withdraw from his positions, he reacted with fury, believing that the British positions were impregnable and could be held. 'Winston got on the telephone with Gen. Paris & put the fear of God into him,' reported Asquith. Churchill's censure was misplaced. Paris was a veteran officer whose judgment was proved correct within hours. The Belgian defences were crumbling under the German onslaught, Antwerp was about to fall, and Rawlinson's reinforcements and the promised French troops were miles away and never arrived.

When the city fell on the night of 10 October 1914, the cost of the vain attempt to defend it by the untrained bluejacket soldiers of

Churchill's Royal Naval Division was high: 57 dead, 158 wounded and 936 captured on a train and put in a German POW camp. In addition two battalions totalling some fifteen hundred men got lost during the retreat and ended up in neutral Holland, where the Dutch were obliged to intern them for the duration of the war. The retreat in the dead of night was utter confusion as Antwerp burned brilliantly and all roads leading from the city became clogged with fleeing refugees carrying or pushing carts filled with what little was left of their lives. 'Antwerp that night was like several different kinds of Hell,' wrote Rupert Brooke, 'the broken houses and dead horses lit by an infernal glare. The refugees were the worst sight . . . old men crying and the women with hard drawn faces. What a crime!'

The British government angrily blamed the French for failing to reinforce the city and for placing Britain's troops there in great peril. Those closest to the Antwerp venture, including Kitchener, Grey and Asquith, firmly believed that the week-long delay in the German capture of the city had bought vital time to secure the Channel ports. Asquith was persuaded by the reliable Hankey that Churchill's actions had not been in vain, preventing the Germans from linking up their forces at grave expense to the Allies.

Others were less charitable. Churchill's godson and biographer, the second Earl of Birkenhead, thought his request to exchange the Admiralty for a military command 'wholly adolescent in character' and felt that it placed 'a devastating question mark against his judgment and the sudden impulses of his mind', being suggestive of 'an excitable boy who had been reading too many adventure stories . . . [and] a measure of Winston's utter absorption . . . in exchanging an office desk for a battlefield, and the romanticism which made him long to command great armies in war'.

Churchill's enemies emerged in full angry flow in both Parliament and the Conservative press, which savagely skewered him; the editor of the *Morning Post*, the newspaper for which he had written so many dispatches from the Sudan and South Africa, attacked him as a 'dictator' run amok in an Admiralty 'governed no longer by a Board of experts, but by a brilliant and erratic amateur'.

Other newspapers came to his defence, and the public was left to wonder who was right. Denunciations of Churchill continued unabated, from Conservatives who derisively referred to him as the 'amateur

Commander-in-Chief of the Navy' to behind-his-back criticism from Asquith based on disturbing first-hand reports from his son, Arthur, who had participated in the defence of Antwerp as a junior naval officer. The prime minister always had mixed emotions about his volatile first lord. While he greatly admired his initiative and audacity, he was uneasy about his excesses. Knowing full well the risks of sending untrained reinforcements into Antwerp, Asquith angrily called it *'wicked* folly . . . nothing can excuse Winston (who knew all the facts) from sending in the two Naval Brigades.'

Although the British government was clearly lacking in strong leadership, for Churchill to abandon all he had worked so long and hard to create – and was now responsible for – was arguably utter recklessness. It remains a profoundly troubling notion that he should even consider forsaking his post as first lord of the Admiralty in the autumn of 1914 to command a lost cause that held every possibility of death or capture. When everything pointed to a long and costly conflict, it was another example of heart over head and common sense at a time of deep crisis.

Thus Antwerp ranks high on Churchill's list of failures. One representative view of the affair was that of his daughter Mary Soames, who argued that rather than being tagged 'an irresponsible adventurer', her father should have been praised for his presence, which 'undeniably stiffened the resistance of the Belgians; and, by delaying the capitulation of the city, [rendered] a signal service . . . to the Allies'. Nevertheless, she conceded, 'Both to his wife and his colleagues it seemed crystal clear that Winston's sense of proportion had deserted him,' and that he had lost sight of his ministerial responsibility for a 'rash and ill-conceived request'. Although it remains indisputable that his presence helped to buy the besieged city some time, whether or not that extra time was significant in securing Dunkirk remains an open question. The two divisions sent by Kitchener to Zeebrugge and Ostend may well have been the real deciding factor.

Violet Asquith had a quite different view of Antwerp, writing, 'No event in his whole career, with the one exception of Gallipoli, did him greater and more undeserved damage.' She questioned Churchill's obsession with trading the Admiralty for a military command at the front, calling it 'the choice of a romantic child'. With the war barely two months old, 'he had served it with the passion of a lover and the dedication of a friar.' How could he even consider such a choice?

The reasons for the storm of recrimination over Antwerp are absolutely clear: he had made so many enemies over the years in his climb to power, dating from his first days as a war correspondent, that invariably his every action was both scrutinized and, even when successful, often harshly criticized. He was already a lightning rod of greater proportions than his flamboyant father. His immediate and rather small circle of friends was loyal, but in others Churchill seemed to inspire cruel invective; whether this was out of jealousy, fear or loathing of him for having deserted the Conservative Party a decade earlier, it was all ammunition that Tory newspapers gleefully exploited.

Although apparently heedless of where his priorities lay, Churchill wrote defiantly in 1923: 'I cannot feel that I deserve the reproaches and foolish fictions which have been so long freely and ignorantly heaped upon me . . . At each stage the action which I took seemed right, *natural* and even inevitable.'

Only years later would he somewhat disingenuously note that he should never have gone to Antwerp and ought instead to have remained in London and 'endeavoured to force the Cabinet and Lord Kitchener to take more effective action than they did . . . Instead I passed four or five vivid days amid the shells, excitement and tragedy of the defence of Antwerp. I soon became so deeply involved in the local event that I had in common decency to offer my resignation of my office as First Lord of the Admiralty to see things through on the spot.'

He would also write: 'Those who are charged with the direction of supreme affairs must sit on the mountain-tops of control; they must never descend into the valleys of direct physical and personal action.' Indeed Churchill never lost his desire for soldiering, and at Antwerp he indulged his passion for a desperate venture. His offer of resignation had nothing to do with his sense of duty as first lord and everything to do with an opportunity once again to engage in soldiering, this time in command. During the Second World War, with considerable nostalgia, Churchill admitted to his favourite battlefield commander, Field Marshal Sir Harold Alexander: 'I do envy you, you've done what I've always wanted to do – command great victorious armies in battle . . . I got very near to it once, in the First World War, when I commanded those forces at Antwerp. I thought it was going to be a great opportunity.'

Yet after his return from Antwerp Churchill was unrepentant and persisted in his quest for a military role in the war, once more pleading with Asquith to be relieved of his duties as first lord of the Admiralty in exchange for a military command. Asquith again declined, reminding him that he could not be spared. Asquith paints us an astonishing picture of Churchill's single-mindedness: 'He scoffs at that, alleging that the naval part of the business is practically over . . . His mouth waters at the thought of Kitchener's Armies. Are these "glittering commands" to be entrusted to "dug-out trash", bred on the obsolete tactics of twenty-five years ago, mediocrities who have led a sheltered life, mouldering in military routine? For an hour he poured forth a ceaseless invective and appeal, and I much regretted that there was no shorthand writer within hearing . . . A political career was nothing to him in comparison with military glory.'

As Churchill was returning from France on the morning of 7 October, Clementine gave birth to a daughter, Sarah, the Churchills' third child. While she was recuperating at home, the foreign secretary Sir Edward Grey emerged from a cabinet meeting and wrote to Clementine to extol her husband's virtues, saying that he felt 'a glow imported by the thought that I am sitting next a Hero. I cant tell you how much I admire his courage & gallant spirit & genius for war. It inspires us all.'

A more sobering assessment of Churchill's Antwerp venture invites a different conclusion: he had allowed his craving for adventure and military glory to override his primary responsibility of supervising the Royal Navy in the first desperate months of the gravest war in his nation's history.

21

'Damn the Dardanelles!
They will be Our Grave'

When I finally decided to go in, I went in whole hog, totus porcus.
— Churchill, testimony to the Dardanelles Commission

By the end of 1914, all hope of an early end to the war had faded away. Both the eastern and the western fronts were frozen in deadlock, and there had yet to be a decisive confrontation between the two powerful navies for control of the sea. The foolish assumption by so many that the war would be over by Christmas was a distant memory. After only five months at war British deaths had already climbed to nearly six figures (95,654), and the conflict had quickly evolved into a deadly one of stalemate and attrition, with little hope of resolution. Men died from endless artillery shells that exploded indiscriminately, from the use of poison gas and from machine guns that cut down anyone missed by the artillery fire. In the nearly five hundred miles of trenches, the numbers killed on both sides were stupefying.

The deaths of soldiers in combat is an inevitable and painful part of war. The First World War carried that precept to heights yet undreamed of. Soldiers became little more than participants in a numbers game, and casualties, whether from death or loss due to wounding or for other reasons, were callously categorized as 'wastage' by the British War Office – a term carried over into the Second World War and one Churchill detested as much as he did 'bodies'. As William Manchester points out, there were so many troops manning the extensive trench lines that there was one soldier for every four inches of trench line – more than seven million men. 'In the course of an average day on the western front, there were 2,533 men on both sides killed in action, 9,121 wounded, and 1,164 missing.'

Prime Minister Herbert Asquith described sitting in the cabinet room at No. 10 in the gloomy days of December, and being reassured by observing the lights blazing across Horse Guards Parade in Churchill's office. 'I see the Admiralty flag flying & the lights "beginning to twinkle" from the rooms where Winston . . . [and his two chief assistants are] beating out their plans.'

Churchill had turned forty in November, and at this point in his life, one of the few people with genuine insight into his character was Asquith's wife Margot. 'What is it that gives him his preeminence?' she wrote in her diary. 'It is certainly not his mind. I said long ago and with truth Winston has a noisy mind. Certainly not his judgment . . . It is, of course, his courage and colour – his amazing mixture of industry and enterprise . . . He never shirks hedges or *protects* himself – though he thinks of himself perpetually. *He takes huge risks.* He is at his very best just now; when others are shrivelled with grief – apprehensive . . . and self-conscious morally; Winston is intrepid, valourous, passionately keen and sympathetic, longing to be in the trenches – dreaming of war, big, buoyant, happy, even. It is very extraordinary. He is a born soldier.'

Britain was in dire need of a winning strategy. To date the war had been a series of disjointed military operations decided and carried out primarily by Kitchener and Churchill. Something better was required, and in November 1914 the War Council was created, in modern terms a war cabinet, chaired by the prime minister. The successor to the Committee of Imperial Defence, it was supposed to provide high-level direction and decision making; instead it quickly grew into an unwieldy bureaucracy of committees and subcommittees, creating what came to be called 'Defence by Committee'. Under Asquith's lackadaisical leadership its two most powerful figures remained the same two men who had dominated from the outset of the war. Too often, as such organizations tend to do, it deferred to either Churchill or Kitchener, rubber-stamping decisions, offering no alternatives, hearing only what it wanted to hear when its members ought to have been asking challenging questions. The Dardanelles Commission would later place a share of the blame upon the War Council, and Churchill candidly told the commission, 'I have often heard the cabinet say: "We do not wish to be told about this." '

With the cabinet thus bereft of direction, what passed for strategy by both the French and the British military commands was simply the use of overwhelming force to break the stalemate on the western front by killing more Germans than the Germans killed Tommies and *poilus*. Small wonder that the War Council recoiled from the costly approach of outslaughtering the enemy and sought better alternatives.

The only other key figure in the British government besides Churchill who might have advanced new ideas that would bypass the trenches and the barbed wire was Lord Kitchener, but the old field marshal, schooled in the now antiquated Victorian way of war, lacked ideas and was baffled by this form of warfare. However, the secretary of state for war was the most powerful figure in the War Office, and no one dared oppose his approach, which focused on maintaining the status quo on the western front.

With the government staggering under the weight of the mounting futility and casualties, Churchill had a clear vision of what he believed needed to be done. What Asquith never quite realized was that his purpose was nothing less than to direct the war, and if not to direct it, then strongly to influence British strategy. First lord of the Admiralty was one of the most powerful positions in wartime in a rather diffident British government, and Churchill acted as if he were the only person competent enough and with sufficient foresight to run the war. Thus, with the land war hopelessly deadlocked, and with Germany refusing to co-operate with his desire for the Royal Navy to engage the High Fleet in a showdown on the high seas, he began to seek other alternatives. 'The Baltic', he said, 'is the only theatre in which naval action can appreciably shorten the war.'

Fisher ridiculed the notion of fighting a decisive campaign in France, pointing out with great accuracy that a British army sent to Europe would inevitably become bogged down supporting the French in a suicidal Continental war. Although Churchill fervently embraced it, the architect of the Baltic strategy was Fisher, who in 1907 had proposed a nearly identical plan in which the British would control the island of Sylt, in the North Sea off the coast where Germany and Denmark meet, and force the German High Fleet to sea, and to battle. This, Fisher believed, would open up the Baltic and permit further operations against Berlin, only eighty miles inland from the coast of Pomerania.

With both Fisher and Churchill attracted to operations in the Baltic, in August 1914 Asquith granted permission to pursue the idea with the

Russian commander in chief, Grand Duke Nicholas, to whom Churchill telegraphed a proposal for a joint operation to seal off the Baltic with the Royal Navy, attack Kiel and its canal, and drive the German fleet into the sea and into the battle he believed would be decisive. Churchill also proposed landings along the coast of Pomerania, thus drawing off large numbers of German troops from the western front. The operation would also turn the flank of the German army holding a line running generally south from Danzig, and, best of all, open up Berlin to attack. The Russians liked the idea but were unable to support such an undertaking, and the concept died.

Towards the end of 1914 Churchill also proposed another scheme, a variation of the Baltic idea, that called for seizure of the island of Borkum (situated off the coast of Holland), as a jumping-off point for an invasion of Schleswig-Holstein, with the similar aim of striking for Berlin and drawing off large forces from the western front. Kitchener had no troops to spare for such endeavours, and this idea soon ended when Grand Duke Nicholas pleaded for assistance against the Turks in the Mediterranean.

Churchill's Baltic plan was derided by many of the key figures within the Admiralty, including Jellicoe and Beatty, who argued that the fleet could not have survived passage through the narrow Denmark Strait (the 'Belts') because the Germans had mined them. After the war it was revealed by Tirpitz that mining did not occur until shortly after May 1915. The German general staff also revealed that it had greatly feared such an attack, and the chief of the German naval staff expressed 'grave anxiety' over the threat posed by a combined Anglo-Russian naval offensive in the Baltic. (With typical bluntness Fisher, in 1918, railed that the failure to undertake the Baltic operation was 'only a tiny bit of the congenital idiocy that has marked the whole conduct of the war'.)

The truth was that operations in the Baltic were a concept far too daring for its time and, given the shortage of available manpower and the timidity of the army leadership regarding fresh ideas (with the exception of Sir John French, who wholeheartedly supported the Fisher–Churchill initiative), simply not within the mental capability of most of the British generals, admirals and politicians of the time. It was only when he could not muster support for a Baltic operation that Churchill began seeking alternatives to a prolonged Continental war.

*

There was further controversy that involved the Admiralty in the autumn of 1914. With the war going badly and with criticism of both Churchill and the Royal Navy mounting, scapegoats were needed. One was quickly found when the first sea lord, Prince Louis of Battenberg, despite being one of the navy's outstanding sailors, was unceremoniously and shamefully obliged to resign his post in October, primarily because of his Germanic roots and the German accent that he had never lost, but also because Churchill sought a more vigorous and imaginative man to head the Royal Navy.

Among the first to demand his removal was Lord Charles Beresford. Churchill fired back in defence of Prince Louis, but when Asquith supported him only halfheartedly, Churchill decided the time had come to replace him, making him the third first sea lord to lose his job during his tenure. Prince Louis also became the victim of a witch hunt and was hounded from office by a mistrustful press and a public unduly influenced by his Germanic name rather than by his deeds and loyal service to the Crown and the country. The king asked Prince Louis to change his family name from Battenberg to Mountbatten. (His son, also named Louis, would carry the family name to a place of honour in the nation that had spurned his father.)

Whatever Prince Louis's real and perceived failures, they were just as much Churchill's responsibility. Churchill, however, had already made up his mind to bring back Fisher as his first sea lord, along with Sir Arthur Wilson in an advisory role. While the reappearance of Fisher as the navy's top admiral was generally hailed in the press and within the government, *The Times* approved for an entirely different reason: he would help rein in Churchill. Others saw the Fisher–Churchill relationship as potentially explosive. Rear Admiral Rosslyn Wemyss, a Beresford protégé and future first sea lord, opined, 'They will be thick as thieves at first until they differ on some subject, probably as to who is number 1, when they will begin to intrigue against each other.'

King George strenuously objected to Fisher's reinstatement on the grounds that the admiral was too old (he was seventy-three) and too disruptive a figure, and he strongly urged Churchill not to proceed but was told by Asquith, 'Winston won't have anyone else.' During an audience with the king Churchill hinted that he would resign his office if denied. An eyewitness recorded that Churchill said 'he would not be sorry to leave the Admiralty as its work was uncongenial to him; he wanted to go to the War & fight and be a soldier.' The King recorded in his diary: 'I did all I could to prevent it . . . I think it is a great mistake . . . At the end I had to give in with great reluctance.'

Although Churchill got his way, he lived to regret his decision. He thought he could manage Fisher, and Fisher likewise thought he could manage Churchill. Thus, heedless of the warnings, Churchill plunged ahead, convinced he had the right man at the right time. In theory the idea made sense, but in practice it committed the two most massive egos in British public life to a devil's pact. The decision to recall Fisher would prove to be among the most important – and ultimately disastrous – made by Churchill as first lord of the Admiralty.

At first everything worked just as Churchill had hoped, but within a short time of his reinstatement Fisher was privately complaining to his old friend Hankey that Churchill was frequently overruling him. Churchill later referred to himself and Fisher as 'the port and starboard lights' of the Admiralty. 'As long as the port and starboard lights shone together,' wrote Churchill, 'all went well.'

The days were frantic. 'I have never lived such a concentrated life as during the months before Winston came to grief,' recalled Eddie Marsh, who opened a small bar in his room, to which the navy brass would retire to indulge in a 'quick one' around midnight, primarily to enable them to keep up with Churchill. 'We began the day around nine o'clock, and went on usually until one or two the next morning.'

As had long been expected, Turkey entered the war on 29 October 1914 on the side of Germany by declaring war on Russia, bombarding Odessa and launching an ill-advised and costly military campaign in the Caucasus. One of the primary goals of the Allies became knocking 'the sick man of Europe' out of the war. The French were tied down defending their homeland, and Russia had its hands full after disastrous losses at Tannenberg and further grave losses during the Battles of the Masurian Lakes. The defeat of Turkey raised the possibility in the minds of Churchill and others of opening up a whole new avenue of attack on Germany, possibly through the Balkans. The dissolution of the already tottering Ottoman Empire also offered the inducement of bringing Italy, Bulgaria and Greece on to the Allied side.

As 1914 was drawing to a close, morale within Asquith's government was at an all-time low even as the mobilization and training of more men continued. Asquith wrote on 29 December: 'When our New Armies are ready . . . it seems folly to send them to positions where . . . in Winston's phrase, they will "chew barbed wire" or be wasted in futile frontal attacks.' The possibility of an alternative strategy was given impetus on New Year's Day 1915 by a personal plea from Grand Duke Nicholas, whose call for the Allies to threaten Constantinople was a spur to British action.

With stalemate now a terrible fact of life, it was inevitable that other means of winning the war would be examined. Churchill and the Admiralty were still smarting over the failure of the Royal Navy to prevent the escape of the German cruisers *Goeben* and *Breslau*, which had rather easily fled from the western Mediterranean in August and reached sanctuary in Constantinople. It was expressly because of the deadlock in France that a number of people in the government began looking to the Balkans and the eastern Mediterranean for possible alternatives. In addition to Churchill, Lloyd George and Maurice Hankey were now eyeing military action against Turkey. Even Kitchener, whose success as a military commander was founded on the principle of overwhelming force, was receptive to an initiative in the eastern Mediterranean.

Their focus was on one of the world's major strategic waterways, the Dardanelles, which divides Europe and Asia. On the northern side of the strait is the rocky Gallipoli Peninsula, the southernmost tip of what was then Bulgaria, an inhospitable wasteland of rocky hills and scrub. To the south lies the fertile basin of the plains of Troy. The entire area is a cradle of ancient history. The legendary Bronze Age city of Troy, founded in 3000 BC, its siege the subject of Homer's epic *The Iliad*, is a mere four miles south of Cape Helles. Militarily the Dardanelles had importance dating to at least the fifth century BC, when an army of the Persian king Xerxes crossed the strait by building a bridge of boats en route to do battle with the Greeks.

The Dardanelles, the only sea route to Constantinople, the Black Sea and the Caucasus, runs for some thirty-eight miles from Cape Helles on the Mediterranean end to the Sea of Marmara on the eastern end, thence to the Bosporus and the great city then called Constantinople. For most of its first fourteen miles the Dardanelles widens from slightly over two miles at the western entrance to four-and-a-half miles. At that point it becomes The Narrows, in ancient times called the Hellespont, barely 1,750 yards in width and overlooked on the Gallipoli side by high cliffs that form a natural defensive position and in 1914 were dotted with forts and blockhouses.

In retaliation for Turkey's declaration of war, Churchill ordered the Royal Navy's Aegean Squadron to bombard the outer forts of the Dardanelles on 3 November 1914, knocking out the heavy guns of the fortress of Sedd-el-Bahr on the European side of the entrance to the strait. Although an event of scant military significance, it convinced Churchill that the employment of naval force might accomplish a great deal more.

At the first meeting of the new War Council on 25 November, Churchill pressed for 'an attack on Gallipoli peninsula. This, if successful, would give us control of the Dardanelles, and we could dictate terms at Constantinople.' Although he still strongly favoured the Baltic initiative, it was clear by the beginning of December 1914 that he too had an alternative in mind. On 5 December Asquith recorded that 'he wants to organize a heroic venture against Gallipoli and the Dardanelles: to wh I am altogether opposed.'

In response to Grand Duke Nicholas's urgent appeal, by early 1915 the Dardanelles was viewed as an opportunity to knock Turkey out of the war with a single blow. The reasoning was perfectly straightforward: control of the Dardanelles and the Gallipoli Peninsula would not only force Turkey out of the war but also open up the Black Sea to important resupply of the Russians, as well as keeping the vital Mesopotamian and Persian oilfields out of German hands.

Although Churchill had yet to give up on the Baltic enterprise and the capture of Sylt, on 3 January he questioned Vice Admiral Sackville Hamilton Carden, the commander of the British battle force blockading Cape Helles: 'Do you consider the forcing of the Dardanelles by ships alone a practicable operation.' Carden replied on 5 January that while it was impossible to rush the Dardanelles, 'it might be possible to demolish the forts one by one.' On 13 January Churchill told the War Council that he believed a plan could be developed for the systematic reduction of all the forts within a few weeks: 'Once the forts were reduced the minefields would be cleared, and the Fleet would proceed up to Constantinople.'

Once planted, the seeds of a naval expedition to penetrate the Dardanelles, gain access to the Sea of Marmara and seize the Bosporus and Constantinople grew exponentially. The idea was to employ a fleet of outmoded pre-dreadnought battleships, which the Royal Navy could

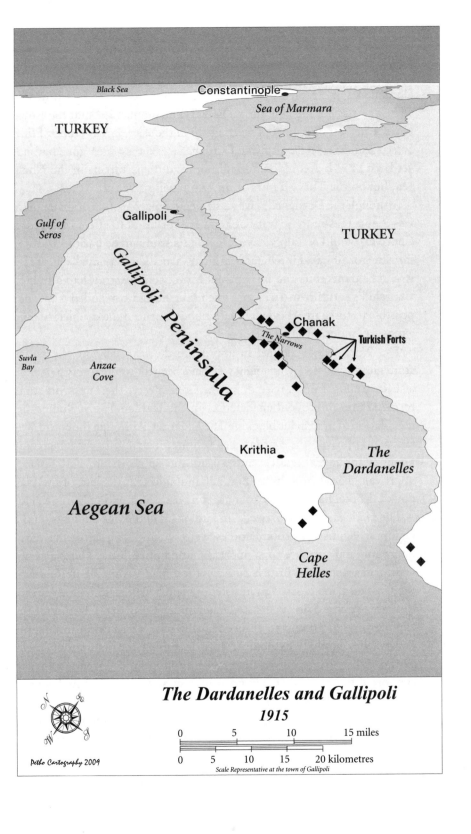

Black Sea

Constantinople

Sea of Marmara

TURKEY

Gulf of
Seros

Gallipoli

TURKEY

Gallipoli Peninsula

Chanak

The Narrows

Turkish Forts

Suvla
Bay

Anzac
Cove

Krithia

The
Dardanelles

Aegean Sea

Cape
Helles

The Dardanelles and Gallipoli
1915

| 0 | 5 | 10 | | 15 miles |

| 0 | 5 | 10 | 15 | 20 kilometres |

Scale Representative at the town of Gallipoli

N
W E
S

Petho Cartography 2009

afford to lose. Fisher embraced the concept of an immediate joint naval–ground attack before the Turks could strengthen their defence of the Dardanelles and replenish ammunition for their guns. In fact it was he who, at a further meeting on 12 January, recommended that the Royal Navy's 'newest and most powerful ship in the fleet, HMS *Queen Elizabeth*, should be sent out to the Dardanelles. Her 15-inch guns had not yet been fired but could be tested, not on dummy targets in the North Sea, but on the Turkish forts at the Dardanelles.'

Although the Dardanelles was a strategic prize beyond compare, there was ample reason to be wary of a naval expedition to effect its capture. Churchill would certainly have known of a study made back in 1906 by the director of naval intelligence which warned that 'a naval[-only] raid would be dangerous and ineffective.' Moreover, the strait had attracted Churchill's scrutiny in 1911, at which time he had concluded it was not possible to force the Dardanelles. 'Nobody', he told the cabinet, 'would expose a modern fleet to such perils.'

The War Council dallied in approving the plan, sought alternative strategies and missed what might well have been the opportunity to launch a successful operation. In so doing the Council gave the Turks vital time to mend and improve their defences in the Dardanelles, including the installation of minefields blocking The Narrows. Although the entire War Council approved the Dardanelles venture, it would never have come about without Churchill's enthusiasm and sponsorship, and Fisher's approval. 'The Admiralty', Churchill announced at the end of the long day of debate, had decided 'to make a naval attack on the Dardanelles'.

The plan was gravely flawed. Instead of simultaneous landings on the Gallipoli Peninsula, ground forces were to land only after the naval operation and too late to support the attempt to force The Narrows. Churchill wanted the British 29th Division made available to join with the Greeks, a move strongly resisted by Kitchener, who had no troops to spare. Yet the British persisted in an undertaking that left undone the capture of vital ground to ensure that the navy's success in forcing the Dardanelles would be exploited. More disturbing, the first serious cracks in the Fisher–Churchill relationship now appeared. Fisher, who had supported the plan, suddenly got cold feet and opposed any diversion of naval assets from the protection of Britain's home waters, writing to Jellicoe (who had been appointed to command the Home Fleet): 'I just abominate the Dardanelles operation, unless a great change is made and it is settled to be a military [army] operation, with 200,000 men in conjunction with the Fleet.' To add fuel to the flames, Fisher wrote a scathing memo condemning the operation and insisted that Churchill present it to the War Council. When Churchill attempted to persuade Fisher to change his mind, the feisty first sea lord wrote out his resignation. Forced into a humiliating position by Fisher's sudden intransigence, and desperate for what he termed 'unity of purpose', Churchill presented the memo to Asquith on the morning of 28 January. Despite Fisher's protests, however, Asquith decided that the operation should proceed.

Churchill's position on the Dardanelles was in evidence at the series of fateful meetings of the War Council held on 28 January. He had come to believe that the navy could successfully go it alone, with landings by ground forces on the Gallipoli Peninsula to come only after the navy was triumphant, and then primarily to mop up any leftover Turkish resistance and act as a police force. Churchill later testified before the Dardanelles Commission that while landings at Gallipoli might have provided a greater military benefit than the naval attack alone, a successful forcing of the Dardanelles would produce 'revolutionary effects at Constantinople and throughout the Balkans [and] seemed to me to make it worth while to try the naval plan'.

As the War Council met, Fisher sat silently. His opposition was apparent when he arose from the conference table, turned his back on the group and stood gazing out of a window. When Kitchener went to speak with him, the old admiral (not for the first or last time) said he would have to resign. In later sessions held that day it was decided that the plan was too important not to be carried out, and during the afternoon session Fisher did an abrupt about-turn and threw his support behind the venture. Hankey wrote that following a day of exhausting meetings the War Council was ripe for consensus; after hearing Churchill expound on the Dardanelles, it formally embraced the operation and 'turned eagerly from the dreary vista of a "slogging match" on the Western Front to brighter prospects in the Mediterranean'.

Asquith, however, came away troubled by the 'the growing friction between Winston and Fisher', and by the way each 'gave tongue to their mutual grievances'. Fisher complained about their 'fierce rows' and the next morning told Lord Esher that he was pessimistic: 'He finds Winston very brilliant, but too changeable; he has a different scheme every day.' The only person capable of stopping the Dardanelles and Gallipoli was Asquith, whose misgivings had been heightened by Fisher's sudden and vociferous opposition. But the prime minister did not act, nor did he demand answers to the tough questions that ought to have been asked before the operation was sanctioned. Although partly a reflection on his leadership – as weak as Churchill's was strong – his failure to do so was also a result of the practice of British politicians in 1915 to cede military judgments to the military.

Lost in the euphoria of the pending great naval operation was the hard fact that no troops were allocated actually to capture the terrain once the navy had forced the Dardanelles. Historians ever since have asked the question no one answered at the time: just how was a naval force expected to capture Gallipoli?

With the approval of the plan, the only likely outcome was failure. Other than Fisher's vacillating utterances, no one spoke out to ask the hard questions, such as what would be the likely consequences of failure, or why there were to be no concurrent amphibious landings on the Gallipoli Peninsula. Churchill and others believed the Dardanelles to be a low-risk operation, whose failure would have only minimal impact on the war and on British prestige.

Churchill, however, had far grander, incredibly optimistic aspirations for the operation. Before the plan had even been formalized, Violet Asquith had never seen him happier or more fulfilled; he talked endlessly about what it would accomplish. When the fleet broke through the Dardanelles, the Greeks and the Bulgarians might join Britain in attacking Turkey; the Balkan states might well unite to drive the Turks from Europe, and of course it would open the door to the Black Sea and aid to Russia: 'I seized upon it . . . Its possibilities seemed endless and he unrolled them before my dazzled eyes . . . He painted with a masterbrush upon his glowing canvas a vision of the Fleet appearing at the Golden Horn.'

Fisher's last-minute objections merely put him at odds with Churchill; they failed to sway Churchill's vibrant predictions of British glory. Fisher's instincts were deadly accurate, but his wild unpredictability and his reputation for abrupt changes of direction caused the British leadership to ignore his latest outburst. Churchill later bluntly told the Dardanelles Commission, 'When I finally decided to go in, I went in whole hog, totus porcus.'

*

The forcing of the Dardanelles was preceded by various attempts to knock out the Turkish forts by means of a sledgehammer approach, using the heavy guns of British warships. The assaults on the forts guarding the strait began on 19 February, when the navy launched the first of a series of attacks to break through the Dardanelles with a fleet of ageing sacrificial lambs.

The initial forays in late February and early March resulted in the fall of the outer forts at the entrance to the Dardanelles, which were captured by a small contingent of Royal Marines and bluejackets of Churchill's naval reserve. Less successful were the first attempts to clear the series of minefields laid at various points across the strait to block any attempt to force The Narrows. The supporting minesweepers were actually a small flotilla of twenty-one unarmed, minimally protected fishing trawlers, manned by naval reserve ratings who were North Sea fishermen in civilian life. The trawlers had been retrofitted to perform minesweeping, and although their crews were courageous, their vessels were wholly ineffective and too underpowered to move at more than a snail's pace against the strong currents of the strait. Because of the trawlers' extreme vulnerability several attempts were made to penetrate the strait and begin clearing the minefields at night, under the noses of the Turks. Each failed when batteries of searchlights emplaced overlooking the minefields for just such a contingency suddenly illuminated the trawlers, which were then subjected to heavy fire and forced to withdraw. By the seventh attempt on the night of 10 March, only a handful of mines had been cleared. Shortly before the last serious attempt just over a week later, Hankey sounded an ominous note of warning in a memo to Asquith: the navy's success would now require the use of land forces.

Churchill became gravely concerned about the slow progress and cabled Carden with the intention of lighting a fire under the admiral to encourage him to take greater risks in clearing the minefields and 'to press the attack vigorously', calling the rewards 'great enough to justify loss of ships and men'.

Supported by the battleship *Cornwallis*, a light cruiser, and four destroyers, a far more determined attempt was made to clear the minefields on the night of 13 March, but this, too, failed amid a blizzard of onshore fire that pinpointed the minesweepers under the glare of searchlights. Increasingly frustrated because none of the sweepers had actually been lost, but with no real idea of the difficulties they had encountered in the cauldron of fire, Churchill again cabled Admiral Carden, this time demanding results. 'Two or three hundred casualties', he wrote, 'would be a moderate price to pay for sweeping up as far as The Narrows . . . This work has to be done whatever the loss of life and small craft and the sooner it is done the better.'

On 16 March Carden resigned his command, citing ill health but chiefly owing to the intense pressure from Churchill and his own loss of nerve. He was immediately replaced by his second in command, Vice Admiral Sir John N. de Robeck, an experienced sailor who had seen the Dardanelles operation turn into a dangerously uncertain situation and was equally fearful of a bad outcome.

With no pretence at surprise, the main naval offensive to force the Dardanelles took place in broad daylight on the morning of 18 March. The battleship HMS *Queen Elizabeth* led an Anglo-French armada of sixteen battleships (four French and twelve British) into the strait towards the deadly minefields of The Narrows in the strongest and – as it turned out – the final attempt to thrust the fleet through the strait.

The Narrows was protected not only by the mobile Turkish shore batteries but also by a deadly minefield ten rows deep, numbering 373 mines. Heavy fire from the shore batteries and forts sank one French and two British battleships and severely damaged three others before the armada could thrust through The Narrows and gain access to (and safety in) the Sea of Marmara. It was an unequal fight. The helpless minesweepers were never able to clear any of the mines before being forced to withdraw under heavy fire. Although Commodore Roger Keyes, de Robeck's chief of staff – a daring, aggressive risk taker and an astute sailor and perhaps the truest believer in Churchill's plan to force the Dardanelles – was convinced the attack would succeed if pressed, his superior thought otherwise and, having lost roughly one-third of his ships, de Robeck withdrew the fleet. Except for a rescue operation to save the crew of the battleship HMS *Irresistible*, mortally damaged by a mine, the Dardanelles operation was over, with losses of more than six hundred killed.

Neither de Robeck nor Fisher, who supported his admiral's judgment, had any inclination to launch a further naval offensive; instead both of them gambled on the success of the Gallipoli landings to accomplish what the navy had not. The consensus among the ground and naval commanders on the spot was that any further attack was hopeless unless the mobile batteries were taken out by ground troops. The Allied commander of the Mediterranean Expeditionary Force was one of Churchill's oldest military friends, Ian Hamilton, who witnessed the naval attack and apparently agreed with de Robeck's assessment, thus setting the stage for a ground campaign on the Gallipoli Peninsula.

Churchill obstinately insisted that a further determined effort to penetrate The Narrows would bring success. Indeed the Turks and the Germans fully expected the British to succeed in forcing the Dardanelles and after the war expressed surprise that they had not made a more determined attempt to do so. Churchill sensed that it was simply a lack of resolve and drafted a telegram ordering de Robeck to resume operations in the Dardanelles, but Fisher intervened, fiercely objecting to Churchill's proposed order and forcefully arguing that such decisions were the prerogative of the responsible commander and not of a government minister. The telegram to de Robeck was never dispatched. After the war Churchill lashed out at Fisher, writing that the old admiral had put himself 'in a position where if the military attack failed he could say, "I was always against the Dardanelles – see my memorandum of February 27," and if it succeeded, "I was always in favour of a joint operation – see my letter to the First Lord of January 4" '.

Although he favoured continuation of the operation, Asquith refused to overturn Fisher's military judgment, leaving Churchill high and dry – and deeply frustrated. On 5 April Fisher wrote a barbed note to Churchill pointing out, 'You are just simply eaten up with the Dardanelles and cant think of anything else! Damn the Dardanelles! They will be our grave.' He went on to point out one of the great truths of the First World War: that Britain was too late in the Mediterranean, 'but we are "too late" ALWAYS!' Captain Richmond may have said it better when he declared in disgust in 1914: 'There is no doubt we are the most appalling amateurs who ever tried to conduct a war.'

In March 1915 there was ample sea power available. The Dardanelles task force consisted of fifteen battleships, two battle cruisers, six light cruisers, twenty-four destroyers, ten submarines, three monitors, fifty-two minesweepers, seven fleet sweepers, one aircraft carrier and a host of smaller supporting craft. However, even if – as Roger Keyes had urged – a renewed attack had taken place, its likelihood of success would have remained questionable without ground support and without clearing the deadly minefields of The Narrows.

One of the lessons of war learned and relearned since 1915 is that operations like the Dardanelles rarely, if ever, succeed without ground or air support, preferably both. No aircraft has ever captured terrain, nor a ship captured a city. In this instance even if the fleet had successfully penetrated the Dardanelles, its essential resupply by mostly unarmed ships would have been costly unless the shore batteries were permanently disabled – which would have required ground troops. For a purely naval operation to have any chance of success, it would have had to be undertaken in late 1914 or early 1915, before the Turks had laid their minefields and improved their shore defences.

In his desire to make something happen in the Mediterranean, Churchill ignored (or perhaps forgot) his own warning about the Dardanelles, written in 1911. His attempt to place blame for the failure of the operation on others, while ducking his own culpability, must now be viewed as entirely self-serving. In microcosm the Dardanelles fiasco represented everything that was at once brilliant and flawed in Churchill. The idea was audacious, the reward of potential significance and the result execrable. Overly dazzled by the prospects of a great prize, he and the War Cabinet seem never to have seriously considered the price to be paid if the plan failed. Hankey implored Churchill to delay until a joint ground and naval operation could be launched, 'but he wouldn't listen, insisting the navy could go it alone.' With bulldog determination Churchill ploughed ahead, Hankey believed, because in the wake of his failure at Antwerp, he wanted to pull off a brilliant success, a success he could claim sole credit for masterminding. In the end, as his official biographer points out, 'he now believed that ships alone would be inadequate ... But he so believed in the need for victory that he was prepared to go ahead with plans for an entirely naval attack. However much he continued to argue that the plans might fail, by agreeing to go ahead with them, he made himself responsible for the very disaster that he forecast.'

The tragic story of the Dardanelles concluded with the pronouncement by Kitchener that the responsibility would be taken over by the army through an invasion of the Gallipoli Peninsula. Thus, by a combination of Kitchener's initiative and the Admiralty's refusal (over Churchill's objections) to incur further losses, it was decided to undertake operations on the ground at Gallipoli – a tragedy of epic proportions in the making.

22

The Reckoning

I thought he would die of grief.   – Clementine Churchill

On the evening of 22 February 1915, Violet Asquith dined at the Admiralty with Clementine and Winston. Churchill excitedly revealed details of the forthcoming Gallipoli landings, adding that he had volunteered his now far better-trained and better-equipped naval division to participate. As if to atone for Antwerp, he had grandiose plans for his naval reservists. 'He was in the throes of a "low" Influenza . . . but thrilled at the prospect of the military expedition & full of plans for landing them in Gallipoli when the teeth of the situation had been drawn by the ships – marching them into Constantinople. "That will make them sit up – the swine who snarled at the Naval Division."' Becoming reflective, he declared: 'I think a curse should rest on me – because I *love* this war. I know it's smashing & shattering the lives of thousands every moment – & yet – I *can't* help it – I enjoy every second of it,' words that would soon ring hollow.

Three days later, on 25 February, under a brilliant sun glinting off the frost, the naval reserve was given a grand send-off at its base on the downs at Blandford in Dorset. The entire force of two brigades was drawn up in dress uniforms to parade before the king, who took the salute during the march-past. Churchill sat resplendent on horseback, much like a proud father overseeing his family. The poet Rupert Brooke was ecstatic at the prospect ('I had not imagined Fate could be so benign') and 'filled with confident and glorious hopes', only to become one of the eight thousand British and empire soldiers to perish on the Gallipoli expedition.

The dreadful tale of Gallipoli has become even more controversial than the Dardanelles for the terrible losses of life sustained on its forbidding, rocky terrain, and for the ineptness of its commanders. Had there been no Dardanelles there would not have been the ill-fated multiple landings on 25 April 1915 by Allied troops, 30,500 of them British, Indian, Australian and New Zealand and 16,700 French.

The key to any successful amphibious landing is surprise. At Gallipoli the Turks were not fooled, and when the Allies, commanded by Ian Hamilton, landed, a force of eighty thousand men awaited them. Hamilton had been as reluctant as Fisher and de Robeck to challenge the Dardanelles again, and was thus committed to a land campaign. His invasion plan, consisting of a fake landing by Churchill's Royal Naval Division at Bulair on the northern tip of the peninsula, completely fooled the Turks and the commander of the Fifth Turkish Army, a German officer, General Otto Liman von Sanders. (The chief of the German military mission in Turkey, Sanders was a cavalry officer who had been reassigned from the command of Turkish forces in the Caucasus to play a key role in the defence of the Gallipoli Peninsula.)

The main landings occurred along the southern coast at Cape Helles, and further north from the Aegean Sea by troops of the Australian and New Zealand Army Corps (Anzac), led by the only capable commander in the operation, Lieutenant General Sir William Birdwood. The Anzacs were heavily counterattacked by Turkish troops under the very able Mustafa Kemal, who took the title Atatürk when he became the leader of Turkey after the war.

Badly planned, devoid of reconnaissance and beset with incompetent commanders, the Gallipoli operation quickly unravelled, turning into a murderous stalemate little different from the western front as both sides poured in more and more troops.

The Dardanelles and Gallipoli were examples of the same kind of misjudgments Churchill would repeat in the Second World War: seeing only the positives but never the negatives, and sanctioning operations without a full appreciation of the consequences or the capabilities of the forces available to carry them out. And while culpability for the Dardanelles and Gallipoli may be laid at the door of the entire Asquith government and the means by which it waged the First World War, Churchill was one of its key players and strategists. Their monumental failure bore out Hankey's dire conclusion: 'Behind each episode there lay a whole history of rumour, contradiction, conjecture, indecision, order, counter-order, before the climax was reached, often in a welter of bloodshed and destruction.'

Churchill's response to his critics was his massive six-volume account of the war, *The World Crisis*, the first volume of which was published in 1923; this work has been fairly described as part self-justification, part history and part autobiography. Balfour once said of it that it was 'an autobiography disguised as an history of the universe'. Thus while it is quite true that Churchill's defence of his actions in *The World Crisis* is self-serving, it is also necessary to cut him some slack in affixing blame.

Nearly a century later books, articles and lectures on the subject of the Dardanelles and Gallipoli continue to appear. Their thrust, however, points to multiple culpability, dreadful planning and a total lack of understanding of what amphibious war entailed. The sane voice of Hankey emerges as one of the few with both foresight and rational hindsight.

When informed by Hankey that the Gallipoli landings would prove 'extraordinarily difficult', Churchill dismissed his concerns, claiming that 'he could see no difficulty at all.' Once again his thirst for action appears to have overruled his common sense. Other than Hankey, who had neither the power nor the influence to change events, there was no one to step forward and question the merits of either operation.

What the British government desperately required before launching both the Dardanelles and Gallipoli was a knowledgeable and influential devil's advocate to step forward and ask the hard questions that were never posed. Although he had a strong military background, Churchill, with his impulsive nature, was not the ideal person to fill that role; instead he fell into the trap of false optimism, driven by the need to influence events and change the direction of the war while blind to the maxim that hardly anything in war ever goes according to plan. Intuition played far too large a role in his military decisions and too often led to results like those that were so costly in 1915.

Asquith is equally if not more culpable. In a Gallipoli Memorial Lecture in 1990 the historian Robert O'Neill declared, 'Asquith continued to permit Churchill and Kitchener to enmire themselves, their nation, the Empire and their allies in a swamp which was to claim the lives of 150,000 men, inflict colossal hardship on a further 850,000 . . . inflict misery on thousands of families of the men who died and blight the lives of all those who had to tend the physically and psychologically maimed survivors over the next generation.'

In early May 1915 Churchill and Fisher clashed over the Dardanelles. With Gallipoli rapidly turning into a debacle, the Dardanelles became a sort of classic catch-22. The navy could not clear the minefields without army assistance, and the army was then incapable of providing that assistance. Yet to do nothing was to place Allied ground forces on the Gallipoli Peninsula in even greater jeopardy. Although Churchill had backed off from a renewed attempt to clear the Dardanelles, he was now on the horns of a dilemma. Admiral de Robeck was sympathetic to the plight of the army and asked the Admiralty for guidance: Should he pursue a purely naval attack in the knowledge that the army was in no position to assist?

The result was another half-measure in which Churchill stopped short of another all-out attempt on The Narrows but compromised by encouraging de Robeck to attempt to clear the Kephez minefield and the forts guarding it, the last barrier before The Narrows and its minefields. On the morning of 13 May the battleship HMS *Goliath*, one of the older vessels, was torpedoed while at anchor in Morto Bay inside the Dardanelles by a Turkish destroyer commanded by a German officer, with a loss of 570 men who drowned in the rough current. With that Fisher had had enough. Convinced that success at the Kephez minefield would lead to yet another attempt to penetrate The Narrows – and to further disaster – he strongly hinted that he was thinking of resignation if Churchill persisted. He was supported by Hankey and their shared belief that there had to be success on the ground first.

Churchill attempted to broker a compromise by withdrawing the battleship *Queen Elizabeth*, but to Fisher's mind his relations with Churchill were beyond repair, and with the situation at Gallipoli worsening, he submitted his resignation to both Churchill and the prime minister on the morning of 15 May. Although it was the ninth time the mercurial Fisher had resigned, this time the old admiral would not retract his decision as he had in the past. Despite attempts by his former boss, Reginald McKenna, and others to get him to stay on, he was – for once – adamant that he would not continue to work with Churchill. Asquith refused to accept his resignation and ordered him in the name of the king to remain at his post, and Churchill wrote, appealing to his patriotism to remain, also obsequiously declaring that he had taken his political life into his hands to bring him back as first sea lord.

Fisher was unmoved and wrote back that it was the Dardanelles that had brought about his resignation. Reiterating his mounting concerns about the operation, he reminded Churchill that 'YOU ARE BENT ON FORCING THE DARDANELLES AND NOTHING WILL TURN YOU FROM IT – NOTHING – I know you so well!' His decision, he said, was final: 'I will not remain.' On 17 May he wrote to the prime minister that while he had remained 'in accordance with your wishes', he would not reconsider. 'I now write to say DEFINITELY that I am unable to remain at the Admiralty with Mr Winston Churchill, and will NOT remain after to-day.' True to his word, within hours Fisher had slipped away to Scotland. Despite their falling out, he would later say of Churchill: 'I backed him up until he resigned. *I would do the same again!* He had courage and imagination. *He was a war man!*'

Still shaken, Churchill prepared to move on and proposed reorganizing the Admiralty by bringing back Sir Arthur Wilson as first sea lord. However, Fisher's abrupt resignation was the beginning of the end of Churchill's tenure as first lord of the Admiralty, and of Asquith's Liberal government. The Dardanelles, the disaster unfolding at Gallipoli and Fisher's angry resignation aroused strong Conservative opposition and created a grave political crisis. On 17 May Asquith, persuaded by Lloyd George that he would have to share power in a wartime coalition government, requested the resignation of his entire cabinet. Winston Churchill's removal from the Admiralty was a major condition on which there was to be no compromise by the Conservatives.

When Churchill met with Asquith the prime minister did not close the door on his further participation in the new coalition government. As Asquith was inquiring if he would like a post or would 'prefer a command in France', Lloyd George joined them and proposed that Churchill should accept the post of colonial secretary. Churchill vehemently rejected the suggestion, insisting that any post that would remove him from a direct role in the running of the war was unacceptable. In such circumstances, he much preferred to be given a field command in France. In the end Churchill was given neither a significant post in the new cabinet nor a command in France under Sir John French.

On 18 May Churchill gathered around him his old friend F. E. Smith and Sir Max Aitken, who later took the title of Lord Beaverbrook and would play a key role in Churchill's Second World War cabinet as his minister of aircraft production. Although Clementine disliked him (primarily for his political views, which she abhorred), Aitken was another of those drawn into Churchill's inner circle for his quirky brilliance and nonconformity. It was clear to him how desperately Churchill wanted to keep his post as first lord: 'He was clinging to the desire of retaining the Admiralty as if the salvation of England depended on it.' In a last-minute ploy Churchill even attempted to broker a deal that would keep Fisher aboard. 'Churchill offered Fisher any terms he liked including a seat in the Cabinet, if he would stay with him at the Admiralty,' Hankey recorded in his diary on the evening of 19 May.

Both Winston and Clementine wrote to Asquith. Clementine's letter was blunt and merely angered the prime minister: 'There is no man in the country who possesses equal knowledge capacity & vigour . . . If you throw Winston overboard you will be committing an act of weakness . . . he has the supreme quality which I venture to say very few of your present or future Cabinet possess, the power, the imagination, the deadliness to fight Germany.' Asquith was neither the first nor the last to learn that Clementine Churchill was not just another pretty face – let alone the fool Beatty had called her – and that when the occasion demanded it she had very sharp claws and was unafraid to use them.

Similar approaches by Winston to the Conservatives likewise produced no support for his retention. For one of the few times in his life he begged a political enemy for a chance to keep his job. Churchill had never had any use for Bonar Law, believed he had a second-rate mind and had savagely ridiculed him during the rancorous Home Rule debates. To have expected a sympathetic response was the height of naivety. The game was over.

Asquith had come to the conclusion that Churchill's intrigues and difficult relationships were too harmful to his career. 'I am really fond of him, but I regard his future with many misgivings. I do not think he will ever get to the top in English politics with all his wonderful gifts.' On 21 May, after nearly a week of anguish, Churchill finally grasped that Asquith had no intention of saving him and tendered his resignation: 'I accept your decision. I shall not look back.'

That, of course, was precisely what Churchill did for the remainder of his life. For Clementine Churchill the uncertain days leading to her husband's resignation were a bitter pill like no other. Her daughter

Mary Soames wrote: 'Of all the events they had lived through together, none had been so agonizing as the drama of the Dardanelles ... For long weeks and months thereafter she shared with Winston every anxiety, every brief hope, every twist and turn of the devious course of the crisis.' Fifty years later Clementine's memories were still fresh. 'I thought he would never get over the Dardanelles. I thought he would die of grief.' Eddie Marsh called the blow to Churchill 'a horrible wound and mutilation ... it's like Beethoven deaf.' He angrily blamed Fisher. 'I tore up his photograph.'

Privately Churchill believed that Asquith had shamelessly cast him adrift and made him the sacrificial lamb for the Dardanelles. In the eyes of the British public his removal was seen as the penalty for a failure that, in reality, belonged in equal measure to Asquith himself, to Kitchener and to all who had failed see the flaws in both the Dardanelles and the Gallipoli operations. Churchill's removal forever tainted his political career, and his enemies would employ the Dardanelles to cast doubt upon his character.

Among those not sorry to see Churchill removed from the Admiralty was King George V, who not only thoroughly disliked him personally but also had doubts about his professional competence: 'He is the real danger.' As a former Royal Navy officer the king believed that Britain's naval power had no business being employed in costly gambles like the Dardanelles.

When the end came Churchill had no more fight left and went quietly, bitterly disappointed but realistic. Violet Asquith found him silent and despairing. 'He seemed to have no rebellion or even anger left. He did not even abuse Fisher, but simply said, "I'm finished." ... I suddenly felt hot tears rolling down my cheeks, and there were tears in his eyes too.'

Both at the time and later, this occasion remained one of the saddest days of Churchill's life. Writing in 1916, Shane Leslie said: 'If Winston had died on the day the fleet was mobilized, he would have fulfilled his ambition, which had been to enjoy a decade of power and achievement.' Before Churchill departed his beloved Admiralty, his former bitter foe Lord Kitchener was among many who visited him. 'He spoke very kindly about our work together,' and as he arose to take his leave, 'he turned and said, in the impressive and almost majestic manner that was natural to him, "Well, there is one thing at any rate they cannot take from you. The Fleet was ready."'

Key figures within the Admiralty were happy for Churchill to go, among them Jellicoe, who observed that Fisher had been the only person able to rein in the impetuous first lord. 'Winston Churchill is a public danger to the Empire,' he averred. And 'Beatty spoke for the Grand Fleet when he wrote to his wife, "The Navy breathes freer now it is rid of the succubus Churchill."'

Not everyone jumped on the bash-Churchill bandwagon, however. Among those offering encouragement was the editor of the *Observer*, who wrote, 'He is young. He has lion-hearted courage. No number of enemies can fight down his ability and force. His hour of triumph will come.'

Publicly Churchill defended the Dardanelles and accused Fisher of doing 'his best to ruin an operation which might well have halved the duration of the war, and although incidentally he destroyed my power to intervene decisively in its course.' His later judgment of Fisher was far harsher and more unforgiving than what he wrote in *The World Crisis*. He thought the old admiral had experienced a nervous breakdown and had 'refused to discharge the most necessary duties, even pending the appointment of a successor. He retired to his house, he pulled down the blinds, and advertised the fact that he had gone on strike.'

Years later Admiral of the Fleet Sir Roger Keyes declared: 'The Navy lost in the course of a few days the services of an Admiral who was one of its outstanding figures of the last hundred years ... and of an Administrator to whom it owed, in a great measure, its readiness for war in August 1914.'

In the cabinet reshuffle Churchill was offered the post of chancellor of the Duchy of Lancaster, perhaps the least important office in the British cabinet, where his chief concerns were the administration of the duchy's vast landholdings and the appointment of county magistrates. He accepted this lowly post as a means of keeping his hand in the affairs of government because it at least afforded him a seat on the new coalition War Council, which had been renamed the Dardanelles Committee. This new body fully backed Gallipoli.

Other than retaining his post on the War Council, Churchill was relegated to the status of an unimportant Whitehall bureaucrat with too much time on his hands. He went from one of the most powerful posts in the government, from a grand office in the historic Admiralty building to plain rooms off the Strand, with no power and no real responsibility; this was the greatest disappointment of Churchill's political career. For one so accustomed to the full trappings of power, a more humiliating denouement is difficult to envisage.

Churchill could not abide sitting idly in an office while the war raged in France. 'He will go to the Front,' Violet Asquith (soon to be married and become Violet Bonham Carter) said to her father. 'That is what I believe he intends to do,' replied the prime minister. 'It is a terrible waste. I think he has more understanding of war than any of my colleagues.'

To the present day the Dardanelles and Gallipoli remain raw wounds in the British psyche. At the centre of it all is Churchill who, having sought the mantle of leadership and having almost grasped it, paid the high price of failure. However, for the remainder of his life he worked to clear away the stain the Dardanelles had inflicted upon his reputation, never quite admitting that the concept had been flawed, arguing that his only mistake was in not 'having the plenary authority wh cd so easily have carried it to success'. The six volumes of his *World Crisis* highlight his version of events in what a naval historian has cynically described as 'the Gospel according to Churchill'. Historians have dissected these volumes and cited numerous examples of how *The World Crisis* was a work of self-justification through selective quotation and the omission of relevant facts and documents.

As a young schoolboy Churchill's son Randolph would also be penalized for his father's leading role in the Dardanelles, when others would challenge him with comments such as 'Your father murdered mine at the Dardanelles.'

As the years passed, condemnation continued unabated from various sources, including this in 1931 from one hostile biographer: 'The ghosts of the Gallipoli dead will always rise up to damn him anew in time of national emergency. Neither official historians, nor military hack writers will explain away or wipe the memories of the Dardanelles.'

The Churchill of 1915 was an ego-driven, self-assured man, secure in his beliefs and unmoved by dissent. Although these qualities failed him in the First World War, they would redeem him when a far more mature Winston Churchill held Britain's fate in his hands during its darkest hour. And what he demonstrated in both world wars was that he was not afraid of failure, even though it devastated him in 1915. Both the Dardanelles and Gallipoli provided more than enough blame to go around at a number of levels. Almost nothing was known at the time of amphibious operations, about whose complexity the Second World War taught equally bitter lessons. Finally, in the words of one writer, the real tragedy of Gallipoli 'was that the conduct of the expedition was unworthy of the courage of the troops who were sacrificed upon its altar'.

That June, with nothing of substance to occupy his time, Churchill took up painting as a means of relieving the hurt and the boredom. Recalling that her son had been present during her own painting lessons, and that drawing was one of the few activities he had actually enjoyed as a schoolboy, Jennie had suggested it as a diversion one night at a dinner party. By the following weekend Winston had followed her advice and taken the first tentative steps, at first using a child's paintbox. Much as ideas poured from his brain, paintings soon began flowing from his brush. For someone untutored and with no previous background, his art is a superb visual representation of his inventive mind. Churchill became a rather skilled painter and turned out a large number of oils; he possessed what the noted artist Graham Sutherland described as 'an extraordinary talent'. For the remainder of his life, painting became a relaxing outlet from the many pressures he experienced.

In the summer of 1915 it was therapy that Churchill desperately needed in the wake of his shattering dismissal from the Admiralty. Clementine was enormously encouraged by her husband's new passion – one that, for a change, did not involve risk taking. Violet Asquith thought him like a happy child playing with new toys. Like the man himself, Churchill's paintings were vibrant and filled with strong colours: 'Watching him paint for the first time on that June morning I became suddenly aware that it was the only occupation I had ever seen him practise in silence.' His cousin Clare Sheridan was impressed by his talent and wrote in 1927, 'I am convinced that had he from the first put all his colossal energy and brain into art instead of politics, he would have been very great and would have something more tangible than a mere repute to leave behind him.'

Churchill's dismissal also brought a return of his 'black dog', and painting proved not only pleasurable but also an escape from depression. During the summer of 1915 the Churchills rented a charming farmhouse in Surrey, to which the entire family retreated. His godson has described this period of his life as 'like Napoleon after Waterloo'.

Although painting and his retreat to the countryside provided a refuge of sorts, Churchill could not evade the torment of his exile and his removal from an active role in the war. His bitterness was like an angry sore. Partly it was the disgrace, but mostly it was the ache of losing his influence and power. The plain truth was that Churchill had become irrelevant – and irrelevance was perhaps the most severe retribution that could have been inflicted upon him. 'I am learning to hate,' he told his brother Jack.

His anguish was best reflected in a series of letters written to his friend Archibald Sinclair. In June he wrote, 'I cannot endure sitting here to wait for a turn of the political mind. I do not want office, but only war direction . . . I am profoundly unsettled & cannot use my gift. Of that last I have no doubts. I do not feel that my judgments have been falsified, or that the determined perseverance of my policy through all the necessary risks was wrong. I will do it all again, if the circumstances were repeated . . . I don't think I can go on here. I am not yet decided what to do or which way to turn.' To Jack, who was serving at Gallipoli as a member of Ian Hamilton's staff, he wrote, 'The war is terrible: the carnage grows apace . . . The youth of Europe – almost a whole genera-tion – will be shorn away. I find it vy painful to be deprived of direct means of action, but I bear the pangs because I see and feel the value of my influence on general policy.'

Time did little to heal the raw wound. He languished, gained weight and painted, attacking his canvases in the way he attacked everything he ever did, all the while refusing to believe there was no role for him in the war. From his pen came a steady stream of memorandums, all designed somehow to re-energize his lost power. In late June he presented Asquith with a memo advocating the formation of an Air Department, with unmistakable hints that he should be appointed to head it. There is no evidence that Asquith even bothered to reply.

In the summer of 1915 Churchill began thinking about a return to active military service and the command of a brigade at Gallipoli. When Jack learned of Winston's intention, he wrote to dissuade him. 'I hope you will not attempt such a thing. You would sacrifice such a lot and gain so little.' Instead, he suggested, 'Why don't you get 3 wks leave and get sent out to report on the situation to the Cabinet!!!' The idea appealed, and when in mid-July Kitchener proposed that Churchill visit Gallipoli in an official capacity to assess the situation, he jumped at the opportunity. Although Asquith thought it was a good idea and approved the trip, Ian Hamilton was not at all keen on any visitors from London, not even his old friend Winston Churchill, who never learned of Hamilton's objection. Another who thought it was a bad idea was Roger Keyes. 'He would like to be – Generalissimo – and will be an awful nuisance! . . . I don't know why we should have this difficult situation to compete with in addition to our heavy task.'

When the Tory members of Asquith's cabinet learned of Churchill's proposed mission, strong objections were raised by Bonar Law, who suggested it might provoke a serious crisis, not so much because it involved a British cabinet minister as because that minister was Churchill, who therefore withdrew forthwith. Asquith professed sympathy but lacked the will to overrule Conservative opposition, thus further widening the breach between the two men and leaving Churchill angrier than ever over the rough treatment being meted out to him. It was another bitter disappointment that still rankled in the last years of his life. As the situation at Gallipoli darkened, so too did Churchill's growing isolation from his colleagues.

Asquith had become both wary and weary of Churchill's incessant advice on war matters and of his increasingly strident requests to participate directly in the war. In September, Churchill appealed to him to be given the command of a corps, with the rank of major general. Embarrassed by his request, Asquith referred the matter to an equally uncomfortable Kitchener, who was mindful that he 'could not offend the Army' by showing favouritism to a politician, and the appointment was not forthcoming. Churchill's official biographer points out that by this stage of the war 'many people began to see in him a man of blood. For those who saw him every day he was the "happy man" at the outbreak of the war, the frustrated soldier thirsting for action at Antwerp, the naval enthusiast willing to throw away ships, and in spectacular enterprises, the Cabinet Minister keen to see the war continue in order to provide opportunities for his own fertile imagination. Churchill seemed to have a lust for battle.' Yet it was impossible for him to convey, either to the public or to his colleagues, that he was not really a warmonger but rather someone who was obsessed with being a major player in the conduct of the war.

In November, Churchill asked for and was refused an appointment as governor general and British commander in chief of British East Africa. His proposal to Asquith also included 'a scheme for attacking the Germans with armoured cars', Hankey recorded in his diary.

By late 1915 there was no end even remotely in sight to the stalemate in France, while at Gallipoli the fighting was bitter, exhausting and no less indecisive. Already there was talk of evacuation, which Churchill fought against, arguing at length that rather than being evacuated Gallipoli should be reinforced with yet more troops. Some ideas refuse to die, and Churchill would not give up the notion of forcing the Dardanelles. Calling evacuation a 'terrible decision' that ranked with the loss of Britain's American colonies, he said it was important beyond measure to keep Russia in the war by opening the Dardanelles. 'The one great prize and reward which Russia can gain is Constantinople. The surest means of re-equipping her ... is the opening of the Dardanelles and Bosphorus. With the evacuation of the Gallipoli Peninsula that hope dies.' Although British submarines penetrated the Dardanelles at will and sank numerous Turkish ships in the Sea of Marmara and the Black Sea, this was not enough to change the outcome or to halt the enormous influx of Turkish reinforcements into Gallipoli.

Kitchener, who formally recommended the drastic measure of evacuation on 22 November, was himself on the verge of being sacked over Gallipoli. Churchill's great friend, the well-meaning but wholly ineffective Ian Hamilton, had been relieved of his command in mid-October. Gallipoli required a commander both ruthless and decisive to take charge of the operation. Hamilton was neither.

Gallipoli became yet another costly example of the very failures that had beset the British army during the Boer War: over-confidence and outrageous incompetence. There was the unwarranted conviction that victory was inevitable and that the Turks would simply roll over. 'Men in the ranks', notes the historian Robert Massie, 'looked forward to "bashing Abdul" and "shoving it to Johnny Turk".' At the top, the War Office, on no basis other than arrogant conjecture, had predicted strong opposition to the landings but a collapse of Turkish resistance once the attack forces were ashore.

Krithia, Anzac Cove, Suvla Bay and Helles became the scenes of great courage from the warring sides, but of little else. When the expeditionary force carried out the evacuation of the Gallipoli Peninsula in late December 1915 and early January 1916, it marked the end of a tragic, ill-conceived, horribly executed military venture that would become a byword for failure. As Prince Philip recounted in the 1987 Gallipoli Memorial Lecture: 'The ultimate irony was that the evacuation turned out to be the most successful operation of the whole campaign. Every single soldier and virtually every horse, mule and weapon was taken off the peninsula at the cost of one man slightly injured.' With her typical eloquence, nearly half a century later Violet Bonham Carter would write of Gallipoli that 'the greatest opportunity of the First World War was thrown away by men of little faith . . . History has not yet forgiven us.'

Also in November 1915 the cumbersome and ineffective Dardanelles Commission was reconstituted and downsized as the Cabinet War Committee, with fewer members. Churchill was excluded from its membership. Suddenly he had no voice left in the government; few really cared what he thought or what he said. It was the last straw. 'I had as a Cabinet Minister to watch for six hateful months the great enterprise slowly and shamefully muddled and cast away by half measures and three-quarter measures all taken just too late.' Mired in a meaningless post that left him spiritless, a heartbroken Churchill resigned as chancellor of the Duchy of Lancaster on 11 November 1915, the same day he learned of his exclusion from the new cabinet. He was determined to play a vastly different role in the war he had once helped to mastermind. The time had come for him to return to soldiering.

TOP LEFT: 'Jack', Lady Randolph Churchill and Winston shortly before
Lieutenant Churchill sailed for India with the Fourth Hussars in 1896.
TOP RIGHT: Churchill, at the age of seven.

Lord Randolph Churchill (1849–1895). There is no known
photograph of Lord Randolph taken with his two sons.

TOP LEFT: General Sir Ian Hamilton. **TOP CENTRE:** Sir Bindon Blood.
TOP RIGHT: Lieutenant Winston S. Churchill, Fourth Hussars (1896).

Sir Herbert Horatio Kitchener
(the 'Sirdar').

Violet Asquith
(later Violet Bonham Carter).

TOP LEFT: First Lord of the Admiralty. TOP RIGHT: Admiral of the Fleet John Arbuthnot 'Jackie' Fisher and Churchill after a meeting of the Imperial Defence Committee, 1913. RIGHT: Prime Minister Herbert H. Asquith (1852–1928). BELOW: An early advocate of aviation, Churchill inspects a naval biplane of the Royal Navy Air Service modified to carry a Vickers gun, circa 1914.

During a visit with General Émile Fayolle and other French officers in December 1915, Major Winston Churchill is wearing a *poilu*'s helmet recently presented to him. During his service on the western front the helmet became his trademark. Edward Spiers is third from left.

TOP LEFT: Neville Chamberlain raises his hat to the crowd outside No. 10 Downing Street, 3 September 1939, the day Britain declared war on Germany.
TOP RIGHT: Foreign Secretary Lord Halifax (*left*) arriving at Downing Street on 3 September 1939. In May 1940 Halifax turned down the chance to become Prime Minister in favour of Winston Churchill.

The War Cabinet in the garden of No. 10 Downing Street in October 1941. *Front row, left to right:* Sir John Anderson, Lord President of the Council; Churchill; Clement Attlee, Lord Privy Seal (later Deputy Prime Minister); and Foreign Secretary Anthony Eden. *Back row, left to right:* Arthur Greenwood, Minister without Portfolio; Ernest Bevin, Minister of Labour; Lord Beaverbrook, Minister of Aircraft Production; and Sir Kingsley Wood, Chancellor of the Exchequer.

LEFT: Air Chief Marshal Hugh Dowding, the Commander in Chief of Fighter Command during the Battle of Britain. BELOW: One of Churchill's most painful duties as Britain's war leader was his frequent trips to the sites of the German air raids. Accompanied by US Ambassador John G. Winant (*in hat on left*), he inspected bomb-damaged houses in the hard-hit city of Bristol on 12 April 1941.

BELOW: The first massive Luftwaffe air raid on London occurred on 7 September 1940; London's dock area and Tower Bridge stand out against a background of smoke and fires.

The Chiefs of Staff

TOP LEFT: Marshal of the Royal Air Force Charles 'Peter' Portal. TOP RIGHT: Sir John Dill became the second CIGS to be sacked by Churchill. His greatest contributions followed as Chief of the British Joint Staff Mission in Washington. After his death in 1944, Dill was buried in Arlington National Cemetery, a rare honour for a foreign officer. CENTRE: Sir Alan Brooke. By 1942 Churchill had replaced all of the chiefs of staff except Admiral Dudley Pound (BELOW LEFT), whose untimely death in 1943 led to the appointment of Admiral 'ABC' Cunningham (BELOW RIGHT), the Commander in Chief of the Mediterranean Fleet, later the Allied naval commander in the Mediterranean under General Dwight D. Eisenhower. Led by Brooke, the team of Cunningham and Portal guided the British war effort through the remainder of the war.

The North African desert was known as the graveyard of generals. One who mastered it was the 'Desert Fox,' Erwin Rommel.

British infantry shelters behind a knocked-out Mark III panzer as German artillery fire lands nearby.

The other two were British – both of whom were lost early in the war. The Germans captured Lieutenant General Sir Richard O'Connor in April 1941, while General Sir Archibald Wavell's ill-fated relationship with Churchill resulted in his relief in the summer of 1941 as commander in chief, Middle East. In this photo, O'Connor and Wavell confer near Bardia, Libya, on 4 January 1941, during Operation Compass.

In the Map Room at the Cabinet War Rooms. On Churchill's right is
Captain Richard Pim of the RNVR, the officer in charge of the Map Room.

A solemn church service on the after deck of HMS *Prince of Wales*, in
Placentia Bay, Newfoundland, on 10 August 1941. Standing behind
Roosevelt and Churchill are: Admiral Ernest J. King (USN); General
George C. Marshall (US Army); Field Marshal Sir John Dill (British Army);
Admiral Harold R. Stark (USN); and Admiral of the Fleet Sir Dudley
Pound (RN). At far left is Harry Hopkins, talking to W. Averell Harriman.

23

Penance

When it is all over we shall be proud that you were a soldier & not a politician for the greater part of the war.   – Clementine Churchill

In his letter of resignation to Prime Minister Asquith, Churchill made his future intentions quite plain: 'I am an officer and I place myself unreservedly at the disposal of the Military authorities, observing that my regiment is in France.' Churchill also served notice that he retained a fiery element of defiance: 'I have a clear conscience, which enables me to bear my responsibility for past events with composure. Time will vindicate my administration of the Admiralty, and assign me my due share in the vast series of preparations and operations which have secured us the command of the seas. With much respect, and unadulterated personal friendship, I bid you good-bye.'

He wasted no time. In this respect Churchill was no different from all the other sons of the British upper class who embraced the war, volunteered for service and paid a price as high as, if not proportionally higher than, other elements of society. In 1914 alone 'six peers, sixteen baronets, ninety-five sons of peers and eighty-two sons of baronets had been killed,' states one of Jennie's biographers. In 1915 the war hit close to home with the death of the husband of Churchill's free-spirited cousin Clare, Wilfred Sheridan, who was killed in action in September in the Battle of Loos.

Churchill's goal was immediately to join his regiment, the Oxfordshire Hussars, in France. Following his resignation he spent a chaotic week at his brother's London home as he made final preparations to depart. F. E. Smith visited and recorded that the place 'was upside down while the soldier statesman was buckling on his sword', and upstairs his mother 'was in a state of despair at the thought of her brilliant son being relegated to the trenches. Mrs Churchill seemed to be the only person who remained calm, collected and efficient.'

Two days before his departure he was given a send-off luncheon hosted by his sister-in-law, Gwendeline ('Goonie'), attended by a small circle of friends and, strangely enough, Asquith's wife Margot, who was hardly one of his admirers. Violet Asquith thought it more of a wake than a happy occasion, but despite this she could sense the return of her friend's eagerness to answer the call of danger and adventure.

There was betting in some London circles that Churchill would not return, and his anguished mother was heard to murmur, 'I suppose they hope he will meet a bullet.' Jennie implored her son to temper his tendency towards acts of bravery. 'Please be sensible. I think you ought to take the trenches in small doses, after 10 years of more or less sedentary life – but I'm sure you won't "play the fool" – Remember you are destined for greater things . . . I am a great believer in your star.' Jennie and Clementine joined the ranks of those whose loved ones had gone off to war while they waited at home to face the gnawing apprehension each day of the dreaded telegram or the appearance of a stranger on their doorstep.

On 18 November Major Churchill crossed the Channel, fully expecting to take up duties with his regiment, then billeted well behind the front lines in a French village. Even as a mere major he was no ordinary soldier, and although he had not expected special treatment, was surprised to find when his ship docked in Boulogne that Sir John French had sent a car to fetch him. After briefly reporting to his regiment, he was taken to French's GHQ at Saint-Omer, where he was fêted by the commander in chief as an honoured guest. His billet at GHQ, 'in a fine chateau, with hot baths, bed, champagne & all the conveniences', was more like a five-star hotel than a military headquarters.

Churchill revealed that French offered him a post as an aide (and a life of relative ease and safety) or the command of a brigade at the front. He unhesitatingly chose to accept a command but with the sensible proviso that he first should learn the ropes by joining a front-line unit and experience for himself what life was like in the trenches. He also reassured Clementine: 'You must not let this fret you in the least . . . Do not suppose I shall run any foolish risks or do anything wh is not obviously required.'

Pleased that the army was 'willing to receive me back as the "prodigal son" ', he was determined to make the most of his experience in France. 'I must try to win my way as a good & sincere soldier,' he wrote hours before departing for 'Somewhere in France', as his next letter to Clementine was headed. 'I did not know what release from care meant. It is a blessed peace. How I ever cd have wasted so many months in impotent misery, wh might have been spent in war, I cannot tell.' And while he was more than willing to endure the same hardships as the men at the front, Churchill nevertheless was more than ready to take advantage of the creature comforts offered at GHQ: 'In the intervals between going into the trenches I shall come back for hot baths, etc. to GHQ where I have been told to consider a place always open. French . . . is a good friend.'

What is clear from their many poignant letters is that the war had drawn Winston and Clementine closer together. Danger is a great motivating force, and their expressions of care and love for each other during his months at the front were heightened as never before, bringing out the best in each.

The first days Winston was away were especially hard for Clementine, who, although she did not articulate it, was understandably concerned about her mercurial husband and what he might do to confront danger. 'I long for news of you,' she wrote in her first letter, 'I want to know where you are . . . what you are thinking and feeling . . . Write to me Winston. I want a letter from you badly.'

Given a choice of units, Churchill opted for the Grenadier Guards, and for the next several weeks was attached to the 2nd Battalion, a unit his ancestor John Churchill had once commanded. Lord Cavan, a future field marshal, then commanding the Brigade of Guards, picked this unit because, as he told Churchill, he would learn more from its commander than from anyone else. Not surprisingly his reception was glacial. Military units, particularly combat units where death is an integral part of daily life, are like a family. They take care of their own; they trust only those who have shown their mettle and are innately suspicious of strangers, not least an unproved, high-profile politician like Winston Churchill.

Escorted to his new unit by the divisional commander, Churchill was met behind the lines on an icy November afternoon by the battalion commander, Lieutenant Colonel George Jeffreys, and given a pony to ride to the front. The Grenadiers were in the process of taking up a sector near the village of Laventie. The presence of not only a politician but also a former powerful cabinet minister was greeted with distrust, and Jeffreys made clear his displeasure by saying, 'I think I ought to tell you that we were not at all consulted in the matter of your coming to join us.' Like most soldiers Jeffreys had a deep suspicion of all politicians. Indeed the mere mention of the word 'politician' was generally prefaced with the adjective 'bloody', reflecting an attitude not confined to the officers and men of the Grenadiers. Churchill later likened the experience to that of 'a new boy at school in charge of the Headmaster, the monitors and senior scholars'.

The battalion command post was a thousand yards behind the front lines in the ruins of what was known as Ebenezer Farm. As Churchill settled in, sleet was falling, and the sounds of bullets and of artillery whistling became the music by which the men lived. The trench he was to occupy was a foot deep in water, and he wisely elected to bunk in the battalion signal office.

In the days that followed he learned a great deal and came to regard 'these magnificent Grenadiers' with awe and to discover for himself what life at the front was like. 'I was infinitely amused at the elaborate pains they took to put me in my place and to make me realize that nothing counted at the front except military rank and behaviour.' There were few more miserable places on earth than the front lines of the First World War, where each day was marked by cold, raw weather in winter and extreme heat and rain in summer. Churchill saw first hand, for example, the ravages of trench foot brought on by alternating periods of frost and soaking rains. Gradually, Colonel Jeffreys began to 'forget that I was a "politician"' and to accept him. He 'took immense pains to explain to me every detail of the economy and discipline of his battalion', eventually permitting Churchill to accompany him as he made the rounds of his battalion, sometimes to the accompaniment of bullets whizzing overhead. Any lingering doubts his colonel may have had were erased when Churchill volunteered to spend time in the trenches in order to experience the conditions under which the men lived.

From France came a steady stream of candid letters to Clementine describing in considerable detail what life was like: 'the venomous whining & whirring of the bullets', legions of enormous rats, the cold, the vast amount of work required to make the trenches barely habitable, the water and the muck, the discomfort and the chilling fact that only a handful of the original members of the battalion remained from its earlier combat.

Despite his good intentions of sharing the same hardships as the Grenadiers, Churchill had little stomach for eating military rations. His letters to Clementine were peppered with requests not only for items of clothing, sleeping kit and various types of boots, but also for extra rations of the sort he was accustomed to enjoying: 'Sardines, chocolate, potted meats, and other things that may strike your fancy . . . as soon as possible.'

Where others merely endured he seemed to thrive. 'Amid these surroundings, aided by wet & cold, & every minor discomfort, I have found happiness & content such as I have not known for many months . . . Do you realize what a vy important person a Major is? 99 people out of any hundred in the gt army have to touch their hats to me . . . At this game I hope I shall be as good as any.'

George Santayana once wrote, 'Only the dead are safe; only the dead have seen the end of war.' In November 1915, Churchill narrowly averted death. While he was in a front-line bunker writing a letter, an orderly arrived with a field telegram from the corps commander. Churchill was directed to meet the general, a man he had known for some years, at a certain crossroads, where a vehicle would be awaiting him, at 3.30 that afternoon. 'I thought it rather a strong order to bring me out of the trenches by daylight – a 3 mile walk across sopping fields on wh stray bullets are always falling, along tracks periodically shelled. But I assumed it was something important . . . I started off just as the enemy began to shell the roads & trenches in revenge for the shelling he had been receiving from our provocative and well fed artillery. I just missed a whole bunch of shells wh fell on the track a hundred yards behind me and arrived after an hour's walking muddy wet & sweating at the rendezvous.'

The general never appeared; only a staff officer arrived, on foot, to say that the vehicle had gone to the wrong location, and that in any event their meeting wasn't all that important: the general merely wanted to chat with him 'about things in general & that another day wd do equally well'. A tired, wet and very angry Churchill was obliged to retrace his steps and trudge through the muck in the dark. Believing he had been made a fool of, he soon changed his mind when, upon his arrival back at the front, he was informed that 'a quarter of an hour after I had left, the dugout in wh I was living had been struck by a shell which burst a few feet from where I wd have been sitting, smashing the structure & killing the mess orderly who was inside . . . When I saw the ruin I was not so angry with the general after all.'

Churchill's kit had been blown to pieces, but he was alive – by a miraculous stroke of luck. Clementine must have been horrified by this tale, but Winston exhorted her, 'Now see from this how vain it is to worry about things. It is all chance or destiny and our wayward footsteps are best planted without too much calculation. One must yield oneself simply & naturally to the mood of the game; and trust in God.' In his later reminiscence of the event Churchill seemed to acknowledge life in general as a matter of 'chance', which, he said, 'casts aside all veils and disguises and presents herself nakedly from moment to moment as the direct arbiter over all persons and events'. Of his near brush with death he wrote, 'There came the strong sensation that a hand had been stretched out to move me in the nick of time from the fatal spot.'

Clementine dreaded having Winston in danger and often candidly expressed her feelings. She was particularly concerned that, unlike others, who had been toughened by training and first-hand experience, he had 'gone at one swoop from an atmosphere of hot rooms, sedentary work & Turkish baths to a life of the most cruel hardship & exposure. And besides thinking of me & the babies think of your duty to yourself & your reputation – if you were killed & you had over-exposed yourself the world might think that you had sought death out of grief for your share in the Dardanelles. It is your duty to the country to try & live (consistent with your honour as a soldier).'

On 1 December the Grenadiers were withdrawn to the rear, thus ending Churchill's first experience of trench warfare. Although he had been with the battalion for only ten days, life in the front lines of the First World War made it seem more like a lifetime, especially in view of his near-death experience.

Some days later Clementine learned of the conditions under which Winston and the Grenadiers lived from Lord Esher, who had visited the front. This knowledge left her even more fearful for her husband's life. Her trepidation was that of every wife, mother or friend whose loved one has ever been sent to war. 'I live from day to day in suspense and anguish,' she wrote. 'At night when I lie down I say to myself Thank

God he is still alive. The 4 weeks of your absence seem to me like 4 years – If only my Dear you had no military ambitions. If only you would stay with the Oxfordshire Hussars in their billets – I can just bear it – feeling that you are really happy. I have ceased to have ambitions for you – Just come back to me alive that's all.'

The state of the war at the end of 1915 was as dismal as it had been a year earlier. Deadlock reigned, and only the toll of misery had changed, constantly rising as fast as the gravediggers could carry out their grim work. At sea the Royal Navy had been incapable of halting the enormous losses wreaked by U-boats; nearly nine hundred thousand tons of Allied shipping had been sunk by German torpedoes.

That month also saw the replacement of Sir John French as commander in chief of the BEF. A cavalry officer like Churchill, French was both appalled and drained by the losses sustained by his beloved soldiers. In Whitehall's view French had outlived his usefulness. Though he was a decent, stubborn man, his rancorous relations with Kitchener, his nearly obsessive suspicions of his French ally and his mishandling of the Battle of Loos, a costly and futile offensive in September 1915 that left sixteen thousand British dead and another twenty-five thousand wounded, were enough to convince both Asquith (spurred on by King George, who wanted French gone) and Kitchener that the time had come to replace him. French was removed on the pretext of elevating him to a peerage, and given an inconsequential new post as commander in chief of British home forces. His replacement was another cavalry officer, the intensely ambitious Douglas Haig, a close friend of the king. Haig became the architect of British military strategy and retained the post until the end of the war. He was praised by some but reviled by others for his stubborn insistence on fighting costly battles of attrition, and for his belief that he was being directed in his efforts by divine guidance, thus in his own mind rendering his actions and decisions above reproach. For Churchill, French's departure meant the loss of a friend at court.

The day of his return from the front Churchill wrote that he had spoken with Lord Cavan, who, in what must have been music to his ears, 'spoke of my having high command as if it were the natural thing, but urged the importance of going up step by step'. Cavan strongly suggested he command a battalion first, before accepting any higher command, 'and this is what I think I shall do, if it is open to me.'

Churchill's return to GHQ coincided with the last days of French's command of the BEF. At dinner on 3 December, when Churchill said he preferred to be given command of a battalion, French rejected his proposal and declared that it would be a brigade of the Grenadier Guards, which also meant the fulfilment of his long-standing dream of proving his mettle as a military commander.

Clementine heard from a family friend several days later that her husband was likely to command a brigade. Aware of the furor this assignment might provoke among Winston's enemies, she thought it was a bad idea and vigorously argued against it. 'I prefer you to win your way than to be thought a favourite of the C. in C. I *feel* confidence in your star,' she wrote, '& I know all soldiers who meet you will love you.' Her pleas were in vain; Winston not only was determined to accept a brigade command but had already singled out two friends to fill key posts, Archie Sinclair to be his ADC and a cavalry officer he had taken a shine to, Captain Edward Louis Spiers, to be his brigade major. Spiers was the product of an Anglo-French upbringing and had survived four wounds. He was well regarded by French, Joffre and a number of other high-ranking generals and French political leaders, and was then the commander in chief's liaison officer to the French Tenth Army.

Spiers had not expected to like Churchill. 'Like all young soldiers of those days, I learned rather to despise the politician Churchill who, like myself, a cavalry officer, had wandered off into the unhealthy and noisome purlieus of Whitehall, there to become a noisy show-off.' Spiers was very much a loner, unafraid to speak his mind, and with few friends among his military contemporaries. When Churchill took him up, it was the start of a lifelong friendship. In the coming years Edward Spears (he changed the spelling of his name in 1918) would become one of Churchill's closest confidants and one of the few men he completely trusted. Although flattered by Churchill's offer, Spiers thought it 'absurd', noting in his diary, 'a politician as Brigadier, a cavalryman as Bde Major! Poor Brigade.'

As the days passed without confirmation of his appointment, Churchill prepared to return with the Grenadiers for another tour of duty in the trenches. With time on their hands he and Spiers visited the French sector of the front, where he was presented with a blue helmet of the kind worn by the ordinary *poilu*. The helmet, which became the signature piece of his time at the front, 'will perhaps protect my valuable cranium'. Churchill wore it constantly, and even though it looked oddly out of place, it suited him. 'I look most martial in it,' he declared, 'like a Cromwellian – I always intend to wear it under fire – but chiefly for the appearance.'

His future seemed settled until 15 December, when French returned to London and informed Asquith that he was appointing Churchill to command a brigade. Asquith expressed his delight at the news only to change his mind several hours later, writing a note that read in part: 'The appointment might cause some criticism.' French was to withdraw it. 'Perhaps you might give him a battalion,' Asquith said. French was acutely embarrassed and angry, while Churchill was inclined to believe that Asquith's 'conduct reached the limit of meanness & ungenerousness'.

Asquith's hasty derailment of the appointment came about when he learned that one of Churchill's political enemies, the acting under-secretary of state for war, Sir Charles Hunter, a Conservative MP, had become aware of his impending appointment and would oppose it. Hunter later challenged the appointment in Parliament by inquiring 'if Major Winston Churchill has been promised the command of an Infantry brigade; if this officer has ever commanded a battalion of Infantry; and for how many weeks has he served at the front as an Infantry Officer?' – all questions designed to embarrass Asquith.

Once again Asquith's indifference, and the settling of old scores by his political enemies, doomed Churchill's promotion. His luck and his influence were now in total eclipse. He had fled to France to escape the harsh political infighting of London only to find that he remained such a magnet for controversy that escape was impossible. Asquith's interference he deemed the ultimate betrayal, and his thoughts turned to revenge, 'to stand up in my place in Parliament and endeavour to procure the dismissal of Asquith and Kitchener . . . I shall do it without compunction.' His mood in the ensuing days was despairing. Two of his letters to Clementine were so angry and emotional that he instructed her to burn them.

Although he was largely absorbed in learning his new craft, never for an instant did Churchill forget the humiliation of his removal from the Admiralty. In January 1916 he wrote with undisguised resentment, 'Whenever my mind is not occupied by war, I feel deeply of the injustice with wh my work at the Admiralty has been treated. I cannot help it –

tho' I try. Then the damnable mismanagement has ruined the Darda-nelles enterprise & squandered vainly so much life & opportunity cries aloud for retribution & if I survive, the day will come when I will claim it.' Clementine replied: 'When it is all over we shall be proud that you were a soldier & not a politician for the greater part of the war – soldiers and soldiers' wives seem to me now the only real people.'

He spent another forty-eight hours at the front, joining a night raid into German lines by a patrol of Grenadiers armed with clubs, where they 'beat the brains out of two of them' and captured a prisoner who was dragged back to the British lines. This brief sojourn at the front was also a lesson for Churchill in the messy side of war: the young British officer leading the raid mistakenly shot and killed one of his own men, 'but the others kept this secret and pretended it was done by the enemy ... In the Grenadiers the opinion is that I am to have a division. This they seemed to consider quite reasonable. I shd be happy to take a company but I do not want much to go under fire again – except with a definite responsibility however small.'

French made one final attempt to sponsor his friend's promotion when he met with Haig shortly before turning over his command. Although Churchill knew Haig from his days as a young MP and had suggested to Asquith in October 1915 that he be appointed chief of the Imperial General Staff, he would never have the intimate relationship that he had enjoyed with French. Although the new commander in chief would not assure him of a brigade command, he did agree that Churchill should have a battalion command. Churchill accepted at once but remained stubbornly convinced that 'it would not have been a great mistake for me to take a Brigade.' Haig also agreed to let him have Archie Sinclair or Edward Spiers to fill a key position in his new battalion, although it would later transpire that Spiers could not be spared.

Churchill invited Haig to read a paper he had written on trench warfare, 'Variants of the Offensive', which was based on his recent experience at the front. Haig replied he would be 'honoured' to do so, and Churchill departed 'back on my perch again with my feathers stroked'.

Officers with the requisite influence were permitted to return to England for brief periods of leave, and Churchill spent Christmas at home before returning to await a decision on his future. On New Year's Day 1916 he learned he was to be assigned to the 9th Division, a Scottish unit, and

North Sea

HOLLAND

Zeebrugge
Ostend

Dover

Dover Strait

Calais

Dunkirk

Bruges

Antwerp

Scheldt

Passchendaele

Brussels

Boulogne

Saint-Omer

Ypres

PLOEGSTEERT

Lys Menin

BELGIUM

Lille

Mons

Arras

Cambrai

Abbeville

Le Câteau

Dieppe

Amiens

Somme

Saint-Quentin

Beauvais

Compiègne

FRONT LINE
1916

Soissons

Rheims

Seine

Marne

Paris

FRANCE

Seine

Troyes

N
W   E
S

Western Front
1916

0   50   100   150 miles

0   50   100   150   200 kilometres

Petho Cartography 2009

to be given command of the 6th Battalion, Royal Scots Fusiliers. He was immediately promoted to lieutenant colonel and on 5 January assumed command of his new unit, then billeted in reserve positions in Flanders, in the village of Moolenacker, well behind the front lines. Before departing to take up his new command he wrote to Clementine to ask that she send him a copy of Robert Burns's poems. 'I will soothe & cheer their spirits by quotations from it . . . You know I am a vy gt admirer of that race. A wife, a constituency, & now a regiment attest the sincerity of my choice.'

The distinguished lineage of the Royal Scots Fusiliers goes back to its formation in 1678, and its participation in the Battles of Blenheim and Sevastopol, the Boer War and numerous colonial wars. From 1914 to 1918 eighteen battalions fought in the major battles of the First World War. The 6th Fusiliers was a typical veteran Great War infantry battalion that had suffered severe losses at Loos and later under the most squalid and dangerous conditions in the Ypres salient before being withdrawn into reserve only days before Churchill joined it. The battalion now consisted of a mix of young recruits and some surviving older reservists.

As it had been with the Grenadiers, Churchill's descent upon the 6th Fusiliers was both sudden and unwelcome. News of his imminent arrival spread through the battalion like wildfire, and as the adjutant, Captain Andrew Gibb, would later write, 'A mutinous spirit grew. Everyone liked the old C.O. and nobody could see why any prominent outsider should come in and usurp his place so easily.' It was widely (and correctly) believed that the former CO was being replaced only as a concession to Churchill. The news, recalled another of the regimental officers, Second Lieutenant Edmund Hakewill Smith (a future major general and division commander during the Second World War), was met with 'horror'. Nor did Churchill initially do anything to change that opinion.

The usual low-profile arrival of a new commanding officer did not suit Winston Churchill. His appearance shortly before noon was arguably the most bizarre of any in the First World War. He rode in on a black charger, accompanied by Archie Sinclair and two grooms, also riding black chargers. Behind them was a cart piled high with his luggage, which far exceeded what was permitted under regulations. 'In the rear half,' recalled Hakewill Smith, 'we saw a curious contraption: a long bath and a boiler for heating the bath water.'

Churchill had sent word ahead that he desired to meet his officers at lunch before inspecting his new command. Hakewill Smith related: 'It was quite the most uncomfortable lunch I had ever been at. Churchill didn't say a word: he went right round the table staring each officer out of countenance. We had disliked the idea of Churchill being in command; now, having seen him, we disliked the idea even more. At the end of the lunch, he made a short speech: "Gentlemen, I am now your commanding Officer. Those who support me I will look after. Those who go against me I will break. Good afternoon gentlemen." Everyone agreed we were in for a pretty rotten time.'

The 6th Fusiliers were assembled on a slope when Churchill appeared riding his black charger and began barking out commands: 'Royal Scots Fusiliers! Fix bayonets!' The whole scene was farcical: 'The command could not possibly be carried out from the slope position. A couple of the chaps put their rifles on the ground and pulled out their bayonets; the rest were merely mystified. Eventually [Captain] Gibb persuaded Churchill to call "Order Arms" and to fix their bayonets in the normal way. Winston then inspected the men. Having done so, he gave a cavalry order: "Sections Right!" This meant nothing to the Jocks, who had the sense to stand still and do nothing.'

Churchill was as unimpressed with his new command as the men were with him, and recognized at once that it would be a challenge to whip them into fighting shape. 'This regiment is pathetic,' he wrote to Clementine a day after assuming command, but the officers he thought showed potential. 'The young officers are all small middle class Scotsmen – vy brave & willing and intelligent; but of course all quite new to soldiering. All the seniors & all the professionals have fallen ... The regiment is full of life & strength, & I believe I shall be a help to them.'

For their part the officers found their new commander enigmatic and their introduction to him bizarre. They were summoned, and saluted and shook hands with their new commander. As each did so, 'Winston relapsed into his chair and scrutinized him, silently and intently from head to foot.' No words were exchanged or questions asked. Gibb was undoubtedly not alone in being disconcerted by Churchill. 'I found myself forced to stare hard back at him and trust to time to bring this, like all other trials, to an end.' It was an extraordinary culmination to Churchill's first day as their new commanding officer.

What they all quickly learned, however, was that their new commander completely immersed himself in every aspect of their daily lives. Changes were made, improvements initiated and constant, almost incessant lectures delivered on a variety of subjects. There did not seem to be a single topic with which Churchill was not conversant. The men smartened up, and a sense of order and purpose emanated from the confidence displayed by their leader. One day he assembled his officers and announced in a solemn voice: 'War is declared, gentlemen.' Expecting a lecture on fighting the Germans, they were astonished when Churchill completed his statement: 'on the lice'. There ensued one of the most utterly unusual discourses ever given by any commander.

'With these words', wrote Gibb, 'did the great scion of the house of Marlborough first address his Scottish Captains assembled in council. And with these words was inaugurated such a discourse on *pulex Europaeus*, its origin, growth, and nature, its habitat and its importance as a factor in wars ancient and modern, as left one agape with wonder at the erudition and force of its author.' Thereafter the 6th Fusiliers became, in Gibb's words, 'a liceless battalion', and 'to an unparalleled degree an utterly "deloused" battalion'. History thus records that Churchill won his first battle of the war.

Though he put his troops through bayonet drills, attempts at cavalry drills using ponies and horses were hopeless; few of his charges had ever ridden. Moreover, cavalry drill was hardly a skill required for men whose existence was spent in the trenches. A visit from the corps commander to the battalion assembled for his inspection went flawlessly until the pipe major played a piece called 'The Drunken Piper'.

After their rough introduction to the new colonel, the officers found Churchill a more relaxed and accessible commander. Their resentments at losing their previous commander were quickly forgotten as the new CO made his mark. Gibb would later write that not only did Churchill improve their lot but also 'he improved *on* us.' The transformation that began evolving within a short time of his assumption of command was a triumph for Churchill, who also began to relax his sternness in the officers' mess, where they 'learnt a little of the charm of as distinct from the Colonel . . . and his capacity for coaxing and charming the best even out of the most boorish is a gift which I never ceased to wonder at. He materially altered the feelings of the officers towards him by this kindliness and by the first insight we thus gained into the wonderful genius of the man. And so he began a conquest which when he left us was complete

– a complete conquest achieved in two or three short months and over men of a race not easily moved and won over.' Returning the compliment, Winston wrote to his brother Jack: 'I shall be proud to lead this shattered battalion in the assault.'

Churchill learned the same skills required of his men. Whether it was throwing the the First World War version of the hand grenade, 'a job to be approached gingerly', the firing of a machine gun or calling down supporting artillery fire, he left nothing to chance, soaking up military knowledge as fast as he could find someone to teach him. The battalion billets in the rear, situated amid 'a sea of sopping fields & muddy lanes', were ramshackle farmhouses that offered few comforts better than the trenches. With movement forward imminent, there was little time for him to improve the quality of life. His own billet was a room in one of the farmhouses large enough to hold only his bed.

It was not only his men who came away impressed by Churchill's flair for command. Major Desmond Morton, who would play a supporting role in Churchill's future, was an artillery officer sent to investigate a request from a battalion commander for supporting fire for a trench raid. Upon his arrival he learned that the officer was Churchill, whom he found drawing sketches of the German lines and re-enacting what his ancestor might have done. 'He was "doing a Marlborough", calling up fire, demanding help on the flank, and turning the whole thing into a major campaign, rather than a trench raid of which the object was to capture a few Germans.'

Somewhat surprisingly Churchill was not the harsh disciplinarian his men had expected; in fact, Captain Gibb thought he was far too indulgent in assessing punishments for first-time offenders for such acts as disobeying orders. 'We permanently differed on this matter and I am afraid the men began to realize that they might at least once indulge themselves in the luxury of telling their sergeants to go to hell!' His compassion extended to arranging for diversions such as a sporting event consisting of mule races and pillow fights, and a concert held in a barn. 'Such singing you never heard . . . Poor fellows – nothing like this had ever been done for them before. They do not get much to brighten their lives – short as these may be,' Churchill duly reported to Clementine. Shortly after the battalion moved forward to the front, he hosted a dinner for his officers complete with oysters and champagne. 'I made the officers a little speech . . . & the pipes played doleful dirges; & we sang Auld Lang Syne.'

On another occasion a company runner, a private named Reginald Hurt, encountered Churchill. After saluting smartly the soldier had gone some dozen paces when he was called back and asked why he was limping. 'I explained that my feet were sore because of the bad condition of my boots and that when I had applied for new pair the quartermaster said they would last another three months. The OC took a letter from his tunic pocket, detached the envelope and wrote on it, "Quartermaster Sgt. B. Company, supply bearer with one pair of boots *immediately*," and signed it.' For Churchill, it was small but important gestures like this that won the confidence of his men.

His relations with his higher headquarters were altogether different. He instituted a vigorous campaign to secure long-overdue promotions for his men that were routinely rejected. Churchill fought back with a flood of paperwork and personal visits to harangue the staffs. The usual routine was to refuse his requests in writing. However, it turned out to be far more difficult when the staff was confronted by a determined CO who refused to take no for an answer. Gibb was not alone in his delight at seeing hated staff officers receive a full dose of Winston Churchill.

British soldiers were regularly transported in commandeered London buses, Scottish soldiers rarely. In the move forward to take their new positions, Churchill managed to secure a single bus for his men. Most, however, went like him, on foot, walking mile after mile over the soot-laden roads of this bleak region of Belgium. Wearing his trademark French helmet, Churchill relished the opportunity to lead men into battle at last. Said Captain Gibb: 'Winston was in his element.'

24
'In Flanders Fields'

I never expected to be so completely involved in the military machine. It almost seems to me as if my life in the gt world was a dream.

– Churchill, 13 February 1916

Real danger unnerves most men; it nerved him.   – General Jack Seely

On 24 January 1916 the 6th Fusiliers occupied the small Belgian village of Ploegsteert. With a name too complicated for Scottish tongues to wrap themselves around, the place quickly became known as 'Plugstreet'.

Situated at the southern end of the Ypres salient, the area around Plugstreet was dotted with small farms and dreary surroundings bereft of almost everything but death and misery. Flanders has become a symbol of the enormous sacrifices of the British during the First World War. Nearby Ypres was already a death trap from the battles of 1915. Today there are 170 British military cemeteries added to the Flanders landscape, one of which is in Plugstreet. Among the dead buried there is a sixteen-year-old soldier whose family was denied a pension by a tight-fisted War Office, which ruled that he had been underage, until it finally relented and paid the paltry sum of five shillings a week to his father.

In this war, unlike earlier wars in which he had participated, Churchill was never convinced that he was meant to survive. His letters to Clementine are filled with disconcerting phrases such as 'if I survive'. He would certainly have understood the memorable poem 'In Flanders Fields', written by John McCrae, a surgeon, then a major in the Canadian army, who was later himself among the dead of whom he wrote so eloquently in 1915:

We are the dead. Short days ago
We lived, felt dawn, saw sunset glow,
Loved and were loved, and now we lie
In Flanders fields.

Before first light on the morning of 27 January the 6th Fusiliers relieved another battalion (the 8th Border) and occupied some thousand yards of the front just east of the village. The changeover was flawless, and Churchill proudly wrote to Clementine, 'I don't think the Grenadiers ever did better.' Two headquarters were established: an advanced command post in the ruins of a house named Laurence Farm, some six hundred yards behind the front lines, on the edge of no man's land; and the main battalion CP at a former hospice run by the Ouvier Sisters of Charity, a few hundred yards south of Plugstreet, on the road to Armentières three thousand yards behind the front. There Churchill lived rather well in a bedroom with a view of the front lines. 'Two nuns remained in the building to tend the small chapel, armoured in their faith and indifferent to their exposed position. They welcomed the British troops as saviours of this part of Belgium and made them appetizing soup.'

Despite the nearly constant German shelling it was soon clear that the target was not the hospice but a nearby British artillery battery. However, Churchill would shortly realize that the Germans, when provoked and harassed by the aggressive tactics of his division commander, struck back with fury. Although no one was safe, the incessant noise and danger were part of routine daily life along the Plugstreet front. The fusiliers spent their first days getting acclimatized to their new in-ground residence. Churchill had remarked, 'We will go easy at first: a little digging and feeling our way, and then perhaps later on we may attempt a "deed",' that is, a trench raid on the German lines that the rear-echelon 'warriors' of the Imperial General Staff were fond of ordering but that served little purpose.

Once at the front Churchill seemed to want to wage his own private war. At night he ordered his troops to begin firing their weapons in order to draw German return fire, 'then he would telephone the artillery demanding support and more than once the nocturnal "hate" of the 6th Royal Scots Fusiliers led to a general flare up in the sector.' His popularity with other units in this normally quiet sector can only be imagined.

For a time the men believed that the reason they were shelled a good deal was that the Germans knew of Churchill's presence. He vehemently disagreed, pointing out that he was as unpopular in Germany as he was in England. 'If they knew I was in the line here they wouldn't send over a few shells like this. They would turn on all their guns and blot the place out.'

For the soldiers of the Great War, whether officers or other ranks, merely staying alive in a minuscule and monotonous world of trench life, sometimes under endless shelling, mortar attacks and machine-gun fire, became their only aspiration. Their earlier existence as civilians was but a distant memory. And so it was for Winston Churchill. 'I never expected to be so completely involved in the military machine,' he wrote to Clementine from the trenches. 'It almost seems to me as if my life in the gt world was a dream.'

Churchill did what all good commanders do: he visited the men of his battalion often (usually three times a day), slogging to every corner of his section of the front to see and be seen by his men. Day and night he became a familiar figure easily identified by his distinctive light-blue helmet as he prowled restlessly around his domain, usually taking two hours to inspect the thousand-yard battalion front. During moonlit nights he often tramped the entire ground of the battalion front with Archie Sinclair as his guide, the only danger coming from random bullets. They also ventured into no man's land, as he duly reported to Clementine. The landscape was torn asunder by the shellings, 'shattered buildings, sandbag habitations, trenches heavily wired, shell holes, frequent graveyards with thickets of little crosses, wild rank growing grass, muddy roads, khaki soldiers – & so on for hundreds & hundreds of miles – on both sides Miserable Europe . . . Cd I help to a victorious peace more in the H. of C. than here?' he wondered.

His first venture into no man's land was not without incident. With a revolver strapped to his waist and wearing a waterproof coat, knee-high trench boots and his French helmet, a powerful flashlamp attached to his web belt, Churchill, accompanied by his adjutant, Lieutenant Jock McDavid, had just begun his journey when German machine guns opened fire. The two officers dived into an already crowded shell hole when suddenly a bright light appeared around them. Churchill commanded, 'Put out that bloody light!' only to discover that his own lamp had somehow been turned on in their scramble to safety.

There were numerous other occasions when Churchill boldly ventured into this maelstrom as if once again to test his courage under battlefield conditions. 'It was a nerve-racking experience to go with him,' said Hakewill Smith. 'He would call out in a gruff voice – far too loud it seemed to us – "You go that way, I will go this."' Other times Churchill would call out, '"Come here, I have found a gap in the German wire. Come over here at once!" He was like a baby elephant out in no-man's-land at night. He never fell when a shell went off; he never ducked when a bullet went past at a loud crack. He used to say to me after watching me duck: "It's no damn use ducking; the bullet has gone a long way past you by now."'

One night during an exchange of artillery fire Churchill suggested that he and Gibb view the German lines from the top of a parapet. With bullets zipping all around them he used the occasion to inquire 'in a dreamy, far-away voice, "Do you like War?" As we stood up on the fire-step we felt the wind and swish of several whizzbangs flying past our heads, which, as it always did, horrified me. The only thing to do was to pretend not to hear him. At that moment I profoundly hated War. But at that and every moment I believe Winston Churchill revelled in it. There was no such thing as fear in him.'

Laurence Farm had been heavily shelled and its protective works destroyed when one of the two brigade commanders under whom Churchill served during his tenure with the 6th Fusiliers arrived. This particular general was thoroughly disliked by the fusiliers, so much so that Gibb later recorded never having encountered him 'without conceiving a sincere desire to punch him upon the head', a sentiment shared by most of his colleagues. The general did not like what he saw and berated Churchill, saying that his defensive works were inadequate. 'Look here, Churchill, this won't do, you know. There's no protection here for the men . . . Look at that sentry there – it's dangerous . . . it's positively dangerous.' An annoyed Churchill brusquely replied, 'Yes, sir, but, you know, this is a very dangerous war.'

He worked tirelessly to improve living conditions and increase the men's safety. Nothing took place in the 6th Fusiliers that he was not aware of or did not have a hand in. Under his prodding his men constantly worked to improve the security of their sector and to reinforce the trenches. Whether it was explaining to nervous sentries the importance of their duties or selecting positions that enabled them to perform these duties with a minimum of exposure and discomfort, Churchill never seemed to rest. Although, as Gibb notes, he was 'utterly impervious to all feelings of aversion from the unpleasant sights of war', he was seen 'several times sitting calmly discussing questions of state with "Archie" [Sinclair] in blood-saturated surroundings', yet 'he was always first on the scene of misfortune and did all in his power to help and comfort and cheer . . . If he heard that a man was wounded he would set off at once to see him.'

Another Churchill innovation was to teach the men to sing while they marched. On one occasion he hosted a dinner party at the front attended by his divisional commander and several other VIPs, including two notable flying officers, all of them decked out in their dress uniforms. After dinner Churchill politely inquired if the general and his other guests would care to see his trenches. 'It's a lovely night, though very quiet,' he said, by way of encouragement. On the spot and unable to decline his invitation without appearing cowardly, the men agreed and, led by Churchill, trooped off into the night for an experience they would not soon forget. 'The battalion was delighted with this performance,' wrote Captain Gibb. It was 'a first-rate joke to the jaded infantry to see them all out there tearing breeches and thumbs on the wire; wallowing in mud and cursing over clothes that had never been grovelled in before . . . We were delighted, justifiably as we thought, at seeing them in the trenches, and even having their noses, so to speak, rubbed in them.'

Although he reassured Clementine whenever possible, Churchill's insistence on absolute candour in reporting to her the intimate details of his daily life continued to make her shiver. One example was the day when he wrote of a close brush with death as a German artillery shell crashed through the roof of his advanced command post at Laurence Farm. Churchill, Sinclair and several others had just finished lunch on 3 February when 'there was a tremendous crash, dust & splinters came flying through the room, plates were smashed, chairs broken. Everyone was covered with debris . . . A shell had struck the roof and burst in the next room – mine & Archie's . . . My bedroom presented a woe begone appearance, the nose of the shell passing clean through it smashed the floor and cut a hole in the rear wall.' After ordering their dugout reinforced for just such contingencies, Churchill went on to report that 'I slept peacefully in my tiny war-scarred room last night, after a prolonged tour of the trenches.'

That was not, however, the only occasion on which Churchill escaped death sitting in his chair. One morning, after provocation from nearby British batteries, the Germans replied furiously with their artillery. He was working on correspondence and refining his essay on 'Variants of the Offensive' in his main command post in Plugstreet when the Germans began raining shells on the town. He continued to work, ignoring the fact that they were landing closer and closer to his house. Eventually he paused to observe the firing through the plate-glass window facing the front lines 'as if from a box at the theatre'. At last common sense overtook his tendency to test his bravery and his luck; none too soon he relocated into a second house directly behind his, which was being used as a battalion office, just as Plugstreet was hit with a methodical bombardment that lasted a terrifying hour and a half and gradually tore the town apart. Churchill later returned to his office to encounter a scene of utter devastation. 'The room in which I had been writing was wrecked and shattered. Daylight streamed through a large hole in the brickwork above the bay-window.' A thirty-pound shell had lodged itself in the basement, where a terrified woman and her daughter had taken refuge. It was a dud.

As he began to reassemble his papers from the mess created by the shell, he could not find a classified document 'of extreme importance'. After a diligent search the document remained unaccounted for. Clearly the dud shell had not destroyed it. For the next several days Churchill worried not only that the document had fallen into the wrong hands (spies were suspected among some of the local inhabitants) but that he was very probably in serious trouble over its loss. 'I passed the next three days in helpless anxiety. I reproached myself a thousand times with not having sent the document back . . . Why had I ever let it out of my possession for a second?' Finally, on the third day Churchill happened to reach into the inner breast pocket of his tunic and 'There I found, safe and secure, the paper I had been so feverishly seeking.'

Not everything was a hardship in Plugstreet. 'The life of an infantry colonel in the lines is not at all unpleasant. Creature comforts are not lacking,' Winston wrote to Sunny Churchill shortly after assuming his new command. There was, he said, the 'constant spice of danger', with day-and-night German shelling. One of greatest pleasures was in having his own private bathtub, in which he would bathe once a week in sheer bliss. Situated in his billet and described as looking like 'a greatly magnified soap dish', his bathtub became the envy of everyone. It was maintained by a batman named Witt, whose task it was weekly to fill the tub by lugging heavy pails of steaming hot water. His officers might have been somewhat more aghast at this breach of military custom had they not vied to use it themselves whenever Churchill was away and Witt was dozing off.

Churchill also began painting again during his free moments, mainly scenes of Laurence Farm in which he attempted to capture on canvas the destruction wrought by months of German bombardments. He set up his easel in the courtyard, pockmarked with an increasingly large number of shell holes. For a time he was morose, his anger reflected in an untypical period during which he was uncommunicative, but all of this changed after nearly a week when he admitted he'd been frustrated by his inability to depict a shell hole properly. The results were a stark representation of the scarred landscape. Several of his Plugstreet paintings survive, including one that appears to include Archie Sinclair reading a newspaper outside Laurence Farm. When Sinclair married in 1918 Churchill presented him with the painting.

Privately he continued to rail against the ineptness of the British leadership and to describe what he would do if only given the power to act. Field communications were 'grotesque' and quite rightly were – as they would be in the Second World War – a source of frustration. 'You cannot get through,' he wrote to Clementine. 'This war is one of mechanics & brains & mere sacrifice of brave & devoted infantry is no substitute & never will be. By God I wd make them skip if I had the power – even for a month.'

His contempt was equal parts envy and disenchantment that he was no longer playing an important role. The satisfaction he received from commanding troops notwithstanding, his loss of authority rankled to the depths of his soul. 'There is not one minute in the 24 hours when steps cd not be taken wh wd save life & treasure and hasten the conclusion of the conflict.' Asquith's War Council rarely met, and when it did it proved once again that waging war by committee is folly.

During ten days' leave in England in March 1916, Churchill's anger and his craving to rejoin the political world he had left behind resulted in a speech in the House that was one of the most ill advised he ever made. The occasion was a debate introduced by Balfour on the proposed new naval estimates. It was as if all of Churchill's bitterness and resentment overwhelmed reason and came pouring out in an oration that ended with the fantastic proposal that Fisher be recalled as first sea lord.

Despite their falling out, Churchill never lost his belief in the importance of Fisher, particularly at a time when the war was going so badly. His proposal was greeted with disbelief and ridicule. Criticism rained down upon him in the press and from public officials on both sides of the aisle. Eddie Marsh was reduced to tears, while Violet Bonham Carter thought her dear friend 'must surely be deranged' to believe in Fisher; and her father was left 'speechless' by what he believed had been a 'suicidal' speech. When Churchill met privately with Violet at his mother's Mayfair home a short time later, she found him distraught: 'I saw at once that, whatever his motive, he realized that he had hopelessly failed to accomplish what he had set out to do. His lance was broken.'

Churchill's criticisms that Britain faced losing the war were valid, but it was his bizarre proposal to recall the discredited Lord Fisher that undid the positive aspects of his speech. Most if not all of the goodwill he had earned on the western front was squandered in a single afternoon. The *Spectator* opined: 'To watch this fevered, this agonized struggle to regain the political fortune which the arch-gambler threw away is to witness one of the great tragedies of life,' while an admiral wondered, 'Surely Winston Churchill must be going off his head like his father did?' It was also a reminder to his enemies of how much they despised Churchill, although Margot Asquith thought that 'if he goes back and fights like a hero it will all be forgotten.'

This incident added fuel to Clementine's argument that the timing was simply not right for her husband to return to the political arena. Winston would not hear of it, however, and began making plans to end his military service in France and return to the fray. At Dover, en route back to France on 13 March, he sent a letter to Kitchener requesting permission to resign from his command 'in order to grapple with the political situation at home'. Kitchener passed Churchill's letter to Asquith, who thought it was a bad idea and told Kitchener to make no reply. Once back in Plugstreet, Churchill had second thoughts and immediately withdrew his request, explaining that he preferred to wait and reassess his state of affairs. Asquith was only too happy to keep him in France, and Churchill once again exchanged politics for the business of war. Both his great friend and confidant Archie Sinclair and Clementine counselled against his return to politics while his reputation was so low, and for once he heeded their advice and reconciled himself to attending to his command duties at the front.

During his tour of duty there Churchill became something of a celebrity and a magnet for visiting VIPs. He 'could be viewed, free of charge, in a British trench'. As a mere lieutenant colonel he was obliged to play the game, stand at attention and brief men for whom he had scant regard. To his credit, he endured such indignities with charm and professionalism.

When Sinclair went home to England on leave in March, Churchill insisted he stay with Clementine. 'I can almost see you and Clemmie arriving by the most noble of arguments at the conclusion that I must inevitably stay here till the Day of Judgement,' Churchill wrote to Sinclair a short time after returning to Plugstreet. At one point he expected a promotion to brigade command, but when another officer was given the post he shrugged it off as unimportant; the lure of returning home to political life grew stronger with each passing day.

Throughout these tense months Clementine had been a rock of support and encouragement. She offered outspoken and pragmatic advice to her husband about his political aspirations. One of his various letters to Asquith she deemed too provocative and refused to send it. She was deeply concerned that he would have no real place in either the present or a newer coalition government, the possibility of which was growing daily, with Asquith clearly demonstrating his unfitness to lead. 'The present government may not be strong enough to beat the Germans, but I think they are powerful enough to do you in, & I pray God you do not give the heartless brutes the chance.'

Clementine pressed a strategy of remaining in France until the time was right to come home. 'To gain a share of War direction you are contemplating a terrible risk, the risk of life-long disappointment & bitterness. My darling love – *For once only* I pray be patient. It will come if you wait. Don't tear off the unripe fruit . . . I could not bear you to lose your military halo. I have had cause during the 8 years we have lived together to be proud and glad for you so often but it is this I cherish most of all. And it is this phrase which when all is known will strike the imagination of the people – The man who prepared & mobilized the Fleet, who really won the war for England in the trenches as a simple colonel.'

He was permitted a brief period of leave in London to take part in a parliamentary debate about conscription in late April, but when heavy fighting erupted along the front he was recalled to Plugstreet and the trenches. Yet he knew his days on the western front were numbered. The long-debated decision of when to leave his command was soon made for him when it was decided to reorganize the Scottish regiments. They had suffered such heavy losses that several of their battalions were to be combined, leaving Churchill, as the junior battalion commander, the odd man out and soon to be without a command.

Although he was back in Plugstreet for only a short interval, Clementine's fears were raised to new heights. 'My darling, I am in agony about you. But I cannot believe that after living thro' these dangerous months unscathed these last few days will be fatal to you.' As it had been on innumerable other occasions in this and other wars, Churchill's destiny was to survive, but not without further danger. On 2 May he wrote, 'The Germans have just fired 30 shells at our farm hitting it 4 times: but no one has been hurt. This is I trust a parting salute.'

It was time to return home to the political war. The right moment came on 3 May when his battalion was relieved from the line and sent to the rear, within days to become part of a combined 6th/7th Battalion. He saw Douglas Haig who, Churchill claimed, offered him the command of a brigade, but also pointed out that he could do far more for the war effort in Parliament as an advocate for the enactment of conscription.

Churchill wrote to his corps commander formalizing his decision to return to England. Before his departure he further endeared himself to his fusiliers by taking 'endless trouble' to secure new posts for men being displaced by the amalgamation. He travelled widely, interviewing other commanders and staffs, extracting promises and calling in favours.

On 6 May 1916 he held a farewell luncheon for his officers at Armentières, then took leave of his battalion and the men he had come to love and respect during his brief tenure as their commander. His praise for his Scottish soldiers was boundless, and it was effusively reciprocated.

For a commander whose arrival had been greeted with disdain and low expectations, Churchill demonstrated early on that he came equipped with the necessary spirit, and that he had learned well from the failure of others (in the earlier wars of his experience as well as the current one) to comprehend that soldiers should not be cannon fodder, and that their safety and welfare are paramount. The commander who follows such a course reaps the best effort from his troops when it counts. Churchill's legacy was best summed up by Captain Gibb, who, while admitting that his commander's tactical and strategic abilities had not been tested during his tenure, said,

I am firmly convinced that no more popular officer ever commanded troops. As a soldier he was hard-working, persevering and thorough. The expected fireworks never came off. He was out to work at tiresome but indispensable detail and to make his unit efficient in the very highest possible degree . . . He loved soldiering: it lay very near his heart and I think he could have been a very great soldier . . . We came to realize, to realize at first hand, his transcendent ability . . . And much more, he became our friend. He is a man who apparently is always to have enemies. He made none in his old regiment, but left behind him there men who will always be his loyal partisans and admirers, and who are proud of having served in the Great War under the leadership of one who is beyond question a great man.

It was the highest accolade any soldier or commander could receive. Jack Seely, who had known him for years and seen him under fire, judged that Churchill might well have made a better soldier than politician. 'I am sure . . . if he had foresworn politics and devoted his whole life to the Army, although he would have been far less adequately equipped for the task – for one learns more about men, and therefore about armies, in political life than anywhere else, as Caesar, Marlborough, Wellington and Napoleon well knew and proved – he might nevertheless have commanded all the British forces and, perhaps, the Allied forces as well.'

Having been a soldier and commanded troops in war, Seely understood leadership better than most. He firmly believed that Churchill had the essential qualities of a military leader, in particular because he possessed 'the one vital essential quality in any great commander of men in real war . . . That quality is cool courage and unimpaired judgment under fire . . . seeing his men, being seen by them,' and inspiring them 'with his own will for victory. Churchill had this quality in high degree. Real danger unnerves most men; it nerved him.'

Even during this relatively quiet period of the war, Churchill had seen war's terror and ugliness at the sharp end, had lost a number of men to the bullets and the shells, and went home to England having not only done his duty but done so with honour. Most politicians who start wars rarely experience the results of their actions. Churchill stood tall, as a voice of the men he had led. As a sitting MP he had set an example. Although his prime motivation for serving in France was to rebuild his shattered political career, few others in the Great War could make such a claim.

25

'Winston's Folly'

By 1918 it was a different tale. The folly was seen to apply to the sceptics, not to Churchill. — Lewis Broad, historian

When Churchill returned from his five-and-a-half-month tour of duty as a soldier on the western front, his life had been changed for ever by the experience, giving him a profound respect for the plight of the British soldiers who were fighting and dying there and a mounting frustration over the course of a war seemingly without end.

Yet the past continued to haunt him unremittingly. His first speech in Parliament was a harbinger of just how bad the situation had become. Churchill spoke on the issue of the Military Service Bill that would create conscription but would exclude Ireland, where military service would remain voluntary. While attempting to convince the House that full conscription was vital, he was rudely interrupted by an Irish Nationalist MP, who angrily shouted: 'What about the Dardanelles?', a challenge that 'echoed about the Chamber like a widow's curse'.

One of Churchill's closest friends and one of his few ardent supporters was Lord Fisher, the man who had brought him down. Not only had his bizarre, magnetic relationship with Fisher been renewed, but their bond, once the bedrock of the Admiralty, now seemed stronger than ever. As Churchill existed in an abyss where he was seen but seldom heard, the two men offered each other encouragement at a time when both were pariahs, tainted by the Dardanelles.

Upon his return to civilian life, Churchill became immersed for nearly a year in the government investigation into the Dardanelles and Gallipoli, carried out by the Statutory Committee of Enquiry into the Operations at the Dardanelles. He relentlessly defended his decisions and for years afterward corresponded regularly with Ian Hamilton, who likewise justified his generalship at Gallipoli. In 1917 the committee's preliminary findings indicated that there was more than enough blame to go around. And while Churchill was included, others were named, among them Fisher, Kitchener and Asquith. Fisher and Asquith lobbied hard to prevent publication of the findings. But Lord Kitchener, Churchill's great nemesis and uneasy colleague in the War Cabinet, had been drowned the previous year. He had been en route to Russia in June 1916 on a fact-finding mission aboard a Royal Navy cruiser when, within view of Scapa Flow, the vessel struck a mine laid by a German submarine and sank with heavy loss of life. Kitchener's body was among those claimed by the sea and never recovered. Churchill paid tribute to his old adversary as the 'Constable of Britain', a man whose 'life of duty could only reach its consummation in a warrior's death'.

The year 1916 ended with the creation of a new coalition government headed by Lloyd George. Churchill yearned to return as first lord and, although Lloyd George would have offered him a place in his administration as chairman of the Air Board, Bonar Law and the Conservatives were so adamantly opposed to his being given any appointment whatever that he was left in the political wilderness, a circumstance he was to experience a great deal more of during the inter-war years. When asked by Lloyd George if Churchill would be 'more dangerous *for* you than when he is *against* you', Bonar Law unhesitatingly said, 'I would rather have him against us every time', an attitude shared by other Tories and by leading newspapers that regarded him as a menace. Only history, a dispirited Churchill surmised, would one day vindicate his role in the Great War.

His erstwhile political enemy, the former prime minister Arthur Balfour, with whom he had since mended fences (at least until his parliamentary speech in March 1916), had replaced him as first lord. Balfour failed to grasp the importance of d'Eyncourt's work with the tank, asking the captain, 'Have not you and your Department enough to do in looking after the design and construction of ships, without concerning yourself about material for the Army?' D'Eyncourt 'went at once to Churchill and warned him of what was about to happen. Churchill immediately appealed directly to Balfour, who agreed to allow [tank] experiments to continue. But the enthusiasm which Churchill had imparted to the project was gone.'

There was, however, no end to his ideas, which continued to flow unabated. In his essay 'Variants of the Offensive' he once again proposed the creation of enormous steel shields some fifteen feet long by four feet high that could be pushed by men or by a tracked vehicle that would protect them from machine-gun bullets as they advanced towards German lines. He also advocated the use of shields by individual soldiers, a modern equivalent of those carried into battle by ancient warriors.

He was driven by the appalling casualty rate, and no one in Britain in the First World War offered more ideas for winning the war. Where others were content merely to wage the same battles of attrition over and over again, with the same dreadful results, he was constantly exploring unconventional lines of thought. Above all he was horrified by the needless sacrifice of men for questionable military results. 'The use of force for the waging of war is not to be regulated simply by firm character and text-book maxims,' he said. 'Mechanical science offers on the ground, in the air, on every coast from the forge or from the laboratory, boundless possibilities of novelty and surprise.'

Churchill never envisaged that the tank would transform the war; he thought rather that it would serve as a supporting weapon aiding advances across no man's land. 'Variants of the Offensive' contained several references to the use of tanks on the western front – apparently the first time Haig had been made aware of their battlefield potential. The memorandum seems directly related to Haig's request for one thousand tanks, made to the Ministry of Munitions in February 1916. However, Churchill's view that, once used on the battlefield, tanks would have little future value was not shared by Haig's GHQ. On the contrary it was thought 'that the tank was simply another instrument of war, the best tactics for which would have to worked out by trial and error'.

By 1916 the War Office had at last accepted its potential battlefield benefits. A design breakthrough occurred, and a tank called 'Mother' (later 'Big Willie', derisively named after the German crown prince, Wilhelm – Wilhelm II's eldest son) became the first operational armoured vehicle produced by the British. The machine was equipped with a six-pound gun mounted inside a small turret, and four machine guns. Although the first armoured vehicles were flawed, their employment on a battlefield vindicated Churchill's initiatives in dramatic fashion and forever changed the course of modern warfare. Forty-nine 'Big Willies' participated in the Battle of the Somme that same year, with varied results. There was as yet no doctrine for their use and, instead of attacking en masse as they would in the future, they were deployed individually across the front. Most broke down or became hopelessly stuck in the mud. Nevertheless the few ungainly iron monsters that survived breaking down enjoyed enormous success and terrorized the Germans. One tank led an assault on the town of Flers, which was taken without a single loss, to the cheers of the New Zealand infantry that followed it; another straddled a trenchwork and captured three hundred German prisoners, while a third attacked a German artillery battery before being knocked out. The sight of these astonishing machines, painted in a variety of rainbow colours, stunned the German high command. German troops were ordered to 'hold their ground at all costs and fight to the last man against these new and monstrous engines of war'. The panic created in the front lines by the first tanks ever seen on a battlefield was reported in the German press under the headline 'The devil is coming!'

Churchill, however, had a different view of their use at the Somme, believing that the British had wasted a golden opportunity. 'The immense advantage of novelty and surprise was thus squandered . . . The certainty of a great and brilliant victory was revealed to the Germans for the mere petty purpose of taking a few ruined villages . . . Instead of employing them all at once in dry weather on ground not torn by bombardment, in some new sector where they could operate very easily and by surprise, they were plunged in fours and fives as a mere minor adjunct of the infantry into the quagmires and crater-fields of Passchendaele.'

In Parliament in October 1916 Lloyd George credited Churchill with transforming the ideas of d'Eyncourt and Hankey into reality, but even such public statements of support did little to remove the cloud under which he still lived. Hostile criticism from the Conservatives and their newspapers continued to pour down upon him, unforgiving of the Dardanelles.

Tanks were again employed in November 1917 but this time on the vast scale Churchill had had in mind: massed across a front of ten thousand yards 378 of the machines attacked the weakly held German sector around Cambrai, advancing in some places as deep as four miles into German lines. When these spectacular results became known in England, church bells were rung for the first time since the summer of 1914 – precipitately as it turned out. The British failed to capitalize on the tanks' success, and German counterattacks later that month negated most of their gains. Although the advent of the tank on the battlefields of France did not change the course of the war, the true effectiveness of what had once been dismissed as 'Winston's folly' would be recognized when another world war coined the term 'blitzkrieg' and saw its brilliant employment by innovative commanders such as Guderian, Rommel and Patton.

It was not until July 1917 that Lloyd George felt it politically expedient to end Churchill's exile by appointing him minister of munitions – in virtual secrecy in order to forestall the angry outcry of Conservatives. In time, however, even Bonar Law came to appreciate Churchill's qualities. Still, other critics howled, led by the *Morning Post*, which proclaimed that he had made 'two capital blunders' as first lord: 'Both expeditions were managed more or less personally by Mr Churchill, whose over-whelming conceit led him to imagine he was a Nelson at sea and a Napoleon on land.'

Thus Churchill became responsible for the five million people who manufactured and supplied the vast quantities of bullets, shells, bombs, torpedoes and equipment that were consumed by Britain's giant military machine. In his new post he did a masterful job of meeting the requirements of Haig and the BEF. A harsh taskmaster, he brilliantly recast a clumsy and hugely overstaffed ministry, reducing some fifty departments and working groups, staffed by twelve thousand civil servants, to twelve, and he recruited some of Britain's best brains to advise him. He also broke a series of workers' strikes by aggressively promising to prosecute the leaders and to withdraw the immunity from military service of the rank-and-file workers, thus peacefully ending the unrest.

The horror of trench warfare and the scale of death on the western front far exceeded Churchill's earlier experience of war, leaving him in the unique position of understanding better than any other politician the hardships faced by the men in the trenches. In fact, as with virtually everyone who had served there, the war haunted him and changed his entire outlook. His frustration was in evidence when he spoke to a group of MPs in the summer of 1916 with great emotion and anger: 'I say to myself every day, "What is going on while we sit here, while we go away to dinner, or home to bed?" Nearly 1,000 men – Englishmen, Britishers, men of our own race – are knocked into bundles of bloody rags every twenty-four hours, and carried away to hasty graves or to field ambulances.'

However, when it came to the business of war he was utterly ruthless and had no reservations at all in relation to the manufacture of poison gas shells. During the Irish uprising at Easter 1916 he supported the use of martial law for the purpose of taking hostages and summarily executing them. His cold-bloodedness also extended to support for the employment of aircraft to reduce Sinn Fein's terrorist acts by bombing or the use of machine-gun fire against groups of Sinn Fein observed drilling with or without weapons.

Churchill's strong affection for the Admiralty did not deter him from besting his former colleagues over steel plating for his tanks, which they claimed was necessary to meet shipbuilding needs. As minister of munitions he controlled all raw materials required for war purposes, including steel. However, rather than wage outright war against the admirals, with typical guile he allocated a large enough supply to meet their needs for a time but kept everything else to meet the requirements of the tank programme.

By the early spring of 1918 the war was approaching the four-year mark with no end in sight. Exasperated by the repeated failure of conventional warfare to overwhelm the German trenches through the use of massive artillery and costly infantry attacks, Churchill sent a memo on 5 March to the War Cabinet in which he posed the question of how Britain was to win the war in 1919. Imaginative thinking and novel resources were needed to prevent more of the same useless carnage. Fresh ideas and a new plan were vital instead of merely hoping that something positive would happen 'before we reach the final abyss of general anarchy and world famine'.

He proposed a fivefold increase in the use of poison gas, a fourfold increase in the employment of tanks and a 50 per cent increase in airpower that would bomb German manufacturing targets. 'The resources are available, the knowledge is available, the time is available, the result is certain,' he insisted. 'Nothing is lacking except the will.' Churchill 'was always a 1919 man', pointed out the biographer and former Labour MP Roy Jenkins, 'to some extent foreshadowing his resistance to the opening of the Second Front in 1943, believing that the correct Western Front strategy was to remain on the defensive until the Americans had arrived in massive strength. This view was forestalled by the German offensive in the spring of 1918,' which led directly to the end of the war in November. Summoned to Downing Street to brief Lloyd George, Churchill outlined his ambitious proposal. It called for a massive new programme to build 4,459 tanks by April 1919 and another 4,424 by the following September. Only then should a decisive new offensive be launched that would end the war.

Sir Henry Wilson, the new chief of the Imperial General Staff, initially supported the idea, although with Britain's manpower sapped to breaking point he wondered how on earth he could ever find the hundred thousand soldiers needed to man this new force. A short time later Wilson changed his mind and argued against the use of tanks on the grounds that the Germans could defeat them with the use of mines. Unfazed, Churchill began to search for some means to defeat the mines and in so doing advocated the invention of the anti-tank devices eventually used in the Second World War. Among his ideas was the mounting of probes on tanks to feel out and destroy mines ahead: a precursor to the flail tank. Mines could be blown up by tank rounds fired at them, then defeated by heavily armoured tanks that could roll over and destroy them, or even by a special vehicle towed by a tank, 'which, activated by wires from the tank, could move ahead and by this way explode minefields'.

Churchill's ideas were not readily embraced, nor did Haig ever change his unsuccessful strategy of employing artillery and infantry in massive and costly attacks. The failure of the German general Erich von Ludendorff's great offensive, launched in the spring of 1918, ended both the war and Churchill's initiatives.

In September 1917 Churchill returned to the front lines as a civilian, one of numerous visits he made to France during the final months of the war. He was accompanied as usual by the faithful Eddie Marsh, and as they motored through the devastated countryside, '*Everywhere*', recorded Marsh, were 'the tiny nameless white crosses, single or in clusters, "like snowdrops" as Winston said – and here and there a regular cemetery with larger named crosses'. Churchill soon made it clear that battle had not lost its attraction for him. Near Arras, when he observed shells bursting in the distance, he again demonstrated his compelling need to march to the sound of the guns wherever a battle was being fought. 'Out we got,' said Marsh, 'put on our steel helmets, hung our gas-masks around our necks, and walked for half an hour towards the firing,' with Churchill oblivious to their increasing peril. 'There was a great noise, shells whistling over our heads, and some fine bursts in the distance – but we seemed to get no nearer, and the firing died down, so we went back after another hour's delay. W.'s disregard of time, when there's anything he wants to do, is sublime – he firmly believes that it waits for him.'

His travels took him all over the western front, dining with Haig and other generals and politicians and visiting his old regiment and battlefields such as Vimy Ridge and the Somme, where desolation reigned. His discussions ranged from aerial warfare to the success of the tank on the battlefield the year before and the use of poison gas and of heavy artillery mounted on railway wagons. Near Ypres shells began falling around them as their vehicle negotiated its way around shell holes and the stumps of what had once been trees while Churchill remained heedless to danger.

The Somme in 1916 and Passchendaele (also called the Third Battle of Ypres) in 1917, with their horrific loss of seventy thousand dead and more than 170,000 wounded to gain six miles of useless mud, had taken further toll upon the British. Churchill summed it up with the observation that 'before the war it had seemed incredible that such terrors and slaughters, even if they began, could last for more than a few months. After the first two years it was difficult to believe that they would ever end. We seemed separated from the old life by a measureless gulf.'

By 1918 the war had drained the life from the weary combatants. The BEF in particular never recovered from Passchendaele; its manpower was so badly depleted that it was estimated another 615,000 men would be required just to replace the losses. On 21 March Ludendorff, the German supreme commander, his armies bolstered by the addition of a million men and three thousand guns from the eastern front after Russia – in the throes of revolution – concluded a humiliating peace treaty with Germany – launched the first of a series of great 'all or nothing' counter-offensives across a two-hundred-mile front that came close to success. The Germans outnumbered the British by a remarkable 450,000. The first thunderous attacks by seventy-six German divisions, against the twenty-eight divisions of the Third and the soon to be shattered Fifth Armies, tore giant holes in the British front, killing 7,000 men and capturing 21,000. The 28,000 losses were the worst of any single day in the war except for 1 July 1916, the first day of the Somme offensive.

German gains increased as the BEF was systematically forced to retreat, facing not only the threat of a breakthrough to the sea but a complete collapse of the British front, with all its catastrophic consequences. When the German offensive began Churchill was already in France visiting his old friend and fellow cavalry officer General Henry Tudor, then commanding the 9th Division. He awoke shortly before daylight on the morning of 21 March to the sounds of 'the most tremendous cannonade I shall ever hear'.

Churchill returned to London on 24 March and geared up the Ministry of Munitions to respond rapidly to Haig's pressing need for armaments. As the situation in France grew more dire, Lloyd George unhesitatingly turned to the one man he believed could help bring about a solution, and he asked Churchill to return immediately to France as his personal emissary to evaluate conditions and to persuade the new Allied supreme commander, General (later Marshal) Foch, to come to the aid of the BEF with the French army by counterattacking against what was now an open German flank.

In Paris, Churchill was greeted effusively by the prime minister Georges Clemenceau, who personally took him to meet the senior British and French commanders. After conferring with Haig and promising reinforcements, Clemenceau insisted on seeing the British battlefield at first hand. When he and Churchill reached the British front lines Clemenceau exclaimed, 'Mr Winston Churchill, we are in the British lines. Will you take charge of us? We will do what you say.' Churchill, who needed no further encouragement, replied: 'Where do you want to go?' Clemenceau: 'As far as possible. But you shall judge.' At the age of seventy-six Clemenceau, admiringly nicknamed 'the Tiger', was fearless, and was capable not only of keeping up with Churchill but of actually outdistancing the younger man's own legendary endurance and appetite for danger. The further they moved towards the front lines, the greater the chaos all around them: flashes from French and British gun batteries, projectiles flying overhead, audible rifle fire and the chaos of battle.

Encountering a group of battle-weary British officers, Clemenceau insisted on shaking their hands. 'We gave these officers the contents of our cigar cases,' recalled Churchill. Nearby a shell burst, terrifying a

337

group of horses, one of which, riderless and wounded, 'came in a staggering trot . . . The poor animal was streaming with blood.' Clemenceau calmly and quickly seized its bridle. At this point Churchill had had enough and urged their return to safer environs, imploring the old warrior that putting himself in danger for one day was all right, but that he ought not to make a habit of it. As he wrote to Clementine: 'I finally persuaded the old tiger to come away from what he called "un moment délicieux",' only to have Clemenceau reply, 'C'est mon grand plaisir.' After seventeen hours the usually indefatigable Churchill was worn out; Clemenceau was merely buoyed, alert and fresh. It was one of the few times anyone ever got the best of Winston Churchill on a battlefield.

On his last trip to the front shortly before the war ended, he again courted trouble. The great German counter-offensive had come to naught, and with the imminent surrender of Turkey and Austria, and the end of the war only a matter of time and negotiation with the victorious Allies, Churchill and Eddie Marsh arrived in France on 25 October to tour the areas liberated by the BEF. It was a troubled trip. They were driven from Boulogne in a Rolls-Royce that blew a tyre en route to their destination. Then Churchill gave their chauffeur the wrong directions. Unable to turn around, owing to the hedgerows that lined the road, the Rolls proceeded for a long distance before finding a suitable turning spot. All the while Churchill fumed and cursed, culminating with 'Well, it's the most absolute f—ing thing in the whole of my bloody life.' The following day Churchill toured the front escorted by Archie Sinclair, with whom he got into a flaming row after Sinclair insisted they return by lunchtime as his superior had directed him to do. However, as Marsh recorded in his diary, Churchill 'wanted to go on with the joy-ride indefinitely'. The two men parted on bad terms, with Churchill snapping that it was 'asinine, I shall take no more interest in him.'

On 29 October things got even worse when Churchill's motor car took the wrong road on the way to Bruges and, although they believed they were still some ten thousand yards from the front line, suddenly came under German artillery fire. Shells exploded all around them, and one landed where they would have stopped had Churchill decided 'to make [the] enquiries' he had been inclined to make. At one point they came within two thousand yards of the front lines and once again came under fire. A chagrined Churchill later wrote to Henry Tudor: 'Really I would not have believed that after all these years one would be so stupid as to motor near the Front without knowing exactly how the line ran. However, all's well that ends well.'

On 11 November 1918, the war ended almost as abruptly as it had begun. There was little to cheer. For a small island nation, Britain and its empire had losses totalling more than 900,000 killed and two million wounded. An estimated 200,000 more were captured or missing in action, many of them never recovered from nameless graves in the soil of what had once been peaceful fields. As the chimes of Big Ben were heard signalling the arrival of the eleventh hour of the eleventh day of the eleventh month, crowds began surging on to the streets of London in wild celebration. For Churchill it was a time to reflect on the end of a war that would forever haunt him, a war in which, he said, 'the chains which had held the world were broken . . . Every one had snapped upon a few strokes of the clock . . . and everywhere the burdens were cast down.'

The ringing of the bells of peace ended Churchill's dramatic and traumatic rise and fall from power. The First World War and its consequences left him profoundly disturbed. While the years he spent writing *The World Crisis* were in large part exculpatory, its six volumes were also a thought-provoking examination of the mistakes he believed had led to higher than necessary losses through bad strategy and tunnel vision.

The World Crisis would probably be judged blatant opportunism were it not for the fact that Churchill had advocated ideas that offered some promise of ending (or least mitigating) the slaughter on the western front. Besides its self-justifications the work brims with his ideas of leadership and generalship. The First World War had demonstrated that without a decisive leader no war could be effectively pursued. The military historian David Jablonsky points out: 'As he became more immersed in the total conflict of World War I, Churchill became increasingly concerned that grand strategic policy must dominate military strategy at the highest leadership.' However, 'the civilian apparatus in control at that level in Britain during World War I was lacking,' and there was 'no supreme authority in London as in Berlin . . . It was only one man's opinion against another.'

Having seen at first hand the dreadful results of the Boer War and the

First World War, Churchill was convinced that a political leader must establish strategic policy: that is, where a war would be fought, what it must achieve and how the generals, airmen and admirals must carry it out, and not the other way around as had been the case in the recent war. He was also visionary in his early recognition that joint military operations (air, sea and ground) were essential, a belief later reinforced by his study of history and, in particular, his epic four-volume, 2,050-page biography of the Duke of Marlborough, which he published during his exile from politics in the 1930s.

Churchill also argued compellingly that Britain had squandered its lifeblood needlessly in the pursuit of what has aptly been described as the near-fanatical conception that 'the last man standing in France would be declared the winner'. Perhaps the most valuable lesson he took from the war was 'the importance of preventing the admirals and generals (and budding air marshals) from running their own shows beyond Cabinet control'.

What frustrated him was that both Haig and Kitchener had gambled on success on the western front and refused to consider any alternatives. He reserved his greatest scorn for the folly of conventional thinking when unconventional ideas were desperately required, for the 'needless and wrongly conceived' battles fought between 1915 and 1917. It might not have been possible to shorten the war, but he argued that it could at least have been less costly had there only been the initiative, the wisdom and the courage to seek alternative strategies, 'if only the Generals had not been content to fight machine-gun bullets with the breasts of gallant men, and think that that was waging war'. He lamented, 'The men in power were not wise enough or strong enough to do things the right way, but the right way was there, at certain critical moments, and it was seen to be there.'

He also wrote: 'We had to improvise our armies in the face of the enemy . . . But there never was found the time to train and organize these elements before they were consumed . . . successive half-sharpened, half-tempered weapons were made, were used and broken as soon as they were fashioned' at the Somme and in the mud of Flanders. 'Suppose', he went on, 'that the British Army sacrificed upon the Somme, the finest we ever had, had been preserved, trained and developed to its full strength till the summer of 1917, till perhaps 3,000 tanks were ready, till an overwhelming artillery was prepared, till a scientific method of advance had been devised, till the apparatus was complete, might not a decisive result have been achieved at one supreme stroke?' While acknowledging that there were practical logistical difficulties in mass-producing three thousand tanks by the spring of 1917, he faulted Britain's leadership for not even thinking that way. The irony of Churchill's involvement in the Great War is that despite his near-disgrace and the enormous damage to his reputation inflicted by the Dardanelles fiasco, he had advanced more bold ideas and innovations for winning the war than anyone else in Britain.

For those who fought it the war was a life-altering event. Like so many of his countrymen, Churchill was profoundly influenced by the experience and emerged from it with a clear vision of the essential qualities required of a war leader (and of future generalship, which he would demand, but not always get, during the Second World War). 'Battles are won by slaughter and manoeuvre,' he wrote. 'The greater the general, the more he contributes in manoeuvre, the less he demands in slaughter.'

That vision, it has been argued with considerable justification, was powerfully affected by Churchill's disdain for Great War leadership, the generals disparaged by the late Conservative MP and historian Alan Clark as 'the donkeys', who in the first two hours of the Battle of Loos in 1915 were responsible for losing more British soldiers than both sides lost on D-day in June 1944. In the Second World War, Churchill's experience of war would make him impatiet with the inability of some of his generals to measure up to his demanding standards, and to act with the promptness and élan he deemed essential.

Although he liked Haig personally, and credited him for overseeing victory and for his steadfastness, Churchill singled him out as an example of what was distinctly lacking in British generalship, comparing him to an indifferent surgeon who does not really care if his patient dies as long as the operation itself takes place. Haig, he said, was utterly conventional and devoid of the vision and genius 'which has enabled the great captains of history to dominate the material factors, save slaughter, and confront their foes with the triumph of novel apparitions'.

During the two decades of the inter-war years, much of them spent in lonely political exile, Churchill would brood about and write again and again of the folly of war and of the need to resist the dictator whose meteoric rise to power in what became Nazi Germany threatened world peace and augured yet another destructive war. 'The shadow of victory is disillusion . . . The aftermath even of successful war is long and bitter,' he wrote. The war's appalling cost in lives produced both realism and cynicism. As Jablonsky records: 'He often returned in his writings and speeches to the attritive slaughter of the trenches where combat had been "reduced to a business like the stockyards of Chicago."'

26

'A Hopelessly Obsolete, Old-Fashioned Warrior'

It is doubtful if even Great Britain could survive another world war and another Churchill. – 1925 biography

The horror inspired in Churchill by the First World War never abated, and during the inter-war years it was never far from his mind, whether he was occupied in one of his many official capacities or while he was in the wilderness of political exile in the 1930s. The man who had been called – and would continue to be called – a warmonger by many spent the next twenty years warning of the dangers of totalitarianism presented by the rise of Hitler and the Nazis in the 1930s, and attempting to avoid war. In 1919 he wrote despondently: 'Never has there been a time when a more complete callousness and indifference for human life was exhibited by the great communities all over the world. All over Europe we see the seething scene of misery, torment and malevolence.'

Churchill later expressed misgivings over what had dragged Britain into war; the entente with France, he wrote, 'had led us into a position where we had the obligation of an alliance without its advantages . . . we were morally bound to come to the aid of France.' Yet it was also Churchill who, before the dead had been counted from the First World War, was advocating another war, against the Bolsheviks in Russia, after previously accepting the notion of Russian self-determination. Seek to avoid war, he preached, but should war be the last resort, then wage it vigorously and win; he failed to apply these principles to Russia in the throes of a civil war.

Although he had hoped eventually to return to the Admiralty, Churchill was appointed secretary of state for war after Lloyd George won an overwhelming mandate in the general election of December 1918. In addition to the Paris Peace Conference, one of the highest priorities in 1919 was the virtual dismemberment of the British armed forces, not only demobilization but cutbacks in expenditure. Immediately upon taking office on 9 January 1919, Churchill faced a chaotic situation. The army had blundered by inefficiently demobilizing the huge force that had been created to fight the war. The men were weary and chafing to return to civilian life, but at first only those with essential civilian jobs or with jobs promised to them at home were discharged. There were riots in Britain, a mutiny in Calais by five thousand men, and growing unrest in British encampments in France, Palestine, Greece and Mesopotamia. Although Haig wanted the ringleaders executed, Churchill overruled his former commander in chief and soon resolved the demobilization problem by establishing a judicious policy of discharging the longest-serving men first.

In January 1919 Churchill also became secretary of state for air and head of the Air Ministry that had been created in 1917 to administer the new Royal Air Force. *The Times* expressed concern that the RAF might be merged with the War Office. Churchill, however, quickly declared the independence of both the RAF and the Air Ministry.

Soon after taking office he showed his determination to make the new Royal Air Force a permanent part of the British military structure. Lloyd George, on the other hand, was anxious to economize after the terrific expenses of the war, to which the RAF had been a major contributor in its final months, at a cost of nearly one million pounds a day. One of Churchill's first acts was to appoint Hugh Trenchard, a man he admired and trusted, as the chief of the air staff. One of the original airmen of the Royal Flying Corps, Trenchard had commanded the corps in France from 1915 to 1917. With the benefit of his advice Churchill set about reorganizing and streamlining the RAF to meet Britain's post-war needs. It was an uphill battle to convince civilians with only scant understanding of the potential uses of airpower that it was vital to keep the RAF intact. And while it survived, its heart was all but cut out by its lack of modern flying machines and the unwillingness of successive governments to invest in armaments in peacetime.

It was clear, at least to men like Churchill and Trenchard, that the employment of strategic aircraft would be an important element of future warfare. During the inter-war years the RAF had to fight off repeated attempts by both the army and the Royal Navy to make it a subservient branch of one service or the other. Trenchard's most notable and controversial legacy was one that has persisted to this day: the notion that strategic bombing alone is capable of winning a war. It became a doctrine passed on from one generation of airmen to another and would embroil Churchill in some of the most contentious inter-service battles of the Second World War.

Although Churchill held the dual posts until 1921, Clementine thought that his air appointment was a bad idea, that doing both jobs would give him 'violent indigestion', and that he ought to give up the air post. 'After all, you want to be a Statesman, not a juggler.' Indeed the demands of demobilization proved Clementine right: Churchill spent very little time in his air office, instead leaving his parliamentary secretary and old friend Major General Jack Seely in charge of day-to-day problems. Churchill's tenure as air minister could have been far more productive, but, as he had shown as first lord, his flaws often over-shadowed his brilliance; in the case of the RAF they were glaring. Under the plan produced by the air staff, forty of the proposed 154 squadrons were earmarked for home defence until Churchill, wedded as he became to the big-bomber school of airpower, slashed the squadrons to a mere twenty-four, only two of which were for the defence of Britain. *The Times* had this tart comment on the fruits of his tenure at the Air Ministry: 'He leaves the body of British flying well nigh at the last gasp when a military funeral would be all that is left for it.'

With the rise of the dictators in the 1930s Churchill's attitude changed. When the government announced severe reductions to the RAF in 1933, he spoke out, arguing futilely that Britain was making a mistake in hoping that other nations would give up arms in the spirit of the Geneva Disarmament Conference. 'There is a terrible danger there,' he warned. 'Not to have an adequate air force in the present state of the world is to compromise the foundations of national freedom and independence.'

As secretary of state for war, Churchill proved to be a grave dis-appointment to the army, where he helped undermine his own vision for the development of the tank and the Tank Corps that he had so fully and faithfully backed. Instead, he permitted 'the older school to refashion the Army on "back to 1914" lines – thus missing the best opportunity of reconstructing it on a modern basis.' Nor did he help matters when, as chancellor of the exchequer in the 1920s, he consist-ently cut the army budget estimates, thus impairing the development of a modern tank force. Churchill's cost-cutting may have been politically expedient, but the British military was left the worse for his inaction, unusual behaviour indeed for a man who had played such an important role in the defence of Britain, and who would become a lonely advocate of rearmament in the 1930s.

Just as he had been the prime mover in the creation of a naval staff, Churchill was years ahead of his time when, in 1919, he advocated the creation of a single entity that would encompass the army, the navy and the new Royal Air Force under a single minister of defence. Although the idea had widespread support, the merging of the armed services into a single defence department took place only after the Second World War in both Britain and the United States.

Overall, however, Churchill's contributions to the betterment of both the army and the RAF during his term of office were unremarkable, except for his excellent management of the massive demobilization. 'Neither the Army nor the RAF had any reason to consider that their long-term interests had been improved by Churchill's period in office,' noted Robert Rhodes James.

Although Churchill would later decry Britain's lack of military preparedness, having been part of the problem he cannot escape responsibility. For example, as chancellor in 1925–6 he ruthlessly forced the Admiralty 'to justify every penny of the naval estimates' proposed by the admiral whose career he had helped advance, Sir David Beatty, now first sea lord.

In the spring of 1918 the Allies intervened in Russia to protect its ports and sources of raw materials from the Germans. British troops were in northern Russia guarding the ports of Murmansk and Archangel, while American troops were in Siberia, in part to keep a watchful eye on the Japanese, who had seized Vladivostok and parts of Siberia. With a small military force in place, Britain began supporting the anti-Bolshevik White Russian armies. By year's end a multinational force of some 180,000 troops that included British, Americans, Italians, Greeks, French, Japanese and Serbs had been assembled within and around the borders of Russia.

By 1919, the Bolshevik Revolution having brought Lenin to power two years before, Churchill had found a new cause to champion. He unleashed a torrent of shrill, abusive criticism and dire warnings of 'a disease, a pestilence' of far greater menace than any ever posed by Germany and the kaiser; Lenin and the Bolsheviks were evil men with wicked intentions. It is no small irony that he would later be obliged to embrace Lenin's successor, the duplicitous and malign Joseph Stalin, in a joint crusade against a common enemy, Hitler and the Nazi state.

His outpouring of criticism even dwarfed what he would later say of Adolf Hitler and the Nazi movement. Bolshevism, he declared, was 'foul buffoonery' and the greatest evil. In so doing he once again raised troubling questions about his political acumen, in waging what was soon dubbed 'Mr Churchill's private war'. Even when, later, he was out of office Churchill continued to warn of the 'Red menace' whose risk to Europe he believed far more dangerous than German militarism. In 1919, however, it all but consumed him and he became the West's leading reactionary and anti-Communist.

Churchill's crusade was nothing less than an all-out attempt to involve Britain in the Russian civil war. If he had had his way Major General Edmund Ironside's British forces would have intervened on the side of the White armies. At the Paris Peace Conference Churchill called for a declaration of war by the victorious Allies against the Bolsheviks, and pressed Lloyd George to make an unambiguous decision either to intervene or to get out of Russia. Torn between Britain's war weariness and the Bolshevik threat, Lloyd George instead authorized Churchill to seek guidance from Clemenceau and President Woodrow Wilson in Paris.

While he was en route with Sir Henry Wilson to Paris in a mad dash to arrive before President Wilson departed for the United States on 14 February 1919, their motor car was in an accident serious enough to shatter the windshield and break the steering wheel. Once again Churchill avoided serious injury. But with no encouragement from Lloyd George or Woodrow Wilson, and with Clemenceau shortly to be wounded by a would-be assassin, the question of Allied intervention in Russia was shelved.

Nevertheless Churchill's dire predictions about the fate of Russia were ultimately proved correct. Margaret MacMillan has written: 'In hindsight Churchill and Foch [who also favoured intervention] were right about the Bolsheviks and Lloyd George and Wilson were wrong,' and the new face of dictatorship was Lenin, who 'established a system of terrible and unfettered power which gave Stalin free rein for his paranoid fantasies'. To his critics Churchill's anti-Bolshevik crusade was ample evidence that he was indeed a warmonger hell-bent on involv-ing in more bloodshed a small nation already reeling from history's deadliest war.

As secretary of state for war, Churchill went overseas frequently and also resumed his flying lessons in the summer of 1919. He had often flown back and forth across the Channel as first lord, and as minister of munitions he twice came close to death: once when an engine failed over the Channel but regained enough power to reach land, and again the same day in another plane that also made a successful emergency land-ing. During the Paris Peace Conference he regularly flew between London and Paris, an experience he prized and described as travelling 'as if on a magic carpet'. The lure of the air intensified his aspiration to qualify for his pilot's licence, to Clementine's dismay. Another crash on 18 July might have killed him had his flight instructor not saved the day. Lord Haldane wrote to Churchill the next day imploring him to give up flying: 'These are not the days in which the country can spare you, and to avoid risk becomes in these circumstances a public duty.'

Although giving up flying meant he would never obtain his licence, the accident was of sufficient magnitude to convince even the stubborn Churchill that he might not survive the next accident and that it was indeed time to stop. He continued to fly from place to place as part of his official duties, but thereafter others did the piloting.

In June 1921 Jennie's splendid and colourful life ended when she died at the age of sixty-seven, not long after a serious fall that broke her ankle, resulting in gangrene and the amputation of her left leg. Although she appeared to be recovering, a sudden haemorrhage led abruptly to her death. 'Her sons and sisters were affected almost beyond the grief that is claimed by ties of flesh and blood,' recalled Shane Leslie of his celebrated aunt. 'Winston was bowed under the greatest grief of his life.' At her burial next to Lord Randolph in Bladon churchyard, Churchill wept as her family tossed roses on to her coffin.

Jennie's death was not the only cause of grief for the Churchills. Clementine's brother had committed suicide a short time before, and then came the early death of Marigold, their youngest child, born in 1918 and adoringly nicknamed 'Duckadilly'. Marigold suddenly fell mortally ill and died in August 1921, allegedly from an undiagnosed

progressive septicaemia after nearly a year of throat trouble and coughing that her doctors had not been able to treat properly. The event tore
at the very souls of Clementine and Winston.

Mary, the last of the Churchills' five children, was born in 1922.
She bonded more closely with her mother than did any of the others.
Clementine was not intentionally neglectful of her children, but taking
care of Winston's needs and demands was really all she could cope with
– often at their expense. The great families of history are often touched
by tragedy and dysfunction, and the Churchills were no exception. The
three eldest children, Diana, Randolph and Sarah, all battled the demons
of alcohol, and Diana, who also fought depression, would commit
suicide in 1978 at the age of fifty-four. None enjoyed a particularly
happy life. There was often bickering, sometimes almost explosive,
within the family. Both Winston and Clementine were extremely fond
of their children, but as parents they were poorly equipped to show it,
and as a consequence their children were often uncertain where they
stood.

Randolph would grow into a brilliant but cantankerous adult who
maintained a lifelong stormy relationship with his father. Try as he
might, Churchill found himself in the same sort of relationship with his
son that Lord Randolph had had with him. The filmmaker Jill Craigie
knew the Churchills and said of the unhappy father–son relationship:
'There was a sort of pathos about Randolph.' Underneath the rudeness
were kindness and courage. 'I think he suffered as a result of his father,
because he was terribly fond of him and couldn't get on with him.'
Randolph later found that writing his father's biography was the one
thing that he found fulfilling and worth while.

In September 1922 Winston, without informing Clementine – who was
pregnant with Mary and had strenuously objected to the idea – purchased for five thousand pounds an eighty-acre estate near Westerham
in Kent (some twenty-five miles south of London) called Chartwell
Manor, upon which stood a run-down, rambling and rather unattractive
house. For Churchill, Chartwell, with its many rooms and vast, untamed
and overgrown grounds, was love at first sight, but for Clementine it
was the beginning of a love–hate relationship. The place needed a great
deal of work and would prove, as she had feared, a financial burden on
a growing family whose income was never enough to support their way

of life. Churchill had always been rather cavalier about owing money, but with her Scottish sense of thriftiness Clementine hated debt and the unpaid bills her husband routinely amassed and couldn't be bothered to deal with, leaving her to juggle when there were insufficient funds – which was often.

The house was in terrible shape and had to be rebuilt. The cost of renovating and running Chartwell was enormous. Mary would later remark that Clementine 'never quite forgave him for it'. Despite her disapproval and the strain it caused in their marriage, Chartwell became Churchill's dream home and his refuge, a place where he was the happiest of his entire life. 'It became his workshop – his "factory" – from whence poured his books, articles and speeches, which alone kept Chartwell and the whole fabric of our family life going,' recalled Mary. He enjoyed wallowing in mud and getting his hands dirty and once declared, 'Every day away from Chartwell is a day wasted.'

Chartwell enabled Churchill to indulge his passion for animals. At one time or another he kept sheep, pigs, dogs, cats, polo ponies, chickens, swans, geese and other birds. Once, when a pair of New Zealand swans advanced menacingly towards his literary aide, Denis Kelly, he sprang at them, waving his hat and shouting: 'Don't you dare talk to me like that!' Kelly once asked Churchill why he liked the pigs he kept and was told: 'Because the fish and birds look up to you but the pigs treat you as an equal.'

Churchill lost his seat in the Commons in 1922 and twice failed to be re-elected in the next two years. With the eclipse of the Liberals, the Conservatives, whom Churchill had abandoned so unceremoniously two decades earlier, suddenly began to hold fresh appeal for an opportunistic politician who had lost none of his zeal to be a major player in the political process. In 1924 he regained a seat in Parliament as a Tory. However, the enemies with whom he had fought so many political battles hardly became new allies. They viewed him with the same suspicion as before: as a self-aggrandizing, untrustworthy, ambitious reactionary. Now, however, Churchill had enemies on *both* sides of the floor, and the Liberals had consigned his portrait to a basement storeroom. Nevertheless, when the Conservatives returned to power and Stanley Baldwin became prime minister, he appointed Churchill his chancellor of the exchequer, a post he held from 1924 to 1929. While he was chancellor he returned Britain to the gold standard; he also lost a fortune in the 1929 Wall Street crash, and was nearly killed in another of his many accidents: this time when hit by a motor car in Manhattan.

In 1930, with the Tories out of office, Churchill resigned from the shadow cabinet. Having opposed Conservative plans to offer India limited self-government, he became a backbencher and political outcast. He always regarded inaction as the coin of failure, yet in the 1930s he became an increasingly irrelevant and sometimes tragic figure, shunned by his own party, with only his reputation as an unpredictable maverick intact.

Nevertheless his frequent speeches in Parliament, as they had from the time of his maiden speech in 1901, continued to be crowd-pulling occasions. In the words of one biographer he had become 'a hopelessly obsolete, old-fashioned warrior'. The former diplomat and Labour MP Harold Nicolson said of him in 1931 that he was 'the most interesting man in England . . . a phenomenon, [but] an enigma . . . His dominant qualities are imagination, courage and loyalty, his dominant defect, impatience.'

Though out of political office, and in no small part to support his lifestyle and finance the expense of maintaining Chartwell, Churchill also remained very much in the public eye by writing prolifically, pouring out articles on every conceivable subject for newspapers and magazines. He also wrote a number of books, mostly memoirs, and made a great deal of money from a lecture tour of the United States during which he recouped his considerable losses from the 1929 stock market crash. In 1931 *My Early Life* was published even as he continued working on his massive biography of John Churchill, all but wearing out his typists and literary aides. In 1939 he wrote his life story in numerous instalments for the *Sunday Dispatch*, chronicling his exploits as a young man in the colonial wars and the Great War, each of which tended to present him in a heroic mode.

Though suffering renewed bouts of his 'black dog', which came and went unpredictably, he also began taking more and more serious note of the rise of the dictators: Mussolini, who had established a Fascist state in Italy in the 1920s, Tojo in Japan, Franco in Spain and, most troubling of all, Adolf Hitler in Germany.

Churchill's frequent and cogent warnings of the threat posed by Hitler and Mussolini went largely ignored. His admonitions drew the ire of the Labour Party. (Founded in the early twentieth century, by the 1920s it had surpassed the Liberals as the Conservative Party's principal opposition.) Although accused of warmongering by Labour left-wingers, Churchill was in fact preaching the exact opposite in the early 1930s. While never relenting in his insistence that Germany be prevented from rearming, he also believed that war could be avoided if the victorious nations dealt more fairly with what he said were the legitimate territorial grievances of a crippled Germany. In November 1932 he held out an olive branch, telling Parliament that a lasting reconciliation in Europe was vital: 'The removal of the just grievances of the vanquished ought to precede the disarmament of the victors.' It was better, he said, to reopen discussions than to face the possibility of another war.

In an essay first published in 1925, entitled 'Shall We All Commit Suicide?', he envisaged the consequences 'should war come again to the world'. He warned that another war would not only mean wholesale destruction but, once launched, be uncontrollable. 'Mankind has never been in this position before. Without having improved appreciably in virtue or enjoying wiser guidance, it has got into its hands for the first time the tools by which it can unfailingly accomplish its own destruction . . . Death stands at attention, obedient, expectant, ready to serve, ready to shear away the peoples *en masse*; ready, if called on, to pulverize, without hope of repair, what is left of civilization.' Eight years after Churchill's original warnings were published – and long forgotten – a political upheaval in Germany brought to power a leader who would spark the very conflagration that Churchill had predicted.

The humiliating terms of the Versailles treaty, with its onerous reparations and restrictions, as well as rampant inflation and rising unemployment, enabled Adolf Hitler and his extremists to appeal to German nationalistic emotions and gradually to undermine the parliamentary democracy of the Weimar Republic. As democracy's last remnants were being swept away by Hitler and the Nazis, for Churchill, viewing events in Germany from afar, they rekindled memories of the kaiser and the march of German militarism that had led to the First World War.

As Britain drifted into appeasement, not only did Churchill's warnings about Germany go largely unheeded, but so did his declarations that Britain must rearm. While writing his ancestor's biography, he once again visited the scenes of the Duke of Marlborough's battlefield triumphs and returned to England disturbed by what he had seen. Hitler had taken note of Churchill's warnings, and when an intermediary attempted to broker a meeting between the two in the summer of 1932, when both men were in Munich and staying at the same hotel, Hitler was said to be nervous at the idea of meeting the fiery Englishman and 'rabid Francophile' and preferred to avoid him. Aware of Churchill's antagonism, the führer came to regard him as his greatest enemy in England.

Denying that he was an alarmist, Churchill nevertheless asserted that the various disarmament conferences would not remove the danger of another European war. Germany's increasing demands to be relieved of the burdens of Versailles were leading towards German rearmament, which should not be permitted. In 1932 he warned in Parliament that there was still time 'to revive again those lights of goodwill and reconciliation in Europe', but he added: 'All these bands of sturdy Teutonic youths, marching through the streets and roads of Germany, with the light of desire in their eyes to suffer for the Fatherland, are not looking for status. They are looking for weapons, and, when they have the weapons, believe me they will then ask for the return of lost territories and lost colonies.' By disarming, he declared, Britain was losing its ability to defend itself; 'the responsibility of Ministers to guarantee the safety of the country from day to day and hour to hour is direct and unalienable.' Over and over again came the warnings, such as this one in 1937 at Oxford: 'We must rearm. We must have a defensive alliance with France. We must have co-operation with America as far as she is willing . . . Whenever war threatens or breaks out, we are at the side of the victim and against the aggressor.'

Much to Churchill's consternation Ramsay MacDonald's Labour government in the early 1930s was committed to disarmament and cut Britain's naval strength well below what the admirals believed was the minimum necessary. Churchill forcefully spoke out on its folly – and was ignored.

The danger threatened by National Socialism became a reality in January 1933, when Hitler achieved control of the German government and began the inevitable advance towards rearmament; the loss of civil liberties, as his Nazi thugs ruled the streets; and the persecution of German Jews. And the new chancellor Hitler proclaimed his 'thousand-year Reich' even as MacDonald proposed further disarmament that would seriously reduce Britain's military capital.

While the British and the French struggled with rampant unemployment and other economic problems, Hitler began rearming Germany in defiance of the Treaty of Versailles, secretly building a new air force that eventually reached some three thousand aircraft, and manufacturing large numbers of new tanks. Conscription was followed by a sizeable expansion of the army and by the construction and deployment of submarines, after successfully persuading the Allies to permit alteration of the terms of the Versailles treaty.

In March 1936 Germany seized the Rhineland in a lightning strike by 35,000 ill-equipped, barely trained troops as Hitler declared in the Reichstag that Germany was re-establishing 'the absolute and unrestricted sovereignty of the Reich in the demilitarized zone of the Rhineland'. He also succeeded in convincing the Western powers that his actions were purely peaceful. The first forty-eight hours were crucial. If the French had responded with military force the Germans would immediately have retreated back across the Rhine, seriously compromising the honour of the German army and possibly causing Hitler's ouster from power.

Instead Hitler's bluff worked, as the French failed to retake the Rhineland – which they could easily have done – while Britain likewise stood idly by, intent on not provoking another war. Most British newspapers, including *The Times*, naively excused the matter and criticized 'the sensationally minded' – undoubtedly a barb aimed at Churchill and those who supported his beliefs. Among the British upper class, including Churchill's own cousin Lord Londonderry, there was considerable admiration of and support for Hitler.

Although he had long been out of office as first lord, Churchill remained highly regarded within the Royal Navy and the RAF. Of the many military issues that drew his attention during the 1930s, the RAF and the future role of airpower headed the list. In 1937 some concerned officers, frustrated by the lack of funds and the shortage of spare parts and such vital equipment as bombsights, secretly briefed him on these and other problems in the hope that he could use his influence to rectify matters. It was an endless battle against cutbacks as Churchill argued that Britain was falling too far behind rapidly rearming Nazi Germany. Privately he referred to 'Nazi gangsters' and 'those savages'. Hitler, in turn, regarded Churchill with ever growing loathing.

Major Desmond Morton, the intelligence officer whose friendship with Churchill had been formed on the western front, became an emissary during the inter-war years. As the chief of the Industrial Intelligence Centre, Morton obtained the consent of three different prime ministers (MacDonald, Baldwin and Chamberlain) regularly to pass along highly classified material to him and was astonished by the depth of Churchill's knowledge of defence issues. Although he would turn on Churchill after the Second World War, calling him 'a wild tactician' and 'frequently a crackpot strategist', they were such intimate friends at this time that Morton was a welcome (and frequent) guest at Chartwell. A man of considerable humour and a penetrating mind, he became Churchill's greatest source of information. Churchill may have lacked formal political power in the 1930s but he was one of the best-informed men in Britain.

Prime Minister Stanley Baldwin felt threatened by what began to look like Churchill's shadow cabinet, and when the News Chronicle got wind of the private meetings it trumpeted in a large headline ANTI-BALDWIN SHADOW CABINET MEETS. In the spring of 1936 a disgruntled Henry 'Chips' Channon, a pro-appeasement, anti-Communist MP, complained in his diary about Churchill's current group, known as the 'the House Party'. They were, he wrote, 'the naughty boys, an insubordinate and ambitious group' who were undoubtedly out to concoct 'dark schemes to torpedo the government'. Although officially ignored by the government of the day and powerless to stop the drift towards military disaster amid warning after warning of the growing Nazi menace, Churchill became a sort of elder statesman in exile, receiving a steady stream of high-level visitors from European countries, ranging from a former German prime minister to the French air minister and the Romanian foreign minister, all of whom came to Chartwell for counsel and to discuss the events of the day.

No nation or leader was willing to step forward to challenge Germany and its charismatic dictator, certainly not Britain's vapid leadership of the 1930s. It was a decade the historian Piers Brendon has called the 'Dark Valley', a period of worldwide economic deprivation and joblessness that plagued the Great Powers, while Hitler was secretly but relentlessly rearming Germany, his partner in the new Rome–Berlin Axis Mussolini was gobbling up Ethiopia (Abyssinia) and Japan was bombing and invading China and massacring thousands. In Spain's civil war Franco's Fascists were being supported by Germany's new Luftwaffe, which made use of the conflict as a rehearsal for the forth-coming war. Men like Lloyd George and Churchill 'remained in the wilderness while safe, mediocre, hollow men – MacDonald, Baldwin and Neville Chamberlain – occupied the seats of power'.

War continued to occupy Churchill's thoughts, and his concerns were frequently expressed both in public and in private. A regular visitor to Chartwell during those years was a family friend, Diana Mosley, one of the Mitford sisters and the wife of the former Labour minister and later leader of the British Union of Fascists, Sir Oswald Mosley. Diana later recalled how Churchill 'loved talking about war, it was quite an obses-sion with him . . . He never hesitated to say what he thought of his colleagues. He was extremely indiscreet.' During the Second World War, Churchill would intern both Mosleys as potential enemies of the state. Others who visited him came away either reassured or appalled by, as one visitor put it, 'a hysterical madman or a Prophet of all that is upon us'. But Churchill's influence was so muted that all he could do was continue warning of Germany's sinister intentions and the danger they posed to a peaceful Europe. He wrote an article in the *Evening Standard*, also published in fourteen other countries, arguing that the threatened nations of Europe should band together to avert war and control 'the hideous drift of events' and to 'arrest calamity upon the threshold. Stop it! Stop it!!! Stop it NOW!!!' Stanley Baldwin's private response to Churchill's repeated calls for rearmament typified British lethargy in the mid-1930s: 'While we listen to him in this House we do not take his advice.'

The historian R. A. C. Parker contends that Churchill might have prevented the Second World War had he been in control of British foreign policy and able to forge a grand alliance of European nations around a solid Anglo-French coalition that could have convinced Hitler that German aggression would be strongly resisted. While this remains a tantalizing what-if question, it does suggest that Churchill was Britain's best hope of avoiding the catastrophic war that soon engulfed the world. That there was no one else was both a testament to Churchill and a condemnation of British leadership in the 1930s.

By 1938 Germany was a military colossus that had matched its pre-war scale and was still growing. When Neville Chamberlain signed the ill-fated Munich agreement, Europe was on the brink of a war that no one was able to prevent. Churchill had been a politician for nearly forty years and a soldier, off and on, for even longer. His hopes of ascending to the leadership of Britain had been repeatedly dashed. The long wait, however, was nearly over.

27

The Shame of Munich

Another Great War would cost us our wealth, our freedom, and our culture, and cast what we have slowly garnered of human enlightenment, tolerance, and dignity to different packs of ravening wolves. – *Sunday Chronicle*, 28 July 1935

The men who led Britain in the first forty years of the twentieth century may (or may not) have been good politicians, but with the possible exception of Lloyd George, none would have made good war leaders. Politicians possessing the kind of leadership ability that is required in wartime are rare. During the 1930s none of Britain's prime ministers were men of this ilk. Stanley Baldwin, premier in the 1920s (twice) and the 1930s (in all, seven years and eighty-two days), did a masterly job in orchestrating the abdication of Edward VIII, but when he retired from office in 1937 and was succeeded by Neville Chamberlain, he was the latest in a succession of prime ministers who had not done enough to prepare Britain for war. Baldwin was no friend of Churchill, and the two men exchanged barbs over the years. Yet, despite the bad feeling between the two, Baldwin said of Churchill in 1935, 'If there is going to be a war – and no one can say there is not – we must keep him fresh to be our War Prime Minister.'

Not surprisingly the three 1930s prime ministers – Ramsay Mac-Donald, Baldwin and Chamberlain – represented the anti-war view of a British populace that still recoiled from the horrors of the Great War. The price of fighting a ground war on the Continent had been too high, and alliances were of value only insofar as they kept Britain out of war. As Churchill had once pointed out, for some four hundred years it had been British foreign policy not to permit any one European power to become dominant, and to prevent this 'by weaving together a combination of other countries strong enough to face the bully'.

This is not to say that there was no concern over Britain's rearmament. In the 1930s the government began to focus on the increasing threat of air attack by the rejuvenated Luftwaffe, so much so that in one parliamentary debate in November 1932 Baldwin bluntly asserted 'that there was "no power on earth" that could protect the British people from being obliterated from the skies since "the bomber will always get through"', echoing the words of Hugh Trenchard, the former chief of the RAF and the father of the concept of strategic bombing. However, Baldwin also suggested that the use of such airpower would devastate European civilization. Although the RAF was given increased attention by the Baldwin administration at the expense of the army, Chamberlain, as chancellor of the exchequer, cut defence spending from a recommended £76 million to £50 million. The army, for example, had its five-year funding in the second half of the 1930s cut from a projected £40 million to a mere £19 million.

Churchill, while arguing that, by increased spending on scientific research, a properly constituted RAF could prevent bombers from getting through, also repeatedly pointed out that Britain was underestimating the strength of the Luftwaffe, which, he said, would be twice the size of the RAF by 1937. Baldwin took much of the steam from Churchill's campaign to rearm the RAF by announcing during the 1934 debates that the government would add 'an extra 300 first-line aircraft to maintain the RAF superiority'. Nonetheless, in a lengthy speech in November 1934 Churchill warned the government that Britain faced the danger of aerial attack. Attacks on London would result within seven to ten days in thirty thousand to forty thousand dead or maimed. 'The most dangerous form of air attack', he said, was from incendiary bombs, a chilling portent of the Blitz. Churchill's warnings fell on deaf ears throughout Britain and mostly stirred criticism for what the Liberal Party leader, Sir Herbert Samuel, declared was 'blind and causeless panic'.

Churchill was almost entirely focused on strengthening the RAF and on the great importance of the threat that was still more perceived than actually posed by the Luftwaffe. He had also become a convert to what was believed to be the ultimate deterrent: the potential of strategic airpower to strike decisively at the heart of Germany. The Luftwaffe was not, however, the most dangerous threat to Britain, nor did German military doctrine even focus on strategic bombing. On the contrary, the Germans thought that Trenchard's doctrine of heavy bombers striking at and crippling industrial war-making targets was flawed. Strongly influenced by Trenchard, Churchill was Britain's leading advocate of aerial warfare. But with his fixation on the bombers he neglected the need for developing stronger aerial defensive measures and placing far greater emphasis on the role of Fighter Command. Created in July 1936, Fighter Command was headed by Air Marshal Sir Hugh Dowding, the architect of Britain's aerial defensive system, which in the coming war would employ the use of radar and an innovative method of air control.

Although he was more concerned with strategic bombing, Churchill had not neglected other deadly uses for airpower. The Middle East in 1920 was a mélange of conflict and rebellion that threatened stability and British interests in the wake of the dissolution of the Ottoman Empire. His longtime colleague and former friend General Aylmer Haldane was now commander in chief of British forces in Mesopotamia (the forerunner of the modern state of Iraq). In 1920 the region was in rebellion, and the unrest was rapidly spreading. Churchill was colonial secretary and had responsibility for the region. With British military assets spread thin, there were insufficient troops available for Haldane to suppress the rebellion. Churchill and Trenchard discussed the employment of airpower to help quell the revolt. Britain had a huge stock of poison gas left over from the First World War, and Churchill told Trenchard that the RAF should 'certainly proceed with the experimental work on gas bombs, especially mustard gas, which would inflict punishment on recalcitrant natives without inflicting grave injury upon them'. His rationale displayed a rather benign naivety that a deathless form of warfare could be waged, and 'asphyxiating bombs calculated to cause disablement of some kind but not death' be employed to quell the rebellious tribes. In recent years print and broadcast media have had a field day sensationalizing and speculating from this regrettably worded missive that he wanted the rebels killed.

The real military danger to Britain, however, lay under the sea. The Royal Navy may have been the world's pre-eminent maritime power, but its Achilles heel remained the same as in the Great War: the U-boat, which would once again wreak havoc on Allied shipping during the Second World War.

*

Neville Chamberlain entered No. 10 Downing Street on 28 May 1937, full of confidence, a handsome figure seemingly perfectly suited for the post of prime minister. Instead he became one of the most tragic figures in British political history: a well-meaning politician whose name is now forever linked with appeasement and Britain's downward spiral into war. Chamberlain, a successful businessman who came to politics late in life as lord mayor of Birmingham, seemed enigmatic and colourless, yet behind the gentlemanly façade he was possessed of a sharp tongue and a confrontational manner when friend or foe disagreed with him. He was anti-war, as much on principle as because of the effect of war on business. Like any good businessman, too, he was strong-minded and self-confident, perhaps too much so in his belief as prime minister that his decisions were the right ones and that they should be treated in the same manner as a business decision. Nor was Chamberlain a shrinking violet in his face-to-face dealings with Hitler. But whereas Baldwin was pragmatic in his willingness to alter policy to the needs of the moment, Chamberlain's inflexibility would commit Britain to a ruinous appeasement and precipitate his eventual downfall.

Two more dissimilar men than Chamberlain and Churchill could hardly have existed. Whereas Churchill never lost his Victorian principles and was flamboyant, impulsive, emotional, possessed of a searching and inquisitive mind and sentimentally wedded to the monarchy, the methodical Chamberlain was none of these. 'Winston is a very interesting but a d—d uncomfortable bedfellow,' Chamberlain once wrote. 'You never get a moment's rest and you never know at what point he'll break out.' One lived rigidly in the here and now; the other looked ahead to broad visions. Chamberlain's stiffness and lack of interest in socializing, or even dining out, were in direct contrast to Churchill's extroverted manner, his love of food and drink and his thirst for knowledge and stimulating conversation. One was a brilliant orator who often spoke before a crowded House; the other was so uninspired that members fell asleep during his speeches. 'The Prime Minister has no gift for inspiring anybody,' wrote Harold Nicolson, 'and he might have been the Secretary of a firm of undertakers reading the minutes of the last meeting.' Whereas Churchill seemed happiest during those years when he was working with his hands, laying bricks, painting and engaging in projects to restore Chartwell, Chamberlain was refined and introverted. In 1925 Chamberlain himself summed up the great disparity between the two men: 'I like him,' he said. 'I like his humour and his vitality. I like his courage,' but 'there is somehow a great gulf fixed between him and me which I don't think I shall ever cross.'

Chamberlain's sympathy for Germany over its harsh treatment by the Allies after the First World War led to a policy of appeasement of Hitler in the misguided belief that the German leader could be reasoned with and war averted. Chamberlain was too naive to grasp that reasoned dialogue would have scant effect on Hitler's (or Mussolini's) territorial designs. Anthony Eden, appointed foreign secretary by Baldwin, and a rising star in the Conservative Party, had no such illusions and resigned in protest in 1938 over Chamberlain's policies. His replacement was Edward Wood, Viscount Halifax, secretary of state for war and leader of the House of Lords under Stanley Baldwin. Halifax saw more good than bad in Hitler's Germany, and in 1937 had reported his favourable impressions to the inveterate diarist Chips Channon, who recorded these remarks: 'He told me he liked all the Nazi leaders, even Goebbels, and he was much impressed, interested and amused by the visit. He thinks the régime is absolutely fantastic, perhaps even too fantastic to be taken seriously.'

Sir Samuel Hoare held a variety of high posts in Conservative governments during the inter-war years. Under Neville Chamberlain he served as first lord of the Admiralty, home secretary, lord privy seal and secretary of state for air, and he later strongly defended Chamberlain and his policies. 'He was not an autocrat who imposed his views upon doubting or hostile colleagues. Appeasement was not his personal policy. Not only was it supported by his colleagues; it expressed the general desire of the British people ... While the prime mover, he was never the dictator of the Government's policy ... His colleagues supported him because they agreed with him.'

Despite the support of prominent men like Hoare, there was an emerging band of rebel Tory MPs who not only strongly disagreed with Chamberlain's social and economic policies but also disavowed his foreign policy of appeasing the dictators. This group included Churchill's former parliamentary private secretary Robert Boothby, his friend Leo Amery, Ronald Cartland and the future prime ministers Harold Macmillan and Anthony Eden.

The nadir of Britain's years of appeasement occurred in Munich in September 1938 when Neville Chamberlain etched his name into history by formally acquiescing in a pact that legitimized Adolf Hitler's annexation of Czechoslovakia's Sudetenland. Chamberlain seriously misread the cynicism with which the führer signed a document pledging non-aggression – a promise he had no intention of honouring. When Chamberlain met with him on 15 September at the Berghof, Hitler's Berchtesgaden mountain retreat, he came away with a hopelessly mistaken impression of the German leader, writing to one of his sisters that 'in spite of the hardness and ruthlessness I thought I saw in his face, I got the impression that here was a man who could be relied upon when he had given his word.' Chamberlain believed he was doing the right thing, and that, as the pact specified, differences between the two nations would be resolved not by war but by diplomacy.

If Munich was the culmination of appeasement in the 1930s, and of the misguided belief that dictators like Hitler could be reasoned with, it will be best remembered for Chamberlain's words, 'Peace in our time', uttered when he returned to England to a hero's welcome – words he took to his grave with regret. Whereas Kaiser Wilhelm II was more foolish and headstrong than he was evil, Adolf Hitler and the Nazi tyranny he created represented the very worst of the malevolent side of mankind. The darkness that descended on Europe in the 1930s was but a prelude to the most destructive war in history, a war that dwarfed even the Great War of 1914–18, a war that would wreck Europe and bring about the genocide of its Jews, Gypsies and other minorities, and the displacement of millions.

Munich thus became one of the most ill-fated events in British history – but only with hindsight. At the time Chamberlain's devil's pact with Hitler was viewed quite differently. It represented the feelings of a British populace utterly sick of war. All but one British newspaper warmly supported it. The prime minister's return from Munich on 30 September was greeted as a triumph for Britain that would avoid war. After landing at Heston aerodrome outside London, he read from his copy of the accord before holding it high for all to see. Despite falling rain, crowds lined the streets to cheer him as he was driven to Buckingham Palace where he appeared on the balcony with the royal family, and again as his motor car made its way slowly back to Downing Street. 'It was as if a great national victory had been scored.' He was cheered in Parliament when he gave a pledge that Britain and France would honour their commitment to support Poland. British newspapers applauded, and the public was reassured. Chamberlain dolls appeared in shop windows, and even the former kaiser Wilhelm wrote that the prime minister 'was inspired by heaven and guided by God'.

After meeting with his cabinet Chamberlain sought to emulate Disraeli's famous appearance at the window of No. 10 in July 1878, after he had gained major concessions for Britain at the Congress of Berlin. 'My good friends, this is the second time in our history that there has come from Germany to Downing Street peace with honour,' he declared. These fateful words, which would forever taint his reputation, he had never intended to utter in public. His private secretary (and future prime minister), Alec Douglas-Home, recalled that once inside No. 10 someone had shouted to Chamberlain that he should go to the window and repeat his statement about peace with honour. 'Chamberlain turned on him and said, very sharply, "No. I don't do that sort of thing." Someone persuaded him otherwise . . . and he did it.'

Chamberlain's motives in signing the Munich pact have been misunderstood. That it was appeasement had never crossed his mind. As Brendon explains, 'Contrary to appearances, this declaration did not mark the end of appeasement: it was an attempt to give the policy teeth . . . Chamberlain was trying to draw a line in the sand. The aim was "to constrain and deter Hitler rather than to defeat him".' When he spoke the famous words that would be his political epitaph, Chamberlain actually thought that, having got Hitler to sign the non-aggression pact, if he broke the agreement 'it would be a nail in his coffin . . . particularly with the Americans,' recalled Douglas-Home. What remains puzzling is why Chamberlain or any of his ministers believed that after the seizure of the Sudetenland – followed by the *Anschluss* in March 1938, which left Austria a vassal state of Nazi Germany – Hitler would spare Poland and other nations of Europe from the same fate. Not long after his return from Munich, Chamberlain naively told his cabinet ministers that while Hitler was 'the commonest little dog', he would nevertheless be 'rather better than his word', and had been truthful in stating that he had no further territorial ambitions for Czechoslovakia now that he had the Sudetenland. The paradox of Munich was that both Hitler and Chamberlain believed war could be averted. Hitler came away imbued with the conviction that neither Britain nor France would come to the aid of Poland.

There was no equivocation about what Winston Churchill thought of

Munich: 'You were given the choice between war and dishonour. You chose dishonour and you will have war.' The day after the terms of the agreement became public, he asked his friend Harold Nicolson, then a Labour MP, to come to his London flat. Also present was the former Conservative MP, winner of the 1937 Nobel Peace Prize and one of the architects of the League of Nations, Viscount Cecil of Chelwood (formerly known as Lord Robert Cecil), who was in despair. Nicolson recorded: 'Churchill sat there in his armchair with that utterly blank expression which he sometimes assumes. He then leant forward and his eyebrows rose slightly. "Yes, Bob," he almost hissed, "Yes, I feel despair unutterable. [But] I feel twenty years younger." I knew then that only Churchill could be our leader if war came.'

Mary Soames has written that for her father and those who thought like him, 'the Munich Agreement was an act of shame and betrayal; it represented the final, fatal grovelling to the insatiable appetite of the dictators.' Before Chamberlain had flown to Germany, Churchill said the partition of Czechoslovakia would be 'the complete surrender of the Western democracies to the Nazi threat of force'. Munich and the crisis leading up to the German invasion of Czechoslovakia and its abandonment by both France and Great Britain were a time of torment for Churchill, who wrote gloomily to another old friend, Lord Moyne: 'Owing to the neglect of our defences and the mishandling of the German problem in the last five years, we seem to be very near the bleak choice between War and Shame. My feeling is that we shall choose Shame, and then have War thrown in a little later.'

When the pact was signed, an irate Churchill went public at once with a statement that read in part: 'We must hope that it does not foreshadow another complete failure of the Western Democracies to withstand the threats and violence of Nazi Germany.' He continued to speak out in opposition even though there was a backlash within the ranks of the pro- and anti-Munich Conservatives, and from the public against those who were critical of Chamberlain. Four days after Chamberlain's triumphant return from Munich, Churchill rose in Parliament and, despite a cry of 'Nonsense' and other barbs from Lady Astor, unequivocally condemned the venture as 'a total and unmitigated defeat', noting that diplomacy and alliances that might have reined in Hitler and the escalation of Nazi power in the early 1930s had been irrevocably squandered and were beyond resurrection. His words had a terrible force:

We are in the presence of a disaster of the first magnitude which has befallen
Great Britain and France. Do not let us blind ourselves to that. You must have
diplomatic and correct relations, but there can never be friendship between the
British democracy and the Nazi Power, that Power which spurns Christian ethics,
which cheers its onward course by a barbarous paganism which vaunts the spirit
of aggression and conquest, which derives strength and perverted pleasure from
persecution, and uses, as we have seen, with pitiless brutality the threat of
murderous force . . . We have passed an awful milestone in our history, when the
whole equilibrium of Europe has been deranged . . . This is only the beginning
of the reckoning. This is only the first sip of, the first foretaste of a bitter cup
which will be proffered to us year by year unless, by a supreme recovery of moral
health and martial vigour, we arise again and take our stand for freedom as in
the olden time.

Churchill was not alone in his dismay over Munich. Clementine
Churchill was so angry that she felt like marching on Whitehall and
'hurling a brick through the window of Number 10'. Munich became a
very sore subject in the Churchill household, and on one occasion
Eva Keyes, the wife of Admiral Sir Roger Keyes, made the mistake of
expressing her pro-Chamberlain views at a luncheon at Chartwell, and
learned just how passionate her hostess was on the subject: an infuriated
Clementine reduced the poor woman to tears.

For Duff Cooper, the first lord of the Admiralty, another of
Churchill's friends and a Conservative ally, Munich was the last straw.
Dismayed and frustrated that his attempts at pursuing stronger British
rearmament had been consistently rebuffed, he resigned the day after
Chamberlain's peace pronouncement. Duff Cooper's wife telephoned
Churchill to tell him the news: 'His voice was broken with emotion. I
could hear him cry.' Hugh Dalton, a leading Labour politician and
future member of Churchill's coalition government in 1940, scornfully
called the agreement that 'scrap of paper torn from *Mein Kampf*'.
Moreover, had either Chamberlain or Halifax ever read *Mein Kampf*,
they might have reached very different conclusions about Herr Hitler
and his intentions.

As Europe once again moved towards war, Churchill's rage and
frustration mounted. In public appearances, in Parliament, in notes to
Chamberlain and other ministers and in the newspapers, his repeated
warnings began to gain him support, both in the press and among the

366

British public. Several newspapers declared that it was time to bring Churchill back into the government.

Still convinced even as late as the summer of 1939 that war might be averted and that Hitler could be reasoned with, Chamberlain resisted bringing back into the fold his unrelenting and unforgiving critic, and fended off Churchill's criticisms in Parliament. Meanwhile he shifted position sufficiently to agree to the rearmament proposals of the service chiefs, including the production of Hurricane and Spitfire aircraft.

Sometimes lost in the long-standing controversy over appeasement is the question of what effect Churchill's proposals for rearmament would have had on the Nazi leader. While he was correct to press rearmament, the retaliatory threat posed by Britain's strategic air force was simply not a deterrent to the only person who counted, Adolf Hitler. The historian Sir Michael Howard has pointed out that 'Churchill never showed the slightest interest in pressing for the only kind of rearmament that might have impressed [Hitler], the building up of a large Continental-style army that would have reassured the French and presented the Germans with a real deterrent to initiating a war on either their eastern or western fronts. Nor did Churchill show any interest in building up the navy, to whose obsolescence his own policy, when Chancellor of the Exchequer, had [been] so major a contribution.' In addition, even without a policy of appeasement, a more aggressive rearmament by Britain would not have deterred Hitler; in fact it is arguable that it would merely have hastened his plans, particularly his decision to invade Poland in the wake of British and French guarantees in March 1939. The irony of Churchill's warnings about Germany in the 1930s is that while they were prophetic they were militarily inaccurate: Bomber Command was no deterrent.

A few weeks before Germany invaded Poland, Churchill predicted the fury and horror of what lay ahead if war came. While he still hoped for peace, the signs pointed otherwise, to 'ugly facts and evil signs'. German industry was on a war footing, some two million men were under arms, and 'it is becoming increasingly difficult to see how war can be averted.' 'Should war come,' he wrote, 'whole vast populations will become inflamed personally against one another to a degree unknown for centuries. It will be an inexpiable war.'

In the Far East, by the 1930s Japan had become an imperialist state, isolated from world economic markets, particularly oil, which the United States blocked, and had turned to the dark side in a loose alliance with Germany and Italy. The country's territorial ambitions unsatisfied, Japanese soldiers matched German and Italian aggression with their own brand of terror and death. In 1931 Japan had taken advantage of unrest and civil war in China to annex the semi-independent state of Manchuria, and in 1937 the Japanese army marched relatively unhindered into China, indiscriminately bombing towns and cities, and committing atrocities that culminated in the rape of Nanking, where some two hundred thousand were slaughtered in an orgy of bloodletting.

Not to be outdone by Hitler, a bellicose Benito Mussolini, whom the führer treated more like a servant than an ally, had his own designs for Italian territorial expansion, from the invasion of Ethiopia in October 1935 to the occupation of Albania in 1939. Fascism's ugly hand also provoked the Spanish civil war, which saw extensive German and Italian support for General Francisco Franco's successful bid to win power.

Robert Boothby called 1939:

a hopeless year, during which we drifted slowly, helplessly and inexorably to disaster. As so often Shakespeare has the final comment:

That England, being empty of defence
Hath shook and trembled at the ill neighbourhood . . . [*Henry V*, 1.2]

Thus we stumbled into what it became fashionable to call the 'Bore War' – without arms, without faith, and without heart.

28

'Bring Back Churchill'

Take Winston Churchill into the Cabinet. [He] is the only Englishman Hitler is afraid of. – Count Lutz Schwerin von Krosigk, German finance minister, 1939

In the summer of 1939 a 'Bring Back Churchill' campaign was gathering steam with the same force as the war clouds that hung over Europe. In early August, Churchill recorded a bleak, prescient and disheartening radio broadcast beamed to the United States, in which he described 'a hush all over Europe, nay, over all the world'. It was, he said, 'the hush of suspense, and in many lands it is the hush of fear.' He recalled the summer of 1914, 'when the German advance guards were breaking into Belgium and trampling down its people on their march towards Paris', and praised China for defending itself against Japanese aggression. Then he suggested: 'No one knows whose turn it may be next. If this habit of military dictatorships breaking into other people's lands with bomb and shell and bullet, stealing the property and killing the proprietors, spreads too widely, we may none of us be able to think of summer holidays for quite a while.' He continued with these ominous words:

Listen! No, listen carefully; I think I hear something – yes, there it was quite clear. Don't you hear it? It is the tramp of armies crunching the gravel of the parade-grounds, splashing through rain-soaked fields, the tramp of two million German soldiers and more than a million Italians . . . No wonder the armies are tramping on when there is so much liberation to be done, and no wonder there is a hush among all the neighbours of Germany and Italy while they are wondering which one is going to be 'liberated' next.

Churchill wrote his own scenario for the coming war with the Axis powers. 'Great Britain', he said, 'stands in the midst and even at the head of a great and growing company of states and nations, ready to confront and to endure what may befall. The shock may be sudden, or the strain may be long-drawn: but who can doubt that all will come right if we persevere to the end.'

Even as a lonely outcast a decade removed from a ministerial post, Churchill still had military men gravitating towards him, not only because he was the voice of opposition to Chamberlain's policies and the voice of a militarily strong Britain, but also because of his status as the nation's unofficial warlord during the second half of the 1930s. Under the Baldwin administration a small group of influential Tories met regularly over dinner at weekends to discuss defence matters. They ranged from disaffected senior backbenchers to Neville Chamberlain's brother Austen and Robert Boothby. They would be joined by Frederick A. Lindemann ('the Prof' – elevated to a peerage in 1941 as Lord Cherwell), an eccentric, brilliant, opinionated Oxford don who had been advising Churchill since they first met in 1921. Other than mutually inquiring minds, the two men outwardly appeared to have nothing in common. Lindemann's family roots were Alsatian, and he was a vegetarian who neither drank nor smoked. He ingratiated himself with Churchill by befriending his children (Sarah Churchill could hardly recall an occasion when Lindemann was not at Chartwell), and was warmly welcomed into the Chartwell circle by both Winston and Clementine. Within a short time he had Churchill's ear and became his chief scientific and technological adviser. Although born and educated in Germany, Lindemann was strongly anti-German. His attraction for Churchill stemmed in part from his service during the First World War as a researcher at the Royal Aircraft Factory in Farnborough, where he learned to fly, and from the way, as a physicist, he had developed, personally tested and proved his theory of how to regain control of spinning aircraft. (It has had universal application, and is still used today to prevent stalling.)

The men Churchill invited into his private circle of advisers and confidants each possessed the buccaneering personality he so greatly admired. Another was Admiral of the Fleet Sir Roger John Brownlow Keyes, a bold, gallant sailor who had been Churchill's strongest supporter in the challenging of the Dardanelles in 1915. Keyes had had an adventurous life, rising through the ranks of the navy to command the Mediterranean fleet from 1925 to 1928, and training many of the sailors who came to the forefront in the Second World War. He ended his active career in 1931 at the age of fifty-eight, and his inscription in a book sent to a friend best defines the man: 'He most prevails who nobly dares.' In 1934 Keyes became a Tory MP, as Admiral Lord Charles Beresford had in the years leading up to the Great War. A frequent guest at Chartwell during the 1930s, he became one of Churchill's most intimate naval advisers. Keyes was a strong opponent of appeasement, was proactive about rearmament and rather like Jackie Fisher never hesitated to lash out with stinging criticism of those with whom he disagreed.

Churchill was often invited to places like the RAF air base not far from Chartwell at Biggin Hill (one of the key fighter bases during the Battle of Britain), to be briefed and to observe military exercises. His new residential secretary, Mrs Kathleen Hill, noted how Chartwell 'was as still as a mouse' whenever he was not in residence: 'When he was there it was vibrating.' Nevertheless Churchill remained 'a disappointed man, waiting for the call to serve his country'.

Lindemann, Brendan Bracken and Lord Beaverbrook became fixtures; along with the trusted, and shadowy Desmond Morton, all fed Churchill secret information. Little or nothing went on behind closed doors in Whitehall that he did not become privy to. Morton still believed that Churchill was the one politician in Britain capable of leading the nation in the event of war: 'I regarded Winston as the only man who had the qualities needed for the job.' Nevertheless, until 1939 successive prime ministers resisted offering Churchill any government role.

Another frequent visitor to Chartwell was General Sir Edmund 'Tiny' Ironside, the six-foot-four-inch officer whose colourful career included spying for British intelligence behind the lines during the Boer War, front-line combat during the First World War, and command of the Allied Expeditionary Force at Archangel in 1918. He was also the model for the heroic spy Richard Hannay in John Buchan's novel *The Thirty-Nine Steps*. The friendship between the two went back to the Boer War, and with war clouds growing ever darker they shared a sense of urgency about Britain's preparedness. Inspector general of overseas forces in 1939, Ironside was one of many who thought Churchill might be the next prime minister. An entry in his diary on 25 July 1939 describes a stimulating night of conversation with Churchill that lasted until 5.00 a.m. 'The deed was signed,' he told Ironside, 'and Hitler is going to make war.'

With remarkable accuracy Churchill also laid out exactly what would happen when war came:

He walked about in front of a map and demonstrated his ideas . . . You must be clear on what is going to happen:
(i) The crippling or annihilation of Poland.
(ii) The employment of Italy to create diversions. Mussolini has sold his country for a job.
(iii) The capture of Egypt, chiefly by Italian forces.
(iv) A pressing on to the Black Sea via Roumania.
(v) An alliance with Russia, when the latter sees how the land lies.

Ironside returned to London convinced that Churchill – 'a man who knows that you must act to win' – would have to lead Britain. He had good reason for his own apprehension when he warned the secretary of state for war, Leslie Hore-Belisha, that Britain had no plan and the French had no intention of reacting to an invasion of Poland other than to prepare to defend their homeland, 'and that no plans for anything existed to deal any blow at either Germans or Italians. The [Royal] Navy had no plan and intended to act "according to the circumstance" and not in unison with any of the other arms. Everything was hopelessly defensive everywhere.' For all the promises of mutual support, Britain's preparedness to fight another overseas war was wholly inadequate. Ironside noted in August 1939 that Britain would be able to dispatch only a single corps overseas after twenty-four-days: 'The remainder is all in the air . . . This is a terrible result after all these years of preparation.'

The hypocrisy of Hitler's promise to refrain from further land grabs was revealed in March 1939, when Germany completed the bloodless takeover of Czechoslovakia by seizing Moravia and Bohemia. Panzers rumbling unhindered in the streets of Prague left little doubt about the worth of the Munich agreement. Churchill's stock began rising to the point where even his opponents swung around to the view that perhaps it was time for his inclusion in the Chamberlain government. Even an ardent supporter of Chamberlain like Samuel Hoare acknowledged that it was time to reconsider Churchill's role.

It had taken a great many years, but Churchill was being listened to as never before. Many, even those like the Labour MP Herbert Morrison, who had previously opposed him, now regarded the former pariah as Britain's only possible saviour. It was testament to how far his stature had evolved that Stafford Cripps, a leading left-wing MP who had vigorously opposed Churchill's appeals for Britain to rearm in 1934, was among the converts in 1939. British newspapers loudly asserted that it was time for the government to send for him.

On 22 May 1939, Germany and Italy signed the so-called Pact of Steel, in which each side pledged to come to the aid of the other in the event of war, and agreed that neither side would make peace without the other's consent. While the Pact of Steel was a natural collaboration of two allies, Germany's alliance with the Soviet Union, signed in August, was a cynical agreement between two despotic nations that gravely mistrusted each other. Although it purported 'to strengthen the cause of peace', in reality it was a deal to carve up Poland between them. With both France and Britain signatories to security alliances with Poland, the stage was set for war. All that was required was a match to ignite the fire.

Whereas the First World War could have been averted, neither Britain nor France was equipped either militarily or morally to restrain Hitler's expansionism. As Munich had demonstrated, no European nation – certainly not Britain – was willing or able to stand up to Hitler when it might have mattered, such as during the German reoccupation of the Rhineland in 1936. Instead Hitler proved to be a master poker player and manipulator whose only aces were brinkmanship and the conviction that appeasement by the French and the British governments would trump any notion of retaliatory action against Germany.

By the summer of 1939 Churchill was convinced that it was no longer a matter of if but of when Germany would invade Poland. France was in political and economic disarray, its readiness to act in defence of its treaties doubtful. What, then, was the state of the French military, and how prepared was it to wage war with Germany? These were among the many questions that troubled Churchill that summer. France's defences were anchored on the Maginot Line, a series of intricate fortifi-cations and underground bunkers built during the inter-war years that guarded the frontier with Germany from Luxembourg to Switzerland. Churchill asked his friend Major General Edward Louis Spears, by then a Conservative MP, to use his extensive contacts within the French government to arrange for a formal invitation that would permit him not only to inspect the Maginot Line but also to assess the state of

France's defences. The invitation was soon forthcoming from General Maurice Gamelin, the commander in chief of the French army.

In mid-August, with Spears accompanying him as an adviser and translator, Churchill flew to Le Bourget Airport outside Paris. He was met by Gamelin's deputy, General Alphonse-Joseph Georges, and escorted directly to a restaurant in the Bois de Boulogne, where 'in the divine sunshine we lunched; & talked "shop" for a long time.' Churchill immediately seized on the gravest problem facing the French and quizzed General Georges on what preparations had been made to deal with the obvious weak point of the Maginot Line – the sector where it ended near Montmédy, a town on the German border north-east of the River Meuse. (Thereafter the French border was guarded only by scattered field defences for some two hundred miles to the English Channel at Dunkirk.)

In Churchill's view France was at risk from another German offensive via the Ardennes much like the one that had been so successful in the First World War. Although he also thought that the Germans might violate Swiss neutrality and invade Alsace via Basel, his primary focus was on the Ardennes and the German threat in the enormous heavily forested area where aerial reconnaissance could not detect troop and vehicular movements. The answers Churchill received from Georges were not reassuring. Churchill's mouth pursed, 'his face had ceased smiling, and the shake of his head was ominous when he observed that he hoped the field works were strong, that it would be very unwise to think the Ardennes was impassable to strong forces . . . "Remember," he said, "that we are faced with a new weapon, armour in great strength, on which the Germans are no doubt concentrating, and that the forests will be particularly tempting to such forces since they will offer conceal-ment from the air."' Churchill was also disturbed to discover that the French and the Belgians had no mutual assistance arrangements in the event of a German attack.

In his war memoirs he recalled an old joke that the British always seemed to be preparing to refight the last war but he applied it to the French army as well. 'I knew that the carnage of the previous war had bitten deeply into the soul of the French people. The Germans had been given time to build the Siegfried Line.' He wanted to believe that France's present defences would hold back a German attack, but in his heart he also recognized that its generals were likely to be defensive-minded, particularly when faced with new offensive weapons developed since the Great War. 'The only conclusion to be drawn from these hard experiences was that the defensive was master.'

Churchill's qualms were in fact an articulation of what the French generals either conveniently ignored or simply failed to see: that the Maginot Line would have served a useful purpose in earlier wars but was now an outdated vestige of past siege warfare that the Germans had no intention of attacking. Instead it was merely an obstacle to be circumvented, particularly since its left flank was anchored along the borders of neutral Luxembourg and Belgium. In later discussions Churchill emphasized that parachute operations opened up a whole new set of problems for a defender, and that attacks under the cover of fog (even artificial fog) were also possible.

After spending the night at the plush Ritz Hotel, Churchill and Spears boarded a special train put at their disposal and were sped to eastern France to begin an extensive and physically gruelling tour of the Maginot Line. They may have been the only foreigners actually permitted to see the inside of its recently completed underground sectors, which included its own railway system.

General Georges admitted that he was worried that the Maginot Line lacked depth and required greater fieldworks and powerful reserves to reinforce it. What no one in the French high command was able to grasp fully was that the Maginot Line also instilled a false sense of security. During a discussion of British tank production, Spears recalled a conversation many years before between Churchill and some French officers. 'I remembered how in 1915 I had heard this same Winston developing his theory of "land cruisers" to a French general and his staff on the Vimy Ridge, and how heartily they had laughed after he had gone, at this absurd idea. "Your politicians are even funnier than ours," they had exclaimed.'

On the banks of the Rhine, at Strasbourg, they peered across the river into Germany, where a large sign proclaimed: 'Ein Volk, ein Reich, ein Führer.' Spears and Churchill discussed the military importance of the bridges linking the two nations. When war came Spears thought it would be possible to float mines down the river that could lash themselves around the bridge abutments and blow them up, while Churchill was not convinced but envisaged employing mini-submarines to achieve the same result. Later the idea became one of his pet projects.

Another observation that Spears made during the trip was how physically active Churchill was for a man of sixty-five, and how seemingly inexhaustible was his energy. 'I would watch him eat a chicken for breakfast . . . while he talked, clarifying his ideas by expounding them, or else considering the problems Georges had enunciated, examining them one by one with concentrated intensity that was not only amazing but awe-inspiring.'

Afterwards Winston joined Clementine and their sixteen-year-old daughter Mary for a short holiday at a château near Dreux that belonged to his cousin Sunny's former wife, Consuelo Vanderbilt. Before joining his family, Churchill wrote out his thoughts and observations and had them dispatched by courier the following day to the War Office. Once the snows fell in the Alps, the time would be ripe for Hitler to attack Poland, he wrote. 'During the first fortnight of September, *or even earlier*, these conditions would be established. There would still be time for Hitler to strike heavily at Poland before the mud period of late October or early November would hamper a German offensive there.'

It was not much of a holiday. 'Appreciation of those halcyon summer days was heightened by our consciousness that the sands of peace were fast running out,' recalled Mary. Even the usual relaxation that came from painting was missing this time. Her father's mood was increasingly gloomy. 'One could feel the deep apprehension brooding over all, and even the light of this lovely valley at the confluence of the Eure and the Vesgre seemed robbed of its genial ray. I found painting hard work in this uncertainty,' Churchill wrote. His warnings horrified another of the English guests, who reacted to Churchill's assessment of what lay ahead for France by later loudly remarking, 'Don't listen to him. He is a warmonger.'

Winston cut short his holiday to return to Chartwell, leaving Clementine and Mary behind. On his way through Paris he again met with General Georges, who presented a full assessment of the military picture of both the French and the German armies. The Frenchman told Churchill that although France would never attack Germany first, its armies were quite prepared to defend against aggression. 'If they attack, both our countries will rally to their duty,' he said, words that for the time being reassured his visitor.

On 27 August Churchill summoned Ironside and Spears to Chartwell for discussions. He articulated virtually the same arguments he had made in 1914 – that Britain must have 'a great Army in France' and must mobilize twenty divisions by Christmas – only to be told by Ironside that no such plans existed. Afterwards Ironside scribbled a note to his wife: 'I spent a night with Winston. It was like being in a madhouse. Everybody came down to see him and the telephone never ceased . . . He was like a lion in a cage . . . He has not been asked to come into the government, but the mass of M.P.s are clamouring for it and to kick out Chamberlain if he does not accept him.'

Despite the false hopes generated by Churchill's last meeting with General Georges, his recent inspection of France's defences, particularly what he observed along the Rhine, 'tore to shreds any illusion that it was not Germany's intention to wage war and to wage it soon. There was no mistaking the grim, relentless and barely concealed preparations she was making,' recalled Spears.

Three weeks after Churchill's 'Hush' broadcast, the opening shots of the Second World War were fired when, on Friday, 1 September 1939, Germany began the 'liberation' of neighbouring Poland after trumping up allegations about a Polish incursion into Upper Silesia to seize a German radio station and broadcast a call for the Poles to go to war.

The Nazi juggernaut launched against the Poles in September was far from the mighty military machine it later became. Germany's military growth was still very much in transition, and in 1939 it was ill equipped for all-out war. German industrial and military production still operated on a peacetime footing. As Matthew Cooper points out in his landmark study of the German army, 'The reasons for the German Army's initial victories lay not so much within itself, but in the weakness of its enemies. Perhaps never before in history had the countries of Europe been so ill-prepared for war.' While the Poles fought valiant but ultimately futile battles, the West sat on its hands. The only war the Allies won in 1939 was 'the war of excuses'.

In 1939 and 1940, horses remained a major source of transport. There were shortages of vehicles and guns, and actual panzer production lagged far behind what the West believed to be the case. The illusion of a powerful, modern and well-equipped German military force was fostered by the invasion of Poland and the coining of the term 'blitz-krieg'. Although blitzkrieg was first mentioned in a German military publication in 1935, its first use in the English language occurred in a 25 September 1939 cover story in *Time* magazine.

For this was no war of occupation but one of quick penetration and obliteration – blitzkrieg, or lightning war. Even with no opposition, armies had never moved so fast before. Theorists had always said that only infantry could take and hold positions. But these armies had not waited for the infantry. Swift columns of tanks and armoured trucks had plunged through Poland heralded by bombs raining from the sky.

The term stuck, as Cooper explains: 'Its future was assured, and blitzkrieg quickly evolved from a purely descriptive term into a whole new theory of strategy and tactics, a concept which, ever since, has pervaded all thought and writing on the Second World War.' None of this spared Poland. Cavalry was simply no match for panzers and dive-bombers, and within three weeks Poland had become the latest German vassal state. Hitler went to Warsaw after its surrender on 27 September and declared: 'This is how I can deal with any European city.' It hardly mattered that between them Britain and France had larger military forces at their disposal than the German army of 1939. Of greater significance was that German success had everything to do with the inability of both France and Britain to put teeth into their pledges of mutual security and support.

There was no better example of Britain's unpreparedness for war than its ignorance of the German invasion of Poland on 1 September. Neither the chief of the Imperial General Staff, Lord Gort, nor his War Office staff was even aware of the attack until shortly after 10.00 a.m., when Churchill telephoned Ironside to report that Poland had been invaded. That Churchill knew before Britain's high command was hardly surprising given his extensive network of contacts and friendships.

At 8.30 a.m. Count Edward Raczynski, the Polish ambassador, had telephoned Churchill with the news of the 4.00 a.m. invasion by fifty-six German divisions. Raczynski mistrusted the British government, and his worst fears were realized when for more than forty-eight hours there was no public declaration of either support or war as Chamberlain futilely sought a diplomatic solution. The one person Raczynski trusted was Churchill, hence his decision to alert him that morning.

Although Churchill and Chamberlain were philosophically light-years apart over Nazi Germany, the prime minister had no trouble recognizing that at this time of national crisis he needed his adversary's experience. He had stubbornly resisted calls within his own government that it was time to bring Churchill back into the cabinet. 'If Winston got into the

Government it would not be long before we were at war,' he wrote to his sister in July 1939. In fact, the calls for Churchill's return extended to Germany itself. Count Lutz Schwerin von Krosigk, the German finance minister, had secretly implored a British general on a visit to Berlin to 'take Winston Churchill into the Cabinet'. The visitor had relayed the count's message to the British military attaché, who passed the exchange on to the Foreign Office: 'Churchill is the only Englishman Hitler is afraid of. He does not take the PM or Halifax seriously, but he places Churchill in the same category as Roosevelt. The mere fact of giving him a leading Ministerial post would convince Hitler that we really mean to stand up to him.'

The years of exile were about to end. With Britain again at war, Chamberlain could no longer afford to ignore Churchill. At noon on 1 September the prime minister telephoned him at Chartwell to advise that Parliament, which had been in recess since early August, would assemble at 6.00 p.m., and would he kindly meet with him beforehand at No. 10 Downing Street.

When the two men met later that afternoon, Chamberlain, after making it clear that war was inevitable, asked Churchill to join a small, six-man war cabinet he was forming. Among its other members were to be Anthony Eden and Churchill's old friend Archie Sinclair. Although Duff Cooper believed Churchill should refuse to serve in Chamberlain's government, he accepted at once, believing it was his duty. Chamberlain's invitation to rejoin the government in a capacity yet to be articulated heartened Churchill. Later he recalled sitting in the Commons, 'fearless at the call of honour'.

Both Chamberlain and Foreign Secretary Lord Halifax made emollient statements in the Commons and House of Lords that implied forgiveness if Hitler would withdraw German troops from Poland. This brought howls of outrage: the mood of Parliament was for war. When the Labour Party's deputy leader Arthur Greenwood spoke for the Opposition, the rebel Tory MP Leo Amery shouted, 'Speak for England, Arthur!' and was loudly cheered. Chamberlain feared his government could fall at once. Duff Cooper was now, along with Churchill and the other backbench Tory rebels, among Chamberlain's sternest critics. He believed that Chamberlain's actions had cost him the support of the Conservative Party, and that Churchill could easily have brought down his government by failing to support him – and that he would then have been picked to succeed the embattled prime minister. Churchill, however, had already agreed to serve under Chamberlain, and was obliged to support him. Except for the timing, Duff Cooper's assessment was accurate; Chamberlain would cling to office until May 1940.

The two days between the German invasion of Poland and the British declaration of war on 3 September were trying ones for Churchill, who, pledged to secrecy by Chamberlain, remained at home in London awaiting the prime minister's summons and visibly chafing at the delay. His London flat became a gathering place for Bracken, Boothby, Eden. Duff Cooper. Cooper noted: 'We were all in a state of bewildered rage.' Helpless to influence events, Churchill was reduced to writing to Chamberlain to complain about the delay in his appointment and asserting 'that injury had been done to the spirit of national unity by the apparent weakening of our resolve.'

Despite brilliant sunshine Sunday, 3 September 1939 was one of the bleakest days in British history, a day when, for the second time in twenty-five years, Britain found itself at war with Germany. Chamberlain announced the news to the nation over the BBC at 11.15 a.m., as 'his sad, resigned, melancholy voice, so different from the solid vibrant strength his successor Churchill was to project, rang out throughout Britain'.

Shortly after noon in Berlin, the CBS correspondent William L. Shirer was one of 250 people gathered in front of the Reich Chancellery when nearby loudspeakers suddenly blared the news of Britain's declaration of war on Germany. There was 'not a murmur' from the silent crowd. 'You could see it was still incomprehensible to them that Hitler had led them into a European war.'

Chamberlain's brief announcement was followed by the playing of the national anthem, in the midst of which Britons heard the wail of sirens, which sent them scurrying into air-raid shelters. Ensconced in his nearby flat, Churchill reluctantly agreed to descend into a shelter, but took his time. 'You have to hand it to Hitler,' he said. 'The war is less than half an hour old and already he has bombers over London.' As he reluctantly entered the shelter 'armed with a bottle of brandy and other appropriate medical comforts', he grumbled that the shelter had no telephone or wireless, and his secretaries were directed to ensure that during future air raids there would be ice, soda and whisky for him and 'sherry for the ladies'. Although the air-raid warning turned out to be a false alarm, there would be many actual raids when the Blitz began in a few months.

The mood of the country that September was a combination of dread and resignation. The novelist Margery Allingham wrote to an American friend: 'There was no bravura, no sudden quickening of the blood, no secret feeling of exultation . . . *Land of Hope and Glory* sung with feeling made one feel slightly sick. We seemed to me to be going to war as a duty, a people elderly in soul going in stolidly, to kill or be killed.' After Chamberlain's announcement there was 'only this breathless feeling of mingled relief and intolerable grief'.

During the first days of the war the sun shone gloriously 'with unremitting splendour', wrote John 'Jock' Colville, a twenty-four-year-old third secretary in the Diplomatic Service. He began keeping what would turn out to be one of the war's most important and illuminating diaries. There was 'nothing about the gaily dressed, smiling crowds in the streets to remind us of this great catastrophe – except perhaps for the gas masks slung across their backs and the number of men in uniform'.

When the Commons met at noon on 3 September, just after the all-clear had sounded, the mood was sombre. Though still for the time being a mere backbencher, Churchill was called upon to speak immediately after Chamberlain and a Labour member. In a voice tinged with defiance and resolve, he delivered one of the briefest orations of his parliamentary career. 'We are fighting to save the whole world from the pestilence of Nazi tyranny and in defence of all that is most sacred to man,' he declared. 'This is no war of domination or imperial aggrandizement or material gain; no war to shut any country out of its sunlight and means of progress. It is a war viewed in its inherent quality to establish, on impregnable rocks, the rights of the individual, and it is a war to establish and revive the stature of man.'

His own destiny was something Churchill firmly believed in. 'He believed in his own Star though at times it was terribly obscured,' said Shane Leslie. 'Church-going meant nothing to him but God – yes – provided God would see him through . . . He made mistakes in working out his Destiny. He believed he was destined to take Constantinople by the expedition to the Dardanelles but he was thwarted by Fisher and Kitchener. In the Second World War he took care to have no thwarters. Some months before it broke I found him in prophetic gloom. He could only say, "I know now that it will come to me to deal with Mister Hitler."'

29

'Winston is Back'

*Once again defence of the rights of a weak state, outraged and invaded by
unprovoked aggression, forced us to draw the sword . . . So be it.*
                                                        – The Gathering Storm

When Churchill arrived at No. 10 Downing Street on the afternoon of
3 September, Chamberlain offered him his old post as first lord of the
Admiralty. He accepted at once. At a brief meeting of the new War
Cabinet, Churchill won his first political skirmish when there was a
clash over who would become the new chief of the Imperial General
Staff (CIGS), replacing Field Marshal Lord Gort, who would shortly be
given command of a British Expeditionary Force being sent to France.
Ironside was the War Office candidate, although others in the War
Cabinet preferred Lieutenant General Sir John Dill, an officer considered
better suited to the post. Churchill threw his support behind Ironside,
whose tenure as CIGS would turn out to be brief and less than successful.

Edward Spears was not alone in believing that 'Winston had been
given a Department so that he would be too busy to make a nuisance of
himself . . . Well informed friends told me that I was right . . . Had
he not had his hands full he would have been running the war, and
overshadowing the Prime Minister in a matter of days.'

Churchill's appointment was not universally welcomed. Within the
government and on the backbenches the old-guard Tories viewed him
as an unprincipled scoundrel who had twice deserted his party, and
whose ambition overshadowed his judgment. Some, such as Lord
Erskine, perceived Churchill's criticism of Munich as warmongering by
an overbearing 'self-seeker'. Others pointed to his support for Edward
VIII at the time of his abdication in 1936. That he had, for the most
part, been right in his warnings about the rise of the dictators was

conveniently overlooked. They were put off by his strange mannerisms, by the belief that he drank too much and by the fact that he clearly talked too much, was a fierce opponent when crossed and was a rather ungainly, portly figure whose habitual props were hat, cane and the ever present unlit cigar.

At 6.00 that evening he went directly to his motor car parked outside to inform an anxious Clementine, who had been concerned that Chamberlain would offer her husband 'a silly little job'. With a smile on his face he quickly allayed her anxiety: 'It's the Admiralty. That's a lot better than I thought.' He then strolled the short distance across Horse Guards Parade to the Admiralty, which was already primed for war, surrounded by concertina wire and guarded by armed sentries. A young friend accompanying him exclaimed, 'Great God! What's *that* for?' 'That's to keep me out,' said Churchill.

Met at a concealed side entrance by his secretary, Kathleen Hill, and the officer soon to become his principal naval aide, Captain (later Admiral) Guy Grantham, Churchill charged into his former office like an exploding rocket. His first act upon returning to the scene of so much triumph and tragedy a quarter of a century earlier was to fling open a hidden panel in the wall. Inside was the map he had used every day during his previous tenure. 'The ships', recalled Mrs Hill, 'were still there,' as if frozen in time from when he had last seen them in May 1915.

Churchill's bittersweet return to his old haunt brought back powerful memories that included seemingly never-ending images of the Dardanelles, which remained as fresh in his mind as they had been twenty-five years earlier. 'So it was that I came again to the room I had quitted in pain and sorrow almost exactly a quarter of a century before, when Lord Fisher's resignation had led to my removal from my post as First Lord and ruined irretrievably, as it proved, the important conception of forcing the Dardanelles.'

Not only did Churchill again occupy the same office, but he also inherited problems of equal gravity as the grim shadow of the war ahead lingered over Britain and Europe. So little had changed, in fact, that he felt as if he had never left the Admiralty. 'It was a strange experience, like suddenly resuming a previous incarnation.'

His return also brought a renewed sense of urgency to the hidebound Admiralty, where, except for an entirely new generation of officers, little had changed in the years since he had presided over the reluctant admirals who manned its desks. 'When Winston was at the Admiralty,' Kathleen Hill later related, 'the place was buzzing with atmosphere, with electricity. When he was away on tour it was dead, dead, dead.'

Shortly after his arrival that evening Churchill was introduced to the current first sea lord, Admiral Sir Dudley Pound, a veteran sailor with whom Churchill would develop an excellent working relationship. One of the least-known major military figures of the Second World War, Pound had commanded a battleship at Jutland and had steadily risen through the inter-war years to become C in C Mediterranean in 1936. He never sought publicity or acclaim and was no doubt surprised to find his photograph on the cover of *Time* in April 1940, one of the few times his name came to the fore prior to his untimely death in 1943. Indeed Pound was so self-effacing that his only biographer has noted: 'His name rarely, if ever, features in the popular histories of the war. He did not have the personal appeal of a Beatty, nor had he commanded in a successful battle as both Jellicoe and Cunningham had done. Yet for more than four years this was the man who had held the reins of power in the Admiralty and had been responsible for supreme direction of the Battle of the Atlantic.'

The admirals of the Royal Navy certainly had good reason to be wary of Winston Churchill, whose reputation for meddling in operational matters was well known from his earlier tenure as first lord. Pound had been the object of Churchill's criticism earlier that year for the manner in which he had disposed the Mediterranean fleet after Mussolini's invasion of Albania in April. Although the admirals understood that they had inherited a tough taskmaster, they welcomed Churchill, the man who had been the lonely voice of rearmament in a sea of appeasers. Grantham remembered: 'It made our day, a great relief to everyone. The news shot round the fleet, everyone was cock-a-hoop.' A naval intelligence officer said, 'A doer was going to take over. I think the top brass knew Churchill was going to get them hard at it, and they said, "Well, never mind – it's a good thing."'

Even though Pound had every reason to mistrust his new first lord, this time around there would be no repeat of the disastrous Churchill–Fisher relationship, which still haunted Churchill. Pound was not inclined to be confrontational, believing that it was counter-productive and only made Churchill more obstinate. This, however, is not to imply that Pound was not his own man. As Arthur Marder has written of him, 'Pound feared neither God, man, nor Winston Churchill.' He coped with Churchill about as well as anyone during the Second World War, picking his battles with the first lord but otherwise keeping his own counsel, and wisely refraining from reacting to the harassment or constant nagging that characterized Churchill's leadership.

His previous sour relationships with the various first sea lords and the navy staff during his first tenure were still fresh in Churchill's mind, and in 1939 he was more conscious of the need to make them work better. Still, old habits die hard, and having once called them 'the machinery of negation', he retained a mistrust of the naval planners. Yet his trust of Pound enabled the two men to work together much more effectively than before.

Of his new counterpart, whom he had known previously as a junior member of Fisher's staff, Churchill wrote: 'We eyed each other amicably if doubtfully. But from the earliest days our friendship and mutual confidence grew and ripened. I measured and respected the great professional and personal qualities of Admiral Pound.' Sir Geoffrey Shakespeare, the Admiralty's parliamentary and financial secretary, later recalled Churchill saying to him after that first meeting, 'I like that old man. I can work with him. But why I call him an old man I don't know, because he is younger than I am.' Churchill once said that Pound was one of only three men whom he believed had a like mind; the others were two of the three Bs (Beaverbrook and Bracken) and Field Marshal Jan Smuts, the premier of South Africa. After Pound's death Churchill had a far less rewarding relationship with his successor, Admiral Sir Andrew Browne Cunningham ('ABC'), and was occasionally heard to lament: 'I wish Pound were here.'

Pound introduced Churchill to the other sea lords, and together they held the first, emotional meeting at which he took the chair reserved for the first lord in the Admiralty Board Room. Admiral of the Fleet Lord Fraser (then the third sea lord) recalled him remarking 'what a privilege and honour it was to be again in that chair, that there were many difficulties ahead but together we would overcome them'. Churchill's demeanour was very similar to that of his first meeting with the officers of the 6th Royal Scots Fusiliers in 1916: 'He surveyed critically each one of us in turn and then, adding that he would see us all personally later on, he adjourned the meeting, "Gentlemen, to your tasks and duties."'

The major difference between his two spells as first lord of the Admiralty was that anyone else in a similar situation who had been badly burned by earlier decisions gone wrong might have taken the safe way out and acted with undue conservatism. This was not Churchill's way, and never would be. The gambler and the warrior in him prevailed over the politician protecting his reputation. As first lord in 1939 and 1940 he would hold nothing back in his quest to fight Hitler on the seas. To mark his arrival the Admiralty signalled to the fleet the now famous words: 'Winston is back.'

Before the night was over Churchill was already sending out memos demanding immediate, detailed answers to questions on a variety of subjects ranging from the status of the German U-boat force to the number of rifles the navy possessed. It took only a short time before his memos were christened 'daily prayers', after his often used phrase 'Pray let me have'. Thus were born what became the famous 'Action This Day' minutes that blasted forth from Churchill's desk for the remainder of the war, with comments and demands scribbled in red ink, most requiring a burning of midnight oil in order to comply with a specific command for information. Woe to the individual who sent an incomplete reply – those who did so were soon obliged to find other employment. A red label (later a red stamp) was affixed to these documents, and the recipient was required to give them priority attention. A typical example was a memo he sent to Admiral Fraser, prodding the third sea lord about fitting additional armour plating to certain vessels. The admiral's answer drew the rebuke 'This reply is incomplete.' Why, Churchill demanded, had it taken fifty-three days after war was declared for work to begin on three destroyers, and why hadn't the decision to do so been taken within the first ten days of the war? Excuses, the staff quickly learned, were unacceptable.

Sir Geoffrey Shakespeare's desk would be piled with action memos each morning when he reported for work: 'Most members of the [Admiralty] Board found their desks resembling a flower-bed of pink tulips. Below the pink tabs were written incisive instructions in red ink or sometimes in typescript: "You will report to me by midnight." . . . "I shall require a report every day (or every week)." In the end there were so many "Action This Day" tabs that each lost its special priority.'

An important figure Churchill brought to the Admiralty was Frederick

Lindemann, his confidant and scientific adviser, a man distrusted by some in Whitehall and within the scientific community for his perceived Rasputin-like influence on the first lord. Lindemann gave far more than scientific advice. Churchill called on him to discuss a full range of issues, from economics to various aspects of warfare. His advice, while often innovative and useful, was also sometimes inane nonsense. By virtue of his unlimited access to Churchill, he became one of the most powerful, feared and detested figures in his wartime circle.

With the Prof always in the background to advise him, Churchill wrote a great many wartime minutes dealing with technical matters of which he seemed to have acquired some knowledge or which he believed to be of military value: 'Anything unusual or odd or dramatic intrigued him: Q ships [armed merchant ships used to decoy U-boats into surfacing in order to attack and sink them], dummy ships . . . deception, sabotage, and, no doubt influenced by Professor Lindemann, the application of novel scientific methods.' Some of Churchill's minutes were truly offbeat, but they remained a reflection of his complete involvement in Admiralty affairs. Nothing escaped his attention. Shortly after returning to office he minuted Shakespeare, 'I am concerned about the shortage of fish,' adding that Shakespeare was to determine at once if the Mine Sweeping Division could release any trawlers for fishing purposes. 'We must have a policy of "utmost fish",' he wrote. Representatives of the Admiralty, trade unions, the Ministry of Agriculture and the trawler owners met at once to form the Fishing Promotion Council. 'So a policy of "utmost fish" was fostered by the Admiralty in wartime.' On another occasion Churchill demanded to know the ice conditions at Luleå, a key port in northern Sweden that the Germans were using to ship nearly a million pounds of iron ore through the Gulf of Bothnia to Germany. 'It is very unsatisfactory that we do not know the daily ice conditions at this significant port,' he complained.

Probing questions were asked and no matter was deemed too insignificant: how fast did convoys of merchant ships travel? How were convoys organized and protected? And the most often repeated query of all: why weren't tasks he directed to be carried out accomplished in a more timely manner? No matter what the replies or justifications for delay put forth by his staff, Churchill was rarely satisfied. He also saw things that others missed. While on one of his visits to the primary naval base of the Home Fleet at Scapa Flow, Churchill noticed that the flagship had no telephone connection to shore and ordered that telephone buoys be placed in each port used by the fleet. He also instituted badly needed welfare reforms in what was one of Britain's most desolate military outposts.

On only his third day in office Churchill was already aware that aerial photography by the enemy could establish the location of all Britain's warships. He proposed to Pound the employment of dummy ships, with deck plans that replicated those of real vessels, in order to mislead the enemy into attacking them 'while the real ships are doing their work elsewhere'. Pound agreed, and although only three dummy warships were put into service, and they ultimately proved of little value, the idea was a precursor to the great Fortitude plan of 1944, when dummy vehicles and tanks were created to mislead the Germans into believing that General George S. Patton had an entire army group based in East Anglia to lead Allied amphibious landings in the Pas de Calais instead of the real invasion site, Normandy.

Another of Churchill's mandates was to the director of naval intelligence. 'It is of the highest importance', he wrote on 5 September, 'that the Admiralty [intelligence] bulletin should maintain its reputation for truthfulness, and the tone should not be forced.' Unlike Hitler and Stalin, Churchill insisted on being informed of everything that took place regardless of whether the information was positive or negative.

There was, however, an occasion when the truth conflicted with one of Churchill's convictions. Although he invariably respected anyone who stood up to him and could defend his position, in the matter of the U-boat war he was intransigent. In November 1939 and again in January 1940, he publicly made wildly exaggerated claims about U-boat losses. The Royal Navy, he said, had sunk one-half of the U-boat fleet, a claim firmly and repeatedly disputed by a senior naval intelligence officer who pointed out that the true number was a mere six of fifty-seven German submarines then in service. Challenging Churchill once too often cost Captain (later Vice Admiral) Arthur G. Talbot his job. In April 1940 his refusal to inflate German losses led to his relief several months later at ten minutes' notice. Churchill's motivation for such exaggerations may have come from Lindemann, and undoubtedly stemmed from what he deemed the need to uphold British morale at a time when there was little positive news to report on the war except actions by the Royal Navy.

Although he was no longer the young man who had taken the Admiralty by storm in 1911 – he now walked with a noticeable stoop and had lost a great deal of his hair – Churchill was the same whirlwind of activity he had always been. Too old to play soldier but never willing to surrender his desire to fight, he relished anything that involved him in the war in even the smallest way. One such occasion was in February 1940, as Churchill and Chamberlain were returning from Paris, crossing the Channel in a Royal Navy destroyer. To Chamberlain's chagrin, Churchill, dressed in a navy duffel coat, with a steel helmet on his head and a cigar clamped in his teeth, ordered the Admiralty flag hoisted and left no doubt who was in charge during this voyage. An eyewitness recalls that 'Mr Chamberlain looked decidedly put out, no doubt regarding himself as No. 1 ashore *or* afloat . . . During the crossing a floating mine was sighted. Instantly Winston ordered it destroyed, and it was duly potted by a rifle and exploded with a huge bang. Winston was overjoyed, and no doubt he felt he was really in the war.'

Churchill never thought of himself as merely an administrator, and his imprint on the Admiralty would be one of dominance and involvement in every single aspect of naval affairs. As he had in the First World War, he also made it his business to learn what the army and air force were doing.

Sir Geoffrey Shakespeare thought he was 'superbly equipped by temperament' for war, and that he loved 'the excitements and tense situations which war always brings in its train. "What a dull war this will be," he said to me once with a spark of prophetic intuition. "We have only Germany to fight. Now if we fought Germany, Italy and Japan together, that would be much more interesting."'

Neville Chamberlain soon learned what it meant to have a dynamo like Churchill as one of his ministers. To his growing exasperation a daily flood of letters and minutes filled with suggestions and imperatives descended upon his desk, until the prime minister finally persuaded his first lord to cease sending him correspondence on matters they invariably discussed in person. Privately Chamberlain complained to his sister about how Churchill's late-night work habits had his staff 'dropping with fatigue and Service Ministers worn out in arguing with him. I say to myself this [is] just the price we have to pay for the asset we have in his personality and popularity, but I do wish we could have the latter without the former.'

During one of his visits to Scapa Flow, Churchill astutely observed what no one else had discerned, namely that the dummy ships placed in the anchorage would not fool a German pilot because there were no seagulls hovering around them. 'You will always find gulls above a living ship. But not around a dummy.' He ordered that refuse be dumped in the water around the clock. 'Feed the gulls and fool the Germans,' he demanded.

Perhaps no one else in the government understood the importance of maintaining a state of high morale among the British people. Britain was only in the first days of what Churchill grasped would be a long, hard war. It was essential that spirits be maintained during the dark days ahead. To the Duke of Windsor (the former Edward VIII, in exile on the French Riviera) he wrote: 'We are plunged in a long and grievous struggle. But all will come right if we all work together to the end.' The words 'all will come right' became Churchill's rallying cry. Their origin dated to his experience in the Boer War, when the president of the Orange Free State had frequently uttered the same words to rally the Boer populace. Churchill adopted them as his personal maxim and regularly repeated them throughout the war.

The first eight months of the Second World War have misleadingly been dubbed the 'Phoney War', what Churchill more accurately called the 'Twilight War'. After Poland had come under the grinding heel of German occupation an eerie calm fell over Europe as the armies of Britain and France prepared to face the inevitable invasion of the West. However, there was nothing phoney about the deadly war being waged at sea. Before the end of Churchill's first day in office a U-boat torpedoed and sank the liner *Athenia* in the Atlantic off the Irish coast, in what resembled the sinking of the *Lusitania* in 1915. The *Athenia* incident convinced Churchill and the Admiralty that Hitler intended to wage unrestricted undersea warfare.

As first lord, Churchill had an enormous responsibility for Britain's naval defences. The island nation's economic survival depended on importing goods – fifty-five million tons in 1939 alone. The need for war matériel also burgeoned dramatically, and the world's largest merchant fleet, of more than four thousand vessels, had to be protected. It fell to the Royal Navy to guard not only Britain's entire coastline but also its many seaports and the numerous waterways leading to them.

And while Churchill delved deeply into every aspect of naval operations, administration and training, in operational matters and naval strategy he invariably deferred to his advisers as long as their suggestions were intelligently argued. Old habits, however, die hard, and some never die at all. To Churchill losing an argument was a clarion call to action. The director of naval intelligence, Admiral John Henry Godfrey, was often on the receiving end of theatrics. 'His battery of weapons included persuasion, real or simulated anger, mockery, vituperation, tantrums, ridicule, derision, abuse and tears, which he would aim at anyone who opposed him or expressed a view contrary to the one he had already formed, sometimes on quite trivial questions.'

On technical matters Churchill had no qualms about imposing his will. The Prof and his scientific gnomes devised what was called a naval war barrage, an anti-aircraft device consisting of two-pound bombs attached to parachutes and fired from multiple launchers aboard ships. The idea behind this device was that it would be fired into the air to about four thousand feet when low-flying enemy aircraft were spotted, forming a screen as they drifted down. A plane flying into one of the bombs would set them off. A number of the large, cumbersome launchers were eventually installed ashore and on larger warships, but none ever worked. Everyone but Lindemann and Churchill labelled the idea 'plumb crazy'. One admiral chalked up this futile exercise as 'just part of the price' Britain had to pay 'to keep Winston going'.

As it had in the Great War, the submarine posed the most significant threat to British shipping. While the German surface fleet was an ever dangerous foe, and its ships including the behemoth battleship *Bismarck* were capable of sinking any British warship with their big guns, to defend against and ultimately neutralize and defeat the menace of the U-boat proved to be the gravest challenge facing the Royal Navy in the Second World War. And, as one of the most important means of defeating Germany, Churchill gave it the highest priority.

Churchill's work habits remained the same, and the Admiralty staff learned to expect demands late at night and into the early-morning hours, including the traditional Christmas and New Year's holidays, when he worked long hours at his desk and demanded that his staff do the same. He attributed his ability to cram a day and a half into a single day to his practice of napping 'like a child' in the afternoon for an hour of deep, untroubled sleep – in the nude, a prerequisite he said. The key to a successful day was a combination of his nap and proper eating. 'If you want to work hard, you must eat hard,' he once told his literary aide. Like so many others Pound altered his routine to conform to Churchill's demands, and he too napped in order to keep pace with his energetic new boss, who was often found working as late as 2.00 or 3.00 a.m., by which time his exhausted aides were hinting without success that he ought to bring his workday to a close.

Commencing at 9.00 most evenings, Churchill met with the Admiralty brass until 11.00, when he began dictating speeches, pacing back and forth in bedroom slippers, his arms behind him and a cigar protruding from his mouth, clouds of smoke filling the room. An ever present secretary was required to type as fast as he spoke. The only reprieve came as he read over the pages, occasionally sipping from a glass of whisky.

Rather than go to bed he would often insist on visiting the war room, where he would examine the flags marking the location of every Royal Navy warship throughout the world. One morning at about three o'clock, Churchill demanded of the war room duty officer: 'Where is the Oil?' The perplexed officer, confused by the way Churchill tended to slur his words, replied, 'What oil, sir?' By now thoroughly irritated, Churchill ordered the hapless officer: 'Wake up, I want the Oil [Earl] of Cork and Orrery,' recalled Shakespeare. 'We were dropping with fatigue,' but Churchill insisted on speaking with Admiral of the Fleet William Henry Boyle, the Earl of Cork, a retired admiral (cut from the same energetic cloth as Roger Keyes) and a former commander in chief of the Home Fleet. Throughout the long years of the Second World War, similar scenes would be repeated over and over again. While Churchill thrived on such ungodly hours, those who served him yearned for sleep and hoped, usually in vain, that he would tire and take to his bed. Despite the ordeal of working for him, however, those who served him mostly admired him. One of his civil servants was typical: 'I fell under the spell of this man; totally concentrated, supremely courageous.'

The thrill of being back at the Admiralty was soon tempered when Churchill found that little had changed within the Royal Navy since 1915. Problems abounded, particularly at Scapa Flow.

Inspecting the fleet on 15–16 September 1939 he was astonished to find the same deficiency he had noted twenty-five years earlier: the anchorage lacked anti-submarine booms to protect its four entrances from penetration by U-boats. He was also irate and disgusted that Scapa Flow still lacked adequate anti-aircraft guns (as did almost every coastal city in Britain) and was virtually defenceless against aerial attack. 'Over and over again, all through the years with Winston Churchill,' recalled his bodyguard, 'he has turned his head over towards me, looked up and growled: "If they had only taken the warning when they got it!" '

Despite the misplaced assurance by the Home Fleet commander in chief that the anchorage was safe, a month later its vulnerability was proved when Captain Günther Prien's U-47 managed to penetrate Scapa Flow on the night of 13–14 October and sink the battleship HMS *Royal Oak* with a loss of 833 lives. When Churchill was given the news 'tears sprang to his eyes', recalled his assistant private secretary, 'and he muttered, "Poor fellows, poor fellows, trapped in those black depths." ' Shortly afterwards he returned to Scapa Flow and 'wept over the wreckage'.

30

Warlord in Waiting

He is the only man in the country who commands anything like universal respect.
– Sir John Colville, October 1939

In two world wars Churchill never lost his appetite for the attack, disdaining defence as an occasional necessary evil. When he became first lord of the Admiralty for the second time, his military philosophy had matured in many ways, but in others it had scarcely changed in the years since he had first held the office. His background and experience of war were vastly improved from those of the man who had dared to try to force the Dardanelles in 1915. In other respects, though, he was the same old Churchill, who had not tempered his offensive-minded military philosophy. One of Pound's primary functions – like that of others who served under Churchill during the Second World War – was to curb his appetite for impossible or inappropriate military ventures, a task he fulfilled with his usual quiet but firm manner. Pound became used to the first lord bounding into his office to announce, 'I've got an idea.'

In July 1939 Churchill was already reinventing his First World War notion of a Baltic strategy, telling Ironside during their discussions at Chartwell that he wanted to put a squadron of battleships in the Baltic: 'It would paralyse the Germans and immobilize many German divisions. The submarine had been dealt with and would no longer be a menace. The idea of British ships in the Baltic was revolutionary, and I was very surprised at how Winston was so navally minded. All his schemes came back to the use of the Navy. It ran through my head that here was a grand strategist imagining things, and the Navy itself making no plans whatever.'

Whether he was planning a major naval offensive or the invasion of an obscure and strategically irrelevant island in the Mediterranean or Aegean, inaction was a form of military heresy to Churchill. With Britain again at war with Germany, the Baltic was the place where the Royal Navy could go on the offensive, force its way into its waters and pose a threat to the naval ports along its northern coast, and to German naval operations against the Scandinavian nations.

The admirals were charged with producing a plan that was code-named Operation Catherine, after Catherine the Great because, said Churchill, 'Russia lay in the background of my thought.' On 12 September 1939, Churchill outlined to the Admiralty staff a series of requirements to enable the fleet to gain access to and operate in the Baltic. Winning control of it was 'the supreme naval offensive open to the Royal Navy'. Several battleships were to be transformed into heavily armoured vessels and the fleet was to be accompanied by oil tankers refitted to carry a three-month supply for refuelling. 'The isolation of Germany from Scandinavia would intercept the supplies of iron ore and food and all other trade.' The Germans, he declared, 'would not dare to send them on the trade routes, except as a measure of despair'. Churchill was not pleased with the staff's conclusion that it would take a minimum of six months to mount the operation. Action meant 'now', not six months later. But even as planning went forward, no decision was forthcoming to launch Catherine.

Churchill strongly believed that taking the naval war to Germany's backyard would force its raiders to return for defensive reasons and 'give us measureless relief. If we allow ourselves indefinitely to be confined to an absolute defensive by far weaker forces, we shall simply be worried and worn down ... I could never be responsible for a naval strategy which excluded the offensive principle and relegated us to keeping open the lines of communication.'

Any notion of pursuing such a strategy ended in mid-January 1940, when Churchill was obliged to accede to the concerns of his admirals. Conceptually operations in the Baltic had attractive possibilities; in practice they were logistically impossible in the long term, and, without air cover, potentially lethal.

Where Churchill was dead wrong was in his assertions that the submarine menace no longer existed and that the Royal Navy would therefore continue to rule the seas unrivalled. First postulated in 'A Memorandum on Sea-Power' that was conveyed to Chamberlain in

March 1939, his strategic plan for the employment of the Royal Navy also proved completely erroneous: he intended that the navy would take control of the Mediterranean within two months and believed that Japan would never run the risk of attacking Singapore. With the navy having achieved control of the Mediterranean and deterring Japan in the Pacific, the Baltic was there for its taking as 'the sole great offensive against Germany of British sea-power'.

Churchill's misconception of the U-boat threat was short lived once the war began. Events forced him to make an immediate about-turn, and he soon became deeply alarmed by the submarine menace, and only to a lesser extent by that of surface raiders, and the steps needed to defend against them, later admitting, 'The only thing that ever really frightened me during the war was the U-Boat peril.' The full extent of the threat became clear not only from the sinking of the *Royal Oak*. Upon his return from Scapa Flow, Churchill's train was met at London's Euston Station by a grave-faced Admiral Pound, who reported the sinking of the aircraft carrier *Courageous* in the Bristol Channel by a U-boat, with a loss of more than five hundred lives. These setbacks were the first of many that Churchill would deal with during the war. Three days earlier another tragedy was narrowly averted when the carrier HMS *Ark Royal* was attacked by a U-boat, and was saved only because the torpedoes missed. Although the carrier's escorts swiftly sank the submarine, the attack was clear evidence of the advent of a deadly new sea war.

Churchill's offence-mindedness also led to his refusal to accept the necessity of convoy protection by escorting warships – a system he regarded as too defensive and therefore dubious. He overrode recommendations by an Admiralty committee and a senior admiral that anti-submarine vessels could best protect convoys. Instead he endorsed sweeps for U-boats by fleets of hunter-killer warships that would seek out and destroy them before they could harm unarmed convoys. Such a force, he believed, would employ the Royal Navy's limited resources to the best advantage. He also thought convoys could run the submarine gauntlet by dispersing in individual or small numbers while the hunter-killers searched for U-boats. Although the threat early in the war was not yet extensive – only fifty-seven U-boats were in service, thirty of them at sea when the war began – these submarines soon became a deadly menace, often hunting in wolf packs and sinking hundreds of

British (and later American) merchant ships. This use of hunter-killers was the wrong approach, but it was not corrected until 1942. And while Churchill alone did not bear full responsibility, his relentless quest for action sparked a failed strategy.

In August 1939 Churchill sent for Walter H. Thompson, the retired Scotland Yard Special Branch detective sergeant who had guarded him at home and during his numerous travels overseas to places like Palestine, Iraq and Egypt from 1921 to 1936. They had ridden camels through the desert with Colonel T. E. Lawrence and the Imperial Camel Corps, and dined with Arab sheikhs. Thompson had helped Churchill build a swimming pool at Chartwell and, as his Man Friday, had done virtually everything except take dictation or type his letters. Although his return to Churchill's service was rather less than voluntary, the tersely worded telegram he received on 22 August 1939 left no room for dissent. Thompson was directed to meet him at an airfield near London upon his return from France, yet when Churchill alighted from his plane in full vigour, he merely said: 'Hello, Thompson, nice to see you. Put the baggage in your car and follow us.' Only after they reached Chartwell did Churchill exhibit the other side of his often brusque persona by putting his arm around Thompson in a welcome-back gesture. Thompson was soon formally recalled to duty by Scotland Yard and officially assigned to protect Churchill.

He remained with Churchill throughout the war. 'To be assigned to Churchill is a strain,' he said. 'He will move at a moment's notice. He will move without notice. He is an animal. In war he is particularly feral. Tensions increase around him. And they increase within the men assigned to protect him . . . I was under terrible tension.' Thompson sometimes wondered how women like Clementine and the other wives of famous people coped so well supporting men who worked ungodly hours and frequently upset the best-laid plans for meals and trips. 'Mrs Churchill never showed that she was troubled though circumstance and disappointment have slashed her a thousand times and more. The capacity of the British to endure is not the gift of their men but their women.'

Churchill also began carrying a revolver, and he kept one within reach while he slept but carelessly left it lying around at other times. He took shooting lessons from Inspector Thompson at small indoor ranges. With characteristic bravado and a cigar in his mouth, he proclaimed with roguish delight, 'You see, Thompson, they will never take me alive! I will get one or two before they shoot me down.'

General Edmund Ironside's lament about Britain's lack of preparedness had become a sad reality. The Chamberlain government had made no plan to deal with either German or Italian aggression or with a state of war. Chamberlain's blindness to preparing for war while attempting to prevent it was reflected in the naivety of King George VI, who thought that after occupying Poland, Hitler would make a peace offer and that, rather than reject it, Britain ought to suggest a readiness 'to discuss terms with the German people but not with Hitler or his régime'.

No longer a peacetime prime minister, Neville Chamberlain was hopelessly ill prepared and lacked the state of mind and the resolve necessary to be an effective war leader. Contributing to his irresolution was the fact that there was as yet no unanimity within the British populace for another war; on the contrary, many deplored it and wanted a resolution before it widened. There had been no War Cabinet in place until war was declared, and Chamberlain wallowed in doubt, unable to grasp fully the enormity of the situation. His hostility to rearmament, and the mistaken belief that he could reason with Hitler, had left his idealism shattered. 'How I do hate and loathe this war,' he complained. 'I was never meant to be a war minister.' Hand-wringing, however, was no substitute for preparation, direction and leadership at one of the most critical moments in British history.

With no ground operations against the Germans yet under way, the only action was taking place on the naval front. The Royal Navy in 1939 was primarily fighting a defensive war until plans could be developed to go on the offensive – and some in the government hoped this would never occur while there still existed the possibility of a rapprochement with Hitler. As a consequence, with the war only days old, Churchill was already taking charge of the war effort and quickly becoming a dominant figure within Chamberlain's War Cabinet. In some quarters there was relief that somebody was seizing the initiative, while from others came predictable disparagement of Churchill's presence. Oliver Stanley, the president of the Board of Trade, said scornfully to a colleague, 'Why did he not bring his "World War"?' – a reference to *The*

World Crisis. Another privately commented that Churchill appeared to be writing his new memoirs. The fact that the Royal Navy was the only British armed service actively engaged in fighting the Germans left Churchill in a strong position, and eventually it led to his becoming the *de facto* minister of defence in April 1940.

In yet another example of déjà vu from the Great War, in February 1939 the Chamberlain government had created and authorized the deployment of a British Expeditionary Force (BEF) if war came. By mid-October four of the ten divisions of the BEF had been sent to France. As they had in 1914, they occupied defensive positions guarding the French army's vulnerable left flank in the Pas de Calais, which consisted of a two-hundred-mile front along the border with neutral Belgium. By May 1940 the BEF consisted of nearly 400,000 men, of whom some 237,000 were manning the front lines.

One of Churchill's first undertakings was to oversee the transport of the BEF across the Channel, a task that was carried out successfully without an attack by German U-boats. Although there were insufficient supplies and equipment to support much more than fifteen divisions by the end of the first year of the war, throughout the autumn and early winter of 1939 Churchill lobbied vociferously for a larger BEF, arguing that it was critical to provide a fifty-five-division force to enable the French to withstand a German invasion. He was fed statistics poured out by Lindemann and his team, and, like a prosecutor cross-examining witnesses, bombarded the War Office with data and estimates, demanded answers from other ministers as to how deficiencies were to be remedied, challenged the Air Ministry over what he argued were excessive stocks of ammunition and chastised the army for its lack of ammunition stocks and weapons.

In November, Churchill visited France to discuss naval matters, particularly anti-submarine measures. During his trip he detoured to Amiens to visit (and inspect, even though he had no formal standing with the army) Lord Gort's BEF. Suddenly air-raid sirens announced an engagement between German and British planes. Everyone was hustled into shelter except Churchill, who lay down in the grass to observe the goings-on above. When Inspector Thompson attempted to get his attention by shaking his shoulder and jerking him upright, Churchill angrily thrust him away: 'Keep your head down, you fool! Do you want us to miss everything?' Whereupon he 'plunged into a hedge, parted the foliage and went on watching the show'.

Neville Chamberlain resembled Asquith at the beginning of the First World War. Neither was a dominant figure at a time when Britain urgently needed someone of experience who possessed strong leadership skills and a degree of ruthlessness. Chamberlain had neither the stomach for war nor the habit of decisiveness. War demands extraordinary measures, firm direction and an end to the leisurely pace of politics and business as usual. The foreign secretary, Lord Halifax, was representative of the same gentle, well-meaning but ineffective politicians who had directed the rudderless ship of the Great War prior to Lloyd George. The events of the previous three years were stark evidence of the failure of appeasement. What Churchill observed first hand during the early days of the Second World War was the same drift and indecision that had failed once before.

After some initial waffling the newly formed Land Forces Committee, of which Churchill was a member, recommended what he had been advocating all along: that the army be significantly increased to fifty-five divisions, with at least twenty available to aid the French army. However, no decision becomes reality without the necessary funds, and none were forthcoming until the committee could study the cost of supporting the needs of all three services. Moreover there was resistance, with critics citing the fact that such a large build-up would hurt the expansion of not only the army but also the Royal Navy and the RAF. Churchill retorted: 'Pardon me if I put my experience and knowledge, which were bought, not taught, at your disposal.' He also insisted that Britain had a duty to come to the aid of France in order 'to do our fair share of the actual fighting on land . . . We ought to hurl ourselves into the task with a new surge of impulse, and face all the sacrifices, hardships and exertions which this entails.' Anything less, he argued, 'would be unworthy of our cause, and unequal to our dangers'.

Not only was Churchill dissatisfied with the pace of rearmament, he also contended that Britain and France should immediately go on the offensive in aid of Poland in the form of a first strike by the French, backed by the RAF. Germany's war-making focal point was the Ruhr, which could be attacked by RAF bombers. He also renewed the earlier concept, code-named Operation Royal Marine, of floating mines down the Rhine to destroy bridges (an idea that was quietly shot down by Pound), and even considered smashing the Kiel Canal with bombers. The Chamberlain government, however, never followed through on any of these ideas. By default the only military operations against Germany during the first months of the war were carried out by the Royal Navy.

The war was barely a month old when Harold Nicolson and some others began to see Churchill emerging as the true war leader. On 26 September Nicolson compared Chamberlain and Churchill. The prime minister seemed 'dressed in deep mourning', and when he spoke, 'One feels the confidence and spirits of the House dropping inch by inch.' Churchill sat hunched over beside Chamberlain, 'looking like the Chinese god of plenty suffering from acute indigestion'. When he rose to speak loud cheers greeted him. 'He began by saying how strange an experience it was for him after a quarter of a century to find himself once more in the same room in front of the same maps, fighting the same enemy and dealing with the same problems,' and, after glancing at Chamberlain, he added drolly: 'I have no conception how this curious change in my fortunes occurred.' While the MPs roared, Chamberlain sulked. Whereas Chamberlain's words were usually greeted with near silence, Churchill gave what Nicolson thought was an amazing speech: 'One could feel the spirits of the House rising with every word. In those twenty minutes Churchill brought himself nearer the post of Prime Minister than he has ever been before. In the Lobbies afterwards even Chamberlainites were saying, "We have now found our leader." Old Parliamentary hands confessed that never in their experience had they seen a single speech so change the temper of the House.'

The prospect of Churchill's becoming prime minister horrified others in both the private sector and the government. He was widely criticized when, in the autumn of 1939, he strongly but unsuccessfully advocated that military force be employed against Ireland for failing to permit the Royal Navy to use its western ports as anchorage for anti-submarine vessels, and to establish bases for flying boats (a specialized type of seaplane with a large fuselage for buoyancy) in the search for U-boats. He felt free to meddle in virtually everyone's business, such as asking if the Foreign Office had any plans to replace the British ambassador to Belgium. In a controversial BBC radio broadcast on 20 January 1940 he praised the stout resistance of the Finns to the Russian invasion of their nation: 'Finland shows what free men can do. The service rendered by Finland to mankind is magnificent.' Turning to the neutral nations, Churchill was scornful of their failure to take a stand. 'Their plight is lamentable; and it will become much worse,' he warned. 'Each one hopes that if he feeds the crocodile enough, the crocodile will eat him last.' He ended his broadcast on a positive note, declaring that the oppressed cities of Europe would one day be free of Nazi tyranny. 'The day will come when the joybells will ring again throughout Europe.' Halifax was indignant and complained to Chamberlain that the speech was inflammatory, but Churchill merely turned on the charm and apologized, explaining: 'Asking me not to make a speech is like asking a centipede . . . not to put a foot on the ground.' Although the bureaucrats disapproved of his speech and its fiery rhetoric, it played well to bolster the morale of the British public.

Jock Colville, the young diplomat in the Foreign Office who in September 1939 became one of Chamberlain's assistant secretaries, wrote in his diary on 1 October that he thought Churchill would one day be prime minister, but that 'judging from his record of untrustworthiness and instability, he may in that case lead us into the most dangerous paths. But he is the only man in the country who commands anything like universal respect.' Colville's views represented a growing sentiment, but the last words of his entry for that day proved wishful thinking: 'Perhaps with age he has become less inclined to undertake rash adventures.'

Churchill's blizzard of advice to Chamberlain (particularly his endless advocacy of Operation Catherine) and to other ministers rendered moot the prime minister's original notion that by giving him the Admiralty he would be too busy running the navy to interfere in other matters. Chamberlain received Churchill's memos with cynicism, writing to his sister, 'I realize that these letters are for the purpose of quotation in the Book he will write hereafter.' Nevertheless as time passed relations between the two men improved, and Churchill grew more supportive as he came to see that, however much Chamberlain disagreed with him, he was sincerely pursuing the war, his distaste for it notwithstanding. Although he retained his reservations, Chamberlain accepted Churchill's impulsiveness. 'Winston is in some respects such a child that he neither knows his own motives nor sees where his actions are carrying him.' Geoffrey Shakespeare seconded Chamberlain's opinion. The impulsiveness and nimbleness that daily produced a flood of ideas in the form of 'Action This Day' memos, he said, came 'from the furnace of his mind almost before they [were] tempered by common sense and due reflection'.

Despite the resistance, however, Churchill's first four months as first lord were significant ones for the Royal Navy, which again had a powerful leader to speak on its behalf. His return to the Admiralty in 1939, as the fast-emerging voice of Britain's national defence in what was otherwise largely a vacuum, was both good news and bad: good in that he brought fresh new ideas, a renewed sense of purpose and incredible energy to the Royal Navy; bad in that he also brought back into play unworkable schemes, launched ill-fated ventures and arranged the return to service in various capacities of men from the Great War who might best have been left retired.

In December 1939 the Royal Navy achieved its first success, off faraway Uruguay. In the Battle of the River Plate, British cruisers engaged a formidable German raider, the pocket battleship *Graf Spee*, which had been hunting and sinking British merchant ships in the South Atlantic, and forced it to flee upriver to neutral Montevideo. With its escape blocked, its crew blew up the *Graf Spee* rather than surrender.

The so-called Phoney War also offered false hopes of a peaceful resolution. Churchill viewed the Russo-Nazi pact as positive for Britain in that it would eventually self-destruct, but for the present it would help buy time to rearm. He himself helped perpetuate the fraudulent notion that all would be well by making optimistic statements in Parliament. These statements included claims of Royal Navy accomplishments and corresponding German losses that were sheer fantasy, not least the absurd assertion that the odds that an Allied ship would be sunk were 1 in 500, when in fact shipping losses were high. Between September and December 1939, indeed, 158 British, 17 Allied and 138 neutral merchant ships were lost.

The war which no one had wanted, and which so far had not amounted to much, was about to change. Some in Britain, including Anthony Eden, the bright young diplomat who had resigned as foreign secretary over appeasement, believed that by not acting right away Hitler had forfeited the initiative. What was not known in those first months was that Germany was not yet ready to wage all-out war on the West, and that Hitler was simply biding his time. France had no intention of going on the offensive, and Britain was poorly prepared for another ground war. Thus both Britain and France continued to play the waiting game, with some believing that there never would be a full-scale war. Only later would it become clear that the first ten months of the war were mere skirmishing.

31

The Norway Debacle

Fortunately, one can always count on the British to arrive too late.

             – German colonel

Too many damned strategists . . . have a finger in the pie, all amateurs.

          – General Sir Edmund Ironside

The year 1939 ended without a strategy or a real conception of how the war would evolve in 1940. Save for Churchill, no minister in the War Cabinet could even remotely be regarded as a strategist. Except for the daily grim news broadcast on the BBC of the sinking of British shipping, the Phoney War continued to mislead both the public and some inside the government. Only in the frozen wastelands of far-off Finland was a real ground war raging, as the Finns bitterly resisted Stalin's attempt to overpower his next-door neighbour. With no modern weapons and an army of a mere nine divisions and only forty-eight fighter aircraft against which were arrayed three thousand Russian planes and fifteen hundred tanks, the Finns were in a hugely unequal contest against a force of 810,000 consisting of forty-five divisions of the Red Army. The Finns held out until March 1940, inflicting enormous losses on the Russians, who initially expected that the war would be over in four days.

  Churchill, whose relationship with the BBC was icy, complained that its repeated daily emphasis on British losses was detrimental to morale and pleaded for more restrained announcements. Reflecting on the first months of the war, Jock Colville noted in his diary on 31 December 1939, 'Here at home . . . people seem to be resigned to war without fully realising the hardships which it must, and the physical terror which it may, imply. Everybody is talking gaily about a changing world, a new social order, a complete revolution of national and international ideals;

but do they realize what effect all this, if it comes to pass, will have upon them personally?'

The British public expected a war in which armies clashed, aeroplanes fought in the skies and dropped bombs, and great battles between giant warships took place at sea. Instead there were only the numbing cold and endless days when nothing much occurred. There was also apathy and disgust that Britain was again at war and apprehension over its uncertain future. Rationing was in effect; blackouts had become a new way of life and the freezing cold winter caused more deaths than the war itself. Some three million Londoners – mainly children – had been evacuated from the capital, which was nightly cloaked in darkness, and the National Gallery had removed its precious paintings to sanctuary in Wales. Endless restrictions and directives emanated from the Whitehall mandarins, regulating daily life. As Churchill's daughter writes: '[Britons] complied with considerable goodwill and an astonishing degree of self-discipline. No one doubted that sterner days would come.'

Nor was Britain particularly well prepared to support a wartime economy. Even at full capacity, steel output was only about half that of Germany, and a significant percentage of speciality steels were imported from America. Moreover Britain was completely dependent on imports of machine tools, and aircraft manufacturing was critically short of qualified workers to assemble the planes that would be needed to take on the Luftwaffe, and to replace losses. Even worse was the state of Britain's finances. The Treasury estimated that within three years the balance-of-payments deficit would be so great that gold, dollar and overseas investments would no longer cover it, and, without assistance from the United States, after two years the war effort would have to be severely contracted.

Behind the scenes the notion of making peace with Hitler was simmering among some members of the minority Labour Party and an increasingly vocal number of the ultra-right peace wing of the Conservatives, among them Churchill's cousin, the aristocratic, well-connected, wealthy Lord Londonderry, one of Britain's largest landowners, who was both a friend and a confidant of King George VI. Londonderry was not alone in his pro-Nazi sympathies and desire for friendship rather than war with Germany. One of the principal reasons for keeping open a dialogue was Britain's growing fear that Communism and the Soviet Union posed an even greater danger.

In the autumn of 1939 and well into 1940, Hitler did not discourage peace feelers; on the contrary, he not only welcomed them but also, in speeches and through emissaries, actively waved an olive branch at the Western nations, declaring that he would respect their sovereignty, and even calling for a peace conference. He tended to view Britain as one would a stubborn child, and after a peace offer was rejected in October 1939 remarked: 'They will be ready to talk only after a beating.'

His primary peace emissary was Reichsmarschall Hermann Göring, the head of the Luftwaffe, then the second most powerful figure in the Third Reich. Because he saw no point in a war with Britain and France, Göring had covertly sent a Swedish representative who met with Chamberlain and Halifax shortly before the invasion of Poland in an attempt to avert war. Halifax noted that numerous peace feelers were occurring, 'all of them tracing to Göring', and he was certainly not alone when he said in October 1939, 'We should not absolutely shut the door.' Churchill's attitude to such peace feelers was to reject them categorically, particularly when one of them came after the sinking of HMS *Courageous*.

One of the great what-ifs of the Second World War is how differently it might have played out had France reacted aggressively and attacked Germany in September 1939 instead of timorously awaiting an invasion. At the Nuremberg trials after the war two of Hitler's prominent generals, Alfred Jodl, the chief of Hitler's operations staff, and Wilhelm Keitel, the chief of the supreme command of the armed forces, both revealed that their handful of divisions manning the Siegfried Line would have been no match for the 110 French divisions. Jodl testified that it was 'the inactivity of the Allies that saved Germany from defeat', an assessment echoed by Keitel, who declared that German forces in the West were merely a screening force, 'not a real defence'. And, had France acted, would the generals who despised Hitler and feared the consequences of a war with the West have risen to displace him in 1939 rather than try and fail in 1944?

Although the British army lagged far behind what Churchill believed would be required to fight Germany, other steps were being taken, from the Royal Navy's aggressive pursuit of the U-boats to the initiation of new civil defence measures. Slowly but surely the nation was being converted from a peacetime economy to a war footing. A closely guarded secret, the development of one of the great weapons of the Second

World War – radar (then called RDF, for 'radio detection finding'), the harnessing of radio waves to guide and detect ships and aircraft, and in a variety of other military applications – was finally being actively pursued. Yet instead of being far ahead of Germany and other nations, British radar development had been severely curtailed by budget cuts imposed by Chamberlain on the military in the 1930s.

Churchill had been in office for only five days when he shocked Admiral Fraser, the third sea lord and the navy's comptroller, by demanding: 'Well, Admiral, what is the navy doing about RDF?' Fraser wondered how on earth Churchill even knew of its existence, unaware that this was one of the many secrets conveyed to him in the 1930s. A directive from the new first lord landed on Fraser's desk: 'The fitting of RDF in HM ships, especially those engaged in the U-boat fighting, is of high urgency.' In addition to its other incredibly important uses, radar would eventually prove one of the most decisive reasons why the RAF won the Battle of Britain.

As he had throughout his life, Churchill refused to be ruled by what may be termed the culture of failure: a fear of innovation and boldness that might induce blame or defeat. Neither Hitler nor Churchill belonged to that class; each was prone to aggressiveness and risk, and each thought he knew more about war and the military than his uniformed counterparts. In Hitler's case this belief aggravated a grave mistrust of his generals that embraced fear of a *coup d'état* or possible assassination. In Churchill's it convinced him that he could determine strategy and carry out what were often unconventional, risky military operations.

From the time of his return to the Admiralty, Churchill had been bent on inserting the Royal Navy into the Baltic, and Operation Catherine was a perfect example of his disregard for the possibility of failure. He thought only of success, and rarely if ever concerned himself with the ugly alternative. The Dardanelles and Gallipoli would have reduced most men in a position of power to tentativeness. Although he never forgot the humiliation of 1915, Churchill nevertheless purposely trod where others dared not go.

Although the Admiralty initially supported Catherine, by the end of 1939 Pound made clear the navy's position that 'even if there were adequate fighter protection for the Fleet, and if Russia were on our side and we had the use of Russian bases [neither of which was the case in

December 1939] . . . I consider that the sending of a Fleet of surface ships into the Baltic is courting disaster.'

Rather than hazard the fleet Pound advocated sending a submarine force into the Baltic to accomplish the same purpose. Churchill was not swayed and replied that he was 'very deeply impressed with the risks and dangers of Catherine', but restated his belief that a British fleet in the Baltic would 'act as a magnet to draw in German vessels from the outer seas' and produce 'very great relief'. Pound refused to budge and renewed his opposition by stating that the fleet would be mauled if sent into the Baltic. Churchill reluctantly bowed to the inevitable and admitted that Catherine was simply not possible in 1940.

Another high-risk operation was the plan to intervene in Norway to halt the flow of vital Swedish iron ore that was an essential ingredient in the manufacture of German munitions, and that accounted for an estimated one-half of the twenty million tons required yearly to feed Hitler's growing war machine. (The other half had come from French Lorraine and, since September 1939, was no longer obtainable.) As the war entered 1940 Churchill continued to warn of the urgency of taking action in Norway. 'The effectual stoppage of the Norwegian ore supplies to Germany ranks as a major offensive operation of the war,' he wrote on 16 December, the same day Colville noted that Churchill 'considers it essential to use drastic, and even illegal, methods to prevent ore being shipped from Norwegian ports, and he wants Cabinet authority to lay minefields in Norwegian territorial waters [within the traditional three-mile limit] . . . in order to drive ships carrying iron ore out of territorial waters into the hands of our contraband control.'

On New Year's Day 1940, the War Cabinet met and, as Colville recorded, 'The Cabinet, instigated by Winston, are considering a daring offensive scheme in Northern Scandinavia, which they think might bring Germany to her knees but which also, to my mind, is dangerously reminiscent of the Gallipoli plan.'

The prospect of precious Swedish iron ore falling into German hands continued to obsess Churchill into the early months of 1940. With Catherine now on the back burner, he was free to turn his attention to what he correctly deemed a far more serious matter. Sweden, Denmark and Norway were all officially neutral, each hoping to stave off occupation by Germany. Norway in particular was zealously guarding its neutrality despite the fact that its ice-free port of Narvik had become a funnel for Swedish ore. Situated above the Arctic Circle and close to the nearby Swedish iron mines, Narvik played an especially important role in winter as it represented the only route through which the Germans could keep the ore flowing.

After less than three weeks in office, Churchill began warning the War Cabinet that German ore carriers were taking advantage of Norway's three-mile limit and its neutrality. 'Our policy must be to stop this trade going to Germany.' When the Gulf of Bothnia became icebound, iron ore was transported by rail to Narvik and thence to Germany, exploiting the protection of Norwegian territorial waters to reach North Sea ports. Churchill wanted the iron-ore pipeline shut down but received no support from an indecisive War Cabinet, which was more concerned about violating Norwegian neutrality. In any case, fearful of German retaliation, neither Norway nor Sweden was willing to permit violations of its neutrality. In January 1940 Churchill led a delegation to France in an attempt to persuade the French to engage with Britain in a joint operation to insert troops disguised as volunteers into Narvik, where they would advance across northern Norway into Sweden to take control of the iron ore.

Although he clearly recognized that violating Norwegian and Swedish neutrality might drive either or both countries to join Germany, Churchill wrote on 14 February to his War Cabinet colleagues, 'It has been painful to watch during the last two months the endless procession of German oreships down the Norwegian territorial waters carrying to Germany the material out of which will be made the shells to kill our young men in 1941, when all the time the simplest and easiest of motions would bring it to an end.'

Two days later the neutrality issue came to a head over the *Altmark* incident, a further demonstration of Churchill's doggedness in respect of Norway. The *Altmark* had been a fuel and support ship of the pocket battleship *Graf Spee* during its deadly 1939 rampage in the South Atlantic. After the *Graf Spee* was scuttled, the *Altmark* escaped from Montevideo and become a floating prison for 299 British merchant sailors after the German raider had sunk their ships. Locked up in filthy, foul-smelling conditions, in darkness and on starvation rations, the prisoners had scant hope of rescue. After eluding the Royal Navy for nearly two months in the enormous expanses of the South Atlantic, the

Altmark was attempting to reach the sanctuary of a German port when it was spotted on 16 February by an RAF aircraft in Norwegian territorial waters near Trondheim. If the *Altmark* managed to reach Germany (it was within some two hundred miles of home waters), the British seamen not only would have been interned as POWs but also would have represented a considerable public relations coup for Hitler.

A destroyer flotilla, commanded by Captain Philip Vian, skipper of HMS *Cossack*, was operating in the general area and was ordered to locate the *Altmark*. Although as an auxiliary vessel the *Altmark* was theoretically neutral when the sighting was flashed to the Admiralty, Churchill thought otherwise, and on the morning of 16 February ordered its seizure 'in territorial waters should she be found', calling it 'an invaluable trophy' that was 'violating neutrality by carrying British prisoners of war to Germany'. He was correct; the *Altmark* had housed its guns and was pretending to be an innocent merchant vessel, immune from interference.

On the afternoon of the 16th the *Cossack* sighted the *Altmark*, which immediately sought sanctuary in nearby Jösing Fjord, south of Bergen. Vian used his destroyer flotilla to barricade the mouth of the fjord; then, along with another destroyer, the *Cossack* attempted to enter the fjord but was intercepted by two Norwegian gunboats. The Norwegians not only refused permission to board the *Altmark* but also pointed their torpedo tubes at the British destroyers and threatened to resist, claiming that they had searched the vessel three times and found no POWs aboard. Although the Norwegians had shadowed the *Altmark* during its passage through their territorial waters, none of their boarding parties had actually searched the ship, and these parties had simply accepted the protests of its intimidating captain that it was carrying no prisoners.

When Vian's signal detailing the standoff reached the Admiralty, Churchill immediately went to the war room. 'He called for the Duty Signal Officer and dictated a signal of precise instructions to Vian,' recalled the duty captain that day. 'Get that ciphered up and be quick about it,' he instructed. 'I've told the Secretary of State [Halifax] that those orders are going at a quarter to six unless we hear to the contrary.' Churchill paced up and down chewing on his cigar, his coat tails flapping, before coming to a decision. 'I can't wait,' he announced. 'Get me Lord Halifax.' Within seconds Halifax was on the line. 'We didn't hear what Halifax said to *him* . . . but we heard what he said to Halifax and that was an education.' Halifax promised to respond within ten minutes and did so by supporting Churchill. The orders Churchill sent to Vian were to board the *Altmark*, 'liberate the prisoners and take possession of the ship, pending further instructions'. After the signal had gone and as Churchill was leaving the room, he turned and announced: 'That was *big* of Halifax.'

That evening the two destroyers forced their way into the icebound Jösing Fjord to carry out Churchill's orders. Using their searchlights, as the Norwegian gunboats stood aside, declining to interfere, they boxed in the *Altmark* and ordered its captain to heave to and to prepare to be boarded.

However, before Vian's crew was able to board it, the *Altmark* set its engines to full speed ahead and attempted to ram the British destroyer, but failed thanks to some nifty navigation by the *Cossack*. Although the *Altmark* ran aground on rocks at the end of the narrow fjord, the crew of the *Cossack* managed to secure grappling lines to the German vessel as the two ships came together like wrestlers in a death grip. Vian's crew managed to board, but not without engaging in hand-to-hand fighting and a shoot-out on deck that killed four Germans. Four machine guns and two pom-pom anti-aircraft guns were seized, weapons that had once sprouted on the *Altmark*'s decks. A British sailor called into the hold: 'Are there any English down there?' A joyous response of 'Yes!' prompted another voice on deck to shout: 'Well, the navy's here.' One of the small ironies of the incident is that along with letters of praise Vian received from the public, 'a number wrote to say that, as I had failed to shoot, or hang, the Captain of the *Altmark*, I ought to be shot myself.' As the *Cossack* sped back to Scotland with the rescued sailors, the *Altmark* returned to Germany without its human cargo. The Germans left a sign ashore that read: 'Here on 16 February 1940 the Altmark was set upon by a British sea-pirate.'

In the larger context of the Second World War, the *Altmark* affair was a very minor incident. It was also a classic example of Winston Churchill in action as a war leader: audacious, willing to ride roughshod over the rules of neutrality – and ready unhesitatingly to accept the consequences. It was proof that he had not succumbed to the culture of failure that would have dissuaded others. The *Altmark* was also a rare instance in which he played a direct role in the type of military operation that was so dear to his heart. His signal was sent directly to Captain Vian, bypassing the chain of command and the commander in chief of the Home Fleet, Admiral Sir Charles Forbes, to whom Vian reported. Churchill later admitted his error (to some extent) by acknowledging, 'I did not often act so directly.'

A sense of immense relief and acclaim swept Britain with news of the freeing of the prisoners, which Churchill exploited to help stir the public and the sceptics in Whitehall. And, while the *Altmark* incident was a public relations coup, he understood far better than the majority of Britain's politicians that the real war was yet to come and that so far it was primarily the Royal Navy that was bearing the burden of fighting the Germans. His action also seems to have spoken directly to British patriotism; the war was good versus evil.

The officers and crews of the two light cruisers, HMS *Ajax* and *Achilles*, that had cornered the *Graf Spee* were paraded through the streets of London and acclaimed by cheering crowds. At Horse Guards Parade, with a band playing, they were formally greeted and inspected by the king. The spectacle was witnessed by a large crowd and by Chamberlain, Churchill, Pound, the War Cabinet and the entire Admiralty Board, while the queen observed from a window of the Admiralty. Afterwards they marched to the Guildhall for a luncheon in their honour, at which Churchill delivered one of his patented patriotic speeches that extolled the navy. Closing on a note of triumph, he said: 'The warrior heroes of the past may look down, as Nelson's monument looks down upon us now, without any feeling that the island race has lost its daring or that the examples they have set in bygone centuries have faded.'

He also praised the daring rescue by HMS *Cossack* 'at the very moment when those unhappy men were about to be delivered over into indefinite German bondage' by means of 'the long arm of the British sea power . . . And to Nelson's immortal signal of 135 years ago, "England expects every man will do his duty," there may now be added last week's not less proud reply, "The Navy is here."' The audience roared its approval. For a brief magical moment, the true ugliness of the war to come was forgotten in the euphoria of patriotic celebration. Indeed, the entire day was a wonderful distraction for a city soon to endure hellish punishment from the skies at the hands of the Luftwaffe.

However, Churchill's decision to intervene had other repercussions, setting a course that would end the Phoney War once and for all. The

Altmark incident left no doubt in Berlin not only that Britain had no qualms about violating Norwegian neutrality but that British intentions were to occupy Norway. Hitler called it 'intolerable' and blamed the *Altmark*'s crew for not fighting sufficiently hard to fend off the British. Determined to get there first, he ordered plans to be brought forward for a German invasion of Denmark and Norway in the early spring as a matter of the highest urgency and importance. As for the *Altmark*, Hitler was somewhat philosophical, observing that history never asked the victors who was right or who was wrong.

Although the *Altmark* incident hardened Hitler's resolve to invade Norway, what he had really desired was for Scandinavia to remain neutral, thus averting the commitment of his armed forces to a sideshow that could only detract from his true objective, the invasion and occupation of all of western Europe, then being planned under the code name Case Yellow. As far as Scandinavia was concerned, he wanted it all: a free flow of precious iron ore and the neutrality of Norway, Denmark and Sweden.

The *Altmark* was not the only time Churchill involved himself in operational matters as first lord. He had his own personal map room in the former library of Admiralty House, where, whenever a blockade runner like the *Graf Spee* was located, he would hasten to consult his maps and study the situation. Never content with merely observing and studying, he had to participate actively as if he were in command himself. His naval assistant, Captain Grantham, wrote that 'he would often suggest the type and names of ships which should be employed, regardless of their immediate availability.' Admiral Pound would never openly challenge Churchill but instead quietly ordered the dispositions he and the naval staff deemed appropriate. Despite his penchant for personal involvement, however, Churchill seems never to have overridden the orders of his first sea lord.

At the top of his agenda during the first months of 1940 was the controversial subject of laying minefields to stem the flow of Swedish iron ore. While planning went ahead for mining Norwegian waters and inserting an Anglo-French expeditionary force, arguments raged over the legality of mounting an incursion into a neutral country against the will of its government. The French were equally split, with the new prime minister Paul Reynaud – the latest in a long line of revolving-door leaders of the Third Republic – in favour and the defence minister, Édouard Daladier, opposed.

Undeterred by French indecision and Norwegian resistance to British overtures that were even less welcome after the *Altmark* incident, Churchill remained determined to mine the waters around Narvik and to send an expeditionary force to Norway. By the end of March 1940, both Britain and Germany were completing plans for naval and ground operations in Norway. The difference, as one writer has aptly noted, was that 'the Germans worked faster.' The War Cabinet had finally given its blessing for what Churchill had been advocating for months. An Anglo-French expeditionary force was to land at Narvik, seize the vital railway line from Sweden and eventually take control of the Gällivare iron-ore fields.

On 8 April 1940, the Royal Navy began mining Norwegian waters in and around Narvik, while other vessels were on the move towards Norway for what seemed certain to be engagements with the German navy. They did not have long to wait. Near Trondheim the British destroyer HMS *Glowworm* encountered German destroyers and the heavy cruiser *Admiral von Hipper*, which was escorting a force to Narvik. At this moment the so-called Phoney War became history when, struck by German shells and against all odds, the *Glowworm* rammed the *Hipper* before sinking. The *Glowworm*'s skipper, Lieutenant Commander Gerald Roope, saved many of the men before going down with his ship. The *Hipper* survived, as did 36 of the 149 crewmen of the *Glowworm*. And, in one of the most unusual acts of the war, the *Hipper*'s captain, in a gesture of great respect, sent a recommendation via the International Red Cross that Roope be awarded the Victoria Cross.

Churchill spent most of the day in the Admiralty war room as reports began filtering in of German movements. 'The entire German navy seems to be heading for Norway,' reported Eric Seal, Churchill's principal private secretary. Although it was a tense day at the Admiralty, Churchill was upbeat – not suspecting that the Germans were executing the most daring combined-operations campaign of the war so far.

On 9 April Denmark was overrun by the Germans, but it was Norway that Hitler was most anxious to seize, before the British and French could react. German airborne troops landed in Oslo, where the citizens of the Norwegian capital were subjected to the tramp of goose-stepping German soldiers in their once peaceful streets. Trondheim also fell, and a key airfield at Stavanger was taken by *coup de main*. Throughout 8 and 9 April Churchill remained characteristically optimistic. Colville recorded: 'The First Lord (who at last sees a chance of action) is jubilant and maintains that our failure to destroy the German fleet up to the present is only due to the bad visibility and very rough weather in the North Sea.'

Paradoxically the rough weather favoured the British. The most successful naval battle of the campaign occurred in Narvik Fjord on 10 April, when six British destroyers took on ten German destroyers that were caught refuelling during a blizzard, and sank five of them. Reinforced by a battleship and other destroyers three days later, the British sank five more and at a stroke reduced the German navy's destroyer force by half. Captain Bernard Warburton-Lee, the Welshman commanding HMS *Hardy*, won the first Victoria Cross of the war (posthumously) at Narvik. For the first lord of the Admiralty, Winston Churchill, this seemed a sea battle in the great tradition of Lord Nelson. Sadly, however, it proved the prelude to utter defeat in Norway itself.

Churchill had spent most of 9 April, until well into the night, in the war room. Seal finally had to compel him to stop work and steered him to bed at the usual ungodly hour. 'I was very worried about Winston,' who was 'knocked out last night. I had to manoeuvre him to bed; he had a good night & this morning is in wonderful fighting trim . . . I have to be a sort of nurse at times!! He is very like a spoilt child in many ways.'

The truth was there was very little to be optimistic about on land; the Germans had caught the British completely by surprise. In the days to come Churchill's belief that the Germans had played into British hands was to prove an illusion. From the start British planning was tentative and haphazard. A prime example was the recapture of Trondheim. With the Luftwaffe more and more active, the War Cabinet's decision to land a twelve-thousand-man Anglo-French task force was reversed when the chiefs of staff got cold feet and changed its mission. The force was unwisely split. One landing took place at Namsos, eighty miles north-east of Trondheim, on 14 April, and the second force landed one hundred miles south-west, at Andalsnes, on the 16th. Even Ironside, hitherto one of Churchill's most ardent supporters, had become exasperated and felt compelled to point out his major fault as a war leader. 'One of the fallacies that Winston seems to have got into his head is that we can make improvised decisions to carry on the war by meeting at 5 p.m. each day ... War cannot be run by the Staffs sitting round a table arguing. We cannot have a man trying to supervise all military arrangements as if he were a company commander running a small operation to cross a bridge ... It seems incredible these things should happen.'

Each of the Allied landings came under heavy air attack from the Luftwaffe and from German ground forces. With no supporting air, AA or artillery and no means of resupply, the two British task forces were effectively trapped and quickly obliged to retreat. Churchill grumbled that part of the force should have been left behind to fight as guerrillas, a proposal that Ironside vetoed.

Ironside was not alone in his criticism of politicians involving themselves in matters outside their purview, but he was especially trenchant about the mounting crisis over whether Namsos would have to be evacuated: 'I find people talking about "desperate situations" and of "evacuation" as if it had to be carried out in a minute. Too many damned strategists who all have a finger in the pie, all amateurs who change from minute to minute and are either very optimistic or very pessimistic ... We must get back to allowing the soldiers to make decisions ... Every plan is taken and torn to pieces by a lot of civilian amateurs ... We simply cannot get on with the work ... How can a staff function?' This was certainly not the last time a senior British officer would ask such a question.

An example of Churchill's interference occurred on 21 April, when he wanted to divert troops to Narvik, then later reversed himself and advocated diverting a brigade from the Narvik sector to reinforce Namsos. 'Now he is bored with the Namsos operation and is all for Narvik again,' complained Ironside. 'It is extraordinary how mercurial he is.' The force that landed at Andalsnes was virtually annihilated, and both had to be evacuated on 2–3 May in what was a humiliating precursor on a very small scale to the forthcoming evacuation of the BEF from Dunkirk. A French officer complained, 'The British have planned this campaign on the lines of a punitive expedition against the Zulus, but unhappily we and the British are in the position of the Zulus, armed with bows and arrows against the onslaught of scientific warfare.'

In early May, soon after the withdrawal of British and French troops from Norway, active resistance by the Norwegians ended. German airpower was the decisive factor that the British could not overcome. Without bases in Norway the RAF was unable to compete with the Luftwaffe. Although the Germans were the victors they also suffered the heaviest losses: some 5,500 men and two hundred aircraft along with the disastrous losses to their destroyer fleet and the sinking of the cruiser *Blücher* near Oslo.

Norway was an example of everything a military operation should not be. Major General P. J. Mackesy, the British task force commander, and Admiral Lord Cork, the Royal Navy commander, had differences over the Narvik landings, and relations between the French and the British were frosty. It took Mackesy's replacement by Major General Claude Auchinleck for relations to improve. Moreover, after the German invasion in the West on 10 May operations in Norway were a serious drain on both shipping and supplies needed on the Continent to support the BEF.

Except for the sterling performance of the Royal Navy and the courage of the soldiers on the ground, the Norwegian campaign was easily one of Britain's worst military performances of the war. The army and navy had yet to learn to work together in combined operations with the effectiveness required if Britain was to survive. As for Churchill, he seems to have learned little from the Norway venture; in particular, he did not learn that large-scale military operations cannot suddenly be altered on an impulse without serious consequences.

An American correspondent reported from Norway in the *Chicago Daily News* that the venture was 'one of the costliest and most inexplicable military bungles in modern British history'. It was all that and more. The Norway campaign was uncoordinated, flawed in concept and massively mismanaged by Churchill, who hardly seemed able to make up his mind and, when he did make it up, invariably undermined an already unwinnable campaign by making decisions as if he were the commander in chief, and by violating cardinal principles of war. And while there is a maxim subscribed to by many that war is too important to be left to its generals, Churchill's habits of micromanagement and of bullying his subordinates did nothing to improve his capacity to understand the consequences of his actions. Moreover, the over-the-hill Lord Cork was an uninspired choice to command such a bold operation.

*

As he had been over the Dardanelles, Churchill was unrepentant over the failure of the Norway campaign, blaming it on 'the impotence and fatuity of waging war by committee . . . It fell to my lot . . . to bear much of the burden and some of the odium of the illstarred Norwegian campaign . . . Had I been allowed to act with freedom and design when I first demanded permission, a far more agreeable conclusion might have been reached in this key theatre . . . But now all was to be disaster.' The truth was that Churchill exaggerated the culpability of others and seriously underrated his own responsibility. His rationale for the Norway campaign was not simply the lure of a first-strike victory over Germany. Although he would never admit it, it is difficult to escape the conclusion that the Dardanelles and the redemption Norway might bring him were never far from his mind.

The great irony of the Norway campaign is that instead of crushing his career for the second time, its negative repercussions barely touched its chief instigator. Churchill himself admits as much in his otherwise misleading and self-serving account: 'It is a marvel that I survived and maintained my position in public esteem and Parliamentary confidence.' Norway brought about the fall of the Chamberlain government and the elevation of Winston Churchill to the prime ministership. It has been argued with considerable justification that had the Chamberlain government not fallen when it did as a result of the failure of the Norway campaign, once the battle for France began no one in Parliament would have risked another crisis by attempting to remove Neville Chamberlain. Instead he would have remained prime minister during the crucial summer of 1940 until forced by his cancer to relinquish his office – possibly to someone other than Churchill.

Another unintended consequence of Norway was Hitler's obsession that Churchill would launch another campaign there. To guard against such an occurrence he left half a million troops, strongly fortified coastal batteries and a significant portion of the German navy. Churchill would gladly have obliged him had he not time and again been dissuaded from doing so by the chiefs of staff. Norway remains stark evidence of his tendency to repeat the same strategic mistakes. And while the disastrous lessons of Norway became deeply ingrained in the minds of the men who led and staffed the British military during the Second World War, the man who led them was not fazed by the outcome.

32

The Loneliest Man in Britain

The good clean tradition of English politics [has been sold to] the greatest adventurer of modern political history.   – R. A. Butler

This cannot be by accident. It must be design. I was kept for this job.   – Churchill to Lord Moran

The 'bitter cup' of aggression that Churchill had prophesied in 1938 was filled to the brim on 10 May 1940 when the call finally came for him to step forward and lead his nation at the most desperate time in its history. At sunrise, on what would otherwise have been a glorious spring day, came the grim news of the German invasion of the West.

As was his custom, Churchill had toiled late into the night of 9–10 May. Shortly after 5.30 a.m. an aide bearing a report of the invasion awakened him. By 6.00 he was attending a breakfast meeting at the Admiralty with the secretary of state for war Oliver Stanley and the secretary of state for air Sir Samuel Hoare. Two military decisions emerged from the Admiralty war room. Besides approval of a contingency plan for the dispatch of two squadrons of RAF fighters to France, orders were immediately issued to commence Churchill's long-sought mining of the Rhine, Operation Royal Marine.

As Hoare later wrote of that morning, 'Churchill, whose spirit, so far from being shaken by failure or disaster, gathered strength in a crisis, was ready as always with his confident advice. I shall never forget the breakfast we had with him. It was six o'clock in the morning, after a fierce House of Commons debate and a late sitting. We had had little or no sleep, and the news could not have been worse. Yet there he was, smoking his large cigar and eating fried eggs and bacon, as if he had just returned from an early morning ride.' Churchill nonetheless faced innumerable fresh problems that spring morning. His desk overflowed with boxes of messages from the Foreign Office, the War Office and the Admiralty.

At a chiefs of staff meeting at 7.00 a.m. on the 10th, the news was at best sketchy. Not much was known of the situation on the Continent except that Belgium, Luxembourg, Holland and France were undergoing a massive invasion from the ground and from the air.

The 8.00 a.m. meeting of the War Cabinet was virtually useless and resolved nothing. Churchill had Lindemann demonstrate a model of what Ironside described as a 'homing A.A. fuze' on a nearby table, leading to a tart observation by the information minister, John Reith: 'Do you think this is the time for showing off toys?' The cabinet, Ironside recorded in disgust, 'doesn't know if it is on its head or its heels'.

Despite the confusion in Whitehall, on that historic morning Winston Churchill stood on the brink of assuming the leadership of Britain. The judgments made about him, both favourable and critical, were reinforced by Norway. Despite its inept planning and the unrealistic expectations that doomed it from the outset, Churchill believed it was a risk worth taking. When he spoke during the parliamentary debates following the British withdrawal, he was unrepentant. 'I do not think we ought to have a kind of mealy-mouthed attitude toward these matters. We have embarked upon this war and we must take our blows.' Privately, however, he candidly admitted to Admiral Pound, 'We have been completely outwitted.'

On 7 and 8 May the House of Commons had debated what was officially called the 'inquest on Norway'. Neville Chamberlain's Conservative government faced wholesale rebellion from angry and restless Tory MPs who were no longer willing to support their leader, some of them actually jeering him as he entered the House. Although a number of MPs had their say during the debate, Chamberlain's fate was sealed by three men close to Churchill: Leo Amery, Admiral Sir Roger Keyes and Lloyd George. Entering the House on 8 May in the uniform of an admiral of the fleet, bedecked with medals, Keyes cut a striking figure, and when he rose to speak he played the Nelsonian card, invoking the name of Britain's greatest naval hero. '"I am of the opinion that the boldest measures are the safest," and that still holds good today.' He vehemently attacked the naval staff and declared that Churchill 'did not interfere enough in the making of strategy and, with his adventurous disposition and inventive mind, he should do more.'

Throughout the debate there were whispers of 'What will Winston do?' Churchill may also have been saved by the venerable Lloyd George, who spoke in his defence, bluntly stating, 'I do not think that the First Lord was entirely responsible for what happened there,' and that his loyalty as a member of Chamberlain's government was not an excuse for its failures. Churchill leaped to his feet and, at his pugnacious best, snapped, 'I take full responsibility for everything that has been done by the Admiralty, and I take my full share of the burden.' Lloyd George responded, 'The Right Honourable Gentleman must not allow himself to be converted into an air-raid shelter to keep splinters from hitting his colleagues.' Throughout the lengthy debate, others also spoke in defence of Churchill.

When Churchill's turn came near the end of the turbulent session on 8 May, Chips Channon immediately perceived that 'he was in bellicose mood, alive and enjoying himself, relishing the ironical position in which he found himself: i.e. that of defending his enemies, and a cause in which he did not believe. He made a slashing, vigorous speech, a magnificent piece of oratory,' in which he 'told the story of the Norwegian campaign, justified it, and trounced the Opposition'. Nor did Churchill try to palliate what had occurred, pointing out that, as Edward Spears put it, 'the crude inadequacy of the foundation upon which we were waging war remained glaringly apparent.' Churchill's remarks were in keeping with a long-standing truism of the British way of war. 'We always seem to be waiting, and when we are struck, then we take some action. "Why", it is asked, "is the next blow not going to be struck by Britain?"' The reason, Churchill insisted, was rooted in the previous five years and the failure to maintain air parity with Germany, which 'has condemned us, and will condemn us for some time to come, to a great deal of difficulty and suffering and danger, which we must endure with firmness until more favourable conditions can be established.'

Nevertheless at the last minute Churchill decided to omit an important part of his speech that reflected on his decision making and vision as first lord. His notes read: 'In Naval circles the power of the [German] Air was underrated, and fact that up to present we are fighting largely with ships built with little regard to Air menace, or built before it developed fully, has affected for the time being our Naval strategy.'

This was, in fact, the principal reason why the Norway campaign had failed.

It fell to Leo Amery, who like Churchill had spent the 1930s in the political wilderness, to deliver the *coup de grâce*. A former first lord of the Admiralty and one of the elder statesmen of the Conservative Party, Amery was a formidable figure who had both a friendship and a history of clashes with Churchill. When he rose to speak on 8 May in what Roy Jenkins has called 'the most dramatic and the most far-reaching in its consequences of any parliamentary debate in the twentieth century', it was to deliver a body blow to Neville Chamberlain. Criticizing the failings of 'peace-time statesmen who are not too well fitted for the conduct of war', Amery ended by quoting Oliver Cromwell's memorable words of 1653 to the Long Parliament, which the lord protector thought had become unfit to govern Britain: 'You have sat too long here for any good you have been doing. Depart, I say, and let us have done with you. In the name of God, go!'

The vote was devastating. In a striking, historic display of party disunity, when a vote of confidence was taken near midnight on 8 May what had once been a huge Conservative majority of more than two hundred fell to a scant eighty-one. Many Tory backbenchers had joined with Labour to voice their disapproval, either by voting against the government or by abstaining. 'One young officer in uniform, who had long been a fervent admirer of Mr Chamberlain, walked through the Opposition Lobby with tears streaming down his face, and there were many who fought a similar battle with themselves.' When the vote was announced the House erupted in near-bedlam, with cheering and cries of 'Resign!' followed by the spontaneous singing of 'Rule, Britannia' by a Labour MP, who was joined by the future Conservative prime minister Harold Macmillan. Though visibly angry, a defeated and humiliated Chamberlain nevertheless kept his dignity, and to riotous chants of 'Go! Go! Go! Go!' left the chamber with his head held high.

Throughout the turbulent days of 9 and 10 May, in dining rooms, behind closed doors in the Palace of Westminster and in London clubs, there were small gatherings of various political elements debating and lobbying vigorously either for or against Churchill or Halifax to become the next prime minister. Chamberlain initially refused to concede that he was finished and soldiered on for nearly two days, vainly hoping to establish a coalition government with the Labour Party. However, the

Labour leadership flatly refused to participate so long as Chamberlain remained prime minister.

As the crisis over Chamberlain's future continued to rage within Westminster, Churchill waited in the wings. On the evening of 9 May he spoke on the telephone with his eighteen-year-old son Randolph, who was serving in a Territorial Army unit in Kettering, Northamptonshire, and said, 'I think I shall be Prime Minister tomorrow.'

Chamberlain realized that without the support of Clement Attlee's minority Labour Party, he could no longer govern Britain. By the evening of 9 May he had reluctantly decided that he would have to resign the following day.

The German invasion at dawn on 10 May was the last straw.

The issue of who would succeed Chamberlain remained to be settled. The natural and widely preferred heir apparent to Chamberlain was the foreign secretary Lord Halifax, the quintessential English aristocrat and an astute politician of impeccable reputation: 'a calm, rational man of immense personal prestige and *gravitas*, his career an uninterrupted tale of achievement and promotion'. The other was Winston Churchill, an eloquent, quick-witted but erratic, irrational and over-emotional politician, aptly described as a 'romantic and excitable adventurer, whose life was a *Boy's Own* story of cavalry charges, prison escapes and thirst for action', and a man whose unpredictable temperament and highly questionable judgment were distrusted by his peers. On balance the choice of Chamberlain's successor should have been plain.

Edward Halifax was the clear preference of the majority of Britain's senior leaders and of no less a personage than his friend King George VI. Although he aspired to the highest office, and under other circumstances would undoubtedly have accepted the post of prime minister, to his everlasting credit Halifax was a patriot who did not believe he was the right man to lead Britain in its darkest hour. Despite the support he knew he had, he demurred. As a member of the House of Lords, he felt that 'I should speedily become a more or less honorary Prime Minister, living in a kind of twilight just outside the things that really mattered.'

Halifax believed Churchill should be the man, and proposed his rival for the post. It was, notes Andrew Roberts, Halifax's biographer, 'a supreme act of self-abnegation'. There may well have been a different calculation by Halifax, however – a sense that Churchill would inevitably fail as prime minister: 'Then perhaps, Halifax could step in to clean up the mess and rally the sensible for a sensible peace.'

As word of Chamberlain's impending resignation spread throughout Westminster, there was dismay within his inner circle over Churchill's impending appointment. Jock Colville lashed out at his chief, Halifax, and Oliver Stanley for having 'weakly surrendered to a half-breed American whose main support was that of inefficient but talkative people of a similar type . . . Everybody here is in despair at the prospect.'

After the war Churchill gave his version to his personal physician and confidant Lord Moran (formerly Sir Charles Wilson): 'I was summoned to No. 10. Halifax was there already. I could see from what the Prime Minister said that he wanted Halifax to succeed him. He looked across the table at me, but I said nothing, and there was a very long pause. Then Halifax said that it would be difficult if the Prime Minister were a peer. I could tell that he had thrown in his hand.'

The final meeting of Chamberlain's War Cabinet took place on 10 May. The minutes recorded that the prime minister 'had reached the conclusion that the right course was that he should at once tender his resignation', and that each member should be prepared to do the same once the new premier had assumed office later that day. Yet when Randolph called his father for news, Churchill seemed less certain than he had been the night before: 'Oh, I don't know about that. Nothing matters now except beating the enemy.'

At about five o'clock Chamberlain journeyed to Buckingham Palace, where King George VI sorrowfully accepted his resignation. Both Chamberlain and the king left no doubt that they favoured the courtly foreign secretary to become the new prime minister. When the king was told that Halifax had turned the post down, it was clear to him what he had to do. Nevertheless he was dismayed by the prospect of Winston Churchill as Chamberlain's successor. Not only was the king close to Halifax, but Churchill had deeply angered him by his ill-considered crusade in 1936 in support of his brother Edward VIII's failed bid to marry the American divorcée Wallis Simpson and still retain his crown.

Whether one regards Halifax's decision as heroic or merely pragmatic, it was what led to Churchill's appointment, and ultimately to the timely leadership of Britain by a man whom the foreign secretary basically mistrusted but yet was willing to support because he believed it was the right thing to do. As Andrew Roberts points out, 'Nothing can cast doubt on the central fact that with the ultimate political prize in his grasp, Halifax acted selflessly and put his country before his father's dreams and his own ambitions,' and he 'never once later expressed a word of regret for his decision'.

The tragedy of Neville Chamberlain was that he was the latest in a long line of irresolute peacetime prime ministers who were ill suited to wartime leadership. His fundamental decency and naivety rendered him incapable of being the strong war leader that Britain required in 1940. He wrote his own epitaph as prime minister the day after his resignation: 'The day may come when my much cursed visit to Munich will be understood. Neither we nor the French were prepared for war. I am not responsible for this lack of preparation. I blame no one. None of us is always wise. I did what I thought was right.' Chamberlain would later admit to his sister, 'All my world has tumbled to bits in a moment.' No one ever questioned his patriotism; only his lack of inspired leadership was deplored. Several days after resigning, he admitted to Halifax that 'he had always thought he could not face the job of being Prime Minister in war, but when it came he did; and yet now that the war was becoming intense he could not but feel relieved that the final responsibility was off him.' The paradox of Neville Chamberlain is that he had a stronger, more positive reception in the House after he resigned than he ever had as prime minister.

The summons to Buckingham Palace came at 6.00 p.m. Churchill was on the verge of exhaustion just when he was called upon to assume the leadership of Britain. As he was driven the short distance from the Admiralty to the palace he exchanged no words with Inspector Thompson but instead sat in unusually silent contemplation. 'I was taken immediately to the King.' There were a few awkward moments after he had 'bade me sit down' as he 'looked at me searchingly and quizzically', before inquiring: 'I suppose you don't know why I have sent for you?' Churchill replied, 'Sir, I simply couldn't imagine why.' The king laughed and invited him to form a new administration. Churchill accepted without out further pretence, promising immediately to put together a coalition government, to appoint a new War Cabinet consisting of five or six members, and to submit before midnight at least five names of those whom he intended to bring into his new government.

Privately George VI was both disappointed and extremely wary of Churchill and his buccaneering reputation, and the following day he expressed his personal regrets to Halifax. Although the king was deeply loyal to both Chamberlain and Halifax and unenthusiastic about Churchill, his misgivings proved short lived. Churchill quickly won him over by a combination of charm and performance. By September 1940 what began as formal audiences at the palace had turned into informal, fruitful exchanges over regular weekly luncheons.

As he returned to the Admiralty from his audience with the king, Churchill sat alone and pensive in the back seat of his motor car. The son of Lord Randolph Churchill, who had once told him he would never amount to anything, was returning to the Admiralty as prime minister of Great Britain. Thompson congratulated him, and added: 'I only wish the position had come your way in better times, for you have an enormous task.' 'God alone knows how great it is,' Churchill replied. 'I hope that it is not too late. I am very much afraid that it is. But we can only do our best.' The new prime minister was all too aware of the magnitude of his responsibilities. 'Tears came into his eyes, and as he turned away he muttered something to himself. Then he set his jaw, and with a look of determination, mastering all emotion, he entered the side door of the Admiralty and began to climb the stairs.' For a brief moment, when elation at the realization of a lifetime dream ought to have prevailed, Winston Churchill was quite possibly the loneliest man in Britain.

When he went to bed that night at 3 a.m., he later recorded, he was 'conscious of a profound sense of relief. At last I had the authority to give directions over the whole scene.' All his life he had believed he was walking with destiny: he now faced his greatest test.

In the late-evening hours of 10 May 1940, Churchill and the British people embarked on what would prove to be a long, often lonely but ultimately triumphant ordeal. In the Great War, Churchill had been merely a player; in this war the years of military experience and preparation would serve him well not only as the political leader of his nation – its source of inspiration to resist the terror inflicted upon its people and its cities – but as its military warlord. The ordeal ahead might well have devastated Britain but for one elderly man's supreme will to resist. Although he once said, 'I know now that it will come to me to deal with Mister Hitler,' Churchill had never anticipated having to fight a war on two fronts in 1940: to hold back Germany's attempts to crush Britain, and to fend off those in his own government who would have made peace with the German dictator. It was an extraordinary challenge he had waited all his life to undertake. The historian A. J. P. Taylor would later write of him that when Britain needed him the most he became 'the saviour of his country'.

The date is burned into the memory of every Briton old enough to have understood its significance. Churchill's daughter Mary was at Chartwell and remembers hearing the news announced on the BBC. She prayed. Edward Spears heard the Berlin radio announce Britain's change of government. 'Mr Chamberlain has resigned and is followed by Winston Churchill . . . [the] most brutal representative of the policy of force, the man whose programme is to dismember Germany, this man whose hateful face is well known to all Germans.'

There is no better assessment of what drove Winston Churchill, not only in the Second World War but also throughout his remarkable life, than Harold Nicolson's observation: 'The British, except in moments of danger, are a lethargic race; they do not care for stimulants, they prefer sedatives. They are distrustful of brilliance. They feel more at ease with what they call "sound common sense". Their optimism, which in a crisis becomes a source of strength, degenerates in neutral periods into an ardent desire to believe that nothing unpleasant is likely to occur. Their motto in such periods is "safety first". And Churchill never believed that safety is the highest aim of human endeavour.'

One of his senior military assistants, Ian Jacob, has pointed out that Churchill was 'never an easy member of a team, never prepared to sit back and let things take their course, filled with the eagerness and the imagination of the "war man" surrounded by men of peace, he seemed to rock the boat.' Yet, in his willingness to rock the boat, Churchill was very unEnglish. The presence in the government of a man whom many called an adventurer and a soldier of fortune might have been distasteful in the past, but in 1940 such a person was precisely what Britain required in its leader.

Indeed someone like General George S. Patton would brusquely have declared that what Britain needed in 1940 was a son of a bitch, someone unafraid to make the difficult life-and-death decisions that befall a war leader, to take charge of a nation in a state of disbelief that it was again at war – a war that was not supposed to have occurred after the terrible sacrifices of the 'war to end all wars'. For all his many admirable qualities, Halifax was certainly not a war leader of the ilk required to defeat Adolf Hitler. On 10 May 1940 just such a son of a bitch took charge of Britain's fate when the responsibility to lead the nation was thrust upon Winston Churchill, who would later remark, 'Some people pretend to regard me as the British Lion. But I am not the Lion. I am simply the Roar of the Lion.'

The mood of Britain's military and political leaders was fairly represented by Ironside's observation that 'the only man who can succeed is Winston and he is too unstable, though he has the genius to bring the war to an end.' Chips Channon, the Tory MP and avid supporter of Chamberlain, described 10 May as 'perhaps the darkest day in English history'. His despairing words were as much a reflection of his dismay at the German invasion of the West as they were of Churchill's ascent to the leadership of Britain.

Others, like Edward Spears, were reassured by the news of Churchill's appointment. 'It seemed to me evident that Churchill alone could lead us to safety and eventually to success. That I had long believed his whole career had shaped him for this end reinforced my conviction in ultimate victory.'

The disapproval of the bureaucrats notwithstanding, George Orwell and Sir Charles Wilson may have spoken for Britain of what Churchill would come to epitomize. Orwell observed that Britain finally had 'a leader who understood "that wars are won by fighting"', while Wilson wrote that what the nation required 'was a man utterly blind to reason, a man who refused to see the sound and compelling reasons for despair and surrender'.

The man who had just become prime minister at the moment of the gravest crisis in British history was never in the best of health, smoked far too much, was thought to drink to excess and had been a political outcast for nearly a decade. Now, this controversial figure, whom many thought dangerously unfit to lead Britain, was suddenly charged with as heavy a burden as has ever been placed upon the shoulders of a leader. When he arose on his first morning as prime minister he said to Clementine, 'Only Hitler can turn me out of this job.'

33

'Action This Day'

Winston did not turn the handle of the door of No. 10 Downing Street, and walk in, he threw his shoulder against the door, burst in and took possession before the astonished staff could get their breath. — Lord Moran

The responsibility that Churchill assumed as prime minister was a challenge unlike any other faced by a British leader. He has been aptly described as 'a Prime Minister without a party', because the Conservatives were still led by Neville Chamberlain. Moreover, unlike the autocratic Hitler, who exercised absolute control over German strategy and its military forces, Churchill was obliged to function within the constraints of a democratic system of government that neither gave him complete control nor provided a means for rapid decisions, which in wartime often make the difference between success and failure. For all their considerable differences, the two men had one common trait: unrelenting tenacity. In Churchill's case it became the defining feature of his leadership.

And while his lifelong dream of playing a heroic role had at last come to fruition at the age of sixty-five, his unrestrained behaviour, comprising four decades of controversy, carried with it a price tag: profound scepticism and the widespread belief that he was simply a prime-ministerial caretaker. Because of his self-absorption, his outspokenness and his often contentious positions on matters of state and of governance, Churchill inevitably became the target of critics and revisionists anxious to question his every action and decision, sometimes even his courage. His chequered past posed an added obstacle that would have to be overcome. Some, like J. F. C. Fuller, held the opinion that 'throughout his turbulent life he never quite grew up, and like a boy, loved big bangs and playing at soldiers'.

Though Churchill showed his age, what the British public and the members of the government would see in the weeks and months ahead was a man driven to lead – and to save the nation. It was as if his lifetime of preparation had been intended for a moment of crisis when he could take the reins of leadership. After the war his principal private secretary Sir John Martin remarked to him that life was just not as exciting as it had been. Churchill replied, ' "You can't expect a war all the time." It was said in jest, but indeed for him his five years as war-time Prime Minister were the supreme period of his life.'

Yet one of Churchill's greatest challenges upon becoming Britain's leader in May 1940 was to learn to relate to people, something he had never been particularly good at. Despite his many friends and acquaintances, he was at heart a rather solitary figure with virtually no understanding of the common man. As Lord Moran observed, 'That may sound odd to those who knew him only as a war leader, buoyant, pink and beaming. But the real Winston was a lonely, rather remote figure ... Winston had gone through life as an individual, absorbed in himself, and rapt in his thoughts and plans. He wasn't really interested in other people. They had sensed this, and he had paid the price exacted from those who leave the herd ... The war closed the gap.'

Churchill remarked in his memoirs that when he went to bed at 3.00 the morning of 11 May he felt confident that 'I should not fail.' However, the facts contradict that retrospective statement. When he became prime minister Britain's survival was very much in doubt. Its French and Belgian allies were being overwhelmed by Hitler's panzers, and although a US president would soon begin secretly defying American isolationism by supplying what military help he could under the Lend-Lease pro-gramme, Britain was alone. Prominent members of his own cabinet were openly doubtful about waging a hopeless war and wanted serious consideration given to making peace with Hitler. Moreover Churchill himself was unpopular with a large section of his own Conservative Party. Others who were even less charitable thought a loose cannon had been set free to run the country. Hankey doubted if 'the wise old elephants [Chamberlain and Halifax] will ever be able to hold the Rogue Elephant'.

One of Churchill's first acts as prime minister was to hang a picture of his beloved Mrs Everest in his study at No. 10, an act he had waited all his adult life to carry out. During the five arduous years he spent as wartime prime minister, she was always near him, and her presence gladdened his heart and brought him solace.

British protocol requires that an outgoing prime minister vacate No. 10 forthwith. In a gracious gesture designed to spare Chamberlain further humiliation, Churchill suggested he take as long as he liked before moving out, and he himself spent the first month living and working part of the day at the Admiralty. Lacking universal support within his own party, he made no attempt initially to take over its leadership, leaving Chamberlain as the titular head of the Conservatives. Chamberlain was given the largely ceremonial post of lord president of the Council, and during the few remaining months before cancer claimed his life on 9 November 1940 Churchill was extraordinarily cordial and deferential to the former prime minister. Others were promptly sacked. Ministers not in the cabinet were summoned and advised that they would have to resign in order for Churchill to bring in men from both parties to form his coalition government. An air of uncertainty hung over Westminster. Yet several of Churchill's critics were disarmed by being appointed to posts they had never expected to be given or retained in posts they had expected to be dismissed from. Among them was R. A. 'Rab' Butler, who was kept on until 1941 as under-secretary of state for foreign affairs. When Butler reminded him of their past disagreements, Churchill demurred and smoothly replied, 'But you have invited me to your private residence.'

The Labour leader Clement Attlee became lord privy seal and from 1942 to the end of the war was the deputy prime minister. In both capacities he played a relatively minor role in the conduct of the war, ever present but rarely consulted. He once said to Churchill in the cabinet room, 'Prime Minister, anything more I can do for you?' 'Yes, go,' said Winston – and that was typical. For his part Attlee once confided his opinion of Churchill: 'Fifty per cent of Winston is genius, fifty per cent bloody fool.'

All his life Churchill believed that military service was an essential ingredient of a political career. 'When he came to a powerful station he never cared much – though he sometimes had to condone it – for putting ministers into his government or shadow cabinet who had not exposed themselves to the fire of the enemy in either of the two world wars.'

Churchill appointed A. V. Alexander the new first lord. In doing so he chose a working-class Labour politician who had previously served in the same post in Ramsay MacDonald's government in the early 1930s. Alexander had strongly supported Churchill over Halifax and was rewarded by his inclusion in the new War Cabinet. Described as essentially a yes-man who left Pound and the admirals alone to do their work without undue interference, Alexander nevertheless earned Churchill's trust. As secretary of state for air, Churchill chose his close friend Archie Sinclair. To complete the shake-up of the military posts Oliver Stanley was dismissed as secretary of state for war and replaced by Anthony Eden. Overall the transition to the Churchill administration was smooth and was achieved without undue disruption. Most ministers simply carried on in their previous posts. Keeping such men as Halifax reduced the bruised feelings among Chamberlain's supporters and eased the transition.

In the early days of his tenure, and indeed throughout his time in office, Churchill made a point of deferring to his War Cabinet colleagues far more than might have been imagined. From the outset he gave orders that any directive issued by him would not be deemed valid unless it was in writing. This form of self-imposed discipline effectively put the brakes on his impetuosity, although in truth it never entirely curbed it.

Those who served Churchill during the war invariably faced a high level of pressure from a demanding master. No one (neither aides, stenographers, military men nor ministers) was spared his often impossible demands or his wrath when anyone failed to satisfy him. 'The administration formed by Churchill in 1940 has been described as the "Great Coalition". It may have been great', wrote Robert Boothby, his parliamentary private secretary from 1926 to 1929, when Churchill had been chancellor of the exchequer, 'but it was not a happy government. Most of the ministers lived in constant dread of a red ink minute from the Prime Minister, or the sack; and some of them got both.'

Churchill's inner circle consisted of old friends, cronies and allies, all of them men he implicitly trusted. Principal among this group was Brendan Bracken. Born in Ireland, Bracken had worked in publishing in the 1920s, edited several publications and was elected to Parliament in 1929. A long-standing friend and confidant, and always hostile to appeasement, Bracken had accompanied Churchill to the Admiralty in 1939 as his principal private secretary. He was resented and regarded with suspicion by both Clementine and Randolph, but despite Clementine's misgivings, he was more than a trusted adviser. When Churchill lapsed into periods of his 'black dog' depression it was Bracken who helped restore his equilibrium in ways not even Clementine could do. A lifelong bon vivant, Bracken was in large measure responsible for Churchill's financial success through his contacts in publishing, which helped secure lucrative deals and financial backing in 1937 when Churchill had money problems.

Others whom he appointed included his son-in-law Duncan Sandys (married to his daughter Diana in 1935), after he had been disabled on active service, and his intelligence adviser Desmond Morton, who continued in this role throughout the war. The mercurial Beaverbrook was appointed to head the newly created Ministry of Aircraft Production, where he significantly increased the output of fighters and bombers. Although his contributions to the war effort were noteworthy, he fought incessantly with the Air Ministry and any other agency that opposed him and became such a distraction that Churchill was obliged to sack him in 1941.

Frederick Lindemann continued to serve as Churchill's powerful and controversial scientific adviser. He was both a mathematician and a physicist, and one of his greatest strengths lay in his status as the prime minister's go-between with the scientific community. Someone once said of Lindemann, who was given to outrageous statements, often to provoke others to think, that 'he was marginally to the right of Genghis Khan'. Feared, respected and sometimes detested, Lindemann and Brendan Bracken were the powerful *éminences grises* of Churchill's inner circle and had virtually unlimited access to him.

One of the first people Churchill met upon his arrival at No. 10 was young Jock Colville, who would serve as assistant private secretary to three prime ministers: Chamberlain, Churchill and Clement Attlee. Colville later recalled hearing the news that Churchill was the new prime minister. 'In May 1940, the mere thought of Churchill as prime minister sent a cold chill down the spines of the staff at 10 Downing Street . . . General Ismay had told us in despairing tones of the confusion caused by his enthusiastic eruptions into the peaceful and orderly deliberations of the Military Co-ordination Committee and the chiefs of staff . . . The country had fallen into the hands of an adventurer . . . Seldom can a prime minister have taken office with 'the Establishment', as it would now be called, so dubious of the choice and so prepared to find its doubts justified.' Colville was in the thick of it: 'Churchill arrived on the scene like a jet-propelled rocket. The even tenor of our life was rudely disrupted . . . Many of the familiar faces vanished, and I, being the least important, was taken over with the furniture . . . The pace became frantic.'

The British civil service has a long tradition of overbearing behaviour, of outmanoeuvring, ignoring and sometimes sabotaging appointed ministers. Everything changed on 11 May 1940. The days of peacetime nine-to-five working hours evaporated almost overnight, as did the leisurely pace of life under Chamberlain, to be replaced by a virtual frenzy of activity. Colville would later remark: 'I doubt if there has ever been such a rapid transformation of opinion in Whitehall and of the tempo at which business is conducted.'

Downing Street secretary Marian Spicer, who had served Neville Chamberlain, describes the effect. 'When Mr Churchill took office in May 1940, the whole place exploded. It was as if a current of high voltage electricity was let loose, not only in Number Ten, but throughout the fusty corridors of Whitehall.' Abruptly forgotten were weekends of free time; leave was all but abolished. Early in the war Archie Sinclair offered the suggestion that the civil servants be given some time off, pointing out that one senior executive had gone home on a Friday night on weekend leave and collapsed. An unsympathetic Churchill merely replied: 'Shows what a mistake he made to go on leave.'

Churchill's personal physician Sir Charles Wilson, who was assigned to him out of concern for his health two weeks after he became prime minister, and remained his doctor for the rest of his life, made this trenchant observation of his new patient in 1940:

From the time he marched his toy soldiers in the nursery at the lodge in Phoenix Park, he had loved war and excitement. To him war was an end in itself, rather than a means to an end. It fascinated him. And when he found himself Prime Minister, and it was his duty to conduct a vast conflict nearly single handed, it seemed almost too good to be true . . . The job was made for him, he revelled in it . . . The burden of a Prime Minister is formidable in peace, in war it may well crush a man in the prime of life. Winston in reckless delight doubled the weight he had to carry by his approach to the duties of the office. He had never done anything in moderation. Now his appetite for work was voracious. He turned night into day.

Throughout the war Churchill was surrounded by a dedicated staff of private secretaries and stenographers, all of whom served him well and were never more than a minute or so away. Those new to his service found a great deal to get used to: his seemingly unforgiving persona; having to work incredibly long hours to keep up with a man far older than most; his fierce, single-minded devotion to winning the war. 'He was an alarming master,' recalled John Martin, who entered Churchill's service on 23 May and soon learned the two very contrasting sides of his nature. Late one evening as Churchill waited impatiently for the War Office to clear a message he had drafted for Lord Gort, Martin went to report the lack of response only to be greeted with an angry grunt. Yet 'on another strenuous evening he put his hand on my shoulder and said, "You know, I may seem to be very fierce, but I am fierce only with one man – Hitler."' Indeed Churchill privately reserved the full force of his contempt for Hitler and Benito Mussolini, 'this absurd imposter', a 'whipped jackal, frisking at the side of the German tiger'. When Hitler invaded Russia in June 1941, Churchill derisively called him 'this blood-thirsty guttersnipe' who had launched 'his mechanized armies upon new fields of slaughter'. The depth of Churchill's animosity became abundantly clear during a cabinet meeting in December 1942 when he stated: 'If Hitler falls into our hands we shall certainly put him to death. This man is the mainspring of evil,' and should die in the electric chair, an instrument, he said, that was reserved 'for gangsters'.

Churchill's speech impediment continued to make it difficult at times to understand him. Although he would never admit it, he relied deeply upon these faithful men and women, 'the "Secret Circle" as he called us', said John Peck, a member of this elite group. 'He hated change and new faces around him, and any newcomer was deliberately given a fairly taxing time. But once you were in, you were in totally and uncon-ditionally; you were part of the Churchill family.' He demanded answers even when he knew perfectly well his aides did not have them. Questions such as 'Where is the *Ark Royal*?' could be met with only one of two replies: the correct answer or 'I'll find out, sir.' The aides soon identified which military department duty officer to contact for an answer at any time of day or night.

Working for Churchill was a constant challenge. It was virtually impossible to relax one's guard, particularly when he was in one of his demanding moods. Meetings of the War Cabinet were held almost every day except when Churchill was travelling. Lawrence Burgis, the War Cabinet assistant secretary, offers this description of a typical meeting. 'There he would be, sitting in his chair at the long table . . . either in his siren suit [or] immaculately dressed in a short black coat, striped trousers, silk shirt and bow tie with spots.' The participants were generally forewarned of how the meeting would go. 'As one entered the historic [cabinet] room one could generally tell from the expression on Churchill's face, if the meeting was set for fine, fair, or wet and stormy.'

The endless torrent of 'Action This Day' memos that poured from his inner sanctum became the defining feature of his war ministry. The duties of his aides did not end when Churchill retired in the early hours of each morning, when 'normally you went to his bedroom and you had to stand there while he stripped to the buff and scratched his back with his back-scratcher. And you discussed the affairs of the day.' Demanding though he was on others, Churchill was just as hard on himself, as he revealed in August when he said to Desmond Morton, 'Every night I try myself by court-martial to see if I have done anything effective during the day. I don't mean just pawing the ground – anyone can go through the motions – but something really effective.'

No one wanted to be the first to earn the wrath of the new prime minister. 'Bells rang continuously and staid civil servants were seen to actually run along its corridors; his chiefs of staff, summoned to Churchill's presence at 9:30 P.M., often staggered forth wearily at 2 A.M., protracted sessions which staffers soon dubbed "the Midnight Follies." Intolerant of opposition, Churchill told one official who found his methods cavalier: "I am indeed honored to sit at the same table with a man who so closely resembles Jesus Christ, but I want to win the war." '

Although his style of leadership was challenging, often contentious, his rationale was not to be deliberately obnoxious or to suppress ideas and opinions but rather to ascertain their validity and provoke clear thinking. Much like a tutor who refuses to accept anything but the best from a student, Churchill insisted that ideas be defensible in the courts of oral and written argument. Those who stood the test survived; those who failed rarely returned for encores. What made him so effective was that, despite his harsh methods, politicians and military men would be completely energized in his presence.

His eruptions, which have been aptly characterized as melodramatic, were usually to serve a purpose. Sometimes they were real, at other times merely a theatrical test of the recipient's resolve. Oliver Lyttelton, who served in the War Cabinet, pointed out, 'He did not get angry because others opposed him, but because he could not persuade them.' Moreover, 'In a long experience of him, I have never known an opinion firmly expressed by a colleague go unweighed and unconsidered. Within limits . . . they were more often adopted than discarded . . . Churchill's method to extract and test a man's opinion was to react violently and provocatively. Heat, he believes, refines the metal.' More than once Lyttelton left Churchill believing that his opinion lay trampled in the dust only to learn later that 'he had modified a speech or a telegram to meet the point.'

As prime minister Churchill continued his habit of conducting business in the middle of the night. Within three days of the change of government Halifax was already grumbling that cabinet meetings were ending as late as 1.00 a.m., and hoped in vain 'that we have cured him of that!' What no one cured Churchill of was his cigars, which perpetually filled the cabinet room with smoke. A bucket sat beside his place, into which the butts were carelessly tossed without benefit of aim but generally with accuracy. What Churchill never knew was that the Royal Marines guarding the room supplemented their pay by selling them as souvenirs for tidy sums.

In past governments, ministers briefing the prime minister had routinely been accompanied by aides and advisers, to whom they turned for information or to answer questions. Churchill changed this. Ministers who were not part of the War Cabinet came unattended and were expected to state their own case, in accordance with his belief that a minister who relied on others was not fit to hold office.

Although he was often impossibly demanding, there were lighthearted moments. There was, for example, the late evening in 1943 when one of his military assistants, Leslie Hollis, telephoned the duty officer of the Joint Intelligence Staff to pass along the prime minister's requirement for 'an intelligence estimate of the German reinforcements in Italy as well as the potential for the political collapse of the Italian government.' Churchill wanted the study by 10.30 the next morning. The exasperated navy captain explained that it was an impossible task at such short notice, and said: 'Hollis, why don't you tell the silly old man to go to bed, and we'll get on with it as quickly as we can and probably have it ready by tomorrow afternoon,' not knowing that 'the silly old man' was listening on an extension. Down the line came the voice of Churchill: 'Perhaps it would help in your deliberations if the silly old man came down to help you.' A short time later Churchill appeared in the operations room dressed in his romper suit to explain his requirements, then left, only to open the door a few seconds later to inquire with a twinkle in his eye: 'Would three o'clock tomorrow afternoon be satisfactory to you, Captain?'

Other challenges involved dealing with Churchill's tendency to ignore time and schedules and his chaotic work habits. Sometimes he was still in bed working on a speech when he was supposed to be in the House delivering it. Frequently trips and meetings were ordered at short or no notice; transport was called for but never used. Whether he was overseas in France during May and June 1940, or in Washington, Moscow, Casablanca, Tehran or Cairo, or merely visiting a bombed-out city or a defensive position on the southern coast of England, Churchill travelled constantly.

Work went on in every conceivable manner. While awake, Churchill would work at his desk, in his motor car, even in his bathtub. During his first trip as prime minister to the United States in December 1941, he was so busy that he once had Hollis read secret reports to him while he bathed. As Hollis read, Churchill suddenly held his nose and disappeared under the water 'like a pink, plump porpoise'. Waiting for him to surface, Hollis stopped reading only to see Churchill emerge spluttering and demanding to know why he had stopped. 'Don't you know that water is a conductor of sound?' His often petrified secretaries also became used to being summoned to take dictation from the other side of the bathroom door, which was left ajar while he splashed or dried himself, never stopping his flow of words. Motor-car trips to and from Chequers (the prime minister's official country house in Buckinghamshire) were especially nightmarish for the unlucky stenographer attempting to take dictation while nearly choking on Churchill's cigar smoke. Yet despite the habitually impossible demands he placed on them, his occasional rudeness and his insistence on perfection as he dictated, usually with machine-gun speed, the women who served Churchill's round-the-clock stenographic needs revered their boss. Most were young and had never encountered anyone quite like him. Sir John

Peck relates how, one morning at Chequers, Churchill was propped up in bed, smoking a cigar, working and giving dictation, when the stenographer noticed that the bedclothes were smouldering and about to burst into flame. Too scared to point out the problem, she excused herself and opened the bedroom door hurriedly to signal to several members of his staff. Peck was first on the scene and saw the prime minister puffing away on his cigar while clouds of smoke rose around his shoulders. 'Sir, I think you're on fire.' Churchill replied that yes, he was. 'Would you like me to put you out?' said Peck. 'Yes, please do.' With the fire out, Churchill's dressing gown was eased away and quickly replaced as he went on working as if nothing untoward had occurred.

Although most cabinet meetings were held at No. 10, there were as many as five other venues, including, during the Blitz, stations of the London Underground. Often Churchill would change the venue at the last minute. 'I don't think he ever realized the extra strain this involved on the secretariat, otherwise he would not have done it,' said Lawrence Burgis.

Those meeting Churchill for the first time encountered a rotund man dressed in one of his colourful siren suits, a unique sartorial creation of his own design, which A. J. P. Taylor once described as resembling 'a child's "rompers"'. The siren suit, which dated from his earlier days working on projects at Chartwell, was a rather bizarre, one-piece garment that zipped up the front and, lacking only tools hanging from a belt, might have passed for a boiler suit it.

The uninformed who underestimated him for his eccentric dress and mannerisms quickly paid the price, and those who vacillated either resigned or were replaced by men who knew their position on a given matter and were willing to defend it. Hugh Dalton, a brilliant, acerbic Old Etonian and Cambridge graduate who taught at the London School of Economics and was a major influence in the Labour Party, had no reason to fear dealing with Churchill. Dalton joined Churchill's coalition government as minister of economic warfare on 14 May 1940. He once mentioned to Lord Halifax that he was never certain how to handle Churchill. Halifax replied: 'Always stand up to him. He hates doormats. If you begin to give way he will simply wipe his feet upon you.' Others learned the lesson the hard way. Like his boss, Dalton did not suffer fools and was once called by his adversary, Brendan Bracken, then the minister of information, 'the biggest bloodiest shit I've ever met'. An unperturbed Churchill merely laughed. He loved 'shits' like Dalton, a man with the courage of his convictions. The rebellious side of Churchill led him particularly to like men who had incurred the wrath of bureaucrats or were unorthodox, and 'who could speak up boldly and hold their own in the rough-and-tumble of controversy', recalled Ian Jacob, one of his military assistants.

Not a single moment of his day was ever wasted. When not sleeping he was working, and whether over a meal or travelling, he made use of every waking moment. The use of written memorandums in dealing with Churchill was essential. In the spring of 1940, Clementine told Edward Spears how to get Winston's attention: 'Put what you have to say in writing. He often does not listen or does not hear if he is thinking of something else. But he will always consider a paper carefully and take in all its implications. He never forgets what he has seen in writing.'

During the war ideas flowed from him, often faster than his harried stenographers could write them down. Some of these ideas might be labelled harebrained, but they were the product of a mind that never rested. Some were well ahead of the technology of the time, such as his scheme for sowing the skies with aerial mines on routes taken by German bombers. Others were innovative and well intentioned but impractical. Of the hundreds if not thousands of ideas that he produced during the war, none was greater or more important than his suggestion that artificial harbours (code-named Mulberry) be created to support the D-day landings in Normandy. The idea occurred to him during a visit to Franklin Roosevelt. The President said: 'You know, that was Churchill's idea. Just one of those brilliant ideas that he has. He has a hundred a day and about four of them are good. When he was up visiting me at Hyde Park he saw all those boats from the last war tied up in the Hudson River, and in one of his great bursts of imagination he said: "By George, we could take those ships and others like them that are good for nothing and sink them off shore to protect the landings." I thought well of it and we talked about it all afternoon. The military and naval authorities were startled out of a year's growth. But Winnie was right. Great fellow, that Churchill, if you can keep up with him.'

When the pressure got to Churchill, as it inevitably did on occasion, he would ruminate on the power of the human mind to overcome adversity. In her autobiography his cousin Clare Sheridan remarked that

Churchill 'produced a theory about brains, which, he said, could be put to any use in any channel. Given the brain-power, it was possible, he thought, to switch it on or off at will, as he did for instance from politics to painting . . . But power is more dear to the heart of man than all else – power over the destinies of men and nations!'

She was quite right; power and its applications are among the keys to understanding Winston Churchill. As he once told Robert Boothby, 'It took Armageddon to make me Prime Minister. But now that I am there, I am determined that Power shall be in no other hands but mine. There will be no more Kitcheners, Fishers or Haigs.'

34
Minister of Defence

*Churchill was a frustrated Marlborough, who itched to be both the general on
the field of battle and the presiding genius of the alliance.* – John Keegan

Churchill wholly subscribed to Clemenceau's dictum that 'war is too
dangerous a business to entrust to soldiers.' He was adamant that never
again would British soldiers have to fight terrible battles of attrition.
War requires central direction and he was single-minded in his determination to pilot Britain through the war. At the stroke of a pen he named
himself minister of defence, calling upon the full extent of his previous
military training and experience to guide generals, admirals and airmen
who had no liking for being told what to do by a civilian. His memories
of the Great War still vivid and haunting, Churchill was adamant that
there would be no recurrence of the failures of 1914–18. 'I felt I knew
more about making war than anyone they could make Prime Minister.
For years I had thought about it.'

Throughout the war Churchill was obliged to juggle the roles of
political leader and commander in chief of the British armed forces.
These roles sometimes clashed when a military decision that he had
initiated or approved produced severe repercussions that threatened him
politically. One of his sternest critics was the architect of the BBC, John
Reith, Chamberlain's minister of information in 1940 and minister of
transport from May to October that year. Reith loathed Churchill, and
when it was announced on 11 May that the new prime minister was
assuming the post of minister of defence, he wrote in his diary: 'Heaven
help us.'

Such criticism warrants a brief examination of this question: was
Churchill so in love with war that he merited the label of warmonger?
The answer is no. His fascination with war must not be confused with

a love of war. His experience of seeing death in many grotesque forms was enough to cure anyone's idealism. However, it was the trappings of war that engaged him, and the notion of being a key player in the making of strategy and, if not its chief strategist, at least the overseer of the war's military direction. Although he never admitted his own culpability in the ultimately disastrous Norwegian campaign, it was precisely the lack of central direction that he took immediate steps to cure.

No role required more nerve or was more important than the higher direction of the war, particularly in 1940, when Britain's fate hung in the balance. The alternative was the traditional one of appointing a politician in the War Cabinet to the post, an option which he deemed unthinkable not least because he felt there was no one more suitable than himself. Not only was Winston Churchill's assumption of the role of generalissimo unprecedented, but unlike previous prime ministers in British history who were responsible for the political direction of a war, he would also be, like the US president, the commander in chief of the armed forces. It was an audacious decision that he took without the authority of Parliament.

One of Churchill's first acts was to create the War Cabinet Defence Committee within the War Cabinet. He appointed himself chairman and Attlee vice chairman; the other members were Chamberlain (until his health failed), the three service ministers and the chiefs of staff. Although often ignored or cast in minor roles, Attlee nevertheless 'believed that it was thanks to "Winston's knowledge of military men, his own military experience and flair, his personal dynamism and the sweeping powers that any prime minister can have in wartime if he chooses to use them" that "the deadly problem of civilian-versus-generals in wartime was solved"' – high praise indeed from the Opposition leader.

Churchill privately explained that he had assumed the post solely out of necessity, 'because times were so very bad. It was accepted because everyone realized how near death and ruin we stood. Not only individual death . . . but, incomparably more commanding, the life of Britain, her message, and her glory.' Churchill knew he was bringing to bear the experience, often painful, of an entire lifetime: a knowledge (or at least a perceived understanding) of every aspect of making war, from grand strategy to tactics on the battlefield, from tanks to aircraft carriers, from airpower to submarines and from code breaking to commando raids. It was this knowledge that gave him confidence that he was Hitler's equal – indeed Hitler's superior – and that with enough time and in a military alliance with the United States, he would save his country and win the war. As Sir Charles Wilson observed: 'Mr Churchill had learnt in a bitter school the importance of confronting the world with a bold face. He saw himself as the saviour of his country, a great figure in history, which has always been to him the story of heroes.'

Senior command appointments in the three services first had to pass muster with Churchill. The chiefs of staff submitted the names and résumés of nominees and he would then decide on their suitability. Some, like the admirals Roger Keyes and Lord Louis Mountbatten, he appointed either without reference to or over the objections of his military advisers.

His most important relationship was with his chiefs of staff. Of the three men he inherited in May 1940, only Pound retained his post. The chief of the air staff, Air Chief Marshal Sir Cyril Newall, would be replaced in October 1940 by Air Chief Marshal Sir Charles 'Peter' Portal, and the faithful Ironside, who had never wanted the job of CIGS in the first place, and who was clearly not the right man to lead the army in wartime, was replaced on 25 May by General Sir John Dill in what was to prove a troubled relationship marked by Churchill's increasingly visible disdain. Dill was a superb soldier, and although blessed with common sense, he was, in Churchill's view, too 'soft' to be the wartime CIGS. Unfortunately it soon became clear that the two could not coexist for long. The wartime director of military operations, Major General John Kennedy, was a first-hand observer of the trials and tribulations faced by the men he served. Dill, he said, became exhausted from overwork and constant pressure from Churchill. 'It was he who bore the brunt of Churchill's fury when the latter's multitudinous ideas and projects were opposed by the Chiefs of Staff. On one occasion, after a long argument about some especially unsound suggestion, Churchill accused him to his face of being "the dead hand of inanition".' Another time, as the chiefs departed after a late-night meeting, Churchill dismissively remarked to an associate, 'I have to wage modern war with ancient weapons.'

Churchill was not satisfied merely to take military advice from his chiefs; he was determined to be a major player in the formulation of strategy. To that end he deliberately excluded the three service ministers from his War Cabinet. Thus when the Chiefs of Staff Committee met with Churchill in the chair, they were free to express their views without the encumbrance of their ministers, and he was free to deal directly with them.

He took matters one step further, creating within the War Cabinet office a small military secretariat that reported directly to him as minister of defence, a move designed to pull together Britain's military machine under his central control. The secretariat was headed by General Hastings Lionel Ismay (known familiarly as 'Pug', for his resemblance to one); the other two key players were both colonels: Ian Jacob, a Royal Engineer, and Leslie Hollis, a Royal Marine. This outstanding trio were 'the foundation of Churchill's war machine', as Lawrence Burgis called them. Functioning as the link between the prime minister and the military departments, they meshed superbly and ensured that what might otherwise have been a difficult set of relationships would succeed. Each brought competence, common sense, dedication and an ability to deal effectively with Churchill, who never travelled anywhere without one of them present. These 'three musketeers' handled the prime minister's endless memos and military demands, came to the rescue of the chiefs when he was on the warpath, and managed to defuse countless situations that might have escalated into major issues. No day in Churchill's service was without its challenge. Before each of his meetings with the chiefs of staff, one or more of the three had to brief him. No matter how well versed they were, Churchill would invariably ask a question no one had anticipated.

Ismay was a worthy successor to Hankey and served Churchill with devotion. It was no mean task to please both Churchill and the equally demanding chiefs of staff. In the words of Ian Jacob, 'As the Prime Minister's Chief Staff Officer, and as an additional member of the Chiefs of Staff Committee, Ismay took the knocks from above and below, and worked day and night to ensure that the often exasperating vagaries of the Prime Minister and the sometimes mulish obstinacy of the Chiefs of Staff did not break up the association.' He had to overcome suspicion of his motives and play the conciliator. Colville later paid him the ultimate compliment, noting that Churchill 'owed more, and admitted that he owed [Ismay] more, than to anybody else, military or civilian, in the whole of the war.' To this day Ismay remains one of the most underrated major British figures of the Second World War. Of his wartime boss he said: 'What a unique and brilliant complex. Brave as a lion, tender as a woman, simple as a child.'

Of Churchill's many relationships as Britain's war leader none was more important than that with the chiefs of staff. From the time he became first lord of the Admiralty in 1911, he was accustomed to issuing orders to the military, and the passage of nearly forty years had merely whetted his appetite. 'I readily admit', he later wrote, 'that the post which had now fallen to me was the one I liked the best. Power, for the sake of lording it over fellow-creatures or adding to personal pomp, is rightly judged base. But power in a national crisis, when a man believes he knows what orders should be given, is a blessing.' As a risk taker who rarely had second thoughts, he hardly ever took into account the consequences of failure – he considered only the virtues of success. One of his frequent sayings was 'The enemy should be made to bleed and burn every day.'

While his relations with the military chiefs were often stormy, he trusted and liked them personally. In 1944 he said of them, with tongue in cheek, 'I may lead them up the garden path, but at every turn of the path they have found delectable fruits and wholesome vegetables.'

For all his battles with the service chiefs, Churchill never wanted them to agree with him merely for the sake of placating him. He encouraged dissent, but when they took him at his word they would often infuriate him. At other times Churchill could become petulant, as he did one evening when, miffed that his generals had backed General Dwight Eisenhower rather than him over an issue, he took his theatrical displeasure out on his soup bowl. 'His chin isn't very much above the soup plate,' recalled Eisenhower with amusement. 'He crouched over the plate, almost had his nose in the soup, wielded the spoon rapidly. The soup disappeared to the accompaniment of loud gurglings,' as Churchill deliberately ignored his table companions.

Nevertheless, by his own admission, Churchill was given to interfering in military matters, large and small. Dr Wilson offered an example: 'I gave him some instance of Hitler's meddling in the conduct of a minor incident on the Eastern Front, [and] he said with a great grin, "that's what I do." '

He found it difficult to let go of the Admiralty, and continued issuing directives as if he were still first lord. This led to a nasty spat over the conversion of an older class of battleships into armoured vessels, which were called for by his now discarded Plan Catherine. He complained that the failure to carry out his wishes would provide 'the most melancholy pages of the Admiralty annals'. An admiral summoned to see him wrote, 'I loved him almost at first sight, but he made . . . such astounding statements about naval warfare . . . [that] I still don't know if he was wanting to find out if I was prepared to applaud everything he said or whether he really believes half what he says.'

His years of military service left Churchill with a special fondness for the ordinary men and women of the armed forces. 'When the soldier is at war, his mind should be at peace,' he once told Wilson, who added that Churchill 'likes soldiers about him – they feel he is one of themselves. When he approached one of his generals or admirals he seemed instinctively to expect to like him.' Sometimes, however, there were awkward beginnings when he first met people. At the Cairo Conference in 1943, Churchill encountered for the first time Major General Claire Chennault, Chiang Kai-shek's personal adviser and the colourful commander of the famed Flying Tigers (officially the US Fourteenth Air Force). Chennault, nicknamed 'the Hawk' by *Time* magazine, had been described by Antony Head, a member of the Joint Planning Staff, as 'resembling a Red Indian Chief who had just taken somebody's scalp'. Turning to Ismay, Churchill asked the name of the American officer in a loud voice that was overheard by the US delegation and produced an embarrassed silence, finally broken when he announced: 'I'm glad he's on our side.' The tale of the prime minister and the Hawk soon made the rounds of the US army.

In addition to his love of soldiers and soldiering, Churchill had a romantic's view of their nobility of spirit, once relating the story of a British tank crew who surrendered to the Germans and were saluted and complimented on their courage. 'That is how I like war to be conducted,' he said. He named his favourite cat Nelson. One day Colville entered Churchill's bedroom with an important telegram from Franklin Roosevelt only to find his boss, half naked and down on all fours, peering under a piece of furniture, under which cowered Nelson, who had taken sanctuary there from the noise of nearby anti-aircraft fire. Addressing the cat, Churchill said: 'You should be ashamed of yourself, with a name like yours, skulking under that chest of drawers while all those brave young men in the RAF are up there fighting gallantly to save their country.'

Throughout the war Churchill often appeared dressed in the uniform of one of the armed services. He arrived at Casablanca in early 1943 attired as an air force commodore and, instead of allowing himself to be hustled away in secrecy as his handlers had planned, he insisted on remaining to greet Ismay, who was in another aircraft about to land. Churchill was adamant that he was quite safe disguised in this manner even though his shape ensured that no one was fooled. Ismay remarked that Churchill 'looked like an Air Force commodore disguised as the Prime Minister'.

Much though he loved soldiering and the trappings of military life, its people, the discipline and the company of military men like Alexander and Admiral Lord Louis Mountbatten, Churchill was never quite the expert authority he thought himself. His grasp of individual aspects of war was both brilliant and mercurial, and his instincts about Hitler and his sense of what Britain must do to win the war were correct. Where he sometimes erred was in his desire for action for action's sake, and for peripheral operations such as his relentless advocacy of an invasion of the islands of Pantelleria in 1940 and Rhodes in 1943. Another example occurred before D-day in 1944. With planning well advanced for the most massive amphibious operation in the history of warfare, one evening, out of the blue, Churchill suddenly announced: 'Why are we doing all this? Why are we going to throw away the best of our young men in assaulting a strongly defended enemy coast? Why do we not, instead of invading France, use the territory of our oldest ally, Portugal, and move towards the German border through the Iberian Peninsula?' The CIGS, Sir Alan Brooke, blew his top and chastised Churchill, one of the few occasions during the war when he did so, for wasting valuable time over a half-baked idea that neither the chiefs nor the Americans would even consider. As was his habit when boxed in, the prime minister merely grunted and changed the subject.

What made dealing with Churchill on military matters difficult was his distrust of the fitness of military men. Memories of their incompetence in the Boer War and the Great War left him habitually suspicious until his generals, admirals and airmen could convince him of the worth of their position or line of reasoning. As the war's chief strategist, Churchill was determined that the mistakes of past wars should not be repeated. The acid test was performance, and those who failed to measure up were unceremoniously sacked or, in the case of General Sir Archibald Wavell and his successor in the Middle East, General Sir Claude Auchinleck, transferred to non-fighting positions. At one point during General Sir John Dill's tenure as chief of the Imperial General Staff, Churchill declared: 'We cannot afford to confine Army appointments to persons who have excited no hostile comment in their careers . . . This is a time to try men of force and vision and not to be exclusively confined to those who are judged thoroughly safe by conventional standards.' Time and again Churchill practised what he preached.

However, unlike Eisenhower, who actively sought men under his command who had been athletes, believing that the test of athletics was excellent preparation for leadership, Churchill particularly distrusted such officers. 'I have never known a case of a great athlete being a great general,' he said. 'No prize-fighter has ever been a good general. The only exception might be the Italian Army, where a general might find it useful to be a good runner.'

There was no part of the military spectrum that escaped his attention. Churchill's military mind could be seen in action one day when the minister of supply presented his plan, complete with graphs, for phasing out an old tank model and phasing in a new one. The presentation went well, and the minister assumed he was off the hook until Churchill asked: 'Why are you going to make 550 obsolete tanks? Why?' No one else had considered that this was a bad idea.

Antony Head described his impact on the war planners: 'Nothing would arrive from Winston until noon, then ceaselessly restless inquiries, queries and exhortations. His extraordinary energy galvanized everyone else into doing more than they thought possible. His physique and brain operated on a different tempo. During his waking hours he hardly ever stopped working or thinking of work. If anything had happened to him in the war the results would have been disastrous . . . He also made the whole thing fun with his frequent shafts of humour and his gusto. The majority of the Planners and Chiefs of Staff had no experience of joint operations. Reassurance that particular operations were feasible rested largely on Winston's experience from the First World War.'

Many of his strategic proposals were sound, some utterly brilliant; others, such as his fixation on Norway, were impossible or impracticable. His meetings with the chiefs of staff became mini-battlefields upon which strategy was thrashed out and eventually decided, invariably after endless discussion, argument and a large measure of irritation on both sides. What really mattered was that, however messy the process, the job got done. However, these meetings were the bane of those seeking an orderly procedure. 'Instead there would be exhortations and harangues, stimulating challenges, explosive expostulations,' often with no decision reached after Churchill had rambled on for hour upon hour. On some occasions he would complain that he lacked men with vision and was obliged to deal with defeatists. At such times his wrath would erupt. Did his generals or admirals want to fight or sit? Much of his anger was simply pent-up frustration that Britain lacked the resources to carry out a particular action. Although it often made their lives difficult, the chiefs understood that his complaints were never personal. Despite their frequent arguments and mutual frustrations, Churchill forcefully defended them. 'He would play the termagant . . . but he trusted them to the full, deferred invariably to their considered opinion, gave them immense authority, and spread over them the umbrella of his powerful protection.'

The root cause of their fiery exchanges was Churchill's fondness for advocating risky ventures, combined with his conviction that the chiefs of staff were too passive unless he pushed them hard. 'He called the Planners "the Masters of Negation" . . . His instincts were that boldness and surprise always paid off,' recalled Antony Head. 'He liked to say "Clive on India accepted odds of such and such." . . . Much of his advocacy was a form of thinking aloud, clearing his mind, testing his ideas to destruction, a constant search for the new and unexpected.' Day and night his thoughts and actions were fixed on the war and on besting Hitler and Mussolini. Once, at dinner aboard the liner *Queen Mary* en route to the Quebec Conference in 1943, Churchill used the occasion to re-create cavalry drills using boxes of matches while he gave 'tuneless renderings of the bugle'.

Despite his extensive military experience Churchill remained hopelessly naive about logistics. The entire subject seemed beyond his grasp. He was still a disciple of earlier, less complicated wars, once complaining to Ismay, 'When I was a soldier, infantry used to walk and cavalry used to ride. But now the infantry require motor-cars, and even the tanks have to have horse boxes to take them to battle.' He tried but failed to understand and deeply resented the enormous logistics 'tail' that all modern mechanized armies require. There was an example of this blind spot in the summer of 1944, when he vehemently opposed the amphibious landings in southern France by British and US forces. Churchill badgered Eisenhower to scrap the landings (Operation Dragoon) that had taken months to plan and instead to land in Brittany, which had no suitable beaches and whose ports were still in German hands. A mere eleven days before the landings he sent a telegram to the US chiefs of staff formally proposing this last-minute diversion, hopelessly unable to comprehend the impracticality of shifting a large-scale operation beyond the reach of air cover and its base of operations at the eleventh hour. In the event the proposal was firmly opposed by Eisenhower and brusquely rejected by Roosevelt.

The lessons of the First World War and the appalling wrangling between the soldiers and the politicians had led to the formation in 1923 of the Chiefs of Staff Committee. Each of the service chiefs, including the head of the newly created Royal Air Force, was charged with advising on defence policy in what was the first British example of joint strategy and, in the Second World War, the first example of three-dimensional warfare. Not all went smoothly, and as one of its early secretaries recalled, '[In] the first few years of their existence the Chiefs of Staff were not exactly a band of brothers.' That changed dramatically under Churchill.

Once, after Churchill had criticized the ideas of a young brigadier assigned to Middle East GHQ, the officer hesitantly asked if he might speak frankly. 'Mr Churchill looked at him with wide open baby eyes and said: "Of course – what do you think we have come here for – to pay each other compliments?" He made it his business to get to know really well all the leading soldiers and to impress upon them that they would always be supported, provided their mistakes were towards the enemy . . . No soldier was ever left in doubt as to the precise meaning to be attached to any order he received from Mr Churchill.' Those who dared to stand up to Hitler or Stalin often paid for it with their lives. Few military men came away from a grilling by Churchill without feeling scorched, but they knew they had been in the presence of an extraordinary individual whose only object was victory.

He believed strongly in personal contact and subjected his generals, admirals and airmen to face-to-face meetings so that he could assess them and gauge their sincerity, their competence and their ability to respond to sharp questioning. Those found wanting were given other employment or forcibly retired. Even brilliant officers like Wavell, who was naturally shy and loath to provide the sort of personal information demanded by Churchill, might not fare well. Churchill's inability to appreciate Wavell's qualities certainly contributed to his relief as C in C Middle East in the summer of 1941. Those who spoke well and with frankness tended to fare better. Sometimes the men who had fought the battles were brought in for an audience with the prime minister, whom their first-hand tales both enlightened and enthralled.

Ismay attempted to convey to his military colleagues that 'Churchill could not be judged by ordinary standards . . . He was indispensable and utterly irreplaceable . . . His loyalty was absolute. No commander who engaged the enemy need ever fear that he would not be supported.'

One of the first military decisions taken by the new coalition government was when and where to begin bombing Germany. The decision revolved around whether to concentrate the assets of the RAF by attempting to hamper the German advance in France or to hit strategic oil refineries and railway yards in the Ruhr. Being the first combatant to initiate bombing would clearly provoke retaliation, but it was inevitable that the Germans would in any case eventually begin bombing Britain. While there was ample justification for attacking the Ruhr as a result of German aggression, the question was whether or not it would be better to do so while the Germans' attention was focused on conquering France and Belgium. The larger questions that would soon require resolution were what level of air support to provide the French and how Britain's aerial commitment would affect its ability to defend its own territory. On 13 May it was decided to defer any decision on strategic bombing until the situation in France became clearer.

War waits for no man, and time was of the essence as Hitler's legions continued their unstoppable sweep across the West and in Norway, where the setbacks continued. Within twenty-four hours of Churchill's appointment his new coalition government was in place, with men of all three parties occupying ministerial posts. On 13 May Churchill himself appeared before a divided Parliament to deliver his first and most important speech as prime minister. It was crucial that he establish his authority while at the same time reassuring his detractors, and on this momentous occasion he was asking for a declaration of confidence not in his new government but in his leadership. The ashes from the fire of Chamberlain's fall had yet to cool, and there remained grave distrust of the new premier among MPs of all parties, so many of whom continued to see him as a caretaker. Indeed his position as prime minister would not be entirely secure until the end of 1940.

Churchill, however, failed to act as if he were a caretaker and not only seized the reins of government but also threw down the gauntlet at Hitler's feet in what has become one of history's most admired and most often quoted speeches. His message was to offer reassurance rather than a promise of military victory, which at this critical period could be no more than speculative. Acknowledging that he had 'nothing to offer but blood, toil, tears and sweat', he declared that 'we have before us an ordeal of the most grievous kind. We have before us many, many long months of struggle and suffering. You ask, what is our policy? . . . It is to wage war, by sea, land and air, with all our might and with all the strength that God can give us; to wage war against a monstrous tyranny, never surpassed in the dark, lamentable catalogue of human crime. That is our policy. You ask us what is our aim? I can answer in one word: it is victory.'

For a moment at the end of Churchill's speech there was utter silence before the House exploded in cheers. It was passionate, demonstrative leadership which reached its listeners in a way that no other, certainly not Chamberlain's, could have done. The message was clear: Churchill was in charge. One of those present that day later recounted: 'I understood then why the men of the Tenth Legion loved Caesar.' Churchill knew he had succeeded, and as he exited the House he turned to Desmond Morton and whispered, 'That got the sods, didn't it?'

In the spring and summer of 1940 Britain was, except for France – which was soon to fall under the Nazi boot – friendless and without outside support. Churchill had formed a long-distance friendship with President Franklin D. Roosevelt, but FDR was constrained by America's extreme isolationism. Churchill had nowhere else to turn for help and would soon make it his policy of survival to bring the United States into the war.

As with any good leader, his public face was one of confidence – and in the desperate days of 1940 the will to resist even when the deck seemed stacked against Britain was more bravado than reality. Privately those early days – and the far worse ones to come – were a time of great travail and of concern about whether Churchill could actually hold the country together in its darkest hours. Colville has recorded Churchill's mood swings as he moved from despair to anguish. On 18 May he was 'full of fight and thrives on crisis and adversity'. The following day a preacher at the Church of St Martin-in-the-Fields delivered a pacifist sermon that led Clementine to walk out in anger, and Winston to tell her, 'You ought to have cried "Shame, desecrating the House of God with lies!"' Churchill then directed Colville to instruct the minister of information to have 'the man pilloried'.

Yet for anyone, even Churchill, to have sustained complete optimism in such an increasingly grave situation would have been absurd. Nevertheless, Clementine once said to Dr Wilson, 'You know, Charles, Winston can switch off worries like a tap.' During the war Wilson saw at first hand how 'this defensive mechanism was put to an extraordinary test. Up to a point it appeared to protect him in the cruel days of adversity. I found that he could close his eyes and fall asleep a few minutes after he had been told of some dreadful disaster in the field . . . But it was inevitable that at times the mechanism broke down. Then the feeling that he had been responsible by his decisions for the death of his soldiers and sailors – perhaps unnecessarily – laid siege to his mind. One saw then that it was not vanity that made the PM admit no wrong. He simply could not bear the thought that his own mistakes had led to suffering.' Yet for all the year's tribulations, Churchill came to regard 1940 as the summit of his prime ministership. He was once asked by Wilson's wife Dorothy which year – if he were allowed to relive one twelve-month period – he would choose, not counting the one in which he married Mrs Churchill. '1940 every time, every time,' he promptly replied.

Despite the moments of despair, Churchill's leadership excelled through his ability to keep his feelings strictly private. For the public he exuded only optimism and defiance. During one of his walks from Downing Street to the Admiralty a few days after becoming prime minister, well-wishers greeted him enthusiastically. 'He was visibly moved, and as soon as we were inside the building, he dissolved into tears. "Poor people," he said, "poor people. They trust me, and I can give them nothing but disaster for quite a long time.'

35

The Central War Room

Hardly a month went by when we could not have been wiped off the face of the earth.   – Inspector Walter H. Thompson

One of the war's great secrets was the underground complex beneath Whitehall that Churchill and the chiefs of staff used on numerous occasions, particularly during the Blitz, when London came under almost daily bombing attacks by the Luftwaffe. Until 1981, when the preserved facility was opened to the public, most Britons were unaware of what lay beneath a large government building just around the corner away from No. 10. It went by various names. Officially it was called the Central War Room, but those who worked there called it simply 'the Hole in the Ground' or 'the Hole'.

During the 1930s it became evident that, in the event of war, cities like London would be bombed. By 1937, as the war clouds over Europe grew darker, the spectre of hundreds of tons of bombs raining down on London increased the need for a secure central war room in which the government could function under emergency conditions. When Germany annexed Austria in 1938, it was decided to construct such a facility under an enormous government office building adjacent to St James's Park, from which air, ground and sea operations could be co-ordinated. The complex at No. 2 Storey's Gate consisted of six acres of rooms and corridors designed to be a self-contained complex fifty feet below ground on the same level as the riverbed of the Thames a little to the east.

With the work supervised by Ismay and Hollis, what were formerly storage rooms were converted into a future nerve centre for the government. The walls consisted of rough brick painted a pale yellow, with a cluttered network of steel girders and ventilating ducts throughout. Construction began in June 1938, and to begin with only a few rooms were ready for occupancy, but with the advent of the war the facility was expanded into 150 small rooms that could hold as many as 270 people who might work and sleep for a week without ever seeing the light of day. At first only rudimentary timbers secured the ceilings, but these were soon reinforced with heavy steel beams and concrete. The underground war rooms were thought to be able to survive a direct hit from a five-hundred-pound bomb. Like everyone else, Churchill believed that they could withstand such a blast. In September 1940 a bomb fell close to the complex, on the nearby Clive Steps. It shook the building above, causing Churchill to observe, 'A pity it was not a bit nearer so that we might have tested our defences.' After the war it was determined that even with their concrete-and-steel reinforcing a direct hit would have penetrated the war rooms and probably have killed everyone inside.

There were special rooms set aside for the prime minister and his wife, operational rooms for the war staff who manned the facility, and a large conference room where Churchill could meet with the cabinet and with the chiefs of staff. His small bedroom contained a single bed and top-secret wall maps that were covered by dingy linen curtains when he was not present. He also broadcast most of his speeches to the nation from this room, and Clementine used it to broadcast appeals for aid to Russia. On the small, plain desk were always a notepad and a stack of his 'Action This Day' labels.

During the Blitz it became evident that No. 10 was far too dangerous a place for working and sleeping. One day an incendiary bomb crashed through the roof and into the bedroom of one of Churchill's secretaries, Marian Holmes, who had the good fortune to be elsewhere at the time. The Churchills reluctantly moved to accommodation at what was called the No. 10 Annexe, situated above the underground war rooms. Although fitted with steel shutters, reinforced walls and other security features, the Annexe offered scarcely better protection than No. 10 from bombs or the V-1 flying bombs and V-2 rockets that were unleashed on Britain later in the war.

Churchill would rarely sleep in his underground bedroom unless there was an air raid in progress. One evening the Air Ministry warned of a heavy raid that night, and a worried Clementine insisted that Winston sleep downstairs instead of in the apartment in the Annexe. To her surprise he agreed, duly went downstairs and made ready for bed. When Inspector Thompson attempted to turn off the lights, Churchill demanded he leave them on. A short time later he summoned Thompson, who found him in his dressing gown. 'I have kept my promise to Mrs Churchill,' he said. 'I came downstairs to bed, but now I am going upstairs to sleep.' The Annexe routinely became Churchill's abode of choice for sleeping in peril, rather than in safety downstairs. He also stubbornly insisted on returning to No. 10 'whenever it was reasonably safe to do so, and the sudden changes of venues for meals & meetings produced hair-raising escapes from chaos,' noted John Peck.

Churchill would often delay his nightly walks from No. 10 to the Annexe or into the underground war room until the bombs began falling. Instead of taking the short walk, he would wander into St James's Park and along the Mall, with incendiary bombs falling all around. One evening, to Inspector Thompson's horror, they had just entered the Annexe when an immense explosion erupted outside. Where they had walked barely twenty seconds earlier was now a giant crater. Churchill, of course, had to see it for himself, and as he peered into it, a 'water main burst and we were drenched.' Thompson's wish that this near-death incident might restrain his boss was in vain. 'Hardly a month went by when we could not have been wiped off the face of the earth.'

Early in the war, when the Annexe was still under construction, Churchill was reluctantly persuaded to seek shelter in a disused Tube station near Piccadilly. Even then he would leave before dawn regardless of whether there were still German bombers overhead. He never seemed to worry overly about being bombed, and once quoted the former French president and prime minister Raymond Poincaré, who said, 'I take refuge beneath the impenetrable arch of probability.'

In the event that it became impossible for the government to function in central London, another war room was established and manned in the north-west of the city at Dollis Hill, under the code name Paddock. Plans were drawn up to shift key civil servants, the War Cabinet ministers, the chiefs of staff and the headquarters of the Home Forces. While Churchill admitted that the day might come when such a move became unavoidable, he insisted it would never occur unless Whitehall and central London became 'practically uninhabitable'.

Chequers became too dangerous to occupy during full-moon periods, when it was a visible target for German bombers. On these occasions Churchill made use of an alternative country house at Ditchley Park,

Oxfordshire, the house of a fellow MP. Despite his predilection for seeking out danger, his mind was attuned to finding ways to reduce risk. He believed that the water in the small lakes in St James's Park and in the gardens of Buckingham Palace might serve as a guide to enemy aircraft and suggested that while they might be required to help put out fires, 'Surely it would be possible to camouflage [them] . . . If it did not cost too much it would be worth trying.'

An extensive evacuation plan was drawn up in 1939 to move the government deep into the countryside if the Germans invaded. Code-named Black Move, it envisaged a small government command centre near Worcester. Six motor cars would carry Churchill, his family and the War Cabinet along a predesignated series of routes. Following closely would be a truck crammed with cabinet papers and top-secret documents. Lawrence Burgis believed that, had the Germans invaded, Churchill would not have moved his government to Canada as an ultimate last resort but instead would have died fighting. 'He would have mustered his Cabinet and died with them in a pill-box' in Parliament Square 'rather than that.' To Halifax, Churchill was even more emphatic: 'If they come to London,' he said, 'I shall take a rifle (I'm not a bad shot with a rifle) and put myself in a pillbox at the bottom of Downing Street and shoot till I've no more ammunition, and then they can damned well shoot me.' To an MP he wrote, 'You may rest assured that we should fight in every street in London and its suburbs. [That] would devour an invading army, assuming one ever got so far.'

London was divided into defensive zones; pillboxes and tank traps were set up and trenches dug; and an inner defensive ring was to be manned by a Guards regiment. If it came to street fighting the Germans would have to fight for the city in the same deadly manner as they later did during the Warsaw Ghetto uprising. All open ground that might allow a glider to land was studded with homemade barricades; all road signs were removed throughout the countryside; and citizens were given precise instructions on how to resist both passively and actively.

(Hitler likewise had bunkers constructed for his protection. Whether it was the bunker he stayed in on 10 May near the Belgian border or the numerous others constructed for his safety during the war, he routinely used them while Churchill just as habitually disdained them. The best known was the secret underground complex near Rastenburg, deep in the forests of East Prussia, which became the führer's field headquarters after the invasion of Russia in the summer of 1941; this was the place where on 20 July 1944, Colonel Count Claus von Stauffenberg's bomb, contained in a briefcase, nearly succeeded in killing him.)

When the bombs began falling on London, Churchill told his colleagues in the House of Commons, 'Get used to it, eels get used to skinning.' Blackouts and power failures were facts of life, and although they slowed the business of conducting the war, and alternative sites existed as far away as the Midlands, Churchill never accepted that the government should relocate from London. The bombing took its inevitable toll. Entire rows of houses sometimes disappeared and in the light of day were heaps of rubble under which lay the corpses of those who had not sought sanctuary below ground. The night Churchill first relocated to Piccadilly the Luftwaffe dropped some four hundred tons of high-explosive and seventy thousand incendiary bombs on London.

One evening not long after assuming office in May 1940, Churchill made his first visit to view his new underground domain. The room where he would soon direct meetings of the War Cabinet was forty feet square, with eighteen-inch girders overhead painted red. The room itself was stark and unappealing and had only a minimum number of lights. Dominating the room was a large table covered with black baize, and at one side there was a small desk for a civilian secretary to record notes. Twenty-five places were set for the chiefs of staff and the War Cabinet, as at a dining table, except that instead of plates each place comprised a pad of paper, a sharpened pencil, a small blotter and a small metal tin for paper clips. The uncomfortable chairs were of crude tubular steel, upholstered in green leather. Churchill's chair, made of brown wood, had rounded arms and was, wrote Leslie Hollis, 'The sort of chair the father of a suburban family might use at the head of the table, when presiding over Sunday lunch, a chair of character and authority'. A nearby fire bucket became a depository for his cigar butts. The chairs occupied by the chiefs of staff were labelled with their names. In front of Churchill's seat was a red leather dispatch case, and on each side was a candlestick for use in case of a power failure. There was also a tattered yellow card that read: 'Please understand there is no depression in this House and we are not interested in the possibilities of defeat. They do not exist. Victoria, R.I.'

Beside Churchill's place were an ashtray and the ever present 'action' labels. On the wall directly behind his chair hung a large world map. Above the entrance were red and green lights used to signal an air raid. The only sound was that of ceiling fans that recirculated air. Churchill gazed silently around, then announced: 'This is the room from which I'll direct the war. And if the invasion takes place, that's where I'll sit.'

Merely enduring meetings of the War Cabinet or with the chiefs of staff, held at all hours of the day or night, was a feat. With Churchill puffing on a cigar, Attlee using a smelly pipe and Minister of Labour Ernest Bevin smoking cigarettes, the atmosphere in the room became nearly intolerable. The first lord and first sea lord sat at a small table opposite the prime minister, and its occupants, 'only a couple of feet from the mouth holding the cigar . . . christened it "The Dock" '. During the war 115 (roughly one in ten) cabinet meetings were held in this room.

At the heart of this underground complex was the map room, an operations centre manned around the clock by duty officers of the three armed services. Hotline phones (known as the 'beauty chorus') connected with the war rooms of the service ministries and No. 10 signalled incoming calls by means of flashing lights. Covering the walls were large situation maps displaying the position of every ship in the fleet and of Britain's armies throughout the world. They were updated virtually every hour until the last day of the war. Classified documents, hand-delivered by soldiers of the Grenadier Guards from all over White-hall in plain envelopes, were addressed to George Rance, the custodian of the war rooms. Guardsmen dubbed 'Rance's Guard' were posted outside the entrance to the stairs leading to the cabinet rooms, at the bottom of which were stationed two Royal Marine guards. Outside, a sandbagged machine gun was positioned to cover the entrance. Along one corridor were rifle racks for the officers manning the map room to assist the guardsmen in defending the facility should it be penetrated.

After the United States had entered the war in December 1941, a small room was reserved for Churchill that contained a direct transatlantic telephone link to the White House and Roosevelt. The system was secure, but initially neither man used it much – both were reluctant to discuss highly sensitive matters on the phone. The sound distortion across three thousand miles was such that during their first conversation Churchill's voice sounded like Donald Duck, causing the president to chuckle and the prime minister to fume that he would never use 'that damn thing' again. Eventually the problem was fixed, and the two men did speak occasionally.

Users of the war rooms preferred the map room. Ismay spoke of its fascination: 'You could never pass it without popping in to see the very latest news of the war – the progress of a convoy, how things were going on each land front.' A duty officer went to Buckingham Palace each morning at 10.30 to provide the king with the latest war information.

Whether Churchill was working above or below ground, Inspector Thompson had the unenviable task of reining in the prime minister's desire to expose himself to danger and, when that failed, to curtail his wanderings in St James's Park during air raids. Despite the raids and the blackout that left London in inky darkness, the prime minister was determined to continue his practice of taking his nightly constitutionals in the park. He especially wanted to be outdoors during air raids to view 'the conduct of the war in person'. When the bombs began falling Thompson would beg him to take shelter but would be firmly brushed off: 'I have asked the people of this country to carry on in their homes, in the streets, in the factories, everywhere. If you think I am going to hide in an air-raid shelter, not for you or anyone else will I do it.'

Not even the king could dissuade him. On one occasion when George VI dined at No. 10 there was a large air raid, and without apology Churchill announced: 'I must go out and see how things are going.' The king asked that he not go and was ignored. As Churchill went out the door without his steel helmet, Inspector Thompson placed it on his head only to have his master fling it off. Reminded of the requirement that he wear a steel helmet, Churchill grinned and did as he was told before going off into the night for yet another boyish adventure. On other occasions Thompson resorted to sleeping beside the door to No. 10 to ensure that Churchill could not sneak by him in the night.

Churchill's risk taking was not confined to nightly walks. He frequently spent hours visiting AA gun batteries in the midst of air raids, spurning the armoured car set aside for his use, and travelling instead in an ordinary motor car, trailed only by a police vehicle. Thompson understood that it was impossible to curb his master but knew it was his duty at least to try. At times they exchanged sharp words about his safety until the inevitable moment came when the policeman recognized he had pushed his boss far enough. His face set in his familiar stubborn scowl, Churchill growled, 'I will travel in the same type of car as anyone else in the country. I will not have any privileges. I will take the same chance as anyone else.' Thompson was just as stubborn, and on the night of 11 September 1940 he sent the Prime Minister's regular car away and instead brought around the armoured car he detested, leaving Churchill no other choice except to ride in it. There was an air raid in progress when they arrived at Richmond Park. He spied others driving ordinary vehicles and immediately turned on Thompson and ordered him: 'Send that sardine tin back and don't bring it out again or you and I will part company.' Left unspoken was his belief that a leader should never cower. At the conclusion of his visit Churchill began to enter the near side of his car, the door held open as usual by Thompson, when he unexpectedly changed his mind and walked around to the other side of the vehicle, opened the door and sat down inside. They had moved only a short distance when a bomb exploded so close by that the vehicle became airborne and then skidded on two wheels, narrowly avoiding flipping over. An unperturbed Churchill wryly remarked, 'It must have been my beef on this side that pulled the car down.' When Thompson asked why he had altered his usual routine, Churchill replied that instinct had told him to change sides. With a finger pointed skyward, he said: 'That mission has to be carried out, Thompson.' Often he would apologize to Thompson for taking risks in this way but would shrug off the danger with the comment: 'When my time is due, it will come.'

Arriving back at the Annexe that night the sights and sounds of the anti-aircraft barrage and of bombs exploding kept Churchill outside while deep in discussion with a colleague about how to improve the employment of searchlights. Suddenly there was a frightening screech that Thompson described as sounding 'like Lucifer's chariots'. He grabbed Churchill and flung him to safety, shielding him with his own body just as a large bomb landed near by. Churchill erupted in fury and shouted, ' "Don't do that!" . . . I think he would have hit me with his cane but it was fortunately well lost in the commotion. Then he swore, shook and stamped about and poked his jaw into my face; a whole gush of ugly sounds accompanied the reverberations of the explosion.' Churchill especially hated losing his hat, which usually happened whenever Thompson was obliged to rough him up for his own safety: 'What he would say while searching for it was a sin against the language.'

Among the chief characteristics of US ambassador Joseph P. Kennedy were cowardice, anti-Semitism and a fervent dislike of the British people. He was a strong proponent of appeasement in the late 1930s and prophesied disaster for Britain. After the invasion of the West he was even more certain that Britain stood no chance against Germany and should make peace. The United States, he told FDR, should not involve itself in the war. Whereas Churchill deliberately exposed himself to danger in order to lend moral support to Britain's armed forces, Joe Kennedy later portrayed himself as having survived 136 German air raids, when in fact he retreated nightly to a rented mansion near Windsor, leaving the embassy staff exposed to danger in London. Kennedy had no use for Churchill and telegraphed Roosevelt that 'Mr Churchill's sun is caused to set very rapidly by the situation in Norway which some people are already characterizing as a second Gallipoli.' In July 1940 he scorned Churchill as 'a fine two-handed drinker' whose 'judgment has never proven to be good'. Kennedy's nightly absences did not go unnoticed in Whitehall, where it was scornfully said of him: 'I thought my daffodils were yellow until I met Joe Kennedy.'

By contrast, Churchill, like a true soldier, would turn towards, not away from, danger. As one of his private secretaries noted, he demonstrated the 'unflinching moral and physical courage of a leader who would "never surrender", who took a delight in mounting to the roof in air-raids, and who turned back his car to London from the road to Chequers because the German "beam" seemed to point to a heavy attack on the capital'.

Churchill's night-time forays were not confined to the streets and parks. During air raids the roof of the building housing the underground war rooms contained a special sandbagged emplacement with a bird's-eye view of much of London, from which he could count the number of fires and time the explosions of the ack-ack as it fired into the night sky. Despite Clementine's protests, one particularly frigid night he went to the roof and, ignoring a message from her that he should come down at once, sat down on the chimney and made himself comfortable. Not long afterwards an officer came out to protest, 'What's going on? We can't work. The place is full of smoke and we are coughing our heads off!' On another occasion, as Churchill watched from his rooftop perch during an especially heavy raid, shell fragments began falling; a staff member remarked loudly to another that he was tempting Providence by remaining in harm's way. As he was meant to, Churchill overheard the comment and replied with his patented 'My time will come when it comes,' prompting a voice in the darkness to interject: 'You're probably right, sir, but there's no need to take half a dozen of us with you.' Eventually even Clementine gave up attempting to control her husband's late-night adventures.

Throughout the war Randolph Churchill was frequently seen in No. 10 and the Annexe and often accompanied his father to international conferences, such as Tehran in 1943. In October 1939 he married Pamela Digby, a worldly nineteen-year-old who would divorce him in 1946. Pamela later had numerous liaisons with famous men, including Edward R. Murrow, Baron Élie de Rothschild, the Fiat magnate Gianni Agnelli and Prince Ali Khan. During the war she began an affair with – and some years later married – FDR's special envoy to Britain, W. Averell Harriman, the railway tycoon and former governor of New York. In 1940 she was pregnant with Winston's grandson, who was born in October and christened Winston Spencer Churchill. During the early months of the war Pamela lived at No. 10. She deeply admired her father-in-law, and her recollections of life with the Churchills during the war are instructive. She especially recalled the prime minister's fierce determination to resist – to the death, if necessary. One evening at dinner when the threat of invasion loomed and there was talk of sending children overseas, he said: 'You can each take a dead German with you.' Pamela replied: ' "But, Papa, I don't know how to shoot a gun, I haven't got a gun." He looked at me very severely and said "you can go into the kitchen and get a carving knife," and that was his whole attitude . . . As a family we were very conscious that the war was on our doorstep.'

While Pamela Churchill was loving and supportive of Winston, Randolph was a conspicuous embarrassment to his parents. He drank to excess, was often intoxicated and made repeated scenes, deliberately going out of his way to provoke others. His reckless behaviour added to his father's already heavy burden. Jock Colville was by no means alone in his dislike of Randolph, whom he characterized as 'one of the most objectionable people I had ever met: noisy, self-assertive, whining and frankly unpleasant . . . At dinner he was anything but kind to Winston, who adores him.' Brilliant, bombastic, acerbic and given to unprovoked rages, Randolph Churchill was a study in contrasts. He was a superb orator like his father and, also like Winston, a journalist and politician. (Later he was his father's official biographer, the author of the first two volumes of his life.) He entirely lacked self-control and when this lack was combined with his propensity to over-indulge in alcohol, it made him wildly unpredictable, rude and insufferable. He could be charming one minute and dangerously aggressive the next. His love–hate relationship with his father was trying for all concerned. As his sister Mary wrote, the fact that he was 'throughout his life an easily aroused explosive person' made his relations with his parents exceedingly difficult. The war years were marked by angry scenes and confrontations that 'left lasting scars on his relationship' with both of them.

One of the reasons Churchill disliked going underground to the safety of the war rooms was that it isolated him from sharing the hardships of the fighting men who defended Britain and from the plight of the ordinary Briton. As a good leader must, he kept his true emotions in check. But there were times when the carnage was too awful even for strong-willed men, and the mask would drop, usually only briefly but enough for those closest to him to see behind it. One of his stenographers, Elizabeth Leighton, recalls how despite the loss of life, 'he was always on the cheerful side to raise the people's spirits, and one time, I remember, he came upon some people whose house had been bombed and he spoke in an uplifting way to them. And then a paper blew around and he quickly said: "Hope that's the income tax demand." '

After touring the wreckage of Bristol one weekend, Churchill returned to his special train and used a newspaper to conceal the tears running down his face. Following the first large-scale bombardments of the London docks in September 1940, he made a point of hastening there to view fires burning amid the devastation. At an air-raid shelter where some forty people had been killed by a direct hit, he found a large crowd of mostly poor people. 'One might have expected them to be resentful against the authorities responsible,' recalled Ismay, 'but as Churchill got out of his car, they literally mobbed him. "Good old Winnie," they cried. "We thought you'd come and see us. We can take it. Give it 'em back." ' Tears flowed down Churchill's cheeks. Ismay heard an elderly woman exclaim, 'You see, he really cares; he's crying.' With alacrity Churchill recovered and at breakneck speed proceeded to inspect the area. 'I could never understand how he managed it. He was no longer a young man, and normally he never took any exercise at all . . . And yet, on his inspection visits, he would cover miles of ground at a remarkable pace.'

On this day Churchill insisted on viewing everything, and, as darkness fell, all attempts to persuade him to leave were obstinately rebuffed. Soon, the Luftwaffe returned, and bombs began falling all around them. Feigning innocence, Churchill inquired what they were. Ismay replied that they were incendiaries, and 'we were evidently in the middle of the bull's-eye.' With the streets blocked by rubble it was difficult to manoeuvre the prime minister's car, but eventually, having seen his fill, Churchill returned safely to Downing Street, where ministers and other members of his staff anxiously awaited his return. Ismay was berated for permitting Churchill to put himself in danger. In barrack-room language the normally even-tempered Ismay replied 'that anybody who imagined that he could control the Prime Minister on jaunts of this kind was welcome to try his hand on the next occasion'.

The ordeal of the British people within their own islands began in the summer of 1940 and continued in various forms until nearly the end of the war. Aerial bombing during the Second World War was often highly inaccurate, and the tragic result was that thousands of innocent civilians on both sides of the conflict died. Where houses had once stood there were simply holes in the ground. History has taught us that such acts do not demoralize a population, as one might suppose. On the contrary, they harden resolve. Hermann Göring's air campaign against Britain succeeded in causing a great deal of damage, but the more the Luftwaffe bombed, the more it created an attitude of defiance that mirrored Winston Churchill's own.

36

Disaster in Flanders Fields

His spirit is indomitable and even if France and England should be lost, I feel he would carry on the crusade himself with a band of privateers. – Sir John Colville

In his novel *The End of the Affair*, Graham Greene recalled the grim news from France and Belgium in that dreadful spring of 1940. It resembled, he wrote, a corpse that was 'sweet with the smell of doom'. Since 10 May German armoured columns had struck deep into France and Belgium, and within the first forty-eight hours the Allies had identified 190 German divisions in action. In a repeat of 1914 Hitler's thrust through the Ardennes had caught the French flat-footed.

Churchill might have been amused to learn that despite the burgeoning success of his armies Hitler had moments when his nerves nearly got the best of him. On 17 May, for example, the chief of the general staff of the army (Oberkommando des Heeres, OKH), General Franz Halder, recorded that the führer was 'terribly nervous' and on occasion hysterical, both alarmed by and a victim of his own success. What made those early days of the war in the West so significant was that the decisions made by both Churchill and Hitler directly influenced the outcome of the campaign in France, and thus, to some extent, the entire war.

Although the Allies and the Germans appeared to be evenly matched (3 million soldiers versus 2.7 million), whatever numerical advantage the Allies enjoyed was largely negated by the enormously successful German blitzkrieg tactics and by the surprise attack through the Ardennes. The Luftwaffe had mastery of the air, and with Allied armour widely dispersed instead of concentrated, numbers were meaningless. Nor were the Dutch and the Belgian armies a match for the better-equipped German spearheads that relentlessly forced retreat on all fronts. The vaunted Maginot Line was easily bypassed as the Germans demonstrated the futility of siege warfare in the age of the blitzkrieg.

The ever lengthening arrows on the situation maps depicting the advance of the Germans revealed in stark detail the Allies' predicament. French morale was crumbling as fast as the panzers advanced. With the French army in retreat, Paris was in danger of imminent capture. General Maurice Gamelin, the Allied supreme commander, who had endeavoured to fight the Second World War by adhering to the outdated First World War principle of passive defence and the inviolability of the Maginot Line, had no real grasp of the situation and lacked even a radio, relying instead on motorcycle dispatch riders (some of whom were killed, their messages lost en route) to bring him reports from the front. When General Maxime Weygand replaced him on 19 May it was already too late.

At seven-thirty on the morning of 15 May an aide awakened Churchill. On the telephone was the French prime minister, Paul Reynaud. Their conversation was in English. 'We have been defeated,' said the Frenchman. 'We are beaten; we have lost the battle. The front is broken near Sedan.' More air support was urgently needed. A telegram followed that pleaded for reinforcements: 'The way to Paris lies open. Send all the planes you can.'

Churchill had been in office for only three days when he was confronted by his first significant military crisis. Archie Sinclair, newly installed as the air secretary, and Air Chief Marshal Sir Cyril Newall both warned that sending additional fighter squadrons to France (six had already been sent) was a bad idea, and Churchill agreed with their recommendation. The ability of fighter support to impede the panzers and the German advance was questionable, particularly given the level of air cover provided by the Luftwaffe. That night Lord Gort telegraphed London to request additional air support for the British Expeditionary Force, and the French never let up in their requests, which continued until the fall of France the following month.

Air Chief Marshal Sir Hugh Dowding's Fighter Command was responsible for the air defence of Britain. After Reynaud's plea for more air support on the morning of 15 May, Churchill convened the chiefs of staff to hear Dowding personally advise against sending further squadrons; their dispatch, he argued, would jeopardize his ability to defend

Britain. Half an hour later, when the War Cabinet met, it was agreed to hit the Ruhr that night with one hundred heavy bombers, but to defer sending any further fighter squadrons to France.

The French clung to the misguided belief that the employment of British fighters would make a difference. On the morning of 16 May Gamelin sent a telegram pleading that all would be lost unless ten squadrons were sent at once. Churchill met the chiefs of staff the same morning to consider Gamelin's request. He well understood that it was a grave risk to deplete the aerial defence of Britain at a critical juncture but also that it was necessary to bolster French morale. He asked for six squadrons. While it was agreed that some support was necessary, Sinclair was opposed to sending more than four. A compromise was reached: four would be dispatched, with two others kept in reserve in Britain.

Reassuring an ally in desperate straits by telephone is difficult if not impossible. That afternoon Churchill, accompanied by Dill and Ismay, flew to Paris to assess the situation personally and to exercise his powers of persuasion in an attempt to stiffen the resolve of the French. What he found was far worse than he had imagined. Inside the French capital rumours were spreading like wildfire that the Germans would soon arrive, and the government was already burning its classified documents in bonfires in the French Foreign Ministry in the Quai d'Orsay. He demanded of Gamelin: 'Where is the strategic reserve?' Told there was none, Churchill was dumbfounded, later admitting that it 'was one of the greatest surprises I have had in my life'. He asked when and where the French would counterattack the German flanks around Sedan. Gamelin shrugged. 'Here was the admission of the bankruptcy of a whole generation of French military thought and preparations.'

The French again pleaded for more air support, and although Churchill thought it would not alter the already dire situation of the French army, he reluctantly acceded to their entreaties. That evening he signalled the War Cabinet, seeking their approval for the dispatch of another six fighter squadrons – in addition to the four approved earlier in the day – 'to give the last chance to the French Army to rally its bravery and strength' over the next four critical days, which he deemed 'decisive for Paris and probably for the French Army'.

With considerable reluctance the War Cabinet agreed. The French expected them to be based in France, unaware of the fierce internal battle in London over the employment of British airpower. The air staff compromised: the six squadrons would continue to be based in Britain but would operate from French aerodromes, three in the morning and the other three in the afternoon.

The decision to send more squadrons left Dowding unconvinced that Fighter Command was safe from further commitments in France. He produced a ten-point memo that has become 'one of the most celebrated documents in RAF history' and sent it to the Air Council. (This was the body, consisting of the secretary of state for air, the chief of the air staff and the heads of Bomber, Fighter and Coastal Commands, that determined air policy.) The memo laid out the hard facts: fifty-two squadrons would be required for the defence of Britain, and only thirty-six were immediately available. Dowding did not mince his words. If adequate fighter forces were kept in the UK and the fleet continued to exist, Britain should be capable of carrying on 'for some time, if not indefinitely'. However, if his squadrons were depleted 'in desperate attempts to remedy the situation in France, defeat in France [would] involve the final complete and irremediable defeat of this country.'

Newall and the other chiefs of staff endorsed Dowding's memo, but it never received an official endorsement from the Air Council, whose reply conspicuously failed to address the matter. It was left to Churchill, now back in London, who issued a memo to Ismay on 19 May declaring that 'no more squadrons will leave the country whatever the need in France,' and that if a withdrawal of the BEF proved necessary, it would require strong air support from the RAF. Nevertheless Dowding remained deeply concerned. 'I knew that Churchill was under tremendous pressure from the French . . . What I was so afraid of was that it would go beyond even that, and that what the French really wanted Churchill to do was to give them our whole fighter force, and for it to be commanded by their generals in France. That would have meant the end of the war, because the French had already been beaten.'

It has been argued that Air Chief Marshal Sir Hugh Dowding's pencil won the Battle of Britain. Years later Dowding was asked what was the most important decision he ever made. He replied: 'The decision to ask for an interview with the War Cabinet to prevent our fighters from being handed over to the French.' His assessment that 'no Hurricane sent out there would come back' was entirely accurate; no matter how many aircraft Britain sent, it was too late for the RAF to turn the tide.

*

Colonel General Fedor von Bock's Army Group B was rapidly advancing against the valiant but outmatched Dutch and Belgian armies, while the tanks of Colonel General Gerd von Rundstedt's Army Group A began sweeping westward to pose a growing threat to the Allied left flank. Especially vulnerable was the British Expeditionary Force. As in the First World War the BEF anchored the left flank of the Allied front between the French First Army and the sea, along the border between northern France and Belgium. With only ten divisions (one of which guarded the Maginot Line while three others were barely fit and were installed in a non-combat role), the BEF was deployed in what soon became indefensible positions.

German strategy appeared to be a repeat of 1914 and worked to near perfection. It was to compel the Allies to defend against Bock's armies as they advanced into Belgium, and draw the BEF and the French First Army away from their defensive positions and hold them in place, thus preventing them from posing any threat to Rundstedt's right flank as it advanced deep into France from the supposedly impenetrable Ardennes Forest.

On 19 May nine panzer divisions were lined up some fifty miles due east of the Channel ports, ready to spring a trap that would enclose the BEF and the French First Army. The Allies' problems were compounded by some eight hundred thousand refugees, flooding back north into the very areas they had fled a short time before, and clogging the roads of northern France in a frantic attempt to escape the panzers. The following day some panzer units reached the Somme and were in a position to crush the Allied front. Rather than advance on Paris, they turned north-west and began a dash for the Channel, quickly threatening Gort's vulnerable supply lines and the BEF rear. If Boulogne and Calais fell, the fate of the BEF would be sealed. To the dismay of Churchill and the War Office, by 22 May Gort was already considering withdrawal to the Channel ports as one of the three options facing the BEF. The other two were to remain and fight it out, with the possibility of being isolated and cut off, or to fight their way south and attempt to link up with the French Seventh and Tenth Armies outside the German trap. With some justification Churchill foresaw a retreat to the Channel ports as a disastrous invitation to the BEF's annihilation. However, as events unfolded in the days that followed, there was little that Churchill or anyone else could do about the collapse of the French front. The new British warlord had become a conductor without an orchestra.

Even as the French army was beginning to melt away and the BEF became increasingly exposed, Churchill still thought only of offence, of counterattack. The last thing on his mind was an evacuation. The German army, he insisted in a letter to General Georges, had over-extended itself: 'The tortoise is thrusting its head very far beyond his carapace.'

The 19th of May was a key date in the epic of what would shortly become the desperate evacuation of the BEF from Dunkirk. The French First Army defending the BEF's right flank was in complete disarray, resulting in a dangerously large gap between the two forces, and although the BEF was subordinate to it, there was little contact or guidance for four critical days. On this date Gort was already exploring the possibility of an evacuation from France. His deputy operations officer, Brigadier Oliver Leese, began making contingency plans with the Admiralty for naval support of an evacuation. Yet Gort was in a deep quandary: given that he was under the operational control of the French, he could not make autonomous decisions without London's specific consent.

To deal with the crisis Churchill immediately returned to London from Chartwell, where he had gone to write a speech to be delivered to the nation that evening. When the War Cabinet met later that afternoon it was formally decided that the BEF should turn south and fight its way to Amiens (nearly forty miles away) and resume contact with the French in order to pull together a line of defence. While London remained unaware of the true situation in France, Gort and his principal commanders met that day and privately agreed on a plan to withdraw the BEF to the coast.

That night Churchill made his first broadcast as prime minister in what he called 'a solemn hour for the life of our country and of our Empire . . . and of the cause of freedom'. He did not attempt to disguise what he called 'the gravity of the hour' in France, bluntly noting that the fighting would eventually spread to Britain itself. To lift public morale he pledged that no matter what happened Britain would survive. 'There will come', he said, 'the battle for our island – for all that Britain is and all that Britain means. That will be the struggle.' For the foreseeable future, words would be the only salve Churchill could offer to his beleaguered countrymen. It was on 19 May that Colville's once low opinion of Churchill suddenly changed. 'Whatever Winston's short-comings, he seems to be the man for the occasion. His spirit is indomitable and even if France and England should be lost, I feel he would carry on the crusade himself with a band of privateers. Perhaps my judgments of him have been harsh, but the situation was very different a few weeks ago.'

General Maxime Weygand, the new Allied supreme commander, out-lined a plan on 21 May whereby the BEF and the French First Army on its right would launch a counter-offensive on the 26th. The BEF was directed to spearhead the operation with the aim of linking up on the Somme with a newly created French army that existed only on paper, while the French Seventh and Tenth Armies drove north into the Germans' flank to cut off their advance to the Channel. The Weygand plan was pure fantasy. The French army was already a broken reed, as incapable of carrying out a counter-offensive as the BEF. With the German advance on the Channel ports unstoppable and the French front crumbling, the BEF was dangerously exposed.

The British government's sense of the situation in France was sketchy. Neither Churchill nor the War Cabinet really understood the growing plight of the BEF, and this led to criticism of Gort based in part on Churchill's unfounded belief in Weygand's imaginary plan. To imple-ment the Weygand plan the War Cabinet authorized the issuing of orders to Gort on the evening of 22 May to counterattack towards Amiens with eight divisions. It was falsely believed in London that the BEF counterattack would join a relief force from the south – a force that turned out to be nonexistent. At the BEF headquarters the order was received with incredulity. Gort's chief of staff, Lieutenant General Henry Pownall, called the order 'scandalous' and blamed Ironside and Churchill, later referring 'sarcastically [to] "The Crazy Gang" of British strategy makers in the spring of 1940' as an example of the 'perils of amateur strategy'.

'Can nobody prevent him trying to conduct operations himself as a super Commander-in-Chief?' raged Pownall. 'He can have no concep-tion of our situation . . . How is an attack like this to be staged involving three nationalities at an hour's notice? The man's mad. I suppose these figments of the imagination are telegraphed without consulting his military advisors, indeed it says little enough for them if they had any hand in it'.

The conundrum in all this was not merely Churchill's belief in the Weygand plan but also his utter distrust of the French army and its capability to carry out the northern end of the counter-offensive. The War Cabinet minutes on the morning of 23 May tell the tale. An intense debate ensued when the normally soft-spoken Attlee raised the central question that no one had addressed. 'Are we not in danger of falling between two stools,' he asked, if the Weygand plan failed and the BEF was unable to hold the Channel ports? The question was not answered.

In mid-afternoon Churchill made a statement to the Commons that the Germans were in Abbeville and that heavy fighting was taking place in and around the port city of Boulogne. Although reinforcements were landed at Calais and were at once in contact with German elements three miles outside that city, throughout the day and into the evening the news worsened. Churchill was relying on the promise of Weygand, whose intentions were admirable but who had no capability of restoring the front with what were mostly phantom forces. No one had any real grasp of the battlefield; for one thing, Weygand mistakenly believed that Gort and the BEF, with the sanction of the British government, had abandoned the French army in its hour of extreme need. Yet in London on 23 May it was still assumed that the BEF *could* launch a counterattack.

At his command post in Armentières, Lieutenant General Alan Brooke, the British II Corps commander, recorded in his diary, 'Nothing but a miracle can save the BEF now, and the end cannot be very far off!'

The increasingly grave situation in France was deeply frustrating to Churchill, whose personal support to the beleaguered French leadership was limited to fruitless attempts to bolster the morale of Reynaud and Weygand, and to offer advice on how best to defend against the German invasion. 'In all the history of war, I have never seen such mismanagement,' he railed on 21 May, referring to the ineptness of the French army. Yet it was the tough questioner who never let any of his own off the hook without an exhaustive grilling who let the French off on the basis of a fantastical promise. On the 24th he vented his frustrations on the BEF and the developing situation both in Boulogne, which was captured the next day, and around the next German target, Calais. With no accurate picture of the situation, he demanded that Ismay explain why a regiment of tanks did not attack the lightly held German lines outside Calais and why Gort did not attack the German rear: 'Here is a General with nine Divisions about to be starved out, and yet he cannot send a force to clear his communications. What else can be so important as this? Where could a Reserve force be better employed? This [German] force blockading Calais should be attacked at once by Gort.'

No doubt because he had few other options, Churchill persisted in his misplaced faith in the Weygand plan, based solely on promises rather than facts, and in the French military and political leaders (Gamelin, Weygand, Reynaud and later the First World War hero Marshal Philippe Pétain), who were more intent on blaming Churchill and the British for not supplying fighter aircraft than on acknowledging their own defeatism. After yet another meeting with Churchill, this time in London on 26 May, Reynaud, long since resigned to the defeat of France, returned to Paris with serious doubts about the British leader. Halifax, he said, was the only Briton who 'realizes that some European solution must be reached. Churchill is always hectoring.'

The utter chaos of those early days of defeat and uncertainty was recorded by one of Churchill's official interpreters, Captain Claude Berkeley RN, who noted that while Reynaud was not impressive, 'The PM was terrific, hurling himself about, getting his staff into hopeless tangles by dashing across to Downing Street without a word of warning, shouting that we would never give in, etc.' Yet it was precisely his involvement in events such as this that would drive his chiefs of staff to distraction and earn him the none-too-complimentary sobriquet of amateur strategist.

If there were common threads among the Allies on 23 May they were confusion and misunderstanding, not only between the British and the Belgians but also among the French, all of which was driven by the relentless and seemingly unstoppable German advances in Belgium and northern France.

No commander wants to be the bearer of news that controverts the orders of a higher command. However, by failing to advise London earlier of the gravity of the BEF's situation and not revealing what his plans were until the last minute, Gort unwittingly planted the seeds of unwarranted optimism. Certainly Churchill's understanding was based more on Weygand's promises than on Gort's operational reports. When it was clear that the BEF was in untenable positions, Admiral Sir Roger Keyes, who was officially representing Britain as an adviser to King Leopold III of Belgium, bluntly wrote to Gort that he should 'tell the government to go to the devil, and insist on being given a free hand to extricate your army from the appalling situation into which it has been placed through no fault of yours'.

Although dismayed by the notion of withdrawing the BEF, both Churchill and the War Cabinet belatedly recognized that such a move was likely. Writing as he did to Roosevelt as 'Former Naval Person', Churchill asked for American fighter aircraft, implying, wrote Colville, 'that without them we should be in a parlous state, even though this country would never give up the struggle'. Colville was 'somewhat taken aback' when Churchill handed the message to him and said, 'Here's a telegram for those bloody Yankees. Send it off tonight.' There was, of course, nothing of immediate consequence that Roosevelt could do to help at this critical moment, even if he had had the wherewithal to do it. Later that evening, though, Churchill recalled the telegram, and there is no record that it was ever sent.

On 25 May the Belgian positions adjacent to the BEF had been penetrated and were crumbling, exposing the British left flank, held by Brooke's II Corps. The BEF was now defending an eighty-seven-mile front with a force that could not hold such a thin line for long. With its position untenable, both the BEF and the French First Army on its right faced encirclement as the Germans advanced on Calais. That evening German panzers were closer to Dunkirk than almost all of the BEF. With further British attacks not only impossible but probably suicidal, Gort elected to fall back on the port of Dunkirk and attempt to extract the BEF from France, the only decision logically left to him short of surrender.

One of the most difficult decisions a commander can be called upon to make is disobeying an order when in his judgment it is either illegal or militarily so unsound that it threatens the survival of his command. In Gort's case this meant rejecting the counterattack order and redeploying the BEF in an effort to save it from annihilation. Gort made this fateful decision on his own – one that, had he been a German commander, would have resulted in his summary execution. ('I make decisions; I need men who obey,' Hitler proclaimed in 1940, when he took charge of the war as Germany's undisputed warlord.) For a faithful and obedient soldier it was an exceedingly difficult and courageous choice. Gort believed that even in a best-case scenario the bulk of the BEF and its equipment would be lost. 'I never thought I'd lead the British army to its biggest defeat in history,' he dolefully remarked to his aide-de-camp.

The decision to withdraw the BEF to Dunkirk had terrible consequences for the Belgian army, whose right flank, once protected by British troops, was suddenly exposed. King Leopold's brave little army deserved a better fate, but without the support of the BEF it was compelled to surrender early on 28 May. Gort had not informed the Belgians of the withdrawal of the BEF, nor did King Leopold inform the British of his decision to surrender his army and his nation to spare them further needless bloodshed. Belgian casualties were nearly double those of the British – 7,500 killed versus 3,457. The Belgians could be forgiven their bitterness. The rift among the three allies was evident when Reynaud condemned Leopold for failing to warn the French of his intentions, calling it 'a deed without precedent in history'. It was a criticism the French would soon apply to what was alleged to be British perfidy.

Gort lacked the confidence of Brooke, who regarded him as incapable of understanding the deadly strategic situation faced by the BEF and as immersed in minutiae, best left to his staff, that detracted from his ability to exercise meaningful command. Brooke was particularly critical of the lack of direction from GHQ that followed Gort's decision to withdraw.

The continuing poor communications and lack of information about the status of the BEF led Churchill to issue a spate of memos that day. Why, he demanded of the War Office, had an order been issued to evacuate Calais, and what was Gort doing and why? It took until well into the night before Churchill and the War Cabinet heard from the new vice chief of the Imperial General Staff, Lieutenant General Sir John Dill (soon to replace Ironside as CIGS), who was in France to assess the situation and to report on the extent of the predicament facing the BEF and the French First Army.

Until Dill returned to report that their plight was dire, there still existed in London the conviction that the salvation of the BEF lay in carrying out the Weygand plan. Dill's assessment brought about a belated recognition by the British government that only an evacuation could save the expeditionary force. The decision, which might have enraged Churchill had it been made several days earlier, was now accepted as essential if the BEF was to be saved from annihilation.

On the morning of 26 May the only unresolved question was whether the BEF could even be saved. The conditions for its successful return to England were unpromising. No one – not Churchill, nor Gort, nor anyone else in a position of authority – believed that anything more than a small fraction of the force could be evacuated successfully while under attack. The four divisions of Brooke's II Corps provided a shield as the rest of the BEF began retreating to Dunkirk. On its flank the French Fourth Army commenced a similar retreat. British and French forces were trapped along an axis some sixty miles in length and varying from fifteen to twenty-five miles in width, rapidly being squeezed shut by the combined might of two German army groups. To evacuate the BEF from Dunkirk, where the Luftwaffe had reduced most of the port facilities to rubble, required a force to hold open the corridor to the port.

The officer charged with bringing the BEF home was Vice Admiral Sir Bertram Home Ramsay. Although retired from active service in 1938, Ramsay had been recalled to active duty upon the outbreak of war and assigned to command the naval base at Dover. At one of the most critical moments in British military history he bore the responsibility for masterminding Operation Dynamo, the evacuation of Dunkirk. He was told that the operation would probably last only two days and that he could expect to bring home no more than forty-five thousand troops of the BEF. Fortunately for Britain this monumental task was in the hands of the right man, a tough-minded organizer and one of ablest admirals in the Royal Navy. At this point, however, Ramsay had no idea if he could save the BEF; he knew only that he would do his damnedest.

37

Deliverance

Better it should end, not through surrender, but only when we are rolling senseless on the ground. – Churchill, 28 May 1940

You can never talk to a fool. Hitler spoilt the chance of victory.
– General der Panzertruppen Wilhelm Ritter von Thoma

In May 1940 the ancient city of Calais, the scene of a famous battle in 1558 that had cost the British dearly during the reign of Queen Mary, and of a mutiny by British army veterans in 1919, became a symbol of bravery and sacrifice. The French seaport geographically closest to England, Calais is easily visible from Dover on a clear day. As the evacuation of the BEF was beginning to take place twenty-four miles up the coast, at Dunkirk, Calais was completely encircled and under siege by the 10th Panzer Division. For three days the British, along with eight hundred French troops, fought a bitter street fight, sometimes building by building, and stubbornly defended against the panzers while being relentlessly shelled by artillery and attacked by Luftwaffe dive-bombers.

If the BEF was to have any chance of evacuation, the corridor to Dunkirk had to be kept open long enough for the Royal Navy to carry out Operation Dynamo. The Calais garrison could still have been extracted, but after Churchill and the chiefs of staff had debated the question on the night of 25 May it was decided that it should remain and fight in order to delay the German advance on Dunkirk. The effect of the order was that death or capture were the only two possible outcomes. It fell to Churchill to sanction the decision – and to ask the Belgians, who had been abandoned when the BEF began its retreat into the Dunkirk perimeter, to continue buying time on its behalf.

At 11.23 p.m. on 24 May, the War Office telegraphed the commander of the Calais garrison, Brigadier Claude Nicholson, ordering his small force to continue fighting 'for the sake of Allied solidarity'. When he was handed a copy of the telegram the following morning, Churchill erupted. That British soldiers should be asked to die for such an obscure concept as 'Allied solidarity' was ludicrous and unacceptable. If a sacrifice had to be made, there must be a valid reason. He immediately drafted a revised memo that was sent to Nicholson on the afternoon of the 25th. 'The eyes of the Empire are upon the defence of Calais and his Majesty's Government are confident that you and your gallant regiment will perform an exploit worthy of the British name.'

For Churchill, whose lifelong ambition had been to exercise generalship, the decision to sacrifice the Calais garrison was his first real experience of the gut-wrenching, life-and-death decisions commanders must make in war. As with Antwerp in 1914, it is not unreasonable to believe that if it had been possible he would have taken personal charge of the defence of Calais. In May 1940, however, he had to settle for making a heart-rending decision.

It left him dismayed, at one of the low points of the war. 'The number of troops involved was relatively small,' Ismay would later recall, 'but it is a terrible thing to condemn a body of splendid men to death or captivity. The decision affected us all very deeply, especially perhaps Churchill.' As the battle raged not many miles distant, Churchill carried on as usual – or at least he pretended to do so, deceiving none of his dinner guests that evening. 'One has to eat and drink in war,' he later said, 'but I could not help feeling physically sick as we afterwards sat silently at the table.' Ismay noted that although Churchill repeated those words in his memoir, 'he does not mention how sad he looked as he uttered them.'

To the end of his life Churchill remained convinced that 'Calais made the evacuation of Dunkirk possible. If Calais had surrendered, those [German] tanks and the troops around Calais would have turned on our men retreating to Dunkirk, and they would probably never have got away. It was my decision.'

The sacrifice of the Calais garrison never had quite the historical importance given it by Churchill. The garrison held out valiantly for three days in heavy street fighting, but on 26 May the survivors were encircled in Calais-Nord, the old section of the city. Those who were not killed were gradually rounded up; a few hid and managed a daring escape by sea when a tiny British ship, completely unaware of the situation there, unwittingly entered Calais harbour and rescued some forty-six British troops who had been concealed near the breakwater. Brigadier Nicholson was trapped in the Citadel, a sixteenth-century fortress near the harbour, and surrendered at 4.00 that afternoon. The attempt to hold out had lasted barely eight hours. The heroic garrison had given its all in a magnificent effort. Despite Churchill's belief that it was pivotal, Calais bought little or no time for Dunkirk. The Germans had diverted only the 10th Panzer Division, and it did not become part of the eventual siege of Dunkirk. Nevertheless, those who fought the good fight in Calais never questioned whether they had been sacrificial lambs. One infantryman who spent the war in a German POW camp wrote, typically: 'It would not be easy to find any who regret the days of Calais.' Brigadier Nicholson was not so fortunate; he died in captivity.

Heinz Guderian, the Prussian panzer general whose corps would have advanced on Dunkirk along the coast, was, next to Rommel, one of the most admired German generals of the Second World War. In his post-war memoir Guderian wrote that the heroic British defence of Calais, while worthy of the highest praise, nevertheless 'had no influence on the development of events outside Dunkirk'.

On 5 June *The Times* published this brief tribute from a reader: 'A silence reigned over Calais – Mr Churchill. Dim was the memory of that ancient pain. But, now you have played this most heroic part, we tell all France with pride that once again England has Calais on her heart.'

During the crucial battles in May and early June 1940 both Hitler and Churchill made far-reaching, strategically important decisions. On 24 May, with the entire BEF and thousands of French troops within his grasp, Hitler 'blinked' and dithered, and thereby committed a cardinal sin of war: letting up when you have your enemy by the throat. With the Germans on the verge of squeezing shut the trap at Dunkirk, the unprecedented advance of his armies unnerved the führer. Convinced in the absence of evidence to the contrary that the rapid advance had exposed his armoured spearheads to a counterattack in the difficult terrain of Flanders, with its many marshes, rivers and canals, Hitler halted his vanguard only fifteen miles outside Dunkirk, on the morning of 24 May.

The decision to halt the panzers instead of attacking the BEF and French forces trapped in the cordon was, according to Hitler's Luftwaffe adjutant Nicolaus von Below, 'strongly influenced by the manipulative Hermann Göring, who saw the chance for his airmen to strike a decisive blow against Britain'. According to General Walter Warlimont (the deputy chief of the Operations Staff of the Oberkommando der Wehrmacht, OKW), when Göring reached him on the telephone the afternoon of 23 May he gave Hitler 'an unconditional assurance that he would annihilate the remnants of the enemy'. Below recorded that while Hitler was not altogether convinced by Göring's argument, 'it suited his plans.'

There was another, perhaps overriding reason why Hitler had little interest in the BEF: his aim was the conquest of France, and so far only its northern region had been taken. On paper the French army still had 1.5 million troops under arms, consisting of some sixty-five divisions that had yet to be defeated. With Göring's promise that 'only fishbait will reach the other side', Hitler had reason to turn his attention to making France the latest German vassal state. Thanks to Göring and Rundstedt, the order remained in force for a crucial forty-eight hours.

Despite having everything in his favour and a golden opportunity to annihilate the BEF (the nucleus of the British army in 1940), Hitler ignored the pleas of both General Halder and the army commander in chief, General Walter von Brauchitsch, to attack at once. The führer remained unmoved, deeming the employment of the panzer force in southern France more important. 'The British Army had no relevance for him,' said Below. By the time Hitler permitted Rundstedt to resume his offensive to capture the Channel ports on 26 May, the decision to pull the BEF out at Dunkirk had been taken and the evacuation was already under way. Moreover, despite permitting the resumption of operations against Dunkirk, Hitler decreed that the panzers advance no closer than artillery range.

Of all the wartime directives Hitler issued to German army commanders, few provoked more controversy or outrage. The halting of the panzers was one of the war's great turning points and a stroke of extraordinary good fortune for Churchill and for Britain. After the war a panzer commander, Major General Wilhelm von Thoma, remarked scornfully, 'You can never talk to a fool. Hitler spoilt the chance of victory.' Other reasons have also been advanced for the order, among them that the führer did not want to humiliate Britain. Although the remark is unverified (if authentic, it bespeaks a masterpiece of self-delusion), he is said to have declared several weeks after the event that 'the army is the backbone of England and the Empire. If we smash the invasion corps, the Empire is doomed. Since we neither want nor can inherit it, we must leave it the chance. My generals haven't grasped that.' After the BEF had escaped, Hitler also told General Ewald von Kleist, the commander of the panzer group spearheading the run to the Channel, that 'he had no intention of sending his tanks into "the mud of Flanders. The English won't show up again in this war, anyway."' 'We were speechless,' said Guderian, whose panzers would have led the charge on Dunkirk, his dignity all the greater given that the Army Intelligence Service had accurately predicted no threat from either the French or the British.

Towards the end of the war Hitler defended his decision by declaring, 'Churchill was quite unable to appreciate the sporting spirit of which I have given proof by refraining from creating an irreparable breach between the British and ourselves. We did, however, refrain from annihilating them at Dunkirk.' The truth was that, as a German historian has written, 'Hitler and some of his generals were so fixated on preventing a repetition of the "miracle of the Marne" that they conjured up the "miracle of Dunkirk".'

The BEF would be saved from destruction by Hitler's decision of 24 May 1940. Churchill would never have returned the favour.

Winston Churchill's role at this point in the Battle of France was primarily one of exhortation. He had agreed to the evacuation of the BEF and wrote to Gort on 27 May that 'at this solemn moment . . . we shall give you all Navy and Air Force can do.' Clearly unaware that Calais had fallen, he could not resist giving Gort military advice, recommending various means by which German tanks should be destroyed, noting his concerns about the defence of Ostend and suggesting that 'a column directed upon Calais while it is still holding out might have a good chance.'

As German pressure mounted and the vice around Dunkirk began to tighten on the morning of 26 May, no one knew how many men would be successfully evacuated. Gort believed that the chances of saving his command were slim. To many the term 'evacuation' smacked of defeatism, but whatever one called it there was now a race against time to save as many men of the BEF as possible.

On the 28th Churchill warned Parliament that it 'should prepare itself for hard and heavy tidings'. Later he summoned all ministers of cabinet rank who were not members of the War Cabinet and told them plainly that everything weighed in the balance at Dunkirk. Britain ought to get fifty thousand home, and one hundred thousand would be 'a magnificent performance . . . He was determined to prepare public opinion for bad tidings,' recorded Hugh Dalton, who believed that 'what was now happening in Northern France would be the greatest British military defeat for many centuries.'

With the bad news over and done with, Churchill put paid to the notion of peace with Hitler. No matter what happened at Dunkirk, 'It was idle to think that if we tried to make peace now, we should get better terms from Germany than if we went on and fought it out. The Germans would demand our fleet – that would be called "disarmament" – our naval bases and much else. We should become a slave state . . . On the other side, we have immense reserves and advantages.' Therefore, he said, 'We shall go on and we shall fight it out, here and elsewhere, and if at last the long story is to end, it were better it should end, not through surrender, but only when we are rolling senseless on the ground.'

Churchill recorded that at the conclusion of his passionate oration 'quite a number seemed to jump up from the table and come running to my chair, shouting and patting me on the back.' More important, his performance was an enormous boost that helped solidify his somewhat tenuous position as prime minister. 'There is no doubt that had I at this juncture faltered at all in the leading of the nation, I should have been hurled out of office.'

This meeting was a major turning point for Churchill. Up to then he had been on shaky ground, often rather distrusted despite his brilliant speeches. Many Tories had still believed he would need to be replaced before long. Waiting in the wings in the expectation that Churchill would fail and that he would once again be called upon to lead Britain was Lloyd George – proving yet again the first unofficial rule of politics: that friendship is almost always trumped by self-interest. There were those on both sides of the political divide who believed that the war could not be won and that Britain ought to open negotiations with Hitler before more blood was spilled. At this meeting Churchill had taken a brave and irreversible stand, calmly but forcefully arguing, with some of the most brilliant oratory of his political life, that neither surrender nor negotiation was a viable option.

Although Churchill's position would not be completely secure until the end of 1940, his own 'finest hour' was certainly his determined stance on 28 May, when the only positive news was that an attempt was being made to rescue the BEF from annihilation on the beaches of Dunkirk. The hallmark of great leadership was on full display. Not for an instant did Churchill exhibit the slightest sign that Britain would ever give in to Hitler.

Despite his masterful public display of fortitude, privately Churchill was never particularly successful at concealing his feelings. His moods swung from ebullience one minute to dejection the next, very often when the almost daily setbacks that characterized his first months in office were in evidence. His former daughter-in-law, Pamela Harriman, later recounted how, after Dunkirk: 'He would come into meals and sometimes he'd put his head in his hands and hardly eat, and then he would suddenly say – 'this is one of the hardest times.'

The evacuation of Dunkirk commenced on 27 May when the first 7,669 troops were rescued while Dynamo was still being organized and lessons were being quickly learned. It was immediately clear that there were insufficient naval vessels. The Admiralty initiated emergency measures to locate additional small craft – civilian, navy, anything they could lay hands on. Lifeboats from cruise liners, fishing trawlers, yachts and other pleasure boats of all types, barges, lighters, tugs – anything that floated was pressed into service. This brilliant mobilization of ships was what ultimately made the evacuation of Dunkirk possible. In all 861 Allied vessels participated, of which 693 were British.

After the first few days of the evacuation Churchill's mood brightened. 'At one time I thought we should be lucky if forty thousand men got away. Next morning my price went up. The small boats taking away our army; it is an epic tale.' During these perilous days he visited the Admiralty war room eight to ten times a day. On the evening of 29 May Captain Richard Pim, the officer in charge, asked for and was given permission by Churchill to take four days' leave in order to assist the evacuation. 'I remember his words,' recalled Pim: ' "God bless you; I wish I were going with you myself." '

Yet on 29 May Churchill remained uncertain that the rear elements and those still ashore at Dunkirk would survive. Some 39,000 had been rescued so far and 7,500 were in the process of being rescued. He wrote to Gort: 'If you are cut off from all communication with us, and all evacuation from Dunkirk and beaches had in your judgement been finally prevented, after every attempt to reopen it had failed, you would become the sole judge of when it was impossible to inflict further damage upon the enemy. His Majesty's Government are sure that the repute of the British Army is safe in your hands.' In other words a decision to surrender was in Gort's hands.

Deep beneath Whitehall in the underground cabinet war rooms, staff officers began recording the numbers. They tell a dramatic tale as the evacuation continued beyond everyone's expectations. By the afternoon of 3 June more than three hundred thousand British and French troops had been safely brought to England. On the morning of 4 June the War Office reported: 'The final evacuation of [26,175] French troops was carried out during the night of 3/4 June and operations have now ceased. The Germans are now in the suburbs of Dunkirk.'

The story of Dunkirk is one of exceptional heroism by nameless men and women in a variety of ways. The bravery of the fishermen and small-boat sailors who made countless trips through the deadly magnetic mines in the waters off Dunkirk laid by the Luftwaffe has become legendary. Ships of the Royal Navy carried out two-thirds of the evacuation from Dunkirk's eastern mole, and only during the last four days of Dynamo were the small boats mobilized and able to evacuate some 26,000 directly off the beaches.

The magnificent achievements of the Royal Navy and the heroic boatmen are well known, but the evacuation of the BEF would not have been possible without the RAF, which flew hundreds of sorties to provide air cover and to engage the Luftwaffe fighters whenever they appeared. There were savage air battles as the RAF threw everything it had into protecting the evacuation, suffering heavy losses out of sight of the evacuees. The losses sustained by the RAF in France in seven weeks would turn out to be higher than those incurred during the Battle of Britain.

Churchill understood just how important the RAF contribution was, and paid it high tribute in his 4 June speech. Nevertheless there was an unfortunate and unfounded belief within the BEF and the Royal Navy that, because the RAF was nowhere to be seen, it had therefore not pulled its weight in the evacuation. The facts are that the RAF lost more than 900 aircraft during the Battle of France, of which 477 were fighters that would soon be desperately needed in the Battle of Britain. Dowding's Fighter Command flew 2,739 missions in support of Dynamo, and during the nine days of the evacuation lost 145 aircraft and eighty-eight pilots. The Luftwaffe fared badly during the evacuation, in large part owing to fog and poor visibility that proved a blessing to the British and a curse to the Germans. Even during the two days of good flying weather, the Luftwaffe pilots had encountered furious resistance from guns of the French and British navies, and from the RAF, losing 156 aircraft during the evacuation.

The Luftwaffe's failure to halt the evacuation turned Hermann Göring's pledge to Hitler into little more than an empty boast. Göring's ineffectiveness would have got him sacked and possibly shot in June 1940 had Hitler not been so loyal to his friend and confidant. Like Churchill, he boasted of having played with toy lead soldiers as a boy, but he became an air ace with twenty-two kills in the First World War. Appointed to command the Luftwaffe in 1935, Göring had reservations about Germany's readiness for war and never seemed confident that his air force could actually best the RAF. When war came his declaration that he would dismiss the British proved hollow, and in May 1940 his earlier doubts were realized in the skies over northern France.

Despite that failure, Göring was promoted to the exalted rank of Reichsmarschall, the highest in the German military, which gave him seniority over every other officer in the armed forces. Hitler also named him his successor in the event of his death. (By the summer of 1944 even the führer had lost all faith in his most ardent supporter, who had become a figure of ridicule, his body swollen by obesity and a long-standing addiction to narcotics.)

The last British soldier at Dunkirk on the morning of 3 June 1940 was an aristocratic, unflappable Guards officer in charge of the British rearguard. Major General Harold Alexander, better known as 'Alex', commanded the 1st Division until 31 May, when Gort turned over to his care the command of the defence of the Dunkirk perimeter. Before embarking for England, Alexander instructed the crew of his motorboat to manoeuvre close to shore. With a megaphone in hand, he repeatedly called out in both French and English, asking if anyone was there. Although no one replied, Alexander nevertheless returned to the harbour and made a final tour to assure himself that no one had been left behind. Only then did he embark. In the months ahead he would become Churchill's favourite general, whom the prime minister regarded as the model of a British officer and commander of troops.

Although Churchill had ordered that as many French troops as possible should be evacuated, when Alexander sailed from Dunkirk there were none to be seen. However, of the 60,000 French in the Allied bridgehead protecting the evacuation of the BEF, some 34,000 were left behind. There were bitter recriminations that Britain had deserted France in its most desperate hour, though Admiral Bertram Ramsay's makeshift 'navy' had rescued 123,095 French troops from Dunkirk.

The organizer and commander of Operation Dynamo was destined to play a key role in 1944 as the commander of Allied naval forces for the cross-Channel invasion of Normandy. Ramsay had been under frightful strain throughout the nine days of the evacuation and rarely left his operations room in Dover Castle. When the operation officially ended at 2.23 p.m. on 4 June, he unwound by playing a round of golf at nearby Sandwich, achieving the best score of his life, which he may have regarded as another miracle in a week already filled with them.

Epic tales of Dunkirk continue to fill the history books. The grit and ingenuity displayed by the Royal Navy, the RAF and the civilian sailors manning the small boats, who ferried the men of the BEF to the destroyers and other ships, are deservedly enshrined for ever in British history. Yet many things about Dunkirk were deeply troubling: from the reality that it was made possible only by Hitler's blunder to the fact that the BEF was compelled to abandon most of its precious equipment on the beaches.

James Bradley was a Bren gunner, and his account of surviving Dunkirk was typical:

I think I became a man there . . . Dunkirk changed my character completely. It changed my thinking about soldiering and actually about killing – accepting it as a part of your day, which you would never do otherwise. You fight back the fear, you put a lid on it – it's a way of life that takes over, because you want to survive. The feeling for survival is a wonderful thing.

Lord Gort and his soldiers were treated to a heroes' welcome. Important though it was to have saved the men of the BEF, it was imperative that those who were to lead Britain in the war ahead were also saved. The salvation of the BEF was not lost on the officer who became the new CIGS in December 1941. After the war Brooke reflected: 'Had the BEF not returned to this country it is hard to see how the Army could have recovered from this blow . . . Time and again throughout the years of the war I thanked God for the safe return of the bulk of the personnel of the BEF.'

Despite its portrayal as a miracle of deliverance, Dunkirk was nevertheless a military disaster of the first rank. Much of its ugliness was covered up. Some territorial officers charged with helping to defend the corridor disgracefully deserted their troops to save themselves. This aspect of Dunkirk never appeared in the British official history, and the offenders were later quietly cashiered from the army. Other acts of indiscipline obliged the navy to use armed sentries to control mob scenes at Dunkirk during the first two days of the evacuation – a situation that improved only with the arrival of regular army units. Communications were chaotic, and there was confusion and a lack of co-ordination and direction from Gort's GHQ. The evacuation might well have failed without the cool heads of commanders like Alexander, Brooke and Montgomery, who commanded the 3rd Division and later assumed temporary command of II Corps when Brooke was ordered back to England at the end of May.

Sometimes lost in the story of Dunkirk are the bravery and tenacity of the French troops who held the perimeter while the final evacuation was taking place, and of the French navy, which helped guard the ships in the Channel. They paid a very heavy price to enable the BEF's escape. Those who were not trapped around Dunkirk would put up a valiant defence of France in June. Overall French losses during the Battle of France were staggering: 120,000 dead, 250,000 wounded and 1.5 million taken prisoner. Although Churchill would send more British troops to France after Dunkirk, the French people's bitterness towards their ally would last for generations.

Of the 372 small craft that braved the Channel and German aerial and artillery attacks, nearly 50 per cent were sunk (170 of the 226 British vessels lost during Dynamo). Of the thirty-nine valuable destroyers employed in the rescue, six were sunk and nineteen more damaged, none of which the Royal Navy could afford to lose given the inevitable battles yet to be fought.

And while the men of the BEF were saved, only twenty-two armoured vehicles were lifted to England. Left behind were 2,472 (of 2,794) guns; and 63,879 (of 66,618) motor vehicles were destroyed to keep them from German hands. Also abandoned were 475 tanks, eight thousand Bren guns, ninety thousand rifles and seven thousand tons of ammunition. An OKW communiqué trumpeted the ousting of the BEF from France: 'The great battle of Flanders and Artois is over. It will go down in military history as the greatest battle of annihilation of all time . . . Since our adversaries persist in refusing peace, the fight will continue until they are destroyed utterly.' Halder and Brauchitsch derided this nonsense. On 30 May Halder exclaimed in frustration, 'We must now stand by and watch countless thousands of the enemy get away to England right under our noses.'

For Churchill, and for his beleaguered nation, Dunkirk was a precious gift that would become the nucleus of Britain's salvation.

38

'Don't Give Way to Fear'

It will be the great paradox of history that Britain was never so strong as she was at the moment of her greatest weakness.   – Sir Geoffrey Shakespeare

The BBC announced on 4 June that the 'Dunkirk rescue is over – Mr Churchill defiant.' Had Churchill been in full control politically he would have been able to devote more of his attention to coping with the immense military problems Britain faced. Instead his most important role during these crucial days was to stem defeatism in the British populace. Once released, morale-lowering genies can rarely be forced back into the bottle, and it took every ounce of Churchill's leadership to do this. Putting on a brave face and exhibiting defiance, he rose that evening before a packed House of Commons to deliver the words for which he remains most famous, the landmark 'we shall never surrender' speech that built on his earlier words of 13 May.

The galleries were jammed with peers, VIPs and others lucky enough to gain entry. While praising the courage of the men and women who had brought the BEF home, Churchill stressed that Dunkirk had untold consequences. 'We must be very careful not to assign to this deliverance the attributes of a victory. Wars are not won by evacuations,' he reminded them. 'Our thankfulness at the escape of our Army and so many men . . . must not blind us to the fact that what happened in France and Belgium is a colossal military disaster.' What victory there was, he said, was the magnificent work of the RAF, which had triumphed in 'a great trial of strength'. Moreover he reminded his colleagues of Hitler's intention to invade England, noting that when Napoleon had considered an invasion, he was told: 'There are bitter weeds in England.'

Churchill ended his speech with his memorable and dramatic reminder that it was Britain's national will to resist an invasion:

We shall go on to the end. We shall fight in France, we shall fight on the seas and oceans ... we shall defend our island, whatever the cost may be, we shall fight on the beaches, we shall fight on the landing grounds, we shall fight in the fields and in the streets, we shall fight in the hills; we shall never surrender.

It is the nature of politicians frequently to say things they don't truly mean. But these pronouncements came straight from Churchill's heart; he meant every word and intended to be among those to die defending the kingdom if need be.

Sitting behind the prime minister, one of his sternest critics, Chips Channon, was deeply moved: 'he was eloquent ... Several Labour Members cried. He hinted that we might be obliged to fight alone, without France, and that England might well be invaded. How the atmosphere has changed from only a few weeks ago when idiotic MPs were talking academic nonsense about our restoring independence to Warsaw and Prague.'

Churchill repeated the speech on the BBC that evening. It had been heard in the Commons by the CBS correspondent Edward R. Murrow, who remarked that England would survive only as long as Churchill led it; otherwise, the result would be 'disaster'. 'He told his American audience that "I've heard Mr Churchill in the House of Commons at intervals over the last ten years ... Today, he was different. There was little oratory. He wasn't interested in being a showman. He spoke the language of Shakespeare with a direct urgency such as I have never heard before." '

The speech was also a heroic bluff. Churchill was like a poker player with a busted hand, betting the house that the British people would believe him. In truth, there was almost nothing to back the boast other than great sincerity and the defiance upon which the substance of his fame comfortably rested. It was also a speech no one else would have dared to make in June 1940. With the BEF barely saved from annihilation, his army a broken reed and the United States eighteen months from entering the war, however heroic his pugnacity it was gambler's talk. And it worked. No one else in Britain could have pulled this off, certainly not the gentlemanly Chamberlain or the reserved Halifax.

While the British people were certainly energized by Churchill's defiance of Nazi Germany, they refused to buy into his declaration that Dunkirk was a military disaster. Instead, as one historian has written, 'They much preferred the myth to the reality, and they were not prepared to listen to anyone who sought to puncture their belief, not even Churchill himself. They were a difficult people to feed on lies, but they were perfectly happy to lie to themselves, particularly when that lie held the key to their survival as a nation.' The author Rebecca West seemed to speak for the country when she wrote in a weekly magazine: 'Don't give way to fear.'

The effect of Churchill's oratory was to give the British people a sense of belonging – a sense that they were all in it together – of believing that they too could make a difference, and that their government actually cared about them and their welfare. His genius lay in the ability to strike exactly the right chord at the right moment. In times of crisis it is often small gestures that mean the most, such as Churchill's use of two fingers to signal V for victory, or the defiant raising of the American flag over the smoking ruins of the World Trade Center by New York City firemen in 2001. (As Colville wrote in his diary in 1941, Churchill gave the V sign 'in spite of the representations repeatedly made to him that this gesture has quite another significance!')

Considerably more than the BEF was saved at Dunkirk. The evacuation very probably saved Churchill's job. It also changed the course of the war in several respects: it lifted the British public at a desperate time and as no other event would until the D-day landings in Normandy four years later. It also helped make certain that Britain would fight on rather than enter into peace negotiations with Hitler. Britons now had reason to feel a sense of national pride that was of great value to Churchill in his new role as galvanizer in chief.

Yet behind the mask of Dunkirk's heroics were some of the war's best-kept secrets as the Ministry of Information's propaganda machine worked overtime. That there was at times a sense of demoralization – shown in the way some combatants donned civilian clothing and threw their weapons from the windows of railway carriages carrying them home – was understandably kept quiet. The public knew almost nothing of the ugly truth: of the scenes of indiscipline on the beaches before order was restored; of the lost ships; of the dead who never made it home, many killed in the water or aboard ships hit by an artillery shell or by the Luftwaffe; of the flaming cauldron of gunfire, bombs and crashing artillery shells; or of the cowardice of those who should have led instead of abandoning their men. Problems within the BEF had nearly proved disastrous and ranged from the breakdown of the communications system to confusion and lack of command and control when Gort unaccountably divided his headquarters, leaving his key operations and intelligence staffs at Arras while he moved the remainder some thirty miles north to Lille.

The press was recruited, and Fleet Street willingly co-operated by publishing only positive information. That the BEF was even being evacuated from Dunkirk was not revealed until the BBC broadcast the news on the evening of 30 May. The BEF, the public was informed, 'have not come back in triumph, they have come back in glory'. Yet the British army was now desperately short of guns, ammunition and equipment, and would have to be quickly reconstituted almost from scratch in order to defend against what was thought in early June to be the certainty of a German invasion. Before that, however, there was a second ill-fated military venture in a vain attempt by Churchill to help save France.

The sight of the green fields of England exhilarated Lieutenant General Alan Brooke, who, like most of the returning men of the BEF, desperately needed sleep. Duty required that he confer with Ramsay in Dover and Dill in London before making his way by train, like an ordinary commuter, to his country home in Hampshire, struggling to stay awake so as not to miss his stop.

He was summoned to the War Office on 2 June and informed by Dill that he was to command a second BEF operation in France, where there were still some 150,000 British troops. Churchill's admiration for Lord Gort was boundless, and his blindness to Gort's shortcomings would have ensured his selection to command a second British Expeditionary Force, composed of fighting and support units that had been operating outside the Dunkirk perimeter and had remained in France to aid the beleaguered French army. However, without the support of the chiefs of staff, Churchill's plan for Gort to command this force was derailed and, instead, at Dill's behest, Brooke was given the daunting assignment: 'Return to France and form a new BEF!'

It was, Brooke later said, one of his blackest moments of the war. 'I had seen my hope in the French army gradually shattered throughout those long winter months. I had witnessed the realization of my worst fears regarding its fighting value and morale, and now I had no false conceptions as to what its destiny must inevitably be.' Before departing, Brooke told Eden, secretary of state for war, that to embark on such a venture would accomplish nothing and that, unless there was some particular political advantage, the expedition 'promised no chances of military success and every probability of disaster'.

Brooke was to come under Weygand's command to help save France. He arrived in Cherbourg on the night of 12 June and on the morning of the 14th drove 170 miles from his HQ at Le Mans to Orléans to meet with the French commander in chief. The new plan rivalled the old Weygand plan in its lack of realism. What the French general told him confirmed Brooke's opinion of what lay ahead. The government had fled Paris, there were no reserves, and what was left of the French army was incapable of offering anything more than token resistance for a few more days. The new plan, which Weygand admitted was fanciful, called for a fighting retreat by Anglo-French forces into a redoubt in Brittany. Brooke immediately telegraphed Dill to report the hopelessness of the situation and to request that no more British and Canadian troops be sent to France.

That evening Dill went to No. 10 bearing Brooke's telegram and the bad news it contained. An abysmal telephone connection was made with Brooke, who explained his intention to withdraw his remaining divisions to Le Mans. The sticking point was the 52nd Division. The day before, the gallant Scots Highlanders of the 51st Division had been needlessly sacrificed at Saint-Valéry-en-Caux while awaiting an evacuation that never came, and Brooke was determined not to lose the 52nd in the same manner. Although he persuaded Dill of the validity of his decision, the CIGS said, 'The Prime Minister does not want you to do that.' An angry Brooke replied, 'What the hell does he want?' Brooke suddenly found himself speaking with Churchill, who insisted that the 52nd stay and fight beside the French. It was Brooke's first contact with Churchill, and it did not go well. 'I had been sent to France to make the French feel that we were supporting them,' he recalled. Undaunted by opposing Churchill, the future CIGS responded with firmness and a piercing candour that marked his entire relationship with Churchill. It was impossible, he told him, 'to make a corpse feel': the French army was, to all intents and purposes, dead.

This was a classic conundrum: Churchill was obliged to make a military decision that was at variance with his responsibility as a political leader. Although he understood that the situation in France was essentially hopeless, he could not resist the notion of establishing a redoubt in the Brittany Peninsula in which French and British troops would resist and eventually form the springboard for a renewed offensive against the Germans.

There was a gap in the lines and a division available; why not act to plug it, he demanded? Brooke pointed out that the gap was already forty miles wide and growing by the hour. Inserting the 52nd Division 'would again inevitably result in the throwing away of good troops with no hope of achieving any results'. Their conversation lasted nearly half an hour, with Churchill infuriatingly offering repeated arguments why Brooke should comply with his wishes and insinuating that his commander in France 'was suffering from "cold feet"'. Brooke bluntly said, 'You've lost one Scottish Division. Do you want to lose another?'

Brooke finally wore Churchill down with irrefutable arguments, a practice he would continue when he became CIGS. 'All right,' said Churchill, 'I agree with you.' The withdrawal of the 'other' BEF was officially authorized. Brooke had won because – as the commander on the spot – his judgments were correct and, after the usual test of wills faced by all military men who dealt with him, Churchill accepted them.

Brooke's command of the BEF lasted only five days, but as a result of his initiative and his willingness to stand up to Churchill, approximately 160,000 British and Allied soldiers, including 20,000 Polish troops, were safely returned to England, along with three hundred guns and three combat divisions that would otherwise have met the same fate as the Highlanders. There were, however, very serious losses when the Luftwaffe sank the liner *Lancastria* at Saint-Nazaire, killing some three thousand British soldiers in one of history's worst maritime losses. On Churchill's order, the news of this disaster was suppressed and never reported by the British press. The only 'recognition' Brooke received upon his return was an inquiry by the War Office questioning why he had not saved more equipment. Unrepentant, he maintained that saving lives was more important; equipment could be replaced more easily than men needlessly sacrificed in a lost cause.

Once again wishful thinking trumped reality. Had Brooke not been so forceful and persuasive, further disaster to the BEF might well have occurred. What disturbed him in his first contact with Churchill was the prime minister's interference with his field commander without sufficient knowledge of conditions on the ground, and 'against that commander's better judgement'.

Shortly after his return to England, Brooke was summoned to Downing Street, where he met Churchill face to face for the first of what would be hundreds of meetings during the war. Over lunch he was thoroughly cross-examined about his experience in France. Although he may not have realized it at the time, Churchill was taking his measure, and in the weeks and months that followed it became evident that the prime minister liked what he saw: a forceful and competent soldier who not only knew the business of war but was willing and able to hold his own in the arena of debate. Such men were too few in the summer of 1940.

Dunkirk also changed Churchill's military thinking. His normal combativeness was replaced by the sobering realization that winning the war did not always mean attack, attack – that sometimes defence was necessary. The transition was not easy for a warrior of his ilk.

Dunkirk was a far cry from days earlier when he had urged, even demanded, offensive action when none was really possible. The transition from the static lines of the First World War to a new age of mobile warfare fought under fast-changing conditions with tanks and movable artillery was not easy even for the innovative mind of Winston Churchill. He failed to understand that this new age brought with it a multitude of logistical problems and that, new innovations, tactics and methods notwithstanding, it was necessary to find and appoint men with the ability and experience to make it all work. Appointing the right people would prove his greatest challenge. The lesson for Churchill – one that he never really quite grasped – was that filling the role of de facto commander in chief required more than just an aggressive approach to war. His desire to avoid the mistakes of the static warfare of 1914–18 is understandable; however, the itch to play soldier in chief instead of commander in chief was ever present, and it would take strong men like Brooke and Dwight Eisenhower firmly but judiciously to dissuade him from rash ventures.

*

Hitler's dream was a peace treaty with Britain – on his terms, naturally. The advent of Churchill as the new British leader threw this strategy into doubt. Nevertheless, there were elements within the Conservative and Labour parties that believed Britain's best – and perhaps only – option was to negotiate with Herr Hitler. Calls for peace with Germany had begun almost immediately after the invasion of Poland in September 1939. While grappling with the fall of France, Churchill had either to neutralize the peace wing of his government or give in and side with it.

Thus the most important political issue in the summer of 1940 revolved around whether to enter into a dialogue with Germany to learn what the terms might be, a position supported by both Halifax and Rab Butler. Neither man was an appeaser; rather, they considered themselves realists exploring all options available to Britain. With the fall of France only a matter of time, Halifax in particular dreaded the consequences of the anticipated German saturation bombing of London and other British cities. His vision was that the British way of life and its empire appeared doomed, and, with Britain in the throes of Dunkirk, he sincerely opposed surrender but, as one of his biographers notes, 'saw nothing particularly heroic in going down fighting if it could somehow be avoided'.

Although Dunkirk has been touted as an enduring example of the traditional British stiff upper lip, the truth was that the nine months of the Phoney War had bred complacency, abetted by Neville Chamberlain's public pronouncement that 'Hitler had missed the bus.' Nor did the British public have a clear idea of precisely what the future held. Nevertheless, given the national sense of war weariness, it is not inconceivable that the public would have supported peace over years of conflict that offered no promise that Britain would emerge victorious. Halifax had sounded a warning in December 1939, telling Chamberlain and the War Cabinet that if the time came when France sued for peace with Germany, 'we should not be able to carry on the war by ourselves.'

These fears were very real. The Air Ministry estimated that the Luftwaffe could rain seven hundred tons of bombs a day on London over a fourteen-day period. Casualties in the first six months were estimated at six hundred thousand dead and 1.2 million more injured. 'Cardboard coffins were stockpiled. Sites for mass graves identified,' and some three hundred thousand hospital beds were allocated to handle the wounded. What about Churchill? While he is quite rightly celebrated for his bulldog stance that Britain would fight to the death, he 'did not rule out an eventual negotiated peace treaty, but argued [and is quoted in cabinet minutes as arguing] that "we should get no worse terms if we went on fighting," and that "the position would be entirely different when Germany had made an unsuccessful attempt to invade this country."'' Nor does his denial in the second volume of his war memoirs that he ever considered negotiation ring true: the historian David Reynolds, in his splendid discussion of Churchill's account of the Second World War, calls it 'the most significant cover-up in *Their Finest Hour*'. The move towards exploring a negotiated peace was led by Halifax at three successive meetings of the War Cabinet in late May 1940. If the terms were right and guaranteed full British independence rather than total destruction, even at the sacrifice of some of the empire, 'we should be foolish if we did not accept them,' in order 'to save the country from an avoidable disaster'. The cabinet minutes reflect that Churchill responded with a compromise: 'If we could get out of this jam by giving up Malta and Gibraltar and some African colonies he would jump at it.' Although he deemed it 'most unlikely,' Churchill conceded that should Hitler be disposed 'to make peace on the terms of the restoration of German colonies and the overlordship of Central Europe,' it would be a satisfactory starting point.

His concession notwithstanding, both at his meeting with the noncabinet ministers on 28 May and in the War Cabinet Churchill, with the backing of Chamberlain, Attlee and Arthur Greenwood, the deputy Labour leader and a minister without portfolio, overcame Halifax's initiative. There would be no peace negotiations until such time as the Battle of Britain was won – or lost. In a telegram replying to Churchill's plea for American intervention, Roosevelt had replied that he would not seek the authority from an isolationist Congress to take the country to war. Churchill's telegram had declared that 'in no conceivable circumstances will we consent to surrender.' Nevertheless, describing the present situation as 'this nightmare', he intimated that if US aid were not forthcoming his government might well be replaced by an appeasement administration.

What has been lost in the mythology of Churchill's 'we shall never surrender' approach was the underlying assumption that eventually there would in fact be a negotiated peace with Germany. And while there would not be 'peace at any price', Halifax and Butler insisted in conversations with the Swedish ambassador that hard-liners like Churchill would not be permitted to let Britain fight on if there was a reasonable chance of a compromise peace. Churchill's so-called walk in the garden, at the request of Halifax on 27 May, came after the latter had confided to a colleague, 'I can't work with Winston any longer.' Both men were posturing: Halifax by threatening resignation and Churchill by smoothing troubled waters and placating his foreign secretary. It is not known what they said to each other, but the outcome was that, although Halifax thought Churchill was difficult and exasperating, the two agreed to disagree – which amounted to a victory for Winston in that there was no open rebellion by the peace wing.

Lloyd George also thought there should have been a negotiated peace in 1940. He believed that there was no way Britain could win the war after the fall of France, and that it was even less likely the United States would come to its aid. The views of the two longtime political allies differed over Hitler. Lloyd George mistakenly and foolishly thought that Hitler was rational, even asserting that the German leader was a greater figure in European history than even Napoleon, and that Churchill was wrong to call him a guttersnipe. Yet Churchill instinctively understood what others did not: that Germany had to win the war rather than wait for Britain to lose it. 'Hitler', Churchill said, 'must break us in this island or lose the war.' In the summer of 1940 Germany was not militarily prepared for a long war, and Hitler was gambling on a brief Continental conflict and a negotiated peace with Britain. Churchill also recognized that, even after Austria, Czechoslovakia, Poland and the invasions of Scandinavia and the West, there could never be a compromise with a power-hungry dictator like Adolf Hitler, whose signature on a piece of paper was worthless.

Two giant obstacles stood in Hitler's way: Fighter Command and the Royal Navy. The defences of Britain's shores, however, were woeful. When, in the immediate aftermath of Dunkirk, the Germans did not invade Britain, they provided precious time for the army not only to be revamped but also to prepare coastal defences. The question history has never answered is whether or not what was called Operation Sea Lion would have succeeded.

At least five major figures never doubted that had the Germans wanted to effect landings they could have done so. General Henry H. 'Hap'

Arnold, the commander of the US Army Air Force, visited England in April 1941 and was told by Dill, Beaverbrook, Archibald Sinclair, Air Chief Marshal Sir Wilfrid Freeman – vice chief of the air staff, one of the architects of the revitalization of the RAF in the 1930s – and the first sea lord A. V. Alexander that they all believed that Sea Lion could breach British coastal defences, and that the key to defeating the invasion lay in containing the German beachheads.

Churchill made a series of trips to France in June in an attempt to stiffen the backbone of the French government. Italy entered the war on 10 June, the same day that the French government abandoned Paris and relocated to Bordeaux, declaring the capital an open city. The following day Churchill, accompanied by Ismay, made his penultimate and most important trip to France in a last-ditch effort to shore up what little was left of France's will and ability to fight. Edward Spears observed, 'A miasma of despond had fallen on the conference like a fog.' At a meeting of Churchill, Prime Minister Reynaud and the Supreme War Council in the Loire Valley, General Weygand reviewed the plight of the French army and pressed for an all-out effort by the RAF to come to its aid. Every available aircraft in Britain should be committed to the defence of France, he said. Weygand's plea created one of the greatest crises Churchill was to face during the war, and another of those critical moments when military and political aims were in opposition. While he had pledged Britain's support for France, he was mindful of Dowding's explicit warning that if any further squadrons were deployed to France he could no longer ensure the defence of the British Isles against the coming onslaught of the Luftwaffe. Ismay sat terrified that in his desire to aid his ally Churchill would agree. He needn't have worried. There was a pause before the prime minister responded, saying, 'This is not the decisive point. This is not the decisive moment. The decisive moment will come when Hitler hurls his Luftwaffe against Britain. If we can keep command of the air over our own island – that is all I ask – we will win it back for you ... Whatever happens here we are resolved to fight on and on for ever and ever and ever.' Militarily there was nothing more that Britain could do before the end came in France, and difficult though it was for Churchill to deny his ally further air support, it was one of his greatest and most significant military decisions of the Second World War.

Moved by the Englishman's sincerity, Weygand replied, 'If we capitulate, all the great might of Germany will be concentrated on invading England. And then what will you do?' Ismay describes how Churchill stuck out his jaw and declared that 'broadly speaking he would propose to drown as many as possible of them on the way over' and to 'knock the others on the head as they crawled ashore'. With a wry smile Weygand, referring to the English Channel, said: 'At any rate I must admit you have a very good anti-tank obstacle.' Nonetheless, the French generals believed, 'In three weeks England will have her neck wrung like a chicken.'

In a rare pessimistic mood after his dismal meeting with the French, Churchill grimly observed to Ismay, 'It seems we fight alone.' Ever the optimist, Ismay answered that they would win the Battle of Britain. 'You and I will be dead in three months,' Churchill replied. 'Quite possibly,' said Ismay, 'but we'll have a hell of a good time in those last seven days.'

Paris fell on 14 June, and the following day the French government formally requested permission to violate the Anglo-French accord and seek a separate peace with Germany. When he returned to England shortly before the final death knell rang, Edward Spears reported that the confusion in France was hard to believe.

Paul Reynaud was the only Frenchman to argue against an armistice with Hitler, whom he called 'Genghis Khan'. With no support and his government a shambles, Reynaud resigned and was replaced by the aged Great War hero Marshal Philippe Pétain, who became the leader of the war-time Vichy regime and a symbol of French defeatism. The formal surrender of France in the forest of Compiègne, the site of the German surrender in 1918, on 25 June left Britain alone to carry on.

The fall of France was devastating to British war strategy. It was far more than the defeat of an ally; it signalled a fundamental shift in the balance of power in Europe, turning a regional conflict, which the British, in concert with the French, expected to be able to contain, into a world war. Not only were the British on their own, but until mid-May 1940 the government had not yet taken the first steps towards contingency planning for a war without France. The ignominious collapse of the French army thus destroyed the long-held premise that the two allies were militarily stronger and would prevail. Their mutual defence strategy had been predicated on a combination of strong French land forces, the might of the Royal Navy and the airpower of the RAF. France's surrender not only negated that strategy but also raised the question of whether Britain could and or even should continue to fight alone. Jock Colville wrote that the only person in Britain he had ever heard predict the collapse of the French armies was Ismay. 'The consensus view was expressed by Lord Halifax . . . when he wrote in his diary on 25 May . . . "The one firm rock . . . for the last two years was the French Army, and the Germans walked through it like they did through the Poles."'

The head of Fighter Command, Air Chief Marshal Dowding, was not among those who believed that the surrender of France was calamitous. 'Thank God we're alone,' he said. Dowding had favoured Chamberlain's appeasement of Hitler at Munich for entirely pragmatic reasons, believing it would buy time to build the fighter defence of the Trenchard bomber-oriented RAF. He told Halifax 'how crushing a weight he felt to have been lifted from his shoulders when he heard that the French had asked for a separate armistice. Otherwise, everything must gradually have been drained away from us; it would have made no difference to the issue in France, and when it had suited Hitler to turn all his force against us, we should have had little or nothing with which to meet it.' Halifax asked Dill if he agreed with Dowding's assessment, 'and without hesitation he said that he did.'

To counter the disastrous news in France and put to rest any notion that Britain might follow, Churchill delivered another patriotic speech to Parliament on 18 June that was subsequently broadcast over the BBC. Reviewing all that had transpired he again made no effort to minimize the extent of the dire situation Britain faced. The threat that lay ahead from the air and probably from invasion would be met with every means and would be rebuffed.

'What General Weygand called the Battle of France is over. I expect that the Battle of Britain is about to begin.' Then, in an implicit reference to Hitler and the nations now under the Nazi jackboot, he said:

Upon this battle depends the survival of Christian civilization . . . The whole fury and might of the enemy must very soon be turned on us . . . If we can stand up to him, all Europe may be free . . . But if we fail, then the whole world, including the United States . . . will sink into the abyss of a new Dark Age . . . Let us therefore brace ourselves to our duties, and so bear ourselves that, if the British

Empire and its Commonwealth last for a thousand years, men will still say, 'This was their finest hour.'

France had been engulfed in defeat, and Churchill was determined to show what Hugh Dalton described as defiance, reason and confidence. He had, in effect, 'staked his own survival as Prime Minister upon a strategy of "no surrender" '. Much of the speech was once again sheer bluff and was intended to reassure both his colleagues and the nation, above all by his statement that thanks to the saving of the BEF Britain now had 'in this Island today a very large and powerful military force'. Anything less than optimism, even the slightest hint of failure, would have sent out a defeatist message. Instead Churchill spoke of 'our inflexible resolve to continue the war', and said that his military advisers believed 'there are good and reasonable hopes of final victory.' Anything less was unthinkable. His final verdict was a promise of triumph over adversity. This was leadership of the first order.

39

'What a Summer to Waste on War'

The summer of 1940 seems now like a distant nightmare, enacted under the glare of a blazing sun.
                                                                  – Robert Boothby

Although the full fury of the air war would not occur until September 1940, when Göring unleashed a succession of air raids designed to pave the way for the intended invasion by neutralizing Fighter Command, the Germans began stepping up their air raids in July. Cities all over England were bombed; in East Anglia, in the Midlands and along the south coast, bombs fell and people died.

The commencement of what would be a campaign of bombing and, later, rocket attacks that continued for the next four years was set against the backdrop of a spring and summer that resembled those of 1914. 'What a summer to waste on war. The country looked incredibly lovely and peaceful,' wrote Churchill's private secretary John Martin in his diary.

The summer of 1940 was a call to arms as the remnants of a peacetime army were converted to a wartime force and trained to fight. Filled with men too old for a modern war, the British army had to be rebuilt virtually from scratch. Brooke, Montgomery, Alexander and other former BEF commanders faced an enormous challenge to re-equip and retrain an army capable of defending Britain against invasion. Time was crucial, given the expected German landings. June to August was a period of explosive growth. The army added some 275,000 men and created 120 more infantry battalions, as England became an armed camp. Every available space was used to capacity, parks were turned into training bases, country estates were requisitioned and convoys of military vehicles choked the roads. The army's primary task in 1940 was home defence; later would come training and preparations for reprisal.

Churchill's affinity with Alan Brooke continued to grow. In mid-July the two men spent four productive hours inspecting units of the general's command in southern England. Two days later Brooke was summoned to the War Office and informed by Eden that he was to take command of all Home Forces, succeeding Ironside, who was shunted aside for the second time in two months. Upon Brooke's shoulders fell the entire ground defence of the United Kingdom. When he arrived at his new HQ in London, Brooke was dismayed to learn that there existed no information, and no advice or guidance from his predecessor, only the keys to a Rolls-Royce motor car set aside for his use. 'That was all. Not a word concerning the defences or his policy of defence . . . absolutely nothing!'

Brooke's dismay was not misplaced. The CBS correspondent Edward R. Murrow witnessed 'ancient cannons being hauled out of British museums and dragged down to the beaches', and Anthony Eden reported to Churchill that Britain's newly formed local defence force was then largely 'a "broomstick" army' (in the summer of 1940 one Scottish unit was actually obliged to train with broomsticks, while hoes, rakes and similar implements formed the arsenals of others). Such was the sorry state of Britain's defences that little else was available to these men but First World War rifles being reconditioned for issue. It may have been Churchill himself who renamed them the 'Home Guard', though most Britons affectionately referred to the volunteers – whose age ceiling was sixty-five – as 'Dad's Army'. When Churchill became prime minister their morale was boosted by his words, particularly his 'we will fight on the beaches' speech. 'I can tell you every man there rose in spirits,' said the Home Guard's commanding officer, Lord Willis. 'You could almost measure it. We would have gone down to the beach at the Germans and beat them with broom-handles. Such was the magic effect of Churchill. It was thrilling. It was absolutely thrilling. Before we'd been ambling along under Chamberlain, this funny old man, who seemed to us to represent a past age, and here suddenly was a man talking with vigour and energy and courage. It was remarkable. The effect on morale was unbelievable.' Without the weapons of war he required, Churchill had only one weapon to work with, and that was his ability to sustain the morale of the people with his speeches, and by his presence in the bombed streets and among the men and women who would fight the battles ahead.

Of the men in his War Cabinet, Churchill was closest to Anthony Eden. Having won a Military Cross in the last war, Eden well understood the magnitude of what he and the under-manned and under-armed defenders faced. As each new intelligence report identified more and more barges and other vessels being assembled by the Germans in French ports, the spectre of invasion loomed ever larger. Churchill would later write, 'This was a time when it was equally good to live or die.'

It was also a time to make do with what little they had, and British ingenuity took over. Even the king got in on the act. With an invasion now more probable than theoretical, George VI informed Halifax that he intended to begin taking rifle practice in the gardens of Buckingham Palace, and 'that he always carried a rifle with him now in the car as well as a revolver'. Among other preparations, the citizen-soldiers of the Home Guard were taught how use improvised garrottes made of cheese cutters, and an idea was borrowed from the Finns, who had badly bloodied the Red Army: half a million Molotov cocktails were fashioned to be thrown at the invaders. There was no doubt in anyone's mind, least of all Churchill's, that an invasion would result in enormous casualties on both sides. Even though the Home Guard was at best a ragtag force, the prime minister's words of defiance gave its members a real (if hardly realistic) belief that, although they might be badly armed, they could still fight back. Even the phrase he coined about the Molotov cocktails – 'You can always take [an invader] with you' – gave them heart. Nevertheless Churchill recognized that 'wars are not won by militias,' and this was all the more reason to have avoided losing more regular divisions in France in a hopeless cause.

To help defend against invasion Churchill went so far as to suggest the adoption of a tactic successfully used by the Germans, the creation of formations of 'Storm Troops' or 'Leopards': well armed and equipped with armoured cars and motorcycles, these were to be brigades of 'at least 20,000 . . . drawn from existing units', held behind the beaches, 'ready to spring at the throat of any small landings'. Although Churchill was talked out of the idea by Major General Bernard Paget, chief of staff of Home Forces, it was proposed instead to form smaller 'Tank Hunting Platoons' and other 'Special Irregular Units'. It was galling for Churchill that rearmament in the 1930s had not produced enough weapons to mount the larger units he wanted, yet a number of these smaller units were established within a matter of days after his order.

In late June, Churchill went to see for himself the state of Britain's defences, and what he encountered was hardly encouraging. Touring the south coast of Kent, near Dover, he was briefed by a brigadier whose brigade had only three anti-tank guns to cover more than four miles of coastline precisely where an invasion was thought likely. 'He declared that he had only six rounds of ammunition for each gun, and he asked me with a slight air of challenge whether he was justified in letting his men fire one single round for practice in order that they might at least know how the weapon worked.' Churchill could only reply that 'we could not afford practice rounds, and that fire should be held for the last moment of the closest range.' When the invaders came ashore they would be immediately counterattacked, the defenders would 'leap at [the enemy's] throat, and keep the grip until the life is out of him'.

In early July help came sooner than expected from the United States in the form of two hundred thousand rifles and ammunition, along with five thousand Thompson submachine guns a month. Canada shipped seventy-five thousand rifles. To avoid the wrath of an isolationist Congress, the American arms shipment was strictly a cash transaction. Suddenly those with broomsticks at least had a means to fight back.

That month Churchill made the acquaintance of Major General Bernard Law Montgomery, then in command of the veteran 3rd Division, which had fought exceptionally well in France and was now assigned to defend a sector along England's south coast in and around Brighton. Meeting Montgomery was an unforgettable experience. Churchill had an aversion to generals that dated back to the Boer War, and to the First World War and his dissatisfaction with the irrational tactics used on the western front. In his view most generals were failures and untrustworthy until they proved otherwise. Although the sterling exploits of Brooke, Alexander and Montgomery in France had certainly attracted the prime minister's attention, his cautious attitude towards generals remained.

His opinion could not have been enhanced by his first encounter with Montgomery, who was the very antithesis of his image of how a successful general looked and acted. This diminutive officer exhibited a casual attitude towards military dress, and had a sharply pointed nose and ears that gave the impression they were too large for his head. Though at first sight Montgomery was anything but impressive, first impressions, as Churchill eventually discerned, can be very misleading.

Anyone but a fool quickly understood that he was in the presence of authority, which could be seen in a pair of penetrating grey-blue eyes that fastened intensely on a speaker and could sear like a laser. George Bernard Shaw once described Montgomery as resembling an 'intensely compacted hank of steel wire'.

Indeed Montgomery possessed the aura of authority that all successful commanders seem to have. Although unable to dominate through physical presence as Alexander and Auchinleck did, Montgomery more than compensated by the magnetism with which he influenced those who served under him.

As the blunt-spoken general known more familiarly as 'Monty' escorted Churchill to Brighton pier, he gave the prime minister an earful. Monty had plenty to complain about and to recommend, and he delivered his message to Churchill in a manner that left no doubt where he stood. Why, he asked, was his regular army division, the only truly mobile formation available, stuck in a static role, its capability utterly wasted? 'With all the buses in England,' he insisted, among them the tourist buses that plied the streets of Brighton, 'let them give me some, and release me from this static role so that I [can] practise a mobile counter-attack role.' Montgomery did not stop there. The British army, he judged, was filled with useless, elderly generals who should all be sacked and replaced by capable younger officers, a point already made to Churchill by Ismay and others. In the darkest days of the Blitz, Brooke would remark similarly: 'How poor we are in Army and Corps commanders. We ought to remove several but heaven knows where we shall find anything very much better.'

The first meeting between Churchill and Montgomery was an occasion for two very stubborn, strong-willed, pugnacious men to test and eye each other much like prizefighters before a bout. Despite his experience with outspoken men like Fisher and Keyes, Churchill had never met anyone quite like Bernard Montgomery, a man who both stimulated and impressed with his knowledge and forceful presence, yet who was irreverent, obnoxious and dictatorial, and who aroused Churchill's combative instincts.

The two were polar opposites on the social scale, and as they sat down that evening to dine at Brighton's Royal Albion Hotel, Churchill, with his ever present cigar in one hand and a glass of whisky in the other, asked what Montgomery would have to drink and was astonished when the little general replied, 'Water,' before adding that he 'neither drank nor smoked and was 100 per cent fit'. Taken aback but not to be outdone by this ferret-like, outspoken upstart, Churchill riposted 'that he both drank and smoked, and was 200 per cent fit'. The journalist Bernard Levin became both a friend and an admirer of Montgomery. In the 1970s he asked the field marshal what was the biggest row he'd ever had with Churchill: 'It seems that Churchill had been looking through some lists of equipment landed on the beaches almost immediately after D-Day and found among the stores "Two dentist's chairs". Next time he saw Montgomery, he demanded to know why, at such a perilous moment, precious space had been found for such luxuries.' Monty replied none too diplomatically, 'Prime Minister, a soldier with a tooth-ache is of no use to me – he can't fight. Good morning.'

The officer sitting across from Churchill that evening in Brighton had risen from the relative obscurity of the middle ranks of the officer corps. Despite an impressive record during the First World War that included winning a DSO and being seriously wounded and nearly dying in 1914, like all career officers he had languished during the inter-war years. In a tradition-filled army where being a 'nice chap' was considered a neces-sary stepping-stone to promotion, Montgomery, the habitual outsider, wore his nonconformity like a badge of honour and refused to respect such constraints. Yet, as was said of Admiral Ernest J. King's appoint-ment by FDR as chief of naval operations, Montgomery was not picked for higher command because he was pleasant or a gentleman. In fact what separated Montgomery from most of his peers was that he was utterly unafraid to be unpopular.

Bernard Montgomery was a consummate professional soldier at a time when Britain was desperate, not for chivalry, but for competent battlefield commanders. Indeed one of the ills of the British army was that it was staffed by far too many 'nice chaps' and 'old boys'. No one ever referred to Bernard Law Montgomery as a 'nice chap'. New Zealand's General Sir Bernard Freyberg, a holder of the Victoria Cross, who once called Montgomery a 'little bastard', also proclaimed, 'If Montgomery is a cad, it's a great pity that the British Army doesn't have a few more bounders.' In the hidebound, elitist British army, Montgomery was the ultimate outsider, an anti-authoritarian, black-sheep 'colonial' in an exclusive old boys' club where one's lineage and social standing counted for more than one's ability. An example of Britain's absurd class consciousness was Air Chief Marshal Sir Arthur Tedder's remark that 'the trouble with Monty was that he was anything but a "nice chap".'

In the summer of 1940 the last thing Churchill and the army needed was gentlemen or nice chaps; they needed fighters, and although Churchill does not seem to have recognized it at their first meeting, he had in Montgomery a fighting soldier. The general's official biographer noted: 'Monty's genius – as Rommel's – would be to see, instinctively and in a manner that had eluded the callous commanders of World War I, that great military leadership in a people's century *could* still be achieved, despite the mechanical, inhumane nature of "total war".' During the Second World War Montgomery achieved a reputation for never needlessly squandering the lives of his men. Asked in a post-war television documentary for his reaction to the deaths of soldiers under his command, he replied with the candour for which he was celebrated that their remains would be 'reverently collected and reverently buried'.

Montgomery was the first British general openly to signal his rebellion against the army's staid customs by his refusal to wear conventional military dress. What counted was that he led and that his troops followed. Churchill would later applaud Monty's outrageous behaviour and showmanship. Once, when a critic complained that the general was wearing unauthorized badges on his bush hat, Churchill retorted, 'If I thought that badges would make my other generals as good as Monty I would order them all to wear badges.'

A general who wins is usually forgiven eccentricity, and such would be the case in 1942 when Montgomery won Churchill's heart with his famous victories in the desert. However, in the summer of 1940, Churchill emerged from the first of many encounters with Montgomery failing to see that behind the obvious lack of charm of this common 'little man', whose manners and social graces were not those of the upper class, was exactly the type of leader Britain needed in its time of peril. Churchill saw to it that Montgomery was given the buses he had demanded, yet instead of being given higher commands and a real war to fight, he would languish for more than two years guarding against invasion before being summoned to North Africa in the summer of 1942 to command and revitalize a battered and beaten Eighth Army.

In a series of memos in June, July and August, Churchill laid out in great detail a strategy for defending Britain from invasion. The main invasion sites were thought to be in East Anglia, with secondary landings likely on the south coast and in Scotland. The Royal Navy and the RAF were the first line of defence of the sea, the air and the ports. If the invaders made it ashore, Churchill wanted counterattacks by ten thousand men within six hours and twenty thousand within twelve hours. Minefields were to be laid, tank traps created and other defences established to thwart the invaders. From his fertile mind came a number of brilliant ideas, not all of which were achievable. He wanted, for example, the creation of artificial, heavily armed concrete islands that could be towed out to sea around key ports and sunk, thus becoming torpedo-proof, and 'with regular pens for the destroyers and submarines, and alighting platforms for aeroplanes'. This idea, dating from the First World War, came to fruition in 1944 as the Mulberry artificial harbours towed to Normandy and emplaced off Omaha Beach and the port of Arromanches. Another of Churchill's ideas that proved technically impossible was to pour oil on and set fire to the waters around the invaders and incinerate them. And, at the urging of the CIGS, if the home defenders had exhausted all other options the War Cabinet approved the use of poison gas.

Churchill's restless mind was constantly conjuring new ideas, ranging from strategy and measures to repel invasion to the smallest details. Such thoughts could have come only from one who understood soldiering and the needs of men in combat. Dunkirk was still under way when he instructed Ismay: 'Inquire into the number of German guns now trophies in this country and whether any can be reconditioned for blocking exits from beaches against tanks.' Another memo asked if 'wax could be supplied to troops to put in their ears in order to deaden the noise of warfare'.

Bad as things were in the summer of 1940 while Britain awaited Hitler's next move, Churchill had made considerable progress in stamping his imprint upon the military establishment. He had listened to his airmen, and he had made the difficult decisions advanced first by Gort to save the BEF, and later by Brooke to save the remaining British forces in France to fight another day. That he had resisted his only ally in its darkest hour may have embittered the French leadership, but Churchill the political leader had acted correctly – as Churchill the warlord.

The fall of France left Britain isolated. In David Reynolds's words, 'In less than 40 days a jumped-up Austrian corporal had done what the

Kaiser's best generals failed to achieve in four years.' Churchill was not alone in his belief that Britain's only possible salvation lay in bringing the United States into the war. Amid the almost overwhelming glut of bad news there was a glimmer of hope. Churchill had lit the candle and would be the keeper of its flame. 'We shall never surrender' became the mantra of a small, beleaguered island nation that would stick in Hitler's craw and, with American involvement, eventually bring about his downfall. The road that led along a painful and bloody journey to victory would really begin with the Battle of Britain.

40

'Set Europe Ablaze'

You are to prepare for the invasion of Europe.   – Churchill, to Mountbatten

Dunkirk and Norway seemed to foster Churchill's obstinacy. If the Germans could not be beaten in 1940, then other means had to be found. The successful evacuations of the BEF from France and 4,500 Allied troops from Narvik were barely over when Churchill warned that 'the completely defensive habit of mind, which has ruined the French, must not be allowed to ruin all our initiative.' To that end he instructed Ismay that raiding forces must be organized and put into action against coastal targets in occupied Europe: 'How wonderful it would be if the Germans could be made to wonder where they were going to be struck next.'

The lessons of the Boer War forty years earlier remained fresh in his mind. Commando units must be created, he insisted in a 5 June memo to Ismay, for a system of espionage and intelligence, and for relentless attacks along the coasts of occupied countries. 'Enterprises must be prepared, with specially trained troops of the hunter class, who can develop a reign of terror down these coasts, first of all on the "butcher and bolt" policy, but later on, or perhaps as soon as we are organized, we should surprise Calais or Boulogne, kill or capture the Hun garrison.' The time for 'passive resistance war, which we have acquitted ourselves so well in, must come to an end. I look to the Joint Chiefs of the Staff to propose me measures for a vigorous, enterprising and ceaseless offensive against the whole German occupied coastline. Tanks and AFVs [armoured fighting vehicles] must be carried in flat-bottomed boats, out of which they can crawl ashore, do a deep raid inland, cutting a vital communication, and then back, leaving a trail of German corpses behind them.'

On 5 June one of Dill's military assistants, Lieutenant Colonel Dudley Clarke, a Royal Artillery officer, drew up the outlines of a force to carry out raiding operations. He called them commandos, naming them after the hit-and-run Boer units that had been so successful against the British. Several days later Churchill approved the concept, which resulted in the creation of a new department within the War Office called MO9. The urgency of forming a commando force quickly escalated. Guerrilla raids against the Germans were little more than annoying pinpricks, but they would serve as a visible reminder that although Britain might have been bowed it was not beaten, and was still capable of striking back, even on a small scale.

Although he had resisted appointing the outspoken Admiral Keyes to a post in the Norway campaign, Churchill appointed him to head the new Combined Operations Headquarters (COHQ), which was created for the express purpose of planning commando raids into occupied Europe and for an eventual cross-Channel assault to open a second front into Europe. The men he chose for key military positions were not always effective, and as with Fisher in 1914 his selection of Keyes would end badly. Churchill had trouble understanding that having been a hero in an earlier war did not necessarily qualify a man for a high post in a newer, more modern war. In the case of Keyes, Dill bluntly told Churchill, 'You can't win World War II with World War I heroes.' Such appointments stemmed from his great attraction to men of courage who were possessed of aggressive, self-confident personalities.

From July 1940 to October 1941 Keyes was the ball of fire Churchill wanted, recruiting and training volunteers for the new commando force and outfitting vessels to carry out raids in occupied territory. He established COHQ as a separate and independent military entity that reported only to Churchill, rather than to the chiefs of staff – an arrangement that aroused the ire of the traditionalists. While under Churchill's protective umbrella Keyes blossomed, and the system of mutual inter-service co-operation worked well for a while. However, Keyes and his upstart organization soon ran afoul of the military establishment, and a growing enmity between them and the chiefs and various service staffs, particularly the Admiralty bureaucracy, finally became intolerable.

By the autumn of 1941 Churchill's declining confidence in Keyes persuaded him to make the admiral's post an advisory one under the chiefs of staff. Keyes refused to accept his loss of autonomy and what he regarded as demotion, so Churchill sacked him in October 1941 in what was a painful parting of two old friends whose relationship dated back to the Dardanelles. 'My dear Roger,' wrote Churchill, 'I have to consider my duty to the State which ranks above personal friendship. In all the circumstances I have no choice but to arrange for your relief.'

Keyes's replacement was the forty-one-year-old Lord Louis Mountbatten. Although a junior Royal Navy officer, Mountbatten was precisely the sort of dynamic individual Churchill sought. He had led a destroyer force that screened the evacuation of British and French troops from fogbound Namsos in Norway in late April 1940 and later skippered the destroyer HMS *Kelly*, which was sunk during the evacuation of Crete in May 1941. Although he had lost his ship, Mountbatten emerged a public hero. As with Keyes, Churchill was enticed by the outspoken and opinionated Mountbatten, an officer who had the same sort of high-powered ideas that complemented his own impulsive and aggressive nature.

'You are to prepare for the invasion of Europe, for unless we can go and land and fight Hitler and beat his forces on land, we shall never win this war,' he instructed Mountbatten. 'You must devise and design the appliances, the landing craft and the technique to enable us to effect a landing against opposition and to maintain ourselves there.'

Churchill went on to articulate one of the most important decisions of the war: the creation of combined operations, the element previously missing, whereby air, sea and ground forces worked as a team towards a defined goal. Dunkirk had been the first example of the three services working jointly, and Churchill was determined that the concept should be expanded. Hence his precise instructions to Mountbatten: 'You must take the most brilliant officers from the Navy, Army and Air Force to help our planners to plan this great operation,' he directed. 'You must take bases to use as training establishments where you can train the Navy, Army and Air Force to work as a single entity. The whole of the south coast of England is a bastion of defence against the invasion of Hitler; you've got to turn it into the springboard for our attack.'

Although initially appointed only as an adviser on combined operations to the chiefs of staff, Mountbatten was quickly promoted to the acting rank of vice admiral, lieutenant general in the army and air marshal, and Churchill made him a member of the Chiefs of Staff

Committee. The reaction of the established services to a parvenu organiz-ation that proposed to use elements of each of the armed services was predictable. By their very nature organizations with great historical traditions are loath to cede authority, particularly to one run by an officer of Mountbatten's lowly rank at the time. The chiefs, while sup-portive of Mountbatten's appointment, were not pleased with Churchill's decision to include him as a coequal member of the Chiefs of Staff Committee and as his chief adviser on combined operations, rather than merely having him plan and carry out commando raids and tactics. Mountbatten took full advantage of his new post and became a master at empire building, a skill he perfected two years later in India as supreme Allied commander, South-East Asia Theatre of Operations, where he created and oversaw a bloated staff of over four thousand.

More often than not the chiefs treated Mountbatten with resentment and derision. When interviewed in 1947, he recalled with considerable bitterness: 'My job with Combined Operations was a very difficult one. I was a very junior officer and had very few men under me who weren't my junior . . . the result was [the military establishment] thought I didn't know what I was doing; regarded my headquarters as made up of madmen. Refused quite often to pay attention to what we were doing. Hooted every time we suggested something . . . the Lords of the Admir-alty are called "Their Lordships". They gave us so much trouble, we finally called them "Their Blockships".' Although the evolution of joint operations was a painful one, as Churchill astutely recognized, it was a crucial step towards the winning of the war.

In 1940 the chiefs advised that Britain's only hope lay in 'stimulating the seeds of revolt in the conquered territories'. To accomplish covert guerrilla warfare required an organization very different from Combined Operations. After Dunkirk, Churchill began asking questions about placing agents in the occupied territories. The result was a top-level meeting on 1 July 1940 to create a new organization to carry out sabotage and subversion, to be called the Special Operations Executive (SOE). Before it could come into being there was bureaucratic wrangling over who would control it. Halifax thought it should be under the Foreign Office but was bluntly told by the colonial secretary, Lord Lloyd: 'You should never be consulted, because you would never consent to anything. You will never make a gangster!' Eventually it was agreed that

SOE would, as the intelligence adviser Desmond Morton suggested, 'have a single dictator'. The turf war went on for several weeks before Churchill concurred and on 16 July appointed Hugh Dalton to head SOE. When the War Cabinet approved on 22 July, he turned to Dalton and uttered the celebrated phrase: 'And now, go and set Europe ablaze.'

Dalton possessed the brashness that Halifax lacked and took on the appointment with great enthusiasm, convinced that by the end of 1940 there would be uprisings in the Nazi-occupied countries. Although Churchill's exhortation created a vision of an occupied Europe whose Nazi masters were constantly being attacked and sabotaged, for nearly two years SOE's charge was simply beyond its capability. Both the prime minister and Dalton envisaged making German occupation untenable through sabotage and the diversion of valuable manpower resources, but without agents in place it was a grand yet unfulfilled scheme. When SOE was created there were agents only in the Balkans but nowhere in western Europe; and it was not until early 1942 that there were agents and active underground cells in every part of the enemy-occupied world.

Where Dalton exhibited confidence, Churchill displayed a romanticized view of secret agents and daring sabotage operations. Both men believed it was a business for amateurs, men who brought fresh ideas, intellect and insights and were not bound by the rigid protocol of the military. Unfortunately SOE was created on the false premise that the Germans had succeeded so brilliantly in overrunning Europe because of the successful acts of fifth columnists operating covertly in each country. It was, the SOE historian later declared, sheer mythology.

Established in Baker Street in central London under the cover of Dalton's Ministry of Economic Warfare, SOE was referred to by Churchill as the 'Ministry of Ungentlemanly Warfare'. SOE's functions crossed governmental lines and required support from a number of ministries. Dalton played no role in operational matters. His primary function was that of fighting often bitter bureaucratic wars to protect and preserve SOE from Whitehall poachers who wanted a piece or all of it.

In 1932 three Polish mathematicians succeeded in breaking the 'unbreakable' German Enigma cipher machine. First developed in 1918 primarily for the purpose of keeping bank transactions secret, the portable Enigma used a series of electromechanical rotors that created unbreakable, one-time codes, thus enabling a party at one end to encrypt a message that another machine could then decode, all with complete security. By the mid-1930s the device, whose settings could be changed daily, was in use by all the German armed services and by the security service, the Sicherheitsdienst. During the Second World War, Engima became a primary means of sending and receiving classified messages. Because of its unique capability, the Germans believed the system was foolproof.

The British naval code breakers of the Great War, who operated successfully out of Room 40 in the Admiralty, were replaced in the Second World War by a brilliant group of men and women that by 1945 numbered some ten thousand. They operated from what was called Station X, the British Government Code and Cipher School, a top-secret country facility situated within a large Victorian estate called Bletchley Park, fifty miles north-west of London, in the peaceful countryside of Buckinghamshire. By the summer of 1940 the Bletchley code breakers were routinely reading German signals traffic. Their challenge was monumental. Without knowledge of the settings they would have had to overcome odds of 150 million million million to 1. Because the Germans changed the code key on a daily basis the cryptographers faced the constant challenge of finding and breaking a new cipher key. The process of decrypting, analysing and disseminating the results was still in its infancy. Moreover most of the German signals traffic went not by radio but by landline, and was thus unobtainable. The first Luftwaffe signals were successfully decrypted shortly before Dunkirk, but it was not until the summer of 1941 that the Kriegsmarine signals were broken, followed in 1942 by those of the German army. Eventually the decrypts from the Enigma machine and from other German communications sources were given the code name Ultra. Churchill's eagerness to accept and act on new ideas became one of the hallmarks of his prime ministership. He firmly believed that one of the keys to winning the war was the development of new weapons, specialized equipment and devices that would give Britain an advantage when fighting its bigger and better-equipped enemy. Whether it was supporting top-secret work of the men and women of Bletchley Park in their pursuit of decrypting German message traffic by means of the compromised Engima machine or backing the development of radar, Churchill was an avid enthusiast who threw the full weight of his office behind any project that might provide an edge, no matter how small.

Churchill did not initiate Bletchley Park's code breaking, but he fully embraced it and after he became prime minister he received daily Enigma decrypts. His suspicion of intelligence and its handlers stemmed from the First World War, and his conviction that intelligence officers were intriguers. This distrust merely reinforced his insistence on reading undiluted intelligence. So great was his interest that a system was soon developed whereby each fresh batch of decrypted signals was couriered to MI6, the Secret Intelligence Service. Those of interest to the prime minister were selected, placed in a special box and hand-delivered directly to Churchill, who was the only person in Downing Street with a key to open it. Most of the time all his staff knew was that strange, ancient buff-coloured boxes dating from Victorian times and bearing the initials 'V.R.I.' were being personally delivered to him by his chief spymaster, Brigadier Stuart Graham Menzies, better known as 'C', the code name for the head of MI6. Churchill had an obsessive concern for secrecy, and the secret of Engima was known to only about thirty people in key positions in the government, including the chiefs, their vice chiefs and a mere six ministers. No one else ever had access to the closely guarded secrets within these boxes, and what he shared even with the thirty was highly selective and used in furtherance of his role as Britain's war leader. To protect the secret even more the contents of the daily Ultra box were known within the government by the code name Boniface, and the notion was planted that 'Boniface' was really a British spy operating in Germany. In July 1940 the content of the top-secret boxes was somehow leaked to a Fleet Street newspaper baron, who laudably kept his silence.

Churchill's appetite for intelligence became almost an addiction. Even when travelling overseas he demanded to be kept informed. Prior to the Casablanca Conference in January 1943, Menzies was directed to 'repeat all really important messages to me', and after a week in Morocco Churchill fumed that he was not receiving enough information. 'Why have you not kept me properly supplied with news? Volume should be increased at least five-fold.'

Like so many others Menzies was routinely summoned to No. 10 or the Central War Rooms at short notice late at night for another session of what were dubbed 'the Midnight Follies', only to return home in the dark exhausted, often in the middle of an air raid. As one senior government official remarked: 'Winston, I fear, is no organizer and, by sleeping half the afternoon himself and then flogging tired men to work half through the night, is killing more of his own countrymen than Germans.' Unfortunately Churchill's faith in Britain's intelligence capability as 'the finest in the world' was misplaced and was not alleviated by his inability to perceive that its failures were responsible for a lack of advance knowledge of Germany's aggressive intentions. Churchill also wondered if perhaps 'there is not some hand which intervenes and filters down or withholds intelligence from Ministers'. This, in turn, led to his insistence on seeing raw intelligence for himself.

Soon after taking office in 1940 he ordered the chiefs to review the way intelligence was used in making military decisions, and on 5 November (Guy Fawkes Day) proposed a single secret intelligence service, an idea he had first put forward in 1920 as secretary of state for war. He was rebuffed by the chiefs, who considered it 'very undesirable that a drastic reorganisation of this magnitude should be attempted at the very moment when we are fighting for our very lives'. As a historian of the British secret service has written: 'No British statesman in modern times has more passionately believed in the value of secret intelligence. None has ever been more determined to put it to good use.' Although he tried again in early 1941, Churchill's vision never came to fruition. Still, 'it was under his inspirational leadership and in the finest hour of his long career that the fragmented intelligence services acquired at last that degree of coordination which turned them into an intelligence community.' Nevertheless there was rivalry and infighting, particularly between SIS (MI6) and SOE, but also involving the code breakers at Bletchley Park, the Security Service (MI5), the intelligence services of the army, navy and air force, and the Twenty Committee (XX – the MI5 Double-Cross System that captured and turned German agents, providing successful deception throughout the war). Despite the lack of a single intelligence service, these organizations made important contributions to the war effort.

In September 1941 Churchill paid his first visit to Bletchley Park. Deeply impressed by what he saw, he began referring to the code breakers as his 'hens' or as 'the geese that laid the golden eggs but never cackled', and enthusiastically supported their needs. The British government went to extraordinary lengths to conceal the Ultra secret both during and after the war, and for thirty years none of the great multitude of participants ever uttered so much as a single public word about Ultra until the secret was revealed in 1974 with the publication of Group Captain F. W. Winterbotham's controversial memoir.

Despite Churchill's obsession with secrecy he rather cavalierly breached security on several occasions, one of them in May 1940 during a telephone conversation with Gort, when he announced that he was flying to France. Before he could elaborate further an aide courageously severed the connection. The many security precautions notwithstanding, there was later evidence that the Germans had intercepted his conversations with FDR until approximately February 1944, when a new scrambler system was installed and a key interception station in Holland knocked out by the RAF. Fortunately both men always spoke circumspectly and used code words.

By the summer of 1940 the United States had taken sufficient interest in what the British were doing in the intelligence field for Roosevelt to send his spymaster to London. Colonel William J. 'Wild Bill' Donovan, the organizer and head of the Office of Strategic Services (OSS), the cover name for America's version of SIS, liked what he saw and came away with an agreement on sharing intelligence. As he always did in his dealings with the United States, Churchill handed over only what he wanted to; the rest he shrewdly kept in reserve, remarking to Ismay, 'I am not in a hurry to give our secrets until the United States is much nearer to the war than she is now.'

Another secret organization, dedicated to developing new weapons of mayhem, was an obscure outfit called MD1 (Ministry of Defence 1), originally created in early 1939 in Room 173 of the War Office for the purpose of developing new weapons to be used in special (irregular) operations behind enemy lines. Among its accomplishments was the creation of the limpet mine, widely and effectively used throughout the war in sabotage operations. MD1 recruited wizards and inventive men with an itch to blow up bridges, communications and railways – in other words the very sort of men who appealed to Churchill.

When he became prime minister, Churchill moved quickly to create his own experimental organization and appointed Major (later Major General) Millis Jefferis, a crusty Royal Engineer whom Ismay fittingly called an 'inventive genius', to head it. Jefferis had caught Churchill's attention with his work on the mining of the Rhine, and by his sabotage work behind the lines in Norway blowing up bridges. By the end of the war twenty-six new weapons had been designed by this exceptional group and were in production. The group's output consisted of bombs for aircraft; booby traps; the PIAT, a light, short-range anti-tank gun; naval mines; and the so-called sticky bomb, an anti-tank weapon that was used extensively but not always effectively when, instead of sticking to the side of an enemy tank, as Martin Gilbert has drily observed, 'it stuck to the hand of the thrower, which did not enhance its popularity.' The assistant director, Colonel R. Stuart Macrae, later noted that detractors disparagingly referred to MD1 as 'Winston Churchill's Toyshop'.

The 'Toyshop's' value to the war effort lay in its freedom to invent, to improvise and to avoid the Whitehall bureaucrats who made it their mission to obstruct. Although supposedly under the protection of Churchill, Ismay and Lindemann, inevitably MD1 attracted too much attention in the Ministry of Supply, which resented the fact that it did not control it. In July 1940 it was scheduled for an inspection by a pompous Guards brigadier whose main function seemed to be finding enough evidence to abolish MD1 just when it was heavily involved in a number of important experimental projects. Realizing that inspecting them as they currently functioned would both confuse the brigadier about what they actually did and inevitably invite disbandment, Macrae and the ingenious staff pulled off their finest invention. To ensure that the visiting brigadier was impressed by the immense scope of their work the staff set up fake workrooms in the basement of their workshops, and filled them with instruments and various devices, meters and other scientific paraphernalia. In some rooms he saw men in white coats hard at work testing and working with strange-looking devices. In other rooms there were men in blue coats equally hard at work. As he was escorted through a labyrinth of passages to room after room, the brigadier never realized that in each room he was seeing the same men over and over again. Some changed to coats of a different colour, while others quickly changed their appearance. As he was being escorted down one passage, the group from the room he had just left scooted down another passage and appeared hard at work in a different room when he appeared there. The inspector reluctantly accepted that important work was being carried out, and MD1 lived on, but not without further mischief by the bureaucrats – and always with the protection of Lindemann, who remained its guardian angel for the rest of the war. Had Churchill known of this nonsense, the brigadier would probably have been found new employment counting toilet seats in some remote outpost.

Although MD 1 made a virtually unknown but exceptionally valuable contribution to the winning of the war, not all went according to plan. The Mills bomb (a hand grenade), widely and ineffectively used in the First World War, was in production when Lindemann informed Churchill that he had designed an improved new version. Enthusiastically, Churchill replied, 'Splendid! Splendid! That's what I like to hear. CIGS! Have the Mills bomb scrapped at once and replaced by the Lindemann grenade.' The hapless Dill informed the PM that contracts had already been signed in both Britain and the United States for millions of them, and that it was too late to alter the design. Churchill refused to accept Dill's evidence; however, production of the Mills bomb went forward and Lindemann's version was never employed – a good thing, because its charge was too powerful.

There were other misadventures. In late May 1941 Churchill witnessed the demonstration of a new device called the Beetle, a self-propelled, tracked remote-controlled robot filled with explosives that was intended for use against enemy tanks. On that occasion, instead of advancing, the Beetle turned and made a beeline for Dill, who was obliged to take severe evasive action as the machine relentlessly chased him. It reminded Churchill of an earlier rocket demonstration arranged by Lindemann that also turned out badly when the errant device was launched, rose a hundred feet, turned ninety degrees and headed straight for Churchill. 'Casting discretion aside, Mr Churchill began to run for his life, but the rocket passed low overhead and buried itself in the ground some distance away.' As for Lindemann: 'Damn the man!' growled Churchill. 'I won't speak to him for a week.' But he still returned for demonstrations of new 'toys' whenever possible.

On 9 November 1916 Churchill had written a memo titled 'Mechanical Power in the Offensive' in which he outlined the use of an armoured trench cutter. 'To achieve decisive results we must be able to make an advance of 7,000 or 8,000 yards, thus capturing the whole line of the enemy's guns.' He decreed that the Royal Navy design a trench digger that would assist the infantry moving safely behind it to overcome fixed positions.

Although the idea never took root, a quarter-century had failed to dim Churchill's memories of the First World War – the stalemate, trench warfare and senseless slaughter that had devastated a generation of Britons. Nor had France and Germany lost their reliance on static defence lines. Millions had been poured into France's flawed Maginot Line, which was easily circumvented in May 1940. The Germans had likewise constructed a line – the so-called West Wall (*Westwall*), usually known as the Siegfried Line by the Second World War Allies. Although there already existed less formidable Great War defences called the Siegfried Line along the French border, after seizing the Rhineland in 1936 Hitler reinforced and extended the line to a distance of 392 miles, from Switzerland to the Dutch border. Half a million workers of the Todt Organization (named after Fritz Todt, Hitler's minister of armaments and munitions, who also built the *Autobahnen* in the 1930s) were employed to build a series of deep defensive positions centred on some eighteen thousand trenches, fortified bunkers and tank traps called dragon's teeth, designed to slow (long enough to bring up reinforcements) but not stop an armoured advance. However, at the time it was built between 1936 and 1940, its primary purpose was to protect the Third Reich from an attack from the west while Germany dealt with Poland and, later, Russia. Although such fortifications were daunting in appearance, their existence failed to sway modern battlefield strategists like Patton, who once declared that the Siegfried Line and its static fortifications were 'monuments to the stupidity of mankind'.

It was in this atmosphere of outdated siege warfare and the misguided French Maginot Line mentality that Churchill advanced his idea for a revolutionary new machine specifically designed to enable the infantry safely to breach Germany's vaunted West Wall. The author of the only book ever written on the subject says, 'In 1916 Churchill's trench-cutters would provide a clear line of attack on the German trench positions; now, in 1939, his objective was similar – a concerted attack on Germany's West Wall. A fleet of his "Moles", as he termed them, would advance simultaneously from their base close to the Maginot Line, and cross no-man's-land until they arrived right up against the defences of the West Wall,' the noise of their night-time advance drowned by artillery barrages.

In a near-repeat of his actions in 1915 with the development of the tank, Churchill summoned the director of naval construction, Sir Stanley Goodall, and directed that he and his engineers turn the idea into reality. Such a mechanical device had never been designed before, but by December 1939 the naval engineers, working closely with Ruston-Bucyrus, a Lincolnshire engineering firm that was at the time Britain's principal maker of earth-moving machinery, had not only produced a working model but predicted that, if given the priority and resources by Churchill, as many as two hundred of the machines could be produced by March 1941.

On 12 December 1939 Churchill showed the model, which he called by the code name White Rabbit Number 6, to Ironside, who agreed that such a machine offered tremendous possibilities. The original code name was later changed to Cultivator Number 6, the name by which Churchill always referred to it. However, in February 1940 responsibility for the project was transferred from the Royal Navy to the Ministry of Supply, which created a secret branch, called the Department of Naval Land Equipment, a name that was soon shortened to NLE. The prototype diggers went by the code name NLE and soon came to called simply 'Nellie'.

Constructed in three sections totalling eighty-two feet in length and weighing 130 tons, Nellie was truly gargantuan and in action resembled a ship ploughing through dirt instead of water. Designing, producing and testing a machine of such immense proportions took nearly two years. In great secrecy the test of the prototype was held in a remote corner of a barren heath in Nottinghamshire on 25 July 1941 and again in August for the army general staff.

On 6 November Churchill arrived in Lincolnshire to view a field test at first hand. Obliged to walk half a mile through boggy ground to the site of the test, he refused the Wellington boots set aside for him and arrived in a thoroughly irritable mood, a cigar jammed in his mouth, for his first glimpse of the great mole machine upon which he had pinned so much hope. Like a giant scythe, Nellie obligingly dug an enormous trench five feet deep and more than seven feet wide at a speed of roughly half a mile an hour.

Since the German occupation of France it had become clear that these cumbersome machines would play no active role in a war that was no longer characterized by static front lines. During the trial witnessed by Churchill, the machine became 'an inferno of heat, noise and [oil] fumes'. Despite its problems the test proved that such trenching machines could work – at least under ideal conditions. But in reality they were scarcely more than fantasy. Their cumbersome weight alone made it impossible for them to ford rivers or circumvent obstacles, climb hills or advance on anything other than the sort of level terrain Churchill had seen in the fields of Flanders. In May 1943 the War Office officially cancelled the project, thus ending the strange saga of Nellie. 'I am responsible but impenitent,' he later declared.

With Lindemann in the wings to advise him, Churchill took a passionate interest in technological matters. New weapons and specialized devices had to be invented, manufactured and deployed. Developing them is complicated and time consuming at the best of times, but when Churchill gave such matters his personal attention he tended to cut through the fog of development and bureaucracy. No one in his right mind wanted to face the prime minister's questions or his wrath. He routinely demanded details of the most specific nature and prodded, questioned and encouraged in areas where there were few precedents and little time. Faced with invasion, Churchill directed Lindemann to investigate the use of rockets and what he called 'multiple projectors' guided by radar to attack German bombers even in bad weather; 'the defence against air attack would become decisive,' he said. 'Assemble your ideas and facts so that I may give extreme priority to this business.'

His unqualified support of the scientific community was vital. The best minds in the nation were urgently needed. The employment of scientists and their research and development of new weapons 'should be at the very spearpoint of our thought and effort', he minuted to the War Cabinet.

A noteworthy success occurred with the invention of a method of countering the radio beams employed by the Luftwaffe from beacon sites in France to guide their bombers to British cities and other targets at night. A young scientist, Professor R. V. Jones, the Air Ministry deputy director of intelligence and a former Oxford pupil of Lindemann, discovered that the Germans were operating a system they called *Knickebein* (crooked leg), whereby their bombers followed a radio beam from France. When it intersected with a twin beam to form the apex of a V, it meant they were over their target. Exploiting the *Knickebein* system the Germans could bomb not only by night but also by day in bad weather. Jones discovered that these beams could be deflected or jammed. When Lindemann reported this to a worried Churchill in early

June 1940, he indicated that there appeared to be a means of neutralizing them. A high-level meeting of scientists, Lord Beaverbrook, Archie Sinclair and senior RAF commanders was held in the cabinet room on 21 June. At Lindemann's invitation Jones slipped quietly into the room and was asked to explain his system. Jones suggested that creating false beams would result in the Luftwaffe dropping its bombs early, and jamming its beams would disrupt and confuse it. His idea was greeted with scepticism, but Churchill had seen quite enough wrangling and inaction, and his frustration with the Air Ministry boiled over. Banging the table and growling, the prime minister 'really tore a strip off the Air Staff', said Jones.

With Churchill's backing, Jones's theory was proved correct when RAF aircraft located the beams and soon developed jamming devices that thwarted the Luftwaffe bombers. Instead of bombing cities, the Luftwaffe left large, harmless craters scattered in the British countryside. The Germans soon responded by developing new navigational devices, and the British responded with a countermeasure in one of the great unseen clashes of the war, which became known as 'the battle of the beams.'

Churchill rarely complimented anyone, but he developed a special fondness for R. V. Jones and his contributions to the saving of countless lives. After the war he told Jones that when he had first learned that the Luftwaffe would be able to bomb as accurately by night as by day, 'it was for him one of the blackest moments of the war.'

Churchill's debt to the scientists was huge. Their unique skills proved invaluable in countless ways. Jones's contributions were just beginning; in 1941 he and his team, aided by aerial photographs taken by the RAF, began to map the German radar sites on the French coast. They detected a site on a cliff near the small port city of Bruneval where there was a radar station that was using a new device called Würzburg, which controlled German night fighters sent up to locate and attack RAF strategic bombers. Jones conceived the idea of a commando raid to capture the device, and with valuable reconnaissance information about the site and its defences supplied by the French Resistance a plan was developed by combined operations to land a small parachute force inland, while the RAF conducted diversionary bombing runs near by. The raid, led by Lieutenant Colonel John Frost (who later earned fame in Sicily and at Arnhem), was carried out on the night of

27–28 February 1942 and succeeded brilliantly. An RAF technician dismantled the device and the raiders brought back enough information and parts (along with a captured German operator) to aid materially in the never ending battle of the beams. When Churchill ordered SOE to 'Set Europe ablaze,' the Bruneval raid was a perfect example of what he had in mind: inter-service co-operation and great initiative and technical help from civilians.

Deception is a vital part of warfare. Its principles are 'mystify, mislead and surprise'. During the Second World War the British became masters of deception. Their mastery culminated in 1944 in the greatest deception of all: by creating a phantom army group, commanded by the Allied general the Germans most feared – George S. Patton – they made the enemy believe that the cross-Channel invasion of France would take place in the Pas de Calais. Deception became a vital weapon in the unseen war waged daily by some of the brightest minds in Britain. Like the scientists and code breakers, most were citizen-soldiers who stepped forward and carried out daring, successful deception operations. Most of them remain largely unknown.

Churchill famously remarked to Stalin that in war, 'Truth deserves a bodyguard of lies.' The historian of deception, Thaddeus Holt, points out that this was 'the wrong end of the stick. For deceivers, lies are so precious that they should be attended by a bodyguard of truth.'

41

London Burning

If Hitler fails to invade or destroy Britain he has lost the war.
– Churchill, during a secret session of the House of Commons, 20 June 1940

Before the Blitz and the Battle of Britain came to symbolize the war in the second half of 1940, an equally important event failed to take place. Had Hitler carried out Operation Sea Lion in July, he would have caught Britain at its lowest ebb defensively and given Germany its best and probably only chance of a successful invasion. Instead, Hitler dithered and thereby gave Churchill and Britain precious time to recover from Dunkirk.

Operation Sea Lion and the Battle of Britain were intertwined: for an invasion to succeed, the air war had to proceed through a sustained series of attacks by the Luftwaffe designed to cripple the RAF. The months when invasion threatened, when the Blitz was endured and the Battle of Britain was fought proved to be the most testing time of the war, a time when it was difficult if not impossible to offer much in the way of hope. In July bombs began to fall with regularity on British cities and ports, and invasion was thought to be imminent. In the view of the author C. P. Snow, despite the destruction and the deaths of friends, neighbours and strangers, the British people experienced a sort of 'collective euphoria', a sense of pride in being the underdog and standing up to a bully – and surviving. 'How strange it all is!' wrote Harold Nicolson on 20 July. 'We know that we are faced with a terrific invasion. We half-know that the odds are heavily against us. Yet there is a sort of exhilaration in the air. If Hitler were to postpone the invasion and fiddle about in Africa and the Mediterranean, our morale might weaken. But we are really proud to be the people who will not give way.' Chips Channon likened the summer of 1940 to 'living as people did during the French Revolution – every day is a document, every hour history.' Under Chamberlain or Halifax, such a feeling could simply never have existed. Ian Jacob thought: 'Winston was the only man who could hold the country united.'

Churchill's role at this critical juncture was to hold the ship of state together, to encourage hope and to prepare defences to repel the expected launch of Sea Lion. In the midst of invasion preparations and despite the cloud of uncertainty that hung over Britain, he was already thinking ahead – offensively. On 7 July he sent a blunt memo to Herbert Morrison, the minister of supply: 'What is being done about designing and planning vessels to transport tanks across the sea for a British attack on enemy countries? . . . These must be able to move six or seven hundred vehicles in one voyage and land them on the beach or alternatively, take them off the beaches, as well, of course, as landing them on quays.' What Churchill had identified was the vital need for the specialized amphibious landing craft that would eventually put Allied forces ashore in theatres all over the world. Hardly anyone in Britain would have been thinking so far ahead at such a difficult time, yet once again Churchill's inventive mind was advancing an idea that was to be a key element in eventually winning the war.

He was determined to change the direction of the war. By the summer of 1940 he had already mapped out what Britain would do once it had survived the present crisis. Colville noticed a new exuberance in Churchill: 'Next year we will be building up a great offensive army and we hope to have fifty-five divisions. We shall plan large-scale "butcher and bolt" raids on the continent and Hitler will find himself hard put . . . to hold 2,000 miles of coast line . . . By 1942 we shall have achieved air superiority and shall be ready for great offensive operations on land against Germany.' His forecast was off by a few years, but the results he predicted in the summer of 1940 would come to pass, not in 1942 but in 1944. By 1945 they would turn Germany into the very wasteland he envisaged that summer afternoon.

For Churchill the fear of invasion served a useful purpose. 'It is well on the way to providing us with the finest offensive army we have ever possessed and it is keeping every man and woman tuned to a high pitch of readiness,' wrote Colville. 'We want every citizen to fight desperately and they will do so the more if they know that the alternative is massacre.'

In August, while the RAF fought for Britain's survival in the skies overhead, on the ground Churchill continued refining his ambitious ideas for the coming year. At his instigation the War Cabinet approved the raising of fifty-five divisions and gave permission for Beaverbrook's Ministry of Aircraft Production to increase its monthly quota to some three thousand planes. Even without the United States in the picture, in addition to planning commando raids against European coastal sites he already had thoughts of a landing somewhere in Italy and even (rather prematurely) of recapturing one of the Low Countries or the Cherbourg Peninsula.

By late June 1940 Churchill's chief assistants noted a marked change in their master. Eric Seal, his principal private secretary, remarked how greatly the prime minister 'had sobered down, becoming less violent, less wild and less impetuous'. Ardently believing that it was his duty 'to extricate this country from its present troubles . . . he certainly will kill himself, if necessary, in order to achieve his object.' To the British public he was hopeful, inspiring, a father figure. To the military chiefs and the departments of state, he had become in two short months their leader – not always liked, often criticized, but the one person who held the machinery of war together at the time of Britain's greatest peril.

Not all his decisions were necessarily the right ones; his insistence on knowing every facet of virtually every action taken was often intrusive and even at times counter-productive; but his grip on the pulse of war was exactly the remedy needed for the turmoil of the summer of 1940.

Churchill used the occasion of a secret session of the House of Commons on 20 June not only to offer political reassurance but also to outline the military problems Britain faced. All depended, he said, 'upon the battle of Britain', by which he meant the expected invasion. Later the term would become immortalized in its application to the epic battle fought over England between the RAF and the Luftwaffe. However, in June the most imminent threat came from the sea. What buoyed Churchill was his deeply held belief that 'if Hitler fails to invade or destroy Britain he has lost the war.' The next three months would determine the result. If Britain could hold out, it could survive for the next three years. 'But all depends on winning this battle here in Britain, now this summer.'

Britain's approach to the United States, he said, had to be positive. 'Nothing will stir them like fighting in England,' a heroic struggle he believed would offer the 'best chance of bringing them in'. Much like his earlier speeches, Churchill's bravado and promises were a colossal bluff backed only by his words of hope and defiance – and by trust that the Royal Navy and the RAF could make a difference. No one – neither Churchill nor the best minds in Britain – knew if a German invasion could be repelled. But in June that was not his real objective, which was to persuade his ministers, members of Parliament and the British public to give it their all – or die trying. 'Blood, toil, tears and sweat', he gambled, would turn into 'their finest hour'.

The fall of France led Churchill to make perhaps the most controversial decision of the war. Although the French army had crumbled, the French fleet was large and formidable and consisted of seven battleships, twenty cruisers, two aircraft carriers and several dozen destroyers. Some ships had escaped from France and were berthed in various British ports and in Alexandria in Egypt, while the remainder were in ports in metropolitan France or in French North and West Africa. Churchill was particularly concerned that the large number of warships berthed at Mers-el-Kebir, the military port of Oran in north-west Algeria, might fall into German hands. He was also troubled by the threat posed by two large, modern battleships, the *Jean Bart* (in Casablanca, Morocco's chief port) and the *Richelieu* (in Dakar, capital of Senegal). Neither of them was operationally ready in July 1940; nevertheless, Churchill and the Admiralty dreaded the prospect of the two French ships paired up with the German raiders *Scharnhorst* and *Gneisenau* (or the new super-battleship *Bismarck*, then under construction) to menace convoys in the Atlantic. Churchill was prepared to do whatever it took to prevent the ships berthed at Mers-el-Kebir from leaving and, in enemy hands, tilting the naval balance in favour of the Axis. 'In no circumstances', he told the War Cabinet, 'must we run the mortal risk of allowing these ships to fall into the hands of the enemy. Rather than that, we should have to fight and sink them.'

Churchill was unaware that Hitler had neither the manpower to run these vessels nor any interest in doing so, despite the keen desire of the German navy to add the two battleships to what was an inferior fleet compared with the Royal Navy. However, as long as the French fleet was neutralized and no threat, Hitler promised to leave it alone. Churchill was thoroughly wary of German assurances despite similar guarantees from the French navy minister, Admiral Jean Darlan. Bitter about Dunkirk and the failure to consult him, Darlan distrusted Churchill almost as much as he did Hitler. Nevertheless he assured Churchill on 11 June not only that the fleet would resist surrendering but that as a last resort he would send it to Canada. At one point he was said to have been ready to sail with it to England; instead parts of the fleet were dispatched to ports in North Africa while the remainder were kept in Toulon in southern France. Churchill later asserted that had Darlan brought the world's fourth most powerful fleet to fight alongside Britain he would have become the leader of the French Resistance instead of Charles de Gaulle. 'The whole French Empire would have rallied to him . . . Fame and power . . . were in his grasp.'

After Marshal Pétain had appointed him minister of marine in the new Vichy government, Darlan changed course and insisted that he felt duty bound not to remove the fleet to England. In reality the decision was a bargaining chip in French negotiations with the Germans. Dismayed that the French government had caved in rather than escape to French North Africa and continue the fight, Churchill belligerently broadcast a speech to France in which he insisted that the fleet come over to Britain. Darlan issued secret orders that it should remain in French hands and that each ship should prepare to scuttle itself. 'No orders of any foreign authority will be obeyed,' he directed, thus setting the stage for a tragic denouement.

Dudley Pound and his fleet commanders opposed the use of force and attempted, through informal contacts with the French naval commander at Oran, Admiral Marcel Gensoul, to broker a deal that would avoid bloodshed. A number of options were offered that included fighting on, moving the fleet to a British port and either '[fighting] with us' or handing the fleet over for manning by British crews. The alternatives were unacceptable to the French: demilitarize the fleet at Mers-el-Kebir or scuttle it.

Admiral Gensoul refused to disobey his orders from Darlan, and on 1 July Churchill got his way and the decision to employ force was reluctantly approved by the War Cabinet. The mission of carrying out one of the war's most repugnant tasks fell, in Algeria, to Vice Admiral Sir James Somerville and his Force H, and in Egypt to Admiral Andrew Browne Cunningham, the commander in chief of British naval forces in the Mediterranean.

On the evening of 2 July Pound sent a signal drafted by Churchill to Admiral Somerville that declared: 'You are charged with one of the most disagreeable and difficult tasks that a British Admiral has ever been faced with, but we have complete confidence in you and rely on you to carry it out relentlessly.' Last-minute negotiations with Gensoul failed to produce a compromise. According to Beaverbrook the decision weighed heavily on Churchill. At 2.00 a.m. on 3 July, the two men ventured into the gardens of No. 10, where Churchill spoke movingly of his fateful decision, and wept.

Though horrified by his orders, Somerville complied with them and, at around six o'clock on the evening of 3 July, his ships began shelling the hapless French vessels at Mers-el-Kebir while RAF aircraft from the carrier *Ark Royal* dropped torpedoes. With the exception of the battlecruiser *Strasbourg* and two destroyers, which managed to escape and sail to Toulon, the French warships were either destroyed or crippled during the deadly nine-minute attack. The British suffered no casualties, but the French navy paid a terrible price of nearly 1,297 dead or missing. Nevertheless, only a portion of the fleet was put out of action and a sizeable force remained at Toulon. In Egypt bloodshed was averted when Cunningham managed to secure the internment of a squadron of French navy vessels in the port of Alexandria.

Churchill spoke at length in the House of Commons, calling the incident painful but necessary. Britain would, he declared, 'prosecute the war with the utmost vigour by all the means that are open to us'. At its conclusion MPs stood and cheered, waving papers and applauding their leader. Harold Nicolson recorded that, as he received the ovation, Churchill sat, deeply moved, 'with tears pouring down his cheeks'. Equally moved but for entirely different reasons was Admiral Somerville, whose reaction to killing fellow sailors was one of horror. 'We all feel thoroughly dirty and ashamed,' he said, describing the incident as 'the biggest blunder of modern times', one that 'would rouse the whole world against us'.

Mers-el-Kebir had other incalculable, unintended consequences, the most important of which was that it forcefully established, perhaps once and for all, Churchill's position as the unmistakable political and military leader of Britain. He had done what a Halifax-led government would never have dared, and in so doing had demonstrated just how utterly ruthless and determined he could be in prosecuting the war, even if it meant attacking what had once been, until the creation of the Vichy government, his country's closest ally. He had overruled the admirals and the War Cabinet, and now his control over the military establishment was irreversible. In office for barely seven weeks, he had grabbed power by the throat with the sheer force of his dominating personality. Those who had underestimated him could now hardly be in doubt over who was in charge.

In Washington the message from London was loud and clear: Britain would fight to the bitter end. 'Immense relief spread through the high Government circles in the United States,' Churchill later wrote. 'Henceforth there was no more talk about Britain giving in.' Indeed, 'It exerted a particular effect on Roosevelt,' who now believed that Britain just might turn Churchill's defiant words into action. Although it was politically suicidal for the president to be openly aiding a doomed Britain, Churchill's audacious act nevertheless stiffened FDR's resolve to continue American assistance.

After the heavy losses sustained by the Royal Navy at Dunkirk, Churchill systematically pursued the acquisition of additional destroyers. A great many had to be repositioned in southern England to counter an invasion, leaving convoys without adequate support. In July 1940 more than two hundred thousand tons of shipping were lost to U-boats. 'We can't go on like this,' Churchill wrote. Throughout the summer he and Roosevelt conducted secret negotiations as FDR sought some means of evading the political and legal constraints he faced in an election year.

As his close adviser Harry Hopkins later explained, Roosevelt had adopted 'a "damn the torpedoes" spirit' at a time in American history when isolationism prevailed. It was, wrote Hopkins, 'Roosevelt's first tremendous wartime decision: to back the seemingly hopeless cause of Britain with everything that he could possibly offer in the way of material and moral encouragement ... This decision was entirely on his own. There was no time in his Presidential career when he met with so much opposition in his own official family or when his position in the country was less secure.' Roosevelt contrived to send fifty obsolete First World War destroyers to Britain in exchange for the rights to lease naval bases in the Caribbean and Newfoundland for ninety-nine years, prompting an angry debate in Congress. Of the many debts, monetary and moral, that Britain owed the United States in the Second World War, none was greater than that for FDR's bold and courageous decision to send support vital to its survival.

In Berlin and Paris, Churchill was vilified over Mers-el-Kebir, and the new Vichy government immediately severed relations with Britain. Hitler exploded with rage at British perfidy: this was clearly not the action of a beaten foe seeking rapprochement. Even so, he continued to delude himself that a peaceful solution with Britain might yet be possible, and as his propaganda mouthpiece Joseph Goebbels proclaimed, if Britain rebuffed a final offer it would be dealt 'an annihilatory blow. The English apparently have no idea what then awaits them.' The German press crowed that his own people should hang Churchill in Trafalgar Square.

Hitler's peace overtures got nowhere, and on the evening of 14 July Churchill broadcast to the nation. The thrust of his words, while intended to offer hope to France and reassurance to the United States, again delivered a powerful measure of defiance, a message aimed squarely at Hitler. Should he dare to come to Britain, 'We shall defend every village, every town, and every city. The vast mass of London, fought street by street, could easily devour an entire hostile army; and we would rather see London laid in ruins and ashes than that it should be tamely and abjectly enslaved.' Harold Nicolson was not alone in being enthralled by Churchill's latest speech. 'But really he has got guts that man. Imagine the effects of his speech in the Empire and the U.S.A. . . . What a speech! . . . Thank God for him.'

On 16 July Hitler's directive to prepare for Sea Lion was intercepted by the British code breakers, confirming the urgency of preparing for the worst. The order was merely to get ready for the invasion and outlined preconditions that had to be met before he would authorize its execution. These included keeping the Royal Navy engaged in the North Sea and in the Mediterranean, neutralizing the RAF to the point where it could not inhibit the crossing, and blocking both ends of the English Channel with mines.

The German navy, already hampered by the loss of many of its essential destroyers in the Norway campaign, never liked Sea Lion and was a reluctant participant, in part because it lacked the necessary landing craft and had to resort to using Rhine river barges (easily swamped and not meant for sea employment), tugs, motorboats, trawlers and steamers – everything but real landing craft, which were virtually nonexistent in 1940. Ultimately the plan was scaled down to some sixty-seven thousand troops of nine divisions in the initial landings, which were to take place at sites between Ramsgate and Brighton. An airborne division would land around Dover and Brighton and eventually surround London, where, by this time, it was reasoned, the British government would be prepared to surrender all of Britain.

The plan was deeply flawed. In addition to lacking the right type of sea craft, the Germans had no experience in amphibious landings and would have been thinly spread over too wide an invasion area. Even worse, not only did the weather, the RAF and the Royal Navy pose potential problems but also there would be enormous difficulty in re-supplying the invasion force once it got ashore. Moreover the makeshift vessels had enough trouble carrying troops, much less vital artillery and tanks, both of which were required to sustain a successful landing. The mythology of the German blitzkrieg has overshadowed the truth that in 1940 mechanized vehicles composed only a small fraction of the German army. There was a heavy reliance on horses as transport during the battle for France; each of the 118 German infantry divisions required a minimum of 5,000 horses. To support Sea Lion some 125,000 horses would have had to be moved across the Channel.

Hitler's olive branch became a cudgel on 19 July when, in a widely published address to the Reichstag, he contrasted the choice of peace with 'unending suffering and misery'. Asked a few days later by his chief diplomatic adviser if he cared to respond, Churchill dismissed the idea, scoffing, 'I do not propose to say anything in reply to Herr Hitler's speech, not being on speaking terms with him.'

By 1 August the message that his peace offerings were a waste of time seems finally to have got through to Hitler. On that date he ordered the Luftwaffe 'to use all forces at its disposal to destroy the British Air Force as quickly as possible'. The 5th of August was cited as the date when Hermann Göring could choose to launch 'the attack of the Eagles', which ended up being postponed until the 13th. Within hours the code breakers were circulating the directive. The RAF, already on high alert, stood ready.

The German air offensive would have taken place regardless of Sea Lion, but Göring botched it. His strategy was defective, and his decisions ultimately aided the RAF. Omitting to knock out the key radar sites along the coast that warned of approaching German aircraft was a monumental mistake, as was the failure to focus on a single strategy. Göring seemed unable to make up his mind whether to concentrate solely on neutralizing the RAF or on destroying the British military infrastructure. In the end he accomplished neither.

While Churchill grappled with a myriad of military problems during the summer of 1940, his heart was with the airmen who fought in the skies defending Britain. He fully understood that the Royal Navy was the ultimate bulwark against invasion, but with an invasion now believed to be some weeks off, the real focus of the war in August and the first half of September was in the air. After the RAF had had a particularly successful day defending Britain's skies, Churchill's confidence in the air force was never higher. 'We live on their wings,' he told Beaverbrook.

One night Churchill stopped at Northolt airfield in west London. He and the station commander, driving around the base, pulled up at the canteen and Churchill went inside. Shortly afterwards several men came scrambling out, grabbed rifles and ran to their posts. It struck Elizabeth Layton, who accompanied him that day to take dictation, that it was typical of Churchill: 'Each of us must do our duty to the very best of our ability and knowledge. That's how he was.'

Churchill often expressed concern about airfield defence in the event that enemy airborne troops landed. One morning, accompanied by Dowding's future replacement as the boss of Fighter Command, Air Vice Marshal William Sholto Douglas, he arrived unexpectedly at Northolt, ordered the base commander to sound the alarm for a mock enemy parachute attack, then began touring the base to view the reaction. What he saw left him in a foul mood. Disorder reigned, and no one seemed to know quite what to do. Arriving at the sector where the Spitfires of a volunteer Polish fighter wing were kept in readiness, Churchill saw the pilots standing on top of the berms protecting them, peering skywards and ignoring the elderly Englishman shouting angrily at them to 'Come down at once.' Growing ever more angry and frustrated when they ignored him, Churchill did not realize that most did not speak much English. Next he went into a dispersal hut and encountered another group of Polish pilots playing cards, reading and smoking. Now boiling mad, he demanded of the squadron leader why they were sitting around when enemy parachutists were attacking.

The unruffled Polish commander replied, 'We know it's a false alarm.

If it were not, we'd have been ordered into the air by now.' With Sholto Douglas barely suppressing a grin, the Pole proffered a beautifully bound visitors' book to the glowering prime minister and politely invited Churchill to sign it. He did, and his mood softened when he saw how delighted the Poles were at having acquired his autograph. Moreover it was impossible to be angry with these gallant men who were fighting and dying to protect Britain.

Throughout the long summer Churchill's thoughts were trained on the skies. While at Chequers on weekends when it was deemed safe for him to reside there instead of Ditchley Park, he routinely rushed outside at the sound of Luftwaffe engines overhead. Sometimes appearing only in his dressing gown, minus his false teeth and with or without the tin helmet that his handlers often failed to persuade him to don, Churchill would peer upwards, his cigar pointing the way.

The famous phrase that he applied to the pilots who fought the Battle of Britain originated on Sunday, 15 September, a day when Göring, believing that the RAF was nearly beaten, launched a massive raid. That afternoon, accompanied by Clementine and Ismay, Churchill inspected the underground operations centre of No. 11 Fighter Group in the west London suburb of Uxbridge. Of the many places he visited during the summer of 1940, none inspired and fascinated him more than No. 11 Group, where he frequently turned up unannounced. Commanded by a New Zealand veteran of Gallipoli, Air Vice Marshal Sir Keith Park, it was responsible for defending the primary battleground of London and all of south-eastern England. From here the air battle was controlled by radios and telephones connected to Fighter Command and to each squadron. Park's senior air controllers were all experienced pilots who guided the airmen to intercept the incoming bombers and fighter escorts, as uniformed women of the Women's Auxiliary Air Force (WAAF) moved counters around a huge plotting table that reflected the position of every enemy and friendly aircraft.

Churchill sat spellbound in an observation gallery overlooking the intense activity below, an unlighted cigar in his hand (even he was not permitted to smoke in the command centre). As unit after unit was committed in one of the air campaign's biggest battles, the markers were moved and orders were barked to unseen airmen.

It was the Germans who were on the receiving end of the full wrath of the RAF. The first wave to attack London was met by some two hundred Spitfire and Hurricane fighters during one of the most terrifying days of the war. A second raid later that afternoon was met by three hundred fighters.

At one point, when all of Park's squadrons were committed, Churchill asked him, 'What other reserves have we?' Park replied that there were none. As Ismay watched the markers representing a new wave of German aircraft crossing the Channel being moved around the plotting table, 'I felt sick with fear.' Churchill's experience that afternoon was a deeply emotional one, and it exhausted him. Before departing he made a point of entering the operations room to congratulate everyone personally. During the sixteen-mile journey back to Chequers, he turned to Ismay and exclaimed: 'Don't speak to me; I have never been so moved.' After a few minutes' silence, Churchill spoke again. 'Never in the field of conflict', he said, 'has so much been owed by so many to so few.' When he repeated those words to the world a short time later, the bravery of the RAF took its place in the lexicon of British historical achievement.

Pamela Harriman was asked years later what she thought Churchill meant by this statement; she replied, 'I think he was referring to the pilots . . . He was terribly conscious that he was the person who was instigating them going to their deaths, possibly, and I think this bothered him enormously . . . He'd have liked to have gone into every battle, into every bomber, himself personally.' Such emotion-filled scenes were no coincidence. During the long ordeal of the war there were many more occasions when he was nearly overcome with tears. 'He felt things more than any human being I have ever known and so genuinely and I honestly think that was the way he was able to be such a great leader because he enthralled people with what he himself felt about it.'

After Churchill awoke from a late nap at 8.00 that evening, John Martin entered his bedroom to provide his nightly summary of news from around the world. 'It was repellent,' remembered Churchill; from shipping losses in the Atlantic to unsatisfactory replies to 'Action' notes, there was little good news until Martin said, 'However, all is redeemed by the air. We have shot down a hundred and eighty-three for a loss of under forty.' To cap off a spectacular day, Bomber Command hammered vessels of the German invasion fleet berthed at Antwerp.

History now records that on 15 September the RAF won the Battle of Britain. And while the RAF's claims were wildly exaggerated (the true figure of German losses was closer to sixty), Martin's observation was nevertheless truthful: after weeks of deadly air combat, the air battle of 15 September affirmed to Göring and to Hitler that the RAF was far from beaten. Although 'won' is a relative term, the RAF had fought the Luftwaffe to a standstill – and that was good enough.

This day also had significance far beyond the victory won by the RAF. On 14 September Hitler had decided that although naval preparations for the invasion were now complete, the air situation did not yet meet his prerequisites. In order to keep the pressure on Britain, he did not want to call off Sea Lion, but the events of 15 September strongly suggested sufficient justification for postponing it. Although it was not formally called off until 1943, and the timetable remained open ended, invasion was never again a serious option because Hitler would soon require many of Sea Lion's assets for Operation Barbarossa, the invasion of Russia in June 1941.

Turning the tide of the Battle of Britain neither reduced expectations of invasion nor abated the onslaught British cities and military targets suffered at the hands of the Luftwaffe. The war took on yet another sinister aspect with the coming of the Blitz. Hitler may have lost the initiative, and a peace treaty with Britain may have eluded him, but the punishment meted out for the next nine months was the most devastating of the war. The official commencement of the Blitz is dated eight days earlier, on 7 September, when the Luftwaffe unleashed nearly a thousand aircraft (348 bombers escorted by 617 fighters) that left parts of London burning. Churchill may have wanted SOE to 'set Europe ablaze', but in 1940 and 1941 it was Hitler who set London and a host of other British cities and towns on fire.

From the roof of the BBC the great drama unfolding all around was reported to America by its principal voice in Britain, Edward R. Murrow. Like Churchill, he refused to take cover when the raids occurred. In the deep, rather mournful tones that earned him everlasting fame came nightly broadcasts that began: 'This is London.' Although more than 120 correspondents reported the Blitz, it was Murrow's voice that stood out from the rest. In the United States, Americans sat glued to their radios as he graphically described a faraway, unseen war. Hearing Murrow intone, 'London is burning,' was a stark reminder of Britain's plight. Although numerous other British cities were bombed, from early

September to mid-November London was on the receiving end of 27,500 bombs and incendiaries as its citizens scrambled for shelter. One night a record 177,000 people took sanctuary on the platforms and in the tunnels of the Underground.

By the time the Blitz was deemed over, following an especially heavy raid a year to the day after Churchill became prime minister, three hundred thousand homes had been destroyed or heavily damaged, twenty thousand civilians had died, and numerous churches had been lost and the House of Commons wrecked.

The first big raid of the Blitz was so intense and the night sky so lit up with fire from the docks area that it was possible to read a newspaper. The next morning Churchill toured the shattered docklands, as one eyewitness recorded, 'occasionally dabbing his eyes from time to time with a large white handkerchief clutched in one hand'. An elderly woman shouted, 'When are we going to bomb Berlin, Winnie?' Instantly Churchill swung around and, waving his walking stick in her direction, growled: ' "You leave that to me!" Morale rose immediately; everyone was satisfied and reassured ... The incident typifies the uniquely unpredictable magic that was Churchill. Transformation of the despondent misery of disaster into a grimly certain stepping stone to ultimate victory.'

Despite the rain of devastation upon London in 1940, it was Churchill who gave hope when there was little cause for optimism and certainly nothing to cheer about. After one particularly destructive night of bombing, the king solemnly toured the scene the next morning. Said one Londoner: 'No one cheered because they didn't feel like cheering. But when Churchill came a few hours later, with a cigar sticking out of his fat pink face, a few people cheered and even I felt like cheering.'

During the summer of 1940 there were occasions when Churchill would become momentarily carefree, when high spirits overcame the grim reality of war. He continued his practice of bringing in senior officers in order to grill them. Lieutenant General Sir James Marshall-Cornwall commanded a corps in that summer. Like Montgomery he had had to re-equip and retrain his formations both for defence against invasion and in offensive operations. In late July, Marshall-Cornwall was summoned to Chequers for what he later called the 'Mad Hatter's Dinner Party', and soon earned Churchill's displeasure when he candidly told him that his formations did not possess the weapons claimed by the War Office. Churchill insisted that the numbers on his graphs said otherwise, but Marshall-Cornwall refused to budge and again contradicted him. 'The PM's brow contracted; almost speechless with rage, he hurled the graphs across the dinner-table to Dill, saying: "CIGS, have those papers checked and returned to me tomorrow."'

After dinner Churchill sprang his trap, asking how the general would go about capturing the Italian-occupied port of Massawa in Ethiopia, situated on the Red Sea. With Dill and Ismay looking on nervously, Marshall-Cornwall sensed that he was being baited and deftly pointed out reasons why such an operation was better left to a British offensive from land. 'The P.M. gave me a withering look, rolled up the map and muttered peevishly, "You soldiers are all alike; you have no imagination."' The next day, en route back to London, Dill thanked Marshall-Cornwall for taking the position he did: 'If you had shown the least enthusiasm for the project, I should have been given orders to embark your Corps for the Red Sea next week.' As Churchill's official biographer suggests, it may well have been nothing more than an intellectual exercise and simply a test for a visiting general, yet such comments were invariably taken seriously.

These military mind games continued in other forms, as Brooke discovered one evening at Chequers in early September 1940 while C in C Home Forces. With invasion still expected, Churchill 'placed himself in the position of Hitler and attacked these isles while I defended them. He then revised the whole of the Air Raid Warning system and gave us his proposals to criticize.'

Before 16 September intelligence reports suggested that the Germans would invade within the next week. Brooke felt the full weight of a formidable responsibility and what he later described as a burden that was 'almost unbearable at times'. He understood perhaps better than anyone else that Britain remained dangerously vulnerable and that 'for the present there is nothing to be done but to trust God and pray for his help and guidance.' It was as if the military establishment was holding its collective breath as the days passed and nothing happened except the endless air raids and the continuing struggle in the air between the RAF and the Luftwaffe.

Churchill made it clear that he would employ every means at his disposal to prevent an invasion. His 'we shall fight on the beaches' and everywhere else was more than mere rhetoric. At one point he told a general, 'I have no scruples, except not to do anything dishonourable.' After the war Brooke wrote that his plans for defence had included reliance on 'heavy air attacks on the points of landing, and [I] had every intention of using sprayed mustard gas on the beaches.'

In the end the failure of the Luftwaffe and the fact that Hitler was never more than lukewarm about the invasion plan resulted in one postponement after another. Although Churchill chose to give most of the laurels for the magnificent achievements of 'the Few', in the background lurked the menacing presence of the Royal Navy, a reminder that warfare is not one dimensional. And while an already sceptical Adolf Hitler used the Luftwaffe's failure to win the Battle of Britain as an excuse for postponing Sea Lion, the Royal Navy remained an unacknowledged factor in his decision. 'Air power was irrelevant to a night crossing,' writes Derek Robinson. 'The only relevant force was the Royal Navy. That was why Hitler quit. There was no battle in the Channel, and that was the Royal Navy's "silent victory".'

Hugh Dowding, the airman who masterminded the Battle of Britain, faded into retirement in November 1940 with scant recognition and without promotion to the rank of marshal of the Royal Air Force, an honour routinely given to others who had accomplished far less. Dowding was belatedly asked to write an official dispatch on the Battle of Britain, but it was never published during the war, on the grounds that it might reveal sensitive information to the enemy. After the war the official air force history failed even to mention Dowding, causing Churchill to write angrily to Archibald Sinclair that it was 'a discredit to the Air Ministry . . . What would have been said if . . . the Admiralty had told the tale of Trafalgar and left Lord Nelson out of it?' Churchill, however, bears his own culpability for hardly mentioning Dowding in *Their Finest Hour*, later privately admitting that he had caved in to pressure from the Air Ministry. Vital though Dowding's contributions were to the success of RAF in the Battle of Britain, it was his actions in the spring and early summer of 1940, which kept Fighter Command from losing further squadrons in France, that made possible the Battle of Britain, a fact Churchill conspicuously failed to mention in his war memoirs.

The invasion crisis was not over, merely postponed. Sir John Martin

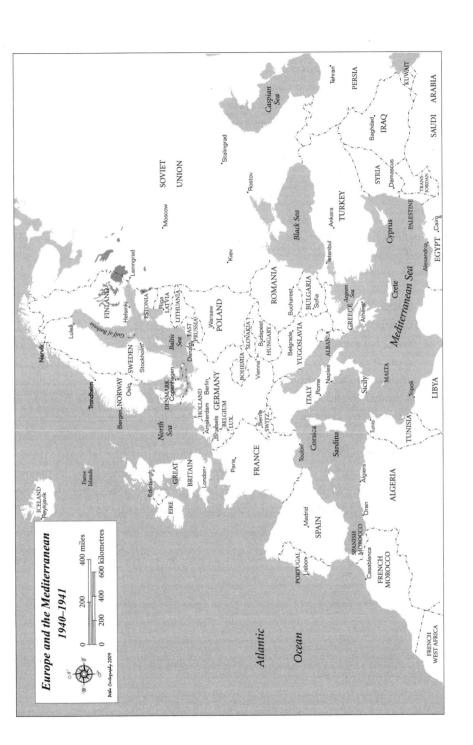

Europe and the Mediterranean 1940–1941

later summed up the summer of 1940 with the remark: 'It may have been Britain's "finest hour", but when we were living through it, it was a time of agony piled on agony.' After the war the playwright Robert E. Sherwood, a keen observer of the war from his perspective as one of Roosevelt's speechwriters, reflected: 'It is perhaps a bit of unnecessarily grim speculation, but I believe there were some in England – and I should not be surprised if Churchill were one of them – who later regretted rather wistfully that Hitler never tried that invasion. As a member of the White House staff remarked later to Hopkins, "it would have been a hell of a fight."'

During the war Group Captain F. W. Winterbotham served as an RAF intelligence officer. In the midst of an air raid Winterbotham was present at a meeting of the chiefs of staff in the Central War Room on the evening of 17 September, shortly after an Ultra intercept revealed that Hitler had postponed Sea Lion. The scene was dominated by 'the extraordinary change that had come over these men in the last few hours. It was as if someone had cut all the strings of the violins in the middle of a dreary concerto.' Churchill beamed, lit a cigar and suggested they all go upstairs for some fresh air.

Ignoring the usual protests that he should not expose himself to unnecessary danger, the party trooped outside and was greeted by the grim scenes of bombs exploding, ack-ack guns firing into the night sky, and 'the red and white glow of the fires silhouetting the tall black trunks of the great trees' in St James's Park. 'It was a moment in history to remember,' wrote Winterbotham, 'and above the noise came the angry voice of Winston Churchill: "By God we'll get the B[astard]s for this."'

42
Wavell in the Hot Seat

He has at least one great general – Wavell . . . But, mark my words, he will get rid of Wavell.
— Lloyd George

In the summer of 1940 the only action was in the Mediterranean, where the three combatants all sought control of war's most valuable resource: oil. The oil in Iran, Iraq, Romania, Kuwait, Saudi Arabia and the untapped potentially rich oil fields of the Caucasus was in 1940 a prize beyond compare. With no oil-producing capability of its own, Germany was dependent on the production of synthetic oil from coal. To fuel their war machines with the real thing, Hitler and Mussolini had first to seize control of the Mediterranean Sea, which for centuries had been the exclusive sphere of the Royal Navy. Britain likewise required oil for its ships, aircraft, tanks and vehicles. In 1940 the Middle East was not a primary source of British oil. To import this commodity some eighteen thousand miles around the Cape of Good Hope was expensive and logistically difficult. Moreover, a shortage of shipping and the U-boat menace effectively shut off the import of Middle East oil. The result was that Britain was forced to rely on the United States to fill its needs. If control of the Mediterranean and the Suez Canal were lost, the results would have given the Axis unhindered access to the Middle Eastern oil fields and brought much of Africa under its control; and with Hitler already planning to attack the Soviet Union in 1941, the southern flank along the Black Sea would have been exposed, provided Turkey was brought into the Axis fold. (Although the Turks had carried out a delicate balancing act in the 1930s and had managed to stay out of the war, Axis control of the Mediterranean would have placed great pressure on Turkey to side with Germany.)

Britain's military presence in the region consisted of the Mediterranean fleet, based in Alexandria, commanded by Admiral ABC Cunningham, one of a group of 'Mediterraneanist' naval officers who believed that it was a higher priority than the Far East. However, with Suez now supplying less than 10 per cent of British imports, voices in London were asking why valuable military assets were being retained that were badly needed in the Far East, and at home.

In 1940 Churchill embraced the Mediterranean as the one place where the Axis could be actively engaged on the ground and at sea. Moreover the British presence in the region made it an attractive alternative to the waiting game he was forced to play until the United States became a full participant. And if there was insufficient economic rationale for defending the Mediterranean, there were certainly strong military reasons – and engaging the Axis there, with the Royal Navy as his cudgel, provided Churchill with a perfect opportunity to take personal control of events. There was no theatre of operations during the Second World War in which he was more deeply involved. The desert generals came under greater scrutiny and pressure than any other element of the armed forces.

Before the fall of France the French fleet had been expected to play a part in keeping the Mediterranean under Allied control. Instead that role had to be filled by Cunningham's fleet in Alexandria and Admiral Somerville's squadron based at Gibraltar, effectively boxing in the Italian navy and keeping its warships from raising havoc in the Atlantic, and enabling the British to defend Egypt and Malta, with its important naval base.

Critics of British strategy in what has been termed Europe's 'soft underbelly' point to Churchill's desire to keep the British Empire intact. However, there were far more important reasons to maintain its presence there and to engage Germany and Italy. If Britain had not remained, it would have lost Egypt and an ill-defended Malta, and Cyprus and Palestine would have fallen, Greece have been imperilled, Gibraltar made all but untenable, and the oil fields opened to Axis use. Hitler's southern flank would have been fully secured, and the entire Middle East turned into an Italian-dominated region. Churchill would have none of it. The debate ended there. The war would be neither won nor lost in the Mediterranean, but it would not be ceded without a fight.

Churchill's views on the war were expounded to Major General

Bernard Freyberg at a dinner at No. 10 Downing Street on 17 July 1940. The New Zealand commander had just returned from the Middle East to take command of the newly formed Second New Zealand Expeditionary Force. Churchill and Freyberg, an Englishman raised in New Zealand, had first met in 1914, when Freyberg had received an officer's commission from the then first lord of the Admiralty and fought at Gallipoli. He was wounded nine times in France, won a Victoria Cross at the Somme in 1916, was awarded four DSOs and the Croix de Guerre and was mentioned in dispatches five times, while becoming one of the youngest general officers in the British army. His service in two world wars made him New Zealand's most renowned and distinguished soldier.

Speaking of his role as minister of defence, Churchill said that he 'had purposely refrained from defining his duties, as he intended to do exactly what he considered necessary'. Then he declared: 'This [meaning England] is the decisive theatre. If we are defeated here, the war is lost.' According to Freyberg, 'He repeated this remark many times during the evening.'

General Archibald Wavell, the commander in chief, Middle East, had recently cabled the chiefs of staff that he might lose Egypt unless reinforcements were forthcoming. If these were provided, supplies and equipment would have to be sent around the Cape by ship, a journey that might take anywhere from 40 to 120 days. The evening ended with Freyberg's echoing the same warning: 'If you are not careful, you will lose Egypt.'

The employment of convoys to the Middle East was but one of numerous bones of contention between Churchill and Wavell. When it was decided in August to send an armoured brigade equipped with the new heavy Matilda tanks, Churchill, backed by Admiral Cunningham, argued that time was critical and wanted them sent by the most direct means, through Gibraltar and the Mediterranean. Wavell regarded the potential loss of an irreplaceable asset as too important to risk and was willing to wait longer to ensure their safe arrival via the Cape. A compromise resulted in the convoy's being sent through the Mediterranean as part of a larger naval force that was able to provide far greater security.

In early August, Freyberg and Churchill again dined together, this time at Chequers. Churchill revealed that he had formulated a strategy for defeating the Italians in the Western Desert. Let them advance as far eastward as Mersa Matruh (a town on the Libyan coast some 250 miles from Cairo) and, with their lines of communication stretched, land a force behind them from the sea and carry out what he called a 'Strangulatory Hernia', a phrase that rather pleased him. Freyberg hammered away at the need to reinforce the Middle East without delay with 'all the aeroplanes, equipment and munitions possible – but above all aircraft'. Churchill replied: 'We cannot increase the number of squadrons in Egypt but we can see that the pilots have good polo ponies.'

The Mediterranean was a militarily rich mother lode that provided Churchill with an endless list of possibilities, leading him to behave, in the words of one cynic, 'like a puppy in a fire-hydrant factory'. Directives and admonishments flowed from his pen in profusion as if he were in the field and directing a forthcoming battle, believing his knowledge superior to and his anticipation of events greater than those of his commanders. Yet one realization was always lacking: it was the commander on the spot who bore the responsibility for failure, not Churchill.

From up and down the army chain of command came complaints that Churchill had no concept whatsoever of either commanders' operational constraints or their logistical problems. Thus by the end of 1940 he had attained a reputation for taking strategic decisions that were more often than not fanciful. Moreover, when operations failed through the ineptness of their commanders, this fuelled the already smouldering fires of distrust and discontent that burned deep within the prime minister over British generalship. In fairness to Churchill, his insatiable quest for action was a direct result of Britain's precarious position, and of his obsession with striking back at Hitler and Mussolini, even if only with pinpricks. In his view failure was never an option but all too often a grim reality. Delay followed by failure was a certain prescription for replacing a commander.

The principal recipient of Churchill's wrath and frustration was Archibald Percival Wavell. The son of a British general, the fifty-seven-year-old Archie Wavell was one of the most remarkable figures in the British army of the Second World War but is now largely neglected by historians. Born in 1883 and commissioned from Sandhurst, he fought with the Black Watch in the Boer War, was wounded at Ypres (where he lost his left eye) in 1915, saw service in Turkey and served under

Allenby in Palestine before being appointed commander in chief, Middle East, in July 1939.

Taciturn to a degree that infuriated Churchill, who judged him aloof and uncommunicative, Wavell was one of the most intellectual men ever to hold high rank in the British army. A poet, essayist, military innovator and teacher, in 1939 he delivered the prestigious Lees Knowles Lecture at Cambridge on the subject of generals and generalship, a lecture which was widely studied and even translated into German. In Wavell, Churchill had a bright, aggressive commander – of the sort that was in desperately short supply in the moribund British army of 1940 and 1941 – to tackle one of the most difficult command assignments ever handed a British officer.

When Wavell assumed command in 1939 there was no strategic plan for any of the three services in the Middle East, and no guidance from London. The three commanders in chief – Air Chief Marshal Sir Arthur Longmore, ABC Cunningham and Wavell – all operated separately under orders from their respective military departments. Fortunately all worked well together.

One of the army's most forward thinkers, Wavell was among those who believed that the lessons of the First World War included shaking 'the last of the Flanders mud out of our minds'. As the senior British army officer in the Middle East, he found himself at one point in the spring of 1941 responsible for the conduct of five military campaigns at the same time. His domain covered an area from the Balkans to the Atlantic, and all of eastern Africa as far south as Rhodesia. It was composed of nine countries spread over two continents, covering an area of eighteen hundred by two thousand miles (more than 3.5 million square miles), from Persia, Palestine, Iraq and Syria to all of Egypt, Suez, East Africa, Cyprus and Malta. Wavell's unbelievably complex responsibilities were not limited to merely the military side. He was also the British proconsul in the Middle East.

His enormous responsibilities were not matched by his pitiful military assets. Totalling less than one hundred thousand, his troops consisted of a five-hundred-man camel corps, colonials with varying degrees of training, cavalry, local defence forces, and immobile garrison troops and a mere twenty-one infantry battalions in Egypt. What little equipment his combat units possessed consisted of obsolete and outdated tanks, artillery and armoured cars. His only armoured division, the 7th Armoured, known as the 'Desert Rats', operated with only 65 of its authorized 220 tanks. Short of tanks, artillery, ammunition, vehicles and anti-tank guns, Wavell's command was surrounded by either hostile or potentially hostile nations; and with France lost as an ally, he faced almost insurmountable problems against nearly five hundred thousand Italian forces massed in Libya and in East Africa.

Wavell took the approach that one of his most important tasks was the defence of the Western Desert. The officer responsible for creating an army out of whatever flotsam could be made available was Lieutenant General Henry Maitland Wilson, the commander of British troops in Egypt and the Sudan. A fifty-nine-year-old infantry officer familiarly known as 'Jumbo', Wilson was a giant of a man with considerable experience as a staff officer. Although never credited with great vision, he brought other excellent traits to his unenviable job. He was calm and steadfast, refused to be pushed around by anyone, including Churchill, and possessed a keen eye for planning, organization and detail. Perhaps most important of all, Wilson was popular with his officers and had a well-earned reputation for backing his subordinates. He was well liked by Churchill, who later promoted him to commander in chief, Middle East, and in January 1944 to the post of supreme commander in the Mediterranean to succeed Eisenhower.

From the scraps tossed to him by Wavell, Wilson organized the Western Desert Force by mixing and matching units, moving vehicles and equipment between units to make up shortages, and generally improvising a small but highly effective fighting force. In command of this improvised desert force was Lieutenant General Richard N. O'Connor, a holder of the DSO who had been mentioned in dispatches nine times during the Great War, and who brought to his unusual task an open and inventive mind. Next to the enormous figure of Maitland Wilson, Dick O'Connor was diminutive and self-effacing, but behind his quiet manner and immense modesty he was a resourceful master tactician prepared (unlike too many generals) to take daring but well-thought-out risks. In the desert war of North Africa, he can fairly be called the British version of Erwin Rommel. Between them Wilson and O'Connor brilliantly carried out Wavell's instructions to plan an offensive against the Italian army in Libya.

Wavell's relationship with Churchill got off to a rocky and perhaps incurable beginning in June 1940, when the prime minister directed that a contingent of some fifteen thousand Australian troops destined for the Middle East be diverted to England, and that eight British infantry battalions be transferred from Palestine to England and replaced with Indian army troops, yet to arrive. Wavell refused, and with the aid of Eden and Dill the order was reversed, arousing Churchill's ire. Churchill complained that Wavell saw matters only from his own perspective and, as for the War Office, 'We are indeed the victims of a feeble and weary departmentalism.' It was Anthony Eden's first taste of Churchill's sharp tongue and ruthless insistence on getting his own way. Eden had recently visited Cairo, understood the seriousness of the situation in the Middle East and backed Wavell's decision not to imperil his already under-manned army.

Wavell was not idle or lacking in offensive spirit, as Churchill seemed to think. On the contrary he was already making plans for offensives in Italian East Africa and in the Western Desert. What he lacked was the resources to carry them out. Things were made worse, not only for Wavell but for other generals with whom Churchill dealt during the war, because the prime minister never grasped that in the harsh and unforgiving wastelands that made up the desert of North Africa the possession of territory other than the seaports was meaningless. What counted was defeating the enemy on a vast battlefield of sand and rock that was devoid of food sources and water but had plentiful heat, insects and sand, properties which sapped the energy and health of the combatants and often turned their equipment into junk. Logistically whatever they possessed had to be transported with them or dropped by air. As one historian has appositely noted, 'The desert war of 1940–43 was fought like a polo game on an empty arena.'

Without substantial reinforcements Wavell lacked the means to go on the offensive; Churchill wanted action, but to get it he had to strip assets from the defence of Britain in order to meet Wavell's needs. From Cairo during the summer of 1940 came a steady stream of requests from the general for troop reinforcements and equipment.

In early August, Wavell was summoned to London to meet with Churchill and the War Cabinet. After an exhausting and dangerous flight, during which his Sunderland flying boat had to evade German fighters off Sicily, he had no sooner arrived in London than he was shown directly into the fateful meeting. As a result of his earlier clash with Churchill over troop deployment, Wavell already had two strikes against him. At this, their first face-to-face encounter, their relationship unravelled. After briefing the War Cabinet on his situation, his problems and his requirements, Wavell was grilled with what he sensed was indifference alternating with animosity. Churchill was heavy-handed and inflexible, as if deliberately making an already tense situation even more hostile. The more they conversed the worse it seemed to get. Churchill – sometimes informed, sometimes uninformed – challenged the general on points large and small, important and petty. He lectured and hectored but rarely encouraged. Wavell did himself no favours by appearing to be utterly detached and without passion behind an emotionless military mask. It frustrated Churchill that he could not penetrate the mask, and this led him to doubt that his general possessed the necessary zeal to succeed. The qualities that should have brought two brilliant men together instead resulted in a disastrous chasm that was never resolved. According to an eyewitness, Wavell's intelligence chief Brigadier John Shearer, the mood became electric, and 'relations between these two magnificent men' were 'irretrievably damaged'.

After this unfortunate meeting Wavell and Dill strolled through the streets of London discussing Churchill. Hurt and angry, Wavell insisted that he would not accept Churchill's invitation to Chequers the coming weekend. Dill replied, 'Archie, no one would deny that you have had unbearable provocation. But he is our Prime Minister. He carries an almost unbearable burden. It is true you can be replaced. He cannot be. You must go to Chequers.' Wavell did his duty but there matters worsened, primarily owing to his inability to communicate well with Churchill. His answers were blunt and to the point, and he saw no reason to elaborate, to cultivate or to develop an understanding, which is what Churchill sought. The result was disquietude on Wavell's part and distrust on Churchill's. Lloyd George foretold Wavell's fate in a conversation with Robert Boothby, who was 'convinced that Churchill alone could save us'. Lloyd George replied that he was probably right, and added, 'But it will be a one-man show. He has at least one great general – Wavell. I was not so fortunate,' he recalled, thinking of his Great War generals. 'But, mark my words, he will get rid of Wavell.' Both Ismay and Jacob thought Churchill would sack Wavell in August 1940 and were surprised when he did not.

Eden sent Churchill a strongly worded note in Wavell's defence. 'Dill and I were much perturbed at your judgment of Wavell. Neither of us know of any General Officer in the army better qualified to fill this very difficult post at this critical time.' Unmoved, Churchill offered the cutting criticism that Wavell was at best 'a good average colonel' who would make 'a good chairman of a Tory Association'. Later still he would deprecatingly refer to him as 'wavering Wavell', just as he would refer to Dill as 'Dilly-Dally'. In his war memoirs Churchill made clear his feelings about Wavell in August 1940 with this less than ringing endorsement: 'While not in full agreement with General Wavell's use of the resources at his disposal, I thought it best to leave him in command.' Eden's conclusion was that 'Churchill never understood Wavell and Wavell never seemed to encourage Churchill to do so.'

Even before the general's aircraft cleared British airspace bound for Cairo, on 15 August, Churchill was dictating a lengthy directive that he expected Wavell to comply with, spelling out in great detail exactly how he was to defend Egypt and the Nile Delta, what forces he was to employ, and even how he was to poison wells in order to deprive the Italians of precious water resources. Such a document from a politician, even someone with military experience like Churchill, was unprecedented. For a war leader to give strategic direction is a necessary and proper function; to delve into tactics and troop dispositions as if he were the commanding general was a clear indication of his distrust – and was unjustifiable. Churchill interfered with every aspect of operations in the Middle East. An example of how deeply he meddled in minutiae occurred after he approved the dispatch of 150 tanks to the Middle East, and then demanded to see the loading tables of the entire convoy sailing to Egypt. Every single item aboard these ships had to be justified and explained to him in detail. Wavell wisely did his loyal best to comply with what he could do, while ignoring what he could not. Had he, for instance, carried out Churchill's instructions to poison the wells, he would have deprived his own army of precious water when the desert army struck back at the Italians.

While it is true that in August 1940 Churchill was already considering replacing Wavell with Claude Auchinleck, he never permitted his lack of confidence in Wavell to prevent him from sending substantial reinforcements for the Middle East, including an armoured division that, against Brooke's advice, was shipped to Egypt, adding desperately needed firepower with its 154 tanks. In addition he pledged that he would send reinforcements from New Zealand, Australia and India.

However, disagreement surfaced even here. Churchill wanted the division transported at once by the shortest means, through the Mediterranean, but the Royal Navy balked and sent the convoy the long way around. When a different convoy was sent to Malta and arrived without loss, Churchill pointed to its success to argue that he had been right.

In 1940 the chiefs of staff were not the brake on Churchill that they became later in the war. With no one capable of restraining him, his tendency to goad his commanders into launching operations he deemed were being unnecessarily delayed had free rein. Had he been more attuned to Wavell he would have found much to like. Both Wavell and O'Connor were avid students of history who had studied Stonewall Jackson's Civil War hit-and-run tactics at staff college. In October 1940 Wavell appeared on the cover of *Time* magazine and was the subject of high praise as 'an unconventional theorist of war'.

Sadly, Churchill never realized that in Wavell he had a general well prepared to conduct mobile operations rather than the setpiece battles favoured by most British commanders. Wavell has been accurately described as a risk taker who employed innovative ideas but was not reckless. However, like many other military men who dealt with Churchill, he got into trouble because he refused to compromise his military judgment merely to placate prime ministerial impatience.

Having studied desert warfare and the mistakes of the past, having read the works of T. E. Lawrence and other military thinkers, Wavell put what he learned to effective use. He took the all-important measure of establishing the necessary logistical bases and lines of communication in Egypt to support and sustain the build-up of his forces, and was instrumental in the creation of what were then called Long Range Patrols, the forerunner of the highly successful Long Range Desert Group that operated behind enemy lines to reconnoitre, deceive and provoke sufficient havoc to convince the Italians that the British were a far larger and more formidable foe than they actually were.

One of the many conflicts between Churchill and Wavell was over British Somaliland, a barren outpost of the British Empire bordering the Red Sea that was attacked on 4 August 1940 by an Italian invasion force of twenty-five thousand men. Churchill was unwilling to cede another piece of the empire without a fight, while Wavell argued that the place was indefensible, with a minuscule garrison of only five battalions. But the general agreed to try even though he believed it was an impossible task. As far back as September 1939 it had been obvious that a British policy of defending the port and capital of Berbera was futile and, as Ismay later put it, would make it 'reasonably certain we would get the worst of both worlds'.

By mid-August 1940 the Italians had compelled another mini-Dunkirk by the Royal Navy. The British garrison was vastly outnumbered defending territory of no strategic value whatever, yet its withdrawal infuriated Churchill. Although Italian losses were about eight times higher, he complained to Eden that British casualties were too low and must therefore suggest a lack of will and leadership on the part of the commander, Major General A. R. Godwin-Austen. In separate memos to Eden he first questioned Godwin-Austen's 'obstinacy and vigour in resistance', then demanded his suspension from duty and the convening of a court of inquiry. His complaints conveniently ignored a memo he had sent to Eden and Dill ten days earlier in which he wrote: 'The evacuation of Somaliland is enforced upon us by the enemy, but is none the less strategically convenient.'

Strategy and courage on the field of battle were two different things for Churchill – the latter often overriding the former. He therefore signalled Wavell, directing him to suspend Godwin-Austen and establish a court of inquiry. He also accused Wavell of breaking his pledge to resist the Italian invasion of Somaliland. Stung by Churchill's ill-considered rebuke, Wavell not only refused to set up the court of inquiry but in his reply also bluntly suggested that 'a big butcher's bill [in defending Somaliland] was not necessarily evidence of good tactics.' Churchill was enraged; Dill later revealed to Wavell that 'this telegram and especially the last sentence roused Winston to greater anger than he had ever seen in him before.' Desmond Morton also noted Churchill's ill temper, and remarked that 'the ill-concealed satisfaction of all three Chiefs of Staff and others who saw this reply did not do anything to mitigate his fury. And, of course, he knew in his heart that Wavell was right and that his own telegram was . . . unforgivable.' However, by standing up to Churchill and defending his subordinate, Wavell sent his own standing with the prime minister plummeting to what has been described as 'the point of no return'.

Churchill does not seem to have given serious thought to the alternative if Wavell had elected to defend British Somaliland and had needlessly lost his entire force. What made his meddling in this instance even more appalling is that it was based solely on the presumption that low British casualties were evidence that the commander had failed to fight hard enough and had thus dishonoured the British army.

Wavell's guarded emotions and his inability to see the need for keeping Churchill happy – and thus off his back – were fatal to satisfying a warlord prone to riding roughshod over others, particularly generals whom he distrusted. In short, Churchill required special handling that Wavell was unwilling to appreciate, despite Dill's advice. Even when Wavell later scored a major victory against the Italians, Churchill managed to find fault.

Benito Mussolini had been waiting for the Germans to invade England, but when there was no invasion by September he ordered Marshal Rodolfo Graziani, the commander of the Tenth Army in North Africa, to invade Egypt with the object of capturing the Suez Canal. On 13 September seven Italian divisions and three hundred tanks struck, compelling O'Connor's undermanned Western Desert Force to fight delaying actions as it retreated into Egypt. In three days the Italians advanced some sixty miles and captured the coastal city of Sidi Barrani. However, instead of advancing towards the British bastion of Mersa Matruh, eighty miles further east, while he still had the initiative, Graziani halted. Plagued by supply shortages and a lack of real mobility, the Tenth Army dug in around Sidi Barrani, inviting a British counterstroke.

Buoyed up by the arrival in late September of those 150 badly needed tanks from England, Wavell ordered his staff to draw up plans for a counter-offensive into Cyrenaica (eastern Libya). Thus was born Operation Compass, a plan to attack the Italian army in the Western Desert that was hatched in the greatest secrecy, its very existence kept from Churchill until Eden conveyed the information to him after visiting the Middle East in late October. Whether or not it was wise for Wavell to have kept Churchill in the dark is debatable; he did so fearing the prime minister's meddling and the inevitable pressure to speed up the operation. When Eden briefed a closed session of the War Cabinet Defence Committee on the plan, 'Every one of us could have jumped for joy,' said Ismay, 'but Churchill could have jumped twice as high.' Purring 'like six cats', the prime minister exclaimed, 'At long last we are going to throw off the intolerable shackles of the defensive. Wars are won by superior will-power. Now we will wrest the initiative from the enemy and impose our will on him.' The plan was approved 'without a moment's hesitation', but, as Wavell had anticipated, signals from the prime minister began piling up on his desk in Cairo, including one on 26 November in which Churchill interjected his own views of how the operation should be carried out. Wavell, he admonished, should have plans 'for moving troops and also reserves forward by sea in long hops along the coast', as well as establishing new bases to supply them.

Britain's fortunes seemed to perk up – particularly at sea. The nucleus of Mussolini's fleet was anchored at the Taranto naval base, the object of a surprise attack by twenty-one Swordfish torpedo bombers launched from the carrier HMS *Illustrious* on the night of 12 November 1940. Three battleships were torpedoed and several others damaged. The following day, fearing further losses, the remaining Italian warships scattered out of harm's way to Naples. At a stroke the threat to British convoys posed by the Italians evaporated, leaving the Royal Navy the dominant naval power in the Mediterranean.

The world took note. In Japan, the architect of Pearl Harbor, Admiral Isoroku Yamamoto, the commander in chief of the Combined Fleet, and his naval planners closely studied the potential of a carrier-based surprise aerial attack. In addition to planting the seeds of what became the Japanese plan to bomb Pearl Harbor, Taranto also demonstrated that the battleship had become increasingly obsolete in modern naval warfare.

Churchill, meanwhile, became fixated on Compass and daily thrust himself into the picture, aiming much of his displeasure at Wavell, who he believed was thinking too small. If Wavell 'is not hurling in his whole available forces with furious energy, he will have failed to rise to the height of circumstances,' he declared, adding, 'I never "worry" about action, but only about inaction.' As he was prone to do, however, Churchill 'magnified the potential results out of all proportion', said General Kennedy, director of military operations. Completely incapable of understanding logistics, 'He fretted at the delays which are inseparable from the preparation of modern fighting forces, and he pressed us incessantly to "grapple with the enemy" . . . [and] refused to recognize the hard realities of the problem of supply in the desert. He urged that operations should begin against Abyssinia from Kenya, regardless of the vast distances.' When Dill interjected facts rather than fantasy, Churchill became petulant, suggesting that British inaction was embarrassing given that the Greeks had successfully resisted an Italian invasion in October.

Churchill began to worry about the defence of Crete, and the War Office was deluged with memos providing very precise instructions about what Wavell was to do, including the exact number of battalions he was to employ in the island's defence. Such blatant interference with Wavell in his role as commander in chief, Middle East, led Dill to convene the chiefs of staff, who met with Churchill almost immediately. In this instance the chiefs prevailed, and a telegram was sent to Wavell that drew his attention to the need to secure Crete while leaving to his discretion the size of the force he employed.

Compass was not Churchill's only fixation. In December, spurred by Roger Keyes, he became obsessed with using a commando force to seize the tiny windswept island of Pantelleria, sixty-two miles off the south-west coast of Sicily and only fifty miles from Tunisia. An island of largely volcanic rock, it offered no particular benefit to the British in 1940, but to Churchill it represented the removal of an obstruction to Royal Navy operations in the Mediterranean. The chiefs pointed out that its seizure not only offered little military advantage but also would have saddled the Admiralty with a far greater defensive problem. Pound and Cunningham strongly objected to the operation and were supported by Dill, who thought it too small a prize to risk failure.

At a contentious meeting on the night of 4 December, Churchill refused to give in without a fight, and considerable time was wasted in argument before the chiefs eventually prevailed. Dill emerged from the encounter so angry at what he deemed Churchill's unwarranted criticism of the army that he stormed out and refused to remain afterwards, even declining to have a drink with him. 'What he said about the Army tonight I can never forgive,' he protested to John Kennedy.

Pantelleria was not the last insignificant island that would obsess Churchill during the war. The Allies eventually captured it in June 1943, by which time its importance had increased because of its valuable airfield, which was needed to support aerial operations against Sicily.

*

The ill feeling between Churchill and Wavell was temporarily forgotten with the launching of Operation Compass in the pre-dawn hours of 9 December. A masterstroke conceived by Wavell and brilliantly carried out by O'Connor, Compass was originally designed to expel the Italians from Egypt and quickly outstripped the expectations of its architects when, with lightning speed, it turned instead into a full-scale offensive. Although it was barely a third the size of the Italian Tenth Army, O'Connor's Western Desert Force slammed through a gap in the Italian flank south of Sidi Barrani and along the coast in a two-pronged attack. Tanks of the 7th Armoured Division and the 4th Indian Division caught the Italians by surprise as they isolated and rolled up their strongpoints, causing chaos and the complete disorganization of Graziani's forces. Compass was the result of six months of hard training and imaginative planning. It was also highly risky and required an approach march of some sixty miles in secrecy that stretched O'Connor's logistical resources to the limit.

At this early stage Wavell modestly called it merely a raid, and what occurred after that would depend on the supply line and the availability of captured petrol to fuel his tanks and vehicles. During the first three days of the operation, ably supported by the RAF and the Royal Navy, O'Connor's tanks and infantry retook Sidi Barrani, captured 38,300 Italians and seized or knocked out seventy-three tanks and 433 guns. The Long Range Desert Group harassed and harried the Italians, creating even more chaos in their ranks. By mid-December the remaining elements of Graziani's disorganized army had retreated into Libya.

The war in the desert offered endless possibilities for men of vision daring to operate without the usual impediments imposed by the presence of cities or civilians. In the vast, empty wastelands of Egypt and Libya, warfare was reduced to its most fundamental elements of fire and manoeuvre. North Africa was a great testing ground where imaginative commanders like O'Connor and, very soon, Erwin Rommel succeeded, while others failed. Compass was also a classic example of successful three-dimensional warfare and battlefield deception. What Wavell had learned from his service under Allenby paid off handsomely.

When reports from Cairo began arriving in London, Churchill had plenty to be pleased about. Only after the magnitude of Compass had become clear did Churchill ask to be given copies of two of Wavell's books, one of which dealt with the campaigns in Palestine.

Although the success of Operation Compass sent a signal, however small, that Britain would fight Hitler and Mussolini to the bitter end, Christmas 1940 became a particularly grim time in London, a city without the voices of children, some 80 per cent of whom had been evacuated to the countryside or to Canada and the United States. Also silent by government order were the church bells, which would be rung only to warn of an invasion. And just as Churchill, and indeed all of Britain, rejoiced over O'Connor's great victory in North Africa, the Germans delivered the strongest reminder yet that control of the war was still in their hands. For three precious days after Christmas they refrained from bombing, but the calm ended with the huge firebombing raid of 29 December that was rivalled only by the Great Fire of 1666. This devastating raid resulted in some fifteen hundred fires, the majority of which were in the hardest-hit area, the City of London, where the flames ravaged one whole square mile, destroying the Guildhall and damaging or destroying other famous landmarks. Amid the flames stood the magnificent spectacle of St Paul's Cathedral, which, although damaged, somehow survived the onslaught to become a symbol of Britain's defiance and resilience. 'The streets were lit up by fires,' recalled John Kennedy. 'The whole horizon was aglow over the City.' The Blitz would continue in full fury until 11 May 1941.

On a positive note, it had become clear by the end of 1940 that Churchill's position as both political and military leader was now securely established. His principal rival, Halifax, was soon to be exiled to Washington, and there was no one else capable of challenging or willing to challenge him. He was the face and the voice of Britain in both word and deed. That Churchill was often irksome, demanding and intolerant was a small price to pay for his heart, his determination and his will to win. Nor had nearly seven months in office softened him in the slightest. Eric Seal's proposal to give the hardworking staff of No. 10 a week off at Christmas merely incensed the prime minister, who decreed that work would go on as usual, with only an hour and half given off to attend religious services.

And what a year it had been. Under Churchill's guidance Britain had survived the fall of France, undergone a seamless change of government, saved the BEF, averted invasion, garnered American aid and held fast in the skies while rebuilding a shattered army and beginning to find men to fight the impending battles. The burden Churchill carried is almost beyond description. To assess his achievements in 1940 one has only to ask this question: what would have happened had he not become Britain's war leader?

Churchill and Eden spoke about 'the dark days of the summer'. As Eden recorded, 'I told him that Portal and I had confessed to each other that in our hearts we had both despaired at one time. Winston said: "yes. Normally I wake up buoyant to face the new day. Then I awoke with dread in my heart." '

During Churchill's first months as warlord he began the process of ruthlessly weeding out and replacing deadwood military officers, re-shaping the three armed services into the most cohesive force in British history. And while some of his appointments were mistaken, under his leadership the services were at last beginning the vital process of working together as a single fighting team. Joint service operations and co-operation had been born at Dunkirk, and despite disasters and defeats that lasted well into 1942, lessons were learned that culminated in history's greatest and most successful amphibious landing in 1944.

Conspicuously missing at the end of 1940 was a strategic plan for victory. When Dill asked Kennedy to prepare a study of how Britain could win the war, the general replied: 'I am sure we can make a plan for not *losing* the war; but the only way to win it quickly is to get America in – we must concentrate on that.' Kennedy was right, and if holding out can be termed a strategy, it was the course Churchill set for Britain. The war could not be won in the Middle East, and while it would not be lost there either, to cede this region to the Axis powers would have been a mortifying setback. Moreover Churchill never equated the need to buy time with inaction. 'War is a constant struggle and must be waged from day to day,' he wrote. 'It is only with some difficulty and within limits that provision can be made for the future . . . Nevertheless, there must be a design and theme for bringing the war to a victorious end in a reasonable period.' There was obviously no such plan at this uncertain stage of the war, and one would not evolve until the United States became a participant.

In December, Churchill wrote to Beaverbrook that he thought things would look much better in a year. As he reminded the House of

Commons, 'It is no good hoping and asking for immediate conclusions. We are still a half-armed nation fighting a well-armed nation.' However, with American aid, 'we hope that we shall become well armed during the course of 1941.' Unfortunately 1941 would not be the year of deliverance.

43

The President and the
'Former Naval Person'

*Nobody enjoyed the war as much as Churchill did. He loved the derring-do and
rushing around. He got Roosevelt all steamed up in his boy's book of adventure.*
— War Correspondent Martha Gellhorn

Winston churchill once said of Franklin Delano Roosevelt, 'No man
ever wooed a woman as I wooed that man for England's sake.'
Churchill's first telegrams to FDR after he became prime minister were
the continuation of a relationship that had begun quite informally in
the summer of 1918, when the two men were introduced to each other
at a banquet held at Gray's Inn in London. Roosevelt was then an
assistant secretary of the navy and Churchill was minister of munitions.
Churchill did not recollect their brief exchange but Roosevelt did,
recalling with some distaste that the Englishman had been rather
brusque, and that ever since 'I had always disliked him . . . He had acted
like a stinker.'

Despite their disparate personalities and Roosevelt's past opinions,
war drew them together in a shared hatred of its horrors. 'I have seen
war on land and sea,' said Roosevelt. 'I have seen blood running from
the wounded . . . men coughing out their gassed lungs . . . the dead in
the mud . . . I hate war.'

In 1933 Churchill hosted a dinner at Chartwell attended by one of
the new president's sons, James Roosevelt. During the meal he asked
each of his guests to articulate his or her fondest wish. When it was his
own turn, Churchill said: 'I wish to be Prime Minister and in close and
daily communication by telephone with the President of the United
States. There is nothing we could not do if we were together.' And,
while this pronouncement may well have been flattery for the ears of
James Roosevelt, there was no mistaking Churchill's growing admiration

for FDR and for his courage in overcoming the crippling affliction of polio to become an effective president.

It is appropriate to call the association of Churchill and Roosevelt 'the special relationship'. However, although they formed a friendship based on a common goal of defeating the original 'axis of evil', there was always an element of wariness between them, hardly surprising given that each possessed a titanic ego. Charming though Churchill was around Roosevelt, he was single-minded. The presidential historian Michael Beschloss observes that 'Churchill pursued this as a courtship. He knew that if there was this relationship, almost like lovers, that Roosevelt might be encouraged to take a couple of chances in helping Britain ... The danger to Churchill was that he was dealing with an American president [who] was immensely cold-blooded. Roosevelt was not likely to be carried away by sentimentality. And the amazing thing is that as canny and at times cynical as Churchill was, he allowed himself to be carried away by Roosevelt in a way that at times in this relationship turned out to be very bruising.'

Roosevelt's anxiety about the rise of German militarism in Europe had by early 1939 become so pressing that he came to see both France and Britain as America's shield and 'front line of defence' while still believing that containing Hitler remained their problem to resolve. Roosevelt's distrust of Chamberlain's leadership added to his fears, 'which is why, on the outbreak of war in Europe, he opened up contacts with Churchill ... inviting him to write personally and outside normal channels concerning "anything you want me to know about"'. Churchill, signing his messages to Roosevelt 'Former Naval Person', willingly obliged. Nevertheless political and national needs came first in their relationship. Some in Washington were wary of Churchill and his reputation as a buccaneer and a heavy drinker. In early 1940 Roosevelt sent Assistant Secretary of State Sumner Welles to Europe and Britain to find out if peace was possible. Although fascinated and impressed by Churchill, Welles thought that he was drunk when they first met but that he appeared to sober up during nearly two hours of non-stop oratory. Other stories of Churchill's reputed drinking made the rounds of Washington, among them gossip from Interior Secretary Harold Ickes, who opined that even though Churchill was supposedly under the influence half the time, he was still the best man in Britain.

In October 1940 Churchill dined with Dowding, Pound and the new chief of the air staff, Air Chief Marshal Sir Charles Portal. Portal had replaced Sir Cyril Newall, whom Churchill had never warmed to and who was elevated to a peerage and conveniently exiled to New Zealand as governor general. As he said good night, Churchill said he was sure that Britain would win the war but confessed he did not then see clearly quite how it would be done. The army was rapidly being transformed, the Royal Navy remained a potent force at sea, and the RAF was intact and would continue strongly to resist the Luftwaffe. In 1941 there would be retaliation on a limited scale. However, until the United States could be persuaded to join the fight, Churchill understood that Britain could not possibly win the war alone.

With the United States neutral for the foreseeable future, gaining precious time to rearm, retrain and continue receiving badly needed armaments remained Britain's greatest need. Major General John Kennedy recalled vividly the occasion in 1941 when Churchill held up his hand, his fingers spread, saying, 'Here is the hand that is going to win the war: a Royal flush – Great Britain, the Sea, the Air, the Middle East, American aid.'

In January 1941 Roosevelt sent Harry Hopkins to Britain as his special envoy. Until briefed by Brendan Bracken, Churchill had never heard of him. Thereafter he made it a point to treat Hopkins as a VIP, and as Ismay records, 'to constitute himself Hopkins' personal guide, philosopher, and friend'. To emphasize his intentions he sent Bracken as his personal emissary to Poole in Dorset to meet Hopkins's BOAC seaplane, which arrived in England from Lisbon on a dismal winter day. The man who emerged from the sea tender seemed ill and near collapse. Escorted by Bracken, Hopkins was led to a Pullman carriage expressly ordered by Churchill. The train arrived at Waterloo Station in the midst of an air raid. Only moments after it had passed through Clapham Junction, a favourite target of the Luftwaffe, hundreds of incendiary bombs fell on the railway line. As he was driven to Claridge's Hotel in the dark, Harry Hopkins found himself experiencing for himself the maelstrom of the Blitz.

Ismay was astonished by Hopkins's 'deplorably untidy' appearance and his obvious debility. 'He seemed so ill and frail that a puff of wind would blow him away. But we were soon to learn that in that sickly frame there burned a fire which no flood could quench. He was completely selfless ... He loathed Hitler ... Not even Churchill was more single-minded than Harry Hopkins that Nazism should be remorselessly crushed.' A key player in the New Deal administration since 1933, when FDR brought him to Washington to take charge of the Federal Emergency Relief Administration during the Great Depression, Hopkins was the president's confidant, adviser and policy maker. Despite his perpetual ill health, he faithfully served Roosevelt as no other. The two men were so close that after the death of his second wife in 1937 Hopkins moved into the White House.

Hopkins's mission was to sound out Churchill and to deliver a personal promise from Roosevelt that, as he told the British leader during their first three-hour meeting at No. 10, 'The President is determined that we shall win the war together. Make no mistake about it. He has sent me here to tell you that at all costs and by all means we will carry you through, no matter what happens to him – there is nothing that he will not do so far as he has human power.'

Privately Hopkins explained his mission to England to Edward R. Murrow. 'I've come here to try and find a way to be a catalytic agent between two prima donnas.' Hopkins believed it was inevitable that these two powerful egos would clash: 'I want to try to get an understanding of Churchill and of the men he sees after midnight.'

What made this fateful meeting even more unusual is that before he arrived in England, Hopkins had had serious reservations about Churchill, whom he saw more as a rival to FDR than as a friend. Churchill would have to show that Britain was doing all it could before Roosevelt would render all-out assistance. Before he left Washington he had been advised by Jean Monnet, a French financier and expert in economic matters, 'to concentrate on Churchill . . . no one else matters.' Hopkins wearied of hearing 'about the almighty Churchill and exclaimed, "I suppose Churchill is convinced that he's the greatest man in the world!"' After their first meeting Hopkins came away convinced of Churchill's sincerity and unwavering commitment to the defeat of Hitler and remarked, 'God, what a force that man has.' After one long evening of food, drink and deep discussion, Hopkins retired to his bedroom, relaxed in a chair and was heard to mutter: 'Jesus Christ! What a man!'

Churchill's wooing of Hopkins paid off handsomely. Despite their diverse backgrounds – Hopkins came from poverty, Churchill from privilege – the two men immediately took to one another. For all his considerable physical weakness, when it came to the war Harry Hopkins fully matched Churchill's intensity. After their first meeting on 10 January, he recorded that Churchill 'believes that this war will never see great forces massed against one another. He took me up to the Cabinet room where there was "a better fire" – and showed me on the map where the convoys are coming through to Liverpool and Glasgow – and the route the German bombers are taking from France to Norway to intercept the ships.'

From doubt came admiration and a bonding of the two men. Hopkins was captivated by Churchill's take-charge approach to the war, which manifestly contrasted with Roosevelt's penchant for relative seclusion, daytime work and a full night's sleep. Whereas FDR left the details of running the war to others, Hopkins saw Churchill in full flow, issuing a flurry of orders, studying maps, being briefed, firing off instructions to generals and ministers, all the while carrying on discussions about the wars and battles of history 'from Cannae to Gallipoli' – and leaving exhausted aides in his wake.

Hopkins was also wined and dined at Ditchley Park, spent three weekends with Churchill at Chequers, and was taken to various places to see the war's effects at first hand. At dinner on a Saturday evening, Churchill launched into one of his eloquent, long-winded monologues, this one tracing the history of the war to the present, what Oliver Lyttelton later wrote was 'the substance of his first two volumes of the Second World War'. Asked what he thought Roosevelt would say 'to all this', Hopkins paused for so long that Lyttelton feared that his reply would not be favourable. To everyone's delight he said that he did not believe the president would 'give a dam[n] for all that. You see, we're only interested in seeing that that Goddamn sonofabitch, Hitler, gets licked.' Lyttelton was not alone in believing that 'at that moment a friendship was cemented which no convulsion ever undermined.' At Dover, Hopkins overheard one worker say to another of Churchill, 'There goes the bloody British Empire.'

At the end of 1940 Churchill appointed Halifax the new ambassador the United States, at a stroke deftly marginalizing Halifax by removing a source of opposition to a post where he would play second fiddle to the prime minister's strong relationship with FDR. Churchill took Hopkins to Scapa Flow to view the fleet and to send Halifax off to Washington with full military pomp aboard the new battleship HMS *King George V*, in what has been cynically described as a 'first-class funeral' for Britain's former foreign secretary.

From his hotel room in Claridge's, Hopkins wrote a letter to Roosevelt that became the glue that would cement the Churchill–Roosevelt relationship. 'The people here are amazing from Churchill down,' he wrote, 'and if courage alone can win – the result will be inevitable. But they need our help desperately, and I am sure you will permit nothing to stand in the way . . . Churchill is the gov't. in every sense of the word – he controls the grand strategy and often the details – labor trusts him – the army, navy, air force are behind him. I cannot emphasize too strongly that he is the one and only person over here with whom you need to have a full meeting of the minds.' Hopkins added: 'Churchill wants to see you – the sooner the better.' He also assured FDR that 'I cannot believe it is true that Churchill dislikes either you or America – it just doesn't make sense.'

Churchill's genuine liking for Harry Hopkins was never more in evidence than in February 1944, when one of his three sons, eighteen-year-old marine private Stephen P. Hopkins, was killed during the invasion of Kwajalein, in the Marshall Islands. Churchill sent this touching note (the lines, from the penultimate scene of *Macbeth*, were rendered by a calligrapher in elaborate antique script):

Stephen Peter Hopkins
Age 18

'*Your son, my lord, has paid a soldier's debt;*
He only liv'd but till he was a man;
The which no sooner had his prowess confirm'd
In the unshrinking station where he fought,
But like a man he died.'
Shakespeare

To Harry Hopkins from Winston S. Churchill
13 February 1944

What made Harry Hopkins such an important element in the Churchill–Roosevelt relationship was summed up by Pamela Harriman: 'Hopkins had the extraordinary ability to make WSC feel Hopkins was working for him at the same time he was working for FDR.'

Shortly after Hopkins returned to the United States, Roosevelt's Republican opponent in the forthcoming election, Wendell Willkie, also visited Britain. Before he departed Washington, Roosevelt asked if would deliver a personal message to Churchill. It was a verse from Henry Wadsworth Longfellow that Roosevelt knew by heart. It would serve as evidence of their growing bond:

Dear Churchill,

Wendell Willkie will give this to you . . . I think this verse applies to you people as it does to us:

> 'Sail on, O ship of state!
> Sail on, O Union strong and great!
> Humanity with all its fears,
> With all the hopes of future years,
> Is hanging breathless on thy fate!'

As ever yours Franklin D. Roosevelt

Touched by Roosevelt's message, Churchill demonstrated his gratitude by reading it on the radio on 9 February, using the occasion to send a further affirmation to Hitler: 'We shall not fail or falter; we shall not weaken or tire. Neither the sudden shock of battle nor the long-drawn trials of vigilance with wear us down.' He concluded by declaring: 'Give us the tools and we will finish the job.'

Thanks to Hopkins's passionate call for American support of Britain Roosevelt managed to get the Lend-Lease Act of March 1941 through a stubborn Republican Congress that was still wedded to a policy of American neutrality. Officially the act authorized FDR to sell, give away, exchange, lease, lend or transfer title to anything that he deemed no longer vital to America's defence. By the autumn of 1941 this was translated into $1 billion in aid for Britain. Lend-Lease also authorized similar support for China, Free France and the Soviet Union and, unlike the arrangement in the First World War, carried no requirement for reimbursement.

A. J. P. Taylor called it 'the most important decision of Churchill's career, and indeed of modern British history'. However, when he accepted Lend-Lease Churchill also ceded economic independence by relying on the United States to provide the means to fight on. What Roosevelt did not offer or intend Lend-Lease to represent was American backing to restore Britain's position in the world. If, as John Maynard Keynes said, 'We threw good housekeeping to the winds,' it hardly mattered, for, in the end, Churchill really had no choice except to ensure Britain's survival by whatever means necessary. And while Lend-Lease ensured a flow of military supplies and hardware to Britain, the United States continued to remain neutral.

Hitler tightened his grip on Europe in 1941. Puppet governments were established, and slave labour was sent to concentration camps, many of them established in occupied countries to facilitate the continued roundup and murder of Jews, Gypsies and other so-called undesirables. Camps such as Auschwitz-Birkenau, Flossenbürg, Mauthausen-Gusen, Dachau and Ravensbrück became images of the worst evils of mankind. There was little Churchill could do about German hegemony except on a small scale against the Axis in the wastelands of northern Africa.

Less visibly, Britain was rapidly losing control of the Atlantic Ocean to German U-boats, auxiliary raiders and, until June 1941, Luftwaffe aircraft based in France and Norway, all of which were feasting on Allied merchant shipping faster than it could be replaced. The shortage of Royal Navy escort vessels enabled Admiral Dönitz's wolf packs to exact a mounting toll on convoys in the icy waters of the North Atlantic. Between September 1939 and the end of 1941, some 2,340 British and other Allied merchant ships were lost, primarily from U-boats and mines.

On the morning of 22 June 1941, the war took a savage turn when Hitler launched Operation Barbarossa, his massive, long-planned invasion of the Soviet Union, thus ending the non-aggression pact that had produced an uneasy, cynical marriage of convenience between the two totalitarian nations, each distrustful of the other even as they eagerly devoured a conquered Poland in 1939. Despite a warning from Churchill in April, Stalin refused to believe that Hitler was planning to invade, convinced instead that it was a ruse intended to bring him into the war.

More than three million German ground troops, supported by nearly 3,400 tanks and two thousand aircraft, swarmed over three fronts extending from the Black Sea to the Arctic, catching the Red Army flat-footed. However, the five-week delay – the invasion had originally been planned for mid-May – ultimately cost the Germans the war on the eastern front. Despite enormous setbacks the Red Army held the line in key sectors and managed to delay the German advance until winter, something Hitler had not planned for. Leningrad would hold out for nine hundred days, and although German spearheads advanced to within fifteen miles of the Soviet capital in October, Moscow also held.

In several respects Barbarossa was a blessing for Britain because it had drawn from France valuable resources that Hitler might otherwise have used to attack England if Sea Lion had been carried out in 1941. But with Hitler now preoccupied with defeating the Red Army, any interest in a cross-Channel invasion simply faded away. And with Russia suddenly an enemy of Germany instead of an ally, the war's entire focus turned eastward, buying crucial time for Britain. Suddenly the British had a new ally, albeit a treacherously unpredictable and uncomfortable one. After months of setbacks, firebombings, blackouts and deprivations, Churchill could declare to the British people, 'We are no longer alone.' Even though Britain had little to give, Churchill promised aid to Stalin.

In August, the face-to-face meeting with Roosevelt that Churchill had long sought was finally arranged. The two leaders agreed to meet in secret at windswept Placentia Bay, the site of the former French capital of Newfoundland. The journey was fraught with risk for both leaders, but for Churchill the possibility of extracting more aid and greater American participation overrode the considerable threat posed by the U-boats. 'Damn the risk,' he said. In the days leading up to his departure he became increasingly energized – almost boyish with enthusiasm. Although Inspector Thompson was not yet privy to the forthcoming journey, Churchill made no attempt to conceal his excitement, which was manifest in rare smiles, mysterious gestures and whispered words to others.

At Scapa Flow he boarded the battleship HMS *Prince of Wales* on 4 August for the five-day voyage to Newfoundland and the first of many meetings with Roosevelt. His usual routine did not change during the voyage; he read and dispatched messages, restlessly prowled the ship and held long meetings with the chiefs and Harry Hopkins, who was returning home from a mission to Russia.

On 9 August the *Prince of Wales* was due to rendezvous with the heavy cruiser USS *Augusta*, which was carrying Roosevelt. At dawn that morning Churchill appeared in his siren suit and stood alone deep in thought on an exposed quarterdeck, peering out to sea through the gloom, as if determined to be the first to spot the *Augusta* and its bevy of escort ships.

As the *Prince of Wales* sailed into the secure anchorage of Placentia Bay, a majestic scene unfolded. It was filled with US navy ships, large and small. At their centre was the *Augusta*, and as the British battleship steamed slowly around it, salutes were exchanged. From the *Augusta* a band played 'God Save the King' and from the *Prince of Wales* came the rousing strains of John Philip Sousa's 'Stars and Stripes Forever'.

Churchill was particularly concerned about the impression he would make on Roosevelt. 'I wonder if he will like me,' he mused to the special envoy W. Averell Harriman, a remark he repeated many times during the conference. (Like Harry Hopkins, Averell Harriman became both a friend and a trusted adviser to Churchill. In early 1941 Roosevelt had instructed him 'to go over to London' as his personal representative 'and recommend everything we can do, short of war, to keep the British Isles afloat'. Harriman also carried out a number of other important missions for Roosevelt, including acting as special envoy to the Middle East and to Moscow. This assignment was followed in 1943 by his appointment as US ambassador to the Soviet Union. During the Second World War, Britain never had a better friend than Averell Harriman.)

Roosevelt likewise wanted to learn everything he could about the Englishman. Secretary of Labor Frances Perkins was one of the few cabinet officers who had actually met Churchill. She described him as 'pigheaded in his own way', a man who kept his word but was not co-operative and often ignored advice; 'he dashes off and does what he wants to do . . . he's a leader rather than a committee man.' Roosevelt just laughed and, more than ever, looked forward to their meeting.

Churchill arrived for lunch with Roosevelt aboard the *Augusta* dressed once again in the dark-blue uniform of an Elder Brother of Trinity House. The ice was broken, and within a short time they were addressing each other as 'Franklin' and 'Winston'. After dinner that evening the president asked Churchill to address the assembled guests on the state of the war, 'sitting if he pleased'. Churchill chose to stand, somewhat formally, and emphasized the importance of England in the war, ending with the belief that the British Empire and the United States would establish an order of peace in the world when the war ended, 'a golden century' of prosperity. Roosevelt echoed his sentiments.

With great ceremony Roosevelt was piped aboard the *Prince of Wales* on Sunday morning, 10 August. Refusing to use his customary wheelchair, the president, assisted by his son Elliott, insisted on walking, willing himself forward on withered, polio-ravaged legs that responded only with the greatest physical effort. That day FDR managed to inspect a guard of honour and walk to the afterdeck, a triumph of courage that left him beaming.

Several hundred sailors of both navies were assembled on the British battleship, and civilian and military VIPs from both nations flanked the two leaders during a religious service carefully orchestrated by Churchill, down to the smallest detail, choosing what hymns would be sung, prayers recited and psalms read by American and British chaplains. In his diary John Martin described how 'hundreds of men from both fleets all mingled together, one rough British sailor sharing his hymn sheet with one American . . . It seemed a sort of marriage service between the two navies, already in spirit allies, though the bright peacetime paint and spit and polish of the American ships contrasted with the dull camouflage of the *Prince of Wales*, so recently in action against the *Bismarck*.'

Sitting in the shadow of the 14-inch guns of the *Prince of Wales*, both men were moved by what was perhaps the most special moment they were ever to share. As the Anglo-American gathering sang 'O God, Our Help in Ages Past' and 'For Those in Peril', concluding with 'Onward, Christian Soldiers', the tears coursed down Churchill's cheeks. Averell Harriman recorded: 'Although he stated he was not religious, he felt a divine power was bringing the two nations together.'

Back home in Britain, Churchill spoke affectingly in a radio broadcast about that special morning, asserting, 'We had the right to feel that we were serving a cause for the sake of which a trumpet has sounded from on high. When I looked upon that densely packed congregation of fighting men . . . facing the same dangers, it swept across me that here was the only hope, but also the sure hope of saving the world from measureless degradation.' In his memoirs Churchill called the occasion 'a great hour to live', but sombrely added, 'Nearly half those who sang there were soon to die.' Roosevelt shared Churchill's feelings and later said of that magical morning, 'If nothing else had happened while we were here, [it] would have cemented us.'

Four days of meetings and fellowship concluded on 12 August with the promulgation of what was called the Atlantic Charter, an eight-point press release that was a declaration of principles rather than a formally signed treaty. Broadly, it stated that neither Britain nor the United States sought territorial aggrandizement, that the nations of the world should have the freedom to choose their own governments, that, in order to enhance their economic advancement, they possessed the right to sail the seas unhindered, and that they must abandon the use of force. The charter did not commit the United States to war, but after Pearl Harbor in December 1941 it served as the basis for the United Nations Declaration, which articulated the war aims of the two Allies who were now joined together in an alliance to defeat the Axis powers.

Although the meeting at Placentia Bay did not result in a commitment that the United States would enter the war, it nevertheless achieved Churchill's goal of meeting the president in person and airing his and Britain's views. Whatever the differences, suspicions and divergent aims that beset them during the war – and there were many – what brought the two leaders together was an unyielding resolve to defeat Adolf Hitler. Ian Jacob's diary, however, reflected only gloom. The US navy, he wrote, believed that the war could be won as long as the Royal Navy did not lose it, and the US army was undermanned and ill equipped in 1941 to fight alongside anyone. Jacob could not find 'a single American officer who showed the slightest enthusiasm to be in the war on our side'.

While much has been made of the two leaders' special relationship and their partnership as allies, Robert E. Sherwood offers a caveat. 'It would be an exaggeration to say that Roosevelt and Churchill became chums at this conference or at any subsequent time. They established an easy intimacy . . . and also a degree of frankness in intercourse, which, if not quite complete, was remarkably close to it.' However, both men were politicians first and friends second, and the interests of their respective countries came first. From their frank man-to-man appraisal of each other they achieved 'a degree of admiration and sympathetic understanding of each other's professional problems that lesser craftsmen could not have achieved'. Roosevelt later gave Churchill the ultimate compliment when, at a particularly dismal time, he ended a cable with 'It is fun to be in the same decade with you.' In the autumn of 1940 Brendan Bracken spoke for both himself and Churchill when he wrote to his friend Eugene Meyer, the publisher of the *Washington Post*, 'England will never forget what America is doing for her.'

One evening Churchill personally introduced Inspector Thompson to Roosevelt, and then left them alone to chat. At one point the president bluntly inquired if Churchill was 'hard to handle.' With equal candour, no doubt recalling his nights guarding Churchill with bombs falling all around, Walter Thompson replied, 'Yes, sir. He's reckless and self-willed. Restraint of any kind is unendurable to him.' Roosevelt asked Thompson to 'take care of him. He's about the greatest man in the world. In fact he may very likely *be* the greatest. You have a terrible responsibility in safeguarding him.'

Eleanor Roosevelt first met Churchill in December 1941 when the two leaders convened a second conference, this time in Washington, and she never warmed to him during his stay at the White House. She thought he was dogmatic and chauvinistic, stayed up far too late at night, drank and smoked too much, and was having an adverse influence on her husband. Her grandson Curtis recalls, 'She saw in Churchill a male tendency to romanticize war . . . She remembered FDR in Europe after the First World War, knowing he would have traded absolutely everything to be one of the heroic soldiers wounded in battle.' The war correspondent Martha Gellhorn had a similar observation about the Churchill–Roosevelt relationship: 'Nobody enjoyed the war as much as Churchill did. He loved the derring-do and rushing around. He got Roosevelt all steamed up in his boy's book of adventure.'

Churchill had a mobile map room that accompanied him on his travels. When he saw it Roosevelt was captivated and ordered one created for him in a coatroom in the White House, which was quickly converted into a near-replica of the underground cabinet map room in London, manned around the clock, complete with maps whose displays were constantly being updated with coloured pins and grease-pencil battle lines. Special pins represented the location at every moment of Churchill, Stalin and the president – Churchill's in the shape of a cigar, Roosevelt's of a cigarette holder. Eleanor Roosevelt happened to peek inside once when the two leaders were deep in a spirited discussion in front of the maps. 'They looked like two little boys playing soldier. They seemed to be having a wonderful time, too wonderful in fact.'

However much Mrs Roosevelt disapproved of Churchill, the time the president and the prime minister spent together in Washington served to cement the relationship begun at Placentia Bay. Roosevelt's parting words in January 1942 were: 'Trust me to the bitter end.'

44
Mediterranean Misadventures

I hope, Jack, that you will preside at my court-martial.
— Wavell to Dill, April 1941,
after Rommel had driven the British from Cyrenaica

The year 1941 began on a high note with O'Connor's triumph in the Western Desert. However, no sooner had the Western Desert Force (now redesignated XXIII Corps) outflanked the Italians than Wavell pulled the rug from beneath him without warning by redeploying the veteran 4th Indian Division to East Africa and replacing it with the Australian 6th Division, a formation with no desert combat experience. This decision, reached even before the launch of Compass, was brought about in large part by pressure from Churchill to open a new front in East Africa in response to earlier successful Italian offensives. O'Connor was shocked and dismayed but carried on with his suddenly depleted force. Under his imaginative leadership, during its two-month, eight-hundred-mile rampage, his corps swept into Libya, giving the Italians no time to regroup before capturing Tobruk and Benghazi, and eventually all of Cyrenaica. O'Connor completed the capture of Cyrenaica by surprising the Italians and cutting off their retreat at Beda Fomm in early February, resulting in the taking of 20,000 POWs, 120 tanks and 200 guns, and leaving the Italian Tenth Army a shambles. Overall some 130,000 Italians were seized, along with 400 tanks and 1,292 guns, in what has been hailed as one of the British army's greatest victories of the war. Eden, back at the Foreign office after Halifax's removal but still closely involved in military affairs, gleefully spoofed Churchill's famous words by remarking, 'Never has so much been surrendered by so many to so few.'

Despite the encouraging news from the Middle East, Churchill remained unpredictable. When Wavell had telegraphed on 11 December 1940 that Sidi Barrani had fallen, Eden telephoned Churchill, who congratulated him on a great victory. The next morning, however, even as O'Connor was on the move, and before he had read a telegram outlining Wavell's future plans, Churchill, without knowledge of events there, complained to Eden that 'we were not pursuing [the] enemy and had much to say about missed opportunities.' Later that day he and Eden had another of their unpleasant encounters in which Churchill again maintained that British Somaliland ought to have been held. Eden voiced his displeasure: 'That is most ungenerous at this moment. You knew that we had not a gun there.' Furious, Churchill snapped: 'Whose fault is that?'

Churchill's congratulatory signal to Wavell on 13 December was an overt reminder of his expectations. 'Naturally, pursuit will hold the first place in your thoughts. It is at the moment when the victor is most exhausted that the greatest forfeit can be extracted from the vanquished.' He followed with a second telegram three days later extolling the 'glorious service to the Empire and to our cause . . . We are deeply indebted to you, Wilson and other Commanders whose fine professional skill and audacious leading have gained us the memorable victory of the Libyan desert. Your first objective must now be to maul the Italian Army and rip them off the African shore.'

Churchill also telegraphed the South African prime minister Jan Christiaan Smuts, one of his closest advisers and confidants during the war: 'Great credit is due to Wavell and Wilson for brilliant planning and execution . . . Wickedness is not going to reign.' The Italians, he predicted, were corn ripe for the sickle. 'Let us gather the harvest.' Smuts was one of modern history's greatest statesmen. An enemy during the Boer War but an ally in the First World War, when he commanded the British army in East Africa, he was not only a warrior but also a humanitarian. He and Churchill had been friends since 1917, when Smuts was a member of Lloyd George's Imperial War Cabinet and was instrumental in the creation of the RAF. As a field marshal in the British army, he filled a similar role in the Second World War as an important member of Churchill's War Cabinet. The League of Nations was built upon his design, and he re-created that role when he advocated and wrote the preamble for the United Nations Charter in 1945. What made Smuts such an important figure during the war was that, unlike men such as Beaverbrook and Lindemann whose advice was not always reliable, he was a steadying influence, someone to whom Churchill could turn for sound military and political counsel.

The great success of Compass was soon overtaken by decisions made by Wavell – and by Churchill – that had a far-reaching impact on the war in the Mediterranean. Wavell's decision to pull the 4th Indian Division eventually left O'Connor unable to continue operations that might otherwise have resulted in the capture of Tripoli and thereby have prevented (with the support of the Royal Navy) Rommel's Deutsche Afrika Korps from using the port city as a staging ground in February 1941. Although O'Connor obtained Wavell's permission to advance on Tripoli, another event would soon derail further British victories in the Western Desert. That event, combined with the reality that his undermanned force was stretched to its limits tactically and logistically, compelled O'Connor to halt his advance at El Agheila, well short of Tripoli.

Mussolini was determined to demonstrate to Hitler that the Italians were capable of achieving a military victory on their own, and on 28 October 1940 Italy invaded Greece from occupied Albania with superior forces. Instead of an easy victory, however, the Italians met strong resistance from the Greek army, which humiliated them by driving them back into southern Albania.

The threat to Greece, and the lure of being able to employ the RAF from Greek air bases to bomb the Romanian oil fields, prompted Churchill to make the most serious strategic misjudgment of the war in February 1941, when he ordered reinforcements sent from the Middle East to Greece in fulfilment of a 1939 undertaking to come to its aid. With German air and ground forces massing in Romania and on the Bulgarian border with Greece, Ultra intercepts pointed to an imminent German invasion of the Balkans. Although initially opposed to diverting any of his precious resources to aid Greece, by February 1941 Wavell had changed his mind and now supported intervention.

In London there was ambivalence over the merits of intervention. The question remained unresolved until well into February. The chiefs of staff were more concerned with securing the Western Desert flank than with aid to Greece, but would later split on the issue. Although the Greek government had refused British help, Churchill began to sway towards sending assistance, and on 12 February directed Wavell 'that your major effort must now be to aid Greece and/or Turkey. This rules out any serious effort against Tripoli . . . You should therefore make yourself secure in Benghazi and concentrate all available forces in the [Nile] Delta in preparation for movement to Europe.' Churchill specified that he 'hoped' Wavell would make available at least four divisions and air support to the Greeks.

In February he ordered Eden and Dill to the Middle East. Dill, however, felt his place was in London and objected to sending aid to Greece. The effect was explosive. 'I could see the blood coming up his great neck and his eyes began to flash.' Churchill growled, 'What you need out there is a Court Martial and a firing squad. Wavell has 300,000 men.' Fortunately Dill did not reply with words he later thought he should have uttered: 'Whom do you want to shoot exactly?'

In retrospect the importance of capturing Tripoli seems obvious. Not only would it have firmly established the British presence both on the ground and at sea and with air bases able to support operations against either German or Italian shipping. Even more important, it would have helped the RAF protect Malta and kept Rommel out of North Africa, with Tunisia the only alternative landing site for the Afrika Korps.

The curious tale of the Greek intervention took another strange turn when Wavell, Dill and Eden all supported it just as Churchill left the door wide open to change course by signalling Eden in Cairo on 20 February: 'Do not consider yourselves obligated to a Greek enterprise if in your hearts you feel it will only be another Norwegian fiasco. If no good plan can be made please say so.' Then he added, 'But of course you know how valuable success would be.' With the decision now taken to send reinforcements to Greece, combat formations were pulled from the desert. This removal disastrously changed the course of the war by spawning disastrous setbacks in Greece and North Africa – and later in Crete.

Initially the Greeks had resisted British intervention on the grounds that it would provoke Hitler into invading, a conviction that was ultimately proved correct when the Germans later declared that they had invaded because Greece had violated its neutrality by accepting British assistance. The Greek army was not large enough or sufficiently equipped to defend its borders with Bulgaria, Yugoslavia and Albania. Allied intervention was contingent upon a joint Anglo-Greek defence of the Aliákmon Line, the most important defensive sector in central Greece and the only place where a reasonable opportunity existed to hold off a superior force. Then, in March 1941, Germany compelled neutral Bulgaria to become an unwilling participant, and the Greeks reversed their previous promise by shifting to the defence of the border area three divisions that had been earmarked to fight alongside a British Expeditionary Force.

Dill and Eden visited Athens in March and were distressed by the Greek reversal. Dill privately acknowledged, 'I am afraid that there will be a lot of bloody noses this spring in the Aegean.' Nevertheless Eden pressed the case for Allied intervention, and it was his support, combined with Wavell's commitment, that carried the decision by the War Cabinet to sanction what was code-named Operation Lustre.

In early April an expeditionary force of sixty thousand British, Australian and New Zealand troops arrived and was deployed along the Aliákmon Line in northern Greece around Mount Olympus. The BEF in Greece was commanded by Jumbo Wilson and included the 6th Australian Division and the New Zealand Division, led by Bernard Freyberg.

The Greek venture was doomed to fail from the outset. The German army invaded Yugoslavia on 6 April and in nine hellish days brutally conquered the country. Luftwaffe bombs savaged Belgrade, and incendiaries killed an estimated seventeen thousand in three days of raids, nearly equalling the eighteen thousand Britons killed during the same period of 1941. The invasion of Greece from Bulgaria the same day was two-pronged, coming first in Macedonia, where the Greek army fought tenaciously along the Metaxas Line. A second Axis force of two Italian armies and a German motorized corps invaded via Albania and Yugoslavia on 18 April. The Germans quickly drove a wedge between the Greek First Army and the British Expeditionary Force, isolating the Greeks, who surrendered on 20 April.

Four days later the Germans launched a second invasion from Yugoslavia. Not only did they possess overwhelming armoured and infantry forces, but the Luftwaffe dominated the skies, outnumbering the eighty mostly obsolete RAF aircraft by ten to one. The Anglo-Greek forces were far too inadequate and had to defend too wide an area ever to have restrained massed, superior German forces that had complete air superiority. When it was put to the test, the notion that an Allied presence might somehow deter Hitler from invading Greece proved fanciful.

Despite fighting in mountainous terrain that usually favoured a defender, the BEF and the Greek army – because they had to fight separate battles – were no match for the Germans, and with no time to prepare defensive positions on the Aliákmon Line the BEF could do no more than slow the German juggernaut. Within forty-eight hours it became clear the BEF would have to disengage or be lost. Unlike the famous battle of 480 BC, when the Greeks heroically delayed the invading Persian army, the 1941 endeavour to emulate the Battle of Thermopylae saw a small force of British, New Zealand and Australian troops fight resolutely and hold up the German advance only long enough to cover the retreat and evacuation of the BEF. Relentlessly hammered by Stukas and Messerschmitts, the BEF retreated to the coast and an improvised emergency evacuation. Athens fell on 27 April, and the Nazi swastika was hoisted over the Acropolis. What had begun as a well-meant gesture to a friendly nation became instead yet another in the litany of British Second World War disasters.

Under pressure as great as that experienced by their Spartan forerunners, for the fourth but not the last time in the Second World War the British pulled off a 'Dunkirk' evacuation. A naval task force of Cunningham's Mediterranean fleet carried out the evacuation of Greece over a period of seven days, commencing the night of 24–25 April. In all 50,672 British and Dominion troops were evacuated, most of them off open beaches. Some twenty-seven thousand were redeployed to Crete; the remainder returned to Egypt. An estimated eight thousand had to be left behind and were captured, along with all but a few of the Greek troops. As in France, everything the troops could not carry had to be abandoned. There was also heavy loss of life when the Germans sank four transport ships and two destroyers.

However noble British intentions, the Greek campaign did not make good military sense and was little more than a futile political gesture. Governments usually cover up defeats and bad news, and the Greek debacle was no exception. It was argued that Britain had done its duty to an ally and despite a strategic defeat had by the law of unintended consequences delayed the invasion of Russia by a crucial five weeks. Even Churchill's reaction was mild when he signalled Wavell his congratulations and declared: 'We have paid our debt of honour with far less loss than I feared.' He naively concluded, 'Feel sure you are waiting to strike a blow. Enemy's difficulties must be immense.' Military forces reeling from a costly emergency sea evacuation are rarely in a position to strike back, and despite offering these words of encouragement Churchill could hardly have believed a British offensive of any kind even remotely possible. Even the usually supportive *Time* magazine commented, 'Wars are not won with return tickets. The British will not win World War II by squeezing miniature forces into defensive crannies at the last moment, and withdrawing them brilliantly. Some sardonic wit in London last week figured out what B. E. F. meant: Back Every Fortnight.'

While the Russians would eventually profit enormously from Hitler's delay in launching Operation Barbarossa in order to deal first with the Balkans, for Britain there were no such benefits. Churchill's decision to reinforce Greece was a catastrophic strategic misjudgment that was expensive in men and equipment and, most important of all, lost the initiative in the Western Desert by weakening Wavell's forces at exactly the wrong moment.

The key players in this debacle bore responsibility: Wavell for embracing it and for offering overly optimistic opinions on the effect on his command of losing the troops sent to Greece; and Eden for believing that the Greeks would jointly defend the Aliákmon Line. Eden not only never adequately evaluated the potential pitfalls of intervening without Greek support but also failed to seek the approval of the Australian and New Zealand governments before committing their troops. Combined with other ambiguities and misunderstandings in Anglo-Greek negotiations, his acceptance of a flawed mission for Allied troops doomed the venture to failure and persuaded Churchill to support intervention when it appears he was prepared to accept a recommendation from his advisers on the spot and from his Middle East commander in chief to call Operation Lustre off.

Churchill's failure to subject the decision to his usual exhaustive scrutiny was out of character. Instead he and the War Cabinet endorsed the recommendations of Eden and Wavell to intervene. In September 1941 Churchill remarked that the decision to send British and Dominion troops to Greece was the only (strategic) mistake his government had made. At the time, however, the blame soon fell on Wavell.

The oddest twist of this unhappy tale is that from the outset Churchill had anticipated that intervention would fail. Harry Hopkins came away from his meetings with him in early 1941 with the clear impression that the prime minister had all but written Greece off. He reported to FDR that Churchill had told him on 10 January that he expected Greece to be lost. 'He knows this will be a blow to British prestige' and 'will have a profound and disappointing effect in America as well'.

Another of Churchill's reasons for supporting the intervention in Greece was that it was hoped the presence of a unified force would draw Turkey out of its neutrality into the war on the Allied side, on the basis of a 1939 agreement with Britain and France that called for assistance in the event that a European power (that is, Germany or Italy) became militarily involved in the Mediterranean. The Turks, however, saw no benefit in involvement and rejected intervention, as did Yugoslavia. Sir Alexander Cadogan, permanent under-secretary at the Foreign Office, wrote that the whole idea was 'a diplomatic and strategic blunder of the first order' that had Eden going 'on a lemon-gathering expedition . . . I *wish* we could have gone on into Tripoli.'

After orchestrating the diversion of British and Dominion forces to Greece, on 18 April Churchill reversed himself and decreed that Libya was now Wavell's chief priority and that 'Crete will at first only be a receptacle of whatever can get there from Greece.' The problem with this directive is that it was a strategy without resources, and an afterthought in the wake of the Greek fiasco. The dynamics of the British situation in North Africa had already changed unalterably with the menacing presence of Lieutenant General Erwin Rommel's Afrika Korps. Rommel and the first combat elements arrived in Tripoli in February 1941.

The setbacks and uncertainties in the Mediterranean, combined with alarming losses of shipping in the Atlantic in 1941, were deeply troubling. Everyone in Whitehall seemed on edge. Churchill was particularly combative and the chiefs were increasingly unhappy. The reasons were not hard to find. British strategy in the Mediterranean in 1941 was centred on North Africa, where Churchill aimed to cut off Rommel's lifeline by sea and, using a fresh flow of armaments and men to reinforce Wavell, contain and destroy Axis forces in the desert. Yet it can be argued that shifting insufficient formations around from place to place, like moving chess pieces or plugging holes in a dyke, was not a strategy, and that attempting to fight in three diverse and distant places at the same time resulted in failure in two of them. Only in East Africa did the British regain lost territory; in the other two, Greece and Libya, the ineffectual support of one imperilled and ultimately lost the other.

During the 1940 campaign in France, Rommel had earned a reputation for boldness, and as a successful maverick commander who seized opportunities that included, whenever necessary, appropriating supplies from adjacent divisions – a practice that nearly earned him a court-martial and did earn his 7th Armoured Division the nickname 'Ghost Division'. Far from the OKH worriers in Berlin who wanted him restrained, in North Africa Rommel was able to give free rein to his penchant for disobeying restrictive orders, seizing the initiative and doing the unexpected that would soon earn him the admiring nickname 'Desert Fox'.

All that mattered was that Hitler admired him, and in March 1941 he awarded Rommel the Oak Leaves to the coveted Knight's Cross he had previously earned in France. 'I picked Rommel because he knows how to *inspire* his troops,' Hitler declared. Operationally and logistically Rommel was nominally under the command and control of the Italian high command; this was something of an irony in that he had fought against the Italians in the First World War. Hitler treated North Africa as essentially a sideshow to bolster the flagging morale of his Italian ally in Libya, and to prevent any further British advances into Tripolitania (western Libya), while the main German effort was directed towards Barbarossa.

Rommel's mission was to provide defensive support against an expected British offensive further into Libya. German intelligence as yet had no inkling that British forces had been recalled and transferred to Greece and East Africa, or that British and Australian forces in Cyrenaica had been ordered to halt and were undermanned, woefully organized and untrained in desert warfare. Worn out from months of unceasing hands-on command, O'Connor had been reassigned to Cairo, and the two senior British commanders facing Rommel were inexperienced and under orders from Wavell to fight a delaying action to Benghazi (and beyond, if necessary) if the Germans attacked.

The first brief skirmish on 24 February between reconnaissance elements of both sides occurred at El Agheila, a small coastal city on the southern lip of Cyrenaica, the furthest point that Rommel was permitted by Berlin to advance to – and coincidentally also the farthest British western outpost.

Churchill had demanded guarantees from Wavell that pulling out troops for Greece would not imperil his forces in Cyrenaica. Ismay recounts that 'Wavell was reassuring' despite growing concern in London over reports of German armoured units and reinforcements disembarking in Tripoli. The British learned through Ultra on 3 March that Rommel was commanding the German force. Wavell, however, seemed confident that the enormous distances and logistical consider- ations that required resupply from Tripoli would inhibit Rommel; there- fore 'no large-scale attack was likely to develop against him *before the end of the summer.*'

Then Rommel rudely shattered this illusion. He began with a small- scale attack on El Agheila on 20 March. Churchill cabled Wavell to say that he presumed 'you are only waiting for the tortoise to stick his head out far enough before chopping it off. It seems extremely important to give them an early taste of our quality.' Neither Churchill nor the chiefs of staff were aware of just how dangerously insecure the western flank had become. However, when Wavell visited Cyrenaica on 17 March, he came away 'anxious and depressed' by the realization not only that, until he saw it for himself, he had not understood the nature of the terrain nor how indefensible it really was, but also that his new desert commander, Lieutenant General Philip Neame, although a brave soldier and the holder of a Victoria Cross, lacked experience in desert warfare and exuded pessimism. Equally troubling were Neame's flawed tactical dispositions, which led to Wavell's frank admission, 'I had nothing left in the bag.'

By stripping his desert force, Wavell had played a very precarious poker hand that was about to be called by Rommel. Wavell admitted his predicament when he replied to Churchill's entreaty to counterattack. Having believed the Italians incapable of a counter-offensive and the Germans unlikely to risk sending a large armoured force to North Africa, he wrote, 'I have to admit to having taken considerable risk in Cyrenaica . . . in order to provide maximum support for Greece.'

Wavell's irreversible miscalculation was made to order for the aud- acious Erwin Rommel. After weeks waiting for a British offensive that never came, Rommel sensed that the British front was thinly held, and that with speed and surprise it was ripe for the taking. Despite orders that he was there only to bolster the Italians, it was simply not Rommel's style to go on the defensive. At the end of March he disobeyed his orders and seized the initiative. The Afrika Korps, although not yet at full strength, slammed into the British in Cyrenaica like a whirlwind. The more the British gave ground, the harder Rommel pushed and the further his tanks and infantry advanced against weak opposition. Benghazi and Gazala fell, and by early April the Afrika Korps was investing the defences of the fortress of Tobruk and threatening to cut off the retreat of the reeling British.

Wavell had every intention of replacing Neame with his best desert general, but instead agreed to O'Connor's request that he function in an advisory role to Neame, who proved no match for battle-tested German commanders. It was a decision both O'Connor and Wavell were to regret deeply. Neame reserved his greatest blunder for the night of 6 April when, against O'Connor's advice, their vehicle took a wrong turn in the desert and sped right into the hands of a German reconnaissance unit. O'Connor remained a prisoner until September 1943, when he escaped from an Italian POW camp near Florence. Although he was never again the same vibrant leader when he became a corps commander in north-west Europe in 1944–5, the seriousness of O'Connor's loss in 1941 was soon borne out by the failures of a succession of revolving-door desert commanders.

The 9th Australian Division defended the fortress of Tobruk, a bleak and unforgiving place more heavily populated by scorpions, mosquitoes, flies and sand fleas than people. Rommel's initial attempts to penetrate the strongpoints ringing the town (strongpoints originally constructed by the Italians) were unsuccessful. For the time being he elected to bypass Tobruk and, after being ordered by Berlin to await the arrival of a fresh panzer division and assemble his forces on the Libya–Egypt border, he drove the remaining British units in Cyrenaica back to Mersa Matruh. Not only were the spectacular gains of Compass lost in a complete reversal of what had begun so successfully the previous December, but the heroic thirty-thousand-man Tobruk garrison was now isolated. It would resist tenaciously for the next 242 days, the longest siege in British military history.

Tobruk now became the linchpin of North Africa, a prize that would frustrate and exhilarate both Rommel and Churchill. Its defence was the one positive thing Churchill could cling to in the summer of 1941. As his countrymen were retreating to Tobruk, the Australian prime minister, Robert Menzies, observed in his diary on 8 April: 'The generals of the War Office are still behind the times. "We have so many divisions" – as if divisions counted. Armour and speed count, and when we catch up to that idea, we will catch up to the Germans. Only tonight I was horrified to hear Churchill saying, apropos of Tobruk to which we are retreating and where we hope to make a stand, "If stout hearted men with rifles cannot hold these people until the guns come up, I must revise my ideas of war." Well, he should revise them quickly!'

Wavell flew into the besieged city on 8 April and ordered it held at all costs, knowing full well that Churchill's anger would be directed at him. Churchill merely cabled, 'Bravo Tobruk! We feel it vital that Tobruk should be regarded as sally-port and not, please, as an "excrescence".' Several weeks later he remarked, more in hope than reality, that Tobruk was 'a speck of sand in the desert which might ruin all Hitler's calculations'. Wavell seems to have had a premonition of his eventual fate. The day before he saw Dill and Eden off to London, he remarked to Dill: 'I hope, Jack, that you will preside at my court-martial.'

The irony of Rommel's success in North Africa in 1941 and 1942 was that he drew more praise from Churchill than from Berlin – where his feats were criticized – and his appeals for more reinforcements to exploit success were rebuffed by the German high command and by Hitler, who had few resources to divert from Barbarossa. The OKH chief of staff, General Franz Halder, regarded Rommel as 'this soldier gone stark mad'.

Churchill was obsessed with both besting Rommel and praising him. Throughout 1941 and well into the summer of 1942, he would decry the inadequacy of British generalship. It was no secret that he longed for British commanders with Rommel's audacity. In January 1942 he took the unprecedented step of heaping praise on the Desert Fox, who had likewise captured the imagination of the British public. In Parliament, Churchill paid what Ismay called 'a handsome tribute to Rommel's leadership' that shocked MPs by its candour. 'We have a very daring and skilled opponent against us, and may I say across the havoc of war, a great General.' In his war memoirs Churchill was unrepentant and again paid tribute to Rommel, praising him for his involvement in the 1944 conspiracy to assassinate Hitler, for which he paid with his life.

'In the sombre wars of modern democracy chivalry finds no place . . . Still, I do not regret or retract the tribute I paid to Rommel, unfashionable though it was judged.'

Churchill wanted the Germans ejected from Cyrenaica without delay, and, to enable Wavell to go on the offensive against Rommel, on 21 April he made the risky decision to give the go-ahead for Operation Tiger, a convoy to deliver 295 tanks and fifty-three Hurricane fighter aircraft to Egypt via the perilous Mediterranean route. As the convoy sailed towards Alexandria, escorted by a carrier and two battleships, 'the PM informed the Cabinet of the timetable, adding "If anyone's good at praying, now is the time."' One ship struck a mine and sank at a cost of fifty-seven tanks and ten aircraft. Churchill thought the loss of these valuable tanks would have far-reaching consequences. What he never quite grasped was that merely sending tanks to Egypt was not in itself an immediate prescription for success. They arrived in poor mechanical shape and had to be retrofitted for desert warfare, and their crews similarly trained. None were fit to be sent on short notice to either the Western Desert or Crete.

The Greek misadventure ended at the same time as Rommel drove the British from Cyrenaica. By early May 1941 British troubles in the Mediterranean were just beginning. A battle loomed in Crete, and it too would end disastrously.

45

Disaster in Crete

My God, it's hell.   – Royal Navy officer

May 1941 was one of the war's worst months. O'Connor's victory in
the desert was but a distant memory, and after the messy end to the
brief Greek campaign Churchill's popularity and his iron grip on a once
highly supportive Parliament had begun to slip. Rumblings of discontent
were heard on both sides of the House of Commons and in the military
departments.

On 3 May Winston and Clementine travelled to Devon, where they
viewed the devastation that had been wrought upon the naval base and
city of Plymouth by five destructive raids in the previous nine days. The
experience left both of them exhausted and cheerless. Added to the
grim sights was the increasing bad news from virtually all parts of
the Mediterranean and the Middle East. Colville recorded his boss as
being 'in worse gloom than I have ever seen him . . . The P.M. said that
this moment is decisive: it is being established not whether we shall win
or lose, but whether the duration of the war will be long or short.'
Earlier that day Clementine had suddenly asked Colville: 'Jock, do you
think we are going to win?' Without hesitation, he replied yes.

That evening, in an effort to mitigate the latest defeat, Churchill
addressed the British people on the BBC, asserting Britain's responsibility to come to the aid of the Greeks 'in their mortal peril'. And while
declaring that he never tried to turn defeats into victories, 'we must not
lose our sense of proportion and thus become discouraged or alarmed,'
he said. 'Nothing that is happening now is comparable in gravity to the
dangers through which we passed last year . . . No prudent and far-seeing
man can doubt that the eventual and total defeat of Hitler and Mussolini
is certain.' Churchill ended his address with the belligerent declaration:

'There are less than seventy million malignant Huns, some of whom are curable and others killable,' compared with the two hundred million people in the British Empire and the United States who would ultimately triumph. In the Reichstag the next day Hitler scorned Churchill's speech as the words of a drunkard and called the British intervention in Greece 'one of the most famous strategical blunders of this war'.

On 7 May Lloyd George made a rare appearance in the House and delivered a lecture about how to run a war that sternly criticized Churchill's leadership. Winston fired back, defending Britain's actions in the Middle East and Greece, and mocking Lloyd George by noting that his was the sort of speech that 'the illustrious and venerable Marshal Pétain' might have made in the dying days of France in June 1940. Churchill also stoutly defended his role as supreme warlord. 'My Right Hon. Friend spoke of the great importance of my being surrounded by people who would stand up to me and say "No, No, No."' Taking a damning swipe at his military, he continued: 'Why, good gracious, has he no idea how strong the negative principle is in the constitution and working of the British war-making machine? The difficulty is not, I assure him, to have more brakes put on the wheels; the difficulty is to get more impetus and speed behind it.' He was, he claimed, surrounded by a number of 'No-men' who resisted him at every turn to 'prevent me from making anything in the nature of a speedy, rapid and, above all, positive constructive decision'. He ended by reminding his colleagues how far they had come since the even darker days of 1940. 'I feel sure we have no need to fear the tempest. Let it roar, and let it rage. We shall come through.'

During the previous nine months Hitler had relentlessly fulfilled his promise to raze Britain's cities, made the previous September when he had unleashed 350 bombers and six hundred fighters on 7 September 1940, the first day of the Blitz. Cities, ports and naval bases were regularly pounded. Luftwaffe targets ranged from Belfast to Liverpool, Manchester, Hull and Newcastle in the north and east and Birmingham, Nottingham and Coventry in the Midlands; in southern England and Wales targets ranged from Bristol, Swansea and Cardiff to Portsmouth, Southampton and Plymouth. The maritime centres on the Mersey, on the Clyde and at Bristol were also hard hit, but as both the capital and the symbol of British defiance London remained the Luftwaffe's main focus. With no end in sight to the death and devastation, 'it was a struggle to breathe,' Churchill recalled. April 1941 was a particularly bad month after two heavy raids claimed the lives of some 2,300 Londoners. And while Sea Lion still remained an option, with Barbarossa about to be launched its likelihood decreased in proportion to the growing doubts in Berlin that the Blitz had accomplished enough to make an invasion possible.

The surge of bad news was beginning to generate criticism of the government and its propaganda that winning was only a matter of time. Brendan Bracken observed that the 'honeymoon period' was over and 'the grim realities of marriage' would have to be faced. The United States remained neutral, and while its eventual involvement was increasingly likely, for the foreseeable future the initiative lay with the Axis powers. Despite Churchill's defiance and his uplifting speeches, the resolve of the citizenry was beginning to crumble under the weight of German bombs.

Saturday, 10 May 1941 marked the first anniversary of the German invasion of the West and of Churchill's prime ministership. Before it ended, this date also became a milestone in the history of the war.

That afternoon Hitler's trusted deputy Rudolf Hess travelled secretly to the Messerschmitt fighter works in Augsburg, donned a flight suit and took off into the evening sky in an Me-110. After piloting his aircraft across the North Sea and penetrating Scottish airspace, Hess baled out near Glasgow and was captured within minutes of landing. His mission, he later informed his captors, was to land near the estate of the Duke of Hamilton, who he wrongly thought could displace Churchill and bring about the installation of a new government that would make peace with Germany. When it became clear that Hess had no official German sanction, he was imprisoned for the duration of the war and later convicted at Nuremberg for war crimes.

While Hess was flying towards Scotland, final preparations were under way at German airfields in France for a night mission. Their destination was London. Shortly after the evening skies had darkened into night around ten o'clock, a massive first wave of 370 German aircraft launched one of the largest and deadliest raids of the war. After a three-week respite from the bombing, Londoners were caught by surprise when sirens signalled the imminent arrival of the Luftwaffe.

The raid of 10–11 May 1941 was one of the most devastating of the war. Incendiary bombs left more than three thousand dead and injured, lit some two thousand fires across the city and destroyed eleven thousand homes and buildings. A direct hit on the Palace of Westminster landed in the historic debating chamber of the House of Commons, leaving it a shattered, charred ruin. Westminster Abbey was also hit and severely damaged by a multitude of fires. Bombs fell on hotels, docks, factories, hospitals, railway stations, the British Museum and Harrods. During the six-and-a-half-hour raid a total of 507 aircraft dropped 711 tons of high-explosive bombs and incendiaries on London. The next morning thick smoke from the fires still furiously burning throughout the city obscured the sky of an otherwise beautiful spring day. London was battered and bloody from its worst night since the great raid of 29 December 1940. What no one knew was that this was the last major Luftwaffe raid on London. A heavy attack on Birmingham on 16 May proved to be the conclusion of the Blitz, but there would be many other smaller-scale raids before the war ended, including retaliatory strikes in 1942 against cities of no military importance such as Bath, Canterbury and York.

One of the first to visit the smoking ruins of Parliament was Churchill, accompanied by Lord Beaverbrook and the journalist Guy Eden, who wrote: 'As we looked at the place that had been the scene of so many triumphs, so many setbacks, so much of his life, I saw tears streaming down Churchill's face. He did not try to stop them, or even wipe them away. Grinding his stick into the charred wreckage, he let his gaze wander slowly round the unfamiliar place that had once been so familiar to him, as if saying a last farewell. For a long time he was silent. Then he turned abruptly, walked out of the wreckage . . . "The Chamber must be rebuilt – just as it was. Meanwhile, we shall not lose a single day's debate through this!" ' True to his word, the House of Commons quickly began meeting in makeshift accommodation, and for the remainder of the war sat primarily in the chamber of the House of Lords.

After his first year in office it is possible to reach some conclusions about Winston Churchill's leadership. He was the quintessential enigma – the most impatient man in Britain, who exhibited the patience of Job over what mattered most: winning a war that was like a marathon, which would neither be won nor lost in the foreseeable future. In everything else he was perpetually impatient, unforgiving of failure and of the real and perceived unwillingness of his military to take risks he believed necessary. Whatever his mistakes in strategy and his incessant involvement in the business of war, his strength lay in his ability to see the larger picture. 'War', he said in 1948, 'consists of fighting, gnawing and tearing, and . . . the weaker or more frail gets life clawed out of him by this method. Manoeuvre is mere embellishment, very agreeable when it comes off. But fighting is the key to victory.' Boldness was also a key element in his philosophy of war, and this explains his partiality for Rommel. Churchill's belief that the summer of 1941 would see the United States enter the war was premature, necessitating a continuation of the strategy of hanging on through a series of defeats and outright disasters.

On 20 May, 8,060 parachute and glider troops of Major General Kurt Student's XI Fliegerkorps, supported by some 650 bombers, divebombers, fighters and transport aircraft, invaded Crete. The Allied commander defending Crete was Major General Bernard Freyberg, whose force of 42,460 British, Dominion and Greek troops (of whom approximately half were in front-line units) was devoid of air, artillery and vital transport support and communications equipment.

The key to the German capture of Crete was to seize and hold the airfields at Heraklion, Rethymnon, Canea and Maleme. Ultra warned Freyberg to expect both airborne and sea landings on 20 May; however, as a First World War infantry general ill versed in aerial and airborne warfare, the New Zealander was convinced that the main invasion would still be by sea.

During the first twenty-four hours the Germans suffered enormous casualties at Heraklion and Rethymnon and barely clung to positions at Maleme. Still mistakenly believing the naval threat paramount, Freyberg held back from counterattacking at Maleme on the night of 21 May, and the last chance to defeat the invasion was lost. The Germans were now in control of the airfield and were able to reinforce Crete with 13,980 troops of the 5th Mountain Division by Junkers-52 troop carriers. As the Ultra historian Ronald Lewin has written, 'Most battles have a central theme. For Crete the theme was airfields, and Freyberg misinterpreted the score.'

Some of the war's fiercest fighting took place on Crete. On 22 May Churchill spoke of the battle in Parliament. 'It is a most strange and grim battle that is being fought . . . Neither side has any means of retreat.

It is a desperate, grim battle . . . which will affect the whole course of the campaign in the Mediterranean.'

The Allies fought bravely and made the Germans pay a fearsome price of some seven thousand killed, but with reinforcements and supplies flooding the island, Crete quickly became a hopeless campaign. When he read reports of the battle, the American military attaché in London concluded: 'This battle must have looked like a rat pit, with men slaughtering each other all over the island.' Unable to recapture Maleme and two other airfields, Freyberg was compelled to retreat into the mountains. On 26 May he signalled Churchill: 'No matter what decision is taken by the Commanders-in-Chief from a military point of view, our position is hopeless.' Predictably Churchill replied that Crete must be held, only to receive a second signal from Freyberg the next day that Crete was no longer tenable and his troops had to be withdrawn or lost.

Fierce battles also raged at sea, where the Royal Navy came under heavy attack by the Luftwaffe, which was able to launch some seven hundred aircraft over Crete, the Sea of Crete and the Aegean.

With disaster looming in Crete, no one felt the pressure more than Jack Dill. 'Do you realize we are fighting for our lives now?' he asked John Kennedy. Unaware that the German invasion of the Soviet Union was only a month away, Kennedy agreed that 'if the Germans were to continue to concentrate their efforts in the Middle East, we should soon have to reckon with the possibility of not being able to hold it.'

Criticism of Churchill was reaching a peak at one of Britain's lowest points of the war. Relations between the prime minister and his generals in May 1941 were increasingly frayed. There was also a classic catch-22: by bombarding Wavell and, later, Auchinleck, with advice and directives (some simply impossible to carry out), Churchill helped them to fail, not only by his incessant meddling but also because he sapped their confidence and diverted their attention from the business of command. The corollary is that, from Churchill's perspective, he meddled because he lacked confidence in them, primarily because of what he regarded as their lack of aggressiveness. Military operations, noted Kennedy, 'were being distorted and coloured by the formidable advocacy of the Prime Minister . . . he was not only advocate, but witness, prosecutor and judge', who sent endless orders and directives to his commanders in chief 'without professional advice'.

On the night of 27 April, well oiled with champagne and in a combative mood, Churchill engaged Kennedy in a furious argument during dinner at Chequers about Wavell and the Middle East. In response to a question about Rommel's potential capability, Kennedy had replied that if the German lines of communication in the Mediterranean were not interdicted, Egypt might be in peril. Churchill flushed and in a fit of temper shouted: 'Wavell has 400,000 men. If they lose Egypt, blood will flow. I will have firing parties to shoot the generals.' Kennedy argued that his assessment had nothing to do with the courage of the British soldiers but was based upon what price would have to be paid to defend the Middle East. He then mentioned that Wavell had a plan to withdraw from Egypt if this was ever necessary. Already afire, Churchill exploded with rage. 'I never heard of such ideas. War is a contest of wills. It is pure defeatism to speak as you have done.'

Brooke was present and later wrote: 'The more Kennedy tried to explain what he meant, the more heated Winston got.' Everyone present breathed a sigh of relief when the dinner finally ended about midnight and the party adjourned to Churchill's study, where many more hours of monologue continued into the small hours. Churchill recalled that in April 1918 Haig might have withdrawn the BEF to the sea if the Germans had broken through, until Foch intervened to declare that there would be no withdrawal. 'That has always been a lesson to me,' he said. In a variation of what he had said some months earlier, Churchill declared, 'My plan for winning the war is this, 1,000 tons of bombs a night on Germany – we are only averaging 50 now – and 20,000 tanks or so, ready to land all along the coasts of Europe.' Without mentioning Wavell by name, he declared, 'The German advance in Cyrenaica was the quintessence of generalship. It is generalship we need in Egypt.'

The Australian prime minister Sir Robert Menzies was a member of the War Cabinet and spent considerable time in London and the Middle East in 1941. He saw both sides of Churchill: the leader he deeply admired for his steadfastness and also the warlord he regarded as a virtual dictator whose courageous leadership was offset by his lamentable strategic sense. 'He does not seem to realize that men without proper equipment, and with nothing but rifles, do not count in modern war – after all, we are not living in the age of Omdurman.' Menzies also remarked that any general who did not plan for such an event as a possible withdrawal from Egypt was not fit for his job.

'Churchill grows on me,' Menzies wrote on 2 March. 'He has an astonishing grasp of detail and, by daily contact with the service headquarters, knows of disposition and establishment quite accurately. But I still fear that (though experience of Supreme Office has clearly improved and steadied him) his real tyrant is the glittering phrase – so attractive to his mind that awkward facts may have to give way.' Nevertheless, observed the Australian, Churchill was adamant he would win in the end. 'Churchill's course is set. There is no defeat in his heart.'

Typical of Churchill's reach into the realm of strategy was a telegram he sent to Wavell in late May: 'Now, before the enemy has recovered from the violent exertions and heavy losses involved in his onslaught upon Crete, is the time to fight a decisive battle in Libya, and go on day after day facing all necessary losses until you have beaten the life out of General Rommel's army.' The telegram drew a rebuke from Dill. Wavell, he suggested, was being unduly interfered with by the prime minister's orders.

For the time being Tobruk was of secondary concern. As the situation in Crete grew worse, Churchill's feelings about Wavell grew proportionally more negative. But other trouble spots in the Middle East also abounded, the latest in Iraq, where a military junta seized power and installed a pro-German Iraqi general as prime minister. In May, Iraqi forces attacked an RAF air base near Ramadi, prompting Churchill to order the 10th Indian Division to land at Basra and an Allied task force diverted from Trans-Jordan to quell the rebellion. The brief and little-known Anglo-Iraqi campaign of 1941 to restore a pro-British government ended in an armistice at the end of the month. It was followed by an invasion in June from Iraq and Palestine of Vichy-controlled Syria and Lebanon, where bitter fighting ensued before Vichy forces capitulated and an armistice was signed in mid-July, restoring stability in a critical area of the Middle East.

Another deadly naval threat loomed in the frigid waters to the west of Iceland, in the Denmark Strait. The world's largest and deadliest warship, the new 42,000-ton German battleship *Bismarck*, and the heavy cruiser *Prinz Eugen* sailed secretly from the Baltic on 18 May and were sighted refuelling in the Norwegian port of Bergen three days later by an RAF reconnaissance aircraft, before slipping away towards Iceland. A Royal Navy battle group that included the battleships HMS *Hood* and HMS *Prince of Wales* was hastily dispatched from Scapa Flow to intercept the *Bismarck* and the *Prinz Eugen* before they entered the North Atlantic and menaced British convoys. On 24 May the combatants found each other some fifty-five miles off the western tip of Iceland. As the *Hood*, already damaged by a shell fired by the *Prinz Eugen*, turned to bring its main armament to bear on the *Bismarck*, it exploded, broke in two and sank within minutes with only three survivors from its crew of 1,418. Although damaged, the *Bismarck* escaped and made a dash for sanctuary in the French port of Brest.

Churchill's exhaustion and increasing testiness often left him unreasonable, particularly in relation to the Royal Navy. He was incensed that the *Prince of Wales* had allegedly failed to press hard enough in the Denmark Strait, though he did not know that it had been badly damaged and most of its armament knocked out of commission. He turned his fury and frustration on the hapless Admiralty and the Mediterranean fleet, whose commander, ABC Cunningham, he berated for '[the fleet's] tendency to shirk its task of preventing a sea borne landing in Crete since Cunningham fears severe losses from bombing'. Churchill was unaware that on 22 May the admiral had signalled his ships: 'Stick it out. Navy must not let Army down. No enemy forces must reach Crete by sea.'

Although Churchill's attitude towards his army generals was mainly one of frustration, his criticism of the Royal Navy was acrimonious and based on the false premise that the admirals were too often loath to risk their ships. When Jock Colville pointed out that the cruisers *Gloucester* and *Fiji* had been sunk, an unsympathetic Churchill snapped, ' "What do you think we build the ships for?" He deprecates the navy's way of treating ships as if they were too precious ever to risk.' Cunningham should have risked everything, insisted Churchill: 'The loss of half the Mediterranean fleet would be worthwhile in order to save Crete.'

Quite the reverse was true. The Royal Navy suffered heavy losses in the Mediterranean, first in the evacuation of Greece, then during the subsequent evacuation of Crete. Cunningham had taken enormous risks, and neither he nor his gallant sailors deserved the abuse heaped on them by Churchill and the Admiralty. Cunningham refused to give in, and in the tradition of great fighting admirals rejected defeatism and led by example, prodding his subordinates even when they flagged and many of his ships were returning shattered, their decks still awash in blood and littered with wreckage. When his surgeon urged that his men desperately needed a rest, 'Cunningham exploded, "I won't have it!" he said.' They would carry on – no more complaining would be tolerated. (Among the losses was the destroyer HMS *Kelly*, commanded by Queen Victoria's great-grandson, Captain Lord Louis Mountbatten, the future head of Combined Operations.)

This was not the only occasion when Churchill was prone to jump to conclusions and criticize his navy before all the facts were known. On 28 March, thanks to a timely Ultra intercept, the Royal Navy scored a major sea victory in the Battle of Matapan, off the southern coast of Greece, sinking two Italian destroyers and three heavy cruisers. Churchill was not the only armchair critic; the dominion secretary, Lord Salisbury, wrote to complain that the Admiralty did not like risking its ships. Instead of putting Salisbury in his place or at least defending the navy, Churchill passed his ill-advised letter to the Admiralty, calling it 'a very important outside opinion' instead of half-baked nonsense that ought to have been discarded in the nearest wastebasket.

The perception that the Royal Navy commanders were unwilling to risk their ships is patently false. Between September 1939 and the end of March 1941, the Royal Navy lost more than 450 vessels of all types, with almost all of these losses due to enemy action, at the cost of thousands of lives. In addition the toll of British, Allied and neutral merchant shipping sunk by the Germans made seafaring all the more deadly. During the battle for Crete a naval officer exclaimed, 'My God, it's hell.' After the heroics of Dunkirk, Churchill might have been expected to temper such criticism, yet his approach to the admirals, generals and air marshals was, simply put: 'What have you done for me lately?' A war for survival such as that fought by Britain tends to inure even the most sentimental of men to demanding something extra from his subordinates. Whatever his private feelings Churchill the ruthless warlord could ill afford the luxury of sentiment, and anything less than perfection brought criticism and renewed demands for success. Because of his bluntness, they were neither always diplomatically phrased nor well received. In the case of Crete his criticism was unfair and misplaced.

In keeping with his insistence that Axis convoys to North Africa be interdicted, when Churchill learned in April that the Royal Navy had allegedly failed to locate an Italian convoy, the Admiralty received a rocket demanding to know why it had not been intercepted. 'This is a serious *Naval* failure,' he fumed. 'Another deadly convoy has got through.' It was soon determined that the convoy had actually turned back and had been intercepted and destroyed. Politicians hardly if ever admit it when they are wrong or out of line, and Churchill's reply to the news was, 'Yes, brilliantly redeemed,' as if finding a convoy in the dead of night with minimal air and sea resources were somehow a given. He remained adamant that Cunningham, whose fleet was, like the army, stretched thinly across an enormous area, should interdict all Axis convoys bound for Tripoli, and that 'the blockading of Tripoli would be well worth a battleship on the active list.'

Other blunt missives raised the hackles of the admirals, but particularly harsh was his disparagement of the Mediterranean fleet. During the battle for Crete, Churchill's prodding led to a signal from the chiefs of staff that, although the fleet was four hundred miles from its nearest air support and under frequent attack by German dive-bombers, all necessary risks were to be taken to prevent further German reinforcement of the island. However, the damage in Crete had already been done; and few reinforcements were getting through by sea. Nevertheless Cunningham kept his dismay at London's lack of grasp of reality in check and reminded his Admiralty masters that he was not afraid of sustaining losses but was duty bound to avoid losses which would cripple his battered fleet to the point where he could no longer maintain control of the eastern Mediterranean.

Churchill was at Chequers on Sunday, 25 May when it was reported that the *Bismarck* had eluded the Royal Navy. Colville recorded, 'A day of fearful gloom ensued.' The previous day Churchill had lamented Wavell's refusal to send tanks to Crete to defend the Maleme airfield. Colonel Robert Laycock commanded the seven-hundred-man Special Air Service commando force sent by Wavell in late April to help defend Crete that later acted as the rearguard during the withdrawal. In July he recounted his experience to Churchill at Chequers and opined that with a dozen tanks at Maleme he could have saved Crete. 'I could almost hear a large nail being driven into Wavell's coffin,' recalled Colville.

Churchill continued firing salvos at the admirals, whom he blamed for losing the *Bismarck* in the Denmark Strait and for failing to land reinforcements in Crete, while at the same time criticizing Wavell for believing he could have landed reinforcements there in the first place. At dinner he opined that the Middle East 'had been very badly managed.

If he could be put in command there he would gladly lay down his present office – yes, and even renounce cigars and alcohol!' A perfectly miserable day ended with Churchill's remark before he retired at 2.15 a.m. that 'these three days had been the worst yet.'

The next day was no better. On 26 May the *Bismarck* was still eluding its pursuers as it raced for the sanctuary of a French port, and the War Cabinet meeting that evening was, Anthony Eden recorded, the worst ever. 'Winston was nervy and unreasonable and everyone else on edge.' A furious argument ensued about whether or not to make public the convoy losses, which Churchill was against publishing. Although he won that argument, he lost another over conscription in Ulster. He then resorted to a tactic he used whenever things did not go his way: instead of the usual histrionics he simply sat in silence for some two minutes while the tension heightened and no one else dared to speak.

Just how tightly wound Churchill was during these trying days is evident from the recollections of his son-in-law, Vic Oliver, the Viennese-born radio actor and comedian who had married his daughter Sarah in 1936 over her father's objections. Churchill was at Chequers for the weekend when he was awakened about seven o'clock on 24 May with the news that the *Hood* had been sunk.

'Her loss was a bitter grief,' he said, not only because so many had died but because the *Hood* was a warship that had been launched in 1920 during his tenure as secretary of state for war and for many years had been the world's largest capital ship and the pride of the Royal Navy. According to Walter Thompson the loss of the *Hood* and of Crete threw him into one of his 'black dog' depressions. 'Churchill went around in a daze.' While they lasted, these periodic episodes took a heavy toll, and there were nights when he was so listless that Thompson sat at his bedside.

Later that morning of 24 May a grim Churchill descended from his study. Averell Harriman's daughter Kathleen saw 'a tear running down his face and it was the saddest sight I'd ever seen . . . His face showed how he suffered.' His mood remained forlorn throughout the day, but no one dared ask him what had brought it on. To help ease the tension Clementine suggested that Oliver play something on the piano, and as he began to play Beethoven's 'Appassionata' sonata, Churchill thundered a demand that he stop at once. When Oliver asked why, he declared: 'No one plays the "Dead March" in my house.' Despite being told the name of the piece, he refused to let Oliver continue, insisting it was a funeral march. When Oliver foolishly attempted to demonstrate the difference, Churchill blew his stack: 'Stop it! Stop it! I want no "Dead March", I tell you.'

Throughout that dismal weekend Churchill was unable to concentrate on getting through the usual mass of paperwork he brought with him whenever he went to Chequers. Most of his time was spent restlessly pacing back and forth in front of a large map of the North Atlantic that was kept current by Churchill's personal assistant, Commander C. R. 'Tommy' Thompson.

On 27 May the search for the *Bismarck* was rewarded when the elusive battleship was sighted some seven hundred miles from Brest. That evening just before dark, a torpedo fired from a Royal Navy Swordfish aircraft crippled it. The next morning the Royal Navy sank the pride of the German navy with the loss of 2,107 lives. In Parliament, just as MPs were about to be informed of its escape, Colville handed Churchill a note. 'I crave your indulgence, Mr Speaker,' he said. There was loud cheering when he announced: 'I have just received news the *Bismarck* has been sunk.'

Andrew Cunningham found himself waging a war on two fronts: with the Germans and with the Admiralty. With the Luftwaffe dominating the airspace in and around Crete, it was painfully clear that the island could not be saved without air support, and to have needlessly sacrificed valuable ships and men merely for the sake of *noblesse oblige* was foolhardy, particularly because he had reported that the Germans were having little or no success reinforcing Crete by sea. And while he was being second-guessed in London, his sailors conducted two successful emergency evacuations without air support, under constant attack by the Luftwaffe, and suffering heavy losses while trying valiantly first to reinforce and then to save Crete. Two thousand sailors were killed, six destroyers sunk (seven more damaged), three cruisers sunk (five more damaged), two battleships crippled and an aircraft carrier put out of action for five months. These were hardly examples of shirking.

When the Admiralty countermanded one of Cunningham's orders with a terse signal, the tenacious admiral had had enough meddling and rescinded their order, bluntly telling London to mind its own business. 'The less said about this unjustifiable interference by those ignorant of the situation the better,' he informed their lordships. What the outspoken admiral said in private can only be imagined. Although never a fan of Churchill, Cunningham later came to appreciate the pressures he faced. 'Those of us who were on the receiving end abroad tended not to make sufficient allowances for the state of mind of politicians and the public at home,' he wrote after the war. 'I had a much greater admiration for Mr Churchill when I found myself close to him as First Sea Lord.'

Cunningham rightly called Greece and Crete 'a disastrous period in our naval history', and wrote to Pound, 'I feel very heavy hearted about it all. I suppose we shall learn our lesson in time that the navy and army cannot make up for the lack of air forces.' He added that he would not be upset if the Admiralty decided to replace him; however, neither Pound nor Churchill ever gave serious consideration to replacing this gallant fighting admiral. Nevertheless Cunningham had every right to be dismayed by 'the disturbing thought that those at home apparently failed to appreciate what our ships and our men had endured'. As far back as June 1940 he had urged, to no avail, the reinforcement of Crete and the establishment of a naval base in Suda Bay. He also pointed out: 'Three squadrons of long range fighters and a few heavy bombing squadrons would have saved Crete for us.'

Freyberg's force lost some thirteen thousand killed, wounded and captured in Crete. In his war memoirs Churchill downplayed the tragedy of Crete as at best a pyrrhic victory for Germany, because it had diverted valuable airborne assets from Barbarossa. Oliver Lyttelton, who was soon to be sent to the Middle East as minister of state, more accurately pinpointed the consequences of losing Crete: 'It brought the Nile delta within the effective range of enemy bombers.' Even though the Germans had suffered heavily and never again employed airborne forces in a major operation, they now controlled the Aegean and prevented the RAF from using Crete to launch air strikes against the Romanian oil fields at Ploesti. No amount of spin by London ever disguised the fact that Greece and Crete were enormously costly and unnecessary disasters.

46

The Endless Desert War

The PM has lost confidence in Wavell – if he ever had any.

– General Sir John Dill

In the spring of 1941 heads began to roll in the Middle East even before the fall of Crete. The first of the senior Middle East commanders to be sacked by Churchill was Air Chief Marshal Sir Arthur Longmore. For some time Longmore had been the object of Churchill's displeasure, not only for his lukewarm support of intervention in Greece but because of the prime minister's belief that the air force had not done enough to support the evacuation. Nor did Churchill like the undiplomatic tone of his insistent but nevertheless legitimate requests for additional assets.

Dunkirk had bred the erroneous assumption by the other two services that the RAF had not done enough, and the Crete disaster exacerbated their resentments and further widened the gulf of misunderstanding. The conviction that the RAF had 'let down the army' was so widespread and so pervasive that airmen were not safe from angry soldiers on the streets of Cairo or even in POW camps, where they were looked upon with disfavour.

What particularly irked Churchill was his misguided belief that Longmore had too few operational aircraft for the numbers of machines and personnel assigned to the Middle East, and that resources were being wasted. Longmore was merely the latest victim of Churchill's inability to understand what it took to keep modern machines of war operational. Longmore's command extended over the same immense geographic area as Wavell's, and involved maintaining an ageing fleet of largely obsolete aircraft under conditions far harsher and more difficult than prevailed in Britain. The RAF Middle East could not be judged by the standards applied to Fighter Command. Heat and sand presented enormous

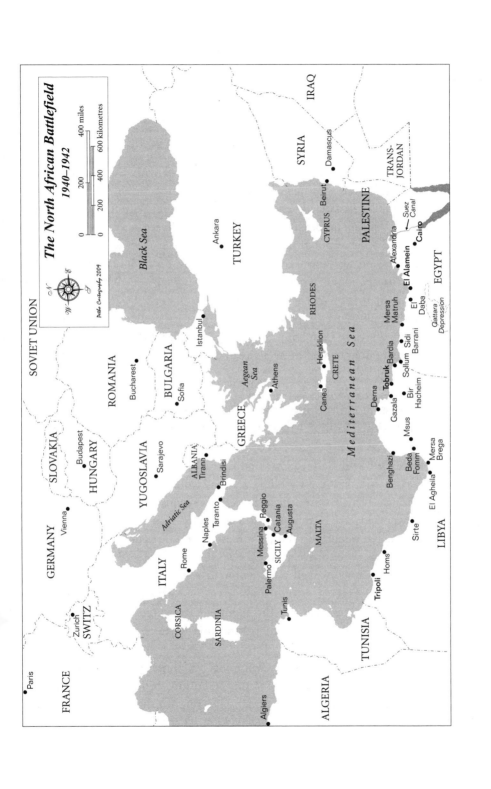

The North African Battlefield
1940–1942

0 200 400 miles
0 200 400 600 kilometres

Peter Cartography 2009

challenges to maintaining aircraft in an operational state. The result was Longmore's dismissal and his replacement by his deputy, Air Chief Marshal Sir Arthur Tedder.

Even before Crete, Churchill had decided to sack Wavell; the only question was when. All along Dill's advice had been, 'Back him or sack him.' Churchill summoned Dill to No. 10 and informed the CIGS of his intention to remove Wavell and replace him with General Sir Claude Auchinleck, the C in C India. The two men would swap jobs, and Churchill sarcastically noted that, once in India, Wavell would no doubt enjoy 'sitting under the pagoda tree'. Dill strongly advised against Wavell's new appointment. 'He has not been there since the last war and has no real knowledge of the problems of the Indian Army . . . His taciturnity alone would be a great handicap . . . Wavell should be brought to England to report and rest.' Churchill adamantly refused and would not even permit Wavell to return to England before taking up his new post, fearing that his popularity with his troops and the British public would draw a storm of criticism upon the prime minister himself.

After deciding to replace Wavell, Churchill left him in command for another month, during which he kept up the pressure on him to relieve the besieged Tobruk garrison. In mid-May, Wavell launched Operation Brevity, a hastily organized operation that made some early gains as far as Sollum and Halfaya Pass on the frontier. Brevity was indeed brief; in less than a day it was solidly repelled with a loss of ninety-six tanks, and the British were forced back into Egypt, while Rommel not only recaptured lost terrain but laid a deadly trap for the next foray by emplacing minefields and 88-mm anti-aircraft guns that were to prove devastatingly effective as direct-fire weapons.

On 15 June Wavell tried again to relieve Tobruk with Operation Battleaxe. Having risked sending such a large number of tanks (his 'Tiger cubs') at great risk through the Mediterranean gauntlet in May, Churchill had envisaged that an armoured tiger would be unleashed. Instead the unsuspecting British drove into the teeth of Rommel's defences along the frontier. Churchill was bitterly disappointed that it had taken so long to mount the operation, believing that it was yet another case of his commanders insisting on 'having the last button sewn on the last gaiter before attacking'. Although there would be other questionable delays in the months ahead, Battleaxe was not one of them. Nevertheless Wavell had clearly articulated a warning to Churchill not to set his expectations too high. The British Matilda Mark I tanks lacked both power and speed against the better armament and mobility of Rommel's panzers. Still, London seemed to think that mounting an armoured offensive was merely a matter of cranking engines and moving out.

To make matters worse, aerial photos and intercepts alerted Rommel that an offensive was imminent. Battleaxe lasted only three days and was a complete disaster. Rommel's dug-in panzers and 88s tore through the Battleaxe force at Sollum with the loss of nearly a hundred British tanks, thirty-six aircraft and nearly one thousand killed, wounded or missing in action. Even if Wavell had commenced Battleaxe sooner, the end result would have been the same.

Churchill was on a rare wartime visit to Chartwell when he received a telegram from Wavell that read: 'I regret to report the failure of "Battleaxe." ' Once again Rommel had established that his battlefield generalship and his innovative use of the 88s were far superior to anything the British could come up with. Battleaxe left Churchill more distraught and frustrated than ever. Sollum pleased Hitler and earned Rommel headlines in Germany and a promotion to full general over the objections of Franz Halder, 'who complained of Rommel's "pathological ambition" '.

Good soldier that he was, Wavell accepted his relief from command with equanimity: 'He had been shaving when the news of the Prime Minister's decision was read to him by his C.o.S. [chief of staff] on the morning of June 22nd, and he had showed not the slightest emotion. "The Prime Minister's quite right," he said. "This job needs a new hand." And he went on shaving.'

Although it was disguised merely as a shift of command to another important post, the fact remains that, short of death, there is no more agonizing experience for a soldier, sailor or airman than to be relieved of command. Churchill's ancestor the Duke of Marlborough may have said it best: 'To relieve a general in the midst of a campaign, that is the mortal stroke.' When he wrote to Dill, Wavell would only comment that he hoped Auchinleck would have better success grappling with Churchill's 'bold and hazardous courses'.

Once formed, Churchill's opinions of people rarely changed, and despite occasional words of public praise his antagonism towards Wavell never mellowed. Instead he spared no effort to demean Wavell's contributions, choosing, for example, to compare him with Rommel, whose only responsibility was tactical. If Rommel could succeed by audacity, why could not Wavell have done the same? Wavell never met the test of Churchill's military philosophy. More than three years after sacking him, Churchill was still unforgiving. At a meeting of the War Cabinet in August 1944, Hugh Dalton recorded that the prime minister 'speaks ill of Wavell. "He was a bad General. He let us down atrociously at Crete. I have been too kind to him." ' His post-war published account of Wavell's relief is equally unsparing.

What Churchill never understood, however, was that to expect victory in such diverse locations as Iraq, Syria, Greece, Crete, East Africa and North Africa without providing the tools to accomplish the job was asking more than any competent commander could deliver with a poorly armed, undermanned, largely conscript army. And, while coming to the aid of Greece was a noble gesture, no consideration seems to have been given to the importance of North Africa as a greater military priority. O'Connor believed that if the RAF and Royal Navy had been committed in support of both a further advance into Libya and the landing of a brigade-size force by sea, Tripoli could have been captured in early 1941 – thus nipping in the bud Rommel's incursion into North Africa. Wavell made the case for such an operation on 10 February but was rebuffed two days later by Churchill, who decreed that 'your major effort must now be to aid Greece and/or Turkey. This rules out any serious effort against Tripoli . . . Our first thoughts must be for our ally Greece.'

Rommel observed: 'If Wavell had now continued his advance into Tripolitania, no resistance worthy of the name could have been mounted against him – so well had his superbly planned offensive succeeded.' The Italian defences around Tripoli were 'totally inadequate'. Rommel articulated what Churchill failed to acknowledge in making his fateful decision to divert forces to Greece: 'When a commander has won a decisive victory – and Wavell's victory over the Italians was devastating – it is generally wrong for him to be satisfied with too narrow a strategic aim. For that is the time to exploit success.' The end result, he said, was that 'history almost invariably finds the decision to be wrong and points to the tremendous chances which have been missed.'

The intervention in Greece was a catastrophic blunder of grand strategy that altered the entire course of the war in the Mediterranean. When he wrote about it in *The Grand Alliance*, Churchill never quite accepted the ultimate responsibility and instead placed blame on the War Cabinet, and on Eden, Dill and, ultimately, Wavell. In 1948 he wrote to his research assistants, 'Wavell spoiled his African show for the sake of the Greek adventure in which he believed and in which he was much pressed by Eden, with the consent of Dill . . . If he had refused to go to Greece, he would not have helped the general show, but would have secured his own . . . His great mistake was allowing the desert flank to be broken in. I would never have gone to Greece if I had not thought the desert flank was secure.'

Churchill was being disingenuous: he was privy to Ultra decrypts that indicated German intervention in North Africa yet he does not seem to have challenged or overturned Wavell's belief that he could hold Cyrenaica with a stripped-down desert force. Moreover, the War Cabinet was prone to accede to Churchill's wishes. Churchill certainly bears a share of the responsibility for both Greece and the Western Desert, but given his difficult relationship with Wavell it is hard to imagine Wavell standing up to him and saying no. Nor is it unreasonable to conclude that if there were to be scapegoats, the scapegoat in chief was not Wavell but Churchill himself. Only after sacking Wavell did he belatedly acknowledge, 'I realized how overloaded and under-sustained General Wavell's organisation was. Wavell tried his best; but the handling machine at his disposal was too weak to enable him to cope with the vast mass of business which four or five simultaneous campaigns imposed upon him.'

If there is a postscript to this unhappy tale it is that, had Wavell done a better job of impressing and communicating with Churchill in August 1940, his tenure as commander in chief, Middle East, might have turned out quite differently. For his part Wavell had put his life on the line and on more than one occasion escaped death or capture. Auchinleck never bought in to Churchill's argument that Wavell was tired; the real reason, he believed, was that his predecessor 'was given impossible tasks'. From the sidelines Brooke observed, 'Why will politicians never learn the simple principle of concentration of force at the vital point and avoidance of dispersal of effort?' Greece was 'a strategic blunder. Our hands were more than full at that time.'

The unsentimental ABC Cunningham was 'desperately sorry' to see his colleague go. 'I had the greatest admiration for Wavell. He was cool and imperturbable when things went wrong, and steadfastly refused to be riled by the prodding messages to which he, like myself, was at times subjected . . . Wavell was always ready to take a chance. Never once did he have the good fortune to fight with all the resources he needed.' The last word on the disastrous first half of 1941 is that Churchill tried to accomplish too much with too little and paid the price.

When he appointed General Claude Auchinleck, Churchill expected a favourable turnaround in British fortunes in the Middle East. Although 'the Auk', as he was familiarly known, had an outstanding record of service in the Indian army, much of it on the North-West Frontier, Dill cautioned Churchill that he might not be the best choice. Auchinleck had been in command of the ill-fated Allied expedition to Narvik in May 1940 and had piqued Churchill by failing to share his enthusiasm for that venture. Yet whatever negative feelings he had engendered in Churchill were replaced by the prime minister's subsequent high opinion of Auchinleck when he commanded the defence of southern England in 1940. Churchill genuinely liked Auchinleck, sent him to the top job in India and was appreciative of his prompt support of intervention in Iraq in May 1941.

An officer of imposing, even noble presence but with little rapport with his troops, Claude Auchinleck was hindered by his long service in the Indian army, which left him with scant knowledge of the mainstream of British army officers. Consequently his choices of senior field commanders and staff officers would prove so ill-starred that in June 1942 he ended up taking personal command of a flagging Eighth Army before he too lost the confidence of both Churchill and his subordinate commanders and became the second commander in chief in a year to be sacked.

To avoid a repetition of the bad relations that had existed between Churchill and Wavell, Dill wrote to Auchinleck and explicitly advised on what he must do to deal effectively with the prime minister. 'The fact is that the Commander in the field will always be subject to great and often undue pressure from his Government. Wellington suffered from it: Haig suffered from it: Wavell suffered from it. Nothing will stop it.' However, to keep Churchill satisfied, Auchinleck had to keep him in the picture by means of frequent telegrams. Ismay offered similar advice, explaining to the introverted Auchinleck that as both prime minister and warlord the extroverted Churchill had a perfect right to be kept fully informed of his plans and actions, and it was vital to act accordingly. 'The Prime Minister is a woman,' advised Ismay. 'You've got to woo him.' Auchinleck never did.

Instead, he resented Churchill's constant interference and refused to humour him, as Dill had urged him to do. Auchinleck's stubbornness not only was his undoing but led to his acceptance of bad advice from staff officers. Whereas Wavell had made better use of them and had been wise enough to separate the useful from the useless, Auchinleck proved too acquiescent. But above all he lacked the foresight to learn from and to counter Rommel's successful tactics. Against the wily and far more resourceful Rommel, Auchinleck's pedestrian attempts, and those of his subordinate field generals, were doomed to fail.

If there was anything to be salvaged from the debacles of Greece and Crete it was that Hitler's intervention in the Mediterranean had no ultimate strategic aim and siphoned off resources into a venture that, without Rommel's initiative in North Africa, led nowhere. Thus, although the events of the first six months of 1941 were costly and humiliating, Churchill's strategic misjudgments were ultimately balanced by Hitler's even greater mistakes.

As the months passed Churchill's well-meant but constant interference began to grate. Colville noted on 19 June: 'The PM does not help the Government machine to run smoothly and his inconsiderate treatment of the Service Departments would cause trouble were it not for the great personal loyalty of the Service Ministers. He supplies drive and initiative, but he often meddles where he would better leave things alone and the operational side of war might profit if he gave it a respite and turned to grapple with labour and production.'

The interaction between Churchill and the generals in 1941, and for the remainder of the war, revolved around the question of whether or not it is possible to provide strategic direction to the military without micromanaging its operations. Churchill obviously did not think so and, lacking sufficient trust in his generals, concluded that only under his tutelage would things get done the way he wanted them done. In short he believed he knew more than his generals, a dangerous assumption but one with elements of truth. However accurate his judgments, his constant interference served to confuse, alienate and ultimately place intolerable pressure on commanders like Wavell. While a few, like Brooke and Montgomery, simply resisted Churchill and got away with it, the majority either could not or dared not do so.

Therein lies the fundamental dilemma of the role of the military in a democracy: generals take their orders from politicians but have the right to expect that their orders are purposeful. The reality is that wars too numerous to mention in the years since the Second World War have proved that more often than not the politicians have got it wrong. What made it so difficult in wartime Britain was that there was no separation (and consequently no counterbalance) between Churchill the political leader and Churchill the warlord. The orders of one were the orders of the other. With no minister of defence to play devil's advocate, the only brake was the chiefs of staff, whose role in that regard became clear very early in the war and was later refined under Brooke. The conundrum is that it is unlikely the war could have been won unless Churchill also filled the role of warlord.

A political and a military hat worn on the same head also created this fundamental problem: what to do when Churchill's views on strategy or his military decisions conflicted with those of his field commanders. Although he had no use for yes-men, when rebuffed, as he was by Wavell in June 1940 over the redeployment of infantry battalions from Palestine to England, he sulked and was unforgiving – in this case for Wavell's having been precisely what he sought in a general officer: someone with military sense who, like Brooke, would stand up to him.

Battleaxe was the first of the back-and-forth battles in the wastelands of North Africa in 1941 and 1942 as Rommel and a series of British generals matched wits. Churchill was impatient, as Ismay put it, to 'try the game again' in the desert. Rommel had become like a bone in his throat, and he wanted Auchinleck to go on the offensive without delay.

Auchinleck's primary task in 1941 was to deal with Rommel, and within a short time of taking over from Wavell was already in Churchill's doghouse. He refused the prime minister's entreaties, insisting it would be November before he could launch his counter-offensive to relieve Tobruk, code-named Crusader. Churchill continued to prod Auchinleck to get on with it. 'While disappointed and alarmed by retardation I fully accept your arrangements,' he wrote with reluctance on 24 October. 'Enemy is now ripe for sickle. I trust this condition will continue . . .

You should not hesitate to press on to Tripoli hot foot upon success if granted. Any lengthy delay will almost certainly close this prospect. You will be justified in running extraordinary risks with your available fast forces while the going is good . . . throw all in and count on me.'

Auchinleck was not alone in drawing fire. Sir Arthur Tedder, the new Middle East air chief, was also soon at odds with Churchill. Brainy and scholarly, Tedder was willing to speak his mind even when it was career suicide. An army officer in the First World War, he had transferred to the new RAF and rose quickly in its ranks. In 1940 he was the director of research at the Air Ministry, where he came into conflict with Beaverbrook over fighter production. He wrote a scathing report in defence of his conviction that as minister of aircraft production Beaverbrook had become a chaotic irritant whose rule was 'based on force and fear'. Tedder's position also brought him into occasional conflict with Churchill. As a strong, even obstinate advocate with a sharp tongue and a reputation for not pulling his punches, he inevitably clashed with the prime minister during the war. When Longmore had asked for Tedder as his replacement, someone else was chosen, but that officer was killed when his plane was shot down – a scenario that would be eerily repeated in North Africa in the summer of 1942. The outspoken Tedder had been effectively exiled to the Middle East, but his appointment was fortunate. His common sense, innovative tactics and organizational skills were put to excellent use.

The British build-up for Operation Crusader – the relief of Tobruk – was at the forefront of Churchill's mind. He relentlessly chivvied Auchinleck for his alleged failure to employ reinforcement tanks and vehicles right off the ship and into combat. Tedder was nearly sacked for observing that the Germans would probably possess 'numerical superiority' – a statement that referred to their ground forces, not the RAF, which he was certain could contain the Luftwaffe. His figures differed from those given to Churchill by the air staff, and they provoked a tempest. Churchill was furious and wanted Tedder's head on a platter.

To resolve the mess Portal, chief of the air staff, sent his deputy, Air Chief Marshal Sir Wilfrid Freeman, to Cairo. An instrumental figure in the rearmament of the RAF during the inter-war years, Freeman voiced support for the embattled Tedder. However, Churchill might well have thrown a monkey wrench into inter-service relations had Tedder not established a good working relationship with Auchinleck. The prime minister sent Auchinleck a pointed reminder that the air was subordinate to the army: 'Do not let any thought of Tedder's personal feelings influence you. This is no time for such considerations.' Then he mischievously invited Auchinleck to inform him if he wanted Tedder replaced, adding that he would appoint Freeman. When Freeman learned of Churchill's backstage manoeuvring, he declared, 'The role of Judas is one I will not fill,' and said he would resign if offered the job.

Auchinleck spiked further intrigue by writing to tell Portal that Tedder 'has been absolutely splendid' and that his relief 'would have been a dreadful mistake'. The crisis passed, but not without leaving Tedder still out of favour with Churchill.

When Crusader was again delayed until mid-November, Churchill wrote none too subtly: 'Feeling here has risen very high against what is thought to be our supine incapacity for action. I am however fully in control of public opinion and of the House of Commons . . . Everything should be thrown into this battle that can be made to play its part.'

In September the desert force was restructured and renamed the Eighth Army. Auchinleck appointed Lieutenant General Alan Cunningham its commanding general. The younger brother of ABC, Alan Cunningham was an artillery officer who had commanded British forces during the successful campaign in East Africa that resulted in the surrender of the Duke of Aosta's Italian army in May 1941, and the restoration of the deposed emperor Haile Selassie to the throne of Ethiopia. Impressed by his performance, Auchinleck appointed Cunningham to command this massive new Allied army, composed of British, New Zealand, Australian, South African, Indian, Polish and Free French units that eventually totalled one hundred thousand men, six hundred tanks and some five thousand vehicles being assembled along Egypt's western border. What Auchinleck actually created was a British panzer army.

Although he projected the very image of a fighting soldier and was described by one of his subordinate generals as 'a magnificent looking chap', Cunningham had never commanded a large force in battle (his command in East Africa consisted of four brigade groups against an inept Italian army in full retreat) and lacked an understanding not only of desert warfare but also of the employment of armour and infantry. Short-tempered and already showing signs of excessive stress, he was at a huge disadvantage by virtue of his inexperience when Crusader was launched. Auchinleck had passed over Jumbo Wilson for the Eighth

Army command in favour of Cunningham, and in so doing perpetrated the first of his ill-fated choices for high command in the desert. For his part Cunningham confidently predicted: 'I am going to seek old Rommel out and destroy him and his armour.'

When it was finally launched in a driving rainstorm on 18 November, Crusader turned out to be a near-disaster, in no small part because British tactics violated the principle of concentration of force. Despite the Eighth Army's great strength there was only the First World War precedent for the employment of tanks as a separate entity against other tanks. O'Connor understood how to employ combined arms effectively, but he was now a POW, and those who followed him repeatedly made the same tactical mistakes – and paid the price. During Crusader, Cunningham split his armour and his infantry, with the result that the Eighth Army's combat power was squandered. Together they would have made a powerful force; fighting separately each was vulnerable. Until they learned the same bitter lesson, the US army in Tunisia would adopt similar tactics in 1943. Rommel later inquired of a captured British officer: 'What difference does it make if you have two tanks to my one, when you spread them out and let me smash them in detail?'

It was just such conventional military thinking by men with little imagination and experience that had led Brooke to bemoan the lack of good senior generals, and Churchill to have become so distrustful of all but the few who proved they were capable of going beyond the orthodox folly of fighting a modern war with outmoded tactics. Those with fresh ideas and open minds, such as the advocates and innovators of mechanization during the inter-war years, like Frederick Pile and Percy 'Hobo' Hobart, were considered mavericks too far outside the mainstream of conventional military thinking. They were not among the 'old boys' who populated the upper ranks of the British army and worried more about their cricket scores and hunting and shooting than about studying and adapting their thinking to the sort of innovative tactics employed by men like Rommel in Germany and Patton and Adna Chaffee in the United States. In light of the failures of well-meaning but unsuccessful commanders like Cunningham, it becomes easier to understand Churchill's frustration and propensity to meddle in matters that he might have ignored had they been in the hands of men he more fully trusted.

Although Rommel had expected a British counter-offensive, Crusader caught him off guard in what turned out to be one of the messiest battles of the desert war, one that has aptly been called 'a battle which both sides deserved to lose'. In theory the combatants were evenly matched, and had it not been for crucial mistakes on both sides, either might have suffered a disastrous defeat. For six weeks the two sides traded blood and terrain, with the heaviest battles fought around Sidi Rezegh. On 24 November Rommel counterattacked, and after his panzers smashed across the Libya–Egypt frontier ('the Wire') into the British rear, he was prevented from having a far more damaging impact only when his fuel ran short and the RAF made further advance too costly.

The Western Desert was unforgiving of those who were not its masters, and within a short time Cunningham lost his nerve and would have halted the offensive and withdrawn the Eighth Army behind the frontier had Auchinleck not intervened at once to save the situation and restore order before the battle fell apart completely. He relieved Cunningham of command two days later. The new commander was Major General Neil Ritchie, and although he proved a better choice than Cunningham in the short run, he too would become yet another failed commander. Only Auchinleck's presence for a crucial ten-day period during the remaining weeks of Crusader saved the day, indeed actually portended a British victory.

The siege of Tobruk was lifted on 28 November, and Benghazi was again in British hands on 24 December. By early January 1942 Rommel had withdrawn the Afrika Korps to El Agheila, in effect ceding all of Cyrenaica to the Eighth Army. This situation was short lived. Reinforced with fresh tanks and armoured cars, Rommel counterattacked on 21 January and by the end of the month had retaken Benghazi and most of western Cyrenaica. The Eighth Army now occupied the Gazala Line, a series of minefields and defensive 'boxes' that extended in an arc more than forty miles out from Tobruk.

Rommel's recklessness would have cost him dearly had the Eighth Army been in better hands. At the unit level the fighting men gained valuable experience in desert fighting, but, despite excellent air support from the RAF, when it came to tactics the British once again demonstrated that without a seasoned commander they were bumbling amateurs in a deadly game in which failure was paid for in blood. With O'Connor a POW, the only general capable of besting Rommel remained on the sidelines in England, largely forgotten and in early 1942 never even remotely considered a future commander of the Eighth Army.

It would take seven months, two more failed commanding generals and near-defeat before he would be summoned to the desert.

In the end stalemate and exhaustion prevailed. Crusader was a British victory only in the sense that Tobruk was relieved and the front extended back into Cyrenaica. The cost to both sides was high: Axis losses were a staggering 32 per cent (38,300 of 119,000), while Eighth Army losses were less than half that (17,700). Both sides lost an estimated three hundred nearly irreplaceable tanks.

Although Operation Barbarossa effectively meant the end of Sea Lion, in the autumn of 1941 Churchill remained deeply concerned that Hitler might yet decide to invade Britain. He wrote to Roosevelt: 'I feel we must be prepared to meet a supreme onslaught from March [1942] onwards.' He was not satisfied that his intelligence estimates adequately addressed Sea Lion and, in one of his shrewdest moves of the war, convened an elite inter-service group of experts to study the problem and report to him. Instead of examining how Britain would defend against Sea Lion, the team did the reverse: it developed a plan of how the *Germans* would carry out a successful invasion, including realistic scenarios of air, naval and ground operations that covered every possible contingency: diversionary landings, likely landing sites and other tactics such as the use of poison gas, saboteurs and airborne troops. One member of this team was Air Marshal (later Marshal of the Royal Air Force Sir) John Slessor, one of the lesser-known but most important figures in the RAF during the war. As a senior air planner, bomber group commander and assistant chief of the air staff, Slessor not only helped forge an effective alliance of the US and British strategic air forces, but as the commander in chief of Coastal Command in 1943 was instrumental in the winning of the Battle of the Atlantic through the employment of long-range aircraft that by mid-1943 were sinking German U-boats at a rate of some seven a month. Slessor always believed that Hitler's insistence on neutralizing the RAF in the summer of 1940 prior to Sea Lion was a fatal mistake, and that 'if he had steeled himself to lose say 200,000 men in the attempt – an insignificant fraction of what he later lost before his defeat – he could have effected a lodgement with armoured divisions, and it is difficult to see how that could have failed to be decisive at that time, when our Army was virtually disarmed. The Prime Minister's inspiring words about fighting on the beaches and on the hills were an immense moral tonic . . . but "pikes and maces" are no match for panzer divisions.'

In the autumn of 1941 the former bad boy and rebellious under-achiever returned to Harrow to deliver an impassioned speech to the pupils and staff, pointing out that Britain was poorly armed and faced attack by air and sea. Despite the catastrophic events of 1941 his message was upbeat. 'Do not speak of dark days,' he declared. 'These are not dark days: these are great days – the greatest days our country has ever lived: and we must all thank God that we have been allowed . . . to play a part in making these days memorable for the history of our race.'

Churchill's daughter Mary well remembers what took him to Washington in December 1941. On Sunday, 7 December she was at Chequers with her father, whose dinner guests that evening were Ambassador Gilbert Winant and W. Averell Harriman. Shortly before 9.00 p.m. Churchill's butler, Frank Sawyers, interrupted their conversation to tell him that there would be something on the nine o'clock BBC news about an attack on Pearl Harbor. A radio was brought in just in time for them to hear the news bulletin about the surprise attack early that morning. Harriman recalled that it actually came as a relief. 'We all knew the grim future it held, but at least there was a future now.' He and Churchill both realized that Britain simply could not win by itself. 'At last we could see a prospect of winning,' said Harriman. Churchill immediately placed a call to Roosevelt, who confirmed the worst. Disastrous as it was for the United States, this sudden turn of events was the lifeline Churchill had been hoping for and gambling on for eighteen arduous months. 'No American will think it wrong of me if I proclaim that to have the United States at our side was to me the greatest joy. I could not foretell the course of events. I do not pretend to have measured accurately the martial might of Japan, but now at this very moment I knew the United States was in the war, up to the neck and in to the death. So we had won after all!' That night, Churchill said, 'I went to bed and slept the sleep of the saved and thankful.'

The next day FDR cabled that Congress had overwhelmingly approved a declaration of war against Japan. 'Today all of us are in the same boat with you and the people of the Empire and it is a ship that will not and cannot be sunk.' It was the first step towards what has aptly been called the grand alliance between Britain and the United States.

Although dark times and setbacks lay ahead, the basis for victory would formally exist in January 1942, when the United States and Britain were joined by twenty-two other nations as signatories to the coalition upon which Churchill had pinned Britain's survival.

47
'Colonel Shrapnel'

He is quite the most difficult man to work with that I have ever struck, but I should not have missed the chance of working with him for anything on earth!
— Brooke

By the autumn of 1941 Churchill's lack of confidence in Dill as CIGS had hit new lows and eventually brought about his downfall. It was clear that his days were numbered when Churchill began referring to him by the scornful nickname 'Dilly-Dally' and as 'the dead hand of inanition'. At a late-night session in 1941 Churchill remarked to General Kennedy that although Dill had 'many excellent qualities he had one great failing: he allowed his mind to be too much impressed by the enemy's will.' Kennedy silently disagreed, and 'thought to myself that Dill's powers of resistance to Churchill were proof enough of his moral courage'. However, once Churchill soured on a military man there was no turning back, and his exit became only a matter of time.

On 17 November Churchill informed Dill that he was being replaced. Like Wavell before him, Dill accepted his fate like a good soldier but nevertheless with bitter disappointment. It is no secret that he was tired and, although the experience of being sacked was wrenching, his close confidant, John Kennedy, intuited that deep down he was not sorry to be relieved of the great burden he had carried to the best of his ability for eighteen arduous months. Dill's nerves were stretched to breaking point, and he was at the point of sheer exhaustion, exacerbated not only by his own deteriorating health but also by the grave illness and subsequent death from a series of strokes in December 1940 of his wife, with whom he had had a disappointing marriage. Like Wavell, he was never completely on the same wavelength as the prime minister. Churchill left the impression that Dill was not a strong enough personality; however, the evidence does not support such a contention. Dill's recently released personal papers reveal that he was no doormat. He fought Churchill over issues ranging from protecting Wavell to the invasion of Greece, which he opposed. Although he had become, along with Wavell, Churchill's chief whipping boy, he responded with candour when challenged. Several months before his dismissal, Churchill was actively belittling his CIGS. 'He has now got his knife right into Dill and frequently disparages him,' wrote Colville. 'He says he has an alternative CIGS in mind: Sir Alan Brooke, C-in-C, Home Forces.'

Dill left office with deeply mixed emotions and said of Churchill that, despite the workload he placed upon the staffs of the military departments, he was the greatest leader the country could have had, but that no one would ever portray him as a great strategist. Dill also later told Hankey, 'I want you to understand that never under any circumstances will I serve under that man Churchill again.' Yet Dill's service to Britain was by no means over, and Churchill was wise enough not to cast him aside completely. For his part Dill was able to swallow his pride and selflessly agree to an assignment in Washington to serve as the chief of the British Joint Staff Mission, and later as the senior British representative on the Combined Chiefs of Staff. As Britain's military eyes and ears in the United States, he was exceptionally effective and became a close friend and trusted confidant of the US army chief of staff, General George C. Marshall. At the time of his death in November 1944, Dill had achieved a stature and prominence he was never able to accomplish as CIGS. He was so admired by Marshall and Roosevelt that not only was he was buried in Arlington National Cemetery, the only Briton so honoured, but his grave is marked by one of Arlington's only two equestrian statues.

Churchill chose Brooke as the new chief of the Imperial General Staff. It was his most astute military appointment of the war, and it almost did not occur. He nearly made the disastrous choice of reappointing Lord Gort as CIGS. Gort had served in the post from 1937 to 1939 but had neither the strategic vision nor the gumption to have stood up to Churchill in the most important military post of all. Backed by Beaverbrook, Churchill also considered Dill's deputy, Sir Archibald Nye, a highly regarded officer who had risen through the ranks from private in the First World War to lieutenant general in 1941. Archie Nye was a man of quick mind, exceptional character and courage; his only draw-back was that he was a relatively junior officer and would have had trouble controlling men like Montgomery, Wavell and Auchinleck with far longer service and higher rank. Eventually Churchill elected not to pursue Gort and instead began favouring Brooke.

On 16 November 1941 Brooke was summoned to Chequers and invited to replace Dill, whom Churchill called 'a tired man'. Brooke later recorded that for a few moments there was a dead silence that Churchill misunderstood. 'Do you not think you will able to work with me?' he asked. Brooke assured him that was not the reason. 'There is no doubt that I was temporarily staggered by the magnitude of the task I was undertaking . . . Added to that was the certain trial of working hand in hand with Winston in handling the direction of the war. I had seen enough of him to realize his impetuous nature, his gambler's spirit, and his determination to follow his own selected path at all costs.' Brooke accepted and was left alone in Churchill's study to reflect before rejoining the other guests. 'I am not an exceptionally religious person, but I am not ashamed to confess that as soon as he was out of the room my first impulse was to kneel down and pray to God for guidance and support in the task I had undertaken.'

The appointment of Brooke (who became Lord Alanbrooke after the war) was also something of a departure for Churchill from his usual preference for dashing commanders. Brooke was not dashing, nor did he display the debonair manner of a soldier like Alexander, an intrepid sailor like Mountbatten or Keyes or an unconventional warrior like General Orde Wingate. Officers like Brooke and Montgomery were all business and had no apparent sense of humour or time for the kind of small talk that Churchill thrived on. Without his uniform, Brooke could just as easily have passed for a banker or a barrister. What Churchill gained was more important: in Brooke he chose a thinking man's soldier.

'Brookie', as he was known to his friends, was, like so many of the war's senior officers, an Ulsterman. Perhaps the best description of him appeared in *The Economist* in 1957: 'In his demanding and abrupt efficiency, he knew when to scold, when to encourage, when to protect. Men admired, feared, and liked him, in that order, perhaps. He became . . . the conscience of the Army: a dark, incisive, round-shouldered Irish eagle, the reluctant chairman of a council of war, frustrating, in selfless but far from patient service, those talents that could not otherwise have forced him into the company of the great captains.'

Although considered abrupt and somewhat dour by those who did not know him well (he was nicknamed 'Colonel Shrapnel' in the War Cabinet offices), Brooke was one of the most consummate and able soldiers of his generation. Possessed of common sense and a background as a low-key, successful fighting commander, he brought to the office of CIGS skills Churchill badly needed. As the spokesman for the chiefs of staff he never hesitated to stand up to the prime minister. He was not only an experienced soldier; he knew what he was talking about and possessed the moral courage to stick to his convictions in the face of Churchill's anger at being contradicted. And while he never liked being overruled, Churchill recognized Brooke's professionalism and respected his willingness to oppose ideas and schemes he deemed wrong. In fact it was precisely because Churchill thought Dill lacked the toughness he wanted from his CIGS that Brooke was chosen to replace him.

Brooke was one of a new generation of Second World War British officers resolutely determined to avoid the mistakes of the 1914–18 leadership. Within six months of assuming office he became the chairman of the Chiefs of Staff Committee and its spokesman. Both Pound and Portal were far less combative, and with Pound becoming increasingly ill from the brain tumour that would compel his resignation a few weeks before his death in October 1943, Brooke filled an enormous void. Both he and his American counterpart, George C. Marshall, were formidable figures who did not suffer fools and were considered aloof by people who did not know them well.

Ismay said of Brooke that 'his selflessness, integrity and mastery of his profession earned him the complete confidence, not only of his political chiefs and his colleagues in Whitehall, but also of all our commanders in the field. On that account alone, he was worth his weight in gold. In the course of my eighteen years' service in Whitehall, I saw the work of eight different Chiefs of the Imperial General Staff at close quarters . . . Brooke was the best of them all.'

Behind the mask of Brooke's public image as a stern, humourless soldier was a passionate bird-watcher and a man of considerable humanity who loathed war, as all good soldiers do. Early in the war he wrote: 'There are times when the madness and the folly of war choke one! Why human beings must behave like children at this stage of the evolution of the human race is hard to understand . . . I am very tired of this war and long for peace.'

Working for Churchill was a trial by fire that spared no one, least of all Alan Brooke. He had no illusions about the difficulty of his task. After nearly two years as CIGS he wondered whether any future historian would ever be able to paint Churchill in his true colours:

It is a wonderful character – the most marvellous qualities and superhuman genius mixed with an astonishing lack of vision at times, and an impetuosity which if not guided must inevitably bring him into trouble again and again. Perhaps the most remarkable failing of his is that he can never see a whole strategical problem at once. His gaze always settles on some definite part of the canvas and the rest of the picture is lost . . . especially if this wider vision should in any way interfere with the operation he may have temporarily set his heart on.

The entire character of the Chiefs of Staff Committee changed with Brooke's appointment. The chiefs gained a new cachet that had previously been missing. With Brooke as their spokesman, the task of reining in Churchill's wilder impulses became more focused and more determined. It also consumed inordinate amounts of time taken from other important pursuits. From the sidelines Charles Wilson saw the battle of wills between Churchill and the chiefs play out:

Common sense, Wavell used to say, is the knowledge of what is and what is not possible, and is the most important quality in a general . . . This in turn depends on a really sound grip of the mechanics of war – topography, movement and supply. Wavell knew that the Prime Minister would not have passed an examination in such matters with flying colours. Common sense had never been Winston's strong suit, and that is why the British and American Chiefs of Staff used to feel a positive sense of disquiet when the PM took an active part in the detailed conduct of the war. Gen. Marshall told me that it had been an important part of their duties to wean Winston from wrong strategic conceptions. This was softened by an affectionate grin as he went on to grumble, 'Winston won't look at things like a man who has been all his life a soldier.' And when I pleaded that he had begun life as a professional soldier, the grin widened. 'You'd not think of consulting Somerset Maugham about your health because he qualified as a doctor fifty years ago!'

What troubled the CIGS was that the PM, with his impulsive nature, tended to arrive at decisions by a process of intuition; he would get a hunch, and once he had made up his mind, it was difficult to induce him to change it. In vain Alanbrooke would plead that it would be prudent to examine the problem systematically and logically. When difficulties were raised the PM lost patience; he saw only victory.

Some of Churchill's most outrageous ideas either came from, or were endorsed by, cronies like Beaverbrook and Lindemann. Desmond Morton claimed that they all came from his brain but that he would often try them out on his closest advisers, who could be counted upon to agree with him without benefit of criticism or real consideration. 'Usually, however, these notions, springing fully armed from him were suddenly shot at the Chiefs of Staff or at the Joint Planners . . . He did not at all like individuals who attacked these ideas of his as soon as they heard of them.'

The result was an inevitable clash with the chiefs that produced arguments that went on for hours. Churchill's love for what Morton called 'funny operations' of the sort created by Mountbatten's COHQ reflected 'his burning desire for ACTION. If the great regular forces and their commanders could do nothing – no matter what the reason – then let us try tricks. He was not a patient man. He also began by thinking that all the "rules of war" adumbrated by his *official* advisors were out of date and fundamentally wrong. He learnt in time that however out of date they were, some of them were of permanent application.'

Tension is an inevitable part of the civil–military relationship. In the spring of 1942, although he still failed to understand some of the problems of modern war, Churchill was right to question Brooke about the presence of 750,000 men in the Middle East, of whom only 100,000 were actually engaged in fighting: 'Explain to us exactly how the remaining 650,000 are occupied.' Given that Rommel was winning victories on a military shoestring, it was a legitimate question that only increased his distrust and his already considerable vigilance.

Although Churchill's criticism usually magnified tensions, it sometimes led to moments of levity. One such example concerned a bombproof building the Admiralty had erected adjacent to Horse Guards Parade that prompted Churchill to observe, 'They have put up a very strong place there – masses of concrete and tons of steel. Taking into account the fact that their heads are made of solid bone, they ought to be quite safe inside.'

The delicate balancing act between Churchill and the chiefs lasted through the war but not without moments of grave crisis, one of which occurred before the second Quebec Conference (code-named Octagon) in September 1944, when the chiefs were collectively on the verge of resigning until Ismay deflected the issues by resigning in their stead – though he was promptly talked out of it by Churchill. 'Winston suspected me for some time of having ganged up with the Chiefs of Staff, but he was distinctly less rough with them from that time onwards,' said Ismay.

The worst outburst of the war between Churchill and the chiefs took place on 4 December 1941 over the ten RAF squadrons he had promised to send Stalin from the Middle East once the campaign in Libya was successful. Although Portal agreed, he cautioned that the offer was too definite. 'This produced the most awful outburst of temper,' recorded Brooke. 'We were told that we did nothing but obstruct his intentions, we had no ideas of our own, and whenever he produced ideas we produced nothing but objections ... Attlee pacified him once, but he broke out again, then Anthony Eden soothed him temporarily ... Finally, he looked at his papers for some 5 minutes, then slammed them together, closed the meeting and walked out of the room! It was pathetic and entirely unnecessary. We were only trying to save him from making definite promises which he might find hard to keep later on ... Such a pity. God knows where we would be without him, but God knows where we shall go with him.'

The problem of containing Churchill's constant attraction to diversionary ventures jeopardized Brooke's policy of closely managing Britain's precious military assets for genuinely important operations. Churchill's continuing obsession with Norway reappeared in the autumn of 1941, while Brooke was still commanding the Home Forces. Although the chiefs had already studied and turned down such a plan, on 3 October Churchill directed Brooke to prepare a detailed plan in one week for an expeditionary force to recapture Trondheim – 'ready to the last button'. The British had neither the resources nor a valid strategic reason for another operation in Norway other than to harass and tie down a German force. Norway in 1941 presented the same problem as it had in 1940: it was beyond the range of adequate air support and therefore a prescription for failure and yet another Dunkirk. Brooke and Dill fought back, insisting with considerable justification that the operation would achieve no real purpose and, in any event, had already been turned down by the chiefs as unworkable because it would have no air support. 'The only reason he ever gave', said Brooke, 'was that Hitler had unrolled the map of Europe, and he would start rolling it up again from Norway.'

Brooke duly carried out his orders, and nine days later there came another stormy session. His plan made the case that the operation would fail for lack of air support. An angry Churchill 'shoved his chin out in his aggressive way and, staring hard at me, said: "I had instructed you to prepare a detailed plan for the capture of Trondheim . . . You have instead submitted a masterly treatise on all the difficulties and on all the reasons why this operation should not be carried out."' Brooke was relentlessly grilled for more than two hours on its every aspect, with Churchill employing sarcasm and scathing criticism in an attempt to poke holes in his reasoning. At one point the prime minister glared at Brooke and declared, 'I sometimes think some of my generals don't want to fight the Germans!' In the end Brooke won the day as Churchill none too graciously conceded defeat – but not before later attempting and failing for a third time to reinvigorate the idea. Brooke later noted that his first major face-to-face battle with Churchill had been good training for the trials that lay ahead of him as CIGS. Nevertheless the battles with Churchill over Norway dragged on, with considerable time and effort wasted planning a risky operation with no viable strategic purpose.

One of the lessons John Kennedy learned that tumultuous night at Chequers in 1941 was what Brooke would practise when he became CIGS. 'Brooke found it an invaluable rule never to tell Churchill more than was absolutely necessary. I remember him once scoring out nine-tenths of the draft of a minute to the Prime Minister, remarking as he did so, "The more you tell that man about war, the more you hinder the winning of it." Nobody who knew Brooke or the Prime Minister would take such a remark as a hundred per cent serious . . . but we were all nervous at times of feeding a new idea into that fertile brain in case it might lead us away from the main stream into irrelevant backwaters.'

Churchill's tendency to wear down his opponents with a combination of intimidation, fatigue and incessant questioning was never successful with Brooke. Time and again sessions like the war of words over Norway were repeated whenever Brooke believed it was the right decision to thwart Churchill or to shelve his unworkable ideas.

It is to his credit that an autocrat like Churchill, so accustomed to gaining his own way, should be drawn to a man with whom he had virtually nothing in common and who could deliver words as sharp as those he himself hurled at others. Had Brooke been less outspoken, he would have been neither as effective nor as respected. Their association got off to a rocky beginning. Churchill was unused to being opposed so forcefully and the sparks would fly, yet the combustible mix somehow worked. Brooke's grasp of facts, his vision and his formidable intellect were every bit a match for Churchill and a lucid counter to his impetuosity. Their relationship, which was to survive until the end of war, while often portrayed as one of love–hate, was rather that of two strong-willed men with a common goal, neither of whom backed away from tackling tough issues and defending his ideas.

Not long after Brooke's appointment Churchill complained to Ismay, 'The CIGS must go. He hates me. I know he does. I can see hatred looking out of his eyes.' Ismay immediately went to see Brooke and relayed Churchill's words. Brooke replied, 'I don't hate him; I *love* him, but the moment I tell him that I agree with him and I don't, that's the time to get rid of me. Then I'm no more use to him.' Ismay asked if he could tell Churchill what Brooke had said. Brooke agreed, and Ismay repeated his remark. 'Churchill's eyes filled with tears, and he gently murmured: "*Dear* Brooke!"'

Their disagreements were at times nothing short of brutal; words that would have seriously wounded lesser men were exchanged in the heat of the moment. Yet such was the magnetic pull of Churchill that he would appoint someone like Brooke who lacked his buccaneering spirit and who had no interest in attaining supremacy. Although he argued and fought with them, 'anyone criticizing the Chiefs of Staff, no matter how high his position', Pound's successor as first sea lord, Andrew Cunningham, would later observe, 'was likely to find the Prime Minister's heavy guns turned against him.'

Like virtually all who served Churchill, Brooke made it clear that the positives outweighed the negatives. In September 1942, for example, he wrote to Wavell:

But is there really anything wrong with our leadership today, can you find a man to lead us with greater courage, greater faith in England, more power of inspiration than the P.M.? He has made mistakes, he will make a good many more, he is difficult in many ways; but taking it by and large I don't think our general strategy has been bad, given our resources . . . and we have certainly had resolute courageous confident leadership at the head. I don't think in this imperfect world we can hope for much more at the present and I believe that . . . we shall come through all right.

What all but wore Brooke out was that he could never escape his master's clutches even when he was able to take a rare Sunday off. Churchill would constantly summon him to the telephone on inconsequential matters that could just as easily have awaited his return. 'My Sundays at home were always subjected to a series of calls throughout the day.'

The first Quebec Conference in August 1943 left Brooke 'absolutely cooked', but even after a particularly demanding day with Churchill he wrote: 'He is quite the most difficult man to work with that I have ever struck, but I should not have missed the chance of working with him for anything on earth!'

Brooke and his colleagues were perpetually exhausted by lack of sleep brought about by Churchill's propensity to work late into the night and to demand that Ismay and the chiefs keep him company. Invariably he ignored all hints that perhaps everyone would be better served by rest. Ismay would often say to him when the bell tolled some early-morning hour: ' "It is getting late, Prime Minister. What about bed?" And always the same retort: "If you do not mind who wins the war, you can go to bed. But I am going to do my duty." And perhaps two hours later, he would turn on me in well simulated anger and say: "You should not have kept me up like this." The schoolboy in him was always coming to the surface. It always will.'

During the war Brooke saw little of his beloved wife, and as a means of relieving the tensions of his job he began keeping a diary that has become one of the Second World War's most revealing windows into the inner councils of the war and its strategy. He wrote of his loneliness and love for his wife, but more important, with unsparing frankness and often with biting criticism, Brooke's war diaries revealed his triumphs, his fears and the frustrations of working for Churchill.

The occasions when an exasperated Brooke would write disparagingly in his diary came mostly at the end of especially punishing late-night sessions. By September 1944 both men were displaying the ill effects of five years of war. To his great credit Brooke never lost perspective: 'Without him England was lost for a certainty, with him England has been on the verge of disaster time and again ... Never have I admired and despised a man simultaneously to the same extent. Never have such opposite extremes been combined in the same human being.'

When Brooke's diaries were published heavily edited in two volumes in the 1950s, they drew a storm of criticism from Churchill's admirers, friends and wartime colleagues for his characterizations of Churchill and other major war figures. Brooke later toned down some his criticism in his post-war 'Notes on My Life', which became part of the published diaries, noting that his criticisms were often written at moments of sheer exhaustion and exasperation.

More often overlooked is that, whereas Brooke acknowledged Churchill's greatness, the feeling was never reciprocated. Once Churchill was asked to respond to a question posed by Dr Wilson: 'Don't you think Brooke is pretty good at his job?' He would respond only after a long pause with the tepid remark: 'He has a flair for the business.' In his war memoirs Churchill barely mentions Brooke. Nevertheless, for all his wrath and impatience when denied or rebuked, Churchill carried out his side of their relationship. When he was asked after the war by Wilson if he had ever considered sacking Brooke, he replied with great conviction, 'Never!' Then, after a long pause, he repeated, 'Never!' Ultimately, however, Brooke's official biographer has concluded that neither man fully appreciated the difficulties under which the other laboured. That these two emotionally very dissimilar men managed to function so well despite the enormous stress to which they were subjected and despite their mutual exasperation is tribute enough to their integrity.

Brooke's appointment came only days before Pearl Harbor. On 8 December, both Britain and the United States declared war on Japan. Pearl Harbor spurred Churchill to travel to Washington to confer with his new ally. On 13 December, accompanied by Beaverbrook and the chiefs of staff (minus Brooke, who remained in London), the prime minister boarded the battleship *King George V* for another risky voyage across the Atlantic. Eight days later he arrived in the United States for what has aptly been called 'the Anglo-American Marriage Ceremony'.

48

Chickens Roosting in the Far East

I can't get the victories. It's the victories that are so hard to get.
                    – Churchill, shortly before the fall of Singapore

Pearl Harbor was not the only military disaster to occur in December 1941. The Japanese army landed an invasion force in northern Malaya on 8 December and began relentlessly advancing south towards the crown colony of Singapore, which was defended by a mixed force of eighty-five thousand British, Indian and Australian troops.

On 10 December, the battleships HMS *Repulse* and HMS *Prince of Wales* (the primary warships of a Royal Navy task force designated Force Z) were sunk by Japanese dive-bombers while returning to Singapore after a fruitless search for the Japanese invasion force. Admiral Tom Phillips, the well-liked commander of Force Z, was among the 840 men who died on the *Prince of Wales*. It was a crushing blow that Churchill took extremely hard. 'In all the war I never received a more direct shock,' he said, deeming it as devastating for Britain as Pearl Harbor was to the United States. His secretary, Kathleen Hill, was in his underground bedroom when he received the news by telephone from Dudley Pound, and she sat silently while Churchill mutely mourned their loss. 'It was a terrible moment,' she recalled, but one that he managed to put behind him, as all good leaders must. In moments of grim humour he would tell his staff: 'We must just KBO – Keep Buggering On.' Hill encountered Dr Wilson and said, 'I think he'd like to see you.' Wilson found Churchill 'slumped over . . . his head was buried in his hands.' Finally, after some moments of silence 'he raised his eyes and looked at me in a dazed way as if he had received a stunning blow between the eyes . . . "You know what has happened. The Repulse and Prince of Wales have been sunk."'

The decision to send the two battleships to the Far East was controversial. Churchill ordered them to Singapore in the autumn of 1941, gambling that they would serve as a deterrent to Japanese aggression in much the same way as the *Bismarck* and the *Tirpitz* had compelled the Royal Navy to tie up large numbers of ships to guard against the menace they posed to Allied shipping. Indeed, in the summer of 1941 he believed that the combination of a fast British fleet based in Singapore and the US fleets at Pearl Harbor and in Manila would deter Japan, both politically and militarily, a calculation that, in retrospect, was naive.

The Admiralty strongly opposed Churchill's decision, as did Smuts, who warned that it was risky to base them in Singapore. Predictably his reaction to the Admiralty's advice was scathing. Under intense pressure, Pound decided he could not stand in Churchill's way and agreed to their deployment.

The aircraft carrier *Indomitable* was to have provided the necessary air cover but never made it to the Far East after being damaged earlier in the British West Indies. Phillips's gutsy but highly risky decision, made on his own, to intercept the Japanese without air cover, proved fatal when Force Z was attacked by a swarm of bombers and torpedo bombers flying from bases in Japanese-occupied French Indo-China. In the hours before the news of their loss reached London, Churchill was already proposing that they either vanish into the Pacific as the *Bismarck* had done in the North Atlantic or sail south and join up with the US Asiatic Fleet. Ismay went to bed the night before and dreamed that the *Prince of Wales* had been sunk, only to learn the next morning that his nightmare had become reality. He recalled feeling numb with the pain of this grievous loss: 'It was a shocking start.' The Japanese had called Churchill's bluff.

With Germany and Italy declaring war on the United States on 11 December, Churchill's long wait was at end, but in the Pacific, he noted, 'Japan was supreme, and we everywhere weak and naked.' Britain's vulnerability was soon proved by the fall of its jewel of the Far East. Japanese forces attacked Hong Kong from the air and the Chinese mainland on 8 December, and for seventeen days the colony's ten thousand defenders held out bravely, but without reinforcements continued resistance became hopeless. To spare further useless bloodshed, the garrison commander surrendered on Christmas Day. Some 6,500 men were captured, a great many of whom would die in brutal captivity under horrific conditions.

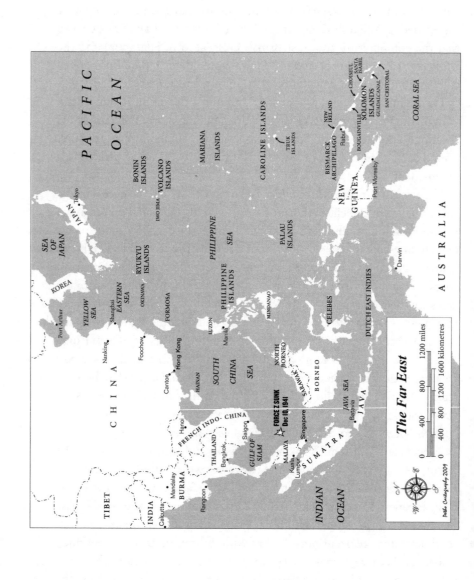

The Far East

Two weeks after Pearl Harbor, Japanese troops landed at Lingayen Gulf on the island of Luzon and quickly marched on Manila. To prevent its wanton destruction, General Douglas MacArthur declared Manila an open city on 27 December and the Philippine capital was occupied on 2 January 1942. MacArthur's forces retreated to the Bataan Peninsula and the island fortress of Corregidor. With defeat inevitable, MacArthur was ordered to Australia and left in the dead of night by motor torpedo boat on 11 March vowing, 'I shall return.' Three months of bitter fighting ensued before the gallant US–Filipino defenders surrendered on 9 April with the loss of 75,000 men, 12,000 of them Americans. Pearl Harbor, the loss of the Philippines and the subsequent Bataan Death March to imprisonment under unspeakable conditions inflicted grievous wounds on the American psyche.

Churchill arrived in Washington on 22 December 1941 for a three-week stay in the White House as Roosevelt's guest. The two continued to warm to each other during a great many hours discussing the war. Evenings were somewhat more informal with FDR making their cocktails himself and Churchill pushing the president's wheelchair from place to place 'as a mark of respect' he likened to 'Sir Walter Raleigh spreading his cloak before Queen Elizabeth'. Despite a common language and heritage, however, there was evidence they were poles apart on a number of fundamental issues. Among them, as Sir Charles Wilson would later write, 'The British Empire was a sin to the Americans, but Roosevelt found Winston an unrepentant sinner ... Lord Halifax has told me that when Winston affirmed to the President that he had not come to Washington to "liquidate the British Empire", the President had a feeling that he was listening to a voice out of the eighteenth century ... "He was a great Tory," the President chuckled indulgently, though he was a little shocked perhaps by his imperialism. Why, he talked about the British Empire as if he was living in the reign of Queen Victoria! And they would never agree about India.' To Eleanor Roosevelt's disgust, Churchill's status as a guest in the White House did not alter his night-owl habits, which kept the president up well beyond his bedtime – nor did it prevent him from barging uninvited into FDR's bedroom at virtually any hour when there was something he wanted to discuss.

Churchill's three weeks in Washington were part of what was known as the Arcadia Conference, the first joint meeting of the newly created

Combined Chiefs of Staff, the term applied to the US and British chiefs of staff operating as a single body to formulate strategic policy and issue guidance to the Allied commanders in chief who would, in due course, be appointed to head the fighting units.

Unlike FDR, who drew back from direct involvement in military negotiations, Churchill was an active participant in Arcadia. Now that the United States was a formal ally, he had to contend with important differences of opinion and strategy, and with the fact that he would not always get his way. The new Combined Chiefs readily agreed that their first priority was the defeat of Germany, and that US operations in the Pacific would hold the line against Japan. How and where Germany was to be defeated remained unresolved and an object of controversy that would drag on well into 1943. In the Mediterranean, however, little would change for most of 1942 until the litany of failed commanders ended and the right man was found to reverse Britain's course and Churchill's fortunes.

American policy during the Second World War was unambiguous and affirmed that direct military action should take priority over political considerations. To that end Marshall and his staff were crafting a plan code-named Sledgehammer, an emergency cross-Channel invasion of northern France in 1942 to relieve the pressure on the Red Army by forcing Hitler to commit troops to the defence of the West.

Although Churchill himself had first conceived of a cross-Channel venture in the black days of 1940 after Dunkirk, the British thought Sledgehammer potentially disastrous and blocked its acceptance. As Marshall noted, 'It appeared that the British staff and cabinet were unalterable in [their] refusal to touch SLEDGEHAMMER ... So we were at a complete stalemate. Churchill was rabid for Africa,' and adamant that the Allies could not and should not mount a cross-Channel invasion in 1942. Failure was unthinkable, Churchill argued; thus the operation should be deferred until the odds favoured the Allies' success. British policy became acceptance of an eventual cross-Channel invasion but opposition to any attempt to carry it out in 1942. Unlike American insistence on a well-defined war strategy, British policy mirrored Churchill's leaning towards opportunism, such as that offered by conducting military operations in the Mediterranean.

Churchill contended that Germany's most vulnerable point was the 'soft underbelly' of the Mediterranean, and his arguments found favour with Roosevelt. Not only was a cross-Channel operation in 1942 impossible, the prime minister declared, it was only in the Mediterranean that an opportunity existed to defeat Axis forces and eliminate Italy from the war, to 'tighten the ring' and prepare for the day a full-scale cross-Channel invasion could be undertaken in 1943. However, Churchill had a much deeper motive: he was deeply distrustful of Stalin and sought to introduce into American thinking a grand strategy that included curbing Russian hegemony and post-war territorial ambitions in eastern Europe.

Marshall opposed Churchill on purely military grounds, arguing that it would be courting disaster to leave the Red Army facing the might of the Wehrmacht unaided; indeed it would be one of history's worst blunders should eight million men be lost because of Anglo-American inertia. Marshall also feared the consequences of becoming bogged down in military operations against the Axis in the Mediterranean, as he believed that the decisive battles of the war would be fought in north-west Europe. Marshall contended that, while Sledgehammer might be 'a desperate operation to save Russia', even if it failed it would serve its purpose by drawing off German forces from the east, thus compelling the Luftwaffe to do battle with the RAF and opening the door to a full-scale invasion in 1943. In addition to Sledgehammer, Marshall proposed two other synchronized plans. They consisted of an enormous build-up of American forces in the United Kingdom (Operation Bolero), considered the first vital step towards the eventual full-scale cross-Channel operation in 1943, which was given the code name Roundup. The British publicly disagreed and privately criticized what they deemed Marshall's political naivety.

Other than the conceptual Germany-first pledge, there was little else to cheer about during Arcadia. The two sides disagreed on the very first issue, the creation of a unified command to engage the Japanese in the South-west Pacific. The British wanted the war run from both Washington and London, a two-headed bureaucracy, while FDR and Marshall strenuously advocated a single, unified commander. With the two sides unable to reach agreement, the matter was consigned to a joint study group.

Although he did not win all of the concessions he would have liked, Churchill cemented his relationship with FDR and won over his new ally by a combination of bulldog dynamism and oratory. Addressing a rare joint session of Congress on 26 December with uplifting words of defiance and confidence, the prime minister brought the legislators cheering to their feet. Of his new ally Churchill would later drily observe, 'Previously we were trying to seduce them. Now they are securely in the harem.'

On the night of 26 December Churchill experienced what he described as 'a dull pain over my heart. It went down my left arm. It didn't last very long ... I thought of sending for you,' he informed Dr Wilson after finally summoning him to his bedside late the following morning. Although he could find no irregularity after examining Churchill's heart, Wilson recognized it as an attack of angina pectoris that would normally have called for six weeks of bed rest. That Churchill would have agreed to such a remedy at a critical stage of the war was unthinkable to both men. To reveal to the world that Churchill had suffered a heart attack would have had disastrous consequences. Wilson was on the horns of a moral dilemma: on one hand, there was little he could do to treat Churchill in Washington; on the other, what if he did nothing and his patient suffered a serious or fatal heart attack? He concluded that Churchill was in no immediate danger and could continue. Churchill convinced himself that the pain was the result of attempting to open a jammed window, and Wilson elected to reassure him that it was nothing serious, but that he should not overexert himself: 'Your circulation was a bit sluggish.' When Harry Hopkins knocked on the door a few moments later, Wilson slipped away to another room.

Churchill kept up his usual taxing schedule; his only concession was to keep Wilson by his side for the remainder of the trip and to take a short holiday in Florida before returning to England. And although a major health crisis was averted during his lengthy stay in Washington (and in Ottawa, where he addressed the Canadian parliament on 31 December), the reckoning was merely postponed for two years. In retrospect it is all the more incredible that a man of Churchill's age, with a failing heart, could function under the extraordinary strains placed upon him as if nothing untoward had occurred. (Churchill's heart attack remained a secret until the publication of Wilson's memoir in 1966.)

During the flight from Norfolk, Virginia, in an American flying boat to Bermuda, where the *Duke of York* lay at anchor to take him back to England, Churchill was invited into the cockpit to take the controls of an aircraft for the first time in many years. With a lighted cigar clamped firmly in his mouth, he flew the big Boeing aircraft for twenty minutes and found the experience exhilarating, although it is doubtful anyone else on board did. Once in Bermuda, he opted to fly back to England on the same aircraft. It was a dangerous decision; there was no air escort for the nearly eighteen-hour trip across the Atlantic, the first ever by the head of a government. Both the official biography and Churchill's Second World War memoir state that off the south-western coast of England at dawn on 16 January the aircraft strayed off course and was some five or six minutes from flying within range of German anti-aircraft batteries in occupied France. An alert Portal is said to have discovered the error and altered the plane's course in the nick of time. The Boeing was soon picked up by British radar and, on the assumption that it was a German bomber flying from Brest, Fighter Command scrambled six Hurricanes with orders to intercept and destroy it. Thirty minutes later the flying boat descended from the clouds and landed safely at Plymouth. The pilot, Captain Kelly Rogers, said to Churchill, 'I never felt so much relieved in my life when I landed you safely in the harbour.' After the war Churchill claimed to have learned the full extent of their close call from the RAF, and made the offhand remark in *The Grand Alliance* that Fighter Command 'had failed in their mission'. This does not do justice to such a close call. However, a recent account of Churchill's wartime travels has thoroughly debunked the story with evidence that his flying boat never came close to the French coast.

Although Churchill returned to England no longer alone, he nevertheless faced a series of setbacks in the Far East and the Western Desert that would leave him reeling. Instead of two there were now three hostile enemies to fight. Japan was flexing its military muscle, with the loss of the *Prince of Wales* and *Repulse* only the beginning.

The Japanese force of 35,000 advancing on two fronts through the jungles of northern Malaya soon posed a grave threat to the island city of Singapore. This was followed by a seaborne invasion that pinned the Singapore garrison inside a perimeter from which there was no escape. As Britain's key strategic naval base, the so-called Gibraltar of the Far East, Singapore was widely believed to have been a fortress, but in reality its defences were pathetically inadequate and incomplete, having been constructed primarily so that its big 15-inch guns could repel a naval attack from the sea. The problem was not that the guns could not be turned around to fire inland – they could – but that they were equipped mostly with armour-piercing shells that were useless against infantry. The irony in this weakness was that it was due, in no small part, to defence cuts made by Churchill while he was chancellor of the exchequer in the 1920s. After years of neglect by successive governments, the bill came due in 1942.

The new commander sent to Malaya in mid-1941 was Lieutenant General A. E. Percival, who did his best to redress Singapore's deficiencies, including warning of the possibility that the Japanese might attempt to 'burgle Malaya by the back door'. That Singapore was vulnerable via the jungles of northern Malaya was no secret, and in the 1930s that prospect attracted the interest of military planners. Airfields were constructed in northern Malaya and manned by units of the RAF and the Royal Australian Air Force (RAAF), but they lacked modern aircraft and proved no match when pitted against the better-equipped and better-trained Japanese air force. An even more candid assessment was sent to London in July 1940 by the secretary of defence of Malaya, who wrote that the real threat to Singapore came from the north, that such a scenario would render the island 'completely useless' – and that disaster would inevitably follow. The report was ignored by the chain of command and probably never reached Churchill. When the Japanese marched on Singapore, not only were its physical defences vulnerable, but its defenders, although large in numbers, were mostly untrained and badly equipped.

A plan called Matador was also in place that called for the defence of the Malay Peninsula from bases to be established some forty miles inside Thailand. These could have impeded the eventual Japanese landings and given the British rather than the Japanese control of valuable Thai airfields along the border with Malaya. However, for Matador to have been effective, these positions would have had to be occupied months in advance, the troops trained and acclimatized to jungle warfare and the RAF/RAAF airfields in northern Malaya operationally beefed up. The War Cabinet gave the go-ahead for Matador on 4 December, but Churchill was reluctant to invade Thailand unilaterally, particularly without a guarantee of American support – against which, before Pearl Harbor, there would certainly have been a backlash in the United States.

Matador was another of Churchill's war decisions in which a political consideration trumped a military judgment. His reluctance to authorize Matador was political, but in retrospect even if the decision had been made two months earlier, when first authorized by the War Cabinet, it would have not saved Singapore. Instead, by 11 December, most of the Allied aircraft flying from bases in northern Malaya had been lost, and with the Japanese air force dominating the air and the invasion force relentlessly advancing south on two fronts, Singapore's fate was already effectively sealed.

One of the decisions made in Washington in early January 1942 was to appoint Wavell the supreme Allied commander for south-east Asia to command British, American, Dutch and Australian forces. The appointment was made under the auspices of the newly created United Nations declaration of 1 January and was called ABDACOM (American–British–Dutch–Australian Command – soon shortened to ABDA). Its mission was to protect the vital Malay Peninsula and the Dutch East India oil fields. Wavell established his new headquarters in Java and faced an impossible task with a command large in numbers but spread across an enormous area; and without cohesion ABDA was essentially a toothless tiger. In his new post Wavell worked feverishly and at times put his life at risk, but there was little he or anyone else could do to halt the Japanese forces bearing down upon the city or to strengthen Singapore's fragile defences.

When he learned the full import of Singapore's increasingly desperate plight, Churchill professed himself 'staggered', dismayed and betrayed by the false picture he had had of its ability to withstand a Japanese siege. 'Now, suddenly all this vanished away and I saw before me the hideous spectacle of the almost naked island and of the wearied, if not exhausted, troops retreating upon it.'

He sent 'a jet of telegrams on Wavell as from a fire hose'. Like a field general he issued detailed orders that spelled out exactly how Singapore was to be defended with mines, artillery, machine guns, field fortifications and searchlights. 'The whole island must be fought for,' he instructed the chiefs of staff, 'and defended to the death,' an order more typical of those commonly issued by Japanese commanders and by Adolf Hitler. Surrender was not an option. 'I want to make it absolutely clear', he telegraphed Wavell on 20 January, 'that I expect every inch of ground to be defended, every scrap of material or defences to be blown to pieces to prevent capture by the enemy, and no question of surrender to be entertained until after protracted fighting among the ruins of Singapore City.'

Although his mind was not yet made up, Churchill already sensed that Singapore could not be held for much longer, and began to turn his eye towards the Japanese threat to Burma, asking the chiefs, 'Was it not only throwing good money after bad' to send reinforcements to Singapore only to see them lost? The problem Churchill faced was to avoid losing both Singapore and the vital Burma Road that served as a lifeline for the resupply of Chiang Kai-shek's Nationalist army in China. Strategically the potential loss of Burma now began to take on even greater importance as the last domino hindering full Japanese control of all of south-east Asia.

With disaster looming in Singapore, Churchill took the audacious step of heading off almost certain political censure. On 27 January he arose in the House to proclaim, 'It is because things have gone badly, and worse is to come, that I demand a Vote of Confidence.' A three-day debate ensued under a continuing cloud of bad news from North Africa and the Far East. Churchill asserted 'that the main strategic and political decision to aid Russia, to deliver an offensive in Libya and to accept a consequential state of weakness in the then peaceful theatre of the Far East was sound, and will be found to have played a useful part in the general course of the War, and that this is in no wise invalidated by the unexpected naval misfortunes and the heavy forfeits which we have paid, and shall have to pay in the Far East.' His confidence in ultimate victory, he declared, was never stronger. And while the vote supported him by an overwhelming 464 to 1, Chips Channon quite rightly pointed out, 'There was no alternative and he knows it. Nevertheless, he is the most inspiring leader we have, and the masses and the Americans both adore him.'

Heading off political trouble was a positive political necessity, but on the military front, with each passing day forlorn hope for a miracle in the Far East gave way to painful reality. Finally, on 14 February, Churchill, having concluded several days earlier that Singapore could not be saved, authorized Wavell to make the final decision when to surrender. Wavell did not hesitate and formally sent permission for Percival to capitulate. With the main water supply to the island destroyed and fuel supplies nearly exhausted, Percival unconditionally surrendered the following afternoon. In the fight to save Singapore nine thousand men had been killed or wounded and 130,000 in the city and in northern Malaya captured, making 15 February 1942 the single worst military setback and one of the most anguished dates in British history. An estimated 57,000 POWs later died in Japanese captivity. Not only was Britain's premier naval base in the Far East lost, but with the exception of India its Pacific empire was now taken by force of arms.

History rarely treats kindly a general who surrenders his command, and General Percival was no exception. Wavell could easily have been the scapegoat for the loss of Singapore, but for perhaps the first time in their unhappy relationship there was harmony between Wavell and Churchill, who praised his efforts, which included nearly remaining in Singapore to bolster Percival and ending up a POW. 'I ought to have known. My advisers ought to have known and I ought to have been told, and I ought to have asked,' Churchill would later write of the painful loss of Singapore. While he appeared to accept some of the blame for Singapore, the larger question revolves around his complete lack of understanding of the nature of the problem. His 'fortress mentality' – the concept that places like Singapore could be defended in a siege-like setting – was the very same Great War thinking he had consistently deplored in others. The stark truth is that the Far East in general and Singapore in particular had been seriously neglected, with no clear definition of responsibility, no tanks or anti-tank guns, and too few, largely obsolete aircraft. The defence of Singapore was predicated on a reliance on air- and naval power, but, without either, the entire burden of defending Malaya fell upon a badly armed and untrained army.

The loss of Singapore was the fault of London, not of its commanders. Despite repeated pleas for modern aircraft and equipment, British policy was deliberately to starve the Far East. Vital assets were either diverted to aid Russia via the convoys to Murmansk or sent to the Middle East. In May 1941 the chiefs warned Churchill that three months' notice would be needed before reinforcements could arrive in the Far East. When he finally decided in mid-December to redress the problem with everything that could be spared, it was too late. Even with reinforcements the outcome would hardly have changed. The Japanese army and air force were better armed and better trained, and were skilled in jungle warfare. The British official history is damning: 'Conditions in Malaya only reflected, if in greater degree, the unreadiness of the whole British people for war.'

Nothing can mitigate the conclusions of Admiral Sir Geoffrey Layton, the former commander in chief of the Eastern Fleet, who candidly reported to Churchill, 'There was only one reason why we lost Singapore, and that is [that] we were unable to provide forces strong enough to defend it.' Churchill immediately suppressed Layton's report on the grounds that 'there is no advantage in circulating this report . . . It should be put by until the end of the war.'

To add to the growing catalogue of bad news, the German battleships *Scharnhorst* and *Gneisenau* and the heavy cruiser *Prinz Eugen* escaped from their sanctuary in Brest on the night of 11 February and made a bold daylight dash up the English Channel the following day. Despite furious pursuit and attacks by Royal Navy motor torpedo boats and RAF aircraft, all three reached the sanctuary of the Elbe river. The British failure to intercept them was not for lack of effort. In the months preceding their escape Brest was heavily targeted by RAF bombers that flew 3,299 sorties, at a cost of forty-three aircraft and 247 lives. Churchill's argument that the raids had forced their dash to Germany was hardly convincing.

The loss of Singapore and the missed opportunity to sink three of the German navy's principal warships represented one of Churchill's lowest points of the war. Violet Bonham Carter found him 'depressed', and 'underneath it all was a dreadful fear', she felt, 'that our soldiers are not as good fighters as their fathers were . . . "In 1915," said Winston, "our men fought on even when they had only one shell left and were under a fierce barrage. Now they cannot resist dive-bombers. We have so many men in Singapore, so many men – they should have done better."' What Violet observed that day was a leader smarting from criticism both in the press and within his government. 'I feel very biteful & spiteful when people attack me . . .' Again & again he said rather wearily "I'm fed up."' But what bothered Churchill the most was contained in the sombre words 'I can't get the victories. It's the victories that are so hard to get.' Violet added that he seemed unable to see that holding trenches in the First World War was not a valid comparison with defending Singapore.

Churchill was prepared to be chided by Roosevelt over Singapore and the so-called 'Channel dash', and wrote frankly: 'When I reflect how I have longed and prayed for the entry of the United States into the war, I find it difficult to realize how gravely our British affairs have deteriorated by what has happened since December seven. We have suffered the greatest disaster in our history at Singapore, and other misfortunes will come thick and fast upon us.' He was pleased when FDR offered only reassurance.

With bad news piling up almost daily, those closest to Churchill saw the heavy toll it was taking. Eden thought he had experienced a stroke, and his daughter Mary has described him as 'saddened – appalled by events [and] desperately taxed'. Adding to Churchill's anguish was his stormy relationship with Randolph, who became deeply resentful that his parents knew of Pamela's continuing affair with W. Averell Harriman and seemed to be siding with their daughter-in-law. A particularly ugly row between father and son that spring left Winston so distraught that Clementine feared for his health.

Singapore was a distant place Britons knew little about, and while its fall shocked the nation Harold Nicolson was not alone in observing that people were more distressed by the navy's failure to sink the *Scharnhorst*, the *Gneisenau* and the *Prinz Eugen*. 'They cannot bear the thought that the Germans sailed past our front door,' he wrote. For the first time there was outright public anger. The first anti-Churchill editorial of the war appeared in the *Daily Mail*. When he addressed the House of Commons a short time later, the prime minister seemed irritable and his comments on the incident unsatisfactory. 'He was not at his best,' recorded Nicolson. 'His broadcast last night was not well liked. The country is too nervous and irritable to be fobbed off with fine phrases. Yet what else could he have said?' Anthony Eden called the first six months of 1942 'a low ebb' in which 'the conduct of the war came under criticism and there was a sense of trouble and discontent.' When he met with Churchill on 16 February Eden was gruffly greeted with: 'I am in a truculent mood.' Over the next several days Churchill shook up his War Cabinet, sacking several members, appointing Attlee deputy prime minister and P. J. Grigg secretary of state for war, and giving up the leadership of the House to Stafford Cripps. 'I was resolved to keep my full power of war-direction,' he later wrote. 'I should not, of course, have remained Prime Minister for an hour if I had been deprived of the office of Minister of Defence.'

His physician had ample cause for concern. Not only had there been his heart attack in Washington but with disaster piled upon disaster in

1942 the threads of hope that had sustained Churchill so well for nearly two years appeared to be deserting him. 'I wish to God I could put out the fires that seem to be consuming him,' Sir Charles Wilson confided to his diary. The loss of Singapore had 'stupefied' Churchill, particularly when he learned of the frailty of its defences. He could not understand why so many troops could not have performed better. 'He felt it was a disgrace. It left a scar on his mind. One evening, months later, when he was sitting in his bathroom enveloped in a towel, he stopped drying himself and gloomily surveyed the floor: "I cannot get over Singapore," he said sadly.'

His broadcast over the BBC about the fall of Singapore was mournful. His boss, noted Commander Thompson, 'sounded desperately tired, and his voice lacked its usual vibrant and challenging ring.' He was frustrated and depressed by the course of the war, and by the mounting criticism of his leadership. Thompson recorded: 'To some of those closest to him he hinted that he was seriously considering handing over his responsibilities . . . He continued to talk dejectedly in this strain for some time.' Alexander Cadogan was not alone in expressing the opinion that in early March there seemed to be no central direction of the war. '[The] War Cabinet doesn't function – there hasn't been a meeting of [the] Defence Committee. There's no hand at the wheel. (Probably due to P. M.'s health). Brendan and Cripps urge that A. [Anthony Eden] should be Deputy Defence Minister.'

Nearly seventy years on it is difficult if not impossible for the historian or biographer to convey a true sense of how overwhelming the pressure was on Churchill during the war's darkest days. To be in his shoes was to face a daily litany of mostly disturbing news of defeat – of the deaths, often in gruesome circumstances, of men and women, civilians and military, who had laid down their lives in defence of Britain. There is no greater burden than to carry the responsibility for thousands of lives that may be saved or lost because of a decision made in a room in Whitehall. For men like Hitler and Stalin, who cared nothing about human life, such losses were almost abstract and carried no burden of conscience. And while Churchill fully understood that loss of life was part and parcel of being both prime minister and defence minister, the responsibility came at a high price in the toll it took upon him both physically and mentally. It was never abstract for Churchill. Each defeat, loss of a vessel or downing of an aircraft was a heavy load he could not share with others, for it was his and his alone. The disastrous events of 1942 might have crushed the spirit of a lesser man. That he was able to bounce back from the worst that war can produce is one of the most important and uplifting aspects of Churchill's war leadership.

He possessed a remarkable ability to put bad news behind him and move on, not with the indifference of a dictator but in the belief that perseverance would overcome adversity. Perhaps only a man of Churchill's extraordinary resilience could have recovered from the combination of extreme overwork, depression and crippling setbacks on Britain's far-flung battlefields. But bounce back he did. By the end of March, he was writing to Smuts: 'Just now I am having a very rough time, but we must remember how much better things are than a year ago, when we were all alone. We must not lose our faculty to dare, particularly in dark days.'

Once again the ideas and demands began to pour forth in seemingly non-stop profusion. Their recipients were worn to a frazzle dealing with them, through late nights and early mornings. Among them were renewals of Churchill's desire to mount an amphibious landing in northern Norway. And once again the idea was debated and rejected by the chiefs of staff, but not without clashes between the stubborn prime minister and Brooke, who in September pointed out that it had been rendered impossible by Operation Torch, the forthcoming Allied invasion of North Africa.

The fall of Singapore was the most important of a series of successful Japanese military operations in early 1942. Java, Sumatra, Borneo, Timor, New Guinea and the Celebes all fell, and by 7 March the entire Dutch East Indies was in Japanese hands. There seemed no battleground that offered any positive news. Action in North Africa was at a standstill, while in the Atlantic shipping losses continued to mount at an alarming rate – the highest of the war. February 1942 saw a new Enigma system initiated by the German navy for its U-boats that Bletchley Park was unable to decipher effectively for nearly eighteen months. The Allies were suddenly blinded to U-boat movements at the worst possible time. With the United States in the war, there were fresh targets for a greatly reinforced U-boat fleet working in wolf packs in the North Atlantic and off the coasts of South America and Africa. British and Allied losses in 1942 were 56 per cent higher than in 1941 (782 British, 987 Allied and

90 neutral merchant vessels totalling 8.3 million tons were sunk, many within sight of the eastern seaboard of North America).

That the Allies were losing the war at sea became one of Churchill's gravest concerns. 'The only thing that ever frightened me during the war was the U-boat peril,' he later remarked. Its effects also worried Dr Wilson, who daily saw the obvious toll it was taking on his health. 'One day [in April 1942] when things at sea were at their worst, I happened to go to the Map-room. There I found the PM. He was standing with his back to me, staring at the huge chart with the little black beetles representing German submarines. "Terrible," he muttered. I was about to retreat when he whipped round and brushed past me with his head down ... He knows that we may lose the war at sea in a few months and that he can do nothing about it.'

As expected, the next British-controlled domino in the Far East to come under Japanese attack was Burma, primarily because of the Burma Road's use as a lifeline to resupply Chiang Kai-shek's army in China via the capital of Rangoon. The defence of Burma was a command muddle typical of the disarray in the Far East. Until mid-December 1941 the responsibility belonged to Far East Command, based in Singapore, but with the creation of ABDA it was transferred to Wavell. When the Japanese invaded Java, Wavell and his staff were forced to flee for their lives. With the abolition of ABDA after a mere five weeks, Burma remained under Wavell in his original capacity as commander in chief, India. It hardly mattered. Burma was ripe for the taking. Its defences were another paper tiger that purported to include a full fighting division which in reality was a ragtag collection of Burmese units augmented by an Indian brigade and two battalions of British infantry.

Churchill was determined to save Rangoon and keep open the Burma Road, but, as with Singapore, resolve and reality were two entirely different matters. The Japanese attacked on two fronts in mid-January 1942. Although every attempt was made to hold Rangoon, it fell on 7 March, but only after the British had implemented a scorched-earth destruction of the port and its main power plant, turning it into a ghost city for the occupying Japanese Fifteenth Army. The fall of Rangoon was merely the opening salvo in a campaign, fought in the mountains and jungles under primitive conditions, that lasted until 1945.

In terms of military strategy the early months of 1942 were little different from those of 1941. Britain had patiently held out until the

United States entered the war. Now that the United States was a full partner and a very general strategy had been mapped out to defeat Germany before Japan, the specifics of how victory would be won remained vague. The chickens had come home to roost in the Far East; North Africa was a stalemate; and the war at sea was going badly. All 1942 promised was yet another year of remaining on the defensive until American military forces could be raised, trained and deployed in support – a forbidding prospect indeed.

49

The Quest for Generalship

I am ashamed. I cannot understand why Tobruk gave in. More than 30,000 of our men put their hands up. — Churchill, 21 June 1942

Even as the dominoes were falling in the Far East, the Mediterranean in 1942 again took centre stage. Crusader had no sooner ended than Churchill began pressing Auchinleck to resume the offensive against Rommel. However, both sides were still licking their wounds and were critically short of supplies and new equipment; they were in no shape to resume the offensive.

Although Churchill heaped praise on Auchinleck's 'persisting will-power' without which 'we might very easily have subsided to the defensive,' the two men had fundamentally different perspectives. Churchill, with Brooke's support, saw the recapture of Cyrenaica and an advance on Tripoli as essential to the security of Malta. The island was like a bone stuck in the craw of the Axis and in 1942 was isolated, increasingly starved of supplies and under aerial siege by Axis bombers that pounded the island round the clock, including thirteen raids in a single night in February. The heavy air campaign against Malta had been unleashed by Hitler's commander of air and land forces in the Mediterranean, the veteran airman and former artillery officer Field Marshal Albert Kesselring. By April an invasion was thought to be imminent; Allied control of airfields in North Africa was of signal importance if the besieged island were to be supported. Malta's very survival was in question.

Churchill was fixated on saving Malta and was prepared 'to run serious naval risks' to save the island he feared would be 'pounded to bits'. Auchinleck, however, viewed Cyrenaica only peripherally, as the western flank of his vast area of responsibility, a sideshow, and a drain on the precious resources of a command that extended eastward as far as Afghanistan. In early 1942 he was far more concerned about his eastern flank and the possibility of a German offensive from the Caucasus against the strategically important Persian oil fields. Nor was Auchinleck acting alone; he had the full backing of the Cairo-based Middle East Defence Committee, which concluded that losing Malta would not be fatal, whereas losing Egypt would render the island untenable.

By March 1942 Churchill was already thinking of replacing Auchinleck with Lord Gort or the deputy CIGS, Archie Nye, an excellent staff officer but an untried commander. Fortunately, with prodding from Brooke, he backed off both ideas and instead sent Gort, as governor general, to Malta, where he performed brilliantly as the personification of British resistance during the siege. One of Brooke's everyday tasks was to temper the increasingly abusive language of Churchill's signals to Auchinleck. While he did his best to shield Auchinleck from the prime minister's wrath, he too was losing confidence in the Auk. 'It is very exhausting, this continual protecting of Auchinleck, especially as I have not got the highest opinion of him.'

Brooke had good reason to be suspicious of Auchinleck's ability to manage the war in the Middle East. Not only was he unwisely obstinate in his relations with Churchill, but he also compounded his problems by lacking ideas on how to fight his enemy or to train his men to do so. To make matters worse, the Eighth Army was badly organized. The practice of employing separate battle groups of infantry and armour (called 'jock columns' or 'brigade groups') – successfully used under entirely different conditions by O'Connor against the Italians – was futile against an experienced commander like Rommel. To be effective in the desert, as already noted, infantry and armour required mutual support. Used independently, each was vulnerable to defeat. The infantry could not effectively fight panzers without supporting tanks, and tanks were at serious risk without infantry to protect them, yet neither Auchinleck nor his staff ever worked this out.

Not only did they fail to comprehend this fatal organizational flaw; they were also unable to issue coherent orders. During the battle for Tobruk they issued either conflicting orders or no orders at all. Freyberg, the New Zealand commander, was scornful. 'General Auchinleck was well known as a bad judge of a man, and he assembled around him a bad staff' – a staff so incompetent that one corps headquarters received three separate sets of orders in a single day, each of which altered the previous policy of defence.

To compound matters Auchinleck made another appalling mistake by leaving Neil Ritchie – originally viewed as a temporary appointment after Cunningham was sacked during Crusader – in command of the Eighth Army instead of replacing him with an experienced commander. A genial, well-liked Scotsman newly promoted to lieutenant general, Ritchie seemed to possess the appearance and the aura of authority vital in any commander. He had served in France under Brooke as his chief of staff, and in the same role under Auchinleck in England. However, since serving in the front lines of the First World War as a junior officer, he had commanded only briefly at battalion level, in Jerusalem in 1938. Although there were better choices available, Auchinleck overlooked the fact that he had placed in command an untested commander, 'an awfully nice chap' who would be completely outmatched when pitted against Rommel. If holding long-winded staff meetings were the mark of a successful commander, then Neil Ritchie would have been very successful indeed. Far more serious was that he was mentally disposed towards retreat and defeat – a fatal flaw in any commander. At a critical time the Eighth Army had as its commander another in a long line of ineffective British château generals dating back to the nineteenth century, men who lacked a clear grasp of the battlefield and its challenges.

Either of the Eighth Army corps commanders would have been a better option than Ritchie, and just as Britain desperately needed a leader like Churchill to take charge of the war in 1940, so too did the Eighth Army in North Africa – Britain's largest and most powerful combat army – need a tough, experienced commander to lead it against Erwin Rommel. Neither Auchinleck nor Ritchie proved to be that officer. While the orthodox Ritchie held his interminable staff meetings and drew up plans to best his opponent, Rommel acted to exploit the weak point of the Gazala Line. Whereas Rommel was ruthless and aggressive, a tough taskmaster who refused to suffer fools, Ritchie was indecisive and unimaginative. In light of such British ineptness it is entirely understandable that Churchill admired Rommel's generalship and secretly wished the German were on his side.

The irony of Auchinleck's decision to keep Ritchie was that he too had serious reservations about his Eighth Army commander but declined to act upon them, fearing that London would send him someone he did not want: specifically Montgomery. The two men had clashed in England, and Auchinleck deemed Monty both difficult and insubordinate. Moreover, having sacked Cunningham such a short time before, he reasoned that replacing the new commander might lower morale. So he let his loyalty to Ritchie overcome his reservations, which he never shared with either Churchill or Brooke. He believed that Ritchie, under his close supervision, could do the job. This unfortunate decision was to bring about Auchinleck's own undoing and one of Churchill's gravest embarrassments of the war.

By the early spring of 1942, Churchill had reached boiling point over Auchinleck's inaction. 'The bloody man doesn't seem to care about the fate of Malta,' he fumed in March. Auchinleck did himself no favours when he resisted Churchill's demand that he come home to England to report on the situation in the Middle East. Claiming that he was too busy, he refused, further infuriating Churchill, who again called for his replacement. And still there was no date forthcoming for an offensive, leaving the chiefs as restive as Churchill and equally certain that Auchinleck was taking too long. Finally, under threat of a direct order from London to mount an offensive, Auchinleck announced plans for operations against Rommel to commence on 1 June, to break out of the Gazala Line and eject what was now called Panzerarmee Afrika from Cyrenaica.

Before the Eighth Army could launch its breakout offensive, on 31 May Rommel struck first at Tobruk's outer defences around the area known as the Cauldron. Although outnumbered two to one, through a series of daring feints and attacks he turned the Gazala Line, by outflanking the defensive 'box' south of the city at Bir Hacheim manned by a Free French brigade. Under cover of a sandstorm he initiated a classic diversion by attacking the heart of the British defences with his Italian divisions, while his German divisions outflanked the British, inadvertently abetted by Ritchie, who believed that Rommel's main attack would be against his main Gazala Line defences. Aptly described as 'like a tiger stalking a tethered goat', Rommel's attack on Tobruk was a combination of stealthy advance followed by the unleashing of his panzers and massive aerial attacks by the Luftwaffe.

Although he had opportunities to hold the Gazala Line by reinforcing the heroic defence of Bir Hacheim by the French, Ritchie squandered them by inaction. It was the type of dithering generalship that made

Churchill gnash his teeth in frustration. Instead of attempting to hold open the supply line to his besieged divisions defending the Cauldron and the 'Knightsbridge boxes' (the code name given to one of the key Tobruk positions), Ritchie ordered two divisions out of the line and sent them to the Egyptian frontier without bothering to enlighten Auchinleck. By mid-June, not only had Rommel turned the Gazala Line, he had also interdicted the coastal road west of Tobruk and converted the city into an inaccessible island.

As he had with so many other places under siege since May 1940, Churchill issued orders that Tobruk was to be held. It was all for nothing. Although outnumbered and sustaining heavy losses in men and machines, Rommel had outgeneralled his opponent and on 21 June captured Tobruk and its South African garrison, bagging 33,000 POWs, two thousand tons of fuel, five thousand tons of supplies and two thousand operational vehicles. A jubilant Hitler promoted Rommel to field marshal while Auchinleck was forced to sack Ritchie on 25 June and assume personal control of the Eighth Army in order to prevent its complete disintegration, as Rommel continued his seemingly unstoppable offensive aimed at capturing Egypt and the Suez Canal. Although Rommel was euphoric at being the youngest officer in the German army to be promoted to field marshal, he told his wife that 'I would much rather he had given me one more division.'

By the end of June the British were deep into Egypt, manning their last line of defence based around a small, fly-infested port 150 miles west of Cairo called El Alamein. Singapore could not have been held, but the fall of Tobruk was preventable if not for the failure of British generalship.

There were many personal low points of the war for Winston Churchill, but the nadir was the fall of Tobruk, which for the first time briefly imperilled his leadership of Britain. He was in Washington at the White House conferring with Roosevelt when the news of its fall was announced over the BBC. Among those in his party was Air Marshal Slessor, who retained vivid memories of 'an evil moment' in a year that was nothing but one disaster after another. When Slessor was ushered into Roosevelt's study a short time later, he saw Churchill 'looking rather crumpled in his siren suit and with a face of gloomy thunder . . . I have seldom been so sorry for anyone.'

The loss of Tobruk could not have come at a worse moment, and Churchill later called it 'one of the heaviest blows I can recall during the war'. Charles Wilson saw him dazed but still full of fight: although Tobruk and the threat posed by Rommel were 'a blow between the eyes . . . Winston refused to take the count . . . There is never a danger of his folding up in dirty weather . . . His brain goes on working as if it were packed in ice . . . The stuff surely is in him; he is built for great occasions.' At that moment, however, Churchill might have disagreed with him.

Ironically, Tobruk promoted his argument with his new American ally that a second front in Europe should be delayed in favour of joint action against the Axis in the Mediterranean, and during the Washington talks he pounded away at this theme. As had been the case with earlier defeats, he never quite understood why this reversal had happened. It was embarrassing enough that this one had occurred while he was in Washington. 'It was a bitter moment,' he later wrote. 'Defeat is one thing; disgrace is another.' With his mood ranging from anger to grim recognition, Churchill exclaimed: 'I am ashamed. I cannot understand why Tobruk gave in. More than 30,000 of our men put their hands up.'

Not only did the loss of Tobruk leave Churchill bitter and dumb-founded, but he returned home to England to face the worst political crisis of his prime ministership. One of his most persistent critics was the Welsh Labour MP Aneurin Bevan, who tartly pointed out that although Churchill won his debates he was consistently losing his battles. 'The country is saying that he fights debates like the war and the war like debates.'

A Conservative MP had tabled a motion that the House 'had no confidence in the central direction of the war'. Among those speaking against Churchill were Admiral Roger Keyes and Leslie Hore-Belisha, the former secretary of state for war sacked in 1940 by Neville Chamberlain. Churchill cut short his visit to the United States and hastened home to begin a two-day debate in the Commons – one that, had he lost the vote, would have ended his tenure as prime minister. The strongest argument mounted against him was that functioning as both prime minister and minister of defence was a task beyond the capacity of one man. Most blamed government incompetence, but one long-standing critic said the blame belonged with Churchill, who patiently waited until the end of the debate to have the last word.

Point by point Churchill struck back with a defence that was more lucid than confrontational. 'When I was called upon to be Prime Minister, now nearly two years ago, there were not many applicants for the job.' Unless there was someone better to replace him, he should be permitted to carry on. The House voted overwhelmingly – 475 to 25 – to defeat the censure motion. It was the last time during the war that Churchill was ever seriously challenged. Nevertheless the experience left him upset and irritated. He said to his secretary Elizabeth Layton that 'he felt like a man who had a group of wasps flying round his head and that he couldn't get on with the important work because of the little stings he was getting.'

Tobruk now joined Norway, France, Dunkirk, Greece, Crete, Hong Kong, Singapore, Burma, *Hood*, *Prince of Wales* and *Repulse* as the latest in the long line of failures that plagued Churchill's first two years as war leader. Before his plummeting fortunes hit bottom there was one more disaster ahead: Dieppe.

On 19 August an Anglo-Canadian hit-and-run raid on the French port city of Dieppe ended in catastrophe when a six-thousand-man amphibious force (five thousand Canadians, a small number of US army Rangers and some nine hundred Royal Marine commandos) was destroyed during a nine-hour battle. The force was supported by 237 landing craft and warships and seventy-four air squadrons, composed of formations from nine Allied nations.

Dieppe was thought to be an easy target; instead it proved to be well defended, not by a low-grade German force but by front-line troops. Allied losses were shocking. Over 70 per cent of those who set foot on French soil that day were killed, wounded or captured. The Canadians lost one thousand killed and another two thousand captured. The Royal Marine commandos and Royal Navy personnel suffered nine hundred casualties. The RAF and Royal Canadian Air Force lost sixty-seven pilots and more than one hundred aircraft.

Originally intended as a means of assessing German defences by seizing a port and gathering intelligence, Operation Jubilee (as the raid was code-named) was the brainchild of Churchill's new chief of Combined Operations, Admiral Lord Louis Mountbatten, who in his new role made it his aim to keep the prime minister happy. When it was first proposed, the idea appealed to Churchill's love of unorthodox raids like the successful hit-and-run attacks on Bruneval and Saint-Nazaire. Mountbatten more than satisfied Churchill's desire for aggressive new blood running the war, but with Dieppe he turned the operation into a mini-invasion that violated every principle of planning, training, intelligence gathering and leadership. The mistakes either perpetrated or condoned by Mountbatten included poor intelligence, a lack of heavy bomber and naval gunfire support, the employment of untested Canadian troops and the appointment of a task force commander with no previous battle or amphibious experience.

Mountbatten had scant grasp of combined operations, and in electing to undertake a raid that never had the slightest chance of success he unwittingly unleashed one of the most ill-conceived operations of the war. Churchill's explication of Dieppe – that 'the grim casualty figures must not class it as a failure' and that it was merely 'a costly but not unfruitful reconnaissance-in-force' and 'a mine of experience' – is both delusional and a vain attempt to justify the operation after the fact. If Dieppe was intended to test the Germans, it turned into yet another painful lesson of the cost of inadequate leadership of good soldiers, glaringly highlighted Allied shortcomings and provided a sobering assessment of just how difficult it was going to be to develop a second-front cross-Channel invasion of France.

Dieppe placated Stalin, whose Red Army was fighting for its life against the Germans, and it also achieved an unintended benefit for Churchill by demonstrating in blood the folly of launching a second front in 1942, which would have ended in a far greater disaster. As he told Stalin, Churchill saw far less risk in committing ten thousand men rather than twelve times that number. However, Mountbatten's alleged assertion that ten lives were saved on D-day for each life lost at Dieppe and Churchill's claim that it was vital preparation for the 1944 cross-Channel invasion have both been entirely discredited.

When it came time after the war to write the Dieppe part of Churchill's memoirs, there were more short memories than helpful records. One astonishing fact was that there was no document that actually showed that the chiefs of staff had approved the raid. A draft report was sent to Mountbatten that cited 70 per cent losses. To exonerate himself from blame, the admiral rewrote the draft into a bland stew that said virtually nothing of substance. And while he was permitted by Churchill to whitewash Dieppe, he did not escape the wrath of at least one powerful

Canadian. Lord Beaverbrook bitterly challenged Mountbatten to his face, declaring: 'You have murdered thousands of my countrymen . . . Their blood is on your hands.' The Canadians have never forgotten or forgiven Mountbatten's role in Dieppe.

One other postscript is that despite his enthusiasm for Dieppe, and as happened with other ventures such as Greece, it was never given the exhaustive attention Churchill customarily gave to forthcoming military operations. He was maddeningly inconsistent during the war in that he sometimes involved himself in micromanaging (such as inspecting the loading tables of vessels), yet on occasions when he certainly ought to have examined an important operation such as Dieppe, he remained uninvolved. Had he taken a hard look at Dieppe, it is reasonable to conclude that he would have detected and reversed Mountbatten's rejection of advice he had received from Montgomery that an airborne force be landed behind the town and heavy bomber support be given, as well as unanswered Canadian pleas for heavy naval gunfire that four destroyers simply could not provide.

While Brooke appreciated the vigour and enthusiasm that Mountbatten brought to Combined Operations, he felt that the admiral unnecessarily inflamed Churchill's propensity for the unconventional. However, he lost the argument to exclude Mountbatten from the Chiefs of Staff Committee, and in December 1942 barely managed to dissuade Churchill from naming him the commander of naval forces for the invasion of France.

In the bitter aftermath of Tobruk, Churchill had yet to come to terms with the underlying reason for its loss: his army commander had been no match for Rommel. Auchinleck likewise failed to realize that ordinary Tommies wanted competent officers commanding them. Until that problem was remedied and first-class generals were placed on the battlefield, there was little to prevent future Tobruks. Soldiers are a brotherhood, and there was nothing wrong with the British soldier that strong leadership could not rectify. Soldiers are rarely if ever deceived by their leaders; they instinctively know when they are well led, and respond accordingly. What existed in the summer of 1942 in the desert of North Africa was not a bad army – it was an army tired of being kicked around by Rommel and desperately in need of resourceful commanders. The problem in June and July 1942 was that such men existed but Churchill had neither identified nor appointed them to key commands. The fall of Tobruk and the imminent threat of losing Egypt finally brought action, but not before Churchill once again nearly indulged his habit of picking the wrong men.

50

Getting it Right

If we cannot stay here alive, then let us stay here dead.   – Montgomery

The capture of Tobruk led Rommel and Hitler to higher ambitions of a successful offensive to annex Egypt, while the German army in the Caucasus drove through Persia and the Middle East to expel the British from the Mediterranean. If Rommel could finish off the Eighth Army, Egypt was ripe for the taking. The Eighth Army was disposed in positions along a loosely held defensive line anchored in the north by the Mediterranean and in the south by three key ridgelines, and the massive Qattara Depression – a gigantic seven-thousand-square-mile hole in the desert. Nearly four hundred feet below sea level, the Qattara Depression is defined by steep escarpments, sand dunes and salt lakes, all of which make it an impassable barrier for tanks and most other military vehicles.

Sensing victory and understanding that this was probably his only opportunity before the Allies reinforced with fresh troops, ammunition and equipment, Rommel continued his offensive against the reeling Eighth Army. That meant attacking even though his supply lines were stretched wire thin, and his forces depleted and utterly spent after some five weeks of near-constant combat in the hellish conditions of the desert of North Africa. The initiative was his, and on 1 July 1942 he attacked British positions along the new Alamein front.

Misnamed the First Battle of Alamein, it was more like Custer's Last Stand – the last defensible position in Egypt. Battles raged throughout the month of July and ended in a draw, which Auchinleck and his chief adviser, Major General Eric 'Chink' Dorman-Smith, treated as a victory. Rommel had failed to seize the key ridgelines, particularly Ruweisat Ridge, and though the Eighth Army had held, it was unable to mount a counter-offensive despite Auchinleck's attempts to reinvigorate his army. 'You have wrenched the initiative from him by sheer guts and hard fighting,' he wrote in a Special Order of the Day, 'You have done much but I ask you for more. We must not slacken . . . STICK TO IT.' It was good propaganda but utter nonsense; the initiative still lay with Rommel who – had his army not been exhausted, desperately short of fuel and supplies and over-extended – would have continued his offensive.

On the battlefield the RAF and tanks and infantry had yet to learn to co-operate in a manner that would bring victory, and while their commanders squabbled and pointed fingers at one another, all chance of success against Rommel was lost. Indeed Auchinleck's senior commanders were in near-rebellion, and the British army had so many desertions from its ranks in Egypt in 1942 that Auchinleck asked London to reinstate the death penalty. Many deserters became freelances who paid local lowlifes to mug and rob their former comrades on the streets of Cairo. In the opinion of Bernard Freyberg, 'The Army had for the moment disintegrated. The system of command had broken down,' and no one seemed to have the necessary grip to stop the slide. Nor could Auchinleck have continued in his dual capacity without both roles suffering: 'You could not combine the duties of C-in-C Middle East with command of an army in the desert.'

With a lull on the battlefield as both sides recuperated, Auchinleck reported to London on 30 July that it would be mid-September before the Eighth Army could again go on the offensive. For Churchill this was the last straw. He was disappointed and angry that Auchinleck had not pressed his attacks. Although Brooke loyally defended his commander in chief, he too had grave doubts about the Auk's performance.

One of those killed at First Alamein was a son of Churchill's first love, Pamela Plowden, now Lady Lytton. When he was informed of the death, Churchill ordered his car brought around and was driven to her home in Hertfordshire to break the sad news to her personally.

In late July, Brooke announced his intention to visit the Middle East to assess the situation there, and shortly before departing wrote to his wife that 'the old ruffian is quite jealous that he is not coming with me!' However, at the last minute the 'old ruffian' decided that he would follow Brooke a day later. Worried that flying at high altitudes would put his famous patient in danger of a stroke, Sir Charles Wilson argued against making the trip, advice that Churchill dismissively ignored.

The day before he departed, Churchill received a box delivered by a courier from MI5. He was travelling under his nom de plume Colonel Warden, and, before changing his mind at the last minute, planned to arrive incognito, with his face hidden by a red beard complete with side-whiskers in order to disguise his presence from prying eyes.

On 2 August he boarded a Liberator bomber named *Commando* for the flight to Gibraltar, his first stop before Cairo. Although in 1943 a specially outfitted American C-54 Skymaster aircraft was furnished by Roosevelt and became Churchill's personal aircraft, this one was frigidly cold with no amenities and sleeping accommodation that consisted of crudely rigged canvas bunks and mattresses dumped on the floor. Meals were taken from picnic baskets and flasks. Before Churchill was allowed to fly he was fitted with an oxygen mask and tested in a high-altitude chamber for a simulated flight at fifteen thousand feet. Even though it worked (after causing some pain due to improper adjustment), Churchill called it a 'damnable muzzle'. Overnight a new mask was created that permitted him both to take in oxygen and to smoke a cigar, an unsafe practice that he consistently followed on other flights.

Auchinleck was still at the front when Brooke arrived in Cairo on 3 August, only hours before Churchill. The CIGS was met at the aerodrome by Auchinleck's chief staff officer, Lieutenant General Thomas W. Corbett, who announced: 'I am to succeed him in command of the [Eighth] Army. In fact, I have been living with my kit packed for the last week.' The news left Brooke shuddering. It was bad enough that Auchinleck had already hired and fired two inept commanders – now he was about to turn the Eighth Army over to yet another officer supremely unqualified to take on Rommel. Thomas Corbett was an Indian army cavalry officer loyal to Auchinleck who had little knowledge of the British army or its officer corps. That Auchinleck would even consider turning the Eighth Army over to someone with no experience outside the Indian army, who could barely find his away around GHQ in Cairo among officers he did not know, and expect him to gain the support and confidence of his subordinates or to fight in terrain alien to him was foolhardy.

Auchinleck was a gallant soldier, but his command selections were his undoing. Even after sacking Ritchie, Auchinleck wrote a glowing report about him. He showed it to Dorman-Smith, who commented after the war to the historian Correlli Barnett: 'Ritchie is like an ox and Rommel hunted him as a tiger might hunt a village buffalo. Wavell would not have put up with Ritchie for five minutes.'

With Churchill sitting in the co-pilot's seat to watch the sun rise, as was his habit on air journeys, the *Commando* arrived over Cairo just after dawn on the morning of 4 August, on the forty-fourth anniversary of the day he had set sail up the Nile to Omdurman with the 21st Lancers. The sight brought back memories: 'In the pale, glimmering dawn the endless winding silver ribbon of the Nile stretched joyously before us. Often I had seen the day break on the Nile. In war and in peace I had traversed by land or water almost its whole length . . . Now for a short spell I became "the man on the spot". Instead of sitting at home waiting for the news from the front I could send it myself. This was exhilarating.' Churchill's arrival in Cairo was to have been kept secret, but as his motorcade was driven into the city he was easily recognized and unable to resist giving the V sign to troops as he passed.

While there is no doubt that Churchill hungered to be near the scenes of combat, his trip to the Middle East to assess for himself what was wrong and how it should be fixed was vitally necessary. After a week of intense meetings and inspections he wrote to Clementine: 'This splendid army, about double as strong as the enemy, is baffled and bewildered by its defeats . . . The more I study the situation on the spot the more sure I am that a decisive victory can be won if only the leadership is equal to the opportunity.'

Churchill was as yet uncertain what he would do to rearrange the Middle East command structure. He conferred with Smuts, who had joined him to offer his usual wise counsel, and met with Auchinleck and others. For two days there were conferences and private discussions but no final decision. Most of his work was done in the British embassy under a large portrait of Lord Kitchener.

He began asking tough questions and seeking ideas on possible replacements for the Eighth Army commander. In the nick of time he and Brooke prevented Auchinleck from appointing Corbett. Brooke's strong objections to him found ready acceptance from Churchill, who called him 'a very small, agreeable man, of no personality and little experience'.

One name began surfacing: Lieutenant General W. H. E. 'Strafer' Gott, the former commander of the 7th Armoured Division, the 'Desert Rats'. A beloved officer then commanding XIII Corps, Gott had been in the desert for nearly three years and had risen spectacularly from lieutenant colonel. He admitted to Brooke not only that he was tired, but that perhaps it was time for 'some new blood. I have tried most of my ideas on the Boche. We want somebody with new ideas and plenty of confidence in them.'

When Brooke expressed his concern about Gott's health and tiredness to Churchill, back came the suggestion that the CIGS take command of the Eighth Army. Brooke was thrilled and sorely tempted by the offer, and later said that it 'gave rise to the most desperate longings in my heart! I had tasted the thrill of commanding a formation in war whilst commanding II Corps in France.' Acceptance would have freed him of the daily grind of the war and of Churchill, but Brooke wisely declined, partly because he believed it would give the impression that he had come to Cairo to depose Auchinleck, but primarily because he recognized that his lack of desert experience made him unsuitable for the post. In his heart, Brooke accepted that his place was to remain as CIGS.

On the morning of 5 August Churchill made the first of many visits to a battle front during the war. He and Brooke flew to a desert airfield west of Alexandria and were met by Tedder, his tactical air commander, Air Marshal Arthur Coningham, and Auchinleck, who escorted his visitors to his command post situated close to the front lines, a crude, fly-infested place. Churchill would later write, with evident distaste, 'We were given breakfast in a wire-netted cube, full of flies and important military personages.'

Auchinleck then escorted Churchill to the front lines to inspect units of the Eighth Army and question their commanders and soldiers. There he met Gott for the first and only time. Churchill liked him at once and had Gott drive him back to the airfield. 'As we rumbled and jolted over the rough tracks I looked into his clear blue eyes and questioned him about himself. Was he tired, and had he any views to give? Gott said that no doubt he was tired, and that he would like nothing better than three months' leave in England . . . but he declared himself quite capable of further immediate efforts and of taking any responsibilities confided to him.' It was enough for Churchill: he had found his new commander.

At first Churchill considered replacing Auchinleck as the Eighth Army commander but keeping him on as commander in chief. That idea was soon scrapped after his visit to Alamein, which left him distinctly unimpressed with Auchinleck's insistence on requiring six weeks to attack Rommel. However, what cemented the fate of both Auchinleck and Dorman-Smith was their obvious lack of enthusiasm for renewing the offensive. Both generals believed they had done well by blunting Rommel's advance and capturing some seven thousand Axis troops. That was not good enough for the offensive-minded prime minister, who was appalled that the Eighth Army had ended up in such dire circumstances in the first place through inept generalship.

Churchill next visited the RAF at Burg el Arab, where he was royally entertained by Tedder and his airmen with a meal sent out from one of Cairo's finest hotels. Dr Wilson was duly impressed by Tedder's flyers: 'These fellows were not groomed in a mess before the war. Their thoughts are not borrowed from others and their speech is forthright. They are critical of the Army, they say what is in their minds without batting an eyelid.'

Churchill returned to Cairo in a rather subdued mood, lost in thought and without speaking a single word. Wilson noted, 'I have a feeling that it is all settled.' Early the next morning an elated Churchill burst into Brooke's bedroom to find his CIGS in the middle of dressing and 'practically naked'. He 'informed me that his thoughts were taking shape and that he would soon commit himself to paper!' A long day of meetings followed. At one point Churchill grumbled, 'There is something wrong somewhere. I am convinced there has been no leadership out here. What has happened is a disgrace. Ninety thousand men all over the place. Alex [General Alexander] told me there are 2,000 officers in Cairo who wear a smart uniform called a gabardine, and that they are called the gabardine swine. There must be no cozening. The Army must understand there are very serious penalties for not doing their duty.'

After hours of discussion with Brooke, Smuts and others, Churchill made up his mind to reorganize the Middle East command into two parts, as Brooke had long urged him to do, with Persia and Iraq split off into a new command. Auchinleck was to be replaced as the Eighth Army commander and offered the post of commander in chief of a new independent Persia–Iraq command.

To take over in Egypt Churchill summoned General Sir Harold Alexander from the Far East. Alexander had carried out the evacuation of the Burma Army from Rangoon in early March 1942 and led the British retreat to India, which, despite the fact that it was another ignominious event, nevertheless saved his force from total defeat, thus earning him the prime minister's gratitude.

Churchill wisely elected to have a clear-out in Cairo. Corbett and Dorman-Smith were both sacked, along with a corps commander, Major General W. H. C. Ramsden. Montgomery had recently been appointed to command British forces in the first joint Anglo-American operation, code-named Operation Torch, an invasion of French North Africa planned for November, but there had been talk of appointing him to command the Eighth Army. To Brooke's surprise, however, Churchill announced that he had settled on Gott. Although he strongly believed that the job ought to have gone to Montgomery, Brooke was not prepared to challenge Churchill and concurred with his decision. To Clementine, Winston wrote with evident satisfaction that in Alexander and Gott he had selected 'an ideal combination': Alexander with 'his grand capacities for war' and Strafer Gott with his 'desert prowess'. Not for the first time Churchill was stirred by appearances.

On 7 August Gott boarded a transport plane at Burg el Arab air base for a routine flight to Cairo. Churchill had flown the same route unescorted two days earlier. On this fateful day tragedy struck when Gott's aircraft was shot down by two German Me-109 fighter aircraft and crash-landed in the desert, where it was strafed and set on fire. Gott and twenty others were trapped inside and burned to death. At a stroke the entire balance of command changed in the Middle East. Though deeply saddened by Gott's untimely death, Brooke was convinced that he had been too tired to have opposed Rommel effectively. 'It seemed almost like the hand of God suddenly appearing to set matters right where we had gone wrong,' he would write after the war.

It fell to Ian Jacob to inform Churchill of Gott's death. 'Winston took the news very hard and was upset,' and was horrified when Jacob said, in his practical way, that there were as many good fish in the sea as ever came out of it. Several months later, as Churchill's plane taxied for take-off after the Casablanca Conference, Jacob overheard Churchill mutter, 'I think it's a pretty straight road now, even the Cabinet could manage it.' His remark was prompted by the knowledge that a plane that had taken off before them had been shot down with several high-ranking staff officers killed in the same tragic manner as Gott.

Once again Brooke had to battle Churchill over who would replace Gott. The prime minister was inclined to stick with appointing a general who had served in the Middle East, and he favoured Jumbo Wilson. Backed by Smuts, Brooke finally convinced Churchill that Montgomery should be summoned to command the Eighth Army. According to Charles Wilson, 'The P.M. took a lot of persuading.' Smuts, Winston wrote to Clementine, 'was magnificent in counsel . . . He fortified me where I am inclined to be tender-hearted, namely in using severe measures against people I like,' an undoubted reference to his soft approach towards Auchinleck. As for Gott's tragic death, 'Here one sees the hand of fate.'

With this historic decision Churchill in effect turned over to a general he did not particularly like the fate of British arms in North Africa, and indeed in all of the Mediterranean. If Montgomery were to fail, he too would fail and most likely would be replaced as prime minister.

Churchill formally sacked Auchinleck on 8 August. He likened the unpleasant task of informing the general of his dismissal to 'killing a magnificent stag'. He delegated it to Jacob, who equated it with 'going to murder an unsuspecting friend'.

Although he had just made two of his most important military decisions of the war and had great sympathy for Auchinleck, Churchill remained fixated on defeating the Desert Fox, who had wreaked such havoc on the Eighth Army, and pointed to his outgoing commander in chief as the culprit. Churchill was grappling with a number of issues, but his overriding concern that day was his obsession with the German field marshal. 'Rommel, Rommel, Rommel,' he growled, pacing up and down his bedroom like a caged lion. 'What else matters but beating him. Instead of which, C-in-C, Middle East sits in Cairo attending to things which a Minister, or a quartermaster, could deal with.'

Auchinleck took his relief with great dignity, but during what Churchill described as 'a bleak interview' formally refused his offer of the new Iraq–Persia command, primarily because he deemed it an insult. He asked to be retired instead. Invited to think it over for several days, he again refused and returned to India, remaining in limbo until June 1943, when he was again given command of the Indian army.

What Churchill never revealed in his version of events was that the War Cabinet had revolted over Auchinleck's proposed appointment to the Iraq–Persia command on the grounds that it gave the appearance of appeasing yet another failed general. Churchill's public and private feelings about Auchinleck were conflicted: the ruthless public warlord was clearly at odds with his private side, which was not fully committed to complete change. In truth he had a far softer spot for Auchinleck than he ever publicly admitted; he once declared, 'At the head of an army with a single and direct purpose he commands my entire confidence. If he had taken command of Eighth Army when I urged him to I believe we would have won the Gazala battle.'

However, his personal inclination to retain Auchinleck in some capacity in the Middle East is not reflected in his telegram to the War Cabinet on 21 August, after he had visited Montgomery at the Alamein front. 'I am sure we were heading for disaster under the former regime,' he wrote. 'The Army was reduced to bits and pieces and oppressed by a sense of bafflement and uncertainty . . . Many were looking over their shoulders to make sure of their seat in the lorry.'

The most troubling aspect of the battle Churchill fought with himself is that he was wrong earlier and quite right in his later judgment that a complete change in the Middle East was absolutely necessary. To have done anything other than institute a clear-out in Cairo would have been a recipe for yet more failure. Nevertheless the decision to remove Auchinleck haunted him, even after Montgomery had won the Second Battle of Alamein. 'It was a terrible thing to have to do,' he told Harold Nicolson. 'We must use Auchinleck again. We cannot afford to lose such a man from the fighting line.' Yet in the same breath he said, 'I saw that Army. It was a broken, baffled Army, a miserable Army. I felt for them with all my heart.'

The arrival of the new command team dramatically changed the Middle East dynamics. Ulster was the breeding ground for many of the most illustrious names of the Second World War: Montgomery, Brooke, Auchinleck, Dill, Gort and Alexander. Unlike his fellow Ulstermen, however, Alexander alone earned distinction as Churchill's favourite general.

A professional soldier since the age of nineteen, Alexander had gained a well-deserved reputation for fearlessness in battle and for being utterly unflappable. In less than a year during the First World War, he rose from platoon leader to battalion commander as one of the youngest lieutenant colonels in the army and – indisputably – the most highly regarded officer of his regiment, the Irish Guards. His success was based on his leadership on the battlefield rather than brilliant planning, on personal example rather than the execution of a well-thought-out strategy. Throughout his career Alexander had simply done what came naturally, with little thought given to the evolving role that an officer assumes as he ascends in rank. And, unlike Montgomery, Alexander personified what a successful British general was supposed to look like.

In the Western Desert in 1942, Alexander and Montgomery made an ideal pair. As his boss, Alexander gave Monty free rein. 'Montgomery', writes Alexander's official biographer, 'was a General who must either be left unpinioned or his neck wrung.' Montgomery typically took full credit for British success in the desert, and although he privately resented it Alexander was quite willing to cede the limelight. 'Montgomery enjoyed adulation; Alexander was surprised and embarrassed by it.'

Alexander's nearly effortless rise to high command and to Churchill's adulation seemed inevitable, a journey that began in the sands of Dunkirk, where (as we have seen) he was the last Englishman to leave France. The story is told of Alexander building sand castles on the beach at Dunkirk at the height of the German dive-bombing and of an excited staff officer rushing up to report, 'Our position is catastrophic,' and receiving the reply, 'I'm sorry, I don't understand long words.'

Alexander possessed an intriguing combination of great courage and a complete lack of intellectual interest or curiosity in the war in which he was playing a major role. He was neither a thinker nor a strategist, but as a role model for the ordinary soldier he was magnificent. He shunned the usual trappings of high command and was known for his modesty. On one occasion he politely ordered the dismissal of a covey of motorcycle outriders who were supposed to clear the road ahead for him with the comment, 'I have a marked objection to clearing my own troops off the road for me.' To his men the general known simply as Alex was a hero – and justly so, not least for his frequent, highly visible presence at the front. 'He not only commanded his men but represented them. He was one of them . . . Instead of a helmet, Alexander deliberately wore his garrison cap with its prominent red band, which usually managed to draw enemy fire whenever he visited the front.'

The very traits that made Alexander a success were also those that led to his greatest failing. His relaxed style of leadership by persuasion was designed to exploit his intuition for the art of the possible, for tactfully handling his subordinate generals in different ways, designed to take advantage of each man's strengths and minimize his weaknesses. Yet this method had mixed results with strong-minded generals like Patton, Montgomery and Mark Clark, who were determined to prevail and often did so by exploiting Alexander's reluctance to impose his will.

The Americans with whom Alexander would soon interact all liked and respected him even when they were angered by his overt bias against American fighting ability. Yet despite his outstanding record there were justifiable doubts about his ability to function as a high-level commander. His command guidance was often so vague that his subordinates were unclear about his intentions. He never fully grasped the reins of high command, and this deeply troubled his superiors, even though Churchill all but idolized him. During the Italian campaign, Brooke would privately question Alexander's fitness for high command on numerous occasions.

In short Alexander was an unfathomable enigma whose admirers ran the gamut from front-line soldiers, who loved him for his courage, to generals who served under him and politicians, like Harold Macmillan, who considered him 'first class'. Others, Brooke and ABC Cunningham among them, saw an entirely different person, as did one of his best division commanders, who wrote of him: 'He is quite the least intelligent commander I have ever met in a high position . . . I found that I could not talk to him for more than five minutes: whereas I can talk for hours to intelligent men. Perhaps it is too harsh to say that he's bone from the neck up, but perhaps it isn't.'

If Churchill was ever aware of Alexander's limitations he never acknowledged them. Their relationship was one of almost reverential awe and envy on Churchill's part and a reserve on Alexander's that guarded his innermost thoughts and beliefs. Around Churchill the general spoke little and offered opinions only when pushed to do so. Churchill once said to him, 'I envy you the command of armies in the field. That is what I should have liked.' Dr Wilson once asked Alexander if Churchill would have made a good general. Alexander sat silent for some time. When Wilson then suggested that Winston was a gambler, Alexander finally admitted: 'Yes, that's true. Winston is a gambler.'

Churchill's relationship with Montgomery was entirely different. When it came to war Montgomery was neither a romantic nor a gentleman like Alexander. Both men were warriors, but it was Montgomery who possessed the more complete understanding of how wars were won. That Churchill's romanticism blinded him to reality was evident on the occasion when Wilson asked him if Alexander was a good general. Back came the reply, 'The best we had, better than Monty.'

Alexander's chief contribution to the desert war was to facilitate the employment of the Eighth Army. He left Montgomery strictly alone to do his job, an instance where his detachment proved to be an asset. Churchill, however, misread his appointment of Alexander and his role in the forthcoming Alamein battles. Even at this stage of the war he either failed to understand or simply ignored the way the chain of command worked, believing that it was essential for Alexander to command both the Middle East and the Eighth Army. 'But, of course,' noted Ian Jacob, 'he didn't understand that it wasn't the C-in-C, Middle East who was going to fight the battle; it was the commander of the Eighth Army, and he couldn't understand this because he said, "But you don't mean to tell me that Alex is going to stay in Cairo – [surely] when the battle impends he'll take the field."' It took Brooke to remind him that Montgomery would fight that battle. 'Winston couldn't understand this at all, he pictured him like Napoleon in Paris . . . about to attack Vienna, or Austria, and making all ready and then at the right moment he takes the field and conducts and wins the battles.'

Given the situation in the Middle East in August 1942, Alexander was an excellent choice. To be effective Montgomery needed a superior who would support him but not meddle or second-guess. Alexander did not interfere, but fully supported his prickly Eighth Army commander's logistical requirements, and otherwise kept his hands off operational and tactical matters while acting as a buffer between Montgomery and Churchill.

Lieutenant General Bernard Law Montgomery arrived in Cairo on Wednesday, 12 August 1942. Having set in motion the new command changes, Churchill had already departed for Tehran before flying on to Moscow to meet with Stalin. Auchinleck's departure from the Eighth Army and Montgomery's assumption of command were not without controversy. The new commander had an uncomfortable meeting with Auchinleck, who elected not to turn over both his commands for another three days – until Saturday, 15 August – an arbitrary decision that made no sense except perhaps to salve his conscience.

When he arrived at the Eighth Army command post to inspect and assess his new command the following day, Montgomery immediately recognized that he did not possess the luxury of waiting another two days until Auchinleck's scheduled handover. There was work to be done immediately. Montgomery liked nothing he heard or saw, from troop morale to the plans for evacuating the Alamein position. He ordered all the plans burned. Unlike Auchinleck, who envisaged the need to evacuate Egypt, Montgomery would not even consider the notion, and upon his arrival drew a line in the sand, informing the men of his new command that they would stand and fight – or die trying. There would be no retreat and no surrender. Moreover the Nile Delta and Cairo were indefensible, and even the notion of ceding the Alamein position was a recipe for more failure – no hint of which, both Alexander and Montgomery acknowledged, could be permitted to infect the minds of the troops. 'I understand there has been a great deal of "belly-aching" out here,' he told his officers and soldiers. 'All this is to stop at once. I will tolerate no belly-aching.' To Jacob it was 'quite clear who means to be master of the Desert'.

Having seen for himself the urgency of shaking up the Eighth Army, Montgomery sent a cable to Cairo announcing that he had taken command on 13 August. Although Auchinleck's feathers were badly ruffled by this audacity, which later became fodder for Montgomery's critics, the new Eighth Army commander could not have cared less. There was no time to waste. Moreover Auchinleck had been sacked and, in reality, was disobeying Churchill's orders by not turning over command of both the Middle East and the Eighth Army at once.

Montgomery quizzed officers he trusted on the state of his new army and concluded it was 'muckage' that needed an immediate shaking up. Major General John Harding described the situation of the Eighth Army and its GHQ in one blunt sentence: 'Nobody knew whether they were standing on their arse or their elbow.' Everything was in disarray, from troop dispositions to artillery support, living conditions and the lack of an army reserve (corps de chasse). 'One officer remembered Monty's address to the troops as "straight out of school speech-day", but he gave the impression that at last someone had "got a grip"' on the Eighth Army.

Montgomery began by shaking his new command to its very foundations. Lieutenant Generals Brian Horrocks and Oliver Leese were summoned from England, each to command a corps, and John Harding was sent from Cairo to command the Desert Rats. Along with Freyberg they became the command backbone of a revitalized army. A few key staff officers were retained, and others were brought in, men Monty trusted who would serve him well for the remainder of the war: Francis de Guingand, his new chief of staff, a young Oxford don named Bill Williams as his intelligence chief (G2), and Charles Richardson, a key planner.

By the time Churchill returned to Cairo on 17 August the transformation had already begun. On 19 August, accompanied by Brooke and Alexander, he motored from Cairo to the Eighth Army HQ at El Alamein, where Montgomery explained how he intended to carry out his directive to expel Rommel from Egypt and Cyrenaica. He not only had begun reorganizing his formations and his artillery for the forthcoming British offensive but also had plans in hand in the event Rommel attacked before he was ready. Although Churchill was disappointed to be informed that it would take six weeks to restructure the Eighth Army, he readily accepted his new commander's judgment, his usual exuberance for combat sooner rather than later mitigated by Montgomery's display of confidence.

The Eighth Army command post had been reconstituted. The crude, fly-infested tents that Montgomery scornfully called a 'meat-safe' had been replaced with vans situated in sand dunes just off the beach, where for a brief period it was a peaceful scene with only the gentle sound of waves breaking near by. Before turning in that night, Churchill collared Brooke for a walk on the beach, 'where he was transformed into a small boy wishing to dip his fingers into the sea! In the process he became very wet indeed!!'

Churchill was astonished by the difference between the full-dress uniform and pith helmet he had been required to wear at Omdurman and the outfits worn by the men of the Eighth Army, who went about nearly naked or dressed in shorts, often hatless. 'I inspected my own regiment, the 4th Hussars . . . near the field cemetery, in which a number of their comrades had been newly buried. All this was moving but with it all there grew a sense of the reviving of the Army. Everybody said what a change there was since Montgomery had taken command. I could feel the truth of this with joy and comfort.'

Churchill's visit to a number of the Eighth Army units was a tour de force that only he could have accomplished with such aplomb. 'The day had been a wonderful example of Winston's vitality . . . He had started the day with a [swim] in the sea; we had then spent a very strenuous day touring the front. This had entailed motoring in clouds of sand, long walks between troops, addressing groups of troops, talks with officers, in fact a non-stop tour of inspection.' To complete his day Churchill insisted on another dip in the sea, naked of course, strictly against Dr Wilson's advice. He arrived on the beach accompanied by Inspector Thompson, who wore a trilby hat and carried an enormous umbrella that shielded his master from the sun. Once again momentarily free of his heavy burden, Churchill threw off his clothes and merrily splashed like a young boy. 'He was rolled over by the waves and came up upside down doing the "V" sign with his legs!' recorded Brooke. Not even the news of Dieppe blunted his feelings of optimism. He seemed to shrug it off, stating that it had been worth the high cost.

His trip to Alamein was also an illustration that in Montgomery he had appointed a general unlike any other he had ever met. At noon that day he lunched with Freyberg at his command post. Suddenly Churchill realized someone was missing. 'Where is Monty?' he asked. Montgomery was outside in his staff car eating sandwiches. When asked why, he replied that it was his policy never to eat lunch with subordinates, and not even the prime minister who had appointed him to his post would compel him to make an exception. Nor would Montgomery subject himself to staying up late to accommodate Churchill. That night he kept to his routine of going to bed promptly at ten o'clock, leaving Churchill bemused but much impressed by the great changes his eccentric new general had accomplished in such a short time. With the same bemusement Churchill would later say of the hero of Alamein: 'Indomitable in retreat; invincible in advance; insufferable in victory!'

Churchill's visit to the Eighth Army wore out the younger Brooke. No sooner had he boarded his aircraft at Burg el Arab for the forty-minute flight to Cairo than Brooke declared, 'I am now going to sleep,' and placing a strip of black velvet cloth over his eyes instantly drifted off and did not awaken until the wheels touched down.

Although exhausted by Churchill's seemingly boundless energy, Brooke was ecstatic about Montgomery's performance and deemed it one of the highlights of his career. 'I was dumbfounded by the rapidity with which he had grasped the situation facing him . . . the clarity of his plans, and above all, his unbounded self-confidence . . . I went to bed that night with a wonderful feeling of contentment,' for perhaps the first time since his appointment as CIGS. That confidence transmitted itself to Churchill, who became infused with the belief that in Montgomery he had finally appointed a commander who would carry out his promises. Monty's presentation to Churchill was so masterful that for one of the few times during the war there was none of the usual scepticism and none of the intense interrogation that most military men experienced. The prime minister cabled Attlee: 'I am satisfied that we have lively, confident, resolute men in command, working together under leaders of the highest military quality.'

Churchill was enjoying himself so much that he began speaking openly of staying until the end of August in order to see the imminent battle – before being dissuaded by Brooke, who heaved a sigh of relief when the prime minister's aircraft lifted off for Gibraltar from the Cairo aero-drome on the morning of 23 August. What could not be revealed was that Churchill's desire to remain was based on advance knowledge of Rommel's intentions, supplied by Ultra.

One reason why Montgomery was such a successful commander is that he never asked his soldiers to do more than they were capable of. He understood that the British army was composed largely of citizen-soldiers. He also possessed genuine confidence, not the pseudo-bravado of his two predecessors, Cunningham and Ritchie. His recipe for success was something Churchill could appreciate: 'The commander of a battle feels very lonely and gets a deep conviction that defeat is inevitable. That is the time when great strength of mind is needed. All you must do is to trust the plan and let the battle win itself. The strength of mind required is simply to do nothing and refrain from dithering.'

Unlike Alexander, who personified a flawless soldierly image, Bernard Montgomery looked nothing like a soldier, especially because of his refusal to wear a conventional uniform. With his small frame, beak nose and rather nasal voice, Monty resembled Brooke in that he seemed more like a banker or shopkeeper than the commander of Britain's largest and most powerful army. Yet Churchill had at last accepted Brooke's judgment, writing to Clementine that in Montgomery 'we have a highly competent, daring and energetic soldier . . . If he is disagreeable to those about him, he is also disagreeable to the enemy.' To his doctor he confided that 'it was plain already that Monty knew the secret of preparing his men for battle.'

Ismay wrote of Churchill's accomplishments during this period of the war: 'many people will always regard the fourteen months which elapsed between the German attack on Russia and the Battle of Alamein as the period of his greatest achievement. In the one case, he steeled a nation to defy defeat; in the other, he laid the foundation of Allied victory.'

Ismay's tribute omits one crucial factor – that, finally, after more than two years as warlord, Churchill had 'awoken to the brutal fact: war on the modern battlefield against a professional and indoctrinated enemy could not be won by appointing friendly faces.' By chance rather than by design, Churchill had at last got it right at a critical moment in the war – at a point when more setbacks like Tobruk might have cost the British the Middle East and Churchill his job. Although he could not know it in August 1942, ahead lay an important turning point of the Second World War for Britain. However, before Churchill could reap the joy of victory that had eluded him since May 1940, he would once again experience helplessness and uncertainty as he feared that his desert army was about to lose yet another vitally important battle.

51
Alamein: The Turning Point

Before Alamein we never had a victory. After Alamein we never had a defeat.

— The Hinge of Fate

Churchill returned to London confident that he had righted the ship in the Middle East. Nevertheless his ambivalent opinion of his new Eighth Army commander was evident when he briefed a group of junior ministers on the war situation. 'We've chosen a new general,' he said. 'I don't think any of you would like the fellow.' Although he never quite got used to Montgomery and found him inscrutable, he was drawn as much to military mavericks as he was to elegant soldiers like Alexander. One such was the fiery, eccentric Orde Wingate, whom he perceived as an officer in the mould of Lawrence of Arabia. Wingate formed and led a guerrilla force in the Sudan and later the deep-penetration Chindit commandos who harassed the Japanese in Burma. During the Second World War those involved in unconventional warfare operations were generally viewed with suspicion. Because he was zealous, dangerously unstable (once nearly committing suicide) and enormously controversial, Wingate had more detractors than supporters. However, in Palestine and the Sudan under Wavell, and later in Burma with Churchill's blessing, he had two powerful admirers and supporters. When he was killed in an air crash in March 1944 Churchill mourned the loss of 'a man of genius who might have become a man of destiny'. Today Wingate's place in history remains the most hotly debated of any British general of the war.

Another was the outspoken Major General Percy 'Hobo' Hobart, an expert in armoured warfare with unconventional ideas that were frequently at odds with those of the rigid hierarchy of the British army. Though he had been one of the early members of the Royal Tank Corps, Hobart's ideas of mechanization, training (in which he excelled) and mobile warfare clashed with those of the old guard, who neither understood nor wanted any part of his notions. Branded as difficult and heretical, he met and instantly established a rapport with Churchill in the 1930s. Despite the label of maverick, Hobart rose to the rank of major general and was commanding the Desert Rats in 1939 but fell foul of his superior, Jumbo Wilson, who distrusted his ideas for the employment of armour and insisted that Wavell sack him. Hobart retired and in 1941 was serving as a lowly corporal in the Home Guard when Churchill rescued him from obscurity and restored him to active duty with his former rank. After he was given command of an armoured division, there was another attempt to get rid of him, this time on medical grounds. When Churchill learned what was afoot he interceded with the War Office. In a sternly worded letter he pointed out that while Hobart 'does not work easily with others it is a great pity we have not more of his like in the Service . . . The High Commands of the Army are not a club. It is my duty and that of His Majesty's Government to make sure that exceptionally able men, even though not popular with their military contemporaries, should not be prevented from giving their services to the Crown.'

In command of the 79th Armoured Division on D-day and in the European campaigns, Hobart more than justified Churchill's intervention. Under his brilliant leadership, and with his incredible drive and innovative mind, a large number of specialized armoured vehicles and items of equipment were designed that were made available to units participating in the invasion of Normandy: these included the DD tanks that could swim, ingenious vehicles designed to carry out engineering tasks, assault bridges, flame-throwing Churchill tanks and tanks with searchlights. Called Hobart's 'Funnies', this immense Noah's Ark of equipment was a vital ingredient in the successful invasion by the Allies in June 1944. Saving Hobo Hobart was one of the finest decisions Churchill made in the war.

Rommel launched his expected offensive against the Eighth Army on 30 August. With the impassable Qattara Depression blocking any flanking movement to the south, his only real hope of blasting through to the Nile Delta meant seizing the key Alam Halfa ridge anchoring the British right flank. Auchinleck, who relied on a more fluid reserve force to counter a penetration of British lines, had never made Alam Halfa a key defensive position, but Montgomery immediately discerned that it was the most vital point for stopping Rommel, and one of his first actions was to reinforce and fortify it. Ultra confirmed Rommel's intentions and the soundness of Montgomery's decision.

For his part Rommel could not afford to wait and thus permit British reinforcements to buttress the Eighth Army's incomplete and vulnerable defences. He believed it was not yet strongly defended, and focused his offensive on seizing Alam Halfa. What he never counted on was that the British now had a commander just as perceptive as himself. The military philosopher Carl von Clausewitz described this trait thus: 'All great commanders have acted on instinct, and the fact that their instinct was always sound is partly the measure of their innate greatness and genius.'

Supported by the RAF, artillery and tanks, the Eighth Army checkmated Rommel during a week-long battle. Alam Halfa achieved Montgomery's goal of preserving the British front and his formations for his forthcoming counter-offensive. It also served to heighten morale in Britain and thrust Montgomery's name into the headlines.

As he began preparing for his own offensive, things began to get sticky. With Montgomery having delivered on his promise to halt Rommel, Alam Halfa left Churchill more eager than ever for an immediate Eighth Army offensive to expel Rommel from Egypt. By 8 September Brooke was already noting that 'my next trouble will now be to stop Winston from fussing Alex and Monty and egging them on to attack before they are ready.' It was, he said, yet another case of what he termed 'a regular disease he suffers from, this frightful impatience to get an attack launched!'

Then came an unexpected dose of disappointment, when Montgomery announced that he required a full moon to coincide with his offensive. The September full moon, he said, did not allow adequate time for the necessary preparations; therefore the attack would not commence until the October full moon – a postponement of seven weeks. For Churchill seven weeks seemed unacceptably long. Moreover, Roosevelt's offer after the fall of Tobruk to send three hundred Sherman tanks and one hundred 105-mm self-propelled artillery howitzers to the Middle East had been eagerly accepted, and their arrival in early September merely increased the pressure from Churchill to mount the Alamein offensive without delay. The pressure Brooke feared came in the form of a cable to Alexander on 17 September in which the prime minister declared: 'I am anxiously awaiting some account of your intentions.' Alexander's virtues as a conciliator were on full display when he travelled at once to the Eighth Army GHQ to meet with Montgomery, who privately insisted that he would not attack in September but would guarantee victory in October. If he were ordered to attack in September he would resign. Montgomery's preparations were devoted to devising an entirely new plan of attack, retraining his army and creating elaborate deception measures designed to confuse Rommel over the location of British units; a host of other measures were also being implemented. Alexander's reply to Churchill made it clear that there would be no offensive in September. Back came an immediate concession: 'We are in your hands.'

Having unreservedly entrusted Britain's fate in North Africa to Montgomery, Churchill could not help retaining grave reservations and his usual impatience at the delay in the launching of Second Alamein until late October. On 30 September Brendan Bracken told Sir Charles Wilson, 'If we are beaten in this battle, it's the end of Winston . . . He's going through a very bad time . . . [and] is finding the suspense almost unbearable.'

Brooke also had to deal with Churchill's latest chapter of the Norway saga: an invasion the prime minister wanted carried out in January 1943. 'He had promised something of this kind to Stalin . . . Now he is trying to drive us into it,' said Brooke. The priority for employment of shipping resources for Torch alone made landings in northern Norway in the dead of winter impossible. Churchill refused to concede the point, and the result was another standoff in which he attempted to outflank the chiefs by trying but failing to persuade the Canadians to mount the operation.

Churchill's impatience over Alamein erupted on 23 September, when he and Brooke tangled in an acrimonious war of words. He showed Brooke a cable he proposed sending to Alexander that was designed to advance the timetable for Alamein. 'I tried to stop him,' a frustrated Brooke wrote in his diary, adding that it would only reveal a lack of confidence in Alexander at a pivotal moment. Churchill 'then started all his worst arguments about generals only thinking of themselves and their reputations, and never attacking unless matters were a certainty, and never prepared to take risks . . . He said this delay would result in Rommel fortifying a belt 20 miles deep by 40 miles broad that we should never break through.' Left unexpressed were Churchill's nagging doubts about whether the average British soldier would measure up in the most difficult challenge of all: defeating Rommel.

Churchill was torn between his long-standing distrust of generals, their promises and their legacy of failure and the reality that he now had in command of the Eighth Army a general who understood what he must do and was preparing to make good on his promises. Churchill's reservations about the quality of his citizen army's performance in the desert were justified, but his focus was misdirected. With proper leadership the British Tommy now responded. Montgomery won over the veterans of the desert with clarity, sincerity and utter honesty. 'He told us everything,' said a regimental sergeant major, 'what his plan was for the battle, what he wanted the regiments to do, what he wanted *me* to do ... What a man!'

Although Churchill had won an enormous victory by persuading Roosevelt to sanction Torch, everything now hinged on the Eighth Army, in the hands of the upstart Bernard Montgomery, stopping Rommel. The autumn of 1942 was a critical time for Churchill. The Arctic convoys to Murmansk were bleeding with heavy losses from U-boats, and, as he remarked to Eden on 1 October, 'If Torch fails, then I'm done for and must go and hand over to one of you.'

Montgomery launched Operation Lightfoot, the Second Battle of Alamein, on the night of 23 October 1942 with the largest artillery barrage of the war. Some 195,000 British and Commonwealth troops consisting of 85 infantry battalions, more than 1,000 tanks, 1,451 anti-tank guns and 908 artillery guns faced off against Rommel's Panzerarmee, numbering just over 104,000, of whom 50,000 were German and the rest Italians, supported by 71 infantry battalions, 496 tanks, 800 anti-tank guns and 500 pieces of artillery.

It was a cat-and-mouse game on both sides. Montgomery used the Australians to deceive Rommel over his intention to launch his main offensive on the British right flank. The air, the massed artillery and the infantry would force a break-in by penetrating Rommel's outer defences, followed by what Montgomery termed a week-long 'dog-fight' to open corridors through the German minefields for his tanks, and then by a breakout that would finish the job.

As prolonged and savage fighting continued and casualties mounted to some ten thousand with no sign of a breakthrough, Churchill's mood grew darker and more explosive, and he demanded and devoured frequent updates for any sign of success. Brooke's own frustrations reached a new high over Alamein when Churchill, now seriously fearing it would fail, began complaining about Montgomery's generalship. Brooke counselled patience, but Churchill and patience were an oxymoron. On 29 October Brooke was summoned and was 'met with a flow of abuse of Monty' before being presented with a scorching telegram Churchill proposed to send to Alexander. 'What was *my* Monty doing now, allowing the battle to peter out (Monty was always *my* Monty when he was out of favour!). He had done nothing now for the past three days . . . Why had he told us he would be through in seven days if all he intended to do was to fight a half-hearted battle?' Churchill admitted he had been influenced by a pessimistic assessment from Eden. Exasperated, Brooke asked Churchill why he had solicited advice on tactical and strategic matters from his foreign secretary instead of from his military men. 'He flared up and asked whether he was not entitled to consult whoever he wished! To which I replied he certainly could, provided he did not let those who knew little about military matters upset his equilibrium.' Brooke also took on Eden, pointing out that his judgments were superficial. Smuts was present and fully backed Brooke, thus averting an even more acrimonious battle between the two.

Before bedtime one night Wilson heard Churchill grunt, 'If this goes on, anything may happen.' Outside the prime minister's bedroom he found Brooke waiting for him. 'Is the P.M. all right, Charles? I thought he was going to hit me when he demanded: "Haven't we got a single general who can even win one battle?" '

What Brooke would admit to no one was that with the outcome of Alamein hanging in the balance, 'I had my own doubts and my own anxieties . . . On returning to my office I paced up and down, suffering from a desperate feeling of loneliness . . . I knew Monty well, but there was still just the possibility that I was wrong and that Monty was beat. The loneliness of those moments of anxiety, when there is no one one can turn to, have to be lived through to realize their intense bitterness.'

Alamein was a battle of attrition in which every foot of ground gained or defended was paid for in what at one point Rommel called 'rivers of blood'. The 'dog-fight' battle dragged on for days. Although Churchill's war memoir fails even to mention it, his anxiety grew graver by the hour in no small part because he had been burned so often in the past by the failure of his generals. Brooke's words fairly describe the agony of doubt that Churchill felt at this precarious moment of the war. As someone who always wanted to be in control of events, he was helpless over Alamein. The fate of the battle was solely in the hands of Montgomery and the men of the Eighth Army. All Churchill could do was wait – and hope.

After days of hard fighting the Eighth Army seized key positions on Kidney and Miteiriya Ridges that compelled Rommel to launch counterattacks, these failed and further depleted his tanks and troops. He believed that Montgomery intended to aim his main attacks near the coast and, in order to prevent a breakout, he concentrated his forces in this sector. On 2 November Montgomery altered his strategy with the launching of Operation Supercharge, an attack further south than originally intended, using British and New Zealand infantry supported by more than a hundred tanks. The overwhelming pressure of Supercharge was too much for Rommel, who was now outnumbered and whose tanks and vehicles were dangerously low on fuel. This was the turning point, and a signal to Rommel that he had lost the battle. By 4 November what was left of his army was in full retreat. Airpower also played an important role and the level of air–ground co-operation was exceptional, all the more so because of the efforts of the two air chiefs, Tedder and Coningham, the commander of the Desert Air Force.

Alamein was the bloodiest battle of the long desert war. Rommel's losses were terrible: nearly twelve thousand killed, wounded or missing and thirty thousand captured, nearly 30 per cent of Panzerarmee Afrika. The battlefield was littered with the wreckage of 350 destroyed or burning panzers. Of the nearly five hundred tanks Rommel had at the start of the battle, a mere eighty were left serviceable. Allied losses of 13,500 killed, wounded or missing added up to nearly 25 per cent of the Eighth Army's infantry strength.

With the eventual success of the Alamein offensive Churchill breathed a sigh of relief, and his mood quickly brightened. 'The victory has brought great joy to the P.M.,' noted Wilson. 'He talks of ringing the church bells all over Britain . . . He will take none of the credit, though the changes he has made in the desert command have been triumphantly vindicated. He is lyrical about Monty and Alex. This victory will silence criticism, and it seems that for the moment all his troubles are at an end.'

There was a brief firestorm in Britain when a photograph appeared in the press of Montgomery with General Wilhelm Ritter von Thoma, the commander of the Afrika Korps and the highest-ranking German captured at Alamein. After his capture Thoma was brought to the Eighth Army command post, where Montgomery accorded him the respect of one honourable professional soldier to another. The two dined that night, and the photograph of the two generals led Brendan Bracken to send Churchill a memo criticizing Montgomery's naivety and saying that it created a bad impression with the public. Churchill merely commented: 'I sympathize with General von Thoma. Defeated, humiliated, in captivity, and,' after pausing for effect, 'dinner with General Montgomery.'

Nevertheless the debt Churchill owed to Montgomery was far greater than merely winning Second Alamein, and the question must be asked: would Roosevelt have backed Operation Torch if Rommel had succeeded in July 1942 and Auchinleck had lost the battle that Montgomery won the following month? This scenario is not without credibility and might have been sufficient to induce Hitler to shift his strategy towards major operations to seize the Caucasian oil fields and towards having these forces join those of Rommel in the Middle East. 'Certainly, this was what Churchill, Brooke, Wavell, Smuts, Auchinleck and others feared,' observes Nigel Hamilton. 'With the unmitigated disaster at Dieppe on 19 August 1942, all hope of a credible second front in Europe would have collapsed, and the leadership of the United States might well have felt justified in concentrating upon a "Japan first" strategy, as Admiral King and other senior American commanders were urging the President.' Even more chilling is the logical result of such a development – namely, had the Axis seized control of the Mediterranean, Churchill would have been far less likely to survive another vote of confidence and thus could well have had to step down as minister of defence and possibly as prime minister.

All of this is conjecture. Churchill later admitted that in September 1942 his position was more vulnerable than at any other period of the war – Tobruk had seen to that, and, even with the success of Alam Halfa, Britain's hold on the Middle East remained at risk – but that after Alamein he never again faced the prospect of losing his job.

Many who served in North Africa and experienced these events at first hand believe that Auchinleck could not have held Alam Halfa.

Supposition or not, it serves to focus on the importance of the Battles of Alam Halfa and Second Alamein, and their importance in the history of the Second World War. On 10 November 1942 Churchill made the now famous, enigmatic observation: 'Now this is not the end, it is not even the beginning of the end. But it is, perhaps, the end of the beginning.' In his war memoirs he said it somewhat more simply: 'Before Alamein we never had a victory. After Alamein we never had a defeat.' He also might have added: 'Before Alamein we were uncertain of our survival in the Middle East.'

There was another factor at play: both Alamein and Montgomery took on heroic status, not only because the battle was a turning point in the war, but also because it had come at the expense of Rommel, who had been elevated to legendary proportions, not least by Churchill himself.

After delaying for a week to be certain that Montgomery's victory at Alamein was indeed secure, Churchill ordered every church bell in England rung on Sunday, 13 November. 'We are not celebrating final victory,' he told Harold Nicolson. 'The war will still be long.' Yet there was at last cause for optimism. Not only had the bleak situation in the Middle East turned dramatically after so many heartbreaking setbacks, but joint Anglo-American operations were soon to get under way in North Africa. The numerous military disasters of 1942 notwithstanding, what Churchill accomplished in that fateful year reveals a great deal about his war leadership. Besides neutralizing Stafford Cripps, who had emerged as a potential threat to replace him, 'he seemed to be 20 men that summer,' writes one of his biographers. 'He defended himself in Parliament ... planned campaigns with his chiefs of staff, dealt with American envoys, flew to Egypt and fired or appointed generals, flew to Washington and worked on Roosevelt, flew to Moscow and did battle with Stalin. Never had he more closely resembled the bulldog that never lets go.' The capstone was Alamein.

52
Ike

He was the most persuasive man I have ever known, and the most persistent.

– Eisenhower

Plucked from obscurity by George Marshall, Dwight David Eisenhower was a rising star in the wartime United States army. A West Point graduate and a career officer since 1915, the man they called Ike missed combat during the First World War, training troops for tank duty in France. Marshall promoted Eisenhower – noted for his great charm, intelligence and all-round efficiency as the army's chief planner – to major general in the spring of 1942 and sent him to London in July to take charge of the growing American military presence in Britain.

Eisenhower had long admired Churchill from a distance. 'Like all other Americans I was familiar with the inspiring leadership he had given his nation from Dunkirk onward,' he later said. 'Some passages were as inspiring to me as to his countrymen. When he came to Washington in December 1941 I was truly anxious to see a man of whom I'd heard so much ... [and] occasionally came sufficiently close to him to be fascinated by his energy, eloquence at the conference table and single-minded purpose of winning the war.'

Three days before his departure for England, Eisenhower's preparations were interrupted by a summons to attend a meeting with the British on a blistering, heatstroke-inducing day in Washington. Present were Marshall, Dill, Brooke and Ismay. It was Eisenhower's first introduction to Pug Ismay, with whom he formed an exceptionally close friendship. The topic was again the thorny issue of strategy: what would be their first joint Anglo-American venture and where would it take place? Churchill was pushing hard for an invasion of French North Africa that would gain the Allies a foothold in the

Mediterranean. Marshall and Eisenhower fought tooth and nail against what Secretary of War Henry L. Stimson had nicknamed FDR's 'secret baby'.

On one point, however, there was complete agreement between the two leaders: there had to be some Allied initiative in 1942. Roosevelt and Churchill met privately at Hyde Park, and Churchill used the occasion to bring his considerable charm and influence to bear on the president to approve an invasion of North-west Africa. Then came the news that Tobruk had fallen to the resourceful and audacious Rommel. And while the increasingly precarious British position in North Africa gave even more leverage to Churchill's arguments in favour of a joint Mediterranean venture, it left Marshall and Eisenhower more dubious than ever about American involvement there.

Before November 1942 British grand strategy had evolved from Churchill's vision of the three Rs: resist, rearm and retaliate. With Operation Sledgehammer likely to be abandoned, it was inevitable that, with no other place in which to initiate operations against the Axis, the Americans should be captive to Churchill's vision. The British argument was that at least in this admittedly secondary theatre, where British forces were fighting for their lives, Anglo-American forces could be employed to harass the Axis and perhaps even win a major victory on the battlefield.

On the basis of a plan drawn up by Eisenhower, Marshall and the US chiefs of staff had a single, unwavering vision for the defeat of the Axis: the liberation of occupied Europe by means of a cross-Channel invasion of France. Anything else was deemed an unnecessary diversion and a sideshow. Although formal approval of a joint Mediterranean venture did not occur until July, Churchill was already preaching to a near-convert. Roosevelt was determined to engage American forces somewhere in 1942, and Churchill's arguments in light of the disaster at Tobruk were tempting him away from Sledgehammer. By the time Eisenhower left for London there still had been no formal decision by the two Allies, but everyone, Eisenhower included, saw the writing on the wall.

When Eisenhower and Mark Clark called on Roosevelt at the White House, Eisenhower was formally introduced for the first time to Winston Churchill, who recalled, 'I was immediately impressed by these remarkable but hitherto unknown men.' Despite the gloom surrounding the fall of Tobruk, Eisenhower detected no hint of pessimism in either Churchill or the president. His full exposure to the charms and manipulative ways of Churchill still lay ahead.

Eisenhower arrived in London at the crucial point when the future direction of Allied strategy hinged upon decisions being made that summer. As the senior American in Britain and unknowing heir apparent to supreme command, he was now engaged in an unlikely military and political partnership. Had the Second World War not erupted, Britain and the United States would never have been allies; their philosophical outlook, even without the inclusion of the strangest of all bedfellows, the Soviet Union, could not have been more contradictory. Bringing together a Communist dictatorship more repressive than Fascist Germany, a colonial power bent on retaining its empire and the free world's bulwark of capitalism was hardly a prescription for a successful military alliance. Into this minefield of intrigue and self-interest stepped Dwight Eisenhower in June 1942, a general dedicated to defeating Germany by any means necessary, who lacked any interest in politics, petty or otherwise.

Eisenhower's new command was called the European Theater of Operations, US Army (ETOUSA), with headquarters at No. 20 Grosvenor Square, in the heart of London's Mayfair.

Winston Churchill was unlike anyone he had ever met. Eisenhower was used to dealing with men with big egos, for whom he mostly had contempt, yet Churchill elicited a wholly contrary response. With the prime minister, Eisenhower found himself up against a powerful personality with a flair for the dramatic gesture – a combination of politician, statesman, warlord and frustrated soldier who would much rather have been on the battlefield commanding troops.

Soon after his arrival the prime minister got into the habit of inviting Eisenhower to lunch once or twice a week at No. 10. On other, less auspicious occasions the general and sometimes his chief of staff, Walter Bedell Smith, and his deputy and old friend, Mark Clark, endured long nights with Churchill at Chequers, whose unheated rooms Eisenhower thought would chill the bones of the dead. (Eisenhower referred to Chequers none too fondly as 'a damned icebox'.)

American visitors to Chequers were intrigued by its halls and rooms decorated with the paintings of long-dead British noblemen and women, most of whose portraits, Commander Thompson pointed out, 'showed the royalty with dirty necks'. Eisenhower and Clark would both come to dread an overnight stay with Winston. On his first night at Chequers, Ike slept in a bedroom that had once been occupied by Oliver Cromwell, which felt as if its absence of warmth had survived the 284 years since the lord protector's death in 1658. The following morning Eisenhower and Clark inspected an impressive guard of honour of tall Coldstream Guardsmen, who provided security for Chequers. As they moved down the line, Churchill leaned out his bedroom window dressed in his night-shirt and shouted, 'Aren't they a fine body of men!'

The one unwritten rule for anyone who dealt with Churchill was to avoid being intimidated. Often exasperated and occasionally irked and exhausted by the prime minister's bulldog manner, Eisenhower never succumbed to his fulminations. (Succumbing was an invariably fatal failing for those who did.) His conversations with Churchill were often tests of will, particularly when the British leader was advocating one of his current ideas for military action.

Churchill was generally popular with American officers. Given the enormous egos of the two men, it was perhaps unexpected that one of his most ardent admirers was Douglas MacArthur. 'If the disposal of all the Allied decorations were today placed by Providence in my hands,' MacArthur told a senior British officer attached to his head-quarters in Australia, 'my first act would be to award the Victoria Cross to Winston Churchill. Not one of those who wear it deserves it more than he.'

From the outset Eisenhower understood perfectly well that he was being thoroughly scrutinized, and that to permit himself to be over-powered by the prime minister's aggressive personality and charm would be disastrous. In the course of 1942 he won over Churchill, and a warm and enduring friendship developed between the two men that survived some bruising encounters.

Churchill was happiest when discussing history and its lessons, and in Eisenhower he found not only a worthy companion but also one of the few who could match him. Once while dining at Chequers, Churchill 'remarked to Eisenhower that he had studied every campaign since the Punic Wars', prompting Commander Thompson to whisper to his neighbour, 'And he's taken part in most of them!'

Evidence of Churchill's genuine fondness for Eisenhower was readily discernible in the prime minister's uncommon gestures of respect, such as seating him to his right at dinner parties, even though protocol dictated that the senior officer or politician present should occupy this position. That Eisenhower was typically junior to most of the officers present made no difference to Churchill. He also developed a habit of walking Eisenhower to his staff car at the end of the evening, a gesture usually reserved for visiting royalty or statesmen.

Nothing, however, could prepare Eisenhower for the full Churchill treatment of unbearably late hours at No. 10 or Chequers as his dinner guests were obliged to sit and squirm on the uncomfortable hardback dining-room chairs while the prime minister pontificated for hours on end. He was also introduced to Churchill's strange evening attire of carpet slippers and a one-piece siren suit that zipped up at the front. Churchill, regularly reinvigorated by food and drink, carried on with great vitality undeterred by the growing fatigue on the faces of his captive audience. Moreover, his method of solving a problem 'by talking it out with anyone who would listen' was a trait that drove Eisenhower to distraction. Although loath to be a part of the prime minister's late-night habits, he too was obliged stoically to endure these ordeals with the same pained expression of resignation and exhaustion as Brooke, Ismay and other senior British officers.

Eisenhower quickly worked out that with Churchill one could never anticipate the direction of his thinking, and that he did not always accept unpleasant news gracefully, often subjecting the hapless messenger to a tongue-lashing. On one occasion Eisenhower witnessed him being briefed on British shipping capacity. 'The picture was not bright, but it was as nothing to the dark annoyance on Winston's face . . . It was easy to see that some outburst was coming.' The speaker referred to British troops as 'bodies', a common practice to avoid having to spell out 'officers, non-commissioned officers and other ranks', a custom Churchill was familiar with. 'How can you use such a disgusting word to describe His Majesty's fighting forces!' he erupted. 'These men are not corpses. I will not have it. Stop it at once.'

From the start of their relationship, Churchill was determined to make the coalition work, once telling Eisenhower that if he had any problem with any member of His Majesty's armed forces, he had merely to inform him and he would personally see to it that the offender was removed or disciplined forthwith. Although Eisenhower never took up the offer, it was a reassuring sign of the prime minister's trust in the American general. United in a common hatred of Hitler and the evils of Nazi Germany, they made a formidable team.

53

Torch and Casablanca

The U.S. regarded the Mediterranean as a kind of dark hole into which one entered at one's own peril.   – Ian Jacob

The year 1943 would begin on a high note for Churchill. Not only did the bleak situation in the Middle East turn dramatically after many heartbreaking setbacks, but with joint Anglo-American operations under way in North Africa, there was cause for optimism that Hitler's proclaimed thousand-year Reich was not invincible after all.

Though in 1942 Britain's task had been to continue to survive in the face of apparently hopeless odds, what Churchill had accomplished in that year was astonishing. However, there was a dark side to his dynamism. He had survived a mild heart attack in December 1941 and, although he himself paid it little attention, his health was a major issue. By the summer of 1942, Smuts was so concerned that he telegraphed Sir Charles Wilson: 'Please continue your efforts for the Prime Minister's health. I feel convinced he cannot continue at present pace without a breakdown. Grave national responsibility rests on you for Leader's health.' When he was shown Smuts's telegram, Churchill quite naturally professed unconcern. 'I am very well,' he said.

For well over two years Britain's survival had depended upon indefinitely postponing a decisive engagement with the German army. Even before Alamein, Churchill and Brooke had pursued a strategy of defeating the Axis in the Mediterranean and Middle East. Churchill persuaded Franklin Roosevelt that the Allies should attack attainable targets in the Mediterranean instead of impossible ones in France.

The Mediterranean campaigns that lasted from November 1942 to the end of the war thus sharply focused on the fundamental differences between a colonial maritime power and an emerging superpower with divergent ideas of how to fight the war. The British considered it both prudent and pragmatic to disperse the Allied effort and take advantage of the opportunities presented in the Mediterranean. While in Moscow, Churchill had explained to a sceptical and bitterly disappointed Stalin that the Allies were not yet ready to invade Europe, that there would be no second front in Europe in 1942 but it would take place in the Mediterranean. He drew a picture of a crocodile in order to illustrate his intention 'to attack the soft belly of the crocodile as we attacked his hard snout'.

Nevertheless the Mediterranean was no easy sell. General Marshall, as the chief American strategist, rejected the devious British approach, which left the Russians taking the main brunt of the fighting – with the opportunity to dominate Europe if they triumphed over Hitler's armies – in favour of a direct assault on Fortress Europe, across the English Channel. 'The Americans thus disliked "side-shows" which to the British were an inherent element of warfare,' the official British historian admitted, 'and the Mediterranean had always seemed to them to bear all the marks of the "side-show".' Every division sent to the Mediterranean 'was a division lost for the main battle'.

Convinced that Operation Sledgehammer was 'dead off and without the slightest hope', the British successfully fended off what Brooke called American rigidity in pushing for a hopeless plan of cross-Channel invasion. Instead they argued that Allied operations in the Mediterranean would not delay a cross-Channel assault beyond 1943, and would provide valuable combat experience for untested American forces.

With FDR's insistence on American involvement in 1942, Marshall was therefore compelled to accept Operation Torch, the Anglo-American invasion of French North Africa in the autumn. In return the British agreed to Operation Roundup in 1943: an infusion of US forces into Britain for the more important invasion of France. To demonstrate good faith Churchill also agreed to the appointment of an American to command the Allied expeditionary force in Torch. As a direct result of their friendship begun several months earlier, Churchill agreed that the appointment should go to Eisenhower.

Churchill relished Torch as a masterstroke that changed the entire course of Anglo-American grand strategy in favour of the British plan of 'tightening the noose' on the Axis. He would have been the first to concede that Roundup would one day have to be mounted, but now it would be carried out according to a British rather than an American timetable. 'A picador strategy was precisely what the British wanted. They did not wish to engage the German army on the Continent until it had been profusely bled elsewhere,' one writer would later comment. If Germany and Russia should bleed each other to death, so much the better for the Western Allies. But Churchill had deeper reasons than simply postponing the final reckoning in France; he wanted full British control of the Mediterranean, with its vital sea-lanes through the Suez Canal to the oil refineries of Iran, and to India and the Far East – which he saw as crucial to the restoration of Britain's ailing empire once the war was over. What he anticipated and Marshall feared was that, once committed, the United States would never be able to untangle itself from the Mediterranean. Ian Jacob would later note in his diary that 'the U.S. regarded the Mediterranean as a kind of dark hole into which one entered at one's own peril.'

Yet enter it the Allies did on the morning of 8 November 1942 when 117,000 of their troops landed simultaneously along a nearly one-thousand-mile coastal front from Algiers and Oran to French Morocco. The Eastern (or Algiers) Task Force was Anglo-American and included 23,000 British troops. The Western Task Force was really an American invasion, commanded by Major General George S. Patton Jr, which seized Casablanca, Safi and Port Lyautey on the Atlantic side of French Morocco.

Churchill was deeply involved in every conceivable aspect of the planning of Torch, which was made far more complex because it was planned in both Washington and London. Eisenhower and Mark Clark spent many of their nights with Churchill, who probed, questioned and one evening summoned both Pound and Mountbatten directly from their beds to No. 10 to answer questions about the convoys. After persuading Pound that the time needed for the operation could be reduced, the first sea lord was dismissed with the admonishment: 'Now, Sir Dudley, you can turn in!' The others present were not so fortunate.

At other times Churchill was impatient and obstinate. It was as if success in Egypt revived the whirlwind of ideas and demands, among them the long-standing insistence on reducing the army's logistical tail in North-west Africa. 'The Army is like a peacock – nearly all tail,' he complained, only to have Brooke remind him: 'The peacock would be a very badly balanced bird without its tail.' While Brooke always countered Churchill's excessive demands, it was Smuts who seemed to have the greatest influence. To end one interminable late-night meeting, as General Kennedy recorded, 'Smuts sent the Prime Minister to bed, like a small boy, and he went off obediently, as though despatched by his mother.'

The situation the Allies encountered in French North Africa was complex and beset with intrigue and a confusion of loyalties among the French military, some of whom remained loyal to Marshal Pétain's Vichy regime, while others supported the Allies. A last-minute ceasefire ordered by Admiral Jean Darlan, the French commander in chief, generally averted bloodshed except at Oran, where the French fought furiously for two days before surrendering to the US 1st Infantry Division.

By late 1942 Rommel had concluded that a continued Axis presence in North Africa was a futile gesture and advised Hitler in person that there was no hope of victory. German forces should be pulled out of North Africa or else they would be destroyed. After the defeat at Alamein, Rommel's desert army was exhausted and critically deficient in manpower, weapons, equipment, food and fuel. Despite mounting evidence that the desert war had turned in favour of the British, Hitler, prompted by the unscrupulous Göring, flew into a rage and without any discussion of the matter summarily rejected Rommel's advice. The Desert Fox was suddenly in bad odour for speaking his mind. Instead, Hitler reacted to the Torch landings by pouring reinforcements into Tunisia. The first of some hundred thousand additional German and Italian troops began arriving there in a steady flow in early November, as the Luftwaffe made Allied movement a costly proposition on land. Meanwhile, at sea German U-boats continued to sink Allied shipping with distressing regularity.

As Allied forces struggled to establish a fully operational front in the forbidding, seemingly endless mountain ranges of western Tunisia, there was nevertheless cause for martial pride in Churchill's war rooms. After Rommel had broken contact with the Eighth Army at Alamein, Montgomery's victorious army pursued his Panzerarmee Afrika relentlessly (if all too deliberately, in Churchill's cavalry-trained eyes) as it retreated towards the Tunisian border. During November and December 1942

Rommel retreated more than eight hundred miles. On 13 January 1943 the Eighth Army closed the books on nearly two years of back-and-forth successes and reverses and captured Tripoli. Ten days later the rout continued, as Rommel's depleted army entered Tunisia to take a stand along the formidable Mareth Line.

The original aim of Allied operations in Tunisia was to secure the ports and lines of communication, and then to trap and destroy Rommel's army in Tripolitania between the Eighth Army advancing from the east and the British First Army advancing from the west. However, the newly created Fifth Panzer Army, commanded by General Hans-Jürgen von Arnim, heavily supported by the Luftwaffe, aggressively disrupted and delayed the Allied advance into western Tunisia. It was one of the few times during the war in the West that the Luftwaffe could claim success. The race for Tunis also became an attempt to beat the winter weather – a race that the Allies lost, obliging Eisenhower (at his headquarters in Algiers) to cancel further offensive operations in Tunisia in 1942 and assume a defensive posture. During the winter of 1942–3, only single British, French and American corps manned the thinly held 250-mile Allied front.

Allied troops and airmen were not lacking in courage, but their inexperience and the unsuccessful results of their first battles left no doubt that there would have to be considerable improvement before they became a match for the veteran German and Italian troops in Tunisia.

In January 1943 Roosevelt, Churchill and the Combined Chiefs of Staff met at Casablanca primarily, as Churchill reminded Roosevelt, 'because we have no [suitable] plan for 1943'. Beyond Torch and a still imprecise commitment to a cross-Channel invasion, the two Allies had yet to agree even remotely on a common strategy to defeat Germany and Italy. Torch had been foisted on an unwilling Marshall by Churchill, abetted by Roosevelt's reluctance for the United States to sit on the sidelines until 1943. At Casablanca, Marshall's hopes for untangling the United States from the Mediterranean were dashed.

In January 1943 Churchill still travelled by air in miserable conditions. The flight from England to Morocco was aboard an unconverted bomber in which most of his party slept in their seats and the only sleeping accommodation was two mattresses slung in the rear of the aircraft, one for Churchill and the other for Dr Wilson (now ennobled as Lord

Moran). While attempting to sleep Churchill burned his toes against some improvised heating elements at the foot of his mattress. Distressed, he shook Portal awake to complain: 'They are red hot. We shall have the petrol fumes bursting into flames. There'll be an explosion soon.' To head off further hazard the heating was turned off, but later Moran was awakened 'to discover the PM on his knees, trying to keep out the draught by putting a blanket against the side of the plane. He was shivering: we were flying at 7,000 feet in an unheated bomber in mid-winter.' Nothing worked. 'The P.M. is at a disadvantage in this kind of travel, since he never wears anything at night but a silk vest. On his hands and knees, he cut a quaint figure with his big, bare, white bottom.'

Stalin pointedly declined to attend Casablanca, but his absence was probably a blessing in that it gave the two Western Allies the opportunity to meet in secret to resolve the many thorny questions left unanswered by Torch. Churchill, the master politician, understood that once it was 'in for a penny' in the Mediterranean, the United States was indeed 'in for a pound', and proclaimed that as soon as North Africa was secure the Allies 'must go forward to the attack on Italy, with the object of preparing the way for a very large-scale offensive on the underbelly of the Axis in 1943'.

Stalin's long shadow was nevertheless present during their deliberations. Although the Red Army would soon win the most important victory of the war on the eastern front at Stalingrad, Stalin had badgered Churchill and Roosevelt during the second half of 1942 to open a second front in the West without delay, and further relieve the pressure upon his hard-pressed armies.

In the autumn of 1942, Churchill had expressed a willingness to mount the Allied cross-Channel invasion in the late summer of 1943, but when it became evident in December that the Tunisian campaign was in trouble, he began to insist on playing out the Mediterranean option – with the invasion of France put back until 1944. Thus, while again affirming the eventual need for the cross-Channel invasion, soon to be given the code name Operation Overlord, he sought to buy time for its planning and preparation by continuing to nibble away at Germany's 'soft underbelly'. The Allies had the Axis on the defensive in the Mediterranean and ought not, he argued, surrender the initiative.

At Casablanca the two Western Allies thus fought a war within a war for control of the direction of their joint effort against the Axis. Churchill and the British chiefs of staff arrived fully committed to the removal of Mussolini and the Italians from the war. Led by Brooke, the British chiefs contended that an invasion of the island of Sicily following the Tunisian campaign was an obvious choice for the Allies to reinforce their success in the Mediterranean and gain a foothold in southern Europe.

The deadlock centred on the timing of Overlord. Marshall was adamant that 'the Mediterranean was a blind alley to which American forces had only been committed because of the President's insistence that they should fight the Germans somewhere.' Marshall's determination to shift Allied forces in North Africa to the United Kingdom was countered by British arguments in favour of Churchill's avowed goal of the 'cleansing of North Africa to be followed by the capture of Sicily'. Although some Americans still held out hope that the cross-Channel invasion could take place in 1943, in the end all the United States got was a promise that it would be carried out in 1944 – an assurance that, contrary to later assertions that Churchill never believed in it, was entirely sincere despite his abiding apprehension about the inevitable cost in lives.

There was also deadlock over the allocation of resources between Europe and the Pacific. In the end the Combined Chiefs reached a compromise on Pacific operations that satisfied Admiral King, and what Churchill loftily proclaimed was 'the most complete strategic plan for a world-wide war that had ever been conceived'. Besides formulating a Europe-first policy, one of its main provisions was – as Churchill had doggedly insisted – the invasion of Sicily. The compromise orchestrated by the British left Churchill's Mediterranean strategy fully intact, American hopes in tatters and Marshall dismayed that he had lost an uneven fight to extricate the Allies from the Mediterranean. (The question of when and where to mount Overlord would not be resolved until the Quebec Conference, held in August 1943.)

Churchill had played his hand masterfully. It was one of the few times during the war when he did not plunge into negotiations, instead staying largely in the background with uncharacteristic patience, leaving it to Brooke and the chiefs to carry out the arduous talks. The 'two emperors' (as Harold Macmillan, newly appointed minister resident at the Algiers headquarters, called Roosevelt and Churchill) and the other high-ranking participants indulged in 'a curious mixture of holiday and business . . . you would see the field marshals and admirals going down to the beach for an hour to play with the pebbles and make sand-castles,' before the debates and discussions resumed each night. Both leaders ignored the dangers of wartime travel. Like Churchill, Roosevelt disregarded pleas that flying was too hazardous. Both men loved adventure tinged with an element of risk, and both benefited mightily from their time away from the heavy burdens of office. 'I have never seen him in better form,' Macmillan said of Churchill. 'He ate and drank enormously all the time, settled huge problems, played bagatelle and bezique by the hour, and generally enjoyed himself . . . The whole affair . . . was a mixture between a cruise, a summer school and a conference.' One day Churchill managed to elude his handlers and leave the compound at Anfa, a holiday resort outside Casablanca where the conference was being held, to stroll around outside. There was a frantic search before the missing prime minister was located sightseeing and safely returned to his villa.

Several other important agreements were concluded at Casablanca: the decision to issue an Allied proclamation that there would be no negotiated peace with Germany, only unconditional surrender; the high priority of defeating the U-boats; and the initiation of a strategic air campaign against Germany.

Casablanca, in sum, was a triumph for Churchill, who spent quality time with FDR in one of the most agreeable settings that either man experienced during the war. Each entertained the other with fine food and conversation, with Churchill often dressed in his siren suit. He reported to Clementine that Casablanca had gone 'in every respect as I wished & proposed . . . The triumphant arrival of the Eighth Army in Tripoli has made it possible for us to obtain practically all the solutions we wished from our American friends.'

54

Down the Garden Path

I suppose that the Americans consider we have led them down the garden path in the Mediterranean – but what a beautiful path it has proved to be . . . How grateful they should be!   – Churchill, July 1943

'You cannot come all this way to North Africa without seeing Marrakech,' Churchill insisted before Roosevelt returned to the United States. With troops lining the road as security, and aircraft constantly overhead, the two leaders set off by motor car on 24 January 1943 for a 150-mile journey that included a stop for a picnic lunch. 'It's the most lovely spot in the whole world,' Churchill reflected on the place he had visited in the 1930s and would subsequently return to numerous times, set in the foothills of the Atlas Mountains. It proved also one the few occasions when he could relax without a care in the world, and it was during this brief respite in Marrakech that Churchill painted the only picture he completed during the war, a scene of the city and mountains that he later presented to Roosevelt.

On their final evening together they toasted each other and sang songs in what was one of the happiest interludes of the entire war for either man. Roosevelt insisted: 'Now, Winston, don't you get up in the morning to see me off. I'll be wheeled into your room to kiss you goodbye.' True to his word the president arrived in Churchill's bedroom the following morning. The prime minister leaped from his bed and, dressed in a bizarre concoction of dressing gown, slippers and an air marshal's cap on his head, insisted on accompanying the president to the aerodrome and boarding his aircraft to see him settled for the gruelling five-day flight to the United States via Brazil. Churchill could not bear to see the president's plane take off. 'It makes me far too nervous,' he said. 'If anything happened to that man, I couldn't stand it . . . He is the greatest man I've ever known.'

Despite entreaties from the Foreign Office to return to London, Churchill flew first to Cairo, then to Adana in Turkey for a brief conference with Turkish leaders in an unsuccessful effort to bring them into the war on the Allied side. When Eden and the War Cabinet protested against his undertaking this unilateral mission, he shot back that he had studied Europe for forty years and would go where he liked. After his return to London, Churchill brushed off complaints about his trip and, as Eden recorded, said that if he had he been killed during his journey, 'it would have been a good way to die and I should only have come into my inheritance sooner.'

Before returning home, however, Churchill ordered his aircraft to fly him to Tripoli, where Montgomery had established his command post. It was here that he uttered these celebrated words through a loudspeaker to the assembled Eighth Army officers and HQ staff: 'Ever since your victory at Alamein, you have nightly pitched your moving tents a day's march nearer home.'

That night came a long-awaited signal from Alexander: 'The orders you gave me on August 10, 1942 have been fulfilled. His Majesty's enemies ... have been completely eliminated from Egypt, Cyrenaica, Libya, and Tripolitania. I now await your further orders.'

The following morning, accompanied by Montgomery and Brooke, Churchill inspected the 51st Highland Division from an open staff car. The division was lined up along the waterfront in parade formation. 'We drove slowly round the line then came back with the men cheering him all the way,' Brooke recorded in his diary. Commander Thompson also described the memorable scene. 'Silhouetted against the clear blue sky, a lone kilted soldier stood motionless on top of Mussolini's triumphal arch as the troops marched past with pipes playing. It was a sight I shall never forget. Nor will the P.M., who was in tears.' During the afternoon Churchill toured the Eighth Army, addressing soldiers, sailors and airmen. 'Everywhere he was cheered to the echo.'

Instead of flying back to London from Tripoli, Churchill ordered his aircraft to Algiers to visit Eisenhower's headquarters just as his staff learned of a possible imminent threat to his life, a development which failed to dissuade him. He was driven from the airport to Admiral Cunningham's villa in a bullet-proof motor car with its windows daubed in mud. His sudden presence unnerved Eisenhower, who feared for his safety and subtly tried (and failed) to persuade the stubborn prime minister to go home. Finally, when Churchill was ready to depart, his plane developed mechanical trouble and he was obliged to spend an additional night in Algiers before everyone connected with his visit to Algiers breathed a sigh of relief as his aircraft, the *Commando*, disappeared into the Mediterranean skies. Not long after Churchill's trip, this aeroplane crashed, killing a different crew.

The apprehension of his ministers notwithstanding, Churchill's lengthy stay in the Mediterranean was a triumph in terms of his strategic aims, and in the inspiration his presence had given to British – and American – forces. Perhaps most important of all, the trip had provided a period of badly needed rest when he could recharge his batteries as he neared the end of his third year as prime minister and warlord.

Though many American planners were left frustrated by Churchill's royal flush at Casablanca, they were forced to think again in mid-February 1943, when General von Arnim and Rommel jointly struck a blow aimed at splitting the Allies in two in North Africa. Surprise attacks at Faid, Sidi Bou Zid and the Kasserine Pass, designed to drive a wedge through American defences and destroying the untested US II Corps that guarded the southern flank in Tunisia, were embarrassing and bloody setbacks for American arms – setbacks that convinced the US high command that, unless there was an immediate improvement in leadership and training, the long-term effects would be disastrous, prejudicing any chance of Overlord's success. Eisenhower dismissed the inept US ground commander and hastily summoned General Patton from Morocco to assume command in early March 1943. Like Montgomery at Alamein, Patton brought about a rapid, dramatic and successful transformation of US forces.

In late March, at El Guettar, Patton's corps won their first victory of the war by defeating a veteran German panzer division. In early April the Eighth Army then cracked the Mareth Line and joined the Allied forces in Tunisia. A month later, Arnim's appeals for food, fuel and ammunition were ignored by Berlin and, with his Army Group Afrika cornered in the Cape Bon Peninsula, he was compelled to surrender its 250,000 survivors, all of whom became Allied prisoners of war – exactly as Rommel had predicted.

Alexander, who had been switched to Tunisia to serve as Eisenhower's army group commander, proudly cabled Churchill to announce that the

Tunisian campaign was over. 'All enemy resistance has ceased. We are masters of the North African shores.'

Hitler's decision to rush German forces to Tunisia and the Allies' entanglement in bitter mountain fighting there had made Overlord impossible to mount in the spring of 1943 – which would have provided crucial summer conditions for the campaign to be waged in France after a successful cross-Channel invasion. This left the Western Allies with two victorious land armies in North Africa, and nowhere to go unless, as Churchill advocated, they were ordered to seize Sicily, land on the Italian mainland – and 'knock Italy out of the war'.

For three months after Casablanca arguments had raged within the Allied high command, as a number of plans for the invasion of Sicily (code-named Husky) were proposed, considered and then scrapped for failing to satisfy everyone. A committee system imposed upon Eisenhower by the British at Casablanca exacerbated the ever widening divisions in what was an entirely British internecine and often acrimonious quarrel between the three force commanders.

If Churchill was often Victorian in his assumptions about modern war, he cannot be blamed for being rendered speechless by the failure of the air, navy and army commanders to agree on an integrated approach to warfare against a highly professional foe such as the Germans. Air Chief Marshal Tedder was insistent on the prompt acquisition of airfields in southern Sicily for his tactical aircraft, while Admiral Cunningham demanded maximum security for his ships by backing a plan for multiple invasions that dispersed the Allied fleet but would have hopelessly weakened the ground forces. Acting in the absence of General Alexander, the designated ground force commander, who conspicuously failed to exert his authority to help bring about a solution to the deadlock, Montgomery contended that the only acceptable plan that would guarantee the success of the invasion was to concentrate all ground forces in the south-eastern corner of Sicily. With time running out, Montgomery's plan was accepted in early May.

The war in the Mediterranean thus assumed its ultimate, sad character: campaigns pursued at the request of the British prime minister, who wanted spectacular performances, but at the cost of British and American lives, limbs and exhaustion, in the dutiful service of a cause that most participants questioned. In this way, after Tunisia, Allied

operations in the Mediterranean were characterized by an unwillingness to assume any undue risk. Mounting evidence of Allied conservatism thoroughly displeased Churchill, however; he could never
understand the reason for it. After receiving a pessimistic signal from
Eisenhower in April, which stated that the planners of Husky feared
failure if more than two German divisions were encountered in Sicily, the
prime minister scathingly signalled: 'These pusillanimous and defeatist
doctrines . . . would make us the laughing stock of the world. What
Stalin would think of this when he has 185 German divisions on his
front, I cannot imagine.' There were no more negative signals from
Eisenhower.

During May and June 1943 Churchill travelled more than 10,000 miles;
these journeys included his third trip to the United States. On 5 May he
boarded the *Queen Mary* under his favourite alias, Colonel Warden.
Converted for military use, the regal liner was painted in muted wartime
colours, and instead of the usual passengers it carried five thousand
Germans destined for American POW camps. Churchill spent most of
the dangerous voyage through the U-boat-infested North Atlantic in
preparation for the forthcoming Trident Conference in Washington. He
ran the stenographers ragged with reams of dictation, and at times of
relaxation played bezique with Averell Harriman. He ordered the life-
boat that had been earmarked for his emergency use mounted with a
machine gun. As he had been during the bleak days of 1940, Churchill
was both defiant and irreverent. 'I won't be captured,' he declared to
Harriman. 'The finest way to die is in the excitement of fighting the
enemy . . . [although] it might not be so nice if one were in the water
and they tried to pick me up . . . You must come with me in the boat
and see the fun.' When word was flashed to his shipboard command
post that Allied troops had sealed off the escape of Army Group Afrika
by capturing Tunis and Bizerte, followed by a message on 13 May from
Alexander that the campaign was over, Churchill was overjoyed and for
the second time in the war ordered that all church bells should be rung
throughout the United Kingdom in celebration.

Halifax had never seen Churchill – who arrived in Washington relaxed
and on a high note of victory – 'in better heart or form, an amazing
contrast to the very tired and nerve-strained PM I saw last August in
England'. Trident, however, was discordant. Churchill, Roosevelt and

the Combined Chiefs failed to reach agreement on the strategic considerations left unresolved at Casablanca, namely what the Allies would do
after Sicily. The bone of contention they gnawed at remained the same:
US opposition to further Mediterranean operations, and the British
belief that the route to success in a cross-Channel invasion of France lay
through Sicily and Italy, which would force Germany to expend its
dwindling military strength defending southern Europe. Brooke and
Marshall clashed. When Marshall expressed reservations about having
acceded too easily to Allied operations in the Mediterranean, there
was a testy exchange between the two. Marshall bluntly reiterated his
disdain for Mediterranean operations, which, he argued, would act like
a 'suction pump' at the expense of the cross-Channel invasion, and also
needlessly prolong the war in the Pacific. He asserted that the Allies were
'now at the crossroads' and implicitly threatened to turn instead to the
Pacific.

The two sides compromised, with the British readily agreeing to Overlord on 1 May 1944, but at the price of continued operations in the
Mediterranean – which would be dictated by Eisenhower. For once the
British were in some disarray when Churchill repudiated the Mediterranean policy decisions over which Brooke had laboured hard to obtain
agreement. Describing it as 'tragic', Brooke lamented, 'There are times
when he drives me to desperation.' Harry Hopkins saved the day by
persuading Churchill to withdraw his alterations.

Churchill also badgered Eisenhower for not moving faster to invade
Sicily – ignoring the fact that an earlier invasion was impossible without
sufficient landing craft, unavailable at that time. The potshots should,
of course, have alerted Eisenhower to Churchill's latest intentions. If
Eisenhower was to be placed in charge, basically, of military strategy as
well as tactics in the Mediterranean, then there was no time to be lost,
Churchill reasoned. Thus, to the dismay of both Brooke and Marshall,
instead of returning to London after Trident, Churchill insisted on flying
to Algiers in order to convince Eisenhower that 'nothing less than Rome
could satisfy the requirements of this year's campaign.' In 1941 and
1942 he had been obsessed with beating Rommel in North Africa, but,
with Rome a prize too large to ignore, he was now determined that the
Allies should set their sights on Italy.

Churchill's arrival in Algiers had been neither anticipated nor scheduled. His purpose was not only to present his case to Eisenhower for the

invasion of the Italian mainland after Sicily, but also to thwart any American attempt to shut down Allied operations in the Mediterranean after the conquest of Sicily. Churchill's last-minute decision to decamp for Algiers has been dubbed the Algiers Conference. An unhappy Marshall, at Roosevelt's insistence, had to postpone a trip to the South-west Pacific to be present to protect American interests.

Eisenhower greeted Churchill and his party at Maison Blanche airfield on 28 May and intended to follow his earlier practice of sharing his car with Marshall in order to be apprised of events before meeting with Churchill. The prime minister, however, ambushed him by insisting on being driven into the city with him, whereupon he immediately began to argue for an Italian campaign and to 'dangle before him the mirage of strategic riches beyond'. Churchill had barely settled into Admiral Cunningham's villa before he met privately with Eisenhower for a second one-on-one session and yet another relentless hammering over Italy.

Handling the demands of such a visitor was not straightforward. During his stay in Algiers rumours circulated on the American side that Churchill habitually drank white wine for breakfast, reinforcing the myth that he was a problem drinker. Commander Thompson noted that when the prime minister was in the Mediterranean he preferred a glass of light white wine instead of tea, which had to be served with canned milk, which he loathed. Otherwise he ate a normal breakfast. 'At home he usually drank a glass of white wine at lunch, champagne at dinner, then a glass of port or brandy afterwards.' Churchill disliked afternoon tea and instead would often have 'whisky heavily diluted with water'. Champagne was difficult to obtain during the war, and at one point Thompson suggested that his boss might consider cutting back to conserve their supply, adding: 'What happens when we run out?' Churchill simply snorted: 'Get some more!'

Whether soaking in the bathtub with pungent cigar smoke filling the air, holding forth at mealtimes or declaiming at formal or informal meetings, Churchill was his usual argumentative, relentless self, cajoling and pleading his case with the fervour of a carnival barker peddling his wares. 'I could not endure to see a great [British] army stand idle when it might be engaged in striking Italy out of the war,' Churchill admitted. Determined to hold operations in Italy to a minimum, but unable to prevent the employment of Eisenhower's military force, which had grown to nearly one million men in the Mediterranean theatre, Marshall kept largely silent, leaving Churchill with the false perception that he accepted the British position.

The Algiers meetings ended with Churchill satisfied that post-Sicilian operations were safe 'in General Eisenhower's hands', and that no formal plan was needed; he would simply use his legendary powers of persuasion to see that Eisenhower followed his wishes. The success of Husky would, he was determined, be best exploited by continuing military operations across the Strait of Messina into southern Italy.

Eisenhower was not the only one Churchill had to convince, however. In order to pacify Stalin, he had had to put the case strongly against Overlord in 1943, arguing that 'I would never authorize any cross-Channel attack which I believed would lead only to useless massacre' – as at Dieppe, where more than a thousand Canadians had been mowed down on the port beachhead in a few hours. Knocking Italy out of the war was the best way the Allies could draw German forces from the eastern front, he assured the Russian generalissimo. Once again Churchill was getting his way.

Churchill enjoyed Algiers so much that he remained for eight days, later recalling, 'I have no more pleasant memories of the war.' His host, who was left to worry constantly about the security of his VIP guest, lost more than his usual share of sleep. Even a ploy by Eisenhower's naval aide, Commander Harry Butcher, who paraded around in his bathrobe, yawning loudly, failed to move the oblivious Englishman to his bed at a civilized hour during the usual late-night meetings.

If Churchill could have remained to witness the invasion of Sicily in July, he surely would have. At last, however, he departed. This time on the return trip to England, he flew in a new four-engine York transport, specially retrofitted for his use, which included a small private cabin and a galley. The assigned mess steward was not a chef and was dozing in the galley when he was suddenly and rudely awakened by a growling voice. Peering at him was Churchill without his dentures. 'I want some soup, hot, clear soup, and I want it now!'' The flustered steward managed to produce something more or less resembling soup that did little to satisfy Churchill. Thereafter a proper galley was installed, and a qualified chef travelled on board to satisfy his exacting gastronomic demands.

*

The invasion of Sicily began on the evening of 10 July 1943 with US airborne and British glider landings to seize key targets in the southern part of the island as part of a bold night operation, the first of its kind ever attempted. Churchill spent a restless night at Chequers awaiting news. His daughter-in-law, Pamela, kept him company, and the two passed the time playing cards as one or another of his private secretaries updated him through what Averell Harriman has described as 'a very tense and tortuous night'. 'So many brave young men going to their deaths tonight,' he intoned. 'It's a grave responsibility.' At 4.00 a.m., when word finally came that the landings were taking place, Churchill went straight to the Chequers war room and began peppering his aides with questions they were unable to answer until further updates came in.

Inexperience, friendly fire, wind and enemy flak were a fatal combination that turned the airborne and glider stage of Operation Husky into a first-class disaster for both forces. The amphibious invasion, however, was a great success. The Eighth Army landings were so effective that Montgomery ordered his two corps commanders to push inland and up the coast towards Catania without delay. After fighting off counterattacks against Patton's US Seventh Army, the two Allied armies were soon firmly in control of bridgeheads and in Sicily to stay.

The Sicily campaign was brief and bloody. Hitler acknowledged that Axis forces had no hope of reversing the Allied invasion, but despite the generally feeble resistance of the Italians, the Germans had no intention of ceding Sicily without a fight. By early August the Germans had undertaken a succession of skilful delaying actions by using the mountain terrain to maximum advantage before carrying out one of the most successful strategic withdrawals in military history across the Strait of Messina.

The Allied air forces made a halfhearted and largely futile effort to interdict the evacuation, and the final days of the battle for Sicily were a dismal conclusion to a campaign that had been beset from the start by controversy and by indecisive leadership from Alexander, who left the conduct of the campaign largely to Montgomery and Patton. The Allies needlessly prolonged the reduction of Sicily by fighting a frontal battle of attrition. The result was that a German army corps that never exceeded sixty thousand men and was devoid of air and naval support managed to delay two Allied armies whose combined strength exceeded

480,000 troops for thirty-eight days in terrain every bit as inhospitable as they would find ahead of them in Italy.

The invasion of Sicily hastened the downfall of Benito Mussolini and his Fascist government, both of which were deposed in late July. Within weeks the new Italian leader, Field Marshal Pietro Badoglio, began secretly negotiating an armistice with the Allies, which led to Italy's unconditional surrender on 8 September 1943. But it did nothing to convince sceptics that fighting German forces in Italy, should Hitler choose to reinforce his troops there, would be any easier.

In July, Secretary of War Henry L. Stimson travelled to London for what turned out to be stormy talks with Churchill, who sent out decidedly mixed signals about future strategy and for the first but not the last time spoke of the English Channel 'full of the corpses of defeated allies', causing Stimson to challenge his commitment to Overlord. 'We went at it hammer and tongs,' said Stimson, who left Britain deeply troubled. Stopping in Algiers to brief Eisenhower, he recounted that 'the Prime Minister was obsessed with the idea of proving to history that invasion of the Continent by way of the Balkans was wise strategy and would repair whatever damage history now records for Churchill's misfortune at the Dardanelles in the last war.' Moreover Stimson 'seemed apprehensive lest the PM would seek to avoid the commitment of the British and American governments to invade France next spring'. He concluded that Churchill might well sabotage the American force buildup in Britain in favour of Mediterranean diversionary operations.

Behind the slow but seemingly inexorable success of Allied forces in the Mediterranean, a veritable chasm was growing in terms of strategy. Roosevelt, Churchill and the Canadian prime minister William Mackenzie King, together with the Combined Chiefs, again met, this time in August 1943 in Quebec for the Quadrant Conference. Yet again they clashed over the scope of future operations in the Mediterranean before finally agreeing that Overlord would take precedence, but that operations would continue into Italy proper. Seven divisions were to be transferred to the United Kingdom to prepare for the cross-Channel attack; Eisenhower would thus have to fight on the mainland of Italy with considerably reduced forces and logistical support.

For the time being at least Churchill was therefore able to keep alive a significant Allied presence in the Mediterranean. His arguments for expanding operations in the eastern Mediterranean, however, were met with a cold rebuff. The United States had no interest in or intention of furthering Britain's post-war aims of empire, or of becoming bogged down in yet another dead-end military campaign that detracted from Overlord. With the bit firmly between his teeth, though, Churchill refused to let go of the idea of opening a new front.

What was lacking at Quebec and indeed throughout the Italian campaign was a statement of Allied grand strategy. If the political goals were vague, even less clear were the aims of the forthcoming military operations. Each side, wrote an American official historian, viewed grand strategy 'through different spectacles'. Churchill's Mediterranean strategy envisaged continued Allied operations into Italy, including an offensive that would carry the forces into the country's northern provinces so that the Allied air forces could be employed in a direct support role in Overlord operations. Marshall did everything within his power to put the brakes on British zeal for a fully fledged campaign in Italy. The inevitable result was that the Allied forces got the worst of both worlds. A land campaign in Italy was launched that became more an improvisation than a deliberate strategy, with no clear and common vision of how best to defeat the main enemy: Hitler's Germany.

What did emerge from Quebec, at least, was affirmation by the Combined Chiefs that Overlord would occur in May 1944. Until then Allied strategy was to keep the Wehrmacht in Italy fully committed, so that its veteran divisions could not be shifted to France to help repel the cross-Channel invasion.

Churchill was an impossible leader to argue with, however; his 'hunt and peck' strategy had successfully driven Italy out of the war, he argued, so it was surely an opportune moment to seize a very important military and political objective that was certain to alter the course of the war in the Mediterranean. That prize was Rome, and by his forceful intervention the prime minister had seen to it that his trusted lieutenant, Harold Alexander, would make Rome his number-one priority. Although his primary mission in Italy was, according to the Quebec agreement, meant to be diversionary rather than suck in more troops and resources, Churchill relentlessly pressed Alexander to act offensively and capture Rome by the end of the year, warning that if its liberation were prolonged, 'no one can measure the consequences.'

It would take until June 1944 for Alexander to fulfil Churchill's dream. If the Eternal City was important to the Allies as the capital city of their former enemy, the Italians, it was of even greater importance to their continuing enemy, the Germans – who would therefore fight fiercely to deny the Allies such a prize. The elimination of Rome from the Axis sphere of control would send a signal to the rest of the world that the Western Allies were serious in demanding unconditional surrender; Berlin, which was being pounded by the round-the-clock combined bomber offensive, would be next. Tying down German forces by compelling the Germans to defend Rome, as agreed at Quebec, was not Churchill's idea of military strategy; he was convinced that boldness would bring swift victory in Italy. He therefore argued that, instead of landing in the toe of Italy and crawling up the leg of the mainland 'like a harvest bug', the Allies should 'strike boldly at the knee' of Rome. This was all very well, except that his bold strikers would have no air cover. Landings in the vicinity of both Naples and Rome were considered but exceeded the operational range of Allied aircraft based in Sicily – a range that barely gave sufficient time for minimal support at Salerno, south of Naples: the site selected for Operation Avalanche on 9 September.

After the Quebec Conference, Churchill went to Washington for more talks with Roosevelt. On 7 September he travelled to Boston to deliver a speech at Harvard University. Landing on the mainland of Italy was, he said in a cable to London, 'the biggest risk we have yet run, though I am fully in favour of running it', yet the recently concluded armistice that had brought Italy to the Allied side 'would be blown sky high if we lost the battle and were driven back into the sea'. As the date for the invasion approached, Churchill grew increasingly restless and preoccupied with Salerno. 'That is where his heart is,' recorded Lord Moran. 'As the appointed day draws near he can think of nothing else. On this landing he has been building all his hopes ... It *must* succeed ... He talked of meeting Alex in Rome before long – the capture of Rome has fired his imagination; more than once he has spoken about Napoleon's Italian campaign.'

Churchill's failure to read Hitler's mind, as opposed to his secret signals, was nearly disastrous. When Italy surrendered on 8 September, Hitler reacted with unbridled fury. The fall of Mussolini led to the implementation of contingency plans for a series of military actions to be taken in the event of an Italian collapse. German troops poured into Italy under the pretence of reinforcing Kesselring in the event of an Allied invasion. 'Overnight, Italy went from German ally to German-occupied country. Now it was about to become a battleground in a grinding war of attrition whose costs were justified by no defensible military or political purpose.'

The landing at Salerno on 9 September by Mark Clark's Anglo-American Fifth Army was badly planned and bitterly contested – and it nearly failed. Despite Allied air superiority and overwhelmingly superior firepower, the Germans controlled the high ground and the exits from the invasion beaches. Without the timely support of the navy the invasion force might not have survived.

While a guest at Roosevelt's country home at Hyde Park, New York, Churchill followed the progress of the invasion with growing apprehension, grumbling that such events always seemed to occur when he was with the president. With no positive news from Italy, Churchill grew more and more irritable. 'I have never seen him more on edge during a battle,' observed Moran. Churchill also wondered if Alexander was 'on the spot' and doing all he could to salvage the landings, unaware that his favourite general was doing nothing to influence the outcome.

During the train journey to Halifax, Nova Scotia, from where he was to sail for home aboard the battleship HMS *Renown*, Churchill became so alarmed by the situation that 'I had a strong impulse to fly to our headquarters in Italy. I restrained it, but not without some help from others.' Instead he settled for urging Alexander to involve himself in the battle. He admitted to memories of Suvla Bay on the Gallipoli Peninsula in 1915, when the British invasion force sat for three days and allowed the Turks to reinforce the battlefield and blunt the invasion. He also recalled how more recently Auchinleck had remained in Cairo while the Battle of Gazala raged in the desert and was lost. He implored Alexander to take charge of Salerno.

Alexander obligingly sent Churchill increasingly optimistic daily reports while he was at sea, but although the general's presence on the battlefield was reassuring, he exerted no appreciable influence on the outcome of the battle. After numerous German counterattacks had failed to push the Allies back into the sea (thanks in part to courageous action by General Clark, who took personal command of the beachhead), Kesselring elected to withdraw and establish his principal defences in the Liri Valley at Cassino. With obvious relief that disaster had been averted, Churchill sent Eisenhower a telegram of congratulations in which he misquoted the Duke of Wellington: 'It was a damned close-run thing.'

Dudley Pound became so gravely ill at Quebec with stroke-like symptoms that were soon diagnosed as a brain tumour that he resigned as first sea lord and was succeeded by ABC Cunningham. Death came quickly – almost fittingly for a British admiral – on Trafalgar Day, 21 October. Churchill had always had a soft spot for Pound and mourned the loss of one of the three men – the others were Beaverbrook and Smuts – who he said meant the most to him. In a moment of deep reflection a few days later he said to Moran, 'Death is the greatest gift God has made to us.'

At Salerno the Allies opened their campaign in Italy without a clear idea of why they were there. Except for Churchill's fixation on the liberation of Rome, neither Eisenhower nor Alexander had ever defined the Allied mission in Italy. Thus the campaign was already adrift before it even began. It was left to the outspoken Montgomery to pose the question no one had articulated: what was their strategic objective?

As Churchill had instinctively known, once the Allies landed on the mainland of Italy (rather than simply threatening to do so), the United States would be forced to invest in the campaign – an outcome that General Marshall had vainly attempted to thwart. What Churchill failed to accept were the casualties that would be incurred. During their twenty months in Italy the Allies fought one bloody battle after another, for reasons no one ever fully understood. Allied strategy in Italy seemed to be not to win, but rather to drag out the war there for as long as possible and in so doing to keep Kesselring's army group from being dispersed to fight in France. One historian has said of the Italian campaign, 'Few soldiers of World War II experienced the kind of deadening, soul-destroying fighting that characterized' the Great War. 'Most of those who did experience it fought in Italy' – Churchill's chosen battlefield, and one that simply distracted the Allies from their real task: crossing the English Channel and opening the endlessly delayed second front.

55
Amid the Ruins of Carthage

Can't you do anything to stop this?   – Churchill to Lord Moran

The near-debacle at Salerno failed to dampen the Allies' belief that Rome would fall within the next six weeks. Kesselring not only failed to play that hand but also managed to persuade Hitler to defend Italy below Rome, at Cassino, where a massive mountain range and the Rapido and Liri rivers formed ideal defensive positions. The soundness of Kesselring's judgment was soon borne out by the deadly and prolonged stalemate that not only kept the Allies pinned down from September 1943 to mid-May 1944, but inflicted increasingly heavy casualties at a time when there were other options available to the Allied leadership. By the autumn of 1943 the Italian campaign was already slipping into a bloody standoff.

Despite the shaky beginning of the campaign, Brooke and Churchill believed that it was a necessary precursor to Overlord and a means of fully engaging German forces in Italy that would otherwise have been sent to defend France from the invasion they anticipated some time in 1944. For Churchill the Mediterranean strategy reflected his philosophy that military forces should always be actively engaged in fighting the enemy. Nor was Italy his only focus: his eye was on what he deemed another prize, this one in the eastern Aegean.

Almost until the end of 1943 the question of who would command Overlord remained unresolved. By December it had become critical that a supreme commander be named without delay. Both Marshall and Brooke coveted the post, and before the Quebec Conference it had been assumed that the supreme commander would be British, partly in return for Eisenhower's selection in the Mediterranean in 1942, but mainly because Overlord would be mounted from Britain, and British forces would play a dominant role, at least initially. In July, Churchill told Brooke that he wanted him to take the invasion command, only to change his mind at Quebec for the same reasons Roosevelt eventually did over Marshall. Roosevelt's change of heart was induced by a warning from Secretary of War Stimson that 'the shadows of Passchendaele and Dunkirk' would be eclipsed by the notion that the war could be won via the Mediterranean and the nonexistent 'soft underbelly'.

On 17 November Churchill and the British chiefs of staff were in Malta. At dinner Churchill candidly discussed the Overlord command, and spoke of his acute embarrassment at having to tell Brooke that he would not have it after all; he pledged his full support for Marshall, pointing out that a British officer would naturally take control of Allied operations in the Mediterranean. Brooke's bitter disappointment is reflected in his diary: 'Not for one moment did he realize what this meant to me. He offered no sympathy, no regrets.' Swallowing his pride, Brooke – as Marshall would do a short time later when FDR pulled back from appointing him – carried on like the good soldier that he was.

Whereas Roosevelt left matters of strategy to his generals, Winston Churchill used every possible means to persuade the Combined Chiefs to bend to his will. He also tried but generally failed to exert the same influence over Eisenhower as he did over his own generals, admirals and airmen. A not inconsiderable portion of Eisenhower's time was spent dealing with Churchill, often to curb the prime minister's adventuresome approach to war.

Churchill's tendency to clutch at straws led to an especially stormy conflict in the autumn of 1943, when his inability to sway the US chiefs of staff to the British point of view, and his increasing irritation with the flagging Italian campaign, led him to champion a British invasion of the German-held Greek island of Rhodes, the largest of the Dodecanese Islands, an Italian possession in the eastern Mediterranean off the coast of Turkey. He argued passionately that the boldness of such an operation would pay off by dragging Turkey into the war and setting the Balkans ablaze.

Such diversionary operations violated the agreements reached at Quebec, which limited future Allied military operations in the

Mediterranean. From the American point of view Churchill's enthusiasm for this scheme smacked of yet another excuse for evading or delaying Overlord. He later candidly admitted that his arguments produced 'the most acute difference I ever had with General Eisenhower', who success-fully argued that Allied resources in the Mediterranean were not suf-ficient to carry out operations in both Italy and the Aegean: 'We must therefore choose between Rhodes and Rome. To us it is clear we must concentrate on the Italian campaign.' This issue also left Marshall more determined than ever that nothing should detract from Overlord, with Brooke fuming that the American chiefs were shortsighted. Although he would soon criticize Churchill for pursuing a strategy that the United States simply would not agree to support, Brooke believed that the prime minister had failed to make the Americans see the light. 'We should have been in a position to force the Dardanelles by the capture of Crete and Rhodes, we should have the whole Balkans ablaze by now, and the war might have been finished in 1943!!! Instead, to satisfy American shortsightedness we have been led into agreeing to the withdrawal of forces from the Mediterranean for a nebulous second front, and emascu-lated our offensive strategy!! It is heartbreaking.'

The prospect of turning Churchill loose in the Balkans left his ally unalterably opposed to his scheme. 'The Americans', recorded Ismay, 'were up in arms at once. They were still haunted by the ghost of Gallipoli and suspected Churchill, in spite of his protests that we were with them in OVERLORD "up to the hilt", of an attempt to get a footing in what they regarded as his favourite hunting-ground, the Balkans.'

The Rhodes venture was typically Churchillian: bold, imaginative and opportunistic, 'an immense but fleeting opportunity', he said. 'It was intolerable that the enemy, pressed on all fronts, could be allowed to continue to pick up cheap prizes in the Aegean.' Yet underlying the drama over Rhodes was the spectre of the Dardanelles. One can detect in Churchill's insistence in going ahead without American support a strong whiff of 1915 – a chance to redress the single greatest setback of his military and political career. The official British naval historian points out that Churchill's 'hope of bringing Turkey into the war, which was the principal plank on which he rested his case, was an illusion; for the Turks could not have defended themselves as long as the Germans held Greece and most of the Aegean Islands'. Churchill's inducements to enter the war on the side of the Allies failed to persuade the Turks to abandon their long-standing policy of neutrality. Undeterred, he stubbornly took his case directly to Roosevelt, who replied that there would be no diversion of forces that would imperil either the Italian campaign or Overlord.

Although he agreed with his basic premise, Brooke feared that Churchill's dogged pursuit of the invasion of Rhodes would upset the delicate balance of US–British relations and detract from operations in Italy. 'I can control him no more,' he wrote despairingly. 'The Americans are already desperately suspicious of him and this will make matters worse . . . He has worked himself into a frenzy of excitement about the Rhodes attack, has magnified its importance so that he can no longer see anything else and has set his heart on capturing this one island even at the expense of endangering his relations with the President and the Americans and the future of the Italian campaign. He refused to listen to any arguments or to see any dangers!' Brooke called it Churchill's 'Rhodes madness' and regarded his state of mind as 'in a very dangerous condition . . . God knows how we shall finish this war if this goes on.' Moreover, the question Churchill never addressed was this: even if the islands of Rhodes and nearby Leros were successfully occupied, what strategic difference would it have made as long as the Germans remained in control of Greece and the Aegean and had air support available to wreak the same damage on the Royal Navy as it had in 1941? Roosevelt posed the right question: 'Strategically, if we get the Aegean islands, I ask myself where do we go from there and vice versa where would the Germans go.'

Against the advice of his chiefs of staff, Churchill refused to concede his vision of a quick, cheap victory in the Dodecanese and the entry of Turkey into the war and elected to act unilaterally. After the 8 September armistice, a far smaller German garrison had overcome the thirty-thousand-man Italian garrison on Rhodes. Churchill remained intransigent, and although an immediate invasion of the island was out of the question, he nevertheless directed Jumbo Wilson to send a British force to the Dodecanese. In September, spearheaded by British Special Air Service (SAS) and Special Boat Service units, Operation Accolade was launched: Wilson dispatched a brigade-sized force of some four thousand British troops to seven of the Dodecanese Islands and to Samos, a large island in the eastern Aegean. The most important island was Kos, which possessed a vital tactical airfield without which the Allies could not provide air support to the ground forces. 'We rely on you to defend this island to the utmost limit,' Churchill cabled the British commander on 3 October. 'Tell your men the eyes of the world are upon them.' It was all bravado; isolated and without air or naval support, the British garrison had no chance whatsoever of holding out. The following day Kos fell and the garrison was captured. Instead of ordering the withdrawal of the remaining British forces on the other islands, Churchill stubbornly ordered Leros and Samos to hold out and would not be dissuaded from the notion that an invasion of Rhodes was still possible. On 9 October he cabled Wilson: 'It is clear that the key to the strategic situation in the next month in the Mediterranean is expressed in two words "Storm Rhodes". Do not therefore undertake this on the cheap.'

Churchill should have realized that Hitler could not afford to have a belligerent Turkey nipping at his heels along his southern flank. The Germans had a powerful air presence in the Aegean, and as long as they controlled Rhodes, Turkey would remain neutralized. Thus Churchill's gamble failed at great cost. Leros fell in mid-November. Between Kos and Leros some 4,600 British troops were captured. It was Norway, Greece and Crete redux, an appalling waste of good men, equipment and ships and yet another demonstration that inadequate peripheral operations were a prescription for failure. Overall the British lost some 4,800 men in the abortive Dodecanese campaign, and the Greek navy and the Royal Navy suffered heavy losses: six destroyers and two submarines sunk, four cruisers damaged and ten smaller craft sunk.

Undeterred, Churchill refused to back off from his insistence on Rhodes and a Balkan campaign. The issue arose during the first of two conferences held in Cairo, one before and one after the Tehran Conference with Stalin. The first Cairo Conference, 22–26 November 1943, ranked as the most contentious yet between the Combined Chiefs. Churchill persisted with his argument that Rhodes should be invaded. 'It got hotter and hotter,' recalled Marshall. Finally the American chief of staff had had enough and exploded. 'Not one American soldier is going to die on that goddamned beach,' he thundered to the horrified assemblage.

'Mr Churchill later told me he thought [my failure to agree with military operations in the eastern Mediterranean] was one of my major wartime mistakes,' Eisenhower later said, noting that he had not agreed with Churchill in 1943 nor did he do so in hindsight. The incident was a prime illustration, he said, of 'the great differences that, from beginning to end, existed in [British and American] methods . . . of waging war'. It was another unfortunate example of how Churchill's good intentions could be overridden by flawed military judgment. The only fire he lit in the Balkans in an attempt to open a third front in the autumn of 1943 burned out, leaving the bitter ashes of another unnecessary debacle. He was in a depressed mood when he confided his disappointment to Averell Harriman. 'He had just been turned down by Roosevelt . . . [and] complained bitterly that they weren't going to let him have even a few of his own British battalions in the eastern Mediterranean to do what he considered important.' Privately he bemoaned the entire affair and ordered a study of what the British could accomplish unilaterally in the Balkans were 'we masters of our own destiny'.

Churchill neither forgave nor forgot being snubbed by his ally. His war memoir was uncharacteristically harsh and blithely ignored the truth in favour of carping that it was the fault of the United States, a 'rebuff to fortune not to pick up these treasures'. In an early but later amended draft he described Eisenhower as 'obdurate' and 'unreasonable'. 'I remained – and remain – in my heart unconvinced that the capture of Rhodes could not have been fitted in.' It was, he said, 'one of the sharpest pangs I suffered in the war'.

With typical candour Montgomery summed up Churchill's Aegean misadventure in a letter to Brooke. 'It has puzzled me for a long time as to why we want to start "frigging about" in the Dodecanese. The party has ended in the only way it could end – complete failure.'

In the autumn of 1943 British divisions outnumbered American divisions by more than two to one, with British commanders in control of ground operations. Yet that preponderance was only fleeting. America's colossal industrial output was nearing its zenith, and the mobilization of its armed forces was producing a massive build-up of US forces in the United Kingdom for Overlord. The British failure in the Aegean was also glaring evidence that Churchill's role as a prime architect of the war was on the wane and would by 1944 descend into near irrelevance. With British forces falling under American strategic control, this realization became painfully evident to him at Tehran in late November and early December 1943 during the first meeting of the Big Three.

At the Tehran Conference (Eureka), Overlord was at the top of the Russian agenda. For more than a year Stalin had been badgering his two allies to open a second front in Europe and to name its commander. At one point the surly Russian bluntly demanded of Churchill: 'Do the English believe in Overlord, or do they not?' Churchill never liked being put on the spot, but in this instance he replied without hesitation to Stalin's obvious challenge: 'Provided the conditions previously stated for "Overlord" are established when the time comes, it will be our stern duty to hurl across the Channel against the Germans every sinew of our strength.'

Churchill stubbornly refused to alter his vision of capturing the Aegean islands, prying open the Dardanelles and persuading Turkey to enter the war as an ally. Neither Roosevelt nor Stalin showed any enthusiasm for bringing Turkey into the war and opening the Dardanelles to resupplying Russia. Instead Churchill's doggedness reinforced American suspicions that the ghosts of Gallipoli were clouding his real commitment, and that his claim of being 'up to the hilt' for Overlord was lip service. Roosevelt and Stalin joined in defeating Churchill over his Aegean strategy. Tehran also left no doubt that the prime minister would thereafter play a secondary role in the conclusion of the war. His diminished significance among the Big Three was painfully clear when the Italian campaign was relegated to third place after Overlord and a subsequent invasion of southern France.

'There I sat with the great Russian bear on one side of me, with paws outstretched, and on the other side the great American buffalo, and between the two sat the poor little English donkey who was the only one who knew the right way home.' The alliance may have been grand, but Churchill's role in it had become inconsequential – and he felt deep resentment. He had demonstrated his ability to rebound from defeat, but what he could not overcome or accept was the spectre of irrelevance. 'Britain had stood alone in 1940; increasingly by the end of 1943, she had to stand aside. It was not so much the "Big Three" as the "Big Two and a half".'

Tehran was a wake-up call of sorts for Churchill. 'I realized for the first time what a very *small* country this is.' The powerful leader who in 1941, after one of the chiefs had suggested that Britain ought to continue its long-standing 'kid gloves' policy towards the United States, had proclaimed, 'Oh! That is the way we talked to her while we were wooing her; now that she is in the harem, we talk to her quite differently,' had lost much of his former clout. The wicked smirk of 1941 had turned into grudging realization of his lowly standing in the Big Three pecking order.

Churchill was accompanied by his daughter Sarah, and his mood during the difficult days negotiating with Stalin and Roosevelt prompted the remark: 'War is a game played with a smiling face – but do you think there is laughter in my heart?' As Brooke would later write, 'He hated having to give up the position of the dominant partner which we had held at the start.'

His single-minded pursuit of the unattainable verged on hubris and deeply frustrated the chiefs of staff. 'There are times when I feel that it is all a horrid nightmare which I must wake up out of soon,' lamented Brooke. 'All this floundering about, this lack of clear vision, and lack of vision!' in which Churchill examined 'war by theatres and without perspective, [and] no clear appreciation of the influence of one theatre on another'. Endless meetings and discussions failed to instil in the prime minister what the chain of military command meant. 'Winston's views on command always remained confused throughout the war. He could not or would not follow how a chain of command was applied. He was always wanting a Commander-in-Chief to suddenly vacate his post,' as he had most recently with Jumbo Wilson over the Dodecanese, 'and concentrate on commanding one individual element of his command at the expense of all the rest.'

Churchill's sixty-ninth birthday on 30 November came at the end of one of his bleakest periods of the war. The chiefs of staff trooped into his bedroom to wish him well and, as Cunningham recalled, 'We had the idea of singing "Happy Birthday to you"; but decided it was beyond our capability.' Had they carried out their intention it surely would have been one of the war's unmatched moments. Then again, perhaps it was just as well they did not.

At the second Cairo Conference in December, the decision over who would command Overlord could no longer be deferred. Since the commander would be an American, the decision was up to Roosevelt, who understood how badly Marshall wanted the command but in the end felt he could not afford to lose the services of his chief of staff. Instead he decided that the new supreme commander would be Dwight Eisenhower.

Was Eisenhower acceptable to the British? he asked Churchill, who graciously replied that the British would warmly entrust their fortunes to him.

Equally pressing but left unresolved was who would command what was called the British Liberation Army for Overlord. Churchill strongly preferred Harold Alexander, as did Eisenhower, who openly championed him to command Overlord. At Quebec, Churchill had spoken of appointing Alexander. Brooke liked him personally but was determined to block his appointment. 'I shudder at the thought of him as Supreme Commander! He will never have the personality or vision to command three services!' Alexander, the CIGS decided, should stay in Italy. The War Cabinet might well have supported Churchill, but the unanticipated appointment of Eisenhower produced fresh concern about the British ground command for Overlord, particularly because with the appointment also came temporary command of all Allied land forces. The secretary of state for war, Sir James Grigg, outlined the cabinet members' position in a signal to Brooke in Italy, explaining that Eisenhower's appointment made them nervous. The War Cabinet, he said, 'are disposed to think Montgomery would be a better choice . . . Some ministers, myself included, also prefer Montgomery to Alexander on our judgment of their military merits for the job.'

Churchill began to see the advantages of keeping Alexander in Italy, where his influence with the Americans could be put to better use than with Montgomery, particularly regarding his pursuit of further operations in the Balkans. Nevertheless, shortly before Christmas the command question was finally resolved and the new appointments were announced. Montgomery would command the Overlord ground forces and be replaced as Eighth Army commander by Lieutenant General Oliver Leese. Alexander would remain in Italy. Admiral Sir Bertram Ramsay, the naval architect of Dunkirk, and Air Chief Marshal Sir Trafford Leigh-Mallory were confirmed as the Overlord naval and air commanders.

After the war Brooke wrote that he had no misgivings about his decision to block Alexander's appointment. 'There is no doubt that he held some of the highest qualities of a Commander: unbounded courage, never ruffled or upset, great charm and a composure that inspired confidence in those around him. But when it came to working on a higher plain, and deciding matters of higher tactics and strategy he was at once out of his depth, had no ideas of his own, and always sought someone to lean on . . . Fortune favoured me and I was able to retain him in Italy.'

By the time of Tehran, Churchill was showing disturbing signs of weariness. Feeling cornered by Stalin and Roosevelt, he was plainly tired by the experience and suffered from a nagging sore throat and at times found speech difficult. On the evening of 29 November Moran found him speaking in a tired voice with his eyes closed, a black cloud of depression hanging over him, part resentment and part anger and considerable fatigue. 'I want to sleep for billions of years . . . When I consider the vast issues, I realize how inadequate we are,' he murmured.

The toll the war had taken was obvious and troubling to everyone around him. At times he was too worn out even to bother drying himself after bathing, instead simply wrapping a towel around himself and flopping on his bed. Another night Moran entered his bedroom to find him sitting with his head in his hands. 'I have never felt like this before,' he complained. 'Can't you give me something so that I won't feel so exhausted?' As he had in Washington in December 1941, Moran found himself caught in another medical dilemma. 'I am afraid of nothing but his heart,' he wrote on 8 December to Smuts. 'If that lasts, he will last. There is no medical remedy, if he goes on racing the machine it may give in . . . all that can be done is to persuade him to give moderation a chance in all things, what he has never yet done. There is nobody around him or in Cabinet who has any influence on him, I believe you are the only person he listens to.'

On the morning of 11 December Churchill took off from Cairo for Tunis, where he was to stay in Eisenhower's villa in nearby Carthage, but for never explained reasons his aircraft was diverted to a desolate, unmanned airfield some forty miles from his destination. While awaiting transport Churchill sat forlornly in a cold wind on his own luggage, his face shining with perspiration. He looked ghastly and was 'chilled to the bone'. Eventually he was flown to Tunis, where Eisenhower met him. On the drive to Carthage, Churchill made a rare admission: 'I am afraid I shall have to stay with you longer than I had planned. I am completely at the end of my tether.'

The illness that his doctor had dreaded came suddenly in the early morning hours of 12 December, when Brooke was suddenly awakened 'by a raucous voice re-echoing through the room with a series of mournful, "Hullo, Hullo, Hullo!"' It was Churchill 'in his dressing gown with a brown bandage wrapped round his head, wandering about my room. He said he was looking for Lord Moran, that he had a bad headache.'

That bad headache was the first symptom of extremely serious trouble. The diagnosis was pneumonia and possible pleurisy, but of greater concern was Churchill's heart. His temperature hovered around 101 degrees, and his pulse was racing and irregular. Moran immediately sent for both a heart and a lung specialist, but by 15 December the prime minister's condition had worsened and at 6.00 that evening he had a mild heart attack. 'My heart is doing something funny,' he told his doctor – 'it feels to be bumping all over the place.' The newly arrived Royal Army Medical Corps heart specialist, Brigadier Evan Bedford, gave him digitalis to slow his heart rate. Moran confided to Harold Macmillan that he believed his famous patient could have died the previous night. Inspector Thompson was detailed to sit outside his bedroom and report any change in his condition. At one point a sleepless Churchill declared: 'I am tired out, body and soul, and spirit.' When Thompson attempted to reassure him, Churchill seemed glassy-eyed and unsure of where he was. Told he was in Carthage, he said, 'What better place could I die than here? Here in the ruins of Carthage?' His daughter Sarah kept him company and somewhat distracted him by reading aloud *Pride and Prejudice*. Yet at one point he remarked: 'If I die, don't worry – the war is won.'

Earlier on the 15th, weak and suffering from lack of sleep, Churchill had rather plaintively cabled Roosevelt that he was 'stranded amid the ruins of Carthage ... with fever which has ripened into pneumonia'. His condition was not helped by the arrival of Randolph Churchill, whose visits to his father invariably led to acrimony. 'His presence will do no good, as he will talk to his father about French politics!' complained Macmillan. 'I could not keep him out Winston's bedroom,' said Moran. 'Once there he would work up a row in no time.' John Colville noted that 'Randolph is causing considerable strife in the family,' and at one point recorded that Churchill 'almost had apoplexy over some of his comments about the French'.

Rather miraculously Churchill was soon out of danger and indeed was making a remarkable recovery. Although he no longer seemed in danger of dying, he nevertheless remained fatigued, listless and in need of complete rest. To those around him this was not the same dynamo they were used to serving at all hours of the day and night. The usual spark had been temporarily extinguished.

Churchill's condition was deemed so serious that the unusual step was taken of summoning Clementine to his bedside. She flew from England aboard an unheated aircraft, cocooned in a padded flying suit to ward off the cold, arriving on 17 December. Winston was overjoyed to see his wife, but Clementine wryly remarked: 'Oh, yes, he's very glad I've come, but in five minutes he'll forget I'm here.'

One night Moran was summoned to Churchill's bedside. 'He appeared distressed and there were tears on his cheeks. At length I was able to get out of him that he had had a bad dream. He saw the battleships *Renown* and *Prince of Wales* sinking and when they were gone a great number of men's heads bobbing up and down in the water, until after a time he could see nothing but the smooth surface of the oily sea.'

Churchill was a difficult patient. Although his pneumonia was brought under control, his doctors attempted to keep him in bed for another fortnight to reduce the chances of further cardiac fibrillation. When Dr Bedford proffered this advice, the prime minister's face turned red with rage and he became almost violent, rejecting their counsel out of hand.

By Christmas Day his fever was down, and he was well enough to preside over a large luncheon. Clementine and Alexander were among those attending a Christmas church service with the Coldstream Guards in a corrugated tin hut normally used to store ammunition and supplies. At the very moment the chaplain was pronouncing the blessing and the bells of Carthage Cathedral were pealing near by, 'a white dove, which had been roosting on a beam in the shed, fluttered down' and came to rest on the altar. Behind Clementine a Guardsman whispered that it must be a sign of peace. When she told Winston, his response was to scoff that it was 'an ecclesiastical hoax!' and nothing more than a trick perpetrated by the chaplain. Neither God nor religion had ever played a meaningful role in Churchill's life, and such symbolism had no place even at a moment of great crisis in his life.

On 27 December, although still rather frail, he was deemed well enough to travel to Marrakech to recuperate. Drawn up outside his villa was a guard of honour of Coldstream Guardsmen. 'I had not realized how much I had been weakened by my illness. I found it quite a difficulty to walk along the ranks and climb into the motor-car.'

Over the years his visits to the 'Red City' (so named because of its striking red and ochre walls) had energized him. Marrakech was a sanctuary where he could relax, paint and momentarily escape the intense pressure of a distant war. Installed in the same jewel-like villa in which he had been Roosevelt's host, Churchill was attended around the clock by a large contingent of clerks and aides. His days were filled with long hot baths and frequent picnics complete with white tablecloths, while at night he listened raptly on a gramophone to recordings of two Gilbert and Sullivan operettas given to him for Christmas by his daughter Mary. 'On the whole one of the happiest hours I have had in these hard days!' he told her.

At no other time during the war was Churchill so carefree as he was during the three nearly idyllic weeks he spent 'in the lap of luxury thanks to overflowing American hospitality'. He was closely monitored by his doctor, who felt an enormous burden lifted from his shoulders as his famous patient benefited from the fresh mountain air and a less taxing workload. Despite his marvellous recovery, however, Churchill still had problems walking, and on occasion had to be tugged and hauled up a steep trail after a picnic by soldiers using the tablecloth as a pulley around his ample body.

One evening in Marrakech, Duff Cooper's wife, Diana, recorded a sombre conversation she had had with Clementine about the forthcoming post-war years. 'I never think of after the war,' she said, 'You see, I think Winston will die when it's over.' Clementine seemed resigned to what she saw as their fate. 'You see, he's seventy [sic] and I'm sixty and we're putting all we have into this war, and it will take all we have.'

Reflecting on Churchill's illness, Lord Moran wrote: 'I remember thinking at Carthage – it must have been about the fifth day of Winston's illness – I'd not give him more than a fifty-fifty chance. I guess we're running it pretty fine. However, Winston had nine lives, and when it was all over and he was [up and] about again, I expected to find him on top of the world. It did not happen like that.'

Even in the luxurious surroundings of Marrakech, Churchill could not entirely escape a number of vexing problems that ranged from Stalin to the faltering campaign in Italy. Officers trooped to his villa from Italy and Tunisia and were grilled, sometimes at his bedside, a sign that while he still required considerable relaxation in order to recover, his mind was seeking solutions. On 27 December Moran noted in his diary words that would prove fateful: 'The P.M. has a bright idea. He is organizing an operation all on his own. He has decided that it should be a landing behind the lines at Anzio.'

56
The Strategic Air Campaign

Our plans are to bomb, burn, and ruthlessly destroy in every way available to us the people responsible for creating this war. — Brendan Bracken

The most savagely debated military aspect of the Second World War was – and remains – the bombing of cities by both sides. Beginning in the late summer of 1940 the Germans launched the Blitz against London and other cities with massive air raids. That August, Churchill ordered the RAF to retaliate by bombing Berlin. 'Now that they have begun to molest the capital, I want you to hit them hard,' he directed the chief of the air staff, 'and Berlin is the place to hit them.' That air raid infuriated Hitler and unleashed a war in the skies that did not end until the last major British raid in late April 1945. The principle of mutual restraint was completely lost; cities burned and people died – in large numbers.

At the end of May 1940 Churchill asked the chiefs of staff if Britain could win the war. They replied that upon economic factors rested 'our only hope of bringing about the downfall of Germany'. However, British estimates of Germany's economy were well wide of the mark. Germany was not particularly well geared for war as a result of Hitler's belief that it was not necessary to disrupt the civilian economy to achieve victory in limited campaigns such as the one fought in Poland in 1939 and in the West in May and June 1940.

What eventually became the strategic bombing campaign of 1943 had its roots in Churchill's belief in airpower and the harsh reality that there were no other options available to retaliate against Germany. 'The Navy can lose us the war,' he wrote in September 1940, 'but only the Air Force can win it. Therefore our supreme effort must be to gain overwhelming mastery in the Air.' While the men and machines of Fighter Command were the key to Britain's salvation, 'The Bombers alone provide the means of victory. We must therefore develop the power to carry an ever-increasing volume of explosives to Germany, so as to pulverize the entire industry and scientific structure on which the war effort and economic life of the enemy depend.' It was, he added, the only means by which Britain could 'hope to overcome the immense military power of Germany'. The problem however was that the RAF lacked the necessary long-range bombers and guidance systems in 1940, and it was not until 1943 that a major air offensive was begun in conjunction with the US strategic air forces.

So ineffective was Britain's long-range bomber capability during those early months of the war that even in daylight RAF aircrews had trouble finding their targets, and when they did find a target, their bombs rarely hit anywhere near it. The official air historians later observed: 'When war came in 1939 Bomber Command was not trained or equipped to penetrate into enemy territory by day or to find its target areas, let alone its targets, by night.'

With the United States some eighteen months away from entering the war, Churchill articulated to his minister of aircraft production, Lord Beaverbrook, his belief that the only means by which Hitler could be defeated was by undermining Germany's will to fight by attacking and destroying its war-making capability, and by what he described as 'an absolutely devastating, exterminating attack by very heavy bombers from this country upon the Nazi homeland'. Britain's bomber force, he said in July 1941, must be twice as large as the Luftwaffe's by the end of 1942. The chiefs of staff also bought in to the idea that aircraft production was Britain's highest wartime production priority, so that the RAF could conduct a massive bombing campaign aimed at the annihilation of Germany's war economy. An enormous part of Britain's industrial output was devoted to supporting the campaign. Initially attempts were made to pinpoint military and industrial targets such as the all-important ball-bearing plants at night, but by all accounts the strategy was a miserable failure. Despite the dropping of increasingly large tonnages, bombing proved so inefficient and so few targets were hit that British strategy evolved into that of area bombing.

Although he had vigorously pursued launching the air campaign, by September 1941 Churchill presciently recognized that despite the exaggerated claims by the RAF, 'It is very disputable whether bombing by itself will be a decisive factor in the present war . . . The most we can say is that it will be a heavy and, I trust, a seriously increasing annoyance.' A short time later he warned Portal: 'I deprecate placing unbounded confidence in this method of attack.' Even if every city in Germany 'were rendered largely uninhabitable, it does not follow that the military control would be weakened or even that war industry could not be carried on.' He concluded with a blunt reminder: 'He is an unwise man who thinks there is any certain method of winning this war, or indeed any other war between equals in strength. The only plan is to persevere.' As the war progressed, Churchill's assessment was proved accurate despite the claims of the bomber barons that airpower alone could win the war.

Churchill's attitude towards bombing civilian targets changed dramatically from that of January 1940, when he soundly condemned the German bombing of Poland's cities as 'a new and odious form of attack', but he rejected the bombing of German cities in reprisal. His first reference to the bombing of civilian targets came on 28 September 1940 in a memo to Ismay which stated that 'the possibility of our having to retaliate on the German civil population must be studied, and on the largest scale possible. We should never begin, but we must be able to reply. Speed is vital here.' The Luftwaffe bombing of Britain drew Churchill away from his earlier desire to spare civilian targets. In the summer of 1941, he declared in a speech in London, 'If the people of London were asked to cast their vote whether a convention should be entered into to stop the bombing of all cities, the overwhelming majority would cry, "No".'

He told the House of Commons, 'As the year [1941] advances, German cities, harbours and centres of war production will be subjected to an ordeal the like of which has never been experienced by any country in continuity.' During his visit to Washington in May 1943 he made similar remarks in a speech to Congress about Japan, whose cities he said should be reduced to ashes, 'for in ashes they must surely lie before peace comes to the world.'

The allegation that Churchill's advocacy of the bombing of such targets amounted to a war crime raises the same moral question that has been debated since 1945 over American use of the atomic bomb on Hiroshima and Nagasaki. Churchill did not think in such terms. He believed he had a war to fight, a war which Britain did not start and from which it was suffering grievously, and that whatever measures were necessary to win it were reasonable. The British policy of massive retaliation continued to the end of the war. As minister of information, Brendan Bracken put it even more starkly at a press conference in Canada in August 1943: 'Our plans are to bomb, burn, and ruthlessly destroy in every way available to us the people responsible for creating this war.'

Although morality and legality were considered, they were certainly not hotly debated questions during the war. As the architect of the strategic bombing campaign, Churchill understood the implications of his strategy and its awful cost. Had the bombing campaign been more successful, there might have been less hand-wringing at the carnage wreaked upon the German populace and its cities, but the bitter truth is that, on the whole, it often failed. The comprehensive post-war US Strategic Bombing Survey concluded that strategic bombing was ruthless, inaccurate and ineffective, and resulted in the needless 'mass slaughter of men, women and children'.

In 1940, without the United States, Britain's only recourse in Europe was to initiate the bombing of cities. Shipping losses in the North Atlantic were growing to horrendous proportions and imperilled the 43 million tons of supplies per month that Britain required. Churchill was unduly optimistic about the results he expected to achieve. Mannheim, for example, was bombed on 16–17 December and achieved little. 'Few lessons were learned.'

One of the insidious myths of the Second World War is that Ultra alerted Churchill in advance of the Luftwaffe raid on Coventry on the night of 14–15 November 1940, and that, to protect the secret, he permitted the raid to occur without alerting city civil defence administrators. The raid, one of the war's heaviest, all but destroyed Coventry, but it was not because of Churchill's alleged desire to protect Ultra. It took many years of attacks by his critics before the truth emerged. Although intercepts referring to a forthcoming raid the Germans had code-named Moonlight Sonata were made in advance of the raid, they did not pinpoint the target, and the conclusion reached by the air staff that it was likely to be London proved erroneous. The real culprit, explains the Ultra historian Ronald Lewin, was a clear moonlit night and wholly inadequate ground and air defences that included no counter-measures to deal with a new system devised by the Germans to improve upon their inefficient *Knickebein*. That the slur upon Churchill continues to rear its ugly head from time to time is a clear example of how difficult it is to dispel long-established myths, particularly sensational ones.

The funeral of Neville Chamberlain, who had died the previous Saturday, took place earlier that day in a frigid Westminster Abbey, whose windows had been shattered by Luftwaffe bombs. Churchill was among the pallbearers. It occurred to Colville that 'a judiciously placed bomb would have had spectacular results.'

The air war against Germany escalated dramatically in 1943. From the time Air Chief Marshal Sir Arthur 'Bomber' Harris became the autocratic boss of Bomber Command in February 1942, he enjoyed the full backing and protection of both Churchill and Lindemann. His reputation as a forceful commander was well earned. Once, when a policeman stopped his Bentley for speeding one night and chidingly warned him that he might kill somebody by driving so fast, Harris retorted: 'Young man, I kill thousands of people every night!'

Harris zealously carried out a controversial War Cabinet directive drafted by Lindemann that called for the deliberate targeting of German cities. The use of area bombing was aimed at destroying both German industrial capacity and the morale of its civilians by making them homeless. In May 1942 Harris launched the first thousand-bomber raid, which wrought heavy destruction on Cologne and displaced thousands who fled the city. Thereafter the firebombing of German cities became an accepted practice.

The entry of the United States into the war enabled both countries to mount a powerful around-the-clock air campaign. The architects of strategic bombing were Harris; his American counterpart, Lieutenant General Carl A. 'Tooey' Spaatz; and Spaatz's predecessor, Lieutenant General Ira Eaker. Along with the chief of the US Army Air Forces, Henry H. 'Hap' Arnold, the bomber barons zealously and sincerely believed that a round-the-clock strategic bombing effort would bring Germany to its knees without the need for a major ground campaign in Europe. Airpower alone, they argued, could do the job. With Churchill's backing, for nearly two years Harris had been on a personal crusade. He initiated relentless night attacks against industrial targets in Germany, Italy and the Balkans, coupled with the systematic area bombing of high-density population centres such as Berlin, Hamburg, Nuremberg and, in February 1945, Dresden. Recent accounts of the air war have focused on the morality of the terror bombing of civilian targets like Hamburg and Dresden, both of which were destroyed in RAF raids, resulting in an estimated 50,000 deaths in Hamburg and 25,000–35,000 in Dresden.

Bomber Command relentlessly destroyed Hamburg in late July and early August 1943, leaving the city a charnel house. The cost of such raids in lost lives and aircraft was astronomical, with ninety-five RAF bombers lost in a single night raid on Nuremberg on 30 March 1944. In 1943 Bomber Command flew 64,528 sorties and dropped two hundred thousand tons of bombs on German targets. The likelihood that an RAF or USAAF bomber crew would survive to complete the required number of combat missions was frighteningly low. The men of Bomber Command none too affectionately referred to their commander as 'Butcher' Harris.

In November 1943 Spaatz confidently predicted that when round-the-clock bombing operations were launched the following spring from both England and Italy, 'Germany will give up within three months.' The great combined Anglo-American strategic-bombing offensive against German industrial, war-producing targets was code-named Pointblank. At Casablanca the Combined Chiefs of Staff issued what was known as the Casablanca directive, which called for the destruction and dislocation of Germany's war-making capacity. It was refined in June by the Pointblank directive, whose top priority was the destruction of Hitler's aviation industry, as well as the weakening of the Luftwaffe's fighter capability, so that the Allies would gain critically important air superiority when Overlord was carried out.

While in Washington in May 1943, shortly before the official launch of Pointblank, Churchill remarked at a joint press conference with FDR that 'the air weapon was the weapon these people chose to subjugate the world . . . And it is an example of poetic justice that this should be the weapon in which they should find themselves most out-matched.'

Both Harris and Spaatz misused Pointblank. Harris paid it lip service but used its authority to carry out his own idea of smashing German cities through a policy of relentless attacks against urban targets. The bombing of aviation-industry targets became almost incidental. In November 1943 Harris went so far as to make an extravagant claim to

Churchill: 'We can wreck Berlin from end to end if the USAAF will come in on it. It will cost between 400 and 500 aircraft. It will cost Germany the war.' Neither Portal nor Churchill supported Harris's fantastical scheme, which had absolutely no chance of ending the war. Even with Berlin in ruins in 1944 and 1945, the war went on.

Churchill's role in the bombing of Berlin was ambiguous. Harris did carry out a bomber offensive against the German capital from November 1943 to March 1944, and while the prime minister showed little interest in Pointblank, he was enthusiastic about avenging the destruction of British cities, and about turning Berlin into the same fire-ravaged ruin as Hamburg. The air campaign against Berlin was deadly both to the RAF and to Berliners. The aircrews experienced intense flak and enormous losses but scored few successes.

Pointblank ultimately worked after a fashion but in a manner entirely removed from its original concept. Daylight bombing by the US Eighth Air Force and night bombing by the RAF failed to destroy German aircraft production or to materially weaken the Luftwaffe. However, the relentless air campaign obliged Luftwaffe fighters to do battle, and in so doing the Germans suffered irreversible losses in the one priceless asset they could not replace: their battle-tested pilots.

In the months preceding Operation Overlord there occurred the fiercest controversies of the war. When Eisenhower became supreme commander in January 1944, it was already clear that Pointblank had failed and that, unless reined in, the air barons would continue pursuing their own agenda at the expense of Overlord.

The only air plan that existed for Overlord vaguely proposed minimal measures for air support during a two- or three-week period before D-day in order to knock out coastal defences and prepare the way for the invasion force. When first briefed on air operations, Eisenhower was not reassured by his own air commander, Air Chief Marshal Sir Trafford Leigh-Mallory, who predicted that it was still uncertain if the Allies would even gain air superiority before Overlord was launched.

Professor Solly Zuckerman, a renowned zoologist turned bombing expert, whom Tedder had brought back to England from the Mediterranean specifically to help devise bombing policy for the invasion of France, was horrified by the inadequacy of the original Overlord air plan, and its failure to consider how the air forces could possibly provide the necessary support in the likely event of bad weather. Nor had the planners seemed to appreciate that targeting only Normandy would have alerted the Germans to the fact that it was to be the site of the Allied landings. The gravest danger was not the D-day landings but German reinforcements speeding to Normandy to seal off the Allied beachhead with larger forces than the Allies could insert across the Channel.

A bombing committee representing all players in the air war convened under the auspices of Leigh-Mallory's Allied Expeditionary Air Force and began drafting alternative proposals that called for a wide-ranging, systematic bombing campaign to knock out the entire French railway transportation system. Thus was unveiled what has been called the Transportation Plan, a scheme that quickly exploded into one of the most rancorous, controversial strategies of the war, pitting Eisenhower against Churchill and the airmen over control of the air forces for the invasion.

The essence of the Transportation Plan was a strategic-bombing campaign to destroy the French rail network, bridges and choke points to prevent Normandy from being reinforced after D-day, while at the same time providing the Germans with no indication of where the invasion would occur.

Churchill turned against the plan when Harris insisted that it would cause high civilian casualties. Spaatz and Harris would not renounce their wildly inaccurate 'private conviction that Overlord was a vast, gratuitous, strategic misjudgment, when Germany was already tottering on the edge of collapse from bombing'. An escalating war of words, between the airmen and Churchill on one side and Eisenhower, his deputy Tedder, Zuckerman and Portal on the other, turned the controversial Transportation Plan into an intra-Allied free-for-all. More than thirty years later Zuckerman would write of still being 'utterly amazed by the nonsensical arguments about the plan'.

Try as he might, Eisenhower could not avoid direct conflict with Churchill over control of the air forces. The bomber chiefs, backed by most in the Air Ministry and Professor Lindemann, rose as one in fierce and formidable opposition, proclaiming that such operations would be a gross misuse of the strategic air forces. The prime minister and the members of his War Cabinet despised the plan primarily on humanitarian grounds.

Eisenhower had to put out the fires of opposition from Churchill but also those raging between the airmen. Spaatz opposed the Transportation Plan and fought to retain his autonomy instead of being placed under Leigh-Mallory's operational control while the plan was carried out, and Harris inflamed matters by damning Leigh-Mallory to Churchill, likewise arguing that he should not be given control of the strategic bombers. Eisenhower was not only in the middle of a monumental intramural war but no closer to resolving his problems. It took until the end of March for a compromise to be brokered when Eisenhower agreed to appoint Tedder to control air operations, which effectively excluded Leigh-Mallory from the chain of air command.

By early April, shortly before the Transportation Plan was to have been implemented, it had yet to be approved. Outside Eisenhower's Supreme Headquarters Allied Expeditionary Force (SHAEF) almost no one liked it. Its formidable opponents now included Churchill, Eden, the majority of the War Cabinet, Harris, Spaatz, Jimmy Doolittle (the commander of the US Eighth Air Force), the Joint Intelligence Committee, the Ministry of Economic Warfare and a host of other critics in the Air Ministry. The deck appeared stacked against Eisenhower.

Churchill was openly hostile to the plan. On 5 April, during the most rancorous confrontation yet, it was debated before the Prime Minister's Defence Committee. Churchill appeared in his siren suit, carrying a cigar and a large tumbler of whisky. The meeting was so charged that by the time it ended, well after midnight, he had consumed neither the whisky nor his cigar. If the plan was adopted, an animated Churchill charged, it would inevitably result in the 'cold-blooded butchering' of helpless French civilians, his anger raised several degrees by arguments over the accuracy of a prediction of 80,000–160,000 casualties. It was clear to Zuckerman that the prime minister's opposition was being fuelled by Lindemann. Brooke also opposed the plan for the same reason, although admitting after the war that he had made a mistake in not backing Tedder. When he learned that Montgomery was insisting on the bombing of villages to create roadblocks that would impede German units sent to reinforce Normandy, Churchill was irate. 'I can still hear the fury in Winston's voice,' recalled Zuckerman, 'as he barked "Who is Montgomery that he can *insist*?"' Churchill then turned his anger on Tedder. On this occasion even the strong-willed and normally unflappable airman was shaken 'by the personal hostility which Winston had directed at him as the night wore on'. Tedder had already made up his mind to resign his post as Eisenhower's deputy if the plan was rejected, and idly wondered if he would soon be a civilian growing tomatoes in his garden.

Despite Churchill's furious opposition and the almost universal condemnation, Tedder and Eisenhower were adamant that, risky or not, the Transportation Plan was vital. Eisenhower disputed the British casualty figures as 'grossly overestimated. The French people are slaves. Only a successful OVERLORD can free them,' he wrote to Churchill. He also wrote to Roosevelt and Marshall, 'I have stuck to my guns because there is no other way in which this tremendous air force can help us, during the preparatory phase, to get ashore and stay there.' Major General Pierre Koenig, the commander of Free French forces, supported Eisenhower. 'This is war and it is to be expected that people will be killed . . . We would take twice the anticipated loss to be rid of the Germans,' he declared. Even the normally stubborn de Gaulle also signed on, and in so doing effectively undermined Churchill's opposition.

The intramural war did not end there. There was infighting between the two prima donnas of the air forces as bitter as their common opposition to outside control of their bombing operations, and the Transportation Plan. Bomber Harris's single-minded obsession with destroying Germany's cities conflicted with the Americans' insistence that precision bombing of German industrial infrastructure was the correct approach. Zuckerman could have been forgiven for thinking he was back in the London Zoo, where he had written a landmark book, *The Social Life of Monkeys and Apes*.

A lesser man might well have caved in to Churchill, but Eisenhower refused to allow the Transportation Plan to be held hostage either by the prime minister or by the warring airmen with their own divergent agendas. Not for the first time thoughts of resignation crossed his mind. He had long since wearied of dealing with 'a lot of prima donnas', and although the notion of an actual resignation only weeks before the most critical operation of the war was unthinkable, he seemed fully prepared to use the threat to gain control of the airmen. 'By God,' he told Tedder, 'you tell that bunch that if they can't get together and stop quarrelling like children, I will tell the Prime Minister to get someone else to run this damn war! I'll quit.'

Throughout April the debate raged, estimates were revised and targets

741

were altered, and the plan limped forward. Churchill and his committee gave provisional approval for the bombing on a week-to-week basis, until early May, when the plan was finally and grudgingly approved. Nevertheless Churchill never lost his distaste for the scheme, and his demands for repeated consultations were a perpetual source of irritation to Eisenhower. The prime minister complained to a sympathetic War Cabinet that he had failed to understand 'that our use of air power before "Overlord" would assume so cruel and remorseless a form'. Clearly 'a great slaughter would inevitably result' unless Roosevelt intervened to stop it. The War Cabinet supported him in one of the few instances of their involvement in a strategic military decision. An appeal to Roosevelt backfired, however, when FDR refused to intervene, in what was a tacit rebuke to Churchill. 'Terrible things are being done,' Churchill wrote to Anthony Eden in late May, and to Tedder he avowed that the RAF was 'piling up an awful load of hatred.'

Despite Churchill's misgivings the Transportation Plan was a major factor in the eventual success of Overlord. The Allied air forces bombed the French railway system into a vast 'railway desert' of smashed rail lines, bridges, depots and equipment, while Leigh-Mallory's tactical aircraft destroyed anything that moved. By mid-May the German Transport Ministry attested to the success of Allied bombing by reporting that the widespread destruction had caused 'critical dislocation of traffic'.

It was the bombing of Dresden in February 1945 that ultimately led Churchill to distance himself from Bomber Harris and the legacy of destruction wrought by the policy of area bombing. Whether fairly or unfairly, Sir Arthur 'Bomber' Harris became a reviled figure for carrying out – perhaps too enthusiastically – the policy of his government. The men of Bomber Command, so many of whom lost their lives, were justifiably bitter that they never received formal recognition of their efforts from the British government in the form of the campaign medal routinely given to those of the other armed services. Harris fought without success for their recognition, which sadly and rather disgracefully has never been forthcoming. Colville recalls being surprised 'by the apparent equanimity with which [Churchill] received an account of what befell Dresden in 1945'. Nevertheless Churchill seems to have developed a case of cold feet over that city. On 28 March he minuted the chiefs and Portal to question the 'bombing of German cities simply for the sake of increasing the terror . . . The destruction of Dresden remains a serious query against the conduct of Allied bombing. I am of the opinion that military objectives must henceforth be more strictly studied in our own interests rather than that of the enemy.' Portal rejected this opinion outright, Harris fired back, and when the chiefs met on 30 March it was formally noted that 'the Prime Minister has instructed that his minute on bombing policy should be withdrawn.' On 1 April 1945 Churchill removed all reference to Dresden. 'By this date the issue was largely academic. For all practical purposes the war in Europe was over.'

Whatever Churchill's public or private misgivings over Dresden and the strategic air campaign, after the war he sent an unambiguous note to a former Bomber Command staff officer: 'We should never allow ourselves to apologize for what we did to Germany.'

57

Stranding the Whale

Legend has it that Nero fiddled at Anzio while Rome burned. In 1944, it appears that General Lucas fiddled at Anzio while Winston Churchill and General Alexander burned. – Felix L. Sparks (US Army company commander at Anzio)

Alexander's ground force in Italy was being relentlessly stripped for Overlord, resulting in good intentions being overcome by a lack of manpower and other resources necessary to carry out a successful campaign where vile weather and harsh terrain favoured Kesselring's army. By the end of 1943 the Allied advance was stalled some ninety miles south of Rome in the Liri Valley, where Kesselring had established his defences along what was called the Gustav Line, a bulwark centred on the town of Cassino and on the heights above the town that were dominated by the imposing medieval Benedictine monastery of Monte Cassino. With the Allies inching towards a winter stalemate, Churchill became more and more frazzled and frustrated. He badly wanted Rome, and its liberation now seemed more and more unlikely in the foreseeable future.

By November, Eisenhower and Alexander had come to the conclusion that the stalemate halting the advance to Rome could not be broken unless the Allies initiated an amphibious outflanking move and drew away German troops manning the Gustav Line. An operation was planned to land a corps-size force of some sixty thousand US and British troops behind enemy lines at the coastal cities of Anzio and Nettuno, thirty-five miles south-west of Rome. Lack of confidence and the imminent withdrawal of landing craft for the Normandy invasion left the Anzio landings uncertain until late December, when Churchill became involved and put pressure on the Combined Chiefs to delay the return of these craft to the United Kingdom. Now that he was beginning to recover from his illness, Italy, not Overlord, became his chief focus.

Eisenhower and Alexander had first discussed the feasibility of such an operation on 24 October 1943, at a command conference in Carthage. In early November the subject was again discussed. There were enormous problems to overcome, not least of which was retaining the necessary landing craft. Clark's Fifth Army was tasked with planning and carrying out what was designated Operation Shingle, and while an outline plan was drawn up, it was for only a single division. There was little conviction that it would ever be carried out, and no enthusiasm on the part of the air and naval commanders. With the Fifth Army exhausted from months of bitter combat, Clark did not press the matter. Anzio appeared to be a dead issue until Churchill intervened.

Brooke had just returned from a week-long tour of the Italian front when he met with Churchill on 18 December. He deliberately refrained from discussing his pessimistic outlook on the campaign with Churchill. 'I knew from experience that it would be fatal to draw his attention to such defects. He would only want to rush into some solution which would probably make matters worse . . . I had to keep all these misgivings to myself and look for a cure.' That cure, as it had for several months, included finding a means of carrying on the campaign in Italy without creating 'an almighty row with the Americans', particularly in view of Eisenhower's lack of interest in a long-drawn-out struggle in Italy.

From his sickbed in Carthage Churchill cabled the chiefs on 19 December: 'The stagnation of the whole campaign on the Italian front is scandalous' and fulfilled 'my worst forebodings. The total neglect to provide the amphibious action on the Adriatic side and the failure to strike any similar blow on the west have been disastrous.' The campaign was of course anything but 'scandalous'; instead it was a victim of Allied priorities and the exigencies of fighting in some of the world's most forbidding terrain and in foul weather.

By Christmas Eve Churchill was feeling much better when he met with Alexander, Jumbo Wilson and Tedder to discuss how to obtain the necessary landing craft to mount Shingle. From the outset the operation's basic premise was faulty, namely that a two-division force would be sufficient to cut off at least a portion of Kesselring's forces. However, no one – not Churchill, nor Alexander nor Clark – questioned the assumptions about what Anzio was likely to accomplish. While it was important to assess what the operation might do to the Germans, no one apparently ever took serious note of the enemy's options or Kesselring's likely response.

Churchill began to envisage much wider results, but achieving them required landing craft. As we have already seen, the chronic shortage of adequate landing craft during the war once led him to complain that 'the destinies of two great empires seemed to be tied up in some God-damned things called LSTs'. He enthusiastically cabled Roosevelt that Anzio 'should decide the battle of Rome and possibly achieve destruction of a substantial part of [the] enemy's army'. Roosevelt agreed to defer the withdrawal of fifty-six landing craft earmarked for Overlord until mid-February 1944.

Marshall drafted the American reply but bluntly warned Churchill that American agreement to Shingle was 'on the basis that Overlord remain the paramount operation and will be carried out on the date agreed at Cairo and Teheran'. Marshall later said, 'I doubt if I did anything better in the war than to keep Churchill on the main point (he always wanted to take side shots). I was furious when he wanted to push us farther in the Mediterranean.' The news was music to Churchill's ears, and for the rest of December Anzio dominated his agenda. 'I had of course always been a partisan of the "end run", as the Americans call it, or "cat claw", which was my term.'

The seeds of trouble were sown in the final days of December, when Churchill made fallacious assumptions about Anzio, among them that it was only necessary to put the invasion force ashore with four days of supplies, and thereafter the LSTs would be withdrawn. The battle itself would be over in a week to ten days. Churchill's vision of a quick, cheap victory at Anzio was fantasy and ran counter to everything he had been told about the difficulty of effecting a link-up between the Shingle force and the Fifth Army driving north from the Cassino front. Blinded by the allure of breaking the deadlock and attaining the prize of Rome, Churchill all but dismissed its military drawbacks as examples of the usual negative thinking of generals, admirals and planners – those 'masters of negation'. He signalled Roosevelt, 'I thank God for this fine decision which engages us once again in whole hearted unity upon a great enterprise . . . Here the word is "Full steam ahead."'

Churchill single-handedly elevated Shingle from the wastebasket of discarded plans to the centrepiece in Italy, and in the process turned it into more of a political football than a military operation. Instead Anzio offered a unique opportunity for Churchill the politician to fulfil his lifelong fantasy of taking charge of a military operation and – at least temporarily – playing the role of a commanding general, a role for which he would never admit he was wholly unqualified. With Brooke now back in London and supportive of Shingle, there was no one else to curb his appetite. Brooke's role proved unfortunate, and Churchill later made him an accessory to his decision: 'We agreed on the policy, and also that while I should deal with the commanders on the spot, he would do his best to overcome all difficulties at home.' Thus the one person with the influence to have killed Shingle instead gave it his blessing.

From a military perspective the operation would have made better sense if an entirely American force had carried it out, because differing equipment, guns and ammunition would make the task of the logisticians far more complicated. Churchill would not hear of it and insisted on British participation and a share of the credit. Otherwise, he said, there would be 'a feeling of bitterness in Great Britain when the claim is stridently put forward, as it surely will be, that "the Americans have taken Rome."' The result was the creation of an Anglo-American invasion force of sixty thousand troops under the command of US Major General John Porter Lucas. The final plan allocated Lucas ten days of supplies, after which he would be on his own. Left unresolved by Alexander and Clark was exactly what Lucas was to accomplish after he landed at Anzio.

Shingle thus became driven by outside factors and by a chain reaction of mistakes and faulty assumptions. The limitations imposed on the size of the operation by logistics and the availability of combat units and landing craft ensured that it would be neither fish nor fowl. Yet its success was conditional on adequate combat strength – which was never provided. To make matters worse the Allies were again violating the principle for which Montgomery had unsuccessfully fought tooth and nail: that commanders, not staff officers, and certainly not politicians, should plan battles.

There were critics of the operation, but their reservations were squelched. The matter was beyond dissent although ABC Cunningham's cousin John, who had replaced him as naval commander in chief in the

Mediterranean, had suggested that 'this operation is fraught with great risks,' only to be told by Churchill, 'Admiral, of course there is risk, but without risk there is no honour, no glory, no adventure.' Alexander's chief of staff, Lieutenant General John Harding, remarked that 'John Cunningham crumpled up because no admiral of the fleet could admit he wasn't interested in honour, glory or adventure.' Churchill's distrust of admirals extended to those he regarded as insufficiently aggressive. John Cunningham was the polar opposite of his fiery cousin – calm, thoughtful and cautious. Neither naval Cunningham appealed to Churchill: ABC had an acid tongue and was willing to challenge him; and he did not place John 'among the brightest luminaries' of the navy.

Among Anzio's dissenters was its commanding general, who was excluded from a conference held in Marrakech in early January 1944. Although there was a star-studded cast in attendance, neither Clark nor Lucas was even invited, and each was permitted only to send several staff officers who had no voice. Anzio thus became unique for another reason: it was planned with its commanding general largely filling the role of spectator while others sealed his fate.

Left with no one to offer any meaningful dissent, Churchill took charge like a commanding general and passed judgments; 'although physically almost prostrate I wielded at this moment exceptional power,' he wrote in an unpublished draft of his memoirs. While his doctor kept a close eye on his patient, Anzio energized him as nothing else could have done. Instead of weeks of dreary recuperation he had a major operation of war into which he could sink his teeth. As his thoughtful biographer Robert Rhodes James observed of Churchill, 'He sees himself moving through the smoke of battle – triumphant, terrible, his brow clothed with thunder, his legions looking to him for victory . . . with himself cast by destiny in the Agamemnon role.'

Although he would have relished leading Allied troops into the Anzio beachhead, Churchill nevertheless took great satisfaction from playing an important, almost heroic role in its planning. Optimism is a vital trait in any successful commander – those who expect to lose invariably do. And Churchill did not expect to lose – his optimism over Anzio at a high pitch, he was fully prepared to earn the laurels of praise for masterminding Shingle and winning Rome. What he never considered were the consequences of failure.

Lucas's two representatives argued for a postponement from 22 to

25 January so that a rehearsal could be conducted. Without the slightest idea of the state of training of the invasion force, Churchill retorted that all troops were trained and needed no rehearsal. When it was pointed out that one of the two invasion formations, the veteran US 3rd Infantry Division, had lost so many experienced personnel that it now had few trained in amphibious operations, Churchill insisted that one experienced officer or non-commissioned officer in a platoon was adequate.

Once the questions of landing craft and a two-division force were resolved, the extensive documentation of this period suggests no questioning of the operation's potentially negative side. No probing what-if questions were either asked or debated. Hardly anyone dared challenge Churchill or the assumptions on which Shingle was based. The few who did were junior staff officers whose misgivings were quickly dismissed or ignored. As he had on so many occasions, Churchill simply steamrollered opposition. 'Can't I ever get any commanders who will fight?' was his standard refrain when anyone opposed one of his ideas. 'You don't care if we lose the war,' he said to one officer. 'You just want to draw your pay and eat your rations.'

Having brushed aside all criticism of Shingle at a second Marrakech conference in January, Churchill said to his military assistant, the newly promoted Major General Leslie Hollis, 'Now that's decided we must tell the Chiefs of Staff.' Reminded that Shingle came within the purview of the Combined Chiefs of Staff, he snapped, 'No! The British Chiefs of Staff are, by agreement, responsible for the Mediterranean area.' Well, replied Hollis, that being the case, the War Cabinet must approve Shingle. 'What is the quorum for the War Cabinet?' Churchill demanded. 'Two,' replied Hollis. 'Well, then, I have beside me Lord Beaverbrook [now lord privy seal]. Are you in favour, my Lord?' With Beaverbrook's affirmation, and without reference to either the chiefs of staff or the other members of the War Cabinet, Shingle was signed and sealed, leaving only its delivery up to the generals. Before the conference broke up, Churchill said to Alexander: 'I do hope, General, that when you have landed this great quantity of lorries and cannon you will find room for a few foot soldiers – if only to guard the lorries.'

This was not the only occasion on which Churchill would employ devious means of bypassing the chain of command. The following month he sent a note to Jumbo Wilson: 'While I do not wish to interfere with your direct communications to the Combined Chiefs of Staff, you are free if you wish to let me see privately beforehand what you propose to send, by using secret intelligence channels.'

His elation was evident in a masterfully exaggerated telegram to Roosevelt on 8 January: 'A unanimous agreement for action as proposed was reached by the responsible officers of both countries and of all services as a result of two conferences. Everyone is in good heart and resources seem sufficient. Every aspect was thrashed out in full detail.'

Two days after the second Marrakech conference Alexander chaired the final commanders' conference before Shingle. The operation, he declared, would take place as scheduled on 22 January, and there would be no further discussion of the matter. Quoting Churchill, he said, 'It will astonish the world,' and added, 'It will certainly frighten Kesselring.' Lucas left the meeting feeling 'like a lamb being led to the slaughter' and in his diary noted: 'This whole affair had a strong odor of Gallipoli and apparently the same amateur was still on the coaches bench.'

A week before Shingle, Clark launched a bloody and ill-fated attempt to establish an Allied bridgehead north of the Rapido river that would have cracked the Gustav Line. Its failure negated the entire premise of the outflanking move at Anzio and ensured there would be no early link-up between the Anzio force and the remainder of Fifth Army. Without a specific mission and without an adequate force, Anzio was doomed before the first LST sailed from Naples.

The landings at Anzio and Nettuno took place as scheduled on 22 January, with only token opposition. Hollis reported this to Churchill, 'whose face glowed with delight'. 'We have landed at the mouth of the Tiber . . . at the throat of Rome.' When Hollis pointed out that the Allies were still thirty-five miles from Rome, his face clouded over in evident displeasure. Hollis was sharply reminded that he ought to have taken the trouble to measure the distance on a map before 'supplying him with such false and disturbing information'. Hollis had worked for Churchill too long not to know how the game was played. He returned to the map room, waited a short time, then returned to tell his master: 'You are quite right, Prime Minister, I was wrong. We are *not* thirty-five miles from Rome. We are thirty-four-and-a-half miles away.' Beaming with pleasure, Churchill replied, '*Exactly*, I *knew* I was right.'

Although Kesselring had long expected the Allies to launch an amphibious attack somewhere near Rome, the Shingle landings nevertheless took the Germans by surprise. Still, they had made plans to react at short notice to any Allied amphibious landings, and within hours divisions from northern Italy, Germany, Yugoslavia and France were on the move to Anzio. Kesselring's immediate concern was to contain the Allied beachhead, and he thrust every unit near Rome into the breach to block an Allied advance to the Alban Hills. The Allies were not to be permitted to establish themselves along this crucial terrain, and against the advice of his generals Kesselring rushed reinforcements from the Cassino front to Anzio.

While Kesselring's decision proved correct, Lucas was faced with impossibly difficult choices. His force of 36,000 was too small to capture Rome, hold the vast area of the Alban Hills and still defend the beachhead and its crucial logistical lifeline, the port of Anzio. He could do one or the other, but not both. He elected to undertake no major offensive action until the security of the beachhead was assured.

By midnight on 22 January Kesselring had moved twenty thousand reinforcements to the vicinity of Anzio, and in the days that followed the Germans' build-up continued at a relentless pace until by the 29th they had massed nearly seventy thousand troops, supported by large numbers of tanks and artillery in a tight band across the Anzio beachhead. It was only a matter of time before they initiated a powerful counterattack to drive the Allies back into the sea.

This was a decisive moment in the war in Italy. Instead of a dagger aimed at Rome, Anzio turned into a colossal liability for the Allies, who were obliged to rush reinforcements from the south to meet the threat of the massive German build-up. Instead of one stalemate at Cassino, the Allies now found themselves deadlocked on two widely dispersed fronts.

Brutality has always been a hallmark of warfare, and the war of 1939–45 raised the ugliness of war to previously unequalled heights. However, of its many battles and campaigns, for sheer desperation and intensity what began at Anzio in January 1944 was in a class by itself.

From London, Churchill observed the events in Italy with mounting trepidation that failure would have an adverse, if not fatal, impact on the success of Overlord. When it became clear that the Anzio force was not advancing to capture the Alban Hills, telegrams flew back and forth between London and Alexander's HQ at Caserta. Anzio became the dominant theme of the prime minister's weekly cabinet meetings, and he began bemoaning a great opportunity squandered. Brooke shared his uneasiness as headlines in British newspapers became grimmer, and suggestions of another Dunkirk in the making more prevalent. Anzio also shook Churchill's faith in Alexander. By early February, Colville was noting his master's dismay. 'It was strategically sound and it had a perfect beginning. He cannot understand the failure to push inland from the beach-head. While the battle still rages he is refraining from asking Alexander the questions to which the P.M. can find no answer, but his great faith in A., though not dissipated, is a little shaken.'

In the ensuing weeks the inability of those in London to comprehend Anzio became apparent. 'Why, if we had superior numbers of fighting troops . . . some 15 to 20,000 more in the Bridgehead than those opposing us – a larger number of tanks; quality if not superiority in guns; and complete control of the air, it was not possible for us to attack,' Churchill complained. What no one, not even Brooke, seemed to understand was that the desperate battle to avoid annihilation had enfeebled the Allied infantry battalions. Armour was ineffective, and the rugged terrain made offensive action with inadequate forces impossible. With no one around him to offer a counterpoint or act as a brake on his impulsiveness, the prime minister remained convinced that he was simply being fed excuses.

Churchill applied the carrot rather than the stick to Alexander, suggesting that he take a more active role, that perhaps he had hesitated to exert his authority because he was dealing with American commanders. He viewed Lucas as a plodder completely lacking in aggressive spirit, and suggested that if Alexander was dissatisfied with his performance, 'you should put someone there who you can trust.' To Sir John Dill in Washington, Churchill privately expressed his disappointment in both Alexander and Clark, both of whom should not 'urge' but 'order'. Behind the scenes a battle of wills took place between Clark and Alexander, neither of whom had a high opinion of the other. Alexander told Clark that he feared a disaster at Anzio and had no confidence in Lucas. For a time Clark was reluctant to relieve Lucas, believing he had been handed a no-win mission, but as the situation in the beachhead worsened, he soon changed his mind.

The Germans launched a huge counter-offensive on 16 February, and five days of desperate battles ensued as US and British troops fought bravely to save the beachhead in one of the most desperate and bloody battles of the war. Although another Dunkirk was narrowly averted, Lucas was relieved of command and replaced with the aggressive and respected Lucian K. Truscott.

At one point, when the situation was at its gravest, Churchill might have intervened with his own scheme had not Brooke quashed it. The best solution, he had argued, was for Alexander to take personal charge at Anzio, with Jumbo Wilson replacing him as commander of Allied land forces in Italy. There were occasions during the war when Brooke completely lost his temper with Churchill – and this was one of those times. Exasperated by the prime minister's meddling, the CIGS pointed out that such a move not only usurped Alexander's authority but would have placed him in the absurd position of reversing roles and becoming Clark's subordinate. Churchill relented, and to Brooke's relief the matter died.

On 11 April Alexander travelled to London to tell him that there would be no breakout offensive at Anzio and Cassino until at least mid-May, and no junction of the two forces before the first week in June. 'We are bogged down in Cassino, and indeed, in Italy,' wrote Sir Alexander Cadogan in his diary. 'It looks to me like a Passchendaele, beloved of Generals.' As much as he detested delay for any reason – even mention of the words 'delay' or 'postponement' was enough to set him off – Churchill was obliged to accept the inevitable. He cabled Roosevelt that Alexander had 'defended his actions or inactions with much force, pointing out the small plurality of his army . . . the vileness of the weather and the extremely awkward nature of the ground.'

Of the many military operations that Churchill had a hand in, none was more frustrating than Anzio. Nothing would dissuade him from the belief that victory had been squandered by Lucas's failure to advance on Rome and the Alban Hills. To Smuts he confided: 'Naturally I am very disappointed at what has appeared to be the frittering away of a brilliant opening . . . I do not in any way however repent of what has been done.'

Despite repeated reassurances from Alexander, Churchill's frustration at the inability of the Allied military commanders in Italy to break the stalemate and capture Rome led to his now famous remark about Anzio:

'I thought we were landing a Tiger cat; instead all we have is a stranded whale.' 'My confidence in Alexander remains undiminished,' he cabled Smuts. However, that confidence was tempered by a degree of scepticism: 'if I had been well enough to be at his side as I had hoped at the critical moment I believe I could have given the necessary stimulus. Alas for time, distance, illness and advancing years.' Churchill had been the prime minister for nearly four years, and it was hopeless for anyone to try to convince him that a politician – even an extraordinarily powerful warlord – had no business being anywhere near a general exercising command in battle.

To a man the veteran British and American commanders who fought at Anzio, even those who severely criticized Lucas's leadership, believed that to have attempted to hold the Alban Hills would have been military folly. A British division commander expostulated: 'We could have had one night in Rome and 18 months in P.W. camps.' George Marshall also supported this view with an indisputable rationale: 'We could have advanced to the Alban Hills, but . . . for every mile of advance there were seven or more miles added to the perimeter.'

With the Allies never quite sure of their purpose in Italy, Anzio was doomed to failure long before the first landing craft descended on the beaches. Not for the first nor for the last time, the Allies did not take into account the ability and willingness of German commanders like Rommel and Kesselring to react in ways that did not match their preconceptions.

The siege of Anzio lasted 125 days, its combatants virtual prisoners locked in a life-and-death struggle from which there seemed no escape except via a hospital or a body bag. The Allies lost seven thousand killed, and 36,000 more were wounded or reported as missing in action; thousands more were killed at Cassino. In May, after months of stalemate at Anzio and at Cassino, Alexander launched a massive two-pronged offensive. Unable to contain the Allies, Kesselring realized that there was nothing to be gained by fighting for Rome or by its destruction, and declared it an open city, leaving only minimal forces to cover a fighting retreat into northern Italy and his troops' final stand on the Gothic Line in the Apennines.

On 5 June 1944 the limelight briefly focused on the capture of Rome. Newspaper headlines trumpeted the fall of the Eternal City after a prolonged and bloody struggle, but its liberation was all but forgotten the following day with the dramatic news that the Allies had invaded France.

Churchill defended his role over Anzio by declaring, 'My personal efforts did not extend to the conduct of the battle.' Shingle was far too complex an operation for all its threads to be tied only to him, but unlike Alexander, who later admitted that Anzio was a bluff that had been called by Kesselring, Churchill took credit for its parentage but was unwilling to accept any responsibility for its illegitimacy. Nevertheless, in a rare moment of candour in September 1944 while aboard the *Queen Mary* en route to Quebec, he blurted out, 'Anzio was my worst moment of the war. I had most to do with it. I didn't want two Suvla Bays in one lifetime.'

58

Overlord at Last

I am in this thing with you to the end, and if it fails we will go down together.
– Churchill to Eisenhower, before D-Day

By mid-January 1944 Churchill was well enough to return to London, where he threw himself back into the daily grind as if he had never been ill. He held weekly conferences about all aspects of the forthcoming invasion of France, and the hopes of some that he would slow down and perhaps mellow were immediately and often rudely disabused by a torrent of 'Action This Day' directives that flowed in all directions, demanding information and immediate response.

Although Churchill understood Overlord's necessity, once proclaiming that it was 'the greatest event and duty in the world', he still sought means of avoiding what he was afraid would be horrendous losses. A large part of that concern stemmed from his belief that the only way the war could be lost was on the impending second front. There are countless examples of his fears. The initial fear was not of failing to get an invasion force ashore in Normandy but of failing to hold the bridgehead. 'I do not doubt our ability to get ashore and deploy,' he wrote to Roosevelt in October 1943. 'I am however deeply concerned with the build-up and with the situation that may arise between the thirtieth and sixtieth days,' and he also articulated his fear that it might 'inflict on us a military disaster greater than that of Dunkirk. Such a disaster would result in the resuscitation of Hitler and the Nazi regime.' However, as the time for the invasion drew near his fear of a stalemate changed into fear of D-day itself and the price in blood that would have to be paid to get ashore.

As the level of American commitment to the war grew, so too did the disparities between the United States and Britain. They were never more evident than in Churchill's attempt to distort and manipulate Allied grand strategy. After Salerno, Alexander had written a gloomy assessment contending that the build-up of Kesselring's forces gravely imperilled the future of the Italian campaign. Eisenhower sent the report to both Churchill and FDR but disagreed with Alexander's conclusions, arguing that keeping German divisions tied down in Italy could only benefit Overlord. Both at the time and in his memoirs Churchill deliberately suppressed Eisenhower's remarks in an effort to add emphasis to his desire to do what Alexander Cadogan called 'nourishing' the Italian campaign and pursuing his single-minded strategy in the eastern Mediterranean. When they learned of Churchill's duplicity, US officials were outraged. Henry Stimson angrily wrote in his diary that it demonstrated Churchill's determination 'to stick a knife in the back of Overlord'. Revenge came at Tehran when the US returned the favour by affirming the Quebec agreement and blocking Churchill's attempted strategic manoeuvrings to bolster Italy and pursue the Dodecanese initiatives.

Sir Ian Jacob offers a rationale for Churchill's military thinking. 'He tended to think in terms of "sabres and bayonets", of old-fashioned sieges, of thousands of men manning the ramparts with rifles and fighting to the death, in hand-to-hand combat if need be. Nor', continued Jacob, 'did he understand the concept that modern infantry without the backing of armour and artillery had very limited power. In short Churchill's thinking sprang directly from his experience and knowledge of the Great War. He did not fully realize the change that had taken place since then in large-scale warfare. The development of armoured divisions, of self-propelled artillery, of mechanical transport and of great tactical air forces . . . robbed the static machine-gun of its mastery of the battlefield.' Churchill's Great War mentality never adapted to the dramatic changes in warfare that had altered the landscape of the modern battlefield. 'Yet Churchill, right up to the summer of 1944, feared the crystallization of a front in France, and a repetition of the vast casualties of 1916 and 1917 in trying to break through.'

Nor did he quite grasp the dramatic changes in naval warfare. While he well understood the menace of the submarine, Churchill thought battleships still ruled the sea, when real naval power lay with the aircraft carrier and its ability to deliver lethal air strikes against enemy ships, as the US navy had demonstrated at Midway Island in June 1942.

Churchill's inability to comprehend modern warfare was in direct contrast to his amazing grasp of its technical side: his frequent probing questions to Portal about a wide variety of technical matters, his interest in radar and navigation in the air and at sea, and a host of other subjects. His best-known and greatest contribution to Overlord came in the form of championing the creation of the Mulberry artificial harbours. This was a project that he threw his full weight behind. In July 1917 he had written a paper submitted to Lloyd George, in which he had outlined his idea of a mobile harbour of flat-bottomed barges that could be emplaced off a hostile shore to form an artificial harbour.

Although the paper had nothing to do with the Second World War Mulberry, the concept was revived in a modern form in 1941 and turned into reality in 1944. One of the vital concerns of the Overlord planners was not simply getting ashore but ensuring a means of resupplying the expeditionary force by sea. The idea was already under consideration and being hotly debated in 1942 when Churchill intervened with a minute to Mountbatten that demanded action: 'They must float up and down with the tide . . . Let me have the best solution worked out. Don't argue the matter. The difficulties will argue for themselves.'

The resulting Mulberry artificial harbours were a feat of engineering genius and one the greatest achievements of Overlord. Constructed in both Scotland and England, two were created for eventual emplacement offshore, one each in the US and British landing sectors. A truly gigantic undertaking, the floating harbours could be towed from England and sunk off the Normandy beaches. Each consisted of 150 prefabricated concrete breakwaters, two hundred feet long, that comprised some two million tons of concrete and steel. Once in place, along with a large number of obsolete merchant ships also to be sunk to form a secure breakwater, the Mulberries offered places where vessels could dock and unload cargo that would be transported ashore along floating jetties and pontoon bridges.

The American Mulberry was damaged beyond repair in a great storm that battered Normandy shortly after D-day; however, the British Mulberry at Arromanches survived and was immensely successful. Over one hundred days more than 2.5 million men, five hundred thousand vehicles and 4 million tons of equipment and supplies were landed in Normandy via the Mulberry.

*

Although Overlord dominated everything else in the West during the first six months of 1944, Churchill raised other issues. As it had throughout the war, an oft debated subject made an unwelcome return visit to the limelight in the form of Operation Jupiter, Churchill's unremitting obsession with amphibious landings in Norway. As they had been in the past, the chiefs were adamantly opposed, and for the same reasons: the idea was logistically unsupportable and there was neither the manpower nor the sea transport available; every asset in Europe was committed to Overlord or in Italy. The result was a number of stormy sessions before the idea was again shelved.

Then, in the midst of the planning for Overlord, Churchill began bombarding the chiefs with his idea that the Allies should land two armoured divisions at Bordeaux or some other appropriate landing place in south-western France approximately twenty to thirty days after D-day. In what was code-named Operation Caliph, the divisions would be transported by sea from Morocco and once ashore would spread havoc behind the German lines. They would be followed later by the employment of commandos, and all of this would 'arouse widespread revolt', disrupt the Germans and significantly aid the Allies in Normandy. Churchill's rationale was that there would be excess British forces available from both the Overlord landings and the later invasion of southern France, Operation Anvil. The joint planners opined that the plan could be carried out only if Anvil was cancelled. However, as Churchill had already learned, Anvil was championed by Eisenhower and backed by Washington, and although he would argue for its cancellation until shortly before it was carried out in August, there would be no troops drawn from this source. A disappointed Churchill looked ten years older, recorded his stenographer Marian Holmes.

By 1944, as Britain entered its sixth year of war, Churchill was showing signs of being deeply fatigued by the weight of his responsibilities. His lack of stamina and enthusiasm was apparent to everyone around him. The normally reserved Clement Attlee sent him a stern rebuke for failing to familiarize himself with papers submitted for his attention and for his loss of control of the 'reins of government'. Even his oratory in Parliament lacked its usual vigour and bite. During meetings with the chiefs and the War Cabinet he displayed an increasing loss of focus. He would sleep until nearly noon on occasion, was forgetful at Prime

Minister's Question Time in the House of Commons and lacked his usual *joie de vivre*. He admitted to Brooke that although 'he could still always sleep well, eat well and especially drink well . . . he no longer jumped out of bed the way he used to, and felt as if he would be quite content to spend the whole day in bed.'

When Churchill convened a meeting of the chiefs on 28 March, Brooke found him 'in a desperately tired mood. I am afraid that he is losing ground rapidly. He seems quite incapable of concentrating for a few minutes on end, and keeps wandering continuously.' Nor did his first radio broadcast to the nation in more than a year go well. Harold Nicolson wrote, 'People seem to think that Winston's broadcast last night was that of a worn and petulant old man.' Nicolson was also 'sickened' by the ingratitude that a 'terribly war-weary' country was exhibiting towards the hero of 1940–1.

As the date for Overlord drew nearer, Churchill's mood was bleaker than ever. On every side he was being rebuffed. His challenges to Anvil and Eisenhower's pre-Overlord bombing plan were falling on deaf ears, and Italy was mired in stalemate and beset by mounting casualties. His scheme to invade the northern tip of the island of Sumatra and yet another attempt at invading Norway were rejected by the chiefs of staff. Physically he was near the end of his endurance, a condition exacerbated by the rejection of his ideas and plans, and the bleakness the future seemed to hold. In retrospect it was miraculous that he had held the reins so firmly for nearly four years of mind-numbing responsibilities and burdens that would have crushed others half his age. Neither the problems he faced nor the responsibilities he carried on his shoulders ever abated for so much as a single day.

Relations between Churchill and Brooke suffered the longer the war went on, as much from fatigue as from mutual exasperation. Although he had been appointed CIGS for his acumen and strength of character, Brooke eventually came to resent playing Churchill's foil. There is a great deal to the suggestion that Brooke viewed his role as having evolved from that of *consigliere* to that of nanny. What particularly irked him was that, despite Churchill's growing experience of war, he never evolved as a strategist, instead regressing and in the process appearing at times to have consumed too much alcohol at meetings with the chiefs.

The strain affected everyone, not least the chiefs of staff, who were fighting a war and sometimes a second one with their prime minister.

Unending pressure, stress and far too little sleep were their lot. Each attempted to escape the pressure cooker of London and the close proximity to Churchill, who believed everyone in the government ought to be available at his beck and call at any hour of the day or night. On his few days off at home in the countryside, Brooke rarely escaped without either a telephone call or a summons from Churchill – usually both. One weekend in early 1944 the chiefs collectively decided to take a badly needed weekend off to go fishing in Scotland. Knowing full well what his reaction would be, they deliberately kept this information from Churchill. Inevitably Hollis received a telephone call from the prime minister, who was at Chequers. Mr Churchill would be most pleased if Hollis would convey his best respects to the CIGS and ask if he would come down, as there were some matters he'd like to discuss with him. Told that the CIGS was out of London and not available, Churchill asked for the chief of the air staff. He was informed that Portal too was out of London and unavailable. The same information was repeated as Churchill asked for the first sea lord. 'And what might they be doing?' he inquired. His hand forced, Hollis replied, 'Prime Minister, they are fishing.' The wires between Whitehall and Chequers lit up as Churchill exclaimed: 'Fishing, fishing, they are fishing when there is a great war going on with one of the greatest build-ups going on for the greatest invasion in history, they go fishing!' Churchill then asked if General Ismay could come down, and Hollis had to reveal that he too was away in the country. In desperation Churchill sighed and said, 'Well, Hollis, perhaps you could come down.'

It was not merely the key players who were showing war weariness; by 1944 the British public was feeling its long-term effects, and with no light at the end of the tunnel, even the collective defiance of the early years was becoming lost in a cloud of fatigue and uncertainty.

What made Churchill unique was his ability to bounce back from adversity, and despite his battles with ill health and overwork, there were occasions when he was his old self – eager, articulate and at the top of his game. His loss of stamina and focus notwithstanding, his insistence on being personally involved in every aspect of the war continued with the Overlord planning. One of the senior planners recalled how he would direct Ismay: ' "Pray let us have a certain plan by next week." We would send something back. The PM would remark: "I see that the Ministry of Negation has successfully marshalled bellyaches as usual." Six out of ten of his ideas were good. If we could get the PM interested in our projects everything was fine. He would see that everything was obtained to carry through the ideas.'

In March the Germans began stepping up air raids on London, and as he had done throughout the war, whenever word came of an impending raid, instead of heading for shelter, Churchill strapped on his tin helmet and climbed directly to the roof to view the event for himself, declaring, 'Let 'em come. We can deal with 'em.'

At 9.00 a.m. on 15 May King George VI, Churchill, Smuts, the chiefs of staff and the entire complement of senior Allied commanders assembled at Montgomery's headquarters in St Paul's School in West, London, in a top-secret room guarded by military policemen, for the final Overlord command briefings. Eisenhower, Montgomery and the other component commanders each rose in turn and, standing before a large terrain model of the Normandy landing sites, gave a briefing on their part of the operation. Montgomery was particularly clear and impressive, 'quite first-class', in Ismay's view. Although Montgomery's presentation was the essence of simplicity and clarity, from defining the problem to stating how Overlord would successfully solve it, one of the senior air marshals noted that Churchill constantly interrupted him with questions 'which seemed designed to show his [own] knowledge of strategy and tactics'.

The day's events concluded with short speeches from George VI, Smuts and Eisenhower. Then it was Churchill's turn. He rose and, gripping his lapels firmly, addressed the silent room. 'I am hardening on this enterprise,' he declared. 'I repeat, I am *now* hardening towards this enterprise.' What Churchill meant and how his remarks were interpreted were two different things. Ismay recorded that the expression was one the prime minister used frequently with him and that 'I had taken it to mean that the more you thought about it the more certain you were of success.' Although Churchill's statement appears to have employed a purely British turn of phrase meant to convey precisely what Ismay understood it to convey, it did not come across as such to Eisenhower, who interpreted it as a sign that the prime minister hadn't previously believed in Overlord. Privately dismayed by Churchill's speech, he thought it sent the wrong message. 'I then realized for the first time that Mr Churchill hadn't believed in it all along and had had no faith that it would succeed,' he later revealed. 'It was quite a shocking discovery.'

Churchill's closing remarks were a reflection of his disdain for what he regarded as a failure of leadership at Anzio. 'Let us not expect all to go according to plan,' he said. 'Flexibility of mind will be one of the decisive factors. We must not have another Anzio ... where we cannot advance twelve miles. Risks must be taken. Rommel cannot afford to concentrate *all* his forces against Overlord.'

Eisenhower closed the meeting by observing, 'In half an hour Hitler will have missed his one and only chance of destroying with a single well-aimed bomb the entire high command of the Allied forces.'

Yet Churchill's fears persisted. Not long before D-day, he said to his staff one evening, out of the blue: 'Why are we doing all this? Why are we going to throw away the best of our young men in assaulting a strongly defended enemy coast? Why do we not, instead of invading France, use the territory of our oldest ally, Portugal, and move towards the German border through the Iberian Peninsula?'

In an unpublished post-war memoir, Eisenhower recorded how he would sometimes find Churchill in a pessimistic mood. 'Time and again he would express his forebodings ... He spoke of visions of beaches choked with the bodies of the flower of British and American youth and of the tides running red with their blood ... At some point in such a conversation he would break in with an enthusiastic word of approval of our plans, proving that he was not pessimistic by nature.'

Less than a month before D-day, Churchill and Eisenhower lunched privately. With tears in his eyes the prime minister declared, 'I am in this thing with you to the end, and if it fails we will go down together.' Eisenhower noted that many weeks passed before he began to see a sign of confidence in the operation from Churchill. Only if the Allies could secure a sizeable portion of the Normandy coast and the Cotentin Peninsula, would he 'at that point publicly say that Overlord had been a well-conceived and worthwhile operation, "And, my dear General, if by the time the snow flies you can have restored her liberty to our beautiful Paris, I shall proclaim to the world that this has been the best conceived and most remarkably successful military operation of all history." ... One day he gave me a hint of a possible cause for these statements, saying, "I'd not want history to record that I agreed to this without voicing my doubts."'

*

In the critical week before D-day Eisenhower and admirals Ramsay and Cunningham had to contend with Churchill's dogged intention of viewing the invasion from the cruiser HMS *Belfast*. The notion first surfaced on 25 April when Churchill told Colville. 'He would be among the first on the bridgehead,' he said, 'if he possibly could – and what fun it would be to get there before Monty.'

An exasperated Eisenhower firmly told the prime minister that he would not sanction his presence at the edge of the battle. Churchill rejoined that as minister of defence he had a duty to take part, insisting he would circumvent Eisenhower's authority by going as a crew member. 'It is not part of your responsibilities, my dear General,' he said, 'to determine the exact composition of any ship's company in His Majesty's Fleet.' Eisenhower conceded his inability to stop Churchill but 'forcefully pointed out that he was adding to my personal burdens in this thwarting of my instructions'. King George VI learned of the prime minister's intention and tried to put a stop to it. In a heartfelt letter hand-delivered from Buckingham Palace, the king pointed out that of course he would never presume to interfere in the affairs of his government's principal minister. However, should Churchill carry out his intention, he too would feel obliged to witness the invasion, as the (titular) head of Britain's armed forces. Like a spoiled child Churchill petulantly argued and quibbled with the king. The entire affair was irrational and reflected Churchill's hubris at its very worst. To have placed himself foolishly in danger, and to have vexed and diverted his senior commanders and others with such nonsense at one of the most critical moments of the war, was inexcusable. Moreover, as Admiral Ramsay pointed out to both the king and Churchill in the underground map room on 2 June, the *Belfast* would run considerable risks from mines, air attack, torpedoes and possibly shore batteries. Also, the ship would be too far offshore for anyone on board to witness more than a small fraction of the invasion, so they would learn more by remaining in the map room. Churchill rejected both the king's and Ramsay's advice, and George VI returned to Buckingham Palace empty-handed and deeply frustrated by the prime minister's insistence on going for a joy ride in the Channel. Although bitterly disappointed and rather resentful, Churchill finally conceded. In his post-war memoirs his disappointment and abiding defiance left no doubt that he had 'deferred to the Crown, not to Eisenhower'.

On 3 June Churchill and Smuts were inspecting British troops along the south coast; that evening the prime minister, without warning, visited Eisenhower's invasion headquarters at Southwick, primarily to 'pour the heat on Ike' for refusing to countenance his participation in D-day, and to take one last crack at persuading the supreme commander to change his mind. Eisenhower, though sympathetic, was annoyed and refused. Churchill left as 'peevish' as he had been when he arrived.

Early on 4 June, the south coast of England was awash in a heavy rainstorm, visibility in the Channel was limited to yards and the air forces were grounded. Word was flashed that Eisenhower had postponed the invasion for at least twenty-four hours, perhaps longer. Overlord was on hold. The window of opportunity for a full moon (which was required for the airborne and glider operations on both flanks of the invasion front) would expire after 6 June. The tension rose everywhere, from the lowliest private, seasick on a landing craft awaiting news of the invasion, to the many military headquarters, and to No. 10. The one facet of the invasion over which no one had any control had taken centre stage.

Early the next morning Eisenhower's meteorologists predicted a narrow window of opportunity: the weather would improve just enough to carry out Overlord. Making the most important and courageous military decision of his career, Eisenhower announced to his assembled generals, admirals and airmen: 'OK, we'll go.' The invasion was set for the morning of 6 June.

At midday on 5 June, Churchill invited the chiefs for lunch. Brooke found him in a 'very highly strung condition' but was astonished at his 'over optimistic' mood 'as regards prospects of the cross Channel operation . . . Similarly in Italy he now believes that Alex will wipe out the whole of the German forces!' Admiral Cunningham recorded that the prime minister was 'very worked up about Overlord and really in almost a hysterical state. He really is an incorrigible optimist.' It was all an act befitting a leader in a time of crisis. Exuding a confidence he surely did not feel, Churchill was actually beset by doubt. The night of 5 June was easily the most nerve-racking of the war. While Eisenhower smoked his way through pack after pack of cigarettes, Churchill remained on edge; all his long-standing fears of a bloodbath came rushing back in a nightmarish vision. He haunted the map room and, before retiring for a sleepless night, sombrely said to Clementine, 'Do you realize that by the time you wake up in the morning twenty thousand men may have been killed?'

Brooke's own sense of gloom on the eve of D-day was reflected in his diary: 'I am very uneasy about the whole operation. At the best it will fall so very very far short of the expectation of the bulk of the people, namely all those who know nothing of its difficulties. At the worst it may well be the most ghastly disaster of the whole war. I wish to God it were safely over.' Only Montgomery, Ramsay and Franklin Delano Roosevelt displayed no outward signs of strain.

Hundreds of thousands of Allied troops and masses of military hardware were crammed on ships and landing craft that had embarked after Eisenhower's 'Go' order on what he would later term 'the great crusade'. The cross-Channel operation that Churchill had envisaged in the dark days of 1940, but had secretly hoped would never be necessary, was about to be unleashed. Of the landings both sides knew were coming, Rommel said, 'The first 24 hours of the invasion will be decisive . . . The fate of Germany depends on the outcome . . . For the Allies, as well as Germany, it will be the longest day.' For Winston Churchill, there was only loneliness, and a knot in his gut that made the seemingly endless late night and early morning hours of 5/6 June 1944 the longest night.

59
Summer of Discontent

Ike said no, continued saying no all afternoon, and ended saying no in every form of the English language at his command.
— Eisenhower's aide on his continuing verbal battle with Churchill

In spite of the bloody battle for Omaha Beach, the D-day invasion was a stunning success. On 6 June, 130,000 Allied ground troops and 23,000 airborne and glider troops were landed in Normandy, and Churchill's nightmarish vision of the English Channel running red with the blood of corpses was averted. The Allies won the battle of the beaches, and among the German commanders only Rommel realized its profound implications.

The morning of 6 June found Churchill in the underground map room, his eyes glued to the large wall map where the staff was plotting the course of events every few minutes as fresh updates were flashed from France. He broke away to report to the House of Commons at noon. At lunch with the king he related what he knew and that afternoon the two men motored, first to Leigh-Mallory's air HQ in Uxbridge, then later to Eisenhower's headquarters in St James's Square for a further update from his staff. Communications in 1944 were crude; information was hard to come by and usually hours out of date. On 6 June Churchill and George VI had to be satisfied that the markers on the maps showed the Allies holding their own.

Churchill lost no time badgering Eisenhower to let him visit Normandy, and on 12 June, accompanied by Smuts and Brooke, he boarded a Royal Navy destroyer at Portsmouth for the three-hour trip. Also accompanying Churchill were Marshall and Admiral Ernest J. King, the US chief of naval operations, who had arrived in London on 8 June. The English Channel was an awe-inspiring mass of ships of every description, as were the two Mulberry harbours. 'It was a wonderful sight to see this city of ships stretching along the coast for nearly fifty miles,' Churchill telegraphed Stalin. The visitors were put ashore at Courseulles and met on the beach by Montgomery. Crammed into jeeps, they were driven to his command post in the grounds of the Château Creully, three miles behind the front lines. Despite the war raging not far away, Normandy seemed little affected. Crops were growing in the fields and farm animals were in evidence, prompting Churchill to comment to Brooke, 'We are surrounded by fat cattle lying in luscious pastures with their paws crossed!'

Inside a caravan converted into a mobile operations room, Montgomery used a large map of Normandy to brief them on the situation and his future plans. As they left for lunch Smuts suddenly turned to Montgomery's aide-de-camp, Captain Noël Chavasse, and murmured to the astonished aide that there were Germans close by. Told that the area had been thoroughly secured, Smuts said, 'There are Germans near us now . . . I can always tell.' As he spoke he stared at a nearby clump of rhododendrons and laurel bushes. Two days later two armed and frightened German paratroopers gave themselves up. They had been hiding there for days and were hungry and soaking wet. Had they acted as Hitler would have demanded, they were close enough to have wiped out Churchill and his party.

The château had been heavily bombed the night before, and there were numerous visible craters. At lunch in a tent Churchill asked if the front was a continuous line. Told no, Churchill inquired, 'What is there then to prevent an incursion of German armour breaking up our luncheon?' Montgomery could only reply that he 'did not think they would come'. Churchill suggested that Montgomery was taking too great a risk if he continued making a habit of being so close to the front. It was a strange but thoughtful turnabout by a man who routinely exposed himself to danger.

Before embarking for home, Churchill detoured to visit the British Mulberry at Arromanches and a smaller neighbouring port, where, to the horror of his Royal Navy escort, Vice Admiral Sir Philip Vian (of *Altmark* fame in 1940), he climbed to the top of a lighthouse to obtain a better view, leaving himself dangerously exposed to shellfire. But when Vian attempted to coax him down, 'Churchill took not the slightest notice.' He was dissuaded from boarding a nearby warship firing its

14-inch guns, but before his destroyer left the battle zone he 'suggested' that its gunners ought to fire at the enemy. After six rounds were duly fired beyond the beachhead, he exclaimed: 'Who knows? We may have just killed a German general capable of winning the war for them.' Delighted that he had for the first time witnessed one of His Majesty's ships firing 'in anger', Churchill slept soundly during the return voyage to Portsmouth.

His relief at the success of Overlord quickly waned a week later when German V-1 flying bombs began raining down on south-east England from missile sites mainly in the Pas de Calais. As a weapon of terror the flying bombs, known as doodlebugs or buzz bombs, were (like the later and more sophisticated V-2 rockets) inefficient, often landing harmlessly in fields. Nevertheless this fresh wave of random terror served significantly to unnerve a war-weary British populace that thought its ordeal from the air had ended. Morale plummeted; no one was spared. During the first eighty days of Hitler's new terror campaign, of the 8,000 flying bombs launched against Britain, 2,300 struck in and around London. While most were shot down or fell harmlessly in rural areas, enough got through to prompt a massive, high-priority but largely futile effort to destroy the hardened launch sites. The worst incident occurred in London on Sunday, 18 June when a V-1 hit the Guards Chapel filled with worshippers, killing or maiming nearly two hundred servicemen and members of their families. Clementine was in nearby Hyde Park visiting her daughter Mary, who was serving with an anti-aircraft battery, and both were horrified to witness the black object suddenly descend from the sky and explode.

Anti-aircraft guns blasted some forty V-1s a day from the skies, but not all could be shot down. On 19 July Brooke recorded about twelve landing near him, one of which came so close to his London quarters that it forced him to take cover on the floor behind his bed.

Finding some means of countering the buzz bombs became Churchill's overriding priority. The V-1 attacks had a greater effect on British morale than had the Blitz, not only because of the sense of helplessness they created but also because – in scenes reminiscent of the darkest days of 1940 – they forced the evacuation to the countryside of nearly 1.5 million Britons. As the attacks worsened, the pressure increased upon Eisenhower to finish off the German army in Normandy and overrun and capture the missile sites. By early July, Churchill was aware that the newer and more deadly V-2 was imminent and was beside himself with distress that it might well be capable of delivering biological agents. Brooke described as 'ghastly' a late-night meeting on 6 July with the chiefs, Eden, Attlee and Oliver Lyttelton (the minister of war production) that began at 10.00 p.m. and lasted until 2.00 a.m. Churchill arrived exhausted and 'in a maudlin, bad tempered, drunken mood, ready to take offence at anything, suspicious of everybody, and in a highly vindictive mood against the Americans'.

He was scathingly critical of Montgomery over the bitter fighting and lack of progress in Normandy, and his rage and frustration boiled over during one of the war's stormiest meetings. And, in a chilling minute to the chiefs, he momentarily flirted with a gruesome idea that one of his biographers has correctly defined as 'a spiritual nadir'. He demanded that they consider drenching Germany with poison (mustard) gas. 'It is absurd to consider morality on this topic when everybody used it in the last war without a word of complaint from the moralists or the Church . . . If we do it, let us do it one hundred per cent . . . I want the matter studied in cold blood by sensible people and not by . . . psalm-singing uninformed defeatists.' Three weeks later the chiefs summarily rejected his minute on the grounds that there was no evidence of German intentions to make use of biological weapons. Churchill was unconvinced, 'but clearly I cannot make head against the parsons and warriors at the same time.'

This episode occurred at one of his lowest moments of the war. He was beset by a variety of tribulations: the stagnating situation in the Normandy bridgehead, his profound dismay over his diminishing role in the war and not being in control of events, what he deemed American intransigence over the forthcoming invasion of southern France, and the endless V-1 attacks. 'I do not see why we should always have all the disadvantages of being the gentlemen while they have all the advantages of being the cad.' He did, however, qualify the possible use of poison gas. He would not employ it, he said, unless it was a matter of life and death for Britain or unless it would shorten the war by at least a year. The issue died of inertia and was never again raised.

There is a great deal to observe of Winston Churchill in 1944–5 that is reflective of a leader on a downward spiral, whose powers and influence were nearing rock bottom. Failing health, frustration, bad temper, loss of concentration and bone weariness, combined with a determination to remain relevant, were all very much in evidence. Yet in spite of – or perhaps because of – his declining role, Churchill refused to accept anything less than the same punishing grind he had imposed on himself from the day he had returned to the Admiralty in September 1939. The question that must be asked is how he managed for so long to endure the interminable grind that would long since have broken an ordinary man. The gifts of spirit and perseverance that had been bestowed on him were not everlasting, and in the summer of 1944 evidence of their departure was manifested by his rapidly diminishing ability to control events and influence the conduct of the war.

Eisenhower and the US chiefs of staff deemed a secondary invasion of the French Riviera essential. They were adamant that a need existed to divert German attention and troops from Normandy during the critical days immediately after the D-day landings. The result was code-named Anvil (redesignated later in 1944 as Dragoon to prevent a suspected compromise), and it became the most hotly debated Allied operation of the war.

The two major issues that set Churchill and Eisenhower at loggerheads during the war were the Dodecanese and Anvil/Dragoon. Eisenhower never wavered, convinced that the Allies in France required additional ports, particularly Marseille, and that Anvil would serve to protect the right flank of the Allied armies during their broad advance towards Germany. The invasion of the Riviera, Eisenhower insisted, would proceed as scheduled.

The British case hinged on the Mediterranean strategy, and the conviction that too much had already been invested in the Italian campaign to rob it of the potential to end the war in Italy at the very moment when the Germans were in disarray after the fall of Rome. The subject produced some of the most acrimonious exchanges between Roosevelt and Churchill. A series of harshly worded cables flew between London and Washington as Churchill argued doggedly but ultimately in vain against pulling troops from Italy, where, he insisted, victory was at hand. 'We have immense tasks before us,' he telegraphed to Roosevelt on 23 June. 'Indeed, I cannot think of any moment when the burden of war has [lain] more heavily upon me or when I have felt so unequal to its ever-more entangled problems.'

On 28 June Churchill issued a fervent plea to Roosevelt that no troops or landing craft be pulled from Italy. 'Let us resolve not to wreck one great campaign for the sake of another. Both can be won.' The Italian campaign, he said, offered 'dazzling possibilities', whereas the landings in southern France would 'relieve Hitler of all his anxieties in the Po basin' and serve no useful purpose in aiding Eisenhower's forces in northern France.

Uppermost in Churchill's mind were the political benefits he foresaw from a successful thrust through the Ljubljana Gap to seize Vienna before the Russians arrived. What he never accepted was that keeping Alexander's army group intact would not have overcome the problems encountered during the deadly Allied advance into northern Italy during the summer of 1944. Neither Churchill nor Alexander ever defined how such a military operation might actually have been carried out through the exceedingly difficult terrain of the Apennines and the even more daunting Slovenian mountains, all the while overcoming German resistance. Eisenhower refused to have anything to do with an offensive through 'that gap whose name I can't even pronounce', and repeatedly refused to scrap Dragoon despite a chorus of pleas in the days and weeks before the operation.

Roosevelt rejected Churchill's attempts to spike the invasion with a pointed reminder that 'a straight line is the shortest distance between two points', a none-too-subtle admonition that the road to Berlin ran through France and western Europe, not Italy and the Balkans.

Backed by the British chiefs, Churchill became increasingly hostile to an operation that would cripple his 'soft underbelly' strategy, and continued fervently to pursue the cancellation of Anvil/Dragoon. There ensued a war of words between Eisenhower and the stubborn Briton to whom the word 'no' was merely a challenge rather than closure. The debate pitted Marshall and Eisenhower against Churchill and Brooke in a battle of the heavyweights that occupied centre stage for some eight months. For Eisenhower, Anvil/Dragoon became the most trying and rancorous aspect of his relations with the British leader. Although the debate was billed as a military quarrel over strategy, it was actually a political clash of wills between Roosevelt and Churchill, with Eisenhower caught in the middle.

The operation stuck like a bone in Churchill's throat – the more he objected and argued for its cancellation, the more stubborn became

American resistance. In July his frustration and anger at being rebuffed boiled over. Brooke found him spoiling for a row with the president and ready to send Roosevelt 'an awful telegram' that the CIGS realized would split the coalition. It demanded better treatment from the United States, 'otherwise it would be necessary . . . to devise some other machinery for conducting the war, including the separation of the commands in the Mediterranean.' Although he was dissuaded from sending this incendiary message, Churchill was adamant that 'Alexander is to have his campaign,' and directed the chiefs to inform his American ally that 'we have been ill treated and are furious.' His resentment culminated in an angry denunciation of Hap Arnold, Ernie King and George Marshall as 'one of the stupidest strategic teams ever seen. They are good fellows and there is no need to tell them this,' he wrote (sentences he excluded from his memoirs). Although Churchill backed off from his threat to split up the Mediterranean, it was a last-gasp attempt to inject a stronger British influence into a war over which he had ceded strategic control to his powerful ally.

On 5 August he arrived at Portsmouth for lunch with Eisenhower to reopen the debate in yet another last-ditch effort to persuade the supreme commander to cancel the Riviera landings and, he said, reap far greater rewards by leaving Alexander's divisions intact for operations in northern Italy and Yugoslavia. Their meeting consumed some six hours, and the more Churchill cajoled and pleaded, the more strongly Eisenhower resisted. His aide noted, 'Ike said no, continued saying no all afternoon, and ended saying no in every form of the English language at his command . . . Ike's position was that sound strategy called for making the Germans fight on as many fronts as possible . . . Ike argued so long and patiently that he was practically limp when the PM departed.'

Those for and against the landings formed strange alliances. The only leading Briton favouring them was Admiral Bertram Ramsay; arrayed with Churchill in opposition, holding that they were unnecessary and ought be cancelled, were Eisenhower's own chief of staff, Bedell Smith, and his close friend ABC Cunningham. Eisenhower stood firm in the knowledge that he had the full backing of Marshall, King and Arnold, and – most important of all – of Roosevelt. 'I will not repeat not under any conditions agree . . . to a cancellation of Dragoon . . . I have never wavered for a moment,' he stubbornly informed Marshall, who told Dill, 'Only over my dead body will you get a change of outlook.'

It hardly mattered that only the previous day, before visiting Eisenhower, and a mere eleven days before the landings, Churchill had attempted to alter Dragoon by signalling the US chiefs of staff to propose a last-minute shift of the operation from the Riviera to Brittany, whose ports were still in German hands; several of these ports would hold out until the end in May 1945. The folly of attempting to shift a large-scale operation beyond the reach of air cover and its base of operations to German-held Brittany was apparently lost on the prime minister, whose proposal was opposed by Eisenhower and rejected by Roosevelt. With only a week left before the date of the landings, Churchill appeared finally to have caved in, cabling the president, 'I pray God that you may be right.'

Yet on 9 August the debate resumed at No. 10, where Eisenhower was obliged to endure a fresh Churchill harangue as the impassioned prime minister declared that the Americans were 'bullying' the British and, having become 'a big strong and dominating partner', were failing to listen to the strategic ideas of their ally. Therefore 'he might have to go to the Monarch and "lay down the mantle of my high office".' For more than two years Eisenhower had experienced every variation of Churchill's wiles, and he recognized at once that the prime minister was bluffing and refused to budge. Two days later he wrote to Churchill to reassure him that 'I do not for one moment believe that there is any desire on the part of any responsible person in the American war machine to disregard British views, or cold-bloodedly to leave Britain holding an empty bag in any of our joint undertakings.'

Despite Eisenhower's affirmation of their strong personal relationship, nothing could mask the fact that Britain was now irretrievably the junior partner in the alliance it had once dominated. Their differences notwithstanding, the great debate between the irresistible force and the immovable object was at last mercifully ended. When Ismay came to dinner on the day of the Riviera landings, he and Eisenhower could look back on the American general's draining experience with Churchill with humour, much like 'two admiring sons discussing a cantankerous yet adorable father'.

In light of the Allies' later failure to secure the port of Antwerp, which did not become operational on their behalf until December 1944, Eisenhower's refusal to cancel Dragoon proved prophetic. The destruction wrought by the Transportation Plan did not include the French railway system in the Rhône Valley, and the great port of Marseille not only was captured undamaged but became a logistical bonanza and a primary means of resupplying Eisenhower's armies during the autumn and winter of 1944–5.

On 15 August two thousand Allied ships bearing 151,000 American, British, Canadian and French soldiers appeared off the Côte d'Azur, the largest such force ever to sail the Mediterranean. Nice, Saint-Tropez, Cannes and the other plush resorts that lined the Riviera coastline, once noted for their expensive yachts and amenities fit for royalty, became the landing sites for what has been called 'the other D-day'. Their formerly immaculate beaches were now fortified with pillboxes, gun emplacements, mines, booby traps and underwater metal stakes.

Churchill had left London on 10 August for an extended visit to Italy and the Mediterranean: his antipathy to the landings was not sufficient reason for him to miss a great military operation. On the morning of the 15th he witnessed from the deck of the destroyer HMS *Kimberley* what he had been denied in June in Normandy. He was still asleep when the landings commenced, but he later appeared on deck, a cigar in his mouth. American GIs on nearby landing craft recognized him and cheered, 'Winnie! Winnie!' They had no inkling that, if Churchill had had his way, none of them would have been there that day. Unyielding to the end, he wrote to Clementine, 'One of my reasons for making public my visit was to associate myself with this well-conducted but irrelevant and unrelated operation.' His scornful opinion of Dragoon notwithstanding, he was disappointed that he had not boarded a landing craft to gain a better view of the landings. 'I could have gone with perfect safety very much nearer the actual beaches.' He had to admit that the invasion was flawlessly carried out, 'like a piece of clock-work'. Too flawlessly – he eventually found the landings boring and retired to his cabin to read a novel. Eisenhower merely breathed a sigh of relief that he had survived yet another trial by fire from the obstinate prime minister.

After watching the Riviera landings Churchill travelled to Italy to confer with Alexander, inspect troops of several nations and swim in the Blue Grotto on Capri and in the Bay of Naples. Dressed in a semi-uniform complete with decorations on his left breast pocket, binoculars, cane, pith helmet and the ever present cigar, and accompanied by Alexander, he became a familiar figure in a number of front-line units. He visited Cassino, pulled the lanyard to fire a round from a howitzer and everywhere went as close to the front as the generals would permit. His headquarters was a comfortable villa in the medieval Tuscan city of Siena not far from Alexander's headquarters. His occupancy included sharing space with an invasion of hornets one night at dinner, and a resident mouse that 'with unfailing regularity ... took up its position every night on a curtain rod in the drawing-room and sat for hours surveying the Prime Minister with close interest'. Nevertheless his resentment over the withdrawal of Allied forces for Dragoon remained like a festering sore.

He also visited his old regiment, the 4th Hussars, shortly before it was committed to the battle for the Gothic Line. After he had landed with Alexander at an airfield near the Adriatic coastal city of Ancona and began advancing towards where the regiment was lined up to greet him, Churchill came to an anti-tank ditch that was part of the airfield's defences. Undaunted, 'he plunged down into it to the obvious distaste of Field Marshal Alexander, who was, as always, elegantly attired. Nevertheless Alexander ... and various aides-de-camp followed. It was just as well, for when the Prime Minister attempted to climb *out* of the anti-tank ditch, he found it beyond his powers and only combined heaving at his not inconsiderable posterior by the Commander-in-Chief and other lesser military mortals succeeded in extricating him.' The unabashed Churchill proceeded with his inspection, and then summoned everyone to gather around while he stood atop a jeep and delivered a well-received pep talk.

His Italian trip stirred renewed hope of a thrust by Alexander through the Italian Alps to capture Vienna. In a telegram to Smuts he complained that the stagnating advance in northern Italy was the result of the weakening of the Allied forces in Italy. Removing troops for Dragoon had permitted the Germans to withdraw and send to France three divisions 'which would not have happened if we had continued our advance here in the direction of the Po and ultimately on the great city [Vienna] ... Even if the war comes to a sudden end there is no reason why our armour should not slip through and reach it as we can.' Although Brooke opposed Dragoon, he saw the folly of an attempted thrust to Vienna and thought that both Churchill and Alexander were naively optimistic. On 23 June he had pointed out that the earliest a campaign could be mounted would be some time in the winter of 1944–5. 'It was hard to make him realize that if we took the season of the year and the topography of the country in league against us we should have 3 enemies instead of one.' Capturing Vienna was a visionary idea, but was unlikely to be achieved. The Ljubljana Gap, which the Allies would have to traverse, was easily defended along virtually impassable roads in the dead of winter.

The 26th August marked the start of a new Allied offensive, and Churchill was eager to see it for himself. 'I took him right up to the front line,' said Alexander. 'You could see the tanks moving up and firing and the machine guns in action a few hundred yards ahead of us. It fascinated him – the real warrior at heart.' Of his day at the front Churchill later remarked that it was 'the nearest I got to the enemy and the time I heard the most bullets in the Second World War'.

Alexander confided to Lord Moran that it was important to keep Churchill cheerful, adding that when he was not depressed he made good things happen. 'The Prime Minister', he said, 'knows so much about our job that he was the first to see that we should be well on our way to Vienna if only the Americans would be sensible.' The long days and nights together in August 1944 cemented the deep feelings each man had for the other. Moran saw it as a courtship in which Alexander went out of his way to accommodate Churchill, to bring in those he most wanted to meet and to keep him happy by frequent trips to the front: 'Alex knows his man. The P.M. never tires of playing at soldiers – the nearer the real thing the better. This grim expedition, he said, had helped him to grasp more clearly how we were winning the war ... Alex's little plot has been laid with great care, but in any case it was bound to succeed. The P.M. can never say no to Alex, whatever he asks; he keeps a place for him in his heart, apart from the others.'

Eisenhower was not the only Allied commander in the prime minister's doghouse in the summer of 1944. Montgomery ran into trouble in Normandy for instilling false hopes in the minds of Churchill, Eisenhower and the other senior commanders that he would capture Caen on D-day. Bitter German resistance stalled the Allies on both flanks of the Normandy bridgehead, and advances, whether measured in yards or miles, were paid for in blood. The build-up of troops and supplies was seriously impeded when one of the most severe storms in forty years lashed Normandy on 19 June. Nearly eight hundred ships were either beached or lost, and the American Mulberry artificial harbour off Omaha beach was destroyed and never replaced. What has been called the 'Great Storm' virtually shut down the war for three days and destroyed more shipping than the Germans had during the entire campaign. Losses in matériel amounted to more than 140,000 tons. Omaha Beach was strewn with the carcasses of ships lying on their sides in the sand, victims of nature's unforgiving fury.

Its effects on manpower were equally dire. Before the storm the strength of the British Second Army was already behind schedule, and the gap increased to three divisions by the time the storm finally abated on 22 June. 'I thank the gods of war that we went when we did,' said Eisenhower, relieved that he had not postponed D-day until the next full moon on 19 June. Churchill lamented to Eisenhower, 'They have no right to give us weather like this.' Ike's son, John, a newly commissioned West Point graduate, witnessed the exchange and remembers thinking 'that Churchill and General George Patton had an attitude in common. Dedicated to their respective missions, each seemed to feel that the Almighty had an obligation – a personal obligation – to render all necessary assistance to their accomplishments.'

Once the storm had passed, the enormous build-up of troops and supplies resumed, but there was little forward progress and as the campaign edged into July the pivotal city of Caen still held out, a symbol to Montgomery's critics of everything that had gone wrong with the campaign. Indeed, by D+30 days there was every sign of a stalemate on both flanks of the Allied bridgehead. High up the chain of command nerves became frayed and sharp words were uttered that it was all Montgomery's fault. It had apparently never dawned on him that his promise on 15 May would be used as a wedge by his enemies, primarily Tedder and Coningham, his old nemeses from the desert, in an attempt to rid themselves of the general they detested. Politically, stalemate in Normandy was a worrying possibility for Churchill that would have given Hitler an enormous bargaining chip in any negotiations to end the war and left all of western Europe vulnerable to conquest by the Red Army.

In mid-July, Montgomery launched Operation Goodwood, a massive tank offensive south-east of Caen. Designed to break the German defences on the Allied left flank and permit a thrust down the open plain beyond to

Falaise, Goodwood failed, and although the German army paid a terrible price in blood carrying out Hitler's orders to stand and fight to the death, the stalemate effectively continued on the eastern flank. Goodwood also created the worst crisis yet in Anglo-American relations by providing ammunition to Montgomery's critics at SHAEF and in London: that he had needlessly forfeited yet another opportunity to win a decisive battle and should be sacked. Although Eisenhower was under pressure to dismiss Montgomery, he declined to accept Churchill's standing offer to remove any British commander who did not measure up.

Churchill made his second visit to Normandy on 20 July, the same day that Colonel Count Claus von Stauffenberg's bomb wounded but failed to kill Hitler in his underground bunker at Rastenburg. The trip was preceded by a nasty spat with Brooke after Montgomery had asked Eisenhower to keep visitors away from his HQ. In so doing so he had Churchill primarily in mind, wanting to be free from the distractions that were invariably accompaniments of a visit by the prime minister. When Churchill learned of it he exploded in 'an ungodly rage!' and demanded of Brooke, 'What was Monty doing dictating to him, he had every right to visit France whenever he wanted . . . He would not stand it. He would make it a matter of confidence.' Alarmed by the pickle Montgomery had inadvertently got himself into, Brooke flew at once to Normandy and had him draft a note to Churchill stating that he had not known of his wish to visit and was pleased to invite him. When he received Montgomery's note all the sound and fury quickly evaporated. He telephoned Brooke to say how pleased he was with the letter 'and felt rather ashamed of himself for all he had said!! . . . What a storm in a teacup.'

During his Normandy visit Churchill inspected the British Mulberry, slept aboard the light cruiser HMS *Enterprise*, visited various air and ground units and was taken on a hedgehopping aerial tour by Air Vice Marshal Harry Broadhurst (the British tactical air commander) in his personal captured Fiesler Storch observation aircraft. Ismay and Commander Thompson carried out their own tour and were taken to task by Churchill when he learned that they had been closer to the front lines than he had.

Churchill wisely never permitted himself to be drawn into the intrigue over Montgomery, and there is no evidence that he ever considered sacking him.

*

After more than two months of bitter and bloody fighting in Normandy the Germans finally broke. On the western flank at the end of July, Lieutenant General Omar Bradley initiated Operation Cobra and US forces spearheaded by Patton's Third Army broke the back of the German defences and poured through a gap at Avranches. With the Third Army loose on the plains of southern Normandy, Montgomery launched an offensive to capture Falaise. Hitler played directly into Allied hands by ordering an ill-conceived and ruinous counter-offensive against the US First Army at Mortain. Paris was liberated and the German commander surrendered the city on 25 August, thus fulfilling Churchill's fervent hope to see it free well before the first snowfall. Also by late August the bulk of the German army in Normandy had been either killed or captured. Only remnants escaped across the River Seine, most with only whatever equipment and weapons they could carry on their backs.

The great victory in Normandy sent Allied spearheads into Lorraine and Belgium. Hitler had lost over a million men on both the eastern and the western fronts, including three hundred thousand killed, wounded or missing in France, while the war at sea was all but lost. Until the supplies ran out, and the four Allied armies ground to a halt a few weeks later, the war seemed nearly over. Only Churchill seems not to have been taken in by the razzle-dazzle, warning that the future remained uncertain. 'It is at least as likely that Hitler will be fighting on the 1st January [1945] as that he will collapse before then. If he does collapse before then, the reasons will be political rather than purely military.'

On 1 September Eisenhower assumed command and direction of the ground war from Montgomery, a decision greeted by the British press as a national slap in the face and only partly assuaged when Churchill announced Montgomery's promotion to field marshal. Eisenhower's post-Normandy strategy called for a broad advance by the Allied armies into Germany, and despite strong British protests he rejected outright Montgomery's plan for what he termed a single 'full-blooded' thrust towards the Ruhr industrial complex. Brussels was liberated by the British Second Army on 3 September but neither its commander, Lieutenant General Miles Dempsey, nor Montgomery ordered the capture of the vital Scheldt estuary, which remained in German hands, thus preventing the opening of the great port of Antwerp. The weeks that followed saw a return to the sort of painfully slow, bloody warfare fought in Normandy as German units heeded Hitler's order to fight to the bitter end to prevent Antwerp from becoming an Allied staging area for the final battle for Germany.

The original Allied blueprint for fighting the war in north-west Europe was predicated on an orderly German retreat across Normandy, and a solid defence of the Seine river line, not a rout such as had occurred as a result of the great American breakout from the Cotentin Peninsula at the end of July 1944 by the First and Third US Armies and the sudden entrapment of Field Marshal Günther von Kluge's Army Group B in the Falaise pocket. Stunning as the Allied victory in Normandy was, there no longer existed the luxury of a pause at the Seine while the Allied armies regrouped, advanced their logistical bases further forward and made plans to resume offensive operations towards Germany. From the North Sea to the Swiss border, British, Canadian, Polish and American forces had advanced as many as five hundred miles from their sources of supply, most of which were still located near the Normandy beaches.

The acrimonious debates over strategy in the late summer and early autumn of 1944 were largely a reflection of the fact that the Allied campaign was now more logistical than tactical. The voracious appetite of the increasing numbers of Allied divisions and support troops dictated what could be accomplished on the battlefield. Lost in the great debates over strategy in the ensuing half-century and more is the truth that the broad-versus-narrow-front argument between Eisenhower and Montgomery was a conflict of ideologies over the best way to win the war rather than a clash of personalities.

On Sunday, 17 September the Allies launched the most daring military operation of the war. Dubbed Market Garden, it employed three airborne divisions and ground forces to gain a bridgehead across the Rhine at Arnhem. If successful, it would mean that the heavily defended Siegfried Line could be bypassed and Germany could be invaded where it was most vulnerable, perhaps finishing the war by the end of 1944. The British 1st Airborne Division was dropped at Arnhem; however, Allied intelligence failed to heed reports from the Dutch underground that a German panzer corps was bivouacked near by. The 1st Airborne was quickly pinned down in the town and Lieutenant Colonel John Frost's 2nd Parachute Battalion was the only British unit to reach and secure the vital Arnhem Bridge, where it awaited relief from a ground force that was to link up with it.

The success of the operation hinged on the ability of the British XXX Corps to relieve the lightly armed airborne troops by rapidly advancing from Eindhoven along the only highway to Arnhem. Two US airborne divisions were dropped along the route to secure other vital bridges over the Meuse, and over the Waal at Nijmegen. The ground force encountered heavy resistance, and before it could reach the Rhine the Germans recaptured Arnhem Bridge, where Frost's paratroopers had gallantly held out for four days before being overwhelmed and compelled to surrender.

By 25 September the operation had failed. Of the ten thousand men who had landed at Arnhem on the 17th, fourteen hundred had been killed and more than six thousand taken prisoner. The 1st Airborne ceased to exist as a fighting unit. Although the heroic stand of Frost's battalion at Arnhem Bridge was one of the legendary episodes of the Second World War, the Allies failed to establish their objective of a bridgehead north of the Rhine, in what has come to be known as 'a bridge too far'. Operation Market Garden thus became mythologized as the latest example of the incongruous British practice of turning military disasters such as Dunkirk into glorious occasions.

The chief supporter of this myth was Churchill, who learned the news on 26 September, the day he returned to Britain aboard the *Queen Mary* from the second Quebec Conference. The heroics at Arnhem Bridge appealed to his romanticized view of war. After Smuts had telegraphed with condolences over the failure of Market Garden, Churchill immediately replied: 'I think you have got Arnhem a little out of focus. The battle was a decided victory . . . I have not been afflicted by any feeling of disappointment over this and am glad our commanders are capable of running this kind of risk.'

Neither the brave British paratroopers nor the Polish Parachute Brigade, which fought to save them, would ever have conceded that Arnhem was anything but a tragedy. Montgomery's later claim that 90 per cent of Market Garden's objectives had been attained was as meaningless as Churchill's claim of victory. Without a bridgehead over the Rhine, Montgomery's narrow front died ingloriously, leaving in its wake the stark reality that any prospect of ending the war in 1944 had been lost.

60

Victory

The mission of this Allied Force was fulfilled at 0241, local time, May 7th, 1945.
– Eisenhower

For the remainder of the war Churchill's role as warlord remained largely inconsequential. The military effort was firmly in the grasp of Dwight Eisenhower, who was calling shots that Churchill did not always approve of but could do little to change. On the occasions when he attempted to outflank Eisenhower by appealing directly to Roosevelt, he was rebuffed. A good deal of his frustration revolved around Britain's loss of empire and the secondary role now being played by the British army. 'The only times I quarrel with the Americans are when they fail to give us a fair share of opportunity to win glory,' he wrote on 6 April 1945 to Clementine, who was in Russia on an extensive five-week goodwill tour in her capacity as head of the Red Cross Aid to Russia Fund. 'Undoubtedly I feel much pain when I see our armies so much smaller than theirs. It has always been my wish to keep equal, but how can you do that against so mighty a nation?'

While many began to see that the war was virtually over, Churchill's prediction came true in the autumn of 1944. The German army may have been in complete disarray and seemingly without hope, its losses breathtaking, having escalated to 900,000 on the eastern front and another 450,000 in the west, but there remained some 3.4 million troops, more than a million of whom were to be committed by Hitler to the defence of the Reich on the western front.

What ultimately ensured that there would be no victory in 1944 stems from the very makeup of the Anglo-American coalition. Had the United States allied itself with a smaller and weaker partner, Eisenhower might have felt justified in a single-thrust military operation in the autumn of

1944, but so long as Winston Churchill led Britain, such a decision was unimaginable. Nevertheless both Montgomery and Churchill had disagreeable but unmistakable evidence that this was now an American-dominated war and that they were virtually powerless to influence its outcome. The real beneficiaries of the Allied blunders of September 1944 at Antwerp and Arnhem were Adolf Hitler and his beleaguered but as yet unbeaten army.

By autumn it was clear the war would extend into 1945. The Allied armies advanced but were eventually stalled on the border of the Reich by a combination of increasingly foul weather and intensified German resistance. In early December, Eisenhower cabled Churchill that he and Tedder were coming to London and would like to provide an update on SHAEF's situation and current plans. Brooke's diary recorded that the meeting took place in Churchill's map room on 12 December where 'Ike explained his plan which contemplates a double advance into Germany, north of [the] Rhine and by Frankfurt. I disagreed flatly with it and accused Ike of violating principles of concentration of force, which had resulted in his present failures . . . discovered that Ike now does not hope to cross the Rhine before May [1945]!' Brooke was so disheartened that, not for the first time, he 'seriously' considered resigning. 'I feel I have utterly failed to do what is required.'

Churchill seemed distracted and despite his impassioned arguments declined to back Brooke. The following day he meekly explained to the CIGS that he felt obliged to support Eisenhower, 'as he was one American against five of us with only Tedder to support him. And also he was his guest. I think he felt I had been rather rough on Ike.' But he had been sufficiently alarmed by Brooke to convene a meeting of the War Cabinet the following day. Although the 'date of May [1945] for the crossing of the Rhine had a profound effect on the Cabinet', noted Brooke, there was little the British could do to influence the course of events in Europe.

In a gloomy telegram to Roosevelt, Churchill complained of his disappointment and anxiety over the failure of the Allied armies to drive to the Rhine and the lack of progress in Italy, which he blamed on 'the weakening of our forces for the sake of "Dragoon" . . . the escape home of a large part of the German forces from the Balkan peninsula [and] frustration in Burma'.

Roosevelt did not share Churchill's pessimism and reminded him, 'We

are winning on every front of our global battleline except in China . . .
Our agreed broad strategy is developing according to plan. You and I
are in the positions of our Commanders in Chief who have prepared
their plans, issued their orders, and committed all of their resources to
battle according to those plans and orders. For the time being, it seems
to me the prosecution of the war and the outcome of battles lie with
our field commanders, in whom I have every confidence.' Despite the
'exasperating delays', the situation was 'now brighter than it has been
for some time'.

On 16 December 1944, in an all-out gamble to compel the Allies to sue
for peace, Hitler ordered the only major German counter-offensive of
the war in north-west Europe by three armies (more than a quarter of a
million troops). Its objective was to split the Allied armies by means
of a surprise blitzkrieg thrust through the rugged, heavily forested
Ardennes to Antwerp, marking a repeat of what the Germans had done
twice previously – in August 1914 and May 1940. Despite Germany's
historical penchant for mounting counter-offensives when things
looked darkest, the US commander, Bradley, miscalculated and left the
Ardennes lightly defended by only two inexperienced and two battered
American divisions.

The once quiet forest became bedlam as American units fought desperate battles to stem the German advance at St Vith, Elsenborn Ridge,
Houffalize and, later, Bastogne, where the 101st Airborne Division was
surrounded, its commander issuing a one-word refusal to surrender that
has become a symbol of defiance: 'Nuts!' As the German armies drove
deeper into the Ardennes in an attempt quickly to secure vital bridgeheads west of the River Meuse, the line defining the Allied front on the
map took on the appearance of a large protrusion or bulge, the name
by which the battle would forever be known.

The northern half of the Bulge was chaotic, and on 18 December
Eisenhower made the courageous decision to appoint Montgomery to
take command and restore order over what was a predominantly
American sector. The Germans' shortage of crucial fuel and the gallantry
of American troops in the frozen Ardennes proved fatal to Hitler's
ambition somehow to snatch, if not victory, at least a draw. Patton's
remarkable feat of turning his Third Army from Lorraine to relieve
the besieged town of Bastogne was the key to thwarting the German

counter-offensive. Before the Bulge was finally sealed on 16 January 1945, the battles that raged for six weeks in the Ardennes were among the bitterest and bloodiest of any fought in the West. Casualties on both sides were appallingly high. The Battle of the Bulge earned the dubious distinction of being the costliest battle ever fought by the US army, which suffered more than one hundred thousand casualties.

As Eisenhower contemplated the forthcoming invasion of Germany, the lingering arguments from the previous year resumed. Hitler misread the Allies' will to continue on the offensive, believing he would be given a respite that would enable him to reinforce the crumbling eastern front. Eisenhower, however, had no intention of easing up and was determined to pursue the advantage by attacking across the same broad front he had created the previous September.

Eisenhower's broad-front strategy, the autumn stalemate and the Battle of the Bulge all produced a chorus of criticism and distrust in Britain. For Eisenhower it was merely the latest example of the growing and now blatant British scepticism about him since he had assumed command of the land battle from Montgomery. What had once been subtle criticism now bordered on open contempt. Churchill, who had just been to France to visit the headquarters of both commanders, poured oil on troubled waters by sending Roosevelt a glowing endorsement of Eisenhower on 6 January 1945. 'CIGS and I have passed the last two days with Eisenhower and Montgomery and they both feel the battle very heavy but are confident of success. I hope you understand that, in case any troubles should arise in the press, His Majesty's Government have complete confidence in General Eisenhower and feel acutely any attacks made on him. He and Montgomery are very closely knit and also Bradley and Patton, and it would be disaster which broke up this combination . . . [that] has, in nineteen forty-four, yielded us results beyond the dreams of military avarice . . . I have a feeling this is a time for an intense new impulse, both of friendship and exertion, to be drawn from our bosoms and to the last scrap of our resources.'

Churchill's peace offering to FDR notwithstanding, British criticism of Eisenhower reached a new high during the prime minister's visit, when, for the first time, Alexander's name surfaced as a possible replacement for Tedder as the deputy supreme commander. Aware of Eisenhower's rapport with Alexander, Churchill cleverly used the occasion to put forth an ill-conceived plan to replace Tedder. Churchill believed that Alexander's mere presence at SHAEF would inevitably lead to the creation of a British general in the *de facto* role of ground commander in chief.

Eisenhower did not refuse Alexander outright but implied that, if Churchill carried out the plan, he would not change the present command structure. Not only would there be no ground commander, but Alexander might find his new duties 'of less influence than he should properly have'. The letter was a bombshell and it detonated when Brooke informed Churchill that Eisenhower proposed 'to employ Alex in the back areas if he comes to him as a Deputy!' In the end the scheme simply faded away. Montgomery was in favour of leaving the Allied team unchanged, and Brooke was satisfied that no change was needed. Only Churchill was miffed, but he glossed over it by remarking that transferring Alexander would merely be 'a waste of Field Marshal Alexander's military gifts and experience'.

Churchill was not at all happy with the situation in the Far East. His goal was to ensure that British colonies would return to British rule after the war, particularly Singapore, which had become a thorn in his side after its humiliating loss in 1942. 'The British contribution to the recapture of our Empire is minute,' he complained to the chiefs on 6 July 1944. 'The shame of our disaster at Singapore could ... be wiped out by our recapture of that fortress.' However, he had no real leverage over what was primarily an American theatre of war. Roosevelt was already on record about granting Philippine independence and was against the return of Indo-China to France. Churchill ran into opposition to his plan to recapture the tip of northern Sumatra as a stepping-stone to Singapore and to increase the British offensive presence in Burma. When the chiefs pointed out that Britain did not have sufficient forces to deploy to the Far East until the war in Europe ended, they met fierce opposition and bitter recriminations. But what Churchill could not alter was a critical drain on British fighting manpower that simply could not be remedied. The barrel had been nearly emptied in supporting the primary campaigns in the Middle East, Italy and western Europe. Moreover, his dreams of great British victories in the Far East in 1945 were washed away on the borders of Germany at the end of 1944, with the war in Burma contributing nothing to the final victory over Japan.

There was one final tempest over command before the war ended. Montgomery's protégé and replacement as Eighth Army commander was Lieutenant General Sir Oliver Leese. Like Alexander, Leese was a Guards officer with extensive command and combat experience. In September 1944 he was appointed commander in chief of Allied Land Forces South-East Asia, where he violated the age-old tenet 'If it ain't broke, don't fix it.'

Lieutenant General Sir William Slim was one the most effective but least-known British commanders of the war. He took command of the Fourteenth Army in October 1943 and turned it into a highly effective fighting force that recaptured Rangoon and defeated the Japanese army in Burma. Leese foolishly decided to relieve the popular Slim and replace him with an officer of his own choosing. During the subsequent uproar there were threats of mutiny and mass resignation by many of Slim's officers. Mountbatten, the supreme commander, declined to back Leese, and a short time later the order was reversed. Slim survived and was promoted to full general, and at the end of June 1945 it was Leese who was sacked.

Although Slim is regarded as Britain's most outstanding army commander of the Second World War, Churchill barely knew who he was, an indication of how in the final stages of the war he tended to pay scant attention to the war in Burma. When Slim launched a daring and enormously successful offensive in November 1944 around Imphal and Kohima to reopen the Burma Road and oust the Japanese from central Burma, neither a tired, inattentive Churchill nor Brooke showed the slightest sign of the usual angst that preceded a major military operation.

Any doubts that there would be an easy resolution to the war were erased when the Big Three met at the Crimean resort city of Yalta in early February 1945 and reiterated their long-standing demand to accept only unconditional surrender. Churchill and a seriously ailing Roosevelt, who had only weeks to live, agreed on the partitioning of Germany, which included the establishment of four zones of occupation – French, American, British and Russian – when the war ended. In return for a Russian commitment to join the war against Japan, the borders of eastern Europe were realigned. Stalin's assurances of free elections in the liberated nations of eastern Europe proved worthless, leading to what Churchill later called in his 1946 Fulton, Missouri, speech an 'iron curtain' descending across the Continent, separating the West from the sphere of Soviet domination. In the aftermath of Yalta, Soviet betrayal of the accords was imminent. Anthony Eden foretold the future when he exclaimed in dismay, 'My God, what a mess Europe is in! What a mess!' The Big Three communiqué spelling out that post-war Germany was to be dismembered merely reinforced Hitler's intention to fight to the bitter end rather than surrender.

At Yalta, John Martin noted the changes in Churchill. As he reported to Lord Moran, the quality of his work had deteriorated in recent months. 'He had got very wordy and bored the Cabinet by talking the whole time. Martin said one subject would get into his mind and he could think of nothing else. He would talk for hours . . . [and] sit up half the night over papers and documents and then have to do it all over again in the morning.' As his attention flagged so too did his energy.

Despite his physical and mental weariness, to the end of the war Churchill continued to visit battlefields, as if drawn by some magnetic force to danger. His fearlessness was never in doubt, but as always the difference between courage and imprudence was often indistinguishable. By routinely sticking his neck out, he apparently failed to recognize that he was too important to become just another casualty of war.

By March 1945 Eisenhower was commanding the largest Allied force ever assembled: nearly 4 million US, British and Canadian troops in three army groups, seven field armies, twenty-one corps and seventy-three divisions were poised to launch the final offensive that would finish off Nazi Germany and end the war. By VE (Victory in Europe) Day these numbers would grow to 4.5 million and ninety-one divisions.

Churchill witnessed the launching of Operation Plunder on the night of 23 March. This was Montgomery's long-awaited blitz-like offensive to secure bridgeheads across the Rhine; it included an airborne and glider operation by two parachute divisions. More than two thousand guns had been assembled to fire on targets that were also plastered by hundreds of RAF bombers. It was the largest military operation since D-day, involving nearly a million troops, and has been criticized as the most overrated offensive of the war. Among a bevy of war correspondents and spectators were Churchill, Brooke and Eisenhower, who arrived at Lieutenant General William Simpson's Ninth US Army headquarters to view the night assault. Churchill was ebullient as he and

Eisenhower watched the display of Allied might. 'My dear General, the German is whipped,' he exulted. 'We've got him. He is all through.'

George S. Patton and Winston Churchill had more in common than merely being tough-minded warriors. Each man had an almost pathological desire to express his contempt for Adolf Hitler in the most impertinent manner possible: Patton by pissing in the Rhine, Churchill by pissing on the Siegfried Line.

Churchill managed the feat on 26 March. Shortly before lunch Brooke saw him strolling a considerable distance away to the banks of the Rhine, where he solemnly relieved himself in the river, his second symbolic gesture of contempt for Adolf Hitler. From a distance Brooke 'felt certain that on his face was that same boyish grin of contentment that I had seen at the Siegfried Line', where three weeks before he had indulged his boyish fantasy of symbolically pissing on Hitler.

During his visit to witness Plunder, Churchill was once again exhilarated at being in close proximity to the guns of war. Brooke recounts how, when Churchill was returning from a visit to Montgomery's HQ, his motor car halted at a bridge over the Rhine, where there were still enemy snipers and artillery. Although the bridge was partially collapsed and boarded over to prevent anyone from venturing on to it, 'Winston at once started scrambling along for some 40 yards . . . Shells began to fall about 100 yards upstream of us. We decided that it was time to remove the PM who was thrilled with the situation and reluctant to leave!' After the war Brooke added a more vivid picture of a scene in which his host, General Simpson, pleaded, ' "Prime Minister, there are snipers in front of you, they are shelling both sides of the bridge, and now they have started shelling the road behind you . . . I must ask you to come away." The look on Winston's face was just like that of a small boy being called away from his sandcastles on the beach by his nurse! He put both his arms round one of the twisted girders of the bridge, and looked over his shoulder at Simpson with pouting mouth and angry eyes! . . . It was a sad wrench for him, he was enjoying himself immensely.'

Churchill's final bitter controversy of the Second World War in Europe was his opposition to the decision by Eisenhower not to advance the Allied armies beyond the Elbe river to capture Berlin. At the time of this decision the four occupation zones of Germany had already been settled. In September 1944, at Quebec, the United States and Britain had approved some of the provisions of the plan – first drawn up in early 1944 by the European Advisory Commission. The real problem was not Berlin but the occupation zones of Germany, which left the German capital a virtual island deep in the Soviet zone – a fact Eisenhower was helpless to alter.

Thus Berlin had already slipped through the crack. Roosevelt thought the Soviets ought to be given a fair chance to implement the Yalta accords and was reluctant to challenge Stalin over Berlin. And when Churchill raised the issue of an Allied race for Berlin, he was soundly rebuffed. The president had been urged by Marshall not to interfere with Eisenhower, and wholeheartedly rejected any attempt to compromise his authority. Marshall and the US chiefs saw little value in making Berlin an objective with the Red Army nearly at its eastern gates. Moreover, with the war against Japan as yet far from won, the United States was anxious to end the war in Europe and begin deploying troops home, and to the Pacific.

Churchill's Balkan strategy of sending Alexander's armies through the so-called Ljubljana Gap and into the plains of the Danube to Vienna had long since been rejected by the United States, and British concerns over Berlin were consigned to the same dustbin. Although Churchill protested that the Allies' failure to take Berlin would 'raise grave and formidable difficulties in the future', Roosevelt endorsed Eisenhower's decision to halt at the Elbe. Churchill and Eisenhower exchanged feisty telegrams over Berlin. Churchill argued fruitlessly that its capture represented 'the supreme signal of defeat to the German people'. When he expressed dismay that His Majesty's forces would be relegated 'to an unexpectedly restricted sphere', Eisenhower replied that he was 'disturbed, if not hurt, that you should suggest any thought on my part to "relegate His Majesty's forces" . . . Nothing is further from my mind.' Exasperated, Churchill turned to Brooke and declared, 'There is only one thing worse than fighting with allies, and that is fighting without them!'

Churchill's entreaties failed either to sway Roosevelt or to alter Eisenhower's intention to halt at the Elbe. Still unwilling to concede defeat, he telegraphed Roosevelt to express the British government's complete confidence in and admiration for Eisenhower. However, 'as the truest friends and comrades that ever fought side by side as allies . . . I say quite frankly that Berlin remains of high strategic importance.' The following day he cabled Eisenhower, 'I deem it highly important that we should shake hands with the Russians as far east as possible.'

On 5 April he again wrote to Roosevelt. He closed with 'one of my very few Latin quotations'. It read: 'Amantium irae amoris integratio est,' which evoked smiles when someone in the War Department translated the phrase and sent it to Eisenhower: 'Lovers' quarrels are a part of love.'

On 25 April 1945 a US infantry division made contact with the Red Army at the Elbe, and in one of the epic moments of the war the eastern and western fronts were joined. Although the end was now only a matter of days, if not hours, away, Churchill was bitterly disappointed at being shut out of the grand finale.

As the Allies swept aside the last resistance in Germany, Alexander's forces broke the winter stalemate on the Gothic Line that had confined them to the Apennines and breached the River Po. Both Germany and Italy now lay in ruins. The remnants of Kesselring's once defiant Army Group C were in full retreat towards the Alps. The end came on 4 May, when the Germans in Italy surrendered unconditionally.

Neither of the dictators who had wreaked so much misery upon the world lived to account for his actions. Mussolini and his mistress, Clara Petacci, were captured by partisans in northern Italy on 27 April and summarily shot; their bodies were taken to Milan and hung by the heels at an Esso petrol station. In his bunker in Berlin, Hitler and his mistress, Eva Braun, committed suicide on 30 April. Their bodies were burned in a funeral pyre in the chancellery garden in a scene befitting a Wagnerian opera. When Colville brought Churchill the news broadcast over German radio of Hitler's death, his response was surprisingly tepid. 'Well, I must say I think he was perfectly right to die like that.'

At Eisenhower's headquarters in Reims at 2.41 a.m., 7 May 1945, Colonel General Alfred Jodl signed the documents of the Act of Military Surrenders of Nazi Germany. At Stalin's insistence the surrender was to take formal effect the following day, 8 May, in Berlin. At 3.00 a.m. Ismay was awakened by the ringing of his telephone. On the other end was Eisenhower, who said, 'They have signed on the dotted line. It's all over.' Shortly before 5.00 a.m. on the 8th Eisenhower cabled the Combined Chiefs of Staff: 'The mission of this Allied Force was fulfilled at 0241, local time, May 7th, 1945. //signed// Eisenhower.' The war that had been thought unwinnable in the dark days of 1940 was mercifully at an end.

On 7 May Churchill hosted a small luncheon for the chiefs of staff, and for Ismay and Hollis. Before they gathered in the garden of No. 10 for a group photograph, Churchill, recorded Ismay, walked round the table, toasting them as 'the architects of victory' and 'raising his glass to each one of us in turn, and at the end of the toasts, he suddenly paused and pointed up to the ceiling. "This is all very well, gentlemen," he said, "but we mustn't forget the One above." ' None of the chiefs responded in kind, even though Churchill 'had himself put out the tray of glasses and drinks, so that Brooke, Portal, Cunningham and Ismay could celebrate this first news with him.' Ismay's administrative assistant, Joan Bright, wrote 'It was a sad example of human imperceptiveness . . . It is possible they were shy, it is certain they were British, it is probable that they reacted as a committee, a body without a heart, and that each waited for the other to take the initiative. Whatever the reason it was an opportunity missed that the Grand Old Man, who had been the architect of the victory they were marking, did not receive a tribute from his three closest military advisers.' Whatever the reasons, it was a depressing finale to the most important set of relationships of the war. Churchill deserved better.

The 8th of May 1945 was VE Day. The weather was glorious, just as it had been on 10 May 1940. Churchill spent most of the morning in bed polishing his victory speech to the nation, to be delivered over the BBC that afternoon from the cabinet room. Speakers were set up in Parliament Square so that the huge crowd could hear him. Promptly at 3.00 p.m. the voice so familiar to Britons spoke words many thought they would never hear. 'Hostilities will end officially at one minute after midnight to-night . . . The German war is therefore at an end . . . The whole world was combined against the evil-doers, who are now prostrate before us.' Calling for the defeat of Japan, whose 'treachery and greed remains unsubdued', Churchill concluded, 'Advance Britannia! Long live the cause of freedom! God save the King!'

After the broadcast it was time to deliver the formal announcement in the House of Commons. Churchill left No. 10 by the garden gate as his staff lined the path and applauded. His secretary Elizabeth Layton detected tears in his eyes. In Horse Guards Parade he climbed into an open motor car for what would normally have been a brief quarter-mile drive to the House of Commons. But not on this day: the crowds were so dense that the journey took some thirty minutes. When he entered the chamber at 3.30 p.m. Churchill was given a rousing ovation as MPs stood and cheered, waving handkerchiefs and order papers. He smiled, gave a half-bow and read the surrender announcement. 'The House was profoundly moved,' wrote Chips Channon, and after Churchill had 'thanked and blessed the House for all its noble support of him through-out these years', he asked that members should 'now attend the Church of St Margaret's, Westminster, to give humble and reverend thanks to Almighty God for our deliverance from the threat of German domi-nation'. Some wept.

The entire House of Commons, some five hundred strong, decamped into Parliament Square, led by the Speaker and Churchill. As church bells pealed and police struggled to clear the way, they walked slowly through the cheering crowd. During the short service of Thanks-giving conducted by the House chaplain, the names of MPs who had died in the service of Britain were read out. Harold Nicolson was among those who wept, while next to him Nancy Astor sniffed, 'Men are so emotional.'

After they had trooped back to the House and formally adjourned, Churchill made his way towards the smoking room amid loud clapping from the crowd. Suddenly a small boy dashed up to him and said, 'Please, sir, may I have your autograph?' After complying, Churchill ruffled the young man's hair and said: 'This will remind you of a glorious day' – as the crowd clapped even more loudly.

A short time later Churchill, the members of the War Cabinet and the chiefs of staff drove at a snail's pace through the cheering people to Buckingham Palace 'to offer their humble duty to the King and congratu-late him on having vanquished his enemies in Europe'. En route the prime minister lit one of his cigars. 'They expect it!' he merrily told Inspector Thompson.

That evening Churchill appeared on the balcony of the Ministry of Health in Whitehall, where an enormous and enthusiastic crowd had gathered. He congratulated Londoners for their courage and persever-ance and proclaimed that they were celebrating 'not a victory of a party or of a class. It is victory of the great British nation ... We were the first, in this ancient island, to draw the sword against tyranny.' When he declared, 'God bless you all. This is your victory,' there was a deafening reply of 'No – it is yours!' Ernest Bevin, the Minister of Labour, led the crowd in singing 'For He's a Jolly Good Fellow'. The occasion ended with Churchill leading the crowd in singing Elgar's 'Land of Hope and Glory'.

Clementine Churchill was still in Russia on 8 May and deeply disappointed at being unable to share her husband's moment of triumph. From Moscow she sent him a brief telegram that read: 'All my thoughts are with you on this supreme day my darling. It could not have happened without you.'

Postscript

I thank God I was given an opportunity of working alongside of such a man, and of having my eyes opened to the fact that occasionally such supermen exist on this earth. — Brooke

Although Churchill had said in 1940 that he would retire after the war to paint and write, he did not do so. Anthony Eden has recorded: 'Winston reiterated that he was now an old man and that he would not make Lloyd George's mistake of carrying on after the war.' That lesson was ignored in the aftermath of the surrender of Nazi Germany, when Churchill called for a general election to be held on 5 July 1945. He expected a grateful nation to respond accordingly and hardly campaigned. The votes were counted on 26 July after the votes of servicemen overseas had come in, and Clement Attlee's Labour Party had won a landslide victory that swept Churchill from office. By the evening he had tendered his resignation to the king. It was a bitter pill. To the end of his life Churchill remained disillusioned by what he deemed repudiation by the nation he had been instrumental in saving.

Although the Second World War was still continuing in the Pacific, it was largely an American endeavour over which Britain had little influence or control. On 27 July 1945 the British chiefs of staff held their final ceremonial meeting with Churchill before he left office. On this day they arrived at No. 10 at 6.30 p.m. 'to confer for the last time with the man with whom they had experienced so much, at whom they had complained so often, whom they had resisted on occasion so stoutly, whom in the last resort they loved so warmly. They were not adroit at graceful gesture, and at least one onlooker [Ian Jacob] was infuriated at their stiffness. They did not raise a glass to Churchill's health. They had no elegant words of sympathy or affection.'

Brooke recorded that it was 'a very sad and very moving little meeting at which I found myself unable to say much for fear of breaking down'. For three-and-a-half years they had worked together, and fought each other over issues each fervently believed in under unimaginable stress that took an enormous mental and physical toll. Brooke's diary of the war may seem unduly harsh, but in the context of the pressure cooker in which he and those in charge of the war existed, it was an outlet, a safety valve in which he could express his innermost feelings, his triumphs and his torments.

Although neither Brooke nor Churchill managed to express his esteem for the other, Churchill wrote three days later to the CIGS: 'I am deeply grateful for all you have done for me and for the country,' prompting Brooke to write candidly in his diary, 'I shall always look back on the years I worked with him as some of the most difficult and trying ones in my life.' He then went to pay Churchill the supreme compliment. 'For all that, I thank God I was given an opportunity of working alongside of such a man, and of having my eyes opened to the fact that occasionally such supermen exist on this earth.'

In 1958 Sir Leslie Hollis, now a full Royal Marine general, who had lived in Churchill's shadow for the entire war, returned to view 'the Hole' deep beneath Whitehall. The visit brought back a flood of memories of the war and of the beehive of activity that had prevailed in its rooms around the clock for more than five years. He found the place just as it had been left on its last day of operation, 15 August 1945, when a ceasefire in the Pacific took hold. The map room where every action across the planet had been recorded and where coloured pins had been moved around on the great maps that filled the walls was eerily silent. No telephones rang; no men and women scurried through its labyrinth of corridors. The trusted and efficient duty officers who had manned this nerve centre of the war so ably had melted silently away. Even the two clocks that had ticked the seemingly endless days of the war were stopped, their hands frozen at five o'clock.

Until resurrected and opened to the public in 1984 as a lasting tribute to and testament of the war, the place was deserted, a secret, mostly forgotten relic. The cabinet room, where so many important and often stormy decisions had been made, still had the nameplates of the members on the black-baize-covered tables as if they might reconvene at any moment. A pile of unused 'Action This Day' sheets lay in front of Churchill's place; the bucket into which his numerous cigars had been discarded stood empty, its contents no longer a source of extra income for Royal Marine guards. As Hollis recalled somewhat sadly, many of those who had regularly met there were now ghosts. 'Yet in the long, silent corridors, the dim lights still burn ceaselessly under their china shades, like lamps lit in memory of great men and great deeds that changed the world.'

Epilogue:
The Last Farewell – A Look Back

Be to his virtues ever kind and to his faults a little blind.
– Sir Henry Thomas Tizard

At the end of each of our lives there is a summing up by those we leave behind. Just as time has softened the passions of many who fought Churchill over political and military issues during his more than sixty years in public life, assessments of the man have ranged from outright admiration to grudging approval and scathing condemnation. The philosopher Sir Isaiah Berlin was once asked why he praised Churchill so highly, and replied, 'In my view, he saved our lives. No man can claim to have done more than that.' However, Lord Boothby's assessment of Churchill was not untypical: 'I just didn't like him as a person very much. I don't think he was a very nice man. I think he was a very great man . . . I shall always be grateful to him . . . for giving me the chance to serve a raging genius which he was.'

While opinions and assessments of Churchill will continue to be voiced, one conclusion is beyond dispute. It is this: his romantic view of war and his inability to understand various aspects of its prosecution notwithstanding, Churchill nevertheless was the only man in Britain who could have led his nation from the dark hours of defeat with unwavering vision and bulldog tenacity.

As with so much else about Churchill, no examination of his role as warlord can ignore the riddle of his genius and his imperfections. They went hand in hand. From the day he took office on 10 May 1940, he was determined to direct the war within the confines of his own vision of the three Rs : resist, rearm and retaliate. Lord Moran saw Churchill at his best, and at his worst, through the good times and the low moments: 'He had been right about the war, he knew better than anyone what ought to be done and he was determined to do what he thought was best. In that mood Winston did not find it easy to stomach strength and independence of character,' especially those shown by Brooke.

One of Churchill's observations in the first volume of his Second World War memoirs dealt with lessons learned from appeasement and the war that ensued. With the coming of the cold war, he pointed out, 'In their loss of purpose, in their abandonment even of the themes they most sincerely espoused, Britain, France, and most of all, because of their immense power and impartiality, the United States, allowed conditions to be gradually built up which led to the very climax they dreaded most. They have only to repeat the same well-meaning, short-sighted behaviour towards the new problems which in singular resemblance confront us today to bring about a third convulsion from which none may live to tell the tale.' How these words apply to the context of the twenty-first century has yet to be determined.

What remains significant is not an interpretation of Churchill but the model he continues to provide for successive generations of democratic leaders. Although, as A. J. P. Taylor wrote, 'he was often rash and impetuous,' and 'a long catalogue of impatient blunders can be drawn against him . . . the fact remains that he won the Second World War. Perhaps he paid an excessive price, but the British people agreed with Churchill that the price was worth paying.'

The arguments over Churchill and his performance as Britain's warlord endure to this day. Some are hagiography, others revisionism. Much of the criticism levelled against Churchill as a strategist is wholly justified. Nevertheless, for all his love of adventure, of great risk and even greater reward, of the exhilaration of viewing war at first hand or in front of a map, he never regarded war as anything but evil. From the time of Omdurman in 1898 he understood its occasional necessity but condemned its wickedness.

Churchill's passion for all things military never diminished. Sir John Peck tells the story of how, in 1945, when Churchill was out of office and living in Hyde Park Gate, Clementine gave a tea party for children. Peck found Churchill sitting before a fire in a large armchair. In the other chair was Peck's young son in exactly the same posture – legs crossed, sitting back. 'And they were having an earnest discussion about tanks or artillery or something of a military nature. And Churchill was quite gravely answering Michael's questions and taking him exactly as if he was with a grown-up. It was my last glimpse of Churchill.'

Churchill may have felt that he failed to meet his own exceptionally high standards for greatness, but historians and biographers have come to very different conclusions about one of the giants of the twentieth century. The critics and revisionists have provided us with unflattering, sometimes venal portraits of him that emphasize his flaws and his failures. Yet what history can never take away from Winston Churchill was his leadership of Britain in the darkest hours of its history. As a benevolent warlord, he led and others followed. This is what great leaders do – and no one did it better during the course of an astonishing life, a life even more amazing considering Churchill's advanced age during the Second World War. War may be a young man's endeavour, but when he was called upon, Churchill responded against phenomenal odds. Ralph Waldo Emerson said, 'To be great is to be misunderstood,' and 'Nothing great was ever achieved without enthusiasm.' Certainly both apply to Churchill.

Perhaps we expected too much of him. History and hindsight are handmaidens that all too often demand perfection from those who have no grasp or experience of the grave burdens that fell upon Churchill's shoulders in 1940.

As his health began to fail towards the end of his life, whether it was from melancholy or the manifestation of his 'black dog', Churchill would sometimes lament his failure to achieve the endgame, the results he had aspired to. He never got over his repudiation by the British voters in 1945, and deemed his inability to restore Britain to a position of power in a world at peace a failure – as if its entire weight rested on his shoulders alone. His long-serving post-war private secretary, Anthony Montague Browne, would remind him of his extraordinary life and achievements – which after the Second World War included the Nobel Prize for Literature – only to have Churchill reply, 'What you say is true, I have worked very hard all my life and I have achieved a great deal, in the end to achieve nothing.' His success in staving off the enslavement of Europe by Adolf Hitler, he felt, had been reversed by the new tyranny of Stalin and a Russian empire that had enslaved many of the nations Churchill had fought so hard to free. The obvious post-war decline into irrelevance of his treasured empire was equally distressing to a Victorian romantic who had dedicated his entire life to perpetuating it.

What Alistair Cooke said of Churchill also bears repeating. 'What we have, in the end, is the phenomenon of an impenitent Victorian who, while never ceasing to yearn for the high noon of imperial Britain had – at a critical time – an intuitive feel for the next lurch of history and was able, with the old weapon of his deeply felt oratory, to goad a sleeping nation to meet it.'

Churchill's final years were a litany of illnesses, and the world mourned when he died peacefully on 24 January 1965, at the age of ninety – seventy years to the day after the death of Lord Randolph Churchill. His state funeral on 30 January in St Paul's Cathedral on a bitterly cold winter day was the first such honour accorded a commoner in the twentieth century, and was seen on television by millions throughout the world. It was also rather Victorian, with its great pomp and flourish, an event seldom seen except when kings or queens die. Churchill would have been pleased with the final tribute paid him both by his nation and by the world, which included the singing of Julia Ward Howe's haunting 'Battle Hymn of the Republic'.

Delegations and VIPs from 112 nations attended, a mark of respect never duplicated before or since. More than 312,0000 people had filed past his coffin during the three days he lay in state in Westminster Hall. Uncounted thousands more lined the route as the cortège made its way to St Paul's and afterwards to Tower Hill, where the cranes along the docks lowered their booms in salute.

In Dallas, at the insistence of his father, a nine-year-old sixth-generation Texan named Keith Grantham watched the funeral on TV. 'I was transfixed by the spectacle of the whole thing. When the ships' cranes bowed my father said that I would never live to see a greater man. In his eyes, and now in mine, Churchill had been responsible for saving the world for the common values that bind the English-speaking world.'

With thousands more lining the riverside, the coffin was placed on board a launch that sailed the short distance up the Thames to Waterloo. There it was carried on to a train for the slow journey home to Blenheim. Fittingly, locomotive no. 34051, which had survived the Battle of Britain, bore a plate reading 'Winston Churchill'. As it passed through each station on its slow journey towards his final resting place in Oxfordshire, large silent crowds paid their respects. From the carriage window one of Churchill's aides saw a man dressed in his old RAF uniform standing on the roof of a small house, saluting; in a field a farmer stopped his work, doffed his cap and bowed his head.

Just as his father had been on a similar frigid January day in 1895, Churchill was laid to rest, in a grave alongside his parents, in the tiny churchyard of Bladon, on the south side of Blenheim Park. Only his family attended the burial ceremony. The horizontal gravestone bears the simple inscription 'Winston Spencer Churchill, 1874–1965'. He had spent his entire life battling the demons of Lord Randolph Churchill; now they too were at last laid to rest, exorcized in death.

Although he was one of the most famous men of the twentieth century, and would be voted 'the greatest Briton' in 2002 by viewers of the BBC, Churchill would have felt equally honoured had he been given a simple soldier's funeral. At an early age he had given his heart to soldiering, and the greatest tribute a military man or woman can be given is to be buried among comrades in arms.

Assessments and tributes to Churchill litter the pages of histories and biographies but, fittingly, it is a soldier's verdict that invites repetition. Major General John Kennedy wrote: 'No soldier ever had more generous and forbearing masters than I. The massive figure of the great Prime Minister towers above them all. Neither his stature nor his place in our annals can be diminished by glimpses of his petulance, or revelations of how difficult it was to chase all the butterflies conjured up and released by his limitless fancy. His glory remains.'

Finally, one can do no more than look back at his extraordinary life and realize again that words alone are insufficient to portray the depth of this man and his life experience. Nevertheless one can reflect upon Winston Churchill's unparalleled life with admiration and awe, and conclude that had he failed in 1940, and not held Britain together until the entry of the United States guaranteed that the war would not be lost, the world would be a very different place today.

Notes

Abbreviations Used in the Notes

BL   British Library
CAC   Churchill Archives Centre, Churchill College, Cambridge
CHAR   Chartwell Papers, Churchill Archives Centre, the Papers of Sir Winston Churchill
        (27 July 1945)
CHC   Clementine Hozier Churchill
CV   Companion volumes
DDE   Dwight David Eisenhower
EL   Dwight D. Eisenhower Library, Abilene, Kansas
EP   *The Papers of Dwight David Eisenhower: The War Years*, ed. Alfred D. Chandler
        Jr, vols 1–6 (Baltimore, 1970).
GCM   General George C. Marshall
GCML   George C. Marshall Library, Lexington, VA
IH   Ian Hamilton Papers, Liddell Hart Centre for Military Archives, King's College
        London
IWM   Imperial War Museum, London
JC   Jennie (Lady Randolph) Churchill
LC   Library of Congress (Manuscript Division)
LHC   Liddell Hart Centre for Military Archives King's College London
LRC   Lord Randolph Churchill
MHI   US Army Military History Institute, Carlisle, PA (www.carlisle.army.mil/ahec/
        MHI.htm)
PRO   Public Record Office – UK National Archives
WC   Violet Bonham Carter, *Winston Churchill as I Knew Him* (London, 1967)
WSC   Winston Spencer Churchill

Introduction: 'Born for War'

xiii *'part of the conduct of war'*: Sebastian Haffner, *Churchill* London, 2003, 17. Haffner's concise biography ranks as one of the most insightful ever written.

xiv *'precipitate a far greater conflict'*: Winston Churchill to his cousin Sunny, the ninth Duke of Marlborough, Nov. 6, 1912, Marlborough Papers, LC.

xiv *'through the smoke of battle'*: William Armstrong, ed., *With Malice Toward None: A War Diary by Cecil H. King* (Madison, NJ, 1971), 300. Cecil King was a strong advocate of British rearmament who wrote extensively of the dangers posed by appeasement of Nazi Germany in the 1930s.

xv *'zip-suit and carpet slippers'*: Brian Gardner, *Churchill in Power* (Boston, 1970; published in London, 1968, as *Churchill in this Time*), xviii.

xv *'greatest of all stimulants'*: David Irving, *Churchill's War: The Struggle for Power* (London, 1989), xiii.

xv *'destiny in the Agamemnon role'*: Quoted in Robert Rhodes James, *Churchill: A Study in Failure, 1900–1939* (London, 1970), 49–50.

xv *'affirmation of nonaggression treaties'*: William Manchester, *The Last Lion: Winston Spencer Churchill: Alone, 1932–1940* (Boston, 1988), 359.

Prologue: 10 May 1940

1 *'before the summer is over'*: William L. Shirer, *The Nightmare Years, 1930–1940* (Boston, 1984), 489–90.

1 *expected destination, Denmark:* Amerika was the name of a town where Hitler fought during the First World War. Descriptions of Hitler's special train are in Nicolaus von Below, *At Hitler's Side: The Memoirs of Hitler's Luftwaffe Adjutant, 1937–1945* (Mechanicsburg, PA, 2001), 18–19, 58.

2 *'Western powers has just started'*: Description of 9/10 May 1940 and quotation in Ian Kershaw, *Hitler, 1936–1945: Nemesis* (New York and London, 2000), 294; and David Irving, *Hitler's War, 1939–1942* (London, 1977), 107–8.

2 *'Proceed brutally'*: Don and Petie Kladstrup, *Wine and War* (New York, 2001), 14.

2 *invaded France by first invading Belgium:* The German strategy that marked the opening of the First World War against France was the brainchild of Field Marshal Alfred von Schlieffen, chief of the German general staff until his retirement in 1906. The Schlieffen Plan was based on the premise that Germany could not afford to attack the strong French fortress defences guarding the Franco-German border. Instead the plan he had devised during his years as chief of staff called for massive attacks through Belgium that would exploit the terrain of the Belgian lowlands, then swing south to attack and capture Paris.

3 *extended into East Prussia:* Jacques Benoist-Méchin, *Sixty Days That Shook the West* (New York, 1956), 68.

3 *'every available aircraft left its field'*: Alistair Horne, *To Lose a Battle: France 1940* (Boston and London, 1969), 210.

3 *'start of the German offensive'*: Ibid., 204, and Richard Collier, *1940: The Avalanche* (New York, 1979), 69.

3 *'dive-bombers were their artillery'*: Len Deighton, *Blood, Tears, and Folly* (New York and London, 1994), 187.

4 *'markings on their wings'*: Norman Moss, *Nineteen Weeks: America, Britain and the Fateful Summer of 1940* (Boston, 2003), 96.

4 *'everything will go all right'*: B. H. Liddell Hart, ed., *The Rommel Papers* (New York, 1953), 6.

4 *he flew into a rage:* Hitler later relented and presented a gold watch to the meteorologist who had issued the prediction of good weather on 10 May.

5 *'fallen into the trap'*: Benoist-Méchin, *Sixty Days That Shook the West*, 75.

Chapter 1: Toy Soldiers

7 *'martial music for his entry'*: Annotated notes of 'Long Shadows' manuscript, Box 35, Folder 3, Sir Shane Leslie Papers, Georgetown University Special Collections. Leslie was the son of Jennie's younger sister, Leonie.

7 *'events leading up to it'*: William Manchester, *The Last Lion: Winston Spencer Churchill: Visions of Glory, 1874–1932* (Boston, 1983), 108.

8 *'another spectacle altogether'*: Simon Schama, *A History of Britain*, vol. 3, *The Fate of Empire, 1776–2000* (New York and London, 2002), 399–400.

8 *'smatterings of respectability'*: Interview with Prof. Roy Foster by Piers Brendon, BREN 1/12, Brendon Papers, CAC.

8 *'like the moon and the sun'*: Shane Leslie, 'The Tragedy of Randolph', Box 44, Leslie Papers.
8 *'the Beautiful, the Witty and the Good'*: G. P. Griggs, ed., *Oswald Frewen, Sailor's Soliloquy* (London, 1961), 13, a memoir based on his unpublished diary and papers. Oswald was the son of Clara Frewen, the 'Good' Jerome sister.
8 *'scornful of those she disliked'*: Shane Leslie, 'Memoir of Jennie Churchill', Box 44, Leslie Papers.
8 *annual regatta at Henley:* William Manchester, in his introduction to WSC, *My Early Life, 1874–1904* (New York, 1996), ix, described Jennie as a beautiful but shallow woman who 'neglected him shamefully' and 'was far more interested in extramarital romance than in motherhood'.
9 *'duty which was to breed Winston'*: Leslie, 'Memoir of Jennie Churchill'.
9 *'could have governed the world'*: Peter de Mendelssohn, *The Age of Churchill: Heritage and Adventure, 1874–1911* (London, 1961), 42.
10 *'but at a distance'*: *My Early Life*, 5.
10 *'dine and even dance!'*: JC to WSC, April 19, 1893, in CV, vol. 1, part 1: *1874–1896* (London, 1967), 375.
11 *'have been invested in my name'*: Shane Leslie, galley proofs of an unpublished biography of Leonard Jerome, Box 65, Leslie Papers. Apparently scheduled for publication in England circa 1948, the galleys have a note attached stating that publication was stopped by Winston Churchill, who, it can be inferred, took exception to his cousin's frank characterization of his parents. Forty thousand pounds in the late 1880s was the equivalent of £1.5 million in 1990. (See Martin Gilbert, *Churchill: A Life* [New York, 1991], 61.)
11 *'the easier that transformation became'*: Leslie, 'Memoir of Jennie Churchill'.
12 *'politically, gallantly, socially'*: Leslie, 'Memoir of Jennie Churchill'.
12 *'real childhood was built'*: Celia Sandys interview, Brendon Papers.
12 *'appears absolutely irrational'*: Winston S. Churchill, *Savrola: A Tale of the Revolution in Laurania* (London, 1900), 41.
12 *soon employed elsewhere:* De Mendelssohn, *The Age of Churchill*, 41. Perhaps the first victim of Winston Churchill's power, the hapless young woman went to work for the family whose son, Clement Attlee, would succeed Churchill as prime minister in the summer of 1945.
13 *'appealed in vain for the police'*: Quote by Shane Leslie, Box 35, Leslie Papers.
13 *'go and worship idols'*: Clare Sheridan, *Nudas Veritas* (London, 1927), 14. Clare Sheridan (1885–1970) was one of Churchill's numerous cousins. In her own way she was just as independent-minded as her cousin Winston.
13 *'Master Winston had spotted her'*: Shane Leslie, 'Winston, a Cousinly Memory', Box 44, Leslie Papers.
13 *'my unworthy productions'*: Unpublished biography of Leonard Jerome, Box 65, Leslie Papers.
13 *'he did not know himself'*: Shane Leslie, *The End of a Chapter* (New York, 1916), 120.
13 *'drunken cabman and a frisky horse!'*: Ibid., 120–21.
13 *'miserable business for us both'*: Shane Leslie, *Long Shadows: Memoirs of Shane Leslie* (Wilkes-Barre, PA, 1967), 20.
14 *'no ordinary child game'*: Sheridan, *Nudas Veritas*, 14.
14 *'waiting for the enemies of England!'*: Leslie, 'Winston, A Cousinly Memory'.
16 *'profession of arms'*: *My Early Life*, 19–20.
16 *'on the nursery floor'*: Ibid., 12.
16 *'spattered with filth'*: Roger Fry quoted in Randolph S. Churchill, *Winston S. Churchill: Youth, 1874–1900* (Boston and London, 1966), 52–53, the first of eight volumes of the official biography, hereafter cited as *Churchill*, vol. 1.
16 *'listening to their screams'*: Ibid.

17 *with predictable results:* Celia Sandys, *From Winston with Love and Kisses: The Young Churchill* (London, 1994), 58.

17 *age of thirty-eight:* Leslie, *Long Shadows,* 21

17 *'one long feud with authority':* Quoted by a fellow student in Sandys, *From Winston with Love and Kisses,* 55.

17 *'any Greek except the alphabet':* My Early Life, 13.

17 *'attitude got on everyone's nerves':* Henry Graf Kessler quoted in Sandys, *From Winston with Love and Kisses,* 58.

17 *'your loving son Winston S. C.':* WSC to JC, Sept. 28, 1893, in CV, vol. 1, part 1, 417.

17 *'It was* horrible': Anita Leslie, *Lady Randolph Churchill* (New York and London, 1969), 97.

Chapter 2: 'A Barren and Unhappy Period of My Life'

18 *'the naughtiest small boy in the world':* V. W. Germains, *The Tragedy of Winston Churchill* (London, 1931), 13.

18 *nearly earned him expulsion:* Sandys, *From Winston with Love and Kisses,* 66.

19 *used daily to check his temperature:* Ibid., 74.

19 *'cursed with so feeble a body':* Ibid., 154.

19 *false impression that he was inebriated: Churchill,* vol. 1, 282.

19 *sent their sons to be educated:* In 2005–6, Harrow had approximately 850 students and fees of nearly £24,000 per annum.

20 *'not with the whole lot':* Leslie, 'Winston, a Cousinly Memory'.

20 *'deepest part of the pool':* 'Memories of Churchill', Charles Eade Papers, CAC.

20 *'most suitable victim to hand':* Leo S. Amery, quoted in E. D. W. Chaplin, ed., *Winston Churchill and Harrow* (London, 1941), 21–22.

20 *'some of his best jibes':* Ibid., 22.

20 *'older boy's English essays':* Celia Sandys, *Churchill: Wanted Dead or Alive* (New York and London, 2000), 33.

20 *'kept back at end of term':* Personal examination of the Harrow punishment book, Nov. 17, 2003. Churchill's offences were fairly ordinary, and he was merely one of a great many other Harrovians who were routinely punished for a wide range of violations of school rules. A maximum of eight strokes of the cane seems to have been the most severe physical punishment administered by Dr Welldon. That Churchill earned seven strokes on two occasions is indicative of the seriousness of the offences.

21 *'painful duty to swish* you': Leo Amery, *My Political Life,* vol. 1, *England Before the Storm, 1896–1914* (London, 1953), 40.

21 *'displeased with you':* De Mendelssohn, *The Age of Churchill,* 69.

21 *were sometimes shattered:* Shane Leslie, 'Winston's Bibliography', Box 44, Leslie Papers.

22 *'were really cowed':* Leslie, 'Winston, a Cousinly Memory'.

22 *'my father is out of office':* Leslie, *The End of a Chapter,* 120.

22 *'throughout Churchill's life':* Ronald Lewin *Churchill as Warlord* (London, 1973), 3.

22 *kissed his beloved nanny goodbye:* Leslie, *Long Shadows,* 21.

22 *'sought to expose my ignorance':* My Early Life, 15.

22 *'which is a noble thing':* Ibid., 16–17.

23 *'Why, he's last of all!':* Ibid., 16.

23 *'history work he has done for me':* H. O. D. Davidson to JC, July 12, 1888, in *Churchill,* vol. 1, 109–10.

23 *throughout Europe in 1890:* The original copy of 'The Influenza' is in the Harrow Archives.

23 *'Who fought and conquered well':* Ibid., and Gilbert, *Churchill: A Life,* 26.

23 *appropriate sartorial splendour:* Sandys, *From Winston with Love and Kisses,* 117.

24 *no role in his life:* Ibid., 165.

24 *'by taking this line'*: JC to WSC, Dec. 8 and 15, 1891, *Churchill*, vol. 1, 154, 156.
24 *'Your loving son, Winny'*: Sandys, *From Winston with Love and Kisses*, 165–67.
25 *tutelage of his French master*: Ibid., 167.
25 *during the summer break*: *Churchill*, vol. 1, 135; and Sandys, *From Winston with Love and Kisses*, 148.
25 *own form of the Holy Grail*: Shane Leslie, 'The Tragedy of Randolph', Box 44, Leslie Papers.
25 *kaiser's helmet and his boots*: Ibid., 141–43.
26 *'always awkward or foolish'*: *My Early Life*, 40.
26 *'going to be some good'*: Lady Soames interview, Brendon Papers.
26 *'in his entire lifetime'*: Interview of Winston Churchill (grandson) by Piers Brendon.
26 *'comprehension of all my affairs'*: *My Early Life*, 32.
26 *'your greatest enemy'*: JC to WSC, June 12, 1890, *Churchill*, vol. 1, 124–25.
26 *'who returned that hate'*: WSC to JC, June 19, 1890, ibid., 125–26.
28 *'The Battle Hymn of the Republic'*: Sandys, *From Winston with Love and Kisses*, 121.
29 *'It was young Winston'*: Jim Golland, *Not Winston, Just William?* (London, 1988), 29.
29 *'took his opponents by surprise'*: *Churchill*, vol. 1, 171.
29 *complete with military dispositions*: In 1947 Robert Somervell's son donated Churchill's paper to Harrow. In the 1870s and 1880s Russian incursions into Central Asia were regarded by Britain as a threat to the North-West Frontier of India. In 1885 the two countries clashed between Afghan and Russian outposts at Pendish; thus it was likely that any writer wishing to describe an imaginary battle would select Russia as the probable adversary.
29 *'best narcotic in the world'*: Ibid.
30 *'would have been a joy to me'*: *My Early Life*, 38–39.
30 *'fit him for Oxford'*: Leslie, *Long Shadows*, 22.

Chapter 3: Sandhurst

31 *one-quarter of its population*: Schama, *A History of Britain*, vol. 3, 264.
31 *Crimean War against Russia*: David French, *The British Way of War, 1688–2000* (London, 1990), 120.
31 *'so-called* pax Britannica*'*: Niall Ferguson, *Empire* (New York and London, 2004), 211.
32 *'learned on the hunting field'*: David Cannadine, *The Decline and Fall of the British Aristocracy* (New York and London, 1999), 264.
32 *'an officer second'*: Ibid., 265.
32 *'without being a gentleman'*: James, *Warrior Race*, 326.
32 *'send a policeman and have it arrested'*: Manchester, *The Last Lion: Visions*, 220.
33 *'degenerate into a bookworm'*: Lawrence James, *Warrior Race: A History of the British at War* (New York and London, 2001), 437.
33 *tribute to the British character*: Roughly half the officer corps was recruited from graduates of Sandhurst and Woolwich; the other half came mainly from the militia, and a small percentage from universities and other ranks of the army. (David Chandler, gen. ed., *The Oxford Illustrated History of the British Army*, [Oxford, 1996], 193.)
34 *competitive written examination*: 'History of the Royal Military Academy Sandhurst', on the official RMA Web site: www.sandhurst.mod.uk/. Parents were responsible for tuition, board, uniforms, books and other required items.
34 *'all depends on yourself'*: *Churchill*, vol. 1, 172; and Welldon to WSC, Sept. 10, 1892, ibid., 173.
35 *'probably within the hour'*: *My Early Life*, 30. Churchill was not, as he claimed, bedridden for three months after the accident. It was at least two days before the surgeon arrived from London, far too late to have saved Churchill's life had a kidney actually been ruptured. WSC later wrote that he had had 'a flash' of inspiration that if he leaped on to the top of a young fir tree that was near the level of the footbridge, he would be able 'to

slip down the pole-like stem, breaking off each tier of branches as one descended, until the fall was broken. I computed it. I meditated' – and nearly killed himself.

35 'acting as such': Lord Dunraven (Windham Thomas) to LRC, Churchill, vol. 1, 181–82.

35 'very firm handling': W. H. James to LRC, March 7, 1893, CV, vol. 1, part 1, 371.

36 as a cavalry cadet: His marks placed him 95th of 389 candidates, his near undoing his usual bête noire, Latin, in which he was placed sixth from the bottom.

36 'shabby unhappy & futile existence': LRC to WSC, Aug. 9, 1893, CV, vol. 1, part 1, 390–91.

37 'infantry regiment of the line': Churchill, vol. 1, 189.

37 'I have a fresh start': WSC to LRC, Aug. 14, 1893; and WSC to JC, Aug. 14, 1893, ibid., 192.

38 'especially Tactics and Fortification': My Early Life, 43.

39 'almost every week': Ibid., 59.

39 face being cut off: JC to WSC, May 17, 1894, CV, vol. 1, part 1, 394.

39 'never do anything right': WSC to JC, Sept. 17, 1893, ibid., 413–14.

39 'I am 50 years old': Ibid.

40 'and so recovered the watch': WSC to LRC, April 22, 1894, Churchill, vol. 1, 172, 212.

40 'is vastly your superior': LRC to WSC, April 21, 1894, ibid., 211.

40 'write long letters to you': Ibid., April 13, 1894, 210.

41 'going into the 4th Hussars': My Early Life, 61–62.

41 'like Aladdin's Cave': Ibid., 59.

41 some other neurological disorder: John H. Mather, MD, 'Lord Randolph Churchill: Maladies et Mort', Finest Hour (Winter 1996–7). See also the Churchill Centre website, www.winstonchurchill.org/.

41 'swiftly fading shadow': My Early Life, 49.

41 'see him as he is': JC to Mrs Moreton Frewen (Jennie's sister Clara), Nov. 18, 1894, CV, vol. 1, part 1, 534–35.

42 'hope you will be pleased': WSC to LRC, Dec. 9, 1894, ibid., 540.

42 'laid that weary brain to rest': Churchill, vol. 1, 251, description from his massive two-volume biography of his father, published in 1906.

42 'under biographical protection': Leslie, Long Shadows, 25.

42 'This I have tried to do': 'Some Memories by Churchill', compiled by Charles Eade from WSC's articles and speeches, Eade Papers.

42 'spread like a glittering pall': Gilbert, Churchill: A Life, 49. Although contemporary views now dispute the idea that the cause of Lord Randolph's death was syphilis, Churchill once told his Second World War confidant Lord Moran that he believed his father had died from the disease. 'He had been telling me of the debauchery of Victorian times. One night Lord Randolph got drunk and was horrified when he woke in the morning to find a strange woman in his bed. From this woman of the streets he contracted syphilis.' ('Father and Son', Box 93, Moran Papers.)

43 'gutters of Monte Carlo!': 'Father and Son', Box 93, Moran Papers.

43 as a cavalry officer: The Duke of Cambridge was a classic example of the stagnation that gripped the army of the Victorian age. He held the army's highest office for thirty-nine years and refused to retire or resign until 1895, when he was finally driven from office at the age of seventy-six.

Chapter 4: A Young Man on the Make

44 for his uniforms: Manchester, The Last Lion: Visions, 219.

44 very disagreeable personality: Richard Holmes, In the Footsteps of Churchill: A Study in Character (New York and London, 2005), 35.

45 half the army was based overseas: Douglas S. Russell, 'Lt. Churchill, 4th Queen's Own Hussars', and article published by the Churchill Society, Oct. 1995. See the Churchill Centre website: www.winstonchurchill.org.

45 *'indeed would never be uttered'*: John Keegan, *A History of Warfare* (New York and London, 1993), xv.

45 *paid nearly twice as much:* Russell, 'Lt. Churchill'. Private soldiers were paid what amounted to starvation wages. A recruiting sergeant once commented, 'It was only in the haunts of dissipation or inebriation, and among the very lowest dregs of society, that I met with anything like success.' (Manchester, *The Last Lion: Visions*, 221.)

45 *regimental cavalry officer:* Roy Jenkins, *Churchill* (London, 2001), 21.

47 *'now opened upon me'*: Ibid., 64.

47 *'Well, we shall see'*: WSC to JC, Aug. 16, 1895, *Churchill*, vol. 1, 249.

48 *'become cruel and squalid'*: *My Early Life*, 65.

48 *'Men, Money and Machinery'*: Ibid., 66.

48 *'sure was impossible, has happened'*: Ibid., 66–67.

49 *'claimed to love so much'*: Holmes, *In the Footsteps of Churchill*, 35. Shortly before her death in July 1895, Churchill did send Mrs Everest a small sum during her recovery from a broken arm. (CV, vol. 1, part 1, 244.)

49 *'darling precious boy'*: Sandys, *From Winston with Love and Kisses*, 192.

49 *maintain the grave: Churchill*, vol. 1, 246. Jennie did not attend Mrs Everest's funeral.

49 *'dear and dutiful woman'*: WC, 27; and Leslie, *Long Shadows*, 18.

50 *'older nations of the earth'*: WSC to Jack Churchill, Nov. 15, 1895, CV, vol. 1, part 1, 599–600.

50 *'man who does not rebel': Churchill*, vol. 1, 260.

51 *'death and wounds'*: *My Early Life*, 76.

51 *'hurry of disembarkation'*: Ibid., 77.

52 *'I had hitherto done'*: Ibid., 83–84.

52 *'sit in our saddles'*: Ibid., 80.

52 *'even for a Churchill': Churchill*, vol. 1, 266.

53 *'and far less stable'*: Ibid., 267.

53 *'bricks at the Monroe Doctrine'*: *New York World*, Dec. 15, 1896; and *New York Herald*, Dec. 19, 1896, CV, vol. 1, part 1, 619–22.

53 *'in a painful dilemma'*: Sir H. Drummond Wolff to WSC, Feb. 17, 1896, ibid., 664–65.

55 *'iron despatch box'*: WSC to JC, Aug. 4, 1896, CV, vol. 1, part 1, 675–76.

55 *'month away from here'*: Ibid.

55 *reply from Lady Randolph: Churchill*, vol. 1, 278.

Chapter 5: The Jewel of Empire

56 *'the miracle of the world'*: Lawrence James, *The Rise and Fall of the British Empire* (New York and London, 1994), 217, 219.

57 *'peril, violence and effort'*: *My Early Life*, 102. What Churchill experienced was most likely a recurrent dislocation. This injury is due to a torn shoulder capsule. Surgery today is very successful, but no such treatment was available in Churchill's day and dislocations typically did not heal well on their own.

59 *'burning heat and dust'*: Gen. Sir George Barrow quoted in James, *Warrior Race*, 433–34.

59 *'live no better than we'*: *My Early Life*, 103.

60 *'the serious purpose of life'*: Known as the game of kings, polo is one of the world's most ancient sports and is thought to be the oldest team sport, originating in the sixth century BC in Persia. Well before the British first discovered polo in India in the 1850s, the sport had already been judged useful for training cavalrymen. A polo field still survives in Tamerlane's palace grounds in Samarkand.

60 *'elephants and their salutations'*: *My Early Life*, 119–20.

61 *'He slashes the ball'*: *The Churchill Years: 1874–1965* (New York, 1965), 70; and Manchester, *The Last Lion: Visions*, 241–42.

62 *'heart to write more'*: *The Churchill Years*, 105; and JC to WSC, Feb. 26, 1897, CV, vol. 1, part 2, 741.

62 *'will remain true to death'*: WSC to Pamela Plowden, Nov. 28, 1898.
62 *'discovering his virtues'*: Gilbert, *Churchill: A Life*, 174.
63 *'lay it at your feet'*: *Scotsman*, Dec. 3, 2003.
63 *'keep him in his place'*: John Gibson Lockhart, 'Young Churchill', in Peter Stansky, ed., *Churchill: A Profile* (New York, 1973), 12.
64 *'keep me down like that'*: Ibid., and Sir Robert Baden-Powell, *Memories of India* (Philadelphia, 1915), chap. 3. Baden-Powell's version is that Churchill emerged and said, 'It is no use sitting upon me, for I'm India-rubber.'
64 *'not slow in coming'*: 'Some Memories' (of Churchill), Eade Papers.
64 *for his lost education*: See Carlo D'Este, *Eisenhower: A Soldier's Life* (New York, 2002).
64 *'with which he sought enlightenment'*: Earl of Birkenhead (Freddy Smith), *Churchill, 1874–1922* (London, 1989), 64. Freddy, Churchill's godson, was the son of one of Churchill's oldest friends, F. E. Smith.
65 *Churchill's state of mind*: WSC to JC, April 14, 1897, CV, vol. 1, part 2, 753.
65 *'not such a bad day either'*: *My Early Life*, 108.
65 *'will not relax your efforts'*: *Churchill*, vol. 1, 291.
65 *a Scottish battalion in 1916*: Ibid., 300–301.
66 *rough-and-tumble sport of polo*: Ibid., 291–93.
66 *'likely to be very valueless'*: Extracts from letters, WSC to JC, Nov. 4 and 18, 1896, CV, vol. 1, part 2, 696–704.
67 *'Responsibility is an exhilarating drink'*: WSC to JC, Feb. 12, 1897, CV, vol. 1, part 2.
67 *'officers in my rank'*: Ibid., Feb. 18, 1897.
67 *'it is not a pleasant one'*: JC to WSC, Feb. 26, 1897, CV, vol. 1, part 2, 741.
67 *find him a sponsor*: WSC to JC, Apr. 21, 1897, CV, vol. 1, part 2, 754–56.
67 *'see the fun and tell the tale'*: *My Early Life*, 121.
68 *'stood Sir Bindon Blood'*: Ibid., 122.
68 *pension of five hundred pounds per year*: Extracted from the County Clare Library website, 'Clare People – Col. Thomas Blood', www.clarelibrary.ie/.

Chapter 6: A Taste of War

70 *intention to remain permanently*: Between 1863 and 1901 there were some twenty frontier wars in this region.
70 *'savages of the Stone Age'*: WSC, preface to *The Story of the Malakand Field Force* (London, 1898).
72 *'in the army are worth'*: WSC to JC, Aug. 17, 1897, *Churchill*, vol. 1, 334.
72 *'because of the risks I run'*: Ibid., 336.
73 *'by time, and by practice'*: Alexander Hamilton, *The Federalist*, No. 25, Dec. 21, 1787.
73 *to the North-West Frontier*: Ted Morgan, *Churchill: The Rise to Failure, 1874–1915* (London, 1984), 98.
73 *'it must be avenged'*: WSC to Jack Churchill, Aug. 31, 1897.
73 *'light of other days'*: *My Early Life*, 124.
74 *'on your head like a nightmare'*: Ibid., 132.
74 *'And he shall keep who can!'*: Sir Bindon Blood, *Four Score Years and Ten*, vol. 2 (London, 1933), 2.
75 *'attraction of its own'*: *My Early Life*, 126–27.
75 *'ought to be kicked'*: Ibid.
75 *'white officer in the East'*: Ibid.
75 *'killed in the preceding week'*: Ibid., 128.
76 *'very cruel people'*: WSC to Lt. Reginald Barnes, Sept. 14, 1897.
76 *'some very serious work'*: Bindon Blood, *Four Score Years and Ten*, 2.
76 *'in punitive devastation'*: *My Early Life*, 147.
78 *meant to his career*: WSC to JC, Sept. 19, 1897.

78 'to be done again': WSC to Frances, Duchess of Marlborough, Oct. 25, 1897, CV, vol. 1, part 2, 810–11.
78 'big dinner or some other function': WSC to JC, Sept. 19, 1897.
79 'merely love of adventure': Ibid., Oct. 2, 1897.
79 'life size and flesh colour': Ibid.
79 'necessity of some things': Ibid.
79 'more dreadful state of barbarism': Frederick Woods, ed., Young Winston's Wars: The Original Despatches of Winston S. Churchill, War Correspondent, 1897–1900 (New York and London, 1972), 9.
79 'man's only necessities': Ibid.
80 'so prosaic an ending': Ibid.
80 'what shadows we pursue': The Story of the Malakand Field Force, chap. 12.
80 'two ordinary subalterns': Churchill, vol. 1, 349.
80 'DSO [Distinguished Service Order]': Bindon Blood to Col. John Brabazon quoted in Manchester, The Last Lion: Alone, 258.
81 'one which I aim to repeat': WSC to Lord William Beresford, Nov. 2, 1897, CV, vol. 1, part 2, 822.
81 'appointments in India depend': Ibid., 823.
82 Victorian standards of gentlemanly conduct: Manchester, The Last Lion: Alone, 259–60.
82 his inability to join it: Churchill went so far as to request a personal interview with the adjutant general, who was the highest authority in India for such matters. 'He declined point-blank to receive me, and I then began to realize my quest was hopeless.' (My Early Life, 153.)
82 'who is also a gentleman': WSC to JC, Dec. 2, 1897, CV, vol. 1, part 2, 834.
83 'very much overrated man': Churchill, vol. 1, 363.
83 test the system any further: My Early Life, 152.
83 'phrase or fact weeded out': WSC to JC, Dec. 31, 1897. Not only was Jennie instructed to find him a suitable publisher, but Churchill demanded (not once but twice) that she 'verify my quotations'.
83 received any additional payment: Gilbert, Churchill: A Life, 86.
83 'Up to date (of course)': WSC to JC, Jan. 26, 1898.
83 'did not think I possessed': WSC to JC, Dec. 22, 1897.
84 'given to man on earth': WSC to JC, May 16, 1898, CV, vol. 1, part 2, 933.
84 'few casualties and little glory': The Story of the Malakand Field Force, 294. Also quoted in David Jablonsky, Churchill, the Great Game and Total War (London, 1991), 197, n. 144. There were other lessons of war that Churchill took to heart, including a compassion for the underdog that was exemplified by his great interest in the scandalous court-martial of Captain Alfred Dreyfus in France, which he described as 'that monstrous conspiracy'. (Jablonsky, 35.)
84 'that is warlike and brave': Quoted in Jablonsky, Churchill, the Great Game and Total War, 35; and The Story of the Malakand Field Force, 208.
84 'believed he had deserved': Churchill, vol. 1, 355.

Chapter 7: Soldier of Fortune

85 'push and persuasiveness pull it off': My Early Life, 157.
86 'Government of India and your regiment': Ibid., 158.
86 characterized Churchill himself: WSC to JC, Mar. 31, 1898, CV, vol. 1, part 2, 906–09.
86 'prodigy would go far': Gen. Sir Aylmer Haldane, A Soldier's Saga (Edinburgh, 1948), 119.
87 jihad (holy war): The term 'Dervish' dates back to the twelfth century and is used here to denote men of religious fanaticism who are ready and willing to die for their particular cause, whether it is against infidels such as Britain and France or against other Muslims. The armies the British fought in the Sudan in the 1880s and 1890s were generally referred

to by this term. (See Richard Holmes, *The Oxford Companion to Military History* [Oxford, 2001], 255–56.)

87 *every single member of his relief expedition:* James, *The Rise and Fall of the British Empire*, 275.

87 *reinstate Anglo-Egyptian rule:* See ibid., chap. 7, for an excellent description of the British control of Egypt and the troubles in the Sudan.

88 *of his Railway Battalion:* Churchill devotes an informative chapter to the building of the Sudan Military Railway. See chap. 8 in the abridged edition of *The River War* (London, 2000) and vol. 1, chap. 9, of the original 1899 edition, published in two lengthy volumes totalling nearly 1,000 pages. Because of the book's length the numerous subsequent editions have been published in a condensed version, of which the 2000 edition cited here is an example.

88 *'serious occupation every day':* WSC to JC, Oct. 25, 1897, CV, vol. 1, part 2, 811.

88 *wife of an army general:* Ibid., Jan. 10, 1898 (855–56), and Anita Leslie, *Lady Randolph Churchill*, 243–44. Churchill's letters to his mother exhorting her to arrange for his assignment to Egypt continued almost endlessly until his return to England from India.

88 *'nothing but shame and disappointment':* Ibid., Mar. 22 and 25, 1898.

89 ' *"Untidy", "Slovenly", "Bad" ':* My Early Life, 154–55.

89 *any of her future debts:* WSC to JC, Jan. 30, 1898, CV, vol. 1, part 2, 870–71.

89 *'a dirty taste in my mouth':* Jenkins, *Churchill*, 37.

89 *'disfigure my first attempt':* CV, vol. 1, part 2, May 22, 1898, 936.

90 *death for his subordinates:* Alan Moorehead, *The White Nile* (New York and London, 2000), 368–69.

91 *treated them with complete disdain:* Philip Magnus, *Kitchener: Portrait of an Imperialist* (New York, 1959; London, 1958), 118.

91 *with extreme ruthlessness:* Ibid., 78.

91 *those of a war correspondent:* Norman Rose, *Churchill: The Unruly Giant* (New York, 1994), 49.

91 *'had to make his name':* Churchill, vol. 1, 383.

92 *Kitchener wasn't buying it:* Various telegrams in July 1898 to and from Kitchener in CV, vol. 1, part 2, 948–49.

92 *with his name on it:* My Early Life, 161.

92 *'to be within [my mother's] reach':* Ibid., 163

92 *'not fail to let me know':* Ibid., 164.

93 *'will be useful to me':* WSC to Lord Salisbury, July 18, 1898, *Churchill*, vol. 1, 378–79.

93 *'detestable French sailors':* WSC to JC, July 30, 1898, CV, vol. 1, part 2, 952.

94 *'do not want to be recalled':* Woods, *Young Winston's Wars*, xiii–xx; and WSC to Aylmer Haldane, Aug. 11, 1898, CV, vol. 1, part 2, 963–65. In each of his dispatches Churchill addressed his supposed recipient as 'My dear'.

Chapter 8: Omdurman

(Churchill's dispatches to the *Morning Post* are in Woods, *Young Winston's Wars*. The dates of the dispatches cited are when Churchill actually wrote them, not when they were published in London, often several weeks later. Except as noted, all correspondence is in CV, vol. 1, part 2.)

95 *'would have been Winston's':* My Early Life, 168. The Grenfell family paid an exceptionally heavy price for their military service. Robert Grenfell's two younger brothers, one of whom won a Victoria Cross, were both killed in the First World War.

96 *wilderness of deepest Africa:* Dispatch, Aug. 31, 1898.

96 *'a moment's peace':* My Early Life, 169.

97 *'swift abundant Nile':* Ibid., 173.

97 *'all one's thoughts':* Dispatch, Aug. 15, 1898.

99 *trek through the wilderness:* Ibid., Aug. 20, 1898.

99 'may induce them to pause': WSC to Aylmer Haldane, Aug. 11, 1898.
100 exceeded those of the Mahdi: Moorehead, The White Nile, 307.
100 'scrutinizing the bank with their guns': Dispatch, Sept. 5, 1898.
101 'impression of a lifetime': Ibid.
101 'to try my best': WSC to JC, Aug. 26, 1898.
101 'at their present rate': My Early Life, 176–77.
102 'all these military magnates': Ibid., 178. A week earlier Churchill had not been so optimistic and was convinced there would be heavy losses. (WSC to JC, Aug. 26, 1898.)
102 Lieutenant David Beatty: My Early Life, 179–80.
103 'element in a splendid game': Ibid., 180–81.
103 'I was in great awe': WSC to Ian Hamilton, Sept. 16, 1898.
103 'Messenger of God': John Pollock, Kitchener: Architect of Victory, Artisan of Peace (New York, 2001), 131.
103 'load and press the trigger': G. W. Steevens, With Kitchener to Khartum (New York Edinburgh and London, 1898), 263. George Warren Steevens was regarded as one of the Victorian era's top correspondents. He covered the Dreyfus trial in France, reported from the United States and Germany, and reported on wars in Greece and later in South Africa, where he died in 1900 from enteric fever. (See CV, vol. 1, part 2, 981 n. 1.)
104 'not a battle but an execution': Moorehead, The White Nile, 370.
104 'tossing and collapsing': WSC, The River War (2000 ed.), 194–95.
104 'such monstrous perfection': Ibid. (1899 ed.), vol. 2, 118–19.
104 'The Maxim gun and they have not': Quoted in Holmes, The Oxford Companion to Military History, 672.
104 mortal agony where they fell: According to Pollock the body count Kitchener ordered after the battle was 10,883, but this does not account for dead removed from the battlefield by relatives in the immediate aftermath of the battle, so the true number was even higher. (Pollock, Kitchener, 138.)
105 'given "a good dusting"': Moorehead, The White Nile, 371.
105 'suffering, despairing, dying': The River War (1899 ed.), vol. 2, 118–19.
105 'one of extreme peril': Ibid. (2000 ed.), 215.
107 'Dervishes could be seen': WSC to Ian Hamilton, Sept. 16, 1898.
107 account of Omdurman: Steevens, With Kitchener to Khartum, 273.
108 at close range: Ibid., 273–75.
108 'other parts of the body': Dispatch, Sept. 6, 1898.
108 'went Heaven knows where': WSC to Ian Hamilton, Sept. 16, 1898.
109 'had been killed or wounded': Dispatch, Sept. 6, 1898.
109 'forty years ago': WSC to Sunny Churchill, Sept. 29, 1898, Marlborough Papers, LC.
109 'devour me like wolves': Birkenhead, Churchill, 82.
109 'I shall live to see': WSC to Ian Hamilton, Sept. 16, 1898.
109 'science over barbarians': The River War (2000 ed.), 218.
110 'only a fool would play at': Dispatch, Sept. 6, 1898.

Chapter 9: David versus Goliath

(Unless otherwise cited WSC's correspondence is in CV, vol. 1, part 2.)
111 'as a racial prerogative': Niall Ferguson, Empire (New York and London, 2004), 221.
111 'match their firepower': Ibid. 226. In 1888 Kaiser Wilhelm II had seen an exhibition of the Maxim gun and its firepower, declaring: 'That is the gun – there is no other.'
112 'Kitchener and other officers to tears': Ibid., 283; and Moorehead, The White Nile, 373.
112 'Surely he [Gordon] is avenged': Moorehead, The White Nile, 373.
112 the car bomb: Ibid., 383.
113 Royal College of Surgeons in London: Ibid., 372.
113 where they had fallen: Medical care in the British army of Victorian times was appallingly bad. Disease alone killed a great many soldiers. To be wounded was to face pain

beyond description and, all too often, a horrible death. Amputation was common. (See James, *Warrior Race*, chap. 4.)

113 *unconvinced that he had acted with propriety:* Pollock, *Kitchener*, 150.

113 *White Paper to that effect:* Magnus, *Kitchener*, 136.

114 ' *"Can I ever forget?" '*: Dispatch, Sept. 10, 1898.

114 *'sometimes filthy tasting':* Ibid.

114 *'will count for much':* WSC to Sunny Churchill, Sept. 29, 1898, Marlborough Papers.

114 *'brave men who fall in war':* *The River War* (1899 ed.), vol. 1, 441.

114 *'glory of the game':* Manchester, *The Last Lion: Visions*, 280.

114 *'as ever walked the earth':* Dispatch, Sept. 10, 1898.

115 *'very high at such moments':* WSC to JC, Sept. 17, 1898.

115 *'even that not completely':* Birkenhead, *Churchill*, 83.

115 *'would have been one of these?':* *The River War* (1899 ed.), vol. 2, 162; and WC, 25.

115 *ordering them back to Egypt:* Moorehead, *The White Nile*, 371 n. 3.

115 *'has yet produced in England':* *The River War* (1899 ed.), vol. 1, 161.

116 *on the part of the British commanders:* Peter Burroughs, in Chandler, *Oxford Illustrated History of the British Army*, 181. One of the cavalry units at Balaklava was the 4th Hussars.

116 *'blood was much strengthened':* WSC to Ian Hamilton, Sept. 16, 1898, IH.

117 *'no more copy for the journalists':* Dispatch, Sept. 12, 1898.

117 *'undying genius entitles us':* Linda Colley, *Captives: The Story of Britain's Pursuit of Empire and How Its Soldiers and Civilians Were Held Captive by the Dream of Global Supremacy, 1600–1850* (New York and London, 2002), 376.

117 *'whenever bullets were in or about':* Leslie, 'Winston, A Cousinly Memory'.

117 *accorded the battle honour 'Khartoum':* J. M. Brereton, *A Guide to the Regiments of the British Army* (London, 1985), 64–65.

118 ' *"by long slow marches" to Atbara':* Gilbert, *Churchill*, 100.

119 *'no Army at all!':* Prince of Wales to WSC, Oct. 6, 1898.

119 *'[Churchill] thinks about':* Anonymous letters to the editor of the *Army and Navy Gazette*, dated Dec. 17 and 24, 1898, CV, vol. 1, part 2, 999–1000.

119 *reprimanded the army:* WSC to the editor, *Army and Navy Gazette*, Jan. 8, 1899, ibid.

120 *encouraged or multiplied:* De Mendelssohn, *The Age of Churchill*, 573 n. 20, quoting Churchill's essay on Sir John French in *Great Contemporaries* (London, 1937).

121 *'how to perform his duties':* Haldane, *A Soldier's Saga*, 130–31.

121 *'uniform & medals for the last time':* WSC to the Duchess of Marlborough, Mar. 26, 1899.

121 *'would like to have both':* *My Early Life*, 211.

122 *'nothing but ambition to cling to':* Birkenhead, *Churchill*, 85.

Chapter 10: The Boer War

124 *'for the human race':* Schama, *A History of Britain*, vol. 3, 360.

124 *'right to rule the world':* Ferguson, *Empire*, 202.

125 *one hundred thousand casualties:* Gregory Freeman-Barnes, *The Boer War, 1899–1902* (Oxford, 2003), 86. Six thousand were killed in battle and another sixteen thousand died from wounds and disease.

126 *'we must fight the Boers':* Churchill, vol. 1, 435. Churchill would call the liberation of Natal from the Boers 'an Imperial debt of honour'. (WSC, *The Boer War* (London, 2002), 21.)

126 *'ill effect on your political fortunes':* Arthur Balfour to WSC, July 1899, *My Early Life*, 227.

127 *'more than an average person':* WSC to JC, Oct. 25, 1897.

127 *higher for other war correspondents: Churchill*, vol. 1, 437.

127 *governor general of the Cape Colony:* Manchester, *The Last Lion: Visions*, 292.

128 *first dispatch for the* Morning Post: Dispatch, Oct. 26, 1899, quoted in *Churchill*, vol. 1, 440. (Copies of Churchill's dispatches, unless otherwise cited in this chapter, are in the 'South Africa' section of Woods, *Young Winston's Wars*.)

128 *before they had even arrived: My Early Life*, 236–37.

128 *wanderings just before his death:* Celia Sandys, *Churchill: Wanted Dead or Alive* (New York and London, 1999), 36.

128 *'Shy he was not':* Morgan, *Churchill*, 128.

129 *'his own age, or younger':* Sandys, *Churchill: Wanted Dead or Alive*, 22.

129 *450,000 men to the conflict:* Freeman-Barnes, *The Boer War*, 24.

130 *'they will emerge victorious':* WSC to JC, Nov. 3, 1899.

130 *'name of the Lord on [their] lips':* Dispatch, Nov. 5, 1899.

130 *'sea-sickness and perpetual nausea':* WSC, *The Boer War*, 18.

130 *paralysed his right leg:* Reginald Barnes survived his wounds from the Boer War and later rose to become Major General Sir Reginald Barnes, retiring after the First World War. (Sandys, *Churchill: Wanted Dead or Alive*, 39.)

131 *'give me a good show':* De Mendelssohn, *The Age of Churchill*, 146.

131 *'pleasant and grassy uplands of Natal':* John Black Atkins, *The Relief of Ladysmith* (London, 1900), 59.

131 *fall victim to a Boer attack:* Ibid., 65–67.

132 *twenty miles north-west of Estcourt:* Morgan, *Churchill*, 130.

132 *'by the time I am forty':* J. B. Atkins, *Incidents and Reflections* (London, 1947), 125.

132 *'fulfil its purpose':* Ibid., 23.

133 *belief in an early death:* Ibid., 24.

133 *'into military terms':* Ibid., 126.

133 *colourful dispatches for the* Morning Post: Sandys, *Churchill: Wanted Dead or Alive*, 36.

133 *'too direct and frank to flatter':* Mortimer Menpes quoted in ibid., 34.

134 *' "By jove, he's done it" ':* K. M. Clegg to Randolph Churchill, Feb. 1963, quoted in *Churchill*, vol. 1, 340.

134 *'Prime Minister of England one day':* Recollections of Capt. Douglas Gilfillan, Imperial Light Horse, CV, vol. 1, part 2, 1153.

134 *'No exchange of Prisoners':* WSC to Sir Evelyn Wood, Nov. 10, 1899, CV, vol. 1, part 2, 1059.

134 *'on those who surrendered':* Sandys, *Churchill: Wanted Dead or Alive*, 40.

135 *signal messages back to Estcourt:* A later version of the armoured train employed on 15 Nov. 1899 had its locomotive cloaked in heavy rope chains, and was aptly dubbed 'Hairy Mary'. (Ibid., 45.)

135 *exposed targets for a Boer marksman:* WSC, *The Boer War*, 36, based on his dispatch of Nov. 20, 1899 from Pretoria.

135 *far greater chance of survival:* Morgan, *Churchill*, 130.

136 *went back to sleep:* De Mendelssohn, *The Age of Churchill*, 147. Peter de Mendelssohn's account is based on the memoirs of Atkins, *Incidents and Reflections*, 127–28, and Amery, *My Political Life*, vol. 1, 117.

136 *'accepted the invitation without demur':* Haldane memoir, quoted in *Churchill*, vol. 1, 447.

Chapter 11: The Great Escapade

137 *'both sides of the railway':* De Mendelssohn, *The Age of Churchill*, 148. The original source of this quotation is Leo Amery, *My Political Life*, vol. 1, 117.

138 *'twice on the same day':* Churchill, *The Boer War*, 38; and Sandys, *Churchill: Wanted Dead or Alive*, 49.

139 *'brave man but a damned fool':* Capt. James Wylie of the Durban Light Infantry quoted in Sandys, *Churchill: Wanted Dead or Alive*, 50.

139 *'were not greater'*: WSC to the Prince of Wales, written in Pretoria on Nov. 30, 1899, CV, vol. 1, part 2, 1080–82.
139 *'poor beggars to their fate'*: Sandys, *Churchill: Wanted Dead or Alive*, 53.
140 *'began to pour with rain'*: Dispatch written and sent from Pretoria on Nov. 20, 1899.
140 *'lords' sons every day'*: Ibid.
141 *other captured British officers*: The Business of War: The War Narrative of Major General Sir John Kennedy (London, 1957), 316.
141 *win a seat in Parliament*: Sir James Aylmer L. Haldane, *A Soldier's Saga* (Edinburgh, 1948), 147. Smuts also admitted that he had had second thoughts about Churchill's arguments and had signed an order for his release only to have Churchill escape before it could be delivered.
141 *might be unjust after all*: Atkins, *The Relief of Ladysmith*, 194–95; and WSC, *The Boer War*, 49.
141 *'interesting for my paper!'*: Atkins, *Incidents and Reflections*, 74–75. Peter de Mendelssohn notes that 'These sayings have become famous, and no biographer of Churchill can afford to omit them; but Churchill himself does not mention them, and it is likely as not that they are apocryphal.' (*The Age of Churchill*, 149.) However, given that Atkins was a scrupulously honest reporter, there is no reason to doubt their accuracy.
141 *'fifty men would have been'*: Quoted in Gilbert, *Churchill: A Life*, 111.
142 *'engine-driver will get the V.C.'*: Thomas Walden to JC, Nov. 17, 1899, *Churchill*, vol. 1, 452.
142 *War Office was not interested*: Sandys, *Churchill: Wanted Dead or Alive*, 69–70. In 1910, when he was home secretary, Churchill lobbied hard on behalf of Wagner and the fireman, Alexander Stewart. Both men were awarded the Albert Medal for their valour on 15 November 1899. The medal was initiated in March 1866 in honour of Queen Victoria's late husband, Albert, the Prince Consort. Although it was originally established to recognize heroic deeds in saving life at sea, in 1877 its criteria were broadened to recognize similar life-saving acts on land.
142 *next day's march began*: Ibid., 72.
142 *'who were downcast and dejected'*: Ibid., 74–75.
143 *'all else is favour'*: Dispatch, Nov. 20, 1899.
143 *'procure my release'*: WSC to JC, Nov. 18, 1899. By the time this letter reached London on New Year's Day 1900, Churchill had long since escaped from Pretoria.
143 *'might have been shot at once'*: Michael Paterson, *Winston Churchill: Personal Accounts of the Great Leader at War* (Newton Abbot, 2005), 151, and *My Early Life*, 253.
144 *'I am in this place!'*: Interview of Chris de Souza (grandson of Louis de Souza) for BBC documentary on Churchill, WCHL 15/2/86, CAC.
144 *under no circumstances be released*: Quotation by a Boer officer in a letter to F. W. Reitz, the Transvaal state secretary, in Sandys, *Churchill: Wanted Dead or Alive*, 86.
144 *'think how little time remains'*: WSC to William Bourke-Cochran (his host in New York City in 1895), Nov. 30, 1899.
144 *'regaining my freedom'*: WSC, *London to Ladysmith* (London, 1900), 70.
144 *feather in his own cap*: My Early Life, 266.
145 *their means of escape*: Churchill later claimed that the wall was ten feet high; however, it was later examined and found to be approximately six feet high. Moreover, it would have been nearly impossible to carry out such a feat without assistance. (Letter of L. C. B. Howard to Randolph Churchill, CV, vol. 1, part 2, 1133.)
145 *'it had to be drunk'*: Haldane, *A Soldier's Saga*, 156.
145 *'did not go according to plan'*: Ibid.
146 *'less fitted for the job'*: Robert Lewis Taylor, *Winston Churchill* (New York, 1952), 183.
147 *'for help and guidance'*: My Early Life, 276.
147 *'gurglings from time to time'*: Ibid., 275.
149 *'we will see you through'*: Reminiscences of John Howard in the *Johannesburg Star*,

Dec. 11, 1923, in CV, vol. 1, part 2, 1125; and Alexander J. P. Graham, *The Capture and Escape of Winston Churchill* (Salisbury, Rhodesia, 1965), 8, copy in WCHL 2/8, CAC.

149 *was obliged to confide:* L. C. B. Howard (son of John Howard) to Randolph Churchill, May 31, 1963, CV, vol. 1, part 2, 1132.

150 *'export to Lourenço Marques':* Graham, *The Capture and Escape of Winston Churchill,* 10.

000 *cold tea and a revolver:* Ibid., 11.

150 *'Goods arrived safely':* Ibid., 11–13. Burnham was later suspected of involvement in Churchill's escape and was tried, but he was able to convince the court that he was on legitimate business in Lourenço Marques.

150 *'I visit Pretoria. – Churchill':* WCHL 2/2, CAC. Both telegrams were dated December 1899.

150 *'bid you a personal farewell':* Churchill to Louis de Souza, Dec. 11, 1898, copy in *Churchill,* vol. 1, 478–79.

151 *strains of 'Rule, Britannia':* Sandys, *Churchill: Wanted Dead or Alive,* 136–38.

151 *'Thank God – Pamela':* Churchill, vol. 1, 489.

151 *'God that looks after Winston':* Leslie, *The End of a Chapter,* 125.

151 *'Correspondent of the day':* De Mendelssohn, *The Age of Churchill,* 156.

151 *'nothing can keep them back':* Captain Percy Scott to WSC, March 24, 1900, CV, vol. 1, part 2, 1160.

Chapter 12: 'The Red Gleam of War'

(WSC's dispatches cited herein are in Woods, *Young Winston's Wars.*)

153 *'appears to be, out here':* Gen. Sir Redvers Buller to Lady Theresa Londonderry, Dec. 26, 1899, CV, vol. 1, part 2, 1093.

153 *'Boer military genius':* Atkins, *The Relief of Ladysmith,* 192–95.

154 *'frankness and perfect manliness':* Mortimer Menpes, *War Impressions* (London, 1901), 124–27.

154 *'might care to give me':* Churchill, vol. 1, 492.

154 *'had paid his brother's debts':* J. B. Atkins quoted ibid., 495.

154 *'reputation behind the kopjes':* Leslie, *The End of a Chapter,* 162.

155 *'And Tommy can never forget':* The full quote is in Sandys, *Churchill: Wanted Dead or Alive,* 134–35.

155 *'Sir Reverse Buller':* Freeman-Barnes, *The Boer War,* 45–47.

155 *he paid serious attention':* My Early Life, 234.

156 *'They do not exist':* Queen Victoria quoted in Freeman-Barnes, *The Boer War,* 47.

156 *'red gleam of war':* Dispatch, Jan. 22, 1900.

156 *captured – all for nothing:* Freeman-Barnes, *The Boer War,* 49.

156 *'the pitiful and the sublime':* Dispatch, Jan. 22, 1900.

156 *'Queen's latest recruit':* Ibid., Jan. 25, 1900.

157 *'here I stay – perhaps forever':* WSC to Pamela Plowden, Jan. 28, 1900, CV, vol. 1, part 2, 1146–47. He added to her discontent by writing, 'I am really enjoying myself immensely and if I live I shall look back with much pleasure upon all this.' Only Churchill could look at the experience of a brutal war such as this one and use the word 'pleasure'.

157 *'The war is vy bitter':* WSC to Pamela Plowden, Feb. 21, 1900, ibid., 1151.

157 *'close to a great event':* Dispatch, Mar. 9, 1900. It took eighteen thousand troops finally to break the four-month siege of Ladysmith.

158 *dispatch of 9 March 1900:* In 1946 Gough examined a copy of *My Early Life* in the Imperial War Museum and made numerous marginal comments in pencil in the book that contradicted Churchill. See Paterson, *Winston Churchill,* 111–12 and 168–69; *My Early Life,* 325–26; and dispatch, March 9, 1900.

158 *brushes with death had only begun:* Churchill reported to his aunt Leonie that he had been under fire 'in forty separate affairs' in the Boer War, and 'one cannot help wondering how long good luck will hold.' (WSC to Mrs Jack Leslie, May 15, 1900.)

159 *'a most exciting adventure'*: *My Early Life*, 338–41. Churchill thought Trooper Roberts should have received the Victoria Cross for his bravery, and though it is not known if he was recommended for it, Roberts did receive the Distinguished Conduct Medal (DCM) in 1907, at least in part owing to the intervention of Churchill, then the under-secretary of state for the colonies. Churchill also sent Roberts a token ten-pound reward. At the time the DCM was the highest decoration for bravery a private soldier could receive, other than the Victoria Cross.

159 *'so near destruction'*: WSC to JC, May 1, 1900, CV, vol. 1, part 2, 1172.

159 *'already mine as a right'*: Col. Neville Chamberlain to WSC, April 11, 1900; and WSC to JC, May 1, 1900.

159 *have got over the snub*: *My Early Life*, 334.

159 *'glide away past our noses'*: Ibid., 352.

160 *newly liberated prisoners cheered*: Diary of Augustus M. Goodacre, quoted in *Churchill*, vol. 1, 512.

161 *'so nothing happened'*: Sir Ian Hamilton, *Listening for the Drums* (London, 1944).

161 *fired at him in anger*: *My Early Life*, 353–54.

Chapter 13: Lessons Learned

162 *each side killed the other*: J. F. C. Fuller quoted in Freeman-Barnes, *The Boer War*, 8–9 and *My Early Life*, 356.

163 *' "We are good friends now" '*: Pollock, *Kitchener*, 212.

163 *something he never forgot*: Sandys, *Churchill: Wanted Dead or Alive*, xxxi.

164 *'unforeseeable and uncontrollable events'*: *My Early Life*, 232.

164 *'among veteran commanders'*: WSC, 'Sir John French', in his *Great Contemporaries* (New York, 1991), 47.

164 *calling it 'ungenerous'*: *My Early Life*, 299–300. General Sir Hubert Gough wrote that he had encountered WSC during the siege of Ladysmith: 'He showed me some cuttings, not in the least abashed, and said: 'Look at these – you see people are talking about me already.' He did not seem to mind what they said so long as he got the publicity.' (Paterson, *Winston Churchill*, 164.)

165 *'even the war was forgotten'*: Sandys, *Churchill: Wanted Dead or Alive*, 99, quoting Adrian Hofmeyr, *The Story of My Captivity* (London, 1900), 132.

165 *self-centred young civilian*: Morgan, *Churchill*, 136–37.

165 *interview him about his escape*: Haldane, *A Soldier's Saga*, chap. 25.

166 *'I didn't like his manners'*: Interview of Don Burnham, WCHL 15/2/86.

166 *Howard had vanished*: CV, vol. 1, part 2, 1133–35.

166 *'Dec. 13, 1899'*: Ibid., 1136.

167 *his capture had been miserly*: *Sunday Dispatch* (London), Oct. 22, 1939. In a recent landmark book on how Churchill wrote his own best-selling six-volume account of the Second World War, the historian David Reynolds has shown how Churchill manipulated events to suit his own point of view, and had no intention of leaving 'his reputation to "history", without being one of the historians'. (David Reynolds, *In Command of History* [New York and London, 2004], 41.) In the case of the Botha myth, Churchill's son and granddaughter have debunked this tale in their accounts.

167 *later editions of the book*: Morgan, *Churchill*, 137. The book in question was *Twice Captured*, by Lord Rosslyn, published by William Blackwood.

168 *'night of the 12th'*: WSC memorandum, written in 1912 when he was first lord of the Admiralty, quoted in *Churchill*, vol. 1, 484. Randolph Churchill believed it was written in connection with the *Blackwood's* libel case.

168 *'not having played the game'*: Diary of Gen. Sir Aylmer Haldane, Haldane Papers, National Library of Scotland, quoted in CV, vol. 1, part 2, 1115.

168 *'ignore that quality'*: Gen. Sir Aylmer Haldane to Lord Knutsford, April 22, 1931, WCHL 2/3, CAC.

169 *'a soldier or a mere word-painter'*: *Spectator* review of May 26, 1900, quoted in de Mendelssohn, *The Age of Churchill*, 161.

169 *in the early 1900s*: Diary of Sir John Colville, Sept. 20, 1940, Colville Papers, CAC.

169 *'In peace, Goodwill'*: *My Early Life*, 330–31.

169 *'I could do both'*: Ibid., 331. Churchill's suggested inscription was never used for the First World War memorial, and only when his history of the Second World War was published did it become a vital part of each of the six volumes. (*The Age of Churchill*, 161.) His private secretary, Edward Marsh, was present when he uttered this remark after the First World War. 'I wish the tones in which he spoke this could have been "recorded",' he wrote, 'the first phrase a rattle of musketry, the second "grating harsh thunder", the third a ray of sun through storm-clouds; the last, pure benediction.' (Edward Marsh, *A Number of People: A Book of Reminiscences* [New York and London, 1939], 152.)

169 *feelings were palpable*: Atkins, *The Relief of Ladysmith*, 193.

169 *'In Durance Vile'*: *My Early Life*, chap. 20.

170 *in the new century*: WSC, *The World Crisis*. vol. 1, *1911–1914* (New York, 1923), 9–10.

Chapter 14: Star Bright

171 *Lord Wolseley in the chair*: Leslie, 'Winston, A Cousinly Memory'.

171 *'bit short on brains'*: Ralph G. Martin, *Jennie: The Life of Lady Randolph Churchill: The Dramatic Years, 1895–1921* (New York, 1971), 144.

172 *affairs with a number of women*: Ibid., 349.

172 *marriage was dissolved in 1914*: Anita Leslie, *Lady Randolph Churchill*, 298, 336–37.

172 *'future Prime Minister of England'*: Haffner, *Churchill*, 27.

173 *'Randolph's boy'*: Randolph S. Churchill, *Winston S. Churchill: Young Statesman, 1901–1914* (Boston, 1967), 6, hereafter cited as *Churchill*, vol. 2.

173 *very uncommon politician*: When it came to public speaking, the son emulated his father, even down to the deliberate manner of his usually dramatic delivery, the pauses at key points, the impression that it was extemporaneous when, in fact, it had been carefully written over a period of days (and sometimes weeks) and endlessly revised and rehearsed.

173 *campaign for seats in Parliament*: Manchester, *The Last Lion: Visions*, 259n.

174 *'exhaustion of the conquerors'*: All quotations from Churchill's lengthy speech are in Hansard, May 13, 1901.

175 *'meet the threat'*: Rose, *Churchill: The Unruly Giant*, 102–3.

176 *'than serve in Heaven'*: Leslie, 'Winston, A Cousinly Memory'.

176 *'heads of the tall poppies'*: *Churchill*, vol. 2, 174.

176 *when Churchill evaded them*: Leslie, *Long Shadows*, 29.

177 *'until 1940 to 1945'*: 'Lord Quickswood', notes by Lord Moran on Hugh Cecil, Box 55, Moran Papers.

177 *party members and the Tory press*: Haffner, *Churchill*, 35.

178 *admission to an exclusive polo club*: Stuart Ball, *Churchill* (New York and London, 2003), 30.

178 *' "W.C. without a seat?" '*: Ibid., 29.

178 *'Must everyone hate my Winston?'*: Leslie, 'Winston, A Cousinly Memory'.

178 *deemed a devious self-promoter*: H. W. Brands, *T.R.: The Last Romantic* (New York, 1997), 662–63.

178 *whom he would infuriate*: King Edward VII to Lord Crewe, circa March 1906, *Churchill*, vol. 2, 180.

179 *'with care and even with ceremony'*: Marsh, *A Number of People*, 151.

179 *'at least of Topography'*: Ibid., 167.

179 *'Winston no convictions'*: *Churchill*, vol. 2, 239.

179 *'it served him well'*: WC, 167.

180 *'seemed to bring them on'*: File K-5/2/3, Box 62, Moran Papers.

180 'at all in such moments': Box 94, Moran Papers, diary, Aug. 14, 1944; Gilbert, *Churchill: A Life*, 167; and Mary Soames, *Clementine Churchill* (New York and London, rev. ed. 2002), 77–78. Mary Soames is convinced that painting, which her father first took up in 1915, was wonderful therapy that enabled him to grapple with his demons. (See chap. 22.)

181 'light of genius': WC, 281.

181 *whom she gently rebuffed: Churchill*, vol. 2, 244; Nathan Miller, *Theodore Roosevelt: A Life* (New York, 1992), 325n.

181 'not likely to contact either!': Leslie, 'Winston, A Cousinly Memory'.

181 'I would drink it': This is one of Churchill's best-known quotations, but for many years. it was believed to be apocryphal. It was also thought by some to have been said by F. E. Smith – a man every bit as witty as Churchill. However, Sunny Churchill's former wife, Consuelo Balsan (the daughter of the railway tycoon William Vanderbilt), verified its authenticity in her book *The Glitter and the Gold* (London, 1953). 'In *Nancy: The Life of Lady Astor*, [author] Christopher Sykes confirms Consuelo Balsan's account. "It sounds like an invention but is well authenticated." ' (Source: www.winstonchurchill.org/.)

181 *daughter of a Scottish laird: Churchill*, vol. 2, 240.

182 'nothing but ill': Ibid., 241.

182 'I am a glowworm': WC, 15–16.

182 'very companionable one': Mary Soames, ed., *Winston and Clementine: The Personal Letters of the Churchills* (Boston: 1998; published in London as *Speaking For Themselves*), xvi. This book is a comprehensive and touching portrait of her parents and their fifty-year marriage that spares neither in its honesty.

182 'her belief in his destiny': Ibid., xvii.

182 'steadfast and pugnacious courage': Marsh, *A Number of People*, 154.

183 pale-pink silk underwear: WC, 230.

183 *rarely repeated, of crossing her:* There were other occasions on which Clementine put her foot down. During one of her husband's voyages to the Mediterranean while first lord of the Admiralty, she refused to permit a live turtle to become Winston's soup du jour that evening. (Marsh, *A Number of People*, 244.)

184 *nights of non-stop monologues:* One of those taking note of Churchill's taste for monologues was a family friend, Diana Mitford. 'Churchill tended to talk at her rather than with her.' Diana married Sir Oswald Mosley, who became Britain's leading Fascist. Both Diana and Oswald Mosley were interned during the Second World War (from 1940 to 1943) in Holloway Prison. (Interview with Diana Mosley, BREN 19, Brendon Papers.)

184 *have shared with Clementine:* Violet Bonham Carter to Venetia Stanley (Clementine Churchill's cousin), Aug. 14, 1908, Mark Bonham Carter and Mark Pottle eds., *The Letters and Diaries of Violet Bonham Carter*, vol. 1, *Lantern Slides, 1904–1914* (London, 1996), 162; and Soames, *Winston and Clementine*, 73.

184 'penitent pigs or pugs': Soames, *Winston and Clementine*, xiv.

184 'lived happily ever after': *My Early Life*, 372.

Chapter 15: The Odd Couple

185 'his descent from Marlborough': Paul Addison, *Churchill: The Unexpected Hero* (Oxford, 2005), 58, quoting Labour politician J. .R. Clynes.

185 *as his personal guest:* The British monarchy's web of German connections in 1906 was made more tangled by the marriage of Queen Victoria to Prince Albert of the German House of Saxe-Coburg-Gotha. Victoria's successor was her son, Edward VII, whose nephew was Kaiser Wilhelm II, the son of Edward's sister, Princess Victoria, who had married the German crown prince Frederick III. Queen Victoria's Hanoverian dynasty had begun with the accession in 1714 of King George I, a German.

186 ' "Exercise a wise discretion" ': Sir Henry Campbell-Bannerman to WSC, Aug. 25, 1906, CV, vol. 2, part 1: *1901–1907*, 574.

186 'German Army before mobilization': WSC, Amid These Storms: Thoughts and Adventures (New York, 1932; published in London as Thoughts and Adventures), 76.
186 example of royal privilege: Ibid., 78–79.
186 'fools in the world again': De Mendelssohn, The Age of Churchill, 125.
187 'was a notable event': Ibid.
187 'to study so pleasantly': WSC to Kaiser Wilhelm II, n.d., but apparently well after his return to England in Sept. 1906, Churchill, vol. 2, 192.
187 'between that army and England': Ibid., 191.
187 'supervision of that sea': Leslie, The End of a Chapter, 123.
187 exercises he attended in May 1909: Jenkins, Churchill, 203.
188 'flowering – in bright red blossom': WSC to CHC, May 30, 1909.
188 were regarded as heretics: James, Warrior Race, 439.
188 'enormous advance upon 1906': Amid These Storms, 81.
189 'wicked folly & barbarism it all is': WSC to CHC, Sept. 15, 1909.
189 like no other in its history: Arthur J. Marder, From the Dreadnought to Scapa Flow, vol. 1, The Road to War, 1904–1914 (London, 1961), vii.
190 'rests the British Empire': Arthur Herman, To Rule the Waves: How the British Navy Shaped the Modern World (New York and London, 2004), 480.
190 'I would have had you shot': Morgan, Churchill, 477.
190 'ruthless, relentless and remorseless!': Ibid., 478.
190 'Moderation in war is imbecility': Jan Morris, 'Fisher's Face', Quarterly Journal of Military History (Autumn 1993).
190 faster battle cruisers: Massie, Dreadnought, 782.
190 'clearing away the cobwebs': Prof. Arthur Marder quoted in Geoffrey Penn, Fisher, Churchill and the Dardanelles (Barnsley, 1999), 4–5. Arthur Marder is widely regarded as the dean of historians of the Royal Navy.
191 domination of the seas: Herman, To Rule the Waves, 479–80.
191 'navy were on guard': Massie, Dreadnought, 501.
192 'guts of the British sailor': Penn, Fisher, Churchill and the Dardanelles, 2.
192 ' "sparks from the same fire" ': Jan Morris, Fisher's Face: Or, Getting to Know the Admiral (New York and London, 1995), 229.
192 'I reflected on it often': The World Crisis, vol. 1, 73.
193 bitter feud in 1915: Arthur Marder, ed., Fear God and Dread Nought: The Correspondence of Admiral of the Fleet Lord Fisher of Kilverstone (London, 1952–9, 3 vols.), vol. 2, 17.
193 'their homes a dunghill': The World Crisis, vol. 1, 73.
193 'into intense activity': Ibid., 75.
193 'and . . . he refused it': WC, 159.
194 'upon purely public grounds': WSC to Herbert Asquith, March 14, 1908, CV, vol. 2, part 2: 1907–1911, 754–55.
194 'offered ample scope': WC, 159–60.
194 gone to Reginald McKenna: Ibid., 159.
194 international trade routes: Massie, Dreadnought, 685–86.
195 'we finally compromised on eight': Herman, To Rule the Waves, 484.
196 'with open arms': The World Crisis, vol. 1, 37–38. The naval historian Jon Sumida has written that the Churchill–Fisher dispute of 1909 was really about 'Churchill's trepidation with regard to the devious and hazardous course being pursued by the First Sea Lord.' (Jon Sumida, 'Churchill and British Sea Power, 1908–29', in R. A. C. Parker, ed., Winston Churchill: Studies in Statesmanship [London, 2002], 8.)
196 'better for us all': Sumida, 'Churchill and British Sea Power, 1908–29', 9; Fisher to WSC, Mar. 2, 1910, and WSC to Fisher, Mar. 3, 1910, in CV, vol. 2, part 2, 988–89.
196 'Winston thinks with his mouth': Jenkins, Churchill, 188.
197 with a dog whip in Bristol: Ibid., 185–86.
197 'England of George V': Morgan, Churchill, 312.

197 *'with equal persuasiveness'*: Ibid., 313.
197 *'Still I think I could do it'*: De Mendelssohn, *The Age of Churchill*, 103.

Chapter 16: 'Alarm Bells Throughout Europe'

198 *promise even greater ones:* David Fromkin, *Europe's Last Summer* (New York, 2004), 17.
199 *'butt ends of our rifles'*: Massie, *Dreadnought*, 175.
199 *'mastery of the world'*: Ibid., xxii.
199 *'most brilliant failure in history'*: Ibid., 106.
199 *rulers of the Holy Roman Empire:* Hagen Schulze, *Germany: A New History* (Cambridge, MA, 1998), 169–70.
200 *stronger than that of Britain:* Herman, *To Rule the Waves*, 473.
200 *'North Sea foam'*: Massie, *Dreadnought*, 164.
200 *cautious* Realpolitik *to an expansionist* Weltpolitik: Golo Mann, *The History of Germany Since 1789* (New York, 1968), 262.
201 *was in fact a menace:* Manchester, *The Last Lion: Visions*, 350.
201 *regarded it as a hostile act:* The Anglo-German naval race resulted in 60 per cent larger battleships, on which the British eventually mounted 15-inch guns that fired massive shells weighing more than nineteen hundred pounds. (Archer Jones, *The Art of War in the Western World* [New York, 1987], 432.)
201 *'Europe began immediately to quiver'*: *The World Crisis*, vol. 1, 43.
202 *'edge of the precipice'*: Ibid., 49–50.
202 *it would pay the price:* WSC notes of conversation with Sir John French, Aug. 10, 1911, CV, vol. 2, part 2, 1107–08.
202 *'jolly well mistaken'*: WSC to CHC, July 4, 1911.
203 *on D+33 days:* Ibid., 508–9; and Morgan, *Churchill*, 331. The complete text of WSC's memo of Aug. 13, 1911, is in *The World Crisis*, vol. 1, 60–64.
203 *'anything at all about the subject'*: Diary of Gen. Sir Henry Wilson, quoted in Morgan, *Churchill*, 331.
204 *future battles might be fought:* Barbara Tuchman, *The Guns of August* (New York and London, 1962), 49–50.
204 *'march in heavy black'*: Ibid.
204 *potential war with Germany:* *The World Crisis*, vol. 1, 53.
205 *'he feared nothing – absolutely nothing'*: Ibid., 80.
205 *testy exchange ensued:* Ibid., 51–52; and de Mendelssohn, *The Age of Churchill*, 539–40.
205 *'only he had the key!'*: Marder, *From the Dreadnought to Scapa Flow*, vol. 1, 244. This same arcane view informed the policy of Wilson's predecessor, Jackie Fisher.
205 *'Cabinet or otherwise'*: Penn, *Fisher, Churchill and the Dardanelles*, 11.
205 *'cocksure, insouciant and apathetic'*: Rose, *Churchill*, 107.
205 *'suicidal folly'*: Sir Peter Gretton, *Former Naval Person: Winston Churchill and the Royal Navy* (London, 1968), 47.
206 *now a motive for action:* Richard B. Haldane Viscount Haldane, *An Autobiography* (New York and London, 1929), 227–28; and de Mendelssohn, *The Age of Churchill*, 542.
206 *'persuade or induce others'*: *The World Crisis*, vol. 1, 65–66.
206 *'fatal to our country'*: WSC to Lloyd George, Aug. 31, 1911.
207 *disastrously in the Boer War:* Chandler, *Oxford Illustrated History of the British Army*, 216–17.
207 *afraid of criticism:* Ibid., 217, 220.
208 *'sleep quietly in your beds'*: Fisher quoted in Massie, *Dreadnought*, 450.
208 *'in fact a British possession'*: Sir Charles Dilke cited in Herman, *To Rule the Waves*, 475.
209 *'to be rid of the radical'*: Haffner, *Churchill*, 38.
209 *more even-handed custodian:* Jenkins, *Churchill*, 205.

209 *'power had been set up'*: *The World Crisis*, vol. 1, 68.
209 *'message of reassurance'*: Ibid., 68–69.
210 *'pour into it everything I've got'*: WC, 249.

Chapter 17: First Lord of The Admiralty

211 *'and the dedication of a friar'*: WC, 361.
211 *rooted in the Churchill legend*: The official biographer Martin Gilbert notes in *In Search of Churchill* that this phrase is just one among many legendary sayings attributed to him whose authenticity has never been proved (232). In 1955 Churchill's post-war private secretary, Anthony Montague Browne, asked him if the statement was true and was told: 'I never said it. I wish I had.' (*Finest Hour* [Spring 2006], 13.)
212 *since the time of Nelson*: Massie, *Dreadnought*, 396–97.
212 *scripted and predictable*: Gretton, *Former Naval Person*, 55.
212 *'bow-and-arrow epoch'*: Marder, *From the Dreadnought to Scapa Flow*, vol. 1, 8.
212 *resistance to change*: Stephen Roskill, *Churchill and the Admirals* (London, 1977), 29.
212 *location of the kaiser's fleet*: Massie, *Dreadnought*, 769.
213 *luxury he did not enjoy*: *The World Crisis*, vol. 1, chap. 4.
214 *called him a 'Lilliput Napoleon'*: Addison, *Churchill*, 67.
214 *dragged on like marathons*: Holmes, *In the Footsteps of Churchill*, 113–14.
214 *'small aspect of the question'*: William Brett, Viscount Esher (1852–1930) quoted in James, *Churchill: A Study in Failure*, 52.
215 *'dating from Nelson's time'*: Manchester, *The Last Lion: Visions*, 433.
215 *'a Royal pimp'*: Ibid., 440.
216 *over such matters*: Churchill did not have a particularly high opinion of George V and wrote contemptuously after he had inspected the fleet in May 1912, 'The King talked more stupidly about the Navy than I have ever heard him before. Really it is disheartening to hear the cheap & silly drivel with wh he lets himself be filled up.' (WSC to CHC, May 12, 1912.)
216 *'is a perfect fool'*: Adm. Earl Beatty to his wife, May 27, 1912, Penn, *Fisher, Churchill and the Dardanelles*, 22.
217 *'which he did not'*: Sumida, 'Churchill and British Sea Power, 1908–29', 10.
217 *over the horizon*: Massie, *Dreadnought*, 782.
217 *'redesigned to fit them'*: *The World Crisis*, vol. 1, 123; and Massie, *Dreadnought*, 781–83.
218 *Anglo-Persian Oil Company*: Massie, *Dreadnought*, 785.
218 *backbone of the Royal Navy*: Ibid., 782.
219 *'understanding, and it failed'*: Tuchman, *The Guns of August*, 52–53.
219 *'strain grows greater'*: WSC speech in Glasgow, Feb. 9, 1912, cited in Robert Rhodes James, ed., *Churchill Speaks, 1897–1963* (New York, 1998), 221. Churchill's strong words were a direct reaction to a speech made by the kaiser when opening the Reichstag. He read about it in a London newspaper and thought it provocative.
219 *'greatest possible help'*: *Churchill*, vol. 2, 546.
219 *'laid down by her'*: James, *Churchill Speaks*, Mar. 18, 1912.
220 *to the negotiating table*: *Churchill*, vol. 2, 551–52.
220 *issue of naval security*: Sumida, 'Churchill and British Sea Power, 1908–29', 10–11.
220 *'have got to the end'*: Speech to the Royal Academy, May 4, 1912, in James, *Churchill Speaks*, 239–40.
220 *'passed from the world'*: *Churchill*, vol. 2, 553.
220 *'only thirty months!'*: *The World Crisis*, vol. 1, 93.
221 *'I will not describe what followed'*: WC, 283–84.
221 *'place in the sun'*: Herman, *To Rule the Waves*, 473.
221 *with the ambitious Wilhelm*: Massie, *Dreadnought*, xxi, xxiii–xxxiv.
222 *'probing, pertinent and detailed'*: Ibid.

222 *'become a water creature'*: Churchill, vol. 2, 558.
222 *of the Royal Navy men*: Roskill, Churchill and the Admirals, 22; and Gretton, *Former Naval Person*, chap. 4.
223 *'had rendered his report'*: Marder, From the Dreadnought to Scapa Flow, vol. 1, 255.
223 *'Why didn't you lock him up?'*: Gretton, *Former Naval Person*, 76.
223 *'as almost indecent'*: Ibid., 75.
223 *'menace of approaching war?'*: The World Crisis, vol. 1, 119.
224 *'barely find the target at all'*: Massie, Dreadnought, 786–88; quotation on 788.
224 *mock charge with sabres flashing*: Diary of Violet Asquith, June 2 and 3, 1912. A full description of WSC's 1912 cruise is recorded in Bonham Carter and Pottle, *Lantern Slides*; and in WC, chap. 19.
224 *'all over to play the part'*: Gretton, *Former Naval Person*, 76.
225 *'nestling towns sky-high'*: WC, 275.
225 *'inner needs of your soul'*: WSC to CHC, Nov. 3, 1913.
225 *'for her – except Clemmie'*: WSC to Sunny Churchill, Nov. 6, 1912, Marlborough Papers.

Chapter 18: Lighting the Bonfire

226 *'L'avion c'est zéro!'*: The Last Lion: Visions, 443–44; and Tuchman, *The Guns of August*, 239.
226 *'avail ourselves of his knowledge'*: Report of CID Sub-Committee on Aerial Navigation, Feb. 25, 1909, CV, vol. 2, part 3: *1911–1914*, 1874.
227 *'young Englishman can adopt'*: WSC to Second Sea Lord, Dec. 1911, Churchill, vol. 2, 678.
227 *first experimental craft*: The World Crisis, vol. 1, 313.
227 *the aircraft carrier*: Churchill, vol. 2, 679–80.
227 *'schoolboys with a new toy'*: Lewis Broad, Winston Churchill: The Years of Preparation (London, 1963), 150. The Royal Engineers formed the first army aviation unit in 1911. The problem faced by the British was a lack of trained pilots. In 1912 the army had fewer than a dozen, compared with the French, whose Flying Service already had some 263.
227 *Britain's military aviation*: John Edward Bernard 'Jack' Seely (1868–1947) was a cavalry officer in the Boer War, in which he won a DSO. He was elected to Parliament in 1900 as a Conservative, but like his friend Churchill, whom he had met in South Africa, he defected to the Liberals in 1904. He was secretary of state for war from 1911 to 1914 and during the First World War commanded a Canadian cavalry brigade, ending the war as a major general.
228 *aegis of the CID*: Although a subcommittee of the CID chaired by Richard Burton Haldane laid down the criteria for what was to be called the Flying Corps, consisting of a naval wing, a military wing and a central flying school to train pilots, in reality there was no one in charge of this multi-headed beast – with the result that each service largely went its own way. (Sir Maurice Dean, *The Royal Air Force and Two World Wars* [London, 1979], 7–8.)
228 *'fleet in the reconnaissance role'*: Churchill, vol. 2, 679.
228 *'expect blooms in a month'*: Lt (later Adm.) Richard Davies, RN, in memoir of Churchill's flying experience by Group Capt. Ivon Courtney, Churchill, vol. 2, 681–82.
228 *its several airships*: Ibid., 680–81.
229 *any longer than necessary*: Ibid.
229 *'swearing to a standstill'*: Andrew Boyle, Trenchard (London, 1962), 36.
229 *before galloping away*: Ibid.; and Morgan, Churchill, 91–92.
230 *'impatient for a good pupil'*: Pelling, Churchill, 168; and Manchester, *The Last Lion: Visions*, 446.
230 *'have taken a different turning'*: Boyle, Trenchard, 107.
230 *had even been born*: Manchester, The Last Lion: Visions, 449.

230 *'alive & on the wing'*: WSC to CHC, Oct. 23, 1913.
231 *by installing weapons: Churchill*, vol. 2, 683.
231 *'don't fly any more just now'*: Sunny Churchill to WSC, Mar. 12, 1913; and Soames, *Clementine Churchill*, 115.
231 *'can I go on liking him'*: Manchester, *The Last Lion: Visions*, 447.
231 *'your career & your friends'*: F. E. Smith to WSC, Dec. 6, 1913, *Churchill*, vol. 2, 687.
231 *'vexed with me'*: WSC to CHC, Nov. 29, 1913.
232 *killing all aboard*: Broad, *Churchill*, 247–48.
232 *'well-known landing places exist'*: WSC minute, March 5, 1914, *Churchill*, vol. 2, 676.
232 *'Your loving Clemmie'*: CHC to WSC, June 5, 1914.
233 *'rejoice & relieve your heart'*: WSC to CHC, June 6, 1914.
233 *'I am so sorry'*: Ibid.
233 *by competitive examination: The World Crisis*, vol. 1, appendix A, 507.
234 *'even for a few hours'*: WC, 229, 277 and 288–89.
234 *'concentrate your attention'*: Ibid., 278–79.
235 *'lifelong dialogue'*: Soames, *Winston and Clementine*, xiii.
235 *extravagant Admiralty estimates*: Morgan, *Churchill*, 400–401; John Grigg, *Lloyd George: From Peace to War, 1912–1916* (London, 1997), 134–35; and *Churchill*, vol. 2, 636–37.
236 *'I believe I am watched over'*: WSC conversation with George Riddell, Jan. 18,1914, in Morgan, *Churchill*, 402.
236 *£4 to £5 million*: Ibid., 403.
236 *'so far been ineffectual'*: WSC quoted in Massie, *Dreadnought*, 854; and *The Times*, March 18, 1914.
237 *at Spithead on 19 July*: Martin Gilbert, *Winston S. Churchill: 1914–1916* (London, 1971), 3, hereafter cited as *Churchill*, vol. 3.
237 *whatever unfolded in Europe*: Robert K. Massie, *Castles of Steel* (New York, 2003), 17.
238 *'act upon it without hesitation'*: Tuchman, *The Guns of August*, 92.
238 *'of its kind ever devised'*: WSC to CHC, July 24, 1914.
238 *'give them a good drubbing'*: Ibid., July 24 and 28, 1914.
239 *supported British intervention*: WSC's letter to Arthur Ponsonby and his note to Lloyd George are in *Churchill*, vol. 2, 699, 701.
239 *admiring his enterprising conduct*: Miller, *Theodore Roosevelt*, 541 n. 1.
239 *'tomorrow morning'*: Michael and Eleanor Brock, eds., *H. H. Asquith: Letters to Venetia Stanley* (Oxford, 1985), letter of Aug. 4, 1914, 150–51.
240 *'Prepare, prepare!'*: *The World Crisis*, vol. 1, 192.
240 *'irrespective of party politics'*: Michael Howard, *The First World War* (Oxford, 2003), 31.
240 *night of 3 August 1914*: Mark Bonham Carter, ed., *The Autobiography of Margot Asquith* (Boston, 1962), 291.
240 *'lifted their hats in silence'*: Ibid.
240 *'numbness in my limbs'*: Ibid.
241 *of No. 10*: Ibid., 297.
241 *'at the declaration of war'*: Leslie, *The End of a Chapter*, 121.

Chapter 19: The Architect of War

242 *surely be over by Christmas*: Michael Howard, *War in European History* (Oxford, 1976), 112.
242 *wounding another twenty-one million*: Fromkin, *Europe's Last Summer*, 5.
242 *'paid for its protection'*: John Keegan, *The First World War* (New York, 1999), 426.
243 *1,700,000 Russians*: There has never been a definitive count of the number of First World War casualties, not least because the great numbers of missing (many never found) need to be factored in.

243 *'tragedy in human history'*: *The Economist*, Aug. 14, 1914.

244 *unsuited to that role*: Grigg, *Lloyd George*, 173; and Robert O'Neill, 1990 Gallipoli Memorial Lecture, 'For Want of Critics: The Tragedy of Gallipoli', *The Straits of War: Gallipoli Remembered* (Phoenix Mill, 2000), 78.

244 *breaking the deadlock*: For an excellent summation see Correlli Barnett, *The Swordbearers: Studies in Supreme Command in the First World War* (London, 1963), 104–05.

244 *'those difficult early days'*: Lord Hankey, *The Supreme Command* (London, 1961), 185–86.

245 *'crush the Rhine fortresses'*: Arthur Balfour quoted in *Churchill*, vol. 3, 72.

245 *suffered 740,000 dead*: Howard, *The First World War*, appendix 2, 146.

246 *'as soon as possible'*: *Churchill*, vol. 3, 65–66.

246 *'it is possible to imagine'*: Rear Adm. Sir Murray Sueter, *The Evolution of the Tank: A Record of the Royal Naval Air Service Caterpillar Experiments* (London, 1941, rev. ed.), 242.

246 *'would pray for is Peace'*: Asquith to Venetia Stanley, Sept. 16, 1914, Brock and Brock, *H. H. Asquith: Letters to Venetia Stanley*, 243. Other citations in this chapter are from this source.

246 *take from the First World War*: Kennedy's remark was part of a speech he was to have delivered at the Dallas Trade Mart on 22 November 1963.

246 *'exercise real power again'*: Asquith to Venetia Stanley, July 31, 1914.

247 *'preserve me from the politicians'*: Gilbert, *Churchill: A Life*, 267; Gilbert, *In Search of Churchill*, 175; *Churchill*, vol. 3, 21; *The World Crisis*, vol. 1, 202; and Pollock, *Kitchener*, 174.

248 *'like rats from a hole'*: Speech to all-party rally, Sept. 21, 1914, James, *Churchill Speaks*, 300.

248 *'not quite a gentleman'*: Morgan, *Churchill*, 455.

248 *'that could cross trenches'*: Sueter, *The Evolution of the Tank*, 15.

248 *'climb like the devil'*: F. Mitchell, *Tank Warfare: The Story of Tanks in the Great War* (London, 1933), 4. Although Swinton's rather ostentatious claim to be the father of the tank has been disproved, he does deserve credit for being 'the first British officer to set down in writing a definite concept of what tanks were needed for and how they ought to be employed'. (See J. P. Harris, *Men, Ideas and Tanks: British Military Thought and Armoured Forces, 1903–1939* [Manchester, 1995], 33, 47.)

249 *'bullet-proof shields and armour'*: Herbert Asquith, the Earl of Oxford, *Memories and Reflections, 1852–1927* (London, 1928), vol. 2, 'Contemporary Notes', Dec. 30, 1914, 62.

249 *a simple extension of logic*: Broad, *Winston Churchill*, 153.

249 *first War Office field trials*: WSC to Asquith, Jan. 5, 1915, and memos from the Dept of the Master General of Ordnance, Feb. and March 1915, *The World Crisis*, vol. 1, 75–76; and Pollock, *Kitchener*, 462.

250 *ripping out the tracks*: Sueter, *The Evolution of the Tank*, 50.

250 *'has ever been found practicable'*: *The World Crisis*, vol. 1, 77.

250 *chaired by d'Eyncourt*: *Churchill*, vol. 3, 536.

251 *shortened to 'tanks'*: Gilbert, *Churchill: A Life*, 298.

251 *'stupid Caterpillar landships'*: Ibid., 243–44.

251 *'Winston's folly'*: Broad, *Winston Churchill*, 245.

251 *eighteen of the new land ships*: Sueter, *The Evolution of the Tank*, 66; and Broad, *Winston Churchill*, 245.

252 *'certain it can be done'*: Sueter, *The Evolution of the Tank*, 53.

252 *'wish to see these trials'*: Ibid., 66; and Broad, *Winston Churchill*, 244.

252 *'your best brains into this'*: Broad, *Winston Churchill*, 244.

252 *design of the first tanks*: Harris, *Men, Ideas and Tanks*, chap. 1.

253 *'converted into practical shape'*: Ibid., 33.

253 *all things monetary flowed*: *The World Crisis*, vol. 2, *1915*, (New York, 1923), 78.

253 '*BROKEN BRITISH REGIMENTS*': Morgan, *Churchill*, 449.
254 'trust your further forecast!': *Churchill*, vol. 3, 64.
254 '*your courage & resolution*': Ibid.
254 '*first aspect was thrilling*': *The World Crisis*, vol. 1, 280–81.
255 '*passage [to France] of the Expeditionary Force*': Ibid., 27–28. The original intent was to establish the new naval air base at Ostend, but after only a few days a decision was made to use an aerodrome at Dunkirk instead.
255 *Churchill's pre-war flight instructors*: *Churchill*, vol. 3, 65–67.
255 *their home bases in Germany*: WSC to Director, Air Department, Royal Navy, Sept. 1, 1914, Sueter, *The Evolution of the Tank*, 28.
255 *first year of the war*: *The World Crisis*, vol. 1, 314.
255 *with Maxim fire*: *Churchill*, vol. 3, 68–69.
256 *bolster French morale*: Ibid., 73.
256 '*I acted for the best*': *The World Crisis*, vol. 1, 322.
256 '*few of them back again*': Asquith to Venetia Stanley, Sept. 19, 1914.
257 *his cousin and his officers*: Manchester, *The Last Lion: Visions*, 496.
257 *Germans scarcely noticed*: Ibid.
257 *Winston's 'own little army'*: Ibid.; WC, 348; and *Churchill*, vol. 3, 73–74.
257 *face a real enemy*: Asquith to Venetia Stanley, Sept. 19, 1914.
257 '*Mon Dieu!*': Manchester, *The Last Lion: Visions*, 496. Kay Halle, *Irrepressible Churchill* (Cleveland, 1966), 75. Trinity House was incorporated by a royal charter from Henry VIII in 1514 for the purpose of establishing and maintaining aids to navigation such as lighthouses, light vessels, buoys and beacons, and as the pilotage authority for London. It was supervised by a board of ten Elder Brethren, and it was in the uniform of an Elder that Churchill appeared in Antwerp on 3 October 1914. It was a rather unusual choice given Churchill's lifelong penchant for wearing the uniforms of various military services, but seems to reflect his role as the custodian of the Royal Navy, and thus of the sea. (See the official Trinity House website: www.trinityhouse.co.uk/.)

Chapter 20: Churchill's Private Army

258 '*beginning of the World*': CHC to WSC, Sept. 19, 1914. Churchill obtained both Kitchener's approval and that of Sir John French for his visit to the BEF in late Sept. 1914. (CV, vol. 3, part 1: *July 1914–April 1915*, 140–41.)
259 '*cast in the Napoleon mould*': James, *Churchill: A Study in Failure*, 78.
259 '*pistol leveled at the English coast*': Wilson, *After the Victorians*, 134. Wilson is quoting a passage from Morris Jastrow, *The War and the Bagdad Railway* (Philadelphia and London, 1918), 97.
260 '*WE MUST HOLD ANTWERP*': WSC to Sir Edward Grey, Sept. 7, 1914, CV, vol. 3, part 1, 97.
260 *help defend the city*: Brock and Brock, *H. H. Asquith: Letters to Venetia Stanley*, 259 n. 7.
261 '*up to the sticking point*': Asquith to Venetia Stanley, Oct. 3, 1914, ibid., 260.
261 *took second place*: Edwin Samuel Montagu (1879–1924) was an affluent Liberal MP and a crony of Asquith, who served as financial secretary to the Treasury on three different occasions between 1914 and 1916. His marriage to Venetia Stanley left Asquith crushed. (See Brock and Brock, *H. H. Asquith: Letters to Venetia Stanley*, part 1; and *Churchill*, vol. 3, 329 n. 1.)
261 '*We're going to save the city*': Quote by E. A. Powell, in Birkenhead, *Churchill*, 316 and n. 8, citing Powell's book, *Fighting in Flanders*.
262 '*I don't know*': Diary of Capt. (later Adm. Sir) Herbert William Richmond, Aug. 20, 1914, in Arthur J. Marder, *Portrait of an Admiral: The Life and Papers of Sir Herbert Richmond* (Cambridge, MA, 1952), 100.
262 '*control land operations as well*': *Churchill*, vol. 3, 50.

NOTES

263 'Churchill's Innocent Victims': Ibid., 47–48.
263 'enemy's opening jaws': Admiral Sir William M. James, 'Churchill and the Navy', in Charles Eade, ed., Churchill – By His Contemporaries (New York, 1954), 115.
263 available at that point: Letter, former seaman Henry Stevens to Martin Gilbert, Churchill, vol. 3, 108–09.
263 hardly an optimistic sign: Churchill, vol. 3, 108.
263 'eating an excellent dinner': Morgan, Churchill, 461.
264 nation's forces during the Second World War: Ibid.
264 'detached force in the field': Telegram, WSC to Asquith, sent at 8.00 a.m., Oct. 5, 1914, in CV, vol. 3, part 1, 163.
264 'necessary military rank': The World Crisis, vol. 1, 351.
264 'roars of incredulous laughter': James, Churchill: A Study in Failure, 80.
265 'under that shellfire': Churchill, vol. 3, 115.
265 'lunatic hands at this time': Richmond diary, Oct. 4, 1914, ibid., 111–12.
265 'glad when he departed': Able Seaman (later Wing Commander) Jack Bentham to his father, Churchill, vol. 3, 119.
266 'starching & ironing the Belges': Ibid., 117.
266 'against any onslaught': Gen. Jack Seely, quoted in Birkenhead, Churchill, 315.
266 'for a couple of days': Churchill, vol. 3, 120.
266 'dashing through the water': Addison, Churchill, 74.
267 'What a crime!': Rupert Brooke quoted in WC, 358–59; and Morgan, Churchill, 465.
267 'command great armies in war': Birkenhead, Churchill, 316–17.
267 'brilliant and erratic amateur': Morning Post, Oct. 23, 1914, quoted in Addison, Churchill, 73.
268 'two Naval Brigades': Broad, Winston Churchill, 157; and Asquith to Venetia Stanley, Oct. 13, 1914. Asquith also noted that one of the reserve units was commanded by Churchill's erstwhile stepfather, the ex-Guardsman George Cornwallis-West, whom Asquith described as 'incompetent & overbearing & hated impartially by both officers and men.' (Colin Clifford, The Asquiths [London, 2003], 236–37.)
268 'rash and ill-conceived request': Soames, Clementine Churchill, 131–32. Richard Holmes makes the same point, that 'it was not his job to be there, and his offer to surrender control of the largest military force available to Britain in order to take command of a certainly doomed defence is a damning comment on his sense of proportion.' (In the Footsteps of Churchill, 108.)
268 real deciding factor: Holmes, In the Footsteps of Churchill, 108–09.
268 'dedication of a friar': WC, 354, 361.
269 'natural and even inevitable': The World Crisis, vol. 1, 358.
269 'through on the spot': WSC, Amid These Storms, 16–17.
269 'physical and personal action': Ibid., 17.
269 'to be a great opportunity': Field Marshal Earl Alexander of Tunis, conversation with Martin Gilbert, 1968, Churchill, vol. 3, 111n.
270 'in comparison with military glory': Asquith to Venetia Stanley, Oct. 7, 1914, Brock and Brock, H. H. Asquith: Letters to Venetia Stanley, 266; also Asquith, Memories and Reflections, vol. 2, 42. See also WC, 354–55; and Alan Moorehead, Gallipoli (New York and London, 1956), 37.
270 'It inspires us all': Sir Edward Grey to CHC, Oct. 7, 1914, Soames, Clementine Churchill, 132.

Chapter 21: 'Damn the Dardanelles! They Will be Our Grave'

271 '1,164 missing': Manchester, The Last Lion: Visions, 506, 508.
272 'beating out their plans': Asquith to Venetia Stanley, Dec. 21, 1914, Brock and Brock, H. H. Asquith: Letters to Venetia Stanley, 334. Other citations in this chapter are from this source.

830

272 *'He is a born soldier'*: Diary of Margot Asquith, Nov. 30, 1914, CV, vol. 3, part 1, 283–84.
272 *'Defence by Committee'*: Stephen Roskill, *Hankey: Man of Secrets*, vol. 1, *1877–1918* (New York and London, 1970), 145.
272 *'to be told about this'*: Rose, *Churchill*, 147.
273 *status quo on the western front*: Penn, *Fisher, Churchill and the Dardanelles*, 97.
273 *'shorten the war'*: Rose, *Churchill*, 133.
273 *suicidal Continental war*: Marder, *From the Dreadnought to Scapa Flow*, vol. 1, 386–87.
274 *the concept died*: *Churchill*, vol. 3, 52–53.
274 *'conduct of the war'*: Diary of Admiral Hugo von Pohl, and Fisher letter, March 1918, both quoted in Penn, *Fisher, Churchill and the Dardanelles*, 102.
275 *head the Royal Navy*: Prince Louis's connection to the British royal family was through his wife, Princess Victoria of Hesse, one of Victoria's granddaughters. (A more complete description of Prince Louis is in Philip Ziegler's superb biography of his son, *Mountbatten* [London, 1985].)
275 *'intrigue against each other'*: Quoted in James, *Churchill: A Study in Failure*, 76.
276 *'fight and be a soldier'*: Account of Lord Stamfordham (Arthur John Bigge), George V's private secretary, quoted in *Churchill*, vol. 3, 151. Also Asquith to Venetia Stanley, Oct. 19, 1914.
276 *'with great reluctance'*: WC, 363–64.
276 *frequently overruling him*: Asquith, *Memories and Reflections*, vol. 2, 'Contemporary Notes', Jan. 20, 1915.
276 *'all went well'*: *The World Crisis*, vol. 1, 406.
276 *'one or two the next morning'*: Marsh, *A Number of People*, 246.
276 *Greece to the Allied side*: Before Turkey entered the war, Churchill favoured an invasion of the Gallipoli Peninsula by Greek troops; however, the king of Greece had blood ties to the German royal family, and Russia vetoed the idea, fearful that a Greek army might capture Constantinople. Thus, the playing of the so-called Greek card died. (Morgan, *Churchill*, 522–23.)
277 *'futile frontal attacks'*: Asquith, 'Contemporary Notes', Dec. 30, 1914, 62.
277 *plains of Troy*: The name 'Dardanelles' is derived from a mythical Trojan called Dardanus.
278 *'dictate terms at Constantinople'*: Notes of Maurice Hankey, quoted in Manchester, *The Last Lion: Visions*, 515.
278 *'I am altogether opposed'*: Asquith to Venetia Stanley, Dec. 5, 1914.
278 *'a practicable operation'*: Telegram WSC to Adm. Carden, Jan. 3, 1915, in CV, vol. 3, part 1, 367.
278 *'proceed up to Constantinople'*: Minutes of the War Council, Jan. 13, 1915, in ibid., 409–10.
280 *'Turkish forts at the Dardanelles'*: Sir Martin Gilbert, 'What About the Dardanelles', *Finest Hour* (Spring 2005), 26–27.
280 *'dangerous and ineffective'*: Adm. of the Fleet Sir Julian Oswald, 'Gallipoli: A View from Seaward', 1999 Gallipoli Memorial Lecture, in *The Straits of War*, 169. This book is a compendium of the series of Gallipoli Memorial Lectures delivered annually at Holy Trinity Church, Eltham, from 1985.
280 *'to such perils'*: Manchester, *The Last Lion: Visions*, 515.
281 *'in conjunction with the Fleet'*: Fisher quoted ibid., 525.
281 *'try the naval plan'*: WSC testimony to the Dardanelles Commission, 1916, *Churchill*, vol. 3, 274.
281 *'brighter prospects in the Mediterranean'*: Hankey, *The Supreme Command*, 265–66; and Pelling, *Winston Churchill*, 191.
281 *'different scheme every day'*: *The Last Lion: Visions*, 526–27; Fisher to Jellicoe, Jan. 29, 1915, and diary of Lord Esher, Jan. 29, 1915, CV, vol. 3, part 1, 470; and Brock &

Brock, *H. H. Asquith: Letters to Venetia Stanley*, Jan. 28, 1915, and 407 n. 4. It was also at this meeting that Churchill vented his feelings over the growing German U-boat attacks. 'Winston is very strong for retaliating on the Germans by methods of barbarism,' a reference to the British practice during the Boer War of incarcerating both Boer civilians and POWs in concentration camps. (Asquith to Stanley, Jan. 28, 1915.)

282 *'whole hog, totus porcus':* WC, 373, 375.

283 *strong currents of the strait:* Massie, *Castles of Steel*, 454.

283 *use of land forces:* Roskill, *Hankey: Man of Secrets*, vol. 1, 153, 163.

283 *'loss of ships and men':* Ibid.; and *Churchill*, vol. 3, 337.

284 *'sooner it is done the better':* Massie, *Castles of Steel*, 454.

285 *'my letter to the First Lord of January 4':* The World Crisis, vol. 2, 275.

285 *'but we are "too late" ALWAYS!':* Fisher to WSC, Apr. 5, 1915, *Churchill*, vol. 3, 385–86; and CV, vol. 3, part 1, 770.

285 *'tried to conduct a war':* Marder, *Portrait of an Admiral*, 23, Sept. 24, 1914.

285 *host of smaller supporting craft:* Penn, *Fisher, Churchill and the Dardanelles*, 159.

286 *price to be paid if the plan failed:* Ibid., 133.

286 *'disaster that he forecast':* Churchill, vol. 3, 311.

Chapter 22: The Reckoning

287 *would soon ring hollow:* Diary of Violet Bonham Carter, Feb. 22, 1915; and Pottle, *Champion Redoubtable*, 25.

287 *perish on the Gallipoli expedition:* WC, 382.

289 *'bloodshed and destruction':* Hankey, *The Supreme Command*, 182.

289 *'history of the universe':* Geoffrey Best, *Churchill: A Study in Greatness* (London, 2001), 83.

289 *'no difficulty at all':* Gen. Sir Hugh Beach, 'The Murderous Responsibility', in *The Straits of War*, 9–10.

290 *'over the next generation':* Robert O'Neill, 'For Want of Critics . . . The Tragedy of Gallipoli', in ibid., 79.

290 *drowned in the rough current:* Massie, *Castles of Steel*, 483.

291 *'I will not remain':* Fisher to WSC, May 16, 1915, CV, vol. 3, part 2: *May 1915–Dec. 1916*, 891–92.

291 *'will NOT remain after to-day':* Fisher to H. H. Asquith, May 17, 1915, ibid., 900.

291 *'He was a war man!':* Fisher to Lord Cromer, Oct. 11, 1916, Marder, *From the Dreadnought to Scapa Flow*, vol. 2, *1914–1916* (London, 1965), 293. Marder points out: 'When [Roger] Keyes remarked (November 1915) that Churchill had "nursed a viper" when he had recalled the old Admiral in 1914, he snapped, "And I would do it again; he brought such fire and vigour into the production of ships." '

291 *field command in France:* Churchill, vol. 3, 448; and *The World Crisis*, vol. 2, 366.

292 *'salvation of England depended on it':* Sir Max Aitken quoted in *Churchill*, vol. 3, 455.

292 *'deadliness to fight Germany':* CHC to Asquith, May 20, 1915, ibid., 459. Asquith never replied to Clementine's letter, but he remarked to Venetia Stanley that he had received 'the letter of a maniac'.

292 *height of naivety:* Max Aitken tried without success to warn Churchill that he hadn't a hope of persuading the Conservative leader, Bonar Law, to permit him to retain the post of first lord.

292 *'all his wonderful gifts':* Asquith, *Memories and Reflections*, vol. 2, 'Contemporary Notes', Mar. 25, 1915, 82.

292 *'I shall not look back':* Churchill, vol. 3, 465.

293 *'devious course of the crisis':* Soames, *Clementine Churchill*, 141.

293 *'he would die of grief':* Related by CHC to Martin Gilbert, quoted in *Churchill*, vol. 3, 473, and Soames, *Clementine Churchill*, 141.

293 *'it's like Beethoven deaf':* Churchill, vol. 3, 473. Also quoted in Richard Hough, *The Greatest Crusade: Roosevelt, Churchill and the Naval Wars* (New York and London,

1986), 93. During the Second World War Churchill made similar admissions about the Dardanelles to his personal physician, Lord Moran.

293 *'I tore up his photograph'*: Marsh, *A Number of People*, 247.

293 *gambles like the Dardanelles*: Kenneth Rose, *King George V* (New York and London, 1984), 189–90.

293 *'tears in his eyes too'*: WC, 427.

293 *'decade of power and achievement'*: Leslie, *The End of a Chapter*, 124–25.

293 *'The Fleet was ready'*: *The World Crisis*, vol. 2, 374–75. Although Churchill would continue to disagree with Kitchener during the brief period that he served in Asquith's cabinet, he never forgot the old general's act of kindness in his moment of despair.

294 *'public danger to the Empire'*: Jellicoe to Ian Hamilton, May 19, 1915, Hamilton Papers, LHC.

294 *'rid of the succubus Churchill'*: Richard Hough, *The Great War at Sea, 1914–1918* (Oxford, 1983), 167.

294 *'hour of triumph will come'*: Ibid.

294 *'he had gone on strike'*: Churchill, 'Lord Fisher and His Biographer', in *Great Contemporaries*, 219.

294 *'war in August 1914'*: Adm. of the Fleet Sir Roger Keyes quoted in Marder, *From the Dreadnought to Scapa Flow*, vol. 2, 293. Original citation in Keyes, *Naval Memoirs*, vol. 1 (London, 1934), 455–56.

294 *appointment of county magistrates*: A full description of the Duchy of Lancaster can be found on the internet at www.duchyoflancaster.org.uk/.

295 *'any of my colleagues'*: WC, 451. In November 1915 Violet married Maurice Bonham Carter, her father's private secretary, nicknamed 'Bongie'. He had been Violet's suitor for a number of years before she agreed to marry him.

295 *'carried it to success'*: Quoted in Rose, *Churchill*, 157.

295 *'Gospel according to Churchill'*: Penn, *Fisher, Churchill and the Dardanelles*, 237.

295 *relevant facts and documents*: For examples of the views of various critics see ibid.; and James, *Churchill Speaks*, 317–19.

295 *'murdered mine at the Dardanelles'*: Rose, *Churchill*, 158.

295 *'memories of the Dardanelles'*: James, *Churchill Speaks*, 318.

296 *'sacrificed upon its altar'*: Philip J. Haythornwaite, *Gallipoli 1915* (Botley, Oxford, 1991), 10.

296 *child's paintbox*: Martin, *Jennie*, vol. 2, 373.

296 *his inventive mind*: Churchill's paintings have been preserved in a superb book: David Coombs with Minnie Churchill, *Sir Winston Churchill: His Life and His Paintings* (Philadelphia and London, 2004).

296 *'extraordinary talent'*: Birkenhead, *Churchill*, 401.

296 *'practise in silence'*: WC, 493–94.

296 *'leave behind him'*: Sheridan, *Nuda Veritas*, 133.

297 *'like Napoleon after Waterloo'*: Birkenhead, *Churchill*, 400.

297 *'I am learning to hate'*: Rose, *Churchill*, 156.

297 *'which way to turn'*: WSC to Archibald Sinclair, June 9, 1915, Thurso Papers, File 1/1, CAC.

297 *'influence on general policy'*: WSC to John Churchill, June 19, 1915, CV, vol. 3, part 2, 1042.

297 *appointed to head it*: Memo, written some time in late June 1915, 'Notes on the Formation of an Air Department', Asquith Papers. Also quoted in CV, vol. 3, part 2, 1099–1100.

298 *'situation to the Cabinet!!!'*: Churchill, vol. 3, 505.

290 *'our heavy task'*: Roger Keyes to his wife, July 18, 1915, Paul G. Halpern, ed., *The Keyes Papers*, vol. 1, *1914–1918* (London, 1979), 163. Churchill was not alone in his disillusionment over the failure of the Dardanelles operation. Keyes wrote to Ian Hamilton

on 27 April 1917: 'I hold no brief for Winston Churchill, but to me too . . . *it is torment to think of what might have and should have been.*' (389.)
298 *still rankled:* WC, 441.
298 *showing favouritism to a politician:* Pelling, *Churchill*, 208.
298 *'lust for battle':* Churchill, vol. 3, 480.
299 *'that hope dies':* WSC memorandum on the Dardanelles, Oct. 15, 1915, CV, vol. 3, part 2, 1220–23.
299 *'shoving it to Johnny Turk':* Massie, *Castles of Steel*, 479.
299 *collapse of Turkish resistance:* Ibid., 479, 481.
300 *'one man slightly injured':* Prince Philip, Duke of Edinburgh, 'Ends and Means', 1987 Gallipoli Memorial Lecture, in *The Straits of War*, 36.
300 *'not yet forgiven us':* WC, 458.

Chapter 23: Penance

(Unless otherwise stated, the letters exchanged between Winston and Clementine Churchill are in The Papers of Clementine Ogilvy Spencer-Churchill, Baroness Spencer-Churchill of Chartwell, Churchill College Archives [CSCT 1 and CSCT 2]).
301 *'I bid you good-bye':* WSC to H. H. Asquith, Nov. 11, 1915, CHAR 28/154.
301 *one of Jennie's biographers:* Elisabeth Kehoe, *The Titled Americans* (New York, 2004), 290.
302 *'collected and efficient':* Soames, *Clementine Churchill*, 151.
302 *call of danger and adventure:* WC, 456–57.
302 *'he will meet a bullet':* Leslie, 'Winston, A Cousinly Memory'.
302 *'believer in your star':* Martin, *Jennie*, vol. 2, 374; also in Kehoe, *The Titled Americans*, 309.
302 *'not obviously required':* WSC to CHC, Nov. 18, 1915.
303 *'is a good friend':* Ibid., letters of Nov. 18 and 19, 1915.
303 *'from you badly':* CHC to WSC, Nov. 19, 1915.
304 *men of the Grenadiers:* Birkenhead, *Churchill*, 407.
304 *'monitors and senior scholars':* Amid These Storms, 101.
305 *'as soon as possible':* WSC to CHC, Nov. 22, 1915.
305 *'as good as any':* Ibid., Nov. 23 and 25, 1915.
305 *'seen the end of war':* George Santayana, 'Tipperary', in *Soliloquies in England*, quoted in Michael Takiff, *Brave Men, Gentle Heroes* (New York, 2003), 546.
306 *'with the general after all':* WSC to CHC, Nov. 25, 1915. There are two versions of this tale: one in his letter to Clementine, the other in *Amid These Storms* (107–10), written in 1932. In the latter he suggests that the shell that would have killed him arrived some five minutes after his departure, whereas in his letter it was approximately half an hour. What is not at issue is his narrow escape from death.
306 *'and trust in God':* WSC to CHC, ibid.
306 *'from the fatal spot':* Amid These Storms, 106, 110.
306 *'honour as a soldier':* CHC to WSC, Nov. 28, 1915.
307 *'alive that's all':* Ibid., Dec. 17, 1915.
307 *'if it is open to me':* WSC to CHC, Dec. 1, 1915.
308 *'who meet you will love you':* CHC to WSC, Dec. 4, 1915.
308 *'become a noisy show-off':* Max Egremont, *Under Two Flags: The Life of Major General Sir Edward Spears* (London, 1997), 41.
308 *'Poor Brigade':* Diary of Edward Louis Spiers, quoted in *Churchill*, vol. 3, 598.
308 *'chiefly for the appearance':* WSC to CHC, Dec. 12, 1915.
309 *'meanness & ungenerousness':* Ibid., Dec. 18, 1915. Churchill pointed out to French that, after his resignation from the Admiralty, Asquith had offered him the command of a brigade. Now that Churchill had become a political liability it was clear that Asquith was cutting his losses.

309 *designed to embarrass Asquith:* Soames, *Clementine Churchill,* 168; and Hansard, vol. 78, col. 2218.
309 *'do it without compunction':* WSC to CHC, Dec. 15, 1915.
310 *'when I will claim it':* Ibid., Jan. 10, 1916.
310 *'now the only real people':* CHC to WSC, Jan. 12, 1916.
310 *'definite responsibility however small':* WSC to CHC, Dec. 15, 1915.
310 *he had enjoyed with French:* Churchill, vol. 3, 543–44.
310 *'take a Brigade':* WSC to CHC, Dec. 18, 1915.
310 *'my feathers stroked':* Ibid. The memo to Haig is in CHAR 2/68.
312 *'sincerity of my choice':* Ibid., Jan. 1, 1916; Birkenhead, *Churchill,* 415.
312 *major battles of the First World War:* J. M. Brereton, *A Guide to the Regiments of the British Army* (London, 1985), 163–64.
312 *'usurp his place so easily':* Andrew Dewar Gibb (first published anonymously as Captain X), *With Winston Churchill at the Front* (London and Glasgow, 1924), 10. Later editions of this charming memoir revealed the author's real name. Gibb later became Regius professor of law at Glasgow University, and the prominent and highly respected leader from 1936 to 1940 of the Scottish National Party (SNP), formed in 1934 to advocate Scottish independence.
312 *'heating the bath water':* Related by Edmund Hakewill Smith in *Churchill,* vol. 3, 631.
313 *'pretty rotten time':* Gilbert, *In Search of Churchill,* 91–92. Hakewill Smith (1896–1986) was a Sandhurst graduate who served with the Royal Scots Fusiliers from 1915 to 1919. In 1947 he served as the president of the military court that tried and convicted Field Marshal Albert Kesselring for war crimes while commander in chief of German forces in Italy in 1944.
313 *'stand still and do nothing':* Hakewill Smith quoted in *Churchill,* vol. 3, 632.
313 *'shall be a help to them':* WSC to CHC, Jan. 6, 1916.
313 *'all other trials, to an end':* Gibb, *With Winston Churchill at the Front,* 19–20.
314 *'utterly "deloused" battalion':* Ibid., 21–23.
314 *'The Drunken Piper':* Ibid., 40.
315 *'not easily moved and won over':* Ibid., 24.
315 *'shattered battalion in the assault':* WSC to Jack Churchill, Jan. 14, 1916, CV, vol. 3, part 2, 1373.
315 *'capture a few Germans':* Maj. Desmond Morton quoted in Birkenhead, *Churchill,* 424.
315 *'go to hell!':* Ibid., 418–19; and Gibb, *With Winston Churchill at the Front,* 77.
315 *'short as these may be':* WSC to CHC, Jan. 17, 1916.
315 *'we sang Auld Lang Syne':* Ibid., Jan. 23, 1916.
316 *'and signed it':* Gilbert, *In Search of Churchill,* 100–101.
316 *'Winston was in his element':* Gibb, *With Winston Churchill at the Front,* 49–50, 51.

Chapter 24: 'In Flanders Fields'

317 *'if I survive':* 'Darling – Do you like me to write these things to you?' Winston once naively wrote to Clementine. 'They are the ordinary incidents of life here – they are dangerous; but not vy dangerous. The average risk is not great – I wd not write to you about them if I thought the account wd cause you extra anxiety. But I think you like to know the dimensions of the dangers, & what they are like.' (WSC to CHC, Feb. 1, 1916.)
318 *'In Flanders fields':* A veteran of the Boer War, John McRae (1872–1918) saw death at first hand as a surgeon in a dressing station during the First Battle of Ypres in 1915. His anguish when face to face with the dead and dying became the basis of a poem he scribbled one day after being deeply affected by the death of a lieutenant, who had been both a friend and a former student of his. McCrae thought little of his scribbling and tossed it away. It was saved by a fellow officer and eventually printed in *Punch* in December 1915.
318 *'made them appetizing soup':* Birkenhead, *Churchill,* 419–20.

318 *'flare up in the sector'*: William Sholto Douglas, *Years of Combat* (London, 1963), 128.
319 *'blot the place out'*: Gibb, *With Winston Churchill at the Front*, 74–75.
319 *'world was a dream'*: WSC to CHC, Feb. 13, 1916.
319 *'H. of C. than here'*: Ibid., March 17, 1916.
319 *' "past you by now" '*: Hakewill Smith quoted in *Churchill*, vol. 3, 657–58.
320 *'as fear in him'*: Gibb, *With Winston Churchill at the Front*, 69.
320 *'this is a very dangerous war'*: Ibid., 65. Churchill's commanding general lived a comfortable life in the relative safety of the rear. Those who did so in the First World War had little idea of what life in the front lines was like and were held in contempt by ordinary soldiers.
321 *'at once to see him'*: Ibid., 73–74.
321 *'rubbed in them'*: Ibid., 89–91.
321 *'tour of the trenches'*: WSC to CHC, Feb. 4, 1916.
322 *'above the bay-window'*: *Amid These Storms*, 118.
322 *'so feverishly seeking'*: Ibid., 115–20. Although he did not specifically say so, it seems clear that the document in question dealt with the development of the tank.
322 *day-and-night German shelling*: WSC to Sunny Churchill, Jan. 12, 1916, Marlborough Papers.
323 *presented him with the painting*: *Churchill*, vol. 3, 658–59; and Coombs, *Sir Winston Churchill: His Life and His Paintings*, 17, figs. 6, 7, 8.
323 *'even for a month'*: WSC to CHC, Feb. 8, 1916.
323 *'conclusion of the conflict'*: Ibid. This letter was written while Churchill was in temporary command of his higher headquarters while the brigade commander was away. His temporary status was as close as he ever got to general officer status.
324 *recalled as first sea lord*: James, *Churchill Speaks*, Mar. 7, 1916, 350.
324 *had been a 'suicidal' speech*: *Churchill*, vol. 3, 721–22; and WC, 475–77.
324 *'His lance was broken'*: WC, 480.
324 *'like his father did?'*: Penn, *Fisher, Churchill and the Dardanelles*, 230.
324 *'all be forgotten'*: *Churchill*, vol. 3, 476.
325 *returning to Plugstreet*: WSC to Archibald Sinclair, Mar. 16, 1916, Thurso Papers.
325 *'heartless brutes the chance'*: CHC to WSC, April 12, 1916.
325 *'as a simple colonel'*: Ibid.
326 *'will be fatal to you'*: Ibid., April 28, 1916.
326 *enactment of conscription*: *Churchill*, vol. 3, 759.
327 *'beyond question a great man'*: Gibb, *With Winston Churchill at the Front*, 109, 111. Gibb also wrote: 'I cannot conceive that exceptionally creative and fertile brain failing in any sphere of human activity to which it is applied.'
327 *'Allied forces as well'*: J. E. B. Seely (later Lord Mottistone), *Fear and Be Slain: Adventures by Land, Sea, and Air* (London, 1931), 262.
327 *'it nerved him'*: Ibid.

Chapter 25: 'Winston's Folly'

329 *'like a widow's curse'*: *Churchill*, vol. 3, 762.
330 *by the sea and never recovered*: Pollock, *Kitchener*, 481–83.
330 *'consummation in a warrior's death'*: *The World Crisis*, vol. 3, *1916–1918* (New York, 1927), part 1, 35.
330 *regarded him as a menace*: *Churchill*, vol. 3, 822–23.
330 *his role in the Great War*: Ibid., 826. Churchill lobbied unsuccessfully to have the papers of the investigating Dardanelles Commission made public, but Asquith refused, undoubtedly because of the impact they would have had upon his own reputation. Lloyd George permitted their publication in 1917.
330 *'to the project was gone'*: Ibid., 537–38; and Eustace Tennyson-d'Eyncourt, *A Shipbuilder's Yarn* (London, 1948).

331 *'into battle by ancient warriors'*: WSC memorandum, 'Variants of the Offensive', WO 158/831, PRO.
331 *'novelty and surprise'*: *The World Crisis*, vol. 3, part 1, 60–61.
331 *across no man's land*: Harris, *Men, Ideas and Tanks*, 53–54.
331 *Ministry of Munitions in February 1916*: Ibid. From WSC's 'Variants of the Offensive'.
331 *'by trial and error'*: Harris, *Men, Ideas and Tanks*, 73.
332 *'monstrous engines of war'*: Mitchell, *Tank Warfare*, 34.
332 *'crater-fields of Passchendaele'*: *The World Crisis*, vol. 2, 89–90.
332 *unforgiving of the Dardanelles*: Churchill, vol. 3, 810–11.
333 *most of their gains*: Howard, *The First World War*, 369–71.
333 *angry outcry of Conservatives*: When Churchill met with Lloyd George on 16 July 1917, he was asked what post he wanted and unhesitatingly replied, 'Minister of Munitions.' (Martin Gilbert, *Winston S. Churchill, 1917–1922* [London, 1975], 3–5, 28, hereafter cited as *Churchill*, vol. 4.)
333 *'Napoleon on land'*: Ibid., 29.
333 *ending the unrest*: Broad, *Winston Churchill*, 237–38.
334 *'or to field ambulances'*: Gilbert, *In Search of Churchill*, 101.
334 *had no reservations*: Holmes, *In the Footsteps of Churchill*, 135; Gilbert, *Churchill: A Life*, 422.
334 *requirements of the tank programme*: Broad, *Winston Churchill*, 238.
335 *end of the war in November*: Jenkins, *Churchill*, 333.
335 *'this way explode minefields'*: Churchill, vol. 4, 72–74.
335 *'larger named crosses'*: Marsh, *A Number of People*, 257.
336 *'it waits for him'*: Ibid., 259.
336 *'by a measureless gulf'*: *The World Crisis*, vol. 4, part 2, 509. Also cited in Jablonsky, *Churchill: The Making of a Grand Strategist* (Carlisle Barracks, PA, 1990), 15–16.
337 *first day of the Somme offensive*: Keegan, *The First World War*, 395–96; John Grigg, *Lloyd George: War Leader* (London, 2002), 444; and *Churchill*, vol. 4, 79.
337 *'I shall ever hear'*: *Churchill*, vol. 4, 79.
338 *on a battlefield*: A full account of Churchill's extraordinary day in France on 30 March 1918 is in *Amid These Storms*, 'A Day with Clemenceau'.
338 *'take no more interest in him'*: Extracts from the diary of Edward Marsh, quoted in *Churchill*, vol. 4, 154–55.
339 *'all's well that ends well'*: WSC to Gen. H. H. Tudor, Nov. 4, 1918, CHAR 2.
339 *'the burdens were cast down'*: *The World Crisis*, vol. 4, part 2, 542–43.
339 *'one man's opinion against another'*: Jablonsky, *Churchill: The Making of a Grand Strategist*, 51–52.
340 *politics in the 1930s*: *Marlborough: His Life and Times* was published in four volumes between 1933 and 1938.
340 *'declared the winner'*: Algis Valiunas, *Churchill's Military Histories* (Lanham, MD, 2002), 69.
340 *'beyond Cabinet control'*: Best, *Churchill*, 83.
340 *'that was waging war'*: *The World Crisis*, vol. 4, part 2, 348.
340 *'it was seen to be there'*: Valiunas, *Churchill's Military Histories*, 68.
341 *'at one supreme stroke?'*: *The World Crisis*, vol. 4, part 2, 61–62. In 'Plan 1919' Lieutenant Colonel (later Major General) J. F. C. Fuller, then a staff officer at Tank Corps Headquarters, advocated a similar idea he believed would win the war by employing some 2,000 massed tanks. (John Terraine, *The Smoke and the Fire: Myth and Anti-Myths of War, 1861–1945* [London, 1980], 155–56.)
341 *not even thinking that way*: *The World Crisis*, vol. 4, part 2, 347–48.
341 *on D-day in June 1944*: Alan Clark, *The Donkeys* (New York and London, 1965), ix.
341 *élan he deemed essential*: The historian John Terraine contends that Churchill's denigration of British generalship in the Second World War stemmed from unfairly belittling the First World War generals for having done their duty and bringing to this new war

rather 'profound reservations', with Wavell and Auchinleck becoming 'the chief recipients of the latter', (*The Smoke and the Fire*, 215.)

341 *'triumph of novel apparitions'*: WSC, 'Douglas Haig', in *Great Contemporaries*, 146.

341 *'stockyards of Chicago'*: Jablonsky, *Churchill: The Making of a Grand Strategist*, 62.

Chapter 26: 'A Hopelessly Obsolete, Old-Fashioned Warrior'

343 *'another world war and another Churchill'*: James, *Churchill Speaks*, 318, quoting an unnamed American historian.

343 *'misery, torment and malevolence'*: William K. Klingaman, *1919: The Year Our World Began* (New York, 1987), 382.

343 *'come to the aid of France'*: *The World Crisis*, vol. 1, 205.

344 *longest-serving men first*: Klingaman, *1919*, 41–42.

344 *RAF and the Air Ministry*: WSC memo, Jan. 12, 1919, *Churchill*, vol. 4, 197.

344 *one million pounds a day*: Boyle, *Trenchard*, 327.

345 *'a Statesman, not a juggler'*: CHC to WSC, Mar. 9, 1919.

345 *'all that is left for it'*: Basil Liddell Hart, 'The Military Strategist', in A. J. P. Taylor, ed., *Churchill Revised: A Critical Reassessment* (New York, 1969; published in London as *Churchill: Four Faces and the Man*), 200.

345 *'national freedom and independence'*: Martin Gilbert, *Winston Churchill: The Wilderness Years* (Boston, 1982), 58, hereafter cited as *The Wilderness Years*.

345 *'on a modern basis'*: Liddell Hart, 'The Military Strategist', 200–201.

346 *rearmament in the 1930s*: Ibid., 201.

346 *'by Churchill's period in office'*: James, *Churchill: A Study in Failure*, 161.

346 *now first sea lord*: Holmes, *In the Footsteps of Churchill*, 152.

347 *'for his paranoid fantasies'*: Margaret MacMillan, *Paris 1919: Six Months That Changed the World* (New York, 2002; published in London as *Peacemakers*), 82.

348 *'in these circumstances a public duty'*: Lord Haldane to WSC, July 19, 1919, *Churchill*, vol. 4, 210.

348 *time to stop*: Soames, *Clementine Churchill*, 218.

348 *others did the piloting*: WSC, *Amid These Storms*, 196–97. It was Churchill's second brush with death in 1919. A short time earlier he and his pilot narrowly avoided crashing at low altitude when they became lost in fog over France.

348 *'greatest grief of his life'*: Shane Leslie quoted in Martin, *Jennie*, vol. 2, 400.

349 *souls of Clementine and Winston*: Soames, *Clementine Churchill*, 229–30. There is no documented cause of Marigold Churchill's death, although biographers have speculated about everything from meningitis (highly contagious and very unlikely given that no one else exposed to her seems to have been infected) to strep throat. A more likely cause is diphtheria, which often starts as a very sore throat and progresses to respiratory compromise and death. There was no treatment for diphtheria in 1921.

349 *fulfilling and worth while*: Jill Craigie interview, BREN 1/12, Brendon Papers. One of the first British female film directors, Craigie (1914–99) was also a successful actress and author, and an expert on the suffragette movement. She married the future Labour Party leader Michael Foot in 1949.

350 *'never quite forgave him for it'*: Mary Soames interview, BREN 1/2, Brendon Papers.

350 *'fabric of our family life going'*: Soames, *Clementine Churchill*, 249.

350 *'treat you as an equal'*: Denis Kelly Papers, DEKE 2, CAC. Churchill steadfastly refused ever to permit any of his livestock to be slaughtered. Only twice were there exceptions, once when Clementine cooked a goose. Winston could not bear to carve it, saying: 'He was a friend of mine.' Another was an incorrigibly ill-tempered ram named Charmayne that once butted Churchill from behind, knocking him to his knees, much to the delight of his young children.

351 *'old-fashioned warrior'*: Haffner, *Churchill*, 83, remarking on the generally held public opinion of Churchill in 1936.

351 *'his dominant defect, impatience'*: Harold Nicolson, quoted in James, *Churchill: A Study in Failure*, 239.

352 *'disarmament of the victors'*: *The Wilderness Years*, 55.

352 *'what is left of civilization'*: *Pictorial Weekly*, Feb. 24, 1934. The editors billed it as 'perhaps the most powerful plea for peace ever penned in our time'.

353 *preferred to avoid him: The Wilderness Years*, 50–51. The intermediary was Ernst 'Putzi' Hanfstaengl, who was half American, had studied in the United States and graduated from Harvard, and was a friend of both FDR, then governor of New York, and Hitler, whom he would later serve as foreign press chief. Hanfstaengl's association with Hitler began in 1922. (See also Ian Kershaw, *Hitler, 1889–1936, Hubris* [New York and London, 1998], 158.)

353 *'direct and unalienable'*: WSC parliamentary speech, Nov. 23, 1932, Hansard.

353 *'against the aggressor'*: *The Wilderness Years*, 176.

354 *to rectify matters:* The navy's confidence in Churchill as an unofficial friend in the high court of politics was expressed in the spring of 1937 when a young naval officer on the staff of the Naval Air Division, Louis Mountbatten, the son of his former first sea lord, sent Churchill a detailed set of notes asking for his help in an organizational dispute within the government over control of certain types of aircraft that the navy wanted under the Fleet Air Arm.

354 *'those savages'*: *The Wilderness Years*, 181.

355 *best-informed men in Britain:* The Industrial Intelligence Centre, the secret agency that Desmond Morton headed in the 1930s, was set up 'to discover and report the plans for manufacture of armaments and war store in foreign countries', Richard Holmes suggests not only that the three prime ministers of the 1930s (MacDonald, Baldwin and Chamberlain), none of whom had any love for him, authorized the disclosure of highly classified information to Churchill, but that they might have given him such extraordinary access to restricted data to sound unofficial warnings of the Nazi menace which they could not express officially during an era of isolation and strong anti-war feelings. (*In the Footsteps of Churchill*, 189–90.)

355 *'torpedo the government'*: Diary of Sir Henry Channon, May 26, 1936, Robert Rhodes James, ed., *'Chips': The Diaries of Sir Henry Channon* (London, 1993), 61.

356 *'occupied the seats of power'*: Piers Brendon, *The Dark Valley: A Panorama of the 1930s* (New York, 2000), 192.

356 *'He was extremely indiscreet'*: Lady Diana Mosley interview, Brendon Papers.

356 *'we do not take his advice'*: London *Evening Standard*, April 3, 1936, CHAR 8; and *The Wilderness Years*, 154–55.

356 *would be strongly resisted:* R. A. C. Parker, *Churchill and Appeasement* (London, 2000), ix.

Chapter 27: The Shame of Munich

358 *'packs of ravening wolves'*: Holmes, *In the Footsteps of Churchill*, 169.

358 *'our War Prime Minister'*: 'Action This Day', Spring 1940, Churchill Centre: www.winstonchurchill.org.

358 *'face the bully'*: Graham Stewart, *Burying Caesar: The Churchill–Chamberlain Rivalry* (New York and London, 2001), 257.

359 *concept of strategic bombing:* Ibid., 210.

359 *devastate European civilization:* Holmes, *In the Footsteps of Churchill*, 168.

359 *mere £19 million:* Ibid.

359 *'maintain the RAF superiority'*: Stewart, *Burying Caesar*, 215.

359 *portent of the Blitz:* Hansard, Nov. 28, 1934.

359 *'blind and causeless panic'*: Stewart, *Burying Caesar*, 215.

360 *war-making targets flawed:* The legacy of the Trenchard doctrine that strategic bombing alone could win wars became like a disease that infected future generations of airmen who fostered the same belief not only in the Second World War, but in later wars such as

Vietnam, where American airpower conspicuously failed either to deter or to destroy North Vietnam's war-making capability.

360 *'grave injury upon them'*: Christopher Catherwood, *Churchill's Folly: How Winston Churchill Created Modern Iraq* (New York, 2004), 85. The letter to Trenchard in which Churchill outlined the use of poison-gas bombs is dated Aug. 29, 1920 (CHAR 16/34).

360 *quell the rebellious tribes:* Holmes, *In the Footsteps of Churchill*, 168.

360 *wanted the rebels killed:* Catherwood points out that Churchill's idea of using poison gas came on the heels of the assassination of British officials in Mesopotamia, and was also made to help redress the shortage of British troops. He also notes that most of the numerous television documentaries unfailingly point out Churchill's use of poison gas but fail to mention that he did not want anyone killed as a result. The post-war British army was spread too thin across the empire and dealing with the rebellion in Ireland. 'We are at our wits' end to find a single soldier,' said Churchill. 'It seems to me so gratuitous that after all the struggles of the war, just when we want to get together our slender military resources . . . we should be compelled to go on pouring armies and treasures into these thankless deserts.' (WSC to Lloyd George, Aug. 31, 1920, Catherwood, *Churchill's Folly*, 87.

361 *friend or foe disagreed with him:* Lynne Olson, *Troublesome Young Men* (New York, 2007), 90.

361 *'what point he'll break out'*: Jenkins, *Churchill*, 416.

361 *'minutes of the last meeting'*: Nigel Nicolson, ed., *Harold Nicolson, The War Years, 1939–1945, Diaries and Letters* (New York, 1967), vol. 2, 35, diary entry of Sept. 20, 1939, hereafter cited as Nicolson diary.

362 *'I shall ever cross'*: Stewart, *Burying Caesar*, 40.

362 *'to be taken seriously'*: Channon diary, Dec. 5, 1937, James, *'Chips'*, 141.

362 *they agreed with him'*: Viscount Templewood (Sir Samuel Hoare), *Nine Troubled Years* (London, 1954), 375.

363 *'he had given his word'*: Manchester, *The Last Lion: Alone*, 339.

363 *'victory had been scored'*: Stewart, *Burying Caesar*, 309.

363 *'guided by God'*: Derek Robinson, *Invasion, 1940* (New York and London, 2005), 15.

364 *'peace with honour'*: Stewart, *Burying Caesar*, 309–10.

364 *'and he did it'*: Interview of Lord Home, WCHL 15/2/12, CHAR. Chamberlain's 1938 Christmas card was a photo of his aircraft in flight to Munich – another rusty nail in his legacy. (Schama, *A History of Britain*, vol. 3, 501.)

364 *'rather than to defeat him'*: Brendon, *The Dark Valley*, 546.

364 *'particularly with the Americans'*: Lord Home interview, WCHL 15/2/12.

364 *he had the Sudetenland:* Manchester, *The Last Lion: Alone*, 339.

365 *'could be our leader if war came'*: Harold Nicolson, 'Portrait of Winston Churchill', unpublished ms., Columbia University Rare Book and Manuscript Library.

365 *'insatiable appetite of the dictators'*: Soames, *Clementine Churchill*, 308.

365 *'Nazi threat of force'*: Manchester, *The Last Lion: Alone*, 342.

365 *'War thrown in a little later'*: Martin Gilbert, *A History of the Twentieth Century, 1933–1951* (New York and London, 1998), 197. Lord Moyne (Walter Edward Guinness) was sent to Egypt in 1942 as minister resident in the Middle East. He was assassinated in Cairo in November 1944 by Zionist terrorists of the notorious Stern Gang.

365 *'violence of Nazi Germany'*: Manchester, *The Last Lion: Alone*, 339–40.

366 *'in the olden time'*: Hansard, Oct. 5, 1938; also in James, *Churchill Speaks*, 653–62, and Churchill, *Blood, Sweat, and Tears* (New York, 1941), 53–66.

366 *reduced the poor woman to tears:* Soames, *Clementine Churchill*, 308.

366 *'I could hear him cry'*: The Wilderness Years, 234.

366 *'paper torn from Mein Kampf'*: Schama, *A History of Britain*, vol. 3, 499.

367 *'so major a contribution'*: Michael Howard, 'The End of Churchillism? Reappraising the Legend', *Foreign Affairs* (Sept./Oct. 1993).

367 *guarantees in March 1939:* Ibid.

367 'It will be an inexpiable war': 'The Hush in Europe', Daily Mirror, circa July–Aug. 1939.

368 'and without heart': Robert Boothby, Recollections of a Rebel (London, 1978), 133, 135.

Chapter 28: 'Bring Back Churchill'

369 'to be "liberated" next': 'A Hush over Europe', Aug. 8, 1939, broadcast to the United States, James, Churchill Speaks, 689–92.

370 'persevere to the end': WSC, Step by Step (New York, 1939), 324.

370 'who nobly dares': Quote from 'Roger Keyes', at www.combinedops.com, a website that chronicles the history of Combined Operations Headquarters during the Second World War.

371 most intimate naval advisers: Roskill, Churchill and the Admirals, 83.

371 'call to serve his country': Kathleen Hill quoted in Gilbert, Churchill: A Life, 579.

371 'qualities needed for the job': Desmond Morton quoted in Thompson, Churchill and Morton, 29.

371 'Hitler is going to make war': Diary of Edmund Ironside, July 25, 1939, in R. Macleod and Denis Kelly, eds., Time Unguarded: The Ironside Diaries, 1937–1940 (New York, 1962), 83, hereafter cited as Ironside diary.

372 'sees how the land lies': Ibid.

372 'hopelessly defensive everywhere': Ibid., July 26 and 27, 1939.

372 'all these years of preparation': Ibid., Aug. 16, 1939.

373 from Luxembourg to Switzerland: In the late 1960s I was stationed with the US army in Germany, not far from the French border. One of the monthly get-togethers of a group called the Allied Officers' Club (consisting of American, French, German and Canadian officers) was a tour of a bunker of the Maginot Line, near the town of Biche, which was still in the condition it had been in during the Second World War. Someone asked a young Luftwaffe officer how the Germans had succeeded in overcoming the Maginot Line. With a wry smile, the officer replied simply: 'We landed behind it.'

373 commander-in-chief of the French army: Egremont, Under Two Flags, 143.

374 'concealment from the air': Maj. Gen. Sir Edward Spears, Assignment to Catastrophe, vol. 1, Prelude to Dunkirk, July 1939–May 1940 (London, 1954), 6–7; and WSC to CHC, Aug. 14, 1939.

374 'defensive was master': WSC, The Gathering Storm (Boston, 1948), 473–6.

375 'they had exclaimed': Ibid.

375 'Ein Volk, ein Reich, ein Führer': Manchester, The Last Lion: Alone, 494.

376 'amazing but awe-inspiring': Spears, Assignment to Catastrophe, vol. 1, 10.

376 'German offensive there': The Gathering Storm, 383–84.

376 'hard work in this uncertainty': Ibid., 400.

376 'He is a warmonger': Sir Evan Charteris (1864–1940), a barrister and biographer, quoted in Soames, Clementine Churchill, 313–14.

376 for the time being reassured his visitor: The Gathering Storm, 400–401.

377 no such plans existed: Ironside diary, Aug. 27, 1939, 90 and The Gathering Storm, 401.

377 'does not accept him': Letter, Edmund to Lady Ironside, Aug. 28, 1939, Misc. 11/221, IWM.

377 'preparations she was making': Spears, Assignment to Catastrophe, vol. 1, 9.

377 'ill-prepared for war': Matthew Cooper, The German Army, 1939–1945: Its Political and Military Failure (London, 1978), 117.

377 'the war of excuses': John Mosier, Cross of Iron: The Rise and Fall of the German War Machine, 1918–1945 (New York, 2006), 130.

377 'cover story in Time magazine': Karl-Heinz Frieser, The Blitzkrieg Legend: The 1940 Campaign in the West (Annapolis, MD, 2005), 4.

378 *raining from the sky:* 'Blitzkrieger', *Time*, Sept. 25, 1939; and Cooper, *The German Army*, 116. Cooper points out that, contrary to popular myth, although the word 'blitzkrieg' is Germanic, the concept is not. 'German military manuals both before and during the war may be scoured in vain for any mention of it.' 'Lightning war' dates back to the fourteenth century and the ruler of the Ottoman Empire, Sultan Bayezid I (*circa* 1360–1403), who employed what he called 'the thunderbolt' (*yilderim*) form of rapid attack.

378 *'writing on the Second World War':* Cooper, *The German Army*, 116.

378 *'any European city':* Gilbert, *A History of the Twentieth Century*, vol. 2, 278.

378 *alert him that morning:* Manchester, *The Last Lion: Alone*, 518–19.

379 *'stand up to him':* Gilbert, *Churchill: A Life*, 616.

379 *'the call of honour':* *The Gathering Storm*, 409.

380 *'weakening of our resolve':* *The Wilderness Years*, 264–65. Churchill's letter was written on Sept. 2. See also *The Gathering Storm*, 406–07.

380 *'rang out throughout Britain':* Donald Cameron Watt, *How War Came* (London, 1990), 601.

380 *'into a European war':* Shirer, *The Nightmare Years*, 454.

380 *'sherry for the ladies':* Tom Hickman, *Churchill's Bodyguard* (London, 2005), 82–83; and *The Gathering Storm*, 408.

381 *'relief and intolerable grief':* Brian Gardner, *Churchill in power*, 1968), 20.

381 *'number of men in uniform':* Diary of Sir John Colville, Sept. 10, 1939. The diary is in the Colville Papers, CAC, and has also been published as *The Fringes of Power: Downing Street Diaries, 1939–1945* (London, 1985).

381 *'revive the stature of man':* James, *Churchill Speaks*, 693.

381 *'deal with Mister Hitler':* Leslie, *Long Shadows*, 275–76.

Chapter 29: 'Winston is Back'

382 *'So be it':* *The Gathering Storm*, 410.

382 *'matter of days':* Spears, *Assignment to Catastrophe*, vol. 1, 27.

382 *overbearing 'self-seeker':* Andrew Roberts, *'The Holy Fox': The Life of Lord Halifax* (London, 1991), 186.

383 *'better than I thought':* Hickman, *Churchill's Bodyguard*, 83.

383 *'That's to keep me out':* Manchester, *The Last Lion: Alone*, 543.

383 *'forcing the Dardanelles':* Ibid., 547; and *The Gathering Storm*, 410.

384 *'dead, dead, dead':* Gilbert, *In Search of Churchill*, 164.

384 *'Battle of the Atlantic':* Robin Brodhurst, *Churchill's Anchor: Admiral of the Fleet Sir Dudley Pound* (Barnsley, 2000), 7.

384 *'"it's a good thing"':* Hough, *The Greatest Crusade*, 125.

385 *'neither God, man, nor Winston Churchill':* Arthur J. Marder, *From the Dardanelles to Oran* (New York and London, 1974), 110. Also in Brodhurst, *Churchill's Anchor*, 119; and in various other sources. The original source, however, is Marder.

385 *characterized Churchill's leadership:* Marder, *From the Dardanelles to Oran*, 110.

385 *'personal qualities of Admiral Pound':* *The Gathering Storm*, 410.

385 *'younger than I am':* Sir Geoffrey Shakespeare, *Let Candles Be Brought In* (London, 1949), 228.

385 *'I wish Pound were here':* Marder, *From the Dardanelles to Oran*, 111, quoting Sir John Colville.

385 *'your tasks and duties':* Adm. of the Fleet Lord Fraser quoted in ibid., 106. Chap. 4 has also been published separately as *Winston Is Back: Churchill at the Admiralty* (London, 1972).

386 *'Winston is back':* Although Martin Gilbert has never located the famous 'Winston is back' signal in the Admiralty Archives, and calls it 'folklore', its authenticity has never been successfully challenged. Not only does Arthur Marder accept its authenticity, but Gilbert himself also quotes the signal in *Churchill: A Life*, 624. Despite its lack of a

paper trail, there seems little doubt of its authenticity. Among others, Adm. Andrew B. Cunningham, then the commander in chief, Mediterranean, notes in his autobiography, 'We received the signal "Winston is back" . . . the evening of September 3rd with considerabled satisfaction.' (*A Sailor's Odyssey* [London, 1951], 217.) Pound's biographer suggests that Pound himself must have originated the signal and that 'it was as much a warning as a greeting.' (Brodhurst, *Churchill's Anchor*, 118.)

386 *'Pray let me have'*: Gretton, *Former Naval Person*, 259.
386 *quickly learned, were unacceptable*: WSC minutes to Adm. Bruce Fraser. Oct. 24, 1939, CHAR 19/3.
386 *'lost its special priority'*: Shakespeare, *Let Candles Be Brought In*, 231.
387 *'Admiralty in wartime'*: *The Churchill War Papers*, vol. 1, 262–63.
387 *'at this significant port'*: WSC to Adm. John Henry Godfrey, Dec. 20, 1939, CHAR 19/3.
387 *most desolate military outposts*: Hough, *The Greatest Crusade*, 133.
388 *'should not be forced'*: WSC to Adm. John Henry Godfrey, Sept. 6, 1939.
389 *'really in the war'*: Capt. J. S. S. Litchfield quoted in Marder, *From the Dardanelles to Oran*, 107–8.
389 *'much more interesting'*: Shakespeare, *Let Candles Be Brought In*, 230–31; and Marder, *From the Dardanelles to Oran*, 108.
389 *'latter without the former'*: Stewart, *Burying Caesar*, 394.
390 *'fool the Germans'*: WSC to Dudley Pound, Sept. 5, 1939, ADM 205/2, PRO; and Hickman, *Churchill's Bodyguard*, 86.
390 *repeated them throughout the war*: Martin Gilbert, *Winston S. Churchill: Finest Hour, 1939–1941* (London, 1983), 13, hereafter cited as *Churchill*, vol. 6.
390 *unrestricted undersea warfare*: Readers interested in a detailed month-by-month account of the Royal Navy in the Second World War should consult www.naval-history.net/, an exceptionally informative website.
390 *waterways leading to them*: Rose, *Churchill*, 310.
391 *'quite trivial questions'*: Adm. J. H. Godfrey quoted in Marder, *From the Dardanelles to Oran*, 109.
391 *'to keep Winston going'*: Ibid., 115–16.
391 *his staff do the same*: Jenkins, *Churchill*, 561.
391 *'you must eat hard'*: Denis Kelly memoir, Kelly Papers.
392 *commander in chief of the Home Fleet*: Shakespeare, *Let Candles Be Brought In*, 67–69. The war room's official title was the Operational Intelligence Centre.
392 *'concentrated, supremely courageous'*: Frank W. Mottershead, private secretary to the permanent secretary, Admiralty, 1939, *The Churchill War Papers*, vol. 1, 545, and n.
393 *'when they got it!'*: Thompson, *Assignment Churchill*, 131.
393 *'in those black depths'*: *Churchill*, vol. 6, 62. The author of the quotation was John Higham, a senior Admiralty civil servant.
393 *'wept over the wreckage'*: Hickman, *Churchill's Bodyguard*, 85.

Chapter 30: Warlord in Waiting

394 *'I've got an idea'*: Hough, *The Greatest Crusade*, 130.
394 *'making no plans whatever'*: Ironside diary, July 25, 1939.
395 *'background of my thought'*: Marder, *From the Dardanelles to Oran*, 140.
395 *'measure of despair'*: WSC minute of Sept. 12, 1939, *The Gathering Storm*, 692–94.
395 *'open the lines of communication'*: WSC to Dudley Pound, Dec. 11, 1939, ADM, 199/1928.
396 *'of British sea-power'*: Reynolds, *In Command of History*, 114–17. Churchill had been first lord for a mere four days when he instructed the Admiralty staff to devise 'a plan for forcing a passage into the Baltic'. The original memorandum is in PREM 1/345, PRO.
397 *British (and later American) merchant ships*: Admiral Karl Dönitz, the head of the

Kriegsmarine, believed that by attacking merchant shipping from other nations of the British Empire and from the United States he could isolate and strangle Britain by cutting off its sources of war matériel and by sinking Allied shipping faster than it could be replaced. By war's end the Germans had commissioned nearly nine hundred U-boats.

397 *assigned to protect Churchill:* Hickman, *Churchill's Bodyguard,* 79–80.

397 *'under terrible tension':* Thompson, *Assignment Churchill,* 213.

397 *'their men but their women':* Ibid., 127–28.

398 *'before they shoot me down':* Ibid., 129.

398 *'not with Hitler or his régime':* Lord Hankey quoting King George VI in Roskill, *Hankey: Man of Secrets,* vol. 3, *1931–1963* (London, 1974), 429.

398 *'to be a war minister':* Schama, *A History of Britain,* vol. 3, 504.

399 *be writing his new memoirs:* Churchill, vol. 6, 15.

399 *minister of defence in April 1940:* Hough, *The Greatest Crusade,* 133.

399 *ammunition stocks and weapons:* A thorough analysis of Churchill's attempts to force the government to come to grips with the enormous problems it faced is in Patrick Cosgrave, *Churchill at War,* vol. 1, *Alone 1939–40* (London, 1974), chap. 6.

400 *'went on watching the show':* Thompson, *Assignment Churchill,* 136; and Hickman, *Churchill's Bodyguard,* 86.

400 *that had failed once before:* Churchill, vol. 6, chap. 1.

400 *'not taught, at your disposal':* 'Action This Day', Autumn 1939, Churchill Centre, http:/www.winstonchurchill.org/.

400 *'unequal to our dangers':* War Cabinet Paper, Feb. 8, 1940, CAB 66/5, PRO.

401 *never followed through on any of these ideas:* Rose, *Churchill,* 313.

401 *'change the temper of the House':* Diary of Harold Nicolson, Sept. 26, 1939, *The War Years,* 37.

402 *'ring again throughout Europe':* BBC speech, Jan. 20, 1940.

402 *'foot on the ground':* Roberts, *'The Holy Fox',* 189. The full text is in James, *Churchill Speaks,* 697–700.

402 *morale of the British public:* 'He is too belligerent for this pacifist age,' noted Harold Nicolson, but 'once anger comes to steel our sloppiness, his voice will be welcome to them, at the moment it reminds them of heroism which they do not really feel.' (Nicolson diary, Jan. 20, 1940, 59.)

402 *'undertake rash adventures':* Colville diary, Oct. 1, 1939.

402 *'Book he will write hereafter':* Chamberlain to his sister Hilda, Sept. 17, 1939, quoted in Reynolds, *In Command of History,* 112.

402 *'actions are carrying him':* Ibid.

403 *'common sense and due reflection':* Shakespeare, *Let Candles Be Brought In,* 66.

403 *138 neutral merchant ships were lost:* Rose, *Churchill,* 314, and Office of War Information (OWI) bulletin, Nov. 28, 1944, 'Allied Merchant Ship Losses, 1939–1943'.

Chapter 31: The Norway Debacle

405 *'a finger in the pie, all amateurs':* Ironside diary, April 23, 1940.

406 *'on them personally?':* Colville diary, Dec. 31, 1939.

406 *sanctuary in Wales:* Richard Collier, *1940: The Avalanche* (New York and London, 1979), 7. In January 1940 there were an average thirty-three deaths a day from the cold.

406 *'sterner days would come':* Soames, *Clementine Churchill,* 318.

406 *to be severely contracted:* Clive Ponting, *1940: Myth and Reality* (Chicago and London, 1990), 31, 45–46.

406 *rather than war with Germany:* Charles Stewart Henry Vane-Tempest-Stewart, the seventh Marquess of Londonderry (1878–1949), was the enormously wealthy heir to an Ulster fortune who earned a dark, if long-forgotten, place in history as an ardent supporter of Hitler. Both related to and a friend of Churchill, he was Ramsay MacDonald's air minister in the early 1930s. Londonderry's story is sadly typical of a generation of aristo-

crats spawned by the Great War who badly misconstrued both Hitler and his intentions and believed that Germany had been given a raw deal at Versailles. See Ian Kershaw's excellent biography, *Making Friends with Hitler: Lord Londonderry, the Nazis and the Road to War* (New York and London, 2004).

407 *'only after a beating'*: Collier, *1940*, 6.

407 *'not a real defence'*: Richard Lamb, *Churchill as War Leader* (New York and London, 1991), 15.

408 *being actively pursued*: Roskill, *Hankey: Man of Secrets*, vol. 3, 466.

408 *to him in the 1930s*: Churchill was made aware of radar's existence within twenty-four hours after successful experiments in July 1935 demonstrated its capability of detecting aircraft with radio waves. (Manchester, *The Last Lion: Alone*, 573.)

408 *'is of high urgency'*: WSC to Adm. Bruce Fraser, Sept. 8, 1939, CHAR 19/3.

408 *'is courting disaster'*: Pound to WSC, Dec. 31, 1939, ADM 205/4; also Marder, *From the Dardanelles to Oran*, 145, and *The Churchill War Papers*, vol. 1, 589–91.

409 *'very great relief'*: WSC to Pound, Jan. 1, 1040, ADM 205/4.

409 *not possible in 1940:* WSC and Pound memos are in *The Churchill War Papers*, vol. 1, 644–46, and Marder, *From the Dardanelles to Oran*, 146.

409 *no longer obtainable*: Marder, *From the Dardanelles to Oran*, 148.

409 *'our contraband control'*: Colville diary, Dec. 16, 1939.

409 *'the Gallipoli plan'*: Ibid., Jan. 1, 1940.

410 *'trade going to Germany'*: War Cabinet minutes, Sept. 19, 1939, CAB 65/1, PRO.

410 *'bring it to an end'*: WSC War Cabinet paper, Feb. 14, 1940, CAB 66/5.

411 *'prisoners of war to Germany'*: WSC minute, Feb. 16, 1940, CHAR 19/6.

412 *by supporting Churchill:* Harold Nicolson noted in his diary on Feb. 20, 1940: 'Winston rang up Halifax and said, "I propose to violate Norwegian neutrality." ' After the parliamentary session on Feb. 20, 'Winston, when he walks out of the House, catches my eye. He gives one portentous wink.' (*The War Years*, 59.) Lord Camrose, a close friend of Churchill, wrote down Halifax's version of their conversation: 'We are sitting opposite the *Altmark*,' said Churchill, 'and there are two Norwegian gun-boats facing us, with their torpedo tubes trained on our boats. These are the instructions we propose to send and I want your approval.' (Lord Camrose [William Ewart Berry, editor in chief and owner of the *Daily Telegraph and Morning Post*], quoted in *The Churchill War Papers*, vol. 1, 773.)

412 *'pending further instructions'*: According to Captain Vian, a second signal from the Admiralty instructed him that if prisoners were found he was to seize and bring home the *Altmark* 'as a prize', and if not, the officers were to be seized and brought to England, 'in order that we may ascertain what has been done with the prisoners'. This was followed by yet another signal that directed: 'Sail as soon as you have recovered prisoners. Leave the ship.' (Sir Philip Vian, *Action This Day: War Memoirs* [London, 1960], 29.)

412 *'That was big of Halifax'*: 'Winston and the Altmark', account by A. V. Alexander, MSS. 5/4/1, Alexander Papers, CAC. A Labour MP and a former first lord under Ramsay MacDonald, Alexander succeeded Churchill as first lord and was one of his principal supporters in his bid to become prime minister. There is a discrepancy in the various accounts of the *Altmark* incident in relation to the date that it was first spotted. Some have it as 14 February and others the morning of the 16th. The *Altmark* entered Norwegian territorial waters on 14 February but remained undetected until the 16th. It sent a signal on entering Norwegian waters, and it is likely that this signal was intercepted and became the basis for the aerial search by the RAF.

412 *'ought to be shot myself'*: Vian, *Action This Day*, 30.

412 *without its human cargo:* It is not clear whether Churchill was praising or mocking Halifax. His biographer, Andrew Roberts, believes it was praise for the foreign secretary's prompt agreement to violate another nation's neutrality in the belief that it would send a strong message to Berlin. In his diary on 17 February, Halifax wrote that the rescue was 'a very fine performance and quite in the Elizabethan style'. (Roberts, *'The Holy Fox'*, 193; Manchester, *The Last Lion: Alone*, 622–23; 'Winston and the Altmark'; Vian, *Action*

This Day, chap. 3; and *Churchill*, vol. 6, 151–54.) In *Hitler's War, 1939–1942* (83), the revisionist historian David Irving, basing his remarks on what he cites as the report of the incident by the captain of the *Altmark*, criticizes the British and puts forward a completely unproved allegation that the Germans aboard the *Altmark* were unarmed and that the ship and its crew were looted.

412 *'by a British sea-pirate'*: Vian, *Action This Day*, 31.

413 *'act so directly'*: Marder, *From the Dardanelles to Oran*, 140.

413 *audience roared its approval*: WSC's Guildhall speech and description of the events at Horse Guards Parade are in *The Times*, Feb. 24, 1940, and are reprinted in *The Churchill War Papers*, vol. 1, 793–94.

414 *highest urgency and importance*: J. R. M. Butler, *Grand Strategy*, vol. 2 (London, 1957), 115.

414 *who was wrong*: Irving, *Hitler's War, 1939–1942*, 82.

414 *orders of his first sea lord*: Marder, *From the Dardanelles to Oran*, 137 and n. 65.

415 *'the Germans worked faster'*: Haffner, *Churchill*, 96.

415 *awarded the Victoria Cross*: After the war Roope was posthumously awarded the VC in 1945.

415 *once peaceful streets*: Collier, *1940*, 52.

416 *'weather in the North Sea'*: Colville diary, April 9, 1940.

416 *'spoilt child in many ways'*: *Churchill*, vol. 6, 223.

417 *'these things should happen'*: Ironside diary, April 14, 1940.

417 *'How can a staff function?'*: Ibid., April 23, 1940.

417 *'how mercurial he is'*: Ibid., April 22, 1940.

417 *'onslaught of scientific warfare'*: Colville diary, May 3, 1940.

418 *'bungles in modern British history'*: Leland Stowe quoted in Gardner, *Churchill in Power*, 35.

419 *'all was to be disaster'*: *The Gathering Storm*, 580.

419 *'public esteem and Parliamentary confidence'*: WSC quoted in Hankey, *Man of Secrets*, vol. 3, 465n. Churchill's original manuscript read that he did not know how he survived, 'while all the blame was thrown on poor Mr Chamberlain'. (See Reynolds, *In Command of History*, 126.)

419 *someone other than Churchill*: François Kersaudy, *Norway 1940* (London, 1990), 227.

419 *significant portion of the German navy*: Ibid., 226.

Chapter 32: The Loneliest Man in Britain

420 *mining of the Rhine, Operation Royal Marine*: Manchester, *The Last Lion: Alone*, 675.

420 *'from an early morning ride'*: Templewood, *Nine Troubled Years*, 431–32.

421 *'time for showing off toys?'*: Ibid.; and John Reith diary, May 10, 1940, Charles Stuart, ed., *The Reith Diaries* (London, 1975), 250.

421 *'its head or its heels'*: Ironside diary, May 10, 1940.

421 *'we must take our blows'*: Hansard, April 11, 1940; and Hough, *The Greatest Crusade*, 147.

421 *'We have been completely outwitted'*: Hough, *The Greatest Crusade*, 147.

422 *'he should do more'*: John Charmley, *Churchill: The End of Glory* (New York, 1994), 501.

422 *'hitting his colleagues'*: Spears, *Assignment to Catastrophe*, vol. 1, May 8, 1940, 123–24.

422 *'trounced the Opposition'*: Channon diary, May 8, 1940.

422 *'remained glaringly apparent'*: Spears, *Assignment to Catastrophe*, vol. 1, May 8, 1940, 127–28.

422 *'conditions can be established'*: WSC speech, May 8, 1940, Hansard; also quoted in *The Churchill War Papers*, vol. 1, 1241.

422 *'time being our Naval strategy'*: *Churchill*, vol. 6, 304–05; and CAB 9/139.

423 *'In the name of God, go!'*: Hansard; also quoted in Stewart, *Burying Caesar*, 410.

423 *against the Government or by abstaining*: Among those who voted against the government was a young newly elected MP named John Profumo who was casting his first vote. As secretary of state for war in the early 1960s, Profumo would be at the centre of one of the worst spy scandals in British history.

423 *'similar battle with themselves'*: John W. Wheeler-Bennett, *King George VI* (New York, 1958), 440.

424 *'be Prime Minister tomorrow'*: Churchill, vol. 6, 305.

424 *could no longer govern Britain*: Gilbert, *A History of the Twentieth Century*, vol. 2, 303.

424 *'tale of achievement and promotion'*: Roberts, 'The Holy Fox', 1.

424 *highly questionable judgment*: Ibid.

424 *'things that really mattered'*: Diary of Lord Halifax, May 9, 1940, Hickleton Papers, Borthwick Institute of Historical Research, University of York.

424 *'act of self-abnegation'*: Roberts, 'The Holy Fox', 2.

425 *'for a sensible peace'*: Schama, *A History of Britain*, vol. 3, 508.

425 *'despair at the prospect'*: Colville diary, May 10, 1940.

425 *'thrown in his hand'*: Box 81, Moran Papers.

425 *'except beating the enemy'*: Churchill, vol. 6, 306.

426 *'regret for his decision'*: Roberts, 'The Holy Fox', 206–7.

426 *'what I thought was right'*: Lady Oxford (the former Margot Asquith), May 11, 1940, Gardner, *Churchill in Power*, 40.

426 *'to bits in a moment'*: Stewart, *Burying Caesar*, 437

426 *'final responsibility was off him'*: Halifax diary, May 14, 1940.

426 *into his new government*: The Gathering Storm, 665; and Wheeler-Bennett, *King George VI*, 444n.

427 *'we can only do our best'*: Thompson, *Assignment Churchill*, 165.

427 *'began to climb the stairs'*: Hickman, *Churchill's Bodyguard*, 91.

427 *'over the whole scene'*: The Gathering Storm, 667.

428 *'saviour of his country'*: A. J. P. Taylor, *The War Lords* (New York and London, 1978), 98.

428 *She prayed*: Lady Soames interview, Brendon Papers.

428 *'well known to all Germans'*: Spears, *Assignment to Catastrophe*, vol. 1, 134.

428 *'highest aim of human endeavour'*: Harold Nicolson, 'Portrait of Winston Churchill'.

428 *'rock the boat'*: Jacob interview, Mar. 13, 1969, JACB 4/10, Jacob Papers, CAC.

429 *'bring the war to an end'*: Ironside diary, May 3, 1940.

429 *'leadership of Britain'*: James, 'Chips', 248.

429 *'conviction in ultimate victory'*: Spears, *Assignment to Catastrophe*, vol. 1, 134.

429 *'reasons for despair and surrender'*: Schama, *A History of Britain*, vol. 3, 510, and notes, Box 62, Moran Papers.

Chapter 33: 'Action This Day'

430 *led by Neville Chamberlain*: Reynolds, *In Command of History*, 277.

430 *sometimes even his courage*: One particularly vicious attack on Churchill in 2002 alleges that he fled London to stay with a wealthy friend in the countryside whenever Enigma provided him with advance information about a bombing raid on the capital. According to the author, 'the allegation has now been in print for fifteen years, and I have never seen it addressed by the Great Man's defenders, let alone rebutted.' This absurd allegation ignores the fact that Enigma decrypts of German message traffic that emanated from Bletchley Park were not real-time, and were received by Churchill well after the fact, and the fact that the Luftwaffe did not routinely announce in advance when and where it would conduct its raids. (See Christopher Hitchens, 'The Medals of His Defeats', *Atlantic Monthly* [April 2002]).

430 *'playing at soldiers'*: Maj. Gen. J. F. C. Fuller quoted in David Jablonsky, *Churchill, the Great Game and Total War* (London, 1991), 96.

431 *'supreme period of his life'*: Sir John Wheeler-Bennett, ed., *Action This Day: Working with Churchill* (London, 1968), 'Sir John Martin', 139.

431 *'The war closed the gap'*: Box 58, Moran Papers.

431 *'I should not fail'*: *The Gathering Storm*, 667.

431 *'hold the Rogue Elephant'*: Hankey to Sir Samuel Hoare, May 12, 1940, Beaverbrook Papers. Also quoted in Martin Gilbert, *The Churchill War Papers*, vol. 2, *Never Surrender*, May 1940–December 1941 (New York and London, 1995), 15.

432 *'your private residence'*: Channon diary, May 15, 1940, James, *'Chips'*, 253.

432 *and that was typical*: Lord Home interview, WHCL 15/2/12, CAC.

432 *'fifty per cent bloody fool'*: Clement Attlee comment, Box 93, Moran Papers.

432 *'either of the two world wars'*: Churchill, vol. 1, 348.

433 *'some of them got both'*: Boothby, *Recollections of a Rebel*, 169.

434 *when Churchill had money woes*: Charles Edward Lysaght, 'Bracken: The Fantasist Whose Dreams Came True', The 2001 Brendan Bracken Memorial Lecture, Churchill College, reprinted in *Finest Hour* 63 (2001).

434 *'right of Genghis Khan'*: Thomas Wilson, *Churchill and The Prof* (London, 1995), 8–9.

435 *'find its doubts justified'*: Wheeler-Bennett, *Action This Day*, 'John Colville', 48–49.

435 *'The pace became frantic'*: John Colville, *Footprints in Time* (London, 1976), 75.

435 *'at which business is conducted'*: Wheeler-Bennett, *Action This Day*, 'John Colville', 49.

435 *'fusty corridors of Whitehall'*: Marian Spicer interview, WHCL 15/2/55, CAC.

435 *'made to go on leave'*: Letter, Leslie Hollis to Lawrence Burgis, May 3, 1955, BRGS 1/2, Burgis Papers.

435 *'He turned night into day'*: Box 59, file K5/6/1, Moran Papers.

436 *a minute or so away*: In his younger days Churchill could be far harsher on his stenographers. When he was chancellor during the 1920s, one of them became so exasperated she threw her shorthand pad at him – and, was, of course, summarily sacked. (Letter, Hollis to Burgis, May 3, 1955, Burgis Papers.)

436 *'"with one man – Hitler"'*: Sir John Martin, *Downing Street: The War Years* (London, 1991), 6.

436 *'new fields of slaughter'*: Jablonsky, *Churchill, the Great Game and Total War*, 94.

436 *reserved 'for gangsters'*: Notes by the deputy cabinet secretary, Sir Norman Brook, WM (42), 168th Meeting, Dec. 14, 1942, PRO. In April 1945, with the Third Reich crumbling into extinction, the subject of what to do with Hitler and the principal Nazi leaders again arose, and again Churchill expressed his belief that they should be put to death and that a trial 'will be a farce . . . Indictment: facilities for counsel. All sorts of complications ensue as soon as you admit a fair trial. I agree with H.O. [Home Secretary Herbert Morrison] that they shd. be treated as outlaws. We shd, however, seek agreement of our Allies.' The meeting was attended by Churchill's close friend and ally, Field Marshal Jan Smuts, the prime minister of South Africa, who declared that summary executions would set a dangerous precedent. (WM [45] 43rd Meeting held on April 12, 1945, CAB 195/1.) This information was not made public until Jan. 1, 2006, and was the first indication of how the British government contemplated dealing with Hitler and the Nazi leaders.

436 *any time of day or night*: John Peck, *Dublin from Downing Street* (Dublin, 1978), 68–69.

437 *'discussed the affairs of the day'*: John Peck interview, WCHL 15/2/14.

437 *'but something really effective'*: Wheeler-Bennett, *Action This Day*, 'John Colville', 112.

437 *'"I want to win the war"'*: Collier, 1940, 65.

438 *'to meet the point'*: *The Memoirs of Lord Chandos* (London, 1962), 172–73. Before becoming Viscount Chandos after the war, Oliver Lyttelton (1893–1972) held a variety of posts in Churchill's coalition government. In later life he was the first chairman of London's Royal National Theatre.

438 *'cured him of that!'*: Roberts, *'The Holy Fox'*, 210.

438 *souvenirs for tidy sums:* James Leasor, *War at the Top* (London, 1959), 10. When the battleship HMS *Prince of Wales* took Churchill to Placentia Bay in August 1941, his cigar wrappers and butts were collected and given to the crew as souvenirs. One can only imagine what they would bring on eBay today.

438 *not fit to hold his office:* 'The Memoirs of Lawrence Burgis'.

439 *'satisfactory to you, Captain?'*: Jablonsky, *Churchill, the Great Game and Total War*, 145–46.

439 *Churchill travelled constantly:* Colville, *Footprints in Time*, 76–77.

439 *'water is a conductor of sound?'*: Leasor, *War at the Top*, 31.

439 *his flow of words:* Mrs Chipps Gemmel, who took dictation for Churchill's war memoirs, had a similar experience. 'You'd stand outside,' she recalled, 'and you'd hear these wonderful bathroom noises.' Other times he would dictate in a car or a swaying jeep, as a hard-pressed secretary fought to get the words down correctly. (Chipps Gemmel interview, WCHL 15/2/63.)

439 *choking on Churchill's cigar smoke:* Colville notes that there were occasions when a stenographer had to be revived with brandy after enduring a motor-car trip with Churchill. (*Footprints in Time*, 77.)

440 *nothing untoward had occurred:* Peck interview, WCHL 15/2/14. Another aide, Patrick Kinna, recalls an occasion when Churchill rather dramatically announced one day as he was reading papers in bed that the papers ought to be burned lest they fall into enemy hands. As Kinna attempted to burn them in the fireplace the room filled with smoke and soot – the chimney was blocked. Churchill exploded with anger, then finally saw the funny side and had the windows opened to air the room. (Kinna interview, Brendon Papers.)

440 *'he would not have done it'*: 'The Memoirs of Lawrence Burgis'.

440 *'wipe his feet upon you'*: Ben Pimlott, ed., *The Second World War Diary of Hugh Dalton, 1940–1945* (London, 1986), Nov. 14, 1940, hereafter cited as Dalton diary.

440 *the hard way:* Churchill's harsh treatment of his subordinates led Clementine to write him a letter on June 27, 1940, imploring him to curb his irascibility and rudeness. Although there is no record of any reply, Churchill's daughter believes her father took the rebuke and advice seriously. (Soames, *Winston and Clementine*, 454.)

441 *one of his military assistants:* Wheeler–Bennett, *Action This Day*, 'Sir Ian Jacob', 173.

441 *'he has seen in writing'*: Spears, *Assignment to Catastrophe*, vol. 1, 101.

441 *'keep up with him'*: Francis Perkins, *The Roosevelt I Knew* (New York, 1946), 307.

442 *'destinies of men and nations!'*: Sheridan, *Nudas Veritas*, 133–34.

442 *'Kitcheners, Fishers or Haigs'*: *Finest Hour* (Spring 2007), 54.

Chapter 34: Minister of Defence

443 *'presiding genius of the alliance'*: John Keegan, in his introduction to Keegan, ed., *Churchill's Generals* (New York and London, 1991), 15.

443 *'I had thought about it'*: Post-war conversation, Box 58, Moran Papers.

443 *'Heaven help us'*: *The Reith Diaries*, May 11, 1940, 250.

444 *war's military direction:* Sir Maurice Dean points out: 'Had Churchill been appointed Minister of Defence in 1936 the results would have been unfortunate. He would in all probability have made a good Minister from some points of view but come 1940 disaster would have struck just the same and he would have been discredited. His great advantage and the supreme gift he brought to Britain was that he came with clean hands.' (*The Royal Air Force and Two World Wars* [London, 1979], 103.)

444 *Opposition leader:* WSC, *Their Finest Hour* (Boston, 1949), 18–19; and Christopher Andrew, *Her Majesty's Secret Service* (New York and London, 1986), 485.

444 *'and her glory'*: Moran Papers.

445 *'story of heroes'*: Ibid.

445 *decide on their suitability:* PREM 3/3/10B.

445 'with ancient weapons': Kennedy, The Business of War, 60.

446 set of relationships would succeed: 'The Memoirs of Lawrence Burgis'.

446 'break up the association': Wheeler-Bennett, Action This Day, 'Sir Ian Jacob', 164–65.

446 'whole of the war': John Colville, The Churchillians (London, 1981), 124.

446 British figures of the Second World War: Holmes, In the Footsteps of Churchill, 207.

447 'simple as a child': Quoted in 'Lord Ismay', Box 60, Moran Papers.

447 'should be given, is a blessing': Their Finest Hour, 15.

447 'bleed and burn every day': Jacob interview, WCHL 15/2/9.

447 'delectable fruits and wholesome vegetables': Wheeler-Bennett, Action This Day, 'John Colville', 61.

447 ignored his table companions: Conversation with Alistair Cooke, General Eisenhower on the Military Churchill (1967 ABC television documentary), Eisenhower General File, GCML.

447 'that's what I do': 'WC's attitude to soldiers', Box 60, Moran Papers. Gen. Lyman L. Lemnitzer, the post-war NATO supreme commander, knew Churchill personally and was once asked if Churchill liked 'to tinker with military plans and move divisions around on a map'. Lemnitzer replied, 'Divisions, hell. He liked to move battalions, but then all politicians do, don't they?' (Herb Puscheck, West Point, class of 1958, anecdote related by Richard F. Reidy, Jr.)

448 'pages of the Admiralty annals': Roskill, Churchill and the Admirals, 109–10.

448 'half what he says': Adm. J. C. Tovey to Andrew Cunningham, Oct. 17, 1940, Cunningham Papers, BL.

448 'expect to like him': Box 60, File K-4/2, Moran Papers.

448 rounds of the US army: Time, Dec. 6, 1943; and Antony Head interview, CLVL 3/5, Colville Papers.

448 'war to be conducted': WSC quoted in Moran, Churchill, 416.

448 'save their country': Colville, Footprints in Time, 118.

449 'disguised as the Prime Minister': Gerald Pawle, The War and Colonel Warden (London, 1963), 3. 'Colonel Warden' was the favourite of the many aliases under which Churchill travelled. Pawle's intimate account is based on the recollections of Commander. C. R. Thompson, one of Churchill's personal assistants, whose job it was to oversee the prime minister's travel.

449 'grunted and changed the subject': Gen. Sir David Fraser interview, BREN 1/12, Brendon Papers.

450 'safe by conventional standards': Douglas MacGregor, 'Fire the Generals', article written for the Straus Military Reform Project at the Center for Defense Information in Washington, DC, 2006. Quotation is from James Mann, Rise of the Vulcans (New York, 2002), 63.

450 'useful to be a good runner': Kennedy, The Business of War, 80.

450 this was a bad idea: Jacob interview, WHCL 15/2/9, CAC.

450 'experience from the First World War': Antony Head interview.

451 for hour upon hour: Lewis Broad, The War That Churchill Fought (London, 1960), 59.

451 'his powerful protection': Ibid., 58.

451 'new and unexpected': Antony Head interview.

451 'tuneless renderings of the bugle': Ibid.

451 'take them to battle': Hastings Lionel Ismay, The Memoirs of Lord Ismay (London, 1960), 270.

452 rejected by Roosevelt: Both Churchill and Brooke either misunderstood Eisenhower, who never agreed to switching the invasion from the Riviera to Brittany, or deluded themselves into believing he agreed with them. To the contrary, Eisenhower fought tooth and nail against any change of venue or cancellation of the operation, believing (correctly as it turned out) that it was vital to gain and maintain additional ports, particularly Marseille, and that it would serve to protect the right flank of the Allied armies during

their broad advance toward Germany. See Carlo D'Este, *Eisenhower: Allied Supreme Commander* (London, 2002), chap. 43.

452 *'not exactly a band of brothers'*: Ismay, lecture to the Imperial Defence Committee, Nov. 1956, Ismay Papers, LHC.

452 *'order he received from Mr Churchill'*: Ibid.; and *The Memoirs of Lord Ismay*, 269–70.

453 *'he would not be supported'*: *The Memoirs of Lord Isman*, 269–70.

453 *situation in France became clearer:* War Cabinet minutes, May 13, 1940, CAB 65/13.

454 *'Our aim is victory'*: David Reynolds observes that 'total military victory over Germany had never been a British aim in 1939, let alone after France fell.' (Reynolds, *From World War to Cold War* [Oxford, 2006], 112.)

454 *'That got the sods, didn't it?'*: Quoted by James in *Churchill Speaks*, 704.

455 *'the man pilloried'*: Colville diary, May 18 and 19, 1940.

455 *'mistakes had led to suffering'*: Box 62, Moran Papers.

455 *'1940 every time, every time'*: Ibid.

455 *'disaster for quite a long time'*: *The Memoirs of Lord Ismay*, 116.

Chapter 35: The Central War Room

456 *'the Hole'*: Gardner, *Churchill in Power*, 52. Today what is called the Churchill Museum and Cabinet War Rooms is operated and maintained by the Imperial War Museum. Readers unable to visit this superbly preserved facility in person can take a virtual tour of the war rooms and the new Churchill museum (opened in 2005) on the internet at cwr.iwm.org.uk; click on 'Virtual Tour'.

457 *'might have tested our defences'*: Lawrence Burgis to Leslie Hollis, May 3, 1955, Burgis Papers.

457 *'Action This Day' labels:* Pawle, *The War and Colonel Warden*, 81.

458 *'I am going upstairs to sleep'*: Thompson, *Assignment Churchill*, 212.

458 *'hair-raising escapes from chaos'*: Sir John Peck quoted in *Churchill*, vol. 6, 783.

458 *'off the face of the earth'*: Hickman, *Churchill's Bodyguard*, 105–06. Description of the war rooms is from Simpkins, *The Cabinet War Rooms*; the Hollis memoir; and post-war newspaper descriptions. See also the papers of Wing Commander J. S. Heagerty, Ref. No. 94/40/1; and Miss G. I. Hutchinson, Ref. No. 94/42/1, IWM. Heagerty was one of three duty officers in charge of the war rooms, chosen for their loyalty.

458 *'impenetrable arch of probability'*: Colville diary, Jan. 24, 1941.

458 *London became 'practically uninhabitable'*: *Churchill*, vol. 6, 781.

459 *'would be worth trying'*: WSC to Ismay, Oct. 24, 1940, CHAR 20/13; and *The Churchill War Papers*, vol. 2, xii and 995–96.

459 *cabinet papers and top-secret documents: Churchill*, vol. 6, 601.

459 *'rather than that'*: Burgis memoir.

459 *'damned well shoot me'*: Earl of Halifax, *Fullness of Days* (New York, 1957; published in London as *Fulness of Days*, 226.

459 *'assuming one ever got so far'*: Moss, *Nineteen Weeks*, 192–93.

459 *resist both passively and actively:* Ibid.

460 *'eels get used to skinning'*: Pawle, *The War and Colonel Warden*, 80.

460 *seventy thousand incendiary bombs on London:* Ibid., 82.

461 *signal an air raid:* Peter Simpkins, *The Cabinet War Rooms* (London, 1983), 42.

461 *'that's where I'll sit'*: Leasor, *War at the Top*, 60.

461 *'christened it "The Dock" '*: 'The Memoirs of Lawrence Burgis'.

462 *two men did speak occasionally:* Warren F. Kimball, ed., *Churchill & Roosevelt: The Complete Correspondence*, (London, 1984) vol. 1, *Alliance Emerging*, xx–xxi.

462 *'anyone else will I do it'*: Hickman, *Churchill's Bodyguard*, 105.

462 *sneak by him in the night:* Ibid., 102–03.

463 *'same chance as anyone else'*: Ibid., 106.

463 'has to be carried out, Thompson': Ibid., 107–08.

463 'it will come': Thompson, *Assignment Churchill*, 211. Walter Thompson's relations with Clementine suffered from his constant presence at her husband's side for more than twenty years. She regarded him as an irritant who was much too privy to the intimate details of the Churchill family's daily life for her liking and demonstrated it by refusing to feed him and banning him from sleeping at Chartwell until Winston found out and overruled her. (217–18.)

463 'sin against the language': Ibid., 210–11.

464 *exposed to danger in London*: Geoffrey Perret, *Jack: A Life Like No Other* (New York, 2001), 92.

464 'as a second Gallipoli': Nigel Hamilton, *JFK: Reckless Youth* (New York and London, 1992), 324.

464 'never proven to be good': Charmley, *Churchill: The End of Glory*, 429.

464 'until I met Joe Kennedy': Robinson, *Invasion, 1940*, 42.

464 'attack on the capital': Wheeler-Bennett, *Action This Day*, 'Sir John Martin', 146.

464 'coughing our heads off!': Elizabeth Leighton interview, WCHL 15 series, CAC.

465 'half a dozen of us with you': Pawle, *The War and Colonel Warden*, 82.

465 'war was on our doorstep': Pamela Harriman interview, WCHL 15/2/3. War extended to moments of relaxation when make-believe war games took place. Someone had given Churchill a Chinese chequers board, and when he learned that his daughter-in-law knew how to play, he insisted that she oppose him and that they would replay the American civil war, with Averell Harriman's daughter Kathleen as the North. Churchill then went on to describe the various moves that had to be made and what general she was playing, and warned of various ploys to look out for. (Kathleen Harriman Mortimer interview, Brendon Papers.)

465 'Winston, who adores him': Colville diary, June 29, 1940.

466 'relationship' with both of them: Soames, *Clementine Churchill*, 452. During the early years of the war, Randolph joined Colonel Robert Laycock's new commando force and was posted to the Middle East, where, in May 1942, he persuaded Major David Stirling, the Scottish laird who founded the Special Air Service (SAS), to let him join a small raiding party of the Long Range Desert Group in an abortive mission to Benghazi harbour. Unfortunately Randolph, who desperately wanted to become a good soldier and to demonstrate his courage, mostly bounced around from one minor military posting to another during the war, usually wearing out his welcome by word and by deed, his great potential wasted through anger, bad behaviour and excessive drinking.

466 ' "income tax demand" ': Elizabeth Leighton interview.

466 *running down his face*: Pamela Harriman interview.

467 'at a remarkable pace': *The Memoirs of Lord Ismay*, 183–84.

467 'on the next occasion': Ibid., 184.

Chapter 36: Disaster in Flanders Fields

468 'with the smell of doom': Graham Greene's 1951 novel *The End of the Affair*, quoted in Roberts, '*The Holy Fox*', 210–11.

469 'is broken near Sedan': *Their Finest Hour*, 42.

469 'Send all the planes you can': Moss, *Nineteen Weeks*, 104.

470 *fighter squadrons to France*: War Cabinet Confidential Annex, May 15, 1940, CAB 65/13.

470 *in reserve in Britain*: Stephen Bungay, *The Most Dangerous Enemy* (London, 2000), 99.

470 'French military thought and preparations': Horne, *To Lose a Battle*, 394.

471 *other three in the afternoon*: Bungay, *The Most Dangerous Enemy*, 99–100.

471 'celebrated documents in RAF history': Ibid., 100.

471 'defeat of this country': Dowding memo quoted ibid.

471 *air support from the RAF*: WSC memo to Ismay, May 19, 1940 quoted in *The Churchill*

War Papers, vol. 2, 91. Churchill's decision came over the strong objections of Professor Lindemann, who argued that the war would be won or lost in France. (Bungay, *The Most Dangerous Enemy*, 101.)

471 *'French had already been beaten'*: Dowding quoted in Robert Wright, *Dowding and the Battle of Britain* (London, 1969), 118.

471 *'handed over to the French'*: David E. Fisher, *A Summer Bright and Terrible* (Emeryville, CA, 2005), 119.

471 *to turn the tide*: Bungay, *The Most Dangerous Enemy*, 101.

473 *'far beyond his carapace'*: Colville diary, May 18, 1940.

473 *evacuation from France*: Nigel Hamilton, *The Full Monty: Montgomery of Alamein, 1887–1942* (London, 2001), 330–31.

473 *withdraw the BEF to the coast*: Ibid., 331.

473 *'That will be the struggle'*: WSC speech, May 19, 1940.

474 *'different a few weeks ago'*: Colville diary, May 19, 1940.

474 *towards Amiens with eight divisions*: War Cabinet Confidential Annex, 7.30 p.m., May 22, 1940, CAB 65/13.

474 *'perils of amateur strategy'*: Brian Bond, ed., *The Diaries of Lieutenant-General Sir Henry Pownall*, vol. 1, *1933–1940* (London, 1973), xxvii.

474 *'if they had any hand in it'*: Pownall diary, May 23, 1940.

475 *hold the Channel ports?*: War Cabinet minutes, meeting of 11.30 a.m., May 23, 1940, CAB 65/7, quoted in Cosgrave, *Churchill at War*, 209.

475 *'cannot be very far off!'*: The war diary of Lt. Gen. Sir Alan Brooke (later Field Marshal Lord Alanbrooke), May 23, 1940, Alanbrooke Papers, LHC. A published version of the diaries is Alex Danchev and Daniel Todman, eds., *War Diaries, 1939–1945, Field Marshal Lord Alanbrooke* (London, 2001).

475 *ineptness of the French army*: Colville diary, May 21, 1940.

476 *'attacked at once by Gort'*: WSC memo to Ismay, May 24, 1940, CHAR 4/150.

476 *'Churchill is always hectoring'*: Reynaud quoted in Norman Gelb, *Dunkirk* (London, 1989), 143.

476 *'never give in, etc.'*: Gilbert, *Churchill: A Life*, 649–50.

477 *'no fault of yours'*: Roger Keyes to Lord Gort quoted in Gelb, *Dunkirk*, 118.

477 *'Send it off tonight'*: Colville diary, May 19, 1940.

477 *no record that it was ever sent*: Ibid.; and Kimball, *Churchill & Roosevelt*, vol. 1. There is no record of this telegram in the voluminous WSC–FDR correspondence during the Second World War.

477 *Germany's undisputed warlord*: Cooper, *The German Army, 1933–1945*, 243, and chap. 17.

478 *his aide-de-camp*: Gort quoted in Collier, *1940*, 87.

478 *7,500 killed versus 3,457*: Mosier, *Cross of Iron*, 142.

478 *alleged to be British perfidy*: Horne, *To Lose a Battle*, 541.

Chapter 37: Deliverance

480 *symbol of bravery and sacrifice*: Calais was an ancient battleground, scene of the year-long siege by the British in 1346–7 during the Hundred Years' War.

481 *'worthy of the British name'*: *Their Finest Hour*, 81–82.

481 *'as he uttered them'*: *The Memoirs of Lord Ismay*, 131.

481 *'It was my decision'*: Moran, *Churchill*, 292. In 1943, en route to the Quebec Conference aboard the liner *Queen Mary*, Churchill noticed that Antony Head was wearing the Military Cross and asked where he had got it. 'Boulogne, Prime Minister,' replied Head. 'If I'd had my way you'd be dead,' Churchill said, 'and walked on.' (Head interview, CLVL 3/5, Colville Papers.)

482 *concealed near the breakwater*: Walter Lord, *The Miracle of Dunkirk* (New York, 1982), 67–68.

482 'regret the days of Calais': L. F. Ellis, *The War in France and Flanders, 1939–1940* (London, 1953), 169.

482 'events outside Dunkirk': Gen. Heinz Guderian, *Panzer Leader* (London, 1952), 120.

482 'has Calais on her heart': Letter to the Editor from J. C. Squire, *The Times*, June 5, 1940.

483 'remnants of the enemy': Walter Warlimont, *Inside Hitler's Headquarters, 1939–45* (London, 1964), 98.

483 'it suited his plans': Nicolaus von Below, *At Hitler's Side* (London, 2001), 60–61.

483 German vassal state: Robinson, *Invasion, 1940*, 33.

483 'spoilt the chance of victory': Goerlitz, *History of the German General Staff*, 376.

484 'haven't grasped that': Kershaw, *Hitler, 1936–1945: Nemesis*, 295.

484 'in this war, anyway': Walter Goerlitz, *History of the German General Staff, 1657–1945* (New York, 1956), 376.

484 either the French or the British: Frieser, *The Blitzkrieg Legend: The 1940 Campaign in the West* (2005), 292.

484 'annihilating them at Dunkirk': Warlimont, *Inside Hitler's Headquarters*, 42.

484 'miracle of Dunkirk': Frieser, *The Blitzkrieg Legend*, 292.

484 never have returned the favour: One evening in 1941, Churchill observed to Major General John Kennedy, the director of military operations, 'Once you grab the enemy by the nose, he will be able to think of nothing else.' (*The Business of War*, 80.)

484 'have a good chance': WSC to Lord Gort, May 27, 1940, CHAR 20/14.

485 'rolling senseless on the ground': Dalton diary, May 28, 1940.

485 'hurled out of office': *Their Finest Hour*, 100.

485 trumped by self-interest: Holmes, *In the Footsteps of Churchill*, 203. Holmes also points out, 'As late as 1942 he [Lloyd George] was still conspiring with a group that included future Prime Ministers Harold Macmillan and Alec Douglas-Home, to replace Winston.'

486 'one of the hardest times': Pamela Harriman interview, WHCL 15/2/3, CAC.

486 'it is an epic tale': Moran, *Churchill*, 292.

487 'going with you myself': Recollection of Capt. Richard Pike Pim, May 29, 1940, *The Churchill War Papers*, vol. 2, 193.

487 'safe in your hands': WSC to Lord Gort, May 29, 1940, PREM 3/114/9.

487 'suburbs of Dunkirk': War Cabinet Daily SITREPS, March 22–June 9, 1940, CAB 100/3. The British official history records, 'When the operation ended 338,226 had been evacuated – 308,888 of them in the ships under Admiral Ramsay's orders. Nearly 100,000 had been lifted from the beaches.' (Ellis, *The War in France and Flanders, 1939–1940*, 247.) The War Office figures reflect that approximately 331,251 Allied troops were rescued, and another 4,000 were delivered to the port of Cherbourg and several other ports still in French hands. The numbers vary depending on the account and were always subject to revision.

487 directly off the beaches: Ponting, *1940*, 91.

487 during the Battle of Britain: Reynolds, *From World War to Cold War*, 25.

488 needed in the Battle of Britain: John Strawson, *Churchill and Hitler* (New York, 1998), 262.

488 145 aircraft and eighty-eight pilots: John Terraine, *The Right of the Line: The Royal Air Force in the European War, 1939–1945* (London, 1985), 157.

488 during the evacuation: John Mosier, *The Blitzkrieg Myth* (New York and London, 2003), 146.

489 Only then did he embark: Gelb, *Dunkirk*, 298.

489 123,095 French troops from Dunkirk: Lord, *The Miracle of Dunkirk*, 276.

489 week already filled with them: Ibid., 269.

490 'survival is a wonderful thing': 'James Bradley's Dunkirk', WW II People's War, BBC archives, www.bbc.co.uk.

490 'personnel of the BEF': Alanbrooke, 'Notes on My Life'.

490 their troops to save themselves: Ponting, *1940*, 92.

490 *1.5 million taken prisoner*: Ibid., 95.

491 *battles yet to be fought*: *Their Finest Hour*, 102.

491 *seven thousand tons of ammunition*: Andrew Roberts, *A History of the English-Speaking Peoples Since 1900* (London, 2006), 273. E. M. Fraser, the director of statistics in the War Office, later told Cecil King, the editor of the *Daily Mirror*, that 'the Dunkirk episode was far worse than was ever realized even in Fleet Street.' Morale among returning men of the BEF was low; some threw their weapons from the windows of railway carriages; others 'sent for their wives with their civilian clothes, changed into these, and walked home!' (Armstrong, ed., *With Malice Toward None: A War Diary by Cecil H. King*, 85.)

491 *'they are destroyed utterly'*: Cooper, *The German Army, 1933–1945*, 236.

491 *'right under our noses'*: Franz Halder diary, May 30, 1940, quoted ibid., 236.

Chapter 38: 'Don't Give Way to Fear'

492 *'her greatest weakness'*: Shakespeare, *Let Candles Be Brought In*, 261.

493 *'we shall never surrender'*: Speech to the House of Commons, June 4, 1940, Hansard.

493 *'independence to Warsaw and Prague'*: Channon diary, June 4, 1940, James, *'Chips'*, 256.

493 ' *"I have never heard before"* ': Joseph E. Persico, *Edward R. Murrow: An American Original* (New York, 1988), 165.

494 *'survival as a nation'*: Prof. Duncan Anderson, 'Spinning Dunkirk', published June 2, 2004, on the BBC website: www.bbc.co.uk/history/worldwars/wwtwo/dunkirkspinning09.shtml.

494 *'Don't give way to fear'*: Moss, *Nineteen Weeks*, 195, quoting *Time and Tide* magazine, June 8, 1940.

494 *'has quite another significance!'*: Colville diary, Sept. 25, 1941.

495 *thirty miles north to Lille*: Ponting, *1940*, 91.

495 *'come back in glory'*: Ibid., 92.

495 *not to miss his stop*: Churchill gave wholly insufficient recognition in his war memoirs to Admiral Ramsay's role in the evacuation of Dunkirk, barely mentioning his artful handling of Operation Dynamo in *Their Finest Hour*.

496 *'destiny must inevitably be'*: Alanbrooke, 'Notes on My Life', June 2, 1940.

496 *'every probability of disaster'*: Ibid.

496 *all intents and purposes, dead*: Ibid., June 14, 1940.

497 *'Do you want to lose another?'*: David Fraser, *Alanbrooke* (London, 1982), 168.

497 *Churchill accepted them*: Ibid; and *Churchill*, vol. 6, 544–46.

497 *never reported by the British press*: Moss, *Nineteen Weeks*, 177–78.

497 *sacrificed in a lost cause*: Fraser, *Alanbrooke*, 170.

498 *'against that commander's better judgement'*: Alanbrooke, 'Notes on My Life', June 14, 1940; and Fraser, *Alanbrooke*, 168.

499 *London and other British cities*: Reynolds, *In Command of History*, 169.

499 *'could somehow be avoided'*: Roberts, 'The Holy Fox', 221.

499 *Britain would emerge victorious*: Geoffrey Best, *Churchill and War* (New York, 2006), 114–15.

499 *'on the war by ourselves'*: Ponting, *1940*, 102, quoting from the minutes of Dec. 7, 1939, in CAB 65/2.

499 *handle the wounded*: Robinson, *Invasion, 1940*, 21.

500 *'invade this country'*: Best, *Churchill and War*, 103, quoting from CAB 63/13.

500 *'from an avoidable disaster'*: Reynolds, *In Command of History*, 169. In his original draft of *Their Finest Hour*, Churchill was critical of Halifax's willingness to 'buy off' the Germans and felt that he had not been 'tough' enough. He was persuaded by Ismay to avoid unnecessarily embarrassing Halifax. Reynolds points out, 'Halifax was not treacherous, but he was naive.' (171.)

500 *'satisfactory starting point'*: Ibid., 169–70.

500 *take the country to war*: FDR to WSC, June 14, 1940, PREM 3/468.

500 *replaced by an appeasement administration*: WSC to FDR, May 20, 1940, in Kimball, *Churchill & Roosevelt*, vol. 1, 40.

500 *chance of a compromise peace*: Reynolds, *In Command of History*, 170.

501 *rebellion by the peace wing*: Jenkins, *Churchill*, 605; John Lukacs, *The Last European War* (New Haven, 1976), 96–97; and David Dilks, ed., *The Diaries of Sir Alexander Cadogan, 1938–1945* (London, 1971), May 27, 1940, 291.

501 *come to its aid*: John Grigg interview, Brendon Papers.

501 *call him a guttersnipe*: Lukacs, *The Last European War*, 97.

501 *'lose the war'*: WSC speech in House of Commons, June 18, 1940, Hansard.

502 *containing the German beachheads*: Reynolds, *From World War to Cold War*, 98.

502 *'conference like a fog'*: Maj. Gen. Sir Edward Spears, *Assignment to Catastrophe*, vol. 2, *The Fall of France, June 1940* (New York, 1955), 156. Spears was Churchill's personal emissary to the French government and was present at all of the prime minister's meetings in May and June 1940.

503 *'good anti-tank obstacle'*: *Their Finest Hour*, 155; *The Memoirs of Lord Ismay*, 140; and Spears, *Assignment to Catastrophe*, vol. 2, June 11, 1940, 158.

503 *'those last seven days'*: Quoted in Holmes, *In the Footsteps of Churchill*, 207–08. In a similar frame of mind, Churchill had written to Stanley Baldwin on June 4: 'We are going through vy hard times & I expect worse to come . . . Though whether we shall live to see them is more doubtful.' (Quoted in Reynolds, *In Command of History*, 172.)

503 *was hard to believe*: Nicolson diary, June 19, 1940.

503 *alone to carry on*: French losses during the Battle of France were enormous: ninety thousand dead and another two hundred thousand wounded. Some 1.5 million were sent to POW camps in Germany, where most were forced into slave labour.

503 *into a world war*: Reynolds, *From World War to Cold War*, 26.

503 *airpower of the RAF*: Ponting, *1940*, 101–02.

503 *'they did through the Poles'*: Ibid.

504 *'Thank God we're alone'*: Wright, *Dowding and the Battle of Britain*, 130.

504 *'he said that he did'*: Halifax, *Fullness of Days*, 228.

505 *defiance, reason and confidence*: Dalton diary, June 18, 1940.

505 *'strategy of "no surrender" '*: Charmley, *The End of Glory*, 419.

505 *triumph over adversity*: WSC speech in House of Commons and to the nation, June 18, 1940.

Chapter 39: 'What a Summer to Waste on War'

506 *'glare of a blazing sun'*: Robert Boothby, *I Fight to Live* (London, 1947), 221.

506 *Martin in his diary*: Martin, *Downing Street: The War Years*, 7.

506 *preparations for reprisal*: David Fraser, *And We Shall Shock Them: The British Army in the Second World War* (London, 1983), 83–85.

507 *'defence . . . absolutely nothing!'*: Alanbrooke, 'Notes on My Life', July 20, 1940.

507 *'dragged down to the beaches'*: Persico, *Edward R. Murrow*, 164.

507 *'morale was unbelievable'*: Interview of Lord Willis, WCHL 15/2/57.

508 *'good to live or die'*: *Their Finest Hour*, 279.

508 *'as well as a revolver'*: Halifax diary, June 1940. The queen told Harold Nicolson that she too was learning to shoot a revolver and was being given instruction each morning. 'I shall not go down like the others,' she declared. (Nicolson diary, July 10, 1940.)

508 *thrown at the invaders*: Robinson, *Invasion, 1940*, 108.

508 *'always take [an invader] with you'*: Robert Rhodes James, *Anthony Eden: A Biography* (New York and London, 198), 233.

508 *days after his order*: WSC memo to Ismay, June 18, 1940, CAB 69/1; and *Churchill*,

vol. 6, 568–69, 574. Bernard Paget, later a full general, succeeded as C in C, Home Forces, when Brooke became CIGS in December 1941.

509 *'of the closest range'*: *Their Finest Hour*, 167.

510 *'hank of steel wire'*: George Bernard Shaw quoted in Nigel Hamilton, *Monty: The Making of a General, 1887–1942* (London, 1981), 7. It would be hard to find two more dissimilar men than Montgomery and GBS, yet when the two met for the first time in 1944 they connected to an unusual, almost electric degree. (See Hamilton's *Monty: Master of the Battlefield, 1942–1944* [London, 1983], 546.)

510 *'a mobile counter-attack role'*: Hamilton, *The Full Monty*, 363.

510 *'find anything very much better'*: Arthur Bryant, *The Turn of the Tide, 1939–1943* (London, 1957), 239.

510 *Churchill's combative instincts*: Hamilton, *The Full Monty*, 364.

511 *'200 per cent fit'*: Ibid., 363.

511 *'Good morning'*: Article by Bernard Levin in *The Times*, March 31, 1976, reprinted in *British Army Review* (Autumn 2006).

511 *unafraid to be unpopular*: A point made to me by Col. Douglas MacGregor (USA), April 2001.

511 *'few more bounders'*: Quoted in Colin F. Baxter, *Field Marshal Bernard Law Montgomery, 1887–1976: A Selected Bibliography* (Westport, CT, 1999), 5.

511 *'anything but a "nice chap"'*: Related to Patton by Gen. Walter Bedell Smith, Patton diary, May 5, 1943, Patton Papers, LC.

512 *'nature of "total war"'*: Hamilton, *The Full Monty*, 559.

512 *'collected and reverently buried'*: Levin, *British Army Review*.

512 *'all to wear badges'*: Shelford Bidwell, 'Monty, Master of the Battlefield or Most Overrated General', *RUSI Journal* (June 1984).

512 *needed in its time of peril*: Hamilton, *The Full Monty*, 364.

512 *south coast and in Scotland*: Robinson, *Invasion, 1940*, 106.

513 *'noise of warfare'*: Colville diary, May 29, 1940.

513 *'achieve in four years'*: Reynolds, *From World War to Cold War*, 26.

Chapter 40: 'Set Europe Ablaze'

515 *'to be struck next'*: WSC to Ismay, June 4, 1940, CHAR 20/13.

515 *'German corpses behind them'*: Ibid., June 5, 1940.

515 *successful against the British*: Although the term has remained a byword for units that operate behind enemy lines, during the Second World War the British designated them Special Air Service and Special Boat Service units.

516 *raids in occupied territory*: Roskill, *Churchill and the Admirals*, 110–11.

517 *'arrange for your relief'*: WSC to Adm. Sir Roger Keyes, Oct. 10, 1941, ibid., 208.

517 *'springboard for our attack'*: Thames Television interview of Adm. Lord Louis Mountbatten, *The World at War, 1939–1945*, IWM.

518 *called them "Their Blockships"'*: Mountbatten interview, Feb. 1947, Pogue Interviews, MHI.

519 *'have a single dictator'* Dalton diary, July 1, 1940.

519 *'set Europe ablaze'*: Ibid., July 22, 1940.

519 *the enemy-occupied world*: Ibid., xxii; and Andrew, *Her Majesty's Secret Service*, 476.

519 *protocol of the military*: Jablonsky, *Churchill, the Great Game and Total War*, 147.

519 *sheer mythology*: M. R. D. Foot, 'SOE', *The Oxford Companion to World War II* (Oxford, 2005), 1019.

520 *countryside of Buckinghamshire*: The intelligence-collection effort was massive. The code breakers worked at a frantic pace to break the daily ciphers and keep the messages flowing. The handling, sorting and distributing became almost as much of a challenge as the actual code-breaking operations.

520 *was thus unobtainable: Churchill*, vol. 6, 610.
521 *for the head of MI6:* Colville, *The Churchillians*, 58. The boxes used to convey the decrypts were so old that on one occasion a bottom fell out when it was being handled by John Peck, spewing secret documents all over the floor.
521 *mere six ministers: Churchill*, vol. 6, 613.
521 *spy operating in Germany:* Ibid., 611–13.
521 *kept his silence:* Lord Camrose, the proprietor of the *Daily Telegraph* and the *Sunday Times*, somehow learned of 'the contents of those buff boxes which "C" sent to the PM'. (Colville diary and *The Fringes of Power*, 422 and n.)
521 *'at least five-fold':* Andrew, *Her Majesty's Secret Service*, 486. The notion that Churchill was interpreting raw intelligence horrified Bletchley Park, and to convince him that he would be better served by receiving intelligence estimates they deluged him with material. Eventually he accepted a reduced amount of raw material and daily estimates prepared by the intelligence tsars.
522 *'his own countrymen than Germans':* Anthony Cave Brown, *'C': the Secret Life of Sir Stewart Menzies* (New York and London, 1987), 292–93.
522 *'withholds intelligence from Ministers':* Andrew, *Her Majesty's Secret Service*, 448.
522 *'fighting for our very lives':* Ibid., 485; and F. H. Hinsley, *British Intelligence in the Second World War*, vol. 1 (London, 1979), 291.
522 *'into an intelligence community':* Andrew, *Her Majesty's Secret Service*, 486.
522 *contributions to the war effort:* Ibid., chap. 14.
522 *enthusiastically supported their needs:* Wladyslaw Kozaczuk and Jerzy Straszak, *Enigma: How the Poles Broke the Nazi Code* (New York, 2004), 65; and *Churchill*, vol. 4, 612.
523 *Winterbotham's controversial memoir:* F. W. Winterbotham, *The Ultra Secret* (London, 1975).
523 *used code words:* Jablonsky, *Churchill, the Great Game and Total War*, 148–9.
523 *'than she is now':* WSC minute, July 17, 1940, PREM 3/475.
523 *who appealed to Churchill:* Col. R. Stuart Macrae, *Winston Churchill's Toyshop* (Kineton, 1971), chap. 5.
524 *Norway blowing up bridges: Churchill*, vol. 6, 746.
524 *'did not enhance its popularity':* The Churchill War Papers, vol. 1, 257 n.2.
524 *'Winston Churchill's Toyshop':* Macrae, *Winston Churchill's Toyshop*, vii.
524 *rest of the war:* Ibid., 81–84.
525 *its charge was too powerful: Churchill*, vol. 6, 684 n.1.
525 *new 'toys' whenever possible:* Pawle, *The War and Colonel Warden*, 109.
525 *overcome fixed positions:* WSC memo of Nov. 9, 1916, quoted in John T. Turner, *'Nellie': The History of Churchill's Lincoln-Built Trenching Machine* (Lincoln, 1988), 16–17.
526 *drowned by artillery barrages:* Ibid., 21.
527 *produced by March 1941:* Ibid., 29–30.
527 *offered tremendous possibilities:* Churchill briefly describes the project in *The Gathering Storm*, appendix J, book 2.
527 *called simply 'Nellie':* Turner, *'Nellie'*, chap. 6.
528 *strange saga of Nellie:* Ibid., 73. Photographs of the field test for Churchill on Nov. 6, 1941 (and the earlier field tests in the summer of 1941), are in the IWM photograph collection.
528 *'responsible but impenitent':* Ibid., chap. 9; and *The Gathering Storm*, 715.
528 *'priority to this business':* WSC to Prof. Lindemann, June 29, 1940, CHAR 20/13.
528 *minuted to the War Cabinet:* WSC memo, Sept. 3, 1940, CHAR 66/11; *Churchill*, vol. 6, 770; and Jablonsky, *Churchill, the Great Game and Total War*, 180.
529 *'strip off the Air Staff':* R. V. Jones, *The Wizard War* (New York, 1978; published in London as *Most Secret War*), 102; *Churchill*, vol. 6, 582; and *Their Finest Hour*, 383–88. R. V. Jones was also instrumental in the development of 'Window', the use of packets of aluminium foil (chaff) dropped from aircraft that gave the impression of non-existent bombers on the German radar, which in turn led their AA guns to fire at thin air.

529 *'blackest moments of the war'*: Jones, *The Wizard War*, 107–8.
530 *never ending battle of the beams:* There is an excellent account of the Bruneval Raid on the Combined Operations website: combinedops.com/Bruneval.htm.
530 *remain largely unknown:* Thaddeus Holt, *The Deceivers: Allied Military Deception in the Second World War* (New York and London, 2004), 1.
530 *'bodyguard of truth'*: Ibid., 72 n.1.

Chapter 41: London Burning

531 *'will not give way'*: Nicolson diary, July 20, 1940.
532 *'every hour history'*: Channon diary, June 20, 1940, James, *'Chips'*, 259.
532 *'hold the country united'*: Ian Jacob quoted in Colville diary, July 11, 1940.
532 *'landing them on quays'*: WSC memo to Herbert Morrison, July 7, 1940, CHAR 20/13.
532 *envisaged that summer afternoon:* Colville diary, July 12, 1940. Churchill's attention to the smallest detail was evident in his concern that Eden's predecessor as secretary of state for war, Hore-Belisha, had abolished the army brass bands, which he deemed important for keeping up morale.
532 *'alternative is massacre'*: Colville diary, July 12, 1940.
533 *some three thousand planes:* Bungay, *The Most Dangerous Enemy*, 389.
533 *or the Cherbourg Peninsula:* Tim Clayton and Phil Craig, *Finest Hour* (London, 1999), 282.
533 *'achieve his object'*: Colville diary, June 25, 1940.
534 *'bringing them in'*: Churchill, vol. 6, 576–80.
534 *in favour of the Axis:* Annex to War Cabinet minutes of June 22, 1940, CAB 65/13.
534 *'fight and sink them'*: Ibid.
535 *'were in his grasp'*: *Their Finest Hour*, 230.
535 *for a tragic denouement:* Robinson, *Invasion, 1940*, 88.
536 *'carry it out relentlessly'*: Pound to Somerville, July 2, 1940, PREM 3/179.
536 *fateful decision, and wept:* Maxwell Philip Schoenfeld, *The War Ministry of Winston Churchill* (Ames, IA, 1972), 14.
536 *'pouring down his cheeks'*: Nicolson diary, July 4, 1940.
536 *'whole world against us'*: Robinson, *Invasion, 1940*, 91.
537 *'talk about Britain giving in'*: *Their Finest Hour*, 239.
537 *Churchill's defiant words into action:* Robert E. Sherwood, *The White House Papers of Harry L. Hopkins*, vol. 1 (London, 1948), 150.
537 *'country was less secure'*: Ibid., 150–51.
538 *'what then awaits them'*: Kershaw, *Hitler, 1936–1945: Nemesis*, 301.
538 *in Trafalgar Square:* Robinson, *Invasion, 1940*, 93.
538 *'tamely and abjectly enslaved'*: BBC speech, July 14, 1940.
538 *'Thank God for him'*: Nicolson diary, July 14, 1940.
539 *moved across the Channel:* Robinson, *Invasion, 1940*, 209–10. By the war's end the German army employed 2.7 million horses, or about twice the number used in the First World War.
539 *'speaking terms with him'*: Churchill, vol. 6, 672, and Colville diary, July 24, 1940.
539 *postponed until the 13th:* Moss, *Nineteen Weeks*, 260.
540 *'We live on their wings'*: Overheard by Colville and noted in his diary, July 16, 1940.
540 *'That's how he was'*: Elizabeth Nel (*née* Layton) interview, Brendon Papers.
540 *dying to protect Britain:* Anecdote related by William Sholto Douglas (Marshal of the Royal Air Force Lord Douglas of Kirtleside) in *Combat and Command: The Story of an Airman in Two World Wars* (New York, 1966; published in London as *Years of Combat* and *Years of Command*), 496–98. The story of the role and achievements of the gallant exile Polish airmen, soldiers and sailors has yet to be fully told.
541 *replied that there were none:* Although Park had no more reserves of his own, there were other units available to provide support. (Douglas, *Combat and Command*, 418.)

542 *congratulate everyone personally:* Holmes, *In the Footsteps of Churchill,* 219.

542 *'so many to so few':* The Memoirs of Lord Ismay, 179–80. Upon hearing Churchill's speech extolling 'the few', one airman is reputed to have remarked: 'That must refer to mess bills.' (Schama, *A History of Britain,* vol. 3, 522.)

542 *'he himself felt about it':* Pamela Harriman interviews, WCHL 15/2/3 and BREN 1/ 11, Brendon Papers.

542 *'loss of under forty':* Their Finest Hour, 337; and Martin, *Downing Street: The War Years,* 25–26.

543 *reminder of Britain's plight:* See Persico, *Edward R. Murrow,* chap. 13, for an excellent description of both Murrow and his broadcasts and what it was like in London during the Blitz. Murrow was so well respected by the British that in 1943, with Churchill's approval, Minister of Information Brendan Bracken invited him to become director general of the BBC. Murrow was intrigued but declined. (205–06.)

543 *tunnels of the Underground:* During the First World War there was only one civilian death for every seventy-five military deaths, compared with one civilian death for every three military deaths during the first fourteen months of the Second World War. (William K. Klingaman, *1941* [New York, 1989], 7.)

544 *House of Commons wrecked:* Philip Ziegler, *London at War, 1939–1945* (New York and London, 1995), 117–18, 161.

544 *'stepping stone to ultimate victory':* Recollection of Sept. 8, 1940 by Samuel Battersby, a government censor, in letter to Martin Gilbert, April 6, 1977, *The Churchill War Papers,* vol. 2, 788–89.

544 *'even I felt like cheering':* Ziegler, *London at War,* 164.

544 *'returned to me tomorrow':* Gen. Sir James Marshall-Cornwall quoted in *Churchill,* vol. 6, 683–85.

545 *'Red Sea next week':* Lamb, *Churchill as War Leader,* 57–58.

545 *were invariably taken seriously:* Churchill, vol. 6, 683–85 and 685 n.

545 *'his proposals to criticize':* Alanbrooke diary, Sept. 6, 1940.

545 *'for his help and guidance':* Ibid., Sept. 8, 1940; and 'Notes on My Life'.

545 *'mustard gas on the beaches':* Moss, *Nineteen Weeks,* 192; and Alanbrooke, 'Notes on My Life', July 22, 1940.

546 *'Royal Navy's "silent victory"':* Robinson, *Invasion, 1940,* 267–68.

546 *'left Lord Nelson out of it?':* Fisher, *A Summer Bright and Terrible,* 262.

546 *pressure from the Air Ministry:* Reynolds, *In Command of History,* 187. Equally ludicrous was Churchill's claim to Dowding in 1942 that he was unaware of his retirement until reading about it in the newspapers. Given his iron control over appointments and his involvement in every facet of the armed services, to have said this to Dowding was insulting and unworthy of the airman's service to Britain. (Fisher, *A Summer Bright and Terrible,* 261.)

546 *in his war memoirs:* David Fisher writes, 'If Churchill had had his way, the valiant Few who won the Battle of Britain would have been the futile Too Few who would have lost it.' Dowding later commented only that 'you couldn't expect the man to admit that he nearly lost us the Battle of Britain before it began.' (*A Summer Bright and Terrible,* 262.)

546 *'agony piled on agony':* Martin, *Downing Street: The War Years,* 6.

548 *'hell of a fight':* Sherwood, *The White House Papers of Harry L. Hopkins,* vol. 1, 151.

548 *'get the B[astard]'s for this':* Winterbotham, *The Ultra Secret,* 81–82; and Moss, *Nineteen Weeks,* 345–46.

Chapter 42: Wavell in the Hot Seat

550 *Far East, and at home:* Douglas Porch, *The Path to Victory: The Mediterranean Theater in World War II* (New York, 2004), Introduction.

550 *would have none of it:* Ibid., 83–84.

551 *renowned and distinguished soldier:* After the war Freyberg became governor general of New Zealand.

551 *'many times during the evening':* Paul Freyberg, *Bernard Freyberg, VC: Soldier of Two Nations* (London, 1991), diary, July 17, 1940, 225.

551 *provide far greater security:* W. G. F. Jackson, *The North African Campaign, 1940–43* (London, 1975), 23.

552 *phrase that rather pleased him:* Freyberg diary, Aug. 3,1940, Freyberg, *Bernard Freyberg, VC,* 228.

552 *'pilots have good polo ponies':* Ibid.

552 *'in a fire-hydrant factory':* Quoted in Porch, *The Path to Victory,* 105.

553 *'mud out of our minds':* Harold E. Raugh Jr, *Wavell in the Middle East, 1939–1941* (London, 1993), 13.

554 *defence of the Western Desert:* Ibid., chap. 4.

554 *highly effective fighting force:* Correlli Barnett, *The Desert Generals* (rev. ed. London, 1983), chap. 1.

555 *already undermanned army:* James, *Anthony Eden,* 233–34; Churchill, vol. 6, 477; WSC minute in CHAR 20/13; and Colville diary, June 6, 1940.

555 *to carry them out:* Raugh, *Wavell in the Middle East,* 65.

555 *'on an empty arena':* Barnett, *The Desert Generals,* 23; and Raugh, *Wavell in the Middle East,* 68.

556 *'irretrievably damaged':* Ronald Lewin, *The Chief: Field Marshal Lord Wavell, Commander-in-Chief and Viceroy, 1939–1947* (London, 1980), 36–37. The quotation is based on Shearer's unpublished memoir.

556 *'You must go to Chequers':* Ibid., 38. Two years later Brooke relayed a similar message, telling Wavell that should he take umbrage every time Churchill abused him, he would have to resign at least once a day. (See Victoria Schofield, *Wavell: Soldier and Statesman* [London, 2006], photograph caption opposite 320.)

556 *'get rid of Wavell':* Boothby, *Recollections of a Rebel,* 147.

556 *surprised when he did not:* Raugh, *Wavell in the Middle East,* 81. An indication of just how far apart the two men were after their disastrous meeting can be found in Ian Jacob's opinion that Churchill thought that Wavell was 'a rather dumb Scotsman'. (Ibid.)

557 *'at this critical time':* Churchill, vol. 6, 731–32.

557 *'chairman of a Tory Association':* Ibid., 732.

557 *Dill as 'Dilly-Dally':* D. R. Thorpe, *Eden* (London, 2003), 243.

557 *'leave him in command':* Their Finest Hour, 425.

557 *'encourage Churchill to do so':* Anthony Eden, *The Reckoning* (Boston and London, 1965), 153.

557 *explained to him in detail:* Kennedy, *The Business of War,* 61.

557 *New Zealand, Australia and India:* James, *Anthony Eden,* 238.

558 *he had been right:* One of the Royal Navy's major problems in the summer of 1940 was the shortage of destroyers for convoy escort duty. Too few had been built in 1938, for financial reasons, and valuable vessels were lost in early sea battles and at Dunkirk. Until the arrival of the fifty obsolete American destroyers 'lent' to Britain by FDR there were simply not enough to go round. All required maintenance and retrofitting and only nine were available for service by the time British naval construction was beginning to fulfil its requirements.

558 *'an unconventional theorist of war':* Time, Oct. 14, 1940. In March 1941 the US army's prestigious *Military Review* called Wavell Britain's 'Soldier of the Hour', praising him for breathing 'new life, inspiration and confidence into the British Empire throughout the world'. (Quoted in Raugh, *Wavell in the Middle East,* 1.)

559 *'worst of both worlds':* Memo, WSC to Eden, Aug. 25, 1940, CHAR 20/13; and *The Memoirs of Lord Ismay,* 194.

559 *'none the less strategically convenient':* Memo to Eden and Dill, Aug. 15, 1940.

559 *'ever seen in him before':* Lewin, *The Chief,* 25.

559 *'telegram was . . . unforgivable'*: Thompson, *Churchill and Morton*, letter of Aug. 21, 1961, 174–75.

559 *'the point of no return'*: Lewin, *The Chief*, 25.

560 *managed to find fault*: Ibid., chap. 2.

561 *'impose our will on him'*: *The Memoirs of Lord Ismay*, 195.

561 *'but only about inaction'*: PM personal minute, Dec. 7, 1940, PREM 3/288.

562 *'regardless of the vast distances'*: Kennedy, *The Business of War*, 62. Churchill did admit that Wavell's problems were much like those Britain faced over the allocation of precious assets to its allies: 'There were too many little pigs and not enough teats on the old sow.'

562 *force he employed*: Ibid., 61.

562 *'I can never forgive'*: Ibid., 63.

562 *obsess Churchill during the war*: Ibid.

564 *'aglow over the City'*: Ziegler, *London at War*, 144; and Kennedy, *The Business of War*, 70.

565 *'dread in my heart'*: Eden diary, Dec. 19, 1940, *The Reckoning*, 211.

565 *'we must concentrate on that'*: Kennedy, *The Business of War*, 65.

565 *'in a reasonable period'*: WSC to FDR, Dec. 16, 1941, in Kimball, *Churchill & Roosevelt*, vol. 1, 294–308. Churchill's telegram is a fifteen-page blueprint for how he envisaged the war would be fought.

565 *United States became a participant*: Professor Eliot Cohen points out, 'Churchill's profound sense of the uncertainties inherent in war suggests that he would have found the notion that one could produce a blueprint for victory at any time before, say, 1943 an absurdity bred of unfamiliarity with war itself.' (*Supreme Command: Soldiers, Statesmen, and Leadership in Wartime* [New York, 2002], 109.)

565 *look much better in a year*: WSC to Lord Beaverbrook, Dec. 15, 1940, CHAR 20/4.

566 *'during the course of 1941'*: WSC speech, Dec. 19, 1940, Hansard.

Chapter 43: The President and the 'Former Naval Person'

567 *'acted like a stinker'*: FDR quoted in Jon Meacham, *Franklin and Winston* (New York, 2003), 5. When the two men again in August 1941 in Newfoundland, Roosevelt was piqued that Churchill had forgotten their 1918 encounter.

567 *'I hate war'*: Ibid., 7.

567 *'if we were together'*: Ibid., 37, based on the reminiscence of Kay Halle, 'a young American heiress with whom Randolph Churchill had fallen in love and once rashly tried to marry'.

568 *'to be very bruising'*: Michael Beschloss interview, Brendon Papers.

568 *their problem to resolve*: Reynolds, *From World War to Cold War*, 170.

568 *' "want me to know about" '*: Ibid., quoting FDR to WSC, Sept. 11, 1939, in Kimball, *Churchill & Roosevelt*, vol. 1, 24.

568 *best man in Britain*: Reynolds, *From World War to Cold War*, 172.

569 *how it would be done*: Colville diary, Oct. 13, 1940.

569 *'the Middle East, American aid'*: Kennedy, *The Business of War*, 79.

570 *should be remorselessly crushed*: *The Memoirs of Lord Ismay*, 213–14.

570 *moved into the White House*: From 1935 to 1938 Hopkins headed the Works Progress Administration, the agency whose mission was to find work for 3.5 million unemployed American workers. Roosevelt appointed him secretary of commerce in 1938, a post he held for only one year, owing to overwork and poor health.

570 *'he has human power'*: WSC, *The Grand Alliance* (Boston, 1950), 23.

570 *'sees after midnight'*: Sherwood, *The White House Papers of Harry Hopkins*, vol. 1, 237.

570 *'greatest man in the world!'*: Ibid., 233. Monnet had been in London since 1939 to help co-ordinate the war production of France and Britain. With de Gaulle's blessing, Churchill sent him to Washington in August 1940 to assist in the acquisition of war supplies. Monnet

soon became an adviser to FDR and one of the most convincing voices for American rearmament of Britain. After the war he was the architect of European unity.

570 *'what a force that man has'*: Joseph P. Lash, *Roosevelt and Churchill, 1939–1941: The Partnership That Saved the West* (New York, 1976), 277.

570 *'What a man!'*: Ibid., 282.

571 *'to intercept the ships'*: Folder 12, Box 56, Harry Hopkins Papers, Georgetown University Special Collections.

571 *exhausted aides in his wake*: Sherwood, *The White House Papers of Harry Hopkins*, vol. 1, 242.

571 *'no convulsion ever undermined'*: *The Memoirs of Lord Chandos*, 166–67.

571 *'bloody British Empire'*: Colville diary, Jan. 24, 1941. When told by Colville what Hopkins had overheard, Churchill replied: ' "Very nice." I don't think anything has given him such pleasure for a long time.'

571 *'for Britain's former foreign secretary'*: Jenkins, *Churchill*, 649.

572 *'it just doesn't make sense'*: Harry Hopkins to FDR, circa Jan. 14, 1941, Box 56/Folder 12, Hopkins Papers.

572 *'But like a man he died'*: WSC to HH, Feb. 13, 1944, Folder 15, Box 1, Hopkins Papers.

573 *'he was working for FDR'*: Quoted in Meacham, *Franklin and Winston*, 98.

573 *'As ever yours Franklin D. Roosevelt'*: Ibid., 95. The verse is from Longfellow's 1849 poem 'The Building of the Ship.'

573 *'we will finish the job:* Ibid.

574 *whatever means necessary:* A. J. P. Taylor, 'The Statesman', in *Churchill Revised*, 52.

574 *from U-boats and mines:* Losses are based on data furnished to the US Office of War Information by the British government. In addition, the British also cited the loss of 747 neutral ships during the same period. Losses are from both enemy action and marine risk. (OWI document 3789.) Britain was solely dependent on resupply by sea, hence German naval strategy was to force its surrender by sinking Allied shipping in amounts equal to its monthly needs for survival.

575 *'Damn the risk'*: Hickman, *Churchill's Bodyguard*, 130.

575 *whispered words to others:* Thompson, *Assignment Churchill*, 224.

576 *bevy of escort ships:* Description in H. V. Morton, *Atlantic Meeting* (New York and London, 1943), 86; and Meacham, *Franklin and Winston*, 107.

576 *looked forward to their meeting:* Lash, *Roosevelt and Churchill*, 392.

576 *as 'Franklin' and 'Winston'*: Meacham, *Franklin and Winston*, 107–9.

577 *Roosevelt echoed his sentiments:* W. Averell Harriman memo of WSC and FDR meeting, Aug. 9, 1941, Box 160, Harriman Papers, LC.

577 *beaming triumphantly:* Pawle, *The War and Colonel Warden*, 128.

577 *'action against the* Bismarck': Martin diary, Aug. 10, 1941, *Downing Street: The War Years*, 58.

577 *'bringing the two nations together'*: Harriman memo, Aug. 9, 1941.

577 *'from measureless degradation'*: Broadcast to the nation, Aug. 24, 1941, James, *Churchill Speaks*, 768–69.

577 *'were soon to die'*: *The Grand Alliance*, 432.

578 *'would have cemented us'*: FDR quoted in Doris Kearns Goodwin, *No Ordinary Time* (New York, 1994), 267.

578 *formally signed treaty:* Had the Atlantic Charter been a formal treaty, Roosevelt would have had to submit it to the Senate to be ratified. As Robert Sherwood remarks, even though it was simply mimeographed and released, 'its effect was cosmic and historic.' (Sherwood, *The White House Papers of Harry Hopkins*, vol. 1, 363–64.)

578 *'in the war on our side'*: Jacob diary, Aug. 11, 1941, Jacob Papers; and *Churchill*, vol. 6, 1161.

578 *'could not have achieved'*: Sherwood, *The White House Papers of Harry Hopkins*, vol. 1, 364.

578 *'same decade with you'*: Ibid., 365.
578 *'what America is doing for her'*: Brendan Bracken quoted in Meacham, *Franklin and Winston*, 75.
579 *'responsibility in safeguarding him'*: Thompson, *Assignment Churchill*, 238–39.
579 *'boy's book of adventure'*: Both quotes in Goodwin, *No Ordinary Time*, 310.
580 *'too wonderful in fact'*: Ibid., 311.
580 *'Trust me to the bitter end'*: Quoted in Martin Gilbert, *Winston S. Churchill*, vol. 7, *Road to Victory*, (London, 1986), 43.

Chapter 44: Mediterranean Misadventures

581 *'by so many to so few'*: Charles Messenger, *The Chronological Atlas of World War II* (New York, 1989), 54.
582 *'Whose fault is that?'*: Eden diary, Dec. 12, 1940, *The Reckoning*, 209.
582 *'off the African shore'*: WSC to Wavell, Dec. 13 and 16, 1940, PREM 3/309 and CHAR 20/14.
582 *'Let us gather the harvest'*: WSC to Field Marshal Smuts, Dec. 13, 1940, PREM 4/43B.
582 *support to the Greeks*: WSC to Wavell, Feb. 12, 1941, CAB 69/2.
584 *'Whom do you want to shoot exactly?'*: Kennedy, *The Business of War*, 75.
584 *'how valuable success would be'*: WSC to Eden, Feb. 20, 1941, CHAR 20/49.
585 *'this spring in the Aegean'*: Dill quoted in Klingaman, *1941*, 116.
585 *same period of 1941*: Ibid., 168.
586 *most of them off open beaches*: Viscount Cunningham of Hyndhope, *A Sailor's Odyssey* (London, 1951), 357. Only fourteen thousand were embarked from wharves and jetties; the rest had to be ferried by small boats of all types pressed into service. British warships carried enormous numbers of troops; in some cases more than eight hundred were crammed aboard destroyers.
587 *'Enemy's difficulties must be immense'*: WSC to Wavell, May 1, 1941, CHAR 20/49.
587 *'Back Every Fortnight'*: 'Too Many of Them', *Time*, May 5, 1941.
587 *mistake his government had made*: Foot, *The Oxford Companion to World War II*, 104, 106.
588 *'in America as well'*: Schoenfeld, *The War Ministry of Winston Churchill*, 106, and Sherwood, *The White House Papers of Harry Hopkins*, vol. 1, 240.
588 *involved in the Mediterranean*: Charles Cruickshank, *Greece, 1940–1941* (Newark, DE, 1976), 14.
588 *'gone on into Tripoli'*: Dilks, *The Diaries of Sir Alexander Cadogan*, March 1, 3, 1941, 360.
588 *'get there from Greece'*: Lewin, *The Chief*, 116.
588 *Axis forces in the desert*: Jackson, *The North African Campaign, 1940–43*, 111.
589 *'how to inspire his troops'*: Lewin, *The Chief*, 123.
589 *untrained in desert warfare*: David Fraser, *Knight's Cross: A Life of Field Marshal Erwin Rommel* (London, 1993), 221.
589 *if the Germans attacked*: Ibid., 219–21, 231.
590 *'before the end of the summer'*: *The Memoirs of Lord Ismay*, 201.
590 *'taste of our quality'*: WSC to Wavell, Mar. 26, 1941, CHAR 20/49.
590 *'nothing left in the bag'*: Raugh, *Wavell in the Middle East*, 186.
592 *'Well, he should revise them quickly!'*: 'Robert Menzies' 1941 Diary' (April 8), www.oph.gov.au/menzies/. The Menzies website also states: 'The original diary is held by the National Library of Australia and was published in full by the Library under the title *Dark and Hurrying Days* in 1993, edited by Allan Martin and Patsy Hardy.'
592 *'as an "excrescence"'*: WSC to Wavell, April 14, 1941, quoted in *The Grand Alliance*, 211.
592 *'ruin all Hitler's calculations'*: Colville diary, May 3, 1941.

592 *'preside at my court-martial'*: Eden, *The Reckoning*, 279.

592 *'soldier gone stark mad'*: Jackson, *The North African Campaign, 1940–43*, 110, 114.

592 *'a great General'*: Phillip Knightley, *The First Casualty* (London, 1982 ed.), 290; and *The Memoirs of Lord Ismay*, 272. The title of Knightley's landmark book is taken from a 1917 remark by Senator Hiram Johnson of California, 'The first casualty when war comes is truth,' a statement as apt today as it was nearly a century ago.

593 *'unfashionable though it was judged'*: *The Grand Alliance*, 200.

593 *'now is the time'*: Letter, Burgis to Hollis, May 3, 1955, BRGS 1/2, Burgis Papers.

593 *far-reaching consequences*: With great concern, Churchill remarked to Colville, 'The poor Tiger has already lost one claw and another is damaged.' (Colville diary, May 9, 1941.) Data on Operation Tiger is from Correlli Barnett, *Engage the Enemy More Closely: The Royal Navy in the Second World War* (New York and London, 1991), 367–68.

593 *Western Desert or Crete*: Jablonsky, *Churchill, the Great Game and Total War*, 164.

593 *drove the British from Cyrenaica*: Although Rommel's critics in Berlin were disapproving of his success in the first German action in North Africa, their reaction was reminiscent of an event in 1945 when Patton was chastised for capturing the German city of Trier against orders. When reminded of this, Patton signalled his superiors, inquiring if they wanted him to give it back.

Chapter 45: Disaster in Crete

594 *he replied yes*: Colville diary, May 2, 1941.

595 *would ultimately triumph*: WSC speech, May 3, 1941, Klingaman, *1941*, 214.

595 *'blunders of this war'*: Hitler quoted in ibid.

595 *'We shall come through'*: WSC speech in the House of Commons, May 7, 1941, Hansard.

596 *'struggle to breathe'*: *The Grand Alliance*, 114.

596 *would have to be faced*: Colville diary, April 23, 1941.

596 *at Nuremberg for war crimes*: Kershaw, *Hitler, 1936–1945: Nemesis*, 369–70. Hitler disavowed Hess and declared him insane. After the war Hess was incarcerated in Berlin's Spandau prison until his death in 1987 at the age of ninety-three.

597 *incendiaries on London*: Gavin Mortimer, *The Longest Night* (New York and London, 2005), 333.

597 *otherwise beautiful spring day*: Colville diary, May 11, 1941.

597 *Bath, Canterbury and York*: On 28–29 March 1942 the RAF heavily bombed Lübeck, the historic centre of the medieval Hanseatic League, on the dubious grounds that it was being used to supply the eastern front. In reprisal, between April and June 1942 the Germans launched a series of deadly raids, vowing to bomb every city starred in Germany's *Baedeker Guide to Britain*.

597 *'single day's debate through this!'*: Guy Eden, *Portrait of Churchill* (London, 1945), 64.

598 *'key to victory'*: Reynolds, *In Command of History*, 244.

598 *'misinterpreted the score'*: Ronald Lewin, *Ultra Goes to War* (London, 1978), 158.

599 *'campaign in the Mediterranean'*: Hansard, May 22, 1941.

599 *'all over the island'*: Brig. Gen. Raymond E. Lee quoted in Klingaman, *1941*, 265.

599 *'our position is hopeless'*: Ibid., 266.

599 *'not being able to hold it'*: Kennedy, *The Business of War*, 124.

599 *'without professional advice'*: Ibid., 114–15.

600 *'shoot the generals'*: Ibid., 105–06.

600 *'more heated Winston got'*: Alanbrooke, 'Notes on My Life', April 27, 1941.

600 *'along the coasts of Europe'*: Kennedy, *The Business of War*, 107.

600 *'generalship we need in Egypt'*: Ibid.

600 *not fit for his job*: Raugh, *Wavell in the Middle East*, 154, and Kennedy, *The Business of War*, 115. Menzies was ousted from office in August 1941, but after the war regained

office to become the longest-serving prime minister in Australian history (Dec. 1949–Jan. 1966).

601 *'no defeat in his heart'*: Menzies diary, Mar. 2, 1941.

601 *'out of General Rommel's army'*: WSC to Wavell, May 28, 1941, Dill Papers, LHC.

602 *'must reach Crete by sea'*: Cunningham, *A Sailor's Odyssey*, 373.

602 *'too precious ever to risk'*: Colville diary, May 22, 1941.

602 *'in order to save Crete'*: Ibid., May 25, 1941.

603 *no more complaining would be tolerated*: Oliver Warner, *Cunningham of Hyndhope* (London, 1967), 154–55. Respect for Cunningham was so high that one of his fleet admirals, Sir Bernard Rawlings, had engraved on his tombstone the words 'One of Cunningham's Captains'. (158.)

603 *into the nearest wastebasket*: Roskill, *Churchill and the Admirals*, 184.

603 *cost of thousands of lives*: A complete list of all vessels and where and how each was lost can be found at www.naval-history.net/WW2BritishLossesbyDate.

603 *'My God, it's hell'*: Klingaman, *1941*, 266.

604 *'convoy has got through'*: WSC 'Action This Day' minute to Pound and A. V. Alexander, April 14, 1941, CHAR 20/36.

604 *were somehow a given*: Roskill, *Churchill and the Admirals*, 182.

604 *'on the active list'*: Ibid., 183.

604 *control of the eastern Mediterranean*: Cunningham, *A Sailor's Odyssey*, 375–76.

604 *'driven into Wavell's coffin'*: Colville diary, May 25, 1941.

605 *'worst yet'*: Wheeler-Bennett, *Action This Day*, 'John Colville', 62.

605 *no one else dared to speak*: Eden, *The Reckoning*, diary, May 26, 1941, 285. See also Dilks, *The Diaries of Sir Alexander Cadogan*, May 26, 1941, 381.

605 *'went around in a daze'*: *The Grand Alliance*, 308; and Thompson, *Assignment Churchill*, 220.

605 *sat at his bedside*: Hickman, *Churchill's Bodyguard*, 140.

605 *'showed how he suffered'*: Kathleen Harriman Mortimer interview, Brendon Papers.

606 *no "Dead March", I tell you'*: Vic Oliver, *Mr Showbusiness* (London, 1954), 143–44. A slightly expanded version of this episode is also in *Churchill*, vol. 6, 1094.

606 *loss of 2,107 lives*: There were only 115 survivors of the *Bismarck*.

606 *'Bismarck has been sunk'*: Nicolson diary, May 27, 1941.

606 *out of action for five months*: Brodhurst, *Churchill's Anchor*, 190.

607 *'of the situation the better'*: A. B. C. Whipple, *The Mediterranean* (Time-Life World War II series, 1981), 100.

607 *'as First Sea Lord'*: Pawle, *The War and Colonel Warden*, 105 and n. 1 quoting letter from Cunningham to Cmdr Thompson.

607 *'lack of air forces'*: Cunningham to Pound, May 30, 1941, Ms. Add. 52561, Cunningham Papers, BL.

607 *'our men had endured'*: Cunningham, *A Sailor's Odyssey*, 390.

607 *naval base in Suda Bay*: Roskill, *Churchill and the Admirals*, 181.

607 *'saved Crete for us'*: Cunningham to Pound, May 30, 1941, quoted in Barnett, *Engage the Enemy More Closely*, 364. Although it is generally agreed that Crete could not have been held, what is remarkable is that Freyberg and his outmatched force fought as well as they did. Through Ultra intercepts, Freyberg was warned of an impending attack, but the code breakers drew conclusions that led him to believe his greatest threat came from a seaborne invasion rather than from the air. Moreover, Freyberg had no experience of using Ultra and was forbidden to reveal it to his intelligence staff or to obtain advice. His decision to concentrate on a seaborne invasion was based on the historical precedent that 'in the whole course of history no island had ever been captured except from the sea . . . This was something Freyberg could not lightly disregard.' (Ralph Bennett, *Ultra and Mediterranean Strategy* [New York and London, 1989], 57–58, and chap. 2, passim.)

607 *'effective range of enemy bombers'*: *The Memoirs of Lord Chandos*, 220.

Chapter 46: The Endless Desert War

608 *looked upon with disfavour:* Denis Richards, *The Royal Air Force, 1939–1945*, vol. 1, *The Fight at Odds* (London, 1974), 335.

610 *criticism upon the prime minister himself:* Dill to WSC, June 21, 1941, Box 7, Dill Papers, LHC.

610 *'last gaiter before attacking':* The Memoirs of Lord Ismay, 209.

611 *'failure of "Battleaxe"':* Barrie Pitt, *The Crucible of War: Auchinleck's Command* (London, 1986), xiv.

611 *'Rommel's "pathological ambition"':* Porch, *The Path to Victory*, 234.

611 *'And he went on shaving':* Barrie Pitt, *The Crucible of War: The Western Desert 1941* (London, 1980), 310.

611 *'that is the mortal stroke':* The Duke of Marlborough quoted in *The Memoirs of Lord Ismay*, 272.

611 *'bold and hazardous courses':* Kennedy, *The Business of War*, 134. Churchill glossed over Wavell's removal in a telegram to Roosevelt on 4 July. 'Wavell has a glorious record . . . He has also borne up well against German attacks and has conducted war and policy in three or four directions simultaneously . . . I must regard him as our most distinguished general. Nevertheless . . . we felt that, after the long strain he had borne, he was tired, and a fresh eye and unstained hand were needed in this most seriously menaced theatre.' (WSC-FDR, July 4, 1941, PREM 3/305.)

612 *'too kind to him':* Dalton diary, Aug. 3, 1944. Lord Moran also pinpointed this tendency, noting in his diary on Jan. 18, 1943, 'Winston, like the President, is apt to form an impression of a man by his surface markings. I am sure he has no idea that Wavell could out quote him in the English poets – one would have expected it to be a bond between them; the PM only sees a very silent, very dour Scot, with an eye missing, and a generally gloomy demeanour, that has a depressing effect on him, and for that matter on the President too; he believes Wavell is "finished".' (Box 60, Moran Papers.)

612 *is equally unsparing:* The Grand Alliance, 349–45.

612 *incursion into North Africa:* Barnett, *The Desert Generals*, 63.

612 *'for our ally Greece':* WSC to Wavell, Feb. 12, 1941, CAB 69/2.

612 *'chances which have been missed':* B. H. Liddell Hart, ed., *The Rommel Papers* (New York, 1955), 94–96.

613 *'desert flank was secure':* WSC memo, Nov. 30, 1948 quoted in Reynolds, *In Command of History*, 233.

613 *'campaigns imposed upon him':* WSC quoted in Barnett, *The Desert Generals*, 77.

613 *'was given impossible tasks':* Auchinleck quoted ibid., 77.

613 *'full at that time':* Alanbrooke, 'Notes on My Life', Nov. 11, 1941.

614 *'all the resources he needed':* Warner, *Cunningham*, 160.

614 *by means of frequent telegrams:* Dill to Auchinleck, June 26, 1941, quoted in full in Kennedy, *The Business of War*, 134–36.

615 *'You've got to woo him':* Jablonsky, *Churchill, the Great Game and Total War*, 124; and *The Memoirs of Lord Ismay*, 269–70.

615 *were doomed to fail:* David Fraser, *And We Shall Shock Them* (London, 1983), 160–61; and Hamilton, *The Full Monty*, 376.

615 *'with labour and production':* Colville diary, June 19, 1941.

617 *'count on me':* WSC to Auchinleck, Oct. 24, 1941, CHAR 20/44.

617 *put to excellent use:* Air Chief Marshal Foxley Norris, 'Tedder', in Field Marshal Lord Carver, ed., *The War Lords* (London, 1976), 488–89.

618 *he would appoint Freeman:* WSC to Auchinleck, Oct. 16, 1941, CHAR 20/20.

618 *'would have been a dreadful mistake':* Denis Richards, *Portal of Hungerford* (London, 1977), 236.

618 *out of favour with Churchill:* Terraine, *The Right of the Line*, 354–56; and Richards, *Portal of Hungerford*, 235–37. The brouhaha began with Tedder's figures relating to air strengths; when the airman submitted revised figures, Churchill noted that they were not much different from the originals, thus bringing to an end an absurd episode of wasted time and unnecessary finger-pointing.

618 *'made to play its part'*: WSC to Auchinleck, Oct. 16, 1941, CHAR 20/20.

619 *'destroy him and his armour'*: Barnett, *The Desert Generals*, 90.

619 *'smash them in detail?'*: Rommel quoted in Jackson, *The North African Campaign*, 183.

620 *'both sides deserved to lose'*: Terraine, *The Right of the Line*, 356.

621 *less than half that (17,700)*: Jackson, *The North African Campaign*, 181.

622 *'no match for panzer divisions'*: Sir John Slessor, *The Central Blue: Memories and Reflections* (London, 1956), 393.

622 *'history of our race'*: Harrow speech, Oct. 29, 1941, Harrow archives.

622 *'see a prospect of winning'*: W. Averell Harriman, with Elie Abel, *Special Envoy to Churchill* (New York, 1975), 112; and John Martin diary, Dec. 7, 1941, CAC.

622 *'So we had won after all!'*: *Their Finest Hour*, 606.

622 *'saved and thankful'*: Lady Soames interview, Brendon Papers.

Chapter 47: 'Colonel Shrapnel'

624 *'the dead hand of inanition'*: Danchev and Todman, *War Diaries*, xv.

624 *'his moral courage'*: Kennedy, *The Business of War*, 78–79.

624 *only a matter of time*: It is now known that Dill's fatigue derived in part from ill health as much as from the strain of bearing the weight of Churchill's frequent wrath against the chiefs for opposing him.

624 *for eighteen arduous months*: Kennedy, *The Business of War*, 179.

624 *had a disappointing marriage*: Alex Danchev, 'The Strange Case of Field Marshal Sir John Dill', *Medical History* (July 1991).

625 *he was no doormat*: In 1999 Dill's family donated an important cache of his papers to the Liddell Hart Centre for Military Archives. These papers, once thought nonexistent, contain his correspondence to and from Churchill in 1940 and 1941 while he was CIGS. An inventory of this collection is available on the internet at www.kcl.ac.uk/lhcma/info.index.shtml.

625 *'Sir Alan Brooke, C-in-C, Home Forces'*: Colville diary, Sept. 28, 1941.

625 *as a great strategist*: Kennedy, *The Business of War*, 74.

625 *Combined Chiefs of Staff*: Before sacking Dill, Churchill considered making him the governor of Bombay. (Alanbrooke diary, Nov. 16, 1941.)

625 *Arlington's only two equestrian statues*: It is now known that Dill died from aplastic anaemia that did not respond to treatment. See Danchev, 'The Strange Case of Field Marshal Sir John Dill'. Photographs of Dill's grave can be viewed on the internet at www.arlingtoncemetery.net/jgdill.htm. The only other equestrian statue in Arlington is that of Civil War general Philip Kearney. Equally unprecedented was a joint resolution of Congress to commemorate Dill's service to the United States, as was the posthumous award of the (American) Distinguished Service Medal in 1945.

626 *'task I had undertaken'*: Alanbrooke diary and 'Notes on My Life', Nov. 16, 1941.

627 *'company of the great captains'*: 'Statesman and Soldier', *The Economist*, Feb. 23, 1957; also quoted in Danchev and Todman, *War Diaries*, xv.

627 *chosen to replace him*: Ibid.

627 *'best of them all'*: *The Memoirs of Lord Ismay*, 318.

628 *'long for peace'*: Alanbrooke diary, Oct. 19, 1940.

628 *'temporarily set his heart on'*: Ibid., Aug. 30, 1943.

628 *'as a doctor fifty years ago!'*: Box 63, Moran Papers.

629 *'he saw only victory'*: Ibid.

629 *'as they heard of them'*: Sir Desmond Morton to R. W. Thompson, July 9, 1960, Box 1, R. W. Thompson Papers, LHC.

629 *'were of permanent application'*: Ibid.

629 *his already considerable vigilance:* Holmes, *In the Footsteps of Churchill*, 233.
630 *'to be quite safe inside':* Kennedy, *The Business of War*, 157, July 29, 1941. Kennedy recorded that the staff of the War Office were greatly cheered when the prime minister aimed his criticism at the navy, 'who, we thought, usually got off more lightly than we on our side of Whitehall'.
630 *'from that time onwards':* Letter, Ismay to Eden, Jan. 7, 1964, Ismay Papers, LHC.
630 *'we shall go with him':* Alanbrooke diary, Dec. 4, 1941.
631 *'rolling it up again from Norway':* Alanbrooke, 'Notes on My Life', Oct. 4, 1941.
631 *lay ahead of him as CIGS:* Fraser, *Alanbrooke*, 194–95; Alanbrooke diary and 'Notes on My Life', Oct. 12, 1941.
631 *'main stream into irrelevant backwaters':* Kennedy, *The Business of War*, 108.
632 *tell Churchill what Brooke had said:* Fraser interview, BREN 1/12.
632 *'he gently murmured: "Dear Brooke!" ':* Fraser, *Alanbrooke*, 295.
632 *'heavy guns turned against him':* Cunningham, *A Sailor's Odyssey*, 585.
633 *'come through all right':* Brooke to Wavell, Sept. 11, 1942, File 6/5, Alan Brooke Papers.
633 *'calls throughout the day':* Brooke, 'Notes on My Life', Sept. 19, 1942.
633 *'for anything on earth!':* Alanbrooke diary, Aug. 30, 1943.
633 *'It always will':* Ismay recording for the National Broadcasting Co., Nov. 1954, Box 2, Ismay Papers.
634 *'in the same human being':* Alanbrooke diary, Sept. 10, 1944.
634 *other major war figures:* Brooke's biographer makes an important point about the diaries. 'They were written for the eyes of his wife alone – "my nightly talk with you on paper." . . . A diary is evidence of the state of mind of the writer on a particular evening. It is imperfect evidence of the facts it records and can imperfectly reflect the writer's true self . . . Diaries do not argue – they assert, with brevity and exaggeration the emotion and prejudice of the minute.' (Fraser, *Alanbrooke*, 196.)
634 *barely mentions Brooke:* Danchev and Todman, *War Diaries*, xix.
634 *' "Never." Then after a long pause, he repeated, "Never!" ':* Moran, *Churchill*, 713.
634 *under which the other laboured:* Fraser, *Alanbrooke*, 295–96.
635 *'the Anglo-American Marriage Ceremony':* Jenkins, *Churchill*, chap. 35.

Chapter 48: Chickens Roosting in the Far East

636 *'Keep Buggering On':* Churchill, vol. 1, 1273.
636 *'Repulse and Prince of Wales have been sunk':* Box 58, Moran Papers.
637 *'It was a shocking start':* The Memoirs of Lord Ismay, 242.
637 *'we everywhere weak and naked': The Grand Alliance*, 620.
639 *'would never agree about India':* Commentary, Box 62, Moran Papers.
639 *something he wanted to discuss:* Meacham, *Franklin and Winston*, 141.
640 *cross-Channel invasion in 1942:* 'George C. Marshall Interviews and Reminiscences for Forrest C. Pogue', GCML.
641 *full-scale invasion in 1943:* Ibid.
642 *'securely in the harem':* Jenkins, *Churchill*, 676.
642 *before returning to England:* Diary, Dec. 27, 1941, Box 59, Moran Papers; *Churchill*, 16–17; and Richard Lovell, *Churchill's Doctor: A Biography of Lord Moran* (Melbourne, 1993), 163–65. Lovell, a surgeon and professor of medicine, supports Moran's decision to let Churchill continue without further treatment in Washington and to send him to a heart specialist when they returned to London.
643 *close to the French coast:* Churchill, vol. 7, 42; *The Grand Alliance*, 710–11; and Brian Lavery, *Churchill Goes to War: Winston's Wartime Journal*, Annapolis, MD, 2007.
644 *'burgle Malaya by the back door':* Schofield, *Wavell*, 225.
644 *probably never reached Churchill:* Lamb, *Churchill as War Leader*, 188–89. The minister, C. A. Vlieland, was a civil servant who had served in Malaya since 1915. When his prescient report was ignored, he resigned his post.

645 'troops retreating upon it': WSC, The Hinge of Fate (Boston, 1950), 49.
645 field fortifications and searchlights: Kennedy, The Business of War, 196.
646 'ruins of Singapore City': WSC to Wavell, Jan. 20, 1942, CHAR 20/68B.
646 control of all of south-east Asia: Churchill, vol. 7, 48.
646 'to pay in the Far East': Ibid., 51.
646 'Americans both adore him': Channon diary, Jan. 29, 1942; James, 'Chips', 319.
647 'I ought to have asked': Reynolds, In Command of History, 296.
647 could arrive in the Far East: J. R. M. Butler, Grand Strategy, vol. 3, part 2 (London, 1964), 403.
647 'whole British people for war': Ibid., 420.
648 'end of the war': Lamb, Churchill as War Leader, 187. Layton's highly damaging report became another of the tens of thousands of documents that were eventually consigned to Britain's National Archives, where they were embargoed for fifty years. The embargo was later relaxed to thirty years, at which time historians began to mine the Second World War files. Moreover, as Lamb points out, 'No official enquiry has ever been conducted into the débâcle of the Malaya campaign.' Although earlier information would still have been too late to have made a difference, it was not helpful that his friend Duff Cooper, Churchill's resident minister for Singapore, failed to alert him to the island's grave deficiencies, which, as a former first lord of the Admiralty, Cooper ought to have seen and reported.
648 sanctuary of the Elbe river: On 12 February alone, the RAF employed hundreds of aircraft (242 from Bomber Command and 398 from Fighter Command) but was unable to prevent their successful escape. A full account is in Barnett, Engage the Enemy More Closely, 447–53.
648 forty-three aircraft and 247 lives: WSC statement in the House of Commons, Feb. 17, 1942, Hansard.
648 ' "they should have done better" ': Violet Bonham Carter quoted in Nicolson diary, Feb. 12, 1942.
648 with defending Singapore: Bonham Carter diary, Feb. 11, 1942, in Pottle, Champion Redoubtable, 236–37.
649 'thick and fast upon us': Meacham, Franklin and Winston, 171–72. Churchill also made a rare admission to Roosevelt, noting on 20 February that he found it 'difficult to keep my eye on the ball'.
649 'appalled by events [and] desperately taxed': 'Action This Day' (Winter 1942), the Churchill Centre, www.winstonchurchill.org.
649 Clementine feared for his health: Soames, Clementine Churchill, 352–53.
649 'what else could he have said?': Nicolson diary, Feb. 16, 17, 1942.
649 'I am in a truculent mood': Eden, The Reckoning, 372.
649 'office of Minister of Defence': The Hinge of Fate, 91.
650 'seem to be consuming him': Moran, Churchill, 32.
650 ' "I cannot get over Singapore," he said sadly': Ibid., 27.
650 'in this strain for some time': Pawle, The War and Colonel Warden, 163–64.
650 'should be Deputy Defence Minister': Dilks, The Diaries of Sir Alexander Cadogan, March 2, 1942, 438.
651 'particularly in dark days': Ibid., 167.
651 the eastern seaboard of North America: Churchill, vol. 7, 68–69; 'Allied Merchant Ship Losses, 1939–1943,' OWI 3789. The worst month was May 1942, when 120 ships were sunk – a loss of 601,509 gross tons. (See The Hinge of Fate, table on 126.)
651 'can do nothing about it': Moran diary, circa April 1942, cited in Moran, Churchill, 32. Although there is no date shown for this quotation in the book, Moran also mentions that Churchill told him that shipping losses for February and March 1942 were 640,000 tons. The losses cited in The Hinge of Fate, table on 126, are 641,000 tons.

Chapter 49: The Quest for Generalship

654 *fundamentally different perspectives:* Barnett, *The Desert Generals*, 125.

654 *The heavy air campaign against Malta:* In March an average of 159 sorties per day were flown against the island. In February 1942, a total of 2,497 aircraft bombed Malta; in March that number doubled to 4,927.

654 *'pounded to bits':* *The Hinge of Fate*, 304–05.

654 *render the island untenable:* Barrie Pitt, *Churchill and the Generals* (New York and London, 1981), 99; and Reynolds, *In Command of History*, 585 n. 24.

655 *'highest opinion of him':* Alanbrooke diary, March 24, 1942.

656 *previous policy of defence:* Freyberg, *Bernard Freyberg, VC*, 381; and Hamilton, *The Full Monty*, 477–78.

656 *under Auchinleck in England:* Barnett, *The Desert Generals*, 123–24.

656 *very successful indeed:* John Bierman and Colin Smith, *The Battle of Alamein* (New York and London, 2002), 154–55; and Porch, *The Path to Victory*, 267.

657 *both difficult and insubordinate:* Bierman and Smith, *The Battle of Alamein*, 157.

657 *could do the job:* Barnett, *The Desert Generals*, 135.

657 *attacks by the Luftwaffe:* Bierman and Smith, *The Battle of Alamein*, 181.

658 *'given me one more division':* Samuel W. Mitcham Jr, *Rommel's Desert War* (New York, 1982), 86.

658 *'been so sorry for anyone':* Slessor, *The Central Blue*, 412–13.

659 *'for great occasions':* Moran diary, June 23, 1942, and notes, Box 58, Moran Papers.

659 *'disgrace is another':* *The Hinge of Fate*, 383.

659 *'put their hands up':* Moran diary, June 21, 1942, Box 58, Moran Papers.

659 *'war like debates':* Schama, *A History of Britain*, vol. 3, 534.

660 *was ever seriously challenged:* Parliamentary speech, July 2, 1942, Hansard.

660 *'little stings he was getting':* Elizabeth Nel (*née* Layton) interview, Brendon Papers.

660 *nine Allied nations:* Foot, *The Oxford Companion to World War II*, 298–99.

661 *twelve times that number:* Hamilton, *The Full Monty*, 430.

661 *have both been entirely discredited:* Lamb, *Churchill as War Leader*, 172. For a full account of Dieppe, see Brian Loring Villa, *Unauthorized Action: Mountbatten and the Dieppe Raid* (Toronto, 1988). Lamb's harsh but fair judgment is that 'the British handed to the Germans on a plate twenty-eight of their most modern tanks and much other war booty which provided complete information about up-to-date radios, infantry weapons and tactics.'

662 *'their blood is on your hands':* Lamb, *Churchill as War Leader*, 173.

662 *simply could not provide:* Ibid., 172.

Chapter 50: Getting it Right

664 *expel the British from the Mediterranean:* Kershaw, *Hitler, 1936–1945: Nemesis*, 523.

664 *last defensible position in Egypt:* Auchinleck's supporters have praised what has passed into British myth as First Alamein. However, both Field Marshal Lord Harding and General Sir Charles Richardson, who was in charge of future operational planning (GSO 1 [Plans]) for the Eighth Army, have derided it as hardly more than improvisation. 'All I was aware of was a chaotic series of attacks scraped together, which to my mind at the time could scarcely have been said to have succeeded,' said Richardson. 'I can state from my continuous presence as GSO 1 (Plans) throughout those weeks, that no battle entitled to the name "First Alamein" ever took place.' (Hamilton, *The Full Monty*, 509; and Gen. Sir Charles Richardson, *Flashback* [London, 1985] 105.)

665 *'stick to it!':* Auchinleck's July 25 Order of the Day quoted in Bierman and Smith, *The Battle of Alamein*, 208.

665 *on the streets of Cairo:* Porch, *The Path to Victory*, 299.

665 *'army in the desert':* Freyberg quoted in Hamilton, *The Full Monty*, 477.

665 *break the sad news to her personally:* John Grigg interview, Brendon Papers. Churchill also wrote a poignant letter of condolence to Pamela Lytton on 19 July 1942 that read in part: 'My heart bleeds for you. Both your gallant, splendid sons have given their lives with all their hope and promise for our country and its cause. I pray you may be comforted.' The Lyttons' elder son Viscount Knebworth had been killed in a flying accident in 1933.

666 *his presence from prying eyes:* Pawle, *The War and Colonel Warden,* 189–90.

666 *mattresses dumped on the floor:* Memoir by Air Commodore John L. Mitchell, 'The Diary of a Navigator on the Prime Minister's Private Aircraft, 1943–5', MISC 59, CAC. On one occasion the crew chief came upon the prime minister smoking a cigar while oxygen hissed from a portable tank. Horrified, the airmen snatched the cigar from his mouth before disaster could overtake them.

667 *'with Ritchie for five minutes':* Correspondence between Eric Dorman-O'Gowan (formerly Dorman-Smith) and Correlli Barnett, Barnett Papers, BRNT 3, CAC.

667 *'This was exhilarating':* The Hinge of Fate, 456.

667 *V sign to troops as he passed:* Pawle, *The War and Colonel Warden,* 190.

667 *'equal to the opportunity':* WSC to CHC, Aug. 9, 1942.

667 *'no personality and little experience':* Hamilton, *The Full Monty,* 481.

668 *'plenty of confidence in them':* Bierman and Smith, *The Battle of Alamein,* 214.

668 *remain as CIGS:* Alanbrooke diary and 'Notes on My Life', Aug. 3, 1942; and Fraser, *Alanbrooke,* 282–83. Fraser notes that Brooke's natural cold-bloodedness and circumspection would have made it difficult for him to relate to soldiers who demand that their commanders identify with them and their plight.

668 *'important military personages':* The Hinge of Fate, 458.

668 *'responsibilities confided to him':* Ibid., 458–59.

669 *first place through inept generalship:* Bierman and Smith, *The Battle of Alamein,* 217.

669 *'without batting an eyelid':* Moran diary, Aug. 5, 1942.

669 *'not doing their duty':* Ibid., Aug. 6, 1942.

670 *'where we had gone wrong':* Bierman and Smith, *The Battle of Alamein,* 219–20; and Alanbrooke, 'Notes on My Life', Aug. 7, 1942.

670 *same tragic manner as Gott:* Burgis 'The Memoirs of Lawrence'.

671 *'sees the hand of fate':* Moran diary, Aug. 21, 1942; and WSC to CHC, Aug. 9, 1942.

671 *'murder an unsuspecting friend':* Jacob diary, Aug. 8, 1942, Jacob Papers.

671 *'quartermaster, could deal with':* Ibid. Also quoted in John Connell, *Auchinleck* (London, 1959), 710.

671 *asked to be retired instead:* Reynolds, *In Command of History,* 307. The Persia–Iraq command went instead to Jumbo Wilson.

671 *given command of the Indian army:* Bierman and Smith, *The Battle of Alamein,* 220–21.

672 *'won the Gazala battle':* Ibid.

672 *'their seat in the lorry':* Ibid., 307-08.

672 *'with all my heart':* Nicolson diary, Nov. 6, 1942.

673 *'his neck wrung':* Nigel Nicolson, *Alex: The Life of Field Marshal Earl Alexander of Tunis* (London, 1976), 196.

673 *'surprised and embarrassed by it':* Ibid, 199.

673 *'I don't understand long words':* Charles J. Rolo, 'General Sir Harold Alexander', *Britain* (July 1943).

673 *'off the road for me':* Nicolson, *Alex,* 280.

673 *'whenever he visited the front':* C. L. Sulzberger, *A Long Row of Candles* (New York, 1969), 230.

674 *high command on numerous occasions:* Brooke's doubts about Alexander's fitness for high command are reflected in many unflattering entries in his diary.

674 *'but perhaps it isn't':* William J. McAndrew in the *Toronto Globe & Mail,* Aug. 30, 1986.

674 *'Winston is a gambler':* Moran diary, Aug. 20, 1944, Gilbert, *Churchill: A Life,* 171.

675 *'better than Monty':* Ibid., 174.

675 *'conducts and wins the battles'*: Jacob interview, WCHL 15/2/9.

675 *between Montgomery and Churchill:* Alexander quickly noticed the low morale of the troops of his new command. There were no signs of cheerfulness, and discipline was sloppy. Troops turned their backs on his staff car and refused to salute it, a sure sign that all was not well. (See Barrie Pitt, *The Crucible of War: Montgomery and Alamein* [London, 1986], 3.)

676 *'no belly-aching'*: Hamilton, *The Full Monty*, 533.

676 *needed an immediate shaking up:* Gen. (later Field Marshal Sir) John Harding quoted in Nicolson, *Alex*, 190.

676 *'on their arse or their elbow'*: Hamilton, *The Full Monty*, 505.

676 *on the Eighth Army:* Porch, *The Path to Victory*, 300.

677 *'became very wet indeed!'*: Alanbrooke diary, Aug. 19, 1942.

677 *'with joy and comfort'*: The Hinge of Fate, 517.

678 *' "V" sign with his legs!'*: Brig. Bill Williams interview, WCHL 15/2/32; and Alanbrooke, 'Notes on My Life', Aug. 20, 1942.

678 *worth the high cost:* The Hinge of Fate, 511.

678 *'insufferable in victory!'*: Halle, *Irrepressible Churchill*, 219.

679 *since his appointment as CIGS:* Alanbrooke, 'Notes on My Life', Aug. 19, 1942.

679 *'of the highest military quality'*: Telegram, WSC to Clement Attlee, Aug. 21, 1942, *The Hinge of Fate*, 521.

679 *morning of 23 August:* Alanbrooke diary, Aug. 24, 1942. During his stop-over at Gibraltar, Churchill chafed at being confined for his own protection in Government House and failed in a bid to be allowed out to roam disguised as an Arab or an Armenian suffering from a toothache.

679 *Rommel's intentions, supplied by Ultra:* A full account of Ultra's role is in Bennett, *Ultra and Mediterranean Strategy*, chap. 6.

679 *'refrain from dithering'*: 'Before I Forget', memoir of Combined Ops, 1941–1945, Vice Adm. Hughes-Hallett, Hallett Papers, CAC.

680 *'disagreeable to the enemy'*: WSC to CHC, Aug. 9, 1942.

680 *'preparing his men for battle'*: Moran, *Churchill*, 68.

680 *'foundation of Allied victory'*: The Memoirs of Lord Ismay, 282.

680 *'appointing friendly faces'*: Hamilton, *The Full Monty*, 504.

Chapter 51: Alamein: the Turning Point

681 *'would like the fellow'*: Pawle, *The War and Colonel Warden*, 202.

681 *'man of destiny'*: John W. Gordon, 'Wingate', in John Keegan, ed., *Churchill's Generals* (New York and London, 1991), 277.

682 *'giving their services to the Crown'*: Ibid., 203.

682 *Allies in June 1944:* Kenneth Macksey, 'Hobart', in ibid., chap. 13. Hobart's 'Funnies' were offered to the American invasion force commanded by Lieutenant General Omar Bradley, but with the exception of the DD tanks the offer was foolishly refused.

683 *'get an attack launched!'*: Alanbrooke diary, Sept. 8, 1942.

684 *'We are in your hands'*: WSC to Alexander, Sept. 23. 1942; Bierman and Smith, *The Battle of Alamein*, 241–42; and The Hinge of Fate, 588.

684 *'suspense almost unbearable'*: Moran diary, Sept. 30, 1942.

684 *mount the operation:* Alanbrooke diary, Sept. 15, 1942, and subsequent entries.

685 *defeating Rommel:* Jackson, *The North African Campaign*, 265–66.

685 *'What a man!'*: Pitt, *The Crucible of War: Montgomery and Alamein*, 15.

685 *'hand over to one of you'*: John Harvey, ed., *The War Diaries of Oliver Harvey* (London, 1978), Oct. 2, 1942. Also quoted in Jenkins, *Churchill*, 703.

685 *500 pieces of artillery:* Jackson, *The North African Campaign*, 284.

686 *battle between the two:* Alanbrooke, 'Notes on My Life', Oct. 29, 1942.

686 *' "who can even win one battle?" '*: Moran, *Churchill*, 76.

686 *'realize their intense bitterness'*: Alanbrooke, 'Notes on My Life', Oct. 29, 1942.

687 *Eighth Army's infantry strength*: Bierman and Smith, *The Battle of Alamein*, 334.

687 *'troubles are at an end'*: Moran, *Churchill*, 77.

688 *'dinner with General Montgomery'*: Bierman and Smith, *The Battle of Alamein*, 329; and Halle, *Irrepressible Churchill*, 220.

688 *'were urging the President'*: Hamilton, *The Full Monty*, 549.

688 *prospect of losing his job*: Moran, *Churchill*, 77. In 1953 Churchill admitted to Lord Moran that September and October 1942 were the most anxious months of the war he had experienced. (71.)

689 *'never had a defeat'*: *The Hinge of Fate*, 603.

689 *not least by Churchill himself*: Raymond Callahan, *Churchill and His Generals* (Lawrence, KS, 2007), 146.

689 *'The war will still be long'*: Nicolson diary, Nov. 6, 1942.

689 *'bulldog that never lets go'*: Haffner, *Churchill*, 130.

Chapter 52: Ike

690 *'and the most persistent'*: Merle Miller, *Ike the Soldier as They Knew Him* (New York, 1987), 383.

690 *wartime United States army*: Portions of this chapter appeared previously in slightly altered form in Carlo D'Este, *Eisenhower: A Soldier's Life* (New York, 2002), chaps. 27, 28.

690 *'purpose of winning the war'*: Eisenhower, unpublished manuscript, furnished to the author by John S. D. Eisenhower. Begun in 1967 as an informal memoir of Ike's wartime relations with Churchill and Marshall, the manuscript was never completed.

691 *victory on the battlefield*: Michael Howard, *The Mediterranean Strategy in the Second World War* (London, 1968), 7–9. The essays that make up this book were the Lees-Knowles Lectures delivered at Trinity College, Cambridge, in 1966.

691 *'hitherto unknown men'*: *The Hinge of Fate*, 384.

692 *either Churchill or the president*: Dwight Eisenhower, *Crusade in Europe*, (New York and London, 1948), 58.

692 *bones of the dead*: Harry Hopkins found Chequers so bone-chillingly cold that he hated the place 'more than the devil hates holy water', and wore an overcoat in an attempt to keep warm. (Diary of Capt. Harry C. Butcher [Eisenhower's naval aide from 1942 to 1945], Sept. 21, 1942, Butcher Papers, EL.)

693 *'showed the royalty with dirty necks'*: Ibid.

693 *'fine body of men!'*: Mark Clark, *Calculated Risk* (New York, 1951), 33.

693 *'deserves it more than he'*: Gilbert, *Churchill: A Life*, 730.

693 *'in most of them!'*: Pawle, *The War and Colonel Warden*, 307–08. Churchill overheard Thompson's remark and groused, 'I'm not as old as all that.'

694 *visiting royalty or statesmen*: Kay Summersby, *Eisenhower Was My Boss* (New York, 1948), 20.

694 *other senior British officers*: Gen. Walter Bedell Smith to George C. Marshall, July 1942, quoted in Miller, *Ike the Soldier*, 383.

694 *'Stop it at once'*: Quoted in transcript of DDE conversation with Alistair Cooke, *General Eisenhower on the Military Churchill*, GCML.

Chapter 53: Torch and Casablanca

696 *'I am very well'*: Moran, *Churchill*, 70.

697 *'attacked his hard snout'*: *The Hinge of Fate*, 481.

697 *'lost for the main battle'*: John Ehrman, *Grand Strategy* (London, 1956), vol. 5, 115.

697 *cross-Channel invasion*: Alanbrooke diary, July 15 and 17, 1942. Historians have argued for more than half a century about Churchill's motives in North Africa, with some

insisting it was primarily an aversion to a second front and its likely butcher's bill. Others, such as Sir Michael Howard, have made a strong case for the Mediterranean. The historian Colin Baxter writes, 'Michael Howard argued that Churchill's advocacy of the North African campaign, rather than displaying an obsession with 'sideshows', was more an indication of his eagerness to grapple with the Germans on land at the only place then available [where] Britain had a real chance of success.' (Colin Baxter, 'Winston Churchill: Military Strategist?" *Military Affairs* [Feb. 1983].)

698 *'profusely bled elsewhere'*: Peter Andrews, 'A Place to Be Lousy In', *American Heritage* (Dec. 1991).

698 *'at one's own peril'*: Operation 'Symbol', Jacob diary, CAC.

698 *were not so fortunate*: Pawle, *The War and Colonel Warden*, 202.

699 *'bird without its tail'*: Kennedy, *The Business of War*, 274.

699 *'despatched by his mother'*: Ibid.

699 *rejected Rommel's advice*: Liddell Hart, *The Rommel Papers*, 365; and Kershaw, *Hitler, 1936–1945: Nemesis*, 546.

701 *'big, bare, white bottom'*: Moran diary, Jan. 13, 1943.

701 *'underbelly of the Axis in 1943'*: Churchill, vol. 7, 253.

701 *Germany's 'soft underbelly'*: Overlord was the best known of the many code names given to military operations in the Second World War. As he had with Torch, Churchill personally selected Overlord from a list of some 9,000 potential code names provided for him in his capacity as minister of defence.

701 *surrender the initiative*: For a full account of Churchill's Mediterranean strategy, see *Churchill*, vol. 7, passim.

702 *'fight the Germans somewhere'*: Fraser, *Alanbrooke*, 314.

702 *'capture of Sicily'*: Jacob diary.

702 *'had ever been conceived'*: Bryant, *The Turn of the Tide*, 559.

703 *discussions resumed each night*: Harold Macmillan, *War Diaries* (London, 1984), diary entry, Jan. 26, 1943, 8–9.

703 *'summer school and a conference'*: Ibid., 9.

703 *'from our American friends'*: WSC to CHC, Jan. 24, 1943.

Chapter 54: Down the Garden Path

704 *presented to Roosevelt: The Hinge of Fate*, 694–95; and Coombs, *Sir Winston Churchill: his Life and his paintings*, 163.

704 *'greatest man I've ever known'*: Meacham, *Franklin and Winston*, 212–13.

705 *'come into my inheritance sooner'*: Eden, *The Reckoning*, 421–22.

705 *'day's march nearer home'*: Roger Parkinson, *A Day's March Nearer Home* (London, 1974), 74.

705 *'await your further orders'*: Pawle, *The War and Colonel Warden*, 229.

705 *from an open staff car*: After its surrender to Rommel at Saint-Valéry-en-Caux in 1940, the division was reconstituted and fought its first battle at Alamein with distinction.

705 *'cheering him all the way'*: Alanbrooke diary, Feb. 4, 1943.

705 *'who was in tears'*: Pawle, *The War and Colonel Warden*, 229.

705 *'cheered to the echo'*: Ibid.

708 *'I cannot imagine'*: A full account of both the planning and the Sicily campaign are in Carlo D'Este, *Bitter Victory: The Battle for Sicily, 1943* (New York and London, 1988.)

708 *'see the fun'*: Harriman and Abel, *Special Envoy*, 205.

708 *'last August in England'*: Lord Birkenhead, *Halifax* (London, 1963), 537; also cited in *Churchill*, vol. 7, 410.

709 *'drives me to desperation'*: Alanbrooke diary, May 24, 1943.

709 *'this year's campaign'*: Churchill, vol. 7, 414.

710 *protect American interests*: During Churchill's flight to Algiers via Newfoundland and Gibraltar his aircraft was struck by a bolt of lightning that awakened him from a sound

sleep. Although reassured by the pilot that all was well, 'Afterwards I learned that there had been a good deal of anxiety.' (*The Hinge of Fate*, 813.)

710 *'strategic riches beyond'*: Geoffrey Perret, *Eisenhower* (New York, 1999), 221.

710 *'Get some more!'* Pawle, *The War and Colonel Warden*, 238–39.

710 *'striking Italy out of the war'*: The Hinge of Fate, 826.

711 *accepted the British position*: Ed Cray, *General of the Army: George C. Marshall, Soldier and Statesman* (New York, 1990), 400–401.

711 *into southern Italy*: Churchill, vol. 7, 424.

711 *assured the Russian generalissimo*: Ibid., 431.

711 *'memories of the war'*: Ibid., 421.

711 *usual late-night meetings*: Butcher diary, May 30, 1943.

711 *exacting gastronomic demands*: Mitchell, 'The Diary of a Navigator'. In 1944 the York was replaced by a far more luxurious American Douglas C-54 Skymaster aircraft that Churchill used for the remainder of the war.

712 *further updates came in*: Pamela Harriman interview, WCHL 15/2/3.

712 *across the Strait of Messina*: The Germans had saved not only themselves, but virtually every weapon and vehicle capable of being ferried to mainland Italy: nearly 55,000 troops, 9,789 vehicles, 51 tanks and 163 guns.

713 *left Britain deeply troubled*: Godfrey Hodgson, *The Colonel: The Life and Wars of Henry Stimson, 1867–1950* (New York, 1990), 269–70.

713 *'invade France next spring'*: Harry C. Butcher, *My Three Years with Eisenhower* (New York, 1946; published in London as *Three Years with Eisenhower*), 373.

713 *Mediterranean diversionary operations*: Lamb, *Churchill as War Leader*, 225.

714 *role in Overlord operations*: Maurice Matloff, *Strategic Planning for Coalition Warfare, 1943–1944* (Washington, DC, 1959), 162.

714 *'measure the consequences'*: Churchill, vol. 7, 483.

715 *'at the knee' of Rome*: Kennedy, *The Business of War*, 294–95.

715 *'driven back into the sea'*: Churchill, vol. 7, 489.

715 *'Napoleon's Italian campaign'*: Moran diary, Sept. 7, 1943.

716 *'military or political purpose'*: David M. Kennedy, *Freedom from Fear: The American People in Depression and War, 1929–1945* (New York and London, 1999), 596.

716 *nothing to influence the outcome*: Moran diary, Sept. 13, 1943.

716 *involve himself in the battle*: Reynolds, *In Command of History*, 391–92; and Ismay, *The Memoirs of Lord Ismay*, 320.

716 *in the desert and was lost*: WSC, *Closing the Ring* (Boston, 1951), 142.

717 *'damned close-run thing'*: Butcher diary, Sept. 23, 1943.

717 *meant the most to him*: Ibid.

717 *'gift God has made to us'*: Moran diary, Oct. 24, 1943.

717 *delayed second front*: James L. Stokesbury, *A Short History of World War II* (New York, 1980), 299.

Chapter 55: Amid the Ruins of Carthage

719 *nonexistent 'soft underbelly'*: David Eisenhower, *Eisenhower: At War, 1943–1945* (London, 1986), 21–22; and Henry L. Stimson and McGeorge Bundy, *On Active Service* (New York, 1948), 436–38.

720 *'concentrate on the Italian campaign'*: Quoted in Churchill, vol. 7, 526.

720 *American chiefs were shortsighted*: In recent years numerous British accounts and memoirs have stressed that Churchill and Brooke were indeed committed to Operation Overlord. An equal number of American participants were of the opposite view. In an unpublished memoir, Eisenhower described how Brooke privately expressed deep misgivings about the cross-Channel venture and spoke favourably of a 'thrust and peck' strategy of hammering Axis flanks to the benefit of the Red Army, whose responsibility,

he said, should be the destruction of Hitler's land forces. Brooke later claimed that Eisenhower had obviously misunderstood him.

720 'It is heartbreaking': Alanbrooke diary, Nov. 1, 1943.

720 'favourite hunting-ground, the Balkans': The Memoirs of Lord Ismay, 336.

720 'cheap prizes in the Aegean': Churchill, vol. 7, 523.

720 'most of the Aegean Islands': Roskill, Churchill and the Admirals, 222.

721 'to see any dangers!': Alanbrooke diary, Oct. 8, 1943.

721 'if this goes on': Ibid., Oct. 7, 1943.

721 'where would the Germans go': FDR to WSC, Oct. 8, 1943; Kimball, Churchill & Roosevelt, vol. 2, Alliance Forged, 505–06.

722 'undertake this on the cheap': WSC to Jumbo Wilson, Oct. 9, 1943, CHAR 20/120.

722 4,600 British troops were captured: Anthony Rogers, Churchill's Folly: Leros and the Aegean – The Last Great British Defeat of World War Two (London, 2003), 234.

722 ten smaller craft sunk: Barnett, Engage the Enemy More Closely, 684.

722 'die on that goddamned beach': George C. Marshall interviews. According to Marshall, Churchill was so shocked by his outburst that Ismay 'had to stay up with him all night'.

723 'of waging war': DDE manuscript, 'Churchill and Marshall', Box 8, Post-Pres Papers, EL.

723 'what he considered important': Harriman and Abel, Special Envoy, 272–73.

723 'we masters of our own destiny': Reynolds, In Command of History, 378–79.

723 'suffered in the war': Closing the Ring, 218.

723 'complete failure': Montgomery to Brooke, Nov. 18, 1943; Hamilton, Monty: Master of the Battlefield, 455 n. 2.

724 'every sinew of our strength.': Moran, Churchill, 137; and Closing the Ring, 373.

724 'Big Two and a half': Thorpe, Eden, 291–92.

724 'very small country this is': Ibid., 291.

725 Big Three pecking order: Bryant, The Turn of the Tide, 282.

725 'laughter in my heart?': Sarah Churchill, A Thread in the Tapestry (New York and London, 1967), 71.

725 'we had held at the start': Alanbrooke, 'Notes on My Life', Nov. 18, 1943.

725 'expense of all the rest': Ibid.

725 'beyond our capability': Cunningham, A Sailor's Odyssey, 588.

726 entrust their fortunes to him: DDE, Crusade in Europe, 227. 'I feel I could not sleep at night with you out of the country,' FDR candidly told Marshall. Roosevelt's close adviser, the playwright Robert Sherwood, thought it was one of the most difficult decisions ever made by the president. (Goodwin, No Ordinary Time, 478; and James McGregor Burns, Roosevelt: The Soldier of Freedom [New York, 1970], 415.)

726 'command three services': Alanbrooke diary, Nov. 18, 1943.

726 'military merits for the job': Cable, Grigg to Brooke, Dec. 15, 1943, PREM 3/336/1.

727 'retain him in Italy': 'Notes on My Life'. That Brooke was able to forestall Churchill over Alexander owed much to Clement Attlee, who was manning the ship of state in England while Churchill was on his lengthy trip, and supported Montgomery over Alexander.

727 'how inadequate we are': Moran diary, Nov. 29, 1943.

727 'won't feel so exhausted?': Lovell, Churchill's Doctor, 223–24.

727 'only person he listens to': Ibid., 224.

727 'end of my tether': Pawle, The War and Colonel Warden, 273; and Closing the Ring, 421.

728 'had a bad headache': Alanbrooke diary, Dec. 12, 1943.

728 slow his heart rate: Digitalis (also called foxglove) is a strong natural herbal used to treat an irregular heart rhythm.

728 'body and soul, and spirit': Thompson, Assignment Churchill, 285.

728 'Here in the ruins of Carthage?': Ibid.

728 *'the war is won'*: Churchill, vol. 7, 606.
728 *'ripened into pneumonia'*: Ibid., 607.
728 *'row in no time'*: Box 60, Moran Papers.
728 *'comments about the French'*: Colville diary, Dec. 21 and 22, 1943.
729 *'he'll forget I'm here'*: Moran, *Churchill*, 152.
729 *'surface of the oily sea'*: Box 62, Moran Papers.
729 *'perpetrated by the chaplain'*: Pawle, *The War and Colonel Warden*, 279; Soames, *Clementine Churchill*, 382; and Colville diary, Dec. 25, 1943.
729 *'climb into the motor-car'*: *Closing the Ring*, 439.
730 *'in these hard days!'*: Churchill, vol. 7, 634.
730 *'overflowing American hospitality'*: WSC to FDR, Dec. 28, 1943, C-524; Kimball, *Churchill & Roosevelt*, vol. 2, 638. After Torch, Marrakech came under the Americans' control, and during the extended stay of their famous guest he was guarded day and night and secluded from the local citizenry. It was thus unlikely that Churchill knew of the problems his hosts faced in attempting to control the city's 28,000 registered prostitutes. (Rick Atkinson, *The Day of Battle* [New York, 2007], 321.)
730 *around his ample body:* Leasor, *War at the Top*, 270.
730 *'it will take all we have'*: Soames, *Clementine Churchill*, 386–87; and Lady Diana Cooper, *Trumpets from the Steep* (London, 1960), 182. His true age was sixty-nine.
730 *'It did not happen like that'*: Box 60, Moran Papers.
731 *'behind the lines at Anzio'*: Moran diary, Dec. 27, 1943.

Chapter 56: The Strategic Air Campaign

732 *'the place to hit them'*: Churchill, vol. 6, 757.
732 *in large numbers:* Keith Lowe, *Inferno: The Fiery Destruction of Hamburg, 1943* (New York and London, 2007), 51.
733 *'military power of Germany'*: WSC memo of Sept. 3, 1940, quoted ibid., 85–6.
733 *US strategic air forces:* Ponting, 1940, 219–20.
733 *'let alone its targets, by night'*: Ibid., 220; and Charles Webster and Noble Frankland, *The Strategic Air Offensive Against Germany 1939–1945*, vol. 1 (London, 1961), 125.
733 *'upon the Nazi homeland'*: WSC to Beaverbrook, July 8, 1940, quoted in Reynolds, *From World War to Cold War*, 85.
733 *by the end of 1942:* Ibid., 86.
733 *supporting the bombing campaign:* Max Hastings, *Bomber Command* (New York and London, 1979), 126.
733 *evolved into that of area bombing:* The bombing of German targets was so inefficient that any bomb dropped within five miles of its intended target was absurdly claimed as a hit.
734 *'The only plan is to persevere'*: WSC minutes to Portal, Sept. 27 and Oct. 7, 1941, CAB 120/300. Also cited in Churchill, vol. 6, 1205–06.
734 *bombing of German cities in reprisal:* WSC speech in the Free Trade Hall, Manchester, Jan. 27, 1940, quoted in A. C. Grayling, *Among the Dead Cities* (New York, 2006), 187.
734 *'Speed is vital here'*: WSC to Ismay, Sept. 28, 1940, CHAR 20/13.
734 *'majority would cry, "No"'*: WSC speech in County Hall, London, July 15, 1941, quoted in Grayling, *Among the Dead Cities*, 187.
734 *'any country in continuity'*: Ibid.
734 *'peace comes to the world'*: Ibid., WSC speech of May 19, 1943.
735 *'creating this war'*: Ibid., 188.
735 *'men, women and children'*: Ibid., 280.
735 *'Few lessons were learned'*: Jenkins, *Churchill*, 641.
736 *their inefficient* Knickebein: Lewin, *Ultra Goes to War*, 99–103.
736 *'had spectacular results'*: Colville diary, Nov. 14, 1940.
736 *'thousands of people every night!'*: Quoted in Lowe, *Inferno*, 56.

736 *ground campaign in Europe*: A full account of Pointblank and the Allied strategic air campaign is in Hastings, *Bomber Command*.

737 *leaving the city a charnel house*: Keith Lowe's *Inferno* is the newest and perhaps best book yet written about the destruction of Hamburg.

737 *Nuremberg on 30 March 1944*: Ten additional aircraft were lost when they crashlanded back in England.

737 *bombs on German targets*: Hastings, *Bomber Command*, 268 and appendix A, 427.

737 *'within three months'*: Harry C. Butcher diary, Nov. 23, 1943, EL.

737 *Overlord was carried out*: Hastings, *Bomber Command*, 218, 221.

737 *'find themselves most out-matched'*: Churchill, vol. 7, 414.

738 *'cost Germany the war'*: Bomber Harris quoted in Hastings, *Bomber Command*, 306.

739 *'edge of collapse from bombing'*: Ibid., 327.

739 *'arguments about the plan'*: Solly Zuckerman, *From Apes to Warlords* (London, 1978), 236. Portal initially opposed the Transportation Plan but was eventually persuaded of its necessity. As a sitting member of the Combined Chiefs of Staff, he was a respected figure and his word carried considerable weight.

740 *critics in the Air Ministry*: Ibid., chaps. 12 and 13, passim.

740 *whisky nor his cigar*: Ibid., 247.

740 *mistake in not backing Tedder*: Arthur Bryant, *Triumph in the West* (London, 1959), 182.

741 *tomatoes in his garden*: Foreign Secretary Anthony Eden was also firmly opposed to the plan and did his best to emasculate it on the grounds that it would have a detrimental effect on Britain's post-war relations with France. (Eden, *The Reckoning*, 522–25; and Zuckerman, *From Apes to Warlords*, 251.)

741 *'OVERLORD can free them'*: DDE to WSC, April 5, 1944, in EP, vol. 3, 1809–10.

741 *'get ashore and stay there'*: Forrest C. Pogue, *The Supreme Command* (Washington, DC, 1954), 131.

741 *'be rid of the Germans'*: Ibid., 132.

741 *and the Transportation Plan*: Spaatz argued that the Overlord bombing violated the Pointblank directive and he countered with what was called the Oil Plan, a scheme for the systematic destruction of Germany's synthetic-petroleum capacity, which he said would win the war. Spaatz's Oil Plan was also designed to steal the limelight from Bomber Harris. (Hastings, *Bomber Command*, 328–29.)

741 *had written a landmark book*: *The Social Life of Monkeys and Apes* (London, 1932).

741 *'I'll quit'*: Perret, *Eisenhower*, 267.

741 *tacit rebuke to Churchill*: Churchill, vol. 7, 739.

741 *'awful load of hatred'*: Ibid., 784.

742 *'critical dislocation of traffic'*: 'Report of Recent Attacks on Railways', issued by the German Transport Ministry, May 15, 1944, cited in L. F. Ellis, *Victory in the West*, vol. 1 (London, 1962), 111.

742 *has never been forthcoming*: Richards, *Portal of Hungerford*, 325–26.

742 *'what befell Dresden in 1945'*: Wheeler-Bennett, *Action This Day*, 'John Colville', 86.

743 *'that of the enemy'*: Frederick Taylor, *Dresden* (New York, 2004), 375.

743 *'policy should be withdrawn'*: Ibid., 379.

743 *'war in Europe was over'*: Schoenfeld, *The War Ministry of Winston Churchill*, 100–101. Lowe has an excellent assessment of the moral issue in relation to the bomber war. (*Inferno*, chap. 24.)

743 *'what we did to Germany'*: Hastings, *Bomber Command*, 126.

Chapter 57: Stranding the Whale

744 *'and General Alexander burned'*: Carlo D'Este, *Fatal Decision: Anzio and the Battle for Rome* (New York and London, 1991), 264.

745 *'look for a cure'*: Alanbrooke, 'Notes on My Life', Dec. 18, 1943.

745 *long-drawn-out struggle in Italy:* Alanbrooke diary, Oct. 25, 1943.

745 *'have been disastrous':* C. J. C. Moloney, *The Mediterranean and Middle East,* vol. 5 (London, 1973), 588.

746 *'at Cairo and Teheran':* FDR to WSC, Dec. 27, 1943, R-427, in Kimball, *Churchill & Roosevelt,* vol. 2, 636.

746 *'farther in the Mediterranean':* Forrest C. Pogue, *George C. Marshall: Organizer of Victory, 1943–1945* (New York, 1973), 330–31.

746 *'which was my term':* Closing the Ring, 427.

746 *' "Full steam ahead" ':* WSC to FDR, Frozen No. 949, PREM 3, 248/1.

747 *'all difficulties at home':* Closing the Ring, 428.

747 *'Americans have taken Rome':* WSC to Jumbo Wilson, T-66A/34, Jan. 18, 1944, PREM 3, 248/2.

748 *'honour, glory or adventure':* Oral history interview of Field Marshal Lord Harding of Petherton, Dept of Sound Records, IWM.

748 *'brightest luminaries' of the navy:* Roskill, *Churchill and the Admirals,* 217.

748 *draft of his memoirs:* Reynolds, *In Command of History,* 392.

748 *'in the Agamemnon role':* James, *Churchill: A Study in Failure,* 49–50.

749 *'eat your rations':* Atkinson, *The Day of Battle,* 322.

749 *'if only to guard the lorries':* Pawle, *The War and Colonel Warden,* 284.

749 *'secret intelligence channels':* WSC to Jumbo Wilson, Feb. 8, 1944, in Reynolds, *From World War to Cold War,* 125.

750 *'on the coaches bench':* Diary of Maj. Gen. John Porter Lucas, Jan. 10, 1944, and 'From Algiers to Anzio', an unpublished manuscript based on his diaries, Lucas Papers, MHI.

750 *'Exactly, I knew I was right':* Leasor, *War at the Top,* 271–72.

752 *'is a little shaken':* Colville diary, Feb. 4, 1944.

752 *'possible for us to attack':* D'Este, *Fatal Decision,* 265.

753 *becoming Clark's subordinate:* Alanbrooke diary and 'Notes on My Life', Feb. 16, 1944.

753 *'Passchendaele, beloved of Generals':* Dilks, *The Diaries of Sir Alexander Cadogan,* Mar. 25, 1944, 613.

753 *'nature of the ground':* WSC to FDR, Apr. 24, 1944, in Kimball, *Churchill & Roosevelt,* vol. 3, *Alliance Declining,* 111.

753 *'what has been done':* WSC to Smuts, Feb. 27, 1944, No. T. 413/4, PREM 3, 248/7; and *Closing the Ring,* 493.

754 *'is a stranded whale':* Ibid. There are other variations of this well-known quotation. According to Brooke the prime minister told the chiefs of staff on Feb. 29, 1944: 'We hoped to land a wild cat that would tear out the bowels of the Boche. Instead we have stranded a vast whale with its tail flopping around in the water!' (Alanbrooke diary; also quoted in Bryant, *Triumph in the West,* 160.)

754 *'illness and advancing years':* Reynolds, *In Command of History,* 391.

754 *'added to the perimeter':* Maj. Gen. W. R. C. Penney, commander of the British 1st Division, quoted in D'Este, *Fatal Decision,* 405; and Marshall interview with Forrest C. Pogue, part 2, MHI. Others such as Generals Lucian K. Truscott, Ernest N. Harmon and G. W. R. Templer echoed this view.

755 *'conduct of the battle':* WSC to Smuts, *Closing the Ring,* 493; and Callahan, *Churchill and His Generals,* 173.

755 *responsibility for its illegitimacy:* The historian David Reynolds is unequivocal: 'The Anzio landing of January 1944 was a desperate, half-baked, and ill-supplied effort by Churchill to regain the initiative.' (*From World War to Cold War,* 124.)

755 *'two Suvla Bays in one lifetime':* Moran, *Churchill,* 188. Two days before the landings, Brooke wrote: 'I feel a special responsibility for it . . . It may fail, but I know it was the right thing to do.' Whether Brooke would have been as supportive had he actually been a party to the planning is less certain.

Chapter 58: Overlord at Last

756 *information and immediate response:* Pawle, *The War and Colonel Warden*, 291.

756 *would be horrendous losses:* *Closing the Ring*, 420.

756 *on the impending second front:* Leasor, *War at the Top*, 269.

756 *'Hitler and the Nazi Regime':* Reynolds, *In Command of History*, 381; and *Closing the Ring*, 313.

757 *Dodecanese initiatives:* Reynolds, *In Command of History*, 381–82; and Dilks, *The Diaries of Sir Alexander Cadogan*, Oct. 27, 1943, 570–71.

757 *'trying to break through':* Wheeler-Bennett, 'Sir Ian Jacob', *Action This Day*, 200–202.

758 *'will argue for themselves':* Philip Ziegler, *Mountbatten* (London, 1985), 207; and WSC minute to Mountbatten, May 30, 1942, PREM 3/216/1. The need to create artificial ports was one of the important lessons of the Dieppe fiasco in 1942, after which it became clear that heavily defended ports like Cherbourg might not be captured (and usable) for some weeks.

758 *jetties and pontoon bridges:* For an excellent description, diagrams and photographs see the 'Mulberry Harbours', at the Combined Operations official website: www.combine-dops.com/Mulberry%20Harbours.htm.

758 *Normandy via the Mulberry:* Ibid.

759 *his stenographer Marian Holmes:* Churchill, vol. 7, 669.

759 *'reins of government':* Schama, *A History of Britain*, vol. 3, 535.

760 *'whole day in bed':* Alanbrooke diary, May 7, 1944.

760 *'keeps wandering continuously':* Ibid., March 28, 1944.

760 *hero of 1940–1:* Nicolson diary, March 27, 1944, 356; and Jenkins, *Churchill*, 733.

760 *meetings with the chiefs:* Danchev and Todman, *War Diaries*, xviii. The editors point to several entries in Brooke's diary in which he comments on this. (See Dec. 20, 1944, and April 17, 1945.)

761 *'perhaps you could come down':* Joan Astley interview, Brendon Papers.

762 *'carry through the ideas':* Brig. (later Lt Gen.) Kenneth R. McLean interview with Dr Forrest C. Pogue, March 11–13, 1947, MHI.

762 *'strategy and tactics':* ACM Trafford Leigh-Mallory, 'Impressions of the Meeting Held at St. Paul's School on May 15, 1944', AIR 37/784, PRO.

762 *'certain you were of success':* Ismay Papers. Churchill also used the term in a telegram to Marshall on March 11, 1944. (*Churchill*, vol. 7, 705–06.)

762 *'quite a shocking discovery':* DDE, *Crusade in Europe*, 269.

763 *'all his forces against Overlord':* Allied Expeditionary Air Force Historical Record, AIR 17/1057.

763 *'high command of the Allied forces':* Ibid.

763 *'through the Iberian Peninsula?':* Gen. Sir David Fraser interview, Brendon Papers.

763 *'not pessimistic by nature':* DDE unpublished manuscript, EL.

763 *' "we will go down together" ':* Butcher, *My Three Years with Eisenhower*, 458.

763 *'without voicing my doubts':* DDE unpublished manuscript, EL.

764 *'get there before Monty':* Colville diary, April 25, 1944.

764 *joy ride in the Channel:* Wheeler-Bennett, *King George VI*, 603. A full account of Churchill's confrontation with the king is in chap. 9, 600–606.

764 *Churchill finally conceded:* Pawle, *The War and Colonel Warden*, 301, and DDE, *Crusade in Europe*, 276.

764 *'not to Eisenhower':* David Eisenhower, *Eisenhower: At War*, 243; and *Closing the Ring*, 622–24.

765 *'incorrigible optimist':* Alanbrooke diary, June 5, 1944; and Cunningham diary, June 5, 1944, BL.

766 *'may have been killed?':* Pawle, *The War and Colonel Warden*, 302.

766 *'it were safely over':* Alanbrooke diary, June 5, 1944.

Chapter 59: Summer of Discontent

768 *'for nearly fifty miles'*: WSC to Stalin, June 18, 1944, CHAR 20/166.

768 *'with their paws crossed!'*: Bryant, *Triumph in the West*, 214.

768 *'I can always tell'*: Pawle, *The War and Colonel Warden*, 303.

768 *exposed himself to danger*: Hamilton, *Monty: Master of the Battlefield*, 644–45; and WSC, *Triumph and Tragedy* (Boston, 1953), 12.

769 *return voyage to Portsmouth*: Pawle, *The War and Colonel Warden*, 303–04; and *Triumph and Tragedy*, 13.

769 *from the sky and explode*: *Triumph and Tragedy*, 39–40.

769 *floor behind his bed*: Alanbrooke diary, July 19, 1944.

770 *'mood against the Americans'*: Ibid and 'Notes on My Life', July 6, 1944.

770 *'psalm-singing uninformed defeatists'*: WSC minute to the COS, July 6, 1944, CAB 120/775, quoted in Holmes, *In the Footsteps of Churchill*, 311–12.

770 *use of biological weapons*: Ibid., 265–66.

770 *'warriors at the same time'*: WSC minute, Jul. 29, 1944, CAB 120/775.

770 *by at least a year*: WSC minute, July 6, 1944, to the Chiefs of Staff Committee, Holmes, *In the Footsteps of Churchill*, 311.

770 *was never again raised*: Churchill, vol. 7, 865.

771 *influence the conduct of the war*: Richard Holmes points out that Churchill's behaviour on the day of the debate on the employment of poison gas 'suggests that the galling experience of playing second fiddle in an orchestra brought into existence by his efforts, and of seeing himself gradually written out of the score, had become too much for him'. (*In the Footsteps of Churchill*, 267.)

771 *'ever-more entangled problems'*: WSC to FDR, June 23, 1944, in Kimball, *Churchill & Roosevelt*, vol. 3, 203.

772 *Eisenhower's forces in northern France*: Ibid., June 28, 1944, 214–20. Churchill wrote as both prime minister and minister of defence.

772 *not Italy and the Balkans*: FDR to WSC, July 1, 1944, ibid., 232.

772 *Eisenhower caught in the middle*: Warren F. Kimball, *Forged in War: Roosevelt, Churchill and the Second World War* (New York, 1997), 259–60.

773 *more stubborn became American resistance*: Bryant, *Triumph in the West*, 183; and Ehrman, *Grand Strategy*, vol. 5, 259.

773 *(sentences he excluded from his memoirs)*: Callahan, *Churchill and His Generals*, 180.

773 *'when the PM departed'*: Butcher diary, Aug. 5, 1944; Miller, *Ike the Soldier*, 675; and Perret, *Eisenhower*, 300–301.

773 *'get a change of outlook'*: DDE to GCM, Aug. 5, 1944, *EP*, vol. 4, 2055–56; and Ehrman, *Grand Strategy*, vol. 5, 255.

774 *'you may be right'*: Ehrman, *Grand Strategy*, vol. 5, 362–67.

774 *'mantle of my high office'*: Butcher diary, Aug. 11, 1944; and Pogue, *The Supreme Command*, 225.

774 *'any of our joint undertakings'*: DDE to WSC, Aug. 11, 1944, *EP*, vol. 4, 2065.

774 *'cantankerous yet adorable father'*: Butcher diary, Aug. 15, 1944.

774 *autumn and winter of 1944–5*: Williamson Murray and Alan R. Millett, *A War to Be Won* (Cambridge, MA, 2000), 433.

775 *'like a piece of clock-work'*: WSC to CHC, Aug. 17, 1944.

776 *'Prime Minister with close interest'*: Pawle, *The War and Colonel Warden*, 313.

776 *well-received pep talk*: Strawson, *Churchill and Hitler*, ix.

776 *'reach it as we can'*: WSC to Smuts, Aug. 25, 1944, CHAR 20/170.

777 *'3 enemies instead of one'*: Alanbrooke diary, June 23, 1944.

777 *in the dead of winter*: Sir Michael Howard has concluded that, of the Allies' options in the summer of 1944, Anvil was the better alternative. 'An effective case has still to be made that there could have been any more rapid or economical way of winning the war.' (Quoted in Nicolson, *Alex*, 305.)

777 'real warrior at heart': Churchill, vol. 7, 915.
777 'most bullets in the Second World War': Triumph and Tragedy, 122.
777 'apart from the others': Moran diary, Aug. 20, 1944; Gilbert, Churchill: A Life, 170–72.
778 full moon on 19 June: J. M. Stagg, Forecast for Overlord (London, 1971), 126.
778 'assistance to their accomplishments': John S. D. Eisenhower, Strictly Personal (New York, 1974), 67.
779 who did not measure up: Carlo D'Este, Decision in Normandy (New York, 1983), chap. 22.
779 'What a storm in a teacup': Ibid. 397.
779 than he had: Pawle, The War and Colonel Warden, 309.
780 'political rather than purely military': WSC minute, Sept. 8, 1944, Churchill, vol. 7, 943.
782 'running this kind of risk': Cable, WSC to Smuts, Sept. 25, 1944, CHAR 20/172; and Triumph and Tragedy, 200.

Chapter 60: Victory

783 'against so mighty a nation?': WSC to CHC, April 6, 1945, 523.
784 'failed to do what is required': Alanbrooke diary, Dec. 12 and 13, 1944.
784 course of events in Europe: Ibid.
784 'frustration in Burma': WSC to FDR, Dec. 6, 1944, Kimball, Churchill & Roosevelt, vol. 3, 434–35.
785 'has been for some time': FDR to WSC, Dec. 7, 1944, ibid., 446.
785 predominantly American sector: On Dec. 20, at Brooke's urging, Churchill telephoned Eisenhower and urged him to place Montgomery in command of the northern half of the Bulge. It should be noted that Eisenhower had actually appointed Monty two days earlier, on Dec. 18. (See Churchill, vol. 7, 1107; and Alanbrooke diary, Dec. 20, 1944.)
786 'last scrap of our resources': WSC to FDR, Jan. 7, 1945, Kimball, Churchill & Roosevelt, vol. 3, 498–99.
786 as the deputy supreme commander: Tedder's role in SHAEF was never clear. He acted as a sort of minister without portfolio, admired by many, distrusted by others. Eisenhower never really gave Tedder a function other than that of adviser and roving ambassador for SHAEF.
787 'than he should properly have': John Martin, Box 59, Moran Papers.
787 'comes to him as a Deputy!': Alanbrooke diary, Feb. 20, 1945.
787 'Alexander's military gifts and experience': D'Este, Eisenhower, 678.
787 'recapture of that fortress': Lamb, Churchill as War Leader, 205; and CAB 79/77.
787 final victory over Japan: Ibid.
788 attention to the war in Burma: Callahan, Churchill and His Generals, 233. Slim is never mentioned by name in Churchill, vol. 7, and while Churchill extolled Slim and his army in Triumph and Tragedy he did so only after being prompted as a result of slighting the Fourteenth Army's accomplishments in his earlier volume Closing the Ring. (See Callahan, 210, 233.)
788 preceded a major military operation: 'In truth, London's interest was not much greater than Washington's in what had become almost a private war between Fourteenth Army and its Japanese opponents,' writes Raymond Callahan (Churchill and His Generals, 228). An excellent account of the war in Burma is in Callahan's chap. 8.
789 'What a mess!': Anthony Eden, March 1, 1945, quoted by Harold Nicolson in Churchill, vol. 7, 1238.
789 rather than surrender: Kershaw, Hitler, 1936–1945: Nemesis, 778.
789 'again in the morning': Comments by John Martin, Box 59, File K5/5/1, Moran Papers.
790 'He is all through': WSC quoted in Charles B. MacDonald, The Mighty Endeavor (New York, 1969), 449
790 symbolically pissing on Hitler: Alanbrooke, 'Notes on My Life', March 26, 1945. Ralph

Martin was a combat correspondent for the GI newspaper *Stars and Stripes*. Martin learned of Churchill's visit to the Ninth Army on 3 March and was present the day he inspected the great dragons' teeth that guarded the German frontier. Before beginning his tour of the Ninth Army front, the army commander, Lientenant General William H. Simpson, asked Churchill if he cared to use a lavatory. Without hesitation Churchill asked, 'How far is the Siegfried Line?' Told it was about a thirty-minute journey, he declined the offer of a lavatory. 'He came [to the Siegfried Line] with an entourage of about twenty cars, and it seemed that all of them were generals . . . And sure enough, there he comes with his cap and a cigar and trooping around . . . inspecting all these tank traps—and it came time to have a pee.' Solemnly, Churchill turned to the horde of photographers that accompanied them and said: 'This is one of the operations connected with this great war which must not be reproduced graphically.' Martin was standing next to Churchill, 'and I could see the glint in his eye and this puckish grin when he said: 'Let's do it on the Siegfried Line' and that was marvelous . . . Here [were] all of us lined up, all these Generals and me and Churchill, everybody all peeing on the Siegfried Line . . . There couldn't have been a more symbolic picture of the entire war . . . The look on his face will always stay with me.' To a man, they obeyed. (Ralph Martin interview, WHCL 15/2/6, CAC.)

790 *'enjoying himself immensely'*: Alanbrooke diary and 'Notes on My Life', Mar. 25, 1945.

791 *'Nothing is further from my mind'*: D'Este, *Eisenhower*, 693.

791 *'fighting without them!'*: Ibid.

792 *'as far east as possible'*: WSC to FDR, April 1, 1945, in Kimball, *Churchill & Roosevelt*, vol. 3, 603–04; and WSC to DDE, April 2, 1945, in Bryant, *Triumph in the West*, 444.

792 *'are a part of love'*: DDE to WSC, April 1, 1945; *EP*, vol. 4, 2573; and Pogue, *The Supreme Command*, 443–4.

792 *eastern and western fronts were joined:* After the war Bedell Smith observed: 'The line of the Elbe was decided on as a primarily military tactical matter. We frankly wanted water between us and the Russians . . . We needed a definite line of demarcation. The Elbe was the most convenient one. Berlin had ceased to have military value.' (Walter Bedell Smith, Pogue interviews, MHI.)

792 *now lay in ruins:* The Italian campaign incurred 312,000 Allied casualties that included 31,886 killed. German losses have never been fully calculated but are known to be approximately 435,000. Most of the 214,000 missing have never been accounted for and are presumed to be dead. (See Carlo D'Este, *World War II in the Mediterranean* (Chapel Hill, NC, 1990), chap. 14.)

792 *'right to die like that'*: Colville diary, May 1, 1945.

792 *'It's all over'*: The Memoirs of Lord Ismay, 394.

793 *'//signed// Eisenhower'*: D'Este, *Eisenhower*, 704.

793 *'mustn't forget the One above'*: The Memoirs of Lord Ismay, 395; Leasor, *War at the Top*, 293; and *Churchill*, vol. 7, 1339.

793 *'celebrate this first news with him'*: Churchill, vol. 7, 1339.

793 *'three closest military advisers'*: Joan Bright Astley, *The Inner Circle: A View of War at the Top* (London, 1971), 206.

793 *'God save the King!'*: WSC broadcast, May 8, 1945. The entire text is in James, *Churchill Speaks*, 859–61.

794 *detected tears in his eyes:* The Memoirs of Lord Ismay, 395; and Elizabeth Nel, *Mr. Churchill's Secretary* (London, 1958), 177.

794 *'threat of German domination'*: James, *Churchill Speaks*, 861.

794 *through the cheering crowd:* St Margaret's Church lies between Westminster Abbey and the Houses of Parliament and is an Anglican church founded in the twelfth century. In 1614 it became the official parish church of the House of Commons. Among those married there were Samuel Pepys in 1665 and Winston and Clementine Churchill in

1908. The church was badly damaged in 1941 and restored. (The official website is at www.westminster-abbey.org/st-margarets/.)
794 *'Men are so emotional'*: Nicolson diary, May 8, 1945. Nicolson also recorded his reaction: 'Damn her.'
794 *clapped even more loudly*: Ibid.
794 *'vanquished his enemies in Europe'*: The Memoirs of Lord Ismay, 395,
794 *'Land of Hope and Glory'*: Thompson, Assignment Churchill, 305–06; Churchill, vol. 7, 1447–48; Nel, Mr. Churchill's Secretary, 177–88; Ismay, The Memoirs of Lord Ismay, 395–96; and Pawle, The War and Colonel Warden, 373.
795 *'happened without you'*: Soames, Clementine Churchill, 413.

Postscript

796 *'carrying on after the war'*: Eden, The Reckoning, 145. Brendan Bracken also believed in 1940 that 'the moment the war is over Winston will want to retire . . . He wants out of politics' (Nicolson diary, July 18, 1940). During the war the chiefs of staff met some two thousand times; however, not every meeting included Churchill. (See Richards, Portal of Hungerford, 344.)
796 *'words of sympathy or affection'*: Fraser, Alanbrooke, 502.
797 *'exist on this earth'*: Alanbrooke 'Notes on My Life', July 27, 1945; and Fraser, Alanbrooke, 502.
797 *mostly forgotten relic*: Although the principal war rooms were turned into a museum in 1948 they were little known and until opened for public view in 1984 could be visited only by special appointment.
798 *'deeds that changed the world'*: Leasor, War at the Top, 9 and 293.

Epilogue: The Last Farewell

799 *'to his faults a little blind'*: Ronald W. Clark, Tizard (Cambridge, MA, 1965), 416.
799 *'raging genius which he was'*: Boothby interview, WCHL 15/2/68.
800 *'independence of character'*: Moran, Churchill, 719.
800 *'to tell the tale'*: The Gathering Storm, 41.
800 *'price was worth paying'*: Taylor, 'The Statesman', in Churchill Revised, 59.
801 *'last glimpse of Churchill'*: Sir John Peck interview, Brendon Papers.
801 *'achieved without enthusiasm'*: Emerson, 'An Essay on Self-Reliance'.
801 *'to achieve nothing'*: Anthony Montague Browne interview, Brendon Papers.
802 *'sleeping nation to meet it'*: Alistair Cooke, 'Churchill at the Time: A Retrospective', Proceedings of the International Churchill Societies, 1988–9.
802 *'never duplicated before or since'*: Forty years after his death, once secret papers in the PRO/National Archives, code-named Operation Hope Not, revealed that the planning for Churchill's funeral began in 1953 and was refined over the next ten years. During these years the queen took a personal interest in the details of the plan. See www.News.Scotsman.com/24 Jan 2005.
802 *'bind the English-speaking world'*: 'Memories of Churchill's Funeral', On This Day (Jan. 30, 1965), BBC website: news.bbc.co.uk/onthisday/hi/witness.
803 *bowed his head*: Wheeler-Bennett, Action This Day, 'Sir Leslie Rowan', 265.
803 *'Churchill, 1874–1965'*: Twelve years later a new inscription was added: 'Clementine Ogilvy Spencer Churchill, 1885–1977'.
803 *'His glory remains'*: Kennedy, The Business of War, 356.

Sources and Selected Bibliography

Unpublished Sources, United Kingdom

Archives, Harrow School
Winston Churchill papers and records; school records.

Borthwick Institute, University of York
The papers of Lord Halifax (Hickleton Papers).

British Library, Colindale, London
Newspaper archives.

British Library, London
The papers of Admiral of the Fleet Viscount Cunningham of Hyndhope.

Christ Church, Oxford University
The papers of Marshal of the Royal Air Force Viscount Portal of Hungerford.

Churchill Archives Centre, Churchill College, Cambridge
The principal sources of information about Winston Churchill and his life are contained in the multitude of collections in the Churchill Archives Centre, beginning with the Churchill Papers. Encompassing more than two thousand boxes, the collection is divided into two parts: the Chartwell Papers (CHAR), which encompass his life from birth to the summer of 1945; and the Churchill Papers, which date from the period beginning on 27 July 1945. The papers primarily used in the research and writing of *Warlord* are the Chartwell Papers (cited as CHAR). An inventory of both sets of papers can be viewed online at the Churchill Archives Centre website: www.chu.cam.ac.uk/archives/.

Additional collections used include the papers of A. V. Alexander, Correlli Barnett, Piers Brendon, Lawrence Burgis, Clementine Churchill; the diaries and papers of Sir John Colville, Sir William Deakin, Charles Eade, Air Marshal Sir Thomas Elmhirst, Admiral John Henry Godfrey, Grace Hamblin, Ambassador Pamela Harriman, Vice Admiral John Hughes-Hallett, Lieutenant General Sir Ian Jacob, Denis Kelly, Elizabeth Layton, Henry David Reginald (Viscount) Margesson, Sir Edward Marsh, John Martin, Air Commodore John L. Mitchell; the memoirs of Lady Onslow, Admiral Sir Manley Power, Major General Sir Edward Spears, Inspector Walter Henry Thompson, Lord Thurso (Archibald Sinclair), Marshal of the Royal Air Force Lord Trenchard and Group Captain Hugh Williamson.

Oral histories in the WCHL series: Julian Amery, Sir George Anderson, Maurice Ashley, Colonel A. M. Barne, Lord Boothby, Don Burnham, Winston S. Churchill, MP (grandson), Sir John Colville, William Deakin, Chris De Souza, General Sir David Fraser, Cecily Gemmel, Alexander J. P. Graham, Lord Hailsham, Kay Halle, Grace Hamblin, Pamela Harriman, Lord Home, Sir Ian Jacob, R. V. Jones, Denis Kelly, Patrick Kinna, Elizabeth Layton, Ralph Martin, Sir John Peck, Lady Portal, Lady Soames, Marian Spicer, Brigadier Bill Williams and Lord Willis.

The Piers Brendon interviews: Julian Amery, Joan Astley (Bright), Sir Isaiah Berlin, Anthony Montague Browne, Senator Harry Byrd Jr, Winston Churchill, MP (grandson), Jill Craigie, John S. D. Eisenhower, George Elsey, Sir Michael Foot, Professor Roy Foster, General Sir David Fraser, Fred Friendly, John Grigg, Lord Hailsham, Grace Hamblin, Ambassador Pamela Harriman, Lord (Denis) Healey, Sir Robert Rhodes James, John Keegan, Patrick Kinna, Elizabeth Leighton, Kathleen Harriman Mortimer, Lady Diana Mosley, Sergeant E. Murray, Elizabeth Nel, Wendy Reves, Curtis Roosevelt, Celia Sandys, Lady Soames.

Imperial War Museum, London
Various unpublished letters, memoirs and papers in the Department of Documents, and oral history transcripts from the Thames Television series, *The World at War*; cabinet war rooms documents of Wing Commander J. S. Heagerty; Admiral of the Fleet Sir Algernon Willis memoirs; General Sir Leslie Hollis unpublished memoir; Field Marshal Lord Ironside papers; miscellaneous memoirs, letters and papers; photographs in the Department of Photographs.

Liddell Hart Centre for Military Archives, King's College London
The diary and papers of Field Marshal Lord Alanbrooke; the diary and papers of General Sir Ian Hamilton; the diary and papers of Sir Ian Jacob; the papers of Field Marshal Sir John Dill, Field Marshal Lord Ironside, General Sir Hastings Ismay, Major General Sir John Kennedy, Sir Basil Liddell Hart, General Sir Beauvoir deLisle, Colonel Roderick Macleod, R. W. Thompson; the diaries of Lieutenant General Sir Henry Pownall.

Miscellaneous Sources
Unpublished manuscript of General of the Army Dwight D. Eisenhower; 'Operation Symbol', diary of the Casablanca Conference, and 'Operation Bracelet', Middle East diary, August 1942, furnished to the author by the late Lieutenant General Sir Ian Jacob.

National Archives (Public Record Office), Kew
Select cabinet papers (CAB series), Admiralty papers (ADM series), Air Ministry papers (AIR series), prime minister's papers (PREM 1, PREM 3, PREM 4 and, for Desmond Morton correspondence and minutes, PREM 7) War Office papers (WO series).

Royal Air Force Museum, Hendon
The papers of Marshal of the Royal Air Force Lord Trenchard.

Royal Archives, Windsor
The diary and papers of King George VI.

Wellcome Library for the History and Understanding of Medicine, London
The Papers of Lord Moran (Sir Charles Wilson). When Lord Moran published his memoir, *Churchill: The Struggle for Survival, 1940–1965*, in 1966 it aroused a firestorm of criticism, primarily from Churchill's close friends and associates. There was also stinging condemnation from members of the medical profession, who believed that Moran had crossed the line of patient confidentiality with his revelations of Churchill's health problems during the final years of his life. The Moran Papers contain several of the harshest letters of censure I have ever seen. There is, however, little controversy over Moran's diary and observations of Churchill during the Second World War. In his extensive collection Moran drew many conclusions about his famous patient, and while not all of them are accurate, his intimate contact with him, particularly late at night when Churchill was inclined to reveal things he would not say to anyone else, was unique. An inveterate diarist, Moran tended to write down his observations. That some were written at later dates provoked strong objections and criticism, particularly from members of Churchill's inner circle. Nevertheless, such is the importance of Moran's extensive collection (and his book) that no biographer can afford to ignore his exceptional insights into Churchill's character, thoughts and opinions.

Unpublished Sources, United States

Manuscript Division, Library of Congress, Washington, DC
The papers of Charles Richard John Spencer-Churchill (nicknamed 'Sunny'), the ninth Duke of Marlborough (1871–1934), were originally deposited in the Library of Congress in 1929. A lengthy article in the *New York Times* on 9 January 1929 cited the event and noted: 'The Marlborough collection given to the Library of Congress sheds light on British social and political life of a past era.' The collection was never accessioned and reposed on the storage shelves of the Manuscript Division of the Library of Congress until 2001, when it was discovered by the Library's modern military historian, Dr Daun Van Ee. The collection includes revealing letters from Churchill to his cousin Sunny, who become a close friend. In particular Churchill's previously unknown letters written after the Battle of Omdurman offer a valuable window into his mind and his experience of war. In 2004 the Library of Congress mounted a successful exhibition on Churchill that included input from the Marlborough Papers.
The papers of Moreton Frewen; the papers of W. Averell Harriman.

Churchill Archive, Westminster College, Fulton, MO
Churchill letters and photographs.

George C. Marshall Research Library, Virginia Military Institute, Lexington, VA
Alistair Cooke interview, *General Eisenhower on the Military Churchill*, for ABC television network.

Georgetown University Special Collections, Washington, DC
The papers of Harry L. Hopkins; the papers of Sir Shane Leslie.

Still Photo Branch, National Archives II, College Park, MD
Selected photographs.

US Army Military History Institute, US Army Heritage & Education Center (AHEC), Carlisle, PA
Documents, files, letters pertaining to Churchill's military experience.

Published Sources

The official biography, *Winston S. Churchill*, comprises eight volumes, of which seven (listed below) are relevant to this work. The biography was begun by Churchill's son, Randolph S. Churchill, who wrote the first two volumes; the final six were completed by Martin Gilbert after Randolph's death in 1968.

By Randolph S. Churchill
Vol. 1, *Youth, 1874–1900*. Boston: Houghton Mifflin, 1966.
Vol. 2, *Young Statesman, 1901–1914*. Boston: Houghton Mifflin, 1967.

By Martin Gilbert
Vol. 3, *The Challenge of War, 1914–1916*. Boston: Houghton Mifflin, 1971.
Vol. 4, *The Stricken World, 1916–1922*. Boston: Houghton Mifflin, 1975.
Vol. 5, *The Prophet of Truth, 1922–1939*. Boston: Houghton Mifflin, 1977.
Vol. 6, *Finest Hour, 1939–1941*. London: William Heinemann, 1983.
Vol. 7, *Road to Victory, 1941–1945*. London: William Heinemann, 1986.
There are also a number of companion volumes of supporting letters and documents:

Edited by Randolph S. Churchill
Companion Volume 1, Part 1, 1874–1896. London: William Heinemann, 1967.
Companion Volume 1, Part 2, 1896–1900. London: William Heinemann, 1967.
Companion Volume 2, Part 1, 1901–1907. London: William Heinemann, 1969.

Companion Volume 2, Part 2, 1907–1911. London: William Heinemann, 1969.
Companion Volume 2, Part 3, 1911–1914. Boston: Houghton Mifflin, 1969.

Edited by Martin Gilbert
Companion Volume 3, Part 1, July 1914–April 1915. London: William Heinemann, 1972.
Companion Volume 3, Part 1: August 1914–April 1915 and *Part 2, May 1915–Dec. 1916.*
London: William Heinemann, 1972.

The Churchill War Papers
Vol. 1, *At the Admiralty, Sept. 1939–May 1940.* New York: W. W. Norton, 1993.
Vol. 2, *Never Surrender, May–December 1940.* New York: W. W. Norton, 1995.
Vol. 3, *The Ever-Widening War, 1941.* New York: W. W. Norton, 2000.

Books by Winston S. Churchill
Savrola: A Tale of Revolution in Laurania. New York: Random House reprint, 1956.
The Story of the Malakand Field Force: An Episode of Frontier War. London: Longmans,
Green & Co., 1898.
The Boer War. London: Pimlico, 2002.
Great Contemporaries. New York: W. W. Norton, 1991. Reprint of 1937 edition.
The River War: London: Prion, 1997. First published in 1899 by Longmans, Green & Co.
in 2 vols.
The World Crisis, 6 vols. New York: Charles Scribner's Sons, 1923–7.
My Early Life, 1874–1904. New York: Touchstone Books, 1996. First published in the
United States in 1930 as *A Roving Commission: My Early Life.*
Amid These Storms: Thoughts and Adventures. New York: Charles Scribner's Sons, 1932.
Step by Step, 1936–1939. London: Odhams Press, 1939.
Blood, Sweat, and Tears. New York: G. P. Putnam, 1941.
The Second World War, vol. 1, *The Gathering Storm* (1948); vol. 2, *Their Finest Hour*
(1949); vol. 3, *The Grand Alliance* (1950); vol. 4, *The Hinge of Fate* (1950); vol. 5,
Closing the Ring (1951) and vol. 6, *Triumph and Tragedy* (1953). Boston: Houghton
Mifflin.

Articles by Winston S. Churchill
'Can We Defend Ourselves?' *Pictorial Weekly,* 10 March 1934.
'Charge of the Twenty-first Lancers.' *News of the World,* 27 January 1935,
'Defence Not Defiance.' *Pictorial Weekly,* 13 January 1934.
'How I Escaped from the Boers.' *Johannesburg Standard and Diggers' News,* 23 December
1899.
'Must Civilisation Crash?' *Pictorial Weekly,* 24 February 1934.
'My Escape from the Boers.' *Strand,* December 1923 and January 1924.
'My Escape from Pretoria.' *News of the World,* 10 February 1935.
'My Life Story.' Series of articles in the *London Sunday Dispatch,* 1939.
'Plugstreet.' *Nash's Magazine,* April 1924.
'The Hush in Europe.' *Daily Mirror,* July–August 1939.

Selected Bibliography

Of the multitude of books about Churchill that have been used in the research and writing
of this volume, several stand out for their readability and for their insights. I commend them
to the attention of anyone who wishes to read more about Churchill. William Manchester's
two volumes *The Last Lion: Visions of Glory, 1874–1932* and *The Last Lion: Alone,
1932–1940* are both superbly researched and written. Manchester set the gold standard for
biographies of Churchill, and his two volumes are profoundly perceptive, not only about
Churchill but also about the times in which he lived. Another excellent but relatively little
known biography of Churchill's early life is Peter de Mendelssohn's *The Age of Churchill:
Heritage and Adventure, 1874–1911.* Like William Manchester, de Mendelssohn originally

intended to write Churchill's life in three volumes but was able to complete only the first volume before his death in 1970.

There is no better window into the mind of Churchill than Violet Bonham Carter's *Winston Churchill as I Knew Him* (published in the United States as *Winston Churchill: An Intimate Portrait*). Her perceptions and portrayal of Churchill and his triumphs and failures are matchless.

Although little known outside Britain, where it was published in translation in 2003, Sebastian Haffner's *Churchill* is a brief but penetrating biography. In his introduction, Professor Peter Hennessy notes that Haffner, the pseudonym of Raimund Pretzel, an exiled German journalist who fled Nazi Germany in 1938 and later became editor in chief of the *Sunday Observer*, 'had a gift for capturing episode, personality, and context . . . There is not a dull page or a stale metaphor in the book.'

Robert K. Massie's *Dreadnought* and *Castles of Steel* provide a remarkable depiction of the naval struggle between Britain and Germany before and during the First World War, and of Churchill's role as first lord of the Admiralty. Massie's grasp of history and his superb narrative make him one of our greatest living writers.

Last, I highly recommend Sir Martin Gilbert's *In Search of Churchill*, a fascinating and revealing account of his years working under Randolph Churchill and his research and writing of the remaining six volumes of the official biography.

Addison, Paul. *Churchill: The Unexpected Hero*. Oxford: Oxford University Press, 2005.
Amery, Leo S. *My Political Life*. Vol. 1, *England Before the Storm, 1896–1914*. London: Hutchinson, 1953.
Andrew, Christopher. *Her Majesty's Secret Service: The Making of the British Intelligence Community*. New York: Viking, 1986.
Armstrong, William, ed. *With Malice Toward None: A War Diary by Cecil H. King*. Madison, NJ: Fairleigh Dickinson University Press, 1971.
Ashley, Maurice. *Churchill as Historian*. New York: Scribner's, 1968.
Asquith, Lady Cynthia. *Diaries, 1915–1918*. New York: Alfred A. Knopf, 1969.
Asquith, H. H. *Memories and Reflections, 1852–1927*, vols. 1 and 2. London: Cassell, 1928.
Astley, Joan Bright. *The Inner Circle: A View of War at the Top*. London: Hutchinson, 1971.
Atkins, J. B. *Incidents and Reflections*. London: Christophers, 1947.
——. *The Relief of Ladysmith*. London, Methuen, 1900.
Ball, Stuart. *Winston Churchill*. New York: New York University Press, 2003.
Bardens, Dennis. *Churchill in Parliament*. New York: A. S. Barnes & Co., 1969.
Barker, Elisabeth. *Churchill and Eden at War*. London: Macmillan, 1978.
Barnett, Correlli. *The Desert Generals*. Rev. ed. London: George Allen & Unwin, 1983.
——. *Engage the Enemy More Closely: The Royal Navy in the Second World War*. New York: W. W. Norton, 1991.
Below, Nicolaus von. *At Hitler's Side: The Memoirs of Hitler's Luftwaffe Adjutant, 1937–1945*. London: Greenhill Books/Lionel Leventhal, 2001.
Bennett, Ralph. *Ultra and Mediterranean Strategy*. New York: William Morrow, 1989.
Benoist-Méchin, Jacques. *Sixty Days That Shook the World: The Fall of France, 1940*. London: Jonathan Cape, 1963.
Berlin, Isaiah. *Mr Churchill in 1940*. Boston: Houghton Mifflin, 1948.
Best, Geoffrey. *Churchill: A Study in Greatness*. London: Hambledon & London, 2001.
——. *Churchill and War*. New York: Hambledon & London, 2005.
Bierman, John, and Colin Smith. *The Battle of Alamein*. New York: Viking, 2002.
Birkenhead, Earl of. *Halifax: The Life of Lord Halifax*. Boston: Houghton Mifflin, 1966.
——. *Churchill, 1874–1922*. London: Harrap, 1989.
Bond, Brian, ed. *The Diaries of Lieutenant General Sir Henry Pownall*. Hamden, CT: Archon Books, 1973.
Bonham Carter, Mark and Mark Pottle, eds. *Lantern Slides: The Diaries and Letters of Violet Bonham Carter, 1904–1914*. London: Weidenfeld & Nicolson, 1996.

Bonham Carter, Violet. *Winston Churchill as I Knew Him*. London: Pan Books, 1967.

Boothby, Robert John Graham. *My Yesterday, Your Tomorrow*. London: Hutchinson, 1962.

———. *Boothby: Recollections of a Rebel*. London: Hutchinson, 1978.

Brendon, Piers. *The Dark Valley: A Panorama of the 1930s*. New York: Alfred A. Knopf, 2000.

Broad, Lewis. *The War That Churchill Waged*. London: Hutchinson, 1960.

———. *Winston Churchill: The Years of Preparation*. London: Sidgwick & Jackson, 1963.

Brock, Michael and Eleanor, eds. *H. H. Asquith: Letters to Venetia Stanley*. Oxford: Oxford University Press, 1985.

Brodhurst, Robin. *Churchill's Anchor: Admiral of the Fleet Sir Dudley Pound*. Barnsley: Leo Cooper, 2000.

Bryant, Arthur. *The Turn of the Tide*. London: Collins, 1957.

———. *Triumph in the West*. London: Collins, 1959.

Bungay, Stephen. *The Most Dangerous Enemy: A History of the Battle of Britain*. London: Aurum Press, 2001.

Butler, J. R. M. *Grand Strategy*. Vol. 2, *September 1939–June 1941*. London: HMSO, 1957.

Calder, Angus. *The People's War: Britain, 1939–1945*. New York: Pantheon, 1969.

Callahan, Raymond. *Churchill and His Generals*. Lawrence: University Press of Kansas, 2007.

Catherwood, Christopher. *Churchill's Folly: How Winston Churchill Created Modern Iraq*. New York: Carroll & Graf, 2004.

Charmley, John. *Churchill: The End of Glory: A Political Biography*. New York: Harcourt Brace, 1993.

Churchill, Sarah. *A Thread in the Tapestry*. New York: Dodd, Mead, 1967.

The Churchill Years: 1874–1965. New York: Viking Press, 1965.

Clayton, Tim, and Phil Craig. *Finest Hour*. London: Coronet Books, 1999.

Clifford, Colin. *The Asquiths*. London: John Murray, 2003.

Cohen, Eliot. *Supreme Command: Soldiers, Statesmen and Leadership in Wartime*. New York: Free Press, 2002.

Collier, Richard. *1940: The Avalanche*. New York: Dial Press, 1979.

Colville, John. *The Fringes of Power: Downing Street Diaries, 1939–1955*. London: Hodder & Stoughton, 1985.

———. *The Churchillians*. London: Weidenfeld & Nicolson, 1981.

———. *Footprints in Time*. London: Collins, 1976.

Connell, John. *Auchinleck*. London: Cassell, 1959.

———. *Wavell: Supreme Commander*. London: Collins, 1969.

Coombs, David, with Minnie Churchill. *Sir Winston Churchill: His Life and His Paintings*. Philadelphia: Running Press, 2004.

Cooper, Matthew. *The German Army, 1939–1945: Its Political and Military Failure*. London: Macdonald & Jane's, 1978.

Cornwallis-West, Mrs George. *The Reminiscences of Lady Randolph Churchill*. New York: Century Co., 1908.

Cosgrave, Patrick. *Churchill at War: Alone, 1939–1940*. London: Collins, 1974.

Cowles, Virginia. *The Kaiser*. New York: Harper & Row, 1963.

Cruickshank, Charles. *Greece, 1940–1941*. Newark: University of Delaware Press, 1979.

Danchev, Alex, and Daniel Todman, eds. *War Diaries, 1941–1945: Field Marshal Lord Alanbrooke*. London: Weidenfeld & Nicolson, 2001.

Dean, Sir Maurice. *The Royal Air Force and Two World Wars*. London: Cassell, 1979.

D'Este, Carlo. *Decision in Normandy*. London: Collins, 1983.

———. *Bitter Victory: The Battle for Sicily*. London: Collins, 1988.

———. *Fatal Decision: Anzio and the Battle for Rome*. New York: HarperCollins, 1991.

———. *Eisenhower: A Soldier's Life*. New York: Henry Holt, 2002.

Dilks, David, ed. *The Diaries of Sir Alexander Cadogan, 1938–1945*. London: Cassell, 1971.

Douglas, William Sholto. *Years of Command*. London: Collins, 1966.

Eade, Charles, ed. *Churchill by His Contemporaries*. London: Reprint Society, 1955.

Eden, Anthony (Earl of Avon). *The Reckoning*. Boston: Houghton Mifflin, 1965.

Eden, Guy. *Portrait of Churchill*. London: Hutchinson, 1945.

Egremont, Max. *Under Two Flags: The Life of Major General Sir Edward Spears*. London: Orion, 1997.

Ehrman, John. *Grand Strategy*, vol. 5. London: HMSO, 1956.

Ferguson, Niall. *The Pity of War*. London: Allen Lane, 1998.

———. *Empire*. New York: Basic Books, 2002.

Fisher, David E. *A Summer Bright and Terrible: Winston Churchill, Lord Dowding, Radar, and the Impossible Triumph of the Battle of Britain*. Emeryville, CA: Shoemaker & Hoard, 2005.

Fisher, John Arbuthnot. *Fear God and Dread Nought*. Vol. 2, *Years of Power, 1904–1914*. Edited by Arthur J. Marder. London: Jonathan Cape, 1956.

Fraser, David. *Alanbrooke*. London: Collins, 1982.

———. *And We Shall Shock Them: The British Army in the Second World War*. London: Hodder & Stoughton, 1983.

———. *Knight's Cross: A Life of Field Marshal Erwin Rommel*. London: HarperCollins, 1993.

Frieser, Karl-Heinz. *The Blitzkrieg Legend: The 1940 Campaign in the West*. Annapolis, MD: Naval Institute Press, 2005.

Fromkin, David. *Europe's Last Summer*. New York: Alfred A. Knopf, 2004.

Gardner, Brian. *Churchill in Power: A Study in Reputation*. Boston: Houghton Mifflin, 1970. (Published in the UK as *Churchill in His Time: A Study in Reputation, 1939–1945*. London: Methuen, 1968.)

Gelb, Norman. *Dunkirk*. New York: William Morrow, 1989.

Gibb, Andrew Dewar. *With Winston Churchill at the Front*. London and Glasgow: Gowans & Gray, 1924. (Also published anonymously by Captain X.)

Gilbert, Martin. *Winston Churchill: The Wilderness Years*. Boston: Houghton Mifflin, 1982.

———. *Churchill: A Life*. New York: Henry Holt, 1991.

———. *In Search of Churchill*. New York: John Wiley & Sons, 1994.

———. *A History of the Twentieth Century*. Vol. 1, *1900–1933*. New York: Avon Books, 1997.

———. *A History of the Twentieth Century*. Vol. 2, *1933–1951*. New York: William Morrow, 1998.

Golland, Jim. *Not Winston, Just William?* London: Herga Press, 1988.

Goodwin, Doris Kearns. *No Ordinary Time*. New York: Simon & Schuster, 1994.

Graham, Dominick, and Shelford Bidwell. *Tug of War: The Battle for Italy, 1943–45*. New York: St Martin's Press, 1986.

Grayling, A. C. *Among the Dead Cities*. New York: Walker & Company, 2006.

Greacen, Lavinia. *Chink: A Biography*. London: Macmillan, 1989.

Gretten, Peter. *Former Naval Person: Winston Churchill and the Royal Navy*. London: Cassell, 1968.

Grigg, John. *Lloyd George: From Peace to War, 1912–1916*. London: Penguin, 2002.

Haffner, Sebastian. *Churchill*. London: Haus Publishing, 2003.

Haldane, Sir James Aylmer L. *A Soldier's Saga*. Edinburgh: William Blackwood, 1948.

Halifax, Earl of *Fullness of Days*. New York: Dodd, Mead, 1957.

Hamilton, Nigel. *The Full Monty: Montgomery of Alamein, 1887–1942*. London: Penguin, 2001.

Harriman, W. Averell, with Elie Abel. *Special Envoy to Churchill*. New York: Random House, 1975.

Harris, J. P. *Men, Ideas and Tanks: British Military Thought and Armoured Forces, 1903–1939*. Manchester: Manchester University Press, 1995.

Harrod, Roy. *The Prof: A Personal Memoir of Lord Cherwell*. London: Macmillan, 1959.

Harvey, John, ed. *The Diplomatic Diaries of Oliver Harvey*. New York: St Martin's Press, 1970.

Hastings, Max. *Bomber Command*. London: Pan Books, 1981.

Herman, Arthur. *To Rule the Waves*. New York: HarperCollins, 2004.

Hickman, Tom. *Churchill's Bodyguard*. London: Headline, 2005.

Higgins, Trumbull. *Winston Churchill and the Dardanelles: A Dialogue in Ends and Means*. New York: Macmillan, 1963.

Hinsley, F. H. *British Intelligence in the Second World War*. Vol. 1. London: HMSO, 1979.

Hoare, Samuel John Gurney, Viscount Templewood. *Nine Troubled Years*. London: Collins, 1954.

Hodgson, Godfrey. *The Colonel: The Life and Wars of Henry Stimson, 1867–1950*. New York: Alfred A. Knopf, 1990.

Holmes, Richard. *In the Footsteps of Churchill*. New York: Basic Books, 2005.

Holt, Thaddeus. *The Deceivers: Allied Military Deception in the Second World War*. New York: Scribner's, 2004.

Horne, Alistair. *To Lose a Battle: France 1940*. Boston: Little, Brown, 1969.

Hough, Richard. *The Greatest Crusade: Roosevelt, Churchill, and the Naval Wars*. New York: William Morrow, 1986.

———. *Winston and Clementine: The Triumphs and Tragedies of the Churchills*. New York: Bantam, 1991.

Howard, Michael. *The Mediterranean Strategy in the Second World War*. New York: Frederick A. Praeger, 1968.

———. *War in European History*. New York: Oxford University Press, 1976.

———. *The First World War*. Oxford: Oxford University Press, 2002.

Hunter, Ian, ed. *Winston and Archie: The Letters of Winston Churchill and Sir Archibald Sinclair, 1915–50*. London: Politico's Publishing, 2004.

Ismay, Hastings Lionel. *The Memoirs of General Lord Ismay*. London: William Heinemann, 1960.

Jablonsky, David. *Churchill: The Making of a Grand Strategist*. Carlisle, PA: Strategic Studies Institute, US Army War College, 1990.

———. *Churchill, the Great Game and Total War*. London: Frank Cass, 1991.

———. *Churchill and Hitler: Essays on the Political-Military Direction of Total War*. Portland, OR: Frank Cass, 1994.

Jackson, Julian. *The Fall of France: The Nazi Invasion of 1940*. Oxford: Oxford University Press, 2003.

Jackson, W. G. F. *The North African Campaign, 1940–43*. London: Batsford, 1975.

James, Lawrence. *The Rise and Fall of the British Empire*. New York: St Martin's Press, 1994.

———. *Warrior Race: A History of the British at War*. New York: St Martin's Griffin, 2004.

James, Robert Rhodes. *Churchill: A Study in Failure, 1900–1939*. London: Penguin, 1981.

———. *Anthony Eden: A Biography*. New York: McGraw-Hill, 1987.

——— ed. *'Chips': The Diaries of Sir Henry Channon*. London: Phoenix, 1996.

——— ed. *Churchill Speaks, 1887–1963: Collected Speeches in Peace and War*. New York: Barnes & Noble Books, 1998.

Jenkins, Roy. *Churchill*. New York and London: Macmillan, 2001.

Jones, R. V. *The Wizard War: British Scientific Intelligence, 1939–1945*. New York: W. W. Norton, 1978.

Kee, Robert. *Munich: The Eleventh Hour*. London: Hamish Hamilton, 1988.

Keegan, John, ed. *Churchill's Generals*. New York: Grove Weidenfeld, 1991.

———. *The First World War*. New York: Alfred A. Knopf, 1999.

———. *Winston Churchill*. New York: Viking Penguin, 2002.

Kehoe, Elisabeth. *The Titled Americans: Three American Sisters and the British Aristocratic World into Which They Married*. New York: Grove Press, 2004.

Kennedy, John. *The Business of War*. London: Hutchinson, 1957.

Kersaudy, François. *Churchill and de Gaulle*. London: Collins, 1990.
——. *Norway, 1940*. New York: St Martin's Press, 1991.
Kershaw, Ian. *Hitler, 1936–1945: Nemesis*. New York: W. W. Norton, 2000.
——. *Making Friends with Hitler: Lord Londonderry, the Nazis, and the Road to War*. New York: Penguin Press, 2004.
——. *Fateful Choices: Ten Decisions That Changed the World*. London: Allen Lane, 2007.
Kimball, Warren F. *Churchill & Roosevelt, The Complete Correspondence*. 3 vols. London: Collins, 1984.
Klingaman, William K. *1941*. New York: Harper & Row, 1989.
Kozaczuk, Wladyslaw, and Jerzy Straszak. *Enigma: How the Poles Broke the Nazi Code*. New York: Hippocrene Books, 2004.
Lamb, Richard. *Churchill as War Leader*. New York: Carroll & Graf, 1991.
Lash, Joseph P. *Roosevelt and Churchill, 1939–1941: The Partnership That Saved the World*. New York: W. W. Norton, 1976.
Lavery, Brian. *Churchill Goes to War: Winston's Wartime Journeys*. Annapolis, MD: Conway and US Naval Institute Press, 2007.
Leasor, James. *War at the Top*. London: Companion Book Club, 1959.
Leslie, Anita. *The Fabulous Leonard Jerome*. London: Hutchinson, 1954.
——. *Lady Randolph Churchill: The Story of Jennie Jerome*. New York: Scribner's, 1969.
Leslie, Shane. *The End of a Chapter*. New York: Scribner's, 1916.
——. *The Film of Memory*. London: Michael Joseph, 1938.
——. *Long Shadows*. Wilkes-Barre, PA: Dimension Books, 1967.
Lewin, Ronald. *Churchill as Warlord*. New York: Stein & Day, 1973.
——. *Ultra Goes to War*. London: Hutchinson, 1978.
——. *The Chief: Field Marshal Lord Wavell*. London: Hutchinson, 1980.
Liddell Hart, B. H., ed. *The Rommel Papers*. New York: Harcourt, Brace, 1953.
Lord, Walter. *The Miracle of Dunkirk*. New York: Viking, 1982.
Lovell, Richard. *Churchill's Doctor*. London: Royal Society of Medicine, 1992.
Lowe, Keith. *Inferno: The Fiery Destruction of Hamburg, 1943*. New York: Scribner's, 2007.
Lukacs, John. *Five Days in London, May 1940*. New Haven: Yale University Press, 1999.
——. *The Last European War*. New Haven: Yale University Press, 2001.
Luvaas, Jay. *The Education of an Army: British Military Thought, 1815–1940*. London: Cassell, 1965.
Lyttelton, Oliver, ed. *The Memoirs of Lord Chandos*. London: Bodley Head, 1962.
Macleod, Roderick, and Denis Kelly, eds. *Time Unguarded: The Ironside Diaries 1937–1940*. New York: David McKay, 1962.
Macmillan, Harold. *The Blast of War, 1939–1945*. London: Macmillan, 1967.
——. *War Diaries: Politics and War in the Mediterranean, January 1943–May 1945*. London: Macmillan, 1984.
MacMillan, Margaret. *Paris 1919: Six Months That Changed the World*. New York: Random House, 2002.
Macrae, R. Stuart. *Winston Churchill's Toyshop*. Kineton: Roundwood Press, 1971.
Manchester, William. *The Last Lion: Winston Spencer Churchill: Visions of Glory, 1874–1932*. Boston: Little, Brown, 1983.
——. *The Last Lion: Winston Spencer Churchill: Alone, 1932–1940*. Boston: Little, Brown, 1988.
Marder, Arthur J. *Portrait of an Admiral: The Life and Papers of Sir Herbert Richmond*. Cambridge, MA: Harvard University Press, 1952.
——. *From the Dreadnought to Scapa Flow*. Vol. 1. *The Road to War, 1904–1914*. London: Oxford University Press, 1961.
——. *From the Dardanelles to Oran*. New York: Oxford University Press, 1974.
Martin, John. *Downing Street: The War Years*. London: Bloomsbury, 1991.

Martin, Ralph G. *Jennie: The Life of Lady Randolph Churchill: The Romantic Years, 1854–1895*. Englewood Cliffs, NJ: Prentice Hall, 1969.
——. *Jennie: The Life of Lady Randolph Churchill: The Dramatic Years, 1895–1921*. New York: Prentice Hall, 1971.
Marsh, Edward. *A Number of People: A Book of Reminiscences*. New York: Harper, 1939.
Massie, Robert K. *Dreadnought: Britain, Germany and the Coming of the Great War*. New York: Random House, 1991.
——. *Castles of Steel*. New York: Random House, 2003.
May, Ernest R. *Strange Victory: Hitler's Conquest of France*. New York: Hill & Wang, 2000.
Meacham, Jon. *Franklin and Winston*. New York: Random House, 2003.
Mendelsson, Peter de. *The Age of Churchill: Heritage and Adventure, 1874–1911*. New York: Alfred A. Knopf, 1961.
Moir, Phyllis. *I Was Winston Churchill's Secretary*. New York: Wilfred Funk, 1941.
Moorehead, Alan. *Gallipoli*. London: Hamish Hamilton 1956.
——. *The White Nile*. New York: Harper Perennial, 2000.
Morgan, Ted. *Churchill: The Rise to Failure, 1874–1915*. London: Triad/Panther, 1984.
Mosier, John. *The Blitzkrieg Myth*. New York: HarperCollins, 2003.
——. *Cross of Iron: The Rise and Fall of the German War Machine, 1918–1945*. New York: Henry Holt, 2006.
Moss, Norman. *Nineteen Weeks: America, Britain, and the Fateful Summer of 1940*. Boston: Houghton Mifflin, 2003.
Nel, Elizabeth. *Mr Churchill's Secretary*. London: Hodder & Stoughton, 1958.
Nicolson, Nigel, ed. *Harold Nicolson, Diaries and Letters, 1930–1939*. London: Collins, 1966.
——, ed. *Harold Nicolson, The War Years, 1939–1945*. New York: Atheneum, 1967.
——. *Alex: The Life of Field Marshal Earl Alexander of Tunis*. London: Weidenfeld & Nicolson, 1973.
Olson, Lynne. *Troublesome Young Men: The Rebels Who Brought Churchill to Power and Helped Save England*. New York: Farrar, Straus & Giroux, 2007.
Oxford, Earl of (H. H. Asquith). *Memories and Reflections, 1852–1927*, vol. 2. Boston: Little, Brown, 1928.
Parker, R. A. C. *Churchill and Appeasement*. London: Papermac, 2000.
——, ed. *Winston Churchill: Studies in Statesmanship*. London: Brassey's, 1995.
Parkinson, Roger. *A Day's March Nearer Home*. London: Hart-Davis, MacGibbon, 1974.
Paterson, Michael. *Winston Churchill: Personal Accounts of the Great Leader at War*. London: David & Charles, 2005.
Pawle, Gerald. *The War and Colonel Warden*. London: Harrap, 1963.
Pelling, Henry. *Winston Churchill*. New York: Dutton, 1974.
Penn, Geoffrey. *Fisher, Churchill and the Dardanelles*. Barnsley: Leo Cooper, 1999.
Perret, Geoffrey. *Jack: A Life Like No Other*. New York: Random House, 2001.
Pimlott, Ben, ed. *The Second World War Diary of Hugh Dalton, 1940–1945*. London: Jonathan Cape, 1986.
Pitt, Barrie. *The Crucible of War: Western Desert 1941*. London: Jonathan Cape, 1980.
——. *The Crucible of War: Anchinleck's Command*. 2nd ed. London: Macmillan, 1986.
——. *The Crucible of War: Montgomery and Alamein*. 2nd ed. London: Macmillan, 1986.
——. *Churchill and the Generals: Their Finest Hour*. London: David & Charles, 1988.
Pollock, John. *Kitchener: Architect of Victory, Artisan of Peace*. New York: Carroll & Graf, 2001.
Ponting, Clive. *1940: Myth and Reality*. Chicago: Elephant, 1993.
Porch, Douglas. *The Path to Victory: The Mediterranean Theater in World War II*. New York: Farrar, Straus & Giroux, 2004.
Pottle, Mark, ed. *Champion Redoubtable: the Diaries and Letters of Violet Bonham Carter, 1914–1945*. London: Phoenix, 1999.

Raugh, Harold. *Wavell in the Middle East, 1939–1941*. New York and London: Brassey's, 1993.

Reynolds, David. *In Command of History: Churchill Fighting and Writing the Second World War*. London: Allen Lane, 2004.

——. *From World War to Cold War: Churchill, Roosevelt, and the International History of the 1940s*. Oxford: Oxford University Press, 2006.

Richards, Denis. *Portal of Hungerford*. London: William Heinemann, 1977.

Richardson, Gen. Sir Charles. *Flashback: A Soldier's Story*. London: William Kimber, 1985.

Roberts, Andrew. *'The Holy Fox': The Life of Lord Halifax*. London: Weidenfeld & Nicolson, 1991.

——. *Eminent Churchillians*. London: Weidenfeld & Nicolson, 1994.

——. *Hitler & Churchill: Secrets of Leadership*. Weidenfeld & Nicolson, 2003.

——. *A History of the English-Speaking Peoples Since 1900*. London: Weidenfeld & Nicolson, 2007.

Robinson, Derek. *Invasion, 1940*. New York: Carroll & Graf, 2005.

Rogers, Anthony. *Churchill's Folly: Leros and the Aegean*. London: Cassell, 2003.

Rose, Norman. *Churchill: Unruly Giant*. New York: Free Press, 1995.

Roskill, Stephen. *Hankey: Man of Secrets*. Vol. 1, *1877–1918*. London: Collins, 1970.

——. *Hankey: Man of Secrets*. Vol. 2, *1919–1931*. London: Collins, 1972.

——. *Hankey: Man of Secrets*. Vol. 3, *1931–63*. London: Collins, 1974.

——. *Churchill and the Admirals*. London: Collins, 1977.

Sandys, Celia. *From Winston with Love and Kisses: The Young Churchill*. London: Sinclair-Stevenson, 1994.

——. *Churchill: Wanted Dead or Alive*. New York: Carroll & Graf, 2000.

Saward, Dudley. *'Bomber' Harris*. London: Sphere Books, 1985.

Schama, Simon. *A History of Britain*. Vol. 3, *The Fate of Empire, 1776–2000*. New York: Hyperion, 2002.

Schoenfeld, Maxwell Philip. *The War Ministry of Winston Churchill*. Ames: Iowa State University Press, 1972.

Schofield, Victoria. *Wavell: Soldier and Statesman*. London: John Murray, 2006.

Seely, J. E. B. *Fear and Be Slain: Adventures by Land, Sea and Air*. London: Hodder & Stoughton, 1931.

Sheridan, Clare. *Nudas Veritas*. London: Thornton Butterworth, 1934.

Sherwood, Robert E. *The White House Papers of Harry L. Hopkins*. Vol. 1, *September 1939–January 1942*. London: Eyre & Spottiswoode, 1948.

——. *The White House Papers of Harry L. Hopkins*. Vol. 2, *January 1942–July 1945*. London: Eyre & Spottiswoode, 1949.

Shirer, William L. *The Nightmare Years, 1930–1940*. Boston: Little, Brown, 1984.

Simpkins, Peter. *Cabinet War Rooms*. London: Imperial War Museum, 1983.

Slessor, Sir John. *The Central Blue: Memories and Reflections*. London: Cassell, 1956.

Soames, Mary. *Clementine Churchill*. London: Doubleday, 2002.

——, ed. *Winston and Clementine*. Boston: Houghton Mifflin, 1998.

Spears, Edward. *Assignment to Catastrophe*. Vol. 1, *Prelude to Dunkirk, July 1939–May 1940*. London: William Heinemann, 1954.

——. *Assignment to Catastrophe*. Vol. 2, *The Fall of France, June 1940*. New York: A. A. Wyn, 1955.

Stansky, Peter, ed. *Churchill: A Profile*. New York: Hill & Wang, 1973.

Stewart, Graham. *Burying Caesar: The Churchill–Chamberlain Rivalry*. New York: Overlook Press, 2001.

Storr, Anthony. *Churchill's Black Dog and Other Phenomena of the Human Mind*. New York: Grove Press, 1988.

The Straits of War: The Gallipoli Memorial Lectures 1985–2000. New York: Sutton Publishing, 2000.

Strawson, John. *Churchill and Hitler in Victory and Defeat*. New York: Fromm International, 1998.

Stuart, Charles, ed. *The Reith Diaries*. London: Collins, 1975.

Sueter, Rear. Adm. Sir Murray. *The Evolution of the Tank: A Record of the Royal Naval Air Service Caterpillar Experiments*. London: Hutchinson & Co., rev. ed., 1941.

Taylor, A. J. P., ed. *Churchill Revised: A Critical Reassessment*. New York: Dial Press, 1969.

Taylor, Frederick. *Dresden*. New York: HarperCollins, 2004.

Terraine, John. *The Smoke and the Fire*. London: Book Club Associates, 1980.

———. *The Right of the Line: The Royal Air Force in the European War 1939–1945*. London: Hodder & Stoughton, 1985.

Thompson, R. W. *Churchill and Morton*. London: Hodder & Stoughton, 1976.

Thompson, Walter H. *Assignment Churchill*. New York: Farrar, Straus & Young, 1955.

Thorpe, D. R. *Eden*. London: Chatto & Windus, 2003.

Tuchman, Barbara W. *The Guns of August*. New York: Macmillan, 1962.

Turner, John T. *'Nellie': The History of Churchill's Lincoln-Built Trenching Machine*. Lincoln: Society for Lincolnshire History & Archaeology, 1988.

Valiunis, Algis. *Churchill's Military Histories*. Lanham, MD: Rowman & Littlefield, 2002.

Vian, Philip. *Action This Day: A War Memoir*. London: Frederick Muller, 1960.

Warner, Oliver. *Cunningham of Hyndhope*. London: John Murray, 1967.

Watt, Donald Cameron. *How War Came*. London: Mandarin, 1990.

Wheeler-Bennett, John W. *King George VI*. New York: St Martin's Press, 1958.

———, ed. *Action This Day*. London: Macmillan, 1968.

Wilson, A. N. *After the Victorians: The Decline of Britain in the World*. New York: Farrar, Straus & Giroux, 2005.

Wilson, Charles M. M., Baron Moran. *Churchill: The Struggle for Survival, 1940–1965*. London: Constable, 1966.

Wilson, Theodore A. *The First Summit: FDR and Winston Churchill at Placentia Bay, 1941*. Boston: Houghton Mifflin, 1969.

Wilson, Thomas. *Churchill and the Prof*. London: Cassell, 1995.

Acknowledgments

My decision to write about Churchill was not taken without some trepidation. To write biography is serious business, particularly when the subject is someone of the great stature of Winston Churchill. General Claire Chennault's biographer, Martha Byrd, said it best when she observed: 'To write an individual's biography is a joy, a privilege, and a sobering responsibility.'

In my first six books, Churchill played varying but invariably important roles. However, I was also mindful of the enormous and still growing number of biographies that have appeared over the years. It seemed pointless to invest the time and effort unless there were uncharted waters. A careful analysis of the Churchill literature revealed how little of it has focused exclusively on his military life – hence my decision to write about the military life of one of the twentieth century's most important figures.

Warlord has been a major undertaking I could not have successfully completed without the help and encouragement of a great many friends and colleagues. It is with immense pleasure that I take this opportunity to thank all those who have contributed so much in the way of assistance, advice and fact checking during the nearly six years it has taken to produce this book. To undertake a work of this scope involves many individuals and public and private institutions. As I have noted in an earlier work, what has proved so rewarding is how generously so many have given of their time and talents.

I begin with an incalculable debt to my longtime friend, mentor and colleague Nigel Hamilton, who played an instrumental role in sharpening my focus, offering wise counsel and critiquing the manuscript. Nigel's support and encouragement have played a major part in the research and writing of *Warlord* for which I am eternally grateful.

My research trips to the United Kingdom were greatly facilitated by the friendship, generosity and hospitality of my dear friends Harry and Sue Brack and Geoffrey and Anne Perret. They not only provided safe haven but also enabled me to get the most from what was invariably a gruelling schedule.

A very special acknowledgment to my hometown institution, the Mashpee (Massachusetts) Public Library, for which I have the privilege of serving as a trustee. Director Helene Defoe, Technical Services Librarian Bridget Bontrager and the wonderfully efficient staff have gone out of their way to lend support. I thank them, one and all. Over the years they continue to play an invaluable part in each of my books.

Once again, my friend and personal physician Dr William E. Litterer of Falmouth, Massachusetts, provided valuable medical advice.

Dr Daun Van Ee, the Modern Military Historian of the Library of Congress, has been an invaluable guide to collections both inside LC and at other institutions, as have the efficient and ever helpful staff of the Manuscript Division. Thanks to Sir Max Hastings, who cast his expert eye over several of the chapters. Dr David Jablonsky likewise shared his deep knowledge of Churchill and kindly critiqued the First World War chapters.

At the US Army War College, Carlisle Barracks, Pennsylvania, I am extremely grateful for the support and encouragement of Colonel Leonard J. Fullenkamp, USA, Ret.; William G. Pierce, the director of its outstanding military history programme; and Colonel Kevin J. Weddle, USA, Ret., its former director. Special thanks to Len for reading and critiquing parts of the manuscipt.

As he has in the past, my old friend the historian Roger Cirillo has been of immeasurable help in ways almost too numerous to count. I extend my deepest gratitude to Roger, who has freely shared his astonishing knowledge of military history and of the Second World War.

My sincere appreciation to Arthur Herman, who read and critiqued the First World War chapters. My friend Colonel James N. Pritzker, the president of Chicago's Tawani Foundation and founder of the Pritzker Military Library, kindly provided me with a set of *The World Crisis*; and my longtime friend Edward C. Tracy, the Executive Director of the Tawani Foundation and the library's former executive director, also has his fingerprints on this book.

Special thanks to Eric Weider, CEO and publisher of *Armchair General* magazine, and to its editor-in-chief, Colonel Jerry Morelock, USA, Ret., for their unflagging support of my work, for their interest in this book and for providing me with a monthly column on their website.

The assistance provided by the archivists and staffs of the following institutions is gratefully acknowledged.

In the United Kingdom:

The staff of the archives and manuscripts reading room of the Wellcome Library for Understanding of Medicine and Science, London, and the current Lord Moran for access to and permission to quote from his father's papers; the staff of the Liddell Hart Centre for Military Archives, King's College London; the Manuscript Division of the British Library; the archivists and staff of the Royal Air Force Museum, Hendon; the Royal Archives, Windsor; the Borthwick Institute of Historical Research, University of York; Christ Church, Oxford; the Keeper and staff of the National Archives, Kew (formerly the Public Record Office); and the Imperial War Museum Department of Photographs, Department of Printed Books and Department of Documents.

At Harrow School, the archivist Rita Gibbs was exceptionally helpful and provided access to the rarely seen student punishment book.

I am deeply indebted to Allen Packwood, director of the Churchill Archives Centre at Churchill College, Cambridge. Allen and his superb staff were unfailingly helpful, enabled my research in a variety of ways and offered advice that pointed the way to collections important to my research and to making the most of my time there.

In the United States:

Nicholas Sheetz and the staff of Special Collections, Georgetown University Library; and Ellen Hall and her fine staff of the Kreitzberg Library, Norwich University.

At the US Army Military History Institute, Carlisle Barracks, Pennsylvania, chief archivist David A. Keough, the wizard of the archives, and Dr Richard J. Sommers have been of immense help for a great many years, as have Louise Arnold-Friend and the other members of this tremendously talented and helpful staff.

Before he became editor-in-chief of *Armchair General* magazine, Jerry Morelock was the Executive Director of the Churchill Memorial and Library at Westminster College, Fulton, Missouri. My thanks to Jerry and his deputy, John Hensle, for their assistance.

Others whom I thank for their assistance: Andrew Roberts; Professor David Reynolds; Antony Beevor; David Bennett; Sir Alistair Horne; the late Lieutenant General Sir Ian Jacob; Richard F. Reidy Jr; Dr Edward M. 'Mac' Coffman; Joel, Danny, Steve, Doug, Phil and Peter at Gold's Gym; Steven Ossad; the late Robin Neillands; and Danny Mulligan.

Keith Lowe, editor at Orion Books and the author of *Inferno: The Fiery Destruction of Hamburg, 1943*, was especially helpful and critiqued the air chapter.

Zachary Bathon did a fantastic job of tracking down photographs in the United States, as did Cecilia Mackay in the United Kingdom.

Special thanks to my talented cartographer, Jason Petho, who drew the maps.

I have been privileged to work with two outstanding and caring editors to whom I owe a debt of gratitude for their counsel, criticism and enduring patience during the years it has taken to research, write and edit this book. Tim Duggan at HarperCollins and Stuart Proffitt at Penguin/Allen Lane believed in the book, and it is through their efforts that it has come to fruition. Thanks also to assistant editor Allison Lorentzen at HarperCollins for her dedicated work in producing *Warlord*.

Behind every successful author are the unseen but nevertheless enormously important contributions of a talented copy editor. For the fourth time I've been especially blessed to have Susan H. Llewellyn as my copy editor. She has smoothed out the rough edges, corrected my lapses with great effectiveness and immeasurably contributed to making this book the best it can be. My thanks also to Peter James for his fine work copy editing the UK edition.

Last but not least, two very special people made this book possible: My agent, Michael Congdon, has been a tower of strength, a friend and a constant purveyor of wise counsel and encouragement. My wife, Shirley Ann, has been there for me with love and encouragement as well as providing a superb sounding board for ideas. Much of what has gone into this book is the result of her advice.

As always, any mistakes of fact or interpretation are my responsibility.

Carlo D'Este
Cape Cod, Massachusetts
June 2008

The author gratefully acknowledges the following authors, publishers and institutions for permission to reprint excerpts from original and previously published material:

Randolph S. Churchill, *Winston S. Churchill, Companion Volume 1, Part 1, 1874–1897 and Companion Volume 1, Part 2, 1897–1900*, published by William Heinemann, 1967, copyright 1967 C&T Publications Ltd. Used by permission of Curtis Brown Group Ltd, London.

Curtis Brown Group Ltd, London, for permission to reprint from published works by Sir Winston Churchill on behalf of the Estate of Sir Winston Churchill, copyright Winston S. Churchill.

Hodder & Stoughton for permission to reprint extracts from the diary of Sir John Colville in the Churchill Archives Centre, Churchill College, Cambridge.

Simon & Schuster for permission to reprint extracts from Winston Churchill, *My Early Life*, Touchstone edition published by Simon & Schuster, 1996 © 1930 renewed 1958 by Winston Churchill.

The Trustees of the Liddell Hart Centre for Military Archives, King's College London, for permission to reprint extracts from the diary and papers of Lord Alanbrooke.

The Master, Fellows and Scholars of Churchill College, Cambridge, for permission to reprint extracts from the papers of Baroness Spencer-Churchill.

Lord Moran for permission to reprint extracts from the papers of his father, Sir Charles Wilson (Lord Moran), in the Wellcome Library for the History and Understanding of Medicine, London.

Young Winston's Wars: The Original Despatches of Winston S. Churchill War Correspondent, 1897–1900, by Winston S. Churchill, edited by Frederick Woods, copyright © 1972 by the Chartwell Trust, © 1972 by Frederick Woods. Used by permission of Viking Penguin, a division of Penguin Group (USA), Inc.

Constable & Robinson Ltd for permission to reprint extracts from Lord Moran, *Winston Churchill: The Struggle for Survival, 1940–1965*, published by Constable & Company, 1966, & by Constable & Robinson, 2006.

The Controller of Her Majesty's Stationery Office for permission to reproduce Crown copyright material.

Index